S0-ABJ-961

MILADY'S
STANDARD

Comprehensive Training for
Estheticians

MILADY'S
STANDARD

Comprehensive Training for Estheticians

Janet D'Angelo

Paula S. Dean

Sallie Dietz

Catherine Hinds

Mark Lees

Erica Miller

Alexandra Zani

THOMSON

DELMAR LEARNING ™ Australia • Canada • Mexico • Singapore • Spain • United Kingdom • United States

Milady's Standard: Comprehensive Training for Estheticians

MILADY STAFF:

President:
Susan L. Simpfenderfer

Executive Production Manager:
Wendy A. Troeger

Executive Marketing Manager:
Donna J. Lewis

Acquisitions Editor:
Pamela B. Lappies

Production Editor:
Eileen M. Clawson

Channel Manager:
Stephen G. Smith

Developmental Editor:
Judy Aubrey Roberts

Text Design and Composition:
Thompson Steele, Inc.

Cover Design:
Spiral Design Studio

Photograph and art credits on page xxv.

COPYRIGHT © 2003 by Milady, an imprint of Delmar, a division of Thomson Learning, Inc. Thomson Learning™ is a trademark used herein under license

Library of Congress Cataloging-in-Publication Data

ISBN-13: 978-1-56253-805-7
ISBN-10: 1-56253-805-5

Printed in the United States of America
6 7 8 9 10 XXX 09 08 07

For more information contact Milady,
Executive Woods, 5 Maxwell Drive
Clifton Park, New York 12065-2919

Or find us on the World Wide Web at http://www.milady.com

All rights reserved. No part of this work covered by the copyright hereon may be reproduced or used in any form or by any means—graphic, electronic, or mechanical, including photocopying, recording, taping, Web distribution or information storage and retrieval systems—without written permission of the publisher.

For permission to use material from this text or product, contact us by
Tel   (800) 730-2214
Fax   (800) 730-2215
www.thomsonrights.com

NOTICE TO THE READER

Publisher does not warrant or guarantee any of the products described herein or perform any independent analysis in connection with any of the product information contained herein. Publisher does not assume, and expressly disclaims, any obligation to obtain and include information other than that provided to it by the manufacturer.

The reader is expressly warned to consider and adopt all safety precautions that might be indicated by the activities herein and to avoid all potential hazards. By following the instructions contained herein, the reader willingly assumes all risks in connection with such instructions.

The Publisher makes no representation or warranties of any kind, including but not limited to, the warranties of fitness for particular purpose or merchantability, nor are any such representations implied with respect to the material set forth herein, and the publisher takes no responsibility with respect to such material. The publisher shall not be liable for any special, consequential, or exemplary damages resulting, in whole or part, from the readers' use of, or reliance upon, this material.

CONTENTS IN BRIEF

Part I Ancient History—Modern Times   2

Chapter 1   A Journey through Time: Esthetics Then and Now   4

Part II The Natural Sciences   24

Chapter 2   Anatomy and Physiology of the Skin   26
Chapter 3   Body Systems   50
Chapter 4   Bones, Muscles, and Nerves of the Face and Skull   68
Chapter 5   Bacteriology and Sanitation   78
Chapter 6   Nutrition   90

Part III The Treatment Room   104

Chapter 7   Room Furnishings   106
Chapter 8   Technological Tools   116
Chapter 9   Basics of Electricity   136
Chapter 10   First Impressions—Setup and Supplies   146

Part IV Gathering Information   160

Chapter 11   Skin Types and Conditions   162
Chapter 12   Health Screening   170
Chapter 13   Skin Analysis   184

Part V The Facial   194

Chapter 14   Anatomy of a Facial   196
Chapter 15   Men's Facials   228
Chapter 16   Postconsultation and Home Care   236

Part VI Advanced Sciences   244

Chapter 17   Disorders and Diseases   246
Chapter 18   Pharmacology   270
Chapter 19   Product Chemistry   282
Chapter 20   Advanced Ingredient Technology   302

Part VII Advanced Skin Care   308

Chapter 21   Aging Skin: Morphology and Treatment   310
Chapter 22   Sensitive Skin: Morphology and Treatment   340
Chapter 23   Hyperpigmentation: Morphology and Treatment   356
Chapter 24   Acne: Morphology and Treatment   364
Chapter 25   Ethnic Skin: Morphology and Treatment   390
Chapter 26   Exfoliation   396
Chapter 27   Holistic/Alternative Skin Care   418
Chapter 28   Advanced Home Care   426

Part VIII Epilation   438

Chapter 29   Methods of Hair Removal   440
Chapter 30   Waxing Procedures   458

Part IX Makeup Artistry   484

Chapter 31   Color Theory, Facial Features, and Setup   486
Chapter 32   Makeup Applications   516

Part X Spa Body Treatments   538

Chapter 33   The Value of Body Services   540
Chapter 34   Body Treatments   556

Part XI Advanced Clinical Skin Care   574

Chapter 35   Career Opportunities in Medical Esthetics   576
Chapter 36   Plastic and Reconstructive Surgery   582
Chapter 37   Patient Profiles   596
Chapter 38   Pre- and Postoperative Care   610
Chapter 39   Camouflage Therapy   622

CONTENTS

Part I   Ancient History—Modern Times   2

Chapter 1   A Journey through Time: Esthetics Then and Now   4

Introduction   5

Career Options   6

Aesthētikos   7

Ancient Surgery and Remedies   9

Roots of Esthetic and Spa Therapies   11

Transition to Western Medicine   17

Evolution of American Skin Care   18

Pioneers of the Twentieth Century   20

The Future   20

Emergence of Industry Conferences   21

Part II   The Natural Sciences   24

Chapter 2   Anatomy and Physiology of the Skin   26

Introduction   27

Skin Function   27

Cell Physiology and Biochemistry   30

Specialized Cell Function and Tissues   32

Layers of the Skin   39

Chapter 3   Body Systems   50

Introduction   51

Endocrine System   58

Circulatory System   60

Immune System   63

Chapter 4   Bones, Muscles, and Nerves of the Face and Skull   68

Introduction   69

Bones of the Skull   69

Muscles of the Face, Neck, and Scalp   69

Nerves   73

Nerve Motor Points of the Face and Neck   75

Chapter 5   Bacteriology and Sanitation   78

Introduction   79

Microorganisms   79

Sterilization   80

Policies and Procedures   84

Chapter 6   Nutrition   90

Introduction   91

Macronutrients   91

Micronutrients: Vitamins   94

Minerals   100

How Much Nutrition Do You Need?   101

Nutrition and Esthetics   101

Part III   The Treatment Room   104

Chapter 7   Room Furnishings   106

Introduction   107

Facial Chair   107

Operator Chair or Stool   109

Maintenance of Furniture, Equipment, and Countertops   110

Ergonomics   110

Utility Carts   114

Chapter 8   Technological Tools   116

Introduction   117

Skin Analysis Equipment   117

Skin Care Machines   119

Microcurrent Machines   128

Other Tools and Accessories   129

Chapter 9   Basics of Electricity   136

Introduction   137

Basics of Matter: The Atom   137

Circuits   142

Basic Forms of Electricity   143

Esthetic Machines   144

Safety   144

Chapter 10   First Impressions—Setup and Supplies   146

Introduction   147

Elements of Meet and Greet   147

Facial Bed Setup   149

Supplies   152

Product Masks   155

Dispensary   156

Safety   157

End of the Day   158

Part IV   Gathering Information   160

Chapter 11   Skin Types and Conditions   162

Introduction   163

Skin Types   163

Skin Conditions   167

Chapter 12   Health Screening   170

Introduction   171

Health Screening Questionnaire   171

Chapter 13   Skin Analysis   184

Introduction   185

Skin Analysis Tools   187

The Analysis Procedure   188

Record Keeping   189

Closing the Analysis   189

Final Review   192

Part V   The Facial   194

Chapter 14   Anatomy of a Facial   196

Introduction   197

Products Used in Facials   197

General Facial Steps   201

Facial Massage   215

The Basic Facial   220

The Minifacial   225

Chapter 15   Men's Facials   228

Introduction   229

Men's Skin Care Products   229

Professional Treatments for Men   231

Chapter 16   Postconsultation and Home Care   236

Introduction   237

Closing Consultation   237

Developing Long-Term Programs   239

Achieving Results   239

Follow-Up   239

Home Care Products   239

The Home Care Guide   241

Part VI   Advanced Sciences   244

Chapter 17   Disorders and Diseases   246

Introduction   247

Common Dermatological Terms   247

Lesions   248

Common Conditions and Diseases of the Skin   254

Common Allergens in the Skin Care Business   259

Contagious Diseases   260

Other Diseases of the Skin   263

Autoimmune Diseases   266

Chapter 18   Pharmacology   270

Introduction   271

Over-the-Counter and Prescription Drugs   271

Skin Lightening Products   275

Corticosteroids   276

Prescription Steroids   276

Allergic Reactions, Hives, and Redness   276

Retinoids   277

Drugs for the Treatment of Rosacea   279

Antibiotics   279

Chapter 19   Product Chemistry   282

Introduction   283

Basic Chemistry   283

Cosmetic Ingredients   286

Chapter 20   Advanced Ingredient Technology   302

Introduction   303

Food and Drug Administration Regulations   303

Serums   303

Delivery Systems   304

Improving Cell Metabolism and Oxygenation   306

Nature versus Biotechnology   306

Part VII   Advanced Skin Care   308

Chapter 21   Aging Skin: Morphology and Treatment   310

Introduction   311

Intrinsic Aging   311

Extrinsic Aging   315

Sunscreens   322

Analysis of Sun-Damaged Skin   325

Treatment Concepts for Sun-Damaged Skin   330

Advanced Mature Skin Treatments   332

Chapter 22   Sensitive Skin: Morphology and Treatment   340

Introduction   341

Barrier Function and Sensitivity   341

Analysis of Sensitive Skin   341

Irritants and Allergens   344

Rosacea   347

Aging and the Sensitive Skin   348

Salon Treatment for Sensitive Skin   355

Chapter 23   Hyperpigmentation: Morphology and Treatment   356

Introduction   357

Analysis   357

Treatment for Hyperpigmentation   359

Chapter 24   Acne: Morphology and Treatment   364

Introduction   365

What Causes Acne?   365

Hormones and Acne   368

Stress Factors   370

Foods and Acne   371

Cosmetics, Skin Care Products,
  and Acne   371

Grades of Acne   371

Concepts of Acne Management   373

Analysis and Treatment of
  Problem Skin   376

**Chapter 25   Ethnic Skin:
              Morphology and Treatment   390**

Introduction   391

Black Skin   391

Asian Skin   393

Hispanic and Native American Skin   394

Chapter 26   Exfoliation   396

Introduction   397

Mechanical versus Chemical
  Exfoliation   397

Mechanical Exfoliation   398

Chemical Exfoliation   401

Enzymes   416

Chapter 27   Holistic/Alternative Skin Care   418

Introduction   419

Psychological Benefits of
  Holistic Practices   419

Mind-Body Connection   419

Methods of Holistic Therapy   420

Chapter 28   Advanced Home Care   426

Introduction   427

Understanding Your Client   427

Advanced Product Types and Features   427

Introducing Advanced Products
  to the Client   428

The Home Care Treatment Form   429

Advanced/Enhanced Selling   429

Sample Advanced Product Plans   432

Part VIII   Epilation   438

Chapter 29   Methods of Hair Removal   440

Introduction   441

Morphology of Hair   441

Differences in Hair Growth
  and Characteristics   444

Hair Removal   445

Furniture and Accessories   451

Tools and Supplies   451

Sanitation   453

Room Preparation   453

General Hair Removal (Waxing)   455

Chapter 30   Waxing Procedures   458

Introduction   459

Eyebrow Shaping   459

Waxing the Ear   459

Waxing the Upper Torso   459

Waxing the Leg   478

Ingrown Hair Service   478

Part IX   Makeup Artistry   484

**Chapter 31   Color Theory, Facial Features,
              and Setup   486**

Introduction   487

Color Theory   488

Facial Proportion and Shape   491

Facial Profile   494

Choosing and Using Makeup Products   501

Makeup Tools   509

Chapter 32   Makeup Applications   516

Introduction   517

The Makeup Work Area   517

Client Consultation   517

The Closing   518

Choosing a Makeup Product Collection   529

Makeup Services   530

Beyond the Basics   535

Part X   The Spa Body Treatments   538

Chapter 33   The Value of Body Services   540

Introduction   541

Who Can Do Body Treatments?   541

Concerns   542

Client Health   543

Body Treatment Principles   544

Hydrotherapy   545

Service Treatment Protocols   545

Techniques for Body Treatments   546

Body Masks and Wraps   549

Aromatherapy   552

Other Performance Ingredients   553

Chapter 34   Body Treatments   556

Introduction   557

Client Charting and Consultation   557

Body Treatments   557

Spot Treatments   561

Paraffin   564

Combination Services, Packages,
and Marketing   564

Body Massage   565

Shiatsu, Reflexology,
and Similar Energy   568

Home Care   571

Part XI   Advanced Clinical Skin Care   574

**Chapter 35   Career Opportunities in
Medical Esthetics   576**

Introduction   577

Joining a Medical Team   577

Esthetician as a Resource   579

**Chapter 36   Plastic and Reconstructive
Surgery   582**

Introduction   583

The Disciplines   583

Common Types of Plastic Surgery   583

Facial Procedures   583

Body Procedures   589

Chapter 37   Patient Profiles   596

Introduction   597

Preoperative Preparation   597

Postoperative Care   597

Survivors of Domestic Violence   597

Elderly   597

Physically Challenged   598

Mentally Ill, Obsessive-Compulsive,
and Self-Abused   598

Pre- and Postoperative Care   598

Medical Documentation   601

Chapter 38   Pre- and Postoperative Care   610

Introduction   611

Procedures and Treatment Plans   611

Treatments Defined   615

Chapter 39   Camouflage Therapy   622

Introduction   623

Short-Term Use of Camoflage Therapy   623

Makeup Applications for Specific
Cosmetic Procedures   623

Medical Applications   627

FOREWORD

When I was invited to write the foreword for the new *Milady's Standard: Comprehensive Training for Estheticians,* I hesitated before accepting this honor. I am not an educator, a cosmetologist, a student, or a product manufacturer. I am *in* the beauty business, not *of* the beauty business.

My role in the education of estheticians actually began on October 31, 1994. This was the day the American Aestheticians Education Association (AAEA) was incorporated as a nonprofit association in the state of Texas for the sole purpose of bringing classroom education without product bias to estheticians in the United States.

Prior to starting AAEA, and in the course of my professional experience over the years, I fell in love with estheticians and education for estheticians in all categories. AAEA has been very successful in bringing quality education to esthetics. The organization continues to grow daily through educational opportunities at major medical and spa conferences and trade shows.

In September 1999 I took part in an exciting event in Atlanta, Georgia, which would lead to the creation of content for a new, generic educational product, *Milady's Standard: Comprehensive Training for Estheticians.* I was invited to participate in a three-day focus group organized by Milady, involving intensive brainstorming with other estheticians and educators in the skin care field. During the three days, we had extensive dialogue, group interaction, shared experiences, compared education opportunities, and explored a ton of information, both current and obsolete. This is an experience I will never forget and for which I will be eternally grateful.

In every profession, quality continuing education is vital. Students should be taught by instructors who are both dedicated and qualified. Educational material should be current. The skin care industry has grown and continues to grow at such a rapid pace, particularly in the medical and clinical esthetics field, that it is difficult to keep up. New equipment, new modalities, new cutting-edge products, as well as a proliferation of trade shows from coast to coast make this an exciting, and challenging, field.

The future of esthetics is literally in the hands of the estheticians. The future of estheticians is in the hands, hearts, and minds of the educators who prepare them for the jobs and opportunities that lie ahead. Schools must be equipped with the best educational materials and staffed by knowledgeable educators. *Milady's Standard: Comprehensive Training for Estheticians* raises the bar for educational products, and I look forward to a new era of esthetics education filled with the challenges of the new knowledge and opportunities brought forth with this product.

Bonnie Day
Founder, American Aestheticians Education Association

PREFACE

Welcome to the *New* World of Esthetics

You are about to embark on a wonderful journey that takes you into the innovative world of skin care. *Milady's Standard: Comprehensive Training for Estheticians* unveils the most up-to-date, scientific, and practical information on the biology, physiology, and pathology of the skin. It offers a complete step-by-step approach for facial and body treatments in 39 chapters. A series of 12 videos and a student CD-ROM provide important reinforcement for what is learned in the classroom.

The concept for *Milady's Standard: Comprehensive Training for Estheticians* arose from the need for straightforward, well-organized information that could be easily read and assimilated by students. After receiving numerous requests over the years for more comprehensive educational materials for skin care, we conducted a focus group attended by ten of the nation's skin care experts and educators to formulate a plan for this new product. We then surveyed educators from across the country, asking them what needed to be included, in what order, and to what depth of coverage. Finally, we sent the draft and final manuscripts to yet more subject-matter experts to ensure the accuracy and thoroughness of the new material. What you hold in your hands is the result of this extensive research and review process.

Milady's Standard: Comprehensive Training for Estheticians was written *for* estheticians *by* estheticians. A unique approach for teaching esthetics, it contains data that is integrated and delivered via a three-tiered process: scientific, technical, and practical "hands-on." Interwoven throughout are ideas and insights to help you master scientific background, skin analysis, and the ability to conduct long-term age-management programs with your clients. Each chapter also integrates business and communication essays to help new estheticians communicate well with clients, coworkers, and employers, and to promote a complete understanding of the business of skin care. These essays, called Skills for Success, cover everything from professional appearance to interviewing tips to resume-writing hints. They provide tools that will unlock the doors to your success.

Additionally, this new product serves as a review and reference for all licensed skin-care specialists. To meet the needs of growing salons, spas, and medical esthetics, our aim is to help prepare you for a career that requires multifaceted skills. You are invited to stretch and challenge your abilities to bring your knowledge into the new millennium. As the industry continues to grow, state regulations and licensures will most likely undergo additional changes as well. We must be prepared to learn as much as we can to continue the growth that was started more than 80 years ago in the United States.

You are the future of our industry. Remember that you are the master of your own skills and destiny. Continue to learn, share, and grow. We commend you for choosing this prestigious career!

CONTENTS

Part I — Ancient History—Modern Times — 3

Chapter 1 — A Journey through Time: Esthetics Then and Now — 4

Introduction 5
Career Options 6
Aesthetikos 7
Ancient Surgery and Remedies 9
Roots of Esthetic and Spa Therapies 11
Transition to Western Medicine 17
Evolution of American Skin Care 18
Pioneers of the Twentieth Century 20
The Future 20
Emergence of Industry Conferences 21

Part II — The Natural Sciences — 25

Chapter 2 — Anatomy and Physiology of the Skin — 26

Introduction 27
Skin Function 27
Cell Physiology and Biochemistry 30
Specialized Cell Function and Tissues 32
Layers of the Skin 39

Chapter 3 — Body Systems — 50

Introduction 51
Endocrine System 58
Circulatory System 60
Immune System 63

Chapter 4 — Bones, Muscles, and Nerves of the Face and Skull — 68

Introduction 69
Bones of the Skull 69
Muscles of the Face, Neck, and Scalp 69
Nerves 68
Nerve Motor Points of the Face and Neck 75

Chapter 5 — Bacteriology and Sanitation — 78

Introduction 79
Microorganisms 79
Sterilization 80
Policies and Procedures 84

Chapter 6 — Nutrition — 90

Introduction 91
Macronutrients 91
Micronutrients: Vitamins 94
Minerals 100
How Much Nutrition Do You Need? 101
Nutrition and Esthetics 101

vii

How to Use the Student Course Book

Designed for use in the classroom, the Student Course Book provides the information students need for licensure success and the training they need to excel in today's competitive, fast-growing professional market.

Milady's Standard: Comprehensive Training for Estheticians contains 11 parts broken down into 39 chapters.

■ Part I, Ancient History-Modern Times, introduces the reader to the concept of skin care, providing an in-depth look at the history of esthetics and its changing face in today's world.

■ Part II, The Natural Sciences, lays the foundation for solid, comprehensive skin care education, covering the natural sciences, including anatomy and physiology, body systems, bacteriology and sanitation, and nutrition.

■ Part III, The Treatment Room, acts as a guided tour through a well-equipped skin care salon, highlighting furniture, equipment, tools and supplies, as well as room setup procedures. A thorough overview of the principles of electricity is also included.

Outstanding **full-color photographs** and **illustrations** highlight step-by-step skin care techniques for over 50 different procedures, clearly demonstrating the points being made.

■ Part IV, Gathering Information, opens with the techniques of assessing and identifying skin types and conditions and introduces the importance of health screening and the proper techniques for skin analysis.

■ Part V, The Facial, begins the hands-on, step-by-step procedures for the different types of facials, including men's facials. These chapters are key to the fundamentals of skin care training.

■ Part VI, Advanced Sciences, presents comprehensive coverage of skin disorders and diseases, a thorough introduction to pharmacology and product chemistry, and an overview of advanced ingredient technology.

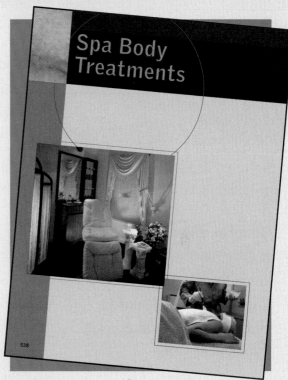

Spa Body Treatments

■ Part VII, Advanced Skin Care, discusses the effects of aging and sun damage on the skin and how to analyze and treat damaged or sensitive skin. It provides step-by-step treatments for sensitive, ethnic, acne-prone, and aging skin. Exfoliation techniques and alternative skin care options are also covered.

■ Part VIII, Epilation, highlights the different methods of hair removal and covers FDA regulations, as well as several techniques for waxing using step-by-step procedures.

■ Part IX, Makeup Artistry, offers an in-depth look at the principles of color, face shapes, and makeup tools and products, as well as step-by-step applications of basic makeup techniques.

■ Part X, The Spa Body Treatments, provides an overview of the value of spa treatments, the principles and protocols involved in treatments, and marketing techniques.

■ Part XI, Advanced Clinical Skin Care, offers a glimpse into the world of clinical skin care, including career opportunities for the esthetician, surgical treatments, pre- and post-operative care, and camouflage therapy.

Features

Innovative features in *Milady's Standard: Comprehensive Training for Estheticians* stimulate critical thinking, develop technical expertise, and encourage students to absorb and apply information presented in the text.

Chapter objectives open each chapter and introduce the main areas targeted for mastery, providing a checkpoint for study and a tie-in to crucial assessment skills.

Key terms are boldfaced and defined the first time they are used in the text.

A running **glossary** appears in the text margin where key terms first appear. It includes complete definitions for easy reference.

Discussion questions at the end of each chapter provide an opportunity for students to assess their understanding of the content and better define areas needing additional study.

References, Additional Reading, and **Helpful Websites** at the end of the chapters document the theoretical basis for each chapter and provide additional resources for continued study.

Helpful **"tip" boxes** offer practical information, shortcuts, and critical advice regarding safety, skin, home care, and more.

Skills for Success, written by Janet D'Angelo, are industry essays illustrating the many communication, business, and retailing skills needed by the esthetician, including topics such as telephone etiquette and exuding confidence around clients.

Step-by-step procedures present over 50 skin care procedures covering everything from the purpose of the procedure, to room and client setup, to supplies and tools, and recommended home care.

Supplemental Materials

Milady's Standard:
Comprehensive Training for Estheticians
Exam Review

The *Exam Review* serves as a convenient preparatory tool for students studying to take the licensure exam for esthetics. With 1,500 questions from all chapters of the Student Course Book, this resource provides students with a comprehensive review of the necessary material. The familiar multiple-choice format imitates that of the state licensure exam to orient students to the types of questions they can expect on the actual exam. An answer key at the back of the book allows students to check accuracy, identify weak areas, and monitor their progress during the review process.

Milady's Standard:
Comprehensive Training for Estheticians
Student CD-ROM

This companion to the Student Course Book helps students prepare for their licensure exams. Complete with rationales for the 1,500 *Exam Review* questions, the CD-ROM is a valuable resource to identify weak areas and reinforce concepts from the Student Course Book. The 50 video clips provide visual reinforcement of the techniques and methodologies presented in the text. Students can use the pronouncing glossary during their course work, when preparing for their licensure exams, and throughout their professional careers, making this a key technological resource.

Milady's Standard:
Comprehensive Training for Estheticians
Web Tutor

This on-line resource provides students with quality supplemental material to use with each chapter of the Student Course Book. Containing content unavailable elsewhere, the Web Tutor provides Chapter Learning Objectives, Online Course Preparation, Study Sheets, Glossary, Flashcards, Frequently Asked Questions, Discussion Topics, On-line Chapter Quizzes, and Web Links for each chapter. *Milady's Standard: Comprehensive Training for Estheticians Web Tutor* is offered on the WebCT or Blackboard platforms.

Milady's Standard:
Comprehensive Training for Estheticians
Leader's Manual

Written by Kathy Driscoll, an esthetics educator experienced in curriculum development, this complete resource features the necessary components to facilitate instruction. The full-color Student Course Book has been reduced to 70 percent to include educational commentary, theory, and convenient annotations to the text.

Key Features

■ Lesson plans help with organizing and presenting the material, and activities provide opportunities to expand the content and further develop skills.

■ Transparency and handout masters are handy time-savers that can aid the instruction process.

■ All components are conveniently packaged in a sturdy three-ring binder for use and reuse throughout the curriculum.

■ Includes a CD-ROM Computerized Testbank that contains 700 multiple-choice, fill in the blank, true/false, and matching questions that correspond to material in the Student Course Book. These questions are in addition to the 1,500 questions found in the *Exam Review* and Student CD-ROM, and are an invaluable tool to create quizzes and tests, helping to prepare students for their licensure exams. The program automatically records test results for each student.

Milady's Standard:
Comprehensive Training for Estheticians
12-Tape Video Library

This set of 12 videotapes includes eight hours of guided demonstration, visually expanding on the content provided in the Student Course Book. Each segment opens with an overview of the procedure being addressed and highlights the specific steps of the procedure. Students learn the tricks of the trade from recognized professionals in the industry as they demonstrate each technical skill in real-life spa and school situations. In addition to demonstrating each procedure, the segments present tips and tricks for preparing clients, using down time between steps, and addressing applicable business and communication skills. Variations and extensions of many procedures are also demonstrated to provide additional skills and techniques beyond the basics.

The series contains 12 tapes, covering eight hours of procedures, tips, and topical discussions by the authors, and the 45 step-by-step procedures coordinate with the content in the Student Course Book. Well-known skin care professionals, who authored the corresponding content in the Student Course Book, present additional variations and extensions of the procedures. Each video is approximately 25 to 45 minutes long.

ACKNOWLEDGMENTS

The authors and editors at Milady recognize with respect and gratitude the following educators and professionals who have played a part in the development of this program:

Focus Group Participants

Rhonda Allison
Owner
Rhonda Allison Skin Therapies
Dallas, Texas

Bonnie Day
Founder
American Aestheticians Education
Association
Carrollton, Texas

Sallie Deitz
Clinical Esthetician
Center for Facial Plastic and Laser Surgery
Bellingham, Washington

Kathy Driscoll
Owner
Houstonian Spa
Houston, Texas

Mary Ellen Gardner
Educator
San Jacinto College North
Crosby, Texas

Patricia Heitz
Owner and Director
Christine Valmy School for Esthetics
Albany, New York

Catherine Hinds
Founder
Catherine Hinds Institute of Esthetics
Boston, Massachusetts

Joyce Sciamanna
Educator
Burlington County Institute of Technology
Mt. Holly, New Jersey

Alexandra Zani
Practitioner and Educator
Carrollton, Texas

Reviewers

Stacy Heatherly
Image Enhancers
Papillion, Nebraska

Carol Thomson Micciche
Lancaster School of Cosmetology
Lancaster, Pennsylvania

Judy Wait
Lytles Redwood Empire Beauty College
Windsor, California

Kari Battuello
Kimberley's – A Day Spa
Latham, New York

Brenda Scharman
Cameo College of Beauty and Skin
Salt Lake City, Utah

Patti Ferraro
Paul Ferraro Salon
Boca Raton, Florida

Paula Michal, R.N.
Herbert M. Janklow, M.D.
Santa Barbara, California

Martha Phillips
Ford Beauty Academy
Boardman, Ohio

Karen Wallace
Grace College of Cosmetology
Cleveland, Ohio

Elizabeth Crilley
Middle Bucks Institute of Technology
Richboro, Pennsylvania

Pamela Gregory
Davidson County Community College
Greensboro, NC
Joseline H. Glenn
Skyline College
San Leandro, California

Barbara Bealer
Allentown School of Cosmetology
Bethlehem, Pennsylvania
Sharon MacGregor
Beauty School of Middletown
Middletown, New York

Renee Poignard
International School of Skin and Nail Care
Atlanta, Georgia

Elizabeth L. Larsha
International School of Skin and Nail Care
Atlanta, Georgia

Ron Deering
Aesthetics Institute of St. Louis
St. Louis, Missouri

Rose Policastro
Capri Institute of Hair Design
Little Ferry, New Jersey

The following manufacturers and suppliers have graciously provided supplies, products, and equipment for use during the photo shoot as well as for our video production. We are grateful for their generosity:

Brushes by Karen, Inc.
Cosmetic Brushes and Accessories
Mineola, New York
Info@Brushesbykaren.com

Qosmedix
A Division of Qosina
Edgewood, New York
Info@qosmedix.com

Mehaz, a professional line of implements made in Solingen, Germany
Los Angeles, California
www.mehaz.com

Correlations, Inc.
Fredericksburg, Texas
www.Correlationsinc.com

Mark Lees, Inc.
Pensacola, Florida
www.marklees.com

Living Earth Craft
Rohnert Park, California
www.livingearthcrafts.com

Here's the Rub
Warminster, Pennsylvania

Star Linen Company
www.starlinen.com

Silhouet-Tone
St. Albans, Vermont

Aesthetics Complete, Inc.
King of Prussia, Pennsylvania
www.aestheticscomplete.com

Special thanks to:

Lansdale School of Cosmetology, Esthetics
Instructor Faith Gilmartin
Jean Madeline Education Center for Cosmetology
Pier 1
Sondra Enck, esthetician
Pearl Bailey Anderson, esthetician

Photograph and Art Credits

Ch. 1, Fig. 1-1, photo by Stock Studios Photography.

Ch. 1, Fig. 1-13, photo courtesy of Jane Crawford, Jane Crawford & Associates.

Ch. 5, Fig. 5-9, photo courtesy of Randall Perry Photography.

Ch. 7, Fig. 7-8, photo by Stock Studios Photography.

Ch. 11, Fig. 11-2, photo courtesy of Marlene McHugh Pratt.

Ch. 11, Fig. 11-3, reprinted with permission from the American Academy of Dermatology. All rights reserved.

Ch. 13, Fig. 13-1a, photo courtesy of Amy Gleason.

Ch. 17, Figs. 17-1, 17-9, 17-10, 17-12, 17-13, 17.34, 17.36, and 17.39, T. Fitzgerald, *Color Atlas and Synopsis of Clinical Dermatology*, 3e, 1996. Reprinted with permission of The McGraw-Hill Companies..

Ch. 17, Figs. 17.2, 17.4, 17.5, 17.6, 17.7, 17.8, 17.11, 17.14, 17.15, 17.16, 17.17, 17.18, 17.19, 17.20, 17.21, 17.22, 17.23, 17.24, 17.25, 17.26, 17.27, 17.28, 17.29, 17.30, 17.31, 17.32, 17.33, 17.35, 17.37, and 17.38, reprinted with permission from the American Academy of Dermatology. All rights reserved.

Ch. 21, Figs. 21-11, 21-12, and 21-13, reprinted with permission from the American Academy of Dermatology. All rights reserved.

Ch. 22, Fig. 22-5, reprinted with permission from the American Academy of Dermatology. All rights reserved.

Ch. 22, Fig. 22-8, photo by Dzaman Photography.

Ch. 23, Fig. 23-3, reprinted with permission from the American Academy of Dermatology. All rights reserved.

Ch. 24, Fig. 24-5, T. Fitzgerald, *Color Atlas and Synopsis of Clinical Dermatology*, 3e, 1996. Reprinted with permission of The McGraw-Hill Companies.

Ch. 24, Figs. 24-9a, 24-9c, and 24-9d, reprinted with permission from the American Academy of Dermatology. All rights reserved.

Ch. 25, Figs. 25-2 and 25-3, reprinted with permission from the American Academy of Dermatology. All rights reserved.

Ch. 27, Figs. 27-1 and 27-4, photo by Stock Studios Photography.

Ch. 32, Figs. 32-6, photo courtesy of Melissa Newton Hayes.

Ch. 33, Figs. 33-3, 33-4, 33-5, 33-7, 33-8, 33-11, and 33-12, photos courtesy of Randall Perry Photography.

Ch. 33, Figs. 33-2 and 33-9, photos by Stock Studios Photography.

Ch. 34, Figs. 34-2, photo courtesy of Randall Perry Photography.

Ch. 35, Figs. 35-1, 35-3, 35-4, and 35-5, photos courtesy of Sherrer Photography.

Ch. 36, Figs. 36-2a, 36-2b, 36-6a, 36-6b, 36-14a, 36-14b, 36-16a, 36-16b, 36-18a, 36-18b, 36-20a, and 36-20b, photos courtesy of David P. Rapaport, M.D., New York, NY.

Ch. 36, Figs. 36-4a, 36-4b, 36-12a, 36-12b, photos courtesy of R. Emil Hecht, M.D.

Ch. 36, Figs. 36-9a, 36-9b, photos courtesy of Jeffrey S. Epstein, M.D. F.A.C.S., Facial Plastic Surgeon, Miami, FL.

Ch. 36, Figs. 36-10a, 36-10b, photos courtesy of Robert Harris, M.D.

Ch. 37, Figs. 37-1 and 37-2, courtesy of Sherrer Photography.

Ch. 38, Figs. 38-1, 38-2a, 38-2b, 38-2c, 38-3a, 38-3b, 38-3c, and 38-4, courtesy of Sherrer Photography.

Ch. 39, Figs. 39-1a, 39-1b, 39-2a, 39-2b, photos courtesy of Susan Lindsay, Clinical Esthetician and Esthetic Rehabilitation Specialist, Edmonds, WA.

All other photos by Larry Hamill, Artist & Photographer.

ABOUT THE AUTHORS

Milady's Standard: Comprehensive Training for Estheticians was written by seven of the best and brightest industry experts in the field today.

Janet D'Angelo, M. Ed.

As contributing author and an editor for this text, Janet D'Angelo is a marketing communications and public relations specialist with more than 20 years of experience in the beauty, skin care, and education fields. She is a nationally recognized educator and speaker and is also a licensed esthetician with hands-on experience in developing a skin care practice. As founder of J. Angel Communications, D'Angelo is a well-respected consultant for the health, beauty, and wellness industry.

Paula S. Dean

Paula Dean is a regular lecturer and educator at national and international esthetic trade shows, educational venues, and world-class spas. As vice president of Expertise by Erica T. Miller & Associates, Inc., she is also an accomplished makeup artist, esthetician, massage therapist, and CIDESCO Diplomat—which was received in Amsterdam, The Netherlands. This pioneer in the development of professional skin care, makeup, and psychological "wellness" enhancement in the spa, salon, and health care professions still enjoys clowning around—as a professional hospital clown for various medical centers in Texas.

Sallie Dietz, B.A.

Whether she's developing or researching new products; providing advanced, therapeutic, or clinical treatments; or publishing her quarterly newsletter, *Your Skin*, clinical esthetician Sallie Dietz is committed to educating and servicing her clientele. Her Web site, DermaCenter.com, promotes beauty products, services, and education, and to that end, she works as a consultant for estheticians, nurses, and physicians. She is certified in lymphatic drainage massage, microdermabrasion, and advanced chemical peels. Dietz practices with the Center for Facial Plastic and Laser Surgery in Bellingham, Washington. She is also a member of both the American Aestheticians Education Association (AAEA) and the American Society of Esthetic Medicine (ASEM).

Catherine Hinds

Inspired by the lure of economic independence in the 1960s, Catherine Hinds has cleared the landscape and paved the road for American estheticians for the last four decades. Bringing seven salons to fruition in Boston and New York, Catherine acquired knowledge and expertise that turned her toward education. In 1979, she sold her salons and founded the Catherine Hinds Institute of Esthetics, which became the first accredited esthetics school in the country in 1983. Hinds weaves European techniques into American technology. The institute has programs in basic and advanced esthetics and offers the first accredited spa therapy and modern esthetics programs in the United States. Catherine Hinds is the recipient of *Dermascope* magazine's Legend Award and has been named Woman of the Year and Esthetician of the Year by the American Salon Owners Association.

Mark Lees, Ph.D.

Renowned skin care specialist Dr. Mark Lees has over 20 years of experience gleaned from his award-winning, CIDESCO-accredited day spa and salon in northwest Florida. In response to his own search for quality products to treat acne-prone, sensitive, and sun-damaged skin, in 1983 Dr. Lees founded his own products company, Mark Lees Skin Care, Inc. This in-demand lecturer regularly teaches classes at professional beauty and medical conventions, consumer and women's groups, and major universities at home and abroad. In addition to his contribution to this text, Dr. Lees has authored another book, *Skin Care: Beyond the Basics* and dozens of articles for industry trade magazines. He is president of Esthetics Manufacturers and Distributors Alliance (EMDA) and is the recipient of numerous prestigious awards for his contributions and expertise in the field of skin care.

Erica Miller

Founder and president of the company Expertise by Erica T. Miller & Associates, Inc., Erica Miller is an internationally acclaimed educator who brings over 25 years of experience as a licensed esthetician, massage therapist, and CIDESCO Diplomat to this project. Voted one of the five most prominent women in American esthetics by *Salon News* magazine, she has served as a consultant and educational trainer for many of the nation's most prestigious spas, as well as major national and international corporations. Miller is an accomplished author and editor, having written three other books in addition to her contributions to this project: *Day Spa Operations, Day Spa Techniques,* and *Shiatsu Massage.* She is also the former editor-in-chief of Dermascope magazine and has produced a series of training videos for facial and body treatments.

Alexandra Zani

A licensed cosmetologist, esthetician, and spa therapist, Alexandra Zani has an extensive background in medical esthetics, pre- and post-surgical treatments, business communications, and organizational development. She is the corporate esthetician for Creative Beauty Innovations (CBI) in Carrollton, Texas, and manager of education and product development for CBI's professional division. A former business owner, Zani has served as a consultant in the spa and medical esthetics industries and has authored numerous articles for *Skin, Inc., Les Nouvelles Esthetiques,* and *Dermascope* magazines.

Ancient History—Modern Times

PART I

Part Outline

Chapter 1   A Journey through Time: Esthetics Then and Now

In order to learn about esthetics today, it helps to study the practice of skin care in the past. The care of the skin has been one of humanity's concerns since the dawn of recorded history. Inseparable from other physical concerns, it was considered a part of overall health treatment, since health and beauty were synonymous.

Contemporary skin and body care therapies are rooted in ancient civilization's ability to ward off disease in order to live a long, healthy life. In early civilizations, health was customarily focused on maintaining body balance and harmony through total well-being practices.

In Part I, you will find a sweeping history of esthetics, which oftentimes mirrors the history of medicine. You will read about the ancient Chinese and their theory of energy, and the Egyptian discovery of essential oils. The Greek theory of health using the four humors will be presented, along with a description of the great Roman baths. Indian culture contributed ayurvedic medicine, which is enjoying a new prominence in contemporary health and wellness circles, just as shea butter, first used centuries ago in Africa, is found in many contemporary skin products. Part I covers this and more, concluding with brief profiles of the many pioneers of what we now call esthetics.

Chapter 1
A Journey through Time: Esthetics Then and Now

Chapter Objectives

After reading this chapter, you should be able to:

- Identify industry trends and statistics.
- List career choices for estheticians.
- Define *esthetics* and its relationship to health care.
- Describe the history of skin care and its development into the modern day skin care industry.
- List the contributions of twentieth century pioneers.

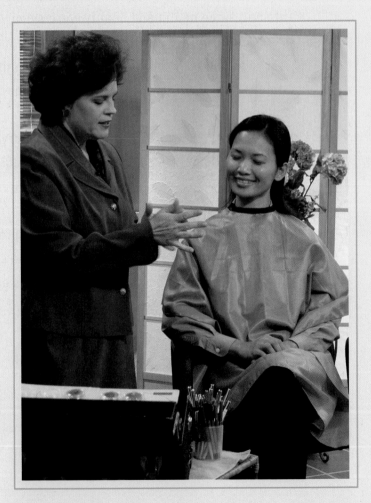

Chapter Outline

Introduction
Career Options
Aesthētikos
Ancient Surgery and Remedies
Roots of Esthetic and Spa Therapies
Transition to Western Medicine
Evolution of American Skin Care
Pioneers of the Twentieth Century
The Future
Emergence of Industry Conferences

Introduction

Once viewed as a casual luxury for the rich and famous, the past 30 years of professional skin care have brought us far beyond the traditional service. All sorts of facial and massage services can be found inside busy shopping areas, airports, corporations, spas, salons, dedicated wellness centers, and medical offices. The trend toward wellness has given the esthetician visibility and recognition to a degree that was not available 10 years ago. No doubt, this evolution will continue and it will offer the esthetician more exciting opportunities.

During the last decade, we have witnessed the transition of esthetics from a minor role in the beauty industry, dominated mainly by hair care, into specialized services found in elegant, full-service salons, day spas, and wellness centers. Marketing efforts are focused on integrating beauty, health, and wellness, and on building relationships with the consumer. The integration of European modalities of spa water therapies such as body wraps, hydrotherapy, and Vichy showers has resulted in a more holistic approach to skin and body care. It is now recognized that ambiance and décor play important roles in creating a mood that promotes relaxation and rejuvenation (Figure 1–1).

Some skin care operations have separated from busy hair salons to provide a more peaceful setting. Day spas have emerged by expanding hair services into a full-service business offering skin and body care (Figure 1–2). They may include facials, massages, body wraps, makeup, natural therapeutic pedicures and manicures, and a full array of products for after-treatment and home care.

With the emphasis steadily growing from basic beauty to wellness and health, the "medi-spa" has emerged as an integral part of esthetics. In this baby boomer-driven economy, there is a greater need for people to maintain a competitive edge in the American workforce. Boomers seek ways to keep their appearance looking younger, including maintaining a healthy body. Medical esthetic services—laser hair removal, vein treatments, photo facial rejuvenation, plastic surgery, and liposuction—are combined with pre- and post-operative care as well as anti-

Figure 1–1 Jean Paul Spa, Albany, NY.

Figure 1–2 An example of a well-organized esthetics retail center.

aging facial and body treatments. Many estheticians obtain advanced training in order to work with physicians and plastic surgeons.

Rising health care costs and the presence of Health Maintenance Organizations (HMOs) foster the search for preventive and alternative care. A few pioneering U.S. hospitals have attached a dedicated spa facility offering massage therapy, pre- and post-surgical facials, water therapies, and other services for both patients and the general

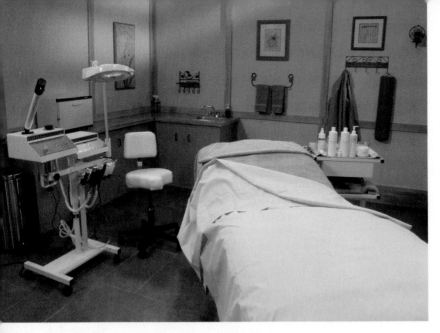

Figure 1–3 A typical skin care treatment room.

- The average life span in the 1800s was 25 years. In 1900 it increased to approximately 48. At the beginning of the twenty-first century the average life expectancy is between 78 and 87 with predictions of it increasing to 100 years or more in the future.

In this busy modern world we live in, exposure to too much sun, pollution, and work-related stress, and the demands for effective skin care ingredients and state-of-the-art in-clinic corrective treatments are challenging skin care chemists and manufacturers. Once thought of as a luxury, facial and spa services are now considered an integral part of an overall health care program.

Career Options

As a licensed skin care professional, your career options are plentiful. You have chosen a most challenging and rewarding career in a high-profile market. Some possibilities for a rewarding career follow:

- licensed esthetician, working in a skin care salon or day spa (Figure 1–4)
- a cosmetic buyer or beauty advisor in a department store
- manufacturer's representative for a skin care line

public (Figure 1–3). Advances in aging research and the discovery of new ingredients, delivery systems, more refined plant extraction methods, and the introduction of antioxidants has resulted in many new high-performance products. A new generation of skin care has emerged as an innovative frontier for results-oriented correction.

Given the changing times, we must strive for a complete understanding of skin science, analysis, and mastery of tools, treatments, product chemistry basics, and knowledge of business concepts. Clients prefer long-term comprehensive age management programs. Consider the following:

- In the U.S. alone, 50% of the population turned 50 years of age in the year 2000. That is one baby boomer turning 50 every seven seconds.
- During the next 20 years, 40 million women will enter menopause.
- A recent survey by Pricewaterhouse-Coopers indicated that 47% of baby boomers are utilizing spa services. Women account for approximately 80% of U.S. spa goers. Men are increasingly participating in specialized men's services, which include antiaging and stress reduction, microdermabrasion, and hair removal.
- One-third of American adults have used alternative treatments for health care purposes.

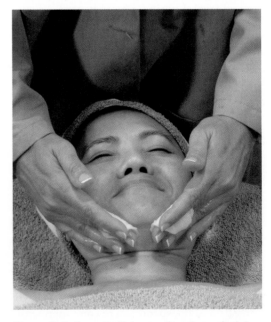

Figure 1–4 An esthetician performing a facial.

Figure 1–5 Makeup artist.

- makeup artist in a salon, department store, modeling agency, or in the entertainment industry (Figure 1–5)
- salon or spa director or consultant
- educator or school director
- assistant to a dermatologist or cosmetic surgeon
- on-site esthetician specializing in pre- and post-operative care
- skin care specialist in a hospital setting (Figure 1–6)
- corrective skin care specialist or makeup artist for patients with burns and disfigurement
- micropigmentation specialist
- corporate esthetician advising research and manufacturing

Figure 1–6 Medical esthetician.

- beauty editor or writer
- freelance writer and lecturer

Whatever career avenue you choose, it is important to master the basics of skin anatomy and physiology, to understand how to perform a thorough skin analysis, and then to proceed with an appropriate treatment based on the needs of your client. Your choice of long-term management program depends on your client's health, age, environmental exposure, and lifestyle.

Personal success depends on many factors: balancing a thorough knowledge of the technicalities of skin care with professionalism, a positive attitude, and dedication to your chosen profession. Mastery means rising above your perceived limitations and going forward no matter how tough the challenge.

> Mastery means going beyond what we know . . . pushing through our perceived limitations . . . and achieving what we were told would be the impossible. Then practice, practice, practice. A. J. Zani

Aesthētikos

The word *esthetics* originates from the Greek word **aesthētikos,** which means perceptible to the senses. An esthetician (also spelled aesthetician) is a person who is devoted to, or professionally occupied with, the health and beauty of the skin. Additionally, aesthētikos means to have an appreciation of beauty. An esthetician enhances and corrects the beauty and health of the skin through the application of products using numerous techniques and tools. A makeup artist works with color and shading (pigment and hues) and brush strokes to create an esthetically pleasing appearance.

A massage therapist performs numerous types of massage techniques and helps to alleviate or reduce stress, joint pain, and stiffness. Water therapies and body wraps support circulation and detoxification. Therefore, increased well-being enhances the appearance of a client. A plastic surgeon may mend a broken nose, resulting in recontouring the esthetic appearance of the nose. Performing a face-lift enhances the esthetic look of an aging face.

aesthētikos
Perceptible to the senses.

Professional Image
Aptitude + Appearance + Attitude—How Do You Rate?

As "professionals" it is expected that we are knowledgeable in a certain area and possess specific skills or techniques that are representative of our training. When we enter a profession we also assume all the responsibilities associated with upholding the standards of that profession. Individually and collectively, we are all responsible for maintaining the integrity of the field.

From core competency (aptitude) to personal presentation (appearance) and conduct (attitude), how you are perceived is a reflection on the entire profession you represent. Once you have graduated from esthetics school you will be expected to have certain knowledge about skin care. This does not mean that you are expected to have the answer to every question put before you by a client. Learning is an ongoing process, and it will take time to become "an expert" in the field.

Your job as a professional esthetician is to promote beautiful and healthy skin. You have been trained to analyze skin conditions and to perform treatments to achieve results. Clients will rely on you to provide them with accurate information about their individual skin care needs. They will expect you to keep them advised of the best treatment methods and products to achieve their goals. This means being knowledgeable about all the services and products you currently offer as well as keeping abreast of new and innovative techniques.

Building the client's confidence in your professional abilities requires you to express your knowledge in a way that builds trust. How do you accomplish this? Display your credentials in a prominent place. Frame your diploma and hang it, along with your license and any other certificates that demonstrate your expertise and commitment to excellence in the field. Find out which organizations are committed to the growth of your profession and join them. Advertise your affiliation with these groups. Attend continuing education seminars and workshops to keep abreast of new information in the field and exhibit certificates of participation. Subscribe to trade publications and build a pool of information based on your own reading and research. Become involved in community projects that demonstrate your willingness to share your professional exper-

tise. As you continue to make these efforts, clients will begin to view you as an authority.

Another important aspect of presenting a positive professional image is your appearance. If you are not "walking the talk" you will have failed to instill a belief in the efficacy of what you do. Estheticians work to attain clean, beautiful, and healthy skin. The first question to ask yourself in terms of appearance is, Do I reflect the basic tenets of the work I do? Clients will have greater faith in your methods if you also ascribe to their use. Taking care to maintain your own skin shows clients that you believe in the value of what you do.

Estheticians are in close, physical contact with clients. They must also take care to maintain a clean, healthful appearance and environment. Take a quick inventory. Do you appear neat and clean at all times? Is your breath fresh and your body free from offensive odors? Are your nails well groomed and manicured? Is your clothing in alignment with being a health practitioner—clean and unobtrusive? Is the environment you practice in sanitary and free from contaminants? Do you change linens and towels after each client? Do you sanitize all instruments and disinfect the area after each treatment? Do you wash your hands often and take care to protect clients by wearing gloves when working on their skin?

Your attitude completes the way you present yourself as a professional. It is a code of conduct. Esthetics is a service industry, requiring careful consideration of others. As a professional esthetician you are expected to be courteous, pleasant, and respectful of the needs of others, treating clients with kindness and dignity. You must work to develop good communication and people skills and be invested in providing quality customer service. This means showing up on time, staying on schedule, being attentive to the needs of others, practicing confidentiality, and doing good work.

Taking time to evaluate your aptitude, appearance, and attitude on a regular basis will keep you at the top of your mark. Learning to look critically at yourself is a necessary part of professional development. When done with a conscious effort to improve your skills and increase client satisfaction, the entire profession benefits.

Ancient Surgery and Remedies

Egyptian and Greek physicians had little knowledge of the *cause* of disease. Many cures were unsuccessful. Healing treatments were based on limited scientific knowledge, and few operations were performed because surgery was very painful. Without anesthetic, a surgical patient could die from shock or infection. Plants were used as remedies for many illnesses (Figure 1–7). Eyebright was used to make an eyewash to soothe inflammation. Hyssop was prescribed for coughs and other chest infections, and was considered a "holy herb." Mullein was also used for the treatment of coughs, and is still used today. Garlic was used to soothe sore throats and bruises.

Cleanliness, Health, and Beauty

Early civilizations had an obsession for cleanliness, as demonstrated by the bathing customs of the Egyptians, Greeks, and Romans. The life span of women was around 35 years and men about 44 years. It was imperative that these civilizations found ways to ward off typhoid, dysentery, tuberculosis, and other illnesses. Bathhouses were part of the social life and preventive care programs were followed by everyone. Bathing was an invigorating process that began in a warm room with tepid water. Next, the bathers moved to a steam room where the water was very hot. They ended with a plunge into cold water.

The spa was once a place of medicine and embraced nutrition, water therapies, and herbal remedies for the relief or cure of health problems and chronic conditions. Massages were performed to help relieve fevers, headaches, and partial paralysis. Beauty and health rituals were an indicator of health and vitality. Skin and hair care treatments included mudpacks, oils, herbs, olive oil, and fragrances. **Henna** was used to color wigs and hair as well as for dyeing fabrics.

Earth, water, plants, pigment, straw, wood, metal, and cloth were used to make everything from internal medicines and building materials, to bath potions, accessories, and body adornments. Many of the herbs, minerals, and plant extracts are used today in modern aromatherapy. Table 1–1, on page 10, lists materials and how they were used for beauty and healing.

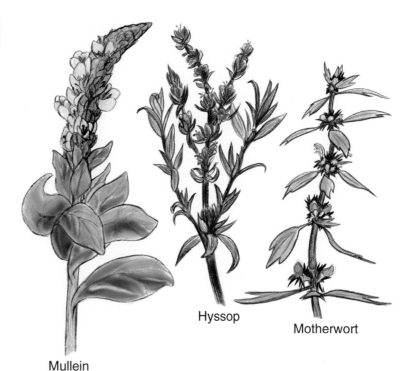

Figure 1–7 A collection of herbs used in skin care and holistic preparations such as masks, cleansers, and remedies.

Hyssop

Motherwort

Mullein

Balance and Harmony

Beauty is more than skin deep. A prevailing theme throughout most ancient cultures was balance and harmony, which lead to health and beauty practices that played important roles in the quest for disease prevention and longevity. The study of ancient practices shows that modern day skin and body care therapies are rooted in ancient civilization's ability to ward off disease in order to live a long, healthy life. Health was customarily focused on maintaining balance and harmony in the body through total well-being practices. Although ancient medicine and traditions such as the Chinese, Ayurvedic (India), Persian, Greek, and Roman created preventive and healing practices, anatomy and the origin of disease were not fully understood. It is surprising, however, to find that each civilization had a common thread of maintaining health by preventing disease. Philosophies and practices were shared as populations expanded. In each town, there were large **pharmacopoeias** filled with herbal remedies. These authoritative books provided healing and preventive mixtures that cultivated more research, writings, and the opening of medical schools.

henna
A reddish hair dye obtained from the powdered leaves and shoots of the mignonette tree, an old world shrub of the loosestrife family.

pharmacopoeias
Authoritative publications designating the properties, actions use, dosage, and standards of strength and purity of drugs.

Table 1–1 Materials Used in Ancient Times

Material	Uses
Almond oil	Used in cooking, herbal remedies, and to rub on the body as perfume
Ambergris	Waxy substance found floating in tropical seas; was made into beads with scented gums
Beeswax	Used for mixing herbs and making molded candles
Berries	Used for paint, dyes, and makeup
Hemp	Grass used for making rope, baskets, boats, and furniture
Henna	Plant dye used for coloring wigs and hair, fabrics, hands, and feet
Kohl	Derived from material related to arsenic and tin, kohl was used for eyeliner
Lamp black	Collected for eye shadow or coloring for brows and lashes; soldiers placed it under the eyes to prevent sun glare
Olive oil	Body emollients, used for bathing instead of soap, cooking
Sour milk	Used for bathing, and refining and softening skin

Ancient healers were also close to their patients and believed that nothing must be done to cause injury. This was the philosophy of the famous physician Hippocrates who said, "Doctors could not understand the parts of the body until they understood the whole system." This was the beginning of integrative practices and the holistic approach to wellness.

Early medical systems and philosophies were practiced and recorded by Ayurvedic (India) practitioners, the Greeks, the Romans, the Chinese, and down through the nineteenth century. The mind, body, emotions, and the spirit were often the focus of earlier health practices. Each physician, alchemist, and researcher, philosopher, and scientist shared parallel views of how the body was to function at its optimum. They all espoused different theories with the common thread that harmony and balance were necessary for the survival and health of the body, mind, and emotional energy systems. Ancient teachings encouraged health through meditation, exercise, and a proper regimen of food and a balanced lifestyle. Slowly, advances in medical practice and science came each century with more research and experiments. Frenchman Louis Pasteur's nineteenth-century works in fermentation led to his theory that microorganisms were the cause of disease and infection. Subsequent findings by other bacteriologists proved that particular microorganisms caused disease.

Ancient health practices relied on knowledge of herbal and botanical remedies that extended benefits to the internal body. Early alchemists (chemists) knew how to mix and extract compounds. They researched the development of precious medicinal potions and kept their research, documented writings, and herbs in large pharmacopoeias. Physicians and healers of the day depended on the findings of these alchemists as well as their own experiments.

Twentieth-century researchers, scientists, and herbalists continued to document and publish the historical and therapeutic aspects of indigenous components and methods of body care. The study and use of herbs, essential oils, muds, salts, seaweeds, mineral springs, sulphur springs, and ocean water therapies such as thalassotherapy, and others are now more clearly defined and used for formulations and spa treatments.

As we search the vast frontier of internal peace and wellness, ancient teachings and traditions are resurfacing and are being integrated into modern day health care. Research institutes such as the Institutes of Health in Bethesda, Maryland—Division of Alternative Studies, the World Health Organization, and the American Massage Therapy Association Foundation continue to document scientific data supporting the benefits of alternative therapies. These organizations study the potential usefulness of these modalities in order to evaluate and examine their safety and efficacy. Today, we are fortunate to be part of a growing trend of full-service salons, health spas, medical spas, and wellness centers.

Roots of Esthetic and Spa Therapies

According to the research and writings of spa consultant Monica Tuma Brown, the word *spa* may be an acronym for the Latin phrase *sanitas per aquas*. The term *spa* was first adopted by a famous resort founded in 1326, in the wooded hills of the Ardennes of Belgium, near Liège. The word did not come into common use until Emperor Charles IV discovered the great Bohemian spa at Carlsbad. Spas were placed over hot springs, near peat bogs, or even near the ocean. They were considered places for healing and warding off disease. They had (and some still do) medical staff available for health advice. In the exploration of ancient cultures, it is apparent how much their early practices have contributed to our modern approach to health, beauty, and wellness.

Chinese Culture

Ancient Chinese civilization began about 8,000 years ago. The Chinese people were enclosed by mountains, deserts, and ocean and had little contact with the rest of the world. Each Chinese era was referred to as a dynasty. Emperors and their officials were responsible for setting up the social structures, laws, military, education system, and creating industry such as building roads, canals, and defense walls.

In ancient China, grooming practices and clothing told a story about the wearer's place in society. Asians are known for beautiful costumes, celebrations, clothing, and artwork. The ancient tradition of Japanese geisha, while still in practice today, has greatly diminished from earlier times. A geisha's makeup and elaborate mode of dress are based on old Japanese customs. Older bathing recipes made from Chinese herbs or sake, a Japanese wine, have been revived and used in exquisite formulas.

Chinese Medicine

Traditional Chinese medicine can be traced back to about 2900 B.C. The first contribution

Figure 1–8 Yin and yang are two principles in Chinese philosophy whose interaction influences the destinies of all creatures and things. Yin is negative, dark, and feminine; yang is positive, bright, and masculine.

to medicine is found in the writings of Fu Xi around 2953 B.C. He wrote the book on which the principles of Chinese medicine were based. Called the trigrams, they represented aspects of nature according to **yin and yang** (Figure 1–8). The symbols yin and yang are used to define and explain the nature of all phenomena. Each subsequent dynasty proposed medical theories based on the trigrams.

Medical information written by the Yellow Emperor was found in the Han dynasty tombs. A work entitled the *Nei Ching Su Wen* or *The Yellow Emperor's Classic of Internal Medicine* established the need for a positive physician-patient relationship. This comprehensive document included information on drugs, surgery, medical theory, spirituality, the life force, the balance of yin and yang, the five elements (wood, fire, metal, air, and water), and the four seasons of healing.

The Chinese believed that the cause of disease was imbalance. They believed that prevention is better than trying to cure illness. They spoke openly about tranquil, moderate exercise with seasonal diets. They stressed the importance of a serene mind. The task of a Chinese practitioner has always been to restore harmony and balance, thus enabling the body's natural healing mechanisms to work more efficiently. While Western medicine divides the body into parts, Chinese methods are based on the belief that illness is the interruption of a vital life force called **qi** or **chi** (pronounced chee).

yin and yang
Two principles whose interaction influences the destinies of creatures and things. The yin is the negative, characterized as dark and feminine. The yang is the positive, bright, and masculine.

qi (also chi)
A life-force energy throughout all organs of the body. Taoists believe good health depends on a free circulation of qi.

By restoring this energy flow, health is restored in the body (as well as in the mind).

The Chinese used three main treatments for the body: herbal cures, acupuncture, and moxibustion. Acupuncture is a treatment for pain and illness in which thin needles are positioned just under the skin at special nerve centers around the body. Moxibustion involved burning a small amount of a dried herb called *moxa* at the site of the acupuncture point. It helped to spread healing and warming throughout the body. The Chinese were considered experts in prescribing herbs and in the practice of acupuncture. They discovered the body's natural 24-hour cycle referred to as **circadian rhythms** (Figure 1–9). Among other things this rhythm determines the time that we sleep and the time that we awaken.

A highly respected Chinese scholar, Confucius, taught, "The body was a gift from your parents. It is considered disrespectful not to take care of yourself."

circadian rhythms
The body's natural 24-hour cycle.

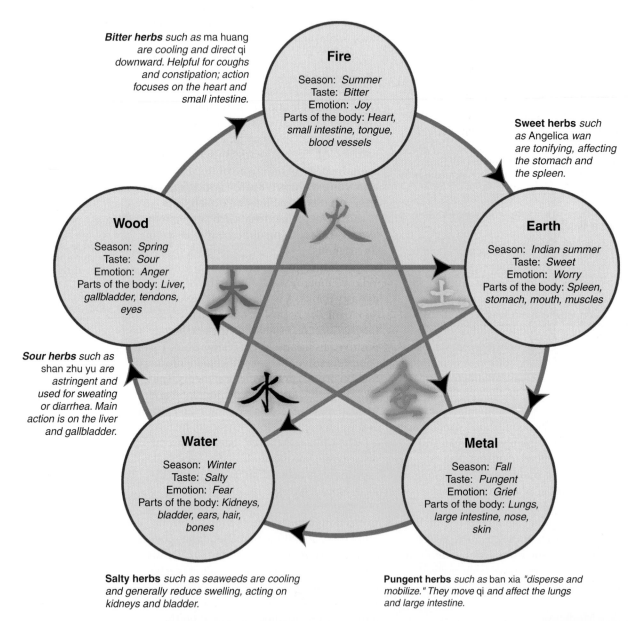

Bitter herbs such as ma huang are cooling and direct qi downward. Helpful for coughs and constipation; action focuses on the heart and small intestine.

Fire
Season: *Summer*
Taste: *Bitter*
Emotion: *Joy*
Parts of the body: *Heart, small intestine, tongue, blood vessels*

Sweet herbs such as Angelica *wan* are tonifying, affecting the stomach and the spleen.

Wood
Season: *Spring*
Taste: *Sour*
Emotion: *Anger*
Parts of the body: *Liver, gallbladder, tendons, eyes*

Earth
Season: *Indian summer*
Taste: *Sweet*
Emotion: *Worry*
Parts of the body: *Spleen, stomach, mouth, muscles*

Sour herbs such as shan zhu yu *are astringent and used for sweating or diarrhea. Main action is on the liver and gallbladder.*

Water
Season: *Winter*
Taste: *Salty*
Emotion: *Fear*
Parts of the body: *Kidneys, bladder, ears, hair, bones*

Metal
Season: *Fall*
Taste: *Pungent*
Emotion: *Grief*
Parts of the body: *Lungs, large intestine, nose, skin*

Salty herbs *such as seaweeds are cooling and generally reduce swelling, acting on kidneys and bladder.*

Pungent herbs *such as ban xia "disperse and mobilize." They move qi and affect the lungs and large intestine.*

Figure 1–9 The Chinese model of health represents five elements that form a network of relationships. The red arrows show how one element gives rise to another, while the gray arrows indicate how one element controls another.

Hebrew and Egyptian Culture

Hebrew traditions contained many laws to ensure health and to prevent disease. Precautionary isolation, quarantine, and the burning and boiling of clothing or utensils were often the remedy for the prevention or spreading of disease. Aromatics, such as frankincense, myrrh, galbanum, cinnamon, cassia, and rosemary were used for anointing and healing the sick. Unknown at the time, these crushed plants or essential oils contained antibacterial properties that helped prevent disease.

Knowledge of herbal remedies and formulations spread throughout ancient Europe during the time of the Egyptians. The Egyptians invented some of the earliest cosmetic, fragrance, and herbal preparations used for personal health remedies, religious ceremonies, and burial rights. Their focus on cleanliness gave rise to the building of an elaborate system of baths that were later expanded upon by the Greeks and, especially, by the Romans. Toiletries and bath potions were all part of this system. There was great emphasis on fragrance and lavish adornments.

The Egyptians were the first to develop methods for extracting herbal and flower essences through a system of distillation. To this day, **distillation** is the main method of extracting essential oils. Precious essences were used to make fragrant oils, ointments, and lotions. Steam is passed over the leaves and flowers, sometimes under vacuum or pressure, so that the essential oils within them are vaporized. The gaseous mixture of oil and water is collected and cooled in a condenser, returning the oil-water mixture to liquid form. Essential oils are insoluble in water. They are lighter than water and float to the top for easy collection. Because they do float, they are called **essential oils**. They are far from true oils because they have a complex molecular structure that contains many properties such as being antiseptic, or anti-inflammatory.

In 1862, recordings found on Egyptian papyri dating to about 1600 B.C. indicated that many common herbs, such as garlic and juniper, have been used medicinally for about 4,000 years. These recordings indicated that both medicine and surgery were extensively practiced. Many prescriptions were listed that included minerals, plants, and animal by-products. Hemp was used for eye problems. Poppy extracts were used to quiet crying children.

There is much information stemming from folklore regarding the discovery of ingredients and compounds used for the body. One documentary has it that slave girls washing clothes at the river's edge found that their feet, when immersed in the mud, became soft and white. This prompted them to use the mud on their face and hands.

Known for her elaborate lifestyle, Cleopatra, Queen of Egypt (51 B.C.), applied clay from the Nile River to her face and soon enhanced this experience by persuading palace alchemists to mix their secret blends of herbs and essential oils into this earthly mud concoction for added benefit. She indulged in enticing bath oils, milk baths, and fragrances. She adorned her head with elaborate wigs and clothing pieces. Kohl was used as eye makeup, which was placed on the eyelids to emphasize that area. Lashes and brows were darkened with soot from oil lamps. Materials and colors for face makeup, wigs, and clothing were derived from various plants, berries, and lead. Needless to say, many of these beautifying materials would not be acceptable by today's standards of cosmetic safety (Figure 1–10).

distillation
A main method of extracting essential oils.

essential oils
Oils that are lighter than water.

Figure 1–10 An example of an Egyptian woman typical of her time, wearing various adornments.

Greek Culture

Hippocrates (468–377 B.C.), a famous physician and teacher of medicine in the fifth century, gained a reputation as the ideal physician who was devoted, kind, and skillful. He came from a family of physicians and founded several schools of medicine. Hippocrates headed one school on the island of Cos. Many writings have been attributed to Hippocrates and his teachers. The theory of **four humors**—blood, phlegm, yellow bile, and black bile—determined a person's constitution, temperament, and health (Figure 1–11). Part of the healing of an individual was to balance the humors. All foods and herbs were listed by fundamental qualities—hot, cold, dry, or damp. He theorized that keeping these qualities in balance, as well as taking plenty of exercise and fresh air, maintained good health and allowed most diseases to cure themselves.

The Greek physician Claudius Galenus (A.D. 131–199) opposed this practice and reworked many of the old Hippocratic ideas, including reformulating the theory of humors. His writings became the standard medical texts for the Roman, Arab, and medieval physicians. Galenus has been cited as creating the first cold cream by mixing 12.5% beeswax and 50% olive oil together. Later, other natural oils such as almond oil were used, but these oils easily spoiled. In 1907, mineral oil replaced previously used oils and was found to be highly stable, requiring no preservatives.

The Greeks were brilliant artists and sculptors who made an association between appearance, character, and personality. Known as the Theory of Physiognomy, it was the study of a systematic correspondence of psychological characteristics to facial features or body structures. Busts, as well as full human sculptures, were skillfully designed following these principles. To this day, these guidelines are utilized in modern art and design, sculpturing a face during plastic or reconstructive surgery, and in makeup artistry.

Like their predecessors, the Greeks continued to design beautiful baths. They formulated elaborate fragrances and designed accessories such as hairpieces and other adornments for hair and clothing. They used **vermilion**, a red pigment, for lip and cheek color and created facial preparations from white lead.

Roman Culture

Roman culture followed the traditions of the Egyptians and Greeks. Roman armies used mineral springs for treating battle fatigue, rheumatism, and gout. The Romans, however, are most known for creating more elaborate baths with separate facilities for men and women. Steam therapy, body scrubs, massage, and other physical therapies were all available at the bathhouse.

The Romans excelled in public hygiene. They drained swamps to prevent disease. When building a town, it was placed away from any areas that had disease potential. They developed an aqueduct system to carry clean water and an elaborate sewer system to remove waste. Waste was drained away from the town and into the Tiber river (this obviously would not be done today!).

Scientists such as Pliny the Elder (A.D. 23–79) wrote 37 volumes of scientific writings covering topics such as geography, animals, botany, medicine, art, and architecture. Seven volumes covered the medicinal qualities of herbs, vegetables, and minerals. Pliny was cautious of herb sellers and physicians who touted the miracles of herbal remedies as a cure-all. He felt that these claims were unfounded and that the individuals promoting them were quacks.

Roman scientists and physicians were responsible for continuing the development of herbal health remedies. They created pharmacopoeias containing writings on hundreds of plants and their uses.

As the Romans moved west across the English Channel, they built walled cities such as Londinium in A.D. 60, known to you today as London, England. Elaborate baths were built in the countryside over hot sulphur springs. Beautiful mosaic tiled floors and pools expanded across an entire town. They offered steam therapy, body scrubs, massage, and physical therapies. Today, one can visit Bath, England, where the natural, hot bubbling sulphur waters are still considered quite healing for all sorts of body ailments despite the unpleasant odor emanating from the waters.

Whether in Europe or in their newly conquered lands, the Romans continued to practice the art of their ancestors, designing even greater masterpieces of art, tapestries, tiles, and baths. They built roads and highly crafted buildings. They brought herbal and beauty

four humors
Blood, phlegm, yellow bile, and black bile.

vermilion
A chemical compound of mercury and sulfur, originally obtained by grinding pure cinnabar; it is now created synthetically.

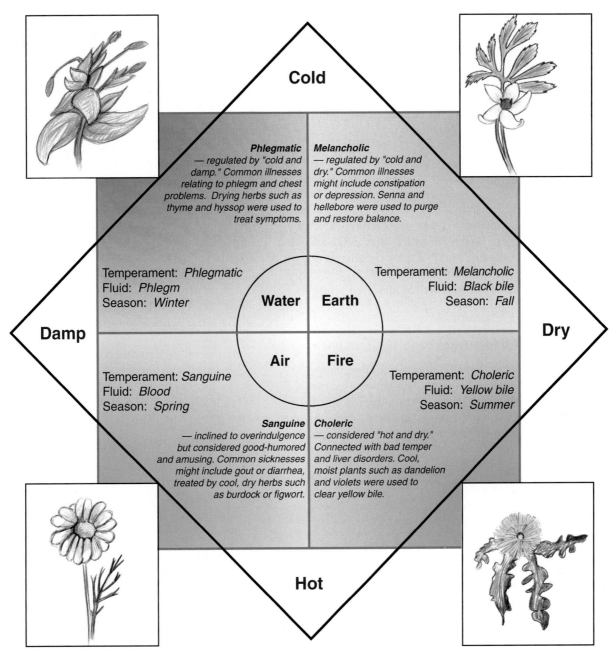

Figure 1–11 Hippocratic Model of Humors.

technology to enhance their own health and well-being. In approximately 454 B.C., Roman men began shaving off their facial hair, and a clean-shaven look became fashionable.

Indian Culture

Ayurveda (eye-ur-vayda) comes from two Sanskrit words—*ayur*, or life, and *veda*, or knowledge. Called the science of longevity or science of life, it is also interpreted to mean

knowledge of how to live. Ayurvedic medical texts date back to around 2500 B.C. Ayurveda is one of the world's oldest and most complete systems of natural healing, containing great wisdom for all humanity. Ancient India developed a coherent medical system that is still in practice today. Ayurvedic medicine is based on the belief that patients are responsible for their own preventive care and restoration.

Illness was seen as an imbalance and herbs and dietary alterations were used to

ayurveda
The science of longevity or the science of life.

restore equilibrium. As in both the Greek and Chinese models of health, ayurvedic principles emphasize treating the whole person using appropriate remedies for the mind, body, and spirit. This could include meditation, physical exercises, or herbs that are targeted toward the correction of some particular ailment.

Many ayurvedic treatments such as the pancha karma—five purification treatments—are part of a medical detoxification therapy. They are widely performed in spas and wellness centers today. Other specialized treatments assist in stress reduction or skin correction, all of which increase balance and harmony. Many of these treatments are based in the use of essential oils and herbal compounds as well as lifestyle alterations (Figure 1–12).

Middle Ages

After the fall of the Roman Empire in A.D. 476 bathing no longer was a daily ritual in Europe. During the era called the Dark Ages, plagues and other diseases were rampant and devastated entire villages. In

1399, bathing became law when King Henry IV decreed *"The Order of the Bath,"* which required all nobleman and women to bathe frequently.

Medical schools quickly spread throughout Europe. The School of Salerno, a very famous medical school in Italy, taught the Hippocratic principles of good diet, exercise, and fresh air. During this era, however, healing and herbalism were largely in the hands of the Church. Monasteries grew medicinal herbs and the monks and nuns tended to the sick. Healing remedies, combined with prayer, were very much part of the philosophy of curing a patient. All recordings were done in Latin, the official language of the Church. There were surgical procedures for plastic surgery, for example, correcting a cleft palate. There were also remedies using antibacterial herbs or minerals such as garlic and cooper salt mixtures.

In the 1500s, Paracelsus wrote the *Doctrine of Signatures,* which maintained that the outward appearance of a plant gave an indication as to the ailments that it could cure.

African Culture

African traditions included wearing colorful fabrics and adorning the face and body with color and design. Jewelry was made from bone and metal, and provided unique distinctions from tribe to tribe. Traditional African medicine practices are believed to be about 4,000 years old. These remedies spread throughout an entire continent. Many aspects of diverse healing systems are part of African medicine: herbalism, divination, and harmony. They defined health as balance and harmony, a basic system of ideas about the world. Anything that disrupts the natural order of the body and its structures is said to be sickness, including breaking social codes or order.

The Africans have many traditions that are unique to each tribe. The Nigerians use a system of color. For example, the color of chalk (white) represents purity and wholeness; the appearance of redness represents a transition or danger; and black represents human chaos. The study of African medicine and tradition is lengthy. One wonderful ingredient found in many skin care remedies, Shea butter, *Butyrospermum parkii,* is derived from the African Shea (Karite) tree nut. It has been a traditional compound for cen-

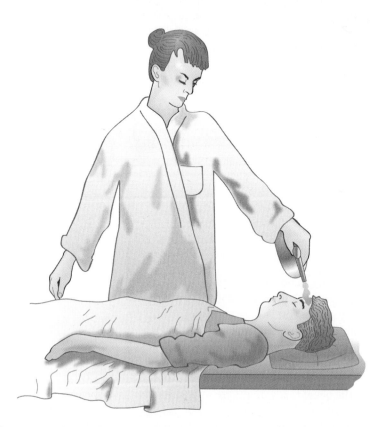

Figure 1–12 Ayurvedic oil treatments are relaxing and purifying to the client.

turies and is used for healing purposes as well as for its skin softening ability. It is still used today in spa body treatments.

Victorian Age

It is widely known that different cultures influenced cosmetic and health practices. From the Middle Ages to the Renaissance, the Elizabethan Age and the Age of Extravagance, beauty practices included the use of fragrant oils, intricate hairstyles, wigs, eye makeup, and highly colored preparations for the lips, cheeks, and eyes. Health and beauty rituals changed and altered to blend with the tradition of each era. A more austere period occurred during the reign of Queen Victoria (1837–1901). Makeup and elaborate clothing were discouraged and the look of both men and women was plain and austere. To preserve the health of the skin, beauty masks and packs were used. They were made from ingredients such as honey, eggs, milk, oatmeal, fruits, and vegetables. Today, we still use many facial and skin care preparations made up of many of the same products.

Native American Culture

Native Americans used colorful beads, headpieces, and specially designed clothing in tribal ceremonies. They believe in being in harmony with their surroundings, respecting all natural earth systems that supported them. They built many encampments on mineral springs. They discovered and used vapor caves, built steam baths, and participated in an early morning plunge into a cold river to invigorate the body.

Earlier settlers from England and Europe suffered from many illnesses and even malnutrition. Native American Indians sometimes came to their rescue by providing healing herbal remedies. Wound healing remedies such as flax seed and yucca were presented to help stop infection and death. As witnessed with earlier history, lack of knowledge concerning bacteria and body anatomy gave rise to superstition and unfounded practices. One of the most profound afflictions that reappeared many times throughout history was the hallucinogenic effects of ergot, a mold found in rye. It caused terrible mental affliction to those who were affected by it, causing hysteria and convulsions. The fear and ignorance of local authorities caused the death of many sufferers who were labeled witches or possessed by evil. Probably the most famous example of this tragedy were the witch trials of Salem, Massachusetts.

American Waters

Early settlers found that there were many mineral springs in America. According to the research of Monica Tuma Brown, in the late 1600s early New England settlers made pilgrimages to Stafford Springs, Connecticut, which is believed to be one of the first American spas. In the following centuries, many fine resorts and spas appeared along the East Coast and other areas of the country east, and eventually west, of the Mississippi. Some included Sulphur Springs, West Virginia; Hot Springs, Virginia; Excelsior Springs, Missouri; Saratoga Springs, New York; Bedford Springs, Pennsylvania; and Glenwood Springs, Colorado. Water therapies were highly accepted and documented in early U.S. texts. In 1927 some of these therapies were well defined by a U.S. physician, William Edward Fitch. He promoted the idea that all medical schools should teach **hydriatics**, which is the study of the physiological and therapeutic properties of mineral waters upon the body. In the late 1940s spa medicine was newly defined as a pampering, beauty experience. It no longer held the esteem of being part of the health care system.

hydriatics
The study of the physiological and therapeutic properties of mineral waters upon the body.

Transition to Western Medicine

By the end of the seventeenth century, the perfumery and distillation industries attracted large commercial enterprises in France. This ultimately began to redirect the original focus of essential oils and botanicals. The idea of disease prevention dissolved into the lucrative business of perfumery. The tradition of the interrelatedness of body and spirit, and the interdependence of medicine and psychology, was forgotten. The medical and preventive focal point of herbs and aromatics was lost.

Treatments went from the hands of the individual chemists and researchers and into a new realm of "professionals." Technical chemistry came into existence and speculation gave way to logic and deductive reasoning. Nineteenth-century chemists were able to identify the various components of the oils and lay out the foundation for their properties. With this information, synthetic counterparts could be made. The growth of the modern day drug industry was based on these findings. By the mid-twentieth century, the role of essential oils was focused on perfumes, cosmetics, and foodstuffs.

During the mid to late nineteenth century and the early twentieth century, the focus of perfumery as well as the inception of new medical societies both in England and the U.S. replaced the traditions of homeopathy and herbal medicine. Allopathic, or Western, medicine no longer accepted anything that could not be proven scientifically. Medicine became segmented, leaving behind many of the earlier traditions of treating the body holistically.

Many of these earlier traditions are once again reappearing. Armed with knowledge of anatomy and physiology and the science behind them, earlier medical models have reappeared and have bridged into modern day health care. The skin care industry both in Europe and North America continues to research technologies that combine modern science and the natural components to help improve the health of the skin. Spas integrated with both herbal and essential oils and traditional medicine are finding their way throughout North America.

Evolution of American Skin Care

Science/Medicine

- **1846**—Theron T. Pond in New York developed witch hazel extract, used primarily as a household remedy for gunshot wounds, sunburn, and other lesions. In 1875, he expanded the product line to include Pond's Extract Soap, Vanishing Cream, and Cold Cream.

- **1951**—Researchers G. S. Berenson and G. E. Burch determined that water could penetrate the stratum corneum layer of the skin, and the "moisturizer" was born.

- **1952**—The Food, Drug, and Cosmetic Act (FDCA) outlawed misleading claims in advertising and harmful ingredients in cosmetic products.

- **1960s**—Aida Grey developed a mask featuring salicylic acid for exfoliation.

- **1967**—Robert Deimer developed Derma Analysis, a precise method for analyzing skin that became an industry standard.

- **1983**—Dr. Eugene J. Van Scott and Dr. Ruey J. Yu began Herald Pharmacal, the original licensee to manufacture glycolic acid products for cosmetic use under their U.S. patent.

- **1985**—Ortho Pharmaceuticals launched Retin-A, a vitamin-A based drug for the treatment of acne.

- **1990**—California dermatologist Dr. Howard Murad launched his line of skin care products with the introduction of Alpha Hydroxy Acids (AHAs) to the professional skin care industry.

- **1991**—Herald Pharmacal launched M.D. Formulations, a collection of glycolic acid preparations, to the esthetics and dermatologist markets.

- **1995**—FDA approved Renova, a wrinkle cream developed by Ortho Pharmaceuticals. It is classified as a drug because it causes cell changes.

Beauty

- **1890s**—Personal bath and cosmetic care for the general public was introduced by *Vogue* and *Harper's Bazaar*.

- **1902**—Sears, Roebuck & Company advertised a bust cream as well as other personal care products.

- **1902**—Helena Rubinstein left her home in Poland to establish her first beauty salon in Australia.

- **1910**—Taking on the fictitious name of Elizabeth Arden, Canadian-born Florence Nightingale Graham moved to New York and opened her first salon named The Red Door.

- **1915**—Max Factor developed Flexible Greasepaint, the first makeup ever developed for film to make actors appear more natural on screen.

- **1920s**—Aida Grey founded her own cosmetic and skin care line, using natural ingredients in her products in spite of the introduction of synthetics and petrochemicals by manufacturers during the 1950s.

- **1932**—Charles Revson, with his brother, Martin, and chemist Charles Lachman, started the Revlon Company in New York, which developed the first homogenized liquid makeup.
- **1938**—Max Factor launched his revolutionary pancake makeup, the first water-soluble cake foundation for Hollywood.
- **1946**—Estée Lauder started her company with a jar of skin cream developed by a chemist uncle. Her unique marketing concept offering "a free gift with purchase," revolutionized the sale of skin care products and fragrances.
- **1968**—Adrien Arpel started her own cosmetics business in New York City. She was the first to introduce professional skin care into department stores.
- **1970**—Oil of Olay became an instant household phrase.
- **1970s**—The first waterproof mascara was launched by Helena Rubinstein.
- **1980**—Lydia Sarfati started her company, Repêchage, where the four-layer masque became a revolutionary esthetics treatment based upon biomarine technology.

Education

- **1946—CIDESCO (Comité International D'Esthétique et de Cosmétologie)** was formed in Zurich, Switzerland, to give estheticians the opportunity to exchange experiences with their colleagues of other countries. In the 1980s, it set up a curriculum for schools to teach a solid spa therapy course. A diploma was awarded to those who could pass the rigorous test. According to some sources, the CIDESCO diploma represents the most prestigious qualification in the field of esthetics and beauty therapy. It is the equivalent of a master's degree for esthetics. There are more than 140 CIDESCO schools worldwide requiring 1200 hours of study.
- **1966**—Romanian-born Christine Valmy opened the first esthetics school in the U.S., having developed the first-ever vocational course for scientific facial treatments and makeup.
- **1976**—Robert Deimer founded the American Institute of Aesthetics, the first postgraduate school for esthetics in the U.S.
- **1978**—CIDESCO diplomat Carole Walderman began the Von Lee International School of Esthetics in Baltimore, MD.
- **1979**—The Catherine Hinds Institute, the first state-accredited esthetics school, was founded in Massachusetts.
- **1980s**—Sylvie Hennessey developed a curriculum of study for advanced graduate training in esthetics.
- **1980s**—The International Dermal Institute was founded in Los Angeles, CA by Jane Martin and Raymond Wurwand as a post-graduate training facility for estheticians.
- **1985**—CIDESCO USA, Aestheticians International Association (AIA), and the Skin Care Association of America (SCAA) merged to form the Federation of American Esthetics (FAE).
- **1985**—CIDESCO diplomat Barbara Salomone founded the Conservatory of Esthetics with six campuses across the U.S.
- **1985**—Annette Hanson opened her postgraduate training center, Atelier Esthetique, located in the Empire State Building in New York City. Hanson developed the 600-hour curriculum for the New York State's esthetics license in 1993.
- **1994**—Bonnie Day started the American Aestheticians Education Association, designed to bring advanced education to estheticians and spa therapists.
- **2001**—Utah became the first state to pass a bill offering two levels of licensure for estheticians—basic and master levels.

Publishing

- **1975**—*Dermascope* magazine, one of the first skin care magazines published for the esthetics professional, was begun by Ron Renee as a four-page newsletter. Renee was the founder of The Aestheticians' International Association, an organization for skin care professionals.
- **1979**—Milady Publishing Company, an imprint of Delmar Learning, published the *Standard Textbook for Professional*

CIDESCO (Comité International D'Esthétique et de Cosmétologie)

International organization formed in Zurich, Switzerland, in 1946, to give estheticians the opportunity to exchange experiences with their colleagues in other countries.

Estheticians by Joel Gerson. His book pioneered standards for teaching skin care in schools and for state board examinations.

- **1979**—Aida Grey published *The Aida Grey Beauty Book* with Lippincott Williams and Williams.

- **1985**—Publisher Dr. Jean Legrand purchased the rights for the American version *of Les Nouvelles Esthetiques (LNE)*, first published in France in the 1940s. The magazine brought new information to the growing American market.

There are many influential people who have made, and continue to make, major contributions to our industry. During the past five years, many dedicated individuals have worked diligently with state boards to obtain separate licensing for estheticians. There are postgraduate schools in many states and the education of American estheticians will continue through the new millennium.

American and European skin care visionaries spoke of something greater than performing "just a facial." Combined services for total well-being was the outcome of combining European healing modalities, including spa water therapies, and scientific skin care technologies. It is these earlier pioneers and visionaries whom we must not forget, including the esthetic professionals who followed through the 1980s and 1990s. Current industry leaders carry the torch for many of us who continue to research and seek technological developments that make major contribution to the world of aging and preventive care.

Pioneers of the Twentieth Century

In 1928, French chemist René-Maurice Gattefosse pursued his interest in the healing properties of essential oils and extracts. Upon receiving a ghastly burn on his hand in his lab, he immediately plunged it into a lavender extract. To his surprise, the burn healed with continual application of the lavender. He pursued more experiments with essential oils. He believed that the essential oils were more effective than their synthetic substitutes. The constituents of essential oils interact with the body's chemistry in a direct manner, affecting certain organs or systems.

Dr. Jean Valnet used essential oils in basic programs to help treat psychiatric disorders.

He believed that there should be no gap between a traditional natural approach to healing and one that is more analytical—Western medicine.

Madame Marguerite Maury was greatly influenced by the work of Dr. Valnet. She applied his theories to beauty therapies and found that correctly selected essences could address skin correction. She set up the first aromatherapy clinics in Paris, Britain, and Switzerland. Two prestigious awards were given to Ms. Maury for her work in essential oils and cosmetology.

European pioneers who arrived on American shores after World War II left their mark in molding and forming the future of esthetics in the United States. Their knowledge of healing body therapies linked the more American clinical approach to facial treatments to what it is today. Many individuals contributed to building a foundation for our current esthetics industry. While we do not have room to highlight everyone, those individuals are deeply acknowledged for their contribution.

The Future

The future of esthetics is here and now. It did not arrive easily. Along with the major contributions already mentioned, it is interesting to hear how our current colleagues moved through the realm of twentieth-century growth.

According to a leading veteran esthetician and business consultant, Douglas Preston, of Preston Wynne Learning Systems, and president of an award-winning day spa,

In the l970s and 1980s, estheticians were essentially the pioneers who were first to carry the "cosmetician" professional role into something more sophisticated, specialized, and decidedly separate from traditional beauty services. . . . (We) saw the emergence of treatment products as the new focus for major cosmetics companies. . . . I remember the day Shiseido informed me to place emphasis on skin care products rather than makeup during my department store customer appointments. Suddenly I was an "expert" in a discipline about which I knew very little. This directive force launched my esthetics career.

. . . Treatments were still a novelty and condition-specific approaches in salon facials were just beginning to develop. Acne, not yet as well managed as it is today, was a chief impetus for bringing new clients into the salon.

Since most states had one domain of licensing—cosmetology—skin specialists basically received most of their training in a school of cosmetology, with an emphasis on hair design and chemical services. Thirty hours of skin care was on the curriculum in most cosmetology schools. Many estheticians traveled hundreds of air miles to and from various conferences and advanced training just to learn more about their profession.

Pioneering medical skin specialist and international consultant, Jane Crawford, of Jane Crawford & Associates, performed esthetic programs in the 1980s in the maternity department of a North Carolina hospital (Figure 1–13). The services were well received and to this day are still supported by the hospital administration. She recalls that

We needed more advanced training since what we knew were basic treatments only. We searched for new products to meet our needs. Many of us introduced alphahydroxy acid (AHA) peels (also known as glycolic acid peels) as a way to advance our treatments. Most estheticians were found in skin care clinics, destination day spas, and salons.

Figure 1–13 Jane Crawford, president of Jane Crawford & Associates, international consultant and a pioneering medical skin specialist.

During the 1970s and 1980s, few protocols for facial treatments were written for more challenging skin conditions in the average salon. Most of the time, clients ended up in a medical office because they did not have anywhere else to go. This situation forced many cosmetologists to seek out further education so that they could perform treatments addressing these specialized needs, thus bridging their work with their medical counterparts. During the mentioned eras, research for medicine was taking place throughout the world. Some of these discoveries would later be incorporated into medical and skin care products.

Emergence of Industry Conferences

By the late 1980s, trade shows emerged separately from the traditional hair shows. Numerous European skin care companies and American companies spread across the floor of convention halls, showing a plethora of the latest product technology and with upgraded packaging to meet the American market. Advanced equipment and furniture were displayed as well.

During those earlier years, it was obvious to vendors that it was difficult to sell a product when their potential buyer—the esthetician or salon owner—had very little background in cosmetic science as well as little understanding of the histology of the skin. Many didn't even understand how to run a profitable business. Many products with more advanced ingredients were based on a science that was often beyond the understanding of the average American esthetician or body specialist. There needed to be a greater emphasis on education; hence, trade shows became a forum to spread the message.

Some idealists, however, felt that the emphasis was on product and not necessarily on education. While this may have been the case, experience has shown, that product line developers are often the experts who research and understand the qualities and properties of their ingredients. There are a few major cosmetic and skin care manufacturers throughout the United States. One manufacturer may produce products for hundreds of different brands. Some product lines may own laboratories and manufacturing.

Different manufacturers maintain libraries of data on research of raw materials. Most follow FDA guidelines for manufacturing, meaning that there are checks and balances along the entire manufacturing process. This includes standards of sanitation and cleanliness. Many cosmetic chemists are highly skilled professionals who work with and compose thousands of ingredients and formulas annually. They constantly update research documents on the latest raw materials.

The mid- to late 1990s gave rise to more trade shows and conventions where estheticians could spend an intensive weekend cramming in knowledge and perusing the latest in skin care technologies. Some of the shows provided pre- and post-show classes by leading experts, many of whom were the manufacturers. This prompted more educational seminars by leading experts who learned their trade through years of experience. Some experts had developed their own product line.

Small "advanced training centers" emerged throughout various parts of the country. More cosmetology schools, including junior colleges, put in a separate esthetic curriculum within their cosmetology department. During the past 30 years, many pioneering individuals took on the role of establishing schools, professional product lines, and advanced training centers. These notable individuals also gave up their time to educate across the country.

According to Preston,

> The 1990s were a "coming of age" for the modern esthetician . . . the American skin care professional was more experimental and confident . . . performing advanced exfoliation treatments, high-performance home care products, and crossover paramedical services. Estheticians . . . were required to keep apace of rapid changes within the skin care industry . . . were finally becoming true career professionals and businesspeople. The day spa phenomenon tremendously boosted consumer awareness of skin care services, and an increasingly savvy and financially fortified client began to swell the appointment schedules."

Summary

Modern skin and body care is rooted in ancient civilizations' philosophy of total body harmony. The prevention of disease was a main focus in the medicine and health care systems that existed in each civilization. Hundreds of herbs and essential oils were studied and documented. Early chemists and physicians worked together to maintain health and beauty. Along with preventive health care, beauty was also a mainstay within earlier cultures. Hairpieces, jewelry, clothing, makeup, sculptures, paintings, and architecture were all part of earlier societies. Much of this changed during the Dark Ages, where studies became secluded deep within the cloisters and monasteries. The monks took many of the materials, transcribing them into books of medicine. Overwhelming plagues and illnesses spread throughout the world. With this, the earlier traditions and systems of hygiene were no longer as prevalent.

Preventive health care continued as more institutions of higher learning and hospitals that cared for the sick were built. As medicine took on new forms, a transition came during the 1800s, when emphasis was turned to a lucrative perfume industry. Traditional health care methods were no longer considered credible and were discontinued.

What is important to note is that the earlier spas had been institutions of health and total wellness. In the later part of the nineteenth and early twentieth centuries, they no longer had this emphasis or even credibility. A once health-oriented environment was transformed into a beauty spa. While part of health care is definitely relaxation and stress reduction, the emphasis on returning spas back to their more holistic approach is on the rise in the U.S. In other parts of Europe, "taking of the waters" or the "cures" are part of national health care systems. Skin care is very much a part of this system.

The pioneering work of a few estheticians, who had full European training in both skin and spa modalities, resulted in a few separate institutes of skin care studies. It is from these roots that modern day skin care evolved. It is more than a pampering and feel-good session. With the re-emergence of a total service environment, whether in a full-service salon, day spa, medical spa, or destination spa, the choice for a more corrective and long-term skin management program is possible.

Discussion Questions

1. Ancient civilizations recognized the therapeutic aspects of indigenous components in creating a balanced and harmonious lifestyle. Discuss how these are still relevant to esthetics in today's spa environment.

2. Create a time chart tracing the evolution of skin care chronologically, noting the major contribution of each historical period and culture.

3. Significant strides have been made in skin care in the United States during the twentieth century. Name five American pioneers in skin care from this period and state the importance of their work.

4. The baby boomer population has had a significant impact on the field of esthetics. Explain the benefits of a good skin care program specific to this population.

5. Select three career opportunities that appeal to you and determine the value that you will bring to each as a licensed esthetician. Investigate additional skills that may be required to pursue your interests.

Additional Reading

Brown, Monica Tuma. 2001. "Spa and Medicine, Mindful of the Past, Movement of the Future, Part 1." *Spa Management Magazine*, April: 9–35.

Brown, Monica Tuma, and Christian Pascal. 1966. "Botanical Bliss" *Massage & Bodyworks*, Spring: 8–13.

———. 1995. "Evolution & Essence of Spa Therapies." *Massage & Bodyworks*, Summer: 53–55.

Crawford, Jane. 2001. "The Potential of Medi-Spas." *Skin Inc.*, May: 47–48.

Ergil, Devin V., et al. 1997. *Ancient Healing, Unlocking the Mysteries of Health & Healing Through the Ages*. Lincolnwood, Ill: Publications International.

Frawley, David. 1997. *Ayurveda and the Mind, The Healing of Consciousness*. Twin Lakes, Wis.: Lotus Press.

Hammer, Leon. 1990. *Dragon Rises—Red Bird Flies, Psychology of Chinese Medicine*. Barrytown, N.Y.: Station Hill Press.

Hoffman, David. 1996. *The Complete Illustrated Holistic Herbal*. New York: Barnes & Noble.

Joshi, Sunil. 1997. *Ayurveda & Panchakarma*. Twin Lakes, Wis.: Lotus Press.

Kamin, Amy R. 2001. "The Future of the Clinical Spa." *Skin Inc.*, May, 50–54.

Lauder, Estée. 1985. *Estée, A Success Story*. New York: Random House.

Lawless, Julia. 1995. *The Illustrated Encyclopedia of Essential Oils*. New York: Barnes & Noble.

Lockie, Andrew, and Nicola Geddes. 1995. *Homeopathy, The Principles & Practice of Treatment*. New York: DK Publishing.

Mason, Sara. 2001. "Spa Profile: Beyond." *Skin Inc.*, May, 74–78.

Pascal, Christian, and Monica Tuma Brown. 1993. "Our Skin & the Sea." *Les Nouvelles Esthetiques*, September: 56–60.

PDR People's Desk Reference for Essential Oils. 1999. Orem, Utah: Essential Science Publishing.

Ody, Penelope. 1993. *The Complete Medicinal Herbal*. New York: DK Publishing.

———. 2000. *Complete Guide To Medicinal Herbs*. New York: DK Publishing.

Porter, Roy. 1997. *Medicine: A History of Healing: Ancient Traditions To Modern Practices*. New York: Marlow & Co.

Time Life Books, ed. 1997. "What Life Was Like [series].ˆ Alexandria, Va.: Time Life Inc.

Warrier, Gopi, and Deepika Gunawant. 1997. *The Complete Illustrated Guide To Ayurveda*. Rockport, Mass: Element Books.

Helpful Web Sites

http://www.dermascope.com (Aesthetics International Association [AIA])

http://www.salonprofessionals.org (The American Aestheticians Education Association [AAEA], Bonnie Day, 972-394-1740)

http://www.salonprofessionals.org (CIDESCO, Beauty Therapy Association, N.C.A.—CIDESCO Section, U.S.A.)

http://www.dayspamagazine.com (*Day Spa Magazine*)

http://www.dermascope.com (*Dermascope Magazine*, 20th Anniversary Issue, [1996])

http://www.lneonline.com (*Les Nouvelles Esthetiques*)

http://www.SkinInc.com (*Skin, Inc. Magazine*)

http://www. miami.edu/touchresearch/ index.html (Touch Research Institutes, University of Miami School of Medicine)

The Natural Sciences

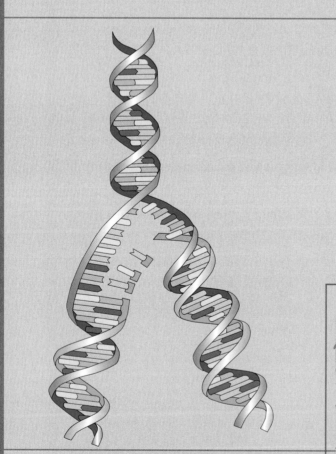

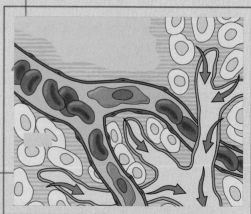

PART II

Part Outline

Chapter 2   Anatomy and Physiology of the Skin

Chapter 3   Body Systems

Chapter 4   Bones, Muscles, and Nerves of the Face and Skull

Chapter 5   Bacteriology and Sanitation

Chapter 6   Nutrition

Building a solid foundation is the core of any career. In skin care, as in the other health-related professions, the practical, hands-on work is the final result of months and months of preparation. One must possess a basic understanding of *what* is underneath the hands—in this case, the skin with all of its complexities—before the hands can be effective. While the excitement of being a new student can sometimes cause one to be more focused on what the hands can do, the student must first be willing to use the mind to comprehend and study the underlying principle that make esthetics a viable profession. This text places a great deal of emphasis on the basic skin care sciences because they are the foundation on which you will implant and build the information in subsequent chapters.

In the chapters that follow, you will learn about the largest sensory organ in the body, the skin, and how it functions and is supported by body systems and structure. The microscopic world of bacterial organisms will be explored as you learn about sanitation and how it can impact the skin. Finally, you will learn the importance of good nutrition and how what goes into the body affects the skin.

Chapter 2
Anatomy and
Physiology of the Skin

Chapter Objectives

After reading this chapter, you should be able to:

- Explain the basic principles of the function of the skin.
- Describe the anatomy and function of the cell and describe each part of the cell.
- Name the different types of tissues and their functions.
- Identify various cells and their functions within the skin.
- Differentiate the layers of the skin: epidermis and dermis.

Chapter Outline

Introduction
Skin Function
Cell Physiology
 and Biochemistry
Specialized Cell
 Function and Tissues
Layers of the Skin

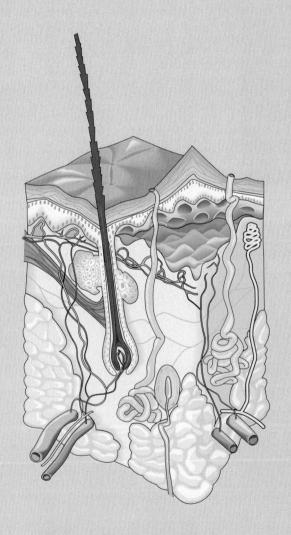

Introduction

A thorough understanding of the science of the skin and the systems that affect it is essential to your success as a professional esthetician. **Esthetics** (aesthetics) is a branch of anatomical science that deals with the overall health and well-being of the skin, the largest organ of the human body. Our contributions play an important role in correcting and maintaining the skin's balance and integrity.

Whenever the skin is touched, pressed, soothed, or receives internal nutrients or topical products, the body's neurological and biological functions are affected. Smells, sounds, and textures all affect our well-being. Touch is so important that the University of Miami has dedicated an entire division to scientific studies on this topic. Massage, therapeutic touch, the growth of newborns, recovery from disease, and the effects of touch on cancer patients are just some of the topics that have been studied. The skin has the ability to alter its appearance through emotional states, overall health, or reveal signs of various disorders. It is a remarkable organ that connects us to the outside world.

When we perform facial or body treatments, our therapeutic touch interacts with the skin (Figure 2–1). When there is a need for skin correction—acne, dryness, aging, stress—experience has shown that the skin responds favorably when it is treated as part of a directed program of facial care. This may be combined with medical intervention when necessary.

Understanding the basic principles of anatomy and physiology greatly contributes to your ability to perform an accurate face analysis. It influences your aptitude to make proper choices in treatment and products. Throughout this course, we consistently refer to numerous stimuli that make a difference in the skin's integrity. Do not be too worried about trying to understand everything in the first reading. As you progress, all segments of this text will fall neatly into place, providing a harmonious and integrated understanding of the whole. Combining practical hands-on experience with consistent referral back to each chapter, along with your own research,

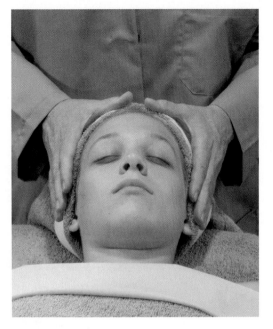

Figure 2–1 Touch is important in the treatment and overall health of the skin.

> **esthetics (aesthetics)**
> A branch of anatomical science that deals with the overall health and well-being of the skin, the largest organ of the human body.

helps foster greater insight. This text will serve as a reference source for you throughout your entire career.

Skin Function

Proper body performance is dependent on all systems working together harmoniously. The skin functions as a system with many parts operating seamlessly to support and protect the body (Figure 2–2). A highly complex organ, the skin is self-repairing and protective. It serves as the interface for the body. It acts as a barrier, preventing transport of harmful materials as well as water loss. Adult skin weighs roughly seven pounds and is approximately 48 inches wide by 96 inches long. Accounting for approximately 15% of body weight, the skin weighs approximately 6.6 lbs. Each square inch contains approximately 15 feet of blood vessels, 12 feet of nerves, 650 sweat glands, and 100 oil glands. It contains more than one-quarter of all the blood in the body, and half the primary immune cells. Thickness varies depending on location. Skin on the back is the thickest; the skin on the eyelids is the thinnest.

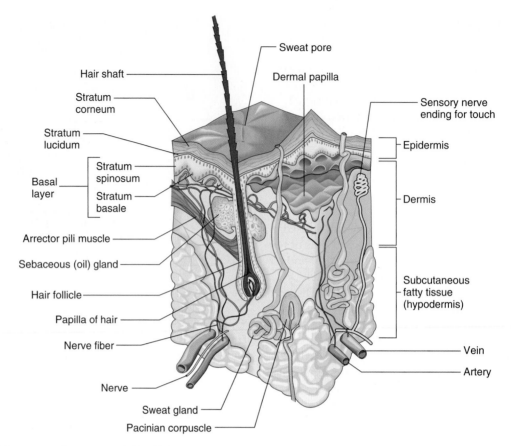

Figure 2–2 Structures of the skin.

Protection

The skin serves as a barrier to protect the inner parts of the body. It discourages and helps prevent invasion by microorganisms. It provides a cushion against physical trauma to protect the bones, muscles, and internal organs. The skin acts as a barrier to help prevent irritating chemicals from entering the body. Outer skin structures protect against windburn and dryness. The skin also keeps water from leaving the body. Water makes up approximately 60% of an adult's body weight. It is a major component of all the cells and is vital for life.

Temperature Regulation

The skin helps to regulate body temperature by warming and cooling the body. During exposure to cold, the body is kept warm through a decrease in blood flow to the skin's surface. Body fat serves as insulation to keep the body warm. When the body is hot, the skin manufactures sweat, which evaporates, allowing the body to cool. Blood vessels dilate in order to assist in cooling the blood.

Healing

The dermis of the skin has the ability to self-heal, repairing tears and injuries. When injured or impaired, the outer skin can perform biochemical reactions to restore itself. The skin manufactures melanin, the body's natural sunscreen, to protect itself against injuries that are caused by exposure to the sun's ultraviolet light.

Immunity

A primary importance of the skin is its immune system. The skin is the largest organ for immune response and function. It contains numerous **immune cells** to help identify, block, control, and eradicate germs and microorganisms from affecting the skin and

immune cells
Cells that help identify, block, control, and eradicate germs and microorganisms from affecting the skin and entering the body.

SKILLS ● FOR ● SUCCESS

Licensing and the Law

Many estheticians enter training with a limited understanding of licensing laws. For those who happened upon the career without the benefit of a historical perspective, you should know that in the United States esthetics evolved from the field of cosmetology. It has only been in the last 20 years or so that estheticians acquired the right to a separate license.

However, today there are many schools that offer only esthetic training and are not linked to a cosmetology school or program. These esthetic training schools operate separately and are responsible for establishing their own credentials. Nevertheless they may be governed by the same state agency as a cosmetology school, for example, the State Board of Cosmetology. But, it is important to note that not all states are subject to specific laws or practices regarding esthetics training.

You should be currently enrolled in a school that has been inspected and licensed by a state governing board. Your school may even be accredited by a federal agency such as the Department of Education. If you are unsure, you may want to ask the director of your school for credentials that define the school's status.

Schooling is one matter. When it comes to individual licensing, there may be an entirely different set of circumstances depending on the state you reside in. Today, most states do have separate licensure for estheticians; however, there are still some states with minimal licensing laws or none at all. Therefore, you may not have the opportunity to obtain a license in the state you work in. If in doubt, you should check with your state licensing board to understand what the law is in your state.

Generally speaking, if your state does offer an esthetic license you can expect to obtain what is known as "reciprocity" from state to state. That is, once you have earned a license in a particular state, you can apply for comparable licensing in another state. However, here is the dilemma: The number of hours required to become a licensed esthetician can vary from state to state. Most states require a certain number of clock hours, not course or credit hours, to take the licensing exam. For your own protection you should be aware of the number of hours required in your state or any other state you may wish to work in. If these are not agreeable, you should seek assistance from the state governing board to determine your eligibility to work.

You also want to be aware of any laws that may prevent you from establishing your own business, if that is your goal upon graduation. Certain states have levels of licensure. This may put you in the position of having to undergo an apprenticeship or to work under another established professional for a certain period of time before going out on your own. You will want to find out just who you can work under in those circumstances.

If all this talk of licensing and laws gives you the jitters, keep in mind that licensing laws are put in place to protect the consumer. They also uphold the standard of a profession. Just as you would not want to see a physician who does not have a valid medical license, you would not want someone practicing skin care without an esthetic license.

There are also legal and insurance issues. Always stay within the boundaries of your training. In case of mishap or malpractice you want to make sure you are protected and do not run the risk of losing the license you worked so hard to earn.

The following Internet addresses may be helpful when it comes to understanding licensing requirements and laws:

http://www.beautytech.com
http://www.skininc.com
http://www.milbank.org

entering the body. The body's immune function will also react to allergens and irritating substances.

Sensory

The skin contains many nerves that detect cold, heat, pressure, and pain. Nerves also are responsible for signaling other nerves to facilitate muscle movement.

Cell Physiology and Biochemistry

Cells are referred to as the basic building blocks of the human body. Their main job is to manufacture protein, which becomes the building material for making the tissues and larger organs that make up the human body. As the basic unit of all life, cells are powerhouses of activity. Understanding the cell is critical to comprehending the overall functioning of the skin and the body. Internal and external stimuli, including the environment, nutrients, drugs, skin treatments, and products all affect these microscopic units.

Bacteria and some other organisms called **protozoa** are one-celled organisms (Figure 2–3). They are able to exist as a single cell because they have, within that one cell, all the systems necessary to keep them alive.

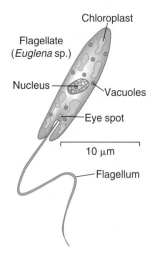

Flagellate (*Euglena* sp.)

Chloroplast

Nucleus

Vacuoles

Eye spot

10 μm

Flagellum

Figure 2–3 Protozoa are one-celled microscopic organisms that can cause diseases in humans. They have a well-defined nucleus with no cell wall, and a tail-like appendage that aids in movement.

cells
The basic building blocks of the human body that manufacture protein; they become the building material for making tissues and larger organs that make up the human body.

protozoa
One-celled organisms.

selective permeability
The characteristic of letting some substances in and shutting out others.

nutrients
Foods that have been broken down by the stomach and intestinal system so they may be absorbed and used by the body.

The cells of the human body cannot live independently, at least not for very long. Each cell contains mechanisms to process food, oxygen, water, and waste. Cells can be *specialized*, meaning that they have a specific function to perform.

Biochemical Manufacturing

Some skin cells manufacture biochemicals that cause other functions to occur. The skin can also manufacture enzymes that break down molecules and destroy cells.

The Cell as a Factory

Cells are busy factories that actually process food, oxygen, water, and waste, almost as if they were separate organisms (Figure 2–4). Despite being microscopic, they are a vital part of a much bigger system. When workers are sick or on strike, the factory cannot produce its product. Cells likewise are fundamentally important to the function of the entire body and its ability to live. Therefore, we must understand cell function prior to understanding the role of the skin.

Cell Membrane

The cell membrane is an outside barrier that helps contain the cell parts (Figure 2–5). This membrane is an important part of the cell. Think of the cell membrane as the skin of the cell, just as our skin is the protective barrier for our body.

Cell membranes are made of fats (lipids) and proteins, which can be permeable, which means that substances can pass through the membrane. More specifically, the cell membrane possesses a characteristic called **selective permeability**, which means that it has the capacity to let some substances in and shut others out.

Membranes allow **nutrients** to pass into the cell. Nutrients are foods that have been broken down by the stomach and intestinal system so that they can be absorbed and used by the body. They are delivered throughout the body by the bloodstream. Water and oxygen, which are vital to life and perform numerous functions, are also allowed into the cell. As a result of nutrient processing, the cell conversely uses the membrane to dispose of waste material, such as carbon

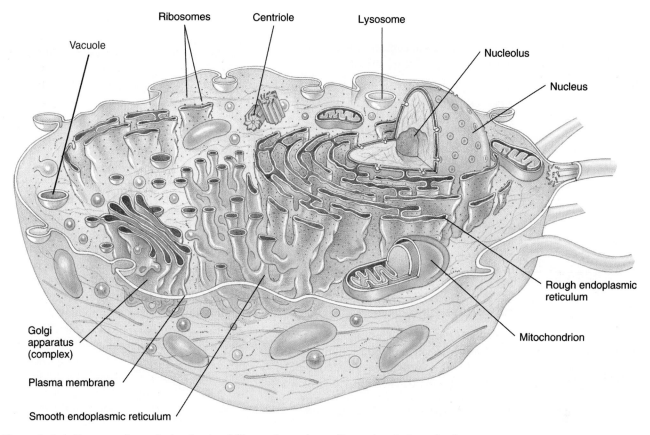

Figure 2–4 A diagram of a typical animal cell illustrating a three-dimensional view of cell ultrastructure.

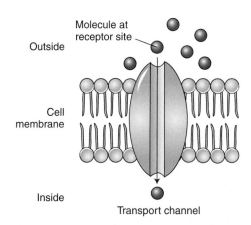

Figure 2–5 The cell membrane regulates substances that flow in and out of the cell. It has receptors to allow specific molecules to enter such as hormones, nutrients, and oxygen.

dioxide. Blood is responsible for bringing nutrients, oxygen, and water to the cell. It is also responsible for carrying away the waste materials.

Another important part of the cell membrane are the small structures that protrude

out of the membrane like antennas or satellites on top of a building. These structures are called receptor sites. Their function is to receive signals from other parts of the body in the form of biochemicals and hormones.

Cytoplasm

Inside the cell very small parts, referred to as organelles, float within a jellylike, watery fluid called cytoplasm. Each organelle has a specific function, just as a factory has different machines designated for specific purposes.

Mitochondria

Mitochondria are organelles responsible for producing energy for the cell. They break down nutrients that the blood has delivered, mainly sugars, fats, and parts of proteins called **amino acids,** into smaller units that are used by the cells for energy. Mitochondria utilize nutrients and oxygen to manufacture **adenosine triphosphate (ATP),** the substance that provides energy to

amino acids
A group of molecules used by the body to synthesize protein.

adenosine triphosphate (ATP)
A substance that provides energy to the cell.

the cell. ATP is produced in all cells that produce energy for the body in general. It also converts oxygen to carbon dioxide, which is a waste product that we breathe out.

Endoplasmic Reticulum

The endoplasmic reticulum is a series of small canals within the cytoplasm. They allow structures and substances to move around within the watery, jellylike cytoplasm. Similar to the way the bloodstream distributes nutrients and oxygen to the cells of the body, the endoplasmic reticulum serves the same purpose within the cell. It allows substances to move in and out of cell organelles.

Ribosomes

Ribosomes are organelles that are attached to the endoplasmic reticulum. Ribosomes help build proteins that are required for different cell functions. They function as a workshop, where parts are built for future use.

Lysosomes

Lysosomes are sacs that produce powerful enzymes that help to break down large molecules of nutrients into smaller chemical structures that can be used for various functions. Additionally, they are responsible for the degradation of dangerous materials such as bacteria, and for the disposal of other unwanted substances and organelles that are worn out. Lysosomes also break down the cell when it dies by producing self-destruct enzymes.

Golgi Apparatus

Discovered in 1898, the **Golgi apparatus** (named after Camillo Golgi, 1844–1926) is an organelle that serves as a storage facility, holding protein for future use. It is also involved in manufacturing other protein substances needed by the cell.

Vacuoles

Vacuoles are holding vats within the cell. They can be used to store and transport water and ingested materials for future use. They also hold waste until it is ready for transport out of the cell.

Nucleus

In the center of the cell, there is a large structure called the cell nucleus. The nucleus can be thought of as the control room of the cell. It is made primarily of proteins, and is responsible for making specific proteins that are needed for cell function and growth. Perhaps the most important role of the nucleus is that it contains the blueprints for the cell, as well as for any future cells that will be produced.

The nucleus contains special fibers called **chromatin**, which are made of nucleic acids and proteins. **Deoxyribonucleic acid (DNA)**, contains coding information that runs the cell, as well as information to pass on to daughter cells (Figure 2–6). The chromatin is responsible for cell duplication and contains all the information about cell function that must be passed on to new cells. Cells divide through a process called **mitosis** (Figure 2–7), in which the chromatin fibers line up in the nucleus and duplicate themselves, and the cell eventually divides into two cells with identical DNA and function.

Genes are part of the DNA in the chromatin. They determine cell traits, and in a bigger sense, the overall genetic characteristics of a human body. When we refer to a characteristic of a person as genetic, we mean that this characteristic is encoded in the person's genes, and has been there since the individual was born. Blue eyes are genetic, as are male pattern baldness and the tendency to have acne or oily skin. All these characteristics are determined by the genes.

Receptor Sites

Cell receptor sites are designed to accept only certain types of signals. The loading dock of the receptor site will only accept selective and specifically shaped substances, which are generally produced by the body. Cell receptor sites may also be influenced by hormones and specific drugs, which work by sending messages to the cells.

Specialized Cell Function and Tissues

Cells often have different functions to carry out within the body. These are referred to as specialized cells. Tissues are groups of cells that carry out the same function. **Epithelial**

---

ribosomes
Organelles that help build proteins required for different cell functions.

Golgi apparatus
An organelle that is a storage facility, holding protein for future use.

chromatin
Special fibers which are made of nucleic acids and proteins.

deoxyribonucleic acid (DNA)
Contains coding that runs the cell, and the information to pass on to daughter cells.

mitosis
The process in which the chromatin fibers line up in the nucleus and duplicate themselves, causing the cell to eventually divide into two cells with identical DNA and function.

epithelial
Tissue that is on the outside of the body's structures.

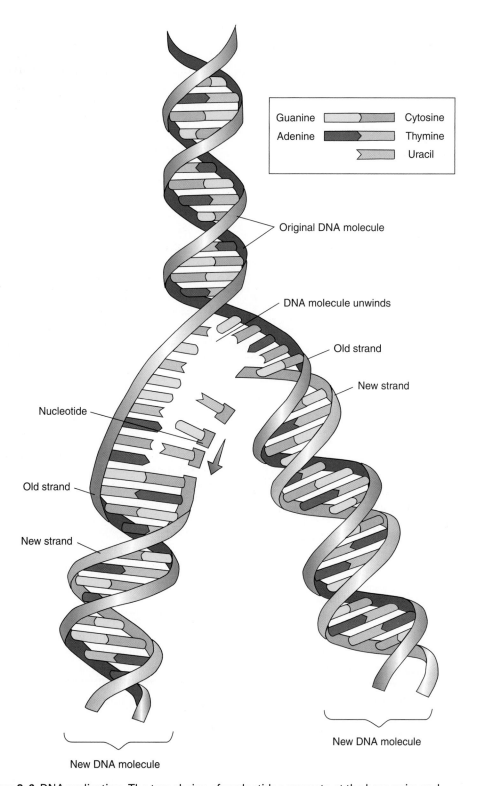

Figure 2–6 DNA replication. The two chains of nucleotides separate at the base pairs and are duplicated.

tissue is tissue that is on the outside of the body's structures. The skin is the very best example of epithelial tissue. **Endothelial** tissue lines the inside of the body and its organs, such as the lungs, stomach, etc.

Muscles

Muscle tissue is made up of three subspecialized groups of muscles: visceral muscles, striated muscles, and cardiac muscle.

endothelial
Tissue that lines the inside of the body, and its organs, such as lungs, stomach, etc.

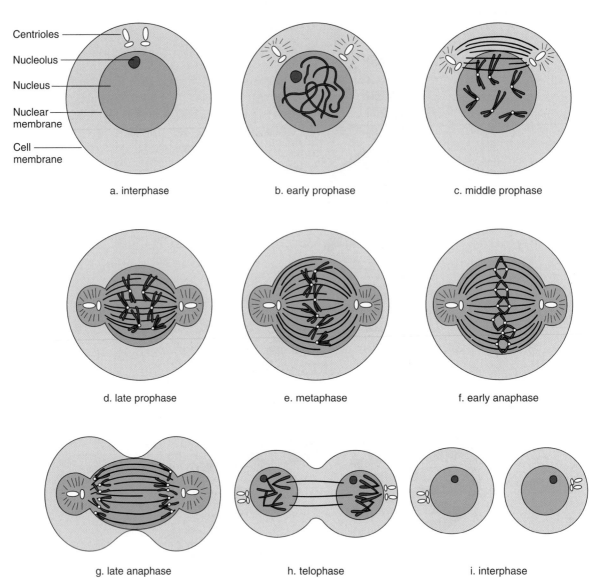

Centrioles
Nucleolus
Nucleus
Nuclear membrane
Cell membrane

a. interphase b. early prophase c. middle prophase

d. late prophase e. metaphase f. early anaphase

g. late anaphase h. telophase i. interphase

Figure 2–7 The phases of cell mitosis.

Visceral Muscles

Visceral muscles are involuntary muscles, which work without us deliberately thinking about their function. They include the muscles that move food through the intestines and the muscles that allow us to breathe. Visceral muscles are also called smooth muscles, because they look smooth, and are even in color (Figure 2–8).

Striated Muscles

Striated muscles contain stripes instead of being smooth (Figure 2–9). These stripes are called **striations**. Better known as skeletal muscles, these are muscles that control voluntary actions, functions that we deliberately make happen. Standing up, chewing food, talking, and walking around the block are all

examples of activities that use voluntary muscles. Although cardiac muscle, which is an involuntary muscle, is also striated in appearance, "Striated muscle" is usually a synonym for voluntary, skeletal muscles.

Cardiac Muscle

A specialized type of muscle, cardiac muscle is involuntary and striated (Figure 2–10). This muscle is responsible for the heart beating to circulate blood around the body.

Tissues

Skeletal tissue makes up the bones of the body, where as **connective tissue** helps to connect the bones and provides a cushion between the bones (Figure 2–11). **Cartilage**

striations
The marks within the muscles that are striped rather than smooth.

connective tissue
Tissue that helps connect the bones, and provide a cushion between the bones.

cartilage
A connective tissue that forms the nose and ears.

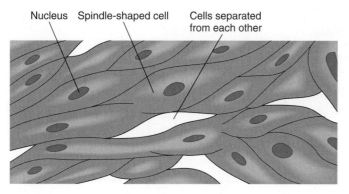

Nucleus Spindle-shaped cell Cells separated
from each other

Figure 2–8 Visceral (involuntary) muscles are located in the intestines; they contract in a wave-like motion to help move food through the intestines for the breakdown and absorption of nutrients.

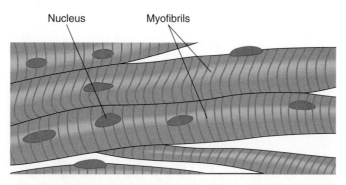

Nucleus Myofibrils

Figure 2–9 Striated muscles are known as skeletal muscles, which control voluntary actions such as moving fingers or walking.

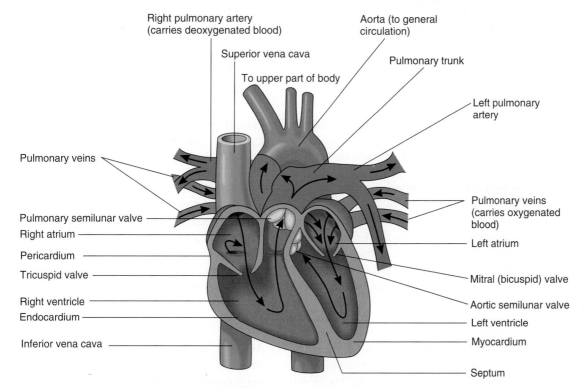

Right pulmonary artery (carries deoxygenated blood)

Aorta (to general circulation)

Superior vena cava

Pulmonary trunk

To upper part of body

Left pulmonary artery

Pulmonary veins

Pulmonary veins (carries oxygenated blood)

Pulmonary semilunar valve

Left atrium

Right atrium

Pericardium

Tricuspid valve

Mitral (bicuspid) valve

Right ventricle

Aortic semilunar valve

Endocardium

Left ventricle

Inferior vena cava

Myocardium

Septum

Figure 2–10 The heart is responsible for bringing oxygenated blood to the cells and returning deoxygenated blood to the lungs.

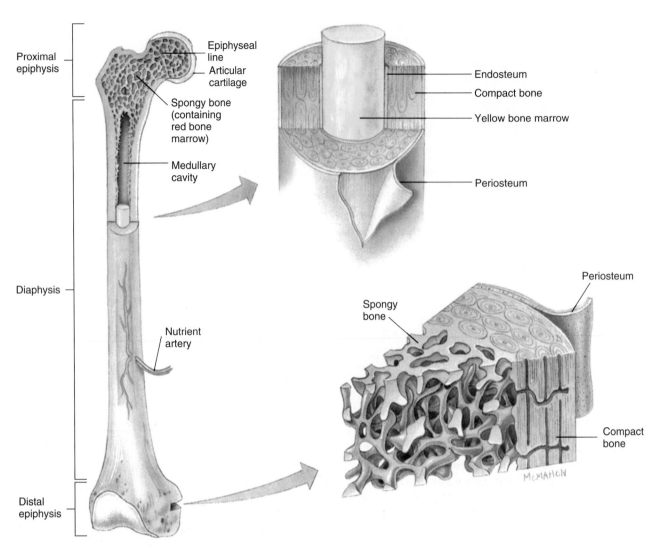

Figure 2–11 Skeletal tissue makes up the bones of the body. A thin covering called the periosteum covers the bone's surface.

ligaments
Tough bands of fibrous tissue serving to connect bones or hold an organ in place.

immune system
Patrols and defends our tissues from invasion by bacteria or other harmful substances.

lymph
Liquid tissue that is fluid and constantly bathes the various tissues of the body.

lymph nodes
Filters within the lymph system.

and **ligaments** are examples of connective tissue (Figure 2–12). Cartilage is what forms the flexible parts of the nose and ears. Cartilage serves as a cushion between bones. Ligaments help hold bones in place.

Blood

Blood is referred to as liquid tissue. There are many subspecialized cells within the blood, including red corpuscles, which are red blood cells that carry oxygen to the cells, and white blood cells or white corpuscles, which help fight infection. Lymphocytes, mast cells, and macrophages are cells in the **immune system** that patrol and defend our tissues from invasion by bacteria or other harmful substances. Blood also contains platelets, which are responsible for clotting when the skin is wounded.

Lymph

Lymph is another liquid tissue. It is fluid that constantly bathes the various tissues of the body. It helps to remove waste and filter it into the bloodstream, where it is eventually excreted as urine. The filters within the lymph system are known as **lymph nodes** (Figure 2–13). Lymph nodes can swell during sickness. This swelling results from collections of waste and dead bacteria from the immune system trying to fight off the infection.

Adipose Tissue

Fat tissue is referred to as **adipose tissue**. It helps cushion the bones and organs of the body. Some fat in the body is necessary for protection.

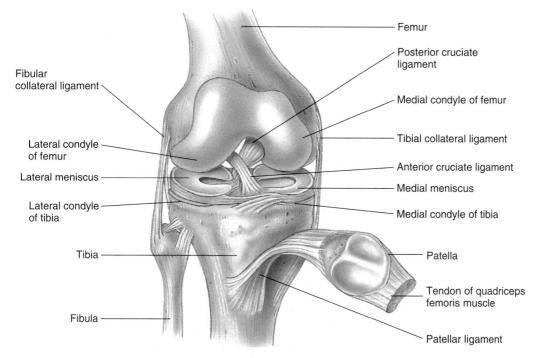

Fibular collateral ligament

Lateral condyle of femur

Lateral meniscus

Lateral condyle of tibia

Tibia

Fibula

Femur

Posterior cruciate ligament

Medial condyle of femur

Tibial collateral ligament

Anterior cruciate ligament

Medial meniscus

Medial condyle of tibia

Patella

Tendon of quadriceps femoris muscle

Patellar ligament

Figure 2–12 Connective tissue helps to connect the bones and provides a cushion between the bones. The knee joint contains cartilage and ligaments with special fluids that lubricate and nourish the joint.

Epithelial Tissues

Epithelial tissue, which is found at the body surface, lines the skin as well as numerous organs such as the mouth, nose, follicle, and other body cavities. Cells in epithelial tissue divide by a process called mitosis. There are two types of epithelial tissue: simple and stratified. **Simple epithelium** consists of a single layer of cells that are called squamous when they are platelike or flattened. Simple epithelium is usually found in areas where substances need to pass through easily. **Stratified epithelium** has more than one layer and is well adapted for protection.

Skin cells in epithelial tissues include flat cells—squamous cells; cube-shaped cells—cuboidal cells; and tall, cylindrical cells or columnar cells. The skin's epidermis is made up of **stratified squamous epithelium** that is in layers. At the base (basal layer) the cells are columnar, at the intermediary level they are cuboidal (Figure 2–14), and at the surface, cells are flattened and considered dry.

Epithelial cells in the epidermis include basal cells, pigment cells called **melanocytes**, sensory cells called **Merkel cells,** and star-shaped immune cells called **Langerhans**. Flattened cells at the skin's surface are called **corneocytes.**

The dermis contains **fibroblasts** responsible for the formation of collagen and elastin which makes up the connective tissue. **Macrophage cells**, **mast cells**, and lymphocytes all make up the immune cells. Fat cells are known as **adipose**.

Only a few years ago, it was believed that the epidermis was composed completely of dead skin cells. While the outer cells of the epidermis are technically dead, there are tremendous numbers of biochemical reactions and activities that are constantly occurring within the epidermal cells.

adipose tissue
Fat tissue that helps cushion the bones and organs of the body.

simple epithelium
Consists of a single layer of cells that are called squamous when they are platelike or flattened.

stratified epithelium
Consists of more than one layer and is well adapted for protection.

stratified squamous epithelium
Consists of more than one layer of cells that are flattened.

melanocytes
Pigment cells that determine the color of the skin and hair.

Merkel cells
Located in the epidermis, these cells are believed to be transmitters of sensory function to lower dermal nerves.

Langerhans
Star-shaped immune cells.

corneocytes
The cells that make up the corneum, or outermost layer of the epidermis.

fibroblasts
Responsible for the formation of collagen and elastin, which makes up the connective tissue.

mast cells
Immune cells.

macrophage cells
Immune cells.

adipose
Fat cells.

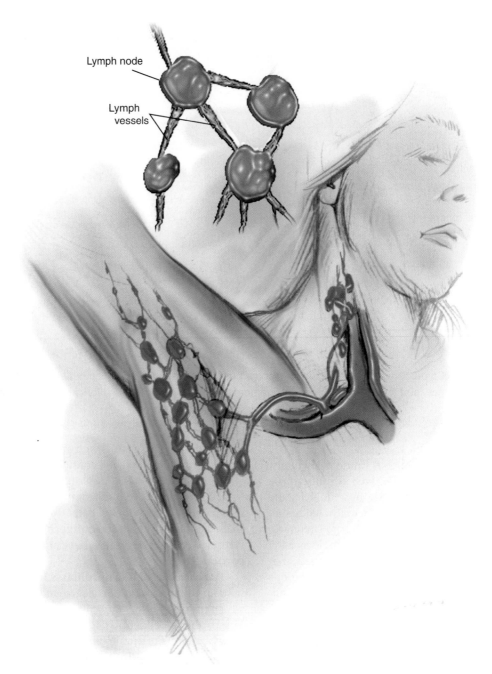

Lymph node

Lymph vessels

Figure 2–13 Lymph nodes are found throughout the body. White blood cells are interwoven with the fibrous mesh inside the node.

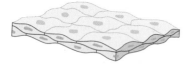

Figure 2–14a Epithelial tissue is responsible for protection, absorption, and secretion. It lines the skin and various organs such as the mouth, nose, and other body cavities. Stratified squamous epithelial cells make up the epidermis.

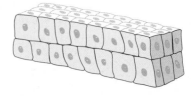

Figure 2–14b Cube-shaped cells are called cuboidal cells and are found in the central area of the epidermis.

Layers of the Skin

Dermis

The **dermis** is the lower, live layer of the skin. Within the dermis are blood vessels, lymph vessels, and the nerves of the skin that sense heat, touch, and pain. Also within this layer are the main structures of the **sebaceous glands** which produce **sebum**, the oily substance that lubricates the surface of the skin and helps to prevent the surface from dehydration. Also living in this layer are the **sudoriferous glands,** which produce sweat. The dermis consists of two layers—the papillary layer and the reticular dermis (Figure 2–15).

Papillary Layer

The upper part of the dermis is called the **papillary layer**, also known as the basement membrane, which connects the dermis to the epidermis. The area of this attachment is also known as the epidermal-dermal junction.

dermis
The lower, live layer of the skin.

sebaceous glands
Glands within the dermis that produce sebum.

sebum
An oily substance that lubricates the surface of the skin and helps prevent the surface from dehydration.

sudoriferous glands
Known as the sweat gland, its main function is to regulate body temperature.

papillary layer
The upper part of the dermis, also known as the basement membrane, that connects the dermis to the epidermis.

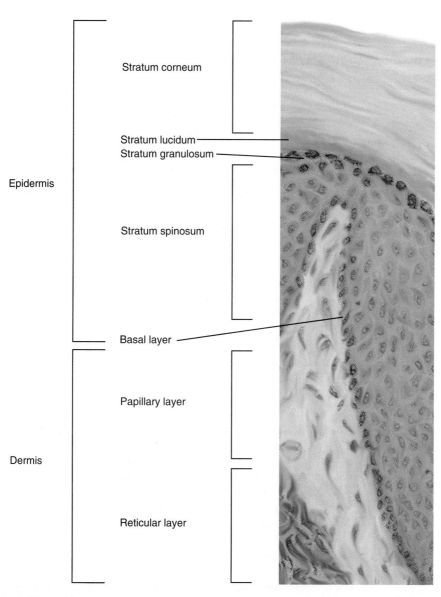

Epidermis
- Stratum corneum
- Stratum lucidum
- Stratum granulosum
- Stratum spinosum
- Basal layer

Dermis
- Papillary layer
- Reticular layer

Figure 2–15 The epidermal and dermal layers of the skin. Note the location of the papillary and reticular layers.

papillae
Small, cone-shaped elevations at the bottom of the hair follicle in the dermis.

rete pegs
The epidermal side of papillae.

basal cell layer
The lower, live part of the epidermis where epidermal cell division occurs.

reticular dermis
The lower part of the dermis.

collagen
A protein that makes up 70% of the weight of the skin; collagen gives skin its strength and keeps it "young."

elastin fibers
Protein fibers that give the skin its elasticity (stretch) and ability to retain its shape.

keloid
A raised scar resulting from an overproduction of collagen.

elastin
The protein in elastin fibers that are responsible for skin's elasticity.

reticulin
Collagen-related fibers that are part of the papillary layer.

Fingerlike ridges called **papillae** form hills and valleys. These ridges are a membrane that attaches to the epidermis. The epidermal side of these ridges is known as **rete pegs**. Within this area are the surface capillaries from the bloodstream that nourish the lower, live part of the epidermis, known as the **basal cell layer**, where epidermal cell division occurs.

It is an interesting fact that scars only form when damage or injury beneath the basement membrane has occurred. Small injuries that we receive as children—minor scrapes and such—rarely form scars, mainly because the basement membrane is still intact.

Reticular Dermis

The lower part of the dermis is called the **reticular dermis,** which contains the larger blood vessels that feed the capillaries in the papillary layer. It is here where **collagen** and **elastin fibers** reside. Collagen and elastin fibers are made of proteins. They are responsible for giving strength, flexibility, and elasticity.

Collagen and Elastin.   Collagen is a protein that gives skin its strength and keeps it "young" (Figure 2–16). It is the main part of the dermis, making up 70% of the weight of the skin, except for water and moisture. Collagen is formed whenever the skin is injured, to help repair the injury. It is the fiber that makes up scar tissue. Overproduction of collagen results in the type of raised scar called a **keloid**.

Elastic fibers contain the protein **elastin**. These fibers give the skin its elasticity or

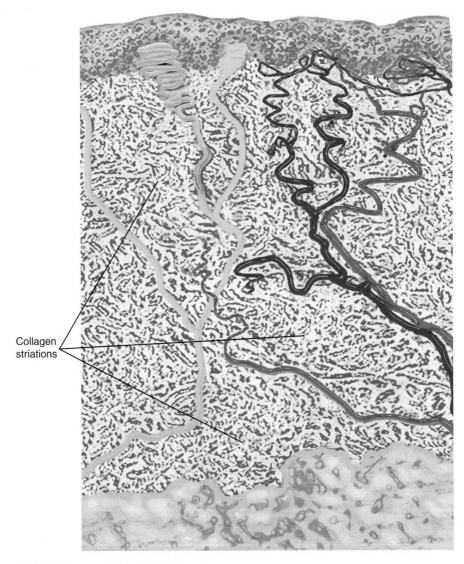

Collagen striations

Figure 2–16 Collagen striations in the dermis.

stretch and the ability to retain its shape. Elastin is present in a much smaller quantity in the skin, about 1 part elastin to 14 parts collagen. A third type of fiber, the **reticulin**, is a collagen-related fiber that is part of the papillary layer.

Collagen and elastin are the fibers that are injured by sun exposure. Alterations caused by sun exposure causes aging. Damage actually occurs to these important fibers over a long period of time. This damage is what causes the wrinkles and sagging of the skin that are associated with aging.

Collagen is produced in the dermis of all body skin by specialized cells called fibroblasts. Fibroblasts are stimulated by many factors, including some topical treatments such as **tretinoin**, better known as **Retin-A**. There is growing evidence that alphahydroxy acids and possibly topical forms of vitamin C may also stimulate these fibroblasts.

Ground substance. Filling the empty space between the collagen and elastin fibers in the dermis is a jellylike fluid known as the **ground substance**. This is made primarily of carbohydrates called **glycosaminoglycans**. Perhaps one of the best known is **hyaluronic acid**, a strong water-binder that helps retain fluid in the dermis. Hyaluronic acid or sodium hyaluronate are common ingredients in moisturizers. These ingredients do a good job of holding water to the skin surface, hydrating dry corneocytes in the corneum, and making dry skin look much more moist and smooth. The hyaluronic acid molecule is so large, however, that it cannot penetrate into the dermis. Sun damage also can cause changes that reduce the hyaluronic acid in the skin.

Subcutis

Underneath the dermis lies a layer of fat known as the **subcutaneous** or **subcutis layer** (sub means under; cutis means skin). This fatty layer provides structure and cushioning between the skin and the muscle layer. As we age, the subcutaneous fat decreases in this layer of the skin, especially after age 70, resulting in a bony look to certain areas of the face.

Nerves

The nerves of the skin are also within the dermis. These nerve endings, known as **sensory nerves,** help the skin to sense

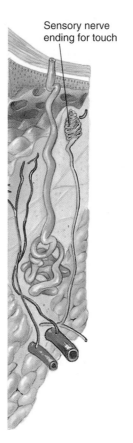

Figure 2–17 Cross-section of the skin showing the nerve endings in the dermis.

touch, heat, pain, and pressure (Figure 2–17). **Pacinian corpuscles** are nerve endings that sense pressure or weight against the skin. The **Meissner corpuscles** detect touch, pressure, and cold. Formerly known as Krause end bulbs, the **mucocutaneous corpuscles** sense pain, as well as pressure. Merkel cells are located in the epidermis and are believed to be transmitters of sensory function to lower dermal nerves.

Epidermis

The epidermis is the outermost layer of the skin. Lying on top of the dermis, the epidermis is our barrier to the outside world. Even though almost all of the epidermis is technically dead, the epidermis provides many immune and protective functions. We are learning more each day about how the epidermis chemically communicates with the dermis, signaling it to perform many important functions.

Sensory nerve ending for touch

---

tretinoin
See Retin-A.

Retin-A
Tretinoin; a prescription cream for acne.

ground substance
A jellylike fluid that fills the empty space between the collagen and elastin fibers in the dermis.

glycosaminoglycans
A group of chemically related polysaccharides that are major components of the extra cellular matrix (ECM) and of connective tissues.

hyaluronic acid
A glycosaminoglycan; a strong water-binder that helps retain fluid content in the dermis.

subcutaneous
(subcutis) layer
The layer of fat underneath the dermis.

sensory nerves
Nerve endings that help the skin to sense touch, heat, pain, and pressure.

pacinian corpuscles
Nerve endings that sense pressure or weight against the skin.

Meissner corpuscles
Nerve endings that help to detect touch, pressure, and cold.

mucocutaneous corpuscles
Nerve endings that sense pain as well as pressure; formerly known as Krause end bulbs.

stratum germinativum
Another term for the basal layer.

differentiate
To continually divide.

keratin
A protein substance which fills the cells as they approach the very outer layer of the epidermis.

stratum spinosum
The prickle cell layer of the skin often classified with the stratum germinativum to form the basal layer; prickle-like threads join the cells.

desmosomes
Small attachments that hold the upper level epidermal cells together.

stratum granulosum
Granular layer of the skin above the stratum spinosum.

intercellular lipids
The substance that fills the space between the upper epidermal cells.

epidermal strata
Cell layers within the epidermis.

The Basal Layer

The basal layer (basal meaning the first, or near the first), formerly known as the **stratum germinativum** (germ meaning seed), is the base of the epidermis, lying just above the papillary dermis. Basal cells continually divide, producing new cells that **differentiate** or become other cells within the epidermis. These differentiated cells migrate toward the surface of the skin. As they migrate, they go through changes that make them more resilient and protective, even if they are dead cells. Almost all cells in the epidermis are known as keratinocytes, meaning that they all produce a protein substance known as **keratin**, which fills the cells as they approach the very outer layer of the epidermis. Keratinocytes make up about 95% of the epidermis. The process of the epidermis manufacturing the protein keratin is known as keratinization.

There are two types of keratin protein—soft and hard. Hair and skin are made of soft keratin. Fingernails and toenails are made of hard keratin. Keratin is produced to provide resiliency to the skin and to protect the inner skin from drying out as well as from injury and reactive chemicals. When you have a small paper cut and accidentally get isopropyl alcohol or lemon juice on the cut, doesn't it sting and burn? This demonstrates two facts—how the epidermis protects the skin from chemical injury, and how thin the epidermis really is.

Stratum spinosum

Just above the basal cell layer is a layer known by several different names. The **stratum spinosum** is also known as the spiny layer and the prickle layer. It is called the prickle or spiny layer because the oval-shaped cells are covered with prickly looking appendages. These tiny hairlike structures on the prickle cells will eventually become **desmosomes** (Figure 2–18), which are small attachments that hold the upper level epidermal cells together. The word *desmosome* is derived from the Greek word *desmos*, which means a band, and *soma*, which means a body.

Stratum Granulosum

The next layer up is the **stratum granulosum**, also known as the granular layer. The cells within the granular layer

Desmosome

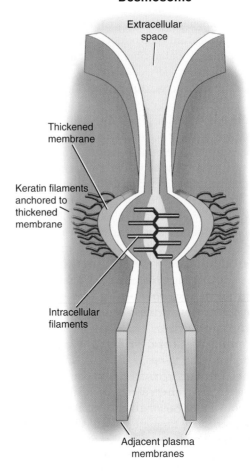

Extracellular space

Thickened membrane

Keratin filaments anchored to thickened membrane

Intracellular filaments

Adjacent plasma membranes

Figure 2–18 Desmosomes are small attachments that help anchor cells to one another.

are grainy-looking cells that are filled with keratin. The nucleus is beginning to fall apart within the cells. Lamellar bodies are present within the granular cells. The Lamellar bodies produce very important **intercellular lipids**, which are the substances that fill the space between the upper epidermal cells. These lipids help form the strong cement structure for the skin's permeability barrier.

Brick and Mortar Concept

The epidermis has been compared to a brick wall. Dr. Peter M. Elias, of the University of California at San Francisco, is credited for the brick and mortar concept (Figure 2–19) of the epidermal cell layers. Cell layers within the epidermis are known as **epidermal strata.** One layer is known as a stratum.

Skin type and condition are discussed in Part IV. It is very important to understand this brick and mortar concept. It is vital to mastering the principles that assist you in choosing the correct treatments and products for your client.

The bricks are the cells, and the mortar is the complex of intercellular lipids that hold or bind moisture in between the epidermal cells. These lipids are responsible for hydration, epidermal firmness, and smoothness. If they are removed or depleted in any way, the skin becomes dry, dehydrated, and more prone to reactivity. These lipids, also known as the intercellular cement, or intercellular matrix, protect against **transepidermal water loss (TEWL)**, which can dehydrate the skin, and also provide protection against invasion of the skin by offending or injuring substances.

This protective ability is referred to as the **barrier function** of the skin. This is an important term, as the barrier function affects both the esthetic and physiological functions of the skin. Keep this fact in mind when studying skin types and conditions. Lipids involved in forming the mortar or intercellular lipids are triglycerides, sphingolipids and glycolipids, also known as **ceramides, cholesterol, phospholipids,** waxes, and **fatty acids**. Do not confuse these lipids with the lipid called sebum, which is secreted from the sebaceous gland in the follicle.

The cell renewal process is responsible for the production of these important lipids. If the cell cycle slows, the production of lipids slows, causing dryness and dehydration. Dehydration of the skin from exposure to cold, dry air—such as frostbite, windburn, or even sunburn—results in damage to the lipid barrier function. The final result is flaking, dryness, a tight or stinging feeling, and redness.

In between the granular layer and the outermost layer of the skin is a clear layer known as the **stratum lucidum** (Figure 2–20). The cells in the stratum lucidum are filled with a substance called **eleidin**, which is involved in the keratinization process. This layer is present in the soles of the feet and the palms of the hands.

Stratum Corneum

The outermost layer of the epidermis, and the layer that estheticians work on directly, is called the **stratum corneum,** made of cells known as corneocytes. Cyte is another term for cell. The study of cells and cellular biology is known as **cytology**.

The corneum is also commonly referred to as the horny layer or cutaneous horn. It is made of flattened keratinocytes, now known as corneocytes. These dead cells are completely filled with keratin. They shed off the skin continuously. The desmosomes, which hold the cells together, have broken loose at this point, making it easy for the corneocytes to slough off. When estheticians perform exfoliation treatments using either mechanical methods such as scrub products, or chemical exfoliants such as alphahydroxy acids, they are helping to remove dead corneocytes.

transepidermal water loss (TEWL)
Dehydration of the skin.

barrier function
Provides protection against invasion of the skin by offending or injuring substances.

ceramides
Lipids involved in forming the mortar or intercellular lipids.

cholesterol
A moisturizer and emollient that acts as a powerful emulsifier in water-in-oil systems; a fat-like substance found in plant and animal cells.

phospholipids
Complex fat substances that, together with protein, form the membrane of all living cells.

fatty acids
Acids derived from the saturated series of open chain hydrocarbons.

stratum lucidum
A clear layer in between the granular layer and the outermost layer of the skin.

eleidin
A substance in the stratum lucidum which is involved in the keratinization process.

stratum corneum
The outermost layer of the epidermis.

cytology
The study of cells and cellular biology.

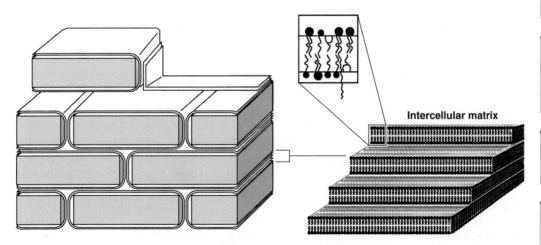

Intercellular matrix

Figure 2–19 The brick and mortar concept of the outermost layer of skin.

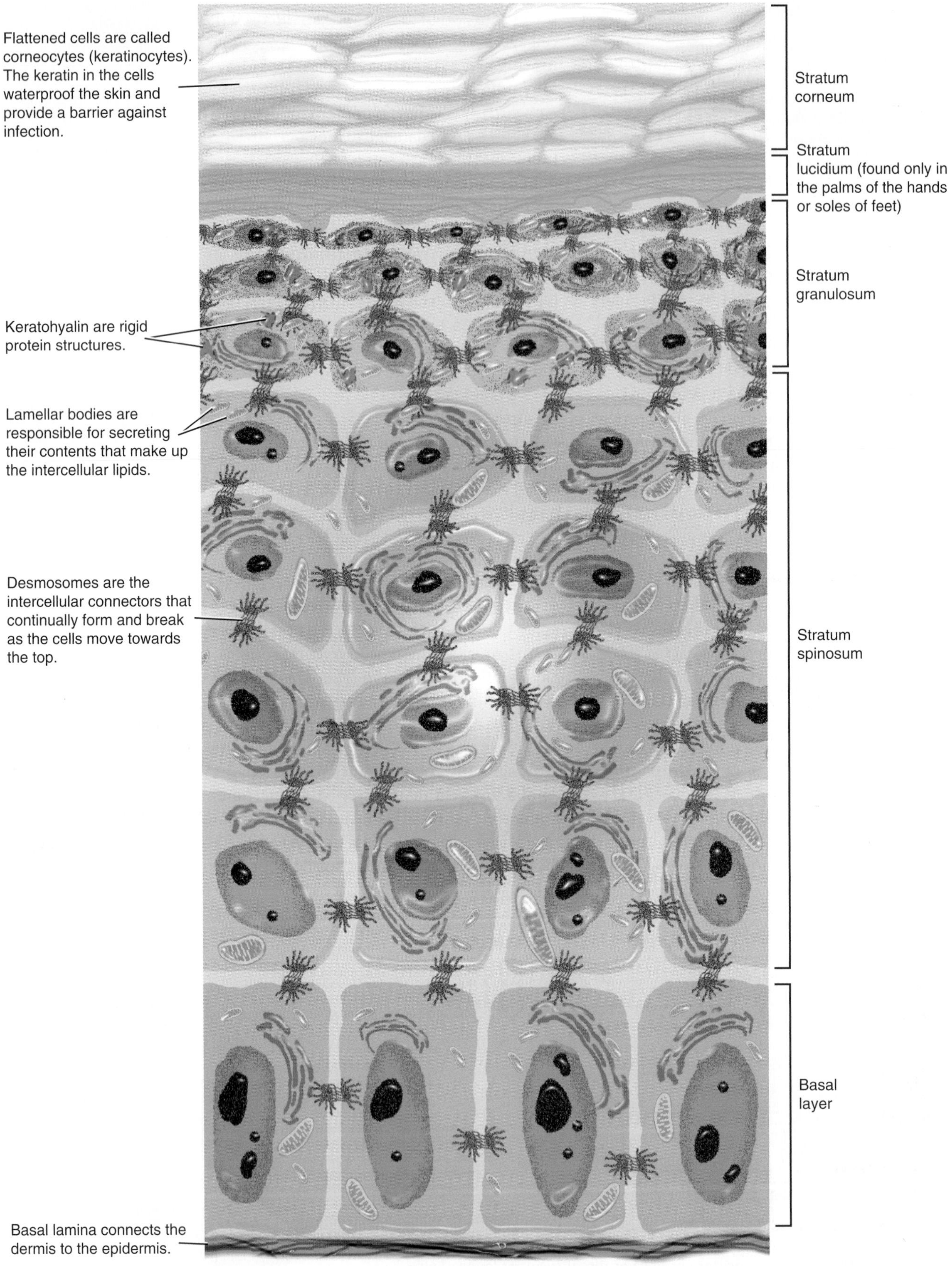

Flattened cells are called corneocytes (keratinocytes). The keratin in the cells waterproof the skin and provide a barrier against infection.

Stratum corneum

Stratum lucidium (found only in the palms of the hands or soles of feet)

Stratum granulosum

Keratohyalin are rigid protein structures.

Lamellar bodies are responsible for secreting their contents that make up the intercellular lipids.

Desmosomes are the intercellular connectors that continually form and break as the cells move towards the top.

Stratum spinosum

Basal layer

Basal lamina connects the dermis to the epidermis.

Figure 2–20 Cell migration from the basal layer to the epidermis.

The Hair Follicle

The hair follicle, also known as the **pilosebaceous unit** or **apparatus**, is the structure in which hairs grow and is commonly known as a pore. Pores may also be referred to as **ostium** (single pore) or **ostia** (many pores). *Ostia* comes from a Latin word *ostiole*, which refers to a small opening such as a pore.

Consumers often use the term *pore* to describe the follicle. They refer to clogged pores, or enlarged pores, which are actually follicles that are impacted with dead cells or solidified sebum. They may be stretched from heavy sebum production or have been permanently distended due to scar tissue in the dermis. The walls of the follicle are somewhat elastic, and adapt to impactions and the amount of sebum traveling through the follicle (Figure 2–21).

At the bottom of the follicle are germinative cells in the papilla of the follicle. This is the area where the hair is produced. Hair is a different form of soft keratin and is completely dead, except for the papilla. The hair itself is called the shaft. The bottom part of the hair that attaches to the papilla is called the bulb.

Sebaceous Gland. Commonly called an oil gland, the sebaceous gland produces an oily, waxy substance called sebum. The exact function of sebum is unknown. Some scientists believe it exists to add additional protection to prevent dehydration of the epidermis, and possibly to provide some lubrication for the hair. Sebaceous glands are present in most areas of the body, except the soles of the feet, the palms of the hands, and the lower lip. There are numerous sebaceous glands on the face, chest, back, shoulders, and scalp. They are generally attached to the side of the follicle. The sebaceous glands empty into the hair follicle canal, called the infundibulum.

Sweat Glands

The sudoriferous gland is commonly referred to as the sweat gland (Figure 2–22). Its main function is to regulate body temperature. Sweat is produced when the body is hot or stressed, and as the sweat evaporates, the skin is cooled. The soles of the feet and the palms of the hands have the most sweat glands in the body skin.

The sucretory coil of the sudoriferous gland is based in the dermis. It is the active

---

pilosebaceous unit (apparatus)
The structure in which hairs grow that is commonly known as a pore; the hair follicle.

ostium
Single pore.

ostia
Many pores.

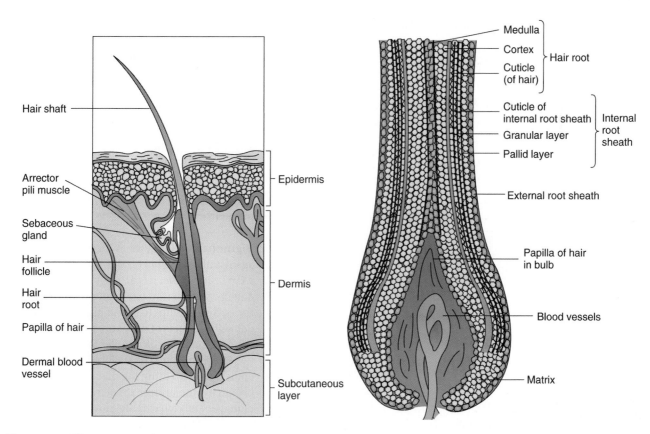

Figure 2–21 The structure of a hair follicle in relation to the sebaceous gland.

part of the gland in terms of sweat production. The sweat leaves the coil and is pushed upward through the sudoriferous duct, a canal leading to the surface of the skin. The main sweat glands are known as eccrine glands.

Apocrine Glands

The sweat glands in the groin and armpits are called apocrine glands. They produce a heavier, fatty type of sweat, which can produce an odor, commonly thought of as body odor, when bacteria are present. The glands in the ear that produce earwax are also apocrine glands.

Specialized Cells in the Epidermis

There are two specialized cells within the epidermis that are very important to its function—melanocytes and immune cells. Melanocytes are responsible for creating pigment that helps protect the dermis (Figure 2–23). Immune cells are made up of Langerhans, macrophages, and masts. The melanocyte is present at the base of the basal cell layer and also in the upper dermis. The melanocyte is responsible for the production of **melanin**, the pigment that gives the skin color. Melanocytes are dendritic cells. They contain small tentaclelike branches, known as dendrites, located at the ends of the cell.

melanosomes
Small granules filled with melanin; manufactured by melanocytes.

melanin
Pigment that gives the skin color.

L-dopa
A biochemical converted from an amino acid called tyrosine.

desquamation
The normal process in which cells move to the surface of the epidermis and shed.

They are not round or oval like many other cells. The melanocytes manufacture small granules, filled with melanin. These are called **melanosomes**. Melanosomes penetrate into the keratinocytes, almost like an injection process. As the keratinocytes are injected with pigment, they continue to migrate to the surface of the corneum, appearing as color in the complexion.

Skin Colors. Skin exhibits four colors: red, yellow, brown, and blue. The hemoglobin in oxygen-carrying blood generates the red color. Yellow colors are found in some of the foods we eat and account for the yellow hue in some skin tones. When oxygen is reduced in hemoglobin and replaced by carbon dioxide, it produces a bluish color. This blue color is seen in the veins. Brown pigment makes up the color found in melanin. There are three types of melanin, known as eumelanin, pheomelanin, and trichochrome.

1. *Eumelanin* is a dark melanin, brown-black in color. It is the type of melanin in black or brown skin, and is also present in black hair.

2. *Pheomelanin* is red-yellow in color and is present in red hair.

3. *Trichochrome* is also a red-yellow pigment that is found in hair.

In black skin, the melanosomes produced are much larger. They are deposited in single, large melanosomes in the cells. In Caucasian skin, the melanosomes are deposited into the keratinocytes in multiple, smaller granules. The process of melanin production is very involved chemically. The simple version is that within the melanocyte, an amino acid called tyrosine is converted to a biochemical called **L-dopa.** During this process, melanin is formed.

Pigment Cells. A tan is the body's defense against ultraviolet rays. While many consider a tan fashionable, it is actually a biological defense system that has been activated. It is the body's attempt to shield itself from the damaging effects of exposure to the sun. When exposed to ultraviolet rays, the rays penetrate through the surface layers of the epidermis, activating the melanocytes to begin producing melanin to shield the cells from damage. Cells eventually move to the surface of the epidermis and are shed in the normal process of **desquamation**. Pigment is also

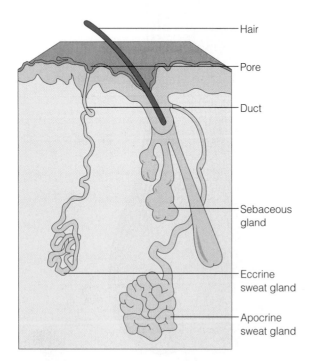

Hair

Pore

Duct

Sebaceous gland

Eccrine sweat gland

Apocrine sweat gland

Figure 2–22 Sweat glands, or sudoriferous glands, are responsible for cooling the body.

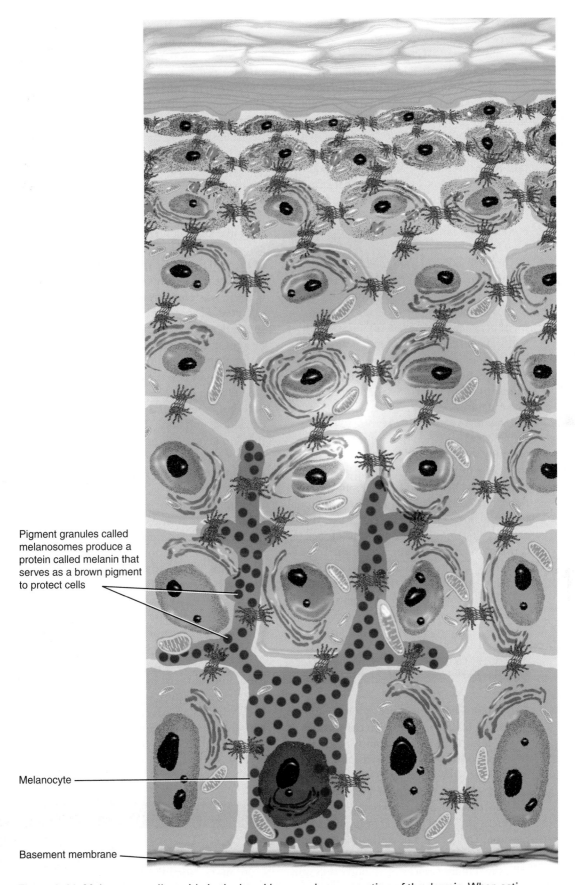

Pigment granules called melanosomes produce a protein called melanin that serves as a brown pigment to protect cells

Melanocyte

Basement membrane

Figure 2–23 Melanocyte cells reside in the basal layer and upper portion of the dermis. When activated by ultraviolet rays, they move their tentaclelike branches between the skin cells to protect them.

laser resurfacing

A surgical process that can stimulate unwanted melanin production. The beams of light emitted from the laser are absorbed superficially by the water in the skin. Depending on the wavelength, it vaporizes a thin layer of skin. When new skin grows back, it is smoother and the scars are much less noticeable.

hyperpigmentation

The overproduction of melanin pigment.

post-inflammatory hyperpigmentation (PIH)

Hyperpigmentation that occurs from irritation.

shed along with the dead corneocytes. This is what causes a tan to fade.

Other stimulants can produce melanin. A surgical process called **laser resurfacing** can stimulate unwanted melanin production. As a defense mechanism, production of melanin is triggered when the skin is chemically insulted through excessive aggression in a treatment, causing inflammation. It is important to be careful with any abrasive treatment or any esthetic procedure that causes cells to shed. These procedures include microdermabrasion and alphahydroxy acid exfoliation treatments, as well as other forms of exfoliation.

In black skin, for example, **hyperpigmentation**, or overproduction of melanin pigment, can result from the overuse of benzoyl peroxide for the treatment of acne, or using too high a strength of benzoyl peroxide. Hyperpigmentation that occurs from irritation, such as these, is known as **post-inflammatory hyperpigmentation (PIH).** Asian, dark Hispanic, and Mediterranean skin types are also prone to hyperpigmentation from injury. The esthetician must treat dark skin types very carefully to avoid problems occurring as a side effect from treatment. Hyperpigmentation can also be caused by hormonal fluctuations, birth control pills, and other hormonal therapies. Pregnancy and menopause can also have hormonal effects that influence or cause hyperpigmentation. The entire mechanism of why hormones affect melanin is not completely understood. Hyperpigmentation from hormonal imbalances happens almost exclusively in women.

Summary

The skin is a very large sensory organ and is the body's main connection to the outside world. It is the very organ that we touch when performing facials. Anything that touches the skin—including heat, cold, a pinprick, being struck by a baseball, and administering topical drugs and skin care products—causes a physical or biological reaction. The skin is a powerhouse of activity. Its normal function is critical for making protein, the building blocks of all body cells and tissue. The main task of the skin is to protect the internal workings of the underlying cells and tissues that make up the body. The integrity of this barrier function is dependent on each cell working to its optimum level. Cells work in units and teams to build the skin layers (epidermis and dermis). Improper cell function leads to the destruction and death of skin cells.

A healthy cell can be compared to a factory with its own workers, suppliers, storehouses, water sources, fuel, and nutrients. The outer wall or cell membrane is tightly controlled through special entryways that look like keyholes. Only recognized substances are allowed into the cell. The quality of the end materials (protein) is solely dependent on the nutrients coming into the cell and the waste materials being properly excreted. Each organelle within the cell must function optimally. The cell membrane must be kept unharmed in order to allow the internal structures of the cell to function effectively and do their jobs.

Cells are specialized in that they make up different types of body tissues such as muscle, blood, and bone. Epithelial cells make up the skin layers. Fibrous tissues called elastin and collagen are made from fibroblasts. Immune cells are called Langerhans, masts, and macrophages.

Whenever there is an interruption in this process, the immune system responds by having sentinel cells guard and destroy any outside invaders. The immune response is critical to warding off external invaders and helping to protect the skin. This is an important fact to clearly understand as you continue to work with the skin. Whenever there is an alteration in the skin's normal function—a cut, bacterial invasion, imbalance of pH, application of a wrong substance, environmental conditions, surgery, laser, or excessive exposure to sun—restoring the skin to its normal health and balance is critical. This is where your job is so important. As a skin specialist, your critical task is to fully understand the very basic unit of all living things—the cell.

Discussion Questions

1. Skin is a highly complex organ. State its primary functions, providing a brief description of each.

2. Cells can perform very specialized roles; however, each cell is uniquely qualified to operate as part of a much larger system. What is the main function of the cell and why is it critical to the esthetician's understanding of the skin and the body? Include in your discussion an explanation of the main components of the cell and what effect they have on cellular function.

3. Healthy tissue and muscle are very important to obtaining vibrant, resilient skin. How does the esthetician work with the body's lymph system to bring about a positive effect on these very specialized cells?

4. List the layers of the skin, describing the importance of collagen and elastin as they relate to healthy skin care and age management. Name at least two topical skin care products or agents that appear to help stimulate their production. By what means are they thought to achieve this goal?

5. Explain what is meant by the "brick and mortar" concept of the epidermis. How does this affect the "barrier function" of the skin and what can estheticians do to minimize dysfunction?

6. Describe the purpose of melanocytes and Langerhans cells in the epidermis. Name several ways in which the function of these cells can be compromised.

7. What role does the endocrine system play in regulating hormone-producing glands? Name the glands that have the most significant impact on proper skin functioning. How do these affect the skin's functioning?

8. What effect does the circulatory system have on maintaining healthy skin?

9. Name the major bones, muscles, and nerves of the head and face. Why is it important for estheticians to have knowledge of these anatomical structures?

Pugliese, Peter. 1991. *Advanced Professional Skin Care.* Bernville, N.Y.: APSC Publishing.

Gerson, Joel. 1999. *Standard Textbook for Professional Estheticians.* Albany, N.Y.: Milady, an imprint of Delmar Learning, a division of Thomson Learning, Inc.

Pugliese, Peter. 2001. *Physiology of the Skin: The Desquamation Process.* Carol Stream, Ill.: Allured.

Additional Reading

Alcamo, Edward. 1996. *Anatomy and Physiology, The Easy Way.* Hauppauge, N.Y.: Barron's.

Campbell, James N. *Endorphins.* (Discovery Channel School, http://www.Discovery.com; original content provided by Worldworldbook/atozscience/e/181150.html, October 21, 2001.)

Clayman, Charles. 1995. *The Human Body, An Illustrated Guide To Its Structure, Function, and Disorders.* New York: DK Publishing.

Gray, Henry. 1991. *Gray's Anatomy.* New York: Random House.

Lee, Deborah. 1997. *Essential Fatty Acids.* Pleasant Grove, Utah: Woodland Publishing.

Lees, Mark. 2001. *Skin Care: Beyond the Basics.* Clifton Park, N.Y.: Milady, an imprint of Delmar Learning, a division of Thomson Learning, Inc.

Montagu, Ashley. 1971. *Touching, The Human Significance of the Skin.* 3rd ed. New York: Harper & Rowe.

Pugliese, Peter. 2001. *Physiology of the Skin II.* Carol Stream, Ill.: Allured.

White, Clifton R., Jr., et al. 1996. *What Does Normal Skin Do?* Vol 1, *Cutaneous Medicine and Surgery, An Integrated Program in Dermatology.* 3–41, 46–56. New York: Simon & Schuster.

Notes

Gümbel, Dietrich. 1993. *Principles of Holistic Skin Therapy with Herbal Essences.* Heidelberg: Haug.

Chapter 3
Body Systems

Chapter Objectives

After reading this chapter, you should be able to:

- Describe the endocrine system and its purpose.
- State the importance of the circulatory system.
- Describe the lymphatic system and its relationship to the body.
- Describe the immune system.

Chapter Outline

Introduction
Endocrine System
Circulatory System
Immune System

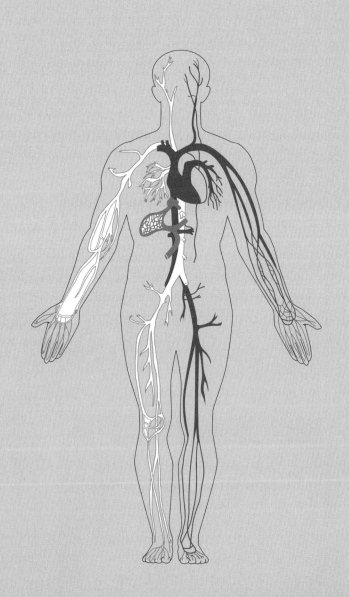

Introduction

In Chapter 2, we studied cells and how they differentiate to make up specific structures such as tissues and organs. In this chapter we will discuss some of the larger body systems that affect the skin. The skin's health is dependent on all internal systems working harmoniously. There are a total of 10 systems, which are outlined below. Each works as a separate unit, yet all are dependent on one another for the physical and biological support of the entire body.

1. The **skeletal system** (Figure 3–1) is the framework on which the rest of the body is built.

2. The **muscular system** makes up approximately half of the body's bulk (Figure 3–2, p. 52–54). Muscles work with the skeletal system and generate energy to move. Muscles make defined movements such as grasping with the hands, lifting, and speaking.

3. The fundamental function of the **circulatory system** (also referred to as cardiovascular) is to pump blood around the body (Figure 3–3). Any pause in blood flow lasting more than a few seconds causes a loss of consciousness. All tissues need a constant supply of fresh oxygen and removal of wastes.

4. The brain is the principal organ of the **nervous system**, which is the basis of consciousness and creativity. Through its connection with the spinal cord and nerve branches, the brain controls all body movements. Additionally, the nervous system works with the endocrine glands to help monitor and maintain other body systems (Figure 3–4).

skeletal system
The framework on which the rest of the body is built.

muscular system
Approximately half of the body's bulk; muscles work with the skeletal system and generate energy to move, make defined movement such as with the hands, lifting, and speaking.

circulatory system
The system that controls the steady circulation of the blood through the body by means of the heart and blood vessels.

nervous system
The basis of consciousness and creativity.

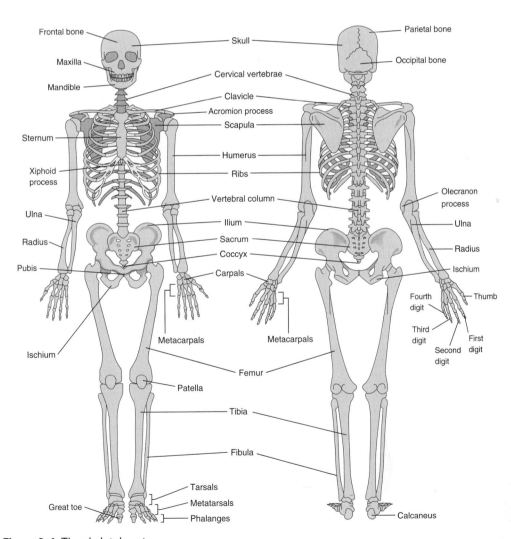

Figure 3–1 The skeletal system.

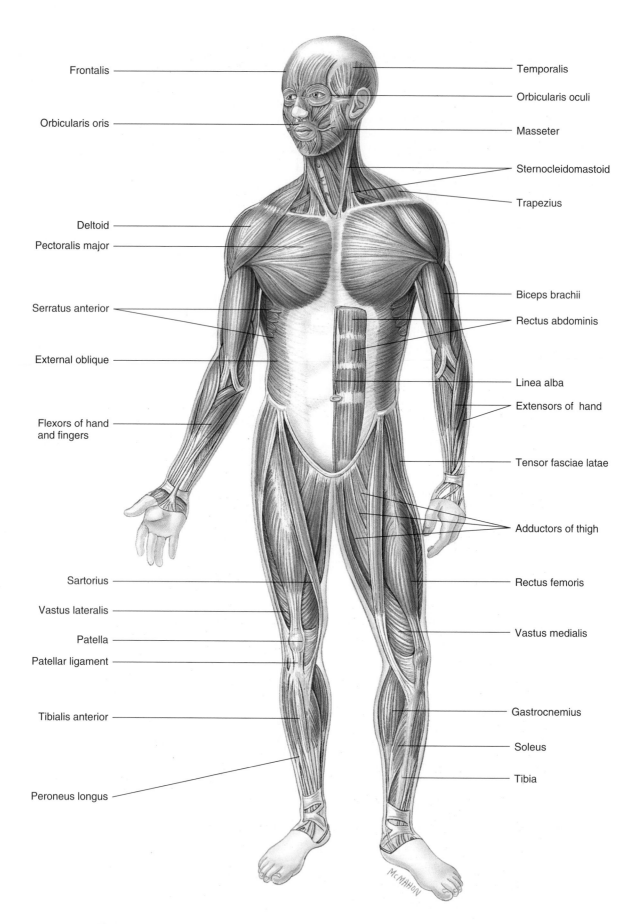

Frontalis

Orbicularis oris

Deltoid

Pectoralis major

Serratus anterior

External oblique

Flexors of hand
and fingers

Sartorius

Vastus lateralis

Patella

Patellar ligament

Tibialis anterior

Peroneus longus

Temporalis

Orbicularis oculi

Masseter

Sternocleidomastoid

Trapezius

Biceps brachii

Rectus abdominis

Linea alba

Extensors of hand

Tensor fasciae latae

Adductors of thigh

Rectus femoris

Vastus medialis

Gastrocnemius

Soleus

Tibia

Figure 3–2 The muscular system.

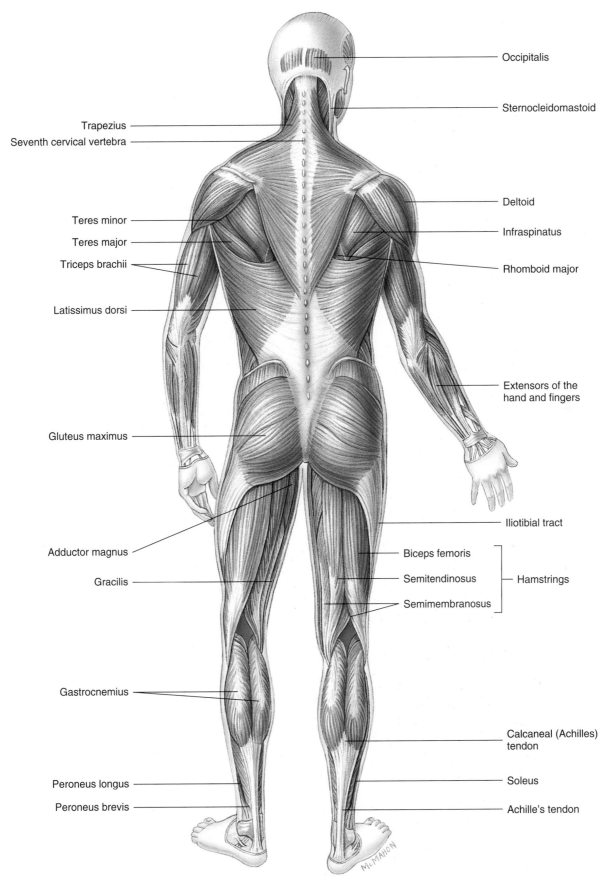

Occipitalis

Sternocleidomastoid

Trapezius

Seventh cervical vertebra

Teres minor

Teres major

Triceps brachii

Latissimus dorsi

Deltoid

Infraspinatus

Rhomboid major

Extensors of the hand and fingers

Gluteus maximus

Adductor magnus

Gracilis

Iliotibial tract

Biceps femoris

Semitendinosus

Semimembranosus

Hamstrings

Gastrocnemius

Calcaneal (Achilles) tendon

Peroneus longus

Peroneus brevis

Soleus

Achille's tendon

Figure 3–2 The muscular system *(continued).*

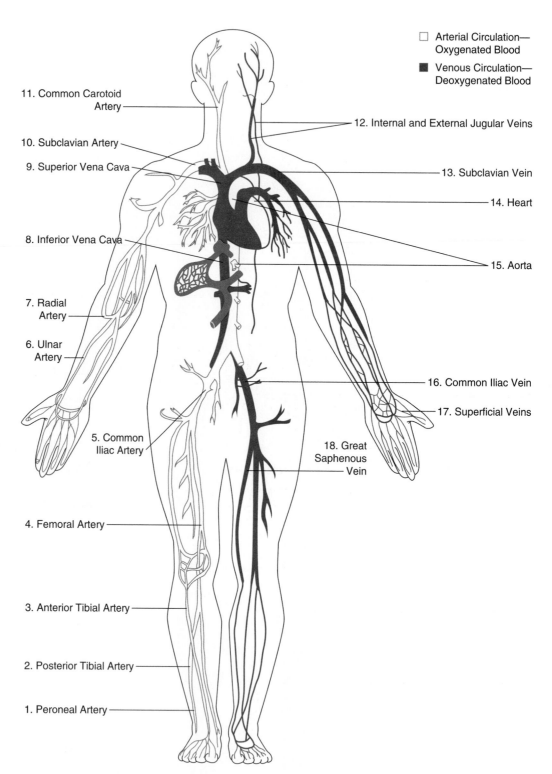

Arterial Circulation—
Oxygenated Blood

Venous Circulation—
Deoxygenated Blood

11. Common Carotoid
    Artery

10. Subclavian Artery

9. Superior Vena Cava

8. Inferior Vena Cava

7. Radial
   Artery

6. Ulnar
   Artery

5. Common
   Iliac Artery

4. Femoral Artery

3. Anterior Tibial Artery

2. Posterior Tibial Artery

1. Peroneal Artery

12. Internal and External Jugular Veins

13. Subclavian Vein

14. Heart

15. Aorta

16. Common Iliac Vein

17. Superficial Veins

18. Great
    Saphenous
    Vein

Figure 3–3 The cardiovascular system.

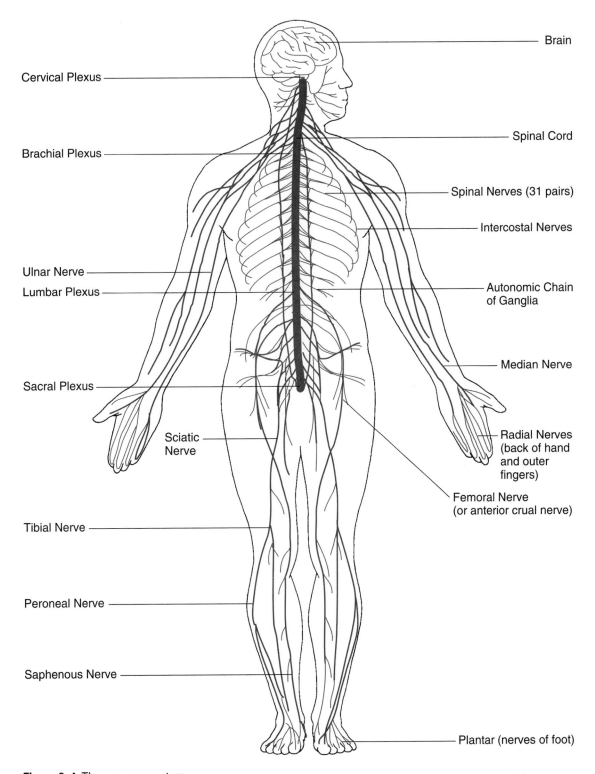

Cervical Plexus

Brachial Plexus

Ulnar Nerve

Lumbar Plexus

Sacral Plexus

Sciatic Nerve

Tibial Nerve

Peroneal Nerve

Saphenous Nerve

Brain

Spinal Cord

Spinal Nerves (31 pairs)

Intercostal Nerves

Autonomic Chain of Ganglia

Median Nerve

Radial Nerves (back of hand and outer fingers)

Femoral Nerve (or anterior crural nerve)

Plantar (nerves of foot)

Figure 3–4 The nervous system.

endocrine system
Regulates most of the hormone producing glands including the pineal gland, hypothalamus gland, pituitary gland, parathyroid glands, adrenal glands, pancreas glands, stomach and intestines, kidneys, and reproductive organs.

hormones
Secretions produced in and by one of the endocrine glands, and are carried by the blood stream and body fluid to another part of the body, or a body organ, to stimulate functional activity or secretion.

antibody
A substance that is formed in response to a foreign body, bacteria, virus, or other toxic substance.

respiratory system
Contains the respiratory tract that works together with the breathing muscles, to carry air in and out of the lungs.

5. The **endocrine system** (Figure 3–5) is made up of several different glands that are responsible for emitting chemical messengers called **hormones**. Hormones circulate in the blood and other body fluids and assist with maintaining an optimal internal environment. The endocrine system initiates the changes that take place in puberty. It also regulates the metabolism.

6. The immune system (Figure 3–6) is the body's defense system, protecting it against foreign invaders that cause infectious diseases. It is a complex system that develops antibodies and also fights off first-time foreign invaders. An **antibody** is a substance that is formed in response to a foreign body, bacteria, virus, or other toxic substances.

7. The **respiratory system** (Figure 3–7) contains the respiratory tract, which works together with the breathing muscles to carry air in and out of the lungs. Oxygen and carbon dioxide are referred to as gases. The cardiovascular system transports these gases to and from body tissue and supplies fresh oxygen. It picks up the carbon dioxide waste and brings it

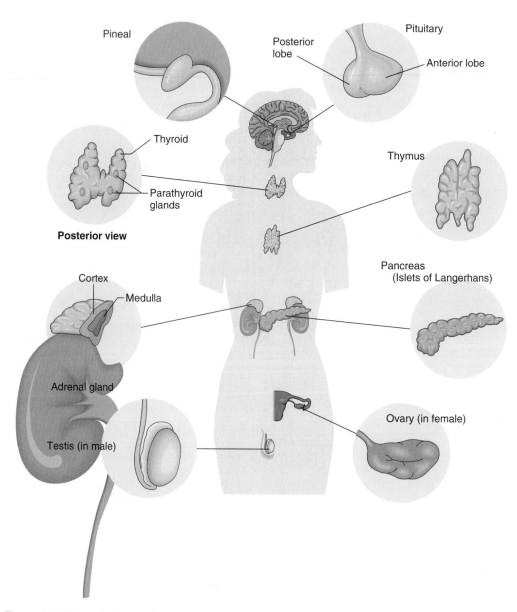

Figure 3–5 The endocrine system.

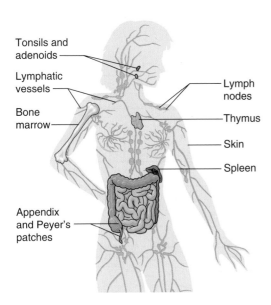

Figure 3–6 The immune system.

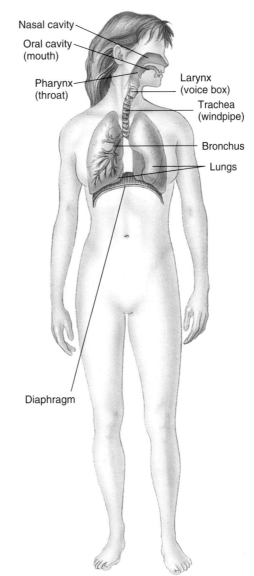

Figure 3–7 The respiratory system.

back to the lungs where is it expelled through the breath.

8. The **digestive system** (Figure 3–8) contains approximately 30 feet of tubing which extends from the mouth to the stomach, and ends at the anus. It has many complex functions that help break down food and separate nutrients, as well as eliminate waste products.

9. The **reproductive system** is a unique system because it deals with reproduction and the continuation of the human species. It is the only system that can be removed without endangering a person's life.

10. The **urinary system** (Figure 3–9) eliminates wastes from the body in the form of a slightly yellow liquid called urine. It helps to maintain the body's water and chemical balance. The production of waste is influenced by blood flow, blood pressure, the endocrine system, and the normal body rhythms and cycles.

Body rhythms are referred to as a circadian cycle. A circadian cycle refers to all the processes take place every 24 hours in an organism. A circadian cycle in the human body determines when we wake, sleep, digest food, rebuild tissue, etc.

The optimum health of the skin and the body is dependent on these systems all working in harmony with one another. Any deviation affects the skin and other organs. While all systems are important to understand and may be affected by your work, we will focus on the endocrine, circulatory, and immune systems. A greater understanding of these systems helps you to grasp the meaning of your treatment work, including massage and how it affects the skin and its health. As you improve your hands-on practice and study of products, you will progressively learn how it is all unified.

---

digestive system
Approximately 30 feet of tubing between the mouth, stomach, and anus responsible for complex functions including breaking down food and separating nutrients, along with eliminating waste.

reproductive system
Deals with the reproduction and the continuation of the human species.

urinary system
Eliminates wastes in the form of a slightly yellow liquid called urine.

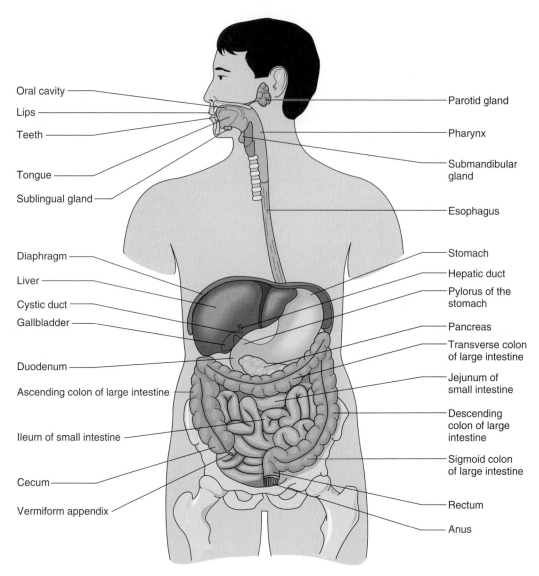

Figure 3–8 The digestive system.

Endocrine System

The endocrine system is responsible for regulating most of the hormone-producing glands. The system includes the pineal gland, hypothalamus gland, pituitary gland, parathyroid glands, adrenal glands, pancreas glands, stomach and intestines, kidneys, and reproductive organs.

Hormones

Hormones are one way that the different tissues, organs, and cells of the body communicate with one another for correct performance. Functions regulated by hormones include metabolism, water and mineral balance, growth and sexual development, and the body's reaction to stress. Hormones reach every part of the body, including skin cells. Skin functions are partially regulated by these chemical messengers.

Sex Hormones

Sex hormones, such as **androgens** in men, are responsible for male characteristics. They are produced in the testes. **Testosterone** is a male sex hormone. In women, the ovaries produce the sex

androgens
Any of various hormones that control the development of masculine characteristics.

testosterone
A male sex hormone.

hormones **estrogen** and **progesterone**. Women have more estrogen, which gives them female characteristics. Estrogens help influence the reproductive system. Progesterone is responsible for building the lining inside a woman's uterus. Overproduction of androgens and progesterone in women can cause acne, breakouts, and excessive facial hair growth.

The sex organs, the **testes** in males and the **ovaries** in females, secrete sex hormones and steroids that have many effects on the skin. The overproduction or underproduction of sex hormones can cause acne, hair growth or hair loss, and unwanted facial hair in women. Sex hormones are responsible for the production of sebum, facial hair growth in men, and the stimulation of collagen production. During menopause, the production of the female hormone, estrogen, decreases. Estrogen benefits the skin in many ways:

- It helps to regulate the size and activity of the sebaceous gland in the follicle (pore).
- It supports the production of important moisture binders such as hyaluronic acid.
- It helps to foster cellular turnover.
- It helps with the manufacture of collagen and elastin by the fibroblasts.

Hypothalamus

The **hypothalamus**, a gland located at the base of the brain, acts as the mastermind or master gland and coordinates hormone production, producing regulatory, or releasing, hormones that travel to the **pituitary gland**. At the site of the pituitary gland, hormones can act directly on, or stimulate, other hormones to perform a direct effect on target glands or tissue cells.

Hormones are transported to specific hormone receptor cells that require them for various functions. Hormones come in contact with the receptor sites, which are like a docking station for an airplane or space shuttle. Once the hormones are recognized, the receptor cells allow these messengers to enter. The messengers activate one or more chemical functions inside the cell, the message is transmitted to the cell's nucleus, and the cell carries out a particular function, as directed by the hormones.

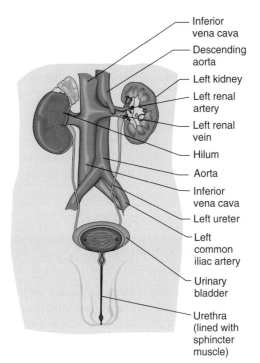

Figure 3–9 The urinary system.

Thyroid Gland

The **thyroid gland** is located in the neck. It regulates the body's metabolism, heart rate, rate of energy used, and calcium. Underproduction of thyroid hormone results in dry, itchy skin and hair breakage. Overproduction of thyroid hormone causes warm and red skin, increased sweating, hair loss, and rapidly growing nails.

Adrenal Glands

The **adrenal glands** are located just above the kidney and secrete **adrenaline** and cortisol, hormones manufactured when the body is under stress. Corticoids, also known as corticosteroids, are very small hormones produced by the adrenal cortex that easily penetrate cells. Corticoids are produced in the adrenal gland. Cortisol is responsible for causing both reactivity to stress and inflammation, and is also responsible for stopping excessive reactions by the body. Laboratory-produced synthetic cortisol is used as a drug to treat inflammation and allergic reactions, and to treat autoimmune diseases such as lupus. There are several types of corticoids that help to regulate the many biochemical reactions responsible for water and mineral balance in the body.

estrogen
A female sex hormone produced by the ovaries.

progesterone
A hormone responsible for building the lining inside a woman's uterus.

testes
Male sex glands that produce reproductive cells.

ovaries
Female sex glands that produce reproductive cells.

hypothalamus
The part of the brain that regulates many metabolic body processes.

pituitary gland
A ductless gland located at the base of the brain.

thyroid gland
Regulates the body's metabolism, heart rate, rate of energy used, and calcium.

adrenal glands
Glands located just above the kidney that secrete adrenaline and cortisol.

adrenaline
A hormone secreted under stress by the adrenal glands; it stimulates the nervous system, raises metabolism, increases cardiac pressure and output, and increases blood pressure to prepare the body for maximum exertion.

Thymus Gland

thymus gland
Responsible for the beginning of the immune system in young persons.

The **thymus gland** signals the development of the immune system in young persons. **T-lymphocytes** are produced in the thymus gland; the "T" stands for thymus. The thymus reaches maturity at puberty and then shrinks until it is undetectable in older adults. Lymphocytes continue to be manufactured in the bone marrow and the lymph nodes where they migrate into the body when needed.

T-lymphocytes
Manufactured in the bone marrow and the lymph nodes where they migrate into the body when needed.

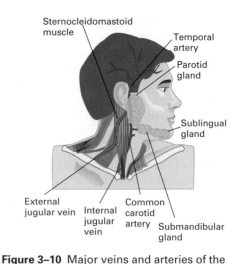

Figure 3–10 Major veins and arteries of the neck.

Circulatory System

aorta
The main artery coming out of the heart.

carotid
The main artery that goes to the head and face.

facial artery
Runs diagonally from the corner of the eye, across the nose to the jawline.

superficial temporal artery
Brings blood to the forehead and scalp.

transverse artery
Supplies the upper cheek and facial sides with blood.

superior temporal vein
Returns blood from the face towards the heart; situated near the temples of the head.

anterior facial vein
Vein located on the anterior sides of the face which drains into the internal jugular vein located on the sides of the neck.

The **circulatory system** originates with the heart and is responsible for moving the blood and lymph throughout the body. It is also referred to as the venal or vascular system. The circulatory system is a network of arteries, veins, and capillaries that nourish, oxygenate, and remove waste and toxins from every living cell in the body. Blood completes a full circuit of the body in approximately one minute. An artery is a tubular, thick-walled, elastic vessel through which oxygenated blood is pumped by the heart throughout the body. Blood is then returned to the heart through vessels called veins. Veins are smaller vessels with moderately thin walls that carry blood in a steady stream from the capillaries back to the heart. Venous blood carries carbon dioxide and waste materials away from the cells. Small branches of the major blood vessels are called capillaries. Capillaries are systems of tiny, thin-walled blood vessels that serve to distribute blood to all the tissues. These vessels can break easily. They are noticeable on the face and other parts of the body such as the legs (spider veins). Capillaries are linked between the arteries and the veins. Blood flows through capillaries to deliver nutrients and oxygen to the living cells in all tissues. These particular capillaries are called arterial capillaries. Capillaries that contain deoxygenated blood with carbon dioxide returning to the heart are referred to as venous capillaries.

The **aorta** is the main artery coming out of the heart. Other arteries branch off the aorta. The main artery that goes to the head and face is the **carotid** (facial) artery, which runs up the side of the neck. The carotid artery then branches into three smaller arteries that supply the facial tissues (Figure 3–10):

1. The **facial artery** runs diagonally from the corner of the eye, across the nose.

2. The **superficial temporal artery** goes to the forehead and scalp.

3. The **transverse artery** (transverse means crossing from side to side) supplies the upper cheek and facial sides.

Blood is returned from the face toward the heart via the **superior temporal vein** (superior means large, on top; temporal means situated near the temples of the head) to the **anterior facial vein** (anterior means near the front). It then connects to the **external jugular vein,** and eventually to the **superior vena cava**, the largest vein returning blood to the heart.

Blood

The blood transports red blood cells, white blood cells, and platelets; delivers nutrients; and removes waste materials (Figure 3–11) In a hospital laboratory, a test tube of blood is often spun to separate the different parts of the blood for study. **Plasma** is the grey-yellow fluid that is observed floating at the top of the tube. Because they are heavier, red and white blood cells and platelets settle to the bottom of the tube.

Blood consists of two types of cells: red blood cells and white blood cells. Red blood

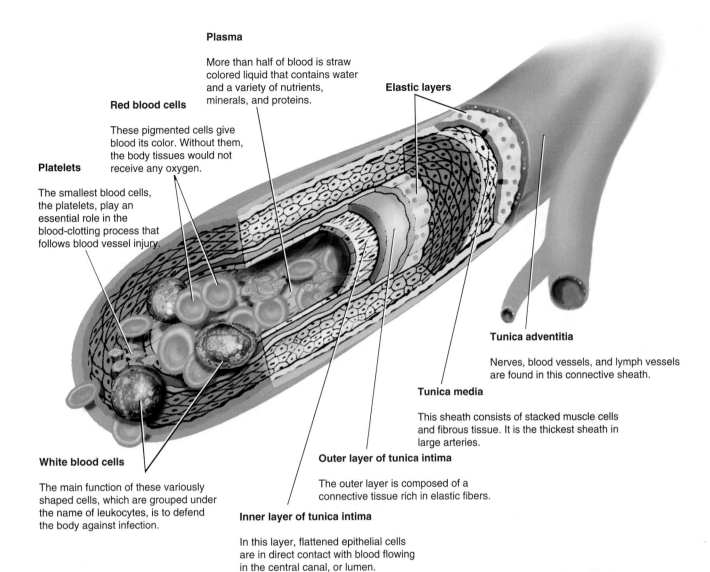

Plasma

More than half of blood is straw colored liquid that contains water and a variety of nutrients, minerals, and proteins.

Red blood cells

These pigmented cells give blood its color. Without them, the body tissues would not receive any oxygen.

Platelets

The smallest blood cells, the platelets, play an essential role in the blood-clotting process that follows blood vessel injury.

Elastic layers

Tunica adventitia

Nerves, blood vessels, and lymph vessels are found in this connective sheath.

Tunica media

This sheath consists of stacked muscle cells and fibrous tissue. It is the thickest sheath in large arteries.

Outer layer of tunica intima

The outer layer is composed of a connective tissue rich in elastic fibers.

Inner layer of tunica intima

In this layer, flattened epithelial cells are in direct contact with blood flowing in the central canal, or lumen.

White blood cells

The main function of these variously shaped cells, which are grouped under the name of leukocytes, is to defend the body against infection.

Figure 3–11 Blood is comprised of red blood cells, white blood cells, and platelets.

cells are responsible for delivering oxygen throughout the body and for removing carbon dioxide from all the cells. White blood cells, known as **lymphocytes,** are the immune cells that assist the immune system to protect and defend the body's cells against disease. **Platelets** are responsible for clotting factors in the blood and are activated when a blood vessel is cut. Platelets help stop bleed-ing during injury. When we cut our finger, the platelets form clumps or clots that become sticky. They mix with the air to form a scab.

The heart pumps blood to the lungs, where oxygen is picked up by the red blood cells and carbon dioxide is removed. The lungs breathe in oxygen and breathe out carbon dioxide. Blood leaves the lungs and returns to the heart, where it is pumped out the other

external jugular vein
The vein located on the sides of the neck that carries blood returning to the heart from the head, face, and neck.

superior vena cava
The large vein that carries blood to the upper right chamber of the heart.

plasma
The pale yellow or gray-yellow protein-containing fluid portion of the blood in which the blood cells and platelets are normally suspended.

lymphocytes
White blood cells formed in lymphatic tissue throughout the body. In normal adults, they make up 22–28% of the total number of leukocytes in the circulating blood.

platelets
Blood cells that aid in the forming of clots.

side of the heart through the arterial system, delivering nutrients and oxygen to cells. Cells deposit waste materials and carbon dioxide in the blood into the lymph, which goes back into the veins through the venous capillaries, and eventually returns to the heart.

Blood circulates through the kidneys, where waste materials and excess water and other fluids are filtered out and deposited in the bladder. Urine is the waste fluid that comes from the bladder. Kidney failure or kidney disease can result in toxins not being filtered from the blood, causing toxicity. Healthy kidneys thoroughly filter the blood and return it clean back to the circulatory system.

Lymphatic System

lymphatic system
Consists of lymph flowing through the lymphatic spaces, lymph vessels, lacteals, and lymph nodes.

manual lymph drainage (MLD)
A specialized advanced form of massage; presurgically, it helps to prepare the skin for a facelift, or other plastic surgery; post-surgery, it helps reduce swelling or edema, dissipates bruising, and encourages the healing process of the skin.

Along the same route as the blood vessels lies the **lymphatic system**. This system is made up of a series of lymph vessels (Figure 3–12) or tubes that carry the lymph, a colorless, plasmalike fluid that bathes tissues and removes wastes and foreign bodies, including bacteria and viruses. It plays a major role in the immune system. Unlike the blood system, the lymph system does not flow both ways. It only flows toward the heart.

Lymph capillaries gather waste materials bathed by the lymph. These capillaries eventually are emptied into larger lymph vessels that connect to the larger blood vessels. On the way to these veins, the lymph passes through networks of lymph nodes, which are masses of lymph tissue serving as filters to remove and kill organisms before they spread to the blood (Figure 3–13). Lymph nodes in the neck area are called cervical nodes. Buccal nodes are lymph nodes that run across the upper cheeks. Parotid nodes are found in the front of the ear. Retroauricular nodes are located in back of the ears and through the scalp (retro means in back of; auricle means the external part of the ear; retroauricular means concerned with the ear). The lymph nodes drain into the thoracic duct, located in the front of the upper chest. This is the main collector or terminal for the body's lymph system.

Lymph nodes occur in groups, with concentrated nodes in the armpits, groin, chest, and neck. Nodes are masses of lymph tissue covered by a fibrous capsule. Lymph nodes become enlarged when an infection exists in the body. Specific lymph nodes will swell with infections in specific areas, for example, the lymph nodes in the neck swell when a throat infection exists or when the individual has the mumps. The tonsils and adenoids are lymph nodes that are often inflamed in children.

Lymph nodes are also referred to as terminals. They can be compared to a waste water treatment plant. Sewer and dirty water is transported through sewer pipes from each home. It stops at a treatment plant (terminal) where it is pumped through filters. The sludge and debris is collected and trucked from the plant where it can be disposed of properly. The filtered water is returned to holding areas for further purification. It continues on to clean water reservoirs where it is tested, treated, and returned for safe use by the community.

A basic understanding of the lymph fluid helps us understand why a lymphatic massage is so helpful during facials, especially for an individual who has a buildup of impurities such as acne or breakouts, or for either pre- or postsurgery. A specialized advanced form of massage, known as **manual lymph drainage** (**MLD**), requires special training to perform. Presurgically, this type of massage helps to prepare the skin for a facelift or other plastic surgery. Postsurgery, it helps reduce swelling or edema, dissipate bruising, and encourage the healing process of the skin. It can be used to help with acne, sensitive skin, and other conditions. Lymphatic drainage may not be performed on individuals with cancer or other autoimmune diseases unless authorized by a physician.

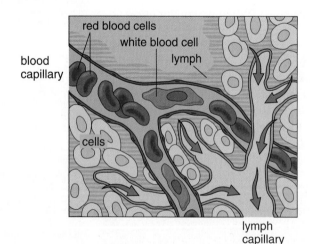

red blood cells

white blood cell

blood capillary

lymph

cells

lymph capillary

Figure 3–12 A lymph capillary vessel.

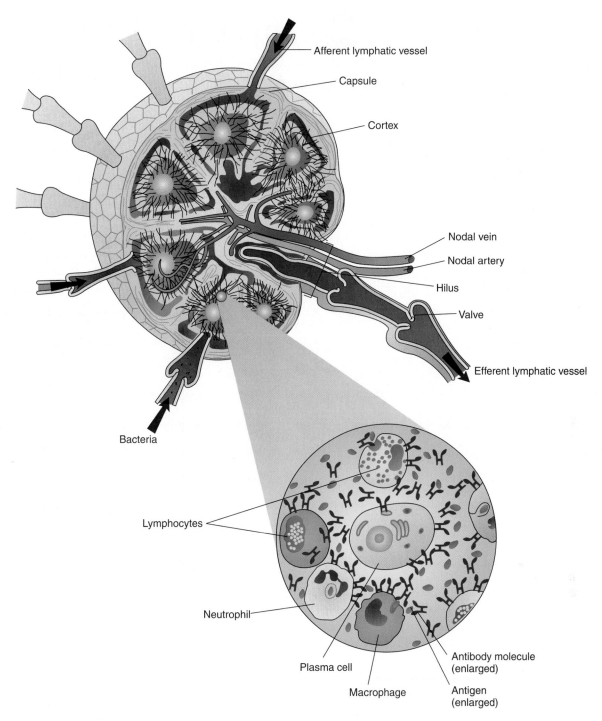

Figure 3–13 labels:
Afferent lymphatic vessel
Capsule
Cortex
Nodal vein
Nodal artery
Hilus
Valve
Efferent lymphatic vessel
Bacteria
Lymphocytes
Neutrophil
Plasma cell
Macrophage
Antibody molecule (enlarged)
Antigen (enlarged)

Figure 3–13 A cross section of a lymph node.

Immune System

The immune system is quite complicated. It is a vital part of our health and without its protection, we would not be able to live. In skin care, it is important to become familiar with the body's immune response. While it may be rare, applying the wrong product to the skin can cause a reaction. Giving a client too many new products at the same time may confuse the skin and create a slight reaction. Anything that is unfamiliar to the skin presents a potential immune response, which is why it is necessary to understand as much about your client's health and skin as possible.

There are basically two forms of immune response in the body:

Nonverbal Communication

Many times it is not what we say, but rather how we say it. There are many facets to communicating well. One of the ways we let others know how we are receiving them is through our body language. Tone of voice and speech patterning are also important.

Paying attention to the nonverbal cues we use can help us improve the quality of our business relations, not only with clients, but with colleagues as well. Take a look at the following list of positive and negative nonverbal cues, and then rate yourself on how well you come across and present yourself to others.

Positive Nonverbal Cues

- Tone of voice is pleasant
- Rate of speech is even
- Tone of voice is moderate
- Maintains good eye contact
- Uses positive gestures such as nodding
- Facial expressions are warm and animated
- Demonstrates positive regard by smiling often
- Body distance is appropriate—neither too close nor too far away
- Uses hand gestures that demonstrate caring, such as touching a client's hand in a supportive way

Negative Nonverbal Cues

- Rate of speech is rapid and jumbled
- Tone of voice is loud and overpowering
- Tone of voice is very soft and unassertive
- Looks away from person when speaking
- Yawns or appears otherwise distracted
- Frowns, or sneers to show disapproval
- Purses lips or folds arms in a put-off manner
- Body distance is uncomfortably close or too far away
- Uses hand gestures such as pointing to scold or embarrass

---

pseudopod
A false foot.

antigen
A foreign invader such as a bacteria, a virus, or other substances that could cause harm to the body.

T-helper cells
A type of white blood cells that signal the immune system within the blood stream to react to the invasion of foreign substances or invading organisms.

1. The antibody immune response. Antibodies are carried in the plasma cells that circulate throughout the body in the lymphatic system and the bloodstream. An antibody is a substance formed in response to a foreign body such as a virus or bacteria.

2. The second response refers to the immune cell response that occurs when an unrecognized foreign substance enters the body. If there are no antibodies already present, the immune cells try to identify and destroy anything that is not recognized. The immune cells also build up new antibodies, which attack and destroy this aggressor if it tries to re-enter the body at a future time.

Immune Response Cells

Langerhans are star-shaped cells manufactured in the bone marrow and found in the lymph nodes and epidermis. Langerhans have cellular projections called dendrites on one end. The other end has a **pseudopod** or false foot, which helps the cell move. The mobility of Langerhans allows them to move in and out of the epidermis shortly after an **antigen** makes an appearance. An antigen is a foreign invader such as a bacteria, a virus, or other substances that could cause harm to the body.

Considered patrol guards or sentinels, Langerhans cells detect foreign substances. They break off a piece of the substance and bring it to a large immune cell called a macrophage, which is found in the dermis and the lymph nodes. Macrophages are programmed to know what is part of the body and what is foreign (macro means large). They give off chemicals that signal another type of white blood cell called **T-helper cells,** which signal the immune system within the bloodstream to react to the invasion of the foreign substance or organisms (Figure 3–14).

Antibody defenses

B lymphocytes recognize the foreign proteins, or antigens, of disease organisms since they differ from natural body proteins. Antigens trigger B cells to multiply. Some develop into plasma cells, which secrete antibodies - proteins that attack and destroy only the antigens.

Memory B cell
These B cells are able to recognize an antigen from a previous infection.

Antigen attacked by antibody

B lymphocyte recognizes antigen

Antigen

B lymphocyte
These cells begin life as stem cells in bone marrow. They develop in the lymph nodes.

Plasma cell

Antibodies

Cellular defenses

T lymphocytes develop inside the thymus gland. "Killer" T cells react to the remains of destroyed specific antigens, attacking them, as well as any infected cells, with powerful proteins called lymphokines. "Helper" T cells activate B and T cells, while "suppressor" T cells inhibit the response of other cells to the invading antigens.

Remains of antigen

Memory T cell
These cells may survive for many years to respond to an attempted second invasion by the same antigen. They mobilize very quickly.

Killer T cell

T cells multiply

Lymphokine

Infected cell

Infected cell and organism destroyed

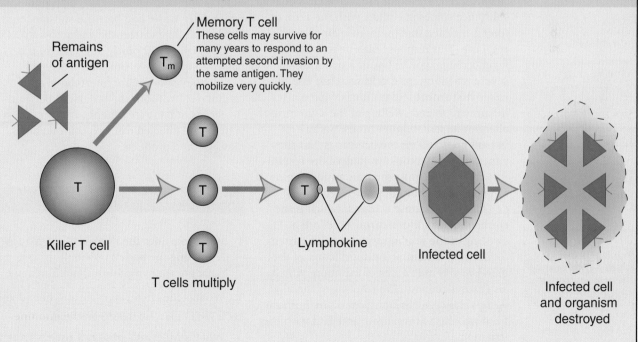

Figure 3–14 The immune response.

autoimmune
An ailment resulting from a breakdown of the body's immune system so that the immune response is directed toward the body's own organs.

lupus
An autoimmune disease resulting in a breakdown of the body's immune system, causing the immune response to be directed toward the body's own organs.

histamine
A chemical that causes inflammation and swelling of the skin during allergic and irritation reactions.

hives
Urticaria; a skin eruption.

urticaria
Red, raised lesions or wheals that itch severely; caused by an allergic or emotional reaction.

There are several different types of T- helper cells. They are produced in the lymph system, the spleen, and the thymus gland. In **autoimmune** diseases such as the HIV virus in AIDS, it is the T-helper cells that are killed by the virus. This is why patients with AIDS cannot defend against common infections such as a cold. A similar response occurs in another autoimmune disease known as **lupus**. An autoimmune disease is an ailment resulting from a breakdown of the body's immune system, causing the immune response to be directed toward the body's own organs, frequently resulting in death.

Macrophage cells alert the T-killer cells, which are headquartered in the lymph nodes. Activated T-killer cells rush to the scene via the bloodstream and kill the invading organism. A third type of T-cell, called T-suppressor cells, signal the T-helper cells that the mission has been accomplished. The T-killer cells are finished with their job and no longer need to be active.

Once an invader has entered the body and been destroyed, special memory cells called B-cells recognize the antigen from a previous illness. They enable the body to respond faster so that the illness is prevented. Antibodies coat bacteria and viruses, causing them to be destroyed. In the event of recurring bacteria, an antibody attaches to the disease organism and destroys it.

Another specialized white blood cell is the mast cell. Mast cells are activated when a substance comes in contact with the skin, or food is ingested that may cause an allergic response. This response may be to food, hay fever, asthma, poison ivy, or a bee sting. In severe reactions, mast cells secrete a chemical called **histamine**. Histamine is what causes inflammation and swelling of the skin during allergic and irritation reactions. Some individuals are so allergic to bee stings that they experience dangerous swelling of the respiratory tract. They must carry an antihistamine to take in case they are stung again.

Another response is **hives**, which is the common term for **urticaria**. Hives are a swelling of the skin in response to an irritant or allergen. Histamine causes dilation of the blood vessels in the area of irritation, which also causes redness. The swelling of the blood vessels allows better transport of the immune function cells to investigate and deal with the irritation.

Summary

The systems of the body are unique and each has a specific role to play. Each of these systems affects the health of the skin because they each have a very important task. All systems working in harmony produces a healthy body and alert mind. When there is illness, the skin tones may appear sallow, with dark circles under the eyes.

The endocrine system is a vital system containing glands that are responsible for producing hormones. Hormones are messengers that deliver instructions to cells. As research continues to uncover the mysteries surrounding hormone function, we know now that they play a large role in healthy skin. Imbalance causes disruption of the normal skin processes. It may manifest as a breakout, sensitive skin, or other symptoms.

The circulatory system is the body's largest internal system and contains the blood that is responsible for delivering nutrients to the cells and carrying away waste materials. Arteries carry oxygenated blood to all the cells and tissues. The veins carry carbon dioxide and wastes back toward the heart. Within the circulatory system lies the lymphatic network. It plays a vital role in keeping disease or foreign substances from harming the body. The blood returning to the heart passes through several lymph nodes, which filter waste and harmful substances. The lymph fluid carries the waste to a main collector called a thoracic duct, where it is passed to the body's elimination organs.

All body systems are interrelated and cannot exist without the others. In performing facials or body treatments, many of these systems are affected through our machines, massage, and products.

Discussion Questions

1. What role does the thyroid gland play in regulating the body's metabolism, and what are the symptoms of malfunction?

2. What is the circadian cycle and how does it affect the function of the body?

3. What is MLD and what is it used for?

4. What role does the endocrine system play in regulating hormone-producing glands? Name the glands that have the most significant impact on proper skin functioning and how they affect function.

5. What effect does the circulatory system have on maintaining healthy skin?

Notes

Clayman, Charles. 1995. *The Human Body, An Illustrated Guide to Its Structure, Function, and Disorders*. New York: DK Publishing.

Ibid, xx.

Ibid, 15.

Ibid, 103.

Ibid, 125.

Additional Reading

Mayo Clinic. 2001. *Your Immune System*. Rochester, Minn.: Mayo Foundation for Medical Education and Research. (http://www.mayoclinic.com)

Pugliese, Peter. 1991. *Advanced Professional Skin Care*, 96–99. Bernville, Pa.: APSC Publishing.

———. 2001. *Physiology of the Skin II*. Carol Stream, Ill.: Allured.

White, Clifton R., Jr., et al. 1996. *What Does Normal Skin Do?* Vol 1., *Cutaneous Medicine and Surgery, An Integrated Program in Dermatology*. 3–41, 46–56. New York: Simon & Schuster.

Chapter 4
Bones, Muscles, and Nerves Of the Face and Skull

Chapter Objectives

After reading this chapter, you should be able to:

- State the significance of the skull and neck bones.
- Identify the function of facial and neck muscles.
- Explain the importance of the nerves throughout the face and neck.

Chapter Outline

Introduction
Bones of the Skull
Muscles of the Face, Neck,
  and Scalp
Nerves
Nerve Motor Points of the
  Face and Neck

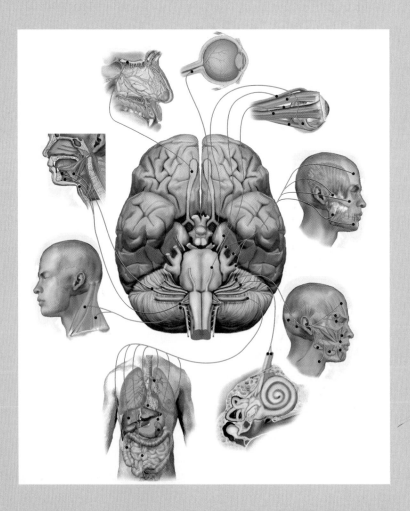

Introduction

Estheticians must understand the bones, muscles, nerves, and nerve points of the head and neck. This chapter focuses on these specific anatomical structures (anatomy of these areas). Knowledge of the muscular structure is important when administering massage techniques, designing corrective makeup, performing newer muscle stimulation techniques, understanding how the face moves, and discussing plastic surgery techniques with both plastic surgeons and clients. This information is also essential when operating more advanced facial esthetic machines for muscle lifting or stimulation.

Bones of the Skull

There are 206 bones in the human body. Bones are made up of fibrous tissues firmly bound together, consisting of one-third **organic** material such as blood vessels and nerves and approximately two-thirds **inorganic** mineral material such as calcium and phosphorous. Organic refers to substances relating to an organ or living tissue. Inorganic refers to substances composed of matter not related to living organisms. The function of bone is to

- give shape and strength to the skull and rest of the body
- protect organs against injury.
- serve as attachments for muscles
- act as levers for all body movements

The entire bone structure of the head, as a unit, is known as the **skull** (Figure 4–1, p.70). An oval bony structure, the cranial vault, shapes the head and protects the brain. The skull is divided into two parts—the cranium and the face. The cranium consists of the eight bones that contain the brain tissue. The face area contains fourteen bones.

Bones of the Cranium

The **occipital bone** forms the lower back part of the cranium. The two **parietal bones** form the sides and top (crown) of the cranium. The **frontal bone** forms the forehead.

The two **temporal bones** form the sides of the head in the ear region, below the parietal bones. The ethmoid bone is a light, spongy bone between the eye sockets, that forms part of the nasal cavities. The **sphenoid bone** joins together all the bones of the cranium. The wavy borders where the bones connect are known as sutures.

Bones of the Face

The two nasal bones are situated at the top of the nose, and form the bridge. Cartilage extends from the nasal bones forming the flexible part of the nose. The lacrimal bones comprise the sockets of the eyes, and are attached to the nasal bone, close to the inside corners of the eyes. Two zygomatic bones form the cheekbones. The two **maxillae** are the upper jawbones, which join to form the entire upper jaw. The **mastoid bone** extends from the temporal bone, and can be felt just behind and over the top of the ear. It extends over the attachment of the **mandible**, which is the lower jawbone, and is the largest and strongest bone of the face.

The following facial bones do not appear on Figure 4–1. Two turbinal bones are thin layers of spongy bone, situation on either of the outer walls of the nasal depression. The vomer is a single bone that forms part of the dividing wall of the nose. The two palatine bones form the floor and outer wall of the nose, roof of the mouth, and floor of the orbits.

Bones of the Neck

The **hyoid** is a U-shaped bone that is located in the front part of the throat, and is known as the "Adam's apple." Cervical vertebrae are found in the neck region at the top of the spinal column. They are small bones that are sometimes injured from impact such as a whiplash, which is caused by a sudden jerking back of the head.

Muscles of the Face, Neck, and Scalp

The muscular system covers, shapes, and supports the skeleton. Its function is to help produce movement. The muscular system

---

organic
Relating to an organ; pertaining to substances having carbon-to-carbon bonds.

inorganic
Composed of matter not arising from natural growth or living organisms; without carbon.

occipital bone
Bone that attaches to the parietal bone and forms the lower back part of the cranium.

parietal bones
Bones that form the sides and top (crown) of the cranium.

frontal bone
The bone that forms the forehead.

temporal bones
The bones forming the side of the head in the ear region, below the parietal bones.

sphenoid bone
Joins together all the bones of the cranium.

maxillae
Two bones that form the upper jawbone.

mastoid bone
Extends from the temporal bone; can be felt just behind and over the top of the ear.

mandible
The lower jawbone.

hyoid
A U-shaped bone that is located in the front part of the throat, and is known as the "Adam's apple."

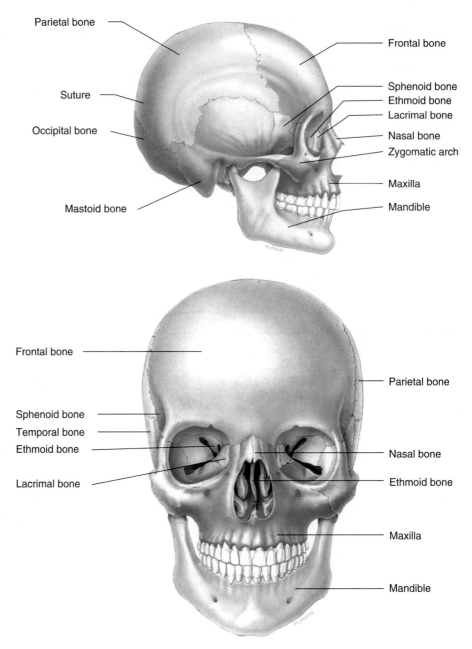

Figure 4–1 The skull bones.

myofibrils
Muscle fibers containing filaments; give muscles their contractible ability.

occipital frontalis
A broad muscle on top of the scalp.

occipitalis
Back of the epicranius; a muscle that draws the scalp backward.

consists of over 500 muscles that range from large to small. They comprise approximately 40% to 50% of the body's weight.

Muscles are contractile fibrous tissue. Body movements are dependent on them. The muscle system works closely with the skeletal and nervous systems for proper operation.

Facial muscles are voluntary muscles that are responsible for facial expressions. They help form and support the skin. They interweave along the facial bones, enabling the face to move in many different ways. Facial muscles also allow for chewing, swallowing, speaking, and other facial movements.

Muscles are made of small protein structures known as **myofibrils**. Muscles move parts of the body, or the face, by means of contraction. An electrical biochemical reaction causes the muscles to contract. Muscles that connect bones are known as skeletal muscles. The central part of the muscle is called the belly. The end of the muscle, which is attached to a stationary bone, is known as the origin. The other end of the muscle, which is attached to the

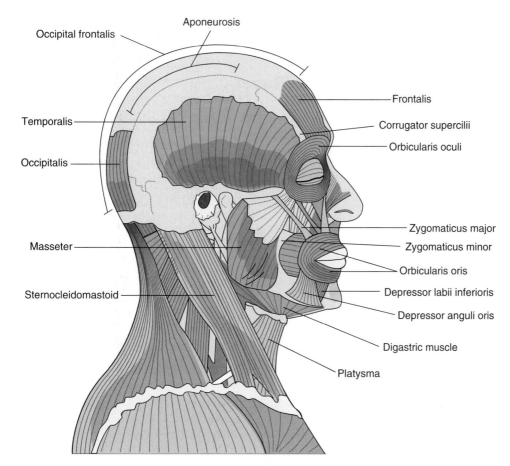

Figure 4–2 Muscles of the face and neck.

frontalis
Anterior or front portion of the epicranium; muscle of the scalp.

aponeurosis
A tendon that connects the occipitalis and the frontalis.

temporalis
Muscles on the sides of the head.

orbicularis oculi
A circular muscle that surrounds each eye.

orbicularis oris
A circular muscle which encircles the mouth.

corrugator supercilii
Facial muscle that draws eyebrows down, and wrinkles the forehead vertically.

Botox®
Botulism toxin which causes temporary paralysis; softens the scowl lines in between the eyes, or the frown lines on the forehead.

zygomaticus major
Muscles in the cheeks which attach the mouth to the upper cheek.

zygomaticus minor
Muscles in the cheeks which attach the upper cheek to the upper lip area.

digastric muscle
Located under the chin; runs the length of the middle of the neck.

bone that moves, is known as the area of insertion.

Facial muscles are layered and lie under the subcutaneous layer of the skin. The upper layers of the muscle structure are responsible for facial expressions, and the lower layers of muscles are responsible for chewing, and movement of the face during talking (Figure 4–2).

Muscles of the Scalp

The **occipital frontalis** is a broad muscle on top of the scalp. It consists of two parts: the **occipitalis,** which is at the base of the back of the skull, and the **frontalis.** Both muscles are connected by a tendon called the **aponeurosis**. The **temporalis** muscles are located on the sides of the head.

Muscles of the Eyebrows

The **orbicularis oculi** is a circular muscle that surrounds each eye. Another circular muscle is the **orbicularis oris,** which encircles the mouth. The muscle that makes the

forehead scowl is called the **corrugator supercilii**, commonly known as the corrugator. This muscle is often injected with botulism toxin, known as **Botox**, which causes temporary paralysis. A Botox injection softens the scowl lines in between the eyes, or the frown lines on the forehead.

Muscles in the cheeks are the **zygomaticus major**, which attach the mouth to the upper cheek, and the **zygomaticus minor**, which attach the upper cheek to the upper lip area. The masseter is the muscle that allows chewing to occur. It runs up and down the face, under the zygomatic muscles. The chin muscles are the depressor anguli oris, which connect the lower chin to the corners of the mouth. The depressor labii inferioris overlaps underneath the angulis oris and the obicularis oris. The **digastric muscle**, located under the chin, runs the length of the middle neck.

Muscles of the Neck

The neck muscles cause the head to move from side to side, and up and down. The muscles that run down the sides of the front

SKILLS **FOR** SUCCESS

Being a Team Player

Team: *Any group organized to work together.*

Team work: *Cooperative effort by the members of a team to achieve a common goal.*

Team player: *An individual dedicated to working cooperatively with others to achieve a common goal.*

Team + Teamwork = Team Player

Are you a team player? Do you enjoy working together with others to achieve a common goal? Or would you rather operate individually, answering only to yourself? Take a few moments to think seriously about these questions—your success in the real world may depend upon it.

Today's spa environment can be hectic and fast-paced. Both clients and employers can be demanding and rightfully so. Treatments are often expensive and clients should expect to receive quality service. Employers also have certain expectations such as increasing business, which depends on each employee promoting and referring clients for additional services. To maintain a stress free and productive work climate coworkers must be able to rely on one other. So unless you are working as a single operator in your own salon, expect your boss to insist on your being a team player.

Most spa operations have little tolerance for individual agendas—they simply cannot afford to undermine the success of the group or alienate clients because of one person's poor conduct. To maintain a positive team atmosphere, each member must be focused on developing the right attitude. The success of any spa depends on each individual developing the following standards.

- **Trust**—Staff members need to know that they can rely and depend on one another.

- **Unity**—Everyone must be united around common goals: providing quality service in a relaxing, supportive, and nurturing environment.

- **Cooperation**—Individuals must pull their own weight and be dedicated to sharing the workload to alleviate stress.

- **Support**—Team members need to express compassion for one another and support one another through difficult times.

- **Responsibility**—Individuals should understand that they need to help one another to achieve common goals and be ready, willing, and able to do so.

- **Genuine caring**—Caring team members demonstrate a genuine interest in nurturing and encouraging one another to do the best job possible.

- **Respect**—The successful team accepts and values one another for their differences.

neck are the **sternocleidomastoid muscles**. These strap muscles are the two cordlike muscles on the front of the neck. The **platysma** extends from the upper chest and wraps the lower cheeks and chin. The platysma is responsible for a firm chin and neck. Stretching and loosening of the neck over the years causes sagging tissue under the chin, which is associated with aging.

Muscles of the Shoulders and Arms

The principle muscle groups attach the arms to the body and permit movement (Figure 4–3, p. 74). These are the muscles that are normally tight and benefit greatly from massage.

The **trapezius** and the **latissimi dorsi** cover the back of the neck and the upper and middle regions of the back. They rotate the shoulder blade and control the swinging movements of the arm. The **pectoralis major** and **pectoralis minor** cover the front of the chest and assist in swinging movements of the arms. The **serratus anterior** assists in breathing and raising the shoulder. There are groups of muscles that extend to the arm. The **deltoid** is the large, thick, triangular-shaped muscle covering the shoulder that lifts and turns the arm. The **biceps** is the two-headed and main muscle on the front of the upper arm. It lifts the forearm, flexes the elbow, and turns the palm upward. **Triceps** is the three-headed muscle that covers the entire back of the upper arm and extends the forearm forward.

The forearm has a series of muscles and strong tendons including the:

- **Pronators**—important since they turn the hand inward, so that the palm faces downward.
- **Supinators**—turn the hand outward, and the palm upward.
- **Flexors**—bend the wrist, draw the hand up, and close the fingers toward the forearm.
- **Extensors**—straighten the wrist, hand, and fingers to form a straight line.

The hand has many small muscles that overlap from joint to joint giving it flexibility and strength. During the aging process, these muscles lose mobility, causing stiffness in the joints and hands. Massage can help relax and maintain pliability of these muscles.

Nerves

There are major nerves within the structure of the face that carry impulses or messages from sensing organs to the brain. Sensory nerves are responsible for feeling pain, pressure, heat, and cold. Motor nerves carry impulses to and from the muscles to the brain. They are responsible for movement. A nerve reflex is the path the nerve travels through, from the spinal cord to the brain, in response to a stimulus. This reflex action occurs, for example, when something hot is touched.

The brain is the largest mass of nerve tissue and is contained in the head. It is the fundamental control center for the body to send and receive messages. Twelve pairs of

---

biceps
The two-headed, main muscle on the front of the upper arm; lifts the forearm, flexes the elbow, and turns the palm upward.

triceps
The three-headed muscle that covers the entire back of the upper arm and extends the forearm forward.

pronators
Muscles that turn the hand inward so that the palm faces downward.

supinators
Muscles that turn the hand outward and the palm upward.

flexors
Muscles that bend the wrist, draw the hand up, and close the fingers toward the forearm.

extensors
Muscles that straighten the wrist, hand, and fingers to form a straight line.

sternocleidomastoid muscles
The muscles that run down the sides of the front of the neck.

platysma
Extends from the upper chest and wraps the lower cheeks and chin; responsible for a firm chin and neck.

trapezius
Muscles that cover the back of the neck and the upper and middle regions of the back; rotate the shoulder blade and control swinging movement of the arm.

latissimi dorsi
A broad, flat superficial muscle covering the back of the neck and upper and middle region of the back, controlling the shoulder blade and the swinging movements of the arm.

pectoralis major
The muscle that flexes and rotates the arm forward and inward.

pectoralis minor
The muscle that draws the shoulder forward and rotates the scapula (shoulder blade) downward.

serratus anterior
A muscle of the chest assisting in breathing and in raising the shoulder.

deltoid
Large, thick, triangular-shaped muscle covering the shoulder; lifts and turns the arm.

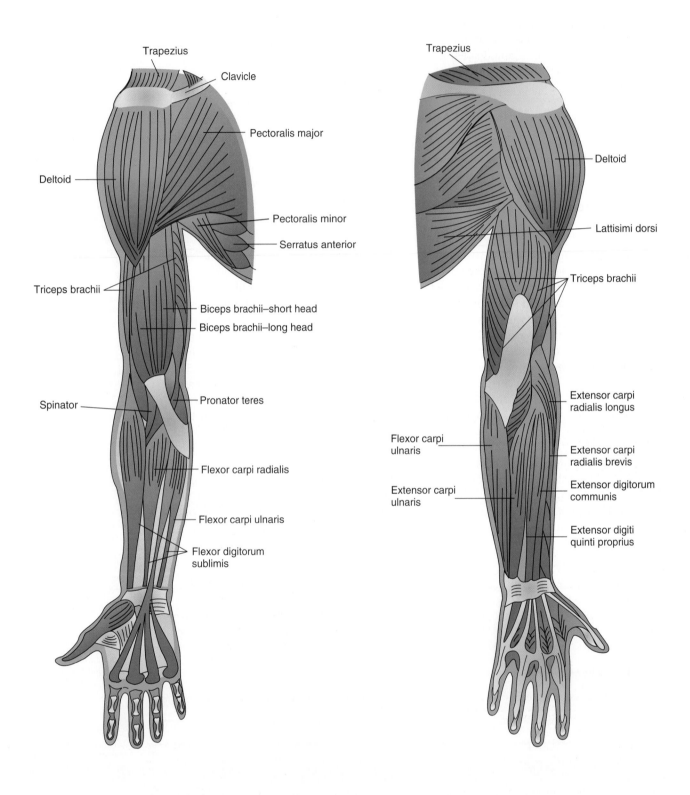

Figure 4–3 Muscles of the shoulders and arms.

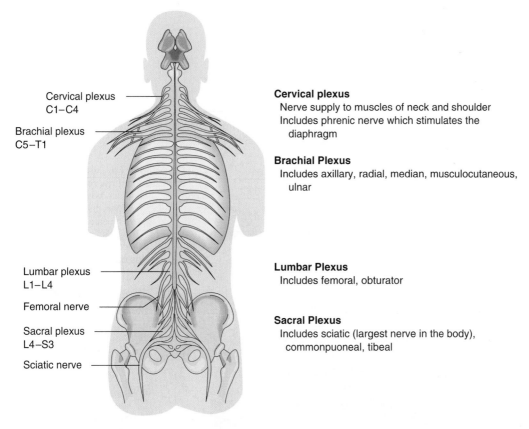

Figure 4–4 Nerves extending from the spinal column.

Cervical plexus
C1–C4

Brachial plexus
C5–T1

Lumbar plexus
L1–L4

Femoral nerve

Sacral plexus
L4–S3

Sciatic nerve

Cervical plexus
Nerve supply to muscles of neck and shoulder
Includes phrenic nerve which stimulates the
diaphragm

Brachial Plexus
Includes axillary, radial, median, musculocutaneous,
ulnar

Lumbar Plexus
Includes femoral, obturator

Sacral Plexus
Includes sciatic (largest nerve in the body),
commonpuoneal, tibeal

cranial nerves originate in the brain, and are distributed to the spinal cord inside a column-like structure.

The spinal cord is made up of 31 pairs of spinal nerves that extend and are distributed from the spinal column to the muscles, skin, and the limbs (Figure 4–4). Nerve impulses are constantly flashing into the brain, and sending chemical signals (messages) to the nerve cables found in the spinal cord. These messages are distributed throughout the entire body into the cells, muscles, and organs, communicating information for proper body function.

Fifth Cranial Nerve

Sensory nerves are branched from the fifth cranial nerve, which is the main sensory nerve of the face, and the motor nerve for the muscles involved with chewing (Figure 4–5, p.76). They affect sensation in the face, and are branched into the mandibular nerve, affecting the jaw and lower face; the maxillary nerve, affecting the midface and cheeks;

and the opthalmic nerve, affecting the eye area and forehead.

Seventh Cranial Nerve

Motor nerves extend from the main facial motor nerve, called the seventh cranial nerve, also known as the facial nerve. This nerve is responsible for facial movements and expressions. It extends from the lower ear and divides into five extended branches. The cervical nerve affects the chin and lower jaw. The buccal nerve extends to the cheeks and upper jaw. The eye and upper cheek contain the zygomatic nerve. The temporal nerve controls the temples and forehead.

Nerve Motor Points of the Face And Neck

Almost every muscle and nerve has a motor point (Figure 4–6, p. 77). Positions vary in location on each person due to the differences in body structure. Pressure or manipu-

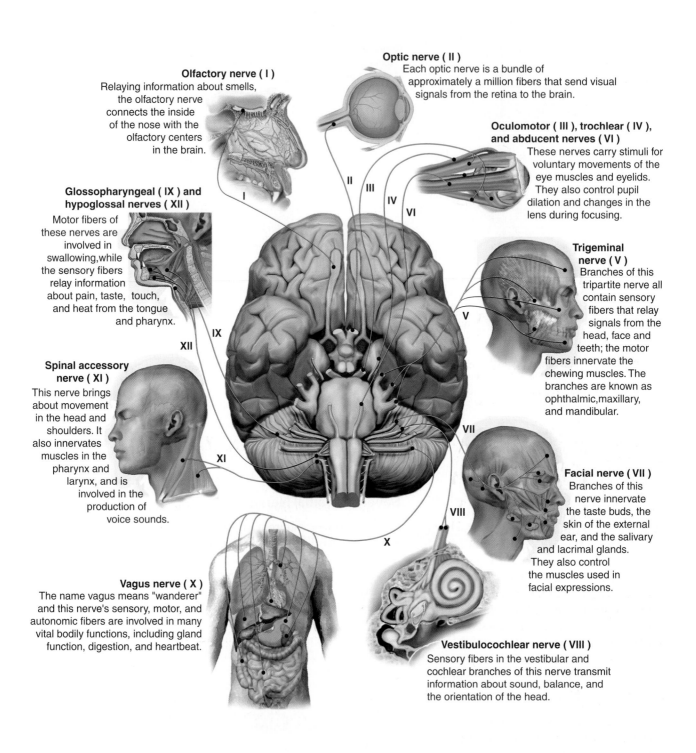

Olfactory nerve (I)
Relaying information about smells, the olfactory nerve connects the inside of the nose with the olfactory centers in the brain.

Optic nerve (II)
Each optic nerve is a bundle of approximately a million fibers that send visual signals from the retina to the brain.

Oculomotor (III), trochlear (IV), and abducent nerves (VI)
These nerves carry stimuli for voluntary movements of the eye muscles and eyelids. They also control pupil dilation and changes in the lens during focusing.

Glossopharyngeal (IX) and hypoglossal nerves (XII)
Motor fibers of these nerves are involved in swallowing, while the sensory fibers relay information about pain, taste, touch, and heat from the tongue and pharynx.

Trigeminal nerve (V)
Branches of this tripartite nerve all contain sensory fibers that relay signals from the head, face and teeth; the motor fibers innervate the chewing muscles. The branches are known as ophthalmic, maxillary, and mandibular.

Spinal accessory nerve (XI)
This nerve brings about movement in the head and shoulders. It also innervates muscles in the pharynx and larynx, and is involved in the production of voice sounds.

Facial nerve (VII)
Branches of this nerve innervate the taste buds, the skin of the external ear, and the salivary and lacrimal glands. They also control the muscles used in facial expressions.

Vagus nerve (X)
The name vagus means "wanderer" and this nerve's sensory, motor, and autonomic fibers are involved in many vital bodily functions, including gland function, digestion, and heartbeat.

Vestibulocochlear nerve (VIII)
Sensory fibers in the vestibular and cochlear branches of this nerve transmit information about sound, balance, and the orientation of the head.

Figure 4–5 The cranial nerves.

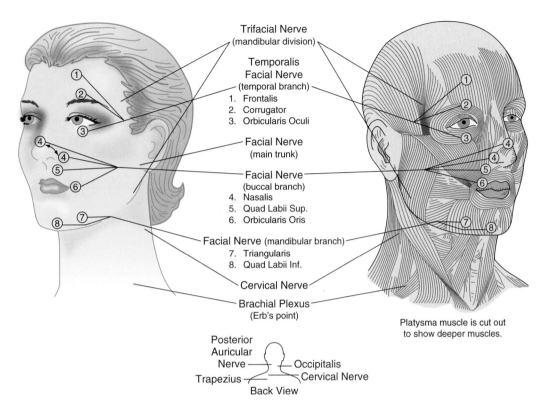

Figure 4–6 Motor nerves of the face and shoulders.

lations over these points induce relaxation. At the beginning of a facial, and to help the client relax, gently press on these points prior to the cleansing process.

Summary

Bone tissue contains nerves, blood vessels, and minerals that all make up the body's skeleton system. Muscles and skin tissue are wrapped over the bones and give it mobility as well as protection. Estheticians play a big role in stimulating muscles and nerves during their work. Any movement that helps increase circulation and flexibility to muscles benefits a client's well-being.

The nervous system is the body's central control center. It originates in the brain. Nerve impulses run along fibers that look like miniature (electrical) cords and distribute messages throughout the body. Impulses are electrical-chemical signals that jump from one nerve ending to another.

Discussion Questions

1. Why is it important for the esthetician to know the anatomical structures of the head and neck?

2. Explain the difference between organic and inorganic.

3. Explain the difference between sensory nerves and motor nerves, including how they function.

4. What is the special significance of the fifth and seventh cranial nerves?

Additional Reading

Becker, Robert, and Gary Selden. 1995. *The Body Electric.* New York: Quill, William Morrow.

Chapter 5
Bacteriology and Sanitation

Chapter Objectives

After reading this chapter, you should be able to:

- State the importance of sanitation and prevention of microorganisms.
- Explain the differences between bacteria and viruses.
- State the importance of sterilization.
- Explain the difference between disinfectants and sterilization.
- Describe the protocols for handling hazardous waste materials.
- Describe how to prevent cross-contamination using the proper equipment and tools.

Chapter Outline

Introduction
Microorganisms
Sterilization
Policies and Procedures

Introduction

Estheticians work on the human body, which makes it essential for them to learn about bacteria and preventing the spread of disease. **Sanitation** is the practice of cleanliness. The practice of esthetics involves following guidelines to prevent the contamination of products and implements. We must prevent the spread of germs from client to client, and from client to the esthetician, and vice versa.

Basic guidelines from both state and federal government authorities have evolved during the past few years, making it mandatory for all health care professionals to practice safe handling of bloodborne materials, instruments, and equipment. These regulations are equally as important to the skin care industry. This information is available from the **Occupational Safety and Health Administration (OSHA),** a U.S. government agency that oversees workplace safety for employees. OSHA has numerous sites on the Internet that deal with specific issues for various occupations. Newer publications focusing on the esthetics industry are also available. Refer to the Additional Reading section at the end of this chapter.

Microorganisms

Microorganisms are germs that live almost everywhere. They cannot be seen with the naked eye. One must use a microscope, and in some cases, an electron microscope, to see them. They are on the surfaces of objects, in and on our bodies, on our skin, and even in the air. Germs in the air are called **airborne microorganisms.** Some microorganisms cause disease; others do not. Microorganisms that cause disease are called **pathogenic microorganisms.** Microorganisms that do not cause disease are known as **nonpathogenic microorganisms.**

Bacteria are an example of one-celled microorganisms (Figure 5–1). Some bacteria cause disease, but other helpful bacteria can actually help us. Digestion of food cannot take place without bacteria. Some vitamin absorption is also dependent on "good" bacteria.

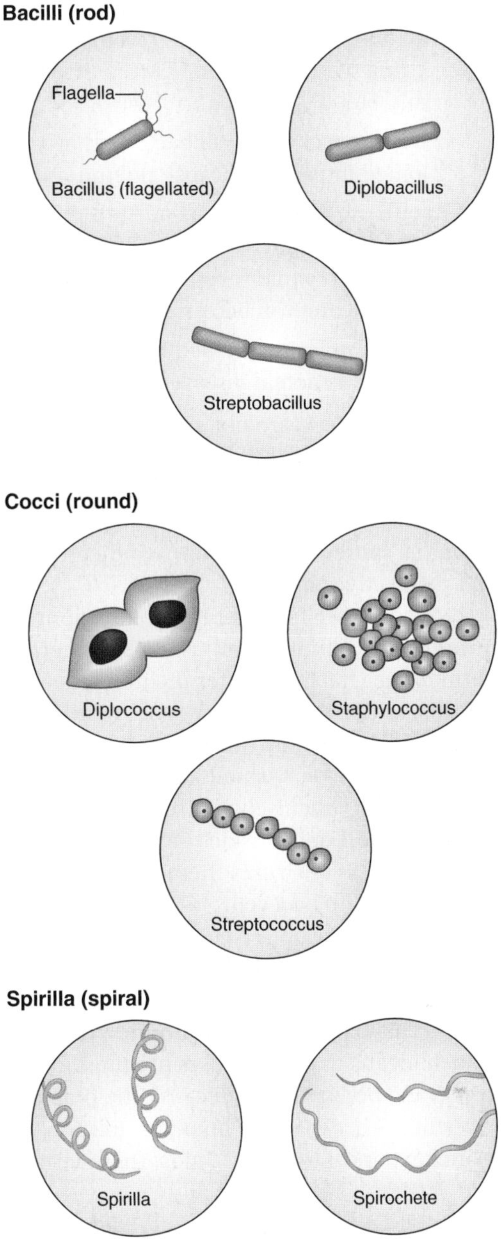

Bacilli (rod)

Figure elements: Flagella, Bacillus (flagellated), Diplobacillus, Streptobacillus

Cocci (round)

Diplococcus, Staphylococcus, Streptococcus

Spirilla (spiral)

Spirilla, Spirochete

Figure 5–1 General forms of bacteria: bacilli, cocci, and spirilla.

Bacteria are divided into three groups: cocci, bacilli and spirilla.

1. **Cocci** are round, pus-producing, pathogenic bacteria that appear in groups or clusters. There are several types of cocci bacteria.

   a. **Staphylococci** are pus-forming microorganisms that are grouped in clusters like a bunch of grapes; found in abscesses, pustules, and boils; sometimes called *staph* (from the Greek *staphyle* meaning bunches of grapes).

---

sanitation
The practice of cleanliness.

Occupational Safety and Health Administration (OSHA)
A U.S. government agency that oversees workplace safety for employees.

microorganisms
Microbe; microscopic plant or animal cell; bacterium; virus; fungi.

airborne microorganisms
Germs in the air.

pathogenic microorganisms
Microorganisms that cause disease.

nonpathogenic microorganisms
Microorganisms that do not cause disease.

cocci
Round, pus-producing pathogenic bacteria appearing in a group.

staphylococci
Pus-forming microorganisms that are grouped in clusters like a bunch of grapes; found in abscesses, pustules, and boils.

Glossary (left column)

streptococci
Pus-forming bacteria arranged in curved lines resembling a string of beads; found in strep throat and blood poisoning.

diplococci
Spherical bacteria that are joined in pairs and cause pneumonia.

bacilli
Rod-shaped bacterium that cause diseases such as tetanus (lockjaw), influenza, typhoid fever, and tuberculosis; the most common bacteria.

spirilla
Spiral-shaped bacteria that cause the venereal disease syphilis.

spores
Tiny bacterial bodies having a protective wall to withstand unfavorable conditions.

mycoses
Fungus-related infections.

fungi
General term for vegetable parasites including all types of yeasts and mildew.

yeast
A substance consisting of minute cells of fungi; used to promote fermentation; a high source of vitamin B.

mold
A fungus growth usually growing in dark, damp places; to form into a particular shape.

Main text (center column)

b. **Streptococci** are pus-forming bacteria arranged in curved lines resembling a string of beads; found in strep throat and blood poisoning.

c. **Diplococci** spherical bacteria that are joined in pairs and cause pneumonia.

2. **Bacilli** are rod-shaped bacterium that cause diseases such as tetanus (lockjaw), influenza, typhoid fever, and tuberculosis; the most common bacteria.

3. **Spirilla** are spiral-shaped bacteria that cause the venereal disease syphilis.

When bacteria are not active, they can form protective shell-like walls called **spores**. Bacterial spores can exist for a very long time, and then become active bacteria again. Bacterial spores are much more difficult to kill than active bacteria.

Mycoses are fungus-related infections. **Fungi** is the plural of fungus, and a general term for vegetable parasites including **yeasts, molds,** and **mildew.** Many types of infection can be caused by fungi.

Viruses are very small particles that cannot survive by themselves. They must exist on a **host cell** or be inside the cell of another organism to live. Viruses themselves are not large enough to be a cell.

Viruses cause both Acquired Immunodeficiency Syndrome (AIDS) and hepatitis, two of the most serious diseases known today. These are both **bloodborne viruses**, which means that the viruses are present in blood and bodily fluids. Because the practice of esthetics occasionally involves unintentional exposure to bodily fluids, these viruses are of great concern.

mildew
A disease of plants or a moldy coating that can appear on walls, fabrics, and the like; usually occurs in damp areas.

viruses
The causative agent of an infectious disease; any of a large group of submicroscopic structures capable of infesting almost all plants and animals, including bacteria.

host cell
A cell that a virus attaches itself to, or lives inside of, in order to live.

Sterilization

Numerous types of chemicals are used for disinfecting and sterilizing. **Sterilization** is the process of completely killing all microorganisms, including bacteria, viruses, fungi, and bacterial spores. Bloody waste is inherent in extraction and hair removal. Scissors, comedo extractors, or any tool that comes into contact with blood or bodily fluids requires sterilization.

The Autoclave

An **autoclave** is an example of an apparatus that uses a heat sterilization process (Figure 5–2). Objects processed in an autoclave are **sterile**, meaning they have no live microorganisms present on them. The autoclave creates an environment in a special chamber that uses very high heat and very high pressure to kill all microorganisms. Autoclaves are always used in hospitals and medical offices, and are used in some spas and salons as well.

Objects such as sponges, comedo extractors, tweezers, and electrolysis needles can be autoclaved. Some items, such as glass electrodes, cannot be autoclaved because they will break. If there is an autoclave in your salon, read the manufacturer's instructions well to find out exactly what objects can and cannot be autoclaved.

bloodborne viruses
Viruses that are present in blood and bodily fluids.

sterilization
The process of completely killing all microorganisms, including bacteria, viruses, fungi, and bacterial spores.

autoclave
An apparatus for sterilization by steam under pressure; it consists of a strong, closed boiler containing a small quantity of water and, in a wire basket, the articles to be sterilized.

sterile
Barren; free from all living organisms; objects that have no live microorganisms present on them.

Figure 5–2 An example of an autoclave.

Disinfectants

Disinfection is the process of killing most microorganisms on hard surfaces. It is not the same as sterilization, because not all bacterial spores are killed during disinfection. Disinfectants are usually chemicals that kill most microorganisms. Unlike sterilization using an autoclave or other approved solutions, disinfectants do not kill bacterial spores. Objects are immersed in the disinfectant for a preset period of time. These chemicals are referred to as **wet sanitizing agents**.

Disinfection is the most commonly used method of controlling microorganisms in the salon. Disinfectant chemicals include **quaternary ammonium compounds (quats), glutaraldehyde, isopropyl alcohol,** and **benzalkonium chloride.** Quaternary ammonia is the disinfectant chemical most often used by salons. Isopropyl alcohol can be used to clean the metal edges of scissors, but it is not as effective as using quats. Check with your supplier

to make sure that whatever you are using is a **hospital-grade disinfectant,** which means that the product has been tested and meets specific standards for killing microorganisms. Hospital-grade disinfectants must kill hepatitis viruses and tuberculosis bacteria. The Environmental Protection Agency (EPA) and the Food and Drug Administration (FDA) regulate all liquid sterilants and disinfectants. Other disinfectants are used to clean countertops and floors. Lysol and Pine-sol are two examples of cleaning products that have a disinfectant that helps kill microorganisms on surfaces. However, in a professional environment, there are hospital-strength disinfectants that are more effective.

Antiseptics are disinfectants designed for use on human skin. They are not nearly as strong as disinfectant solutions, which can be very irritating if used on human skin. Hydrogen peroxide is a good example of an antiseptic.

The instructions for use in Table 5–1 are general guidelines only. Check with your state board of cosmetology for approved sanitizing solutions. Diluted sanitizing solutions may have limited activity after so much time. Always follow the manufacturer's instructions. Many new solutions have appeared on the market and are highly effective.

Disposables

Some utensils used by salons are used once and then discarded in a covered trash receptacle or other container. One-use disposable items include esthetician's gloves, sponges, cotton, cotton swabs, tongue depressors used for product application, paper towels, tissues, and disposable makeup utensils such as mascara wands and disposable lip brushes. Lancets, used to dilate follicles for extraction,

---

hospital-grade disinfectant
Products that have been tested and meet specific standards for killing microorganisms. They must be able to kill hepatitis viruses and tuberculosis bacteria.

antiseptics
Disinfectants designed for use in human skin.

isopropyl alcohol
A homologue of ethyl alcohol; used as a solvent and rubefacien.

benzalkonium chloride
A preservative. With continuous use, it can cause occasional allergic reactions.

---

disinfection
Decontamination, nearly as effective as sterilization, but does not kill bacterial spores; used on hard surfaces.

wet sanitizing agents
Chemicals that objects are immersed in for a preset period of time to sterilize them.

quaternary ammonium compounds (quats)
A group of compounds of organic salts of ammonia employed effectively as disinfectants, conditioners, and other surface-active agents; nontoxic, odorless, and fast-acting.

glutaraldehyde
A dialdehyde used as a germicidal agent to disinfect and sterilize instruments or equipment that cannot be heat sterilized.

Table 5–1 Commonly Used Disinfectants, Sterilizers, and Antiseptics

Disinfectants and Sterilizers

Name	Form	Strength	Use (follow manufacturer's instruction)
Quaternary ammonium compounds (quats)	Liquid or tablet	1:1000	Immerse implements in solutions for 20 or more minutes.
Formalin	Liquid	25% solution	Immerse implements in solution for 10 or more minutes.
Formalin	Liquid	10% solution	Immerse implements in solution for 20 or more minutes.
Alcohol (ethyl or isopropyl)	Liquid	70% or 90% solution	Immerse implements or sanitize electrodes and sharp cutting edges for 10 or more minutes.
Autoclave	Heat sterilizer may be used as steam or dry heat..		Sterilize for 30 minutes

Antiseptics

Name	Form	Strength	Use
Boric acid	White crystals	2% to 5% solution	Cleanse the eye.
Tincture of iodine	Liquid	2% solution	Cleanse cuts and wounds.
Hydrogen peroxide	Liquid	3% to 5% solution	Cleanse skin and minor cuts.
Ethyl or grain alcohol	Liquid	60% solution	Cleanse hands, skin, and tiny cuts. Not to be used if irritation is present.
Formalin	Liquid	5% solution	Cleanse sinks and cabinets.
Chloramine-T (Chlorazene; Chlorozol)	White crystals	1/2% solution	Cleanse skin and hands, and for general use.
Sodium hypochlorite (Javelle water; Zonite)	Liquid	1/2% solution	Rinse the hands.

sharps boxes
Plastic box in which used needles, curettes, and anything sharp is disposed of. The top, when full, can be locked so it cannot be reopened. The full box must be disposed of as medical waste.

contaminated
When an object or product has microorganisms in it.

contamination
Pollution; soiling with infectious matter; the spreading of microorganisms to an object or product.

cross-contamination
Occurs when touching an object like the skin, and then touching an object or product with the same hand or utensil.

spatulas
Flexible implements with blunt blades used for removing creams from their containers without touching them with your hands and contaminating them.

come presterilized, and are used only once and then discarded.

Sharp objects that have been used in skin care procedures, such as lancets or needles, should be discarded in hard containers called **sharps boxes** (Figure 5–3). A sharps box is made of hard plastic to prevent used items exposed to blood or bodily fluids from accidentally cutting or injuring someone. Sharps boxes may be purchased from medical or esthetic supply companies. They must be disposed of according to OSHA guidelines.

Cross-contamination

When an object or product has microorganisms in it, it has been **contaminated**. Any disinfected item that has been touched or exposed to air is also contaminated. **Contamination** is the spread of microorganisms to an object or product. **Cross-contamination** occurs when you touch an object, such as the skin, and then touch an object or product with the same hand or utensil. You must use properly disinfected tools, and must never

touch clean items with hands that have been exposed to the client's skin!

Spatulas are flexible implements with blunt blades used to remove products from jars without touching them with your hands. A product can be safely used after it is removed from the container, as long as it is only used on one client. Once a product has been removed from a jar or container it should never be put back into the container. Spatulas must be properly disinfected or disposed of after each use. Some estheticians use children's tongue depressors as spatulas. These are disposable and are only used once. Plastic spatulas can be disinfected and reused.

Any nondisposable object that touches a client's skin must be properly disinfected before it is reused. Nondisposable items include plastic spatulas, mask brushes, reusable sponges, towels, sheets and linens, machine attachments, electrodes, headbands, and client gowns. Any object that is exposed to blood or bodily fluids must be discarded or autoclaved.

Figure 5–3 Sharp implements such as lancets should be properly disposed of in sharps boxes.

Gloves should be worn during all skin treatments. Microorganisms on the client's skin are tiny enough to penetrate the smallest cut or abrasion that might be on the esthetician's hands. Accidental exposure to bodily fluids does sometimes occur. It can expose the esthetician to bloodborne pathogens such as HIV, herpes simplex, or a hepatitis virus. When performing a facial, and part of the protocol is to massage arms or feet, change your gloves before returning to the face. Gloves are especially important during and after extraction, waxing, and electrolysis (Figure 5–4). It is during these types

of services that the danger of contamination from blood or extraction material is the highest. These are invasive procedures, requiring that minute openings be made in the skin to extract pustules and hair.

Aseptic Procedure

An **aseptic procedure** is the process of properly handling sterilized and disinfected equipment and supplies so that they do not become soiled or contaminated by microorganisms until they are used on a client. The following is a good example of an aseptic procedure:

1. Before beginning any treatment, lay out all implements that you will use during the treatment (Figure 5–5). This would include cotton, swabs, sponges, gauze, brushes, spatulas, tweezers, comedo extractors, electrodes, wax strips, gloves, etc., on a clean towel. To prevent airborne contact cover with another clean towel until you are ready to start the treatment. By prearranging these utensils, you will be less likely to need to open a container to get more supplies. This not only prevents cross-contamination, but is also a more efficient technique. Think of the time you would waste if you had to remove your gloves, resanitize your hands, and go look for more supplies. Once you have begun a treatment, you must never open any package or container or touch a product without a spatula or tongs. Touching any object with gloved hands that have

aseptic procedure
The process of properly handling sterilized and disinfected equipment and supplies so they do not become soiled or contaminated by microorganisms until they are used on a client.

gloves
Should be used during any skin treatment.

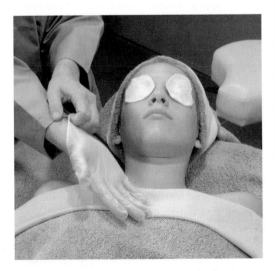

Figure 5–4 Gloves should be worn for both safety and hygiene.

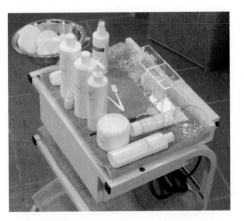

Figure 5–5 Proper handling of equipment and supplies helps prevent contamination.

touched the client will contaminate that object. Any object touched during treatment must be discarded, disinfected, or autoclaved.

2. Aseptic procedure includes using clean towels, sheets, headband or plastic cap, and client gown for each client.

3. The esthetician should wash and sanitize hands after touching a client's hair.

4. The esthetician should apply latex or vinyl gloves at the beginning of every treatment, and wear them throughout the treatment. This is especially important during and after extraction, waxing, or electrolysis.

5. Creams and products should be removed from containers using pumps, squeeze bottles with dispenser caps, or with disinfected spatulas. It is best to remove products before the treatment and place them in small disposable cups. This prevents you from needing to touch bottles or jars with soiled gloved hands. Spatulas should be used once and disinfected.

6. After the treatment is complete, linens should be placed in a covered laundry receptacle. Disposable items should be thrown away in a closed trash container. Sharps should be carefully placed in a sharps box. All items to be reused must be properly disinfected or sterilized. Unused product that has already been removed from a container should be discarded.

7. All surfaces touched during treatment should be wiped down with disinfectant before the next client is seated.

Figure 5–6 Aluminum dry cabinet sanitizers help to sterilize equipment.

Dry Sanitizers

Other common sanitizers are ultraviolet lights or fumigants in commercially available dry cabinet sanitizers (Figure 5–6). The cabinet should be aluminum, which does not rust. Most tools are placed into the sterilizer when wet from rinsing, so wiping the bottom of the sanitizer with a dry cloth is required after each use. The minimal mold that could grow is killed by the heat or ultraviolet lamp used in the sterilizer.

The life span of an ultraviolet lamp is about 6,000 hours depending on the manufacturer, size, and hours of use. Keep a spare ultraviolet lightbulb in your supplies. These lightbulbs are engineered to run when the sanitizer door is closed and to stop when it is opened. This prevents exposure of humans to the ultraviolet light and prolongs the life of the bulb. Popular salon chemical sterilizing agents include fumigants, antiseptics, and disinfectants.

Policies and Procedures

Every organization will have specific policies and procedures to follow for maintaining the cleanliness and sanitation of the premises and equipment. The following describes general guidelines that should be incorporated—at a minimum—into these policies and procedures.

Work Stations

Workstations, stainless steel bowls, and all other supplies should be disinfected with an approved hospital-grade disinfectant (Figure 5–7). Most esthetic suppliers have disinfectant concentrates, trays, and instrument disinfectants. Occupational, Safety, and Health Administration (OSHA) guidelines should be followed for proper disposal of blood borne pathogens and other bodily fluids.

A special spray disinfectant, for use in the treatment room, can be mixed from a disinfecting concentrate available in bulk sizes. Once a week, a measured amount of concentrate is placed into another empty gallon jug and diluted with water. Sprayer bottles for the treatment room are refilled from this solution. This instant disinfectant kills surface microbes and viruses within seconds. Spray the solution on equipment surfaces and counters and wipe dry.

Figure 5–7 Many different types of disinfectants and sterilizer containers are available.

Laundry

Soiled laundry should be handled with gloves, and should be placed in a closed lined receptacle until it is washed. Chlorine bleach serves as a disinfectant for laundry. It is added along with the soap powder. Clean towels should be kept in a closed closet or cabinet until used. Laundry hampers or bins should be cleaned daily with disinfectant. Laundry should be done regularly and not be left for the next day. Fungus and mold can grow in damp linens. Damp linens left in laundry carts used for separating linens will grow fungus not only on the linens, but on the cart as well if the cart is made of a canvas material.

Trash Cans

All receptacles should be made of a non-porous material that can be cleaned and sanitized (Figure 5–8). A very practical receptacle that is most appropriate for treatment rooms is one made of metal and operated by a foot pedal. It can be lined with a disposable plastic bag. These containers help keep contaminated items from being left on the countertop or sink during treatment. The foot pedal allows you to open the container and immediately dispose of contaminated items.

Figure 5–8 A covered, nonporous trash receptacle is a must for every treatment room.

Treatment Rooms

Treatment rooms normally have dim lighting and are often damp from steam or showers (Figure 5–9). If not kept clean and sanitized, mold and mildew quickly grow around sink trim and drains. For example, take a look in your home bathroom, especially if you live in a very warm, humid climate. You may discover molds or mildew growing in the tile grout and under the sealants around the toilet, tub, shower, or sink. If these areas are

SAFETY*Tip*

Contaminated items such as disposable extractors, or bloody cotton or pads, should be placed in a hazardous waste container.

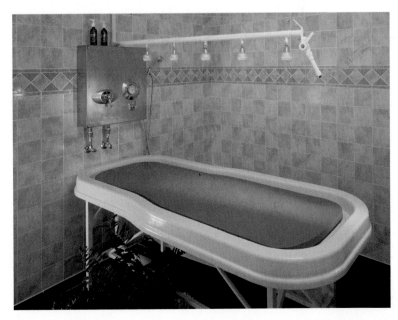

Figure 5–9 Treatment rooms are often damp from steam or showers.

Policies and Procedures

Can you imagine highways without speed limits, airports without traffic controllers, appliances without manuals, trains and buses without schedules, department stores without exchange and return policies, medications without directions, a government without laws? It would be hard to live in a world where people did not know what the rules and regulations are. Businesses also need clear-cut directives. These typically come in the way of policies and procedures.

Successful businesses understand the value of policies and procedures; these "rules" help keep day to day operations running smoothly. Efficiently run organizations let their employees know exactly what behaviors they expect from them and how they would like things done. Ultimately, both of these objectives will enhance client satisfaction.

Whether you work for a small clinic or a large corporate chain, chances are you will receive an employee handbook. Someone in authority should review this information with you. If not, make sure you read it; ignorance is no excuse for being misinformed. The employee manual should provide you with important information, such as the correct protocol for calling in sick or late, how many sick days you are allowed, what holidays the salon is closed, how much vacation time you can accrue, what the dress code is, how the company's insurance plan operates, and who you should direct questions to. If you do not receive such a manual before you begin your employment, be sure to ask how all of these issues are handled.

Some companies may also incorporate a mission statement or philosophy in the employee handbook that lets you know what their vision is. This will help you to decide if you are in sync with the company's long-term goals. If you are working for a large organization you may also receive an organizational chart. This is often helpful in terms of understanding who is in authority across the board and who you report to.

Estheticians must also be aware of safety and health concerns. Working with the public has many rewards, but also carries with it a great deal of responsibility. Smart business managers will want to provide specific guidelines on such topics as sanitation, sterilization, and standard precautions to practice quality control. Employers may also wish to choose a particular approach to introducing consent forms to ensure protection against liability. For aggressive skin care treatments, the employer may include a standard protocol that each practitioner is expected to follow explicitly.

Savvy employers also understand that success depends on consistently good results. Don't be offended if your individuality takes a backseat to predictable outcomes. Adhering to set protocols often ensures a quality standard of care. In the final analysis, these standards may also support team values. Consider that the goal of any successful service business requires each operator to be able to reproduce the same treatment equally well.

not sealed properly during initial installation, or are old, contaminated water can infiltrate under these areas, causing mold and mildew to breed. These areas quickly become unsanitary. Periodically inspect all wet rooms. Watch for rusting, mold, and other signs of deterioration.

Tile Flooring

When building a new facility, ceramic floor tiles as well as the grouting should be sealed with a special nonporous finish found in any hardware store. Unsealed grout is very porous and is a good place for mold or mildew to grow. Make sure your contractor seals adequately and correctly. New rubber floor tiles are less expensive than ceramic. Although the rubber tiles initially have a finish that is applied from the manufacturer, they can become porous through everyday wear. They scratch and can be gouged with furniture. Upon installation, it is a good idea to apply several coats of sealant to keep them in a nonporous state. They are more attractive as well. Correctly sealing new tiles in the beginning makes for less work later.

Air Systems

An air system is a major expense in any facility. When inadequately engineered, it can also be a means to transport allergens and pathogens. Poor circulation, ventilation, and temperature control can be a constant aggravation to both staff and customers. It can also become a health hazard.

Be practical about the placement of air ducts. You do not want cool or warm air to flow directly onto your client. Although it may be more expensive initially, placing both inputs and returns in closed treatment rooms will result in a more comfortable environment that is fresh and healthy. Other closed areas, such as showers and wet rooms, should include ventilation that removes steam. Ceiling grates should be cleaned monthly or sooner if they collect dust. Airborne particles can be transported through these grates if they do not contain proper filters. Even filters do not stop all pathogen and dust particles.

Locations that have or use caustic substances, such as manicuring or hair areas, should have their own ventilation systems. In a spa environment, they should be built away from facial and massage areas. Chemicals from acrylic or regular nail services, as well as hair care products, can cause severe allergic reactions in some sensitive individuals. Just as they should not be exposed to cigarette smoke and other caustic substances, babies and young children should never be allowed in these areas. This means even for a short duration. Many newer facilities include separate rooms behind glass or walls that are specifically ventilated to prevent smells from permeating throughout the entire facility.

Material Safety Data Sheets

Exposure to chemicals is another area of workplace safety concern. Disinfectants are one example of a chemical used in the workplace that could be harmful to workers if misused or accidentally ingested.

Any chemical that is used in the workplace must have a **Material Safety Data Sheet (MSDS)** (Figure 5–10). These forms include information about flammability, toxicity, how to handle spills, and other information about chemicals used in the workplace. The information is compiled by the manufacturers and lists product ranges for ingredient content and associated hazards to combustion levels and storage requirements. Employers are required to have MSDSs for all chemicals used in the workplace. In the esthetics profession, most chemicals used are skin care products, most of which obviously are not harmful, because they are meant to be used on the skin. However, other chemicals used in the salon, such as disinfectants, germicides, and nail chemicals, can be harmful if misused. All these chemicals, regardless of how harmless, must have MSDSs on the premises. Manufacturers are required, if requested by the purchaser, to furnish MSDSs on any salon-use products sold.

Bloodborne Pathogen Act

In 1993, OSHA issued a set of voluntary guidelines designed to reduce the occupational risk or exposure to the hepatitis B virus (HBV). These guidelines were sent to employers in the health care industry and included a description of the disease, recommended work practices, and recommendations for immune globulins and the hepatitis B vaccine.

In 1987, OSHA published the *Federal Register* announcing the initiation of the rule-

> **Material Safety Data Sheet (MSDS)**
> Information compiled by a manufacturer listing product ranges for ingredient content and associated hazards to combustion levels and storage requirements.

Material Safety Data Sheet (MSDS)

Section I

Product Name or Number	Emergency Telephone No.
Manufacturer's Name	Manufacturer's D-U-N-5 No.
Address (Number, Street, City, State, Zip)	
Hazardous Materials Description and Proper Shipping Name (49.CFR 172.101)	Hazardous Class (49CFR 172.101)
Chemical Family	Formula

Section II — Ingredients (list all ingredients)

	CASE REGISTRY NO.	%

Section III — Physical Data

Boiling Point (F) (C)		Specific Gravity (H20 = 1)			
Vapor Pressure (mm Hg) ————		Percent Volatile by Volume (%)			
(psl) ————					
Vapor Density (Air = 1)		Evaporation Rate (= 1)			
Solubility in Water		pH =			
Appearance and Odor		Is material: Liquid Solid Gas Paste Powder			

Section IV — Fire & Explosion Hazard Data

Flash Point (method used)	Flammable limits	LEL	UEL
( )			
( )			
Extinguishing Media			
Special Fire Fighting Procedures			
Unusual Fire and Explosion Hazards			

Figure 5–10 A sample MSDS Product Sheet.

making process. In March of 1992, new regulations on the protection of employees from infection with bloodborne pathogens were released. Compliance to these regulations came into effect in July 1992 and became legally enforceable. OSHA inspectors could conduct unannounced inspections of employers. Through this system of inspection, OSHA has set a national standard of requirements for medical facilities, health care workers, and other stipulated places. Salons are required by OSHA to have a program in place to educate employees about workplace safety. The use of gloves, lab coats, and prevention of contact with bodily fluids are of utmost importance in health care and personal care services environments.

State Laws

Every state has its own laws and rules regarding salon sanitation. It is important to understand and comply with all your state's regulations. Your esthetics instructor can tell you or furnish you with information about the sanitation rules in your state.

Summary

Bacteria and viruses are microscopic and cannot be seen with the naked eye. They can be dangerous when instruments, equipment, and treatment rooms are not cleaned and disinfected properly. Methods of sanitation include using hospital-strength disinfectants. Hospital strength means that the solution kills HIV viruses, hepatitis, and other pathogens upon contact. Sanitation practices for a busy salon or spa are key to reducing the danger of infection. Dark treatment rooms can be an open invitation for microbes and fungus to grow. OSHA has set guidelines for safety in the workplace. It is important to follow these regulations and comply with all safety standards. This ensures a safe work environment for both you and your clients.

Discussion Questions

1. Name three types of bacteria and provide an example of a common illness associated with each.

2. Describe the difference between sterilization and disinfecting.

3. How does the autoclave prevent the transmission of bacteria? Are there any instruments or materials that the esthetician uses that cannot be safely sanitized in the autoclave? List several ways estheticians can prevent cross-contamination in addition to the use of the autoclave.

4. List several common disinfecting agents used in the spa or salon. Why is it important for the esthetician to use a hospital-grade disinfectant? Give an example of how aseptic procedure can be applied to supplies or equipment, laundry, and treatment rooms.

5. Name the government agency responsible for publishing safety guidelines for health professionals. Why should the esthetician be concerned with adhering to these standards?

Additional Reading

Chesky, Sheldon R., Isabel Christa, and Richard B. Rosenberg. 1994. *Playing It Safe: Decontamination, Sterilization and Personal Protection* Clifton Park, N.Y.: Milady, an imprint of Delmar Learning, a division of Thomson Learning, Inc.

Ellzey, Enga, and S.S. Warfield. 1997. *Physician's Guide to In-office Dispensing.* Glen Rock, N.J.: PCI Journal. Available on-line at http://www.pcijournal.com/.

Lees, Mark. 2001. *Skin Care, Beyond the Basics.* Clifton Park, N.Y.: Milady, an imprint of Delmar Learning, a division of Thomson Learning, Inc.

Schoon, Douglas. 1994. *HIV/AIDS & Hepatitis* Clifton Park, N.Y.: Milady, an imprint of Delmar Learning, a division of Thomson Learning, Inc.

Warfield, Susan B. 1997. *OSHA Manual on Bloodborne Pathogens.* Glen Rock, N.J.: PCI Journal. Available on-line at http://www.pcijournal.com/.

Chapter 6
Nutrition

Chapter Objectives

After reading this chapter, you should be able to:

- State the importance of vitamins and minerals in skin care.
- State the importance of proteins, fats, and carbohydrates.
- Explain the functions of lipids, proteins, vitamins, and minerals and the results of their deficiencies.
- Relate information on nutrition to your client.

Chapter Outline

Introduction
Macronutrients
Micronutrients: Vitamins
Minerals
How Much Nutrition Do You Need?
Nutrition and Esthetics

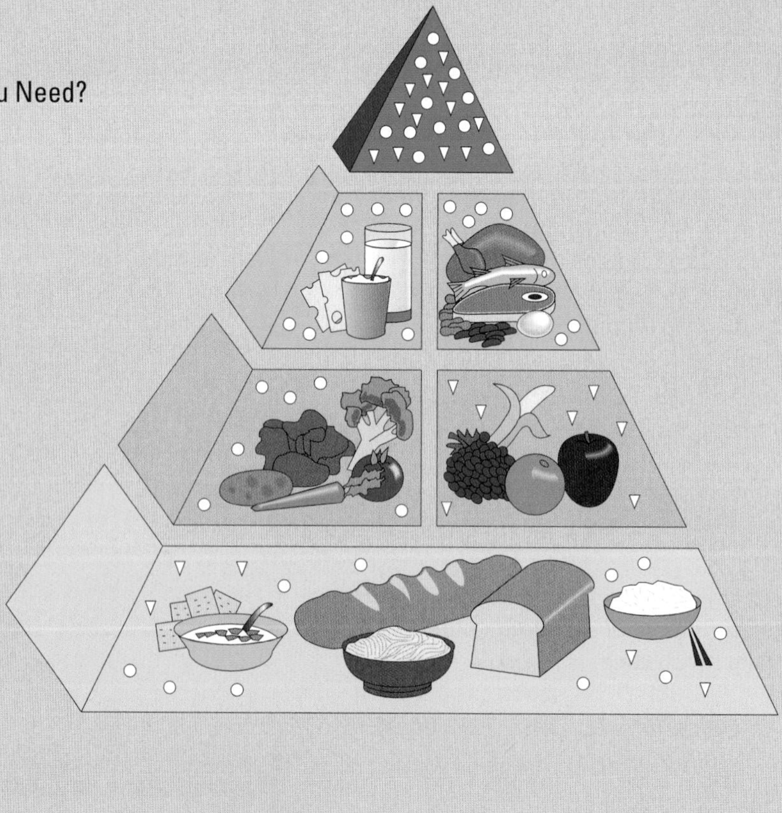

Introduction

All bodily functions, including the building of body tissues, are directly related to nutrition. Foods are broken down into basic molecules that are then delivered to every single living cell in the human body. These molecules are used by the cells to repair damage, form new cells, and conduct all biochemical reactions that run the body's systems. They provide energy for our bodies to perform numerous functions.

You can look at the foods we eat and the water we drink as the basic building blocks of life. Think of the body or the cell as a construction site. All building supplies are contained in the foods we take in.

Estheticians are not dieticians. Dieticians have degrees in dietetics, the science of nutrition. In most states, dieticians are licensed and regulated. Persons who are not licensed or registered dieticians are not usually qualified to give advice on nutrition. Estheticians are not adequately trained in nutrition to be recommending dietary changes to their clients. Clients may have medical conditions, such as diabetes or high blood pressure, that can be negatively affected by misleading advice. However, it is beneficial for anyone interested in, or practicing, health care or personal care services such as esthetics to have a good working knowledge of nutrition, and how the body is affected by foods.

Macronutrients

Nutrients are the basic building blocks necessary for bodily functions, including functioning of the skin (Figure 6–1). The principal

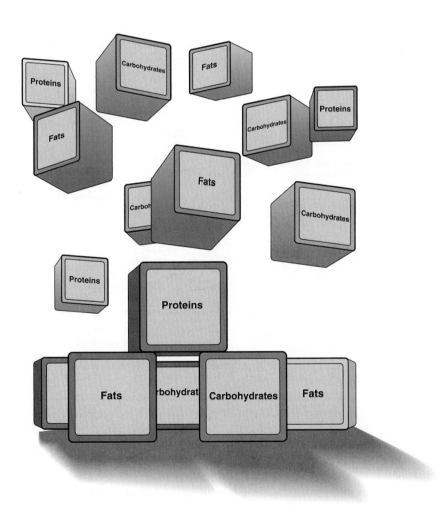

Figure 6–1 Proteins, carbohydrates, and fats are the basic building blocks of nutrition.

proteins

Chains of amino acid molecules, which are used by every cell of the body to make other useable proteins to carry out various functions as required by the cells and the body.

nutrients are proteins, carbohydrates, and fats. They are also called macronutrients, meaning that they make up the largest part of the nutrition we take in.

A fourth, and equally important requirement, is water, which is essential for all bodily functions. An adult body is made up of approximately 60% water. Water is responsible for moving nutrients around the body and into the cells. It is the main ingredient in the fluids that make up the blood, lymph, sweat, and other body fluids.

Proteins

Proteins are basically chains of amino acid molecules, which are used by every cell of the body to make other usable proteins to carry out various functions as required by the cells and the body. Proteins are used in body growth, in the duplication of deoxyribonucleic acid, better known as DNA, the blueprint material that contains all the information that runs the function of every living cell. Proteins are needed to make mus-

cle tissue, blood, and enzymes, as well as the keratin that is present in skin, nails, and hair. Proteins are extensively used by the immune system in defining what is an invader, and how the body will react.

The body can manufacture some amino acids. These are known as nonessential amino acids. Since the body can make these from other bodily chemicals, they do not have to be obtained from eating protein. Essential amino acids are amino acids that must be part of the diet, because the body cannot manufacture these.

Dietary sources for proteins include animal meats as well as fish, eggs, dairy products, and beans (Figure 6–2). Although most vegetables also contain protein, it is a smaller proportion. Vegetarians must be careful to obtain their daily protein requirements. Vegetarians who also consume dairy products have an easier time obtaining a sufficient amount of protein. Vegans are people who eat strictly plant products with no dairy products. Vegans must be especially careful to consume a sufficient amount of protein in their diets.

carbohydrates

The source of nutrition that breaks down the basic chemical sugars that supply energy for the body; frequently called "carbs".

fiber

A slender, thread-like structure that combines with others to form animal or vegetable tissue.

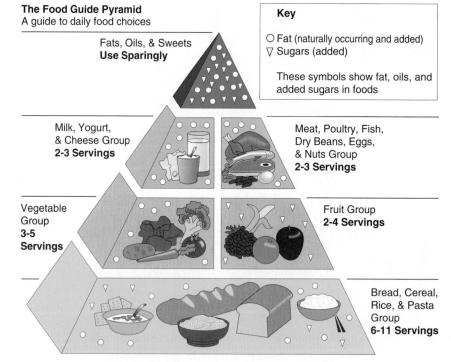

Figure 6–2 The Food Guide Pyramid depicts the number of required servings in each of the five basic food groups.

Carbohydrates

Carbohydrates break down the basic chemical sugars that supply energy for the body. They are frequently called "carbs." The three basic types of carbohydrates are outlined below.

1. Simple sugars are present in table sugar (also known as sucrose), fruit sugars (fructose), and milk sugars (lactose). Simple sugars are always sweet in taste.

2. Starches, which are also called complex carbohydrates, are present in many vegetables and grains. Starch is a white, odorless, granular, or powdery complex carbohydrate that is the chief storage form of carbohydrates in plants, and an important foodstuff.

3. Carbohydrates also include **fiber,** which is necessary for proper digestion. Fiber is made of a carbohydrate called **cellulose,** which is not digested by humans, and is important in helping push wastes out of the colon. Lack of fiber is associated with constipation, and long-term, with colon cancer.

Carbohydrates can be combined with proteins to produce many important body chemicals. Mucopolysaccharides, for example, are important to the skin and are present in the dermis as glycosaminoglycans, the filler water-binding substance between the fibers of the dermis.

The most basic unit of a carbohydrate is **glucose,** the simplest of all carbohydrates. The glucose molecule is what is known as a **monosaccharide** (*mono* means one; *saccharide* means sugar), a one-unit sugar molecule that all cells use for energy. Fruit sugar is a naturally occurring monosaccharide. A **disaccharide** is made up of two molecular sugar units (*di* means two). Lactose and sucrose are both disaccharides. **Polysaccharides** (*poly* is from the Greek *polu,* which means many) are made of a chain of sugar unit molecules. Starch is a digestible polysaccharide, which can be broken down by the digestive system into simpler, usable glucose molecules. Fiber is also a polysaccharide, but is not digestible.

Carbohydrate food groups include simple carbohydrates such as sweets, syrups, honey, fruits, candy, and many vegetables. Starches, polysaccharides that can be broken down into simple sugars, include cereals, breads, and other flour products, potatoes, rice, and pasta. High-fiber foods include grain brans (such as oat bran or wheat bran), whole grain breads, beans (also called legumes), and vegetables such as carrots and corn.

You may notice that some foods are listed in two different categories. This is because there is more than one type of saccharide group in many foods. Potatoes are a starch source and also contain fiber. Fruits and vegetables have both simple sugars and fiber.

Lipids (Fats)

Fats or **lipids** are the third group of macronutrients. Fats can be used as energy, but not as readily as carbohydrates. Although many people associate fats with obesity, some fat is required in the diet, and it is an essential component of good health. Lipids are used by the body to make hormones, to create cell membranes, and they are important for the absorption of the fat-soluble vitamins A, D, E, and K.

The body has the capacity to manufacture fats for use as needed. These can be made from carbohydrates and proteins. One particular fatty acid, **linoleic acid,** is not made by the body, and must be taken in the diet. Linoleic acid is known as an essential fatty acid for this reason. Linoleic acid is used to make important hormones known as **prostaglandins.** Linoleic acid is also a fatty acid that is present in the lipid barrier function of the skin. Linoleic acid is found in oils made from safflower, sunflower, corn, soybean, borage, and flaxseed.

Triglycerides

Fatty acids make up **triglycerides,** which is the main fat in foods. Fatty acids are made up of a chain of carbon atoms. Hydrogen atoms can attach themselves to these carbon atoms, resulting in **hydrogenation.** Hydrogenation is the process that forms what are known as saturated fats, which means that the fatty acid has been saturated with hydrogen. Unsaturated fatty acids are fatty acids that do not have hydrogen atoms attached.

Monounsaturated fatty acids are capable of binding to one location on hydrogen atoms. Monounsaturated fatty acids are present in olive or canola oils. Polyunsaturated

---

cellulose
A carbohydrate that is not digested by humans, and is important in helping push wastes out of the colon.

glucose
The most basic unit of a carbohydrate.

monosaccharide
A one-unit sugar molecule that all cells use for energy.

disaccharide
Made up of two molecular sugar units.

polysaccharides
Made of a chain of sugar unit molecules.

fats (lipids)
The third group of macronutrients. Fats can be used as energy, but not as readily as carbohydrates.

linoleic acid
An unsaturated fatty acid prepared from fats and oils; used as an emulsifier.

prostaglandins
Hormones that are made by linoleic acid and help with blood vessel dilation.

triglycerides
The main fat in foods.

hydrogenation
The result of hydrogen atoms attaching to carbon atoms to form saturated fats.

fats, such as corn oil or safflower oil, are capable of bonding to more hydrogen on the chain of carbon atoms. How this translates into everyday knowledge is that saturated fats tend to be solid in texture. Lard is a classic example, and so is margarine which is made by synthetically hydrogenating oil. Oils are liquid at room temperature, and they are nonhydrogenated or partially hydrogenated.

Fats are very high in calories, which is a measurement of energy potential. Calories are required by the body, and are a measurement of usable energy. A gram of fat has 9 calories, while a gram of carbohydrate or a gram of protein has 4 calories. When people take in too many calories, and do not use them in body functions, the body stores the excess calories as body fat. The body can store fat from any calorie intake above what it uses, but it is easier for the body to make body fat from fat intake than it is to make it from carbohydrate intake. It takes about 3,500 extra calories for the body to store one pound of fat. These extra calories can come from intake of fat, carbohydrates, or even protein.

It is the goal of many dieticians to have Americans take in less than 30% of their entire caloric intake from fats. Only 10% of the calories should come from saturated fat; the balance should come from polyunsaturated and monounsaturated fats. Saturated fats come primarily from meats and dairy products. Polyunsaturated and monounsaturated oils come primarily from vegetable oils. Foods such as pastries, fast foods, fried foods, snack foods (junk foods), and products that contain cream are high in fat and should be eaten in moderation.

Trans Fatty Acids

Recently, much research has been done on trans fatty acids, which are mirror image fatty acids that are produced when polyunsaturated oil is partially hydrogenated. Trans fatty acids can increase the "bad" type of cholesterol in the blood, low-density lipoproteins, and decrease the production of a hormone called prostaglandin which helps with blood vessel dilation. There is growing evidence that trans fatty acids can lead to, or contribute to, heart and cardiovascular disease.

A high-fat diet is associated with heart disease, high blood pressure, and an increased risk of cancer. Animals and humans manufacture cholesterol, a type of steroid alcohol. Only foods from animals

omega-3 fatty acids
A type of fat that is believed to possibly decrease the likelihood of cardiovascular diseases.

arteriosclerosis
Clogging and hardening of the arteries.

contain cholesterol. No plant or vegetable products contain cholesterol. Beef, pork, eggs, dairy products, chicken, and even fish and shellfish contain cholesterol. We do need some cholesterol. It is important for cell membranes, and cholesterol is even a part of the lipid matrix that comprises the barrier function of the epidermis. However, too much cholesterol or fat in the diet can result in high blood cholesterol. These are fats that clog the blood vessels, slowing and blocking blood flow. High levels of blood cholesterol can lead to high blood pressure, heart disease, and stroke.

Omega-3 fatty acids are a type of fat that has drawn much attention recently. Omega-3 fats can possibly decrease the likelihood of cardiovascular diseases. Omega-3 fats, in short, reduce the clotting potential that can lead to **arteriosclerosis,** clogging and hardening of the arteries. Omega-3 fatty acids are largely present in cold-water fish. Salmon is highest in omega-3 acids, but mackerel, tuna, herring, trout, and cod are also high in omega-3. It has been suggested that these fish should be a regular part of the American diet, and should be consumed two to three times a week.

The bottom line is that we should all eat less fat, especially saturated fat that comes primarily from meats. We should set a goal of taking in 30% or less of all our calories from fat. "Good" fats are linoleic acids, essential for good health, and omega-3 fatty acids. We should also be aware of our intake of trans fatty acids and make an effort to limit the amount we eat.

Micronutrients: Vitamins

Vitamins are substances that have no calories and no real nutritional value, yet they are necessary for many nutrients to be properly processed by the body. They are also needed for many processes that are carried out by the cells, and the production of many biochemicals necessary for life. Most vitamins must be part of the diet; the body cannot synthesize vitamins.

Vitamins are required for many chemical reactions that break down and reconstruct proteins, converting amino acids, and synthesizing fatty acids. Many are also involved in energy release from carbohydrates. In short, without vitamins, nutrients cannot be properly broken down, and amino acids and fatty acids cannot be reconstructed as needed by the cells for various biochemical reactions. Without vitamins the body cannot operate, and will eventually die. Vitamins fall into two categories. Fat-soluble vitamins include vitamins A, D, E, and K, and water-soluble vitamins include the B vitamins and vitamin C (Figure 6–3).

Vitamin RDA	Natural Sources	Functions	Deficiency Symptoms
A 5,000 IU	Yellow and green fruits and vegetables, carrots, dairy products, fish liver oil, yellow fruits	Growth and repair of body tissues, bone formation, vision	Night blindness, dry scaly skin, loss of smell and appetite, fatigue, bone deterioration
B1 Thiamin 1.5mg	Grains, nuts, wheat germ, fish, poultry, legumes, meat	Metabolism, appetite maintenance, nerve function, healthy mental state, and muscle tone.	Nerve disorders, cramps, fatigue, loss of appetite, loss of memory, heart irregularity;
B-2 Riboflavin 1.7 mg.	Whole grains, green leafy vegetables, liver, fish, eggs	Metabolism, health in hair, skin, nails; cell respiration, formation of antibodies and red blood cells	Cracks and lesions in corners of mouth, digestive disturbances
B-6 Pyridoxine 2 mg	Whole grains, leafy green vegetables, yeast, bananas, organ meats	Metabolism, formation of antibodies sodium/potassium balance	Dermatitis, blood disorders, nervousness, weakness, skin cracks, loss of memory
B-12 Cobalamin 6 mcg	Eggs, milk/milk products, fish, organ meats	Metabolism, healthy nervous system, blood cell formation	Nervousness, neuritis, fatigue,
Biotin 300 mcg	Legumes, eggs, grains, yeast	Metabolism, formation of fatty acids	Dry, dull skin, depression, muscle pain, fatigue loss of appetite.
Choline (no RDA)	Lecithin, fish wheat germ, egg yolk, soybeans	Nerve metabolism, and transmission, regulates liver, kidneys and gall bladder	Hypertension, stomach ulcers, liver and kidney conditions
Folic acid Folacin 400 mcg	Green leafy vegetables, organ meats yeast, milk products	Red blood cell formation, growth and cell division (RNA and DNA)	Gastrointestinal disorders, poor growth, loss of memory, anemia
Inositol (no RDA)	Whole grains, citrus fruits, yeast molasses, milk	Hair growth, metabolism, lecithin formation	Elevated cholesterol, hair loss, skin disorders, constipation, eye abnormalities
B complex (Niacin) 20 mg	Meat, poultry, fish milk products, peanuts	Metabolism, healthy skin, tongue, and digestive system, blood circulation, essential for synthesis of sex hormones	Fatigue, indigestion irritability, loss of appetite, skin conditions
B complex PABA (no RDA)	Yeast, wheat germ, molasses	Metabolism, red blood cell formation, intestines, hair coloring, sunscreen	Digestive disorders, fatigue, depression, constipation

Figure 6–3 Vitamin Information Chart.

Vitamin RDA	Natural Sources	Functions	Deficiency Symptoms
Pantothenic acid B-15 10 mg	Whole grains, pumpkin and sesame seeds	Metabolism, stimulates nerve and glandular systems, cell respiration	Heart disease, glandular and nerve disorders, poor circulation
C Ascorbic Acid 60 mg.	Citrus fruits, vegetables, tomatoes, potatoes	Aids in healing, collagen maintenance, resistance to disease	Gum bleeding, bruising, slow healing of wounds, nosebleeds, poor digestion
D 400 IU	Egg yolks, organ meats, fish, fortified milk	Health bone formation, healthy circulatory functions, nervous system	Rickets, osteoporosis, poor bone growth, nervous system irritability
E 30 IU	Green vegetables, wheat germ, organ meats, eggs, vegetable oils	Red blood cells, inhibits coagulation of blood, cellular respiration	Muscular atrophy, abnormal fat deposits in muscles, gastrointestinal conditions, heart disease, impotency
F (no RDA)	Wheat germ, seeds, vegetable oils	Respiration of body organs, lubrication of cells, blood coagulation, glandular activity	Brittle nails, and hair, dry dandruff, diarrhea, varicose veins, underweight, acne, gallstones
K (no RDA)	Green leafy vegetables, milk, kelp, safflower oil	Blood clotting agent, important to proper liver function and longevity	Hemorrhage
P Bioflavonoids (no RDA)	Fruits	For healthy connective tissue, aids in utilization of Vitamin C	Tendency to bleed easily, gum bleeding, bruising, similar to vitamin C's symptoms
Calcium 1000–1400 mg	Dairy products, bone meal	Resilient bones, teeth, muscle tissue, regulating heart beat, blood clotting	Soft, brittle bones, osteoporosis, heart palpitations
Chromium (no RDA)	Corn oil, yeast, clams, whole grains	Body's use of glucose, energy, effective use of insulin	Atherosclerosis, diabetic sugar intolerance
Copper 2 mg	Whole grains, leafy green vegetables, seafood, almonds,	Healthy red blood cells, bone growth and formation, joins with vitamin C to form elastin	Skin lesions, general weakness, labored respiration
Iodine .15 mg	Iodized table salt, shellfish	Part of the hormone thyroxine which controls metabolism	Dry skin and hair, obesity, nervousness, goiters
Iron 18 mg	Meats, fish, leafy green vegetables	Hemoglobin formation, blood quality, resistance to stress and disease	Anemia, constipation, breathing difficulties

Figure 6–3 *(continued).*

Vitamin RDA	Natural Sources	Functions	Deficiency Symptoms
Magnesium 400 mg	Nuts, green vegetables, whole grains	Metabolism	Nervousness, agitation, disorientation, blood clots
Manganese 2 mg	Egg yolks, legumes, whole grains	Carbohydrate and fat production, sex hormone production, bone development	Dizziness, lacking muscle coordination
Phosphorus 800 mg	Proteins, grains	Bone development, important in protein, fat and carbohydrate utilization	Soft bones, rickets, loss of appetite, irregular breathing
Potassium 2000 mg	Grains, vegetables, bananas, fruits, legumes	Fluid balance, controls activity of heart muscle, nervous system and kidneys	Irregular heartbeat, muscle cramps (legs), dry skin, general weakness
Sodium 500 mg	Table salt, shellfish, meat and poultry	Maintains muscular, blood and lymph, and nervous systems, regulates body fluid	Muscle weakness and atrophy, nausea, dehydration
Sulphur (no RDA)	Fish eggs, nuts, cabbage, meat	Collagen and body tissue formation, gives strength to keratin	N/A
Zinc 15 mg	Whole grains, wheat bran	Healthy digestion and metabolism, reproductive system, aids in healing	Stunted growth, delayed sexual maturity, prolonged wound healing
Selenium 055 mcg	Whole grains, liver meat, fish	Part of important antioxidant, glutathione peroxidase	Heart damage, reduces body's resistance to chronic illnesses
Fluoride 4 mg	Fluoridated water and toothpaste	Bone and tooth formation	Increased tooth decay

Figure 6–3 *(continued)*.

Fat-Soluble Vitamins

Fat-soluble vitamins are generally present in fats within foods. The body stores them in the liver and in adipose (fat) tissue. Because they can be stored in the body, it is possible to get too much of certain vitamins, namely vitamins A and D.

Vitamin A
Vitamin A is formally known as **retinol**, which you may recognize as an ingredient used in some skin care products designed for aging skin. Provitamins, also called precursors, are vitamin-containing substances, that are converted to the actual vitamin once they are in the body. Betacarotene is provitamin A. Betacarotene is found in colorful vegetables such as carrots, dark green vegetables such as spinach, and in fruits that are orange in color. Liver, fish oils, whole milk, and skim milk that has been fortified, all contain vitamin A. Fortified means that vitamin A has been added to a food product. Most people get about half their vitamin A from retinol, and half from betacarotene.

vitamin A (retinol)
Formally known as retinol, an ingredient used in some skin care products designed for aging skin.

follicular keratinosis
A skin condition resulting from vitamin A deficiency; generally affects the body skin.

retinoids
Skin drugs containing derivatives of vitamin A.

vitamin D
Sometimes called the sunshine vitamin; the skin synthesizes vitamin D from cholesterol when exposed to sunlight.

rickets
The result of a deficiency of vitamin D; seen in children, who do not develop bones normally.

vitamin E
Also known as tocopherol, primarily serves the body as an antioxidant.

tocopherol
Vitamin E; any of a group of four related viscous oils that constitute vitamin E; chief sources are wheat germ and cottonseed oils; used as a dietary supplement and as an antioxidant in some cosmetic preparations.

antioxidants
Substances (such as vitamin E) that protect the body through blocking or counteracting the damaging effects of free radical activity.

Vitamin A is necessary for proper eyesight, especially at night. A deficiency in vitamin A can result in a condition known as night blindness, or the impaired ability of the eyes to adapt to the dark. Vitamin A is also important for the proper maintenance of epithelial tissue, which makes up the surface of the lungs, intestines, mucous membranes, the bladder, and the skin. These surfaces produce mucus, which is important for protection and flexibility. Without vitamin A, a hard substance, keratin protein, which impairs cell function of these tissues, replaces this mucus. It can result in bacterial infection. These surfaces are also a frequent site for cancer development. There is ongoing research to determine the role of vitamin A in cancer. Vitamin A deficiency can result in a skin condition known as **follicular keratinosis,** which generally affects the body skin.

Because the body stores vitamin A, too much can result in vitamin A toxicity. This can be very serious, and can cause hair loss, very dry and cracked lips, and damage to the liver, spleen, and other organs. Persons should avoid taking more than about 15,000 RE (Retinol equivalents) per day. This is generally only a problem when people take too many vitamin A supplements.

Betacarotene is responsible for the bright color of many fruits and vegetables. The carotenes consumed in the diet are very important in controlling free radicals that are formed during biochemical reactions in the body. Current research also points to the possibility that carotenes may play an important role in the formation and function of immune system cells.

Derivatives of vitamin A are used in many skin drugs known as **retinoids.** Tretinoin, better known as Retin-A or Renova, is used to treat both acne and sun-damaged skin.

Retinoids are also used in skin care formulations. Retinol is used to help improve the appearance of sun-damaged skin, and may have applications in other esthetic disorders. Retinyl palmitate polypeptide and betacarotene are also used in skin care, primarily for their antioxidant properties.

Vitamin D
Vitamin D is sometimes called the sunshine vitamin because the skin synthesizes vitamin D from cholesterol when exposed to sunlight. This is not a recommendation for tanning, as the skin is also severely damaged by sun exposure. There are plenty of dietary sources for vitamin D, including fortified milk, fish oils, egg yolks, and butter. Plants are not a good source of vitamin D.

The main function of vitamin D is to enable the body to properly absorb and use calcium, the element needed for proper bone development and maintenance. Deficiency of vitamin D results in a condition called **rickets,** which is seen in children. Children with rickets do not develop bones normally. In adults, a condition called osteomalacia, or adult rickets, is the gradual softening and bending of the bones due to a lack of vitamin D. This disease is more common in women than men, and often first develops during pregnancy. Osteoporosis is a reduction in the quality of bone or atrophy of the skeletal tissue. It is an age-related disorder affecting 20 million Americans, 80% of them women age 45 and older. Lack of vitamin D is a contributory cause of the disorder. Psoriasis also appears to be linked to a lack of vitamin D.

Vitamin D is stored in the body. It is possible to have toxic symptoms from too much vitamin D in the body, although this is a rare problem. Again, most vitamin D toxicity is the result of taking too many vitamin D supplements.

Vitamin E
Vitamin E, also known as **tocopherol,** primarily serves the body as an antioxidant. **Antioxidants** are very important in protecting the body from damage cause by free radicals. Free radicals are wild molecules that steal electrons. Tocopherol helps to scavenge these wild molecules, squelching them so that cell membranes are not damaged. Continual damage from free radicals is associated with many diseases, tumor formation, and the aging process of the body as well as the skin. Vitamin E generally works to protect many tissues of the body from damage so that they can function normally. It is present in vegetable oils and seed oils. Safflower oil is very high in vitamin E concentration. Green leafy vegetables, avocadoes, wheat germ, egg yolks, and butter are also good sources of vitamin E.

Vitamin K

Vitamin K is responsible for the synthesis of factors necessary for blood coagulation. Coagulation is the clotting factor that allows bleeding to stop. Deficiency of vitamin K is rare. It results in hard-to-control bleeding. Vitamin K deficiency can be related to certain disorders that do not allow proper absorption of fats by the intestines. It is found in beans, dark leafy vegetables such as spinach, broccoli, and egg yolks.

Water-Soluble Vitamins

Water-soluble vitamins do not stay in the body for very long. They are not stored in body fat like the fat-soluble vitamins. They include the B vitamins—niacin, riboflavin, thiamin, pyridoxine, folacin, biotin, cobalamine, and pantothenic acid. Vitamin C is also a water-soluble vitamin.

The body must have regular supplies of the water-soluble vitamins because they are used in almost every metabolic reaction and are excreted and not retained by the body. Most of these are easily obtained through many foods.

Vitamin B Complex

Thiamine (vitamin B_1) is present in pork, beef, fortified cereals, whole-wheat products, and nuts. Vitamin B_1 removes carbon dioxide from cells, and converts carbohydrates stored as fat. Beriberi is the disease caused by B_1 deficiency. Beriberi affects the nervous system, and can slow heart the rate as well as cause mental dysfunction. In children it can stunt growth. B_1 deficiency can also be caused by alcohol abuse.

Riboflavin (vitamin B_2) is made up of enzymes that are functional in energy production by cells. Cells use vitamin B_2 to manufacture various amino acids and fatty acids. Deficiency can result in retarded growth, nerve tissue damage, dryness of the skin, and cracks at the mouth corners, known as cheilosis. B_2 is found in milk, meats, liver, and dark green leafy vegetables, broccoli, eggs, salmon, and tuna. Grains and bread are often fortified with riboflavin.

Niacin is a necessary part of many metabolic reactions. Most of these complicated reactions are important in the release of energy from carbohydrates. Niacin is also required for the manufacture of steroids by the body, and the manufacture of red blood cells. **Pellagra** is the disease associated with niacin deficiency. Pellagra can affect the skin, mental functions, and the intestinal tract, and can cause death. Proteins are the best source for niacin: peanuts, beans, milk, eggs, and meats. Some niacin is found in whole grain products, and in enriched foods.

Pyridoxine (vitamin B_6) is important in the metabolism of proteins, both breaking down and reconstructing amino acids, as needed by the body. Several important chemicals, including histamine, are produced in conjunction with vitamin B_6. Deficiency of vitamin B_6 results in many symptoms including poor coordination, mental acuity problems, and can affect levels of white blood cells. Because vitamin B_6 is strongly connected to protein synthesis, many problems are associated with deficiency, having a domino effect on many other reactions. Interestingly, research has been performed on vitamin B_6 and its effect on premenstrual syndrome (PMS) and on mood and irritability. Vitamin B_6 is present in meats, soybeans, fish, walnuts, and in vegetables and fruits such as bananas, potatoes, prunes, and avocadoes.

Folacin, also known as folic acid, is a very important B vitamin. It is involved in processing amino acids, and in transporting certain molecules, which is important for the cells to make a number of important chemicals involved in mental health. Vitamin B_{12} and vitamin C must be present for folacin to work properly. Deficiencies can result in a number of mental problems including moodiness, hostility, and loss of memory. There is a connection between low intakes of folacin and birth defects, as well as colorectal cancer.

Folacin is found, as are many other important vitamins, in dark leafy green vegetables. Asparagus, cantaloupe, sweet potatoes, and green peas are all good sources of folacin.

Cobalamin (vitamin B_{12}) is important in the activation of folacin, proper fatty acid synthesis, and DNA synthesis in conjunction with proper red blood vessel formation by the bone marrow. A disorder known as **pernicious anemia** is caused by a lack of vitamin B_{12}, or from poor absorption of the

vitamin K
Responsible for the synthesis of factors necessary for blood coagulation.

thiamine (vitamin B_1)
Present in pork, beef, fortified cereals, whole-wheat products, and nuts; removes carbon dioxide from the cells, and converts carbohydrates stored as fat.

riboflavin (vitamin B_2)
Comprised of enzymes that are functional in energy production by cells.

pellagra
The disease associated with niacin deficiency; can affect the skin, mental functions, and the intestinal tract, and can cause death.

pernicious anemia
A disorder caused by lack of proper amounts of vitamin B_{12}, or from poor absorption of the vitamin caused by other diseases.

| **biotin** |
| Involved in energy formation by cells, synthesis of both proteins and fatty acids. |

| **pantothenic acid** |
| Important in various processes involved in synthesis of fatty acids, and the metabolism of proteins and carbohydrates. |

| **L-ascorbic acid (vitamin C)** |
| An antioxidant that helps protect the body from many forms of oxidation, and free radical induced problems. |

| **calcium** |
| A mineral the body requires for the formation and maintenance of teeth and bones. |

| **magnesium** |
| Mineral used for energy release and protein synthesis, prevention of tooth decay, and in movement of muscles. |

| **phosphorus** |
| Mineral involved and present in DNA, and in energy release. |

| **potassium** |
| An element, the salts of which are used in medicine; an essential mineral found in vegetables and fruits, necessary to the health of the skin; potassium and sodium regulate the water balance within the body. |

| **sodium** |
| Moves carbon dioxide; regulates water levels and the transport of materials through the cell membranes. |

vitamin caused by other diseases. Absorption of this vitamin decreases with age, making deficiency symptoms more likely in older persons. Liver, salmon, clams, oysters, and egg yolks are some good food sources for vitamin B_{12}.

Biotin is involved in energy formation by cells, as well as the synthesis of both proteins and fatty acids. It is produced in the intestinal tract by microbes ("good" bacteria), but is also present in milk, liver, and other organ meats. Deficiencies are primarily caused by intestinal disorders or from poor absorption. Antibiotics can kill off good bacteria along with the bad ones, and can cause lower levels of biotin.

Pantothenic acid is important in various processes involved in the synthesis of fatty acids, and the metabolism of proteins and carbohydrates. Its role in fatty acid synthesis includes synthesis of hormones, cholesterol, and phospholipids. The latter two make up an important part of the barrier function of skin.

Pantothenic acid deficiency is practically nonexistent. Pantothenic acid is present in many foods but it is not present in fruits. Because it is so widely available through many food sources, deficiencies would be associated with starvation.

Vitamin C

L-ascorbic acid (vitamin C) is an antioxidant, helping to protect the body from many forms of oxidation, and free radical induced problems. Vitamin C performs numerous functions in the body. It is required for collagen formation. Collagen is not only in the skin, but also in cartilage, and supports the discs in the spine. Vitamin C is also functional in preventing breakage of capillary walls that can cause easy bruising, bleeding gums, and even capillary distension. Vitamin C renews vitamin E by allowing it to neutralize more free radicals. Vitamin C helps the body deal with stress, and is easily depleted during times of great stress.

Vitamin C is easily depleted in smokers, which is important because smokers have more free radicals forming in their bodies. It has been suggested that smokers need twice the vitamin C as nonsmokers.

Research indicates that adequate intake of vitamin C may help prevent cancer because of its ability to scavenge free radicals that attack DNA. DNA damage can lead to the formation of cancerous cells. Vitamin C can also kill cancerous cells in the beginning stages, re-establishing a normal state for cells. Vitamin C also helps prevent cardiovascular disease by helping to maintain blood vessel walls, and by preventing oxidation of bad cholesterol, which can lead to clogging in the blood vessels. Studies also show that vitamin C helps reduce the time someone is sick with a cold, and the severity of the symptoms.

Scurvy results from vitamin C deficiency. Symptoms of scurvy include easy bruising, bleeding gums, poor wound healing, and anemia. Scurvy is rare, but can occur in persons with very poor diets, and is occasionally seen in senior citizens. Vitamin C is found in citrus fruits, dark green leafy vegetables, tomatoes, and other fruits and vegetables.

Minerals

Many minerals are required by the body. These are inorganic materials that are required for many reactions of the cells and the body. Most are required in relatively small quantities, but are nevertheless necessary for life. Some of the important minerals required by the body, and their functions are listed below.

- **calcium** is required for the formation and maintenance of teeth and bones. It helps prevent osteoporosis, a degenerative disease that results in brittle bones.

- **magnesium** is required for energy release and protein synthesis, the prevention of tooth decay, and in muscle movements.

- **phosphorus** is involved and present in DNA, and in energy release.

- **potassium** is required for energy use, water balance, and muscular movement.

- **sodium** moves carbon dioxide and regulates water levels and the transport of materials through the cell membranes.

Other minerals needed in the body are trace minerals. These are required in very small quantities. They include iron, iodine, zinc, copper, chromium, fluoride, selenium, and manganese. All of these are necessary for correct body function, and many are present in cells and tissues. Iron, for example, is an important component of red blood cells. It is necessary to properly transport oxygen to the cells.

How Much Nutrition Do You Need?

The answer to this question varies a lot with an individual's age, sex, size, and the individual circumstances of each person. Pregnancy and lactation affect the nutritional needs of a woman. The U.S.D.A. (United States Department of Agriculture) is the governmental department that governs nutrition-related affairs. The U.S.D.A. issues what is known as recommended dietary allowances (RDAs) for certain nutrients, including vitamins and minerals.

The number of calories required to run the body varies with all of the above factors as well. An adult male needs about 2,300 to 3,100 calories per day. An adult female needs about 1,600 to 2,400 calories. Dieticians generally believe that 55% to 60% of all calories should be obtained from carbohydrates, mainly grains, breads, pasta, vegetables, and fruit. Candy is also a carbohydrate, but sweets should be limited to no more than 240 calories per day for women, and 310 calories per day for men. It is also generally accepted by most nutritional authorities that fats should be limited to no more than 30% of the diet. No more than 10% of this should come from saturated fats. Protein requirements make up the balance of the diet, around 15% to 20%. Remember that protein sources, such as meat, also include fats and carbohydrates.

Nutrition and Esthetics

Proper nutrition is a primary factor in maintaining the skin's health. Some foods directly affect certain conditions of the skin, but there are also many myths about food and the skin. An example is the widely held belief that junk food and chocolate can cause or worsen acne. The truth is that junk foods and sweets are unhealthy and should not be consumed in large quantities, but they do not have a direct effect on acne.

On the other hand, it is well known that spicy foods and alcohol consumption can induce rosacea flare-ups. Some women have such low-fat diets that their body fat drops too low, and they have hormonal imbalances that can cause skin problems, including hyperpigmentation and forms of acne.

Unfortunately, some estheticians place too much importance on diet and the skin. With a few exceptions, such as rosacea, what you eat on Friday does not affect your skin on Saturday! This is why it is so important that estheticians have some understanding of the real issues in nutrition.

Obesity and weight loss is a concern of many clients. They may talk to you about their concerns. It is important to remember that although you may be interested in proper health practices, you are not an authority on nutrition. You should not be a source of counsel for persons with nutritional concerns. To do so might endanger your client's health and have legal consequences. All clients who have serious questions about nutritional issues should be referred to a registered dietician. Many spas now offer nutritional counseling with a licensed dietician. This can be a useful service for many clients.

Fad diets are rampant. Every week there is some new magical weight-loss gimmick or plan. The truth about weight loss is:

- There are only three ways to lose weight: burn more calories than you take in, take in fewer calories than you burn, or a combination of both!

- Certain diets can be harmful to the body, and can cause chemical imbalances that can damage the body.

- Vitamins and supplements are not substitutes for proper nutrition. You can get most of the vitamins and minerals you need from a balanced diet.

- Vitamin and mineral supplements have little nutritional value because they do not provide the basics: the carbohydrates, proteins, and fats necessary for life processes. You must take these in as food for the vitamins and minerals to have any effect. In other words, if you look at

zinc
A white crystalline metallic element; used in some cosmetics such as powders and ointments; salts of zinc are used in some antiseptics and astringents.

copper
A metallic element that is a good conductor of heat and electricity.

chromium
A trace mineral, required in very small quantities for correct body function.

fluoride
A trace mineral, required in very small quantities for correct body function.

selenium
In nutrition, an essential mineral found in cereals, vegetables, and fish; preserves tissue elasticity and aids in promotion of body growth.

manganese
A grayish-white, metallic, chemical element which rusts like iron; it is not magnetic.

Ethics

Is it ethical to provide minors with cigarettes, to ask about a prospective employee's personal life, or to discuss a patient's prognosis on the elevator? Many lengthy discussions, covering a wide variety of subjects, have occurred on the topic of ethics.

Ethics refer to standards of moral behavior. These can be quite far reaching. However, when we talk about professional ethics we are talking about a code of conduct that is essential to maintaining the integrity and credibility of a profession.

Unfortunately, in today's society we are witnessing a growing distrust of professionals. One only has to turn on the evening news to learn about the latest misuse or abuse of power. Negative media attention can make it difficult to encourage professional trust but it should not altar our professional conduct.

As professionals we are obligated to uphold a certain ethical standard that protects the consumer. To do this we must be clear about what behaviors are appropriate and which are inappropriate. We must understand what is expected of us and act accordingly. Ethical dilemmas often arise when we are confused or inexperienced about our boundaries or how to handle situations. To avoid problems we must establish and adhere to certain rules or guidelines.

Estheticians are expected to be knowledgeable about skin care. They are trained to perform specialized skin care services. In this role you will be expected to perform certain face and body treatments, as well as advise and educate clients on products and techniques. To do this well you must maintain competency, act responsibly, protect client confidentiality, avoid exploitation, and demonstrate exemplary conduct.

Obtaining the appropriate state license or certificate to practice esthetics is the first step in establishing credibility. But estheticians should also be aware of FDA and other government agencies whose function is to protect the consumer. There are numerous regulations in place to prevent the public from being unnecessarily duped by false claims and advertising when it comes to products and equipment.

As skin care professionals we can all appreciate the consumer who is wary of purchasing "snake oil" or the ubiquitous "miracle in a jar." So how do we gain the public's trust? We begin by being honest and sincere. This helps clients develop trust in our expertise. The following are some general guidelines that will help you maintain credibility and build confidence.

- Obtain the appropriate credentials, licenses, and certificates necessary to practice in your state. State these in an honest and professional manner.

- Join and participate in professional organizations that take an unbiased approach to esthetics.

- Attend as many continuing education seminars as possible. But recognize that one workshop does not make you an expert.

- Know your boundaries. Do only what you are trained to do. Do not offer advice or make recommendations outside your area of expertise. This means understanding when to decline a service or opinion and refer the client to the appropriate professional.

- Keep client relationships professionally friendly. Clients will often confide very personal information. Practice respectful listening and maintain professional boundaries. Do not give advice or share personal information. Do not socialize with clients.

- Be honest and truthful. Do not make false claims about products and techniques. When you don't have the answer don't be afraid to say, "I don't know."

- Do not rely on promotional literature by manufacturers to ensure a product's efficacy. Conduct your own research, particularly on controversial methods or ingredients. Always make sure you can stand behind a product without losing credibility.

- Be open to seeking consultation from more experienced colleagues or other professionals.

- Keep informed. Subscribe to professional trade publications and read as much as possible.

nutrition as building and maintaining a house, the nails (vitamins and minerals) are no good without the wood and the bricks (macronutrients).

- There is no magical ingredient that can cause weight loss without other, sometimes harmful, effects on the body.

- The best way to lose weight, and maintain proper weight, is to adopt a healthy diet along with proper exercise.

We have barely touched on the basics of nutrition in this chapter. If you are interested in this subject, check out nutrition courses at your local community college or university. This will give you a better knowledge base for both nutrition and health issues.

Summary

Basic nutrition is fundamental to the health of the skin. Without the macronutrients, minerals, and vitamins necessary for proper nutrition, deficiencies will affect the skin. Cell function is dependent on balanced and quality nutrients. Good nutrition is fundamental to building tissues and organs. There are many obstacles that may play a role in our nutrition. Diseases or medications that affect our ability to digest food interrupt the normal process of nutrients reaching the bloodstream and consequently, the cells. Ultimately, the skin may lack luster, lose elasticity, or break down. Gaining an understanding of nutrition helps you in your analysis of the skin. It also assists you in performing corrective treatments that help restore the skin's suppleness and vitality.

Unless you are a registered dietitian, it is not appropriate to offer nutritional advice to a client. While you may be qualified to make proper decisions for treatments and products, it is better to recommend someone who is qualified to provide nutritional advice. Keep a list of referrals for your clients.

Discussion Questions

1. Why is it important for the esthetician to have a good understanding of nutrition? Include the importance of professional boundaries in providing quality care to clients.

2. Name the three basic building blocks or nutrients responsible for sound body functioning. Describe their functions and give examples of common dietary sources for each.

3. In general, what effect do vitamins and minerals have on good health and nutrition? As a professional, how can you relate these to good skin care practices?

4. Make a list of all vitamins, differentiating between those that are fat-soluble and water-soluble and describe the health benefits associated with each.

5. What is meant by the term *antioxidants*, and how do they help to promote good skin care?

Additional Reading

Braverman, Eric R., et al. 1997. *The Healing Nutrients Within, Facts, Findings and New Research on Amino Acids.* New York: McGraw-Hill. 2d ed.

Garrison, Robert Jr. 1997. *Nutrition Desk Reference.* 3d ed. New York: McGraw-Hill.

Kirshman, Gayla J., et al. 1998. *Nutrition Almanac.* 4th ed. New York: McGraw-Hill.

Murray, Michael T., 1996. *Encyclopedia of Nutritional Supplements, Essential Guide for Improving Your Health Naturally.* Rocklin, Calif.: Prima Publishing.

Wilcox, Bradley, et al. 2001. *The Okinawa Program, How the World's Longest Lived People Achieve Everlasting Health and How You Can Too.* New York: Crown Publishers.

Willet, Walter C., et al. 2001. *Eat, Drink and Be Healthy: The Harvard Medical School Guide to Healthy Eating.* New York: Simon & Schuster.

The Treatment Room

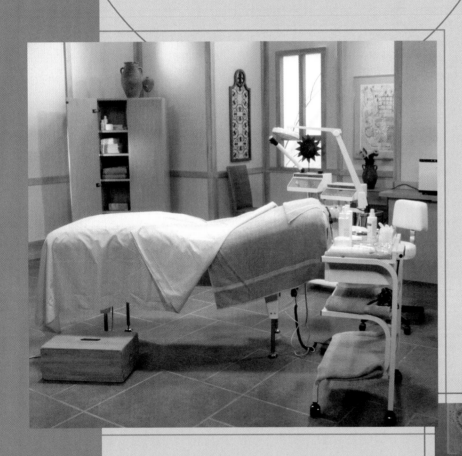

PART III

Part Outline

Chapter 7   Room Furnishings

Chapter 8   Technological Tools

Chapter 9   Basics of Electricity

Chapter 10   First Impressions—Setup and Supplies

The esthetician's primary workspace is the treatment room. To ensure productivity, careful consideration must be given to the location and furnishings of the treatment room. In many salons and spas, one room may serve several purposes. Facial chairs, operator chairs, and equipment must be strategically arranged for comfort, efficiency, and mobility. Supplies and other accessories must be readily available. Technical tools, such as galvanic and high-frequency machines used to perform facial treatments, may require special electrical and safety considerations. In the chapters that follow, you will learn about the primary tools and furnishings needed to set up the basic treatment room. Basic furniture and equipment will be introduced, as well as how to care for and maintain them. You will learn about the technological tools used during in-depth facials and how to use them, as well as the role electricity plays in skin care. Finally, you will see how the importance of making a positive professional impression with the client, through room preparation and the correct use of accessories and supplies, will prepare you for performing a facial.

Chapter 7
Room Furnishings

Chapter Objectives

After reading this chapter, you should be able to:

- Identify how to select ergonomically correct furniture.
- Discuss the importance of the esthetician's well-being.
- Perform a basic room setup.
- Perform proper maintenance on furniture and equipment.

Chapter Outline

Introduction
Facial Chair
Operator Chair or Stool
Maintenance of Furniture, Equipment,
   and Countertops
Ergonomics
Utility Carts

Introduction

Furnishings and equipment play a significant role in operating a successful skin care practice. A carefully planned treatment room should take into account the comfort and safety of both the practitioner and client. A calm and serene environment helps clients relax. A clean and tidy work space contributes to building the client's confidence. The esthetician's supplies and instruments should be stored until needed. The facial chair or bed should be arranged with fresh linens and should be able to support a large person. An adjustable stool allows the practitioner to maintain an ergonomically correct height while working. All equipment, such as the magnifying light, steamer, and hot towel cabbie should be checked regularly to ensure that they are in good working order, and clean, with no oil or finger marks on the finish.

Planning an efficient work space or treatment room depends largely on the focus of the esthetic practice. Each skin care clinic or spa will have its own philosophy or vision which will influence the nature of the services performed by the esthetician. However, the main goal in setting up any practice is to be able to work professionally and efficiently. Eventually, you may choose to open your own business. It is important to become familiar with the basic operational tools necessary to equip a facility. Attending industry trade shows and conducting additional research will help you become aware of the many options in furnishings and supplies that are available today.

Becoming familiar with the many supplies and tools needed to work as an esthetician may be intimidating at first. Your instructor will guide you through this process. Operating the facial chair and doing the practical work of performing facials will soon become second nature. As you discover what is needed to work comfortably and efficiently, you will automatically develop an understanding of what constitutes a good facial room setup. This chapter provides guidelines on how to use equipment and how to set up the treatment room.

Facial Chair

The esthetic chair, sometimes called a facial bed, is the most important piece of equipment in any treatment room—it is where you perform your work (Figure 7–1). Today, there are many different options and styles to choose from, depending on the practitioner's requirements. In selecting an esthetic chair it is important to look at practical features, such as the ability to lower or increase height. This will allow you to perform a more comfortable service.

Facial chairs have undergone many technological improvements over the years. In the early days estheticians used simple inexpensive loungers. These usually came in drab colors such as brown and black and were covered with sheets to improve their appearance. Pillows were used to prop the client up and to position the head to a more comfortable position. Extra padding made the chairs soft and comfy but had to be removed to perform the facial massage. Ultimately the bigger loungers were replaced with more

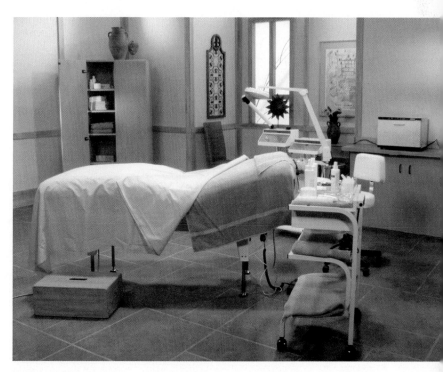

Figure 7–1 The facial bed is the most important piece of equipment in the treatment room.

Booth Rentals

Some skin care clinics, beauty salons, and medical practices offer the esthetician the opportunity to rent space within the facility. This can be a viable option for those with an entrepreneurial spirit looking to test their management skills on a smaller scale. Booth rentals offer practitioners a chance to be their own boss and manage a clientele within certain set boundaries. The esthetician pays a rental fee to operate within the confines of an agreed upon space in an established clinic or salon.

If you are fortunate enough to find such an opportunity within a successfully run business this may be the right arrangement for you. But before you jump into a situation that appears to be lucrative, make sure you gather enough information to make an informed decision. Begin by asking the following important questions:

- Is it legal in my state to rent a booth to conduct skin care?

- What licenses are required to operate my own business?

- Am I covered by my present license to operate on my own?

- Will I be covered by any facility licenses, or will I be completely responsible for my business?

- What insurance protection will I need? What is the cost of that insurance, and does it include malpractice?

- How successful is the business? Is there an opportunity to draw from the existing clientele, or will I need to proactively solicit business for myself?

- Is there an option to share in joint advertising?

- What competition exists within the business itself? For example, how many estheticians are on staff?

- What hours is the establishment open? Are these convenient for me? If not, will I be able to extend my own hours?

- Will I be subject to any other rules or requirements that may impinge upon my freedom?

For the most part, renting booth space is tantamount to running your own business. You have all the responsibilities of being self-employed, but not always all the control. Developing a strategic business plan will be an important factor in your success. As you weigh your options, be careful to assess all the costs associated with conducting business in this manner. Make sure you respect the owner and agree with the philosophy of the establishment before you sign any contracts. And, on that note, you should take care to obtain the appropriate legal advice before signing any legal documents or contracts.

professional chairs. Many clients still preferred the older models—they found the loungers so comfortable!

Modern technology has provided us with many new options (Figure 7–2). Today esthetic chairs or beds are designed to perform multiple tasks and provide flexibility in the treatment room. Some are manufactured with hydraulic motorized adjustments that require electricity to run. They can be quite heavy depending on their engineering complexity. Other chairs are designed with manual hydraulic pedals that assist in chair adjustment and allow the chair to be arranged in several positions or lie flat. Many models can be used for the dual-purpose of facials and massage.

Whether you utilize more sophisticated technology or a simple bed, the most important criterion for any facial chair is how it meets *your fit.* Think of how many hours you will use this equipment. While it is important for the practitioner to be comfortable, the client's needs should not be overlooked. Catering to special concerns such as neck, lower back, and leg problems are common. Heated underblankets, leg rolls, and pillows help you to make each client feel comfortable and nurtured. Tune into the great sighs of relief as you settle the client into a relaxing, safe place. It is comforting to know that the client feels tucked in and cared for right from the beginning.

Estheticians must often use the facial chair to perform other treatments, such as hair removal. Ideally this should be avoided whenever possible, because it destroys the ambiance of the facial treatment room, which is best kept subdued and free of extraneous odors. However, if it is necessary to use the room for other services, be sure to be meticulous about your housekeeping. Protect the facial chair from miscellaneous drips and spills and clean up after each client.

Operator Chair or Stool

The operator's stool should be **ergonomically correct,** that is, healthy for the human spine. A stool with good wheels will help to achieve this. The esthetician needs to be able to move around freely, gaining easy access to

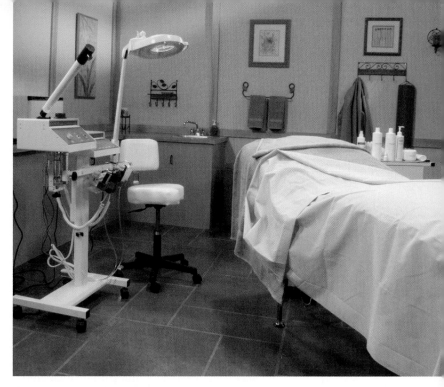

Figure 7–2 A modern treatment room.

products and equipment without distracting the client. Moving up and down frequently or opening and closing doors can cause the esthetician to lose the **treatment rhythm,** the smooth flow of movement that occurs as you perform your facial. A good stool will help you to be comfortable and productive, as well as keep the treatment rhythm flowing (Figure 7–3).

Practitioners can choose from a variety of treatment stools, depending on individual comfort needs. Stools are available with or without back support and may be padded

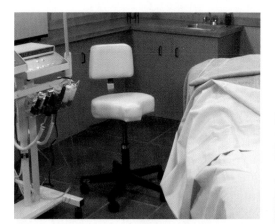

Figure 7–3 Choosing a proper esthetician's stool is very important.

ergonomically correct
Healthy for the human spine.

treatment rhythm
The smooth flow of movement that occurs during the performance of the facial.

with either round, contoured, or saddle style cushions. Manufacturers may offer a choice of furniture coverings. Practicality should be the prime concern when selecting a stool covering for the esthetic treatment room. A sturdy, nonporous, material that is able to withstand a good cleaning is always a good choice. Cushion density is also a factor.

Step Stool

The step stool is often overlooked when it comes to treatment room furnishings; however, it is important to maintaining a safe environment for your clients. In today's society, safety is a big factor and the risk is real. Service providers must practice preventive measures. Providing a step stool to assist clients moving on and off the facial bed may help to avoid an unfortunate incident (Figure 7–4).

Always offer clients the choice of using a step stool, even if they appear quite agile. If necessary, steady the arm and help direct them onto the facial bed. Particularly at the end of a treatment, clients may become disoriented. It is best to assist them to an upright position and once again show them the stool that you have thoughtfully placed under their feet. Have them wriggle toward

the edge of the bed, once again with your hand on their arm. Guide them until their feet touch the step stool and they can transfer their weight onto it.

Maintenance of Furniture, Equipment, and Countertops

With proper care facial chairs and stools will last for years. Always check with the manufacturer for specific instructions before attempting to clean tools and equipment. Then be sure your cleanser is compatible with the manufacturer's recommendations. When in doubt use a mild cleanser that does not leave a film. Avoid caustic substances such as ammonia, window cleaner, scouring powders, and harsh solvents. These can scratch delicate fabrics or ruin vinyl coverings. For extra protection, place a pad or mattress covering over the facial bed and stool.

If the treatment room is furnished with vinyl upholstery, a special word of caution is indicated. Vinyl is particularly susceptible to damage from heating pads and essential oils. Never leave thermal heating elements on an uncovered empty bed. It will cause the upholstery to dry and crack. The oils leave penetrating stains that are permanent. Once the vinyl is damaged it ultimately weakens and must be replaced.

Many other esthetic products can also leave permanent stains or corrode paint. Formica countertops, trolleys, trays, esthetic machines, and steamers have delicate surfaces. It is important to treat them gently. Be careful not to place items that may cause unsightly stains on top of your machines. Do not use scouring powders or abrasives to clean them. Even stainless steel surfaces can become scratched or worn down. However, if properly maintained, esthetics equipment and furniture will last for years and look just as new as the day it was purchased.

Ergonomics

The work of estheticians is repetitive. It is vital to their comfort level and safety to have back support to avoid upper and lower back

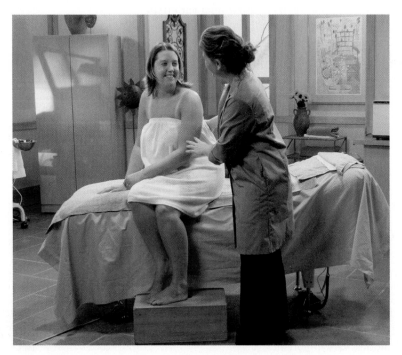

Figure 7–4 Assist the client on and off the facial bed for safety.

Liability

If you goal is to work for someone else, perhaps the furthest thing from your mind is liability. After all, why should you be concerned about protecting yourself against claims if you do not own the business? Shouldn't that be the employer's responsibility? To a certain extent the answer to that question is yes. However, in our litigation-oriented society, being informed about liability should be of concern to all those who service clients.

Today's skin care market is becoming increasingly more focused on providing dramatic results. As a result, estheticians are being asked to use products and techniques that are far more complex. Although the esthetician operating at an entry-level position may not be asked to perform more sophisticated treatments, it is in everyone's best interest to take a cautious approach.

In an ideal situation, you would have numerous opportunities to practice working with a product or technique until you become comfortable. You might even have the opportunity to be closely supervised until you build enough confidence to keep the margin for error considerably low. However, the truth is that most estheticians starting out will not have the luxury of either. To avoid problems, and to ensure the safety of your clients, consider the following:

- Before beginning any new procedure, review the client's history, noting any contraindications.

- If you are in doubt about whether a client is a viable candidate for a particular treatment, seek counsel from a more experienced member of the staff or from the product distributor.

- Use consent forms, which explain the procedure, list the benefits, and clearly state any side effects or possible risks.

- Review the consent form with clients, making sure that they clearly understand what is involved and how to care for their skin after the procedure.

- Have the client sign and date the consent form each time the service is performed.

- If problems do arise, carefully document any side effects on the client's profile card or history.

While no one looks to have a negative experience, keep in mind that accidents do happen. Reactions or sensitivities to products are common, and clients may not always fully disclose their situation. For example, a client may be so eager to obtain a new peel designed to turn back the hands of time, that she forgets to inform the esthetician that she is using products such as Retin A.

You should know that, in some cases, estheticians may still be held liable for errors in professional judgment. Before you begin working for someone else, ask for documentation of their professional liability insurance—no matter what their professional status. Working for a physician does not necessarily guarantee your protection. It also makes sense to inquire about the cost of acquiring additional personal liability insurance. Professional organizations, and your esthetic training school, can be good sources of information on this topic. Don't wait until an unfortunate incident occurs to find out that you are not adequately protected against a client's claim.

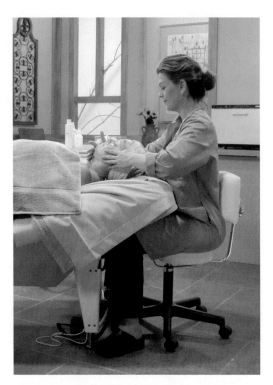

Figure 7–5 Proper positioning of the stool is vital to the comfort level and safety of the esthetician.

height and size of the operator. If the stool does not have a back support, lean back periodically to adjust the spine. Wear comfortable, flat-heeled shoes. Adjust the facial chair so that your wrists are not at an exaggerated angle while performing the facial massage. The head of the client should be aimed at your breastbone. Rest your elbows on the bed near the client's ears so that there is no tension in the shoulders. When performing the facial massage, your hands should be at a 90-degree angle.

Proper clothing and personal grooming is also important. Uniforms should be comfortable and provide good mobility, especially in the shoulder and elbow areas, but should not be too loose fitting. Hair should be up and off the shoulders. Long hair should never impair the esthetician's vision or hang in the client's face. Dangling jewelry is inappropriate and can get caught in the client's hair or hit the client's face.

The esthetician's energy level is also an important factor, especially when working with many clients in one day. Be sure to take scheduled breaks, eat properly, and drink plenty of water. Weather permitting, step outside for a few moments and take a few deep breaths to increase your oxygen level.

Proper hand care cannot be emphasized enough! To prevent injury it is wise to periodically give your hands a rest. Rotate them and perform exercises to ease any stiffness and to maintain flexibility (Figure 7–6a-f).

and neck strain (Figure 7–5). It is important to learn to work sitting down on a stool with an adjustable back. A major contributor to back problems is sitting for long periods of time without a break. To prevent back problems the tension on the stool's back support should be adjusted to accommodate the

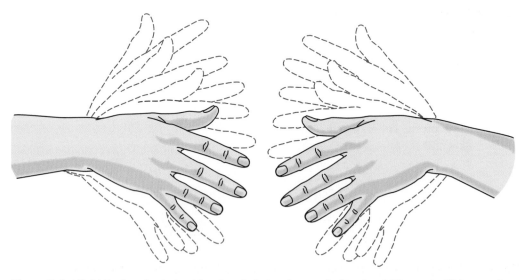

Figure 7–6a Hold the hands at chest level and shake vigorously for about 25 counts. This exercise warms and limbers the hands and increases circulation.

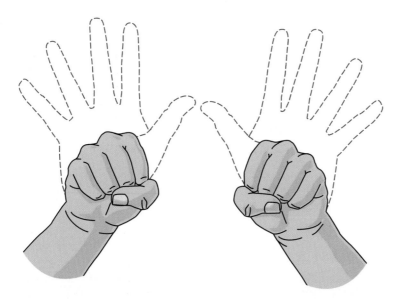

Figure 7–6b Hold the hands at chest level with fists clenched. Make a fist, squeezing as hard as you can, while holding for a count of five. Release the hands, spreading the fingers wide for a count of five. Repeat 10 to 20 times. This exercise is excellent for strengthening the hands and wrists.

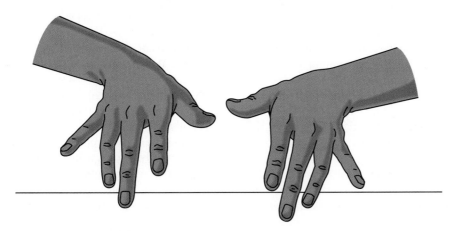

Figure 7–6c Place both hands, palms down, on a flat surface. Tap each finger beginning with the thumbs, and count each finger from thumb to little finger, as it is tapped in rhythm. Count 1, 2, 3, 4, 5. Then, starting with the little finger, tap each finger to the count of 5, 4, 3, 2, 1. This exercise is similar to playing the piano and is especially good for building coordination and hand control.

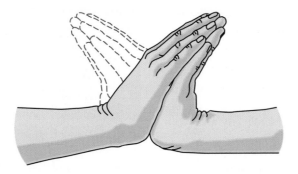

Figure 7–6d Place the palms together at chest level. Keep them together as you bend the left wrist as far back as it will go; then do the same with the right wrist. Keep bending the wrists in rhythm for 20 counts. This exercise strengthens the hands and wrists and makes them more flexible.

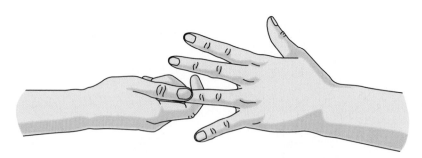

Figure 7–6e Massage each finger, beginning with the thumb of the left hand, rubbing from the base to each knuckle and to the tip, one by one, until each finger has been thoroughly massaged. Repeat the exercise on the right hand. This exercise stimulates circulation, warms the hands, and keeps them supple.

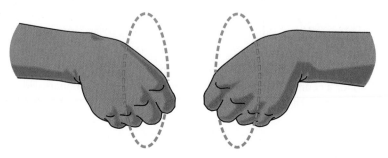

Figure 7–6f Hold the clenched hands at chest level and rotate in circular movements at the wrists for 20 counts. Reverse the rotating movements for 20 counts. This exercise limbers and strengthens the wrists.

Utility Carts

Utility carts help the esthetician organize his work space. There are many styles to choose from, each with certain features and benefits.

Trolleys or utility tables with multiple shelves and wheels provide an ideal workstation. The esthetician's supplies, products, and equipment can all easily be stored within arm's reach. Multitier carts are ideal for storing specialized equipment, such as the Wood's lamp, keeping them within easy reach. Many carts also have electrical power strips that allow several pieces of equipment to be plugged into one wall outlet (Figure 7–7). This helps keep the necessary cords and plugs safely and neatly arranged. It is important to mention that room outlets need to be configured properly to safely handle any high-voltage equipment.

Using a trolley makes the fundamental task of performing a facial treatment that much easier. The arrangement in each salon or spa will dictate protocol for setting up the **back bar,** the place used for organization and storage of professional products used

back bar
The place used for organization and storage of professional products used during the facial.

during the facial. The utility table serves as a useful prop to help keep the esthetician organized. Typically, back-bar items are dispensed in one of two ways (Figure 7–8). They are either stored in the treatment room, or kept

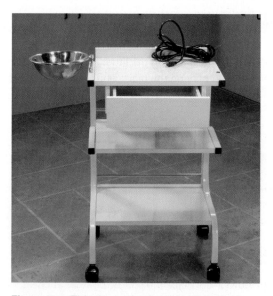

Figure 7–7 This three-shelf cart is electrified and also has an attached bowl to keep water conveniently close.

Figure 7–8 A neat dispensary helps maintain and control inventory.

in another area of the business and dispensed as needed. Space is often a primary consideration when determining which approach is taken.

Summary

The treatment room is the esthetician's primary work space. It should be neat and clean and reflect a professional ambiance. Estheticians work many hours a day in a treatment room. It is important to develop good work habits early on that will sustain health and longevity in the workplace. Practicing ergonomically correct posture while working with clients prevents body fatigue and decreases the risk of injury. Practitioners must also focus on the safety and health of their clients. Assisting clients on and off the facial chair or bed is important in developing a standard of care. The step stool is a handy and practical item that can help prevent mishaps.

Organizing the work space and taking special care to maintain equipment properly allows the esthetician to work efficiently and productively. Taking the time to read and follow manufacturers' directions is important to alleviate unnecessary problems and keep valuable work tools functioning at their best.

In the final analysis, the treatment room offers the client a valuable first impression of your operation. The esthetician should keep in mind that how well this space is maintained is often a good barometer of whether or not the client will return.

Discussion Questions

1. Understanding the basic necessities of a functional work space is an important part of developing a solid business plan. Make a list of the standard furniture necessary for the esthetician to begin practicing, and research the cost of these basic items.

2. Define ergonomics, and explain its relevance to the field of esthetics. How could you go about learning more on this topic? Who might you call upon for direction as you begin your research?

3. Promoting beautiful, healthy skin is the work of the esthetician. To do your job well, you must not only have excellent knowledge of skin, but also knowledge of the proper way to perform certain physical tasks. Focusing on the physical aspect of your job, make a list of general guidelines to ensure your own well-being while working with clients.

4. Client safety is always an import issue in any skin care salon or spa. To avoid accidents, develop a client safety checklist.

5. Taking safety precautions one step further, make a list of emergency numbers in your area and post the list by the telephone.

Additional Reading

Miller, Erica. 1996. *Day Spa Operations.* Clifton Park, N.Y.: Milady, an imprint of Delmar Learning, a division of Thomson Learning, Inc.

Tezak, Edward. 2002. *Milady's Successful Salon Management for Cosmetology Students, Workbook.* 5th ed. Clifton Park, N.Y.: Milady, an imprint of Delmar Learning, a division of Thomson Learning, Inc.

Chapter 8
Technological Tools

Chapter Objectives

After reading this chapter, you should be able to:

- Describe the machines used in skin analysis.
- Identify the machines used in skin care treatments.
- Explain the function and maintenance of each machine.
- Demonstrate galvanic and high-frequency machines.

Chapter Outline

Introduction
Skin Analysis Equipment
Skin Care Machines
Microcurrent Machines
Other Tools and Accessories

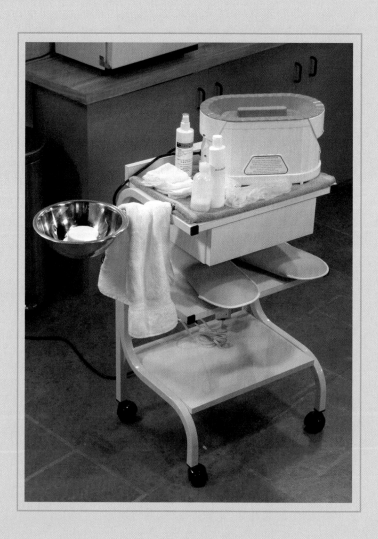

Introduction

Estheticians use several technological tools to enhance their job performance. Although facials can be performed well without the use of electrical devices, the opportunity to correct more challenging skin conditions and achieve greater results is enhanced by tools more powerful than the esthetician's hands.

Whether or not estheticians choose to work with electrically powered equipment, they must keep in mind that there is a direct correlation between all interactions created on the skin and its ability to be healthy and function well. Tools should enhance the esthetician's performance, making the work of performing a correct skin analysis, penetrating products (galvanic), and sanitizing the skin (high frequency) that much easier.

In the rapidly expanding field of skin care, new machines and technology emerge at each trade show, helping you perform your work more precisely and with greater results. Estheticians must continue to be educated on the latest methods in skin care. Although the use of advanced technology such as microdermabrasion requires advanced training and most likely will not be part of your basic course, it is important to be familiar with such trends. The media today has provided clients with far greater access to information, and they will expect you to be knowledgeable about such topics. To maintain professional credibility it is important that you are aware of current trends and technology. Some of the more advanced and innovative skin care treatments used today are briefly mentioned here to familiarize you with the terms and available technologies emerging in the skin care industry.

Skin Analysis Equipment

Analyzing skin requires instruments that provide proper lighting and magnification. The purpose of the analysis equipment is to closely examine the skin. Tools such as the magnifying lamp provide the esthetician with a light source and amplify what is seen (Figure 8–1). Some lights, such as the Wood's lamp, allow you to view even deeper into the skin. Proper lighting is a necessary tool for every treatment room.

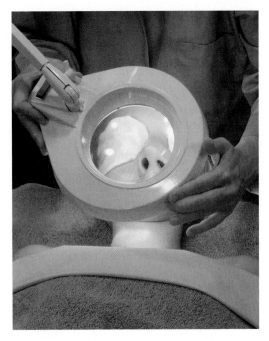

Figure 8–1 The use of a magnifying lamp clearly shows any imperfection, making it easier to conduct a thorough skin analysis.

The Magnifying Lamp (Loupe)

The naked eye is as important as any tool. The magnifying lamp, however, offers a glare-free aid to help the esthetician analyze skin and to treat it. The lamp uses a cool fluorescent light bulb shaped like a thick ring. It is usually protected by a translucent shield or bulb clamps. It is sometimes referred to as a **loupe.** A basic yet required tool, the magnifying lamp contains various powers of magnification known commonly in the industry as **diopter.** The average lamp in the industry comes in 3; 5; or 10-diopter, which means 30X power magnification, 50X power magnification, or 100X power magnification. Many loupes are standardized at 5-diopter. The majority of professionals find that the 5-diopter is sufficient. For the vision impaired, a 10-diopter may be necessary in order to obtain optimal vision. New estheticians may not realize that it is important to be aware of the quality and clarity of the lens as well as its magnification. It is imperative that a quality light is chosen, one that provides you with the most comfortable, clear, and accurate lens. You are using this light many hours of the day. Any distortion will not only add strain to your eyes, it will also make it more difficult to accurately see the skin.

loupe
Another term for a magnifying lamp.

diopter
A measure of the powers of magnification of a magnifying lamp.

Maintenance

Maintenance of magnifying lamps is not particularly involved. Periodically check the screws around the light to ensure that they are not loose. The arm may need tightening as well. Magnifying lamps can last up to 10 years if they are well constructed and well maintained. If they are abused and roughly handled, they will not last very long. If problems do occur, they typically involve the adjustment arm, which allows you to keep the lamp at the correct distance from the client. The spring on the arm can wear out and may break. As with all electrical equipment, the lamp must be respected and used with care. The lamp is in very close proximity to both the practitioner and client, so it is important not to startle the client by shining bright light directly into the eyes, or lose control of the lamp and accidentally strike the client.

There are variations in magnifying lamps. The use of skin scopes, which provide the added advantage of having the client observe what the esthetician sees, is becoming increasingly popular. They are helpful to estheticians in educating clients on skin types and home care.

Wood's Lamp

The Wood's lamp is a medically based tool developed by physicist, Dr. Robert Williams Wood (Figure 8–2). It makes use of a filtered black light that is used to illuminate skin disorders, fungi, bacterial disorders, pigmentation problems, etc. The Wood's lamp allows the esthetician to conduct a more in-depth skin analysis, illuminating common skin care problems, such as pigmentary conditions, that are ordinarily invisible to the naked eye. Although estheticians are not qualified to diagnose diseases or disorders, it is possible to spot a problem and refer the client to a physician. Under no circumstances should an esthetician make a diagnosis concerning a disease or disorder.

The key to using the Wood's lamp effectively is the ability to control the room's lighting. If the room cannot be darkened, there is little or no reason to utilize a Wood's lamp. Additionally, it is best if the Wood's light contains at least two rows of violet light as well as a magnification lens. If the Wood's lamp is being used in conjunction with a

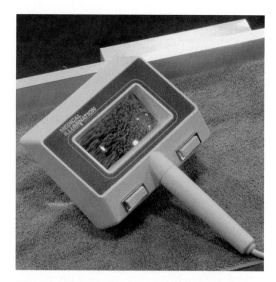

Figure 8–2 A Wood's lamp allows the esthetician to conduct a more in-depth skin analysis.

magnifying light, then it is best to concentrate the role of the Wood's lamp on determining disorders, pigmentary anomalies (irregularities), and degree of oiliness.

Maintenance

Use a camera lens or eyewear cleaner (found in many optical stores) to remove dust and markings from the magnifiers and mirror. The outside should be wiped clean of any finger marks and dust. Do not use any caustic substances (scouring powders or ammonia) on the paint because they can scratch and ruin the finish.

Skin Scopes

Similar to the Wood's lamp, the skin scope analyzer has a deep violet light to show different skin conditions. The light has the ability to penetrate the epidermis, manifesting several different colors on the client's face. The esthetician utilizes two models of the skin scope: a stationary box-type apparatus and a handheld model. The skin scope is a valuable tool that utilizes different colors to help the esthetician identify skin conditions.

How to Use

The stationary skin scope, or scanner as it is sometimes called, is similar to an old time photographic device. The client sits and places the face into a tentlike area. The practitioner sits on the opposite side of the box. A two-way magnifying mirror allows the client and practitioner to view the skin simultaneously through a small magnified window. The colors reflected in the face mirror reflect information about the client's skin (Table 8–1).

The skin scope is a terrific sales and educational tool. It is very effective in demonstrating a variety of skin conditions, such as sun damage. It may also be used as a screening device to raise awareness of skin cancer. The skin scope provides a very real image of what is going on with a particular client's skin. This makes it easy for the esthetician to explain the nature of the client's skin type and condition and to introduce an appropriate treatment plan.

The handheld skin scanner also serves a very useful purpose. This device allows the esthetician to view the progress of more advanced treatments as they happen. It is an excellent analysis tool that has many applications in medical esthetics. It is especially helpful in tracking the penetration depths of chemical peels. The esthetician must be able to control the room's lighting to make use of this device.

Maintenance

Maintain the skin scope just as you would the Wood's lamp.

Skin Care Machines

There are a variety of useful machines designed to enhance the performance of the esthetician. Each provides a specific benefit to the skin and makes clients feel as though they are receiving a specialized service. It is important that you are familiar with how these tools are integrated into the facial experience.

Rotary Brush

Brush machines vary depending on the model. Typically they have two or three small brushes that rotate at different speeds. The main purpose of the rotary brush is to assist in the cleansing process as well as lightly exfoliate the top layer of the skin. The brush stimulates the skin and helps clean and soften excess oil, dirt, and cell buildup.

Table 8–1 Colors and Conditions Depicted by Skin Scopes and Wood's Lamps

Color	Condition
white fluorescent	thick cornea layer
white spots	random horny layer and dead cells, dandruff
blue-white	normal healthy skin
purple fluorescent	thin skin, lacking moisture
light violet	dehydrated skin
bright fluorescent	hydrated skin
brown	sun damage
yellow	comedones

Brushes come in smaller sizes for the face and larger sizes for body areas, such as the back (Figure 8–3).

How to Use

The following steps describe a safe and effective use of a rotary brush (Figure 8–4).

1. Prior to using the brush, perform a light cleansing on the skin.

2. Insert the appropriate size brush for the face into the handheld device.

3. Apply more cleanser onto the skin.

4. Dip the brush into water and begin the pattern of movement at the forehead.

5. Continue the rotation down the cheeks, nose, upper lip, chin, jaw, and neck areas. No pressure should be applied. Allow the rotating brush to do the work. The bristles of the brush should remain straight.

SAFETY*Tip*

Neither the client nor the esthetician should look directly at the light of a skin scope.

Figure 8–3 The brush machine helps cleanse and lightly exfoliate the skin.

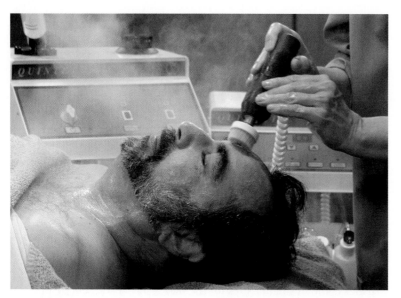

Figure 8–4 To properly use the brush machine, a light touch is used, with no pressure on the skin.

SKINTIP

The rotary brush is not recommended for use on inflamed or acne skin.

6. Moisten the brush before each use to soften the bristles. Dryer skins require a slow, steady rotation. Thicker, oily skins can tolerate a faster speed.

Maintenance

Rotary brush machines come with detachable brushes for cleansing ease. These must be removed after each use, and washed thoroughly with soap and water. After manually cleansing, the brushes should be immersed into a hospital-strength disinfectant and timed according to the manufacturer's instructions. It is important to cleanse, rinse, and store the brushes in such a way that they do not lose their shape when drying. If not kept in a circular shape, they will not rotate properly. Although they can be stored temporarily in a dry ultraviolet sanitizer, the brushes will break down if left in the sanitizer too long. When they are completely dry, transfer them to a closed container.

Vacuum Spray and Suction

The vacuum machine often serves a dual purpose: to vacuum and to spray the skin (Figure 8–5). Glass devices used to suction the skin come in different shapes depending on their use. The vacuum is attached to a hose, which is connected to a machine that contains a small vacuum motor inside. The vacuum serves two main functions. The first is to suction dirt and impurities off the skin. The second is to help reduce the appearance of creases, such as laugh lines, improving the overall appearance of the skin. Suctioning helps to stimulate the skin by increasing blood circulation at the site of treatment. It should not be used on broken capillaries.

The vacuum spray is attached via a hose that is connected to a small plastic bottle with a spray nozzle. This bottle can be filled with a freshener solution or toner to gently mist the client's face after cleansing or other treatment. Spray mists are beneficial in calming and hydrating the skin.

How to Use Suction

Use the vacuum to suction the skin as follows.

1. Attach the appropriate glass tip to the hose.

2. Turn the power on and adjust the suction.

3. Place on the area to be treated then move horizontally on the skin. The finger hole should be covered with the index finger when moving the suction across the skin.

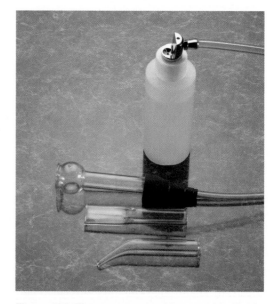

Figure 8–5 The vacuum machine provides both suction and spray features.

Be careful not to use oily product solutions when vacuuming the skin because they can clog the hoses.

4. Gently move the device over the pores. Be sure to include the creases right near the nose.

How to Use Spray

To hydrate the skin, use the following steps.

1. Place a towel under the client's chin or use a small kidney-size bowl.

2. Turn the power on and adjust the velocity of the spray.

3. Hold the spray approximately 12–15 inches away from the face and gently mist.

4. Spray the skin for several minutes to help calm and/or hydrate it.

5. Turn power off.

6. Gently pat in the rest of the product left on the skin.

Maintenance

Clean all glass devices with soap and water and soak them in a hospital-strength disinfectant. Normally a filter is placed at the end of the hose where the hose attaches to an orifice connected to the machine. The filter may have to be changed frequently depending on use. Mineral buildup in the nozzle of the sprayer should be cleaned monthly or more often. It is important to read and follow all cleaning instructions supplied by the manufacturer.

Steamer

Professional steamers come in various sizes and models; however, they all work on the basic premise of boiling water. Water placed inside the steamer is boiled in a separate jar or tank through the action of a heating element or coil. This generates steam that rises and is propelled through a long pipe or arm with a diffuser element at the end of it. The resulting vapor is then directed onto the skin's surface via a nozzle at the end of the arm (Figure 8–6).

There are many benefits to steaming the skin. Steam helps to stimulate circulation. It

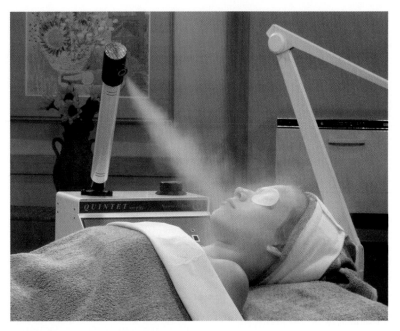

Figure 8–6 The steamer helps to provide stimulation for circulation in the face as well as softens sebum and other debris.

also assists in softening sebum and other debris. The warmth relaxes the skin and tissues, making it easier for the esthetician to extract comedones. Steam also helps to oxygenate the skin. It also has an antiseptic effect on the skin that is beneficial in treating acne and problematic skin due to the presence of ozone, or O_3, in the mist.

Ozone

Have you ever smelled the air after a lightning storm? It has a pure and refreshed quality to it. Air is made up of approximately 20% oxygen (O_2). When lightning crashes through the atmosphere, oxygen ions (molecules) become charged with electricity. This creates ozone (O_3). Ozone molecules (ions) possess antiseptic qualities. These molecules have the power to kill bacteria and other microorganisms.

Although it has the same ionic structure, ozone generated from a steam machine should not be confused with the ozone layer that surrounds the earth. You will learn more about the function of the ozone layer in Chapter 21.

Most steam machines sold in the United States have a very small closed circuit, high-frequency electrical generator built into the area where the steam begins to ascend to the opening of the pipe. Water (H_2O) contains both oxygen and hydrogen. When boiling

SAFETY*Tip*

Do not use steam on skin that is irritated or highly sensitive.

To avoid injury always preheat the steamer *away* from the direction of the client. This is an important safety factor in the event that there is any spitting of hot water caused from buildup of condensation or overfilling the reservoir. Once there is a steady stream of vapor, carefully position the steamer toward the face.

steam passes over this little generator, the water droplets containing oxygen ions (molecules) are charged with electricity. They suddenly disperse, causing a fine cloud mist. This mist contains some O_3, or ozone, which is antiseptic.

How to Use

When using a steamer, always read and follow the manufacturer's instructions. General instructions for use follow.

1. Steam treatments are timed according to the specific needs of the client and the type of facial procedure. Ordinarily, treatment time is between 6 and 10 minutes. The esthetician should be aware that too much steam may actually cause the skin to become dry because the skin overheats and sweats.

2. Use eye pads and place a towel right around the client's neck and shoulder area to protect these areas.

3. Place distilled water into the designated container.

4. Turn the machine away from the client and flip the on/off switch to on. Do *not* turn on the ozone or vaporizer switch, as it is sometimes called, until the steam is coming through the head of the pipe.

5. When the water is boiling and a small amount of steam is noticed from the pipe, flip on the ozone switch and slowly adjust the arm near the client. This will activate the little electrical generator inside the machine. You may hear the sound of a small motor.

6. Steam should be kept at a distance of approximately 15 inches from the face. Place the steamer farther away, if necessary, so that it is warm but not too hot on the face. If placed too close, steam can cause overheating of the skin and possible irritation. Always check the client's comfort level.

7. *Never* put essential oils or herbs directly into the water. Essential oils are highly active. When dropped directly into a closed jar with boiling water, they can cause excessive spitting of water or, even worse, cause the glass to break from pressure. Some steamers are equipped with a wick-type apparatus at the mouth of the nozzle. A couple of drops of essential oil can be placed here. The steam picks up the aroma as it vaporizes out into the room. Other models make use of a special container for herbs. These specialized steamers are normally more expensive; however, they provide the esthetician with the added benefit of incorporating therapeutic herbs into the steaming process.

8. Many machines have automatic regulators that detect the water level. When it becomes too low or empty, a safety switch is triggered, turning off the machine.

9. Note that there is usually a reset button on steamers for additional safety in the event the steamer runs out of water. If the steamer is not running, check the reset button before you call for help and are embarrassed when the manufacturer suggests you push the little red button! The reset button is ordinarily found on the back of the machine.

10. When you are ready to discontinue the steam, turn off the ozone/vaporizer switch *first*, then turn off the on/off switch.

Maintenance

Following several basic guidelines will keep your machine in peak working condition for years. It is simply unacceptable to be careless with this expensive device. At night, empty the jar and let it dry. Make sure that the rubber seal along the rim of the jar is clean. Refill the steamer machine with fresh distilled water each morning. Turn it on to give it a chance to warm up. This will save valuable time when receiving your first client of the day.

To adequately maintain the steamer, follow these guidelines.

• Water used inside the steamer should be as free of chemicals and minerals as possible. Therefore, it is recommended that distilled, not tap, water be used. Most tap water contains chlorine, other chemicals, and mineral deposits.

- Do not leave water in the steamer overnight or on weekends. If the steamer is not emptied regularly deposits can collect on the heater element. Empty the jar and lightly clean with soap and water. Allow the coils to dry.

- Neglected steamers have a tendency to spit hot water due to the buildup of mineral deposits that occur with daily use. Mineral deposits may appear as a white or yellow crusty film on the heating element. These deposits then drop off into the water in the jar or tank, causing a foamy effect. When entering the steam system, it causes spitting. The hot droplets can propel onto the client's face and may cause a serious burn. Some steamer models have solid tanks. You cannot see the element; therefore they need to be routinely cleaned bimonthly. A cleaning solution of plain vinegar and water is indicated.

- To ensure proper usage always read and follow the manufacturer's specific instructions.

Cleaning. The following are general guidelines. Always check with the manufacturer for specific cleaning instructions.

1. Add two tablespoons of white vinegar and fill to the top with water.

2. Turn on the steamer and let it heat to steaming. Do *not* turn on the ozone.

3. Let the machine steam for 30 seconds.

4. Turn off the steamer and let the vinegar solution rest in the unit for 15 minutes. Because vinegar tends to have a pungent smell, clean the steamer in your utility room or in an area away from the treatment rooms. It is a good idea to open a window, if possible, when performing maintenance to avoid fumes traveling to other areas of the salon.

5. Drain the steamer completely and then refill with water. Again let the steamer heat to steaming and operate for approximately 10 minutes. If there is still an odor, drain the unit, and repeat the process.

6. Do not allow the caustic vinegar and water solution to sit on the heating coil without steaming immediately. If left overnight, it will totally corrode the copper coils.

7. The steamer should be trouble free if you follow this cleaning procedure.

SAFETY*Tip*

Never refill cold water into a steamer that is still hot. Allow the steamer to cool off for 10 minutes before refilling it. The sudden change of temperature when the cold water touches the heating element could cause the heating element and/or glass to crack or explode.

Lucas Sprayer

The Lucas sprayer is a convenient handheld device designed to apply plant extracts, herbal teas, essential oils, skin fresheners, and astringents directly to the face (Figure 8–7). This specialized piece of equipment generates a much finer mist than the sprayers previously discussed. Because it emits a cool mist it is particularly beneficial to dehydrated, mature, and couperose skin types.

High Frequency

High frequency is an apparatus that utilizes alternating or sinusoidal current, as explained in Chapter 9. The oscillating circuit passes through a device that allows for the selection of tesla pulse train current. This current can produce a 60,000 to 200,000 Hertz frequency depending upon how it is regulated. Remember that the frequency indicates the repetition of the current per second. Because high-frequency current is

SAFETY*Tip*

Do not overfill the steamer above the maximum level indicator. This can cause it to project a spout of boiling water at the onset of the steaming.

Figure 8–7 The Lucas sprayer applies essential oils, fresheners, and astringents to the face.

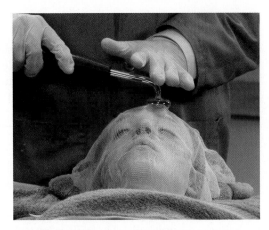

Figure 8–8 The high-frequency machine is a versatile tool in the skin care room.

capable of changing polarity 1,000 times per second, it basically has no polarity and in effect does not produce chemical changes. This makes it physically impossible to penetrate products. Product penetration is achieved with the galvanic method.

The rapid oscillation created by high-frequency does vibrate water molecules in the skin. This can produce a mild to strong heat effect. It is important to note that esthetic high-frequency devices cause a mild effect. An example of a stronger reaction is seen in thermolysis which is used for permanent hair removal. The process of thermolysis is discussed in greater depth in Part VIII.

The high-frequency machine is a useful and versatile esthetic tool (Figure 8–8). It may be applied after extractions or used over a product. It provides the skin therapist with the following benefits.

- has an antiseptic effect on the skin
- stimulates circulation
- helps oxygenate the skin
- increases cell metabolism
- helps coagulate and heal any open lesion after extraction
- generates a warm feeling that has a relaxing effect on the skin

Electrodes

During the manufacturing process, most of the air is removed from high-frequency electrodes creating a vacuum in the tube. The air is replaced mainly with neon gas. However, some electrodes may also contain argon gas. As electricity passes through these gases they emit visible shades of light. Neon gas

produces a pink, orange, or red light. Argon or rarified gas produces blue or violet light. Sometimes these lights are inaccurately called ultraviolet or infrared because of their colors. However, there are no infrared or ultraviolet rays in high frequency.

There are several types of direct or indirect electrodes available with high frequency. Each of these electrodes has unique benefits and features that produce specific physiological reactions in esthetic treatments.

Types of Electrodes

There are numerous shapes of electrodes that come with high frequency (Figure 8–9). Several common applications of their use are illustrated in Table 8–2.

Sterilizing and Maintenance

After each use, clean the glass electrode by wiping it with a solution of soap and water. Do not emerge the electrode directly in water. Then place only the end into a sterilization solution for 20 minutes. Rinse with cool water. Do not get the metal part wet. Dry with a clean towel and store in a covered container. Do *not* place electrodes in an ultraviolet machine or in an autoclave.

Unless they break or are damaged, most electrodes do not need replacing. However, they are very fragile. Take extra care to wrap them in a soft material, then store them in a drawer where they will not be knocked around, damaged, or cracked. Some of the newer machines offer inserts to store the electrodes right on the machine. The high-frequency coil should be replaced after a few years of use if it is losing power. Check with the manufacturer for additional service requirements.

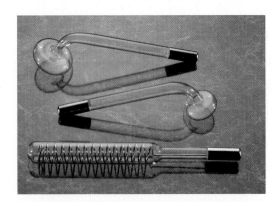

Figure 8–9 A selection of electrodes for the high-frequency machine.

Table 8–2 Common Electrodes and Their Applications

Electrode	Application
Small mushroom 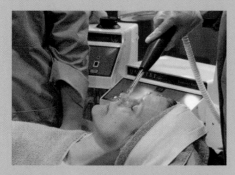 The electrode is used to stimulate the skin during massage.	(Pink/orange light) for sensitive skin *or* (violet light) for normal to oily skin. 1. Place electrode into the handheld device. 2. Adjust the rheostat to the proper setting if the machine is not automatic. 3. Place an index finger on the glass electrode. 4. Apply the electrode directly onto dry skin beginning at the forehead. 5. Glide the electrode over the skin in circular movements (across the forehead area) and then to the nose, cheeks, and chin areas. Sometimes when skin is very clean, the electrode drags. In this case, place gauze between the skin and the electrode. 6. To remove from the skin, place an index finger over the glass and remove it. Turn the power switch off.
Large mushroom 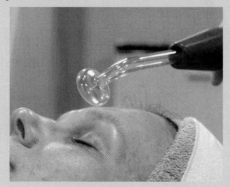 A large mushroom electrode in use on the face.	(Violet light) normal to oily *or* (pink/orange) sensitive 1. The large mushroom is used in the same way as the small mushroom. 2. Another effective way to use this apparatus is to open a piece of cotton gauze and glide the mushroom electrode over the gauze. This produces a small spray of sparks onto the skin. This treatment is ideal for acne or problematic skin. 3. Facial finish: High frequency may be used at the end of a treatment over cream. Place cotton gauze between the cream and the electrode. Glide in circular motions over the entire area.
Indirect electrode (spiral)	Used indirectly to stimulate the skin during massage. This treatment is ideal for sallow and aging skin. 1. Apply cream to the client's face. 2. Give the wire glass electrode to the client who holds it with both hands. 3. The operator places the fingers of one hand to the forehead. 4. With the opposite hand, turn the high frequency on and move to a low setting. 5. Using both hands, perform a piano finger motion, gently tapping the skin. Move around in a systematic manner over the entire face. 6. To discontinue, remove one hand from the skin and turn the power switch off. 7. Do *not* lose contact with the skin during this procedure.
Sparking (glass tip)	A glass tip electrode is used to direct sparking to a specific area such as an acne lesion. It helps disinfect and heal the lesion. 1. Place the electrode into the handheld device. 2. Apply the index finger to the glass electrode and place it on the lesion area removing the finger so that the area is sparked. 3. Place the finger back on the electrode as you move from lesion to lesion releasing the finger in order to spark the skin. This is a quick motion. 4. Remove the electrode from the skin by placing the finger once more on the glass. Turn the power switch off.
Comb electrode (rake)	Directly applied to the face. It may also be used in a scalp treatment. To apply, follow the directions for the mushroom electrode.

Galvanic Current

The galvanic machine converts the oscillating current received from an outlet into a direct current. Electrons are then allowed to flow continuously in the same direction. This creates a relaxation response that can be regulated to target specific nerve endings in the epidermis. Galvanic current is used to create two significant reactions in esthetics: chemical (disincrustation) and ionic (iontophoresis).

Chemical (Disincrustation)

Estheticians use disincrustation to facilitate deep pore cleansing. During this process galvanic current is used to create a chemical reaction that acts to emulsify or liquefy sebum and waste. This treatment is extremely beneficial for oily or acne skin problems because it helps soften and relax the follicle to encourage the easy removal of open and closed comedones.

To perform disincrustation, an acid-based or electropositive solution is placed onto the skin's surface. The solution is purposely formulated to remain on the surface of the skin rather than being absorbed. When conducting disincrustation, the client holds the electrode in a positive polarity. The esthetician makes direct contact with the disincrustator that is set on negative (not positive). This creates a chemical reaction that transforms the sebum of the skin into soap—a process known as **saponification.** Soap is made from fat and lye (sodium hydroxide). When the electrical current interacts with the salts (sodium chloride) in the skin, it creates the chemical sodium hydroxide—or lye. This soapy substance helps dissolve excess oil, clogged pores, comedones, and other debris on the skin, while softening it at the same time. Extractions are then easily performed with less skin irritation.

How to Use Disincrustation

Several types of electrodes are available for the galvanic machine. The most popular are the disincrustator and the ionizing roller. To make proper contact, each electrode must be covered with cotton and the client must hold the opposite pole electrode.

1. Gently cleanse the skin prior to treatment.

2. Instruct the client to remove any jewelry from the hand that will be used to hold the electrode. Cover the electrode held by the client with a moistened sponge or

saponification

A chemical reaction that occurs during disincrustation where a chemical reaction from the current transforms the sebum of the skin into soap.

iontophoresis

The introduction of ions by means of a galvanic current.

SKINTIP

Disincrustation should only be applied to the oily areas of the skin or to areas where there are more sebaceous secretions. Avoid the dryer areas such as the cheeks. Never use disincrustation on the eyelids or the neck. Severe irritation can result.

place a piece of dampened 4" x 4" cotton gauze around the electrode. Give this to the client to hold. This electrode is connected to the red wire.

3. The operator prepares the handheld disincrustator electrode by placing a small, dampened sponge or round cotton pad into the black ring. Slide the ring back onto the electrode.

4. Dip the electrode into the disincrustation solution. Apply the electrode to the client's forehead.

5. Turn the switch to negative and set at 0.05 microamps.

6. Beginning on the forehead, gently rotate the electrode while gliding it over the forehead area and continue in the T-zone area down the nose and onto the chin area (or onto any area that is oily). Avoid the cheeks because they are normally dry.

7. Upon completion, turn the machine off and remove the electrode. Rinse the skin thoroughly with warm 4" x 4" cotton pads. Discard the pads.

8. Proceed with extractions.

Iontophoresis

Iontophoresis means the introduction of ions. This process allows estheticians to transfer or penetrate ions of an applied solution into the deeper layers of the skin by means of galvanic current. Current flows through conductive solutions by means of positive and negative polarities or ionization.

Theoretically, the process of iontophoresis is based on universal laws of attraction. For example, negative attracts positive and vice versa. Similar to a magnetic response, iontophoresis relies on attraction of the poles to create an exchange of negative and positive ions or charges. Once the charge of the solution is determined, the esthetician sets the switch on the machine to the appropriate setting while the client holds an electrode with an opposite charge. When the client grips the handheld electrode, all the water molecules in the skin become charged with the polarity of the electrode. To allow iontophoresis to occur, the client must hold the polarity opposite to the product; otherwise, there will be no attraction. Remember, like polarities do not attract; they repel each other.

To ensure proper connections it is also important that the electrodes are moistened. The client holds an electrode that is wrapped with a moistened cover or sponge. The esthetician then places a sponge or piece of cotton that has been dipped into the ampoule solution onto the electrode before applying to the skin. No metallic electrode should ever be placed directly on the skin. Gels can be used with metallic electrodes as long as the skin is completely covered with the gel.

Reactions to the Skin

Table 8–3 illustrates the possible skin reactions that can occur during ionization.

Polarity of Ampoules

It is important for the esthetician to learn to identify the polarity of an ampoule. Products that have a slightly acidic pH are considered positive. Products with an alkaline (or base)

Table 8–3 Possible Skin Reactions during Ionization

Positive Pole (Anode)	Negative Pole (Cathode)
Causes an acid reaction	Causes an alkaline reaction
Calms or soothes nerve endings	Stimulates nerve endings
Decreases blood circulation	Increases blood circulation, softens and relaxes tissue

tendency are considered negative. If the manufacturer indicates that the product is negative, the esthetician infuses the solution with the electrode set at negative; that is, the esthetician applies the product with the electrode set at negative. The client holds the positive electrode. If the product were positive, the opposite would hold true.

Some manufacturers may include ingredients in the same vial that are simultaneously positive and negative. In this case, the product should be ionized for 3 to 5 minutes on negative and for 3 to 5 minutes on positive. If neither a negative nor positive polarity is indicated for an ampoule, as a general rule the esthetician should infuse first with negative and then positive (Figure 8–10).

The molecular weight of a product is also a factor in permeability. Smaller molecules have greater penetration ability. Larger

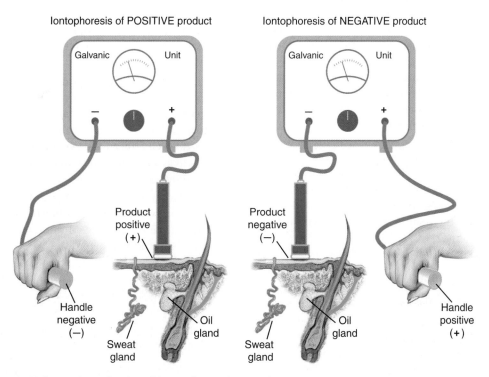

Figure 8–10 Iontophoresis of positive and negative products.

Table 8–4 Iontophoresis

Product Polarity	Client Polarity
Positive (+) cataphoresis	Negative electrode (−)
Negative (−) anaphoresis	Positive electrode (+)
Unknown	3 to 5 minutes on negative
	3 to 5 minutes on positive

cataphoresis
The infusion of a positive product during iontophoresis.

anaphoresis
The infusion of a negative product during iontophoresis.

molecules cannot penetrate. The process of ionic penetration takes two forms: **cataphoresis** refers to infusion of a positive product, and **anaphoresis** refers to infusion of a negative product (Table 8–4).

How to Use Ionization

The proper steps for ionization follow.

1. The client holds the positive electrode.
2. The esthetician applies the product with the electrode set at negative.
3. The esthetician has the option of switching positive and negative poles when infusing solutions, depending on polarity.

Maintenance

Before attempting to clean the electrodes, always read and follow the manufacturer's instructions for cleaning and disinfecting. Detach the electrode cord from the disincrustator. Remove any soiled sponge or cotton cover from the disincrustator and discard. Do not soak the electrode unless directed to do so by the manufacturer. *Never* place the electrode in an autoclave. The black ring can be soaked in a germicidal solution for 10 minutes unless directed otherwise by the manufacturer. In general, when cleaning rollers, detach the metal tip and soak for 20 minutes in disinfectant solution. Carefully spray the tip with a hospital strength germicide and wipe with 4" x 4" cotton gauze that has also been sprayed with germicide. Once again, follow the manufacturer's instructions for cleaning.

Ionto Mask

The ionto mask works with galvanic current and can be used to facilitate either disincrustation (deep pore cleansing) or ionization (penetration of product). Depending on the treatment goals, different solutions can be used to target specific skin conditions. The face is first covered with moistened gauze. This helps direct current to the underlying tissue. The mask is then applied to the face and timed according to treatment parameters. Instead of the client holding an electrode, a wet pad is placed under the shoulder. The mask is then plugged into the source of the galvanic current.

Microcurrent Machines

Modern medicine utilizes microcurrent to treat many conditions such as Bell's Palsy and stroke paralysis. The growing uses of microampere electrical neuromuscular stimulation include healing muscles and wounds, pain control, and even bone fusion. There is even greater potential for this type of therapy. Studies on the use of electrical stimulation have reported the following:

- An increase in DNA protein and collagen synthesis in fibroblasts in vitro in the laboratory.
- Increased healing of ligament injuries. In 1984, Dr. Stanish, the physician for the Canadian Olympic team, found that implanted electrodes delivering specific current hastened the recovery of injured athletes suffering from ruptured ligaments and tendons. He reported a shortened recovery time from 18 to 6 months.

More recent studies on the use of microcurrent on facial muscles have reported the following:

- The ability to reconstruct or reeducate muscle tissue stretching or tightening as necessary. Microcurrent can stretch out cramped and shortened muscles. This works well around the eye, mouth, and forehead areas to reduce fine lines and wrinkles.
- Strengthen and tone loose and slack muscles, for example, around the cheeks, jaw line, and breast, giving a firmer appearance to the face and body.
- Microcurrent stimulates and speeds up the rate at which the skin produces its own connective tissue fibers, for example, collagen and elastin fibers, which are critical to increasing the supportive framework of the dermis.
- Stimulates lymphatic drainage to help eliminate toxic waste from the face and

body. This helps to reduce puffiness and fluid retention particularly around the delicate eye area.

- Improves the overall color and tone of the epidermis, generating a more youthful appearance.
- Causes a regenerative effect, increasing the local metabolism of the skin and muscle tissue, acting as a preventive measure in age management.

What is Microcurrent?

Microcurrent or **wave therapy** devices mimic the way the brain relays messages to the muscles. Considered a passive form of exercise, this therapeutic technique helps stimulate motor nerves to the point where a visible contraction of the muscles can be seen. In the past faradic current has been used to stimulate motor nerves. Faradic current is an intermittent alternating current named for nineteenth-century British physicist Michael Faraday, who discovered the phenomenon in 1831. However, without precise control and careful technique, there is often danger of doing harm to the muscle when using this type of strong current.

Waveform and Shape

Alternating current must have a form. Current intensity is referred to as having a shape such as a square, sine, rectangle, or ramp (Table 8–5). **Waveform** helps determine the strength of the current as well as the length of penetration. When wave energy is introduced to the skin it begins at a certain point, rises, and then drops. The amount of time at peak performance is predetermined by setting and treatment goals.

As mentioned earlier, there are many biological processes associated with electrical impulses. Facial skin tone and muscles are all related to this system. As we age, impulses may slow down causing the skin to sag. Muscles may not completely contract after using them, such as in the case of sagging jowls (jaw muscles). The same effect can be seen on the rest of the body as well. That is why exercise and stretching are so important as one ages.

Microcurrent devices are designed to work in harmony with the natural bioelectrical currents found in the body. Placing two probes on muscle groups begins the process. A specific movement technique is followed. A gel such as a collagen ampoule is placed on the skin prior to beginning the treatment. Current is regulated according to the skin's resistance. This feature is referred to as a current generator, which keeps the current flow at a constant level.

Microcurrent is reported to aid in the healing and repairing of tissue, and to influence cellular exchange, local metabolism, and cellular activity. It works very gently and helps speed up the natural regenerative processes of the body when the correct intensity of current, frequency, and waveform are used. The results may be a more firm appearance and healthier skin.

When using any electrical device it is vital to obtain a complete client health history and conduct a consultation prior to treatment. Estheticians performing such services should receive thorough training that includes clinical practice prior to using any machine.

Other Tools and Accessories

In addition to the machines used directly on the skin, a number of other tools and equipment are used by the esthetician. The paraffin wax heater and hot towel cabinet are necessary for the esthetician to provide the services clients desire. Electric mitts, boots, and blankets soothe and comfort clients in the manner they expect from a facial service.

wave therapy
Also known as *microcurrent*. A passive form of exercise, this therapeutic technique helps to stimulate motor nerves to the point where a visible contraction of the muscles can be seen.

waveform
Helps to determine the strength of the current as well as the length of penetration.

Table 8–5 Common Shapes and Intensities of Alternating Currents

Wave Type	Intensity
Sine wave	Referred to as a mild form, it usually exhibits equal energy levels under positive and negative phases.
Rectangular	Referred to as a sharp form, it has a rapid instantaneous use with a long duration and sharp drop-off.
Square	Same as rectangular; however, the rise duration equals the intensity duration.
Ramp	The rate of the rise is fairly rapid but not instantaneous, but with a sharp drop-off.

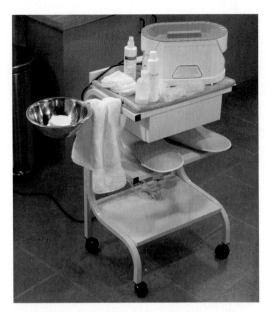

Figure 8–11 A paraffin heater is used to create a warm paraffin mask for hydrating dry skin.

Paraffin Wax Heater

The paraffin wax heater is used to create a warm paraffin mask for hydrating dry skin (Figure 8–11). A perfect stand-in for the galvanic machine, this device provides the esthetician with a treatment that offers quick results for a limited period of time. Heated paraffin is applied to the face, creating a "tent" to hold body heat and perspiration and penetrate underlying products. There is no concern about the products being water soluble. The result is a wonderful hydrating and relaxing treatment that gives clients a quick glowing complexion. Mothers of the bride rave about it!

Paraffin wax heaters are programmed to stay warm at a very safe low level of heat for long periods of time. They must be replenished as you discard the used wax. These heaters tend to take a very long time to heat up in the morning. During the week, the paraffin heaters may be left turned on overnight without ill effect. However, the esthetician is cautioned always to use a professional wax bath machine that emits low heat. *Never* use a substitute heater, such as a crock-pot, which regulates heat differently.

Hot Towel Cabinet

Hot towel or washcloth warmers, called hot towel cabinets or hot cabbies, are commonly found in the esthetic treatment room (Figure 8–12). Hot towels may be used for both face and body treatments. They provide a warm, soothing and softening benefit to the skin and are ideal for removing facial masks.

Maintenance

It is important to keep the hot towel cabinet clean and free of mold or mildew. Daily maintenance includes removing any excess unused towels. The inside of the cabinet should be cleaned with a topical disinfectant or a good 70% alcohol spray. Some cabbies are equipped with ultraviolet lamps; however, these also require a thorough cleansing at the end of the day. Leave the door open at night to allow the cabinet to dry thoroughly.

The Heat Mask

The heat mask utilizes infra-ray heat, a soothing and relaxing heat that penetrates deeply through the layers of the skin. It is placed on top of a nonsterile cotton compress or wrap that has been soaked in a therapeutic solution to create an incubating therapeutic cotton wrap. The heat helps the skin absorb the beneficial ingredients of the mask. Similar to the process that occurs when using galvanic current to perform disincrustation, the infra-ray mask causes saponification. As discussed earlier, saponification creates a soap-like substance through the activity of heat and specialized solutions. A primary benefit of the infra-ray heat mask is its ability to penetrate heat deeply through the layers of the skin. Heat travels down the hair follicles to

Figure 8–12 A hot towel cabinet provides a good supply of warm towels.

the bones of the face, bounces off the bones, and reflects back up to the surface. It opens the sebaceous glands from behind. Therefore, after you remove the heat mask, the tissues of the face retain the warmth stored in the bone structure. This action facilitates deep pore cleansing, softens the skin, and allows extractions to be performed more comfortably. The heat mask provides the esthetician with a simple and reliable therapeutic mechanism that is capable of delivering thermostatically controlled heat to the skin time after time. When performing a heat mask treatment it is not necessary to use the steamer or apply hot towels. The heat mask requires little maintenance when used properly.

How to Use

The use of the heat mask is quite simple and sanitary.

1. Plug the heat mask into the electrical outlet.
2. Place protective vinyl over the cotton wrap.
3. Place the heat mask on the face.
4. Place a Velcro headband under the client's head.
5. Adjust the heat mask to fit the client's face.
6. Set the mask's control to the proper setting.
7. After an appropriate time (10 to 25 minutes), remove the mask and plastic liner, and dispose of the cotton.

Electric Mitts and Boots

Boots and mitts are designed to apply heat to the skin tissues of the hands and feet to encourage circulation and to promote the client's overall relaxation (Figure 8–13). Often billed as a menu add-on, boots and mitts actually perform an important function. The heating of the extremities creates a profound effect on the overall circulation of the blood in the torso and face. This enhances stimulation and increases the benefits of a simultaneous facial or body treatment.

Boots and mitts are also the ideal complement to salon hand and foot spa treatments when used with a therapeutic application of an exfoliating scrub or a mud wrap. They help restore natural skin oils, and soothe tired aching feet and hands.

Figure 8–13 Electric mitts and booties apply heat to the skin, and help the client relax.

How to Use

To ensure professional sanitation standards, boots and mitts are used with plastic disposable liners.

1. Preheat on low to medium. Do not turn dial to hot.
2. Apply lotion on clean hands or feet.
3. Optional: Immerse hands or feet into the paraffin.
4. Slip on plastic liner.
5. Slip on warmed mitts or booties.
6. Time for 10 to 15 minutes.
7. Unplug and pull off mitts or boots.
8. Remove plastic liners.

Spa Thermal Blanket

Spa thermal blankets are used to ensure warmth and comfort during spa body treatments such as herbal wraps, seaweed wraps, and detoxifying treatments. They gently wrap the client's body to create a relaxed and luxurious spa feeling. Spa treatment blankets come in two styles. One incorporates the heating elements within the structure of the

> **SAFETY***Tip*
>
> Whenever working with electrical devices always check cords and connections. Use extra caution when working near water. Use blankets specifically designed to be used around water when working in close proximity to spa water therapies. Always use spa blankets appropriately.

Evaluating Productivity

To the clinic or spa owner, time is money. Although many owners may have entered the field with higher ideals in mind, the bottom line is that to stay in business salons must make money. This means taking a critical look at operating expenses and employee performance.

Today many salons are using information systems to pinpoint operation costs, analyze sales, and measure employee productivity. From a positive perspective this allows businesses to make important decisions in terms of day-to-day operations, such as scheduling, stocking inventory, and budgeting for necessary expenses, repairs, or improvements.

How does the esthetician fit into the revenue equation? With all operational systems in place, your boss may expect you to maintain certain performance standards or reach set revenue goals. Estheticians starting out must get comfortable with the idea of being evaluated in terms of productivity.

To gain a better understanding of how this process works let us take a look at a simple measure of productivity using the number of working hours available divided by the number of treatments that can reasonably be performed, times the cost of the service:

Hours ÷ Number of Services × Cost = Productivity Level

Given a standard 8-hour day, with an hour for lunch, this means the esthetician will have 7 hours in which to perform services. If one hour and 10 minutes is allowed for each facial, the esthetician can reasonably expect to perform 6 facials per day within this time frame. If the salon charges an average of $50.00 per facial, and you work a 40-hour week, your employer can expect you to take in $1,500.00 per week. If the salon pays you $10.00 per hour, plus 10% commission on each facial or service, they must subtract $106.00 per day, or $530.00 per week, to pay your salary.

You may be thinking that the owner is realizing a considerable profit in this situation. However, salary is just one of the employer's expenses. Considering other obligations such as rent, telephone, utilities, insurance, cost of product, repairs, etc., employers may expect more from you, particularly if the operation is small. Of course, productivity measures must also take into account such variables as client cancellations, the economy, and market trends.

For the sake of argument let us compare this very basic model with a more productive day. Let us say that during the 7 hours available for facials, the esthetician also manages to add on several other services, such as an eyebrow wax or a hand or foot treatment, raising service revenue to an average of $75 per client, per hour. In addition the esthetician also manages to sell $100.00 in retail products per client, per hour. Working with these figures, the clinic or spa would then take in $2,625.00 in services, plus $3,500.00 in retail products per week. Given the increased productivity level, the esthetician may now earn $12 per hour and 15% commission on services, plus 10% on retail products. The salon owner would then realize an intake of $6,125.00, and the practitioner's gross pay would be $1,163.75. A win-win situation for both the practitioner and the salon owner.

Smart employers will recognize the value of productive employees and build incentives to increase their revenue performance. They may also realize the value in cooperative efforts, and set not only individual, but team goals allowing practitioners to benefit from each other's productivity. For example, a spa may set a monthly goal of $15,000 in retail sales. If that goal is surpassed employees who reach their individual goals may then become eligible to realize an additional team-based bonus or reward. This would provide added incentive to boost the spa's monthly sales goal.

Whatever the agreement, it is nevertheless important to have a clear understanding of what your employer expects of you from the onset of your employment. It is also reasonable to expect a weekly or monthly report from your employer summarizing your intake, particularly if any commissions are involved. If this is not available, it is wise for the practitioner to take personal responsibility for tracking this information because it may become extremely useful in terms of assessing your overall job performance.

blanket. This is placed on the facial bed underneath the fitted sheet. The other is a professional heavy-duty electric cover that is made especially for those spa treatments that are conducted around water. Choose the one that is most appropriate for your services.

How to Use

All spa thermal blankets should be used according to the manufacturer's specific instructions.

Microdermabrasion

As we enter the twenty-first century the role of the esthetician continues to expand. The public's growing interest in age management, coupled with tremendous scientific advances, has generated a new trend toward integrating beauty, health, and therapeutic services. As a result, estheticians are required to be far more knowledgeable about a greater number of advanced tools and technology. The recent introduction of new treatment tools, such as microdermabrasion has expanded the esthetician's repertoire to include more results-driven services.

Microdermabrasion, a new form of mechanical exfoliation, originated in Europe. Some of the first machines entered the U.S. market around 1995. Today, there are numerous microdermabrasion models available for both the esthetician and physician's use (Figure 8–14). These can be found in the treatment rooms of skin care clinics, spas, and medical offices around the country. The microdermabrasion machine is a powerful electronic vacuum that provides the practitioner with a true mechanical process. The Food and Drug Administration places it in the same category of devices as electric toothbrushes. Microdermabrasion is achieved by spraying high-grade microcrystals, composed of corundum powder or aluminum dioxide, across the skin's surface through a closed stainless steel or glass pressurized wand.

As with any machine, technique plays a vital role in creating a positive outcome. Proper use of the hand piece, rate of crystal flow, and vacuum setting all contribute to a successful performance. It is not necessary to be so aggressive that the client is uncomfortable. A series of treatments that incorporate complementary products, along with a com-

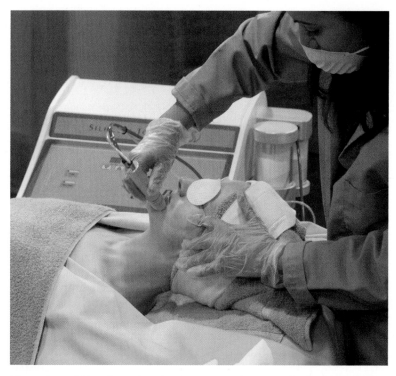

Figure 8–14 Microdermabrasion is a new and popular form of mechanical exfoliation.

plete home care program, is what makes the difference in obtaining the best results. The esthetician's professional expertise in analyzing the skin, and recommending the best program, are what make these wonderful new tools more effective.

Reading a manual does not provide instant experience. Training and certification are absolutely mandatory. Microdermabrasion machines should be used by licensed and trained skin care professionals only. However, rules and regulations warranting their use may vary from state to state. It is important to check with the governing board in your state before incorporating microdermabrasion into your practice.

Benefits

Microdermabrasion can be used safely and effectively on all skin types and colors. It is recommended for treating skins with sun damage, open and closed comedones, fine lines and wrinkles, enlarged pores, and coarse textured skin.

Maintenance

Daily care and proper use prevents unnecessary repairs. Microdermabrasion machines

microdermabrasion
A new form of mechanical exfoliation that uses a powerful electronic vacuum to spray high-grade microcrystals composed of corundum or aluminum dioxide across the skin's surface through a pressurized wand.

Table 8–6 Guidelines for Performing Microdermabrasion Treatments

Microdermabrasion is not recommended for clients with lesions, eczema or psoriasis, inflammatory acne, or infected pustules.
Do not be overly aggressive; this could result in possible skin irritation. It is best to work gradually in a series of sessions.
When working on scar tissue, follow directions precisely. Improperly performed, microdermabrasion could cause irritation and pigmentation.
On sun-damaged or pigmented skin, be cautious not to overablate (exfoliate) during the first two sessions. The skin could end up with more pigmentation and irritation.
Only use crystals recommended by the manufacturer. To prevent the infiltration of moisture, crystals should be kept in an airtight container. Moisture contamination could render crystals unusable.

are relatively simple with internal motors, hoses, filters, and hand pieces. Only use the crystals recommended by the manufacturer. It is not necessary to overuse crystals in order to obtain results. A constant, even flow is the best way to have your treatment be smooth and effective. Crystals should flow onto the skin's surface only. Carefully clean up crystals wearing rubber gloves and a mask.

Lasers

Lasers are a highly versatile energy source used in various capacities ranging from space projects to communications to medicine. The lasers estheticians use are considered medical devices and are the same as those used by a medical doctor. The physician has a very precise tool to perform surgery.

In laser skin resurfacing, pulsed lasers are so precise that they can be directed to "burn" off the surface of the skin without ever touching the lower dermis. Some lasers are attracted to a substance such as melanin, dark hair, blood vessels, skin growths, and pigmentation. They are able to work precisely in a given area with no damage to surrounding tissue.

Lasers produce a powerful beam of light, which creates heat. Some beams are thin enough to make holes the size of a pinhead. Some lasers can pierce a diamond and others can produce a nuclear reaction. Bursts of laser light can record music or store data on a compact disk.

A laser can be used over long distances with no loss of power and are used in fiber-optic communications. Electrical signals are changed into pulses (bursts) of laser light. An optical fiber is about as thin as a human hair and can carry as much information as several thousand copper wires. This allows for a tremendous amount of information to be carried over telephones, television, and other data to be carried relatively inexpensively.

It is not necessary at this stage to learn all the fine details concerning these devices. They are mentioned to familiarize you with the versatile laser technology that will continue to grow.

Summary

Advances in science and technology have generated many new high-performance tools that enhance the esthetician's work. Estheticians must continue their education to keep abreast of the latest developments in therapeutic skin care. In this chapter we have presented an overview of specialized tools and equipment designed to help the esthetician obtain the best results possible in skin care treatments. We recommend that you study Chapter 9 to review the suggested guidelines for operating machinery and practice your skills, until you are comfortable working with equipment.

Discussion Questions

1. Describe how the magnifying lamp, the skin scope, and the Wood's lamp are used to analyze the skin, outlining the most significant features and benefits of each.

2. What is the purpose of a brush machine? Discuss the effect chemical exfoliants have had on the use of this apparatus.

3. Steamers are often thought of as standard tools of the trade in esthetics. What are the main benefits of their use when performing a facial? Make a list of important safety precautions for the client and describe basic maintenance procedures.

4. Describe how heat masks are used to perform skin care treatments. How does this differ from the use of steam?

5. What is the purpose of galvanic current in skin care? Compare the effects of

positive galvanic current (iontophoresis) and negative galvanic current (disincrustation), describing the main benefits and features of each.

6. Why should estheticians use other accessories such as boots and mitts?

7. How has the introduction of microdermabrasion affected the field of esthetics? What skin types or conditions can benefit from its use? Include in your discussion any contraindications to its use.

Additional Reading

Lee, Mark. 2001. *Skin Care: Beyond the Basics.* Rev. ed. Clifton Park, N.Y.: Milady, an imprint of Delmar Learning, a division of Thomson Learning, Inc.

Miller, Erica. 1996. *Day Spa Operations.* Clifton Park, N.Y.: Milady, an imprint of Delmar Learning, a division of Thomson Learning, Inc.

Chapter 9
Basics of Electricity

Chapter Objectives

After reading this chapter, you should be able to:

- Define the basics of atoms, neutrons, and electrons.
- Explain the flow of electricity.
- Identify the differences in direct and alternating current.
- Explain the differences between galvanic and high-frequency currents.
- Discuss the need for safety in the operation of electricity and machines.

Chapter Outline

Introduction
Basis of Matter: The Atom
Circuits
Basic Forms of Electricity
Esthetic Machines
Safety

Introduction

Electricity is energy. It is a fundamental force in nature. Electricity is all around us in our homes, our offices, and treatment rooms. Electricity is used to power our lights, computers, dishwashers, microwave ovens, stereos, and many electrical devices in and out of our homes. It is used to power large factories and power plants. It is used in telephones, cell phones, televisions, radios, and satellites.

Our first observation of an electrical force outside our home most likely was a lightning storm. There is, however, an even greater energy behind the phenomenon of electricity. Electricity and magnetism together make up a greater force called electromagnetism. It is this electromagnetic energy that is responsible for holding together the atoms and molecules from which all matter is composed. Electricity actually determines the structure of every object that exists. It follows the law of attraction. Negative charges attract positive charges. Positive charges attract negative charges. This is the underlying principle in the production of electricity.

Many biological processes within the body are associated with electricity. Chemical electrical signals travel back and forth to the brain along the spinal column, which is connected to the base of the brain (Figure 9–1). These signals travel to nerves throughout the body. They tell the brain what our ears hear, what our eyes see, and what we feel through our fingers and other body parts. Muscle contractions are also stimulated through electrical impulses from the brain. The heart is regulated by electrical signals from the brain. When chemical electrical impulses are inhibited, as in the case of injury or degeneration, nerve impulses may not communicate to the brain as they did prior to the injury.

Electricity is used in medicine and science to conduct research. Magnetic resonance imaging (MRI) allows doctors to look inside the body without surgery. Electron microscopes are able to scan living cells to study detailed characteristics. An electrocardiograph machine records tiny electrical signals from the heart, which helps to diagnose heart disease. Electrical energy in esthetic medicine includes the use of lasers to eliminate superficial spider veins. Lasers that remove hair or rejuvenate the skin also use electricity. Electric stimulators can aid in the healing of a muscle.

Estheticians use electricity to enhance their work with the skin. Electrically-powered skin care machines are used to infuse performance ingredients into the skin, dissolve sebum, cleanse impurities, and strengthen muscles. Galvanic current, high frequency, the steamer, microdermabrasion, wax heaters, towel warmers, and microcurrent machines are all powered by electricity.

In this chapter, we will explore the basics of electricity and how it works. These basics will expand our knowledge in understanding how our machines actually work with the skin.

Basis of Matter: The Atom

An atom is made up of tiny particles called **electrons** and quarks. Quarks make up larger particles called protons and neutrons. In an atom, the proton and neutron make up the tiny core called a nucleus. A proton contains a positive charge. In order to make an atom, it must contain both a nucleus and orbiting electrons. Electrons and neutrons exhibit a property called electricity.

In nature, the earth and moon attract one another. The earth can be thought of as having a positive charge, and the moon a negative charge. The moon stays in orbit around the earth. The earth is analogous (similar) to the nucleus of an atom, and the moon is analogous to an electron. Electricity is electrons in motion. Electrons are the negatively charged particles that orbit the positively charged nucleus (proton) of an atom. A hydrogen atom possesses a single positively charged proton in its nucleus. The hydrogen atom is a very simple form of an atom because it contains just one positive proton and one negative electron (Figure 9–2). It is said to be in equilibrium because the single negatively charged electron orbits the single proton (nucleus). A **state of equilibrium** exists when the number of protons equals the number of orbiting electrons. This atom is considered neutral.

electrons
Negatively charged particles that orbit the positively charged nucleus of an atom.

state of equilibrium
The state that exists when the number of protons equals the number of orbiting electrons.

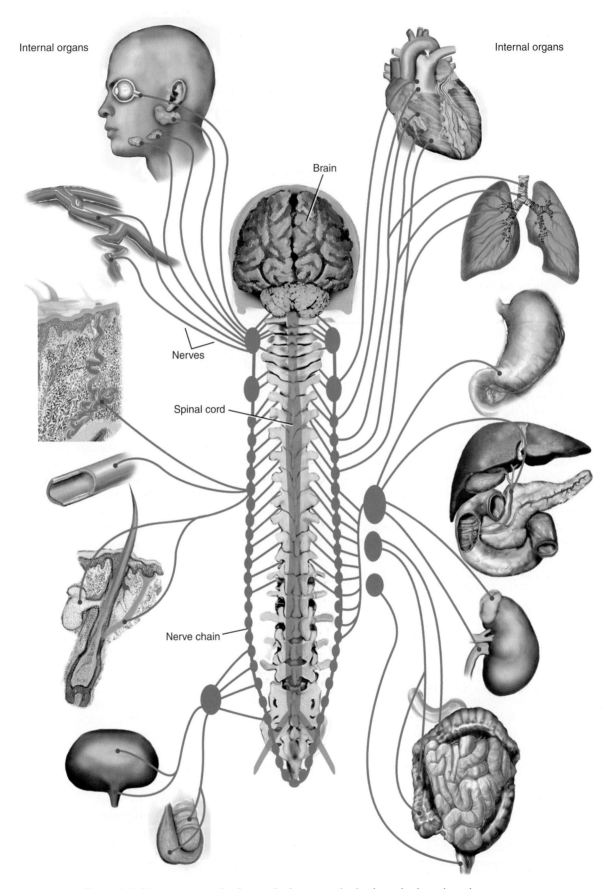

Internal organs

Internal organs

Brain

Nerves

Spinal cord

Nerve chain

Figure 9–1 Nerve communication paths between the brain, spinal cord, and organs.

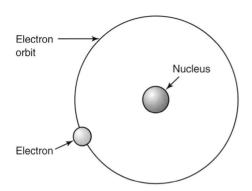

Figure 9–2 A simple hydrogen bond.

Electron Shells

The other basic elements in nature have different and more complex atomic structures. They contain more positively charged protons in their nucleus with an equal number of negatively charged electrons orbiting at various distances from their nucleus in what are called bands or shells.

Not all atoms are as simple as the hydrogen atom. A copper atom contains more than one electron, which orbits the nucleus in shells (Figure 9–3). The innermost shell contains only 2 electrons; the second contains up to 8; the third up to 18. The electrons in the outermost shell are the most important in electricity because they can be displaced very easily. This outer ring, or axis, is called a valence shell. A valence shell can contain one or several electrons. Low valence atoms are attracted to high valence atoms. High valence atoms are attracted to low valence atoms.

We can view the sun as a nucleus around which all 13 planets (electrons) are aligned

and orbit at various distances from one another. Each planet has its own axis on which it rotates around the sun. It is similar in looks to an atom having more than one electron ring. The electrons in the inner orbits are known as **bound electrons**. They are difficult to move from their orbits. Electrons found in the outermost orbit are known as **free electrons** and are more easily moved from their orbits. Free electrons attempt to move to another atom that may have a shortage of electrons.

Ions, Molecules, and Bonds

The way atoms are joined together depends on the amount of electrons that are orbiting in the outermost shell (valence shell). An atom can steal or give away an electron. When the outermost orbit or valence shell gains an electron, the atom takes on a negative charge. If it loses an electron, it takes on a positive charge. Imbalanced atoms that carry an electrical charge are called **ions.** Positive and negative ions attract each other. During this process, they can combine to form solid materials or structures. An example is table salt—NaCl or sodium chloride.

Sodium and chlorine ions are attracted to each other. They become interlocked or bonded because of their strong affinity (Figure 9–4). Each sodium atom gives up one

bound electrons
Found in the inner orbits of the atom.

free electrons
Found in the outermost orbit; they are more easily moved from their orbit.

ions
Imbalanced atoms that carry an electrical charge.

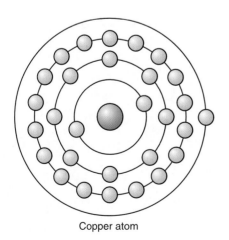

Figure 9–3 Electron shells in a copper atom.

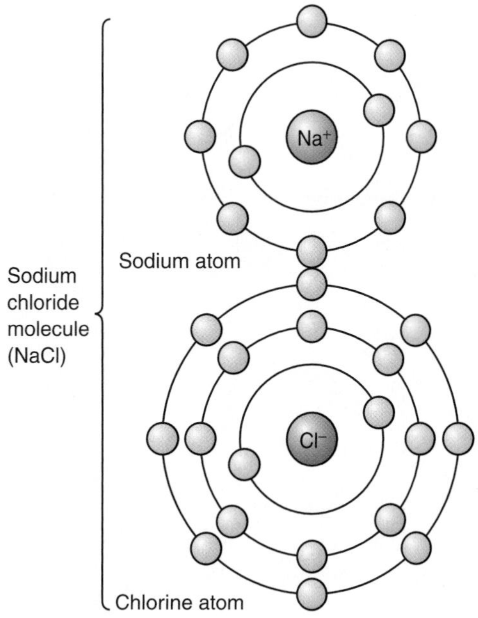

Sodium chloride molecule (NaCl)

Sodium atom

Chlorine atom

Figure 9–4 A sodium and chloride bond.

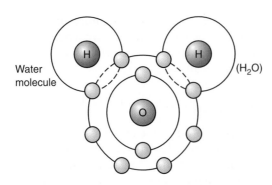

Figure 9–5 A water molecule "sharing" electrons between hydrogen and oxygen atoms.

molecule
Two or more atoms that have become linked.

covalent bond
The sharing of electrons between two atoms.

electron to form a positive sodium ion. The chlorine atom takes on this electron and becomes a negative chloride ion. This trading of negative and positive electrons is known as an ionic bond. When two or more atoms become locked (linked) together, they become a **molecule.**

Another example of an ionic bond is water. Let us look at hydrogen and oxygen. Two hydrogen atoms can share electrons with one oxygen atom and become a water molecule (Figure 9–5). Hydrogen electrons spend more time near the oxygen atom, giving it a lightly negative charge. In turn, the two hydrogen atoms take on slightly positive charges. They are attracted to each other, creating a liquid called water.

A **covalent bond** (Figure 9–6) is formed when two atoms share outer electrons

between them, instead of giving away or taking electrons as in ionic bonding.

The atomic structure of any element determines whether it is either a good conductor, or a good insulator. The more complex elements have several orbits, or shells, located at various distances from the nucleus. It is the outermost, or valence shell, that ultimately determines its conductivity.

When studying electricity, a primary concern is the negatively charged electrons. When we cause a movement, or flow of negatively charged electrons, an electrical current is established. Thus electricity is simply the movement of charges along a conductor such as a copper wire or other metals that allow electron flow.

Because electrons are negatively charged particles, an abundance of electrons on a surface will give that surface a negative electrical charge. A lack of electrons on a surface will give that surface a positive electrical charge.

Charges

Do you recall the study of magnets in a school science class? A magnet has a positive charge (north pole) at one end, and a negative charge (south pole) at the other. You can continuously hook one magnet to the other by using the positive end to attach to the negative end of the next, etc.

The law or principle in this exercise is that positive and negative charges attract

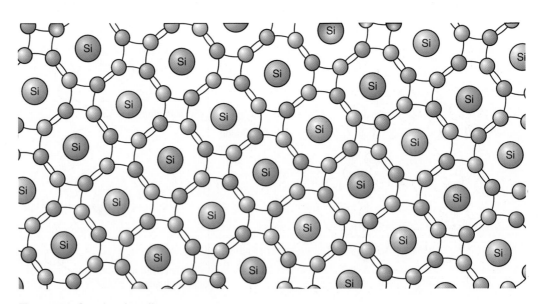

Figure 9–6 Covalent bonding.

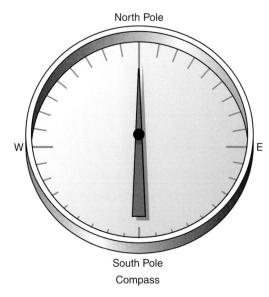

North Pole

W — E

South Pole
Compass

Figure 9–7 Magnetic pull—positive attracts negative.

each other (Figure 9–7). However, if you tried to attach the positive end to a positive end, like charges would not be attracted to one another. The same holds true for attracting a negative charge to a negative charge. There is no attraction. Thus, the law here is that like charges repel (push away) one

another. The power to attract and repel charges is caused by invisible influences called **electric fields.** Around each atomic structure is an electric field.

Conductors and Insulators

Because a copper atom only has one electron in its outer orbit, it can easily be displaced or even have another electron added to it. This results in a material that can carry electrons easily. It is referred to as a **conductor.** A conductor is a material or element that will easily pass an electrical current or flow of negatively charged electrons. It offers little resistance to this flow. Other good conductors are metals such as copper, aluminum, iron, gold, silver, and mercury, all of which have loosely bound outer valence electrons.

If a material has 5 to 8 electrons in the valence shell or is more than half full, it is much more difficult to move the electrons in and out of the outer orbit. The electrons are more firmly bound to the atom. This type of structure makes a good **insulator.** An insulator is a material or element that does not easily pass an electrical current. Good insulators include dry wood, ceramic, glass, and most plastics.

> **electric fields**
> Invisible influences surrounding each atomic structure, having the power to attract and repel charges.

> **conductor**
> A material or element that will easily pass an electrical current or flow of negatively charged electrons.

> **insulator**
> A material or element that does not easily pass an electrical current, such as dry wood, ceramic, and most plastics.

Table 9–1 Summary of Electrical Terms

Term	Description
Ampere	A unit used to measure the rate of flow of an electrical current.
Conductor	A material that electric current flows through without resistance.
Direct current	A current where electrons flow in the same direction. Direct current has polarity. Iontophoresis is an example.
Electric charge	A basic feature of certain particles of matter that causes them to attract or repel other charged particles.
Electric circuit	The path that an electric current follows.
Electric field	The influence a charged body has on the space around it that causes other charged bodies in that space to experience electric forces.
Electrode	A piece of metal, glass, or other conductor through which current enters or leaves an electrical device.
Electromagnetism	A basic force in the universe that involves both electricity and magnetism.
Electron	A subatomic particle with a negative electric charge.
Alternating current	Current that moves in an alternating direction; A to B and B back to A. There is no polarity in alternating current. High frequency is an example of alternating current.
Insulator	A material that opposes the flow of an electric current.
Ion	An atom or group of atoms that has either gained or lost electrons and so has an electric charge.
Kilowatt-hour	The amount of electric energy a 1,000-watt device uses per hour.
Milliampere meter	An instrument for measuring the rate of flow of an electric current.
Neutron	A subatomic particle in the nucleus that has no electric charge.
Ohm	The unit used to measure a material's resistance to the flow of electric current.

(continued)

Table 9–1 Summary of Electrical Terms *(continued)*

Term	Description
Plug	A two- or three-prong connector at the end of an electrical cord that connects an apparatus into an electrical outlet.
Polarity changer	A switch that reverses with the direction of the current from positive to negative and vice versa.
Proton	A subatomic particle with a positive electric charge, located in the nucleus.
Resistance	A material's opposition to the flow of electric current.
Rheostat	A specific control regulating the strength of the current used; a variable resistor.
Static electricity	An electric charge that is not moving.
Voltage	A type of "pressure" that drives electric charges through a circuit.
Watt	A unit used to measure the rate of energy consumption, including electric energy.

Circuits

circuit
The path a current takes as it moves through a system.

voltage
The measured push or rate at which the current is being delivered.

ampere
A measure of the amount of current flowing into a circuit.

ohm
A measure of how much a material resists a flowing current.

A **circuit** is the path a current takes as it moves through a system. When turning on a flashlight, electricity from the battery moves from the battery's negative electrode to the filaments inside the bulb (Figure 9–8). The filament creates a strong resistance to the electrical current. The electrons in the current collide with the atoms in the filament, giving up most of their energy. Released energy creates heat, which causes the filaments to glow. The electrical current returns back toward the positive electrode in the battery. Electricity is stopped when we turn the switch off. The circuit is disrupted.

To have electrical current, two conditions must be present.

1. There must be an electromotive force or push. **Voltage** is the measured push or rate at which the current is being delivered. In a small flashlight or radio battery, the voltage is normally too small to cause any serious harm. If the skin is wet, the salts in the skin create a greater conductor for electrical current. The 120 volts in a household circuit, however, can cause severe injury. A 220-volt circuit allows for even more electrical current to pass. Larger appliances such as clothes dryers, air conditioning units, and electric stoves normally require a 220-volt outlet.

2. There must be a conducting path. A copper wire may be found in the electrical cord of an appliance. The plastic surrounding the wires acts as an insulator.

An **ampere** is a measure of the amount of current flowing into a circuit. The more current flow, the higher the amperes. An **ohm** is a measure of how much a material

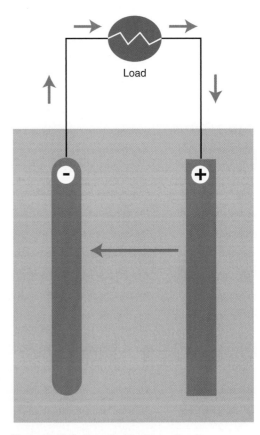

Figure 9–8 A chemical battery circuit.

resists a flowing current. For example, a filament in a light bulb glows because it has a high resistance and gets hot (glows). The support wires underneath have low resistance and do not get hot. The glass that makes the bulb has high resistance; therefore, it is a good insulator (Figure 9–9).

Basic Forms of Electricity

Electricity basically exists in three forms: static, direct current, and alternating current. In skin care, specific forms of electrical currents are used for infusion of products, to cause chemical alterations in the skin, for a specific purpose such as hair removal, for stimulating, and for bactericidal effects.

Static Electricity

When a large number of atoms in an object gain or lose electrons, the entire object takes on an electric charge. A good example of static electricity is walking across a rug on a dry day. This contact produces friction between your shoes and the rug. Electrons from your body are transferred to the rug, giving the body a positive charge. Touch a metal object, such as a doorknob, and you may see a spark or feel a small shock.

Direct Current

Direct current is used often in esthetics. A machine converts the alternating current from an outlet to a direct current. Direct current means that electrons move in one direction only. They move from point A to point B.

An important point is that direct current produces chemicals. This process is actually called electrolysis. While electrolysis is thought of as hair removal, it is actually the chemical reaction that takes place in the skin when an electrode carrying a small amount of current makes direct contact with the skin or into the follicle. For example, galvanic current is a direct current and interacts with the skin to produce an end result.

Let us discuss how current moves in a flashlight. There is a positive electrode and negative electrode located at opposite ends of

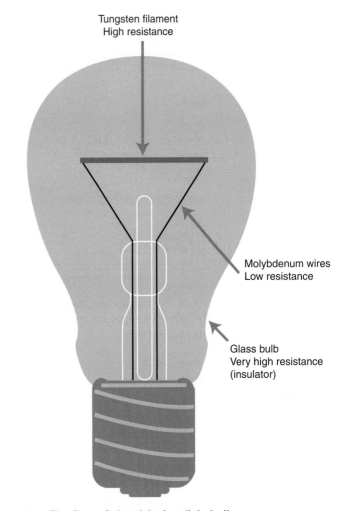

Figure 9–9 The flow of electricity in a light bulb.

the battery. When the switch is turned on, this closes (or completes) the circuit allowing for negative electrons to be released from the negative electrode of the battery. They move up the circuit until they reach the bulb and then return to the positive terminal. When all the available electrons have been used, the battery reaches a state of equilibrium. It is unable to produce electricity. The battery in a flashlight is an example of a direct current (Figure 9–10).

Alternating Current

The flow of electrons takes place in an alternating current; however, it occurs in a different way. Unlike direct current, which flows in one direction, alternating current flows from point A to point B and then back again

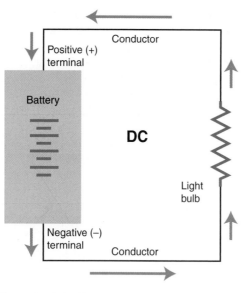

Figure 9–10 In direct current, the electrons move in just one direction. A battery is a typical example of direct current.

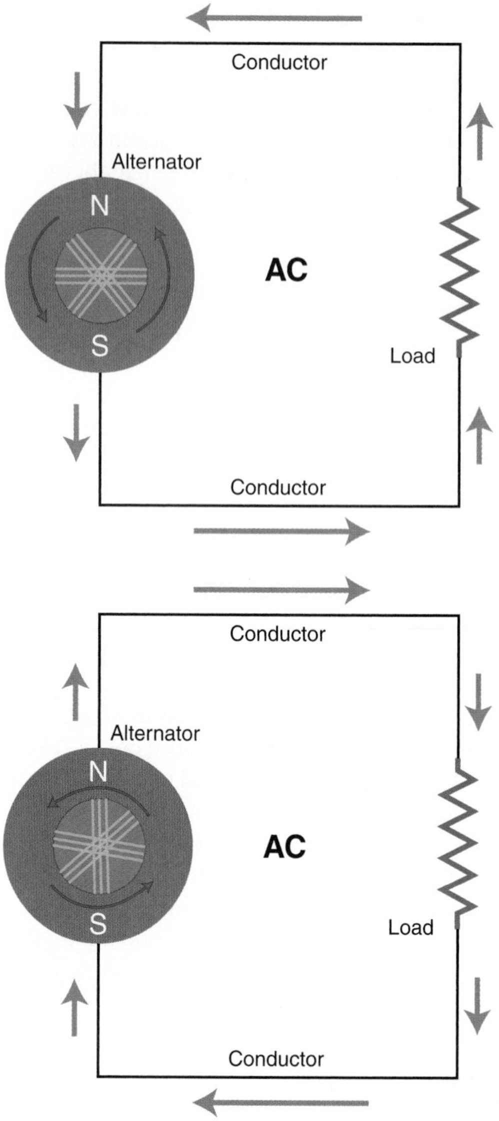

Figure 9–11 In alternating current, the electrons flow in reverse.

sinusoidal
Alternating current.

hertz (Hz)
The rate at which the reversal of direction occurs in alternating current.

from point B to point A (Figure 9–11). This type of current is defined as **sinusoidal**. It is also the current that is used in high-frequency machines. The rate at which the reversal of direction occurs in alternating current is known as frequency or **hertz (Hz)**. Because alternating current reverses direction so frequently, it has no polarity. The important thing to remember is that direct current creates chemical effects. Alternating current does not produce chemicals. Any chemical effects that are created with alternating current when the current is traveling in one direction would be canceled out when the current returns or travels back in the other direction.

Esthetic Machines

Esthetic machines use either direct or alternating current. However, the way in which these currents are processed by the machine are a different story. At this writing, more and more esthetics machines are available to us. It is imperative that we understand them as much as possible, especially, how they are integrated into our facial and body treatments. Normally, a manufacturer or distributor provides training. However, it is important

that we understand the basics of electricity and its effect on the skin. This makes it easier for us to understand the newer technologies.

Safety

The safety of the client and the esthetician is the number one priority when working with electrical devices. It is imperative that we understand how the machines operate.

Direct contact devices must meet certain safety standards as directed by the United States National Electrical Code and the guidelines for manufacturing safe electrical devices. All esthetic and electrical machines must comply with these codes.

Wall outlets should be the three-wire grounded type. Electrical current normally travels on the two flat blade terminals that are plugged into the outlet. The round terminal is the safety device and is connected to a separate wire that is connected to an earth ground. This ensures that your machine is receiving electrical current properly from the outlet. Do not ever try to modify or alter the cord or plug. Do not overload the wall circuits. If you do not have proper outlets, then it is advisable to have them updated. It is not advisable to use an adapter, because there is no way to ensure that it is grounding the machine properly.

Well-manufactured machines normally contain circuit breakers that automatically shut off the machine in the event of a problem. Your client may have an existing health condition, such as a pacemaker, so you should always check with your client before using any kind of electrical apparatus during a treatment.

Summary

Electricity is the flow of negative electrons along a conductor. Beginning with a simple atom, all matter is formed and shaped based on the flow of electrons to and from the valence shell. Matter is everything including the human body, nature, paper, and everything that makes up the planet as well as everything within the universe. Electrons hold a negative charge. Depending on the number of electrons in the outer orbit, an atom will either take from another atom, give away, or share electrons in order to be in balance or neutral. There are basic elements that make up all matter. It is from these that all things are formed.

Electromagnetic energy is based on negative and positive attraction. This is also the basic principle of electricity—the law of attraction. It is actually based on negative and positive charges caused by electron flow, exchange, or sharing. There are three forms of electrical current: direct (DC), alternating (AC), and static. Households in the U.S. currently use 120 volts to an outlet unless a special outlet is installed, such as a 220 volt for clothes dryer or another large electrical appliance.

Understanding the basics of electricity opens the door for greater knowledge of how esthetic machines actually help the skin. Knowledge is power—it is the "electrical" force that takes one to the next level of learning.

Discussion Questions

1. How is electricity used in skin care? What are the two types of electric current found in most esthetic machines?

2. Describe the flow of electrical current.

Additional Reading

Lees, Mark. 2001. *Skin Care Beyond the Basics*. Albany, N.Y.: Milady, an imprint of Delmar Learning, a division of Thomson Learning, Inc.

Roberts, Wallace A. 2001. "Understanding Electrical Currents, Part One," *Dermascope Magazine* (August): 71–76.

Roberts, Wallace A. 2001. "Understanding Electrical Currents, Part Two," *Dermascope Magazine* (September): 65–68.

Wolfson, Richard. 2001. *Electricity*. Discovery Channel School, original content provided by World Book Online, http://www.discoveryschool.com.

Chapter 10
First Impressions— Setup and Supplies

Chapter Objectives

After reading this chapter, you should be able to:

- Explain the importance of first impressions and professionalism.
- Set up a treatment room, including a workstation.
- Demonstrate how to use supplies, accessories, and small equipment.
- Explain the purpose of facial masks.

Chapter Outline

Introduction
Elements of Meet and Greet
Facial Bed Setup
Supplies
Product Masks
Dispensary
Safety
End of the Day

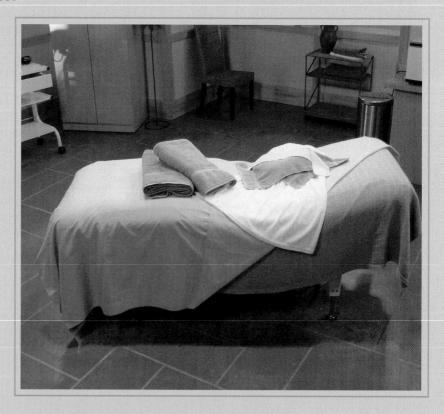

Introduction

First impressions are indeed lasting ones! In esthetics there are many factors that contribute to creating a positive first impression. However, these can be narrowed down to two very important general categories: personal and environmental. Both the esthetician's personal presentation and the ambiance of the facility are equally important in creating a welcoming environment that results in a repeat customer—the main goal in maintaining a successful skin care practice. This chapter provides specific instructions on how to make a positive personal impression and shape your work environment so that it is user-friendly both for the practitioner and client.

Elements of Meet and Greet

Greeting the client in the waiting room with a firm handshake, eye contact, a smile, and a clipboard ready to take the client's history is the first step in building a positive professional relationship (Figure 10–1). The esthetician starting out should understand that physical presentation has a direct correlation to professional impact. While dress codes vary regionally, wearing a uniform—lab coat, jacket, or smock—is the norm. The esthetician should take a minimalist approach in creating a polished and professional personal appearance. It is recommended that you wear little or no jewelry, keep nails short and natural, and use fragrance conservatively.

Your Presentation

You have only one chance to be first! In the first five seconds of meeting a client you will no doubt make an impression that lasts a lifetime. This may be the first time that the client has met an esthetician. The client may not know what an esthetician does or exactly what to expect. How you present yourself is not only a personal statement, it reflects on the industry as a whole. More importantly, it provides clients with an overall first impression of how well they will be treated in the salon or spa.

First time clients to the spa or salon should be given a thorough tour of the facility. Allow an extra 15 to 20 minutes when booking them for a first visit to accomplish this task. The purpose is to familiarize your clients with the salon or spa setting and orient them to the many treatment options that are available. Give them an opportunity to ask questions. Explain the salon philosophies, its market focus, for example, antiaging or stress reduction. Explain the general protocols for an initial treatment, such as filling out a health form. The preplanned script for this tour should be informative and educational. It should be something that is consistent and performed in a predetermined amount of time. Introduce new clients to other members of your team. Taking the extra time with new clients may very well be the means of gaining them as loyal clients. It also serves to put clients at ease. More importantly you have laid a foundation of credibility and professionalism.

This is also an ideal time to assess the client's personality. Is the client an introvert or an extrovert? What can you tell about the client based on her appearance? Relaxed or on edge? Try to guess the client's skin type

Figure 10–1 Greeting the client properly is the first step to building a positive relationship.

Table 10–1 Client Wraps

Item	Description
Client wrap—white terry	A one-piece 100% cotton terry garment that wraps around the client under the arms. Fastens with a Velcro close. It comes in a regular weight or an extra soft, luxurious weight.
Client smock (elastic top)	A one size fits all concept normally made of terry cloth or a cotton blend. Elastic keeps the gown snug. The client slides the one piece over the head.
Gentlemen's jacket	V-neck pullover, usually cotton. One size fits most.

and conditions based on general physical appearance and attitude. When performing the analysis, check yourself out. How did you do?

This is the beginning of whole thinking, perceiving the client as a whole person. It will be extremely helpful in creating a complete assessment of the client's needs and wants. From this assessment you can proceed to make connections between nonverbal cues and reading the client's skin types and conditions gathered from observations under the loupe. Part of understanding the skin is to perceive a greater picture of your client from the moment he or she walks into the waiting or treatment room. As your skills advance, you will begin to make valuable connections between nonverbal cues and skin care needs.

You may find the following five Rs from the nursing field most helpful in working with clients.

1. **Review.** Use your skin analysis to make appropriate treatment and product recommendations.

2. **Reassess.** Visualize and prioritize the path ahead. If the client is a first-time caller, determine whether or not you have addressed the primary concerns.

3. **Reassure.** Highlight treatment goals to build confidence as you perform the service.

4. **Reeducate.** Make sure the client understands the main reasons for conducting the treatment, long term treatment goals, and how to perform a relevant home care program.

5. **Record.** Reference and file important information.

Room Impression

Upon entering the treatment room, the client should see a folded gown neatly placed on

the facial bed. The facial gown is placed under the shoulders and fastened in the front. It is different from a robe, which covers the entire body. Wearing a facial gown, or wrap, as they are sometimes referred to, exposes the face, neck, and décolleté (upper chest, usually referred to in women) making it easier to perform the treatment and massage. There are several styles of gowns available.

Client Wraps

Give the client clear instructions on changing procedures. Some clinics and spas offer lockers to store clients' belongings. Others typically provide two or three clothing hooks located on a wall or on the back of the door (Figure 10–2). Providing cloth-covered clothes hangers and plastic ones with clips for pants or skirts is a nice touch and gives the

Figure 10–2 Make sure a clean gown is placed in the room for each client.

client the message that you really care. They also help keep delicate silks and suits from possible damage.

An additional robe should be made available if clients are receiving other spa services. Place the extra robe in a convenient and easily accessible location in the treatment room, for example, on a hanger, draped over a chair, or on the treatment bed. This gives the client full coverage when moving from room to room.

Give the client privacy to disrobe, unfolding the gown as you reiterate the changing instructions. Instruct the client to remove glasses, contact lenses, jewelry, especially earrings and necklace as these are often contraindicated with many technological tools. Before leaving the room, ask if the client requires any assistance. A footstool should be available in case the client needs assistance getting onto the facial bed.

Facial Bed Setup

Clean linens are the first step in preparing the facial bed or chair. Linen protocols may vary from region to region and are often influenced by climate. In colder climates, you may need more covering. In warmer climates, lighter cotton covers and spreads are sufficient. Sheets are considered a basic item regardless of the temperature.

Each salon or spa will have its own protocol concerning the look of the treatment rooms, including draping the facial chair (Figure 10–3). If none is specified be sure to ask for instructions on the correct placement of sheets and covers. Two basic methods of draping are outlined here. Each is considered

acceptable. Many salons or spas may use elaborate setups dictated by special color themes, fabrics, and other decorating features that are congruent throughout.

Method One: Cocoon Draping

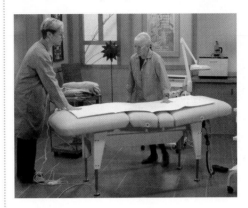

Bed warmer. Some look like a fitted sheet and cover the entire bed, others are more like a large heating pad. They are found in the linen departments of many stores. In either case, a heat regulator dial sets the temperature from low to high. Purchase one that is made to place *under* the client. They range in price from moderate to the more elaborate ones made specifically for spa environments that have more water activity.

Fitted sheet (twin size). This is optional, but if used, place it on top of the bed warmer.

Light blanket. The blanket is placed over the sheet and is used to keep the client warm.

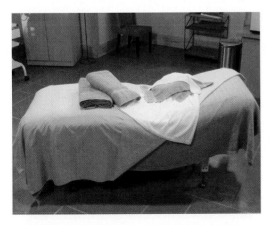

Figure 10–3 Clean linens are the first step in preparing the facial bed.

Flat sheet (twin size). Drape it over the blanket.

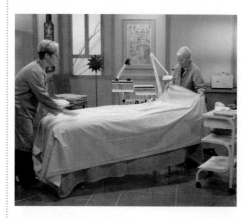

Bath sheet. A large bath towel can also be used. Place it on top of the flat sheet. Leave space at the top for the head/shoulder towel.

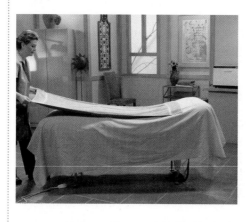

Hand towel. Terry or cotton towel. Place it at the top of the bed in the head/shoulder area.

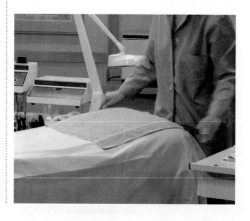

Headband. Position it on top of the towel.

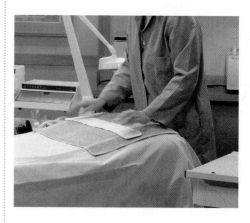

Cotton towel. Fold it in half diagonally, so that there are two "points" at one side. Position the folded edge even with the bottom edge of the headband (points should be facing you).

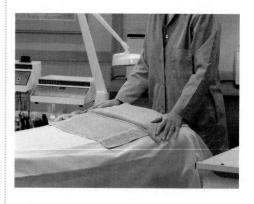

Help the client lie down, with the head centered on the wrap and the headband and the body centered on the bed.

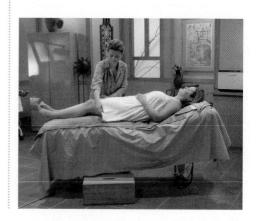

Wrap the head, by drawing up each side of the towel, one side at a time.

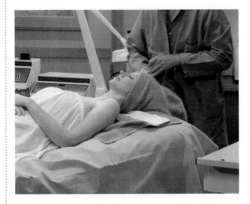

Hold the towel with one hand, bring up the headband and close it securely. Check to make sure that the client is comfortable and the head wrap is not too tight.

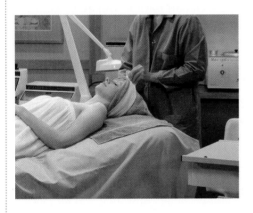

Bring up one side of the sheet and blanket, starting at the feet and legs, tapering the covering at the shoulder. Repeat with the other side.

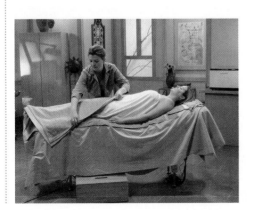

Tuck the blanket under the feet, and place a small hand towel at client's décolleté to protect the cocooned covering from spills.

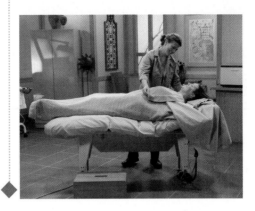

Another method of covering the head is to use a cotton barber towel, folded in half diagonally, and secure with a T pin (wig pin). Just be careful you do not prick your client's scalp!

Method Two: Noncocoon Draping

A quicker, less involved method of draping is the noncocoon draping. This type of covering is used for quick, less involved procedures. In this style, the bed warmer and sheet (either fitted or flat) are the same, but the light blanket is not used. Instead, the client reclines on the bed and a bath sheet is placed lengthwise over her.

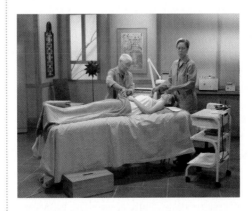

Make certain that the bath sheet covers the client completely, especially the feet.

Next, a small towel is placed over the chest area to protect the covering from spills.

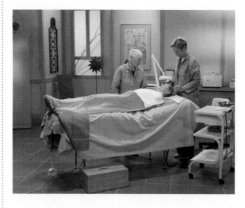

Finally, the head is wrapped and the client is ready to begin.

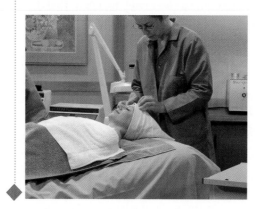

Head Protection

There are numerous head covers and bands from which to choose. Their purpose is to protect the hair from products and water. Hair protection can be a concern to the client. Some bands or covers will flatten the hair. Others provide adequate protection around the periphery of the client's face without crushing the balance of the hair. Be sure to let clients know that their hairstyle may be compromised during the treatment. Some types of hair covers follow:

- Small barber towel—Fold the towel diagonally and drape it around the head. Fasten with a clip or T pin.
- Terry turban—Fully covers the hair and has a stretchable band that stays snug around the face.
- Terry stretch headband—Approximately 4 inches wide, with a Velcro closure.

- Bouffant facial cap—Resembles a shower cap. Made of a light, breathable, meshlike material fitted with elastic. The cap can be molded around the head and is large enough to cover the ears and hair. Because of its ample size, it is comfortable to wear.
- 100% cotton, cream colored "sackcloth" towel—Found in the kitchen towel area of stores. Usually sold in packs of five or six. An economical alternative for covering the head. It can also be used under the head/shoulder area.

To make a head wrap, fold a towel diagonally as a triangle and place it on the bed with the point facing you. Slide it under the client's head to the base of the neck. Take the left corner and bring it all the way around the forehead down the right side of the face. Hold it in place and take the right corner and bring it over past the ear on the left side. Tuck the excess under the towel. Check with the client to be sure it is comfortable. Take the pointed part (facing you) and place it over any visible hair and loosely tuck on the side. The look is clean and neat and will fully protect the hair.

Clients expect a soothing ambiance where they can relax and receive corrective skin care at the same time. It is not recommended to use paper sheets or gowns in a salon environment. They are too noisy and are normally used in a more medical environment. An exception to this rule is the use of small polyguard towels that have a water-resistant backing. These are great for placing under the head to catch debris as it is rolled off during a gommage treatment. After the treatment, the polyguard towel can be carefully rolled off and away from the client. The client is now on the soft cotton towel.

Supplies

Before any procedure can begin, the esthetician must make sure that the room contains every supply that may be needed and that all supplies are organized for ease of use during the facial. Where supplies are stored will depend on the method used for product storage.

Disposables

The list of esthetic disposables continues to grow. Disposable items used in the esthetic practice may be purchased from beauty or

First Impressions

Yes, it is true—that first impression *is* a lasting one. Although many of us may be uncomfortable with the idea of being judged on appearances, in the esthetic industry, keeping up with appearances is considered a core value. Estheticians must be aware at all times of the impression they are giving. From the initial point of contact, whether that is a telephone call or walk-in visit, clients will be forming a reaction to your presentation.

The telephone offers clients a miniview of your business and professional ethic—it is the company's first and foremost marketing tool. Many times estheticians find themselves suddenly thrust into the role of "receptionist." If you think that this responsibility may be delegated to you be sure to review all aspects of telephone courtesy and make sure you become knowledgeable with all the clinic's business practices. Not having the answers to simple questions, such as the cost of services and hours of daily operation, gives clients the impression of incompetence.

Personal appearances are equally important in terms of first impressions. However, when you think about making a positive impression, don't overlook your professional presentation skills. After you take a careful look in the mirror to see that your hair is neatly coiffed, your makeup is carefully applied, your clothes are clean, and your shoes are buffed and polished, give yourself a personal skills inventory. Do you smile and appear friendly? Is your attitude courteous and respectful? Is your posture nonthreatening and considerate? Do you give the client the impression that you are competent? Clients will take all these things into consideration in forming a first impression.

Clients will also be appraising the clinic's appearance. Learn to think about the little things that catch the client's eye. For example, is the room clean, dust and dirt free? Have all utensils been disinfected and sterilized? Are beds neatly draped with clean linens? Do robes, slippers, and towels appear clean and fresh smelling? All these things let the client know that you are invested in their health and well-being.

Whether or not you have control over the entire clinic or spa, take time periodically to rate yourself in the following categories. Diplomatically sharing this laundry list with the powers that be may also help to encourage a unified positive impression.

- Does your clinic or spa feel like a special place? Is service conducted with a smile? Is the décor attractive? Are retail products displayed in an enticing fashion?

- Is the environment neat, clean, and well scrubbed? Dust, dirt, and cobweb free? Tools meticulous? Surfaces sparkling? Disinfected with an antibacterial agent?

- Are rest rooms and locker rooms neat and tidy?

- Does the staff adopt a professional attitude? Are they Prompt? Courteous? Qualified? Welcoming? Helpful?

- Are clients given clear directives and a proper orientation?

- Are product samples and retail merchandise readily accessible?

- Are rooms warm and inviting? Fragrant and refreshing?

- Is music carefully selected to calm and restore the spirit?

- Are clients given creature comforts such as refreshments, robes, and slippers?

- Do reading materials present the image or personality of the clinic or spa and its clientele? Do these include educational materials on skin care?

- Is there a sense of order and organization—a place for everything and everything in its place?

- Is the front desk clearly visible, easily accessible, and clutter free?

- Are clients able to check in and check out with a minimum of effort and confusion?

Once you address all of these points, you can be sure that your clients will enjoy their experience and will return often.

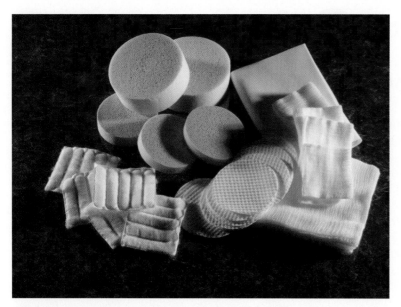

Figure 10–4 Many different types of disposable supplies are used in esthetic treatments.

medical supply houses. Keep in mind that disposables are expensive. Employers may be concerned about the increase in overhead they generate. It is wise to use them prudently. Disposable supplies include swabs, spatulas, condiment cups, foil, lancets, cotton pads, cotton strips, and eye pads (Figure 10–4). Using processed cotton balls is prohibitively expensive. A convenient and inexpensive alternative may be found in using cotton rolls. These can be easily cut into 4" x 4"

pads, strips, and eye pads. These are nonsterile and are not as fluffy, but they are far less expensive than the sterile kind. Cutting them to your specifications is more efficient as well as frugal.

Commonly called 4 by 4s, gauze pads are disposables with many applications in advanced esthetics. Woven 4 by 4s are excellent for applying chemical peels. They are designed for one-time use only, which means that there is no cross-contamination. Disposables should be kept at your workstation on the utility cart in closed jars and restocked daily. Bulk supplies should be stored in a closed cabinet in either the treatment room or in the central dispensary.

Brushes

Brushes come in all shapes and sizes and are used for a wide variety of things (Figure 10–5). Brushes are used to apply professional treatment masks and are useful in administering peels. Small fan brushes are particularly useful where there is a need to apply a product carefully and quickly. Small round brushes are used in the application of makeup. They should be kept thoroughly cleaned, sanitized, and dry.

Palettes

Palettes are used when products are dispersed from a central dispensary that holds large professional size pump bottles of cleansers, toners, and moisturizers. Pumps are a great idea because they prevent contamination and save time. Squeeze bottles provide similar convenience in the treatment room. Palettes are available in metal or plastic. Artists use them for mixing paint colors before applying them to a blank canvas. Palettes come in different sizes and are easy to clean and sanitize. They contain indentations approximately the size of a fifty-cent piece and are ideal for rationing product.

The palette system allows the esthetician to customize facial products to the client's needs and at the same time control the amount of product used. After analyzing the client's skin the esthetician proceeds to the dispensary to fill the palette according to the client's skin type, conditions, and treatment

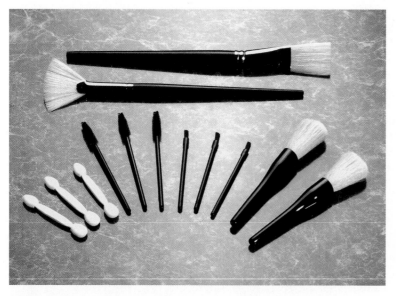

Figure 10–5 Brushes come in all sizes for a wide variety of uses.

requirements. It is useful in controlling wastefulness when the facility has multiple treatment rooms.

Jars and Containers

To maintain an efficient and sanitary setup for dispensing products directly in the treatment room, all back bar containers, bottles, and cylinders should have pumps. When using this method for dispensing products, back bar containers are typically refilled from larger ones that are kept in a locked area.

Other disposables such as cotton, swabs, wooden applicators, and spatulas should be kept in glass sundry jars or stainless steel cylinder containers that are covered with a lid. Acrylic caddy containers are also useful for storing cotton and smaller items. These containers should be neatly arranged and easily accessible on the counter or workstation. To avoid contamination, it is important that you do not place your gloved hand into the jars once you have touched your client's skin. If necessary, remove items from the jars with a set of tongs. It is helpful to prepare a set of brushes, spatulas, cotton, and other necessities on a tray on the counter. This can easily be prepared ahead of time along with the product palette.

In a larger dispensary system, trays can actually be prepared in advance. Trays can be set up for a basic facial or for a more advanced treatment. This takes some planning, but will save a great deal of time and waste. The esthetician merely picks up the newly filled tray with the product palette and carries it back to the treatment room.

Bowls, Sponges, and Sanitation

Small round stainless steel bowls are easy to sanitize and will not break down with sterilizing solutions. They fit neatly into most sinks and can be used to hold esthetic implements before placing them into a sanitizer. Two-ounce, stainless steel cups (often called condiment containers) are an alternative for using a product palette. They are deeper and are less apt to spill. Kidney-shaped bowls fit nicely under the client's neck, and are ideal for rinsing masks and/or other solutions that require cotton wraps or compresses (Figure 10–6).

Figure 10–6 Bowls and sponges are useful in the treatment room.

Sponges

Many salons and spas use disposable precut roll cotton or 4 by 4s for cleansing, product application, and rinsing. However, some estheticians prefer to use sponges. Sponges must be sterilized after each use. If not cleaned properly they can harbor bacteria. Follow the guidelines in Chapter 5.

Do not use sponges to remove lipstick or eye makeup. Apply makeup remover solution to two cotton squares and also place a couple of drops onto small cotton swabs. To remove mascara, hold the pad under the lashes (eyes are closed) and gently slide the cotton swab down the lash and onto the pad. Continue to swipe away from the eye until all the mascara is removed. Remove lipstick with another disposable cotton square.

Product Masks

Product masks come in a variety of treatment-specific formulas. They are infused with high-performance ingredients that are based in clays, herbs, camphor, vitamins, seaweed, algae, aromatherapy oils, honey, mud, and sea salts. Masks are used to target numerous

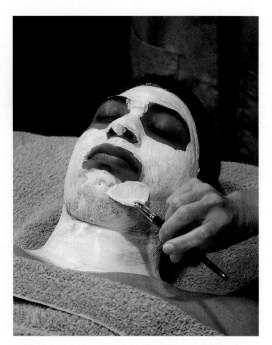

Figure 10–7 Masks are targeted for use with many different skin conditions.

skin conditions. Choose the appropriate mask for your client (Figure 10–7).

Masks are applied in a thin layer with a spatula or brush. Moistened pads soaked in a calming solution such as chamomile are applied to the eyes once the mask is in place. In general masks remain on the face for 10 to 15 minutes. The esthetician can make valuable use of this time to fill in the treatment record chart, plan a home maintenance regimen, or retrieve the recommended products.

To remove the mask fill a stainless steel bowl with lukewarm water, then wipe the mask off with cotton squares or esthetic cellulose sponges. Use the same pattern that you use to cleanse the skin, moving up from the jaw line to the cheeks to the forehead. Rinse the sponges frequently, or discard the cotton with each stroke and use new ones until the job is done.

Dispensary

We present two ways of setting up a dispensary. A **dispensary** is a location where extra supplies and bulk products are kept—usually behind lock and key. These are referred to as

dispensary
An area where extra supplies and bulk products are kept.

model
A design, idea, specific organization, or protocol that is used as an example to copy.

models. A **model** is a design, idea, specific organization, or protocol that is used as an example to copy. This textbook offers several models or examples that you can follow to conduct your work. In this chapter, we showed two models for setting up your facial chair. Practicing these models will help you become familiar with the procedure.

In method one professional back bar products are kept in the treatment room. Products are placed on the shelf of the cart in an organized fashion. Some estheticians place a turntable on the shelf (these may be found in kitchen or retail stores in the organizer section). Products are easily located by just turning the disk (Figure 10–8). Back bar containers normally have pumps or flip caps to dispense the product. They are usually refilled from bulk sizes kept in the dispensary.

Containers housed in the treatment room must be kept meticulously clean and organized to appear professional. Once you analyze the client, take a small amount of each appropriate product and transfer it onto the palette. This eliminates the task of opening and closing containers during your facial.

The main advantage to products being kept in the treatment room is that they are in close proximity to the esthetician. When there is need for an alternative product, it is immediately available for dispensing.

There are also disadvantages to this model. Products tend to look untidy and sometimes the labels are smeared or falling off. A bit of effort is needed to keep the product area neat and clean at all times. There is also a temptation to dispense more product than necessary, thus wasting product.

Method two is based on a medical model. In a medical environment, the physician or nurse may not know what is necessary for the patient until after an examination. They then proceed to the dispensary to obtain a special supply or drug. They may also have to consult with another colleague on an issue concerning the patient. Normally, the dispensary is locked.

In a salon or spa, the esthetician proceeds to the dispensary after the facial analysis. Product is dispensed from the bulk sizes, as needed for the procedure. A small amount is placed on a palette. It should contain the appropriate cleanser, toner, massage cream,

Figure 10–8 Placing products on a turntable on the cart can help the esthetician easily locate the necessary product during a facial.

massage oil, cotton eye rest pads, and mask for the tasks ahead of you. Once the items are placed on the workstation, the facial can begin without interruption.

In a large operation, ownership may feel that it is more economical to dispense from a main area. It also deters theft of products and supplies. Inventory control is easier. A central dispensary area also allows for a confidential interaction with a senior esthetician if there are questions regarding the client's condition or facial procedure. On the other hand, leaving the treatment room may mean loss of time in a busy spa or salon. It may also appear disruptive to the client. The esthetician may have to return to the dispensary if an alternative product is needed.

Safety

Safety is a key concern in the salon. It is particularly important to guard the well-being of clients. Preventing accidents before they occur is important to running a safe practice. Helping clients on and off the facial chair or bed should be standard procedure. Clients may spend an hour or more lying down to receive a service. Particularly after a treat-

ment they may experience some disorientation as they get up off the bed. This is normal. To avoid an accident at the end of a treatment, assist the client in moving off the facial bed. They may need to sit first and then swing around with their legs hanging over the side.

The esthetician must assume responsibility for keeping the environment safe. Good housekeeping can help prevent accidents. Always wipe spills immediately and do not allow trash to accumulate. Hallways should be clear, and equipment kept out of the flow of traffic to ensure a safe exit out of the room. Electrical outlets should never be overloaded. Personal as well as client safety must be considered at all times.

Microwave

Microwaves are convenient for heating absorbent cotton and solutions and for softening hard waxes. At the push of a button, the microwave can also warm facial and body massage creams and oils. Be cautious, however, not to overheat any of these products or they will separate. To avoid becoming an intrusion, the microwave is best kept out of the treatment room.

Laundry

The facial procedure generates a considerable amount of soiled, reusable cloth items such as head wraps, terry cloth towels, sheets, blankets, and bath sheets. Therefore, proper sanitary handling of laundry is important. Ideally, laundry facilities are best kept on the same floor where the laundry is generated. To prevent any noise from permeating into the spa/salon place them in a room that can be insulated with sound barrier wallboard. All laundry should be washed in hot water with chlorine bleach and dried with heat. Once laundered, it should be kept neatly folded and stored in closed containers or in a cabinet until used again, to avoid contamination.

End of the Day

Most salons and spas require that the esthetician leave the treatment room ready for the next day. Whether or not it is a requirement, you should always take time at the end of the day to clean and set up your room. Arrange all tools and instruments needed to perform a basic facial treatment at your workstation, in a neat and orderly manner. As exhausted as you may be after a full day's work, you will thank yourself the next morning.

Do not be surprised if you are asked to arrive thirty minutes prior to opening to prepare for the day. Many salons require employees to arrive early. Consider this time a valuable opportunity to check on your schedule and prepare for your clients.

Summary

Professional presentation has a great deal to do with both client satisfaction and your success. The esthetician's personal appearance and the status of the treatment room both have a considerable impact on creating a positive first impression. The esthetician must take care to make a positive impression, and to practice good communication and customer service skills. A great deal of attention must also be paid to maintaining a clean and organized workspace. Carefully prepared beds with clean linens and personal comfort items help make clients feel welcome and comfortable

The treatment room is not only meant to be inviting to clientele, it must also allow the esthetician to work efficiently and productively. In this chapter we discussed two models for dispensing products. One allows the esthetician to have access to all supplies right in the treatment room. The other model relies on a main dispensary. It is based on a medical model whereby product is dispensed as needed. Advantages and disadvantages of both methods were discussed. The esthetician should be prepared to operate in either situation.

Estheticians make use of numerous items that help them to work effectively day to day. Palettes, stainless steel bowls and cups, brushes, sponges, cotton, and linens all contribute to the efficiency of their service. To promote client safety these tools must be kept sanitized and ready for use.

Ultimately practicing good habits helps to build a good work ethic. At the end of the day, clean and prepare your room for the next day. This saves time and also promotes good customer service.

Discussion Questions

1. Review the process of preparing a client for service, describing the key factors in making the client feel comfortable.

2. Pair up with a fellow classmate and take turns giving each other a tour of your skin care training facility, and preparing each other for a treatment. Discuss those things that made you feel most welcome or uncomfortable.

3. List the "five Rs" and decide what the best method for integrating these into your standard facial procedure would be.

4. Choose the method of draping a facial bed that most appeals to you. Practice your timing so that you can accomplish this task quickly and efficiently between treatments.

5. Discuss the pros and cons of treatment room setup versus dispensary supply control. How might a computer be helpful in tracking inventory and controlling the use of supplies?

6. Keeping supplies and instruments clean and/or sterile is an important issue in today's skin care environment. Discuss the best practices for using sponges, lancets, and disposables in light of this issue.

7. Atmosphere and ambiance are significant factors in the workplace. Make a list of those ingredients that are most important to you in creating a positive and productive work environment.

Additional Reading

Miller, Erica. 1996. *Day Spa Operations*. Clifton Park, N.Y.: Milady, an imprint of Delmar Learning, a division of Thomson Learning, Inc.

Tezak, Edward. 2002. *Milady's Successful Salon Management for Cosmetology Students, Workbook*. 5th ed. Clifton Park, N.Y.: Milady, an imprint of Delmar Learning, a division of Thomson Learning, Inc.

Gathering Information

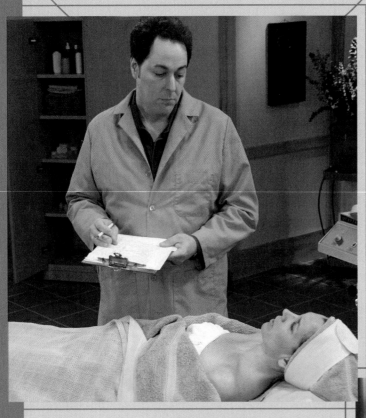

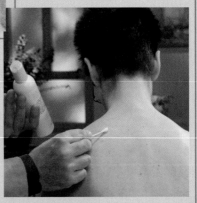

PART IV

Part Outline

Chapter 11 Skin Types and Conditions

Chapter 12 Health Screening

Chapter 13 Skin Analysis

Prior to any facial treatment, the esthetician must obtain and analyze essential data from the client in order to make accurate decisions about recommended services. The client must complete a health history form and answer questions from the esthetician in a client consultation. The consultation is then followed by the performance of an accurate skin analysis.

In Part IV, you will learn methods for gathering this information both from information provided by the client consultation and health history, and from firsthand observation. You will be introduced to the five standard skin types, and the common conditions that occur during different phases of life. This will be followed by instruction on the client health history process, an essential step because of the large role health conditions play in the appearance of the skin, and how it may respond to treatment. The health history will serve as a starting place for the discussion of the preliminary consultation. Finally, you will learn how the esthetician takes this knowledge, and uses it to observe the client's skin using tools such as the Wood's lamp, magnifying lamp, and skin scanner. Part IV concludes with the importance of recording all information on the client's record for future reference.

Chapter 11
Skin Types and Conditions

Chapter Objectives

After reading this chapter, you should be able to:

- Define the five skin types.
- Explain the difference between dry skin and dehydration.
- Explain the difference between skin type and skin condition.
- Describe several skin conditions.

Chapter Outline

Introduction
Skin Types
Skin Conditions

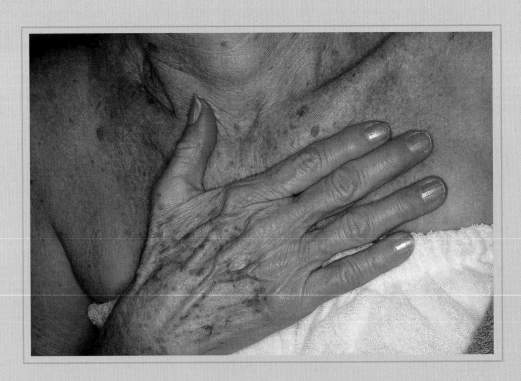

Introduction

Skin type refers to characteristics of the skin from a genetic standpoint. Parents pass on programmed data in the form of DNA that determines a child's skin type. DNA, or deoxyribonucleic acid, is a molecule carried in chromosomes that influences development and characteristics. Traits such as follicle size, skin thickness, circulatory system, and nerve endings are all inherited.

The primary determinant of skin type is **secretions**. They are produced between skin cells and in the sebaceous glands inside the follicles. Secretions determine whether skin is dry, normal, or oily. Normal skin is rare.

The quality and activity level of lipid secretions between the skin cells determine how well the skin retains moisture. These secretions also form the lipid barrier, which is fundamental in establishing whether the skin is normal, oily, or dry. The barrier decreases with aging. Secretions from sebaceous glands move up the follicles to the skin's surface. The activity of these glands determines how much oil is secreted into the follicle. Increased secretions may produce an oily condition on the skin's surface. This activity is predetermined by an individual's genes.

Skin Types

Skin type classifications can be broad. Cosmetic companies tend to simplify them in order to more easily structure their skin care lines. However, the professional system of skin typing is more complex and allows for more precision in the analysis. There are five categories in this system.

1. normal skin
2. normal–combination skin
3. dry/dehydrated skin
4. oily/problem skin
5. sensitive skin

These skin types are not necessarily permanent. Skin sensitivity is a growing area of concern that can affect skin type. Nutritional deficiencies can also affect skin types or conditions. Furthermore, seasonal, hormonal, or environmental distresses and health play a major role in skin types and conditions. This is why a client's health history is so vital.

SKINTIP

While generally considered the ideal or most beautiful skin, normal skin needs the most protection and preservation. The goal is to forestall the aging process by good cleansing and maintaining the skin's balance.

skin type
Characteristics of the skin from a genetic standpoint.

secretions
The primary determinant of skin type. They are produced between skin cells and from the sebaceous glands in hair follicles.

A facial analysis begins with careful observation of the skin prior to cleansing. After a light cleansing, the skin is examined again. The following sections cover the five skin types in more detail. This presentation will focus on the overall face, and will not address specific conditions or problems.

Normal Skin

Normal skin appears to be perfect to the naked eye and a quick touch. While few people have truly normal skin, you will encounter a few who do over the course of your career. The skin is plump, soft, smooth, and has even pores and color tones. It functions well and has no excess oil or dryness.

Treatment

Although normal skin does not need any specific correction, treatments should be applied to maintain the skin's good condition. A daily regimen of cleansing and stimulation with exfoliation of dead cells is important. The skin should also be protected from environmental and treatment damage. For normal skin, an esthetician's goal is to maintain, prevent, and postpone the aging process.

Normal–Combination Skin

Combination skin is partially oily and partially dry/dehydrated. The forehead and central part of the face is known as the T-zone. Due to the increased number of sebaceous glands concentrated in this area, it tends to be oilier. It also generally shows more enlarged pores. The cheeks and outer areas of the face appear more dry, perhaps even a little flaky or scaly. When this area becomes extremely dry or dehydrated, treatment should be a facial for dry skin. Part of this treatment can address the oilier T-zone areas with a special mask applied just in those areas. A proper home care regimen can also address this area.

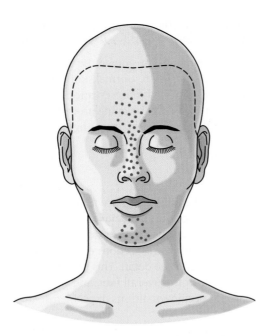

Figure 11–1 The T-zone pore structure.

SKINTIP

Normal combination skin can suffer from excess oil and enlarged pores with areas of dry/dehydrated skin. The goal is to balance the degree of oil and moisture retention.

dehydrated
Lacking water.

Treatment

Combination skin types are sometimes challenging to treat, but most product lines address them. One approach is to first assess the severity of the T-zone area (Figure 11–1). It may require an oily skin mask twice weekly to keep it under control. After cleansing and toning, a specialized product for oilier areas is applied in the T-zone area and followed by a moisturizer for combination skin. Normally, creams in combination skin systems are higher in water content to add the needed moisture. Because there is less oil in the product, it also serves the T-zone area well without adding additional oil. Combination skin care product systems are top sellers in most salons simply because they address the needs of many people.

alipidic
Lacking oil (lipids).

Dry/Dehydrated Skin

Assessing dry versus dehydrated skin types requires several considerations. Ninety percent of this skin type is actually dehydrated skin rather than dry skin. Understanding what causes dry skin is essential. For example, is it a temporary situation? An environmental condition such as hot air (experienced either indoors or outdoors) can easily dry the skin's surface. Circumstances such as lack of water, strenuous exercise, allergy medications, and other factors can all lead to dry skin. These may be temporary conditions that are corrected when the environmental factor is gone. Young, old, oily, or sensitive skin can get dehydrated.

As the skin ages and is damaged by the environment, loss of moisture leads to other conditions. It causes a deterioration of the collagen and elastin fibrils, which results in sagginess, wrinkles, and folds in the skin. Estheticians should treat dry/dehydrated skin with the utmost care because of its disposition for damage. Although it is not always visible on the surface, the underlying skin structures can be damaged.

Dehydrated Skin

Dehydrated skin lacks water. It could be the result of extrinsic damage (e.g., sun) or intrinsic issues (e.g., aging). Dehydrated skin is frequently delicate, thin, flaky, or scaly, and feels tight, dry, and uncomfortable to the touch or when facial expressions are made. Sometimes dehydrated skin looks normal but it has a flaky roughness to it. The skin seems to have fine pores and is prone to fine lines and sun damage.

Dehydrated skin shows early signs of aging and is the most difficult to correct. One would think that just drinking eight glasses of water each day would alleviate the condition. While drinking water is certainly beneficial, it is not necessarily the remedy for dehydrated skin.

Dehydrated skin is more common than truly dry skin. In many cases, however, it is difficult to discern the difference between the two types.

Dry Skin

Genuine dry skin can be classified as oil/dry, dehydrated, or **alipidic** (meaning lacking oil). Dry skin lacks oil. Remember that the lipid barrier helps hold moisture inside the skin. As a person ages or the skin is environmentally damaged, this barrier diminishes considerably. Individuals who had normal to combination skin early in their lives may later

SKINTIP

The primary goal for treating dry and dehydrated skin is to balance the moisture and oil of the skin, soften the texture, hydrate, and moisturize. This skin type needs a lot of moisture and sun protection. Skin can be excessively oily and dehydrated at the same time. It requires a water-based moisturizer.

develop dry skin. In the normal process of aging, a decrease of lipids between the skin cells causes the skin to become consistently dry and dehydrated. The skin requires water and oil to help replenish the moisture barrier.

Treatment. Dehydrated skin requires an assessment of the cause of dryness. The goal in treating dehydrated skin is to increase the moisture or hydration level in the skin. To do this, the treatment must include products that contain ingredients that hold moisture, such as special serums and water-based treatment creams. Other treatments include protection from water evaporation, sun protection, and exfoliation.

Treatment for dry/alipidic skin requires addressing the dehydration and lack of barrier lipids. Antiaging facials combined with well-designed home care products containing both lipids and oil can make a dramatic improvement.

Oily Skin and Dehydration

Oily skin can have intense lipid secretions and yet be dehydrated as well. For example, a teenage player on a sports team sweats a lot during a game and loses moisture. But after a game, the T-zone area is slick with oil. One may conclude that the oiliness indicates a lot of moisture. On the contrary, the player is most likely dehydrated.

Oily skin can have areas of dehydration or moisture loss but still have enough oil. This is considered combination skin. Dry skin (alipidic) is also dehydrated. Dry and dehydrated skin are categorized together. Dry/dehydrated skin may also be considered a condition.

Oily/Problem Skin

Oily skin exhibits an excess of sebum or oil production. The follicle (pore) size appears enlarged. The skin appears sallow, shiny, and thick. Clumping of dead cells and sebum may cause clogging of the follicles, which increases the surface thickness of the skin. This causes a sallow appearance. Additionally, oily skin is more at risk for breakouts.

During skin analysis, an esthetician should consider the overall characteristics of the skin to determine whether it should be classified as an oily skin type. Nose skin that is congested with blackheads or open comedones is associated with an oily skin type. But the number and condition of lesions on the skin can change the designation from oily/problem skin to acne. Acne is a conditional disorder and not a skin type.

Additionally, oily skin is more susceptible to emotional breakouts and is easily affected by intrinsic aging factors such as puberty and hormonal explosions. Younger individuals and those with hormonal fluctuations often experience problematic conditions associated with comedones and pustules. It takes hard work to improve the condition of this skin type. Balancing the excess oil secretions is a daily challenge. The skin requires frequent cleaning. However, there is a tendency to overtreat individuals with surface oil. Excessive treatment can worsen the problem because the body will try to compensate for the oil loss by producing more oil.

Most people with an oily skin type will always have oily skin. The good news for oily skin types is that they are less inclined to form fine lines and wrinkles. The excess oil provides a better moisture barrier, which prevents water loss.

Treatment

The treatment for oily skin is to balance it. First, exfoliate the buildup of keratinized cells. Then, moisturize the surface with a hydrating product for oily skin. Eventually, the oil secretions are brought under control. Treatment of an oily skin type is a constant juggling act of cleansing without overcleansing and providing adequate moisture to avoid overproduction of oil.

An important point for estheticians to remember is how to perform a consultation with a client who has oily skin. Although it may seem unsuitable to use a cream or moisturizer on a client with oily skin, the correct product system can create noticeable improvements. Another point to remember is

Appointment Scheduling

The goal of doing business is to increase business. Estheticians do that by encouraging clients to book appointments on a regular basis. This means that the process of scheduling an appointment should be made as easy as possible for the client. Although most salons today have specific personnel and utilize computer systems to help manage the flow of traffic, estheticians should be aware of their contribution in making the day go smoothly.

As Stephen Covey, author of the national bestseller *The 7 Habits of Highly Effective People* says, "Begin with the end in mind." For the esthetician this means managing time well each day. Staying on schedule is important to business—remember "time is money." Practice good time management skills. No one wants to wait. In our overprogrammed society time is precious to all of us. No matter how flexible someone else's lifestyle may look, you need to be respectful of the fact that clients have other obligations. There are children to attend to, errands to run, social commitments, and other appointments to keep. You also need to be mindful of your coworkers who may also be working on the same client. If you get off schedule they are off schedule, too.

But before you can begin scheduling in an efficient manner, you must understand how long it takes to perform each treatment or service. As an esthetician just starting out, it will take time before you can make quick decisions. Accommodating a client's spur-of-the-moment request for an eyebrow waxing needs to be negotiated carefully or you will find yourself running behind all day. If you cannot service a client comfortably within the time slot allowed, perhaps you can ask the client to reschedule, or recommend another member of the staff who can oblige more easily.

Educating other staff members is also valuable. The most important person in any salon or skin care practice is the person booking appointments. This is usually the receptionist. Take time to inform this person about every aspect of scheduling. If your schedule changes weekly, provide an updated, easy-to-read calendar each week. If there is a monthly rotation, you should get in the habit of supplying your schedule on the first day of each month. If possible have the schedule laminated to avoid damage from accidental coffee spills, and provide a minieasel or stand so that the receptionist can view it easily at the appointment desk. It is also a good idea to give the receptionist a "cheat sheet" that lists timings for each procedure.

Repeat business is essential to keeping your appointment book full. The whole idea is to get clients to plan skin care visits on a regular basis. Encourage your clients to book their next appointment before they leave the salon. An easy way to accomplish this is to create a "prescription slip." As you consult with the client at the end of each service you can list home care products and include a space to schedule their next appointment. They can then bring this user-friendly tool directly to the receptionist, who won't have to trouble you for specifics.

If promotional efforts are not in place where you work, consider talking to your boss about adding incentives for clients to book their next appointment. Offering discounts on a series of treatments, or 10% off the next appointment when booked at the time of service, will encourage repeat business. Frequent buyer programs are another way to add value.

Do your part to take notice of your clients' scheduling behavior and encourage the use of freebies or special values on products and services on your slower days. You can encourage your clients to be more flexible and take advantage of these less desirable times if you provide additional incentive.

Ultimately you are in the driver's seat. You must work hard to maintain good work habits. Check your appointment schedule every day before leaving. If you have a day off call in to see if any new appointments have been booked. Arrive 15 to 30 minutes early to organize your day. Take time to prepare yourself for busy days. Be sure to stock supplies and review each client's history before the day begins. This will save valuable time and make your day go smoothly and efficiently—a real benefit in keeping clients relaxed, happy, and coming back.

SKINTIP

Oily skin should be balanced but not overtreated. Clean the skin but do not strip it. Exaggerated cleansings can increase an oil problem.

to control bacteria growth for oily skin types, because bacteria exaggerates this skin type's problematic nature. The skin should also be exfoliated well without overdoing it. Gentle exfoliation helps to prevent skin buildup.

Oily skin types require consistent maintenance to avoid cell buildup. Gentle exfoliation, good cleansing, and moisturizing help balance the secretions.

Sensitive Skin

Skin types are basically classified as normal, dry, or oily. However, skin care technology has expanded the ability to treat numerous skin types. During recent years, sensitive skin has become its own classification. While sensitivity is a condition that may occur on any skin type, certain circumstances and more at-risk skin can require treatment as a separate type.

Sensitive skin is mostly thin and beautiful. It is pink to red in color, and it is clear with a smooth appearance. A closer look, however, reveals a parchment look or feel. This skin type flushes easily and may feel uncomfortable or painful when touched. Aggravated by topical substances and environmental conditions, sensitive skin requires the utmost care and gentleness.

Do not confuse sensitive skin with skin that is allergic to specific substances. Allergic reactions may occur in all skin types and are due to a specific cause. In contrast, sensitive skin is genetically predisposed or has been sensitized by an aggressive treatment.

During the initial skin analysis, any refined, delicate-looking skin with a tendency

SKINTIP

Treat sensitive skin gently, and give it extra care. Choose products designated for this skin type, and avoid sun exposure and conditions that may cause irritation.

toward redness is safely classified as sensitive. Regard it carefully both in treatment in the and selection of home care products.

Treatment

Today, most product lines recognize the sensitive skin type. Special systems with reduced sensitivity factors are available. Note that sensitizing ingredients such as perfumes and certain preservatives, as well as high ingredient activity may irritate sensitive skin. Improvements in technology and a greater understanding of this skin type have resulted in products that can calm and strengthen the tissue. See Chapter 22 for more details about sensitive skin.

Skin Conditions

When first learning facial analysis, it is easy to identify obvious skin issues. Everyone has a skin type classification; however, not everyone has a skin condition. There is a distinct difference between type and condition.

Conditions occur in many different skin types and include dehydration, dryness, sun damage, hyperpigmentation, telangiectasis, wrinkles, birthmarks, and acne, among others. Acne and its treatment are covered in depth in Chapter 24.

Dehydration and Dryness As a Condition

Key indicators of dehydration are visible fine lines and a sense of tightness on the skin. Also, during consultation a client may state that the skin feels tight and dry. These are all clues to treatment. When you can confidently discern the difference between dryness and dehydration, you can plan a proper course of treatment. It may include more oils and surface lubrication for the dry conditions. More water and specialty hydration serums and masks can correct the dehydration.

Sun and Environmental Damage

Sun and environmental damage appears in many forms. Most often, it appears as dehydration, which can be caused by living and working in a dry, cold climate or by exposure to wind. Typically, dehydration in these instances is more acute than in normal

Figure 11–2 Freckles are an example of hyperpigmentation.

environments. Thus, lubrication and protection are the primary goals.

Hyperpigmentation

Hyperpigmentation is another condition that results from environmental damage. Hyperpigmentation is an excess of skin pigment. Freckles (**lentigines)** are an example of hyperpigmentation (Figure 11–2). They may be caused by sun and environmental damage rather than by genetic predispositions. Another example is a **pregnancy mask**, which is a common, hormonally-determined example of hyperpigmentation that often occurs during pregnancy. It gets worse from sun exposure.

Other hyperpigmentation spots known as melasma or chloasma may appear on the skin as patches or splotchiness (Figure 11–3). Any ultraviolet exposure stimulates hyperpigmentation. Melanin or pigment is a natural protectant from the ultraviolet rays of the sun.

Pigmentation is not always visible to the naked eye. Deeper pigmentation can be seen through a Wood's lamp. It shows up as brownish splotches or dark spots. These spots often disappear when the lamp is turned off. The hyperpigmentation you see under a Wood's lamp is a sign of environmental sun damage. The obvious treatment is protection from further sun damage and constant use of sunscreen. The performance of multiple exfoliation treatments can reduce hyperpig-

mentation. In addition, a brightening product can be recommended for everyday home use.

Telangiectasia

Telangiectasia is a condition involving the circulatory system (Figure 11–4). The symptom is small, red, enlarged capillaries, normally seen on the face and legs. When stress is put on the capillaries, it causes the blood vessel to enlarge or **distend.** Sun exposure, cigarette smoking, alcohol, and poor health can cause this condition. Commonly called **couperose**, this condition manifests as diffused redness on the cheeks, nose, and neck. Sometimes this redness is associated with sensitivity or an allergic response. However, note that this type of redness is different from redness that appears on environmentally damaged or sensitive skin.

Facial Lines and Wrinkles

Dramatic aging occurs in the neck and eye area as a result of sun and environmental exposure. There is an absolute direct correlation between sunbathing and premature aging. Sun is a major factor in damaged skin, which becomes dry, dehydrated, and internally injured. Once the underlying skin structures are damaged, the skin loses its firmness. The result is exaggerated lines, deep furrows, and wrinkles on the face and neck. Therefore, one of the first steps after a skin analysis is to educate the client about sun prevention and protection.

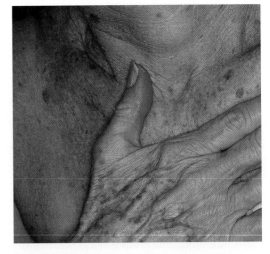

Figure 11–3 Pigmentation such as melasma appears on the skin in patches and is hormonal.

lentigines
Freckles.

pregnancy mask
A common hormonally determined example of hyperpigmentation that typically occurs during pregnancy. It often gets worse from sun exposure.

telangiectasia
A condition involving the circulatory system; small, red enlarged capillaries that normally appear on the face and legs.

distend
To enlarge.

couperose
The common name for telangiectasis.

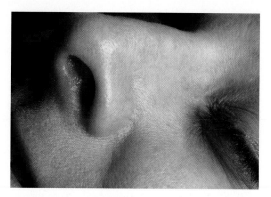

Figure 11–4 Small broken capillaries, or spider veins, often appear on the face and legs.

SKIN TIP

Many conditions such as dry skin are easily treated. An observation of anything out of the ordinary on the skin provides an opportunity to serve a client better. Don't ignore any condition just because you can't identify it. Note it in the client's chart.

The Eye Area

Puffiness, dark circles, and redness around the eyes often result from a person's lifestyle and behavior. For example, fatigue causes dark circles around the eyes. Lymphatic drainage, the application of eye products, and adequate sleep can create esthetic improvements. However, some ethnicities have a natural darkness around the eyes, which is a result of skin pigment rather than lifestyle.

Moles, Birthmarks, Scars, and Warts

Although estheticians technically cannot treat the skin for birthmarks and moles, an analysis should include them. Any unusual mark or growth should be noted in the client's chart. This documentation is a reminder to watch for changes. It is also wise to gently mention it to the client so that a physician can check it. A small mole can one day become cancerous.

Summary

Every skin has a general type and any number of individual conditions. Knowing the five basic skin types—normal, normal–combination, dry/dehydrated, oily/problem, and sensitive—allows you to precisely analyze the skin. Two types, normal–combination and sensitive, have become the mainstays of most treatment protocols and home care product routines. It is generally easier to put a client's initial skin analysis under one of these categories. Furthermore, information about com-

mon skin conditions allows estheticians to serve clients better and helps estheticians determine the correct treatments.

Discussion Questions

1. To aid estheticians in the process of skin analysis, the skin is categorized or classified in several ways. Explain what is meant by *skin type* versus *skin condition.* Provide examples of each.

2. Compare and contrast the differences between *dehydrated* and *dry/alipidic* as skin types and conditions. What are the main causes of each?

3. Discuss the evolution of sensitive skin as a type. How does skin prone to allergic reactions differ from sensitive skin?

4. Write a brief description of the more commonly known skin conditions. What is the best way for the esthetician to classify them when conducting a skin analysis?

Additional Reading

Fitzpatrick, Thomas B., et al. 1997. *Color Atlas and Synopsis of Clinical Dermatology.* 3rd ed. New York: McGraw-Hill Health Professions Division.

Lees, Mark. 2000. *Skin Care: Beyond the Basics.* Clifton Park, N.Y.: Milady, an imprint of Delmar Learning, a division of Thomson Learning, Inc.

Helpful Web Sites

http://www.emedicine.com (eMedicine)
http://www.ucsf.edu (University of California, San Francisco)

Chapter 12
Health Screening

Chapter Objectives

After reading this chapter, you should be able to:

▶ Define the purpose of a health analysis form.

▶ Explain the purpose of each question on the form.

▶ Explain the purpose of a screening consultation.

Chapter Outline

Introduction

Health Screening Questionnaire

Confidential Skin Health Survey

PLEASE PRINT

Today's Date _____

First Name _____ Last Name _____ Date of Birth __/__/__

Street _____ Apt. # _____ City _____ State _____ Zip _____

Phone—Home ( ) _____ Work ( ) _____ Mobile ( ) _____

Dermatologist/Physician _____ Phone ( ) _____

Emergency Contact _____ Phone ( ) _____

Your Occupation _____

Referred By ❏ Friend ❏ Mailer ❏ Walk-by ❏ Yellow Pages ❏ Gift Certificate ❏ Other _____

Esthetician Name _____

---

1. Is this your first facial? ❏ Yes ❏ No
2. What is the reason for your visit today? _____
3. What special areas of concern do you have? _____
4. Are you presently under a physician's care for any current skin condition or other problem? ❏ Yes ❏ No
   What? _____
5. Are you pregnant? ❏ Yes ❏ No
6. Are you taking birth control pills? ❏ Yes ❏ No
   If so, what type? _____
7. Hormone replacement? ❏ Yes ❏ No
   If so, what? _____
8. Do you wear contact lenses? ❏ Yes ❏ No
9. Do you smoke? ❏ Yes ❏ No
10. Do you often experience stress? ❏ Yes ❏ No
11. Have you had skin cancer? ❏ Yes ❏ No

12. Are you now using (or used in the past): ❏ Azelex
    ❏ Differin ❏ Renova ❏ Retin-A
    ❏ Tazarac ❏ Glycolic or alphahydroxy acids
    If so, when and for how long? _____
13. Are you now using or have you ever used Accutane?
    ❏ Yes ❏ No
    If so, when and for how long? _____
14. Do you have acne? ❏ Yes ❏ No
    Experience frequent blemishes? ❏ Yes ❏ No
    If so, how frequently? _____
15. Do you have any allergies to cosmetics, foods, or drugs?
    ❏ Yes ❏ No
    Please list _____
16. Are you presently taking medications—oral or topical?
    ❏ Yes ❏ No If so, please list _____
17. What products do you use presently? ❏ Soap
    ❏ Cleansing milk ❏ Toner ❏ Scrub ❏ Mask
    ❏ Creams ❏ Sunscreen ❏ Other

Please circle if you are affected by or have any of the following:

Asthma	Hepatitis	Metal bone, pins, or plates
Cardiac problems	Herpes	Pacemaker
Eczema	High blood pressure	Psychological problems
Epilepsy	Hysterectomy	Sinus problems
Fever blisters	Immune disorders	Skin diseases—other
Headaches—chronic	Lupus	Urinary or kidney problems

Please explain above problems or list any significant others: _____

I understand that the services offered are not a substitute for medical care, and any information provided by the therapist is for educational purposes only and not diagnostically prescriptive in nature. I understand that the information herein is to aid the therapist in giving better service and is completely confidential.

SALON POLICIES
1. Professional consultation is required before initial dispensing of products.
2. Our active discount rate is only effective for clients visiting every 4 weeks.
3. We do not give cash refunds.
4. We require a 24-hour cancellation notice.

I fully understand and agree to the above salon policies.

_____   _____
Client's signature   Date

Introduction

A client's health affects the skin. Therefore, a health analysis form is the first step in a facial analysis (Figure 12–1). This wealth of written information complements the physical analysis of the entire face, neck, and décolleté. The form is followed by an interactive (or conversational), visual, and tactile analysis. The primary analysis concentrates on the entire face, then evaluates its different parts. While the natural tendency is to focus on obvious conditions, it is advisable to thoroughly survey the overall face and skin type.

The thorough client health history that begins this procedure is called a health screening or health intake form (Figure 12–2). These forms are designed to meet the individual requirements of each practice and the services that are offered. You may have a health survey for each service, such as a facial, massage, wet treatment, or **epilation**—a hair removal treatment such as waxing, electrolysis, or laser hair removal.

Estheticians should never perform a treatment without first obtaining the appropriate health information from a client because of the potential for harm to the client. For example, some drugs are **contraindicated** for treatments, or not safe for use on clients who have a specific condition or are under medical care for a particular situation. A second reason for the health screening form is to obtain information about the history of a client's skin care habits. This history provides clues about a client's interest level in salon skin care treatments as well as guidelines for recommending a home care regimen.

Health Screening Questionnaire

The name, address, and phone numbers of a client should begin the form. Even if you have obtained this information on the phone, this will confirm that the address, phone numbers, and spelling are correct.

Date of Birth

Some clients choose not to reveal their date of birth, but knowing their age allows you to assess the condition of their skin in relation

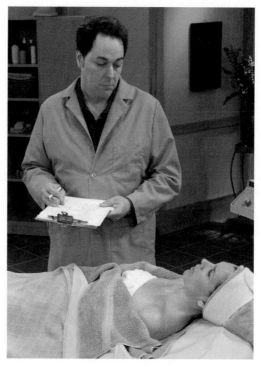

Figure 12–1 It is vital to record a thorough client history before treatment.

to their age. A 50-year-old client who only has expression lines probably has taken good care of his or her skin. A 30-year-old who looks much older and has lines, wrinkling, splotching, and obvious sun damage has severe symptoms for this age.

Occupation

A client's occupation can affect the skin. For example, a client who works outdoors may need additional sunscreen protection or a water-resistant sunscreen. The client also may be more susceptible to sun-oriented exposure problems, such as sunburn, **photoaging** (aging symptoms due to sun damage), or development of skin cancer. Another example is a teenager with acne who works in a fast food restaurant. This client is constantly exposed to greasy air, which may contribute to or worsen the acne condition.

It is also good to know a client's occupation for conversational and consultative reasons. If a client indicates on her health form that she is a physician, she will be knowledgeable about skin conditions, and you should acknowledge this fact. However, you should still conduct a thorough consultation.

epilation
A hair removal treatment such as waxing, electrolysis, or laser hair removal.

contraindicated
Services, activities, or products that can cause side effects or harm, or pose danger to persons who have a specific condition or are under medical care for a particular situation.

photoaging
Aging symptoms due to sun damage.

Confidential Skin Health Survey

PLEASE PRINT

Today's Date _____

First Name _____ Last Name _____ Date of Birth ___/___/___

Street _____ Apt. # _____ City _____ State _____ Zip _____

Phone—Home ( )_____ Work ( )_____ Mobile ( )_____

Dermatologist/Physician _____ Phone ( )_____

Emergency Contact _____ Phone ( )_____

Your Occupation _____

Referred By ❑ Friend ❑ Mailer ❑ Walk-by ❑ Yellow Pages ❑ Gift Certificate ❑ Other _____

Esthetician Name _____

---

1. Is this your first facial? ❑ Yes ❑ No
2. What is the reason for your visit today?
   _____
3. What special areas of concern do you have?
   _____
   _____
   _____
4. Are you presently under a physician's care for any current skin condition or other problem? ❑ Yes ❑ No
   What? _____
5. Are you pregnant? ❑ Yes ❑ No
6. Are you taking birth control pills? ❑ Yes ❑ No
   If so, what type? _____
7. Hormone replacement? ❑ Yes ❑ No
   If so, what? _____
8. Do you wear contact lenses? ❑ Yes ❑ No
9. Do you smoke? ❑ Yes ❑ No
10. Do you often experience stress? ❑ Yes ❑ No
11. Have you had skin cancer? ❑ Yes ❑ No

12. Are you now using (or used in the past): ❑ Azelex
    ❑ Differin ❑ Renova ❑ Retin-A
    ❑ Tazarac ❑ Glycolic or alphahydroxy acids
    If so, when and for how long? _____
13. Are you now using or have you ever used Accutane?
    ❑ Yes ❑ No
    If so, when and for how long? _____
14. Do you have acne? ❑ Yes ❑ No
    Experience frequent blemishes? ❑ Yes ❑ No
    If so, how frequently? _____
15. Do you have any allergies to cosmetics, foods, or drugs?
    ❑ Yes ❑ No
    Please list _____
16. Are you presently taking medications—oral or topical?
    ❑ Yes ❑ No If so, please list
    _____
    _____
17. What products do you use presently? ❑ Soap
    ❑ Cleansing milk ❑ Toner ❑ Scrub ❑ Mask
    ❑ Creams ❑ Sunscreen ❑ Other

Please circle if you are affected by or have any of the following:

Asthma	Hepatitis	Metal bone, pins, or plates
Cardiac problems	Herpes	Pacemaker
Eczema	High blood pressure	Psychological problems
Epilepsy	Hysterectomy	Sinus problems
Fever blisters	Immune disorders	Skin diseases—other
Headaches—chronic	Lupus	Urinary or kidney problems

Please explain above problems or list any significant others: _____

I understand that the services offered are not a substitute for medical care, and any information provided by the therapist is for educational purposes only and not diagnostically prescriptive in nature. I understand that the information herein is to aid the therapist in giving better service and is completely confidential.

SALON POLICIES

1. Professional consultation is required before initial dispensing of products.
2. Our active discount rate is only effective for clients visiting every 4 weeks.
3. We do not give cash refunds.
4. We require a 24-hour cancellation notice.

I fully understand and agree to the above salon policies.

_____   _____
Client's signature   Date

Figure 12–2 Confidential skin health survey.

Referrals

To support the business's marketing efforts, it is appropriate to find out how a new client discovered your services. New clients who are referred by happy clients make great clients! They show more trust, interest, and awareness of what makes a successful esthetic treatment. They are more likely to purchase products and follow instructions.

Some salons offer reward programs for clients who refer new clients. During an initial conversation, asking how a new client heard about you and your services is a great icebreaker. Often, you hear that the client has a friend who has been successful with your programs. Rest assured, clients talk to one another, and a referred client may already know a lot about the program. Nevertheless, always thoroughly explain the program to new clients.

"Is this your first facial?"

Clients who have had previous facial treatments may be familiar with the general procedure. They will most likely inform you about what type of treatment they prefer. They will be able to express what they liked or disliked about their last service. If they were pleased, ask what they liked about the service. This gives you a hint about how to give them a satisfactory experience. If they had a negative experience, they will probably tell you without much coaching. Listen and make a mental note. Clients who receive regular treatments also know more about their skin. Furthermore, some clients have had only basic facial services or a relaxing facial, so estheticians should recommend the appropriate treatment and explain it well.

"Are you under a physician's care?"

This question is intended to bring to your immediate attention any diseases or conditions that may be contraindications for esthetic treatments. Clients who have health problems are usually aware that their issues may be contraindications. Sometimes clients will list that they are under a physician's care when they simply have a regular physician but have no major health problems.

"Are you pregnant?"

Numerous treatments are contraindicated for pregnant women. They should avoid any type of electrical current being applied to the skin—galvanic, high frequency, microcurrent, and others. Avoid any form of chemical exfoliation unless approved in writing by the client's doctor. Keep all written approvals in the client's file.

During pregnancy, many body treatments should also be avoided. Only licensed massage therapists who have been specially trained in pregnancy massage should perform this service. Moreover, estheticians must pay careful attention to the application of certain essential oils that may be contraindicated during pregnancy. Hormone fluctuations due to pregnancy often result in skin changes. Pregnant women may experience an increase in oiliness, flares of blemishes, and hyperpigmentation. Many of these symptoms disappear after the baby's birth.

On the other hand, some women experience excellent skin conditions during pregnancy, also likely due to hormonal changes. Often after pregnancy or after a woman stops breast-feeding, more changes occur. Estheticians may have to work more extensively with a client after childbirth.

In general, simple soothing facial treatments and the avoidance of any aggressive treatment are appropriate for pregnant women.

"Are you taking birth control pills?"

Like pregnancy, birth control pills cause hormonal changes. Birth control pills and other hormone treatments, such as hormone replacement, have been linked to acne and hyperpigmentation. It is appropriate to inquire about hormonal drugs, including birth control pills. Although estheticians are not endocrinologists or gynecologists, they can refer a client to her doctor to discuss how a drug is affecting her skin.

Positive skin changes are also attributed to hormonal therapies. Women on hormone replacement therapy during or after menopause often experience softer skin, reduced appearance of wrinkling, and less unwanted hair. Additionally, a brand of birth control pill, Ortho Tri-Cyclen, has been approved by the Food and Drug Administration for treating hormonal acne. Clients who experience chronic premenstrual breakouts may want to ask their doctors about this pill.

"Do you wear contact lenses?"

Modern long-wearing contact lenses do not generally cause problems for routine facial treatments. However, if a client feels uncomfortable or if an esthetician anticipates performing additional or intensive treatment to the eye area, the client should remove the lenses. Advanced treatments such as galvanic, high frequency, microcurrent, AHA (alphahydroxy acids), BHA (betahydroxy acids), enzyme exfoliants, chemical peels, and microdermabrasion require lenses to be removed. This ensures the safety of the eye and cornea. Estheticians should not take any risks when working around the eye, even if a client insists.

General Medical Conditions and Contraindications

Many medical conditions have no contraindications with esthetic treatments. However, some services, medical conditions, and medicines require more scrutiny to determine what treatments are appropriate.

In general, nonelectrical treatment, light massage, and nonstimulating products are appropriate for almost all clients. You must be careful when using chemical exfoliants, including AHAs, BHAs, and Jessner's exfoliation, among others. Strong masks (such as sulfur or benzoyl peroxide), lymphatic drainage massage, body treatments, acne treatments, electrical treatments, and waxing are service areas that could cause problems for clients with certain health problems (Table 12–1).

When it comes to electrical treatments, the general rule is: When in doubt, don't! This means to be conservative and gentle with treatments until you are sure that a client can tolerate a more intense procedure.

Medications

Clients will generally list oral medications here. Some clients are specific and others are general about their answers. Estheticians do not need to know specific dosages of any drug. Rather, they need to know if any of the medications being taken have contraindications for treatments. Common drugs listed are prescription antacids, hormone replacements, antidepressants, and blood pressure medications. Clients may also list antibiotics they are using for acne or for temporary infections. When a client is taking antibiotics, it is best to avoid any stimulating treatments. There is no general rule about contraindications for antibiotics, but many estheticians avoid waxing, AHA treatments, or other exfoliation treatments on clients using antibiotics.

Topical Agents

Topical agents are products applied to the skin's surface. Topical medications may be OTC (over-the-counter, nonprescription drugs) or prescription drugs. Clients often do not list topical medications because they think of drugs as *internal* medications. This is why health forms should specifically ask about topical medications.

Table 12–1 Electrical Contraindications

Client Type	Precaution
Cardiac patients, especially with pacemaker	Never administer electrical treatments.
Epileptic patients	Epilepsy is a neurological condition resulting in seizure. Never administer electrical treatments.
Pregnant women	Never administer electrical treatments.
Patients with metal implants	No electrical treatments.
Nervousness or numerous health problems	If a client seems nervous about electrical modalities or seems to have many health problems, avoid the treatment.

Chemical Exfoliants

Chemical exfoliants are contraindicated for many clients using topical medications: Retin-A and Renova (both contain the drug tretinoin), Differin (adapalene), Azelex (azelaic acid), Tazarac (tazarotene), or any prescription keratolytic. Prescription **keratolytic** drugs work by peeling off the top cells of the epidermis. Removal of these **keratinocytes** causes the skin to be more **permeable**, or more easily penetrated by chemicals and other substances. These drugs may also cause increased blood flow to the area and may increase the sensitivity of immune and neurological responses, such as pain.

Thus, these drugs make the skin more sensitive and reactive to treatments and skin care products. Exfoliation treatment in the salon or the use of additional exfoliating agents in a home care program should be recommended only if they have been specifically approved by the physician prescribing the topical medication.

Additionally, stimulating treatments, many essential oils, fragranced products, and aggressive massage should be avoided on clients using a keratolytic agent. It is best to use nonfragranced, gentle products. Estheticians should stay away from hard-setting masks or any treatment that releases heat, and they should avoid using alcohol-based products, harsh cleansers, and abrasives both in treatments and products recommended for use at home by the client.

Erythemic skin, or skin that turns red easily during simple esthetic procedures, is a red flag to avoid strong or potentially irritating products or techniques as well as exfoliating treatments.

Specific Drug Questions

The health form should include several specific questions about drugs.

- Are you using Retin-A or Renova?
- Have you ever used Accutane?
- Are you currently using any prescription skin drugs or skin treatments that you have obtained through a physician?

These specific questions are designed to emphasize that it is important to list all drugs that may affect the skin.

Retin-A and Renova, also known as tretinoin, may make the skin reactive to many products and treatments that normally would cause no side effects. Waxing, strong or harsh treatments, abrasives, heat and heat-producing products, aggressive massage, and fragranced or products with drying alcohols should never be performed on clients taking these drugs. It is also important to ask how often the medication is used and how it is applied. Clients may have the medication, but do not use it because of its cosmetic side effects. Some clients use Retin-A as a drying agent for blemishes, which is not its intended use.

Health forms specifically ask whether a client has ever used Accutane. This is a systemic drug that stays in the body for a long time and can make skin sensitive for months after a client stops taking it. Waxing and the same products and treatments contraindicated for Retin-A should be avoided. Because Accutane) affects the skin of the entire body, these treatments and products should not be used anywhere on the skin.

To ensure that clients have reported all the drugs they are taking, the last question requires them to list any products obtained from a dermatologist. Cosmetic dermatologists now dispense peeling agents, AHAs, TCA (trichloroacetic) peels (often combined with Retin-A), and high-percentage hydroquinone products (lightening agents) through their offices. TCA peels provide deeper penetration and will remove larger wrinkles. Dermatologists are administering stronger treatments with potentially greater side effects. Although these are cosmetic treatments and many are not prescription drugs—some are actually cosmetics—estheticians must determine what drugs have been used and whether they can cause side effects.

Systemic Drugs

Drugs taken internally by mouth or injection are called systemic drugs. They travel in the bloodstream throughout the body, and some can affect the skin of the entire body. Accutane is commonly used and probably produces the most skin side effects of any systemic drug. It makes the skin fragile, sensitive, and very reactive. Like a topical medication, Accutane has a keratolytic effect on the skin.

Estheticians should never tell a client to stop using a prescription drug. Rather, the

keratolytic
Drugs that work by peeling off the top cells of the epidermis.

keratinocytes
The top cells of the epidermis.

permeable
Skin that is easily penetrated by chemicals and other substances.

erythemic skin
Skin that turns red easily during simple esthetic procedures.

Initial Consultation

Ask estheticians why they have chosen to practice skin care and chances are they will tell you that they enjoy "helping" people. But before you can begin working with clients you must understand what their needs and concerns are.

The initial consultation is the most important interaction you will have with a client. Information gathered at this point will help you define the client's goals and objectives. Begin by having clients fill out an inclusive profile or questionnaire and take time to review this information with them. Note any unusual problems, such as allergies or medical conditions and seek further clarification as needed without being too invasive. You also want to find out the main reason for the visit. Remember that each client is an individual with her own agenda—whether that is age management, acne control, or relaxation. Clients will be looking to you as the professional to find solutions to their concerns. Once you are clear about what a client is looking for, you can work together to develop a strategy for meeting these needs.

The primary goal of the initial consultation is to establish a bond with the client. This is critical to implementing a plan of action and maintaining a long-term committed relationship. Practicing positive communication skills will be key to this effort. This means showing genuine concern and caring, being an empathetic listener, and demon-strating patience and acceptance. These character traits go a long way in terms of building trust and achieving a positive outcome.

You must also be forthright with clients. Answer questions honestly and to the best of your ability. If you do not have the answer don't be afraid to admit your lack of knowledge. We live in a competitive age where consumers have access to a great deal of information. Expect clients to be informed and acknowledge their initiative. This will only enhance your status as a caring professional and it will ensure client satisfaction and retention.

client should be referred back to a physician if a drug is problematic. For a complete list of drugs, their purposes, and their contraindications, see Chapter 18.

Waxing Contraindications

In the process of depilatory waxing, the wax attaches to the skin's surface. Clients using keratolytics are at especially high risk for injury. Removal of the wax may result in blistering, severe erythema, bleeding, and injuries that may cause scarring. Clients using a topical keratolytic, such as Retin-A, on a specific area should not be waxed or exfoliated in that area. A Retin-A user can have her legs waxed, as long as she is not using the drug on her legs.

Prednisone, a systemic drug often used to treat autoimmune diseases such as lupus, is another drug that can cause systemic side effects and is also contraindicated for waxing.

In general, if a client indicates that she takes any sort of systemic drugs or has any serious medical conditions, estheticians should be very careful using treatments and recommending products. Waxing, in particular, is a service that may cause problems for clients using multiple drugs, being treated for autoimmune disease, or using drugs to treat skin conditions.

Clients with AIDS and Immunodeficiencies

It is illegal to ask clients if they have AIDS or if they are HIV positive. People with AIDS and HIV are protected under the Americans with Disabilities Act (PL 101–336). Some clients may confide in an esthetician that they are HIV positive. This is, of course, a confidential matter, because there are still many prejudices against individuals with HIV and AIDS. If proper precautions are taken (see Chapter 5), estheticians should have no concerns about treating clients with AIDS and HIV.

Persons who are HIV positive frequently experience unusual skin problems. These include severe seborrheic dermatitis, *molluscum contagiosum*, flat warts, flares of herpes I and II, shingles, and unusual rashes. Always refer clients with any of these symptoms to a physician.

SAFETY*Tip*

- Do not perform any treatment when you know a client should avoid a certain type of procedure.
- A systemic drug such as Accutane affects the skin of the entire body. Do not perform waxing anywhere on the body of a client using this drug.

Other immunodeficiencies are caused by chemotherapy or immunosuppressive drugs prescribed after organ transplants or for other medical reasons. Clients with immunodeficiencies are more likely to experience infections and reactions, so treatments should be kept simple and nonstimulating.

Furthermore, clients with cancer may have restrictions on various skin care services, especially massage techniques. In this case, estheticians should contact a client's physician to obtain permission to treat and to find out if there are any specific contraindications. These can vary depending on the type of cancer and the type of treatment.

Note that the National Cosmetology Association offers specialty training in the *Look Good, Feel Better* program for cancer patients. This program teaches cosmetologists, estheticians, and nail technicians techniques used to treat esthetic problems experienced by cancer patients.

Hepatitis

People who have active cases of hepatitis, a disease that causes inflammation of the liver, should not be treated without specific written direction from a physician. On the other hand, some people are hepatitis carriers, which means they do not have the disease, but carry it and may infect others. Carriers may be treated as long as sanitation and aseptic techniques are followed.

Previous Skin Problems

Eczema, **psoriasis**, and seborrheic dermatitis are common skin disorders that clients may indicate they have had or are currently experiencing. All of these conditions tend to be **chronic**, or ongoing. Estheticians should ask whether the client has experienced these conditions on the face. Seborrheic dermatitis

prednisone
A systemic steroid often used to treat autoimmune diseases such as lupus.

eczema
An inflammatory disease of the skin that can cause lesions and painful itching.

psoriasis
A skin disease that causes scaly, red patches on the scalp, lower back, elbows, knees, and chest.

chronic
An ongoing condition.

is the most common disorder to affect the face. In clients who may occasionally experience flares of dermatitis seborrheica, most stimulating treatments should be avoided, as should heavy creams, fragranced products, and intensive massage. Clients with a history of eczema or psoriasis tend to have reactive skin. It is best to treat their skin as you would treat sensitive skin.

Other Medical Problems and Contraindications

Numerous medical problems exist that are not discussed here. Below are some of the more common conditions that affect clients more frequently.

Asthma

Asthma is a chronic inflammatory disease of the lungs, affecting breathing. Estheticians should consider whether to expose a client with asthma to steam during treatment. They should also ensure that a treatment table is properly positioned so that a client's breathing is not impaired.

Lupus

Lupus has two classifications: lupus erythematosus and discoid lupus. Both affect the skin. For more specific information on these two diseases, refer to Chapter 17. Patients with lupus often experience overreaction to treatments. Electrolysis, extraction, waxing, electrical stimulation, and exfoliation should be approached with caution. Many patients with lupus use systemic steroids to control the immune system's overreactions. These patients may experience edema and sometimes acne symptoms as a side effect of steroid treatment.

There is no real rule of thumb regarding the esthetic treatment of patients with lupus. Many clients whose disease is under control respond normally to esthetic treatment and find it very beneficial. Again, it is a good idea to speak with a client's doctor about possible contraindications and necessary precautions.

Fever Blisters and Cold Sores

As long as you follow proper sanitary precautions, a client with **herpes simplex** should not be an issue. Clients with a history of herpes simplex lesions may be sensitive to any stimulating treatment, including microdermabrasion, AHA treatments, and Jessner's exfoliation. These procedures could be stimulating enough to cause a herpetic flare-up. If a client has a history of herpes simplex and wishes to have these types of treatments, estheticians should refer the client to their physician for **prophylactic** (preventive) treatment using antiviral drugs. The client should take the preventive drug for at least one to two weeks before the stimulating treatment is administered.

Chronic Headaches

Persons with chronic headaches may have a **neurological** disorder that affects the nervous system and nerve tissue, which operate by sending small bioelectric charges. Application of any type of electrical modality can aggravate the condition. Therefore, it is best to avoid electrical therapy on clients who experience chronic headaches.

High or Low Blood Pressure

Clients with high blood pressure are more likely to have redness of the face, couperose, and facial swelling. There are no specific contraindications for facial treatment, but heat and stimulants should be avoided, as they would for any skin with redness problems. Clients with high or low blood pressure should avoid body wraps and other body treatments that involve wrapping the body or raising body temperature.

Chronic Blood Disorders

This category includes many different problems, but diseases such as **hemophilia**, in which the blood does not clot normally, are more likely to affect treatment. Other clients may suffer from blood that clots too easily and may be taking blood-thinning drugs such as Coumadin. These types of conditions may cause unpredictable bleeding during routine procedures. Estheticians should check with a client's physician about treating these clients.

"Please list any other health problems."

Asking for nonspecific health problems ensures that a client has told you everything that might be of concern in determining the

---

herpes simplex
A fever blister or cold sore caused by a virus.

prophylactic
Preventive.

neurological
Relating to the nervous system.

hemophilia
A disease in which the blood does not clot normally.

best treatment. Clients occasionally list a condition that is not included among the specific conditions included on the form but may be important.

"Do you have acne or frequent blemishes?"

This is an important question, particularly if a client experiences frequent breakouts but has clear skin at the first treatment. Many clients check yes for this question. In this case, estheticians should discuss the client's history of acne and determine what measures have been taken to control breakouts. The client may have tried an assortment of treatments, medical or cosmetic. Estheticians should also ask the client if she has noticed a pattern to the breakouts The answer may indicated hormonal fluctuations. A related question asks how long the client has experienced blemishes. This information enables you to help the client determine the cause of the condition.

"Have you had facial surgery?"

After some experience in the esthetics profession, you will be able to detect quickly if someone has had plastic surgery. This question allows an opening for a discussion about the client's previous surgery experiences, including what skin care was performed presurgery and postsurgery. Note that clients who have had elective cosmetic surgery are generally more skin care savvy and more knowledgeable about esthetics.

Some facial surgery is not elective. Clients may have had reconstructive facial surgery after cancer or another medical issue. This might include laser treatment for vascular lesions, scar revision for burn or car accident survivors, or dermabrasion for postcystic acne. Some postsurgery patients may seek treatment for the esthetic side effects of bruising, swelling, or redness. Refer to Chapter 36 and the Additional Reading section for more information about this type of treatment.

"Have you had skin cancer?"

Some clients indicate that they have had skin cancer. This is not unusual since skin cancer is the most prevalent cancer in the United States.

There are no specific instructions or contraindications for patients with skin cancer unless they have had surgery recently. In this case, treatments should be delayed until the physician has officially released the client.

Despite the lack of treatment restrictions, estheticians should be aware of patients who have undergone treatment for or have been diagnosed with skin cancer. They inevitably have severe sun damage and therefore have other sun damage symptoms, including additional skin cancers, and actinic keratosis, which requires referral back to the dermatologist. During each treatment, the esthetician should carefully observe the client's skin to detect any changes that require a physician's attention.

"Do you experience stress often?"

Everyone from air traffic controllers to retirees mark yes to this question. Stress is an individual perception or actual reaction to a circumstance that places demands on one's nervous system or body, which produces a response. Although a healthy amount of stress makes people productive and life interesting, too much stress affects a person's health and appearance.

Stress has definitely been connected to both acne and rosacea. In acne, stress is thought to stimulate the adrenal gland, which releases adrenaline that helps us cope. The adrenal gland also releases androgen, a male hormone that stimulates the sebaceous gland. This signals a surge of sebum to be secreted into the follicles, which inflames the follicle and aggravates breakouts.

Stress has been observed to affect **rosacea** in many patients. Rosacea is a vascular disorder that is characterized by flushing of the skin with blood. High blood pressure brought on by stress puts pressure on blood vessels. This can cause flushing of the skin, which leads to a flare-up of rosacea.

Continual stress has additional detrimental effects on the skin. We have all seen friends or loved ones who have been under a lot of stress. They look tired, and their skin can look puffy or discolored. The stress of illness causes similar symptoms on the skin.

rosacea
A vascular disorder characterized by flushing of the skin with blood.

While there is no magic cure for stress, many skin care salons and day spas now offer stress-reducing services such as massage, aromatherapy, and yoga classes. Estheticians can also reduce a client's stress by keeping the home care regimen simple or by performing a special facial massage (when appropriate for the skin).

"Do you have any allergies to any cosmetics, foods, or drugs?"

This question informs you of sensitivities or allergic reactions a client may have to cosmetics, foods, or drugs. Estheticians must respect this information. Many individuals have no known allergies, but they may have allergies they have not yet discovered. Thus, there is no way to completely prevent allergic reactions. People with skin that is thin, dry, and turns red easily are more likely to have allergies and are more reactive to irritants. Clients with histories of nasal allergies and asthma are also more susceptible to cosmetic or topical allergies.

Some individuals are allergic to fragrances, the number one cosmetic **allergen**, a substance that causes reactions for certain individuals. Fragranced products can generate numerous problems for these people, so estheticians should have nonfragranced products available for these clients.

Other frequent allergens are preservatives such as imidazolidinyl urea, quaternium-15, and the paraben group—methyl, ethyl, propyl, and butyl paraben. Commonly used in cosmetics, these preservatives kill bacteria that can contaminate products. Most people are not allergic to them. When allergies to products containing these preservatives occur, dermatological testing is the only way to determine the allergen.

Other fairly common allergens include **benzoyl peroxide**, an ingredient with antibacterial properties used in acne medication, the skin-lightening agent hydroquinone, sunscreen chemicals such as benzophenone-3 or PABA (para-amino-benzoic acid), and plant extracts of various sorts. People even have occasional allergies to ingredients such as aloe vera and **chamomile**, a plant extract with anti-inflammatory properties, which are traditionally used as soothing agents.

A common misconception about allergies is that natural cosmetics are less likely to be allergens. However, natural products are actually more likely to be allergens. These products are made from plant extracts, which are groups of chemicals, and it is very hard to determine which chemical is the allergen. In addition, proteins are the reactive components in many allergens. All plants contain proteins, which are probably the causes of fragrance allergies.

Allergies versus Irritants

While an allergy is an individual reaction to a specific product or ingredient, irritants can cause the same reaction in many clients. For example, exfoliants are frequently irritants. These include benzoyl peroxide, AHAs, sulfur, salicylic acid, resorcinol, and even prescription drugs such as tretinoin. Overuse of AHAs will cause peeling and redness in almost any client, but this is not an allergic reaction; rather, it is an irritation.

Allergies versus Acnegenic Reactions

Clients often confuse pimples they get after using a particular product with allergic reactions. These pimples are more likely caused by acnegenic substances, which are ingredients or products that cause follicular inflammation resulting in a flare-up of acne or pimples. For more on acnegenic reactions see Chapter 24.

Food and Drug Allergies

Clients may list drug reactions. These concern estheticians because some topical agents contain drugs. Food allergies may also overlap with cosmetics. For example, clients who are allergic to almonds should never have almond oil or honey-almond scrubs applied to their skin.

Estheticians should note if clients list salicylate allergies or allergies to aspirin. In this case, avoid products containing salicylic acid, such as wintergreen, willow bark, and Filipendula extract. Use caution with sunscreens, as some are salicylates.

Recording the Allergy

Any indicated allergies should be noted boldly in the client's chart and highlighted with a bright colored pen or a red sticker. This serves as a warning for other staff members

---

allergen
A substance that causes an allergic reaction in certain individuals.

benzoyl peroxide
An ingredient with antibacterial properties commonly used to treat acne.

chamomile
A plant extract with clinically proven anti-inflammatory and repairer properties.

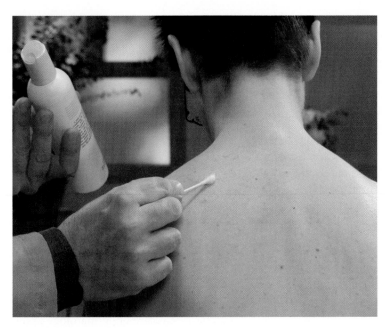

Figure 12–3 A patch test is an important indicator of product sensitivity.

when they assist the client with treatments or retail products. Products containing contraindicated ingredients should be avoided.

General Precautions about Allergies

When a client has a history of many allergies to topical agents, estheticians should initiate special precautions. Perform a **patch test** by applying a small amount of a product behind the ear or on the inside of the arm, or on the part of the skin to be treated. The following day, the client or esthetician should check for any redness or swelling in the area. If there is no redness after 24 hours, have the client apply the product on a small area of the face overnight. If there is still no reaction again after 24 hours, the product can be used in the client's regular program.

Products should be tested one at a time. Despite the effectiveness of the patch test method, there is still no foolproof way of determining allergies (Figure 12–3). Clients may have an allergic reaction at any time to any product, but taking these precautions can prevent most reactions from happening.

"What products do you presently use?"

A client may or may not have had success with the products she is currently using. The answer to this question gives estheticians an idea of the client's current home care program. It provides a wealth of information about a client's habits and her willingness to adapt to a routine, how knowledgeable she is about skin care, and her budget.

For example, if a client is using soap, she probably enjoys the feel of washed skin. An esthetician should recommend a replacement product that produces foam and is easy to rinse off. The client will be more likely to use this type of cleanser.

A client's present skin conditions also indicate the products she uses. If the skin is in great shape, she most likely makes good product choices. If not, which is more likely, she has probably chosen the wrong products for her skin condition or is skipping necessary steps. This gives you plenty of information to assemble a good home care program.

Medical Disclaimer

A **medical disclaimer** is part of the health history form that ensures that the client understands that the treatment she is receiving is for cosmetic rather than medical purposes. The statement also ensures that the client understands that all the information she provides will be kept confidential.

patch test
A test to determine a client's sensitivity to a particular product. A small amount of a product is applied behind the ear or on the inside of the arm and is then checked for a reaction.

medical disclaimer
Part of the health history form that ensures the client understands that the treatment she is receiving is for cosmetic rather than medical purposes.

Salon Policies

Most salons and spas have basic policies listed on the health form. Some salons use an entirely separate form, which is completed at the same time as the health form. This is an agreement by clients that they are fully aware of the salon's business policies concerning no-shows, last-minute appointment cancellations, refund policies, and other house rules. This part of the form makes clients aware of policies from the very first visit.

Screening Consultation

Once a client has completed the health form, an esthetician conducts a short preliminary consultation regarding the answers. You should ask specific questions to clarify the answers. Check to make sure that the client has filled out all sections completely. She must sign the form. If a client is a minor, a parent or legal guardian must provide a signature as well.

If the Client Refuses to Fill Out the Form

Occasionally, a client who is not accustomed to professional skin care services may not understand why you need all this information. Explain that you are trying to provide a complete, professional, and safe service for her, just as her physician or dentist would. Also, explain that certain drugs have contraindications for treatments and that you want to make sure you provide the best treatment possible. Most clients will understand and fill out the form. Clients who still refuse to fill out the form should be politely refused service.

Summary

To ensure the safety of clients, they must complete an initial health analysis form. Health screening is an important procedure to avoid contraindications and to learn more about a client's individual needs and lifestyle. The form asks many questions that inform estheticians about specific treatment information. The form is also the ideal topic of a preliminary consultation, which leads to a thorough analysis, good client communication, and ultimately a more complete and successful skin care program.

Discussion Questions

1. Discuss the value of proper skin analysis. How can this be incorporated into a competitive business plan or strategy? Think about your own personal goals as you approach this task.

2. What are the two most important components of skin analysis? Discuss the best approach to gathering this information.

3. Research the use of health questionnaires in medical skin care or dermatology practices and skin care clinics. How do they differ? How are they the same?

4. Develop a list of commonly known allergens or irritants in products. Find out which agencies or organizations may be helpful in learning more about these topics.

5. Make a list of frequently used terms that imply product safety (for example, "dermatologist tested"). As you do so, develop a dialogue for educating clients on the meanings.

Additional Reading

Boyd, Alan S. 1998. *The Skin Sourcebook*. Los Angeles, Calif.: Lowell House.

Fitzpatrick, Thomas, Johnson, Richard, Wolff, Klaus, Polano, Machiel, and Suurmound, Dick. 1997. *Color Atlas and Synopsis of Clinical Dermatology*. New York: McGraw-Hill.

Fulton, James. 1984. *Dr. Fulton's Step-By-Step Program for Clearing Acne*. New York: Barnes and Noble.

Furman, Rachel. 2000. *Drugs & Cosmetics, Combinations That Can Kill You*. Studio City, Calif.: CRF Publications.

Garrison, Robert, and Somer, Elizabeth. 1995. *The Nutrition Desk Reference*. New Canaan, Conn.: Keats Publishing.

Inwold, D., ed. 2000. *Anatomica*. Willoughby NSW, Australia: Global Publishing.

Kaiser, Jon. 1999. *Healing HIV*. Mill Valley, Calif.: Health First Press.

Kenet, Barney, and Lawler, Patricia. 1998. *Saving Your Skin*. New York: Four Walls Eight Windows.

Lees, Mark. 2001. *Skin Care: Beyond the Basics*. Clifton Park, N.Y.: Milady, an imprint of Delmar Learning, a division of Thomson Learning, Inc.

Leffell, David. 2000. *Total Skin*. New York: Hyperion.

Michalun, Natalia, and M. Varinia Michalun. 2000. *Skin Care and Cosmetic Ingredients Dictionary*. Clifton Park, N.Y. Milady, an imprint of Delmar Learning, a division of Thomson Learning, Inc.

Perricone, N. 2000. *The Wrinkle Cure*. Emmaus, Pa.: Rodale.

Pugliese, Peter. 1991. *Advanced Professional Skin Care*. Bernville, Pa.: APSC Publishing.

Pugliese, Peter. 1996. *Skin Physiology*. Carol Stream, Ill.: Allured Publishing.

Schoon, Douglas. 1994. *HIV/AIDS and Hepatitis*. Clifton Park, N.Y.: Milady, an imprint of Delmar Learning, a division of Thomson Learning, Inc.

Turkington, Carol, and Dover, Jeffery. 1996. *Skin Deep*. New York: Facts on File.

Chapter 13
Skin Analysis

Chapter Objectives

After reading this chapter, you should be able to:

- Explain the concept of the Fitzpatrick Scale.
- Describe the difference between each Fitzpatrick level.
- Describe how to perform an analysis using a Wood's lamp.
- Describe how to perform an analysis using a magnetic light.
- Identify and record analysis findings on chart.

Chapter Outline

Introduction
Skin Analysis Tools
The Analysis Procedure
Record Keeping
Closing the Analysis
Final Review

Introduction

Estheticians need to concentrate on practical observation of the skin. For example, you must understand the structure of a hair follicle and its sebaceous glands, but you must also be able to examine the result of a follicle that is blocked or clogged. Thus, the key to a skin analysis is the visual aspect and the subsequent treatment protocol or plan. The analysis is divided into three categories:

1. Learn to recognize the skin according to the Fitzpatrick Scale.

2. Recognize general skin types.

3. Identify specific skin conditions occurring on the face and with the general skin type

This approach to analysis will help you build a solid method for determining the best approach for selecting an accurate client treatment system and program.

When most estheticians discuss skin typing, they think of oily, dry, or combination skin. When dermatologists discuss skin types, they are referring to a *degree* of hereditary skin coloration (pigment). This ranking of coloration is also representative of a natural tolerance, or lack of tolerance, to the sun and its ultraviolet rays.

The **Fitzpatrick Scale** is a method of skin typing that measures and refers to different skin types' tolerance to the sun's burning rays. Dr. Thomas Fitzpatrick, a renowned dermatologist, developed this scale; hence the typing technique bears his name.

Additionally, both dermatologists and plastic surgeons refer to this scale prior to performing any aggressive peels or light therapies; i.e., the PhotoFacial (Photo Facial is a registered trademark of ECS Medical Systems), laser resurfacing, plastic and corrective surgery, laser hair removal, and varicose vein injections. This information serves as an indicator for determining treatment selection, tolerance level, healing time, and end results.

An esthetician will find this a valuable gauge that assists in determining potential reaction and/or tolerance level associated with facial treatments, especially microdermabrasion, and any other aggressive peel or treatment. It helps in product selection for home care. This is one more tool that adds more credibility to your treatment outcome.

The more natural pigment in the skin, the greater its resistance to sunburn and environmental skin damage. Although dark skin can suffer from both sunburn and sun damage, it has greater resistance to potential damage due to its pigment. The melanin in the skin provides a natural hereditary form of sunscreen. Darker skin types are much less likely to develop sun damage, sun-induced skin cancer, wrinkles, and solar elastosis, a lessening of elasticity in the tissues due to overexposure to sun.

The Fitzpatrick Scale types skin from the lightest, most susceptible to sunburn and sun damage, to the darkest skin coloring, the most resistant to sunburn and cumulative sun damage (Table 13–1). When you analyze skin, you should also note the client's Fitzpatrick skin type (Figure 13–1). Fitzpatrick skin types are referred to with Roman numerals.

Daily sunscreen protection should be worn regardless of coloring. This scale not only indicates sun damage susceptibility, but also serves as a scale of intrinsic sensitivity. While dark skin types can still be sensitive, thinner, type I and II skin types tend to be more reactive to external and topical substances, including exposure to the

Fitzpatrick Scale
A method of skin typing that measures and labels the tolerance of different skin types to the sun's burning rays.

Table 13–1 The Fitzpatrick Scale

Skin Type	Appearance	Reaction to Sun Exposure
Type I	Very fair; red or blonde hair; blue eyes; likely has freckles	Always burns, never tans
Type II	Fair skinned; blue, green, or hazel eyes; blond or red hair	Burns easily
Type III	Very common skin type; fair with any eye or hair color	Sometimes burns, gradually tans
Type IV	Typical Mediterranean Caucasian skin; medium to heavy pigmentation	Rarely burns, always tans
Type V	Mideastern skin types; rarely sun sensitive	Tans
Type VI	Black skin; rarely sun sensitive	Tans well

Figure 13–1a Fitzpatrick Type I—Very fair, red hair, blue eyes, and freckles. Always burns, never tans.

Figure 13–1b Fitzpatrick Type II—Fair skinned, with blue, hazel, or green eyes and blond or red hair. Burns easily.

Figure 13–1c Fitzpatrick Type III—Fair skinned with any color eye or hair color. Sometimes burns, gradually tans.

Figure 13–1d Fitzpatrick Type IV—Typical Mediterranean Caucasian skin; medium to heavy pigmentation. Rarely burns, always tans.

Figure 13–1e Fitzpatrick Type V—Mideastern skin type, rarely sun-sensitive. Tans.

Figure 13–1f Fitzpatrick Type VI—Black skin; rarely sun-sensitive. Tans.

environment, including sun, heat, cold, and wind.

These skin types may also be affected differently by pigmentation disorders. Hyperpigmentation is more likely to affect types IV–VI than the lighter skin types. Certain advanced skin treatments including Jessner's exfoliation (peels), more than 5% benzoyl peroxide, and resorcinol may irritate these skin types and cause or worsen pigmentation. Medically, laser and deep chemical peels are generally reserved for types I–III.

Asian and Hispanic skin types are very susceptible to hyperpigmentation problems. Any injury to the skin can result in hyperpigmentation. Darker skin types produce more melanin than Caucasian skin and are more reactive to stimulation and injuries, including chemical insults from skin care products that are too strong for their skin. Pigmentation resulting from irritation or injury is called postinflammatory hyperpigmentation (PIH).

Skin Analysis Tools

Several tools are available to make a skin analysis easier (Figure 13–2). Two or more of these tools should be employed during the analysis. The most effective devices are your hands, your eyes, and your magnifying lamp. A professional magnifying lamp is critical for examining the skin.

Wood's Lamp

The correct use of a Wood's lamp is essential to performing an accurate skin analysis. The lamp must be used in a dark room. Observations through a Wood's lamp show different skin colorations and reveal a great deal about the skin (Table 13–2). For instance, patches of intrinsic oiliness or sun damage that may not be visible to the naked eye appear under the lamp. Thus, it should be used during every facial to note any new changes in a client's skin.

The colors and descriptions mentioned in Table 13–2 are general. Observation with a Wood's lamp is only part of the entire skin analysis. The crucial point is for the esthetician to make the assessment based on visual assessment, a health form, and conversation with the client.

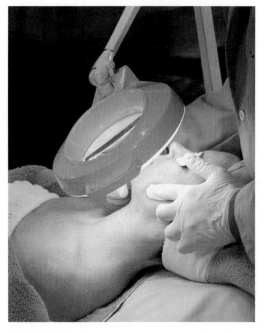

Figure 13–2 A lighted magnifying lamp helps estheticians observe many potential skin problems.

Magnifying Lamp

If a magnifying lamp (also called a mag lamp, mag light, or loupe) is your only tool besides visual analysis, it is used to assess all aspects of the skin. However, the mag lamp is most useful to observe overall skin texture and visible conditions. It helps estheticians observe:

- pore structures: enlarged, tight, and/or clogged
- lines: light dehydration, sun damaged fine lines, and/or deeper lines and wrinkles

Table 13–2 The Wood's Lamp

Skin	What You See
Normal to combination skin	Overall bluish cast
Dehydration to dryness	Color changes from bluish to violet to very deep purple in dehydrated or dry areas
Oiliness	Pinkish to orange dots in oily areas around the nose, chin, and forehead
Hyperpigmentation	Brownish to dark patches in cheeks, forehead, chin, etc., or where lesions have left marks
Hypopigmentation	White patches where pigmentation would normally show darker casts
Other skin disorders	Bright or neon yellow: • Bacteria such as herpes or fungi • Clients on a course of antibiotics or other drug therapy • Lipstick or other cosmetics

- telangiectasia: couperose, distended capillaries, and/or diffused redness
- lesions: comedones, acne, pigmentation, etc.

Skin Scanner

A skin scanner is a great tool for retailing purposes. Because it readily shows skin problems, it is often used at cosmetic counters to help increase the sales of sunscreens, antiaging products, and antioil products. Although it may be considered a gimmick by some people, when used professionally and responsibly, a skin scanner may actually convince a client to take better care of the skin because it clearly shows skin problems.

The Hands

An esthetician's hands are another tool for skin analysis. The hands can assess the texture, temperature, and thickness of the skin. While it may seem like an instinctive tool that is not really part of the analysis process, the eyes and hands are actually some of the greatest and most effective implements for determining skin type and condition.

The Analysis Procedure

The esthetician must be alert to anything that suggests contraindications for treatment or products at all times during a client's appointment. The formal analysis procedure, however, should progress in stages.

Table 13–3 Visual Checklist

• How does the makeup appear? Is it cracked, flaky, or smooth?
• Does the skin appear tight and firm overall?
• What is the condition of the neck and décolleté?
• Is the eye area dry, and does it show dark circles or tightness and wrinkles?
• Are there deep folds around the mouth area?
• Caucasian: What is the skin's color: pink and healthy or flushed? Does it show signs of environmental damage?
• Non-Caucasian: Are skin tones even? Are there areas of hyperpigmentation? Scars?
• Acne: What are the types and locations of lesions, if any?
• Men: Are there in-grown hairs and irritation on the face or neck? Is there a recessed hairline with thicker or pinkish skin (indicative of sun damage)?

Step 1: Initial Impression

A skin analysis begins when a client arrives at the salon or spa and continues until her departure. First, note the client's appearance: clothing, hairstyle and hair condition, makeup, skin (if not wearing makeup), and overall demeanor and gestures. Also observe the arms and hands. This is part of the analysis.

Step 2: Light Cleansing

Once a client is situated after arrival, the skin should be observed prior to cleansing. This informs estheticians about how well the client is performing a skin care routine at home. First, observe the skin when the client is in the facial chair (Table 13–3). After a light cleansing, observe the skin again. Two cleansing options that do not disturb skin other than gently removing surface makeup and debris are described below.

Option 1: The Quick Cleanse
The quick cleanse begins with removal of all makeup to eliminate all pigmented products from the skin's surface. Eye makeup remover is used for eye makeup and lipstick; then a cleansing lotion is used to remove face makeup. Next, moistened eye pads are applied to protect the eyes from the bright light. The analysis proceeds with a mag light and Wood's lamp.

Option 2: The Full Cleanse
The full cleanse is the same as the quick cleanse, except that it adds a step. Following the removal of makeup, the face is sprayed or swiped with facial freshener to remove all traces of residue left from the cleansing. This step eliminates oily residues left on the skin.

Step 3: Observation

After cleansing, estheticians observe the skin using the tools presented in this chapter. They then continue to observe the client's skin throughout the rest of the facial procedure, especially during a client's first appointment. It is possible to notice different information about the skin between the visual analysis and actual hands-on performance of the facial. Note the following questions:

- How does the skin respond when applying each product, beginning with the cleanser and exfoliation products such as the gommage or enzyme?

- How does the skin respond when you apply pressure during the massage?

- How does the skin appear upon completion of the facial?

- As an esthetician becomes familiar with a client's skin, these points help her recommend an ongoing selection of skin correction and home care products.

Keep in mind that a client's first appointment is very important. While all appointments have time constraints, first-time customers need at least 15 extra minutes. This is a critical process in building client confidence and repeat business. Chapter 16 discusses how to conclude a facial session with a postconsultation and home care recommendation.

Record Keeping

Charting and accurate record keeping are the responsibilities of the esthetician. **Charting** is a term in the health care industry that means to record information regarding a patient or client. Whether you work in a salon, spa, or medical office, keeping accurate client records is mandatory. Many professionals fail to reach their optimum potential because they downplay the importance of analysis and charting. But no one can remember all the details about every client.

A chart initially contains health forms, analysis forms, and treatment forms. It also notes what was performed on a client as well as any reactions or other important notes. These written records provide information for other practitioners when you are not available or the client calls during your absence to discuss a concern.

Quality analysis charting objectives include:

- providing legal documentation on a client.

- obtaining a thorough health analysis in order to evaluate the skin and the appro-

priateness of performing a treatment.

- presenting complete details on a client's skin type and current skin conditions.

- documenting the client's home skin care regimen.

- serving as a point of reference when recommending skin care programs.

Each business will most likely develop custom forms to fit its clientele and types of services. This textbook provides generic forms so you can get accustomed to them. While charting may seem overwhelming in the beginning, it becomes second nature after a while. Furthermore, it actually helps you create better programs for your clients. It is an ongoing progress report on your clients and your work.

Chapter 12 presented a confidential health analysis form that is to be completed by the client during a first visit. That form begins an analysis because it provides written information about a client's general health.

This chapter includes a detailed skin analysis form (Figure 13–3). When first learning facial analysis, you may not be able to fill it out completely. But as you learn to identify more skin conditions, the analysis form will make more sense.

The treatment record form is completed after a facial (Figure 13–4). Its purpose is to the keep a continuous record of skin care treatments. Like other forms, it should be kept in a client's chart.

charting
A term in the health care industry that means to record information regarding a patient or client.

Closing the Analysis

A great skin analysis—and the resulting client retention—is based on three simple concepts:

1. Inform the client of what you accomplished in the treatment.

2. Tell the client what you plan to accomplish in the next appointment. State your plan of action and then record it.

3. Don't just sell products. Educate the client about the importance of using home care that conforms to the goals established in the spa or salon treatment.

SKILLS **FOR** SUCCESS

Client Record Keeping

In the service industry there is nothing more important than building client relationships. However, this is easier said than done, particularly if you are employed by a huge organization that services a large volume of clients. How will you remember that Mrs. Jones is allergic to products with bee pollen, cannot tolerate an enzyme peel for more than 4 minutes, and has a dog named Sue that she adores? Take heart; there are several methods that you can employ to save your human computer system from crashing at the worst possible moment.

If you are like many of us you may become overwhelmed at the thought of having to remember lots of details. Practicing good record keeping habits can help eliminate this frustration and at the same time improve customer satisfaction.

Whether you use a computer system or employ a simple note card, taking time to jot down the important facts about a client's visit can make a big difference in terms of building business. Client record keeping should not be confused with a client history intake or questionnaire. Record keeping refers to a method for taking personal notes that helps you do your job better. You should set aside several minutes after each client to perform this task while the information is fresh in your mind. It is often difficult to jog the memory after a long day's work.

Good record keeping can help you

- analyze sales and service.
- track customer trends.
- measure your own performance.
- remember specific dates or anniversaries.
- note a client's special likes or dislikes.
- make clients feel special.
- assist in performing marketing-related tasks.

If your workplace does not provide a specific form for client record keeping, create one of your own and categorize your customers in a special file box. Alphabetical order works best and can save you the time of searching through months or days of paperwork.

Always record

- client's name.
- date of visit.
- products used.
- treatments performed.
- special likes/dislikes.
- a personal anecdote.
- client's special dates; e.g., birthdays.

Ideally, you should be able to enter all information in a computer system that helps you look at information in an organized way. But whatever method you choose, the important thing to remember is to use the information that you worked hard to record. Always take time to review your previous notes before meeting with a client. A simple technique that works well is to organize your notes for the entire workday the night before. Clients will appreciate the special effort you take to show them this personal attention. This will go a long way in building the client relationship and your sales.

Skin Analysis

First Name _____ Last Name _____ Date_____

Performed by _____

1 - PERIPHERAL VASCULAR SYSTEM & ITS DISORDERS
- ❑ Normal _____
- ❑ Erythrosis (permanent redness) _____
- ❑ Couperose (vascular & follicular dilation) _____
- ❑ Telangiectasis (dilated capillaries) _____
- ❑ Cyanosis (bluish/purple coloration) _____
- ❑ Rhinophyma (bulbous nose) _____
- ❑ Erythema (intermittent redness) _____
- ❑ Angioma (red round swelling) _____
- ❑ Telangiectatic wart _____

SKIN ABSORPTION
Winter: ❑ Poor   ❑ Good   ❑ Very Good
Summer: ❑ Poor   ❑ Good   ❑ Very Good

KERATINIZATION
- ❑ Normal
- ❑ Hypokeratinization
- ❑ Furfur (flakes)
- ❑ Squama (scale)
- ❑ Pityriasis (slight patchy)
- ❑ Eczema (crusty inflammation)
- ❑ Psoriasis (open scaled papules)
- ❑ Ichthyosis (fishlike scales)
- ❑ Keratosis senilis(dry brown spot)

2 - LIPID SYSTEM & ITS DISORDERS
- ❑ Normal secretion: Regions(s) _____
- ❑ Little secretion: Region(s) _____
- ❑ Very little secretion: Region(s) _____
- ❑ Excess secretion: Region(s)_____
- ❑ Seborrheic (oily)_____
- ❑ Asphyxiated (dull, accumulation of keratin) _____
- ❑ **Acneic**
- ❑ Many comedones
- ❑ Macula: Region(s) _____
- ❑ Nodules: Region(s) _____
- ❑ Papules: Region(s) _____
- ❑ Pustules: Region(s)_____
- ❑ Papule-pustules: Region(s) _____
- ❑ Vesicula: Region(s)_____

ERUPTION PATTERN
❑ Few   ❑ Many   ❑ Intermittent   ❑ Permanent

Acne Grade
Grade 1: _____
Grade 2: _____
Grade 3: _____
Grade 4: _____
Medically treated? ❑ Yes ❑ No
Prescribed medications _____
Appearance of skin prior to removing make up _____

3 - SKIN HYDRATION
- ❑ Normal hydration
- ❑ Skin-deep dehydration
- ❑ Superficial dehydration
- ❑ Wrinkles Region(s) _____
- ❑ Furrows: Region(s) _____

SKIN SENSITIVITY
- ❑ Normal
- ❑ Reactive
- ❑ Hyperreactive
- ❑ Demography (pressure)
- ❑ Known allergies _____

Intolerant to _____
Pruritus (Itching) _____
Burning sensation _____
Duration of symptoms _____

SKIN THICKNESS
❑ Fine   ❑ Slightly thick   ❑ Thick

GRAIN OF SKIN—Pore size
- ❑ Very fine (not apparent)
- ❑ Fine (visible)
- ❑ Moderate (more visible)
- ❑ Apparent - Severe (very apparent – enlarged)

SKIN TEXTURE
- ❑ Smooth
- ❑ Rough
- ❑ Granular

SKIN TONE
❑ Firm   ❑ Mild lack of tone   ❑ Severe loss of tone

4 - COMPLEXION & PIGMENTATION DISORDERS
- ❑ Milky
- ❑ Olive
- ❑ Reddish
- ❑ Pinkish
- ❑ Slightly amber
- ❑ Amber
- ❑ Yellowish
- ❑ Black
- ❑ Melanocytic nevus (birthmark)
- ❑ Senile lentigo (liver spot)
- ❑ Dark circles (eyes)
- ❑ Chloasma (pregnancy mask)
- ❑ Ephelis (Macula solaris, freckles)
- ❑ Vitiligo (nonpigmented patches)
- ❑ Fair

❑ Other pigmentary spots: _____

Figure 13–3 The skin analysis chart (continued on p. 10).

5 - TAN AND PHOTO TYPES

Phototype	Complexion	Erythema Potential	Tanning Potential	Check
I	Creamy	Always burns easily	Never tans	
II	Light	Always burns easily	Tans slightly	
III	Light/Matte	Burns moderately	Tans gradually	
IV	Matte	Seldom burns	Always tans well	
V	Brown	Rarely burns	Deep tan	
VI	Black	Never burns	Deeply pigmented	

6 - SKIN DISORDERS

❑ None ❑ Nodules ❑ Phlyctena (blister)
❑ Chapping ❑ Eschar (scab) ❑ Excoriation (scratch)
❑ Ulcers ❑ Furuncle (boil ❑ Carbuncle (large boil)
❑ Scars ❑ Cheloids ❑ Stretch marks

7 - SKIN EXCRESCENCES (Growths)

❑ None ❑ Nevus epidermal (mole) ❑ Pigmented hair
❑ Melanocytic nevus (birth mark) ❑ Molluscum pendulum

8 - FATTY INCLUSIONS

❑ None ❑ Milium
❑ Sebaceous cyst ❑ Closed comedones
❑ Open comedones

9 - HAIR SYSTEM

❑ Normal down ❑ Abundant down ❑ Sparse hair
❑ Abundant hair ❑ Hypertrichosis ❑ Folliculitis

Figure 13–3 *(continued).*

Final Review

After each skin analysis, an esthetician should reflect on the following points:

- What did you accomplish today? Be specific.
- What will you do to improve the skin next time?
- What should the client do at home?

Summary

There are three levels of gathering information about the skin. The first is determining its Fitzpatrick type, which has to do with the skin's response to the sun. The next level of information determines its type from a genetic point of view. Final data include the conditions that may fluctuate during environmental changes, or originate from a

Date _____ Esthetician _____	**Comments:**
Today's treatment _____	
Cleanser _____	
Toner _____	
Exfoliation _____ Time _____	
Extraction? ❑ Yes ❑ No _____	
Steam? ❑ Yes ❑ No How long? _____	
High frequency? ❑ Yes ❑ No	
Galvanic? ❑ Yes ❑ No	
Ampoule? ❑ Yes ❑ No What? _____	
Mask? What? _____ Time _____	
Moisturizer? What? _____	
Sun Block SPF _____	

Figure 13–4 The treatment record.

systemic disorder. Systemic means relating to the entire bodily system. For example, manifestation of a visual condition on the skin, such as a breakout, may have to do with what is happening inside the body. In this case it is the activity inside the follicle with an over activity of sebaceous secretions. This may be a result of increased hormonal activity (systemic condition).

A thorough skin analysis is a critical first step in determining the course of action for a client. It not only provides detailed information for choosing the correct skin treatment, but it also helps estheticians recommend a home care regimen. During the analysis, the skin is observed, cleansed, and inspected using tools such as a Wood's lamp, magnifying lamp, or skin scanner. The observations are then noted in the client's chart.

Discussion Questions

1. What is the Fitzpatrick Scale and how is it used by estheticians? By plastic surgeons? By dermatologists?

2. Create a color chart or pyramid associating basic skin types or conditions typically indicated by the Wood's lamp.

Keep this near your lamp until you are able to automatically make these associations.

3. Provide a detailed approach to using the magnifying lamp and/or Wood's lamp. Include the basic differences between the two tools, and how you could use them in combination.

4. How are the esthetician's hands used in analyzing skin types and conditions?

5. How do charting and record keeping help the esthetician in conducting skin analyses? Research the cost of preprinted and computerized materials used for this purpose.

6. Explain the benefits of the quick cleanse and the deep cleanse procedures when performing an analysis. After conducting analyses using each method, note the pros and cons of each.

Additional Reading

Lees, Mark. 2001. *Skin Care: Beyond the Basics.* Clifton Park, N.Y.: Milady, an imprint of Delmar Learning, a division of Thomson Learning, Inc.

The Facial

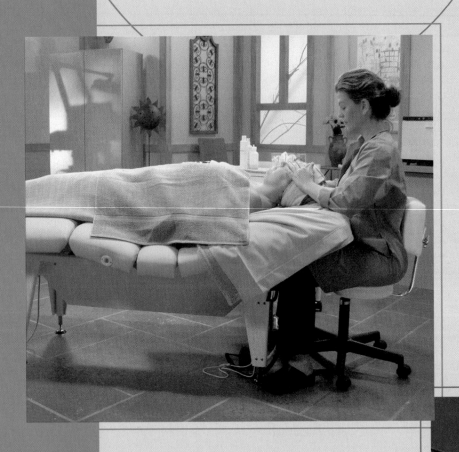

PART V

Part Outline

Chapter 14   Anatomy of a Facial

Chapter 15   Men's Facials

Chapter 16   Postconsultation and Home Care

With today's frenetic lifestyle and changing environment, our bodies are challenged by stress, and our faces serve as a billboard for our health and well-being. Other people see the skin on our faces every day. Maintaining our skin's maximum health not only contributes to its longevity, but improves our general appearance. Regular facials accomplish this maintenance. Deep cleaning, massage, the application of special ingredients, and sun care all contribute to this process.

Part V begins with an introduction to all aspects of the facial. The basic products used in facials are defined, along with their functions, as is the information needed to select a product system for clients. This discussion is then followed by a detailed explanation of the seven phases of a facial, and by the classical methods of facial massage. Step-by-step sequences are presented for the three basic facials, designed for each of the three skin types—normal, normal/combination, and dry/dehydrated skin—and the procedure for a minifacial.

The next chapter addresses skin care for men, an area often overlooked, and contains a chapter with step-by-step instructions for a men's facial. Part V concludes with a chapter on the important closing consultation, the recommendation of a home-care regimen, and following up with first-time clients.

Chapter 14
Anatomy of a Facial

Chapter Objectives

After reading this chapter, you should be able to:

- State the factors used to choose product lines for clients.
- Identify the information an esthetician must know about product lines.
- Explain the functions of basic facial products.
- Describe the benefits of a facial.
- Identify each step of a facial and explain the reason for each.
- Explain the benefits of facial massage.
- Describe the different types of massage.
- Describe the techniques of classical massage.
- Explain the difference between normal/combination and dry/dehydrated skin.
- Identify the three different basic facials and how they differ.
- Describe the basic home regimen following a facial.
- Understand what a minifacial is and when it is used.
- Perform a complete basic facial.

Chapter Outline

Introduction
Products Used in Facials
General Facial Steps
Facial Massage
The Basic Facial
The Minifacial

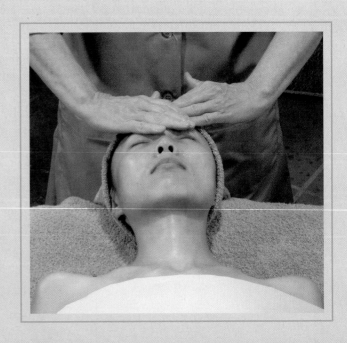

Introduction

When learning about facials, you must first memorize the steps, then master the techniques with your hands (Figure 14–1). As you progress from basic to more advanced treatments, the protocol will change depending on the steps of the corrective treatment. All facial treatments begin with a cleansing and exfoliation, unless otherwise directed. A session is completed with a moisturizer and sunblock. Advanced facial treatments require correct preparation, which also includes a thorough cleansing.

- Regular facials benefit the skin in many ways, including the following:

- The skin is deeply cleansed and exfoliated.

- Blood and lymph circulation is increased, helping to remove impurities.

- The skin is toned and relaxed.

- Numerous performance treatments support and correct skin conditions, including couperose, dry, oily, alipidic, atonic (lacking tone), and dehydrated skin.

- They are considered a preventive measure against prematurely aging skin.

- Estheticians are skin specialists and advisors on the care of the skin (Figure 14–2). They instruct clients on the choices in facials and home skin care regimens. Clients can save money because they are not purchasing every new hype or trend. Rather, they get a regimen customized for their skin.

Products Used in Facials

Most professional skin care manufacturers make products that fit logically into systems that contain targeted ingredients to serve various skin types. They also produce specialized serums, concentrates, and masks that focus on correcting certain skin conditions. For example, if a system is designed for very sensitive skin that is considered couperose, then the selected product components help to calm the skin and address the couperose skin condition. For an acne skin condition, products may contain components that are

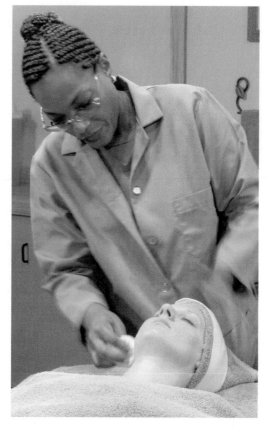

Figure 14–1 It is important to master each of the steps and techniques when learning about facials.

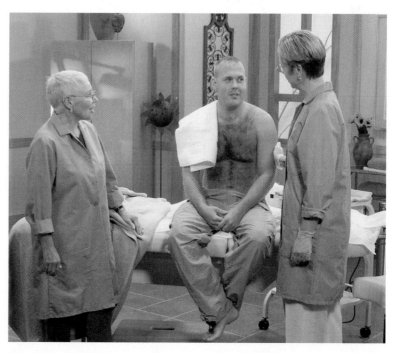

Figure 14–2 Taking time to talk with the client before beginning any treatment will help you determine the client's needs.

Client Retention

There is a lot of competition in the skin care industry today. Skin care clinics and day spas must work hard to attract clients and even harder to retain them once they come through the door. It is up to the salon or clinic owner to bring business in and set the mood or tone of the environment. However, as a service provider you play an important role in maintaining the client relationship.

We live in an age of information. Thanks to numerous technological advancements, we can now access and process important information that allows us to target clients more effectively. But collecting information that helps us to understand the needs and wants of the consumer is futile unless we use it to develop a mutually satisfying relationship.

In today's fast-paced and often impersonal business world many companies are looking to develop a long-term relationship with the consumer. Establishing a real and lasting personal relationship is key to building a clientele in the esthetics industry. The good news is that estheticians are in a prime position to encourage and promote this effort.

Once you have established a positive working relationship with your clients the real challenge begins—keeping them. While there may be a number of reasons why clients initially choose to come to you for service (e.g., convenience, price) there are two main reasons they come back: they respect your professional expertise, and they benefit from the skin care services you provide. Keeping this in mind, let us review several important rules of behavior to keep clients coming back.

1. Avoid becoming complacent.

Estheticians must continually practice quality control. Learn to focus on the needs of the customer and improve your method of delivering or meeting these needs. Clients are paying for your expertise. They expect you to be knowledgeable and professional. This means that you must work hard to keep up with new techniques and methods. You must also practice good business habits. Maintain a professional appearance and environment at all times. Demonstrate your personal commitment to the profession by practicing good skin care habits. Be punctual and pleasant and keep your room clean. If ambiance is lacking infuse your personal work space with candles, music, and pleasant aromatherapy.

2. Give clients what they want.

Clients want skin care programs that are tailored to their unique and individual needs. Listen and respond to these needs. Use consultation time wisely to find out what the client hopes to achieve and determine whether their expectations are reasonable. Let clients know that you are invested in helping them to attain their goals and that you will use your professional expertise to make appropriate adjustments as needed. Avoid disappointment—be clear about company policies, such as cancellations and returns.

3. Make each client feel special.

Consider treating each client as if he or she were a special guest coming to visit your home for the first time. Practice good communication skills, making sure your verbal tone and body language are in alignment. Always welcome clients personally with a warm greeting and address them by name. Offer healthy refreshments, such as flavored sparkling water or fresh fruit. Be sure to take time to review the clients' history before they arrive, and make reference to special

Client Retention (continued)

consideration or tidbit of information that the client has shared with you.

4. Practice respectful listening and caring.

Develop a long-term relationship based on mutual respect and trust. This means listening to your clients' concerns and providing services that address these concerns. Make an effort to attend workshops and seminars that address positive ways to communicate and nurture the practitioner and client relationship. Keep the conversation friendly but professional. Clients will be more inclined to confide needs and concerns if they know you can keep a confidence. Be gracious and let clients know you appreciate the opportunity to work with them. Follow up with a personal phone call or note whenever the client begins a new treatment or home care program.

5. Reward good clients.

Make sure your regular clients receive any special offers or discounts that are available. Give them samples of new products to try. Whenever possible give something away. For example, if they have five consecutive facials, arrange to give them the sixth at no cost. If they refer someone else to you, make sure they are rewarded with a special add-on service or discount coupon. Be as accommodating as possible when it comes to scheduling.

Post these rules in a place that will serve as a reminder. Review them often, and reap the rewards of a satisfied clientele. If you don't, you may find yourself spending your time trying to figure out why your clients are not coming back.

---

antiseptic, calming, hydrating, and that help reduce the occurrence of breakouts. For environmentally damaged skin that is mature and dry, components may be highly nourishing to help replenish moisture and help stimulate cellular turnover and renewal. The system may also include ingredients that help combat pigmentation.

After estheticians consider the type and condition of a client's skin, they can choose specialized products that are formulated to address those needs. This simplifies the selection of products for the esthetician and the client because it removes the confusion created by the large number of products available.

Product Positioning

Estheticians work with many age groups, skin types, and conditions. Therefore, they must understand the entire line of products the spa or salon carries, all of the line's systems, and the function of each product within the systems.

An understanding of ingredient chemistry helps the esthetician understand the differences between performance (active) ingredients and their uses. This information, as well as skin type and condition, allows estheticians to understand the systems and positioning of any professional product line. Each line has unique selling points and product names, but these are details. The key is to study the big picture in order to be able to choose products carefully and to be able to provide customers with the correct products. This proper selection results in fewer product returns and more satisfied clients.

Purpose and Function

The first step in understanding a product line is to understand it from a generic standpoint.

Table 14–1 Products and Their Functions

Product	Function
Eye makeup remover	• Dissolves pigmented products around eyes and lips, yet is gentle for delicate eye area • Softens and moisturizes delicate eye area • Nongreasy formulas are good for contact lens wearers
Cleanser	• Dissolves makeup • Dissolves oil and surface impurities • Has nondetergent cleansing ability
Washable or foaming cleanser	• Acts like soap with a foaming cleansing feel • Cleanses skin without the harshness of soap • Is nonalkaline and easy to use
Freshener or toner	• Removes traces of makeup and cleanser • Readjusts the skin's pH level • Refreshes skin to feel completely clean • Provides moisture • Prepares the skin for application of correction fluid or day or night cream
Day cream	• Protects and nourishes the skin • Softens and moisturizes skin • Provides smooth base for subsequent application of makeup
Sunscreen	• Protects the skin from harmful ultraviolet rays • Some contain moisturizers
Night cream	• Nourishes the skin • Feeds special treatment ingredients into the skin during sleep • Softens and moisturizes skin
Mask	• Blankets the skin to provide special moisture and other performance ingredients • Draws and lifts impurities and/or dead cells • Tightens and tones

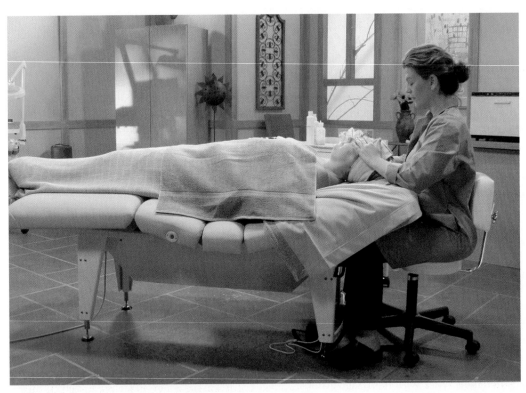

Figure 14–3 The facial process is divided into seven phases.

Table 14–2 Phases of a Basic Facial

Phase I—Light cleansing	• Remove makeup and lightly cleanse the skin.
Phase II—Analysis and consultation	• Use a magnifying light and Wood's lamp to examine the skin. Determine the type of treatment and products to be used.
Phase III—Deeper cleansing and exfoliation, extractions	• Perform a second cleansing with or without brushes; steam at a distance. • Exfoliate; steam may or may not be appropriate for this step. Check the manufacturer's instructions. • Perform extractions. • Use high frequency to disinfect.
Phase IV—Treat and correct	• Apply ampoule with or without galvanic. or • Perform a specialized high-performance treatment, following the manufacturer's instructions.
Phase V—Massage	• Perform massage according to treatment protocols.
Phase VI—Mask	• Apply a mask that is appropriate for the client's skin type and condition.
Phase VII—Completion	• Remove the mask; cleanse away mask residue. Apply an appropriate moisturizer and sunblock.

For example, what is a cleanser and what is its purpose? What is the function of a day cream? Estheticians must be able to explain to their clients the purpose of a product and how it is used. Then they can focus specifically on product lines and choose products to meet their clients' needs.

Table 14–1 shows generic product types and their principle functions. This information is essential for estheticians to know and to be able to explain to their clients.

General Facial Steps

The facial process (Figure 14–3) is divided into seven phases: (1) light cleansing; (2) analysis and consultation; (3) deeper cleansing, exfoliation, and extractions; (4) treat and correct; (5) massage; (6) mask; and (7) completion. Table 14-2 outlines each phase of the facial process and what is involved in each step. As you practice facials, follow this chart to memorize the steps.

This chapter covers the three basic facials, which follow the same phases, outlined in Table 14–2, using different products and techniques. However, in more advanced skin treatments, phases IV, V, and VI can vary, depending on the protocol. In subsequent chapters, other facial treatments are presented with an additional step, client preparation. Other steps may also be added according to the focus of the facial.

Room Setup

Before beginning the seven phases of any facial, the esthetician must prepare the room, whether for the first client of the day or between clients. The necessary steps are listed below.

1. Prepare the facial chair with fresh linens and warm coverings.

2. Fill the steamer with distilled water. When filling the steamer for the first client of the day, turn on the power and preheat it to boiling (no ozone), turn it off, and set it aside. This preheats the water so that it saves time during the actual facial.

3. Prepare the high-frequency machine. Place the glass electrode into the hand device.

4. Prepare the galvanic machine for disincrustation (if this is part of the process for this particular client). Prepare the electrode by placing a small round dampened cotton pad on top of the metal tip and placing the black ring over the cotton pad to hold it in place. Set it aside.

5. Place the face brush into the rotating brush machine.

6. Prepare 3 or 4 rolled face towels dipped in water and aroma essence. Squeeze out the excess water. Place the towels in the hot towel cabinet.

Step by Step The Facial Process

Phase 1: Light Cleansing

Purpose: Perform a light cleansing to remove makeup and surface debris to enable you to do a thorough facial analysis. Remove all makeup thoroughly, especially mascara residue. Mascara residue can continue to dissolve and drip into the eyes, causing irritation. Do not overstimulate the skin at this phase.

Tools and supplies: Sanitized facial sponges or disposable 4" × 4" cotton pads, 2×2s, round cotton eye pads, cotton swabs, stainless steel bowl for water, extractor or cotton swabs, 2 mask brushes, circular palette or condiment cups (stainless steel or plastic), gloves

Procedure

1 Dispense products being used on a circular palette or in condiment cups.

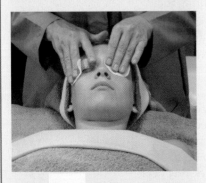

2 Apply eye makeup remover to a moistened cotton pad and gently cleanse the eye area by swiping away from the eye.

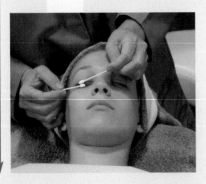

3 For heavy mascara, apply a drop of eye makeup remover on small, dampened cotton swabs. With the client's eyes closed, thoroughly remove the mascara by placing lashes between the swabs and gently swiping down and away from the lash and eye. Change swabs as necessary until all the mascara is removed.

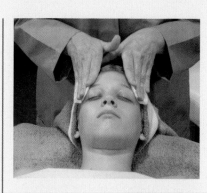

4 Rinse with a 2"×2" moistened pad.

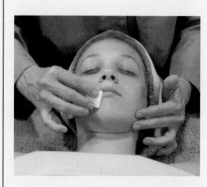

5 Remove the lipstick with makeup remover.

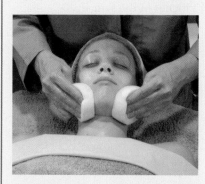

6 Apply a small amount of cleanser, according to skin type, on the entire face and neck. Quickly perform a light cleansing and rinse.

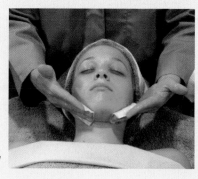

7 Apply freshener to remove excess traces of the cleanser and makeup. Spray or apply the freshener with a moistened cotton pad and wipe.

Phase II: Analysis and Consultation

Purpose: The analysis and brief consultation establish skin type and condition for determining present and future facial treatments. Make mental notes concerning home care products.

Tools and supplies: Moistened eye pads, magnifying light, Wood's lamp, gloves, facial analysis form on clipboard (see Chapter 13)

Procedure

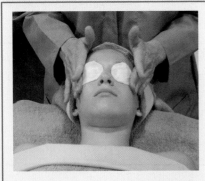

1 Cover the eyes with moistened cotton pads or a similar eye covering.

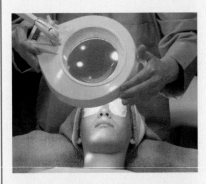

2 Move the magnifying light to within 6–12 inches of the skin.

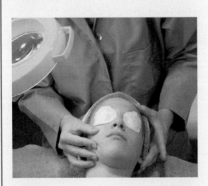

3 Looking through the magnifying light, examine the face, area by area, while touching and determining the texture and pore structure of the skin.

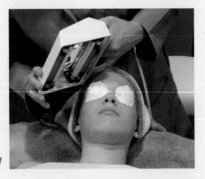

4 Turn the lights off and examine the skin with the Wood's lamp to determine the degree of oiliness, dryness, dehydration, and pigmentation.

5 Briefly converse with the client while analyzing the skin's surface. It may be necessary to ask further questions about the client's skin and health. To facilitate a high-quality analysis, search for as many clues as possible to perform the analysis in a detailed manner. This normally takes about 5–7 minutes, though more experienced estheticians need less time. Make notes on the facial analysis chart if appropriate, then complete the form after the facial.

6 Remove the eye pads and continue your discussion with the client.

Phase III: Deep Cleansing, Exfoliation, and Extractions

Purpose: To continue with a deeper cleansing. This step includes exfoliation to help remove deeper debris, dead skin cells, excess oils, as well as to soften clogged pores and any breakout lesions. Extractions are performed after the cleansing.

Tools and supplies: Brushing equipment, cleanser and exfoliation product (gommage or other)

Procedure—Steamer (Cleansing)

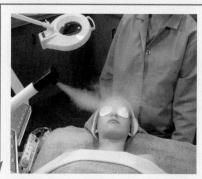

1 Apply eye pads.

2 Turn the steamer switch to on. When the water is boiling, turn on the ozone switch and direct the steamer toward the client's face, keeping it at a distance of about 15 to 18 inches. Adjust accordingly.

Procedure—Brush Machine (Cleansing)

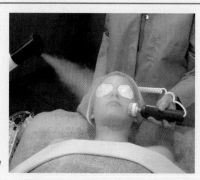

1 Apply deep cleansing solution to the entire face.

2 Dip a small, rotating face brush into water and apply it to the face. Beginning at the neck area, work up the face in a systematic manner.

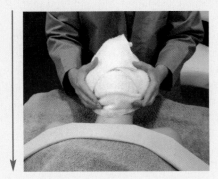

3 Remove the solution thoroughly with warm towels.

4 Proceed with exfoliation.

Procedure—Disincrustation Solution (Exfoliation)

1 Hand the electrode to the client or place it under the client's shoulder.

2 Apply a small amount of solution in the T-zone area—forehead, nose, and chin.

3 Dip the electrode into the disincrustation solution and place it in the center of the forehead

4 Turn on the galvanic current to 0.05 (unless automatic) and adjust it until the client feels a very slight sensation.

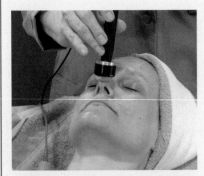

5 Begin rotating and moving the disincrustation electrode across the forehead, down the nose area, and into the chin and jaw areas. Apply it to other areas only if the areas are extremely oily. Perform for approximately 5 minutes.

6 Turn off the galvanic machine and remove the electrodes.

7 Rinse thoroughly with warm towels or pads.

8 Proceed with extractions.

Procedure—Extractions

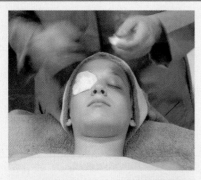

1 Reapply eye pads.

2 Move the magnifying light over the face.

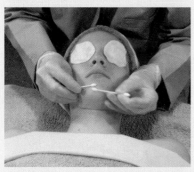

3 Using two cotton swabs or moistened gauze wrapped around the index finger of each hand, begin at the forehead, working down the T-zone and then to other areas of the face and neck, using light pressure. Perform this for approximately 5 minutes. Note that technique is very important. You should not use force, because any discomfort may cause the client to tighten facial muscles. This tension makes extractions more difficult and increases the potential for harming the skin. If more extractions are desirable, the client can return for another deep cleaning.

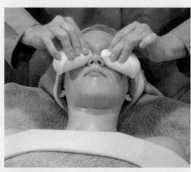

4 Rinse the skin thoroughly with warm water. Pat dry.

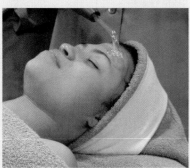

5 Apply high frequency either directly on the skin or over an open 4"×4" gauze. Beginning at the forehead, apply high frequency over the entire face, ending at the chin and jaw areas. Perform for approximately 5 minutes.

6 The skin is now very clean and ready for phase IV.

Phase IV: Treat and Correct

Purpose: To perform a specialized corrective treatment for a specific skin condition. These treatments can include an ampoule that is applied by hand or with galvanic, a collagen sheet, a soft mask, seaweed, or any other high-performance treatment. Follow the manufacturer's instructions.

Tools and supplies: Ampoule

Procedure—Ampoules

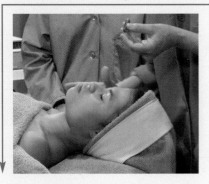

1 Apply the contents of the ampoule to the skin and massage it in until absorbed. Do not perform facial massage at this stage unless indicated in the manufacturer's protocol. Many ampoules and other treatments are water-soluble and must be applied after the skin is totally free of excess oils.

Phase V: Massage

Purpose: A facial massage offers relaxation to the client, stimulates the blood and lymph circulation, stimulates cell turnover, and helps to infuse any ampoule concentrate.

Tools and supplies: Appropriate massage cream or hydrophilic oil (water-soluble oil)

Procedure

1 Use linear movement over the forehead. Slide the fingers to the temples; rotate with pressure on the upward stroke. Slide to the left eyebrow, then stroke up to the hairline, gradually moving hands across the forehead to the right eyebrow.

2 Circular movement: Starting at the eyebrow line, work across the middle of the forehead, and then toward the hairline.

3 Crisscross movement: Start at one side of the forehead and work back.

4 Cheeks: Using a lifting movement, lightly grasp the cheeks between the thumb and forefinger and move from the mouth to the ears, then from the nose to the top of the ears.

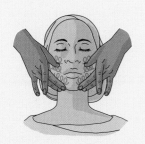

5 Using a rotary movement of the fingers, massage from the chin to the earlobes, from the mouth to the middle of the ears, and from the nose to the top of the ears.

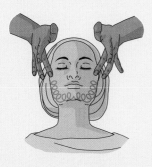

6 Lower cheek movement: Use a circular movement from the chin to the ear and back again.

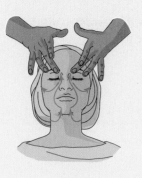

7 Mouth, nose, and cheek movements: Apply light, sweeping movements from the inner corners of the eyes to the outer corners; from the inner corners of the eyes to the chin and back; from the jawline under the ears to the center of the chin and back.

8 Chin movement: Lift the chin, using a slight pressure.

9 Apply light upward strokes over the front of the neck. Use heavier pressure on the sides of the neck in the downward strokes.

10 Using a light tapping movement, work from the chin to the earlobe, from the mouth to the ear, from the nose to the top of the ear, and then across the forehead. Repeat on the other side.

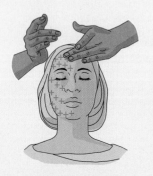

11 Stroking movement: Link and slide fingers to the center of the forehead, then using slight pressure draw the fingers back and forth from temple to temple.

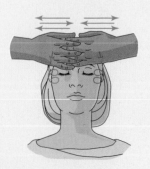

12 Brow and eye movement: Place the middle fingers at the inner corners of the eyes and place the index fingers over the brows. Slide to the outer corners of the eyes, under the eyes, and back to the inner corners, making a complete circle.

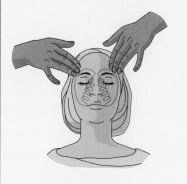

13 Nose and upper cheek movement: Slide the fingers down the nose. Apply rotary movement across the cheeks to the temples and back again, moving gently. Slide the fingers under the eyes and back to the bridge of the nose.

14 Mouth and nose movement: Apply circular movement from the corners of the mouth up the sides of the nose. Slide the fingers over the brows and down to the corners of the mouth.

15 Lip and chin movement: Draw fingers from the center of the upper lip, around the mouth, and under the lower lip and chin..

16 Optional movement: Hold the head with the left hand. Draw the fingers of the right hand from under the lower lip, around the mouth, to the center of the upper lip.

17 Starting at the back of the ears, apply circular movements down the sides of the neck, over the shoulders, and across the chest.

The massage should last approximately 10 to 15 minutes.

Phase VI: Mask

Purpose: Masks add benefit to a facial and differ from a moisturizer or a finishing cream. Masks normally contain concentrated nutrients and other components to help correct the skin. They help soften, moisturize, tone, and tighten the skin. They can also help draw out impurities from oily or problematic skin.

Masks are chosen according to skin type and condition. In a basic facial, it is common to apply a dual mask: an overall mask appropriate for hydrating the dry cheek area and one to treat the oilier T-zone area. Most basic masks have a creamy consistency that remains moist until it is ready to be removed. More advanced masks are applied in a soft form and gradually harden on the skin. These are called thermal masks. They become warm when applied and then cool as they harden. This type of mask helps to infuse beneficial nutrients into the skin. The protocols should be followed precisely for this advanced service.

Tools and supplies: Mask brush, 1 tablespoonful of mask

Procedure

1 Choose a mask that meets the needs of the client's skin.

2 Prepare a small amount of mask (approximately a tablespoonful) in a cup or small bowl and whip until it is fluffy. This allows it to spread easily and reduces product waste.

3 Dip a clean brush into the mask product.

4 Beginning at the neck area, apply a medium thickness (the thickness of a dime) with upward strokes, working up the face to the forehead.

5 Do not apply the mask too near the eyes or nose membranes.

6 Time for 10–15 minutes or according to treatment protocol or the manufacturer's recommendation. Do not let the product dry unless indicated to do so in the manufacturer's instructions.

7 Rinse thoroughly with warm water using a soft rinsing cloth or shammie. Do not overstimulate the skin at this point.

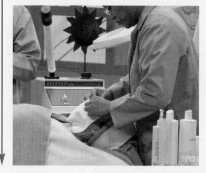

Phase VII: Completion

Purpose: In the final phase, restore and rebalance the skin with a freshener, and moisturize and protect the skin with sunblock. This is also an appropriate stage to speak to the client regarding home skin care. Allow clients a few moments to wake up if they have fallen asleep.

Tools and supplies: Sanitized facial sponges or disposable 4"×4" cotton pads, freshener (toner), eye moisturizer, light moisturizer appropriate to skin type, sunblock

Procedure

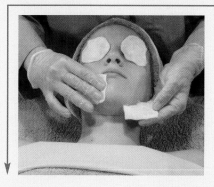

1 Apply a small amount of freshener (toner) to a cotton pad or sponge and swipe the entire face and neck.

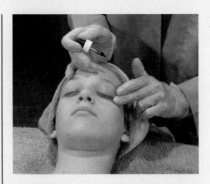

2 Apply a small amount of eye moisturizer around that area.

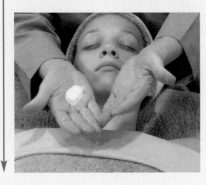

3 Apply a moderate amount of a light moisturizer, according to skin type, to the face and neck.

4 Apply a sunblock.

Figure 14–4 Deciding on the appropriate home care and follow-up products is an important part of the facial process.

Closing/Home Maintenance

This is the appropriate time to discuss the skin treatment with the client, recommend products and their use, and determine when the next treatment should occur (Figure 14–4).

Facial Massage

Massage is one of the oldest therapeutic modalities in the history of medicine, dating back about 3,000 years. It has many known benefits, both physiological and psychological. Therapeutic touch is well recognized and is being taught not only to massage therapists but also to medical professionals. When the hand touches and moves around on the skin, reflex receptors respond by increasing blood and lymph flow. The central nervous system is greatly affected, resulting in a state of relaxation.

Benefits of Massage

Massage is essential to facial treatments because it benefits the client in so many ways. Various techniques are used in salons,

and with practice the esthetician will become expert in giving the best massage for the client's individual needs. A good massage should never be applied too long or too deeply, since that would counteract most of the helpful effects. A proper facial massage can achieve the following benefits:

- relaxes the client
- relaxes facial muscles allowing for better product absorption
- stimulates blood and lymph circulation
- improves overall metabolism, increasing oxygen to tissues
- helps muscle tone
- helps activate sluggish skin
- helps cleanse skin of impurities
- helps slough off dead cells
- helps balance sebum production
- helps with removal of comedones by softening sebum
- helps reduce puffy eye area
- helps relieve muscle tension and pain
- provides a sense of physiological and psychological well-being

A professional facial massage (Figure 14–5) is the difference between having a professional treatment in a salon or spa and a

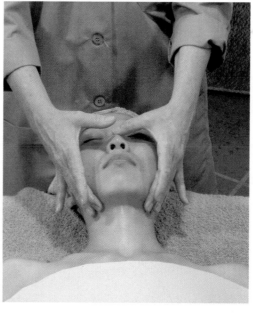

Figure 14–5 A proper massage is the single largest difference between having a professional facial and a home care regimen.

home care regimen. It should not be slighted or overlooked. Facial massage requires consistency in movement. New estheticians must practice until their hand movements are smooth and easily glide from one area to the next.

Hand Mobility

The esthetician's hands should be flexible and relaxed, yet strong, controlled, and supple. Hand mobility is important in maintaining a regular rhythm and regulating the pressure of hand movements. Hand exercises aid in the prevention of repetitive motion disorders, such as carpal tunnel syndrome and other musculoskeletal disorders (MSDs). Many estheticians and therapists are susceptible to MSDs because of repetitive hand movements, muscle and tendon strain, and fatigue due to improper or poor posture. (Chapter 7 describes six of the basic hand-strengthening exercises.)

Types of Massage

There are several different types of massage, based on both body structure and energy. While most massage techniques are based on the classical, or Swedish, massage movements, there are many advanced massage techniques that stimulate and detoxify major organs and nerve centers of the body. Although they require additional training and study, these types of massage are practical for use as part of a facial or body treatment. It is possible to combine many of these message techniques to provide optimal benefit to the client.

- **Acupressure** is the technique of applying gentle but firm pressure to specific points of the body (acupressure points) to release muscle tension and spasm.

- **Shiatsu** is a Japanese technique that combines stretching of limbs with pressure on acupressure points. Many of the motor points on the face and neck are acupressure points and respond to manipulation by the esthetician (Figure 14–6).

- **Reflexology** is a form of massage that manipulates areas on the hands and feet. Although not a part of a facial massage, this type of massage can be used as part of a body treatment.

- **Aromatherapy massage** uses essential oils that penetrate the skin during

---

acupressure
The application of gentle but firm pressure to specific points of the body to release muscle tension and spasm, based on traditional Oriental medicine principles.

shiatsu
A Japanese style of therapeutic massage based on the principles of acupressure.

reflexology
A form of massage that manipulates pressure points on the hands and feet that affect other parts of the body.

aromatherapy massage
Uses essential oils that penetrate the skin during massage movements.

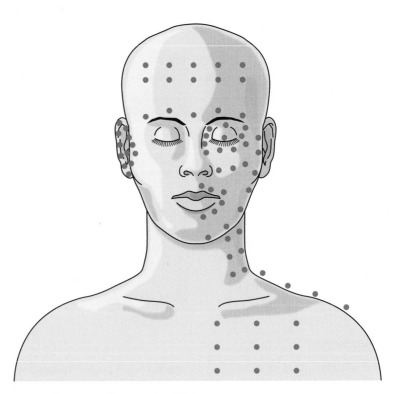

Figure 14–6 Motor points of the face, neck, and chest.

The Brochure or Service Menu

At some point you may be asked to help design a brochure or menu of services. Imagine being able to delight clients with a variety of skin care *choices*. The more choices you offer, the more clients you can recruit. The purpose of a brochure is to help clients understand what services are offered and what options may be available in obtaining these. It should be easy to read and contain all the information necessary for booking an appointment.

The brochure is likely to be one of the most expensive printed materials a skin care clinic or spa will invest in. It is a key presentation piece that determines the way business is conducted. It should be planned thoughtfully, keeping in mind the image you would like to present and who you will be presenting it to, that is, who your customer is. Developing a menu can be fun and exhilarating. As you get caught up in the excitement of deciding what treatments to offer, be sure they are services that *your* clients will be interested in purchasing.

Brochures can be simple or elaborate depending on the size of your business, the size of your staff, and the types of services offered. Full-service skin care clinics or day spas with multiple treatment rooms and water services will naturally have more items to choose from than a one-person operation with one or two rooms devoted exclusively to facial skin care.

But whether a clinic is modest or grand in style, the brochure can still make a big statement. Consider developing a brochure your opportunity to be creative and have fun with it. The important things to consider are clarity, consistency, and legibility.

Developing themes or catchy names for treatments, such as a "Journey into Tranquility" or "Botanical Booster" can make your brochure interesting and turn it into a marketing gem that clients simply will not forget. If you decide to go this route be consistent. Jumping to another style that simply describes a basic facial will be disappointing once you have sparked the client's interest with an imaginative flair.

If you are not creatively inclined, do not despair. Manufacturers often provide interesting names for specialized products and treatments that can be woven into the menu. In either case, you do want to describe treatments in language that the client can understand—do not get caught up in heavy scientific theory.

Establishing a mood or flow to your brochure helps the reader use it more efficiently. Breaking services down to body parts is a good way to do this. Begin with the face and work your way down the body to the fingers and toes. Save special packages or series savings for the end.

A strategically placed logo, thoughtful layout design, legible print type, and visuals will add polish to your brochure. If you can, include attractive photos of the clinic. Photos are a good way to draw the reader into your world, both literally and figuratively.

If space allows, it is good idea to include your vision, or a mission statement, that your customers can identify with. Stating company policy about cancellations, punctuality, pricing, the use of credit cards, and children in the salon are important considerations. Depending on how often you plan to print and review brochure copy, generating a separate price index may be a good idea.

Before going to print, take time to review the details. Do not forget directions, clinic hours, phone numbers, and your address, including e-mail or a Web site if appropriate. Remember to use spell check and always have several proofreaders review the information.

massage movements. These oils are often used during facial massage to promote relaxation.

- **Lymph drainage massage** uses gentle pressure on the lymphatic system to remove waste materials from the body more quickly.

lymph drainage massage
Uses gentle pressure on the lymphatic system to eliminate watery stagnation of tissues from the body and to stimulate the flow of body fluids.

Incorporating Massage During the Facial

A facial massage is always part of a facial. It is performed for approximately 10–15 minutes after the cleansing steps and treatment phase. If the latter step is skipped, the massage immediately follows cleansing.

This chapter contains general guidelines that may vary according to each specialized treatment. A facial massage may change depending on the protocols established by the product manufacturer. The massage stage may also vary for a special massage technique such as the Jacquet (jawk-kay) technique, named for Dr. Jacquet, a French dermatologist, who developed the technique in 1907. Performed for very oily skin, it helps move sebum on the skin's surface, which helps with the cleansing process. During some advanced treatments, massage may not be indicated. Note that massage techniques can be basic or advanced.

Classical Massage Movements

Classical massage movements include effleurage, petrissage, friction, tapotement, and vibration. In all cases, the massage movements chosen by an esthetician should be appropriate to the client's skin type and condition, the amount of treatment time available, and treatment goals.

Effleurage
Effleurage is a soft, continuous stroking movement applied with the fingers (digital) and palms (palmar) in a slow and rhythmic manner (Figure 14–7). The fingers are used on smaller surfaces such as the forehead or face and the palms are used on larger surfaces such as the back or shoulders. Effleurage is often used to open and close most massage sessions and is applied to the forehead, face, scalp, back, shoulders, neck, chest, arms, and hands. It begins to warm and soften the skin while simultaneously

effleurage
First of the classical massage movements, effleurage is a soft, continuous stroking movement applied with the fingers or palms in a slow and rhythmic manner. This movement is often used to open or close the massage session.

petrissage
A deep kneading movement of the skin between the thumb and forefinger. This highly stimulating movement stimulates sebum production, expulses excess oil, and activates sluggish skin.

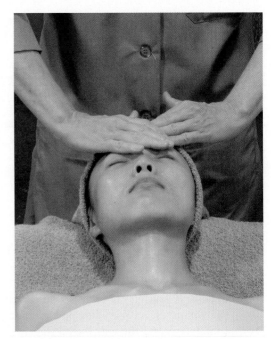

Figure 14–7 Effleurage is a soft stroking movement and is used to open and close most massage treatments.

relaxing the client. To correctly position the fingers for stroking, slightly curve the fingers with just the cushions of the fingertips touching the skin. Do not use the end of the fingertips, since fingertips cannot control the degree of pressure and may scratch the client. To correctly position the palms for stroking, hold the whole hand loosely. Keep the wrist and fingers flexible and curve the fingers to conform to the shape of the area being massaged. Effleurage, the most important of the five movements, is used in conjunction with other types of massage such as shiatsu.

Petrissage
Petrissage is a deep kneading movement that highly stimulates the underlying tissues (Figure 14–8). The skin and flesh are grasped between the thumb and forefinger. As the tissues are lifted from their underlying structures, they are squeezed, rolled, or pinched with a light, firm pressure. Petrissage is performed on the more fleshy parts of the face. The pressure should be light but firm, and the movements should be smooth and rhythmic. Used mostly to stimulate sebum production, it expulses excess oil and activates leathery or sluggish skin.

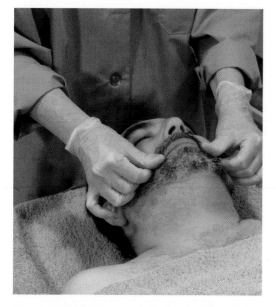

Figure 14–8 Petrissage, a deep kneading of the skin, is used to stimulate sebum production.

Friction

Friction maintains pressure on the skin while the fingers or palms are moved over the underlying structures (Figure 14–9). Friction has a marked influence on the circulation and glandular activity of the skin. Circular friction movements are usually employed on the scalp, arm, and hands. Lighter circular friction movements are generally used on the face and neck.

SAFETY*Tip*

Contraindications for Petrissage
Because of its highly stimulating nature, petrissage is avoided on sensitive skin and on skin with nodules or pustules (in order to prevent spreading infection).

Chucking, rolling, and wringing are variations of friction movements, employed principally to massage the arms or legs. The chucking movement is accomplished by grasping the flesh firmly in one hand and moving the hand up and down along the bone, while the other hand keeps the arm in a steady position. The rolling movement requires that the tissues be compressed firmly against the bone and twisted around the arm or leg. Both hands of the esthetician are active as the flesh is twisted down the bone in the same direction. Wringing is a vigorous movement in which the esthetician's hands are placed a small distance apart on both sides of the arm. While the hands are working downward, the flesh is twisted against the bones in opposite directions.

Tapotement

Tapotement or percussion consists of tapping, slapping, and hacking movements (Figure 14–10). This form of massage is the

friction
Maintains pressure on the skin while the fingers or palms are moved rapidly over the underlying muscle structures. Friction is used to improve circulation and glandular activity of the skin.

tapotement
Often referred to as percussion, tapotement consists of tapping, light slapping, and hacking movements. This form of massage is the most stimulating and should be applied with care and discretion.

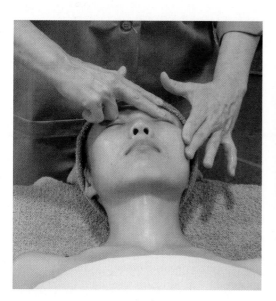

Figure 14–9 Friction massage movements have a marked influence on the circulation and glandular activity of the skin.

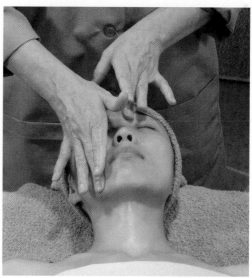

Figure 14–10 Tapotement, a tapping, light slapping, or hacking movement, is considered the most stimulating of the classic movements.

most stimulating and should be applied with care and discretion.

In facial massage, only light, digital tapping should be used. The fingertips are brought down against the skin in rapid succession. This movement is sometimes referred to as a piano movement. The fingers roll and lift without making an actual tapping sound.

Slapping and hacking movements are used to massage the back, shoulders, and arms. In slapping movements, keep the wrists flexible so that the palms come in contact with the skin in light, firm, and rapid slapping movements. One hand follows the other. With each slapping stroke, lift the flesh slightly. Hacking movements use the wrists and outer edges of the hands. Both the wrists and fingers move in fast, light, firm, flexible motions against the skin in alternate succession.

vibration

A shaking movement emanating from the shoulders of the esthetician by rapid muscular contractions in the arms. The ball of the fingertips are pressed firmly on the point of application.

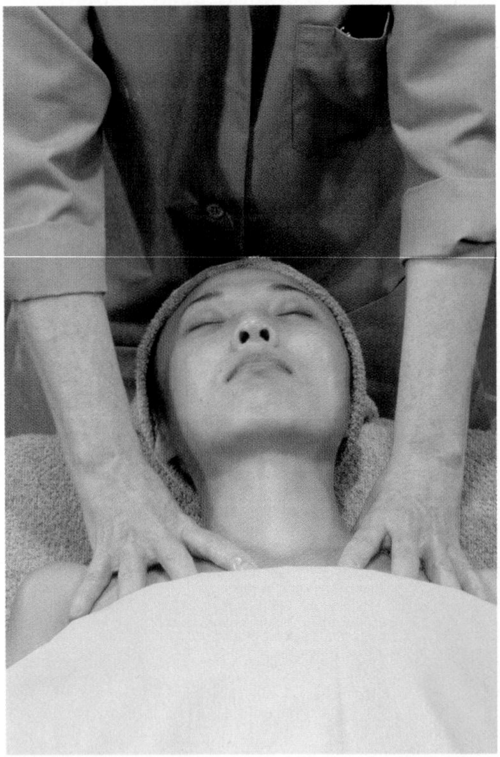

Figure 14–11 Vibration, a shaking movement stemming from the shoulders of the therapist, should be used sparingly. It is also applied using small mechanical facial vibrators.

SKINTIP

- Expert estheticians learn a number of massage patterns for each of the classical movements. Each pattern is chosen according to the function of the movement and the particular skin treatment.
- Effleurage is normally performed in a basic facial. Advanced treatments may require modification for variety.

Vibration

Vibration is a shaking movement emanating from the shoulders and not from the fingertips. It is accomplished by rapid muscular contractions in the arms of the esthetician (Figure 14–11). The balls of the fingertips are pressed firmly on the point of application. It is a highly stimulating movement, but it should only be used sparingly and never for more than a few seconds on any one spot. When properly administered, the vibration method of massage is normally well received by clients. Since the advent of a variety of small facial vibrators, the mechanical (hand) vibration method is rarely used.

The Basic Facial

The three basic facials correspond to the three basic skin types: normal skin, normal/combination skin, and dry/dehydrated skin. While their protocols are similar, each technique has a different purpose. The seven phases of a facial are outlined, highlighting those steps that differ from facial to facial. Note that the facial for normal skin does not include Phase IV, treat and correct. Normal skin is often perfectly balanced and rarely needs correction.

Estheticians must master the basic facials for the three skin types. Once an esthetician has chosen a product line for a client, the appropriate product for the client's skin type can be used in the facial.

Step By Step The Basic Facial

Purpose: A facial for normal skin is performed to deeply cleanse and maintain the skin by exfoliating excess dead cells. The goal is to maintain the smoothness and moisture level. The facial for normal/combination skin rebalances oil and moisture in the skin, removes comedones or other skin blockages, smoothes skin texture, reduces oil in the T-zone, and hydrates. The facial for dry/dehydrated skin exfoliates dead cells, replenishes lost moisture through deep hydrating, and protects by restoring (lubricating) the skin's moisture barrier.

Normal Skin Products: Cleanser and freshener (toner) for normal skin, exfoliation—gommage, massage oil or cream, mask for normal skin, day cream for normal skin, sunblock

Normal/Combination Skin Products: Cleanser and freshener (toner) for normal/combination skin, exfoliation—gommage, massage oil or cream, mask for normal/combination skin, day cream for normal/combination skin, sunblock

Dry/Dehydrated Skin Products: Cleanser and freshener (toner) for dry/dehydrated skin, exfoliation—brushes or gommage, mask for dry/dehydrated skin, day care cream for dry skin, sunblock

Tools and supplies: Sanitized facial sponges or disposable 4"×4" cotton pads, 2×2s, round cotton eye pads, cotton swabs, extractor or gauze for making finger cots, 2 mask brushes, stainless steel bowl for water, gloves

---

Room Setup

1. Prepare the facial chair with fresh linens and warm coverings.

2. Fill the steamer with distilled water.

For normal/combination skin and dry/dehydrated skin

1. Prepare the high-frequency machine. Place the glass electrode into the hand device.

2. Place a face brush into the rotating brush machine.

3. Prepare 3 or 4 rolled face towels dipped in water with a few drops of an aroma essence. Squeeze out the excess water. Place the towels in a hot towel cabinet.

Procedure

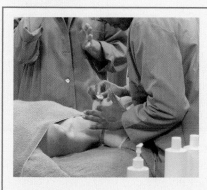

1 Remove eye makeup and lipstick with eye makeup remover.

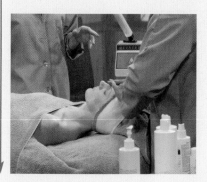

2 Cleanse face with cleanser appropriate to skin type. Remove residue with freshener.

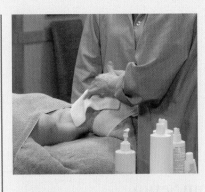

3 Rinse thoroughly with warm sponges or a shammie.

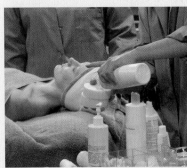

4 Apply freshener to remove any cleanser residue.

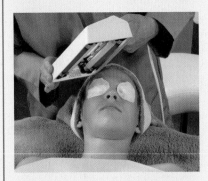

5 Perform a skin analysis.

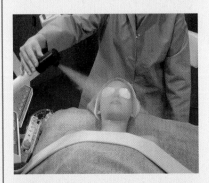

6 Direct steam toward the face. Perform a cleansing exfoliation with a normalizing facial cleanser or gentle exfoliant. Apply exfoliant over the entire face, neck, and décolleté, cleansing in a circular motion with the fingertips.

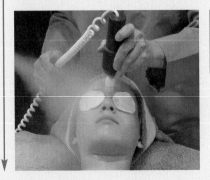

> For normal/combination skin, the rotating brush machine can be used to further cleanse. Men generally appreciate the mechanical brush, since it makes them feel that their skin is better cleansed.

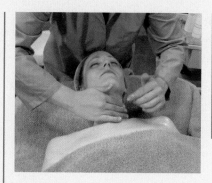

For dry/dehydrated skin, choose from three different exfoliation options:

1. A deep cleansing exfoliation with a soft scrub is appropriate. Apply over face, neck, and décolleté, cleansing in a circular motion.

2. A gommage

3. A soft enzyme peel may be appropriate since it dissolves the dead cells and softens buildup in the follicle.

7   While the steam is still on, thoroughly rinse the skin with warm water and a shammie.

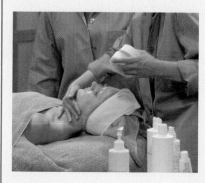

8   Apply freshener for normal skin to remove any excess residue. Make sure the face is quite warm, then remove the steamer.

9   Proceed with extractions (using finger cots, cotton swabs, or metal extractors) for approximately 5 minutes.

Note: This step is performed during the normal/combination facial or the dry/dehydrated facial only.

10   Apply the appropriate disinfecting solution. Apply the glass ultraviolet high-frequency electrode. If using a liquid disinfectant, the glass electrode will slide easily. The electrode can also be applied over a piece of gauze cut to fit the face.

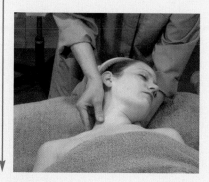

11   Apply a massage product appropriate to the client's skin type and perform 15 minutes of massage. Remove residue with warm moist sponges or a shammie.

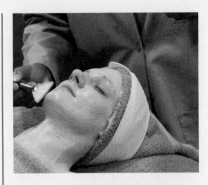

12 Apply a mask appropriate to the client's skin type and let it sit 10 minutes or as indicated in the manufacturer's directions.

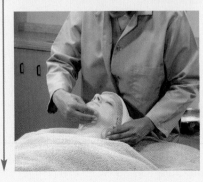

13 Remove the mask by rinsing with sponges or a shammie.

14 Apply a freshener (toner) appropriate to the client's skin type. You may use the spray device on your machine, if you have one.

15 Apply a moisturizer appropriate to the client's skin type. Follow by applying sunscreen. If use of an eye cream is indicated, apply before the moisturizer.

Home Maintenance

Clients should return monthly or bimonthly for good maintenance. If this schedule is too aggressive for clients, suggest having a facial for each season—four times annually—since skin changes with the seasons and clients may need to add a mask targeted to a specific problem. See Tables 14–3, 14–4, and 14–5 for maintenance schedules based on skin type.

The Minifacial

The main differences between a minifacial and a basic facial are time and content. Minifacials take only 25 minutes and don't include all the steps of a full 50-minute facial. The omitted steps are the comprehensive skin analysis, the massage, and other specialized treatments. Deep cleansing and masking are the most important elements of the minifacial, since these produce visible results.

Purpose

The minifacial will introduce a client to a very light, refreshing facial that leads to a rebooking for a more in-depth facial to address specific concerns and conditions.

Procedure

1. Perform a quick cleansing to remove makeup. Rinse well.
2. Analyze with a magnifying lamp.
3. Perform a second quick cleansing with an exfoliant or a deep pore cleanser. Rinse thoroughly.
4. Apply a freshener appropriate for the client's skin type.
5. Apply a moisturizing mask. Time for 5 minutes. Rinse.
6. Apply freshener.
7. Apply day cream and/or sunblock.
8. Recommend a treatment for the client's next visit.
9. Recommend initial home care products and complete the home care guide.
10. Follow up with a new client 1–2 days later and encourage the client to have a full basic facial treatment.

Table 14–3 Home Care Regimen for Normal Skin

	AM	PM
Cleanse—normal	X	X
Freshener—normal	X	X
Mask (1–2 weekly)		X
Moisturize—normal	X	X
Sunblock—SPF 15	X	

Table 14–4 Home Care Regimen for Normal/Combination Skin

	AM	PM
Cleanse—deep pore	X	X
Cleanse—liquid with beads (2 × weekly)		X
Freshener—normal/combination	X	X
Mask—to balance oily skin, hydrate (2 × weekly)		X
Moisturizer—light	X	X
Sunblock—SPF 15	X	

Table 14–5 Home Care Regimen for Dry/Dehydrated Skin

	AM	PM
Cleanse—very dry	X	X
Gentle scrub		Twice weekly
Freshener—very dry	X	X
Mask—to rebalance and hydrate		Twice weekly
Moisturize—nourishing	X	X
Sunblock—SPF 15	X	

Summary

Mastering the basics of a facial is vital for estheticians. Your hand movements are key to building confidence in a great facial. Practice the step-by-step movements presented in this chapter in order. Additionally, each stage relies on understanding specific protocols, tools, and products. Once you become familiar with these, you can learn more advanced techniques. After assessing a client's skin type and condition, an esthetician can identify a product system for a client. Product systems contain variations on several basic types of products that an esthetician must understand in order to best serve clients.

The three basic facials are based on skin type—normal, normal/combination, and dry/dehydrated skin. The treatment for normal skin is a basic facial. Normal/combination skin requires more treatment due to its combination of oil in the T-zone and dryness along the cheeks and the rest of the face. Dry skin, on the other hand, requires exfoliation of the dry skin cells followed by moisture. Facial massage is a vital step in all complete facials and provides many benefits to the skin. It supports the blood and lymph circulation and relaxes and oxygenates the skin. It also prepares skin for specialized ingredients that help soften, hydrate, and prevent evidence of aging.

Perform a minifacial to acquaint a client with the benefits of the facial. Do not offer all phases, such as massage, but encourage the client to rebook a complete facial on another visit.

Discussion Questions

1. Name the basic components of all facial treatments and review the seven phases of the basic facial process. Set a timer and practice these basic elements until you are within the 50-minute range.

2. Collect menus from several established and reputable skin care salons or clinics. From each menu, select three treatments, closely evaluating the "positioning" of each. Can you determine the focus of the clinic's marketing strategy from these treatments?

3. The facial massage provides many benefits to the client that cannot be duplicated at home. Discuss the benefits of massage as they relate to promoting good skin health.

4. Select a product line and choose four essential products that would be most beneficial to each of the following major skin types: normal, normal/combination, dry/dehydrated, oily/problem, and sensitive skin. Discuss your reasoning for each.

5. Understanding the function of specific product prototypes such as cleansers and night creams will help you to understand their function. Choose one of these prototypes and compare at least two different product lines. Are any of the terms used to describe the benefits and features similar? Working in teams, make a list of commonly used adjectives to describe each of the generic prototypes.

6. Discuss the benefits of a systems approach to product selection. How does it help or hinder the esthetician when suggesting products for home care?

7. Identify and list the differences in the three basic facial procedures and explain what factors contribute to them.

8. Until you are accustomed to performing treatments routinely, you may need help remembering the protocols for each of the basic facial treatments. Make a list of key words or phrases to help you remember the basic steps involved in each treatment and place it discreetly in view until you feel more secure.

9. What is the primary goal of the minifacial? Team up with a classmate and develop a dialogue for introducing this procedure to clients, and then practice on each other before trying it out in the student clinic.

10. Review the five "classic" massage movements, describing the specific benefit of each.

11. Develop a generic massage protocol for each of the major skin types, determining any contraindications where appropriate.

Additional Reading

Gerson, Joel. 1999. *Milady's Standard Textbook for Professional Estheticians.* Clifton Park, N.Y.: Milady, an imprint of Delmar Learning, a division of Thomson Learning, Inc.

Hampton, Aubrey. 1991. *Natural Organic Hair and Skin Care.* Tampa, Fla: Organica Press.

Hoffman, David. 1996. *Holistic Herbal, A Safe and Practical Guide to Making and Using Herbal Remedies.* New York: Barnes and Noble.

Lawless, Julia. 1995. *The Illustrated Encyclopedia of Essential Oils*. New York: Barnes and Noble.

Michalun, Natalia, and M. Varinia Michalun. 2001. *Skin Care & Cosmetic Ingredients Dictionary*. Clifton Park, N.Y.: Milady, an imprint of Delmar Learning, a division of Thomson Learning, Inc.

Miller, Erica. 1996. *Salonovations' Day Spa Techniques*. Clifton Park, N.Y.: Milady, an imprint of Delmar Learning, a division of Thomson Learning, Inc.

Murray, Michael T.,N.D. 1996. *Encyclopedia of Nutritional Supplements*. Rocklin, Calif.: Prima Publishing.

Ody, Penelope. 1993. *The Complete Medicinal Herbal*. New York: Dorling Kindersley.

Ody, Penelope. 2000. *Complete Guide to Medicinal Herbs*. 2d ed. New York: Dorling Kindersley.

Tappan, Frances M. 1988. *Healing Massage Techniques, Holistic, Classic, and Emerging Methods*. 2d ed. New York: Prentice-Hall.

Helpful Web Sites

http://www.amtamassage.org (American Massage Therapy Association)

http://www.doctormurray.com

http://www.healthwellexchange.com

http://www.infotrieve.com

http://www.massagemagazine.com (Massage Magazine)

http://www.Miami.edu/touch-research (Touch Research Institute, Miami Hospital)

http://www.naturalhealthmag.com

Chapter 15
Men's Facials

Chapter Objectives

After reading this chapter, you should be able to:

- ▶ Describe the importance of a man's facial.
- ▶ Explain the difference between facials for men and women.
- ▶ Identify the conditions that can occur on a man's skin.
- ▶ Perform a man's facial.

Chapter Outline

Introduction
Men's Skin Care Products
Professional Treatments for Men

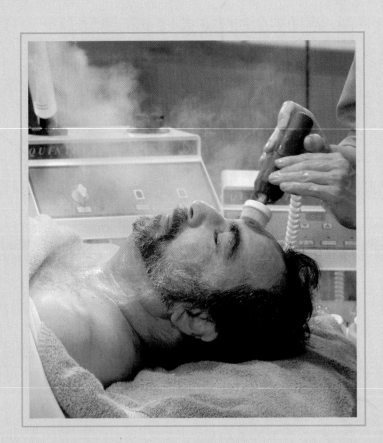

Introduction

Men's skin care is a subject that is not discussed much in most books, videos, and educational seminars. However, it is just as important as skin care for women. In fact, many professionals recognize today that male clients can be better clients than women in some ways. For the most part, male clients are more willing to follow suggestions and generally want a basic, consistent routine. They tend to be loyal customers (Figure 15–1). Male clients also tend to recommend a spa or salon to their friends and associates if they are satisfied with their treatments. The market for men is between 15% and 20% of business, and it is expected to continue growing at a solid pace in years to come. The challenge is to get male clients to come to a salon or spa in the first place. One way to attract male clientele is to offer special services designed just for them.

Men's Skin Care Products

Treatment concepts for men vary from professional to professional. Some feel very strongly that in order to build the male market, one needs to carry a specific line of men's skin care products. Others believe that most lines will work as long as the packaging isn't too feminine (which may put off some males). This concern can be easily overcome by a professional esthetician who has gained a client's confidence and obtained good results for his skin. Obviously, it is easiest if a salon's main product line also includes a men's line. But the market for men's products is still relatively small and it is therefore not cost-effective for many skin care companies. When considering a men's skin care line, there are some key points to keep in mind. These points are discussed below.

No Fluff

Men generally do not want highly fragranced, fluffy products. For example, creams need to be simple, nonfragranced, highly absorbent, with a matte finish. Most men do not like the greasy feeling of some products.

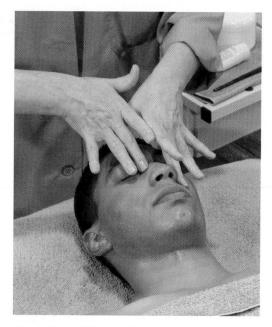

Figure 15–1 Offer specialized services designed just for men.

Simple Routines

Men prefer simple routines and multipurpose products. They would rather have a combined cleanser and toner. They also like the soapiness or foaminess of soaps, so a foaming cleanser is a good choice. They can use a toner as they would an aftershave lotion. They should then use a light moisturizer.

Keep the following tips in mind when working with male clients.

- Tubes are more man-friendly than jars.

- A male client's skin care regimen should begin with only two products, since men prefer very simple and basic routines. If he wants three, add the toner. As he grows accustomed to the regimen and sees favorable results, he will most likely add to his regimen by purchasing a sunscreen, eye cream, and a mask.

- Estheticians should teach male clients that most movements for the beard and moustache area should be done *with* the hair growth pattern. For example, shaving seems to be more effective and closer if it is done against the hair growth instead of with the growth. But the closer the shave, the more sensitivity may be experienced. To calm and soothe the face, men should shave and wash the face in a downward direction.

The Fine Art of Promoting Business

Airlines offer frequent flyer programs, restaurants are famous for early bird specials, cosmetic companies tout free gifts with higher value purchases, department stores offer one-day sales events, etc. The list is endless. The esthetician's goal is to have a full appointment book and increase product sales. No matter what your niche, the bottom line remains to add value and build business.

The whole idea behind promotional efforts is to draw attention to increase the volume of business. However, the goal is not only to attract new customers, but to reward repeat customers. Make it fun and it is a win-win situation for everyone.

In the skin care business you should be looking to accomplish the following:

- Fill slow days, months, or specific time frames.
- Promote *new* services and products.
- Encourage interest in regular treatments.
- Promote retail sales in general.

Particularly if you are in a position where you are the sole skin care practitioner in a larger full service salon or spa, you may be asked for ideas or suggestions on how to promote your services. How do you stimulate excitement in the aesthetic industry? Some methods to consider include the following:

- *Offer frequent customer or membership programs.* Create a frequent buyer system and offer a free treatment after the card is full. Incorporate your business logo as an added marketing bonus.
- *Let clients sample a treatment on a smaller scale.* Offer a minifacial or allow them to take a paraffin hand dip.
- *Promote specials for slower days.* Provide a free additional service, such as a hand or foot massage with the standard facial. Give an additional 10% off services on Mondays.

Present each client with a special gift, such as a retail product you would like to promote.

- *Add value to an existing service.* With any skin care treatment offer a second treatment of choice at half price. You can limit these offerings to specific services. Offer an accompanying retail product at a reduced price when the client purchases a certain treatment
- *Reward customers who refer other clients.* Send them a gift certificate for a service or treatment.
- *Give first time customers a reduced rate on their initial treatment.*
- *Use themes.* Take advantage of months, seasons, and holidays. Promote sunscreen products during the summer months. Offer a discount on moisturizers during the winter. Have a "March make-up madness" sale. Encourage gift certificate purchases on holidays, such as Mother's day.
- *Have a contest.* Use a fish bowl to gather business cards and choose one winner each week or month for a special service. Be smart and make sure everyone gets into your database.
- *Cross-merchandise.* Work with other businesses that complement your services. Offer a discount skin health membership in collaboration with the local gym. Give a discount on a series of treatments to the neighborhood health and nutrition center.

These are just a few suggestions for promoting your services and products. Be creative and be open to implementing successful strategies from larger chains and retail outlets. Just be sure to attach value to your service—consumers often attach the notion of lesser value or suspect fraudulent motives when they see the word *free*.

- Once accustomed to receiving treatments and using products, a man will use an eye cream if he is taught how. While men may be conscious of lines and wrinkles around their eyes, they seldom request an eye product. Estheticians should point out the benefits of this product.

Professional Treatments For Men

While it may be more challenging to enroll a male client into facial work, once he has experienced the benefits, he will probably be a loyal client and trust your advice. Depending on his skin condition, you will be able to perform various treatments (Figure 15-2). Note that most men love steam and the brush machine. Even if a client's skin is slightly sensitive, he will prefer the assertiveness of a brush and foamy cleanser.

There are some other important aspects of men's facials. First, sponges are more appropriate for a man's face. Cotton pads or gauze will grab the beard hair, leaving particles clinging to the face. Also, should a man shave before his facial? While some men prefer to shave because they don't want to show a five o'clock shadow, shaving actually makes the skin more sensitive. On freshly shaven skin, application of exfoliating products, including strong sensitizing agents such as alphahydroxy acids and microdermabrasion, may be contraindicated.

Beards

Professional movements during a man's facial should flow *with* the hair growth. For example, most massage movements in the beard area should point downward not upward. This goes against the typical esthetic procedure of lifting movements up the neck and face. But in this instance, gravity is not the dominant issue. Sensitivity and the tendency for folliculitis (ingrown hairs) are the focus.

Overall, the beard area tends to be relatively sensitive due to overstimulation from shaving lotions that contain perfume, alcohol, or other similar substances. Shaving itself is also quite abrasive to the skin, so men need more protective and healing products.

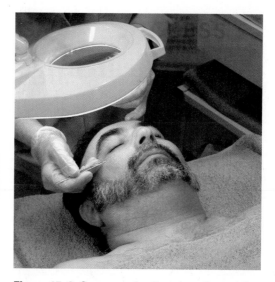

Figure 15–2 Once a male client experiences the benefits of facial work, you may be able to expand treatments.

Folliculitis

Some men are susceptible to a condition known as folliculitis (Figure 15-3), especially if they have very coarse or wiry beard hair. Improper shaving may also cause **folliculitis,** wherein instead of growing up and out onto the skin's surface, hair grows slightly under the skin, causing a bacterial infection. Folliculitis is often accompanied by inflammation and pus. The treatment goal for this condition is to alleviate the irritation, dry up and disinfect the pustules, and desensitize the area. A clear gel mask is probably the most comfort-

folliculitis
A skin condition common in men, where instead of growing up and out onto the skin's surface, hair grows slightly under the skin, causing a bacterial infection.

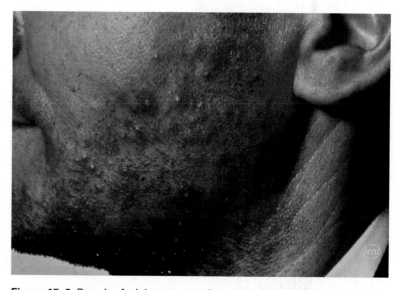

Figure 15–3 Regular facial treatments incorporating masks can help rid clients of folliculitis.

Step *by* Step Deep Cleansing Facial

Purpose: To thoroughly cleanse and hydrate

Products: Milky cleanser, deep pore cleanser, toner, exfoliant, mask for client's skin type, moisturizer, sun block

Tools and supplies: 3 or 4 towels, small sharp scissors for trimming, if necessary, clean sponges, 2×2s for eye pads

Room Setup

1. Prepare facial table to protocol.
2. Place small face brush into brush device.
3. Fill steamer.
4. Prepare high frequency.

Procedure

1 Soak 3 or 4 towels in citrus or menthol and place them in a hot towel cabinet.

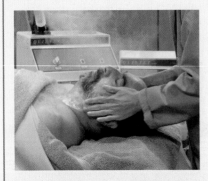

2 Cleanse the entire face with a good cleanser. Work the cleanser into the skin under the beard, with the fingertips. The brush machine may be used, as long as the hair is not long enough to get caught up in the rotation of the mechanical brush. If the hair is too long, work the area by hand. The key is to clean the skin well, under the hair growth, without causing irritation.

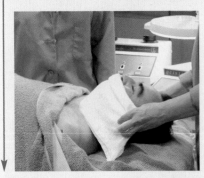

3 Apply hot towels to remove the cleanser and rinse, or rinse well with sponges.

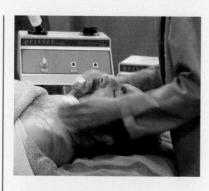

4 Apply freshener and wipe off with sponges, a shammie, or a hot towel. On sensitive skin, use a shammie or soft cloth in the same way. However, the feeling of a hot towel is also very pleasant to a male client.

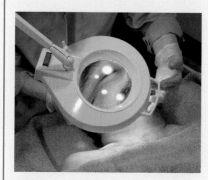

5 Analysis: Follow the same method used for women. Also, analyze the hair growth between the brows and on the nape of the neck, tips of the ears, and nose.

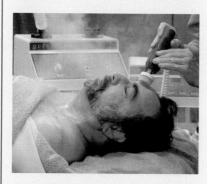

6 Perform a second cleansing with the deep pore or foaming cleanser and brush machine. Do this under steam.

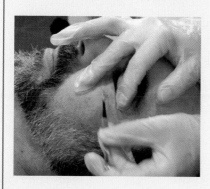

7 Proceed with normal extractions. Men often require a little more time for extractions. A relatively gentle approach is best.

8 Use disinfectant and high frequency.

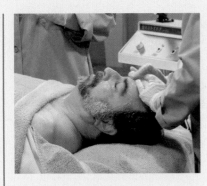

9 Massage is a very important part of the treatment. Perform the massage for 10–15 minutes. Be firm but not aggressive.

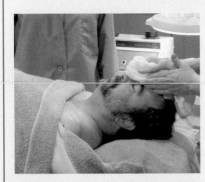

10 Remove massage oil residue from the face with a warm towel since the skin is well stimulated at this point.

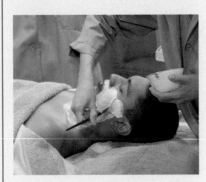

11 Apply a soothing mask for the beard area that helps suppress potential irritation, softens and conditions the beard, and hydrates. The T-zone often requires a different mask to draw and tighten the skin. Time for 7–10 minutes.

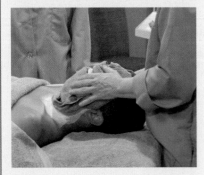

12 Rinse thoroughly, leaving no trace of mask or massage oil on the face, ears, neck, chest, and shoulders.

13 Spray on freshener. Pat the skin until cool.

14 Review and/or recommend a home care regimen. Set goals and rebook the client.

SKIN**TIP**

A shorter beard is more easily treated. You might consider a surcharge for longer beards.

able treatment product for a male client if he chooses to use one. The mask is especially welcome if it has soothing and healing properties.

Pseudofolliculitis, often referred to as "razor bumps," resembles folliculitis without the pus. This condition also results from improper shaving techniques.

Waxing for the Male Client

Men have two particular areas of interest for waxing: the brow area and the nape of the neck (base of the back of the neck). Another treatment area is the back (Figure 15–4). Estheticians must proceed with caution in all cases. Men may have a low tolerance for pain from waxing. The skin may get red and irritated. However, a male client's endurance level will most likely increase once the benefits are experienced, such as a more natural brow line and a smoother nape of the neck. Waxing the nape of the neck has the added value of helping to prevent fraying collars.

Men may also grow wiry hair on the edge of the ears and on the very edge of their nose. This growth tends to increase with age. Unless an esthetician is well trained, it is not advisable to wax these areas! However, removing the external hair is permissible. See Chapter 29 for more information.

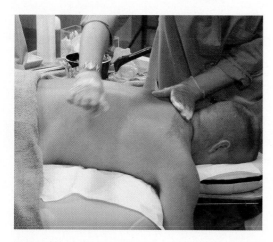

Figure 15–4 Back waxing is a popular treatment for men.

Summary

Men are increasingly having services performed in a salon or spa environment. Like women, they are concerned about aging and tend to be loyal clients once they like a service. Although most skin care lines do not include products geared specifically for men, there are basic products that address their needs. Keep things simple and offer your male clients treatments and products that will give good results. The market for men will continue to grow as they feel more comfortable about receiving spa or salon services.

Discussion Questions

1. Recognizing basic differences between male and female clients is an important factor in meeting the needs of both. Discuss how this understanding can help you attract a male clientele and build a business that satisfies the needs and wants of both populations.

2. Men have different skin care needs than women. Bullet the key points to consider when choosing skin care products for men.

3. In general, how do professional treatments for men differ from conventional protocol?

4. How you present a service is often as important as how well you perform the service. Discuss different approaches to introducing wax hair removal to men. How might your approach to women be different or similar?

5. Explain any additional considerations for a facial designed for men.

Additional Reading

Gerson, Joel. 1999. *Milady's Standard Textbook for Professional Estheticians.* rev. ed. Clifton Park, N.Y.: Milady, an imprint of Delmar Learning, a division of Thomson Learning, Inc.

Chapter 16
Postconsultation and Home Care

Chapter Objectives

After reading this chapter, you should be able to:

- State the purpose and the steps of the postconsultation.
- Describe how to sell a product line to a client.
- Explain the importance of the home care guide.

Chapter Outline

Introduction
Closing Consultation
Developing Long-Term Programs
Achieving Results
Follow-Up
Home Care Products
The Home Care Guide

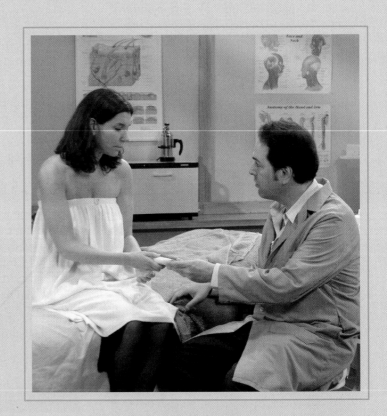

Introduction

A postconsultation provides the opportunity to show clients that you are a true professional who is well educated and concerned about them. This step focuses on the health of the client's skin and takes the mystery out of confusing product selection and treatment options. Reviewing a client's health form and performing the visual examination provide valuable information about skin type and condition. Additionally, the facial session provides a firsthand report about the skin's actual response to a product and treatment. This information is used in the postconsultation.

Closing Consultation

Clients come to estheticians for advice and expertise. Therefore, recommending future treatments and home care products is a vital part of the service (Figure 16–1). You should describe how a specific series can help a client. What will it do for a client's skin?

As one experienced esthetician said,

> I automatically assume the client is going to be with me for a long time, unless they live in another part of the country. I also know that in order for him or her to succeed in our programs, home care is just part of my conversation. Prior to entering the treatment room, I have a mindset that, unless they choose otherwise, the sale is made before they leave. At the close, and after I've reviewed my analysis, I direct my conversation back to their initial concerns. I make a suggested list as to what conditions to treat first. Whatever they choose, it will help the key concern with benefits to the others. I proceed to explain what series A or B will accomplish for them. My next question is what series would work—A or B? I then proceed to review quickly what products would benefit them the most. I have gained their confidence and they are pleased that I was so professional and knowledgeable about their skin concerns.

Maximizing the Postconsultation

Be sure to perform the postconsultation at the end of the facial. This stage allows you to

SKINTIP

For long-term programs, clients benefit most when they follow directions for the home care regimen and keep their treatment appointments.

address a client's initial reasons for seeking treatment by explaining what you found during the skin analysis and treatment.

Use the postconsultation to develop a long-term program of skin correction or preventive care by discussing the high-performance treatments that you offer as well as targeted products. Write down the program, pull products while the client is dressing, then quickly explain the home care regimen. Be sure to include written instructions for home care.

The 5-Minute Close

At the beginning of the facial, you did a brief consultation. You then observed the client's skin throughout the entire facial process, noting any sensitivity or other concerns. You also made a mental checklist of what to recommend for future treatments and products. After the facial treatment, prior to leaving the room, face the client and briefly discuss the skin analysis. Incorporate the following points into your discussion.

- Mention the concerns that were written on the health form, and communicated at the beginning of the facial.

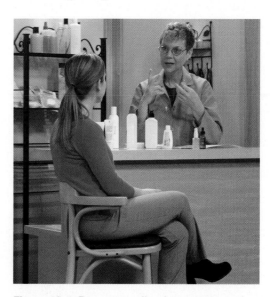

Figure 16–1 Recommending home care products is an integral part of the facial service.

Closing Consultation

Before clients leave the clinic or spa, it is your professional responsibility to educate them on the proper maintenance of their skin. This includes recommending a series of professional treatments and home care products.

Remember that clients come to you because they value your knowledge and expertise in skin care. They expect you to be able to help them sift through the numerous products on the market and recommend the ones that will be most useful to their particular skin type or condition.

Today's savvy consumer is also looking for professional treatments that show an improvement in the condition of their skin. Salon treatments are expensive. Clients are perfectly justified in expecting positive results. Seeking your services is an investment in their skin's health. To provide them with the maximum benefit of any treatment you must outline a course of action that maximizes their efforts.

As esthetic professionals it is our job to review clients' concerns and inform them of the best approach to solving their problems. This should include a written recommendation of products and treatments with specific directions and time frames. For example, how and when to use a daily cleanser, toner, and moisturizer along with appropriate sun protection. Specialized salon treatments, such as peels, can be recommended as a series over the course of several months for the best results.

What if a client is dedicated to using a brand of skin care products that you do not endorse or, even worse, have no knowledge of? Make a point to learn more about the products your client is

using and recommend treatments based on your analysis of the client's skin type and condition. Understand that clients come to us because they want to resolve certain issues concerning their skin. There are any number of products and techniques that can accomplish this goal, but their effectiveness will depend largely on the esthetician's sound and professional recommendations. First build the client's trust in your knowledge and then ease slowly into making changes even if you feel a particular product will produce far more dramatic results.

The smart esthetician knows that new advancements in product and technology will continue to change how we work and what we can accomplish. However, one thing remains constant—the customer's need for accurate information from a trained professional. As a professional esthetician it is your knowledge and expertise of the benefits and outcomes of different treatments and products that will continue to be in demand. Providing this information in a straightforward and user-friendly manner is the goal of closing consultation.

SKINTIP

Do not talk too much during the facial procedure; you want your client to be able to relax and enjoy the treatment.

- Make suggestions about optional treatments and beneficial products.
- Base your conversation on the client's concerns and your own findings. What would the client like to accomplish in the area of skin correction?
- Describe one or two choices of results-driven treatments. Which course of action would the client prefer?

Armed with these answers, leave the room so that the client can dress. Pull the appropriate products, write up a home care regimen, and then greet the client when she leaves the room. Review the directions for the products, and confirm the results to be expected from the next facial (or beginning of a series). Next, escort the client to the checkout area to make the next appointment, and thank her for coming.

Developing Long-Term Programs

The key to a successful skin care program is to see a client for more than one treatment. Since it took years for the skin to become sun damaged, it takes several dedicated skin care sessions to help correct some of the damage. The long-term skin management form (Figure 16–2, p. 240) is an important tool to help provide your client with the best service. This form should be placed in the client's folder. It lists a 12-month program that can be changed and modified as you treat the client over time. It also helps you focus on the needs of a particular client.

Achieving Results

Maximum results cannot be achieved if a client wants clinical treatments but insists on using her own home care products. If a client objects to using home products that you recommend, review what she already uses.

SKINTIP

Record keeping provides ample opportunity to show your expertise to clients. It shows that you take the extra steps necessary to accurately record your findings on the skin analysis form.

Then you can incorporate the products she has, such as cleanser, toner, or even moisturizer, as long as they are appropriate for her skin condition. Recommend the corrective serums or concentrates from your line in order to achieve proper results.

When a customer has used all of the products she already owns, she can replace them with products from your line. Never tell a client to throw out or not use the products she already has at home. In an attempt to correct her skin, she may have made a major investment in products purchased elsewhere.

Follow-Up

A necessary step in establishing a relationship with a new client is to make a follow-up phone call 1–2 days after the service. Estheticians can use this call as an opportunity to check on a client's skin response and to see if the client has questions regarding the new skin care regimen. Note that it is not necessary to call after every subsequent treatment unless a client is having major skin correction work done.

While follow-up is critical, it can be intimidating for new estheticians. Fear of rejection or negativity from the client can cause procrastination. However, while a few clients may grumble, most are impressed that you took the time to call. A brief phone call builds trust and confidence. This follow-up communication can also prevent major problems.

Home Care Products

Estheticians are distinguished from department store salespeople by their expertise; estheticians study, practice, and are licensed to perform treatments and to sell products that cannot be bought at a department store. As a result of this work, estheticians can

Skin Care Management Program for ______________________

Months 1–3	Months 4–6	Months 7–9	Months 10–12
Date ________	Date ________	Date ________	Date ________
Concerns—Conditions	**Concerns—Conditions**	**Concerns—Conditions**	**Concerns—Conditions**
1. ________	1. ________	1. ________	1. ________
2. ________	2. ________	2. ________	2. ________
3. ________	3. ________	3. ________	3. ________
Home regimen	**Home regimen**	**Home regimen**	**Home regimen**
Cleanse ________	Cleanse ________	Cleanse ________	Cleanse ________
Tone ________	Tone ________	Tone ________	Tone ________
Correct ________	Correct ________	Correct ________	Correct ________
Correct ________	Correct ________	Correct ________	Correct ________
Correct ________	Correct ________	Correct ________	Correct ________
Moisten ________	Moisten ________	Moisten ________	Moisten ________
SPF ________	SPF ________	SPF ________	SPF ________
Detail of in-salon program	**Detail of in-salon program**	**Detail of in-salon program**	**Detail of in-salon program**
1. ________	1. ________	1. ________	1. ________
2. ________	2. ________	2. ________	2. ________
3. ________	3. ________	3. ________	3. ________
4. ________	4. ________	4. ________	4. ________
Areas of concern	**Areas of concern/ improvement**	**Areas of concern/ improvement**	**Areas of concern/ improvement**

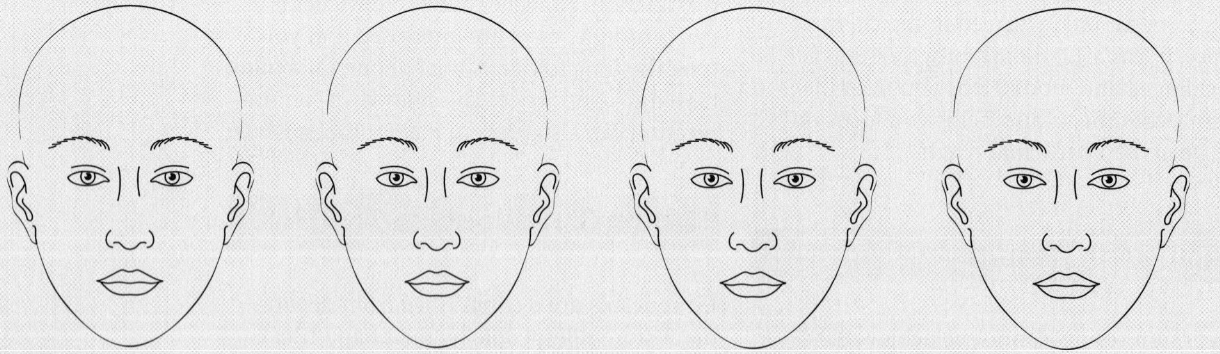

Figure 16–2 Long-term skin management form.

determine the correct course of action in salon or spa treatments and in the choice of products for home care. While you may perform an impeccable facial, in order to provide full service to a client, you must also offer home care, follow-up, and rebooking.

In a successful salon or spa business, approximately 40%–45% of sales should be generated from retail. These goals are easily obtainable with a strategic plan. In treatment procedures, you should recommend the products that will achieve optimum results. For example, when a client has concerns about environmentally damaged skin, high-tech products and ingredients are available to remedy or slow down this process.

Fear of Selling

The way to overcome the fear of selling is to realize that you are serving customers in a clinical environment. They have come to you with concerns about their skin, and your job is to educate them and present a course of treatments and products that will serve their skin care needs. This includes treatments performed in the spa or salon as well as performance products used at home.

Your goal is not to immediately sell a client an entire set of your product line. Rather, estheticians should organize treatments and educate clients about products that will produce results. Begin with a list of the most beneficial products. Write these on the client's home care chart, even if she does not purchase all the products in the first visit. All the products you recommend should produce visible results; this helps build your product credibility.

The ultimate goal is to have clients switch entirely to your product line. Obviously, there is better synergy when using products from one line. While we do not ever guarantee a result, when a customer faithfully keeps on schedule for treatments and follows the home care regimen, the skin will most likely respond well. Clients will be pleased, and the noticeable results will generate more business.

Product Integration

As professionals, estheticians should develop the ideal program for a client, even if it means incorporating some of the client's products into the home care regimen and later replacing them with you products. In

SKINTIP

Never sell by the features of a product. Always educate clients on the personal benefits, and the solutions that will be achieved by using a product.

order to do this, you must understand completely your own product line, its systems, and its unique ingredients.

When you work some of your product line into a client's home care regimen, she gets the message that you are not just out to sell her products. You will also become more comfortable with the idea of sending her home with a regimen. Through this process, selling is transformed into enrollment. The focus becomes enrolling your clients into a healthy, vibrant skin care system so that the skin appears younger and more readily tolerates everyday environmental changes.

The Home Care Guide

The **home care guide** (Figure 16–3) or prescription form, is an important guide to give clients. It provides a detailed routine of when to apply products and in what order. Many concepts and systems for home care guides exist. The form you use should meet the needs of your business environment and client base. Anything a client takes home should professionally represent the business. The following essential elements should be incorporated into anything that a client sees in the salon's repertoire of written materials, including your stationery, brochures, flyers, and other marketing materials.

1. The home care guide should be attractive enough so that clients do not just throw it away.

2. All generic directions should be preprinted to avoid unnecessary writing. A fill-in-the-blank form saves a great deal of time.

3. Estheticians should print all information legibly. Use the names on the product labels to avoid confusion.

4. List your own products in large print, and list the client's own products by initials and in smaller print to de-emphasize those items. In parentheses, list

home care guide
A prescription or guide that provides a detailed routine of when to apply products and in what order.

Your logo

A customized skin care program for _____

Date _____

1. Apply _____ eye makeup remover on a two-sided moistened cotton pad and swipe the eye area in a downward direction. Flip the pad and wipe the eyes until clean. If necessary, turn the pad inside out or use a newly moistened pad and repeat until the eyes are completely clean.

2. Cleanse the face with _____ by applying about a teaspoon of cleanser, massaging the hands together and massaging both hands over the entire face. Massage in circles for about 30 seconds and rinse with warm water.

3. Apply _____ foaming cleanser with moistened fingertips and lather well over the entire face and neck. Massage the face in upward and outward circles. Then rinse with warm water. You can also do this in the shower.

4. Apply _____ freshener on moist sponges and wipe the entire face well, turning sponges until all traces of dirt, oil, and makeup have been removed. Apply _____ freshener again by spraying or by using the fingertips and patting the skin.

5. In the morning, apply a peanut size amount of _____ day cream on a clean, toned (after freshener) face, and massage in well. Wait until dry before applying makeup.

6. At night before going to bed, apply _____ night cream on a cleansed and toned (after freshener) face and neck. Massage it in well. The skin should feel slightly moist but not too greasy. Allow the cream to nourish the skin during sleep.

7. Apply the _____ mask _____ times per week on cleansed and toned skin. When applied with the fingertips, the mask should be the thickness of a dime. Do not allow the skin to show through the mask. Rest _____ minutes and rinse with warm water. Follow with freshener and a night cream.

If you have any questions, please contact your esthetician immediately at _____ .

Figure 16–3 Home care guide.

what you would recommend from your line. It is important to allow clients to use their current products, but they should also start to think in terms of your line.

5. Develop a mark or a code such as a star or asterisk that represents the most important products you want a client to purchase immediately. This will alert the support staff, such as the front desk person, to encourage the client to purchase a particular item. The esthetician may not be available to complete the sale because of other appointments.

6. The chart or form should be printed with at least two carbonless copies so that the client can take one home and the salon or spa can have a copy in the client's file.

In our high-tech, information society, clients are inundated with all sorts of data. Your goal is to support them as simply as possible with as little verbal repetition as possible. Clients are most likely unfamiliar with your products or any professional products for that matter. The terminology may be totally foreign. Do not assume anything. Rather, write down the information as if the client does not know anything about the care of her skin, including the purposes of a cleanser, toner, mask, or serum, and the proper product application. Keep your instructional information generic and precise.

The home care guide should be re-written and updated periodically according to the following guidelines:

- at least 2–4 times a year for seasonal changes in routines
- changes in age and health
- lifestyle changes and adjustments
- to introduce new technology and product developments that are added to your skin care lines

The importance of the home care guide cannot be stressed enough. Many clients will not purchase products, or be bothered with a skin care routine, simply because they are confused and do not understand the value and uses of products. When designed well, the home care form becomes a valuable quick reference tool. It takes the guesswork out of a daily skin care routine.

Summary

Postconsultation and home care is a part of the facial that provides the opportunity to show clients that you care about their skin. Your thoroughness, caring, and professional demeanor build confidence. This step includes performing a closing consultation, developing a long-term program, recommending a home care regimen, and following up with new clients. Additionally, the home care guide serves as a constant reminder of you, your products, and treatments. It also helps facilitate a client's switch to your product line by de-emphasizing their other products.

Discussion Questions

1. The closing consultation is the crux of good home care. Discuss the essential elements that must be incorporated to ensure its success.

2. What is the basic reasoning behind client follow-up? Explain how you will present this to your employer as a regular part of your job description.

3. It is customary for estheticians to generate approximately 40%–45% of sales from retail. Decide how you will meet this goal based on a fixed number of treatments performed each week. Explain how you might customize your plan to meet your client's individual needs and target your client's skin care concerns.

4. What are the primary goals of a home care guide? Based on these principles, develop a user-friendly guide to facilitate the client's success. How will you incorporate any necessary changes?

Additional Reading

Hyatt, Carol, et al. 1993. *When Smart People Fail: Rebuilding Yourself for Success*. New York: Penguin.

Hyatt, Carol, et al. 1997. *The Women's New Selling Game: How to Sell Yourself—and Anything Else*. New York: McGraw–Hill.

Advanced Sciences

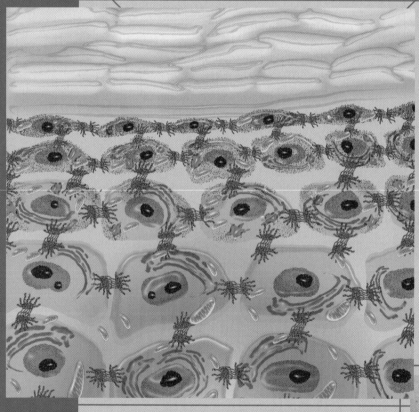

PART VI

Part Outline

Chapter 17 Disorders and Diseases

Chapter 18 Pharmacology

Chapter 19 Product Chemistry

Chapter 20 Advanced Ingredient Technology

Although estheticians are not qualified to treat skin diseases or medical conditions, they frequently come into contact with them and therefore need a basic understanding of these diseases and the drugs used to treat them. Furthermore, estheticians who work with over-the-counter drugs and skin care products or cosmetics need to know the products' intended uses and how they work.

In Part VI you will learn about the common skin conditions that motivate customers to seek professional treatment and how to identify certain medical conditions. In addition to the basic chemical reactions that take place in the skin, Part VI contains a description of over-the-counter and prescription drugs that affect the skin, including the drugs contained in sunscreens and the drugs used to treat acne. You will also learn about developments in the technology of skin care ingredients and products. An explanation of the Food and Drug Administration (FDA) regulations for claims about cosmetics is included, along with information about new skin care ingredients such as serums and polymers.

Chapter 17
Disorders and Diseases

Chapter Objectives

After reading this chapter, you should be able to:

- Explain the different kinds of skin lesions.
- Define common dermatological terms.
- Identify common skin conditions and diseases.
- List common allergens in the skin care business.

Chapter Outline

Introduction
Common Dermatological Terms
Lesions
Common Conditions and Diseases of the Skin
Common Allergens in the Skin Care Business
Contagious Diseases
Other Diseases of the Skin
Autoimmune Diseases

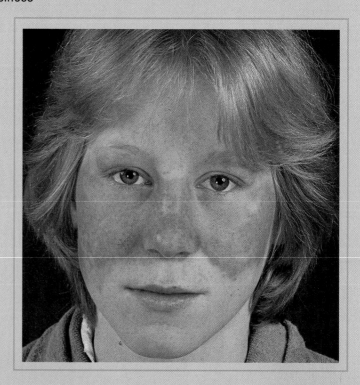

Introduction

Estheticians are in the unique position to observe many disorders of the skin and some skin diseases. They should be able to recognize disorders and diseases that require precautions, that are contraindicated for esthetic treatment, or that require medical referral to a dermatologist, plastic surgeon, or other physician. Some chronic conditions require care from both medical and esthetic professionals; these include acne, rosacea, and skin sensitivities. However, estheticians do not perform treatment for medical reasons, whereas dermatologists are physicians with years of training in the treatment of skin diseases.

Common disorders of the skin are well within an esthetician's scope of expertise. These disorders include oiliness, dryness, clogged and impacted pores, comedones (blackheads), and minor acne problems. Estheticians also administer exfoliation treatments and other treatments to help improve the appearance of aging, sensitive, sun damaged, dry, oily, and combination skin.

Common Dermatological Terms

All estheticians should be familiar with common dermatological terminology used to describe conditions of the skin. Symptoms are described in two ways:

1. **Objective symptoms** are visible, noticeable symptoms such as edema or erythema.
2. **Subjective symptoms** are symptoms that can be felt by the individual but are not detectable through normal observation. Subjective symptoms include pruritis, stinging, burning, and other pains.

Dermatitis

Dermatitis is defined as any sort of inflammation of the skin. It comes in many types, including the following:

Contact dermatitis occurs when the skin comes into contact with a sensitizing agent. As a result there is an immune response, causing inflammation.

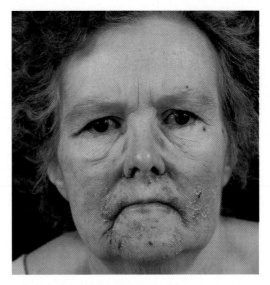

Figure 17–1 Erythema.

Atopic dermatitis is dermatitis that runs in families. It is related to nasal allergies and asthma.

Other Dermatological Terms

Eczema is an advanced, more severe form of dermatitis.

Erythema is redness; a red lesion is said to be erythemic (Figure 17–1). Erythema is caused by **inflammation,** which is swelling caused by the body's response to injury or infection. Inflammation can occur without infection, but infection always includes inflammation. **Infection** occurs when a **pathological,** or disease-producing, organism invades the body.

Keratoses are generally defined as built-up cells. **Hyperkeratosis** means a thickening of the skin due to this mass of keratinized cells, or keratinocytes.

pathological
Disease-causing.

keratoses
Build-up of cells.

hyperkeratosis
A thickening of the skin due to keratinocytes.

objective symptoms
Visible, noticeable symptoms such as edema or erythema.

subjective symptoms
Symptoms that can be felt by the client or patient but are not detectable by simple observation.

dermatitis
Any sort of inflammation of the skin.

contact dermatitis
A form of dermatitis that occurs when the skin comes into contact with a sensitizing agent. As a result there is an immune response causing inflammation.

atopic dermatitis
A form of dermatitis that runs in families. It is related to nasal allergies and asthma.

erythema
Redness indicating inflammation.

inflammation
Swelling.

infection
The invasion of body tissue by bacteria that cause disease.

pruritis
The medical term for itching.

purpura
Any form of lesion caused by bleeding under the skin.

hematoma
A collection of blood under the skin.

ecchymoses
Large bruises.

benign
The term for any condition of the skin that is not cancerous.

malignant
The term for cancerous lesions.

lesion
Any mark, symptom, or abnormality on the skin.

linear
Describes lesions in the shape of a line.

rounded
Describes lesions that are round.

annular
Describes lesions that are ring-shaped.

sepiginous
Describes lesions that are wavy and shaped like a snake.

geographic
Describes lesions that are shaped like a map.

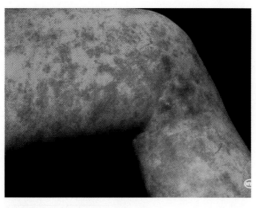

Figure 17–2 Purpura.

Pruritis is the medical term for itching.

Purpura is any form of lesion caused by bleeding under the skin (Figure 17–2). A **hematoma** is a collection of blood under the skin. Bruises are sometimes referred to as purpura or **ecchymoses,** which are larger bruises.

Benign is the term for any condition of the skin that is not cancerous.

Malignant is the term for cancerous lesions.

Lesions

A **lesion** is any mark, symptom, or abnormality on the skin; the term comes from the Latin word *laesio*, meaning to hurt. Lesions can be pigmented marks such as freckles, redness such as telangiectasia, or other blemishes such as pimples (Figure 17–3). The presence of lesions does not mean that the skin is diseased. Lesions may be hereditary freckles or scars from a cut.

There are three types of lesions: primary, secondary, and vascular, each containing a subgroup. Primary lesions are characterized

target
Describes lesions that are shaped like a target. A pustule is a target lesion.

macule
Any sort of flat lesion.

vascular macules
Red or purple spots that remain from former pimples or other injuries.

by flat, nonpalpable changes in skin color such as macules or patches, or an elevation formed by fluid in a cavity, such as vesicles, bullae, or pustules. Some are also elevated, palpable solid masses, such as a papule, plaque, nodule, tumor, or wheal. Secondary lesions are characterized by a collection of material on the skin, such as a scale, crust, or keloid. Secondary lesions are also characterized by a loss of skin surface, such as erosion, ulcer, excoriation, or fissure. Vascular lesions are a change in the tissue characterized by the appearance of small blood vessels close to the skin, such as cherry angioma, telangiectasia, petechia, or ecchymosis.

Shapes of Lesions

Many terms exist to describe the shapes of lesions. They include:

Linear lesions are shaped like a line.

Rounded lesions are round.

Annular lesions are ring-shaped.

Sepiginous lesions are wavy and shaped like a snake.

Geographic lesions resemble a map.

Target lesions look like targets; a pustule is a target lesion.

Macules

A **macule** (Latin for spot) is any sort of flat lesion. This group includes:

Vascular macules: Red or purple spots that remain from former pimples.

Telangiectasia: A condition where small, red, enlarged capillaries appear on the face and legs (Figure 17–4, p. 8).

Petechiae: Tiny, pinpoint, red spots from trauma.

Hyperpigmented macules: Freckles or lentigines (one such lesion is a **lentigo**).

petechiae
Tiny, pinpoint, red spots from trauma.

hyperpigmented macules
A type of macule that includes freckles and lentigines.

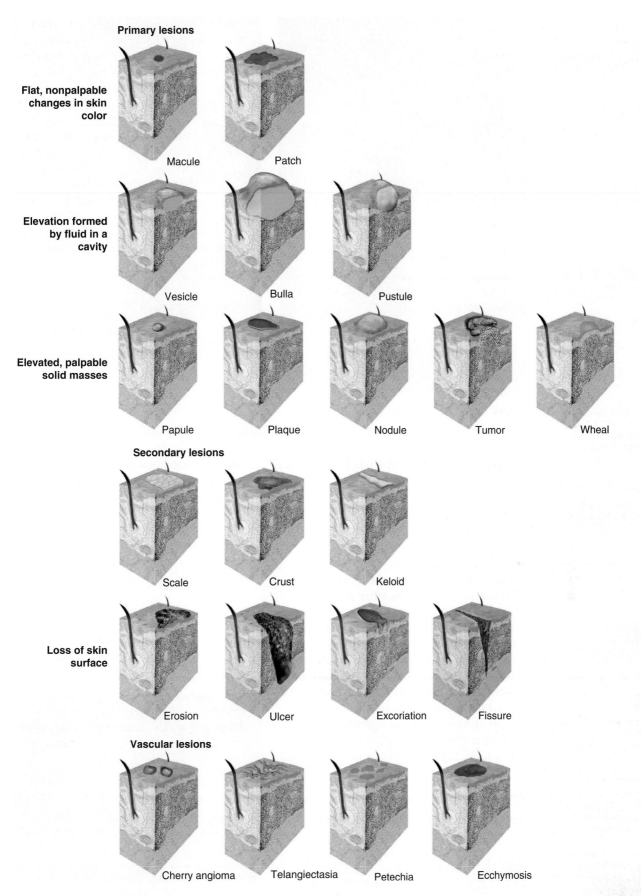

Primary lesions

Flat, nonpalpable changes in skin color

Macule   Patch

Elevation formed by fluid in a cavity

Vesicle   Bulla   Pustule

Elevated, palpable solid masses

Papule   Plaque   Nodule   Tumor   Wheal

Secondary lesions

Scale   Crust   Keloid

Loss of skin surface

Erosion   Ulcer   Excoriation   Fissure

Vascular lesions

Cherry angioma   Telangiectasia   Petechia   Ecchymosis

Figure 17–3 Three types of skin lesions.

lentigo
The singular form of lentigines.

actinic lentigines
Freckles from sun damage.

solar lentigines
Freckles from sun damage.

patches
Macules larger than one centimeter.

open comedo
A blackhead.

comedones
More than one comedo.

closed comedo
A comedo without a dilated ostium or follicular opening. It appears as a small bump just beneath the skin's surface, and generally has no color at all.

milia
Whiteheads.

papule
A type of raised lesion that is usually characterized by red bumps.

pustule
An infected papule.

pus
A fluid that is a product of infection and is a mixture of dead white blood cells, bacteria, blood, and other debris including tissue or cells that have been destroyed by infection.

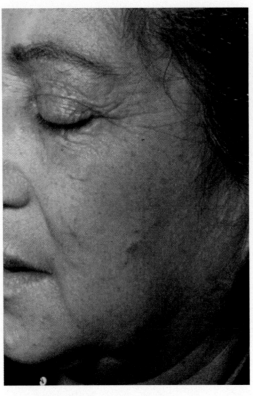

Figure 17–4 Telangiectasia.

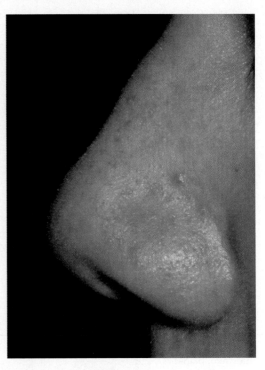

Figure 17–5 Open comedo.

Actinic lentigines or **solar lentigines:** Freckles resulting from sun damage.

Patches: Macules larger than one centimeter.

Comedones

An **open comedo** is commonly known as a blackhead (Figure 17–5). More than one comedo are known as **comedones.** Comedones are a buildup (stacking) of dead cells within the follicle, held together by solidified sebum. An open comedo has a black top caused by lipid (sebum) oxidation, hence its common name blackhead. A **closed comedo** is a comedo without a dilated ostium or follicular opening, which appears as a small bump just beneath the skin's surface. It generally has no color at all.

Milia

Milia are commonly called whiteheads (Figure 17–6). They are very small epidermal cysts that are just under the surface of the skin. They resemble sesame seeds. They are almost always perfectly round. They contain sebaceous secretions and a buildup of dead cells, but they are not necessarily associated with a follicle. Milia often form after a skin trauma or surgical procedure. They are especially frequent after skin resurfacing treatments, such as dermabrasion, chemical peels, or laser resurfacing.

Milia can be removed by gently lancing the very surface of the lesion and gently extracting the contents using cotton swabs or a comedo extractor.

Papules

Papules are raised lesions that are usually red bumps and can easily be felt when

Figure 17–6 Milia.

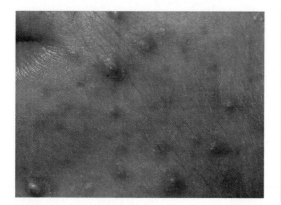

Figure 17–7 Pustule.

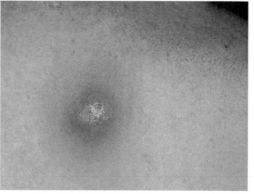

Figure 17–9 Sebaceous cyst.

touched. Acne is one example of papules. A **pustule** is an infected papule (Figure 17–7). It has a head with a white or yellow center, which is pus. **Pus** is a fluid that is a product of infection and is a mixture of dead white blood cells, bacteria, blood, and other debris including tissue or cells that have been destroyed by infection. A **crust** may be seen around different types of infected lesions. Crust is a dried body serum such as dried pus or blood.

Nodules

A **nodule** is a solid bump that you can feel, which is normally larger than one centimeter (Figure 17–8). Nodules may or may not be visible. Some are located beneath the surface of the skin but can be felt. Nodules that are felt and can be lifted away from the skin with two fingers are said to be **palpable**. Nodules can be caused by many different types of problems. They can be scar tissue, infections, fatty deposits, or other conditions. Very large nodules are called tumors.

Cysts, Scales, and Plaques

Cysts are pockets of fluid, infection, or other matter under the skin (Figure 17–9). Many different types of cysts exist, but estheticians are most familiar with acne cysts. Obviously flaky skin cells are called **scales.** They often pile up and are quite obvious on the skin. **Plaques** are lesions that have flat surfaces, yet are raised above the skin. A hive (urticaria), or **wheal** is **edematous**, or swollen, because it is full of fluid (Figure 17–10). **Edema** (rarely spelled *oedema*) means swelling.

Vesicles

Vesicles are blisters, or a separation of the epidermis from the upper dermis caused by fluids released by surface blood vessels. Never peel off a blister, because the top or flap protects the skin from infection. Allow it to dry and heal by itself. Very large vesicles are called **bullae** (Figure 17–11, p. 12).

crust
A dried body serum such as dried pus or blood.

nodule
A solid bump you can feel that is normally larger than one centimeter.

palpable
Describes a nodule that can be felt and lifted away from the skin with two fingers.

cyst
A pocket of fluid, infection, or other matter under the skin.

scales
Flaky skin cells.

plaques
Lesions that have flat surfaces, yet are raised above the skin.

wheal
A plaque that is full of fluid.

edematous
Full of fluid.

edema
Swelling.

vesicles
Blisters, or a separation of the epidermis from the upper dermis caused by fluids released by surface blood vessels.

bullae
Very large vesicles.

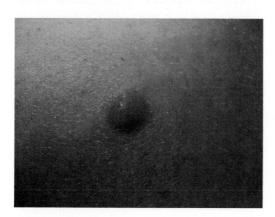

Figure 17–8 Nodule.

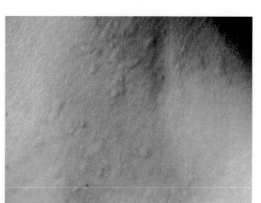

Figure 17–10 Hives.

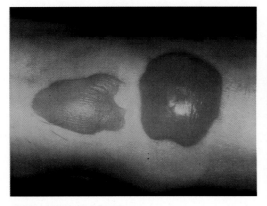

Figure 17–11 Bullae.

scars
Lesions that are visible and that result from injury or infection.

hypertrophic
Describes an elevated scar; overgrowth.

erosion
A type of scar that is a depression in the skin's surface.

hypotrophic
Describes an erosion or depressed scar.

excoriation
A type of scar caused by scrapes or scratches.

acne excoriée
A disorder in which the client purposefully scrapes off the surface skin on all acne lesions.

ulcer
A deep erosion in which the skin surface is destroyed by infection, poor blood circulation, or cancer.

nevus
A mole or birthmark.

vascular
Related to blood vessels.

port-wine stain
A type of birthmark characterized by a large, splotchy, wine-colored mark.

Scars

Scars are visible lesions that are the result of injury or infection. Scar tissue is hardened tissue that has been formed by the body to repair an injury or to heal the tissue. Elevated scars are **hypertrophic**, which means overgrowth (Figure 17–12). A keloid is a larger type of scar that is hereditary and prevalent in black and Asian skin.

Scars can also be the absence of tissue. An **erosion** is a depression in the skin's surface. One example of erosion is a depressed scar called a **hypotrophic** scar.

Other erosions include **excoriations**, which are scrapes or scratches. **Acne excoriée** is a disorder in which the client purposefully scrapes off the surface skin on all acne lesions (Figure 17–13). This disorder is characterized by many scraped-looking flat lesions. They may be red, because the epidermis has been scraped off, or they may be brown, because pigment has formed to protect the injured skin.

An **ulcer** is deeper erosion, in which the skin's surface is destroyed by infection, poor blood circulation, or cancer.

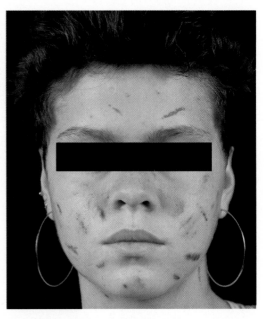

Figure 17–13 Acne excoriée.

Nevi

A **nevus** is a mole or birthmark. Nevi (more than one nevus) are generally pigmented, but they can be **vascular**, or related to blood vessels.

A good example of a vascular nevus is a **port-wine stain**, a type of birthmark characterized by a large, splotchy, wine-colored mark (Figure 17–14).

Figure 17–12 Hypertrophic scar.

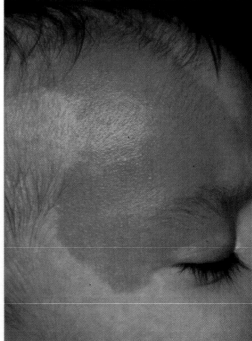

Figure 17–14 Port wine stain.

SKILLS **FOR** SUCCESS

Starting Your Own Business

Are you an entrepreneurial spirit? Have you always dreamed of owning your own business? Perhaps you chose a career in esthetics with just that idea in mind. As the esthetic industry continues to grow at a phenomenal pace, many estheticians enter the field thinking about opening their own skin care practice.

But before you decide on becoming your own boss, take the time to ask yourself three very important questions: What skills are necessary for starting a skin care business? Do I have these skills? If not, how will I acquire them?

Starting your own business requires several important character traits. The first and perhaps most important is having a clear vision of what you would like to accomplish. Why did you decide to become an esthetician? Oftentimes prospective students say they have chosen a career in esthetics because they enjoy working with people. They like the idea of providing a healthful service that makes others feel and look good. Consider whether this will be in alignment with the task of running your own business.

In order to do the actual work of a practitioner and run the business, you will have to be disciplined and focused. This requires tremendous motivation, commitment and energy. Make no mistake about it—there will be long days and many challenges. Are you willing to make the personal sacrifices that will be necessary? Not every day will be easy. Do you have the kind of resilient personality that can overcome adversity and begin each day anew? Growing a business may also demand a great deal of financial sacrifice—are you willing to deprive yourself to achieve your goal? These are the kinds of questions you should begin to ask yourself.

Once you have made the personal commitment to start your own business, you can begin to address the functional requirements. This means developing a strategic plan and organizing a business strategy. Implementing these requires solid business acumen.

Understanding finances is an important aspect of doing business. A careful analysis of start-up costs must be weighed against the effort required to meet these costs over an initial time period. Once you have figured out such expenses as equipment, supplies, rent, utilities, telephone service, insurance, license fees, marketing materials, hiring, training, etc., you must realize the work involved in paying for them. That is, how many services will you need to provide to cover your costs? To be successful you must continually work to meet your expenses and increase profitability.

Conducting day-to-day operations, such as booking appointments, taking inventory, buying supplies, and handling employee issues requires the ability to solve problems on a regular basis. Having a clear vision of how you will manage such tasks will help you address problems before they arise. This means setting standards, policies, and procedures.

Sound like more than you bargained for? If you are really invested in owning your own business, take heart. Perhaps the most important tool in starting your own business lies in recognizing your own strengths and weaknesses. Know that you cannot be all things. While the initial cost may be expensive, the benefits of hiring a business or management consultant, becoming computer savvy, and installing a user-friendly information system could be the wisest investments you make.

Common Conditions and Diseases of the Skin

Literally hundreds of different disorders and diseases can affect the skin. This section describes the most common skin conditions, the ones that estheticians are most likely to see in their practice.

Skin Tags

acrochordons
Skin tags, or small extensions of the skin that look like small tags or flaps hanging off the skin.

skin tags
Small extensions of the skin that look like small tags or flaps hanging off the skin.

Sometimes called **acrochordons, skin tags** are small extensions of the skin that look like small tags or flaps hanging off the skin (Figure 17–15). They can be flesh-colored, brown, or black. They are benign and can be easily removed by a dermatologist. Removal is accomplished with cryosurgery (liquid nitrogen freezing), by clipping off with surgical scissors, or by treatment with an electric needle (electrodessication). Skin tags are more common in women, and many skin tags are associated with obesity. They frequently occur on the neck, under the arms, and around the breasts.

Sebaceous Hyperplasia

Common in clients over 30 years of age, sebaceous hyperplasias are benign lesions that are frequently seen in oilier areas of the face (Figure 17–16). They result from an overgrowth of the sebaceous gland, which causes an elevation of the skin above them. Often donut-shaped, they have been described to appear like tiny volcanoes. They can also be asymmetric, appearing lopsided.

Sebaceous hyperplasias can occur as only one or two isolated lesions or there can be many of them. They often resemble open

keratosis pilaris
A nonpathological condition of the skin, characterized by redness and bumpiness on the cheeks.

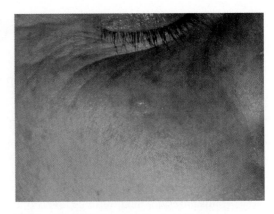

Figure 17–16 Sebaceous hyperplasia.

comedones and are generally esthetically unacceptable. A dermatologist or plastic surgeon, using cryosurgery, electrodessication, or a laser, can remove them. Larger ones must be surgically removed.

Sebaceous hyperplasias are sometimes filled with sebaceous material, and the esthetician may attempt to extract them. Although the sebaceous matter can be removed, the hyperplasia itself will not be removed without dermatological treatment.

Noninfectious Disorders And Diseases

There are many noninfectious disorders and diseases that require care by a skin care professional or physician. Below are some of the more common conditions and a brief overview to help with identification.

Keratosis Pilaris

A nonpathological condition of the skin, **keratosis pilaris** is characterized by redness and bumpiness in the cheeks (Figure 17–17). It is often observed on the upper arms, and

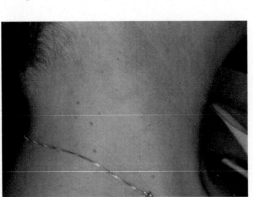

Figure 17–15 Skin tag.

Figure 17–17 Keratosis pilaris.

the skin can feel like sandpaper. The condition occurs more often in persons who have asthma or nasal allergies, and it is more prevalent in young children and pubescent teenagers.

The follicles in keratosis pilaris have small plugs of dead cells. Some theorize that it is caused by small hairs trying to emerge from the follicle, but the follicle is too small, and hyperkeratosis, or a buildup of cells, occurs.

Keratosis pilaris is more of a cosmetic nuisance than anything else. It may itch, particularly if the skin is dehydrated, and it is more likely to occur in cold weather. Keratosis pilaris is best treated with a mild keratolytic product with an alphahydroxy acid such as glycolic or lactic acid. Moisturizers containing these ingredients are helpful. Very gentle abrasive scrub products are helpful as long as they are not applied aggressively. Treatment of keratosis pilaris must be consistent, because it tends to reoccur.

Seborrhea

Seborrhea is severe oiliness of the skin, primarily on the face and scalp. It is common in young males. The term seborrhea is often confused with **seborrheic dermatitis,** which is a common form of eczema that primarily affects oily areas of the face (Figure 17–18).

Seborrheic dermatitis is an inflammatory disorder characterized by erythema and flaking in the oilier areas, such as the hairline, brows, scalp, sides of the nose, and ears. It may appear in one or several of these areas at once. The exact cause is unknown, but it may be related to Propionibacterium acnes or yeast known as *Candida albicans* or pityrosporum ovalli. It also may be hereditary. Why it affects oily areas is unknown. Seborrheic dermatitis may be related to the way the individual's skin clears, or does not clear, the follicles of sebum.

More prevalent in men than women, the odds of having seborrheic dermatitis increase with age. It is also prevalent in people with depressed immune systems, such as AIDS patients, who can have very severe cases of seborrheic dermatitis. Clients with rosacea, acne, and oily, sensitive skin are also likely to have periodic bouts with seborrheic dermatitis. Seborrheic dermatitis can flare up if the client is under excessive stress or during sudden changes of weather.

Figure 17–18 Seborrheic dermatitis.

Lay people and some estheticians erroneously diagnose this as dry skin and apply heavy, and often scented, moisturizers that can worsen the condition. The best course of action is to use very light, fragrance-free products, and hydrocortisone cream or lotion, which is available over-the-counter at up to 1%. Products that are designed for sensitive skin are the best choices. Essential oils have also been known to cause seborrheic dermatitis to flare up.

The condition should be referred to a dermatologist if it does not clear or if it recurs. A dermatologist will treat it with more potent topical or oral corticosteroids. Antiyeast medications, such as ketoconazole, selenium sulfide, and zinc pyrithione, are sometimes used. The latter two may be purchased over the counter (OTC). Some of these chemicals may sound familiar because they are used in OTC products to treat **dandruff**, which is a lay term referring to any condition causing flaking of the scalp. In many instances, dandruff is actually seborrheic dermatitis.

Rosacea

Rosacea is a common skin condition that occurs in adults; it usually occurs after age

seborrhea
Severe oiliness of the skin, primarily on the face and scalp. It is common in young males.

seborrheic dermatitis
A common form of eczema that primarily affects oily areas of the face.

dandruff
A lay term referring to any condition causing flaking of the scalp.

vascular growth factor (VGF)

A biochemical in the skin that is responsible for the development of new blood vessels and may be out of control in clients with rosacea.

demodex

Small mites in the skin, which may be associated with rosacea.

flares of rosacea

Sudden worsening of rosacea or redness.

vasodilation

A sudden dilation of blood vessels.

metronidazole

A prescription antiyeast medication, commercially known as MetroGel®, Metro-Cream®, or Noritate®, used to treat rosacea.

rhinophyma

An enlarging of the nose cartilage, directly related to rosacea.

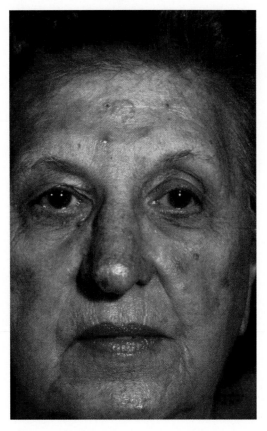

Figure 17–19 Rosacea.

40, but it can begin as early as age 20 (Figure 17–19). It is more common in women than in men and in Fitzpatrick skin types I, II, and III. Rosacea is characterized by chronic diffuse redness such as blushing (without embarrassment), many telangiectasias, and flushing, which is a sudden reddening of the skin. In mild and early cases, the client may only notice bouts of redness that may be triggered by heat or alcohol ingestion. In more severe cases, the client may develop large, sore, acnelike papules and pustules. In very severe cases, cysts can develop, and the client may undergo therapy with isotretinoin, also known as Accutane.

When we think of the late comedian W. C. Fields, we often think of his large red nose. Mr. Fields had rosacea and a severe condition known as **rhinophyma,** which is an enlarging of the nose cartilage, directly related to rosacea. Rhinophyma is more prevalent in men than women, but rosacea is more prevalent in women than men.

The exact cause of rosacea is unknown. It is believed to be hereditary. One theory is that the inflammation is caused by the pres-

ence of small mites, called **demodex**, in the skin. Some experts theorize that rosacea may be related to Helicobacter pylori, a bacterium known to be associated with stomach ulcers. Others think it may be related to the presence of yeast or fungus in the skin. Rosacea may also be related to a biochemical in the skin called **vascular growth factor (VGF)**. VGF is responsible for the development of new blood vessels, and may be out of control in patients with rosacea. None of these theories has been proven, and a combination of these factors may possibly cause and flare rosacea.

We do not fully understand what causes rosacea to flare up, or what causes a sudden worsening or redness. **Flares of rosacea** are caused by anything that causes vascular dilation of the blood vessels in the face. Sun exposure, heat exposure, or extreme temperature changes can cause flaring. Clients should be told to avoid sun at all costs, and that heat may be just as bad. Something as simple as letting a hot car cool before entering can prevent a flare.

Although foods do not affect acne vulgaris, they may affect rosacea. Spicy foods, alcohol, wine (especially red), or hot liquids may cause redness or flaring. Tobacco and caffeine also cause **vasodilation**, or a sudden dilation of blood vessels. Even heat from exercise has been implicated in rosacea flares.

Controlling redness and flares may help to minimize the disease. It is believed that chronic, continual redness may lead to a release of VGF, which may cause the condition to worsen and progress.

Clients with rosacea should be referred to a dermatologist for diagnosis and management. Medical treatment of rosacea is mainly topical treatment with a prescription antiyeast medication called **metronidazole**, commercially known as MetroGel, Metrocream, or Noritate. This substance helps control inflammation to minimize redness and flaring. Patients must be consistent with treatment for good results. In more severe cases of rosacea, dermatologists may prescribe an oral antibiotic to help control inflammation, or they may prescribe isotretinoin (Accutane).

Rosacea is a skin condition where both dermatological and esthetic treatment can be helpful. The right medications and the right skin care products work well together. They help the client with rosacea avoid flaring and worsening of the condition.

The esthetician's role in education of the rosacea patient is also important in treatment. Soothing and calming moisture fluids, particularly those with calming agents, like dipotassium glycyrrhizinate or stearyl glycyrrhetinate may be especially soothing and will calm redness. Serums with grapeseed extract or green tea may also be very helpful in lessening redness.

Rosacea is often termed *dry rosacea* or *oily rosacea*. These are not official dermatological terms, but they group clients with rosacea into two categories. Clients with oily rosacea tend to have bouts of pimples and oiliness. Some clients with oily rosacea may also have periodic occurrences of seborrheic dermatitis. Rinseable foaming cleansers are appropriate for oily rosacea, provided that the cleanser is not harsh or overdrying. Hydrators and moisturizing products should be fragrance-free and properly tested to make sure they are noncomedogenic. Nonstimulating, alcohol-free toner and lightweight broad-spectrum sunscreen are important for these clients.

On the other hand, dry rosacea is often characterized by parchmentlike dehydrated surface skin. It may easily flake and is quickly reddened (becomes erythemic) by harsh treatment or products. It is important to hydrate dry rosacea but avoid anything heavy or stimulating. Lightweight, fragrance-free hydrators and sunscreens are helpful. Antioxidant serums using ingredients such as grape seed extract and green tea are helpful in soothing this reactive skin. Very mild, nonfoaming or nondetergent cleansers are less likely to aggravate this skin condition.

Avoid products that are harsh, abrasive, fragranced, or heavy. Any product that is stimulating or stripping can trigger redness and a possible flare. Alphahydroxy acid (AHA) products can be used on rosacea, providing that they do not have very low pHs. AHA products should not be used during a flare or when the skin is red or agitated.

In addition to avoiding certain products, estheticians should also be aware of what treatments should be avoided for rosacea. Excessive extraction, prolonged steaming, and stimulating massage can all cause blood to flush the skin. Ultrasonic steamers that produce cool steam are helpful and provide needed hydration for these clients without the heat of a regular steamer. A Lucas sprayer (atomizer) is also a good choice. Clients should be educated to avoid heat, spicy foods, alcohol, and other triggers.

Perioral Dermatitis

An acnelike condition, **perioral dermatitis** occurs almost exclusively in women. The age range for these women is generally 20–40 years of age. *Perioral* means around the mouth, and this is exactly where this condition occurs. The nose and nasolabial folds may also be involved.

Perioral dermatitis appears as small clusters of papules. The key word here is "clusters." The lesions look like they are in a group. There is usually erythema over the whole area. Itching and scaling may also occur. Small, pinpoint pustules may also be present.

The cause of perioral dermatitis is unknown. It is theorized to be related to the overuse of moisturizers or heavy moisturizers, fluoride toothpastes, contact with cinnamon oil, and other irritants. The fact that it occurs almost always in women adds hormonal factors to the list. The fact that antibiotics treat it successfully points to bacterial factors.

Administered by a dermatologist, treatment usually involves a several-week course of oral antibiotics such as tetracycline. Topical antibiotics such as clindamycin are also prescribed sometimes. Perioral dermatitis usually clears up in a few weeks with treatment but it often recurs.

Estheticians should advise clients to use a lightweight, fragrance-free moisturizer, preferably one properly tested for irritancy and comedogenicity. They should also be advised not to overapply the moisturizer or any other skin care product. A cleanser should not be harsh and it should be easily rinseable. AHAs should be temporarily discontinued in the area, as should any other exfoliating agent. Perioral dermatitis is not contagious.

Contact Dermatitis

Allergic contact dermatitis (ACD) is one type of contact dermatitis (Figure 17–20, p. 258). It is an allergic reaction in the skin due to contact with a particular substance. The best example of this is poison ivy. ACD occurs when a person who is allergic comes in skin contact with an allergen, the substance the person is allergic to. The immune

perioral dermatitis
An acnelike condition around the mouth that occurs almost exclusively in women.

allergic contact dermatitis (ACD)
A type of contact dermatitis that is an allergic reaction in the skin resulting from contact with a particular substance.

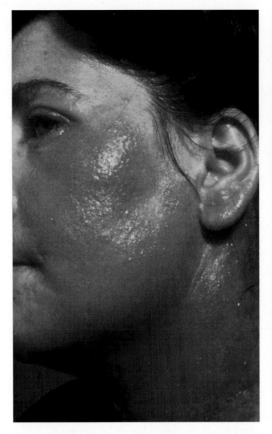

Figure 17–20 Allergic contact dermatitis (ACD).

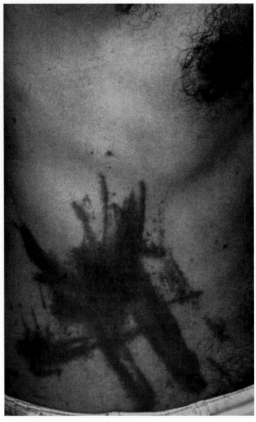

Figure 17–21 Irritant contact dermatitis (ICD).

irritant contact
dermatitis: (ICD)
Dermatitis caused by
exposure to an irritating
chemical.

system reacts strongly, but may not immediately react—it may take up to a few days.

Irritant contact dermatitis (ICD) is dermatitis caused by exposure to an irritating chemical (Figure 17–21). This is more of an irritation than an allergic reaction. One of the main differences between ACD and ICD is that not everyone has an allergy to a particular substance, but everyone will react to an irritant. Anyone who comes in skin contact with a highly acidic material will develop an irritation.

Urticaria

Commonly known as hives, urticaria can flare up from exposure to allergens of various sorts (Figure 17–22). The hive itself is caused by edema and the release of a defensive chemical called histamine. Hives can form very quickly when the skin is exposed to allergens, and they can form during facial treatments, although this situation is rare. If a client has a reaction during a salon treatment, immediately remove all products and

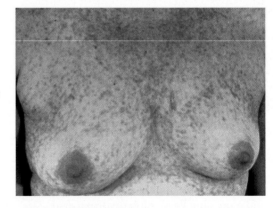

Figure 17–22 Urticaria.

apply a cool, wet compresses. Do not apply other creams or preparations, as they can add to the reaction.

General precautions for clients with a history of urticaria are to adhere to the rules for sensitive skin: avoid heat and sun, avoid fragranced products, avoid stimulating treatments of any type, avoid aggressive treatments, and use products designed and tested for sensitive skin.

Eventually, every esthetician will see a client with allergic contact dermatitis or with irritant contact dermatitis. The most common type of allergen in skin care products and cosmetics is fragrance. On most skin types, fragrance-free products are regarded as the safest products to use. This is especially true on skin with a history of allergic reactions and sensitivities.

Preservatives are another common cosmetic allergen. Some individuals have reactions to formaldehyde-releasing preservatives, such as imidazolidinyl urea, diazolidinyl urea, and quaternium 15. These ingredients do not cause problems for the majority of people, but you may want to avoid them when treating clients with histories of reactions to unknown substances.

An example of irritant contact dermatitis that estheticians often see is clients who overuse keratolytic substances such as benzoyl peroxide or other acne medications. Some individuals are also allergic to benzoyl peroxide.

Atopic Dermatitis

Atopic dermatitis is a genetic skin condition that is prevalent in people with asthma, airborne nasal allergies, and overreactive immune systems (Figure 17–23). Atopic eczema is a severe form of atopic dermatitis.

Most people suffer periodically from atopic dermatitis all their lives. It is quite common in young children. It begins with redness and very itchy skin, which people tend to scratch, creating flaking and dehydration and further irritating the area. In adults, it is more common on the legs, arms, inside of the elbows, and the backs of the knees.

Atopic dermatitis tends to be worse during the colder, winter months. Stress can also be a factor. Additionally, excessive sweating is associated with flare-ups of atopic dermatitis.

Treatment of atopic dermatitis involves the routine use of a fragrance-free, allergy-tested moisturizer, which helps to keep the skin from dehydrating, which can cause more itching. Avoiding excessive bathing with soaps or cleansing agents is also helpful. Medical treatment includes the use of topical

Figure 17–23 Atopic dermatitis.

corticosteroids. Occasionally, oral or steroid injections are given to reduce symptoms.

Psoriasis

Psoriasis is a condition caused by skin cells replicating themselves too quickly, a phenomenon known as **overproliferation** (Figure 17–24, p. 260). Diseases associated with the rate of cell turnover or cell renewal are called **proliferative diseases.** Psoriasis is a hereditary disease that is believed to be associated with immune dysfunction. It is prevalent in people with autoimmune diseases, as well as those with depressed immune systems, such as AIDS patients.

Clients with psoriasis suffer from very red, thickened, scaly patches. The condition often appears on the elbows, scalp, legs, and knees. The patches do not fade quickly and can remain flared for months at a time.

Psoriasis is treated with topical corticosteroids and vitamin A derivatives, and in more severe cases, oral medications are prescribed. One of the drugs used to treat psoriasis is psoralen. Psoralen, a phototoxic drug,

overproliferation
A phenomenon wherein skin cells replicate themselves too quickly; it is associated with psoriasis.

proliferative diseases
Diseases associated with the rate of cell turnover or cell renewal.

pityriasis rosea
A skin condition characterized by red patches of skin that may be round or oval in shape.

herald patch
The first patch that occurs in pityriasis rosea.

dermatosis papulosa nigra
A condition that occurs in black skin and is characterized by many black or brown lesions that look like tiny moles.

warts
Growths caused by a virus called human papillomavirus (HPV).

human papillomavirus (HPV)
The virus that causes warts.

molluscum contagiosum
A viral disease that appears in clusters of small, flesh-colored papules.

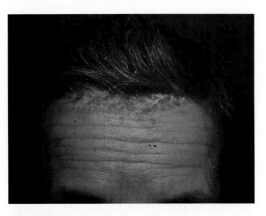

Figure 17–24 Psoriasis.

causes a reduction in the patches when combined with controlled artificial ultraviolet light exposure, known as PUVA treatments.

Pityriasis Rosea

Red patches of skin that may be round or oval in shape characterize a very common condition called **Pityriasis rosea** (Figure 17–25). The patches often have a flesh-colored center or appear to be annular. The first patch that occurs is called the **herald patch**; other lesions appear after it. The pattern of pityriasis rosea on a person's back resembles a Christmas tree. Secondary syphilis can also have this type of pattern, so it is important to distinguish the two diseases. Lesions of pityriasis seldom affect the face.

A virus may be the cause of pityriasis rosea, but this theory is not supported by strong evidence. The condition normally clears up by itself in 6–12 weeks. Itching, which is not always present, can be controlled with mild hydrocortisone creams.

Dermatosis Papulosa Nigra

Dermatosis papulosa nigra is a condition that occurs in black skin and is characterized by many black or brown lesions that look like tiny moles. It is not known to be associated with any cause. A dermatologist can remove the bumps.

Contagious Diseases

Although the skin conditions discussed so far are harmless, some conditions are contagious. Estheticians should be especially aware of these diseases and avoid working on clients with contagious diseases until they have been medically treated and approved for continued esthetic treatment.

Warts

Warts are growths caused by a virus called **human papillomavirus (HPV).** There are two major types of warts: common warts and plantar warts. Plantar warts occur on the soles of the feet. Warts are usually flesh-colored and have a rough, scaly-looking top. Flat warts may be seen on the face.

Since a virus causes warts, antibiotics do not cure them. Doctors sometimes treat warts with repetitive cryosurgery. Over-the-counter products for treating warts contain salicylic acid.

Molluscum Contagiosum

A virus belonging to the pox group of viruses, **molluscum contagiosum** appears in clusters of small, flesh-colored papules (Figure 17–26). They are often confused with milia.

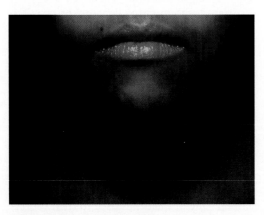

Figure 17–25 Pityriasis rosea.

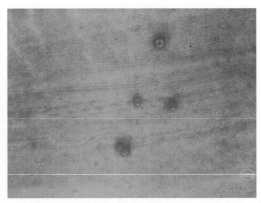

Figure 17–26 Molluscum contagiosum.

Molluscum contagiosum is frequently passed between children through skin contact and between young adults through sexual contact. Lesions occur several weeks after contact, making it hard to identify the source of the infection.

AIDS patients, because of their depressed immune systems, may have hundred of lesions that are often nonresponsive to treatment.

The lesions from molluscum contagiosum can be **autoinfectious**, which means they can spread to other areas on the same person. They generally clear up by themselves within a few weeks but can be treated by a dermatologist if they are persistent. Estheticians may see these lesions on the face, but they can occur on almost any area, including the genitalia.

Herpes Simplex Virus

The **herpes simplex virus 1 (HSV 1)** is the virus that causes **cold sores** and is most often spread by kissing (Figure 17–27). It should not be confused with **herpes simplex virus 2,** the virus that causes genital herpes. Cold sores can occur on or around the mouth and can be painful and look unattractive. They are actually small clusters of blisters. Cold sores are best treated early with a prescription antiviral medication. Itching or burning in the area precedes the onset of a cold sore; this is when medication should be started. Because people often have recurrent cold sores, they should keep medication on hand to take when they first feel a lesion coming on.

Some esthetic treatments, mainly exfoliation procedures, can cause flares of HSV 1. At the initial visit, a client should indicate on the health screening form if she has a history of cold sores. Note this information in the client's record. Clients who have HSV 1 should have pretreatment with an antiviral drug prescribed by a physician before AHA exfoliations, Jessner's exfoliations, microdermabrasion, and other exfoliation procedures. Clients undergoing surgical resurfacing should also have this pretreatment.

HSV 1 is extremely contagious; estheticians should never work on clients who have current HSV 1 lesions.

Impetigo

A bacterial infection of the skin, **impetigo** often occurs in young children and is extremely contagious (Figure 17–28). It is characterized by clusters of very small blisters that develop into weeping, crusty lesions that are filled with bacteria. Scratching them can spread the infection easily. When adults have impetigo, it may be associated with a different problem, such as eczema, where the skin is already broken.

Impetigo is treated with oral antibiotics. Families should be careful to wash their hands with antibacterial soap while a family member is infected. They should not share washcloths or other items that touch the skin of the infected person.

Tinea

Tinea are fungal infections of the skin. Fungi feed on proteins, carbohydrates, and lipids in the skin and other organs. **Tinea pedis** is the medical terminology for athlete's foot, characterized by itching, flaking, and a pink rash (Figure 17–29, p. 262). It occurs most commonly between the fourth and fifth toes, but toenails can also get infected. Athlete's foot is

autoinfectious
Describing a disease that can spread to other areas on the same person.

herpes simplex virus 1 (HSV 1)
The virus that causes cold sores.

cold sores
Sores caused by the herpes simplex virus that can occur on or around the mouth; they can be painful.

herpes simplex virus 2
The virus that causes genital herpes.

impetigo
A bacterial infection of the skin that often occurs in young children and is extremely contagious.

tinea
Fungal infections of the skin.

tinea pedis
The medical term for athlete's foot, a fungus characterized by itching, flaking, and a pink rash.

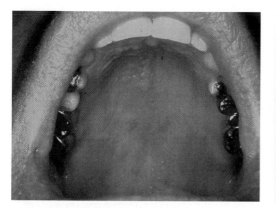

Figure 17–27 Cold sore.

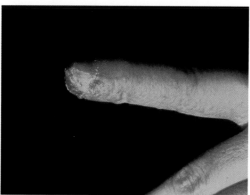

Figure 17–28 Impetigo.

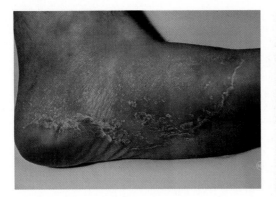

Figure 17–29 Tinea pedis (athlete's foot).

spread in warm, moist environments, such as showers, gyms, and other areas where the public goes barefoot. Wearing slip-ons or slides in these areas will help prevent athlete's foot.

Tinea pedis is easily treated with OTC medications. Sprays, powders, and creams are available containing the active antifungal ingredients clotrimazole, terbinafine, or miconazole. A physician should see clients with recurrent infections.

Tinea Corporis

Tinea corporis is a fungus commonly known as ringworm (Figure 17–30). It occurs in a ringed, red pattern with elevated edges and resembles a worm under the skin. Tinea corporis is most often seen on the body, but it can occur on the face or scalp. These lesions are very itchy.

Tinea corporis is often spread by small children who have contact with dogs and cats. It is treated with the same antifungal agents used to treat tinea pedis. Ringworm is highly contagious, so esthetic treatments should be discontinued until the lesions have cleared up.

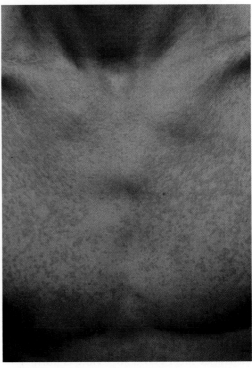

Figure 17–31 Tinea versicolor.

Tinea Versicolor

Tinea versicolor, also known as pityriasis versicolor, is a yeast infection (Figure 17–31). The yeast, **pityosporon**, occurs normally on everyone's skin. It is not known why, but in some people the yeast infects the skin and affects the ability of the skin to produce melanin. The infection is often first noticed when someone has sun exposure, because they tan only in areas where the yeast has not affected the melanin production. Thus, many people erroneously believe that the fungus is caused by the sun or sand at the beach. It is often incorrectly referred to as sun fungus.

Note that the white splotches of hypopigmentation associated with tinea versicolor are more common on the body than on the face. The fungus is treated by applying an antifungal cream such as ketoconazole or selenium sulfide shampoo. Occasionally, oral antifungal medication is prescribed.

Bacterial Conjunctivitis

Bacterial conjunctivitis, or pinkeye, is an extremely contagious disease that is frequently seen in clients. The eyes are red or pink, with a crusty or yellow discharge. The client will complain that her eyelids are stuck

tinea corporis
A fungus commonly known as ringworm.

tinea versicolor
A yeast infection, also called pityriasis versicolor.

pityosporon
The yeast that occurs normally on everyone's skin; it can cause tinea versicolor (pityriasis versicolor).

bacterial conjunctivitis
A disease that causes eye infection; also known as pinkeye.

Figure 17–30 Tinea corporis (ringworm).

together. Pinkeye is easily treated with prescription eyedrops. The client should replace all her eye makeup products immediately and not wear eye makeup while the infection is present. Any implements used by the client around the eye should be sterilized or discarded.

Other Diseases of the Skin

Shingles

Shingles (Figure 17–32) is a skin condition caused by **herpes zoster**, the same virus that causes **chickenpox.** When someone has chickenpox, the virus stays in the body and lives in the nerve tissue. Later in life, it can resurface as shingles. Shingles are characterized by groups of blisters that form a rash and are frequently found on one side of the face or wrapped around one side of the chest or abdomen. Shingles can be very painful, and in severe cases, even after the rash has cleared, the nerves can remain inflamed, a condition known as postherpetic neuralgia. Shingles can occur in any adult but are most prevalent in older people or those with compromised immune systems, including AIDS patients.

Shingles are treated with antiviral medications, commercially known as Zovirax (acyclovir), Valtrex (valacyclovir), or Famvir (famciclovir).

Cellulitis

Cellulitis is a severe bacterial infection of the skin (Figure 17–33). (Do not confuse the

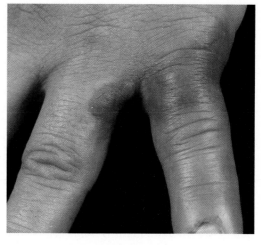

Figure 17–33 Cellulitis.

word *cellulitis* with *cellulite*.) It appears as a large area of red, swollen skin that is hot to the touch. Streptococcus bacteria cause cellulitis, which is often associated with a puncture wound or other cut to the skin. A very severe form of cellulitis, **erysipelas**, can be fatal if not treated soon enough. A physician should immediately see this condition or any condition that seems similar to it.

Folliculitis

Folliculitis is an inflammation of the follicle caused by bacteria or by an irritation (Figure 17–34). *Staphylococcus aureus* and yeast are common bacteria that can cause folliculitis. Irritation that causes folliculitis includes chemical irritations and mechanical irritations.

Chemical irritations are often caused by work-related chemical exposure. Mechanical

shingles
A skin disease characterized by groups of blisters; it is frequently found on one side of the face or wrapped around one side of the chest or abdomen.

herpes zoster
The virus that causes shingles and chickenpox.

chickenpox
A contagious disease occurring most often during childhood; it is caused by the same virus that causes shingles.

cellulitis
A severe bacterial infection of the skin, characterized by hot, swollen skin.

erysipelas
A very severe form of cellulitis that can be fatal if not treated soon enough.

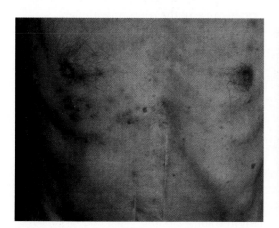

Figure 17–32 Shingles.

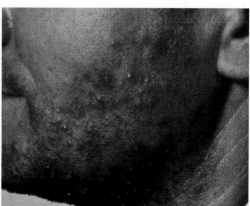

Figure 17–34 Folliculitis.

folliculitis causes hair breakage and ingrown hairs. When a hair is pulled out, torn, or breaks below the surface, the hair can grow into the side of the follicle, causing irritation. The swelling can cut off oxygen to the bottom of the follicle, just like in an inflammatory acne lesion. Anaerobic bacteria then have a perfect environment for growth. This condition is known as pseudofolliculitis barbae.

Pseudofolliculitis barbae is prevented by shaving in the direction of hair growth and not so close to the skin. Electric razors can help, and special razors are available that cut hair above the skin. Ingrown hairs can occur on the face, legs, bikini and groin area, and armpits.

Determining the source of mechanical and chemical irritations results in better treatment. OTC preparations that help prevent ingrown hairs are available and sold by estheticians. These formulations contain salicylic acid, which helps break up the impaction and kills bacteria. In the case of an infection, the correct topical or oral antibiotics can be prescribed after the type of bacteria is identified.

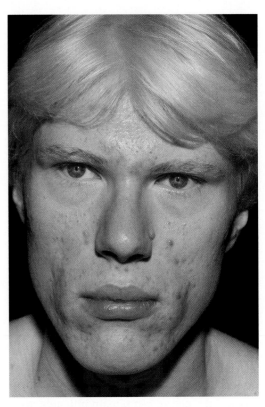

Figure 17–35 Albinism.

Dyschromias

A **dyschromia** is any abnormal discoloration of the skin. Dyschromias may be related to pigment or may be vascular lesions, such as port-wine stains or telangiectasias. Pigment dyschromias are either caused by hyperpigmentation (the overproduction of pigmentation) or hypopigmentation (the absence of pigmentation).

Albinism

Albinism is a hereditary condition in which the body lacks pigment, including the skin, hair, and iris of the eye (Figure 17–35). Persons with albinism are called albinos. An albino has white hair, at any age, and no visible skin pigment, resulting in very light skin. Albinos also have pink eyes, because even the irises have no pigment. Albinos have no natural protection against the harmful effects of the sun and are at particular risk for developing skin cancers.

Vitiligo

Vitiligo is a partial lack of skin pigment that appears as white or light skin patches on normal-colored skin (Figure 17–36, p. 265). The exact cause of vitiligo is unknown. One theory is that it results from an autoimmune disorder that destroys the melanocytes in certain areas. Vitiligo may begin as a small macule of hypopigmentation and spread over a large area. It often occurs in childhood, but it can also affect adults.

Vitiligo can be extremely obvious on dark skin because of the contrast with light patches. Treatment of vitiligo generally has poor results. Techniques involve treatment with topical steroids and a drug called psoralen. Also used to treat psoriasis, psoralen has been used in conjunction with artificial ultraviolet treatments in an attempt to repigment the skin.

In serious vitiligo cases, a drug called monobenzone is used to cause depigmentation of the skin. This results in an irreversible removal of the rest of the pigment. The skin eventually has no pigment, but it is consistent in color.

vitiligo
A partial lack of skin pigment that appears as white or light skin patches on normal-colored skin.

albinism
A hereditary condition in which the body lacks pigment, including the skin, hair, and iris of the eye.

dyschromia
Any abnormal discoloration of the skin.

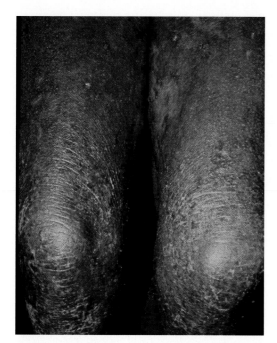

Figure 17–36 Vitiligo.

Estheticians frequently help clients with vitiligo or other hypopigmentation disorders use camouflage makeup to cover and blend affected areas to resemble normal pigmentation.

Hypopigmentation

Hypopigmentation is less than normal pigmentation or the absence of pigmentation. It results either from missing melanocytes or from a disorder that prevents the melanocytes from producing melanin.

Hypopigmentation is sometimes caused by long-term sun exposure. Small white spots may appear on the face or other areas, usually mixed into mottled (blotchy) coloring. This is probably caused by a dysfunction in the melanocytes resulting from sun damage.

Tinea versicolor, the fungus that inhibits the production of melanin wherever the fungus is present, is also a type of hypopigmentation. This condition is reversible; the pigment eventually returns to normal after the fungus is treated.

Hyperpigmentation

Numerous disorders and diseases result in hyperpigmentation, the overproduction of pigment that causes darkening of the skin. It most often occurs in a pattern of splotchy, hyperpigmented macules and patches. Examples of hyperpigmentation include mottling, solar lentigenes, and poikiloderma of Civatte. Mottling is an uneven pigmentation caused by sun exposure, solar lentigenes are sun-induced freckles, and poikiloderma of Civatte is a horseshoe-patterned hyperpigmentation mixed with telangiectasia that appears on the necks of persons with severe sun damage.

Sun exposure can make any form of hyperpigmentation worse, or unresponsive to treatment. Heat exposure, even while wearing a sunscreen, may also make pigmentation worse. It can cause it to recur, or even interfere with treatment.

Hyperpigmentation can also result from injuries, rashes, or chemical irritation. Hyperpigmentation occurs after the original irritation. This condition is known as postinflammatory hyperpigmentation (PIH). Even acne or eczema can result in hyperpigmented macules.

Hyperpigmentation from injuries is especially prevalent in people with darker skin, including Asians, persons of Middle Eastern heritage, and people with black skin. The reason trauma causes hyperpigmentation is that pigment is a defense mechanism of the skin, and if the skin interprets any injury as an invader, melanin can be produced. Estheticians should be especially careful when treating these darker skin types because they are so susceptible to hyperpigmentation. Extraction and exfoliation procedures must be very gentle. Black skin can hyperpigment from overuse of exfoliating agents such as higher strength benzoyl peroxide, which is used to treat acne.

Hyperpigmentation is traditionally treated with an active ingredient called **hydroquinone,** a topical drug ingredient that interferes with the production of melanin by the melanocytes. Hydroquinone is used in 2% concentrations in OTC products that are used and sold by estheticians. Prescription versions used by physicians have 4%–6% concentrations.

Hydroquinone is currently the only drug ingredient approved by the Food and Drug Administration (FDA) for the treatment of hyperpigmentation. However, numerous

hypopigmentation
The absence of pigmentation in the skin, resulting from missing melanocytes or from a disorder that prevents the melanocytes from producing melanin.

hydroquinone
A topical drug ingredient used in medication to treat hyperpigmentation.

other topical ingredients do help to suppress melanin production and have a lightening (sometimes called brightening) effect on hyperpigmentation. These ingredients include kojic acid, arbutin, bearberry extract, asafetida extract, magnesium ascorbyl phosphate (a vitamin C derivative and an antioxidant), azelaic acid, and licorice extract.

Estheticians should use an exfoliating agent in addition to the treatment for melanin suppression in order to rid the skin of dead cells that are already pigmented. These agents typically include glycolic acid and other AHAs, salicylic acid, or prescription tretinoin (Retin-A or Renova). Finally, sunscreen with a sun protection factor of 15 or higher should be applied daily to discourage tanning. Heat exposure should also be avoided.

Melasma

melasma
Common term to describe any disorder of hyperpigmentation; it is frequently used to describe a condition known as pregnancy mask.

Melasma is any disorder of hyperpigmentation, but the term is frequently used to describe a condition known as a pregnancy mask (Figure 17–37). This condition occurs

Figure 17–37 Melasma.

acquired immunodeficiency syndrome (AIDS)
A syndrome caused by a virus that causes the body's immune cells to malfunction, leaving the body unable to defend itself.

almost exclusively in women and is characterized by a dark, splotchy pattern on the face. The skin around the eyes is usually not affected, resulting in white rings around the eyes. The contrast in colors accentuates the splotchiness.

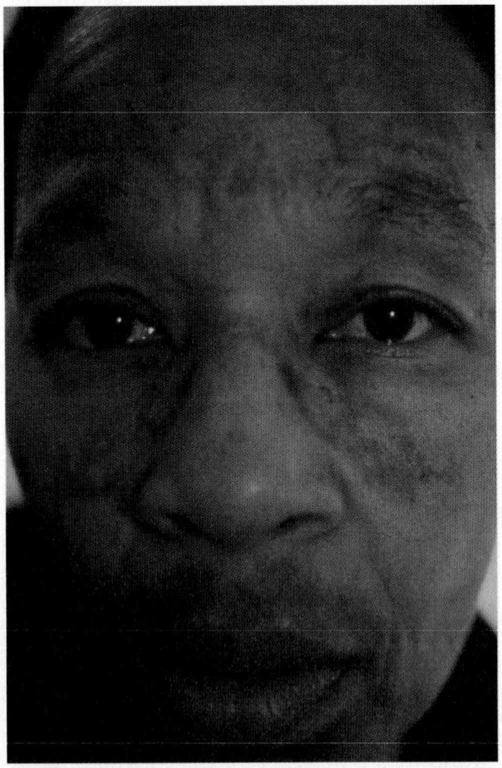

Not all forms of melasma form an entire mask pattern. Some people experience large splotches on the forehead or cheeks. This form of melasma is caused by an imbalance of hormones that triggers melanin production. In some cases, the mask appears during pregnancy but gradually fades, although a pregnancy is not necessary for the condition to occur. Melasma has often been associated with contraceptive hormones (birth control pills) or estrogen.

Autoimmune Diseases

The immune system of the body is responsible for detecting and fighting foreign organisms and inflammations in all of the body's systems, tissues, and organs. A properly functioning immune system allows the body to overcome illnesses—from the smallest pimple to cancer cells.

When someone has a malfunction of the immune system, the system or the person is said to be immunosuppressed, immunocompromised, or has a depressed immune system. Many diseases, such as AIDS, cause depressed immune systems. The treatments for some health problems can suppress the immune system, such as chemotherapy treatment for cancer and immunosuppressive drugs for organ transplant recipients.

Sometimes, the body has diseases or disorders that lead to an overactive immune system. The immune system cannot distinguish between foreign organisms and the body itself, and the immune system attacks the body's own tissues. This is known as autoimmune disease.

AIDS

One of the best examples of immunosuppression is **acquired immunodeficiency syndrome (AIDS)**. AIDS is a syndrome caused by a virus known as the **human immuno-**

SKILLS **FOR** SUCCESS

Referrals

How did you hear about us? This is one of the most important questions you will ever ask your clients. Taking note of how clients find out about you is the first step in developing a system of referrals.

Successful salons understand the value of attracting and keeping clients. They work hard to develop business through marketing and advertising plans. Analyzing these efforts is key to expanding the customer database.

Today, most savvy salons are using computer information systems to track and code clients. Hopefully the skin care clinic you work in is one. If not, you can conduct your own tracking system with a simple notation on your client's data card.

In order to understand where your clients are coming from, you need to ask them. A simple "how did you hear about us?" will help you gain access to important information on how to increase business. Did the client respond to a newspaper ad, see your name in the news, meet you at a business event, or does she work with a friend who is a current client? Entering this information into a database that can analyze your referrals will help you focus your expansion efforts.

The majority of a clinic's referrals are generally "word of mouth." The smart business person (esthetician) knows these clients are precious and valuable assets. They indicate a vote of confidence in your abilities. They should be treated with care and rewarded in tangible ways. Salons often institute a referral reward program offering a special discount to clients who bring in new clients. This can be a free facial, product gift, or discount.

If you note that a good number of your clients are coming from a particular advertising approach you should make sure that it remains in place. Should a group, such as the local chamber of commerce or nail shop, send you a significant number of clients, you should thank them in some tangible way. Perhaps you could invite the staff in for a special day or evening of beauty at a discount rate. Make sure that they have plenty of brochures and business cards on hand for continued referrals.

If you find that your referrals do not cover a broad enough spectrum you may want to pay special attention to building your network. Try to initiate relationships with other professionals who may share the same goals or who can form mutually beneficial alliances. Some connections to consider would be dermatologists, plastic surgeons, massage therapists, nail technicians, chiropractors, and other allied health professionals. Start the process by sending a brief note, business card, and menu of services. Follow up with a phone call to personally introduce yourself.

You might also look to suppliers or vendors who offer an opportunity for cooperative advertising. Making it known that a popular product is available through your clinic or spa will give you a chance to showcase other treatments.

It may seem awkward at first, but many opportunities happen by chance. Always be prepared with your business card and do not be afraid to offer it should someone show an interest in your work—you may just win a client for life!

human immunodeficiency virus (HIV)

The virus that causes AIDS.

deficiency virus (HIV). HIV causes the body's immune cells, or T cells, to function abnormally; thus, the body cannot defend itself properly.

Lupus

Perhaps the best known autoimmune disease, and one that often affects the skin, is systemic lupus erythematosus (SLE), commonly known as lupus. The term *lupus* comes from the Latin term for wolf. It refers to the red marks left on the face of a wolf attack victim. In SLE, the red rash on the face associated with lupus takes a form that resembles a butterfly across the cheeks. The nose is the butterfly's body (Figure 17–38).

Other symptoms include joint pain, hair loss, swelling of the feet and fingers, and visible blood vessels around the nail cuticles. SLE is a serious form of lupus that also affects internal organs. A physician prescribes steroids to help patients manage SLE.

Discoid lupus erythematosus (DLE) is a form of lupus that primarily affects the skin. The skin forms round, firm lesions, called discoids, and red patches with raised red bumps

dermatomyositis

An autoimmune disease that affects the immunity of the body's muscles and causes inflammation.

scleroderma

An autoimmune disease that makes the skin very tight and thick. Internal organs and tissues are also affected.

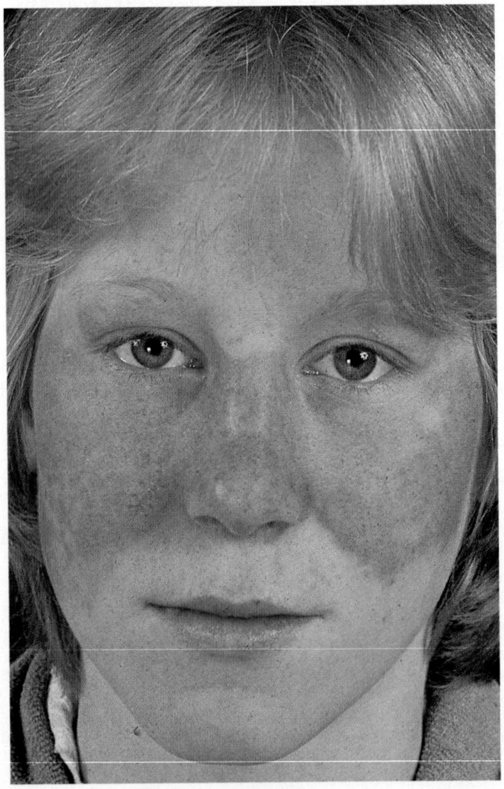

Figure 17–38 Lupus butterfly rash.

around the hair follicles. Rashes typically appear on the face and the back of the forearms. DLE almost exclusively affects parts of the body exposed to the sun. Interestingly, DLE is managed with the same drugs used to treat malaria.

All forms of lupus are flared by sun exposure. In fact, sunburn may trigger the first symptoms. Both SLE and DLE are more prevalent in women.

Treatment

Lupus is not contagious, and because it causes skin sensitivity, redness, and the need for constant sun protection, the esthetician needs to understand it. Estheticians do not actually treat the disease, but they can help treat the skin with products for very sensitive skin. They can also provide appropriate makeup techniques to help clients cover redness. Clients must receive approval from their physicians for esthetic treatments.

The skin of a client with lupus must be treated with ultimate care. Fragranced products, stimulating treatment, and any aggressive treatment must be avoided. Rather, estheticians should offer cool steam with gentle hydrating masks, soothing agents such as green tea, and moisturizers designed for sensitive skin.

The most important treatment is to help clients with lupus choose an appropriate broad-spectrum sunscreen for daily use. Products with physical sunscreens, such as zinc oxide and titanium dioxide, are the best.

Dermatomyositis

Dermatomyositis is an autoimmune disease that afflicts the body's muscles, resulting in inflammation. One symptom is a red or lavender ring-type rash around the eyes, called a heliotrope. This disease is very debilitating due to the muscle inflammation. Like SLE, dermatomyositis is treated with corticosteroid drugs.

Scleroderma

Scleroderma is an autoimmune disease that makes the skin very tight and thick. It has been compared to wearing a glove, because it restricts movement due to the tightness. The thickened skin appears on the face and fingers. Internal organs and tissues are often affected. Scleroderma is twice as common in women as it is in men.

Summary

Clients quickly notice skin conditions, which normally motivates them to seek professional help. Many skin conditions require medical attention, thus estheticians should be required to identify medical conditions such as skin lesions and diseases. They should also be able to identify skin conditions and allergens, and they should be familiar with dermatological terminology.

Discussion Questions

1. Define the parameters of esthetic skin care and dermatological skin care. Discuss why it is important for estheticians to be familiar with medical terminology.

2. Name all the abnormalities of the skin that are considered lesions. Can you think of a way to identify and differentiate these easily?

3. Developing a logical and analytical format to determine the different dermatological symptoms is key to proper skin analysis and treatment. Make a list of questions that might be helpful in querying clients about specific dermatological skin conditions.

4. Discuss the common symptoms associated with seborrheic dermatitis. How is this distinguished from seborrhea? Include in your discussion a list of those most frequently affected by this condition and the best approach to treatment.

5. Explain the origin of rosacea and name those skin types most affected by this condition. What is the best method of treatment?

6. Describe how common allergic contact dermatitis typically presents and discuss common allergens that are often associated with this condition.

7. Estheticians should be aware of those skin conditions that are considered contagious. Develop a list of contagious diseases typically seen on the skin and briefly describe each. Carefully review photos of each.

8. Autoimmune diseases can have a significant impact on the skin. Discuss the best method for treating clients afflicted with the autoimmune disease lupus.

Additional Reading

Fitzpatrick, Thomas B., et al. 1997. *Color Atlas and Synopsis of Clinical* Dermatology. 3d. ed. New York: McGraw-Hill Health Professions Division.

Lees, Mark. 2000. *Skin Care: Beyond the Basics.* Clifton Park, N.Y.: Milady, an imprint of Delmar Learning, a division of Thomson Learning.

Helpful Web Sites

http://www.emedicine.com (eMedicine)
http://www.ucsf.edu (University of California, San Francisco)

Chapter 18
Pharmacology

Chapter Objectives

After reading this chapter, you should be able to:

- Identify the OTC drugs that estheticians use.

- Describe the prescription drugs that estheticians need to understand.

Chapter Outline

Introduction
Over-the-Counter and Prescription Drugs
Skin Lightening Products
Corticosteroids
Prescription Steroids
Allergic Reactions, Hives, and Redness
Retinoids
Drugs for the Treatment of Rosacea
Antibiotics

Sunscreen Ingredients Listing:

ACTIVE INGREDIENTS: Octinoxate, Octisalate, Oxybenzone

OTHER INGREDIENTS: Water (Aqua), Caprylic/Capite, Triglyceride, Butylene Glycol, Steric Acid, Aloe Barbadensis Leaf Juice, Glyceryl Stearate, Propylene Glycol Dicaprylate, Dicaprate, Glycerine, Dimethicone, PEG-100 Stearate, Paraffin, Silk Amino Acids, Glycoproteins, Sphingolipids, Glycosphingo-lipids, Phospholipids, Cholesterol, Sodium Hyaluronate, Sodium PCA, Ceteth-20, Disodium EDTA, Cetyl Alcohol, Carbomer, Triethanolamine, Propylene Glycol, Diazolidinyl Urea, Methylparaben, Propylparaben.

Introduction

Pharmacology is the study of medicinal drugs, how they work, and how they are produced. The U.S. Food and Drug Administration (FDA) states that drugs are intended to treat or prevent a disease or alter a body structure or function.

Over-the-Counter And Prescription Drugs

The United States classifies drugs in two ways: over-the-counter and prescription. **Over-the-counter (OTC)** drugs are available in stores without a prescription. The drugs sold in conjunction with cosmetics and skin care products in stores and salons are over-the-counter drugs. **Prescription drugs** require a written order from a physician. Prescriptions may also be written by dentists, veterinarians, and, in some states, physician's assistants (PAs) and advanced registered nurse practitioners (ARNPs).

A variety of factors determine a drug's classification as prescription or OTC. Almost every new drug ingredient starts out as a prescription drug product. In the United States, when companies develop a new drug ingredient, they must apply for a new drug approval from the FDA. They are required to perform many tests and studies to determine a drug's safety as well as any possible side effects.

Testing for new drugs takes years and requires millions of dollars, and the FDA makes no guarantees that it will approve new drugs. After a drug is approved, it almost always becomes a prescription drug initially. Restricting drugs through prescriptions allows doctors to monitor dosages, results, and side effects. Occasionally, a new drug will be safe for many years, with only minor side effects. It may then go off prescription and become an OTC drug. Many cold medications and antihistamines, as well as the hair growth drug Minoxidil, have gone off prescription.

Drugs that may be addictive, have strong side effects, or have very specific dosing requirements may remain available only by prescription. For example, antibiotics can be overused, resulting in the mutation and development of antibiotic-resistant bacteria. Therefore, the use of antibiotics is restricted to prescriptions.

Once a drug goes off prescription, it can be used in formulations at predetermined levels. The FDA determines these concentration levels, and larger concentrations may remain available only by prescription. Any FDA-registered laboratory wishing to formulate a product using approved OTC ingredients within the approved concentration levels may do so. They must register their plans with the FDA and comply with FDA standards for that drug ingredient. For example, in the United States, sunscreens must have expiration dates and they must have sun protection factor (SPF) testing using at least 20 people in the study.

Some cosmetic laboratories are also FDA-registered OTC labs. These laboratories can make both cosmetic products and topical drugs.

OTC Drugs Used by Estheticians

At least three types of OTC drugs are used and sold by estheticians in the United States. These categories include sunscreens, acne drugs, and lightening products.

Sunscreens
The most common OTC drug product used and sold by estheticians is sunscreen. All sunscreens in the United States are defined as OTC drugs; thus, sunscreens must undergo thorough testing before they are marketed. This testing determines the SPF. In Australia and other countries, sunscreen products must be evaluated to determine how much light is blocked or absorbed before a company is allowed to market them as **broad spectrum,** which means that they screen out a large portion of the light spectrum.

Sunscreens work by absorbing or reflecting ultraviolet (UV) light rays. Most sunscreen ingredients work by absorbing the UV rays.

Physical Sunscreens. Physical sunscreens, or particulate sunscreens, contain reflecting sunscreen ingredients. Only two such ingredients are approved: zinc oxide and titanium dioxide. Particulate sunscreens are in particle form and are actually earth pigments. They work by physically blocking the light or

pharmacology
The study of medicinal drugs, how they work, and how they are produced.

over-the-counter (OTC) drugs
Drugs available in stores without a prescription.

prescription drugs
Drugs that require a written order from a physician.

broad spectrum
A term given to sunscreens based on how much of the light spectrum is blocked or absorbed.

reflecting the light off the particle crystals. They block a larger portion of the light spectrum than other sunscreens, including ultraviolet A rays, (UVA), which most absorbing screens do not absorb.

The original law stated that products containing titanium dioxide or zinc oxide as active ingredients could be called sunblocks. However, the FDA has determined that consumers may assume that all ultraviolet light is being blocked, so the term *sunblock* is no longer allowed. No product blocks 100% of the ultraviolet rays.

Particulate sunscreens have only come into vogue in the last few years. Previously, physical sunscreens could easily be seen on the face. Most of us have seen surfers with white noses that are coated with a water-resistant zinc oxide. This is a very effective sunscreen, but people do not want to walk around with white faces! Fortunately, through technology, we now can "micro-grind" pigments into a very fine powder; this is called the micronization process. On very dark skin types, these pigments are still visible, but they are basically invisible on most skin colors. Particulate sunscreens are also less irritating to the skin than other types of sunscreen.

Chemical Sunscreens. A second type of sunscreen is ultraviolet B (UVB) or chemical sunscreen, which mainly works by absorbing and neutralizing the ultraviolet rays. The term *chemical sunscreen* is slightly misleading, because all sunscreens are chemicals. Chemical sunscreens involve a chemical reaction that absorbs the light, whereas physical sunscreens entail a physical reaction that reflects the light.

The most popular UVB sunscreen is octyl methoxycinnamate, also known as ethyl-hexyl p-methoxycinnamate. Octyl methoxycinnamate is often combined with other absorbing sunscreens, such as octyl salicylate and benzophenone-3, to create a broad-spectrum product. Benzophenone-3 absorbs some UVB and some UVA rays, and octyl salicylate absorbs a different area of the spectrum of UVB light. The combination of all three active sunscreen ingredients improves the spectrum of light absorbed by the finished product.

All sunscreen ingredients have advantages and disadvantages. Absorbing screens are more likely to irritate the skin, and they produce heat while absorbing rays, which can be irritating to some skin. The advantage is that they cannot be seen on the skin.

Physical and chemical sunscreens may be combined into one product. This is an ideal sunscreen because it provides broad-spectrum protection with lower potential for irritation. Octyl methoxycinnamate blended with zinc oxide or titanium dioxide is a good example of such a product.

Sunscreen and the Esthetician

Sunscreens can be formulated in a variety of vehicle bases such as creams, lotions, oils, fluids, and gels. Because many sunscreens are now developed for daily use under makeup, estheticians must find the right sunscreen formulations for a client's skin type. Creams are great for dry skin but are often too heavy for oily or combination skin. Creams may also contain comedogenic emollients that are good for alipidic, dry skin but are clogging to oily and acne-prone areas. Lotions and fluids that are noncomedogenic are better choices for combination and oily skin.

Special conditioners can be added to sunscreens to improve application or provide advantages for certain skin types. For example, green tea or matricaria extract can be added for sensitive skin. Ultralight products have been developed for oilier skin. Most daily use sunscreen products have hydrating benefits.

Another formulation of sunscreen is water-resistant. These are sometimes call waterproof, although no product is completely waterproof. Water-resistant sunscreens are designed for outdoor use, during water sports, or for strenuous activity. They are also sweat resistant. They are required to pass a test that shows that the product is still effective after being submerged in water for 80 minutes. Note that water-resistant products tend to be thicker, heavier, and generally more comedogenic than non-water-resistant products. They are generally less popular as under-makeup products because of their heaviness.

Remember that a client needs to be comfortable with any product she wears all day, every day. Take into account lifestyle needs as well as skin type. Does the client spend all day in an office? Or does she plan to spend a day on a boat in direct sunlight?

Sunscreen Ingredients Listing:

ACTIVE INGREDIENTS: Octinoxate, Octisalate, Oxybenzone

OTHER INGREDIENTS: Water (Aqua), Ca-prylic/Capite, Triglyceride, Butylene Glycol, Steric Acid, Aloe Barbadensis Leaf Juice, Glyceryl Stearate, Propylene Glycol Dica-prylate, Dicaprate, Glycerine, Dimethicone, PEG-100 Stearate, Paraffin, Silk Amino Acids, Glycoproteins, Sphingolipids, Glycosphingo-lipids, Phospholipids, Cholesterol, Sodium Hy-aluronate, Sodium PCA, Ceteth-20, Disodium EDTA, Cetyl Alcohol, Carbomer, Triethano-lamine, Propylene Glycol, Diazolidinyl Urea, Methylparaben, Propylparaben.

Figure 18–1 Ingredients listed for sunscreens must follow specific phrasing approved by the FDA.

All OTC drugs, including sunscreens, have special requirements for labeling (Figure 18–1). Active ingredients must be listed first, followed by the other nondrug ingredients. Sunscreens must also use spe-cially worded directions with phrases approved by the FDA. Cautionary statements such as "reapply after swimming or excessive perspiring," or "do not use on children under 6 months of age," and warnings to discon-tinue use if the skin is irritated, are standard statements and are required by law.

If your spa or salon carries a European skin care line, you should be aware that, in Europe, sunscreens are considered to be cos-metics. However, when they are sold in the United States, they are considered OTC drugs and must comply with all FDA sunscreen regulations. The European line you sell must have proper labeling to be sold in the United States.

OTC Acne Products

The second most prevalent category of skin-related OTC topical drugs is the active ingre-dients for acne treatment. Four ingredients are OTC-approved for acne treatment: ben-zoyl peroxide, **salicylic acid, sulfur,** and sulfur with **resorcinol.** The purpose of these topical drugs is to kill **Propionibacterium**

acnes (p. acnes), the bacteria that cause acne vulgaris, or to help exfoliate follicular hyper-keratosis, which can block pores and cause acne.

Acne is caused by a few different factors. The first factor is hereditary retention hyper-keratosis, which causes a buildup of cells on the walls inside the follicles. This cell buildup mixes with, and is coated by, sebum from the sebaceous gland. Overproduction of sebum by the sebaceous gland is also a hereditary acne factor.

The second factor that causes acne is plugs of dead cells and solidified sebum, which block atmospheric oxygen from entering the follicle. P. acnes bacteria are **anaerobic,** which means they thrive in the absence of oxygen and cannot live in the presence of oxygen. They feed on fatty acids that they break down from the solidified sebum within the follicle. Thus, the plugs produce the perfect thriving ground for the bacteria.

Benzoyl peroxide is the most widely used OTC acne drug. It is both antibacterial, physi-cally killing the acne bacteria, and is also a keratolytic, or exfoliating agent. Exfoliation inside the follicle helps to remove the buildup of dead cells, allowing penetration of atmos-pheric oxygen to kill the p. acnes bacteria. Benzoyl peroxide has a strong drying effect on the skin and may easily irritate skin if it is overused. It can also cause allergic reactions in some people. Estheticians should patch test benzoyl peroxide products, especially on clients with sensitive or reactive skin.

Benzoyl peroxide is used in granular scrubs, rinseable cleansers, spot treatments, masks, and leave-on medications. It is most effective in a leave-on gel formulation. Clients often used benzoyl peroxide directly on pimples to dry them up. However, this ingredient is best used on all areas of the acne-prone skin, as the keratolytic action helps to flush out follicles that will eventually become an acne papule or pustule.

Benzoyl peroxide is classically used in 2.5%, 5%, and 10% concentrations. Recent evidence shows that benzoyl peroxide may be as effective at 2.5% as it is at 10%. Use of 10% concentration has classically been reserved for treating resistant pustular acne, since this concentration can easily irritate the skin. Benzoyl peroxide is also used in pre-scription formulations. A widely used acne

salicylic acid
An OTC-approved ingredient used in the topical treatment of acne.

sulfur
An OTC-approved ingredient used in the topical treatment of acne.

resorcinol
An OTC-approved ingredient used in the topical treatment of acne.

Propionibacterium acnes
The bacteria that cause acne vulgaris.

anaerobic
Existing in the absence of free oxygen.

Follow-Up

We have talked at length about the importance of developing a real and lasting relationship with the client. Nurturing the practitioner-client relationship is key to building a successful practice in the esthetics industry. So how do you bond with your clients?

Think about the significant positive relationships in your life. What goes into being a good friend, parent, sibling, or spouse? How do the important people in your life make you feel special? Extend your thinking to those professional relationships that you would rate as positive. Make a list of things that encourage, nurture, and support the growth of these relationships. Chances are you listed such traits as genuine caring, respectful listening, and spending time together. Now let us focus on how you can use some of these traits to foster the client relationship.

Positive relationships are built on mutual trust, empathy, and caring. Once you have established a working relationship with the client you must focus on maintaining it. An important part of that work is follow-up.

Whether you are dealing with a client for the first or the fiftieth time, following up with them is a valuable way to strengthen the relationship. The key to navigating follow-up is timing.

We have all heard the expression "timing is everything." Just as the physician or nurse schedules a return visit or phone call after a significant procedure or diagnoses, the esthetician must learn to build in a method of follow through. This lets the client know you are a concerned professional. It is also an excellent tool for reinforcing the benefits of a particular treatment or home care regime. The key to success is in timing.

Follow-up should occur anywhere between 24 hours and one week later, depending on the need. If a client has undergone an aggressive treatment that can produce side effects, you will want to check in the next day. If the client started a new home care regime that is more involved than the previous one, call within 48 hours to

make sure she has acclimated well. All other concerns should be addressed within a week's time. This lets the client know you are invested in her success.

You may be wondering how you will ever be able to accomplish this on top of a busy schedule. The key to your success is planning and formulating a structure that works. There are several ways to approach following up with clients.

- Build a weekly or daily call-in hour right into your schedule.
- Set aside a specific time to make phone calls directly to clients.
- Send clients a brief note through regular or electronic mail.

Learning to communicate with clients on a level that is comfortable for them is the cornerstone of a successful follow-up plan. Find out how the client likes to approach tasks. This will help you determine the best method for reaching them. If the client is visual, send her home with a written "prescription" or instructions. Follow-up can be accomplished with a handwritten note that includes additional information or literature.

Is the client a talker? Then a verbal approach would probably work best. Let the client know you schedule a call-in time. You should also initiate a personal call directly to the client.

Before you begin, spend time creating a standard note or voice mail message. This approach will ease the task considerably. If your clinic or spa has its own stationery use it to write notes. If not, find a simple stationery that complements the environment and be sure to include your business card. Arrange packets of information and materials on different topics or products so that you can easily distribute these. This will save you time and effort.

Sound like too much work? Think again. The time and energy you expend in going out of your way is well worth the reward of developing long and lasting relationships with your clients.

topical, Benzamycin, combines the antibiotic erythromycin with benzoyl peroxide in a prescription topical treatment.

Salicylic acid is both an antibacterial and a keratolytic up to a concentration of 2%. It is most often made in gel form, although it may be incorporated in acne cleansers, spot treatments, and toners.

Sulfur is another active OTC ingredient for acne that has been used for many years. Primarily a light peeling agent, sulfur helps to exfoliate the follicle. It is typically used in a 10% concentration, but it may be combined in an 8% concentration with resorcinol in a 2% concentration. Sulfur-resorcinol gels are good alternatives for people who are allergic to, or easily irritated by, benzoyl peroxide. The combination of sulfur and resorcinol is often used in formulations designed for adult skin because many adults find this combination less drying than benzoyl peroxide.

Cleansers for acne treatment may contain any of the four acne ingredients, but one classic formula is a granular scrub with 2.5% benzoyl peroxide. Polyethylene beads are the grains used in this scrub cleanser, which help to mechanically "bump off" dead cell buildup loosened by the treatments. Another classic formula exists without the grains for more sensitive skin. Both types of cleansers contain substantial concentrations of surfactants, producing a foam that helps remove the excess sebum that plagues this skin type. Similar wash formulas are available without benzoyl peroxide for people allergic to benzoyl peroxide. These other washes are not labeled as acne treatments. They contain no approved active ingredients for acne, but are strong detergent cleansers that may be beneficial in removing excess oils.

Spot treatments may include active acne treatment ingredients. These products are designed to be dabbed directly on acne lesions, and are designed to provide overnight intensive drying. They may be lotions, gels, or clay-based creams. Generally, spot treatments are reserved for clients with occasional pimples. Gel medications are used for clients with chronic acne flares.

Masks for acne are almost always clay-based. They may include any of the approved active OTC ingredients but classically use sulfur or benzoyl peroxide. Drying masks, used regularly, can be a beneficial acne treatment at home.

Moisturizers for acne-prone skin may contain salicylic acid. These products help to hydrate, while still providing some exfoliating and antibacterial properties.

Skin Lightening Products

Hydroquinone is the only OTC active ingredient approved for skin lightening. It may be used in concentrations up to 2% in OTC products but is available in 4% concentration through prescription. Hydroquinone works by interfering with the chemical process that causes pigmentation of the epidermal cells.

Hydroquinone is often used in gel formulations also containing glycolic acid, an exfoliating agent that is not an OTC active ingredient. The glycolic acid, which is an alphahydroxy acid (AHA), exfoliates dead surface cells that already contain melanin pigmentation.

Physicians often prescribe a 4% hydroquinone topical treatment such as Solaquin, Lustra, and Melanex combined with Retin-A (tretinoin). This treatment is much more aggressive than the OTC variety.

Hydroquinone causes allergic and irritant reactions in a fairly large number of people. Estheticians should patch test clients before recommending a hydroquinone product for use at home.

Because of these problems with hydroquinone, companies have attempted to develop other ingredients that have similar lightening effects on hyperpigmented skin. Ingredients include magnesium ascorbyl phosphate, bearberry extract, arbutin, asafetida extract, licorice, and kojic acid. Because these ingredients are not officially approved as OTC drugs, companies cannot make "lightening" claims and instead refer to these ingredients as "brighteners." Mixed with an exfoliating agent such as glycolic acid, these products are helpful in making skin color appear more even.

Any treatment that involves an attempt to lighten or reduce hyperpigmented areas must always include the routine use of a broad-spectrum sunscreen with an SPF of at least 15. The sun is the cause of many hyperpigmentation problems.

Note that hydroquinone oxidizes very easily and tends to turn brown in the bottle or jar after opening. Consumers should be instructed not to leave the product in direct sunlight and to keep the product in a cool place, with the bottle securely closed.

Corticosteroids

corticosteroids
Hormones that help to relieve inflammation.

Corticosteroids are hormones that help relieve inflammation. They are used in creams known as steroid creams, corticosteroid creams, and hydrocortisone (cortisone) creams. These are the layperson's terms for drugs that relieve itching and redness.

Corticosteroids are also available as lotions or thick ointments. Hydrocortisone is available in OTC products at up to 1% concentration and is used to treat minor rashes and redness from seborrheic dermatitis, eczema, and atopic dermatitis. It is also used to relieve the inflammation from contact dermatitis, but only after determining and stopping contact with the irritant.

Estheticians may sell or use up to 1% hydrocortisone, but there are many precautions. Hydrocortisone should be used for relatively short periods of time and never on a daily basis for more than 2 weeks at a time, unless otherwise advised by a physician. Hydrocortisone, if overused, can cause the skin to become thin, resulting in long-range problems.

Hydrocortisone is a symptom reliever. It helps stop redness, itching, burning, and swelling, but it does not necessarily stop a disease or disorder. One of the biggest problems with hydrocortisone is that people use it to treat problems that need other medical treatment, and they simply suppress the symptoms. Even symptoms of infections can be masked by hydrocortisone usage. Anytime you notice that a client has chronic skin inflammation, you should refer him to a dermatologist.

Prescription Steroids

antihistamine
A drug that works by blocking the reactions within the skin (histamines) that cause swelling, itching, and redness.

Many drugs prescribed by dermatologists and other physicians often have side effects that affect the skin. Steroids are the most prevalent of these drugs. Different types of steroids are used to treat the symptoms—not the causes—of skin diseases. For exam-

ple, dermatologists who treat rashes and various types of skin inflammation often prescribe corticosteroid topicals. Psoriasis, eczema, dermatitis, severe forms of poison ivy, and severe forms of seborrheic dermatitis are all treated with prescription cortisone products.

Common commercial names for prescription steroids are Temovate, Diprolene, and Psorcon, which are all very potent drugs that are generally not used on the face. They are used to treat body skin problems, such as severe atopic eczema and psoriasis. Elocon and Topicort are other potent cortisone drugs. Aclovate is a cream commonly prescribed for facial use because it is mild and less likely to cause severe side effects; it still should not be used every day.

Prescription cortisones are also available in oral and injectable form. These are generally used to treat more serious diseases because they have many possible side effects. They are only used when a weaker drug will not work. Patients with lupus and other autoimmune diseases frequently take these drugs orally or by injection.

One of the most widely prescribed oral steroids is prednisone. You should watch for this drug on health screening forms and avoid any overly stimulating treatments for these clients. You may also want to ask your client if you can speak to his physician concerning treatments that may or may not be appropriate. Not all clients taking prednisone or other oral steroids have a severe disease. Prednisone is often prescribed in short-term doses, and even chronic sinus conditions can be treated with it.

Allergic Reactions, Hives, And Redness

Allergies and other conditions such as urticaria (hives), itching, and insect bites can be treated with a topical or oral **antihistamine.** These drugs work by blocking the reactions within the skin that cause swelling, itching, and redness.

Prescription antihistamines include astemizole (Hismanil), Zyrtec, Tagamet, and Claritin. A commonly used OTC antihistamine is diphenhydramine, commonly known as Benadryl.

Retinoids

Retinoids are drugs that are related to vitamin A. They normalize many types of abnormal skin problems.

Tretinoin

Perhaps the most well-known retinoid drug is tretinoin, better known as Retin-A. Retin-A is a topical cream, gel, or lotion used to treat acne and sun-damaged skin. The drug was originally designed as a keratolytic treatment for acne because it has **comedolytic** properties, which means it loosens comedones. After years of use to treat acne, it was observed that Retin-A appeared to reduce wrinkles and smooth rough, sun-damaged skin. The drug was studied for its ability to correct the signs of sun damage, and it was determined that histologically, the skin of the patients using tretinoin was more like younger skin— clearer, smoother, and less wrinkled. Pigmentation was more even, and the skin had better coloring.

The company that makes Retin-A, Ortho Pharmaceuticals, subsequently applied to the FDA for a new use for tretinoin: treating the signs of sun damage. After years of testing and study by the FDA, **Renova** was the first drug ever approved by the FDA to treat the visible signs of photodamage.

Despite its benefits, tretinoin requires many precautions. Clients using Retin-A or Renova experience an adjustment phase, during which their skin has side effects including erythema, flaking, burning, and stinging. The drugs also make the skin more sensitive, so many skin care products should be avoided while tretinoin is being used, whether the skin is being treated for acne or sun damage. The products to avoid include:

- Alcohol-based, fragranced, or mentholated products.
- Peeling or exfoliation agents.
- Mechanical scrubs.
- Stimulating products.
- AHAs (unless the prescribing dermatologist approves it).

Certain treatments should also be avoided on clients using tretinoin. Waxing should

never be performed on or near any area treated with tretinoin because it may result in injury and thinning to the epidermis in these areas. Exfoliating salon treatments should also be avoided.

Tretinoin also makes the skin more sensitive to the sun. Sunscreen should be worn every day, and clients should never deliberately expose their skin to the sun. Furthermore, tretinoin and other retinoids should be used at night because exposure to light may deactivate the drug and make the skin more sensitive.

Many products and treatments are appropriate for use with tretinoin. These products include:

- a daily use, nonfragranced sunscreen cream or fluid.
- a mild cleanser, preferably low foaming or nonfoaming.
- alcohol-free and fragrance-free toner.
- a soothing hydration fluid.

Salon treatment for people using tretinoin should be hydrating and soothing. Gentle cleansing with a nonfoaming cleanser, followed by cool steam with a hydrating, nonfragranced fluid is a good start. Extraction should be very gentle, since skin treated with tretinoin tends to turn red easily. The next step should be a light massage with a nonfragranced hydrating fluid, followed by a soothing gel mask to hydrate the skin's surface and ease redness.

Clients tend to be noncompliant with directions for tretinoin treatment. Many people begin turning red and flaking, and they choose to discontinue the treatment. Try to educate clients about the proper use of tretinoin and how to avoid some of the cosmetic side effects.

When AHAs became popular in the early 1990s, cosmetic treatment with tretinoin decreased. Many clients found that they could treat the same cosmetic problems with AHAs with fewer side effects than tretinoin. Although the treatments are not the same, AHAs seem to treat appearance-related problems to the satisfaction of clients.

Other Retinoids

Adapalene, also known as Differin, is another prescription vitamin-A related retinoid used to treat acne. Its actions and

comedolytic
A term meaning that a product loosens comedones.

Renova
The first drug ever approved by the FDA to treat visible signs of sun damage.

adapalene
Also known as Differin, another prescription vitamin-A-related retinoid used to treat acne.

side effects are similar to tretinoin; it may cause inflammation, especially when someone begins using it, and increased sun sensitivity. Treatment precautions for the esthetician are essentially the same as for tretinoin.

Tazarotene, also known as Tazorac, was originally a prescription retinoid for psoriasis but is now used to treat acne. Like other retinoids, it may cause inflammation initially and increased sun sensitivity. The precautions for esthetic treatment are the same as for tretinoin.

Retinol and retinyl palmitate are cosmetic ingredients that are retinoids. Retinol can cause irritation when first used. Retinyl palmitate does not cause any problems, but it does not provide the same favorable appearance changes as retinol.

Accutane

Isotretinoin, also known as **Accutane,** is an oral retinoid used to treat severe inflammatory and cystic acne. Many people consider it a miracle treatment for severe cystic and scarring acne. Isotretinoin is the only drug that actually causes sebaceous glands to shrink and normalize. It also normalizes the hyperkeratosis in the follicle. Many patients have had wonderful results with isotretinoin. On occasion, it may also be used for severe cases of rosacea.

However, Accutane has a tremendous number of esthetic and medical side effects. Medically, it increases lipids or fats in the blood. Patients must have their blood monitored regularly during treatment. Liver and kidney functions are also monitored. There is a risk of developing bone and tendon calcifications.

One of the two major side effects of isotretinoin is that it causes severe birth defects in the children of women taking it.

Therefore, women of childbearing age who take isotretinoin must also use reliable birth control.

The second major side effect of isotretinoin, which has only recently surfaced, is possible mental disturbances associated with an increased risk of suicide. This risk is of particular concern for teenagers taking the drug to treat acne. Investigation into this possible side effect continues.

Accutane also has many side effects that concern estheticians and their clients. The skin of the face, and sometimes of the body, can become very red, sensitive, and dry. Dehydration and flaking is common. For this reason, clients using Accutane should immediately stop using all exfoliating and keratolytic products. Any products containing benzoyl peroxide, sulfur, salicylic acid, resorcinol, retinol, AHAs, and any other exfoliating chemical must also be immediately discontinued, unless otherwise directed by the dermatologist. Furthermore, the same treatments that are avoided for other retinoids should also be avoided for patients taking Accutane.

After the patient has stopped taking Accutane, the effects remain for several months. Eventually, the skin becomes less dry, and some sebum production will resume. Wait several months before resuming any of the above treatments, or check with the client's dermatologist about when these treatments can be resumed. When you resume treatment, do so with extreme caution.

Clients using isotretinoin should be directed toward specific types of products. These products include:

- a mild, nonfragranced, nonexfoliating, nonfoaming, or low foaming cleanser.
- a nonalcoholic, hydrating toner.
- a hydrating, nonfragranced, and non-comedogenic moisturizer.
- a nonfragranced, noncomedogenic, and alcohol-free, SPF-15, broad-spectrum sunscreen.

Additionally, gel hydrating masks designed for sensitive skin help moisten the surface layers in the dehydrated skin of the client using Accutane. Soothing agents such as matricaria, azulene, and green tea extracts help reduce redness and make the skin feel

---

tazarotene
Also known as Tazorac, originally a prescription retinoid for treatment of psoriasis, now used to treat acne.

Accutane
An oral retinoid to treat severe inflammatory and cystic acne.

SAFETY*Tip*

Tips for Treating Clients Using Accutane
- Do not wax any area of the body.
- Do not perform any exfoliation procedure.
- Avoid heat masks or any treatment using heat.
- Avoid drying alcohols in any product.

---

more comfortable. Gel masks do not dry, and they can be used several times a week if needed.

Drugs for the Treatment Of Rosacea

The prescription drug most commonly used to treat rosacea is metronidazole. This is an antiyeast medication that has strong anti-inflammatory properties. It is commercially known as MetroGel, Metrolotion, Metrocream, and Noritate. Metronidazole is a topical drug applied to the face daily to control the inflammation associated with rosacea and to help prevent flares. Metronidazole occasionally causes irritation, especially when a person first begins using it.

The use of metronidazole must be combined with good habits to prevent the flushing caused by rosacea; these habits include avoiding heat, sun, alcohol, spicy foods, and any stimulating products. Cosmetics and skin care products should be fragrance-free and tested for irritancy, and cleansers should be nonstripping. Products that contain soothing agents such as green tea extract or matricaria can help calm skin affected by rosacea. For more severe cases of rosacea, oral antibiotics such as tetracycline or minocycline are prescribed to be used in conjunction with the metronidazole.

Sulfacetamide (Sulfacet, Klaron) is another topical drug frequently prescribed for rosacea. It is used to treat oily, acnelike flares and is also recommended for acne vulgaris.

Antibiotics

The skin can have many types of bacterial infections. Acne is only one kind of bacterial infection, and it is not contagious. Other bacterial infections include impetigo, cellulitis, and furuncles (boils).

Antibiotics are drugs that kill bacteria. They require a prescription because misuse of them can cause bacteria to mutate and become resistant. This is particularly a problem in hospitals, where many bacteria are

present and many antibiotics are used.

Antibiotics come in topical or oral form. Common topical antibiotics are neomycin, polymyxin, and bacitracin. These are available over the counter. Prescription topical antibiotics include mupirocin (Bactroban), topical tetracycline, erythromycin (which can be combined with benzoyl peroxide for acne), and clindamycin (Cleocin). Oral antibiotics prescribed for bacterial skin infections include tetracycline, erythromycin, azithromycin, cephalexin (Keflex), dicloxacillin, and doxycycline (Monodox, Vibramycin).

Antibiotics are sometimes prescribed for their anti-inflammatory benefits. They help reduce inflammation, redness (erythema), and other symptoms.

Antiviral Medications

Skin infections can also be caused by viruses. Common diseases caused by viruses include warts, herpes simplex (cold sores), shingles, and genital herpes. Antiviral medications are used to treat these diseases. Drugs commonly used to treat herpes simplex include acyclovir (Zovirax), famciclovir, penciclovir, and valacyclovir (Valtrex). These are also used to treat herpes zoster, which causes shingles and chickenpox. Like bacteria, viruses can become resistant to these drugs, particularly if they are overused.

Summary

Estheticians need to understand OTC and prescription drugs that can affect clients' skin. The primary OTC drugs used in salons and spas are sunscreen, acne treatments, and hydroquinone. Customers also frequently use corticosteroids to treat skin irritations. Estheticians need to know about the prescription drugs that affect the skin including retinoids, corticosteroids, antihistamines, drugs that treat rosacea, antibiotics, and antivirals.

Obviously, many prescription drugs are not mentioned here. If you have questions about a particular drug that a client is using or possible contraindications, do not hesitate

sulfacetamide
A topical drug frequently prescribed for rosacea.

antibiotics
Prescription drugs that kill bacteria.

Table 18–1 Medications and Contraindications

Agent/Drug/Service	Reason for Use	Effects/Contraindications
Accutane (isotretinoin)	Aggressive, systemic, internal drug for severe nodular acne	Makes skin over entire body fragile, sensitive, erythemic, highly reactive. Do not wax, exfoliate, or use keratolytic drugs.
Antibiotics	Acne, acute infections: bladder, ear, sinus, vaginal, other	Best to avoid stimulating treatments, waxing, AHAs, and other exfoliants. May interfere with normal healing time.
Essential oils (some)	To stimulate	Avoid use with keratolytic drugs.
Fragranced or drying DS or isopropyl alcohols	Used in formulations for antibacterial effect, or as a stabilizer for other ingredients	Avoid use with keratolytic drugs. May dry or irritate.
Keratolytic prescription drugs: Azelex (azelaic acid); Differin (adapalene); Retin-A, Renova (contain the drug tretinoin); Tazorac (tazarotene); others	Topical OTC medications or prescriptions applied to the skin's surface that work by peeling off the top cells of epidermis	Salon or home care: Do not use any chemical exfoliants, AHAs, BHAs (salicylic acid), keratolytic enzymes (papain, bromelain, pancreatin) unless specifically approved in writing by the prescribing physician.
Massage (aggressive)	To stimulate	Avoid. Perform only gentle massage.
Prednisone	Systemic corticosteroid prescribed for asthma, acute allergic reactions, arthritis, lupus, kidney transplants	Skin thinning, reduced healing time, infection masking. No waxing or peels.

to call the client's physician or a pharmacist. You can also refer to the books listed under Additional Reading.

Discussion Questions

1. State the guidelines used by the FDA to distinguish between over-the-counter (OTC) and prescription drugs.

2. What are the three types of OTC drugs used by estheticians in the United States? Describe each briefly.

3. Explain the difference between chemical and physical sunscreens, highlighting the advantages and disadvantages of both. How might this information affect the type of products you recommend to clients?

4. List the four OTC ingredients approved by the FDA for treating acne. Briefly describe the main benefits and features of each along with any contraindications for their use.

5. Describe how corticosteroids are used to treat skin conditions. What precautions must the esthetician take when using or recommending these to clients? The esthetician must also be familiar with prescription forms of corticosteroids. Make a list of common commercial names associated with these drugs for future reference.

6. What is the main purpose for using the family of drugs known as retinoids? Develop a plan for educating clients on proper skin care while using these drugs. What special precautionary measures must the esthetician take when treating clients who are taking oral retinoids such as Accutane?

7. Explain how antibiotics are used to treat bacterial infections of the skin. List those antibiotics commonly associated with bacterial infections, distinguishing between topical and oral medications. (Place an asterisk next to those that are available over the counter.) How does the treatment of viral skin infections differ from that for bacterial skin infections?

Additional Reading

Michalun, Natalia, and M. Varinia Michalun. 2001. *Milady's Skin Care and Cosmetic Ingredients Dictionary*. 2d ed. Clifton Park, N.Y.: Milady, an imprint of Delmar Learning, a division of Thomson Learning, Inc.

Griffith, H. Winter et al. *Complete Guide to Prescription and Nonprescription Drugs*. 2000. Berkley Publishing Group.

Spratto, George R. and Adrienne L. Woods. 2002. *PDR Nurse's Drug Reference*. Clifton Park, N.Y.: Milady, an imprint of Delmar Learning, a division of Thomson Learning, Inc.

Helpful Web Sites

http://www.cosmeceuticals.net
http://www.cosmetic-Information.com
http://www.skin-disease.com

Chapter 19
Product Chemistry

Chapter Objectives

After reading this chapter, you should be able to:

- Explain the elements of basic chemistry.
- Describe the most common cosmetic ingredients.

Chapter Outline

Introduction
Basic Chemistry
Cosmetic Ingredients

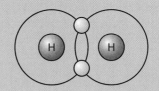

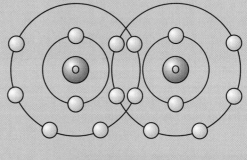

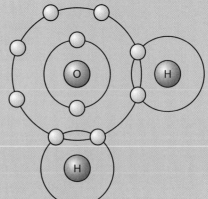

Introduction

The effects of cosmetics and skin care products on the skin are based on chemical reactions. The skin itself is made up of chemicals, and many of its functions are actually biochemical reactions. **Biochemistry** is the study of the chemical reactions that occur within a living organism. Essentially all functions of any living organism represent some sort of chemical reaction.

One myth in the cosmetics world is that chemicals are bad for the skin. Clearly, all skin care products and cosmetics contain chemicals, and while some chemicals can cause irritation and reactions, most of the chemicals in skin care products have a positive effect on the skin. Frequently, the underlying problem in a skin reaction is that the wrong product has been chosen for a particular skin type or condition.

Another myth is that natural ingredients do not contain chemicals. The truth is that natural extracts and substances are groups of chemicals. In fact, one plant extract may contain 250 or more chemicals. Certain plants do contain harmful chemicals: many plants are poisonous, and some, such as poison ivy, cause allergic reactions in people. But these chemicals are not used in skin care products.

Moreover, most chemicals used in manufacturing skin care products and cosmetics are derived from plants. Over one-third of all drugs are derived from plants. Estheticians must be aware that all cosmetics and skin care products are chemicals, whether they are made from natural substances or from laboratory-synthesized ingredients.

Many people have a fear of learning about chemistry. They think that chemistry is difficult and complicated. Although not everyone is meant to be a biochemist, understanding chemistry as an **applied science** (defined as the search for practical uses of scientific knowledge) enables estheticians to understand how chemical substances can change the appearance and condition of the skin.

Basic Chemistry

Chemistry can be compared to a monetary system. In order to make purchases, people exchange money. In order for chemical reactions to occur, chemicals exchange electrons, which are elementary particles consisting of negative charges of electricity. This exchange or sharing of electrons causes changes in chemicals and allows bodily functions to occur. The exchange of electrons is also responsible for the chemistry of many skin care products.

The simplest form of any chemical is called an **element,** which is a chemical that has not reacted with another element. Iron and oxygen are examples of elements. When you expose iron to oxygen, a chemical reaction takes place. This reaction creates rust, which is a **compound**—the product of uniting two or more elements. Rust is a compound called iron oxide, which is used as a cosmetic ingredient to give color to makeup products.

Chemical reactions take place when parts of elements combine with each other. The smallest possible unit of an element is called an **atom** (Figure 19–1). An atom has two major parts: a **nucleus,** which is the center of the atom, and electrons, which revolve around the nucleus.

The nucleus of an atom is made up of particles called **protons** and **neutrons.** Protons have a positive charge, neutrons have no charge, and electrons have a negative charge. Negatives and positives are attracted to one another, which is why electrons orbit the nucleus of an atom. Atoms of different elements vary in the number of electrons and protons they contain. In its most basic state, an atom of a particular element has exactly the same number of electrons as protons.

biochemistry
The study of chemical reactions that occur within a living organism.

applied science
The search for practical uses of scientific knowledge.

element
A chemical that has not reacted with another element.

compound
The product of uniting two or more elements.

atom
The smallest possible unit of an element.

nucleus
The center of an atom.

protons
Particles that make up the nucleus of an atom; they have a positive charge.

neutrons
Particles that make up the nucleus of an atom; they have no charge.

Carbon Atom

Proton

Neutron

← Electron

Figure 19–1 An atom is composed of negatively charged electrons, positively charged protons, and neutral neutrons.

energy levels
The orbits in which electrons travel.

ionic bond
The bond between two ions that have opposite charges.

The orbits in which electrons travel are called **energy levels.** The bigger the atom, the bigger the nucleus, and the more electrons orbit the nucleus. The bigger the atom, the more energy levels, so electrons can orbit on more than one energy level.

Each energy level contains a certain number of electrons. The number of electrons in the outermost energy level determines how this atom will react with another atom. All atoms have a physical need to have a full outer energy level. This is a very basic and important principle of chemistry that you must understand in order to understand chemical reactions. If the outer energy level is almost full, the atom will "want" extra electrons to fill it up. If the outer energy level has only one or two electrons, the atom will "want" to get rid of electrons so that the next energy level down, already filled with electrons, will be its outer level. Atoms are in their most stable state if their outer energy levels are filled with electrons.

For example, table salt is the compound sodium chloride, which is formed by the reaction of the element sodium with the element chlorine. Sodium has only one electron in its outer energy level, and it needs eight electrons in the outer energy level to be stable. Chlorine has seven electrons and also needs an eighth to be stable. So when sodium comes in contact with chlorine, the chlorine will "steal" an electron from sodium, creating a full outer energy level for each element. Because sodium has lost an electron, it has lost a negative particle, and now the whole atom has a positive charge because the atom has more protons than electrons. Likewise, chlorine has gained an electron, making the atom negative because it now has one extra electron. Atoms that have a charge because they have gained or lost an electron are called ions.

Since negative and positive charges are attracted to one another, the ions of sodium and chlorine are now attracted to each other because they have opposite charges. They form an **ionic bond** and become the compound sodium chloride, which has completely different properties than either sodium or chlorine (Figure 19–2). A molecule as been created, which is two or more atoms bonded together by exchanging or sharing electrons.

Another common chemical bond is called a covalent bond. A covalent bond is a reaction where two atoms share electrons instead of exchanging them. An oxygen molecule is an example of a covalent bond (Figure 19–3). Oxygen exists in the atmosphere as O_2, which means that there are two atoms of oxygen that stay together because they are sharing electrons to have a full outer energy

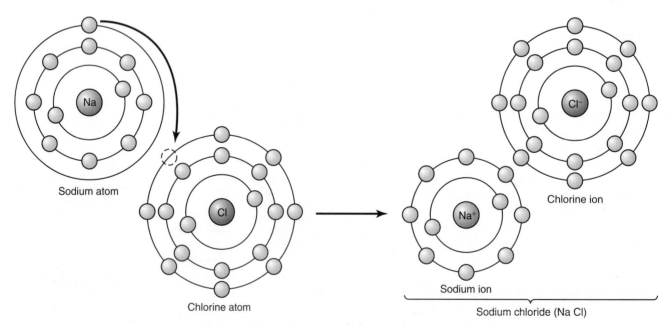

Sodium atom

Chlorine atom

Chlorine ion

Sodium ion

Sodium chloride (Na Cl)

Figure 19–2 Sodium and chlorine atoms forming an ionic bond.

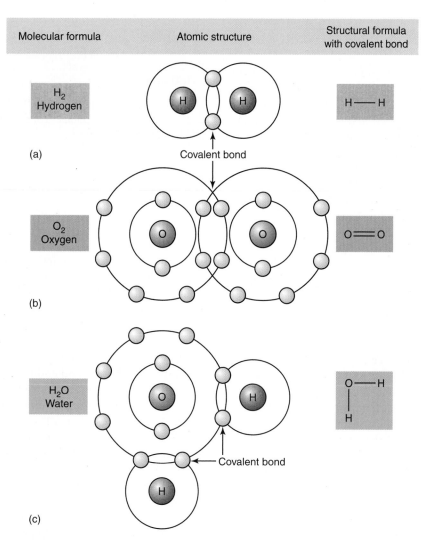

Molecular formula	Atomic structure	Structural formula with covalent bond
H_2 Hydrogen	(a)	H——H
	Covalent bond	
O_2 Oxygen	(b)	O══O
H_2O Water	(c) Covalent bond	O——H H

Figure 19–3 A covalent bond is formed when atoms that share a pair of electrons are both attracted to the shared pair.

level. This type of bond occurs frequently in biochemical reactions within the body.

Frequently, oxygen molecules split into two atoms in the body. One takes all the electrons it can hold in its outer energy level, leaving the other atom missing electrons. This creates positively and negatively charged atoms. The atom of oxygen that is missing electrons will try to "steal" electrons from other atoms. This unstable, thieving oxygen atom is known as a **free radical.** Many types of free radicals exist, but they are all related to oxygen.

Free radicals often attack the lipid cell membrane in the skin. Lipids are a great source of electrons that are easy for free radicals to steal. Once the oxygen atoms steal from the lipid membrane, the membrane is molecularly changed. The membrane then cannot react in the same way it did before. As a result, normal cell function is impaired.

Cells in the body communicate through chemical reactions. If the chemicals or molecules are altered, cell communication is impaired, causing chaos. This inability of a cell to communicate properly is the root of cell damage and dysfunction. When enough of these dysfunctions occur, the body becomes overwhelmed, resulting in disease.

Thus, chemicals are vital in almost every type of body function and reaction. The chemicals used in cosmetics and skin products work by causing chemical changes that help the skin look better.

free radical
An unstable oxygen atom that tries to "steal" electrons from other atoms.

Cosmetic Ingredients

cosmetics

Defined by the FDA as "articles that are intended to be rubbed, poured, sprinkled or otherwise applied to the human body or any part thereof for cleansing, beautifying, promoting attractiveness or altering the appearance."

Cosmetics are defined by the Food and Drug Administration (FDA) as "articles that are intended to be rubbed, poured, sprinkled or otherwise applied to the human body or any part thereof for cleansing, beautifying, promoting attractiveness or altering the appearance." Cosmetics are made from cosmetic ingredients, and every ingredient employed in cosmetic chemistry has some function in the finished product. These ingredients are divided into two basic types: functional ingredients and performance ingredients.

functional ingredients

Ingredients in a cosmetic product that make up the majority of a product and allow products to spread, give them body and texture, and give them a specific form.

Functional ingredients make up the majority of a product. They allow products to spread, give them body and texture, and give them a specific form such as a lotion, cream, or gel.

Performance ingredients cause the actual changes in the appearance of the skin. Examples include glycerin, which hydrates the skin's surface; alphahydroxy acids (AHAs), which exfoliate the corneum, resulting in a smoother look for sun-damaged skin; and lipids, which help patch the skin's barrier. Performance ingredients are sometimes referred to as active agents, key ingredients, or active principals. They are sometimes erroneously called "active ingredients," which is a term reserved for describing drugs, because it is an official term used in the drug industry.

performance ingredients

Ingredients in a cosmetic product that cause a change in the skin's appearance; also known as active agents or active principals.

A third category has been proposed. Products in this category are called **cosmeceuticals,** which are products intended to improve the skin's health and appearance.

cosmeceuticals

Products intended to improve the skin's health and appearance.

FDA Regulations

The FDA does not officially approve any skin care product or cosmetic, although it has an expensive, complicated process to approve drugs. The FDA only regulates cosmetics in terms of safety or claims. Only appearance-related claims can be made for cosmetics, and companies must use ingredients that are generally regarded as safe. The FDA only gets involved in cosmetics regulation if a product makes a drug claim, is not properly labeled, or has been reported as unsafe.

Skin Care Product Ingredients

INGREDIENTS:
Paraffinum Liquidum, Isopropyl Palmitate, Polyethylene, Ceteth-20, Trihydroxystearin, Sorbic Acid, Methylparaben, Butylparaben, Propylparaben, Aroma.

Figure 19–4 Water is usually listed first in many products because it is usually the main ingredient.

FDA regulations for cosmetic labeling state that cosmetic companies must list the company's name, location, or distribution point as well as all the ingredients in the product. This allows consumers to check for ingredients they may be allergic to. Ingredients must be listed in descending order, starting with the ingredient with the highest concentration and ending with the ingredient with the lowest concentration. An exception is made for ingredients that have a concentration of less than 1% of the formula. These ingredients can be listed in any order.

Water is listed first in many products (Figure 19–4). The second ingredient listed is usually a spreading agent or a vehicle that spreads the cosmetic across the skin and helps it adhere to the skin's surface. Ingredients listed next include preservatives and other ingredients that are used in small amounts.

Water

Water makes up a large part of the skin. All cells require water to live, and even dying cells in the epidermis contain water, as does the precious intercellular lipid matrix that we know as the barrier function. Water is also the most frequently used cosmetic ingredient—it is both a vehicle and a performance ingredient. As a vehicle, it helps keep other cosmetic ingredients in solution and helps spread products across the skin. As a performance ingredient, water replenishes moisture in the surface of the skin.

Almost all skin care product are a mixture of oil and water. There are two basic types of creams or lotions: oil-in-water emulsions and

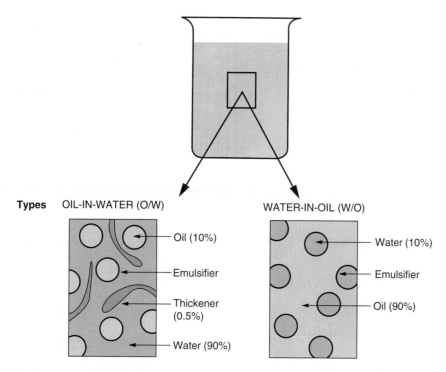

Figure 19–5 Oil and water emulsions.

water-in-oil emulsions (Figure 19–5). **Oil-in-water (O/W) emulsions** are made of oil in a base of mostly water. This is the most common type of lotion or cream. **Water-in-oil (W/O) emulsions** are made of water in a base of mostly oil. These are heavier creams. Products that do not contain any water are called **anhydrous**. These include oil serums, petrolatum-based products such as lip balm and silicone serums. Generally, anhydrous products are designed for very dry skin.

Emollients

Emollients are cosmetic ingredients that are almost always fatty agents. Oils of various sorts, fatty esters, fatty alcohols, fatty acids, and waxes are all emollient ingredients.

Emollients can act as either vehicles or performance ingredients. As vehicles, emollients are the agents that help place, spread, and keep other agents on the skin. For example, emollients in sunscreen cream help spread the sunscreen agents across the skin and hold it in place. Emollients in loose powder help the powder slip evenly across the skin and help it adhere to the skin.

As performance ingredients, emollients lubricate the skin's surface and set up a guard for the barrier function. Emollients lie on top of the skin and prevent dehydration by trapping water, which increases moisture in the epidermis. This technique of moisturization is called **occlusion** (Figure 19–6, p. 288).

Emollients are useful in cosmetics because they fill in gaps in the skin, smoothing over wrinkles and helping to soften the appearance of dry patches by lubricating the surface. They provide a smooth surface for makeup application. Emollients can also add creaminess to products such as lipsticks and creams.

Oils

Many oils are used in skin care. They vary in density, fat content, and heaviness. They also vary in their tendency to cause comedones in oily or acne-prone skin. Different oils are appropriate for different degrees of dryness in the skin. The oils used in skin care products and cosmetics come from many sources.

oil-in-water (O/W) emulsions
Oil in a base of mostly water.

water-in-oil (W/O) emulsions
Water in a base of mostly oil.

anhydrous
Describes products that do not contain water.

emollients
Cosmetic ingredients that are almost always fatty agents.

occlusion
The technique of placing a layer of emollient over the skin in order to keep natural moisture from escaping from the epidermis.

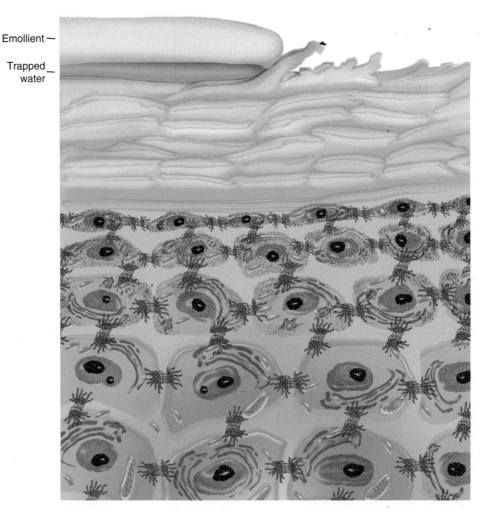

Emollient —

Trapped water —

Figure 19–6 Emollients lubricate the skin's surface and set up a guard for the barrier function in a process called occlusion.

biologically inert
Describes an ingredient that does not react with the chemicals involved in the skin's function.

comedogenic
Describes substances that cause comedones (blackheads).

Oils from the Earth

Mineral oil and petrolatum come from the earth, specifically from petroleum sources. Both of these emollients are time-tested and work as good protection against dehydration. They help build water content in the skin by occlusion. They also help prevent irritant skin contact.

Petrolatum and mineral oil can be combined with water and blended with an emulsifier into a cream, lotion, or fluid. This makes the agent much less oily. Classic cold cream, one of the first moisturizers ever made, was blended with mineral oil. Mineral oil is also the key ingredient in baby oil.

Recently, mineral oil and petrolatum have become less popular, but these two emollient ingredients are probably the most effective protective emollients and two of the safest ones. They are completely nonreactive and are **biologically inert,** which means that they do not react with other chemicals involved in the skin's function. They are used in many prescription ointments routinely applied to skin with serious inflammations such as eczema and burns. Mineral oil and petrolatum can also be used without any preservatives because they do not harbor bacteria or other organisms.

Mineral oil and petrolatum have been rumored for many years to be **comedogenic,** which refers to substances that cause comedones. While these ingredients may be too oily to use on oily, acneic, or combination skin, they do not cause comedones. Much research has been performed to substantiate this fact. However, many manufacturers omit these ingredients in their formulations, mainly because of this erroneous information. This is unfortunate because the manufacturers are omitting some useful ingredients. Consumers, as well as estheticians, have been victims of this misinformation.

Oils from Plants

Virtually dozens of plant oils are used in skin care products, most for their emollient properties, but some for their fragrances, such as aromatic essential oils. Plant oils basically comprise fatty acid components. They mimic human sebum, which is beneficial for alipidic skin, which does not make enough protective and lubricating sebum. The oils work as a protectant to keep the skin from dehydrating.

Plant oils vary in fatty acid content and heaviness. **Coconut oil** and **palm oil** are two of the fattiest and heaviest oils. These oils are the sources of many other emollient ingredients such as cetyl alcohol, oleic acid, stearic acid, and octyl palmitate. Some lighter and less comedogenic natural oils are safflower, sunflower, canola, and jojoba oil.

Other Emollients

Literally hundreds of emollients exist. Some come from natural sources and others are synthesized in a laboratory or derived from other oils or fatty materials.

Fatty esters are produced from fatty acids and alcohols. Esters are easily recognized on labels because they almost always end in a-t-e. They often feel better than natural oils and have a better ability to lubricate evenly. Numerous fatty esters are used; some of the most common ester emollients are tridecyl stearate, propylene glycol dicaprylate/dicaprate, octyl palmitate, octyl cocoate, decyl oleate, isopropyl palmitate, isopropyl myristate, and caprylic/capric triglycerides.

Fatty acids are lubricant ingredients that are derived from plant oils or animal fats. Animal fats are by-products of meat processing. Fatty acids have lost favor in the last decade or two because plant-derived ingredients are more popular. Examples include stearic acid, a major component in many shaving creams, caprylic acid, oleic acid, myristic acid, lauric acid, and palmitic acid.

Note that just because these ingredients are acids does not mean that they are irritating. Corrosive acids such as sulfuric acid are not used in cosmetics. Fatty acids are actually more like oils. They are derived from triglycerides, which are fats from plants or animals, and can give creams a soft feel or can smooth a product's texture. Many fatty acids also help other products adhere to the skin.

Fatty alcohols are fatty acids that have been exposed to hydrogen. They are not drying alcohols like isopropyl alcohol or SD alcohol (SD stands for specially denatured). They have a waxlike consistency and are used as emollients or spreading agents. Stearyl alcohol and cetyl alcohol can be used as **opacifiers,** which means that they cause creams to develop a solid white color, which helps protect skin from ultraviolet light. These alcohols also help improve the feel and texture of creams and lotions.

Emollients and Comedogenicity

Many emollient ingredients can cause or worsen the development of comedones in the skin. These emollients are said to be comedogenic, which means they block pores. **Comedogenicity** is the tendency of any topical substance to cause or to worsen a buildup of dead cells in the follicle, leading to the development of a comedo (blackhead).

Emollients are more comedogenic than any other type of cosmetic ingredient. This is most likely due to the similarity of these oils to human sebum. The fatty acids in many of these oils may also play a role in acne, because Propionibacterum acnes bacteria (the bacteria that cause acne vulgaris) feed on fatty acids as their only nutritional source.

The fact that many emollients are comedogenic is a particular problem. Emollients and spreading agents make up the majority of most products. The more comedogenic ingredients that are in a product, the more likely the product is to be comedogenic.

The frequent misdiagnosis of skin types and conditions, either by consumers or by poorly trained estheticians, causes another problem with emollients. Skin that is clog-prone or acne-prone can also be dehydrated (remember that dry means lacking water; alipidic means lacking sebum). If clients with this skin type uses a comedogenic product with comedogenic oils as major ingredients, they can end up with blackheads and other acne lesions. Acne-prone skin produces sufficient amounts of sebum. The addition of a comedogenic product increases the risk of acne. If the client had dry (alipidic),

coconut oil
A fatty and heavy plant oil.

palm oil
A fatty and heavy plant oil.

fatty esters
Emollients produced from fatty acids and alcohols.

fatty alcohols
Fatty acids that have been exposed to hydrogen.

opacifiers
Fatty acids that develop a solid white color in creams.

comedogenicity
The tendency of any topical substance to cause or worsen comedones (blackheads).

dehydrated skin, there would probably be no problem because the skin lacks sebum.

What Ingredients Are Comedogenic?

Over the last 20 years, much research has been performed on what products are comedogenic. Many oils and other emollient ingredients have been tested to check for comedogenic potential. Some have been found to be very comedogenic, some are likely to cause follicular irritation, and some are unlikely to cause either comedones or irritation.

The concentration of the emollient ingredient in a product plays a factor in its comedogenicity. Oils and emollients have often been tested as single ingredients, in their **neat** form—not combined with other ingredients. As neat ingredients, emollients have a strong tendency to be comedogenic. The comedogenicity factor is usually reduced when other ingredients, such as water, dilute them. However, when some oils are added to neat emollients, they do not alter the comedogenicity at all.

Skin Type and Comedogenicity

Emollients that are comedogenic are generally not intended for clog-prone or acne-prone skin. Oilier skin produces enough of its own emollient, as sebum, and does not need more. But dry or alipidic skin does not produce enough sebum and may need more or heavier emollient ingredients to lubricate and protect the skin from dehydration. This type of skin does not clog easily and is not acne-prone.

Noncomedogenic Claims

The word **noncomedogenic** often appears on the labels of skin care and makeup products. Theoretically, this means that the substance does not cause comedones. Unfortunately, some manufacturers make this claim without adequate testing. Testing is expensive, and some companies simply skip it. Some companies avoid known comedogenic ingredients, but they do not perform testing on their finished products to ensure that they are not comedogenic.

Estheticians should check products for comedogenic ingredients. Unless you know for sure that a product has been tested, you may be accidentally using or selling products that are comedogenic. Ask product manufacturers to explain their testing process for

noncomedogenic claims. If they can explain their testing readily, they are probably doing adequate testing.

Comedogenicity lists, like the one in Table 19–1 are somewhat controversial. Some scientists and cosmetic companies believe that these lists should be reserved for the scientists developing products. They fear that consumers (or estheticians) may not buy a product simply because it contains a comedogenic ingredient found on the list.

Since you cannot be sure whether a product is tested for comedogenicity, you should examine the ingredient labels on products. The labels will give you an idea of whether or not the product is appropriate for acne-prone skin. Because federal law requires the list of ingredients in a product to be in the order of ingredient concentration, you will have an idea about the amount of the comedogenic ingredient relative to other ingredients.

Silicones as Emollients

Silicones are a group of mineral-based substances used in cosmetics as lightweight emollients. They also act as vehicles in some products, including makeup foundations. Silicones have unique properties in cosmetics. They are excellent protectants, helping to keep moisture trapped in the skin, yet allowing oxygen in and out of the follicles. Silicones also add an elegant, nongreasy feel to skin care and cosmetic products.

Three silicone-based ingredients are commonly used as emollients and vehicles—cyclomethicone, dimethicone, and phenyl trimethicone. They are noncomedogenic and have extremely low irritancy potential.

Surfactants

One of the biggest categories of cosmetic ingredients is surfactants. **Surfactants** are chemicals that reduce the surface tension between the skin's surface and the product. These can help the spreadability of skin care and cosmetic products. The main type of surfactant used in skin care products is **detergent.** This is not the type of detergent you associate with washing floors or clothes, but it is from the same chemical family as those cleansers.

Detergents are used primarily in cleansing products. They help reduce the surface

neat
Describes an ingredient that is not combined with other ingredients

noncomedogenic
Describes a substance that does not cause comedones (blackheads).

silicones
A group of mineral-based substances used in cosmetics as lightweight emollients.

surfactants
Chemicals that reduce surface tension between the skin's surface and the product.

detergent
The main type of surfactant used in skin care products.

emulsifiers
Surfactants that keep oils and water blended in a product.

tension of the dirt and oils on the skin's surface, helping to lift them off the skin (Figure 19–7). However, detergents that are too strong or in too heavy a concentration can remove too much sebum and actually damage the lipid barrier function of the skin. This is what causes the skin to feel very dry if a cleanser is too strong or overused.

Detergents are also the agents that cause cleansers to foam. Foam is formed by air coming between the skin and surface oils or debris. The more detergent, the more foam, or the longer the foam stays on the skin.

The most common detergent used in skin cleansers is sodium lauryl sulfate, or sodium laureth sulfate. This is a good cleansing agent, but it is an irritant to sensitive skin. It is being used less and less in skin care products in the esthetics market. It is still frequently used in hair shampoos.

A related, but less aggressive and less irritating detergent is ammonium lauryl sulfate. It is used in rinse-off cleansers for oily to combination skin types. Triethanolamine lauryl sulfate is another related, even less aggressive detergent agent.

People with dry skin require special cleansers with gentle detergents in small concentrations and buffers in the formulation. This allows them to wash their faces and have skin that feels clean without stripping the skin and impairing its important barrier. Cleansers with gentle or low concentrations of detergent surfactants that do not foam very much are called low-foamers.

Decyl glucoside is a fairly new cleansing agent that is much milder than the sulfates. Another detergent frequently used for more sensitive skin is disodium laureth sulfosuccinate. Other common detergents are cocamidopropyl betaine, alpha olefin sulfonate, and cocoamphocarboxyglycinate.

Emulsifiers

Emulsifiers are another category of surfactant. In fact, some of the detergents discussed above can also act as emulsifiers.

Emulsifiers keep oils and water blended in a product. Without emulsifiers, oil and water would separate into layers. This type of separated product is called a suspension. Prior to use, suspensions are vigorously shaken in order to be mixed. If you have ever discovered an old bottle of moisturizer, you may have noticed that it has separated into oil and water. After a few years, emulsifiers can stop

Table 19–1 Common Comedogenic Ingredients

Highly Comedogenic	Mildly Comedogenic (2–3/5 or 1/3)
(4–5/5 or 5/3)	Corn Oil
Linseed Oil	Safflower Oil
Olive Oil	Lauryl Alcohol
Cocoa Butter	Lanolin Alcohol
Oleic Acid	Glyceryl Stearate
Coal Tar	Lanolin
Isopropyl Isostearate	Sunflower Oil
Squalene	Avocado Oil
Isopropyl Myristate	Mineral Oil
Myristyl Myristate	(Please note that mildly comedogenic ingredients are generally
Acetylated Lanolin	not a problem when used in diluted concentrations. Check
Isopropyl Palmitate	to see their ranking of concentration on the ingredient label.
Isopropyl Linoleate	**Noncomedogenic**
Oleyl Alcohol	Glycerin
Octyl Palmitate	Squalane
Isostearic Acid	Sorbitol
Myreth 3 Myristate	Sodium PCA
Butyl Stearate	Zinc Stearate
Lanolic Acid	Octyldodecyl Stearate
	SD Alcohol
Moderately Comedogenic	Propylene Glycol
(3–4/5 or 2/3)	Allantoin
Sorbitan Oleate	Panthenol
Decyl Oleate	Water
Myristyl Lactate	Iron Oxides
Coconut Oil	Dimethicone
Grape Seed Oil	Cyclomethicone
Sesame Oil	Polysorbates
Hexylene Glycol	Cetyl Palmitate
Tocopherol	Propylene Glycol Dicaprate/Dicaprylate
Isostearyl Neopentanoate	Jojoba Oil
Most D & C Red Pigments	Isopropyl Alcohol
Octyldodecanol	Sodium Hyaluronate
Peanut Oil	Octylmethoxycinnimate
Lauric Acid	Oxybenzone
Mink Oil	Petrolatum
	Butylene Glycol
	Tridecyl Stearate
	Tridecyl Trimellitate
	Octyldodecyl Stearoyl Stearate
	Phenyl Trimethicone

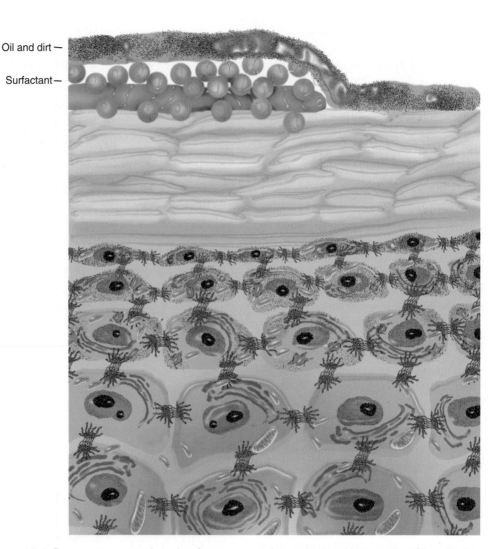

Oil and dirt —

Surfactant —

Figure 19–7 Detergents cause cleansing foam to come between the skin and oils, lifting debris away.

working in a product, causing the oil and water to separate.

Emulsifiers surround oil particles, allowing them to remain evenly distributed throughout the water. When skin care products are mixed, materials that are compatible with oil are mixed in with the oil. These substances are called **oil soluble,** and they are mixed into the oil phase of the product. Substances that are mixable with water are known as **water soluble,** and are mixed in the water phase. When an emulsifier is added to the oil and water phases, the product known as an **emulsion** is formed (Figure 19–8).

Many emulsifiers are used in skin care products. Examples include ceteth 20, glyceryl stearate, diethanolamine cetyl phosphate, beeswax, stearic acid, steareth-

(followed by a number), polyethylene glycol (PEG) (followed by a number) stearate, polysorbates, and C^{12-15} alcohol benzoate. Emulsifiers are also used in food products such as ice cream and candy.

Emulsion Cleansers

Commonly known as cleansing milks, these nonfoaming cleansing products are most often oil-in-water emulsions. They can use natural oils, mineral oil, or other fatty materials as emollients. They are excellent makeup removers and are good solvents for talc and pigments, which are removed more easily with emulsion than with many rinsable foaming cleansers. Emulsion cleansers are generally liquids, but they can vary in thickness depending on the oils and ingredients used in the formulation.

oil soluble
Describes materials that are compatible with oil.

water soluble
Describes substances that are mixable with water.

emulsion
A product containing a mixture of oil and water bound together with an emulsifier.

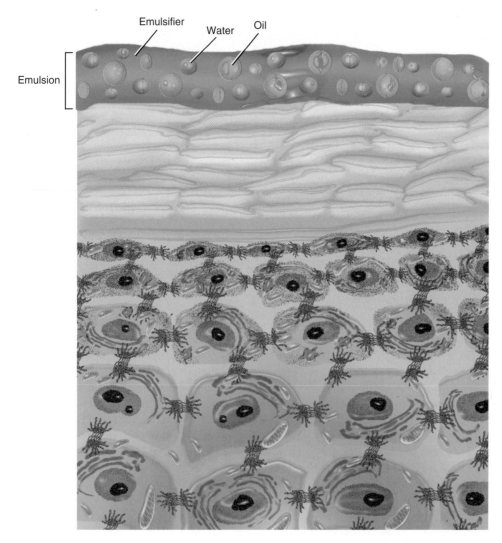

Figure 19–8 When an emulsifier is added to the oil and water phases, an emulsion is formed.

Cleansing milks can be adapted for particular skin types. Soothing agents can be added for sensitive skin, and oil-absorbing ingredients can be added for oilier skin types. Cleansing milks are frequently used for dry skin types and sensitive skin because they do not contain detergents that can damage the barrier function of these delicate skin types. A toner is generally used after a cleansing milk to help remove the excess fatty material left behind.

Thickeners and Texturizers

Certain vehicle ingredients are added to thicken products or to help suspend ingredients that are hard to mix into a product. One example is a **carbomer,** which is used to thicken creams and is frequently used in gel products. Carbomers are usually listed with suffix numbers, such as "carbomer 934" or "carbomer 940," or they may be listed with other suffix numbers that indicate the type of carbomer and the size of the molecule.

Carboxymethyl cellulose, hydroxyethyl cellulose, cellulose fiber, and cellulose gum are all thickeners. Carboxymethyl cellulose is frequently used in gels and gel serums. All of these ingredients are derived from the fibrous matter of plants. Other thickening agents include algin, magnesium aluminum silicate, cetyl palmitate, corn starch, and xanthan gum.

pH Factors and Buffering Agents

The pH scale measures the concentration of hydrogen ions in a substance and determines

carbomer
An ingredient used to thicken creams; frequently used in gel products.

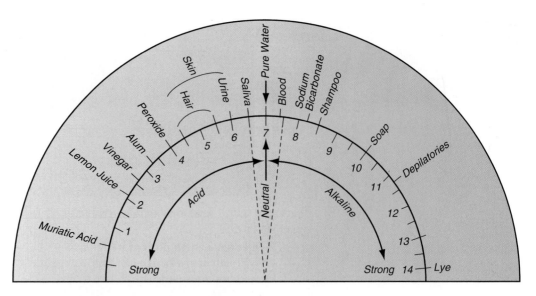

Figure 19–9 Average pH values.

whether a product is acid or alkaline (Figure 19–9). Estheticians must be concerned about pH because products with very low or very high pH values can be harmful to the skin.

The skin produces both sebum and sweat, which create a barrier on the surface of the skin known as the **acid mantle.** The acid mantle is a protective barrier against certain forms of bacteria and microorganisms, and it may be a factor in the natural skin shedding and renewal process.

Water has a pH of 7.0 and is considered neutral—neither acid nor alkaline. **Acids** have pH values lower than 7.0, and **alkalines** have pH values higher than 7.0. Since the pH scale is a logarithmic scale, a change of one whole number represents a tenfold change in pH. That means that a pH of 8 is ten times more alkaline than a pH of 7. A change of two whole numbers represents a change of ten times ten, or a one-hundredfold change. That means that a pH of 9 is 100 times more alkaline than a pH of 7. A small change on the pH scale indicates a large change in the concentration of hydrogen and hydroxide ions.

The mantle of the skin varies in pH between 4.5 and 6.2. When the skin is exposed to low or high pHs, inflammation can occur, along with varying degrees of accelerated exfoliation. Very strong acids, such as sulfuric acid, can produce chemical burns that basically destroy the epidermis. These acids are, of course, never used in esthetic services. Likewise, highly alkaline substances, such as lye, can also produce inflammation and in some cases chemical burns.

Even at levels that are not nearly as severe, variations in pH can damage the barrier function and cause irritation. Because it is so important to keep pHs at a safe level, pH adjusters or **buffering agents** are frequently added to skin care products. These adjusters keep the pH at the correct level to produce the product's desired effect, while keeping the product safe and nonirritating to the skin. Buffering agents include acidifiers such as citric acid or lactic acid and alkaline buffers such as sodium or ammonium hydroxide.

Fragrances

Fragrances are a major aspect of the cosmetics industry. Consumers love wonderful smells, especially in products they associate with relaxation, such as bath oils and bath salts. As soon as consumers open a new product container, they smell it. Fragrances can come from plant, animal, or synthetic sources, but plant oils are especially popular.

Bad smells make a product unpleasant to use, and sometimes fragrances are added to products to cover up an unpleasant smell of an extract or other ingredient. These fragrances are called masking fragrances.

Aromatherapy oils, also referred to as essential oils, are frequently used in skin care products. These highly concentrated plant oils possess properties that have various effects on the skin and can be used to relax or stimulate the mood of the client.

Unfortunately, fragrances often cause allergic reactions. Fragrances are responsible

---

acid mantle
A barrier on the surface of the skin formed by sebum and sweat.

acids
Substances with a pH value lower than 7.0.

alkalines
Substances with a pH value higher than 7.0.

buffering agents
pH adjusters that are added to skin care products.

aromatherapy oils
Highly concentrated plant oils that possess properties with various effects on the skin; also known as essential oils.

Educating the Client

Clients come to you because they want to resolve certain issues concerning their skin. They also value your professional opinion. As esthetic professionals it is our job to review clients' concerns and inform them of the best approach to solving their problems. To carry out this task we must perform a careful analysis of the information presented to us. Critical to this process is the client profile or questionnaire.

We have already reviewed the purpose of the client intake—to gather information, particularly around health concerns, and to develop an understanding of the client's needs and wants. While each esthetician will ultimately develop her own consultation style it is important to remember that the consult and evaluation set the tone for developing a working relationship and educating the client. Most clients are able to tell whether their skin is oily or dry. It is your professional assessment of the various conditions present and the options available to clients for reaching their goals that makes the difference.

But before you begin to offer a detailed evaluation, take time to have the client explain any problems she may be having with her skin and describe what she is doing to remedy the situation. Hearing directly from the client how she is approaching a problem will give you valuable insight into the complexity of her skin care program and how open she is to trying a new format or products. If the client is absolutely in love with the products she is using, not only will it be hard for you to convert her immediately it may also alienate her. Take time to get to know your clients before you dictate a new agenda. Let conversation flow in an easy conversational style, and learn to listen. Trust and bonding are needed before any changes can be made. Your job is not to pass judgment, but to help alleviate the client's concern. Whenever possible make a positive comment, particularly when the client reports something she is doing that is beneficial to the skin.

Once you have developed an easy rapport with the client you can proceed with a thorough analysis of her skin using professional tools of the trade, such as a Wood's lamp and the Fitzpatrick Scale. Learn to use the clients' goals—that is, what they tell you they would like to improve or change about their skin—as a guide to developing a plan of action. Work these into the clinic's offerings, educating the client as you go along. As you build the client's confidence in your technical skills, you can introduce the benefits of an accompanying skin care line.

Lots of estheticians will attempt to educate the client as they perform a service. This is often counterproductive. Give the client an opportunity to relax and enjoy the treatment. You should, of course, introduce each phase of the therapeutic process as you go along; however, it is best to review products and additional treatments or series options when you have the client's full attention. Take the time to write down the process for home care and any additional services in a prescriptive format at the end of the client's visit. This will also serve as reminder of your professional services. It is helpful to provide the client with additional literature to read at home. If this information is not available through product and equipment vendors, consider developing several simple pieces of your own.

The esthetician's primary concern is maintaining the health of the skin. By taking the time to review the process and procedure for new treatments and products you will not only educate clients, but also gain their respect and trust—key ingredients in the therapeutic relationship.

for a significant amount of the skin reactions seen by estheticians, especially in sensitive skin. Fragrances are not generally necessary for a product's effectiveness in terms of improving the condition of the skin.

Fragrance is listed on an ingredient label as perfume, **parfum** (the international term for fragrance), or fragrance. Skin care products that have an odor but do not have a fragrance listed on the label contain some other substance with an odor. Often, they contain a plant extract or another ingredient such as a sunscreen, preservative, or alcohol. Lemon extract, chamomile, and rose oil are examples of ingredients that have a fragrance, even if they have not been added specifically to give the product a fragrance.

Preservatives

Preservatives are an important functional ingredient in many skin care and cosmetic products. Preservatives work to prevent bacteria and other microorganisms from living in a product. They are toxic to the bacteria or release other substances that poison the microorganisms. Without preservatives, products could easily be contaminated with fungi, molds, or other microorganisms that could harm or cause disease in the person using the product.

Preservatives can cause problems in sensitive individuals, and some people are allergic to them. However, many types of preservatives are available, so people with allergies to them do have options. Some common preservatives are:

Butyl paraben

Diazolidinyl urea

Dimethyl oxazolidine

DMDM hydantoin

Ethyl paraben

Imidazolidinyl urea

Methyl paraben

Methylchloroisothiazolinone

Nonoxynol-9

Phenoxyethanol

Propyl paraben

Quaternium 15

Other Preservatives

In addition to fighting bacteria, preservatives can also help protect products from chemical

changes that can affect the action of the product. Antioxidants, substances that inhibit oxidation or reactions promoted by oxygen or peroxides, can be both functional and performance ingredients. They are used to help the condition of the skin, but they are also used to help products retain their properties.

As you have already learned, free radicals cause a process called **oxidation,** the loss of an electron by a chemical. This process damages the lipid membrane of cells. It causes iron to rust, potato salad to turn dark, as well as the blackhead on an open comedo.

Oxidation can also affect creams and other products. Once a product has been exposed to air, it begin to oxidize. Products that turn dark after they have been opened have oxidized. This can affect their performance and can make them smell bad. Products that have a dark color or a bad odor from oxidation are said to be rancid. Creams or any products that contain oils or fats can oxidize easily (which is why the mayonnaise in potato salad oxidizes). However, antioxidants are added to products to prevent oxidation of the fats. They work by chemically stopping the radicals from attacking the fats.

Antioxidants are also used to help improve the condition of the skin. In these products, the antioxidants are used in larger quantities and are often protected by **microencapsulation,** which envelops the antioxidant ingredients in a bubblelike structure. A liposome is an example of microencapsulation. A liposome helps keep the antioxidant from neutralizing before it gets onto the skin and helps it penetrate the surface of the skin better.

Antioxidants that are used to help keep products fresh are not microencapsulated because they must work on the product itself. Common antioxidants include vitamins and vitamin esters such as tocopherol (vitamin E), retinyl palmitate (vitamin A ester), and ascorbyl palmitate (vitamin C ester). Other commonly used antioxidants are butylated hydroxyanisole (BHA), butylated hydroxytoluene (BHT), and benzoic acid.

Color Agents

Color agents serve several purposes in skin care and cosmetic products. In skin care products, they add color, which mainly enhances the visual appeal of the product. In

---

parfum
The international term for perfume or fragrance.

oxidation
The loss of an electron by a chemical.

microencapsulation
When an antioxidant ingredient is enveloped in a bubblelike structure.

color cosmetics, of course, the color agents are responsible for most of the product's cosmetic effects. They give color to products such as eye shadows, lipsticks, and foundations (also called base makeup).

The FDA regulates color agent ingredients very closely. There are two types of color ingredients: certified colors and noncertified colors. **Certified colors** are inorganic are and also known as metal salts. They are called **lakes** and are listed on ingredient labels as "D&C," which stands for "drug & cosmetic." "D&C yellow #5" refers to a D&C color, in this case yellow, and the number associated with the color by the FDA. Certified colors are yellow, blue, red, orange, and green. Certified colors are much more intense than other color agents. They are mostly used in colorful cosmetics, and about 35 exist. These agents can be blended to produce many different colors for cosmetics.

Noncertified colors are organic. They include zinc oxide, iron oxides, carmine, mica, and the ultramarine colors. They are less intense in color than the certified colors. But zinc oxide and iron oxide help with opacity, meaning that they provide a solid color that is not transparent. They are used extensively in coverage makeup products such as foundations. Talc is another principal ingredient used to provide coverage properties to makeup.

Delivery Systems

Delivery systems are chemical techniques using vehicles to make products work. They can be used to spread products, to deliver certain ingredients to certain parts of the epidermis, or to make products adhere better. Generally, complexes of other ingredients or emulsifiers are used to protect ingredients. They can be used to increase product penetration, limit penetration, protect fragile ingredients, or time release ingredients.

The classic example of a specialized delivery system is the **liposome,** which is a microbubble made of lipids that contains ingredients such as hydrators, antioxidants, or alphahydroxy acids (Figure 19–10). The epidermis readily absorbs liposomes. They become a part of the intercellular lipids in the corneum, and they deliver ingredients when they are absorbed. Liposomes by themselves can help improve the barrier function, but they are not listed on ingredient lists. The materials the liposomes are made from are listed. Phospholipids, lecithin, and ceramides are examples of ingredients used in liposomes. Product manufacturers are usually proud of sophisticated technology, and they often explain their use of liposomes in the product information or description.

Another much-publicized delivery system is the **microsponge.** Microsponges are specialized delivery vehicles that release

certified colors
Color agents that are inorganic; also known as metal salts.

lakes
Names for certified colors in cosmetics.

noncertified colors
Color agents that are organic.

delivery systems
Chemical techniques using vehicles to make products work.

liposome
An example of microencapsulation.

microsponge
A specialized delivery vehicle that releases ingredients at appropriate levels or appropriate times.

Liposome

Encapsulation

Instant release

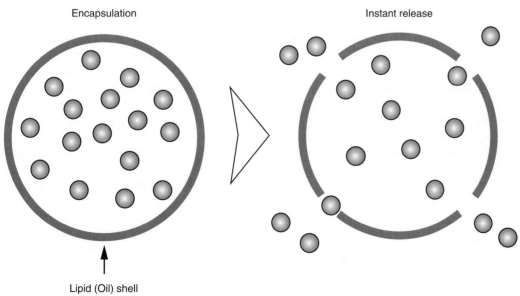

Lipid (Oil) shell

Figure 19–10 A liposome is a specialized delivery system.

ingredients at appropriate levels or appropriate times. Microsponges are used in topical medications as well as in skin care products.

Hydrators and Moisturizers

Hydrators and moisturizers are ingredients widely used in skin care products. Improving the moisture content of the epidermis can improve smoothness, firmness, plumpness, and make the skin look much younger. It can make wrinkles less apparent and can improve barrier function to the point that it decreases skin sensitivity. Properly hydrated skin definitely functions better than skin that is lacking moisture.

There are two types of dry skin: alipidic skin and dehydrated skin. Dehydrated skin is a condition in which the skin is suffering from a loss of water and hydration between the corneum cells. Alipidic skin suffers from a lack of sebum production. Alipidic skin is considered to be a skin type, because it is hereditary, not due to environmental influences. Alipidic skin is often dehydrated, but dehydrated skin is not necessarily alipidic. Even oily or acne-prone skin can be dehydrated.

Two basic treatments exist for dry and dehydrated skin. To treat alipidic skin that is also dehydrated, protective emollients are used to keep natural moisture from escaping from the epidermis by placing a layer of emollient over the skin. This technique is called occlusion, and the emollients— mainly oils, fatty materials such as fatty alcohols or esters—are known as **occlusive agents.**

Hydrators are ingredients that actually attract water to the skin's surface. They can lock water on the skin, improving the symptoms of dehydration. These ingredients are also known as **humectants** or **hydrophilic agents.** There are numerous humectants and hydrophilic (water-loving) agents. They include glycerin, sodium PCA, sorbitol, butylene and propylene glycol, hyaluronic acid (sodium hyaluronate), seaweed extracts, and algae extract. They absorb water from moisture products, and they can attract water from the atmosphere.

Most moisturizing products are basically combinations of emollients and humectants. Thousands of possible combinations exist. These combinations cause the differences between moisturizers. They are also the dif-

ference between creams, lotions, and fluids. Creams have more emollients than lotions or fluids.

Other ingredients can be added to these moisturizing bases. Soothing agents, antioxidants, exfoliating agents, and even sunscreens can customize moisturizers for many skin types and conditions. They can also be specialized for certain areas, such as the eyes and neck, which require more emollients than other facial areas.

Improvement of the Barrier Function

The natural barrier function is primarily made up of lipids. The main lipids in this intercellular barrier matrix are sphingolipids and glycosphingolipids (also known as ceramides), squalane, cholesterol, phospholipids, linoleic acid, and glycerol. They work to prevent moisture loss and act as a barrier against penetration of irritants. Aging and sun damage can break down the barrier.

In addition to moisturizing, occlusive agents can help restore the skin's barrier function by helping to eliminate transepidermal water loss while the barrier is renewing itself (Figure 19–11). Petrolatum or petroleum jelly is probably the best occlusive agent, but it is sticky and unpleasant to use. Still, it is the definite choice for postlaser resurfacing patients to protect against moisture loss while the epidermis is restoring itself.

While the lipid replacement ingredients help to hold water in the skin, they do not attract it. This is why it is so important to use a good humectant product along with lipid ingredients. Natural oils such as borage oil, evening primrose oil, and sunflower oil all have linoleic acid and other lipid components that are beneficial in supporting barrier function (Figure 19–12).

Ingredients for Sensitive Skin

It is vital to know which ingredients to avoid for sensitive skin and which ingredients to use on it. Clients with sensitive skin should avoid fragrance ingredients, aggressive surfactants, stimulants, most exfoliants, highly acidic or alkaline products, formaldehyde-releasing preservatives, and color agents, which are all possible irritants. On the other hand, people with sensitive skin should use soothing ingredients such as chamomile or matricaria extract, bisabolol, azulene, licorice

<occlusive agents>

occlusive agents
Ingredients such as fatty esters that cause occlusion, keeping moisture in the skin.

hydrators
Ingredients that attract water to the skin's surface; also known as humectants or hydrophilic agents.

humectants
Ingredients that attract water to the skin's surface; also known as hydrators or hydrophilic agents.

hydrophilic agents
Ingredients that attract water to the skin's surface; also known as humectants or hydrators.

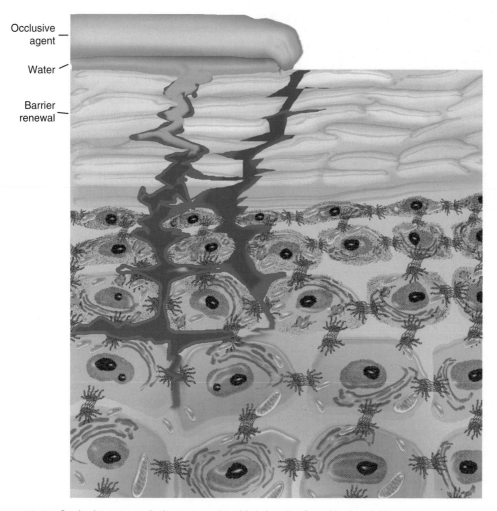

Occlusive agent

Water

Barrier renewal

Figure 19–11 Occlusive agents help restore the skin's barrier function by holding in water.

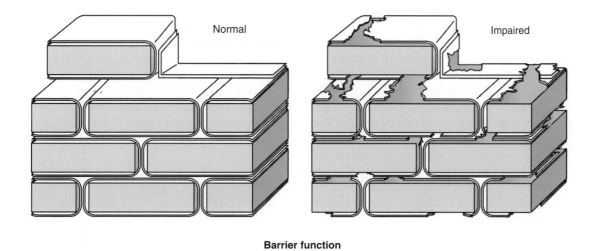

Normal

Impaired

Barrier function

Figure 19–12 Normal versus impaired barrier function.

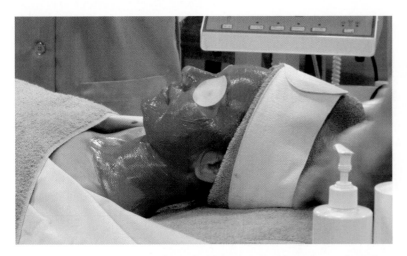

Figure 19–13 Masks are helpful in firming mature skin and as a cleansing agent.

colic, lactic, malic, tartaric, citric, and salicylic acids. These work by loosening the bond between cells in the surface of the corneum. Certain plant extracts, including passion fruit, lemon, and apple extracts, also contain AHAs. Any of these performance exfoliants can be added to gels, lotions, serums, or creams.

Enzymes are also used in exfoliating products, primarily in salon products. Proteolytic enzymes work by dissolving keratin in the surface corneum cells. Examples of these enzymes are papain, bromelain, and pancreatin.

Mask Ingredients

Masks are designed as an intensive treatment for various esthetic problems. Manufacturers can blend almost any performance ingredient into a mask. Because masks are thick and occlusive, their ingredients are more likely to produce immediate esthetic effects.

Two primary types of masks exist: setting masks and nonsetting masks. **Setting masks** harden and dry after a few minutes of exposure to air. These masks are normally used for cleansing, to remove surface dead cells, and to absorb sebum. In addition, they are sometimes used to firm mature skin, and they work by trapping moisture in the surface layers (Figure 19–13). This causes skin to look smoother and firmer, at least temporarily.

Setting masks normally use clays, derived from the earth, as their base. These clays dry when exposed to air, absorb excess oil, and have an exfoliating action. The main clay used in masks is **bentonite,** although **kaolin** is also popular. **Diatomaceous earth,** made from sea algae, is another popular mask base. Zinc oxide is often added to masks for its soothing properties.

Nonsetting masks are primarily moisturizing and soothing masks. They do not harden or dry, and some absorb very readily. These masks are more often intended for dry and sensitive skin types.

extract, dipotassium glycyrrhizinate or stearyl glycyrrhetinate. These ingredients have anti-inflammatory and anti-redness properties. They can be added to any skin care product but are most effective in leave-on products such as moisturizers or serums. Furthermore, specific antioxidant ingredients such as green tea extract and grapeseed extract are also anti-inflammatories due to their properties for controlling free radical reactions.

In sensitive skin, emulsifiers can break up lipids in the barrier function. Some newer sensitive skin moisturizers are made without traditional emulsifiers. A new technique of physical emulsification involves special ingredients, such as many algae derivatives, to provide a well-blended product without using as much concentration of traditional emulsifiers. High-speed blending techniques also help to keep these products well mixed and uniform.

Exfoliation Ingredients

Exfoliation, or the removal of dead corneum cells, can improve the look of most skin types. Mechanical exfoliating ingredients are added to products, often cleansers, to literally knock dead cells off the skin's surface. The ingredients include polyethylene beads, ground nuts such as almonds, various seeds, and hard beads made of hydrogenated jojoba oil. Polyethylene beads and jojoba beads are gentler and not as sharp as ground natural substances.

Exfoliation can also be achieved through chemical action. Alphahydroxy acids (AHAs) and betahydroxy acids (BHAs) include gly-

setting masks
Masks that harden and dry after a few minutes of exposure to air; used for cleansing and removing surface dead cells and for absorbing sebum.

bentonite
The main clay used in masks.

kaolin
A popular clay used in masks.

diatomaceous earth
A popular mask base made from sea algae.

nonsetting masks
Masks that primarily moisturize and soothe.

Summary

Cosmetics and skin care products work by chemical reactions. Therefore, estheticians need a basic understanding of how chemistry works. They should also know how the specific ingredients contained in skin care products and cosmetics react chemically with the skin to produce the desired effects.

Discussion Questions

1. Define biochemistry and discuss common myths that are often associated with "chemicals" in the cosmetics world.

2. Why is it important for the esthetician to have a basic understanding of chemistry? Explain what is meant by the term *applied science* and provide at least one example in your discussion.

3. Explain how normal cell function is compromised by free radicals.

4. Cosmetic ingredients are differentiated in terms of function and performance. Define the terms *functional ingredients* and *performance ingredients* and give examples of each. Explain in your discussion why the use of the term *active* ingredient is considered controversial in reference to cosmetic products.

5. Discuss the distinction between cosmetics and drugs. What is meant by the term *cosmeceuticals*? Look for products and ads that use this term to define cosmetic products. How does the use of this term affect the way estheticians sell professional skin care products?

6. What role does the FDA play in regulating the sale of cosmetic and skin care products? How does this differ from the way drugs are regulated? Discuss how this might affect the role of the esthetician in encouraging consumer awareness and confidence in the efficacy of cosmetic products and treatments.

7. Water is a main ingredient in most skin care products. Explain the difference between oil-in-water and water-in-oil based products. What does the term *anhydrous* mean?

8. Describe the function of emollients in cosmetics and discuss the benefits and features of mineral oil and petrolatum, two of the most commonly used emollients in skin care products.

9. Emollients can come from natural sources or they can also be synthesized in the laboratory. Learning to recognize emollients, such as fatty esters, acids, and alcohols, will help you understand how a product works. Make a list of common fatty esters, fatty acids, and fatty alcohols that are manufactured synthetically.

10. Discuss the role emollients play in encouraging comedogenicity. What is the best approach for the esthetician in determining whether a product will promote comedones or is safe for a client's particular skin type?

11. Describe how surfactants are used in cosmetic products. How could they adversely affect the lipid barrier function of the skin? What can be done to prevent this? How do emulsifiers work as surfactants?

12. Why should the esthetician be concerned with the pH level of a product? How are buffering agents used to adjust pH levels?

13. What does the term *parfum* indicate on a product label? What should the consumer assume if a product is fragrant but does not list this term?

14. Explain how the FDA regulates the use of color agents in cosmetic ingredients.

15. Hydrators and moisturizers are widely used in skin care products to treat dry and dehydrated skin. Describe how occlusive agents and hydrators are used in treating these skin conditions, then see if you can find examples of these on several moisturizing creams or lotions.

Additional Reading

Lees, Mark. 2001. *Skin Care: Beyond the Basics.* Clifton Park, N.Y.: Milady, an imprint of Delmar Learning, a division of Thomson Learning, Inc.

Michalun, Natalia and M. Varinia Michalun. 2001. *Milady's Skin Care and Cosmetic Ingredients Dictionary.* Clifton Park, N.Y.: Milady, an imprint of Delmar Learning, a division of Thomson Learning, Inc.

Chapter 20
Advanced Ingredient Technology

Chapter Objectives

After reading this chapter, you should be able to:

- Describe the FDA regulations regarding cosmetic claims.
- List the new technological developments in skin care and describe their effects on the skin.

Chapter Outline

Introduction
Food and Drug Administration Regulations
Serums
Delivery Systems
Improving Cell Metabolism and Oxygenation
Nature versus Biotechnology

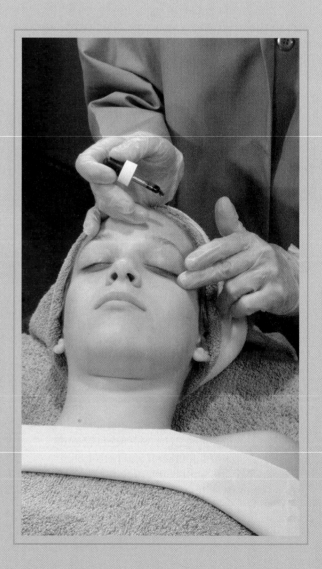

Introduction

In addition to understanding basic chemistry and cosmetic ingredients, estheticians may need to know about newer, more advanced ingredients and treatments. While estheticians may not yet be allowed to claim the actual benefits of these products, they should understand them. Products such as serums, polymers, and glycoproteins, in addition to new delivery systems such as nanosomes, are the results of new skin care technology.

Food and Drug Administration Regulations

The Food and Drug Administration (FDA) views cosmetics according to the Cosmetic Act of 1938, which distinguishes between drugs and cosmetics. Obviously, the technology behind cosmetics has advanced since the act was passed in 1938. Regardless, it is still the operating law today.

Basically, the law views cosmetics as products intended to be rubbed, poured, sprinkled, or otherwise applied to the human body or any part thereof for cleansing, beautifying, promoting attractiveness, or altering the appearance. In contrast, drugs are products (other than food) intended to affect the structures and/or function of the body of humans or other animals.

These definitions are important because they imply that estheticians cannot make claims that a product or treatment can affect the true structure or function of the skin. Estheticians focus on improving the skin's *appearance*.

For example, an exfoliant such as an alpha hydroxyacid (AHA) affects the skin's structure. But estheticians don't actually make that claim. Rather, they say that AHAs exfoliate dead surface cells and improve the appearance of the skin. Is the statement "this cream will make your skin younger" a cosmetic or a drug claim? The statement says that the cream causes a change in the skin's structure, and therefore it is a drug claim. In contrast, the statement "this cream will make your skin younger looking," is a cosmetic claim because it only refers to the appearance of the skin.

Obviously, such claims have fine lines. Until the FDA officially accepts new, proposed categories, such as *cosmeceutical* or *pharmocosmetic,* and allows a broader claim base, estheticians must be content to learn about the new technology. Fortunately, wonderful new ingredients are available that have an amazing impact on the skin's appearance.

Serums

New concepts, ingredients, and treatment technologies are advancing at record-breaking speed. New advances are being developed in laboratories all around the country. Serums are one example of recent advancements (Figure 20–1).

Serums, intensive correctors, and concentrates are user-friendly versions of more traditional ampoules that are available retail. While some companies still have ampoules for professional use, they have switched to serums for home use. The main difference between an ampoule and a serum is probably

serums
A user-friendly version of ampoules that are used for retailing; also called intensive correctors or concentrates.

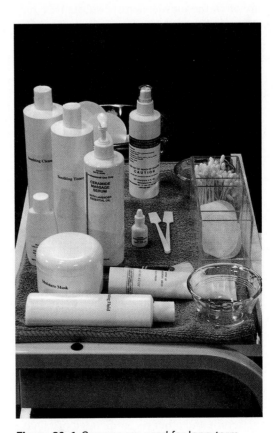

Figure 20–1 Serums are used for long-term specific corrective treatments.

the degree of purity of the ingredients without preservation and intensity. While a professional ampoule is generally intended for an immediate, one-time use, serums or concentrates are intended for a specific corrective treatment used day and night for 30–60 days or more. Serums are still highly active substances, but they are not quite as active as ampoules. Intensive correctors are for home care work and are used in salon treatments as well. They are highly valuable because they help increase the results of an esthetician's work.

In fact, because of newer delivery systems, serums may be just as potent as the more traditional technology used in most ampoules. Almost every major skin care manufacturer today has developed serum technology, and in most home care lines serums are the most active and potent treatments. It is important to study the technology of your specific manufacturer; most of them offer various serums for different skin types and conditions.

Historically, serums have been used to correct targeted issues. Consequently, they are often the most expensive substances in a skin care line and may be overlooked because of their cost. But today's consumer is searching for the fastest, most potent miracle in a bottle. Estheticians should educate clients about the benefits of serums using strategies such as the following:

- Sell the serum as the number one product to buy, and then sell the cream to seal in the serum. Proceed to the cleanser and freshener. While good cleansing is tantamount to a successful skin care routine, it is not usually a perceived need of a client when a specialty product with antiaging benefits is available.

- Estheticians should personally use and understand the benefits of serums. Selling a product's benefits is difficult when you have not used it yourself.

- When performing corrective skin care on your client, especially in a series, create a plan for the home care regimen. Include product systems based on the type of skin correction your client needs. Include the serum and other recommended products in the plan.

nanosomes
Smaller and thinner liposomes, capable of holding more performance ingredients and delivering them more efficiently.

polymers
New, advanced delivery systems with multiple uses.

Delivery Systems

One of the most exciting areas of cosmetic technology today is in the advancement of delivery systems.

Liposomes

A major advancement in delivery systems is in the area of liposome technology. Liposomes are vehicles that transfer important ingredients to the skin by slowly dissolving them over time. When a traditional product is applied to the skin, a certain amount of absorption with some evaporation takes place. Liposome technology helps to stabilize and preserve the performance ingredients so that the skin receives maximum benefit.

Because of the very nature and activity of liposomes, the term does not clearly differentiate between a cosmetic substance and a topical drug. To avoid potential confusion with topical drugs, the term *liposome* is rarely mentioned. Rather, descriptive phrases such as "microspheres of moisture" are more prevalent in media advertising and efficacy claims.

Nanosomes are smaller and thinner liposomes. They are capable of holding more performance ingredients and delivering them more efficiently.

Polymers

Polymers are new, advanced delivery systems with multiple uses. Some companies refer to polymers as *microsponges*, which are small beads with tiny perforations that release substances onto the skin's surface at a microscopically controlled rate.

Dr. Albert Kligman, research dermatologist of the University of Pennsylvania School of Medicine, discovered that advanced polymer systems could safely deliver retinol, a very active substance, in small doses in a time-released mode. This method affects exfoliation and cell renewal without the caustic side effects that occur when retinol is delivered through a traditional medium such as a cream.

SKILLS ● FOR ● SUCCESS

Professional Retail Sales

You are not alone if you are ambivalent about selling products. Most estheticians are uncomfortable with the idea of retail sales. After all, you chose a career in skin care to nurture and encourage healthy skin—not to be a salesperson. So the first challenge you will have to face is changing your perspective about retail sales.

Adjusting your attitude toward retail requires coming to terms with two very important basic principles in esthetics:

1. Selling retail is no different than selling services.
2. Recommending and providing quality skin care products is a professional responsibility.

By choosing a career as a professional esthetician you have made a commitment to promoting clean, healthy, and beautiful skin. You advocate these goals every time you provide a service. Clients choose to purchase your services because they believe in the value of what you do. In reality, you sell the concept of skin care everyday. Understanding that this is a worthy goal, you will begin to realize that clients also expect you to recommend products that keep them in alignment with these objectives.

As you are the *expert* on skin care, clients will come to identify the purchase of skin care products with you because you are the professional. This is a positive association. Products are the professional tools of our trade. They are an integral part of our work. You would not go to a physician or homeopath whose advice and care you respect, have them diagnose a problem or condition, and then refuse to follow up with the prescription or herbal remedy, now would you?

Becoming comfortable with recommending appropriate skin care products is the first step to successful retail product sales. Once you have passed this roadblock you can begin to work on your technique.

You don't have to be "pushy" to sell products. You are the expert; your job is to *educate* clients about the proper use of products. However, to build credibility as a professional you must be honest and sincere. This is easily accomplished when you believe in and understand the products you are using and know exactly what effect they will have on the client's skin condition. Obtaining as much information as possible from vendors and supervisors will help alleviate any pressure you may feel about making the right recommendations. Learning to translate this information into a language that the client can understand comes next. Developing a communication style that is authoritative but nonthreatening will build the client's confidence in you. Practicing a dialogue with your colleagues or someone you trust can generate useful feedback that will help you improve your performance in this area.

Using the products yourself is ultimately the best way to acquire knowledge. Remember that you are the best form of advertisement for any product line that you endorse. If your skin looks good clients will trust the performance of the product.

In products made for oily skin, polymers are actually empty. When deposited onto the skin's surface, they roll around absorbing excess oil and filling the polymeric ball.

Polymers can be made in various sizes and with various porosity levels (permeability), allowing them to perform a variety of surface level functions. This incredible technology now allows a much more effective use of highly active substances on the skin, without being too aggressive.

Improving Cell Metabolism And Oxygenation

A major goal in advanced skin care treatments is to help the skin function at its maximum capacity at any age. When the natural biochemistry of the skin is balanced, it protects the skin properly. It also appears radiant and healthy. Improvements in cell turnover that emulate younger skin, together with enough nutrients to facilitate this process, can slow down the appearance of aging. While it is impossible to reverse major damage, a well-planned skin care management program can reduce the symptoms of aging.

A number of high-tech ingredients serve as antioxidants and actually stimulate metabolic processes. The objective is to use high-powered metabolic stimulants and supporters to improve the skin, reduce fine lines and wrinkles, and to speed up the healthy cell transferal processes. The substances and their functions vary from one ingredient and treatment system to another.

Polyglucans and Beta-Glucans

Biotechnology derives ingredients from plant extracts and other natural substances. Many of these ingredients are used to help strengthen the skin. For example, **polyglucans** and **beta-glucans** are thought to help strengthen the immune system and stimulate the metabolism. They are normally derived from yeast cells and have a natural affinity for the skin. In addition, a polyglucan is a hydrophilic ingredient that attracts water and therefore helps preserve and protect collagen and elastin. Beta-glucans help reduce the appearance of fine lines and wrinkles by stimulating the formation of collagen.

Tissue Respiratory Factor

Tissue respiratory factor (TRF) is also derived from yeast cells and functions as an anti-inflammatory and moisturizing ingredient. TRF, polyglucans, and beta-glucans are powerful antiaging, antiwrinkle ingredients that help the skin stay younger longer.

Glycoproteins

Glycoproteins (glycopolypeptides) are another yeast cell derivative. Studies have found that they have the ability to enhance cellular metabolism, which boosts oxygen uptake in the cell. The revitalizing capacity of glycoproteins strengthens the skin's natural ability to protect itself against damaging environmental influences. Glycoproteins are especially beneficial to skin that appears unhealthy, is dull from smoking, has diffused redness, or has environmental damage. A well-known, trademarked glycoprotein product is Revitalin-BT, which originated in Switzerland.

Coenzyme Q10

Coenzyme Q10 is one of the newest technological breakthroughs in skin care. It has a catalytic effect on skin systems and is a highly prized ingredient that protects and revitalizes skin cells. Q10 is often formulated with other natural protective ingredients to strengthen the capillary network and increase energy to epidermal cells. It is considered a powerful antioxidant. It seems to fortify the skin's immune function and activate metabolic functions. Use of Q10 most often results in the visible reduction of wrinkles and fine lines.

Nature versus Biotechnology

Some of the most effective advanced ingredients are not directly derived from plants. No one can debate the value of natural substances, but we should not be too quick to condemn biotechnological ingredients. Thousands of components called biotechnological ingredients are developed in the laboratory to emulate nature and have been found to be just as efficacious or even better than natural ingredients.

polyglucans
Natural substances derived from yeast cells that help strengthen the immune system and stimulate the metabolism. A hydrophilic ingredient able to absorb more than ten times its weight in water, it can be absorbed into the outer layers of the epidermis due to its extremely small size.

beta-glucans
Ingredients used in antiaging cosmetics to reduce the appearance of fine lines and wrinkles by stimulating the formation of collagen.

tissue respiratory factor (TRF)
A natural substance derived from yeast cells that functions as an anti-inflammatory and moisturizing ingredient.

glycoproteins
Yeast cell derivatives that have the ability to enhance cellular metabolism, which boosts oxygen uptake in the cell; also called glycopolypeptides.

coenzyme Q10
An enzyme that has a catalytic effect on skin systems and revitalizes skin cells.

Natural ingredients can have drawbacks. Many natural things are not always beneficial to people, such as natural diseases. Natural ingredients can cause allergies in people who are sensitive, while the bioengineered versions of the same ingredients may not cause allergies. Moreover, certain bioengineered ingredients are very effective in skin care preparations as cell renewal stimulants.

Sometimes it can be difficult to know when to choose nature over biotechnology. They both make a tremendous contribution to skin care formulations. For this reason, estheticians must stay current on cosmetic chemistry education and the various developments and product lines available. Each professional manufacturer has a unique positioning in the marketplace. Manufacturers also do extensive research and development to bring the latest technologies into cosmetic formulations.

For example, hyaluronic acid, an ingredient used to bind moisture in formulations, was initially derived from roosters' combs. Biotechnological production of this ingredient was developed, and today it is completely derived from synthetic sources for use in cosmetics. The biotechnical version is much more stable and has more effective water-binding capabilities.

The key point is that estheticians must continue to study technology and its advancement because many products and treatments are made up of ingredients from the natural world and from biotechnology.

Summary

The cosmetics and skin care industry is making constant breakthroughs in technology that benefit the skin. Many new ingredients help reduce the signs of aging. Although the FDA restricts the claims manufacturers can make in the United States, these products may actually improve skin structures and functions. Estheticians should always know the most recent biotechnological developments that have an impact on skin care products and cosmetics.

Discussion Questions

1. Explain the difference between ampoules and serums. Discuss the pros and cons of integrating these into a professional treatment and home care program.

2. Modern cosmetics boast many new advances in the area of technology. Discuss major advances in terms of product delivery systems along with product examples. How do the claims enhance the effectiveness of the product?

Additional Reading

Lees, Mark. 2001. *Skin Care: Beyond the Basics*. Clifton Park, N.Y.: Milady, an imprint of Delmar Learning, a division of Thomson Learning, Inc.

Michalun, Natalia, and M. Varinia Michalun. 2001. *Milady's Skin Care and Cosmetic Ingredients Dictionary*. Clifton Park, N.Y.: Milady, an imprint of Delmar Learning, a division of Thomson Learning, Inc.

Advanced
Skin Care

Part VII

Part Outline

Chapter 21   Aging Skin: Morphology and Treatment

Chapter 22   Sensitive Skin: Morphology and Treatment

Chapter 23   Hyperpigmentation: Morphology and Treatment

Chapter 24   Acne: Morphology and Treatment

Chapter 25   Ethnic Skin: Morphology and Treatment

Chapter 26   Exfoliation

Chapter 27   Holistic/Alternative Skin Care

Chapter 28   Advanced Home Care

Many clients seeking the help of an esthetician do so because of advanced skin care conditions, such as sun damage, acne, or hyperpigmentation. These skin conditions are often the result of a combination of environmental, hereditary, and lifestyle elements, and they need to be treated with a program that involves medical, salon, and home care. To successfully treat these conditions, estheticians must be aware of what causes them and what aggravates them, as well as what clears them.

Treating ethnic skin, understanding the differences and the common elements, and how it differs from Caucasian skin is crucial in our culturally diverse society.

Chapter 21
Aging Skin: Morphology And Treatment

Chapter Objectives

After reading this chapter, you should be able to:

- List different examples of intrinsic and extrinsic aging.
- Describe the various forms of sun damage and how to treat them.
- Explain salon treatments for aging skin.
- Identify considerations in choosing a product line.

Chapter Outline

Introduction
Intrinsic Aging
Extrinsic Aging
Sunscreens
Analysis of Sun-Damaged Skin
Treatment Concepts for Sun-Damaged Skin
Advanced Mature Skin Treatments

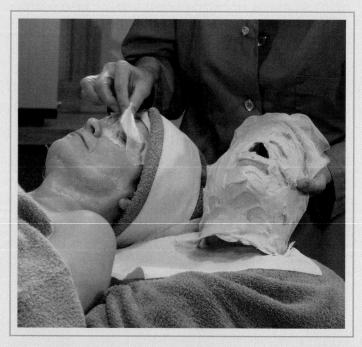

Introduction

When we refer to aging skin, many of us may think of elderly people. However, the skin actually begins the aging process as early as the late teens. In fact, damaging factors that affect premature aging can begin during the childhood years. Symptoms of intrinsic (inherent) aging include the development of expression lines and a loss of elasticity, or sagging skin.

Intrinsic Aging

Intrinsic aging refers to aging that occurs because of heredity, genetic factors, and the general nature of our physiology. We inherit genetic characteristics from our parents that partially determine how our skin behaves throughout our lifetime and how our skin looks as we age. **Genes** are tiny particles on chromosomes that can be thought of as blueprints that help determine many characteristics of our skin, such as skin coloring, certain acne factors, oiliness or dryness, skin sensitivity, and what naturally happens to our skin as we get older. Have you ever noticed how much a child looks like his or her parents, especially as the child becomes an adult? This happens because of genetic information that determines how we look at different ages (Figure 21–1).

Rhytids (rye-tids) is the medical term for wrinkles. Rhytids can be caused by the repetition of facial expressions, but multiple wrinkles that do not develop in the pattern of facial expressions are most likely caused by cumulative sun exposure, which will be discussed later in the chapter.

Expression lines, sometimes referred to as smile lines, scowl lines, or crow's feet (Figure 21–2) are wrinkles or depressions in the skin that develop from muscles repetitively moving in the same direction, repeatedly twisting and bending the skin. Muscles

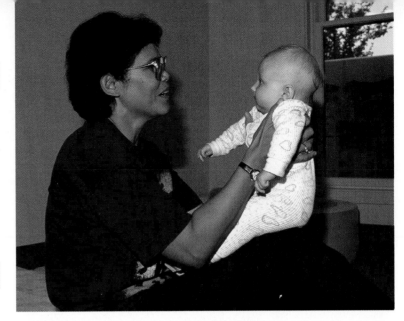

Figure 21–1 Intrinsic aging occurs due to environment, genetics, and lifestyle.

Figure 21–2 Expression lines develop from facial muscles repetitively moving in the same direction.

genes
Tiny portions of chromosomes that determine an individual's features including skin coloring, acne factors, sensitivity, and the aging process.

rhytids
The medical term for wrinkles.

expression lines
Wrinkles or depressions in the skin developed from muscles repetitively moving in the same direction.

of the face are attached to the skin, not to bones as in other parts of the body. Consequently, folds form from the movement of the muscles, which are attached to the skin. Over time, the skin's elastic fibers stretch out to accommodate this constant pulling. This results in sagging facial skin and folds in the patterns of facial expressions. The eyes and the mouth area are especially vulnerable to expression lines caused by smiling. The lines that form from the corners of the nose to the mouth are known as **nasolabial folds** (Figure 21–3). Horizontal lines also frequently form in the forehead due to raising the eyebrows during facial expressions.

People who have very expressive faces definitely develop deeper and more wrinkles than those who have less expressive faces. People who smoke are more likely to develop lines around the mouth, partially from repetitive facial movements and more importantly from free radical damage and other biochemical damage.

Figure 21–3 Nasolabial folds are the lines that form from the corners of the nose to the corners of the mouth.

Expression lines deepen with age. Someone in their teens or early twenties may already have some expression lines that will deepen and increase with age. Individuals who have more expressive faces will develop deeper wrinkles and more of them than a person who is less expressive facially. Smokers are more likely to develop lines around the mouth due to repetitive facial movements (and more importantly from free radicals and other biochemical damage discussed later in this chapter).

Some expression lines develop from pressing on the face in repetitive ways. A person who sleeps on the side presses the face in a folded manner against a pillow for hours at a time. When awakening, the face appears wrinkled or pressed-looking. These wrinkles are most often vertical, instead of a typical facial expression, which is horizontal (Figure 21–4). As soon as the circulation stimulates, much of this pressed look disappears. However, pressing on the face night after night, year after year, eventually causes stretching of the dermal elastin fibers, resulting in a lack of elasticity and vertical wrinkling. Additionally, the fat pad under the epidermis begins to disappear with age, eliminating some of the support that is normally pushing against this pressure. Special pillows are available that discourage side sleeping, keeping the face free from pillow pressure. Other pillows are designed to encourage individuals to sleep on their back facing up.

Gravity is another intrinsic aging factor. Gravity is a force that constantly pulls down on our bodies. It also pulls down on the skin and causes some eventual sagging or **elastosis**, which is the scientific term for lack of skin elasticity. All persons experience some elastosis resulting from the effects of gravity over a period of years. Elastosis usually begins to show slightly in the late twenties or early thirties and is more pronounced during the forties and fifties. Elastosis is made much worse if the skin has been routinely exposed to the sun's ultraviolet rays.

Other parts of the body's skin are subject to elastosis. The skin on the arms, legs, breasts, torso, and buttocks all show varying degrees of reduced elasticity resulting from the aging process. The facial skin, however, is the most likely area to show elastosis, due to repetitive facial movements causing wrinkles, which are made worse by cumulative sun exposure.

nasolabial folds
Lines that form in the skin from the corners of the nose to the corner of the mouth.

elastosis
The loss of elasticity in the skin.

Time and Physiological Changes

Some scientists theorize that there is a pre-programmed factor in aging. We inherit a preset pattern of instructions as to how cells behave over time and, therefore, how our skin looks at different ages. Each year, the scientific community learns more and more about delaying and controlling the aging process. Some conflict exists among scientists as to how much of the aging process is due to predetermined genetic factors and how much is due to damage as a result of sun exposure, abuse, smoking, pollution, and other lifestyle factors or **extrinsic aging factors** (factors that are controllable and not genetically predetermined). At this point in time, we know that some physiological aging changes appear to happen as a result of genetics, and they happen at various times in the course of a lifetime.

The Twenties

From ages 20 to 30, expression lines begin to show because of the loss of collagen, which diminishes about 1% per year beginning in the midtwenties. The skin on the upper eyelid begins to lose elasticity, known as **browtosis**. Fat around the eye may herniate or bulge out of its normal contour, causing fat pockets that result in eyebags. Eyebags can also be accentuated in individuals who suffer from sinus allergies, because chronic stretching of the skin under the eyes from swelling can lead to more elastosis and an increased chance of fat herniation.

The Thirties

In the thirties, gravity begins to take its toll. Drooping of the skin begins as a result of skin stretching and the continued loss of collagen. Cumulative sun damage makes these symptoms much worse and more accelerated.

The Forties

In the forties, elastosis is much more apparent. Lines deepen in the nasolabial folds, and the skin begins to sag at the jaw line, resulting in what is referred to as jowls. Forehead wrinkles develop, although these may occur prematurely, especially in sun-damaged skin.

Menopause

At menopause, a woman begins to produce less and less estrogen. Estrogen is partly responsible for the skin's ability to produce

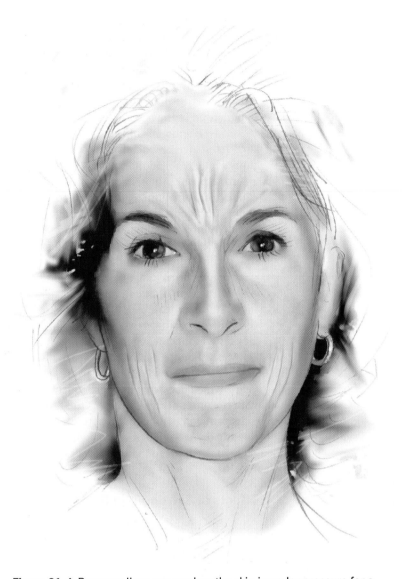

Figure 21–4 Pressure lines occur when the skin is under pressure for a long time.

collagen. As the production of estrogen slows, the skin's ability to repair and replace collagen diminishes. This results in more accentuated wrinkles and elastosis.

Changes in hormone levels at menopause affect lipid production between the skin cells that make up the skin's barrier. Sebum production decreases, causing superficial dehydration on the skin's surface. Women may need to switch to moisturizers, protectants, sunscreens, and other products with a more emollient base. They need the protection provided by silicones, oils, or other protective ingredients that help prevent dehydration.

Women experiencing menopause often report what clients often call "sudden aging." They look in the mirror and they seem to have aged "overnight." This, of course, is not

extrinsic aging factors
Controllable factors that contribute to the aging of the skin, such as sun exposure.

browtosis
The loss of elasticity in the skin of the upper eyelid.

true, but it may seem this way, as hormones influence collagen production and moisturization of the skin. This may make wrinkles and sagging much more obvious.

Menopausal women may also experience a flare in acne, something they may not have experienced in the past. Acne at this point is caused by hormonal shifts that include a drop in estrogen, which keeps follicle secretions in check. In addition, unopposed progesterone triggers the sebaceous gland to produce more sebum, resulting in a possible acne flare. Products must be carefully selected since an esthetician is not only working with a decrease in the lipid barrier that secures moisture, but is concurrently challenged with overactive follicle secretions. As a result, skin can be dry and have acne flares at the same time. Estheticians should recommend products that have been properly tested for comedogenicity.

Many menopausal women begin to see damage from excessive sun exposure over the years, which begins to manifest concurrently with the onset of menopause. What the client may blame on menopause is actually cumulative sun damage effects, complicated and accentuated by menopausal skin problems.

Effects of Estrogen on Skin

Estrogen can affect the skin in various ways. Estrogen

- reduces the size and activity of the sebaceous glands in the follicles.
- is responsible for fibroblast activity.
- stimulates collagen synthesis.
- increases the production of hyaluronic acid (moisture).
- slows the rate of hair growth.
- increases cell mitosis in the epidermis.

The Fifties

morphological
Changes in the shape and form of the face due to gravity and other factors.

The face goes through other **morphological** changes as it ages. Morphological changes are changes in shape and form. In the fifties, cartilage in the nose and ears expands due to gravity, making the nose and ears appear larger in older persons. Wrinkles and elastosis in the neck are also more apparent during the fifties. Bones throughout the body and in the face begin to shrink, removing even more support from the facial skin. This process occurs earlier in women than men (Figure 21–5).

Figure 21–5 In one's fifties wrinkles and elastosis are more apparent and occur sooner in women than men.

After Age 50

Due to a loss of subcutaneous fat (adipose), which is intrinsic, the skin appears thinner in older people. This is particularly true in persons over 70. The bones in the skull, particularly the forehead and cheekbones, may appear more obvious due to the loss of this fatty support.

The Dermis

Histological changes also occur in the dermis as the skin gets older, which helps explain the changes we notice in the appearance of the face, chiefly the loss of elasticity and increased wrinkling. In fact, most of the changes in the physiology of the skin occur in the dermis. As we know from our previous discussion of skin anatomy and physiology, collagen and elastin basically hold the skin together and provide strength and resilience, but they are also constantly broken down and reformed. During the aging process, collagen and elastin replacement rates diminish, collagen at a rate of 1% a year throughout our lifetime. And a lack of elastin and collagen is the main reason for elastosis and wrinkling. Damage to these fibers also advances the appearance of aging skin. This injury can result from natural, intrinsic aging, or it can result from extrinsic factors, such as cumulative sun exposure.

The Epidermis

Although the real physiological changes in the skin occur in the dermis, the epidermis experiences changes that may make aging skin look much worse. If the skin suffers from elastosis and wrinkling, dry, dull, dehydrated, and rough surface skin will accentuate this. Many of these epidermal changes can be treated, controlled, and prevented by the esthetician.

The epidermal skin renewal cycle, normally about 28 to 30 days, slows with aging, and the slowdown becomes more evident in the mid-thirties and forties. As discussed in the section on the renewal process, intercellular lipids hold moisture in the epidermis and are responsible for the visual smoothness and firmness of the skin's surface. They also provide a barrier against irritants and allergens entering the epidermis and causing reactions or damage.

Mitigation in the rate of cell renewal causes clumping of cells on the surface of the skin. Light is reflected unevenly, giving the appearance of dullness. The reduction of lipids results in a decrease of moisture retention in the epidermis. The outcome is dehydration, accentuated wrinkles, and reduced firmness of the skin. The skin develops more fine lines and increases in laxity, or a lack of firmness. It appears saggy, which further accentuates expression lines. It also increases the chances of irritant and allergic reactions, because gaps in the intercellular lipid structure lead to easy penetration of irritants and allergens. Furthermore, increased skin thinness, combined with a poor lipid barrier function, causes older skin to experience more sensitivity.

These effects can be remedied by the regular use of an exfoliant, such as an enzyme or alphahydroxy acids (AHA). Any method of exfoliation, chemical or mechanical, will remove dead surface cells, making the skin appear brighter and more youthful.

Extrinsic Aging

Extrinsic aging is damage caused by outside or external factors. It means superimposing environmental and sun exposure, bad health habits, lack of proper skin care, and improper nutrition onto the chronological aging process. In short, extrinsic aging factors are those factors over which we generally have control. Fortunately, many scientists and dermatologists believe that extrinsic factors may be responsible for 85% of what we see as aging skin symptoms.

Sun Damage

The single biggest factor contributing to premature aging is cumulative exposure to the sun. Repetitive sun exposure causes severe damage to the skin structures, such as destruction and alteration of collagen, elastin, hyaluronic acid, ground substance, as well as damage to blood vessels and cells. Aging symptoms related to sun exposure are referred to as photoaging. General damage associated with sun exposure is referred to as **actinic damage.** The technical term for sun-induced aging symptoms is **dermatoheliosis.**

The sun is very intense light made up of a spectrum of light that contains many different types of rays. The two rays we are primarily concerned with are **UVA** (ultraviolet alpha rays or ultraviolet A) and **UVB** (ultraviolet beta rays or ultraviolet B). The light spectrum is measured in nanometers. For example, the spectrum for UVB rays is approximately 290 to 320 nm, while UVA is 320 to 400 nm. This is important to remember when learning about the spectrum covered by the different sun protection chemicals.

Ultraviolet B rays penetrate the skin, but most stop at the lower epidermis and are reflected and scattered from this point. UVA, however, is a longer, more intense type of ray and penetrates into the dermis, where the elastin and collagen fibers, blood vessels, and ground substance are located.

Located in the basal cell layer of the lower epidermis and in the upper dermis, melanocytes are pigment-producing cells that respond to sun exposure by producing melanin, or skin pigment. Melanin is produced to protect the skin from damage, and one function of melanin is to help the skin reflect these damaging light rays. Increased skin pigments, then, is why sun exposure causes a tan to develop. Tanning is not purely cosmetic, as many people believe; it is a biological function—a defense mechanism manufactured by the body as a shield against damaging invasion.

actinic damage
General skin damage associated with sun exposure.

dermatoheliosis
The technical term for sun-induced aging symptoms.

UVA
Ultraviolet A rays, one type of ray contained in the light spectrum making up the sun's light. Longer, more intense than UVB rays, these penetrate into the dermis.

UVB
Ultraviolet B rays, one type of ray contained in the light spectrum making up the sun's light. Less intense than UVA rays, these only penetrate to the lower epidermis.

Free Radicals

Free radicals are wild molecules or atoms, usually oxygen or an oxygen-based compound, that have lost electrons and are not stable. Oxygen exists in the environment as O_2, or two oxygen atoms with a covalent bond that share electrons. This is the stable form of oxygen. Sun exposure causes this molecule to split, creating one stable and one unstable oxygen atom. This unstable oxygen atom is a free radical, also known as a **superoxide**.

The tendency of all chemicals is to try to reach their most stable state. Because of the loss of electrons, free radicals are desperately trying to regain enough electrons to restabilize themselves. To accomplish this, they will actually steal electrons from other atoms. One of the best sources of electrons is the cell membrane, and superoxide radicals often steal electrons from the lipids in the membrane of the cell. When these electrons are stolen, more free radicals are formed because now the atoms in the cell membrane are missing electrons. The type of free radical formed when the membrane is damaged is called **lipid peroxides.**

Damage to the cell membrane affects the ability of a cell to function properly. The cell membrane is responsible for nutrient, water, and oxygen absorption, as well as the disposal of cellular waste. Also important is that the membrane contains receptor sites that allow the cell to chemically communicate with other cells.

Iron is one of the most reactive elements; it loses electrons, or oxidizes, very readily. Surely you have noticed how easily iron rusts. Rust is a reaction of iron and oxygen that forms iron oxide. In terms of skin, peroxides can react with iron, which is abundantly present in the hemoglobin in blood, to form **hydroxy radicals**, the most dangerous free radical. Hydroxy radicals (abbreviated as -OH) can react with many different molecules, including the DNA in the cell nucleus, causing permanent damage to the cell. Consequently, this causes damage to the DNA in future cells produced through cell division. This is what really causes skin aging!

Free radicals also attack the proteins in collagen through a process known as **crosslinking.** Collagen fibers normally slide over one another to give the skin flexibility.

Crosslinking, however, binds the fibers together, making them inflexible, and resulting in the appearance of old skin. Crosslinking takes years to accumulate, but some crosslinking occurs with any unprotected sun exposure.

Inflammation and Free Radicals. These different kinds of free radicals can cause many problems for the skin, resulting in what is known as **subclinical inflammation.** This is inflammation that is not visually seen, as you would imagine would be the case with most inflammatory conditions. Subclinical means that normal clinical symptoms are not visible. This does not mean that they are not happening; it only means that they are happening at a level that is not showing visible redness and symptoms.

Any skin inflammation is the source of free radical activity. When a skin cell is inflamed, it releases special chemicals that signal the immune system within the blood that it has been damaged. Blood rushes to the site in a large enough response to create redness or inflammation. This may not be as visible in subclinical inflammation. In addition, white blood cells release chemicals that signal to the skin cells to make self-destruct enzymes, primarily elastase, collagenase, and hyaluronidase, that destroy elastin, collagen, and hyaluronic acid, respectively. Increased blood supply and other reactions surrounding skin inflammation help support free radical activity.

It is fair to say that any inflammation can damage the skin, and chronic inflammation will result in skin damage that creates symptoms we think of as signs of aging. It is, therefore, important to treat the skin for inflammation, as well as prevent any occurrence of inflammation. The most prevalent and immediate sign of inflammation from sun damage is redness, or erythema.

Long-Term versus Short-Term Damage

Unfortunately many individuals think that sun damage will never happen to them, but years of nonprotection results in all the symptoms of photoaging: wrinkles, elastosis, pigmentation disorders, roughness, leathery texture, dilated capillaries, and skin cancers.

Long-term sun damage creates a disorganized dermis, which actually thickens from an unsystematic effort to frantically repair dam-

---

superoxide
An unstable oxygen atom.

lipid peroxides
A free radical formed when the cell membrane is damaged.

hydroxy radicals
The most dangerous of the free radicals; they are formed when peroxides react with iron in the blood.

crosslinking
The collagen fibers are bound together by free radicals, making them inflexible, resulting in the appearance of old skin.

subclinical inflammation
Inflammation that is not apparent to the eye; it has no visible symptoms.

age. Think of the dermis as a house that is continually damaged by earthquakes and hurricanes. Crews have tried to repair the structural damage, but never have time to complete the repairs before another disaster happens. After years of this damage, the house is still standing, but it is held together by disorganized, makeshift repairs. Likewise, the dermis is always repairing but cannot undo all the damage of long-term sun exposure.

Short-term damage includes immune suppression of the epidermis caused by repelling macrophages, known as Langerhans cells. This lack of immune function can result in breakouts of herpes simplex virus (HSV), causing flares of fever blisters or cold sores. In fact, people with lupus (an autoimmune disease) are often first diagnosed after a severe reaction from sunburn.

Any sun exposure damages the DNA in the skin. The absence of Langerhans cells causes delays in immediate skin repair. A few days after sun exposure, DNA synthesis and cell division increase dramatically for several weeks. If the DNA is not properly repaired, this affects the blueprint of the cell, which causes defects in proper cell function. Alterations in the DNA and fast replication of damaged cells lead to cancer. Years of repetitive damage, therefore, dramatically increases the chances of permanent DNA damage, leading to dysfunctional cells and an increased probability of skin cancers.

Sunburn. Sunburn is an inflammatory response that occurs after cells are damaged by the sun, mostly caused by UVB rays. In the short term, sunburn results in redness, pain, peeling, tightness, dryness, pigmentation, inflammation, and a burning sensation. Erythema occurs from dilated blood vessels as the blood responds to the invasion of the UV rays. Swelling and blistering takes place, indicating separation of the upper epidermal layers from the lower ones.

Never treat sunburned skin because skin that is reddened from sun is more likely to be reactive to skin care treatments. All treatments should be delayed until the skin is not inflamed. This is especially true for alpha-hydroxy, microdermabrasion, and other exfoliating treatments. Clients with minor sunburns should be advised to apply cool compresses to their skin. They should not apply heavy moisturizers, oil, or butter (an

old wives' tale). A cool bath with a small amount of vinegar may help the skin feel better.

Once the skin has been sunburned, nothing will prevent peeling. After the erythema has subsided, light, fragrance-free moisturizers can be used; fragranced moisturizers can inflame the already irritated skin. Although moisturizers and hydrators may make the skin look and feel better, they will not prevent peeling. You should strongly advise a sunburned client to stay out of the sun completely until all the inflammation is gone and any peeling skin is healed. Further sun exposure on already peeling skin can result in hyperpigmentation and more severe damage.

A physician should see severely sunburned clients immediately, including any sunburn that involves bubbling of the skin or physical symptoms such as fever, nausea, or disorientation.

Other Reactions to Sun Exposure. Polymorphous light eruption (PLE), commonly known as sun poisoning or phototoxic reaction, is a severe reaction that may happen because the client is taking photoreactive drugs such as tetracycline or sulfur. It appears as a rash in the central areas of the face. PLE can also indicate the presence of a disease, such as lupus erythematosus.

Solar urticaria is hives associated with sun exposure. They appear as red, often raised, swollen lesions that may itch severely or burn. They may be indicative of an underlying disease, or they may happen in extremely reactive, sensitive skin. These clients are often aware that their skin has a tendency toward solar urticaria, as one occurrence is often unpleasant enough for the client to avoid a repeat episode.

solar urticaria
Hives associated with sun exposure.

Symptoms of Sun Damage
Sun-damaged skin is not only one isolated symptom. It is always a combination of the symptoms described below, although the number and severity of symptoms will vary with the age of the client and the amount of cumulative sun damage.

In most people, hyperpigmentation is actually the first sign of premature aging related to sun exposure. If you compare the skin of an 18-year-old with that of a 23-year-old, there is usually not much difference in elasticity and smoothness. However, you will

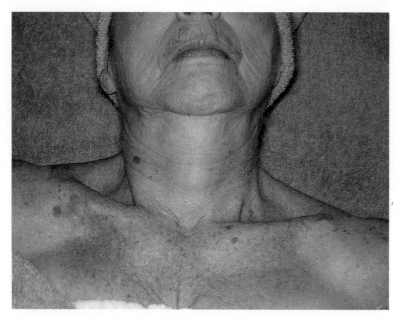

Figure 21–6 Sun-induced freckles, or solar lentigines, are the first sign of premature aged skin.

the yard for hours at a time are exposed to the sun's damaging rays, and it is highly likely that children who are allowed to overexpose their skin to the sun will experience premature aging. There is also a strong probability that they are more vulnerable for developing skin cancer later in life. To prevent this damage, they should be trained to apply a broad-spectrum sunscreen of at least sun protection factor (SPF) 15 on a daily basis.

Also well accepted is the fact that children learn most of their lifelong health habits before age 6. When a child is taught at a very young age to apply sunscreen on a daily basis, he or she is less likely to have sun damage later in life. This child is more likely to learn this important health habit and continue to use sunscreen daily throughout a lifetime. Table 21–1 lists important information about the effects of excessive sun exposure.

Other Pigmentation from the Sun

In more seriously sun-damaged skin, the skin appears very blotchy and mottling increases dramatically. Some seriously sun-damaged skin will also develop spots of hypopigmentation, or lack of pigment. These lighter spots may be accentuated by surrounding dark, hyperpigmented splotching.

Severely sun-damaged skin shows clumps of melanocytes that are very responsive to any further sun exposure. Darkening of these areas may occur readily with more sun exposure. Melasma, also known as a pregnancy mask, can appear in anyone, but women are much more likely to experience it. Melasma is associated with hormonal factors, is accentuated by the sun, and may recur after it has been successfully treated if a woman continues to be exposed to the sun. Heat from the sun is also a factor in hyperpigmented skin and should be avoided.

In older sun-damaged skin, dark splotches of hyperpigmentation can develop on the hands or the face. Commonly known as liver spots, these spots have nothing to do with the liver, except that they may resemble it in color. This condition is sometimes known as chloasma, but it is actually a very intense solar lentigo.

Telangiectasias. Telangiectasias (ta-lang-eck-tazjas) are also erroneously called broken capillaries. Telangiectasia is Greek for dilated blood vessel, and these tiny roadmaplike blood vessels have formed from dilated blood

mottling
A form of speckled hyperpigmentation resulting from sun exposure.

often find a difference in coloring and splotchiness, also known as **mottling**. Mottling is a form of speckled hyperpigmentation.

The first sign of sun-damaged, prematurely aged skin is that it is no longer uniform in color. Sun-induced freckles, called solar lentigines, will be evident (Figure 21–6). Overall, the skin is freckled and speckled, a characteristic caused by clumps of melanin and active melanocytes in the basal layer and upper reticular dermis. These melanocytes have desperately tried to shield the dermis from the sun and are basically working overtime, becoming overly sensitive and responsive to sun exposure. The more damaged the skin, the longer the response time to any kind of treatment.

It is a well-accepted fact among dermatologists and scientists that most of our sun damage occurs before age 18. Children playing in

Table 21–1 Facts about Sun Exposure

80% of lifetime sun exposure occurs prior to age 18.
3% of childhood cancers are skin cancers.
Death from skin cancer occurs at the rate of one death per hour in the U.S.
Skin cancer kills more women in their late twenties and early thirties than breast cancer.
93% of parents do not correctly use sunscreen on their children.
33% of adolescents never use sunscreen.

vessels, almost like small tributaries off a swollen river. Any routine form of vasodilation, meaning any substance that causes dilation of the blood vessels, can cause them. Sun is a major vasodilator, as are alcoholic beverages and tobacco. If you look closely at the skin of a sun-damaged client, you will see both large and small telangiectasias and large areas of very diffuse redness, called couperose. This may be especially obvious in the neck, décolleté, and the chest. It may look like a red area of skin, but on closer examination, you will see tiny dilated blood vessels.

Telangiectasia, diffuse redness, and hyperpigmentation often appear in a horseshoe pattern, with dark areas of hyperpigmentation and redness down the sides of the neck. There is also an obvious fleshcolored or normal-looking pigmentation in the center and under the chin. This condition is known as **poikiloderma of Cevattes,** which is an indicator of severe cumulative sun damage. The shading provided by the chin causes the lighter pigmentation in the center.

Although discussed here in terms of sun damage, telangiectasias can also be caused by constant pressure. A very typical place for telangiectasias is on the side of the nose. These are caused from years of nose blowing and wiping the nose with tissue. Individuals with high blood pressure may also have couperose and telangiectasia.

Larger telangiectasias can be treated with an electric needle, also known as **electrodessication**. In this procedure, a fine needle is inserted into the capillary, and a small current is released, causing a small clot to form in the capillary. This blocks the blood flow from entering the capillary, and the telangiectasia disappears. In most states, a physician must perform this treatment. Plastic surgeons and dermatologists can also treat telangiectasia with lasers that help stop blood flow to these small capillaries.

Estheticians can treat telangiectasia and couperose areas with specialty creams or serums that contain vitamin K, which also helps fade bruises. Some products contain horse chestnut *(Aesculus hippocastanum),* an extract loaded with bioflavonoids that is known in Europe as vitamin P. Bioflavonoids help strengthen the capillary walls. Grapeseed *(Vitis vinifera)* and green tea *(Camellia sinensis)* extracts may also be very helpful for couperose skin.

A relatively new technique for treating telangiectasia involves a machine known as **ultra high frequency**, which releases heat into the tissues, and is quite different from traditional high frequency. Treatments are administered several times a week, with eventual dissipation of the telangiectasia.

It is important to advise clients undergoing treatment for telangiectasia to avoid sun, tobacco, and alcohol. Do not perform stimulating treatments or massages and do not employ extreme temperature changes and heat sources, because all of these cause vasodilation. Clients should also use an SPF-15 or higher sunscreen daily. Sunscreens containing zinc oxide or titanium dioxide may be more effective on clients with couperose skin.

Telangiectasias can re-form very easily, and people who have them tend to have more of them. Obviously a hereditary factor, lighter-colored skin types tend to form telangiectasia easily. Rosacea patients, who also tend to be light-skinned, often have many telangiectasias.

Sun Damage and Wrinkles

We have already discussed wrinkles that form intrinsically. Wrinkles from sun damage are much more severe since overexposure increases the depth of expression lines. Wrinkles and creases also occur in areas that are not normally affected by facial expressions. **Crisscross wrinkling**, which is wrinkling in crossed patterns, is typical in sun-damaged skin (Figure 21–7, p. 320). Wrinkles also occur much sooner in sun-damaged skin.

The thick, leathery skin caused by thickening of the dermis and severe damage to the elastin and collagen fiber networks is more susceptible to wrinkles, and the wrinkles are often deeper than they are on less-damaged skin. **Tactile roughness** or roughness in the feel of the skin, is also associated with sun damage. In addition, neck skin is extremely thin and vulnerable to sun damage. Sun-damaged neck skin will develop pinpoint texture changes and wrinkles that can be compared to the skin of a plucked chicken.

Elasticity and Sun Damage

As a result of free radical attacks (discussed below) that cause ill repair of elastin proteins, sun damaged skin exhibits severe sagging or **solar elastosis.** When you examine a client's skin, gently lift the skin on the

poikiloderma of Cevattes
A combination of hyperpigmentation and telangiectasia formed in a horseshoe pattern, appearing as dark redness down the sides of the neck with a more normal-looking flesh-colored pigmentation under the chin.

electrodessication
A treatment for telangiectasia involving the use of an electric needle inserted into the capillaries to kill the edge of a lesion.

ultra high frequency
A relatively new treatment for telangiectasia that releases heat into the tissues.

crisscross wrinkling
Wrinkling in a crossed pattern typical in sun-damaged skin.

tactile roughness
Roughness to the feel of the skin, also associated with sun damage.

solar elastosis
Severe sagging of the skin resulting from sun-damaged skin.

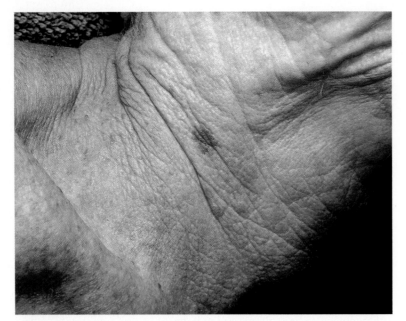

Figure 21–7 Crisscross wrinkling and leathery texture are typical in sun-damaged skin.

Solar Comedones

Severely sun-damaged skin can develop very large comedones, especially on and around the eyelids and on the upper cheek. These very large open and closed comedones are part of a disorder known as **Favre-Racouchot,** or solar comedones (Figure 21–8). This condition occurs mainly in men but is certainly seen in women, and it is directly related to years of sun exposure.

Extraction of these comedones is difficult, especially without bruising this extremely damaged, fragile skin. Typical treatment at home involves alphahydroxy acid gel or dermatologic treatment with tretinoin. Clients with Favre-Racouchot ar generally not very compliant with home care, as they have neglected their skin for many year, and it is hard for them to start taking care of it after so much damage. This skin type frequently also suffers from other sun-damage symptoms.

Seborrheic Keratosis

Keratosis is a pileup or thickening of epidermal cells. Seborrheic keratoses (keratosis is one lesion; keratoses is plural) are surface growths that almost look like scabs on the skin, but they are not malignant lesions. They have been described as looking as if they have been stuck on the skin. They mostly occur on the face and torso of sun-damaged individuals 40 years of age and older, although you may occasionally notice multiple small keratoses in the forehead or around the perimeter of the face. Seborrheic keratoses (seb-o-ree-ic ker-a-toe-sees) are usually brown to dark gray or can be very dark. Smaller, freshly formed keratoses may

cheek of the client and let go. If the skin does not snap back immediately, this skin suffers from elastosis. The skin may look like it is literally hanging off the underlying muscle structure. It is almost always leathery, thick, and hyperpigmented. It may also seem fragile on the surface.

Although elastosis affects all areas of the face, the neck, jaw line, and eyes are most dramatically affected. The neck skin is also stretched by weight gain and loss, and fat pockets under the chin further affect the jaw line and chin. Some of this is, of course, the intrinsic effect of gravity. However, solar elastosis makes the condition much worse.

The epidermis actually thins with cumulative sun exposure. Sun-damaged skin may bruise very easily because of this thinness. Older people with sun damage have frequent bruising, particularly on their arms. Known as **senile purpura**, it probably should be called solar purpura, since the occurrence has a lot more to do with sun damage than chronological age.

Be very careful with extractions and waxing or any other treatment involving pressure on this type of skin. Care should be taken to avoid bruising the skin or injuring small blood vessels that could lead to small red splotches just under the skin. This skin will eventually heal from these temporary injuries if they do accidentally occur, but they are, obviously, not esthetically pleasing to the client.

senile purpura
Easy bruising of the skin.

Favre–Racouchot
Also called solar comedones. Large comedones developed around the eyelids and cheekbones resulting from sun damage. It is more common in men than women.

Figure 21–8 Solar comedones are directly related to years of sun exposure, and occur mainly in men.

be lighter brown with a sallow hue. They usually have a rough texture to the touch. They can be as small as a pea or large as a quarter. Commonly, larger dark lesions occur on the cheekbone of older clients.

Etheticians should always refer clients to a dermatologist or plastic surgeon who will treat the seborrheic keratoses by freezing them with liquid nitrogen. They will then dry up and fall off. To prevent obvious discolorations in the areas from which they are removed, they should be treated while still small.

Actinic Keratoses

Actinic refers to conditions of the skin that result from sun damage. Actinic keratoses are often referred to as precancers by dermatologists. Untreated, these lesions can become a skin cancer called **squamous cell carcinoma**. They often feel s lightly sharp to the touch. Estheticians often notice these lesions during massage because they feel sharp, rough, or prickly when touched or passed over by the fingers. Actinic keratoses occur in areas of the skin that have been chronically overexposed to the skin. They are often pink but may be flesh-colored, and usually appear in areas with other symptoms of sun damage—rough, erythemic, dry, scaly, and hyperpigmented areas. Actinic keratoses are frequently seen on the forehead, upper cheeks, ears, and the temple area, but can occur in any sun-exposed areas. They also often occur on the hands and arms. They frequently feel slightly sharp to the touch and are thus easily located by an esthetician. Normally, actinic keratoses are noted in older clients, especially over the age of 60. They are most likely to be found in individuals with Fitzpatrick Type I, II, and III skin types. The area may look thin and red, with parchment-like dryness.

Dermatological treatment of actinic keratoses includes freezing the area with liquid nitrogen, a technique known as **cryosurgery**. They may also be treated with **curettage**, which is a technique of scooping out the lesion with an instrument called a curette. Tissues are then sent to a pathology laboratory for examination and detection of possible skin cancers or abnormal cell growth patterns.

Persons with multiple actinic keratoses are often treated with a topical drug called 5-fluorouracil, commercially known as Efudex.

The patient at home applies this medication for several weeks. The intent is to peel off the areas of the actinic damage, which will help replace the damaged tissue with more normal tissue. Side effects include extreme redness, stinging and burning, and, of course, peeling. Another drug known as masoprocol is also used to treat extensive actinic keratoses.

Clients cannot have esthetic facial treatments while taking these peeling drugs. A few weeks after the client has stopped taking the drug, the client may begin facial treatments, but the skin should be treated as sensitive skin.

Other Extrinsic Aging Factors

Sun exposure is, by far, the number one cause of premature aging of the skin. It is also the number one cause of skin cancer. A number of other environmental and lifestyle factors affect the skin, including free radicals, smoking, and poor skin care habits.

Smoking and Alcohol

Smoking is a habit that is insulting and injurious to the body in general. Cigarette smoke causes a huge number of free radicals to enter the bloodstream that affect every area of the body, including the skin. Smoking causes depletion of vitamin C in the body, a necessary component for collagen production. It affects blood flow, which affects delivery of nutrients to the skin tissues, oxygen transport, and disposal of cellular waste products. Smokers often have a noticeable yellowish, sallow color to their skin. Some of this may be caused by poor blood flow, but mostly the yellow color is caused by lipofuscin, which is a leftover-type substance produced from oxidized lipids. This is an indicator of how free radicals attack cell membranes. Even if you are a nonsmoker, you are affected by second hand smoke, known as environmental tobacco smoke (Table 21–2, p. 322).

Excessive alcohol consumption also affects all the organs in the body, which, in one way or another, affects the skin. Alcoholics often have very poor nutrition, and the nutrition that the body does get is not properly distributed. In addition, removal of cellular waste is impaired by excessive alcohol consumption.

squamous cell carcinoma
A form of skin cancer resembling a raised, crusty nodule or bump on the skin, caused by cumulative sun damage.

cryosurgery
Dermatological treatment of actinic keratosis involving freezing the area to be treated with liquid nitrogen.

curettage
The technique of removing a lesion with an instrument called a curette.

Table 21–2 Effects of Second Hand Smoke on Nonsmokers

Each year about 3,000 nonsmoking adults die of lung cancer as a result of environmental tobacco smoke (ETS).
ETS causes an estimated 35,000 to 40,000 deaths from heart disease.
ETS causes 150,000 to 300,000 lower respiratory tract infections in infants and children younger than 18 months in the U.S.
Children exposed to secondhand smoke at home are more likely to have middle ear disease and reduced lung function.
ETS increases the number of asthma attacks and the severity of asthma in about 20% of this country's 2 to 5 million asthmatic children.
Secondhand smoke contains over 4,000 chemical compounds, including carbon monoxide, formaldehyde, ammonia, nickel, zinc, acetone, cholesterol, hydrogen cyanide, and formic acid. Four chemicals in ETS are known human carcinogens: benzene, 2-naphthylamine, 4-aminobiphenyl, and polonium-210. The EPA classifies ten other chemicals as probable human carcinogens.

Poor Care

Poor care of the skin is a major controllable factor. Proper use of sunscreens on a daily basis is the best protection against premature aging. Products that are too aggressive, however, damage the barrier function of the skin, leading to inflammation and damage. Chronic use of stripping products should be avoided, as should anything that chronically irritates the skin.

An esthetician is in a wonderful position to educate consumers about proper skin care, and specifically, what can be done to prevent damage to the skin leading to premature aging. Consult with clients to help them choose products and treatments that are beneficial to them both at home and at the salon.

sun protection factor (SPF)

A numbering system applied to sunscreens that indicates how long skin can be safely exposed to the sun without burning and showing redness.

Sunscreens

Sunscreen products are the best protection against sunburn, premature aging, skin cancer, and all forms of sun-induced damage to the skin. They work by either absorbing or reflecting the ultraviolet (UV) rays that come at the skin. By absorbing or reflecting the UV rays, sunscreens prevent the beginning of the free radical cascade of chemical reactions that lead to cell and skin damage.

Absorbing sunscreen ingredients, also sometimes erroneously called chemical sunscreens (all sunscreens are chemicals by definition), work by absorbing and neutralizing the sun's UV rays, whereas physical sunscreen ingredients work by scattering or reflecting the sun's rays. Commonly used absorbing sunscreens include octyl methoxycinnamate, benzophenone-3, avobenzone (Parsol 1789), methyl salicylate, and para-aminobenzoic acid (PABA).

Only two physical sunscreens ingredients are approved for use in sunscreens in the United States, zinc oxide and titanium dioxides, both of which are crystals in the form of a powder. As a result, these sunscreens are opaque and known as particulate sunscreens, meaning that they are particles suspended in a lotion or a cream. You may have noticed that surfers often wear a white substance on their noses; this is zinc oxide paste, a powerful sunscreen. For use in transparent sunscreens, these opaque physical sunscreen ingredients must go through a micronization process to avoid being seen on the skin's surface.

For many years, before we knew the connection between aging and sun exposure, only UVB sunscreens were available. UVB sunscreens were designed mainly to prevent sunburn, because ultraviolet B is mainly responsible for sunburns. Today, sunscreens protect against UVA and UVB rays, and many guides are available to help you decide what level of protection is necessary for various usage and activity levels.

The main visible symptom of sunburn is redness or erythema; therefore, prevention of erythema was the hallmark for developing early sunscreens. Scientists developed tests for sunscreen efficacy that measured time factors in the prevention of redness. The amount of time required to develop erythema, or redness, in the skin is called the minimal erythemal dose (MED). The **sun protection factor (SPF)** is a number that indicates how long skin can be exposed to the sun without burning and showing redness. If a person normally burns in 30 minutes, an SPF-4 sunscreen should allow the person to be exposed to the sun for two hours (40 × 30 minutes) without becoming red or burning.

Sun protection factors, however, do not indicate how much sun damage is being prevented. They only indicate how long a person can receive exposure without burning or becoming red and irritated. They do not measure subclinical irritation or UVA damage, which is less likely to produce visible redness.

Up to a few years ago, people only used or thought about sunscreens when they intended to expose themselves to direct sunlight, for example, going to the beach or deliberately trying to get a tan. Many still believe that they do not need a sunscreen unless they are going to be sitting outside in direct sunlight.

Sunscreens are the very best antiaging treatment available and are the number one tool for the professional esthetician. The best thing you can ever do for clients is to educate them that they must use an SPF-15 or higher sunscreen every single day of their lives. They should also avoid deliberate sun exposure and tanning.

Truths about Sun Damage

Most of our cumulative sun damage occurs from occasional, nondeliberate exposure, which is referred to as casual exposure. This is sun exposure we get from walking the dog, going to the mailbox, walking to work, or even sitting by a window, because UVA rays cut right through glass. Most of our sun damage occurs before we turn 18 years old. This is why it is so important to protect children from sun exposure and to teach them to apply sunscreen every single day. Sun damage that causes what we think of as premature aging occurs over a lifetime, and we must use sunscreens every single day to prevent damage. For someone who is already sun damaged, it may be too late to prevent what has already happened, but is never too late to start preventing further damage.

Shielding Both UVB and UVA

Only in recent years have we come to know that UVA probably causes the most damage to the skin, and it is only in recent years that useable products have been developed to prevent UVA damage. Some ingredients prevent UVB and some UVA, and some overlap. UVA sunscreen ingredients include benzophenone-3 (some UVB and some UVA), avobenzone, and the physical screens zinc oxide and titanium dioxide. UVB absorbing sunscreen ingredients include octyl methoxycinnamate, octyl salicylate, para-aminobenzoic acid (PABA), methyl salicylate, padimate A, padimate O, and homosalate. Many of these have been available for years.

Broad-spectrum sunscreens are products designed to prevent damage from both UVA and UVB rays. Broad-spectrum sunscreens most often contain more than one active sunscreen ingredient. Tests have yet to be approved in the United States, as of this writing, for broad-spectrum sunscreens. Australia, a country with very stringent sunscreen laws, has had broad-spectrum testing for years.

As previously stated, titanium dioxide and zinc oxide are probably the most effective sunscreen ingredients against the widest spectrum of UV rays. They are also the least reactive of all sunscreen ingredients, in terms of allergies and sensitive skin. However, as single active ingredients, these are difficult to formulate in high SPFs in cosmetically acceptable products due to their particulate nature. They must be carefully formulated to distribute the crystals throughout the product, but they have a strong tendency to clump, resulting in unacceptable application and inconsistent SPFs.

To counter this, formulators often use fairly heavy cream bases to keep the crystals properly and evenly distributed. This sometimes makes for a fairly heavy product, which many consumers dislike. The micronization process is helping, though, to make lighter and hopefully more widely used sunscreens.

Commonly, zinc oxide or titanium dioxide is mixed with a UVB sunscreen ingredient, often octyl methoxycinnamate. This is close to an ideal formulation, both chemically and cosmetically. The mixture can shield from a broad spectrum of sunlight, with an effective SPF of 15 or higher, and the product can be lighter and smoother on the skin.

Choosing the Right Sunscreen

The most important thing you can ever do for a client's skin is to help her find a broad-spectrum sunscreen that is used on a daily basis. The best way to ensure that a client will use the product is to make it user-friendly and comfortable to apply and wear. It is important to choose the right sunscreen for the right skin type. It is also important to choose a sunscreen product that is wearable on a daily basis and works well under makeup. Many modern creams and lotions have sunscreens built into the day moisturizer, eliminating the need for two separate products—a sunscreen and a day moisturizer.

Sunscreens are available in lightweight fluids and lotions for oily and combination skin types, as well as heavier creams and lotions for dryer skin types. For oily and acne-prone skin, make sure you choose a sunscreen that has been properly tested to be noncomedogenic. For sensitive skin, make sure the product is fragrance free. A product with physical sunscreen active ingredients will be less likely to cause reactions.

Water-resistant sunscreens have undergone testing to make sure they stay on the skin for up to eight hours in the water, in the rain, or if the client is sweating. These sunscreens are generally not as lightweight or as user-friendly as non-water-resistant sunscreens. Some may be comedogenic if used frequently. However, they are important products for clients who participate in strenuous sports, as well as for people who will be in the summer heat for hours or who will be swimming.

water–resistant sunscreens
Sunscreens that will not wash off the skin for up to eight hours after exposure to water or rain.

Which SPF Is Best?

Among scientists and dermatologists it is generally accepted that an SPF-15 broad-spectrum sunscreen used on a daily basis is good protection for most people. SPFs of 30 and above are available. For clients who are in the sun for long periods of time, or clients who have had previous problems with skin cancer or other sun-related medical problems, an SPF-30 sunscreen may be a better choice. It is recommended that you have a variety of sunscreen products available for sale at your salon or clinic. Many clients may use a lightweight SPF-15 fluid on a daily basis, but may use an SPF-30 for a day at the zoo or a day in the water.

Sunscreen chemicals tend to be irritating, especially to sensitive skin. The higher the SPF, the more sunscreen ingredient in the product. The higher the SPF over 15, the more reactive the product may be to your clients with sensitive skin.

Facts about the Sun

A tremendous amount of misinformation about sun exposure, tanning, and sun damage is out there. As an esthetician, it is your job to help educate your client and squelch misinformation. Once you understand some fundamental facts about the sun and its harmful effects on the skin, you are better able to educate your clients.

- Any tan from the sun is an indication of damage to the cells. The only safe tan is one from a bottle, as in a sunless tanning product. Please remember that "tans" produced by self-tanning products provide no protection against real sun exposure.

- You get sun anytime during daylight hours. You do not have to be bathing in direct sunlight to receive damaging rays. In fact, most of us get most of our sun from walking to the car, playing with our children in the yard, and sitting by the window. There are more skin cancers on the left ear and left arm than on the right for people living in the United States, indicative of sun damage while driving.

- You get sun even in the rain during daylight hours. Clouds only filter a very small amount of UV rays.

- The skin will be more damaged if you are out in the sun between the hours of 10 A.M. and 3 P.M. If you exercise outside, try to do it early in the morning or late in the day.

- Umbrellas and hats do help prevent sun damage, but they are not substitutes for a broad-spectrum sunscreen.

- You will prevent UV damage to the eyes, which can lead to cataracts and other problems, if you wear a good pair of UV filter sunglasses. You will also help prevent squint lines.

- If you are going to be in direct sunlight, apply sunscreen at least 30 minutes prior to going out. This helps allow the sunscreen to absorb properly. Reapply sunscreen at least every 90 minutes while you are still in direct sunlight. One of the worst and most irritating things you can do to the skin is to apply sunscreen after the sunburn has occurred.

- Make sure you apply enough sunscreen. One ounce of sunscreen is the appropriate amount of sunscreen for one application for the average person wearing a swimsuit.

- No amount of moisturizer will make up for or repair the damage caused by sun exposure. Many people incorrectly think that "dryness" is the main effect of sun on the skin. Dehydration is a short-term factor, but the long-range exposure produces the real damage, which a moisturizer cannot fix.

- Tanning booths are not safe alternatives. Tanning beds and booths use UVA to tan the skin. You may not burn in a tanning bed, but you are receiving close-range doses of UVA. Remember the A in UVA is for aging.

- There is no benefit in pretanning in a tanning bed prior going to a sunny location for vacation. You are actually causing more damage to the skin.

Analysis of Sun-Damaged Skin

Most clients over the age of 30 who visit you for treatment will have some symptoms of sun damage. Older clients tend to have more damage, but do not let the client's age fool you. There are many young people who have sun damage problems. It is important to make note of all symptoms of sun damage and to make a proper medical referral when you see a suspicious skin condition.

After thoroughly cleansing the face, look under a magnifying lens and note on a client's record all skin conditions and symptoms, whether they are caused by sun damage or not (Figure 21–9). The first thing you will generally notice is the skin coloring and pigmentation. This will include notation of the client's Fitzpatrick skin type. You may notice melasma, solar lentigines, diffuse hyperpigmentation, hypopigmentation, or areas of splotching. You may also notice seborrheic keratoses.

Gently lift the skin with the thumb and forefinger and let go (Figure 21–10). Does the skin snap back quickly? If it takes any time at all to snap back, the skin is lacking elasticity. Repeat this procedure gently all over the face.

Skin lacking elasticity often feels flabby and soft, instead of firm and tight. You may also plainly notice folds of skin, jowls, and sagging in the neck, jaw line, and eyes. This is elastosis, most often related to sun damage. Obviously, degrees of elastosis vary with age and damage. You will develop a "sixth sense" about aging and sun damage, after practicing for a year or two. You will eventually be able

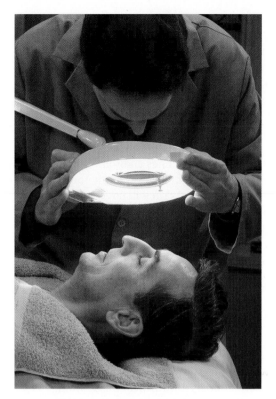

Figure 21–9 Look under a magnifying lamp to thoroughly look for signs of sun damage.

to determine mild, moderate, or severe sun damage quickly.

Are wrinkles only in the expression line areas, or are there wrinkles outside these areas? Are there crisscross wrinkles? How deep are the lines in the eye, forehead, and nasolabial folds? Are there other sun damage symptoms? Sun-damaged skin will have

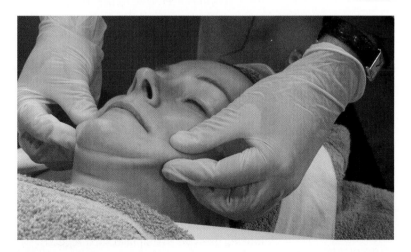

Figure 21–10 The "pinch test" indicates the amount of elasticity in the skin.

deeper wrinkles than normal, nondamaged skin of the same age. Sun-damaged skin will also have wrinkles besides those in the normal facial expression patterns.

Run your fingers over the skin's surface. Does it feel rough or smooth? Soft or leathery? Tactile roughness and a thick, leathery texture are characteristics of sun-damaged skin. Mature skin without sun damage will have expression lines and some intrinsic elastosis but will still feel soft to the touch.

Undamaged skin will have very little, if any, telangiectasia and very little redness. Sun-damaged skin, on the other hand, will have multiple telangiectasias in many areas and will also have areas of diffuse redness. If you look closely at these areas, you will notice very small capillaries. You may also notice mixtures of hyperpigmentation and couperose areas, such as poikiloderma of Cevattes on the neck skin. If you notice any unusual lesions that you have any doubt about, do not hesitate to refer the client to a dermatologist for further consultation.

After properly covering the client's eyes, examine the skin through a Wood's lamp. You will notice large amounts of brown areas under the skin, including freckles. This cannot be detected without the help of the Wood's lamp. If you have a tent-type mirrored Wood's lamp (a skin scope), the client can also observe the damage. You can point out areas of concern for the client.

Skin Cancer

Unfortunately, many clients will have some form of skin cancer. Due to the frequency with which they see clients, estheticians are in a position to detect the first signs of a precancerous or cancerous condition. If you see anything suspicious, refer the client to a dermatologist. Fortunately, skin cancers are curable when they are caught in time. Estheticians are not doctors, and although they do not diagnose skin cancer, it is important to be able to recognize abnormalities so that they can be thoroughly checked by a physician

Signs of Possible Cancer
Always be aware of any new abnormal-looking growths that appear on a regular client. Be especially observant in clients who have a lifetime of sun exposure. Make note of any unusual lesion, and ask the client if he is aware of it. If you are not sure what the lesion is, it is always best to refer the client to a dermatologist.

An area that repeatedly bleeds with no explanation definitely needs to be checked by a dermatologist. You may be cleansing a client's skin and, all of a sudden, see a small rough area bleed. This may be something as simple as a scab from a scratch or a healing pustule, but pimples and scrapes have a definite appearance different from that of rough, actinic damage. Be aware of lesions that do not seem to heal well, because they are another warning sign.

Basal Cell Carcinoma
Basal cell carcinoma is a common form of skin cancer that originates in the basal layer of the epidermis (Figure 21–11). More than 300,000 cases are diagnosed each year. It is more common in Fitzpatrick skin types I, II, and III, but can be seen on skin of any coloration. While this type of cancer mainly occurs in patients over 40 years of age, basal cell carcinoma can occur in individuals in their twenties and thirties. They are often found on the face and other sun-exposed areas. Basal cell carcinomas rarely **metastasize,** or spread to other tissues or organs, so although not life threatening, they can produce unpleasant scarring if they are not detected early.

Several different types of basal cell carcinomas can develop. The most common type is frequently described as a pearl-like bump, usually flesh-colored or slightly pink, often

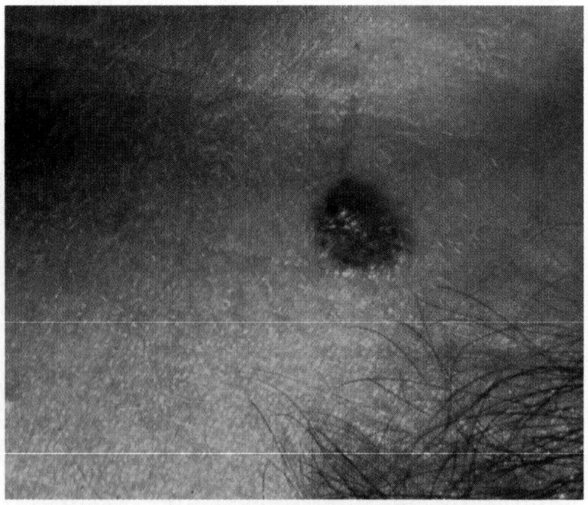

Figure 21–11 Basal cell carcinoma.

---

basal cell carcinoma
A common form of skin cancer that originates in the basal layer of the epidermis.

metastasize
To spread to other tissues or organs.

nodulocystic
Basal cell carcinoma presenting as a pearl-like bump, usually flesh-colored or slightly pink, often with small capillaries running through it. They are generally painless.

superficial basal cell carcinoma
Red, flat, scaly lesions that look much like eczema. Frequently misdiagnosed.

sclerosing
Scarlike; most often occurring on the forehead.

with small capillaries running through it. They are generally painless. This type of basal cell carcinoma is called **nodulocystic**.

Superficial basal cell carcinomas look much like eczema. They are red, flat, and scaly and are frequently misdiagnosed as other conditions. You may notice that this type of lesion hasn't cleared after more than one facial. Recurrent conditions such as this, in the same area, should raise concern. It is important to refer this client to a dermatologist.

Sclerosing or cicatricial basal cell carcinomas look like scars and often occur in the forehead area. You may notice these lesions lingering over time. **Pigmented basal cell carcinomas** have melanocytes involved in the lesions and are dark in color. **Ulcerative carcinomas** are ulcerated and have an indented center.

Basal cell carcinomas are treated with various techniques. A **biopsy**, which is a sampling of tissue taken to analyze in the laboratory, will help determine the type of cancer. Simple lesions can be treated using curettage and **electrodessication,** which is treatment with an electric needle. The lesion is scooped out with a curette, treated with an electric needle to kill the edges, and then retreated.

Recurrent or larger basal cell carcinomas, or ones that have not been caught early, are treated by surgical excision. When larger lesions are removed from the face, facial surgeons or plastic surgeons are frequently consulted, because they are trained to minimize scarring and have more advanced surgical techniques. When large lesions are removed a skin transplant or **graft** may be required. The graft is often taken from a leg, arm, or from skin behind the ear.

More difficult cases of basal cell carcinoma may be treated with **Moh's surgery**, a special dermatological surgical technique used to ensure that all cancerous cells are removed. In this technique, developed by Dr. Frederick Mohs at the University of Wisconsin, tissue samples that have not been completely removed are evaluated for cancer cells. The dermatologist continues to remove tissue until there are no cancer cells seen in the tissue samples.

Squamous Cell Carcinoma
Squamous cell carcinoma, the second most frequently diagnosed skin cancer, is seen in

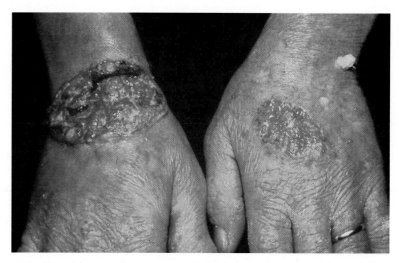

Figure 21–12 Squamous cell carcinoma.

about 100,000 patients annually. It is caused by cumulative sun exposure and is more frequent in severely sun-damaged skin. Squamous cell carcinoma is usually raised, crusty, or warty looking (Figure 21–12). It appears as ulcers or nodular bumps and may bleed easily. These cancers can also be caused by frequent and long-range exposure to certain industrial chemicals.

People with actinic keratoses are more likely to develop squamous cell carcinoma. Squamous cell carcinoma frequently develops on the tops of the ears, on the face, on the lips, and in the mouth. They can also occur on old scars.

Unlike basal cell carcinoma, squamous cell carcinoma can metastasize and spread to other organs as well as deeply within the skin. Fortunately, 90% of squamous cell carcinomas are detected and removed before they spread or recur. Squamous cell carcinomas are more often treated with surgery, or Moh's surgery, than basal cell carcinomas.

Melanoma
The most serious and deadly form of skin cancer is melanoma (Figure 21–13). It is the fourth most prevalent cancer in men ages 50 to 59, and the number one cancer in women ages 25 to 29. Overall, melanoma is the seventh most common cancer in the United States. It has been estimated that as many as one person in 75 will develop melanoma during their lifetime.

Melanoma derives its name from melanocytes, the cells that produce pigment and are responsible for this type of skin

pigmented
Melanocytes are involved in the lesions and are dark in color.

ulcerative
Having an indented center.

biopsy
A sampling of tissue taken to analyze in the laboratory.

graft
Skin transplant.

Moh's surgery
A special surgical technique for the removal of tumors that takes only a minimum of healthy tissue. The tissue is examined prior to removal, is mapped, and then removed bit by bit, until the unhealthy tissue has been completely removed and the site is surrounded by healthy tissue.

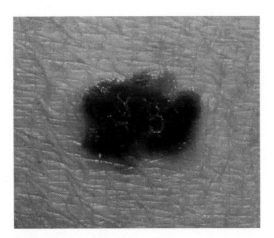

Figure 21–13 Melanoma.

cancer. Melanomas can occur in an existing mole or arise from normal skin. They metastasize quickly and are extremely serious. Approximately 18% of persons with melanoma die from it. Because melanoma spreads so quickly, early detection is essential for treatment and remission.

Several factors may be responsible for melanoma. The tendency to develop melanoma may be hereditary. It may also be related to immune suppression and the presence of many moles (more than 50); more cases occur in blondes or redheads with blue or green eyes. In addition, people with certain types of existing moles or nevi are more likely to develop melanoma. These nevi are referred to as dysplastic nevi (abnormally growing). Furthermore, melanomas may or may not occur on sun-exposed areas. Growing evidence suggests that sun exposure is a major contributing factor, but melanoma can occur on areas never exposed to the sun.

Several major types of melanoma have been identified. The most common are superficial spreading melanoma, nodular melanoma, and lentigo maligna melanoma.

Referred to as the ABCDs of melanoma, four major characteristics are used to detect possible melanoma in a lesion:

1. **A**symmetry—One side of a lesion is not identical to the other side. Normal moles are identical on either side.

2. **B**order—The edges of the lesion are uneven and jagged. The edges of normal moles are smooth and rounded.

3. **C**olor—Multiple colors or colors that fade into one another are typical of melanoma. In normal moles, the color is even.

4. **D**iameter—The diameter of a melanoma is usually at least as large as a pencil eraser.

Not all four characteristics must exist in any single case of melanoma. Evidence of only one of the four characteristics should make one suspicious of a mole or other lesion. However, most melanomas do present more than one characteristic.

Melanomas can occur on the face, trunk, or even in places like the back of the knees or between the toes. This is why estheticians must always be aware of the characteristics of melanoma, as well as other skin diseases. Estheticians may be the first person to see a lesion that requires referral, sometimes even before the client sees it.

Melanomas are treated by surgical removal of the lesion and the immediate surrounding tissue. If a melanoma metastasizes, it often spreads throughout the lymphatic system. As a result, lymph nodes must often be removed if they are affected. Sometimes they are removed in order to see if melanoma has spread. At times, chemotherapy may be used in advanced melanoma cases, along with surgical removal.

If You Find a Suspicious Lesion

You should never panic a client by blurting out that they may have skin cancer. You are not a dermatologist. However, it is certainly okay to say, "I noticed this strange little area that I do not remember seeing before. Have you had this checked by a dermatologist?" If the client has not had the lesion checked, you may say, "I think it would be a good idea to get this checked," or "This may be nothing serious, but I would feel better if you had this checked. Let me give you the names of a couple of dermatologists I know." In other words, let a client know that you are not sure what this lesion is, without panicking the client.

Discussing Aging and Sun Damage With Clients

Being tactful when discussing skin conditions with your clients is extremely important. Always be positive, and speak in an upbeat tone. However, it is equally important to be honest with your clients. It is certainly acceptable to talk about sun damage, and the fact that your client is experiencing the problems that stem from it. When discussing the

Merchandising

The secret to successful merchandising is understanding that it is a sensory experience. Being able to see, touch, smell, and feel a product is an important part of the decision-making process. We are bombarded with sensory stimuli on a daily basis—some pleasant, some offensive. Cooking aromas, traffic fumes, fabrics, fragrances, heat, cold, wind, color—they all serve to heighten our sensory awareness. But, for the most part we have little control over their direct personal impact. When it comes to choosing what we put on our bodies we want to have choices.

As an esthetician you are considered an authority on skin care products. However, in order to be successful in merchandising retail products you must also be realistic. Retail sales are another opportunity for income. Understanding what your clients need and want is an important part of becoming a retail success. Taking care to present merchandise in a positive manner that appeals to a broad range of clients will increase your credibility and your sales.

Although estheticians have uncovered a real share of the product market they are still in competition with larger retail enterprises such as department stores and rapidly growing e-commerce and home shopping ventures. Rather than being intimidated, estheticians must learn to compete.

Estheticians have the advantage of being personally involved with their clients—a key element in today's relationship-oriented selling market. The client has already solicited your professional expertise. Keeping the client on track and informed about products that will enhance the benefits of a clinical program will increase your success rate.

Begin by educating the client. Provide as much visual or print information as possible and position it so that it is easily accessible. The reception and waiting areas are ideal places to hang posters and place brochures and other reading material on products and services. But be creative. Hang information dispensers in the treatment rooms and bathrooms and enclose additional information with the client's purchases. Be sure to alert clients to any specialized training you may have with the products you use. Frame and hang training certificates in a strategic location to add to your professional credibility.

Consider yourself an ambassador and educate your coworkers about the products you use as well. Chances are you may not always be available when a client comes in to purchase or replenish products. Whether they call or come in person, everyone in contact with the client should be informed about retail products. The receptionist is a key person in supplying information. Begin educating your colleagues with a treatment. Allow them to experience the treatment as you teach them about home care and treatment products. Provide samples as well as literature and offer to answer any questions other staff members may have.

As you plan your approach to clients and colleagues, think aesthetically. You are in the business of making individuals look good. That philosophy should extend to all that you do.

Look at designing displays and showcases as an opportunity to use your creativity. Keep these clean, attractive, colorful, and inviting. Make sure you include testers to touch, smell, and try products. Perk things up with attractive posters that display the positive results of using your products.

And do not forget the details. Leaving the salon with a handsomely wrapped package emphasizes the ambiance of a total beauty experience. Incorporating the clinic logo on packaging will also serve as free advertising for your establishment. If available, place new product samples in the package for the customer to try. You may also want to include an invitation for any introductory offers or specials to keep clients coming to you.

topic of aging, avoid expressions like "old" or "wrinkled." "Mature skin" or "sun-damaged" are more appropriate terms. Clients are most likely aware and concerned that they are aging. You should try to explain that the primary factor with aging skin is not the number of years that have passed but the cumulative effects of sun damage.

It is never too late for a person to start taking better care of her skin. While it may be too late to reverse 50 years of sun exposure, most skin will respond favorably to specialized treatments that help correct, moisturize, and soften the condition. Most skin can look younger with your skills and a good home care regimen.

Treatment Concepts For Sun-Damaged Skin

Antiaging is the most researched and developed segment of cosmetic science and product development, primarily due to the aging population of the world and their desire to remain as young and healthy as possible. The following are antiaging tips that estheticians should incorporate into their practices and treatment and should also make clients aware of.

Antiaging Tip #1—Wear Sunscreen On a Daily Basis

Question your clients about current and past sun exposure habits. Badly sun damaged skin is obvious, as is recently tanned skin. It is acceptable to ask the client about recent sun exposure and if she uses a tanning bed. Explain to your client that the best antiaging advice you can give is to avoid sun exposure, and the very best antiaging product is a daily-use broad-spectrum sunscreen.

Explain that modern skin care products are available in various weights and forms, designed for overall skin types and conditions. You should have many sunscreen products of varying weights in lotions, fluids, and creams available for purchase.

Many clients erroneously believe that sunscreens smell like bananas and coconuts, and are oily. This especially concerns oily and acne-prone clients. Your clients may also be concerned about how these products work under makeup. Explain that modern skin

care products are of various weights and product forms, based on their overall skin type and conditions. You should, of course, have many sunscreen products available for purchase, of varying weights in lotions, fluids, and creams. Every "day cream" you carry should have SPF protection.

Explain to your clients the importance of broad-spectrum products. Briefly explain how free radicals are caused by sun exposure and that daily small doses of sun eventually crosslink collagen and elastin fibers. Many skin care companies have brochures, posters, and other educational tools to help you consult with your client. Brochures about sun damage and skin cancer are also available from the American Cancer Society and the Skin Cancer Foundation.

Mentioning to your clients that sun exposure also causes a large number of hyperpigmentation problems may be worthwhile. Hyperpigmentation is of concern to most clients, including younger ones who have not yet started to develop apparent wrinkles.

Antiaging Tip #2—Use Antioxidants Topically and Orally

Whether topically applied or taken orally, antioxidants help protect the skin from free radicals. Antioxidants work by scooping up and neutralizing free radicals. They may work by furnishing electrons to stabilize the free radical, or they can actually change the chemical form of the free radical. Antioxidants are used throughout the body to neutralize free radicals and to protect cells and tissues.

Known to be beneficial in the form of health supplements, the antioxidants vitamin C and vitamin E are utilized in topical skin care formulations to help protect the skin. Modern skin science now understands more about how they work. Together, vitamin C and vitamin E neutralize free radicals. One form of vitamin C, magnesium ascorbyl phosphate, has a melanin-suppressant action and is helpful in treating hyperpigmentation. Beta carotene, a form of vitamin A, is another well-known antioxidant. Superoxide dismutase, and minerals such as zinc and copper, also help prevent reactions from starting.

Other more contemporary antioxidants are grapeseed extract (*Vitis vinifera*) and maritime pine bark extract (also known as its trade name Pycnogenol). They contain proanthocyanidins, which are known to be powerful antioxidants. Another important property is that they help neutralize the most dangerous free radical, the hydroxyl radical.

Another powerful antioxidant that has received much acclaim is Japanese green tea extract (*Camellia sinensis*). Green tea contains components called catechins and polyphenols that are very strong antioxidants.

A current trend is towards broad-spectrum antioxidants, which means combining several different antioxidants that help to protect against various trigger reactions leading to free radical damage. A mixture of topical vitamins, proanthocyanidins, antioxidant plant extracts, and enzymes are known to help protect against cell damage. Their combined action prevents different stages of the free radical reactions that lead to cell damage. Sunscreen protection alone is a good first step in preventing the original creation of free radicals.

Skin care formulations must be developed and packaged correctly to protect the efficacy of the antioxidants. They must also be available in an effective delivery system, such as liposome technology or microencapsulation. Microencapsulation keeps antioxidant ingredients from oxidizing and helps deliver these important ingredients where they are most needed. A sign of oxidation is product darkening in a jar. It is useless to have these powerful antioxidants incorporated into a product if they are not readily available for delivery into the skin.

Antiaging Tip #3—Avoid Irritation And Inflammation

As we have discussed, wherever there is inflammation, there are also free radicals. Any habit, product, or treatment that chronically irritates the skin can be damaging. Avoid sun, heat, smoking, excessive alcohol, and anything that routinely reddens the skin.

In addition to avoiding known irritants, adding soothing agents to help control inflammation prevents trigger reactions that lead to free radical damage. These ingredients include soothing agents such as dipotassium glycyrrhizinate, stearyl glycyrrhetinate, and extracts of licorice (*Glycyrrhiza glabra*), bisabolol, azulene (*Anthemis nobilis*), grapeseed (*Vitis vinifera*), green tea (*Camellia sinensis*), and matricaria (*Matricaria recutita*).

How do you decide which products have the right levels of calming and soothing agents? The best way is to speak with the manufacturer, and then try the product on irritation-prone skin. Well-formulated products will speak for themselves in relieving redness and making the skin feel much less irritated.

Antiaging Tip #4—Protect the Barrier Function of the Skin

We have lready discussed in detail the importance of the barrier function of the skin. The barrier function decreases with age and cumulative sun damage. When the skin has a poor barrier, water can escape from the lower levels (transepidermal water loss), and irritants can penetrate the skin much easier. This can cause inflammation, leading to free radical damage. Further, poor barrier function interferes with the epidermis's ability to hold moisture, resulting in many fine lines, accentuating any dermal elastosis, and making the skin look older and more damaged.

To protect the barrier, avoid exposure to the sun, which causes lipid peroxidation, damage to the lipids that make up the barrier function—the intercellular cement. avoidance of drying factors, including exposure to cold, wind, heat, drying soaps, and aggressive cleansers, will help to protect the fragile barrier.

Skin that is dry often does not manufacture enough sebum to help protect the barrier function by lubricating the surface of the corneum and preventing water loss. One sign of alipidic skin is no visible pores or very small pores. This type of skin is much more likely to dehydrate and suffer damage to the barrier function. Clients with alipidic skin can protect their skin by using products that provide an emollient protection ingredient, such as petrolatum, dimethicone, cyclomethicone, or oils such as jojoba, sunflower, or borage.

Individual lipids can be used in products that can also help reinforce and supplement the barrier function of the skin. Look for ingredients such as sphingolipids, glycosphingolipids, ceramides, phospholipids, cholesterol, squalane, and linoleic acid, all of which are actual components of the natural lipids within the intercellular barrier. These ingredients can be used in almost any type of formulation, including sunscreens, hydrators, eye creams, masks, and concentrated serums.

Antiaging Tip #5—Use Alphahydroxy Acid Gels, Creams, or Lotion

Regular daily use of 8%–10% alphahydroxy acid leave-on products, which may be in the form of gel, fluid lotion, or cream, is one of the most important factors in helping reverse the surface signs of sun damage. Alphahydroxy acids cause epidermal cells to relayer, a process that, over time, diminishes fine lines and surface wrinkles and causes the epidermis to become more even. Alphahydroxy acids also produce much smoother skin and improve hyperpigmentation.

Additionally, as the cell layers renew in a more orderly fashion, lipid production normalizes, which helps enforce the barrier function. As a result, the epidermis retains adequate moisture, increasing the skin's smoothness and firmness.

The appearance of the skin improves fairly quickly when using alphahydroxy acids. More dramatic improvement occurs after months of regular use. It is important to teach your client that improved appearance of sun-damaged skin requires constant routine care.

Choosing the right alphahydroxy product is important. The product must match the skin type. Oily and combination skin are better off with liquid-gel products, whereas lotions and cream versions are more appropriate for dryer skin types. They should be used under sunscreens or hydrators. Because alphahydroxy acids do thin the surface of the epidermis, an SPF-15 broad-spectrum sunscreen should always be used during the day.

Alphahydroxy acids (AHA) are sometimes added to cleansers or toners to improve their efficacy. They are normally used in fairly small percentages and are, of course, rinsed off in this type of product. Because of the small percentage of AHAs in these products, and the fact that the product is removed almost immediately, they do not produce the same changes in the appearance of sun damage as a leave-on product. It is important for your client to understand that products that have a more long-term effect on sun-damaged skin must stay on the skin.

Some AHA products have percentages of AHA exceeding 10% or a very low pH, less than 3.5, which increases the irritancy of these products. The lower the pH of a product, the more acidic it is. Low pHs can produce much irritation, and if the product is used daily, it may produce chronic inflammation. Low-pH, high-concentration AHA products should be reserved for use by dermatologists in the medical treatment of severe sun damage.

The Cosmetic Ingredient Review Board, an industry-sponsored panel of dermatologists and other scientists, has recommended that daily-use consumer AHA products not exceed a 10% concentration and should not have a pH of less than 3.5.

Antiaging Tip #6—Hydrate, Hydrate, Hydrate

Without moisture, the skin could not function, and all the other ingredients we have discussed would be useless. Hydration must be used along with these other beneficial ingredients to achieve the changes desired in the skin's appearance. To help retain moisture in the skin, some products include hydrators, which help bind water to the skin and attract water to the epidermal layers. These agents include ingredients such as hyaluronic acid, sodium hyaluronate, sodium PCA, and glycerin.

Advanced Mature Skin Treatments

Antiaging treatments for mature and wrinkled skin present numerous challenges to both the clients and estheticians. The good news is that many advanced treatment options are available. Review the procedure for a basic facial in Chapter 14 for a foundation; the following treatments are advanced treatments. The treatments described are more technically involved, require more steps, and should offer more immediate results.

Numerous variations on the discussed treatments are available for aging skin. Choices are dependent on the correction goals for your client.

An antiaging treatment is available that concentrates on an oil-based ampoule that incorporates a variety of free radical neutralizers, such as vitamins C, A, and E, along with rosehips (*Rosa canina*), and primrose oil.

Step by Step Mature Skin with Paraffin Mask

Case study: A 55-year-old individual with lines, wrinkles, and dehydrated, dry skin.

Purpose: To force-feed hydrating, softening, and nutritional ingredients into the skin with an occlusive paraffin mask. The heat in the mask causes the ostia and follicles to expand, thereby increasing penetration of nutritional substances. Paraffin masks offer a mummylike effect, causing heat transference and higher absorption of the nutrients applied under the mask. If the client perspires slightly, this is ideal because the ostia and follicles will expand and allow more absorption of ingredients. Due to its occlusive nature, no evaporation takes place in this treatment, and moisture is infused back into the skin at a high rate.

Contraindication: Not recommended for the claustrophobic client or patients with highly sensitive, reactive, or acne-prone skin.

Products: Cleanser and freshener for dry/dehydrated skin, AHA exfoliant or disincrustation fluid, ampoule for skin type, massage cream, and moisturizing cream/sun block

Tools and supplies: Face gauze with cutouts for the eyes, nose, and mouth; and paraffin

Procedure

Cleanse

1 Remove eye makeup and lipstick with regular eye makeup remover.

2 Cleanse the face with a dry/dehydrated skin cleanser or cream. Rinse well. Remove residue with dry/dehydrated skin freshener.

Analyze

3 Perform a skin analysis.

Exfoliation and Extractions

4 Apply AHA exfoliation according to the AHA treatment shown. Time for 5–10 minutes, according to the client's skin condition and comfort level. Rinse well and reuse the skin freshener to remove all residue. If the AHA is too sensitizing for the client's skin type, perform a gommage instead. Rinse well.

5 Steam to soften the skin if it is not contraindicated. While steaming, you may choose to do a hand and/or foot massage.

6 Perform extractions, if applicable. Generally if you have done an aggressive exfoliation you would not use a disincrustant solution. Or you may choose to steam with a disincrustant solution and then perform galvanic disincrustation (−) just prior to the extractions (see oily acne skin treatment in Chapter 24).

7 Apply high frequency.

Treat and Correct

8 Apply a corrective ampoule or serum using galvanic (+) or according to the manufacturer's instructions. Or use high frequency for better penetration of the substance. You may also apply the serum by massaging until it is absorbed. If the client is contraindicated for electricity do not use galvanic or high frequency.

Massage

9 Perform a deeply lubricating and softening massage. If the skin is thin and sensitive, be sure the massage is gentle, utilizing mostly effleurage. If the skin is thick and leathery or deeply wrinkled, do a luxurious oil-based massage that includes deep petrissage. If no surface grit is felt on the skin after the massage, the cream may be allowed to stay on the skin. When leaving cream on the face, be sure the chosen product has nutritional value and is not a "slip-based" massage cream. If it is, remove the residue and apply a generous amount of night cream appropriate for the client's skin, massaging about half of it into the skin.

Paraffin Mask

10 Apply eye cream or gel and cover the area with moistened cotton pads.

11 While some estheticians prefer to paint the paraffin with a brush after placing the dry gauze on the face, a more efficient application is to dip the gauze into the paraffin, being careful to wring out the drippy part at the tip of the gauze. This method prevents cross-contamination of the brushes because they can not easily be washed and sanitized.

12 Apply several dipped pieces of gauze depending on the desired thickness and heat transference. A typical paraffin mask will use three or four layers. If it is winter and the skin is ultra dry, you may choose to apply five or six layers.

13 Time the mask for 10–20 minutes or according to the number of layers. Once the paraffin has cooled, the process is complete.

14 Remove the mask in one piece. Rinse the skin with tepid water.

Complete

15 Cool and tone the skin with a freshener with your machine sprayer or a Lucas sprayer. Pat in well.

16 Apply the balance of the ampoule (if some was saved for this step) or serum.

17 Apply day cream, eye cream, neck cream, and sunscreen as appropriate for the skin.

Step by Step Thermal Mask

Introduction: Thermal masks can have anywhere from two to five layers of treatment substances, creams, and other absorbing masks, depending on the goals of the treatment. They may be in a kit presentation, meaning that all the steps are sequenced, making it easier for the esthetician to perform the treatment.

Thermal masks are great for individuals in cold, wintry climates, but they are especially valuable when a hot and cold effect can further penetrate the underlying substances. They are ideal for mature, dry, dehydrated, and wrinkle-prone skin types.

The action of the mask is twofold. Made from dry minerals, they are usually kept in a sealed, moisture-free pouch. They are activated when mixed with water or with a manufacturer-supplied liquid substance. Upon application, they initially create a heating effect on the skin, which means that the heat causes vasodilation for increased circulation, as well as for expansion of the ostia for better infusions and absorption of the previously applied ampoule and cream. As the mask begins to harden, it cools significantly, rendering tightening and toning effects on the skin. The effect is also referred to as vasoconstriction (from the word *vascular*, meaning vessels). The skin's appearance is refreshed and radiant.

Contraindication: Not recommended for claustrophobic patients or for highly sensitive or acne-prone skin

Purpose: The goal is similar to the previous paraffin treatment in the action of heat. This treatment focuses more on the thermal minerals in the mask to balance and mineralize the skin while force-feeding other active agents into the skin.

Products: Cleanser and freshener for dry/dehydrated skin, AHA exfoliant or disincrustation fluid, massage cream, thermal mask pouch and ampoules, and moisturizing cream with sunblock

Tools and supplies: Face gauze with cutouts for eyes, nose, and mouth; rubber bowl; spatula

Procedure

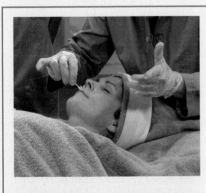

Cleanse

1 Remove eye makeup and lipstick with regular eye makeup remover.

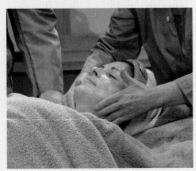

2 Cleanse the face with a dry/dehydrated skin cleanser or cream. Rinse well. Remove residue with a dry/dehydrated skin freshener.

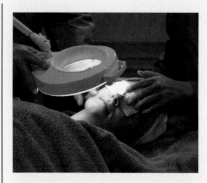

Analyze

3 Perform a skin analysis.

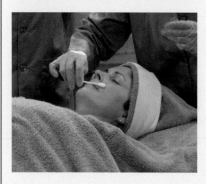

Exfoliation and Extraction

4 Apply AHA exfoliation according to the AHA treatment chosen. Time for 5–10 minutes according to the client's skin condition and comfort level. Rinse well and reuse freshener to remove all residues. If the AHA is too sensitizing for the skin type, perform a gommage instead. Rinse well.

5 Steam to soften the skin if steam is not contraindicated for the skin. While steaming, you may choose to do a hand and/or foot massage.

6 Perform extractions, if applicable. Generally if you have used an aggressive exfoliation you would not use a disincrustant solution. If not, you may choose to steam with a disincrustant solution and then perform galvanic disincrustation (–) just prior to the extractions (see oily acne skin treatment in Chapter 24). Apply high frequency.

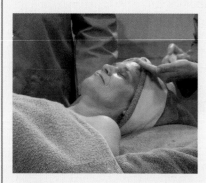

Treat and Correct

7 Apply serums or ampoules either using galvanic (+) or high frequency for better penetration. Or, apply by massaging until the serum is absorbed. If the client is contraindicated for electricity, do not use galvanic or high frequency.

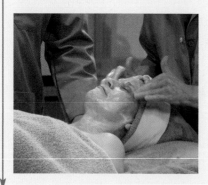

Massage

8 Perform a deeply lubricating and softening massage. If the skin is thin and sensitive, be sure the massage is gentle, utilizing mostly effleurage. If the skin is thick, leathery, or deeply wrinkled, perform a luxurious oil-based massage including deep petrissage. If no surface grit is felt on the skin after the massage, the cream may be allowed to stay on the skin. When leaving cream on the face, be sure the product chosen has nutritional value and is not a slip-based massage cream. If it is, remove the residue and apply a generous amount of night cream appropriate for the client's skin and massage about half of it into the skin.

9 Depending on the manufacturer and treatment concept, either another cream or another cream-based mask is applied. In some cases the massage cream should be completely removed and serum and cream applied again.

Thermal Mask

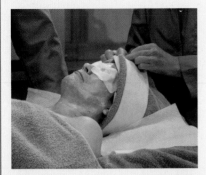

10 Apply eye cream and cover the eye area with pads.

11 Protect the hairline and décolleté areas with a head cap or covering. Place a towel over the décolleté area. The mask should not adhere to the hair or the towel.

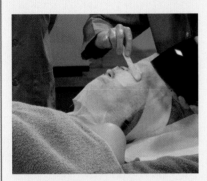

12 Mix the mask immediately prior to applying. For best results, apply the mask quickly, evenly, and thickly. Create a thick lip around the edges so that it can be removed in one piece. Use all the mask powder designated by the manufacturer. A thin mask will not have the layering and thermal value if not used specifically as directed. Apply within 4–6 minutes. The mask should look very smooth and even all around the face, neck, and décolleté.

> Do not wash the residue of this mask down the drain. Scrape out the bowl into the trash can and then rinse the bowl.

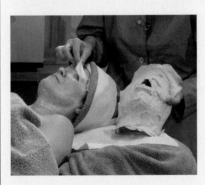

13 The client will rest for 15–20 minutes or until the thermal heating and cooling effect has been completed and the mask has hardened into one piece. To remove, gently loosen both sides of the mask by a sliding a finger between the skin and the edge of the mask. Place fingers under both sides of the mask and rock it gently until it lifts off in once piece.

14 Rinse the skin thoroughly with tepid water and wipe with a freshener.

Complete

15 Use the machine sprayer filled with freshener to cool and tone the skin. Pat well. You may also use a Lucas sprayer if desired.

16 Apply the balance of the ampoule (if a part was saved for this step) or serum.

17 Apply day cream, eye cream, neck cream, and sunscreen as appropriate for the skin.

Antiaging Firming Treatment

Case study: A 45-year-old individual with sun and environmental damage with elastosis.

Purpose: To stimulate the skin's metabolism, increase antioxidant protection, and firm the skin.

Products: Cleanser and freshener, papaya enzyme, protein ampoule, vitamin E oil for massage, moisturizing cream, and sunblock.

Procedure

Cleanse

1   Remove eye makeup and lipstick with regular eye makeup remover.

2   Cleanse the face with cleanser. Rinse well.

3   Remove residue with freshener.

Analyze

4   Perform a skin analysis.

Exfoliate

5   Prepare steam without ionization.

6   Papaya enzyme exfoliation: Mix 2 tablespoons of powder with a small amount of water and mix with a spatula until it reaches the consistency of pancake batter, not too thick and not too thin. Apply with a brush to the face and neck. Time for 10 minutes (or according to the manufacturer's directions) under steam without ionization. Rinse well. Apply the freshener to remove the residue.

Treat and Massage

7   Apply the firming protein serum and massage it into the skin. Use vitamin E oil for the massage and perform a deeply lubricating and softening massage.

Mask

8   Apply an antioxidant firming clay mask to the face, neck, and décolleté.

9   Apply the firming eye gel on the eyes, massage for 5 minutes, apply the eye mask, and let the client rest.

10   Time for 10–15 minutes. Rinse the skin with tepid water and freshener.

11   Using the machine sprayer or a Lucas sprayer, apply freshener to cool, and tone. Pat in thoroughly.

Complete

12   Apply a little more of the firming serum, then the antioxidant serum.

13   Apply firming day cream, eye cream, neck cream, and sunscreen as appropriate.

The primary emulsifying massage product is shea butter, which is known to be healing and conditioning and can reduce fine lines. A complementary eye treatment is offered that has similar ingredients to refine and stimulate the metabolism around the eye area, with the added benefit of tightening the skin.

One line specializes in ceramides, which emulate the intercellular lipids surrounding the epidermal cells. They help strengthen the skin's barrier function and prevent water loss. These particular ceramides are in capsule form; they are single-use polymeric serum applications.

Summary

A variety of intrinsic and extrinsic factors, ranging from genetic predisposition to sun exposure to smoking, affect how our skin looks as it ages. The short- and long-term effects of sun exposure can take the form of burned skin, hyperpigmentation, and a variety of other skin conditions, including cancer. Many products are available to combat free radicals, a decreased lipid barrier, wrinkles, and other signs of aging skin, but the most important practices are avoiding sun exposure and wearing adequate sunscreen at all times.

Discussion Questions

1. Review the symptoms of aging skin, then briefly describe the main benefits of the following advanced skin care treatments: the paraffin mask, the thermal mask, and AHA exfoliation. How would enzymes and/or ampoule treatments enhance these procedures?

2. What is telangiectasias and what factors contribute to its appearance on the face? What are the various treatments, and which are most beneficial?

3. List the various disorders and diseases resulting from sun damage. Discuss the treatments for each and their long-term prognoses.

4. What is meant by *broad spectrum* in sunscreens?

5. Define basal cell carcinoma and squamous cell carcinoma. How do they differ? What are the most common symptoms and treatments?

Additional Reading

Lees, Mark. 2001. *Skin Care: Beyond the Basics*, Clifton Park, N.Y.: Milady, an imprint of Delmar Learning, a division of Thomson Learning, Inc.

Michalun, Natalia, with M. Varinia Michalun. 2000. *Skin Care and Cosmetic Ingredients Dictionary.* Clifton Park, N.Y.: Milady, an imprint of Delmar Learning, a division of Thomson Learning, Inc.

Robinson, Maggie Greenwood. 2001. *Wrinkle-Free: Your Guide to Youthful Skin at Any Age.* New York: Berkeley Publishing.

Helpful Web Sites

http://www.skincheck.com (The Melanoma Education Foundation)

http://www.skincancer.org (The Skin Cancer Foundation)

http://www.dermadoctor.com

Chapter 22
Sensitive Skin: Morphology And Treatment

Chapter Objectives:

After reading this chapter, you should be able to:

- Explain impaired barrier function's relationship with sensitive skin.
- List ways to identify sensitive skin.
- Describe the differences between irritants and allergens.
- Identify key elements in treating sensitive skin.

Chapter Outline

Introduction
Barrier Function and Sensitivity
Analysis of Sensitive Skin
Irritants and Allergens
Rosacea
Aging and the Sensitive Skin
Salon Treatment for Sensitive Skin

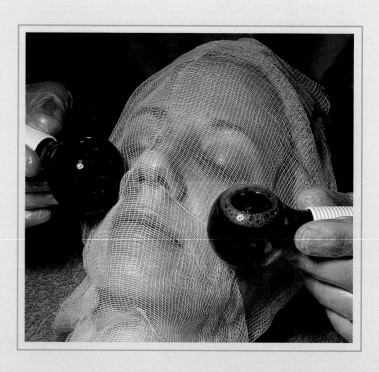

Introduction

Sensitive skin is one of the most difficult skin types to treat. More and more, sensitive skin is considered a type of skin rather than a condition of the skin. Sensitive skin reddens easily from any form of stimulation. It easily flushes, which mean that redness manifests from exposure to heat or cold, touch, stress, or even from embarrassment.

Barrier Function and Sensitivity

Chapter 3 discusses how lipids are formed and how lipids make up the intercellular cement, or the mortar between the bricks, in the epidermis. This lipid complex mortar is the skin's natural barrier that helps prevent dehydration and serves as a protective shield so that irritants cannot easily penetrate the skin. When normal skin is exposed to an irritant, the irritant may be blocked from penetration because the keratinocytes in the epidermis are in good form. When the irritant does not penetrate, it will not activate the immune system, and the skin will not become red and irritated.

Sensitive skin frequently suffers from an impaired barrier function. It may actually have a thinner corneum, or it may not make the normal amount of lipid complex to support the barrier function. This lack of lipid causes gaps between the keratinocytes, known as impaired barrier function. An impaired lipid barrier allows transepidermal water loss, which is responsible for dehydration. It also accelerates the penetration of irritants into the skin's surface, causing irritation or an allergic reaction. These reactions are more likely to occur in someone with sensitive skin, because this type of skin has a more reactive immune or nervous system than normal, nonsensitive skin.

Think of the corneum as a roof on a house. The shingles are evenly layered on a normal solid roof. They are attached in a uniform way and arranged in such a way as to prevent rain from penetrating the roof. A good roof also keeps heat or air-conditioned air from escaping from the house. If the roof is poorly constructed, the shingles may not overlap properly, and there may be gaps between the shingles.

These gaps can be compared to the lack of intercellular lipids between the keratinocytes in the corneum. Air conditioning and heating can easily escape from a house with a roof in ill repair, in the same way that moisture can escape from skin with a poor barrier function. When the roof is thin and in bad repair, the insulation and wiring is more likely to become wet, just like the immune system in the dermis is more likely to be stimulated. When the immune system is activated, the skin can become red, swollen, or inflamed.

Analysis of Sensitive Skin

True sensitive skin is hereditary, although any skin can be sensitive at certain times and under certain conditions. Sensitive skin is more reactive to stimulants, pressure, and changes in products. It is especially more sensitive to heat and sun than normal skin.

When examining sensitive skin under the magnifying lamp, you will notice a pink tone and that the skin appears very thin. In actuality, the slight redness that shows is the blood under the skin. The slightest stimulation to this skin type provokes more redness or other reactions (Figure 22–1).

One technique for testing whether or not skin is sensitive is called **touch-blanching.** On normal skin, you can apply gentle pressure to any area of the face and then release the pressure without seeing any change in the skin color. On sensitive skin, the area

touch–blanching
A technique for testing sensitive skin. Apply gentle pressure to an area of the face and release the pressure. If the skin color changes to white, the skin is sensitive.

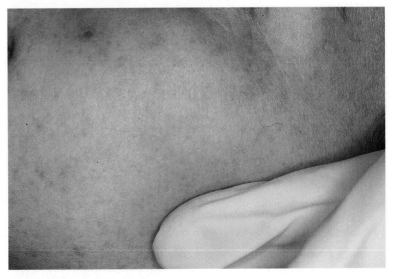

Figure 22–1 The slightest stimulation to sensitive skin provokes redness.

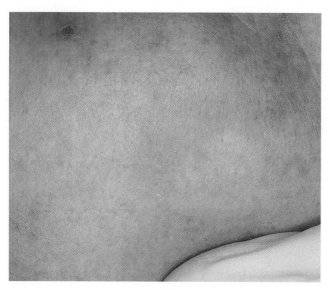

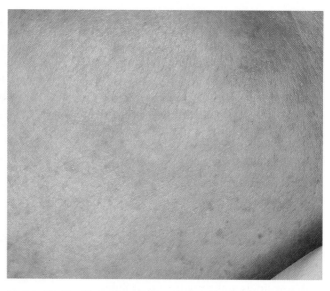

Figure 22–2a In sensitive skin, the area appears whiter than the surrounding skin after pressure has been applied and first removed.

Figure 22–2b The skin quickly regains its pink tone, sometimes becoming darker after pressure.

where the pressure was applied appears white (Figure 22–2a) or lighter in color when the pressure is initially removed. It then quickly regains a pink tone, sometimes becoming pinker for a short time (Figure 22–2b). For example, sensitive skin often reddens during a procedure as simple as a basic cleansing.

Hereditary sensitive skin is most often very light in pigmentation, usually Fitzpatrick type I or II, although very dark skin types can be sensitive too. Sensitive skin

dermatographism
A condition in which the skin swells from the slightest touch or scrape.

generally burns easily in the sun and has trouble tanning. Reactions are less obvious in dark skin, because of pigment. Redness cannot easily be seen on dark skin, but persons of color who have irritations often have other obvious symptoms, such as itching, burning, or swelling.

Telangiectasias (distended capillaries) may be present on sensitive skin, but telangiectasias are not necessarily a sign of sensitivity (Figure 22–3). Telangiectasias may also be signs of sun damage or other extrinsic damage. It is only with other signs of sensitivity, such as thinness and a history of reactivity, that it can be said that truly sensitive skin exists.

Sensitive skin may swell easily when irritated. Hives, also known as urticaria, may form when histamine, a hormonelike substance, is released by mast cells when the skin is irritated. Histamine is released to increase blood flow to an area, and it dilates blood vessels to allow for better transport of immune system blood cells. This, of course, can only add to the redness problems.

Dermatographism is a condition in which the skin swells from the slightest touch or scrape. Clients who are dermatographic will be much more reactive to harsh treatment, including more aggressive physical treatment, such as cleansing with rough sponges, suction machines, brushing machines, or microdermabrasion. Avoid

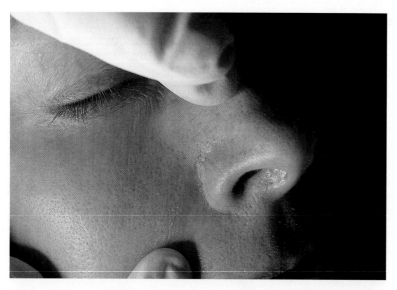

Figure 22–3 Distended capillaries may be present on sensitive skin but are not an indicator.

using these tools and procedures on this type of skin. Individuals with dermatographic skin often have a history of nasal allergies or asthma.

Waxing and extraction almost always cause erythema and some swelling on dermatographic skin (Figure 22–4). These reactions are transient, meaning they generally do not last for very long, usually only a couple of hours. However, it is best to avoid doing anything to aggravate this reactive skin.

Rashes, redness, and swelling are all objective symptoms, or visible symptoms, of sensitivity. These may indicate an allergy to individual ingredients or products. Subjective symptoms of sensitive skin may include pruritis (itching), burning, or stinging. Clients may tell you that they have subjective symptoms without presenting objective symptoms.

Sensitive skin may also be more sensitive to pain than normal skin. Nerve endings and blood vessels on thinner skin are closer to the surface and more sensitive to temperature changes, pressure, and pain.

Clients who have sensitive skin will generally tell you during the preliminary consultation. If you think the skin you are treating is sensitive, be careful about your techniques and what products you use, especially on the first visit. Keep stimulation to a minimum, avoid products containing isopropyl or SD (specially denatured) alcohol, and do not use more aggressive treatments, such as alphahydroxy (AHA) acid exfoliations, granular scrubs, enzyme treatments, or any other peeling treatments, until you can see how the skin reacts to the initial treatment.

Skin may turn red easily during treatment from heat, stimulating massage, essential oils, fragrances, drying masks, extraction, or waxing. While many of these procedures will make most skin types slightly red, sensitive skin may turn very red, swell, and stay red for hours in some cases.

As a general rule, you should approach programs for sensitive skin with care and simplicity. The more products and techniques involved, the harder it will be to determine the aggravating factor if the client has a problem. Likewise, products chosen for use on sensitive skin should have as few ingredients as possible, and they should be irritancy tested by an independent laboratory. Most companies that market products for sensitive

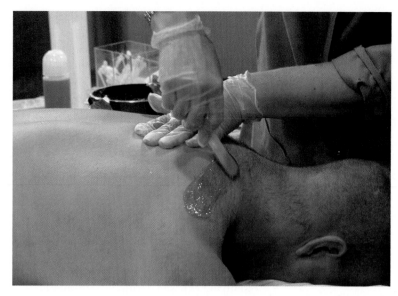

Figure 22–4 Sensitive skin almost always shows redness and swelling after waxing.

skin will state that the products have been tested for irritancy. These tests are run on humans to try to provoke a reaction. Products that do not cause reactions when tested under such stringent conditions are not very likely to cause problems for most clients.

While it is important to look for products that have been properly tested, there is no such thing as a product that is 100% nonallergenic. Every product, no matter how carefully it is tested, can potentially cause a reaction in someone who is allergic to something in it.

Transient Sensitivity

Irritant reactions to skin care products, windburn, sunburn, frostbite, and even itchy winter skin are all examples of sensitivity that is transient. They are not permanent conditions. Environmental damage can happen to any skin type, although hereditarily sensitive skin is even more susceptible.

If you notice flaking, dryness, redness, or other symptoms when evaluating a client's skin, you must be careful with treatment, if you perform treatment at all. Clients will normally tell you what happened if some sort of environmental exposure caused the condition you see.

Environmentally damaged skin represents a damaged, or perhaps even an absent, barrier function. The skin will be extremely sensitive to many substances, heat, cold, and possibly touch. Your client may experience stinging when a moisturizer is applied to damaged skin. This is due to the stimulation of nerve endings in the dermis and the penetration of ingredients within the moisturizer that may be irritating. A moisturizer that never causes problems for a client may, all of a sudden, begin stinging when it is applied to skin suffering from barrier function damage.

Minor dryness can be treated by the esthetician using hydrators and hydrating masks. Stick with fragrance-free products specifically designed for sensitive skin. Do not treat the skin if it is swollen, extremely red, or has blisters or areas of rawness, which is essentially exposed dermis. These clients should be referred to a dermatologist. If you have any doubt about treating a client, err on the side of caution and do not treat the client.

Irritants and Allergens

The main difference between an irritant reaction and an allergic reaction is that an irritant reaction can basically affect any skin type, while allergic reactions affect only certain individuals. An irritant is a chemical or product that can cause irritation in any skin if it is overused in frequency or amount (Figure 22–5). For example, 70% glycolic acid will sting and irritate almost any skin type.

Sensitive skin, however, will be more reactive due to hereditary thinness. Skin that is sensitive because of environmental factors, such as being windburned, will also be more reactive to contact with an irritant. Overuse of benzoyl peroxide can also cause redness and flaking in many skin types, but this is an irritant reaction, not an allergic reaction.

Allergies are the result of the immune system rejecting a particular substance or ingredient. Allergies do not affect every individual; only certain people's immune systems will identify a certain substance as an allergen. The client must have had contact with a substance more than once to have an allergy. The immune system will always react to that substance, or allergen, whenever it comes in contact with it. The immune system has determined, from a previous exposure, that this particular substance is offensive to the body or the skin, and it will always launch an attack when it senses the presence of the allergen. Allergic reactions tend to be more widespread across the skin and more severe in terms of edema (swelling) and erythema (redness). A second difference between allergies and irritant reactions is the time that elapses before a reaction occurs. An irritant reaction happens very quickly, while an allergic reaction can take a few days to appear.

Allergies and irritant reactions are treated in similar ways. The first step is to remove the offending ingredient, product, or substance. If your client is having a reaction, look at the products she is using and see if there is possibly a known irritant among them. Products that can cause irritation frequently include exfoliating or drying agents, absorbing sunscreen ingredients, stimulating ingredients, drying alcohols, and aggressive cleansers that strip too much surface oil. Are any of the products being used too often or is too much being applied?

If you cannot determine the offending product, the best procedure is for the client to discontinue all products until the skin is completely clear. Then, have the client restart the program one product at a time. Each product should be used for a few days, with another product being added if no reaction occurs. When you or a client notices irritation, check to see which product has been added most recently. If a client seems to be having a severe reaction, you should refer her to the dermatologist for possible allergy testing.

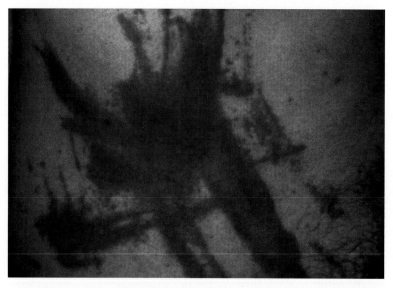

Figure 22–5 Irritant contact dermatitis developed from use of vitamin E.

Handling Difficult Clients

Difficult clients come in many varieties:

Needy
They want you to resolve not only their skin problems but also their personal problems.

Angry
They are overbearing and quick to lose their temper at the least provocation. They are easily insulted, and must be handled carefully.

Manipulative
They are determined to get their way at any cost. They will push you to perform a service that is inappropriate for them just because they have decided they must have it. They may even attempt to engage your coworkers or your boss in the process.

Intimidating
They are the know it alls who have read everything there is to know on the treatment in question and are prepared to tell you how to do your job.

Insecure
They must be reassured constantly. They want to hear that you are doing the right thing, the right way, incessantly.

Critical
They are just waiting for something to go wrong. They watch your every move just waiting for you to trip up. And they are prepared to let you know when that happens.

Problematic
They always have a crisis. They arrive late, forget their appointment, or cannot find their checkbook or credit card when it is time to pay. They have numerous "legitimate" excuses and are capable of throwing everyone in the salon into a tizzy.

The first thing you must realize when dealing with difficult clients is that it is not about you! Do not take it personally. As a service provider working with the public you must be prepared to deal with all kinds of personality types. Not every one who comes into your salon will be easygoing and trust your judgment implicitly. In fact, there may be clients looking to take advantage of the fact that you are a novice.

Setting some basic rules, or coping strategies, will help you maintain control even when you feel like you are going to "lose it."

Respect boundaries.
- Keep conversation on a professional level. Be prepared to steer inappropriate commentary back to the task at hand.
- Do not socialize with clients.
- Do not give personal or health advice.

Post rules in a visible place.
- Make sure the client is aware of the salon's policies. State these verbally and visually with the help of management.

Be assertive.
- State the facts simply, courteously, and succinctly. Repeat as often as necessary.
- Avoid engaging in gossip.
- As harmless as the simplest innuendo may appear, learn to censor your dialogue and think before you speak.

Practice positive communication skills.
- Use language that evokes a positive response. Whenever possible find a middle ground.
- Assure the client as needed.
- Be clear. Practice stating factual information about treatments and techniques in a manner that does not provoke controversy or argument.

Practice active listening.
- Acknowledge concerns and state what you are able to do for them.

There will always be difficult clients. People are multifaceted and complex. While difficult clients do present a challenge, you need to remember that they are still a source of income. Many of them appear as regular clients. Learn to look at them as an opportunity to practice your public relations skills and positive communication skills and it will become a win-win situation for all.

Irritant reactions tend to leave the skin red and flaking, indicative of an impaired barrier function, which means all treatments should be discontinued until the skin has returned to normal. Introducing new treatments or products to irritated skin may be asking for trouble. Skin redness will begin to dissipate when the offending product is removed from home care, but dryness and flaking will remain for a few days after the reaction has stopped.

Cooling the skin with water compresses reduces inflammation. In allergic reactions, use of topical hydrocortisone helps to squelch the reaction. Severe cases must be referred to a dermatologist so that they can be treated with an antihistamine that will help to block the effect.

Clients who have experienced any type of reaction should be advised to stay out of the sun and heat. Strong cleansers should be avoided, because they can strip more lipids from the barrier while the skin is trying to return to its normal state. Many clients will overuse products, and occasionally estheticians become too aggressive with exfoliating and stimulating treatments. Overuse of exfoliating or strong surfactant products can disrupt the barrier function of the skin, thinning the protective barrier that shields the nerve endings and blood vessels from exposure to irritants. It is always better to take a little more time to treat the skin and to avoid irritant reactions from too much treatment or too strong a treatment for the problem.

Mechanical irritation can also occur, especially in sensitive skin. Rather than being caused by a chemical, this irritation is the result of an abrasive, such as a scrub, stiff washcloth, or even microdermabrasion.

Determining whether a reaction is allergic or irritant is sometimes difficult, even for medical experts. Table 22–1 may help you understand some of the differences between allergies and irritant reactions.

Frequent Allergens

Below is a list of frequent allergens. These are all important ingredients in cosmetics, and they do not cause problems for most skin types. However, when a cosmetic allergy occurs, these are some of the ingredients that are the most likely causes. You should be aware of the fact that *any* ingredient has the potential to cause an allergic reaction is some individuals.

> benzophenone-3 (sunscreen)
>
> benzoyl peroxide (acne medication, exfoliant)
>
> color agents
>
> essential oils
>
> formaldehyde-releasing preservatives (imidazolidinyl urea, diazolidinyl urea, DMDM hydantoin, quaternium 15)
>
> fragrances
>
> hydroquinone (melanin suppressant)
>
> lanolin (emollient)
>
> nail products
>
> other preservatives (parabens, methylchloroisothiazolinone, methylchlorothiazolinone)

Table 22–1 Allergies versus Irritants

	Allergies	Irritants
What causes the reaction?	The a rejection of a particular substance by the immune system of the body.	A localized irritation caused by a chemical that burns or overexfoliates the skin.
Who has the reaction?	Only people who have a specific allergy to a particular substance.	Any person can have an irritant reaction if enough of the substance comes in contact with the skin.
Can you have the reaction the first time the skin is exposed to a product or chemical?	No	Yes
Can the entire body be affected by the reaction?	Yes	Not usually
Does the amount of chemical exposure affect the degree of reaction?	Not necessarily. Allergies can occur from a very small amount of exposure.	Yes
Does the reaction usually occur quickly?	No	Yes

paraminobenzoic acid (PABA) sunscreen

paraphenylenediamine (hair dyes)

products containing animal or plant proteins

salicylates (octyl salicylate—sunscreen; salicylic/acid—exfoliant)

Frequent Irritants

Below is a list of frequent irritants. Many of these agents often have important functional roles in skin care products. They may be irritating if they are overused (used too frequently), used in larger concentrations than recommended, or if they are used on skin that is very sensitive or has impaired barrier function. Many of these ingredients can interfere with barrier function if misused or overused. Do not regard these ingredients as problem ingredients. They are only problems when they produce irritancy, and many times they have been misused or applied to the wrong skin type.

AHAs (glycolic, lactic, malic, tartaric acids)

benzophenone-3 (sunscreen)

benzoyl peroxide (acne medication, exfoliant)

detergent cleansers that are too strong

drying alcohols (isopropyl, SD)

drying clay masks

essential oils

exfoliating grains

fragranced products

hydroquinone (melanin suppressant)

low or high pHs (low pHs are pHs below 3.5 in AHA leave-on products; high pHs may be present in aggressive foaming cleansers or disincrustants)

resorcinol

roll-off exfoliators

salicylic acid

sodium lauryl (laureth) sulfate

sulfur

Rosacea

Rosacea is a type of sensitive skin that you may encounter frequently in your practice. Rosacea is a hereditary disorder of unknown origin that results in diffuse redness and sometimes papules and pustules. It most often affects individuals with lighter skin types, mostly people of Northern and Western European descent. Rosacea most frequently appears in individuals in their late thirties or forties, (Figure 22–6), although it can occur as young as the early twenties or as old as the sixties.

Rosacea used to be thought of as a form of acne, but it is now thought to be a vascular disorder. Skin that suffers from rosacea should be treated with many of the same procedures and protocols that you would use for any sensitive skin. Rosacea skin can suffer from bouts of dehydration and irritation, which may be caused by using the wrong products or by aggressive treatment. It is possible to have sensitive skin and not have rosacea, but most clients with rosacea will suffer from sensitive skin symptoms as well.

A red nose and redness across the tops of the cheeks are often the first signs of rosacea. Clients may report becoming red or feeling flushed with heat in the face after drinking wine or eating spicy foods. Spicy foods and alcohol are both vasodilators, which means that they increase blood flow and dilate blood vessels. Heat, sun, and exercise are also

Figure 22–6 Rosacea most often appears in adults in their late thirties or forties.

major vasodilators. These and other vasodilators tend to make rosacea worse.

Besides following the sensitive skin concepts listed below in this chapter, clients should be advised to avoid all of the above-mentioned aggravating factors. For much more on rosacea, see Chapter 17.

Aging and the Sensitive Skin

Concepts of Sensitive Skin Treatment

You must always remember that regardless of the skin type or conditions that may exist, sensitive skin will be more likely to react to any aggressive treatment. It is always best to be conservative and to try the simplest and most gentle treatment first. You may want to get to know the skin before suggesting products that exfoliate or products or treatments that are known to cause irritation.

You must keep in mind that the barrier of the skin is thinner and more fragile in clients with sensitive skin. Nerve endings and blood vessels are closer to the surface. Anything you apply will penetrate faster, and more of the substance may penetrate. Cleansers and exfoliants may further impair the barrier if they are too strong.

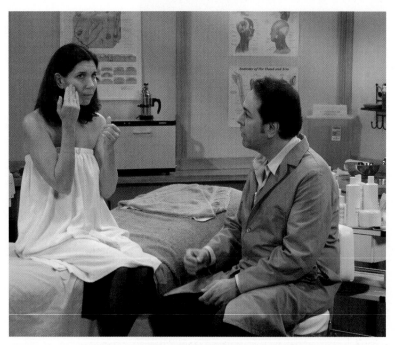

Figure 22–7 A detailed consultation is key to treating sensitive skin.

Consulting with the Client With Sensitive Skin

Clients with sensitive skin may have reservations about skin treatment. Many may have suffered a long time with chronic problems with sensitivity and reactivity. You must be well versed in skin sensitivity to deal with these clients and to be successful in helping them with programs to meet their needs. You must discuss their experiences and what has and has not worked in the past for them (Figure 22–7). They may know specific ingredients that have caused problems or that they have had success with. If they know what products they have had problems with, you must stay away from these ingredients. If they have had success with certain products, you should attempt to find out what, specifically, helped the client.

You should also carry products specifically designed for sensitive skin. These products should be thoroughly irritancy-tested by the manufacturer and, in general, should be fragrance-free and free of other known irritants and frequent allergens.

Sensitive Skin Treatment Tip #1

Use nonfoaming or low-foaming cleansers. Foam helps to determine the amount of detergent in a product. The more foam, the more detergent, and the more oil removed or, in this case, the more lipids removed. Because the barrier is thinner, the lipids within the barrier are more susceptible to destruction by surfactant cleansers. Strong detergent cleansers eat away at the lipid barrier, the mortar between the bricks. This can cause increased absorption of possible irritants and increased water loss, resulting in dehydration. These detergents may be helpful for very oily skin, but they are not appropriate for thin, fragile, sensitive skin. Also make clients aware that traditional soaps are known to cause barrier function loss, and this can affect the skin on the face and the body.

Some cleansers will actually include ingredients such as lipids or oils that help buffer contact with the skin, preventing the removal of the skin's protective lipids and preventing barrier function damage. These products are helpful because they clean the skin without leaving it dry, dehydrated, and irritated.

Sensitive Skin Treatment Tip #2

Reinforce the barrier function with lipid ingredients. Barrier guards such as cyclomethicone, dimethicone, and petrolatum help seal the skin. They lower transepidermal water loss and lessen the chance for irritant penetration. Lipid ingredients help reinforce the barrier itself; glycosphingolipids, sphingolipids, phospholipids, cholesterol, and linoleic acid help supplement the fragile barrier. Oils such as olive, sunflower, borage, and evening primrose also contain natural lipids to support barrier function.

Improving the barrier function of the skin will help the skin look better, reduce redness, and reduce reactivity. It will also significantly improve the hydration level of the skin. Restoration of the barrier function allows the skin to regain its composure and return to a normal, nonirritated state. Always remember, however, that this skin type is prone to barrier function problems, and you must never think of the skin as "normal," at least in terms of reactivity.

Sensitive Skin Treatment Tip #3

Avoid heat and sun. This is a good tip for any skin type, but heat makes sensitive skin especially irritated and, therefore, more reactive to other substances. Heat causes dilation of the blood vessels, redness, and swelling in very sensitive skin. Heat also causes increased dehydration, making the skin dryer, which further impairs barrier function and makes the skin more reactive.

Avoid hot steam during salon treatments because it may make the skin more reactive later in the treatment. In the treatment room, try using cool steam from an ultrasonic steamer that produces a fine, cool mist from ultrasonic vibration rather than from boiling heat.

At home a client should also avoid hot water and prolonged hot baths or showers. This is equally important for sensitive body skin, which can become more dehydrated from exposure to hot water.

Sun should be strictly avoided, because it produces heat that is especially injurious to sensitive skin. Sensitive skin generally sunburns much faster than nonsensitive skin. Daily use of sunscreen is important for all skin types, but it is especially important for sensitive skin in order to avoid redness.

As we have previously mentioned, some sunscreen agents, particularly absorbing screens, can be irritating to sensitive skin. Sensitive skin is more tolerant of zinc oxide and titanium dioxide, the reflective physical sunscreens. These materials work differently than routine absorbing screen ingredients; they reflect, instead of absorb, sunlight. This reflection of the rays decreases the amount of heat absorbed by the skin, and, as we have firmly established, heat is not good for sensitive skin. High SPF sunscreens that contain absorbing screens are more likely to cause irritation because they contain more absorbing (and possibly irritating) sunscreen chemicals.

Often, a product will contain both an absorbing and a reflective sunscreen, such as octyl methoxycinnamate with zinc oxide. When zinc oxide or titanium dioxide is used alone in a formulation, the product must be thicker to keep the sunscreen reflectors properly mixed. By mixing in a little absorbing sunscreen agent, you have a much lighter, more consumer-friendly product. Smaller amounts of absorbing chemicals are less likely to cause irritation. If a client is allergic to a sunscreen chemical, however, any amount of that chemical can cause an allergic reaction.

Sensitive Skin Treatment Tip #4

Avoid known sensitizers and irritants. Besides being more reactive to stimulants, sensitive skin is more likely to have allergic reactions than normal skin. Ingredients known to frequently cause problems and agitate sensitive skin are fragrances, preservatives, many essential oils, large amounts of emulsifiers in creams, detergents (strong surfactants) in cleansers, drying clay masks, SD or isopropyl alcohol, stimulants such as wintergreen, peppermint, or camphor (which, for some skins, can be soothing), and highly acidic or alkaline products.

Exfoliating agents can be used, but should be recommended with great caution for sensitive skin. While exfoliation may be great for normal or nonsensitive skin, it may make sensitive skin more reactive. On sensitive skin, alphahydroxy acids may thin an already poor barrier. If the barrier function is already impaired, low-pH acids can cause irritation and lead to more redness, dehydration, and reactivity. Alphahydroxy products or any other exfoliating product should never be administered on skin that is red, inflamed, or irritated or on skin that has flaking and irritation, a sure sign of barrier function problems. It is best to observe the skin for at least a few weeks before adding any sort of exfoliation procedure. Make sure that the skin is adapting well to the basic products you have recommended, such as the cleanser, toner, and moisturizer, before adding any type of exfoliating agent.

Fragrance

Fragrance is a big part of the cosmetics business. People love products that smell good, and estheticians frequently use aromatherapy for their stress-relieving treatments. Fragrance, however, is also a major cause of cosmetic allergy. Although important from a marketing perspective, in most cases fragrance is an unnecessary ingredient for a skin care product or cosmetic to work properly.

Because many fragrances are major allergens, fragrances should be left out of products designed for sensitive and reactive skin.

Essential Oils and Aromatherapy

Essential oils are concentrated groups of plant chemicals that contain proteins and other potentially irritating or allergy-causing chemicals. They are often stimulating to the circulation and the immune systems, both of which can be problems for sensitive skin.

Figure 22–8 Essential oils and aromatherapy treatments should generally be avoided for sensitive skin.

Figure 22–9 Color agents added to skin care products cause a large share of allergic reactions.

Essential oils and aromatherapy are popular treatments in skin care and have wonderful properties, but they can often cause problems for sensitive skin and generally should be avoided (Figure 22–8).

Color Agents

Color agents cause a good share of allergic reactions and are often unnecessary ingredients that have nothing to do with the proper function of a product (Figure 22–9). While they do make a product look pretty in a bottle, undeniably important for marketing, they serve no purpose in the efficacy of the skin care product and can easily be left out.

Preservatives

Preservatives are important functional ingredients and can be found in most products. Preservatives help keep harmful bacteria out of products. These bacteria can cause skin and eye infections. That is, preservatives are toxic to microorganisms which could contaminate a product.

Some preservatives, called formalin-releasers or formaldehyde donors, work by releasing very small amounts of formaldehyde. These include imidazolidinyl urea, diazolidinyl urea, DMDM hydantoin, and quaternium 15. These preservatives do not cause problems for most clients, but they are worth mentioning because allergies to these are sometimes detected during allergy testing by dermatologists. Any client can have an allergic reaction to any preservative, not just formaldehyde donors. Remember that allergic reactions are individual, not general.

Step ~~By~~ *Step* Treatment for Sensitive Skin

Purpose: To clean and calm sensitive skin

Client Preparation: Have the client complete the health care form. The esthetician performs a brief consultation

Products: Nonfragranced cleanser, sensitive freshener, hydration fluid, gel mask, and sunscreen

Tools and Supplies: Cryoglobes and gauze

Procedure

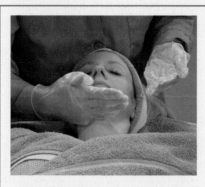

Cleanse

1 Choose a nonfragranced, nonfoaming cleansing milk with a soothing agent such as aloe vera, matricaria, or chamomile. Apply the cleanser directly to facial skin with your gloved hands. Applying the product with sponges could be more irritating than applying it directly with the hands. Using small circular movements and light pressure, use the fingertips to massage the cleansing lotion across the skin, thoroughly covering all areas. Brushing and suctioning should be avoided on sensitive skin.

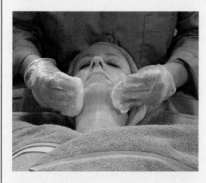

2 Remove the cleanser using cool, wet cotton pads or very soft cloths. Apply a freshener or toner for sensitive skin.

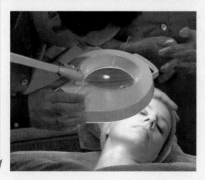

Analyze

3 Carefully examine the skin and record your analysis. Check for undue redness.

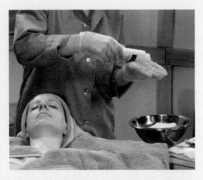

Steam

4 Apply a soothing, nonfragranced hydration fluid to all areas of the face.

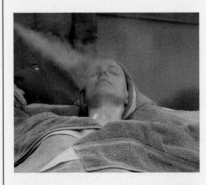

5 Apply cool steam from an ultrasonic steamer or a cool Lucas spray device, if available. If you must use warm steam, make sure the steamer is at least 18 inches away from the face. It is important not to get the face warm or hot. Steam should be applied for about 8–10 minutes if cool steam is used. If warm steam is used, it should limited to 3–5 minutes and applied at a distance so that the face does not become warm.

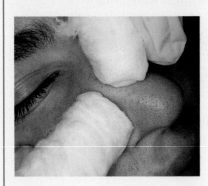

Extract

6 Gently extract impactions or comedones. Do not overextract. Sensitive skin will often redden and sometimes develop pressure urticaria during extraction.

7 After extraction, apply cool, wet cotton compresses and allow them to sit on the skin for several minutes. This is particularly soothing after extraction.

8 Apply a gentle nonalcoholic toner with soothing ingredients such as green tea, chamomile, or aloe vera.

Treat and Massage

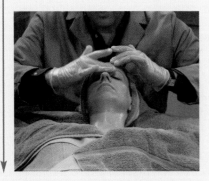

9 Apply a nonfragranced hydrating fluid or lightweight cream to the skin. Again, soothing agents in the fluid or cream will help reduce irritation during the massage. Gently massage the fluid into the skin with gentle pressure and effleurage movements. Very light tapotement may also be beneficial. The massage should be limited to about 5–10 minutes on sensitive skin. If the skin reddens substantially, discontinue the massage. You may need to apply more hydration fluid if it is quickly absorbed. Leave a light coat on the skin when finished with the massage.

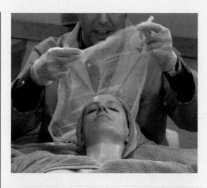

Special Treatment

10 Unfold a 4" × 4" 16-ply gauze square or use a precut gauze face mask, and lightly apply it across the face. Gently secure it to the skin with light pressure.

11 Apply cryoglobes, which are small plastic, Pyrex, or glass, handheld globes that contain a refrigerant fluid that retains the cold. The globes are kept in the freezer so that they are always cold. Gently glide the globes in a symmetrical pattern, making sure you apply the same gliding pattern to both sides of the face simultaneously.

> Should the skin ever develop obvious swelling while being treated, discontinue the treatment, remove all products with cool wet cotton pads, and apply cool wet compresses to the face. Do not continue the treatment that day.

Mask

12 Apply a cooling gel mask to the skin. This mask will help hydrate and cool the skin, reducing redness still left from the treatment. This mask should not harden and should contain ingredients to soothe and hydrate.

13 Apply a cool, damp compress to gently remove the gel mask. Remove all traces of the mask thoroughly.

Complete

14 Reapply a soothing toner as in step 8.

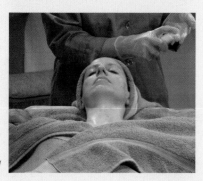

15 Apply a sunscreen containing a physical sunscreen ingredient such as titanium dioxide or zinc oxide. If the skin is still red after treatment, it may be best to wait until the redness has cleared before applying sunscreen. It is best not to apply makeup immediately following a treatment on sensitive skin.

Home Maintenance

Home care for a client with sensitive skin should be carefully designed to avoid agents that can impair the barrier function, and it should have added soothing agents to calm the skin. Obviously, you must avoid any product that has caused the client previous problems.

Keep in mind that sensitive skin is thin, has a fragile lipid barrier, and reacts much more readily than normal skin, so the program should be as simple as possible. Products that are designed for sensitive skin and for which the manufacturer has made irritancy-tested claims, are generally good choices. AHA and exfoliating products should not be used until you have determined that the skin needs an AHA. Any additional products should be carefully introduced only after the initial products are being well tolerated by the client.

The following is a typical program for clients with sensitive skin.

Procedure

Morning

1 Cleanse the face gently with a nonfoaming or lowfoaming, fragrance-free liquid or lotion cleanser that is free of exfoliating agents. Have the client use the fingertips or a very soft cloth, such as a shammie. Only tepid water should be used to rinse the cleanser. Be sure no excess cleanser is left on the skin.

2 Toner or freshener should be alcohol-free and fragrance-free, and it should contain one or more soothing agents, such as green tea extract, chamomile, azulene, matricaria, bisabolol, or aloe barbadensis. If the toner contains a humectant, butylene glycol is a good choice.

3 An antioxidant or soothing serum containing green tea or grapeseed extract will help with redness and serve as a calming agent.

4 SPF-15 sunscreen with physical screening agents such as zinc oxide or titanium dioxide is a good choice. The sunscreen may include soothing ingredients such as green tea, bisabolol, or aloe barbadensis.

5 Eye creams should be carefully chosen. The simpler the formula, the better.

Night

1 Remove makeup with a nonfoaming lotion cleanser, the same as in the morning.

2 Apply toner, as in the morning.

3 Apply a soothing serum, as in the morning.

4 Night hydration should include soothing agents and should be designed to reinforce barrier function and include lipid ingredients. As always, fragranced products should be avoided.

5 Apply eye cream, as in the morning.

6 Apply a gel mask. Choose a gel mask for sensitive skin. It will include hydrators and soothing agents and can be used 2 or 3 times a week. A gel mask does not dry or tighten. Often these masks can be applied when the skin feels flushed or slightly irritated, and they help calm the skin in a fairly short period of time.

Sensitive Skin Treatment Tip #5

Use products that contain soothing ingredients, which may help to squelch or prevent reactions. Aloe vera, chamomile, and bisabolol are standard well-known soothing agents. Some newer ingredients that help to calm and squelch redness and reactivity include stearyl glycyrrhetinate and dipotassium glycyrrhizinate (both from licorice extract), azulene (also known as matricaria extract, a particular type of chamomile), and antioxidants such as green tea and grapeseed extracts. These ingredients may be helpful in reducing redness and discomfort, and they may also prevent irritation. Products containing these extracts can be applied to the skin prior to a procedure to help prevent irritation from the treatment products themselves.

Salon Treatment For Sensitive Skin

Salon treatment for any sensitive skin should be very gentle. The initial treatment should be simple until you are more familiar with a particular client's tolerance level. You should always avoid heat exposure for sensitive skin, although ice cold treatments are not a good idea either. Thin skin has heat and cold nerve receptors closer to the skin's surface and will react more readily. Having all items, including steam, wet towels, and creams, at room temperature or slightly cooler is a good idea.

Excessive use of many techniques should be avoided. Excessive massage, excessive extraction, and excessive cleansing are examples of stripping or overly stimulating treatments that can set off reactive skin. Massage techniques should be limited to light effleurage and light tapotement.

Waxing can also cause problems for sensitive skin. It is best not to wax sensitive skin until you have treated the skin long enough to determine its sensitivity level. Tweezing or electrolysis may be better choices for sensitive skin, although both of these techniques can also inflame sensitive skin. After waxing, it is important to soothe the skin with a soothing agent such as matricaria or green tea, accompanied by cool compresses.

Summary

All skin can be sensitive at times, usually due to environmental damage. Clients with diagnosed sensitive skin, however, often have impaired barrier function and reduced lipid production, making them more susceptible to both allergens and irritants. When treating sensitive skin, use caution when choosing products with additives and preservatives. The simpler the products, the less likely they are to cause problems.

Discussion Questions

1. Describe how the barrier function can be compromised in sensitive skin types. Discuss remedies available to combat this problem.

2. What is the best approach to determining a true sensitive skin type? How can the client questionnaire be useful in this process? Develop a list of specific questions that would be helpful. Be sure to incorporate a measure for transient factors.

3. Explain the difference between irritants and allergens. What is the best approach to take in determining whether a particular product is simply irritating or is actually causing an allergic reaction?

4. Sensitive skin types may be particularly vulnerable to accelerating aging symptoms. How can the esthetician help clients control sensitivity and at the same time address their aging concerns?

Additional Readings

Lees, Mark. 2001. *Skin Care: Beyond the Basics.* Clifton Park, N.Y.: Milady, an imprint of Delmar Learning, a division of Thomson Learning, Inc.

Michalun, Natalia, with M. Varinia Michalun. 2000. *Milady's Skin Care and Cosmetic Ingredients Dictionary.* Clifton Park, N.Y.: Milady, an imprint of Delmar Learning, a division of Thomson Learning, Inc.

Helpful Web Sites

http://www.dermadoctor.com

Chapter 23
Hyperpigmentation: Morphology And Treatment

Chapter Objectives

After reading this chapter, you should be able to:

- List the different types and causes of hyperpigmentation.
- Explain treatment approaches and considerations.

Chapter Outline

Introduction
Analysis
Treatment for Hyperpigmentation

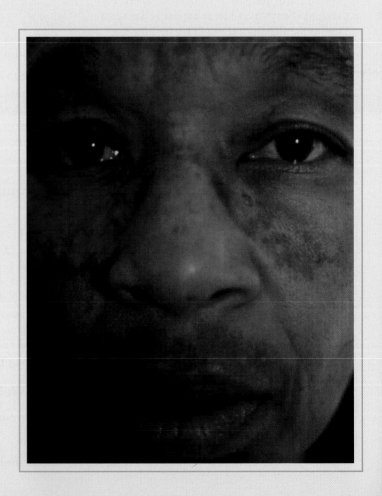

Introduction

The causes and symptoms of hyperpigmentation have already been mentioned in Chapter 17 and Chapter 21. We now need to discuss actual treatment programs for hyperpigmentation, and the role the esthetician plays in the management of hyperpigmentation.

Analysis

During the analysis process, you may notice various hyperpigmentation problems affecting your client's skin. Estheticians should be aware of and look for the following during the analysis process: mottling, chloasma and melasma, sun and heat exposure, skin coloration, hyperpigmentation, and inflammation. These are discussed in detail below.

Mottling

Mottling is freckly hyperpigmentation that does not appear in a pronounced patch, but rather in small freckles that are various shades of brown and tan (Figure 23–1). This is not the same type of freckling that is hereditary, as in red-haired persons, although older, sun damaged clients with hereditary freckles will often have more mottling due to cumulative sun-damage. Sun-induced mottling can be seen in almost any age group, including young people in their late teens and early twenties. As previously mentioned, mottling is the very first sign of sun-induced damage contributing to the process of skin aging.

Mottling responds fairly well to home treatment with a 10% alphahydroxy acid (AHA) gel or cream, along with a sunscreen. The client must also make a commitment to stay out of direct sun in order to maintain the results. Most of the time, a melanin suppressant is unnecessary with this type of hyperpigmentation.

Chloasma and Melasma

Chloasma is often referred to as liver spots, and it occurs on the face, arms, and hands (Figure 23–2). Contrary to folklore, these

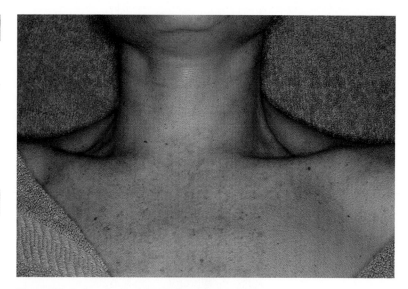

Figure 23–1 Sun-induced mottling is noticeable in any age group.

spots have nothing to do with the liver. Instead, they are spots of concentrated melanin production caused by sun damage.

Melasma can be any form of splotchy hyperpigmentation, but it is seen most often in women in the form of a pregnancy mask (Figure 23–3). The mask pattern can cover the entire center panel of the face, or it may occur as larger splotches in any area, frequently affecting the outer sides of the face. A darkening of the upper lip is also common.

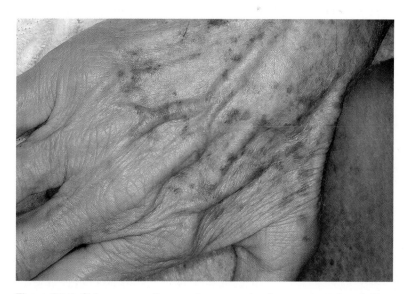

Figure 23–2 Chloasma, or liver spots, are spots of concentrated melanin caused by sun damage.

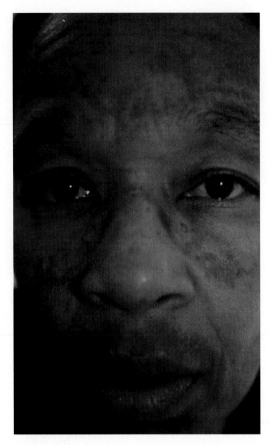

Figure 23–3 Melasma, a splotchy form of hyperpigmentation, can mask the center of the face or cover large areas.

Sun and Heat Exposure

Sun exposure is the major cause of hyperpigmentation problems. Chronic sun exposure causes severe hyperpigmentation, especially on the face, neck, hands, and arms. Clients who have had years of sun exposure will have hyperpigmentation combined with wrinkles, elastosis, and other problems, such as actinic keratoses and skin cancers. However, sun exposure can cause hyperpigmentation at any age.

Wherever a client has a hyperpigmented area, a group of melanocytes in the basal layer or in the upper dermis is overproducing melanin. These melanocytes, which have been stimulated by sun exposure to the point that the skin is chronically hyperpigmented, will always have the tendency to overproduce melanin. Even if the hyperpigmentation is corrected, the melanocytes are still there and can still be easily stimulated.

For clients who already have hyperpigmentation, heat is known to stimulate the melanocytes. An example is a client who is using sunscreen, AHAs, and a melanin suppressant such as hydroquinone but continues to be heat-exposed. In this case, the melanin can recur very readily.

Clients who are being treated for hyperpigmentation must make a strong commitment to avoid any form of direct sun exposure, even if they are wearing a broad-spectrum sunscreen. An SPF-15 or higher sunscreen should be used every single day. Sunscreens that have physical screening agents, such as titanium dioxide or zinc oxide, tend to deflect heat and prevent the skin from getting as hot, in addition to screening damaging UV rays. You should consult with clients who have hyperpigmentation and inform them that they must avoid the sun. Treating hyperpigmentation in a client who will not avoid sun exposure is a futile effort.

Hormone fluctuations, birth control pills, and hormonal therapies can cause, worsen, or sometimes even improve melasma.

Clients with hormonally induced melasma can be treated by the esthetician, but they should also be referred to a gynecologist or an endocrinologist. These clients often need both hormonal and topical treatments to help improve the problem. Although rare, sometimes this type of hyperpigmentation is indicative of a serious hormonal or health problem, so medical referral is important.

Many clients have already discussed their problems with their doctors. The doctor has often established that there is no major underlying hormonal problem. In many cases, the problem is more cosmetic than medical, and some doctors do not take the condition seriously. To the client, however, melasma can be worrisome.

Skin Coloration

Hyperpigmentation can happen in skin of any coloring, but the problem is most prominent in skin of color (Figure 23–4). Darker skin produces larger granules of melanin, and the melanocytes may be deeper in the skin than they are in Caucasian skin. Individuals of Mediterranean, Arabic, or African descent, Asians, and Hispanics very likely to have problems with hyperpigmentation. These clients are also likely to be slow to respond to treatments for hyperpigmentation.

Hyperpigmentation And Inflammation

Inflammation or irritations can often cause or aggravate hyperpigmentation. A classic example of this is hyperpigmentation caused by acne lesions. This is especially prevalent in Asians, Hispanics, blacks, and other people of color.

Clients who have acne excorieé(frequently have problems with splotchy hyperpigmentation. When clients pick at their skin, it causes scratches that are then exposed to sunlight, creating the splotches. For some clients, the process of scratching can cause or aggravate the problem.

Overuse of AHAs or other exfoliating agents to the point of irritation, overaggressive microdermabrasion, or any other harsh treatment that leaves the skin excoriated or chronically irritated can cause or worsen hyperpigmentation. Although exfoliation is a part of the treatment for hyperpigmentation, if the exfoliation is overaggressive, stimulation of melanocytes occurs, and the hyperpigmentation can worsen. If overused, mechanical abrasions or pressure, such as what occurs in the process of microdermabrasion, can also stimulate the melanocytes. All of these trauma-related hyperpigmentation problems are known as postinflammatory hyperpigmentation or PIH.

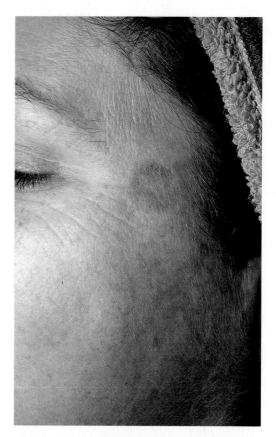

Figure 23–4 Hyperpigmentation can be caused by inflammation or irritation.

Treatment for Hyperpigmentation

The treatment of hyperpigmentation is one of the most difficult treatment plans because variables such as hormones, which estheticians have no control over, must be considered. Treatment of hyperpigmentation must then be looked at from a program perspective by both the esthetician and the client. As we have already mentioned, the first item that should be addressed is a client's sun habits. The client must make a commitment to avoid

sun exposure if any progress is to be made. Use of an SPF-15 or higher sunscreen on all treated areas is an absolute must every single day. Sunscreen for the hands is something that many clients overlook, but hands should always be treated with a water-resistant sunscreen.

AHAs and other exfoliating agents should also be used daily by a client at home on the areas of hyperpigmentation. These agents can be in the form of a gel, lotion, or cream. The AHA should be in a concentration of 8%–10%, and it should be applied twice a day.

AHAs do not treat or inhibit the hyperpigmentation process; they simply remove keratinocytes that already contain melanin. Stained cells are removed through any type of exfoliation. The reason AHAs do a better job than many other exfoliating treatments is that they are applied every day by the client at home, and the cells are constantly coming off the skin's surface.

Keeping Communication Positive

In this fast-paced world we live in it is often difficult to remain positive. With so many sources of negative news throughout the media it can be a real challenge to find something good to say each day. In addition there are personal issues that we may occasionally get caught up in—there are bills to pay, children to tend to, medical emergencies, and obligations to meet. But no matter what concerns we may have, we must remember that clients are coming to us for a professional service. They expect and should receive quality service.

We already know that good communication skills, both verbal and nonverbal, are essential for doing our job well. We also know that in order to develop a positive relationship we must work hard to develop such traits as empathy, respectful listening, and a genuinely positive outlook. Keeping client information confidential and steering clear of gossip are also important in gaining the client's trust. Once you cross either of these boundaries it will be hard to win that trust back. The quality of your language is another important consideration. Avoid using any offensive language, or slang remarks. Your goal should be to appear polished and professional at all times.

The role of an esthetician is a healing and nurturing one. Therefore you must also incorporate an additional set of communication skills to be a supportive helper. When working with clients you will need to learn to:

- Ask open-ended questions.
- Clarify goals by probing and redefining the client's responses.
- Evaluate skin conditions and make positive recommendations.

- Resolve problems to promote a positive outcome.
- Motivate and reassure clients.
- Inform clients about the numerous products and treatments that are available.

To perform these tasks well you should think about the language you use. For example, when evaluating a client's skin type or condition you should frame any negative aspects in the best light possible. Instead of reprimanding the client with sun-damaged skin for spending too much time in the sun, you might consider asking how much time she spends outdoors and offer suggestions for protecting the skin.

You should also get in the habit of paraphrasing and summarizing your communication to ensure that the client understands. Learn to make statements such as: "I am glad you have chosen to purchase a series of facials. This will help us control your acne and keep your skin clean on a regular basis. Between visits it will be important for you to use the cleanser, toner, and blemish lotion we discussed. If you have any questions please do not hesitate to call."

At first these techniques may seem staged or unnatural to you, but as you gain experience, they will become a natural part of your communication repertoire.

Melanin Suppressive Agents

The production of melanin is reduced by suppressive agents interfering with the series of biochemical reactions that lead to its production. Consumers and estheticians sometimes refer to melanin suppressive agents as bleaching agents. This is incorrect. These agents are not bleaches and they do not work by bleaching or fading the melanin. The only FDA-approved ingredient for this purpose is hydroquinone. In the U.S., claims for lightening cannot legally be made by any other agent, and products that do not contain hydroquinone cannot be called lighteners. Hydroquinone is used in over-the-counter formulations at a concentration of up to 2%. Standard prescription versions contain 4% hydroquinone, and some physician-dispensed formulas contain 6% hydroquinone.

Many other agents, however, can also affect melanin production. These agents include kojic acid, azelaic acid, magnesium ascorbyl phosphate, ascorbyl glucosamine, asafetida extract, mulberry extract, bearberry extract, arbutin, and licorice extract. All of these agents contain chemicals similar to hydroquinone in their actions on the melanin process; however, they are not approved to make the claim of lightening. Many companies that manufacture for estheticians include these agents in their formulations for hyperpigmentation. They use these agents in products called brighteners, which is a cosmetic term, not a drug term.

Lightening and brightening agents are available in gel, cream, liquid, or lotion form. Gels are probably the most prominent and, many feel, the most effective. They are best used in conjunction with some sort of exfoliating agent, namely AHA. Many gels contain AHA, most often 10% glycolic acid, and one or more melanin suppressive agents. If a product contains both AHA and hydroquinone, it is not necessary to use another AHA. In fact, using one application of AHA on top of another one can be irritating.

Physicians often use tretinoin with hydroquinone to accelerate the lightening process. This approach reflects the philosophy of using an exfoliant to remove dead cells filled with melanin and a suppressive agent to slow or stop the production of new melanin.

Home Care for Hyperpigmentation

1. A client should cleanse with a product appropriate for her skin type. This may be a foaming or nonfoaming cleanser, depending on the skin type and other conditions, such as oiliness, dryness, or sensitivity.

2. A toner or freshener appropriate for the client's skin type should be applied.

3. An AHA product, usually a gel, of 8%–10% AHA concentration, should be applied. This product may also contain a melanin suppressant such as hydroquinone, kojic acid, magnesium ascorbyl phosphate, or any combination of these ingredients for hyperpigmentation. Some companies will recommend separate products for AHA exfoliation and melanin suppression.

4. A broad-spectrum sunscreen of at least SPF15, preferably with a physical sunscreen agent and a built-in moisturizer, should be applied every day. For people who work outside or are exposed to water, the sunscreen should be water resistant. Water-resistant sunscreen is also a must for hands, if they are being treated.

5. At night, the same basic program should be followed. Sunscreen, of course, is not necessary for nighttime. A good hydrator that is appropriate for the client's skin type should be applied instead.

Salon Treatment

Exfoliating treatments are the key treatment for hyperpigmentation, and the first treatment used is usually an AHA series. Exfoliating the skin surface with concentrated AHAs speeds the process of hyperpigmentation treatment. Getting rid of stained surface cells and cell buildup fades existing hyperpigmentation and makes melanin suppressive products absorb better.

As we have discussed in this and other sections, you should stick to AHA salon treatments that do not exceed 30% concentrations, with pHs no less than 3.0. If the AHA or other exfoliating procedure causes unwanted irritation, hyperpigmentation can actually worsen. The key is to exfoliate with-

Practical Tips for Creating Retail Displays

Many practitioners enjoy the creative aspect of merchandising. If you have an interest in arts or crafts and like to organize, you may want to explore the idea of using these skills to promote retail sales. Most employers will appreciate the extra help and admire your initiative. But before you volunteer your services to your boss, consider developing a strategic plan that takes the following into account:

- **Salon Image.** Owners generally devote a great deal of time and energy to creating a certain look or image for their day spa or clinic. When approaching the task of merchandising, you should be respectful of the mood they have worked hard to develop. Make sure your suggestions flow with the image of the salon rather than compete for attention. If the tone is soft and restful, you can introduce ideas that blend gently with the surroundings, such as natural plants, flowers, seashells and sand, crystals or stones. An atmosphere that is modern and funky may be more open to introducing offbeat items such as retro art, movie icons, or cartoon characters.

- **Mission or Vision.** When promoting retail sales, be sure to take into account the clinic's objectives. If the main focus of the clinic is to provide services that make clients look better, highlighting those products that demonstrate dramatic results will be well accepted. If health and well being are more in sync with the establishment's philosophy, you may choose to focus on the remedial aspects of a product. Choosing promotional language that is in alignment with these goals will also be important.

- **Promotion Planner or Calendar.** Take advantage of natural time lines, such as months, seasons, and holidays to generate automatic retail responses. Holidays are a natural for generating gift certificate— Christmas, Hanukah, Mother's Day, Father's Day, and Valentine's Day all lend themselves easily to sales promotion. When linked to an additional value, such as a stress reduction technique, even less popular dates like April 15— tax return deadline—can turn into a marvelous sales opportunity. Working around relevant skin care concerns such as summer sun exposure or winter dehydration and moisture loss can also be great sales boosters and at the same time demonstrate integrity for what you do.

- **Artful Association.** Generating ideas to create artful and inviting displays can be challenging. To help you decide on a theme, try making a list of all those things you associate with a particular month, holiday, or event. Then look around for simple objects that emphasize the theme. Scan fashion and health magazines, go window shopping, visit department stores, art galleries, or museums to help you get started. Party goods stores are an inexpensive resource for paper products and small theme items such as confetti and balloons. Those with more imagination may also wish to explore thrift shops and yard sales for other interesting art objects.

out irritating and stimulating underlying melanocytes.

Betahydroxy acid (BHA) (salicylic acid) treatments, also discussed in Chapter 14, are also helpful for treating hyperpigmentation. They are an alternative salon treatment; they are not performed at the same time as the AHA treatment series.

For more stubborn hyperpigmentation, advanced procedures such as Jessner's or resorcinol exfoliations can be helpful. This should not be attempted until a less aggressive treatment such as AHA has been tried first. As always, Jessner's and resorcinol exfoliations should only be performed by estheticians thoroughly trained in these procedures.

Patience, Patience, Patience

Hyperpigmentation is a hard to treat condition, and often requires months of treatment to achieve a change in a client's appearance. Clients should be told from the very start of treatment that this is a long-term project, so that they are not disappointed when they have not seen much change after only a couple of weeks. They must also be consulted constantly and understand that they have to be extremely diligent and conscientious about their home care, salon treatments, and habits if they are to see any results. During this time, sun must be avoided completely.

Summary

Hyperpigmentation is one of the most difficult skin conditions to treat, and clients should be aware that results take a long time to see. Sun exposure is a primary cause of hyperpigmentation, and other elements, such as hormones, are beyond an esthetician's control. Treatment should be nonaggressive, nonirritating, and diligent.

Discussion Questions

1. Classify the main types of hyperpigmentation and outline the main reasons for the skin's discoloration, describing these briefly in bullet format.

2. Exfoliating agents are often recommended to treat hyperpigmentation. However, these same agents can also induce a condition known as postinflammatory hyperpigmentation (PIH). Explain the process by which this occurs and what can be done to prevent it.

3. What is the best approach to treating hyperpigmentation? Include a complete treatment program that includes professional treatments as well as a home care regime.

4. Develop a list of over-the-counter ingredients that inhibit the production of melanin. Do you recognize any of these agents in the retail product lines you are currently using? What is the best way to explain to clients how these work?

Additional Reading

Goodheart, Herbert. 1998. *A Photoguide of Common Skin Disorders, Diagnosis and Management.* Philadelphia, Pa: Williams & Wilkins.

Lees, Mark. 2001. *Skin Care: Beyond the Basics.* Clifton Park, N.Y.: Milady, an imprint of Delmar Learning, a division of Thomson Learning, Inc.

Turkington, Carol. 1998. *Skin Deep: An A to Z of Skin Disorders, Treatment and Health.* New York: Facts on File, Inc.

Helpful Web Sites

http://www.dermadoctor.com
http://www.sdefderm.com (Skin Disease Education Foundation)

Chapter 24
Acne: Morphology and Treatment

Chapter Objectives

After reading this chapter, you should be able to:

- Explain how hormones and heredity cause acne.
- Identify the effects of stress on acne.
- List the medical grades given to acne.
- Describe home and salon treatments for acne.

Chapter Outline

Introduction
What Causes Acne?
Hormones and Acne
Stress Factors
Foods and Acne
Cosmetics, Skin Care Products, and Acne
Grades of Acne
Concepts of Acne Management
Analysis and Treatment of Problem Skin

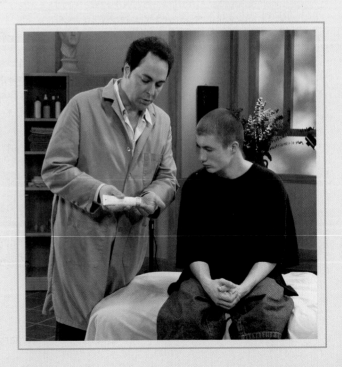

Introduction

People think of acne as a teenage affliction, but acne is a disorder of the skin that can affect people at almost any age and it is often a lifelong battle. Acne can take different forms, and even occasional pimples or breakouts are a mild form of acne. Although most forms of acne can be successfully controlled, because it is a hereditary disorder, clients will have to be aware and conscientious of treatment for many years.

When we say the word *acne*, we are generally referring to the condition known as acne vulgaris, the most common form of acne. Acne can be disfiguring, causing redness, pustules, and, in severe cases, scarring that can last a lifetime. There is no question that acne, although not infectious, contagious, or life threatening, can affect a person's self-esteem and self-perception.

Acne is one of the primary concerns of esthetic clients. Many of the clients you see will have some mild form of acne. In this section, we will discuss the causes and the treatment techniques for managing acne and problem-prone skin.

What Causes Acne?

Acne and pimples have little to do with cleanliness. Although it is important to keep the skin clean, acne is not caused by dirt. Instead, the main causes of acne are heredity and hormones (Figure 24–1).

Acne is a genetic disorder, and it is largely hereditary factors that determine who gets acne. If parents suffer from acne, chances are that their children will also suffer from the condition. People who have acne have a hereditary factor known as **retention hyperkeratosis,** which means that dead cells, or keratinocytes, do not shed off the surface of the corneum and out of the follicles as they do on normal skin.

Corneum cells, as we learned in Chapter 2, are on the very surface of the skin and also form the lining of the follicles (pores). In normal skin, the cells release and shed off the skin's surface, and they also shed off the follicle lining. Retention hyperkeratosis, how-

ever, causes cells to build up inside the follicle and line the follicle wall.

The tendency for people to have heavy sebum production, or oily skin areas, is also hereditary. Sebum is problematic because it waxes over current cell buildup and causes more cell buildup to occur. The sebum itself can also irritate the follicle, causing inflammation. People who experience heavy sebum production tend to have visible oiliness on the surface of their skin. In fact, the oilier the skin, the stronger the tendency for severe acne. Clients are quite aware of this oiliness, and they will often complain of a constant shine and difficulty with makeup adhering.

Oiliness is prominent in the T-zone, the term that refers to the pattern of oiliness on the face. This area includes the forehead, nose, and chin, and may also include the cheeks. With very oily skin, all areas of the face are oily, and the scalp may be oily as well.

Enlarged pores are good indications of oily areas. They are caused by the amount of oil being produced and coming through the

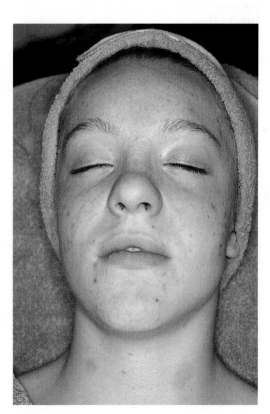

retention hyperkeratosis
A hereditary factor in which dead cells do not shed off the surface of the corneum and out of the follicles, causing acne.

Figure 24–1 The two main causes of acne are heredity and hormones.

infundibulum
The follicular canal.

comedo
A plug of oil and sebum inside the follicle.

microcomedo
The beginning of the plug formation, not visible to the naked eye.

blackheads
When the sebaceous material in an open pore darkens because of oxidation; open comedones.

noninflammatory
Not red or inflamed.

follicular canal, the **infundibulum,** and eventually coating the skin's outer surface.

As cells build up on the walls of the follicle and in the bottom of the follicle, they are mixed with sebaceous matter. This is the beginning of a **comedo,** which is a plug of oil and sebum inside the follicle. Actually, the beginning of the plug formation is known as a **microcomedo.** Microcomedones (plural) are too small and too deep in the follicle to be seen, even with a magnifying lamp. In acne-prone skin, microcomedones are numerous. When enough buildup occurs in the follicle, the plug forms and becomes a comedo.

Two types of comedones exist: open comedones (Figure 24–2a) and closed comedones (Figure 24–2b). Open comedones are commonly known as **blackheads** because the sebaceous material in the follicle darkens when it is exposed to oxygen, a process known as oxidation. (Lipids make up the sebum, and fats oxidize very readily.) It is a common misconception that the black part of a blackhead is dirt. It is not dirt; it is simply oxidized sebum. You can see the level to which oxygen penetrates the follicle by looking closely at an extracted plug. Notice that the top of the impaction is black from oxidation and that the sides of the extracted plug are also somewhat dark. As you observe the part of the plug that was originally at the bottom of the follicle, note that this area has little or no dark color. It has not oxidized because oxygen has not reached this area.

Closed comedones form in the same manner as open ones, except that the ostium, or pore opening, does not dilate. Oxidation is less obvious, and closed comedones are sometimes called whiteheads. They appear as small bumps just under the surface of the skin. If you look carefully at closed comedones, you will notice a very small opening in the lesion. In acne-prone clients, these closed comedones may be numerous. They can appear in any area but are most obvious in the cheek areas. Oxidation, or darkness is not visible, although some oxidation does occur. However, there is no visible dark color in a closed comedo.

Both open and closed comedones are known as **noninflammatory** acne lesions because they are not red or inflamed. They are simply impactions of sebaceous material and dead keratinocytes in a follicle.

Acne Bacteria

Residing at the base of every follicle are bacteria known as Propionibacterium acnes, also referred to as p. acnes. These bacteria are anaerobic, meaning that they cannot survive in the presence of oxygen. Oxygen molecules are very small and move easily in and out of follicles on normal skin. In normal skin, bacteria are constantly dividing and replicating themselves, but they are also constantly being killed by the oxygen that is present in the follicle. In acne-prone skin, the plugs of sebum and dead cell buildup

Figure 24–2a Open comedones are commonly known as blackheads because the sebaceous material in the follicle darkens.

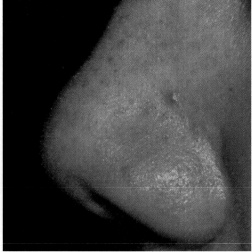

Figure 24–2b Closed comedones are also known as whiteheads.

block the oxygen from reaching the bottom of the follicle, thereby preventing the bacteria from being killed. As a result, the bacteria multiply.

Propionibacterium acnes bacteria also grow because they feed off the sebum within the follicles. They break down the sebaceous secretions into fatty acids, which serve as nutrients for the bacteria. When enough bacteria accumulate in the follicle, along with inflammation from the breakdown of the fatty materials, pressure builds on the follicle wall. Eventually the pressure builds to a point where the follicle wall ruptures. This tear in the wall occurs in the area of the follicle, which is located in the dermis of the skin. Debris from the follicle then spills out of the rupture, debris that includes bacteria, sebum, and dead cells.

The fallout is detected by the immune system of the dermis, which is present in the bloodstream, and white blood cells, or leukocytes, investigate the invasion of the dermis caused by the follicle rupture. At this point, the skin around the lesion and follicle becomes red as the bloodstream brings white blood cells to help fight off the acne bacteria. The redness or erythema is described as inflammation, and the lesion is then known as an **inflammatory acne lesion** or an acne papule. Papules are red, sore bumps that do not have white centers (Figure 24–3).

Pus is a substance that is made up mainly of dead white blood cells that have been killed during the attempt to fight infection. In acne lesions, pus is formed and rises to the surface of the lesion, forming a clump at the top of the distorted follicle. This lesion is known as a pustule, an elevated red lesion with a white center.

The noninflammatory lesion that most often leads to papule or pustule formation or to inflammatory lesions is the closed comedo. Open comedones are not attractive, but generally they do not lead to the formation of inflammatory lesions because oxygen has killed the p. acnes bacteria. It is much harder for oxygen to enter a follicle and kill off the bacteria in a closed comedo with a very small opening to the skin's surface.

A nodule can be any sort of deep lesion in the skin, but the term is frequently used to describe deeper acne lesions (Figure 24–4). They are palpable, which means that they can be felt or palpated easily under the skin.

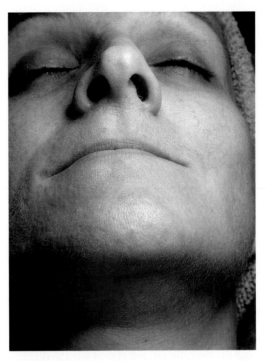

Figure 24–3 Inflammatory acne lesions are red, sore bumps without white centers.

The skin can often be moved or "rolled" over the nodule. Most nodules are at least the size of a small pea and can be somewhat larger.

Cysts are very deep pockets of infection, with large amounts of pus (Figure 24–5, p. 368). In cyst formation, the skin forms hardened tissue in an attempt to wall off the spread of the bacterial infection. The infec-

inflammatory acne lesion
When a lesion becomes red.

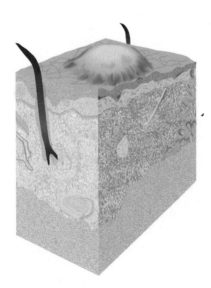

Figure 24–4 A nodule is a deep lesion in the skin that can be felt.

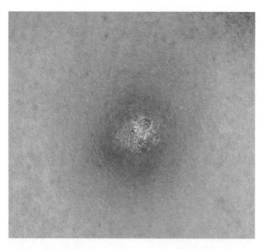

Figure 24–5 A cyst is a very deep pocket of infection containing large amounts of pus.

Hormones are often at the root of acne problems. Male hormones, known as androgens, stimulate sebaceous glands, which cause an increase in sebum production. The specific problem hormone is dihydrotestosterone (DHT), which comes in contact with the receptor sites on the cells of the sebaceous gland. The hormone stimulates the sebaceous gland to produce sebum. Androgens can also cause increased inflammation in follicles.

The first evidence of these sex hormones stimulating the sebaceous glands occurs at puberty. This is the time in life when humans begin secreting substantial amounts of hormones. Puberty generally begins at age 11 or 12. Along with puberty, arrives the formation of other secondary sex characteristics, including hair growth on the body, deepening of the voice in males, and development of breasts in females.

Prior to puberty children have follicles, but they cannot be seen easily with the naked eye. Follicles enlarge and pores appear at the beginning of puberty. As hormones stimulate the sebaceous glands, sebum begins flowing through the follicle, which causes the follicle walls to stretch. This is seen on the skin as more obvious pores. This process usually begins on the nose, then the forehead, the chin, and finally the cheek.

Small comedones may appear on the facial skin of children as early as age 10, normally in the nose area first. Teenage acne can occur in either males or females but tends to be more active and more severe in males. Left untreated, these comedones may become inflammatory lesions.

Treatment for very young clients should be on an as-needed basis. Treatments should be shorter in duration than normal salon cleansing treatments and should focus on loosening and removing comedones. Having the young client begin home treatment for a couple of weeks before having a salon cleansing will help loosen the clogs so that removal is not as difficult or traumatic for the client.

One of the problems with very young clients is their lack of discipline in treating their skin. Young clients with acne are often unlikely to comply with treatment instruc-

pocks
Depressed scars.

tion can destroy dermal skin tissue, which can lead to depressed scars known as **pocks** and the raised scars associated with severe acne. Acne that involves cyst formation is known as cystic acne. Cysts and nodules are too deep to be helped by any sort of surface esthetic treatment. Clients with cystic acne should be immediately referred to a dermatologist for medical treatment.

Clogged Pores

The small impacted follicles that frequently appear in the T-zone of oily skin are not actually open comedones, even though they may have oxidized and have a similar dark top. Instead, many of these small impactions are **sebaceous filaments,** sometimes called clogged pores. Both are a mixture of solidified sebum. The difference between an open comedone and a sebaceous filament is that the comedone will have a large buildup of cells mixed in with the sebaceous plug, whereas the sebaceous filament is primarily just sebaceous secretions.

Sebaceous filaments plaque many clients. They are treated with the same techniques as open comedones, yet they are harder to control. Any client with oily skin or oily areas will have a strong tendency toward developing filaments. Foaming cleansers that help with sebum management and alphahydroxy acid (AHA) gels used at home on a daily basis are helpful in treating and preventing sebaceous filaments.

sebaceous filaments
Small impactions of solidified sebaceous secretions that have oxidized.

tions. These clients should have a very simple program and should receive specific instructions about how to use the products. Remember, these clients are new at treatments and must receive gentle encouragement.

Older teenagers show much more interest in taking care of their skin, because they are more aware of their appearance. Peer pressure to have clear skin helps them comply with the home treatment plan. However, teenagers with hereditary acne problems may feel helpless if the treatment is not effective. Parents should be aware of their child's skin problem and help them receive the proper treatment, so that they are not subjected to the ridicule of their peers or the self-consciousness that accompanies skin problems. The sooner the acne is treated, the less severe it is likely to be (Figure 24–6).

Almost all teenagers experience a few zits. The severity of the problem depends on hereditary factors. Teenagers should begin using products to control oiliness, such as a mild foaming cleanser and mild exfoliants, such as an alphahydroxy acid gel, along with a sunscreen designed for oily skin. They also will need a spot-drying agent to treat pimples as they appear.

Parents will often seek dermatological care for their teenagers before seeking esthetic care. They are often not aware of the treatments available at the skin care salon. It is up to the esthetician to educate the public about the value of proper skin care for teenagers.

Adult Acne

Most forms of adult acne are also related to hormones. Females are more likely to have adult acne than are males. This is mainly due to hormone fluctuations and other factors affecting hormone production, such as birth control pills, pregnancy, lactation, menopause, and hormonal therapy. Improper use of skin care products and cosmetics can also contribute to the problem (Figure 24–7).

Many women who never had acne as teenagers may have chronic breakout problems beginning in their twenties or thirties. **Premenstrual acne,** which occurs in flares usually eight to ten days before a woman's period, is directly related to changes in hor-

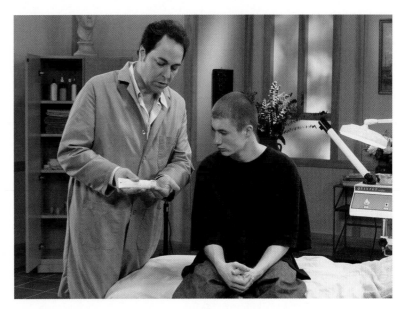

Figure 24–6 A simple program and clear instructions on how to use products help younger clients comply with home treatment.

mones, resulting in increased sebum production and inflammation within the follicles. This inflammation results in **perifollicular inflammation,** which causes swelling inside the follicle. This inflammation can lead to obstruction of the follicle and the creation of anaerobic "pockets" that cause flares of acne.

This type of hormonal acne often affects the chin area and is thus referred to as chin acne. Large, sore papules appear on the jaw line and chin, as well as on the neck and other areas of the face. The reason that the

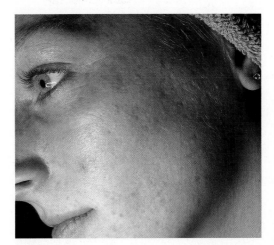

Figure 24–7 Many forms of adult acne are hormone related.

premenstrual acne
Acne that occurs 8–10 days before a woman's period; it directly related to changes in hormones, resulting in increased sebum production and inflammation within the follicles.

perifollicular inflammation
Swelling inside a follicle.

lower face is more affected by these hormonal changes may possibly be related to the larger sebaceous glands in these areas or more active androgen receptors on the glands' cells.

So far, we have been discussing **comedonal acne,** which is the most common form of acne and the type most likely to occur in teenagers. Another form of acne is called **inflammatory acne,** and it is not necessarily related to the formation of comedones in the follicles. Instead, inflammatory acne results from inflammation to the follicle caused by sudden surges of sebum. This type of acne is prevalent in adult women. If you are examining the skin of a client who has few, if any, comedonal lesions but still has acne papules, this is inflammatory acne (Figure 24–8).

Besides being caused by hormonal flares that result in surges of sebum, inflammatory acne is also caused by external topical substances, including some cosmetics and skin care products. In some individuals, certain skin care products can cause inflammation of the follicle, resulting in papule formation. These products are referred to as **acnegenic.** Another common term is comedogenic, which is the tendency of a product to cause or contribute to cell buildup, resulting in the formation of comedones.

Comedogenic reactions may take months to occur, but acnegenic reactions can occur much more suddenly. Sometimes after a facial treatment, especially the first facial treatment, a client will experience a few pimples. This is an acnegenic reaction, most likely caused by irritation from the treatment or from extraction. Any activity that causes perifollicular irritation can cause an acnegenic reaction.

Treatment of Hormonal Acne

Most hormonal acne is fairly minimal and can be treated with the regular procedures described later in this chapter. Clients with severe or repetitive hormonal flares around her menstrual cycle should be referred to a dermatologist or an endocrinologist. The physician will often prescribe or recommend a change to birth control pills that help control hormonal fluctuations and reduce the acne flares. At the time of this writing, only one such prescription drug is approved for this treatment, Ortho-Tri-Cyclen.

Esthetic treatment for hormonal acne should be the same as for any other adult form of acne. Emphasis should be placed on the prevention and control of stressors that increase hormone fluctuations. For clients with premenstrual acne, treatment with deep cleansing and galvanic desincrustation may be helpful, especially if this is done at the halfway point of her menstrual cycle.

Stress Factors

Stress is no doubt a factor in acne. Clients may develop breakouts when they are experiencing many types of life traumas, ranging from final exams to a divorce. Stress actually causes hormonal fluctuations that result in sebum overproduction and inflammation. The gland that responds to stress is the adrenal gland, which is located on top of the kidneys. The adrenal glands secrete a hormone called adrenaline, which is what helps people cope with danger, emergencies, and other stressful events. Whenever you are under stress, adrenaline is being manufactured.

In women the majority of the male hormone androgen is produced by the adrenal gland. When the adrenal gland is stimulated

comedonal acne
The most common form of acne.

inflammatory acne
Acne caused by inflammation within follicles.

acnegenic
Elements that cause inflammation in the follicle and resulting acne.

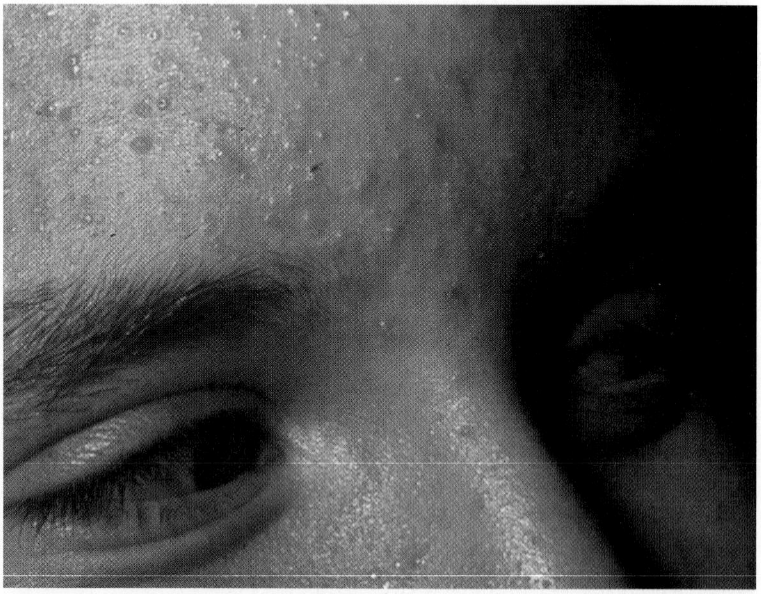

Figure 24–8 Inflammatory acne can be caused by some cosmetics and skin care products resulting in surges of sebum.

by stress, both adrenaline and androgen production is increased. This increases the percentage of the male hormone in the bloodstream, which increases the chances of the sebaceous gland being stimulated.

Foods and Acne

Dozens of myths abound regarding foods that supposedly aggravate acne. Pizza, hamburgers, caffeine, alcohol, and especially chocolate have all been blamed for acne. The truth is that foods have very little to do with acne. Although a diet of mostly pizza, chocolate, and fast food is not particularly healthy for the body, there is no scientific evidence that any particular food causes acne flares. This is not true for rosacea, which, in the past, has been considered a form of acne. Certain foods do flare rosacea.

Clients are more likely to break out from the stress of worrying about eating the wrong food than they are from actually eating it. It is important to encourage your clients to have a healthy diet, but they should not feel guilty or blame the food if they occasionally eat a candy bar or have some pizza. Estheticians should take the opportunity to inform their clients of the truth about acne and foods.

Cosmetics, Skin Care Products, And Acne

As discussed in Chapter 19, emollient ingredients often include fatty ingredients, including fatty acids, fatty alcohols, waxes, oils, and fatty esters. Many of these emollient ingredients are comedogenic and can aggravate acne, and they can also cause or hasten the formation of comedonal lesions. The comedogenic fatty ingredients penetrate the follicle, helping to "wax over" the cell buildup, just as the skin's own sebum does. This can directly contribute to the formation of comedones. Secondly, many of these fatty acids can be irritating to follicles, causing inflammation that can possibly bring on an acnegenic flare.

These ingredients, unfortunately, are often vehicles or spreading agents in the product. This means that they are present in rather large concentrations. Their presence is not always a problem for skin that does not develop clogs easily. Dry, alipidic skin types do not have a tendency for retention hyperkeratosis and may actually need emollient type ingredients to prevent dehydration. Oily and acne-prone skin types, however, manufacture too much of their own emollient and do not need any more from the products used for care and treatment.

Products that cause the most problems for acne-prone skin are moisturizers, sunscreens, serums, and other items that stay on acne-prone areas of the face for long periods of time. Even alphahydroxy products can cause problems if they are contained in a vehicle that is comedogenic.

Makeup products often get overlooked in a comedogenicity assessment. Foundations, powders, and blushes can all be comedogenic. Powders and blushes can be very comedogenic because they are solids pressed together with fatty materials that are semiliquid. These fatty ingredients are pressing agents that help keep the product bound into a cake form and also help the product adhere to the face. Because water or other liquids do not dilute the fatty material, as they would in a moisturizer, the comedogenic effect for acne-prone skin is much stronger in pressed powder products.

Products intended for acne-prone clients should be thoroughly tested for comedogenicity before being marketed. They should also be tested for follicle irritancy, as inflammatory factors can cause acnegenic flares. Unfortunately, there is no law that requires testing, and some companies market their products as noncomedogenic without doing the testing necessary to support the claim. Although many companies try to avoid ingredients that are known to be comedogenic, combining different ingredients may result in an irritating product. It is important that the final product itself is tested. Check with your manufacturer to find out how their products are tested for comedogenicity.

Grades of Acne

Dermatologists refer to the severity of an acne condition in terms of acne grades (Figure 24–9, p. 372). This is a medical

Figure 24–9a Grade 1 acne.

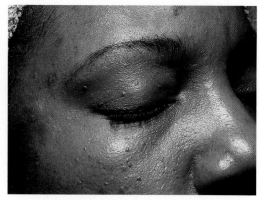

Figure 24–9b Grade 2 acne.

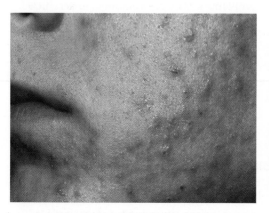

Figure 24–9c Grade 3 acne.

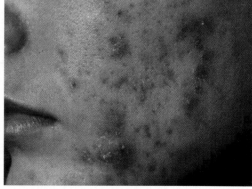

Figure 24–9d Grade 4 acne.

method of describing the type and number of both non-inflammatory and inflammatory lesions on the skin.

- Grade 1 acne is comprised of mostly open comedones, some closed comedones, and few papules and pustules (Figure 24–9a).

- Grade 2 acne has many more open comedones, many closed comedones, and more papules and pustules. Skin appears very bumpy due to the presence of the many closed comedones (Figure 24–9b).

- Grade 3 acne is very erythemic (red) and has inflamed skin with open and closed comedones, and many papules and pustules. This type of acne is what people often think of when they hear the word acne (Figure 24–9c).

- Grade 4 acne is also known as cystic acne and is the worst type of acne vulgaris, with deep nodules, cysts, and scarring.

Open and closed comedones, papules, pustules, and severe inflammation are often present as well (Figure 24–9d).

Grade 1 acne is quite common and is frequently seen in the skin care salon. The client with grade 1 or 2 acne can benefit from extraction of the noninflammatory lesions (open and closed comedones). The client with one or two pimples on a regular basis suffers from grade 1 acne, although it may never be called this. Grade 2 acne is also seen fairly frequently by the esthetician.

Clients with grades 3 and 4 acne must be treated by a dermatologist, but they can also have esthetic treatments. Clients with extremely inflammatory acne need oral or topical antibiotics and more aggressive therapy. Estheticians should refer these clients to a dermatologist for prescription medical treatment. Deep-cleansing treatments by an esthetician can be beneficial and support the medical treatment.

Dermatologists sometimes actually count the active lesions on the face of an acne patient. This is referred to as a lesion count. The number of lesions is factored into the diagnosis to determine the grade of acne. For the esthetician's purposes, this is not practical, but it is information you may need to know if you are speaking to a dermatologist about a client's acne.

Concepts of Acne Management

An esthetician can do nothing to change the hereditary factors that cause acne. A dermatologist or endocrinologist can manipulate hormones, but this is not always successful and, of course, is not the domain of the esthetician. Problem skin and acne can be brought under control, however, to the point where there are no visible lesions for very long periods of time. The client may still have an occasional lesion, but between salon treatments and proper home care programs, problem skin can be managed effectively on a long-term basis. Below we discuss the factors an esthetician has some control over, including topical therapies that can be used by an esthetician in an attempt to control problem skin.

Acne Treatment Tip #1—Eliminate All Comedogenic Products

When you first see a client who has acne-prone skin, you should check to see what products she is currently using. Many closed comedones are often evidence of **acne cosmetica,** which is acne caused or worsened by skin care and cosmetic products. These comedones may appear all over or in specific areas, such as the blushline. Blush is a frequent culprit in cosmetic acne because of the coal tar dyes (also known as D&C red dyes), and the fatty material used to keep the powder blush in a cake. Likewise, pressed foundations, or dry foundations in a pan form, are frequently a problem for acne-prone skin.

Moisturizers and hydrating products that are intended for dry skin, but used by acne-prone individuals, frequently contain fatty acids and other fatty materials that provide emollient properties for dry skin. The oily,

acne-prone skin already produces enough emollient (in the form of sebum), and does not need these fatty substances. The fatty substances flow into the follicles when applied to the skin, adding to the clogging sebum and causing comedones to form.

Often, these moisturizing products with emollients are intended for older skin, which may not produce much sebum. Antiaging products can be formulated without these emollients as well. If your client is both acne-prone and concerned about aging and sun damage, you should have products available that have good antiaging ingredients such as AHAs and antioxidants that have been formulated so that they do not clog acne-prone skin.

One of the most misleading terms used in cosmetics is *oil free*. There are, unfortunately, many oil-free products on the market that are, indeed, free of oils but loaded with fatty esters, fatty acids, and other comedogenic spreading agents. Many of these fatty ingredients are much worse in terms of contributing to clogging. Always encourage clients to look for products that are designed for problem skin and that have been properly tested for comedogenicity and acnegenicity.

Hydrators intended for acne-prone skin should contain water-binding humectants, such as sodium PCA, sorbitol, hyaluronic acid, or glycerin. All of these agents are noncomedogenic and will help add moisture to the skin without exposing it to fatty materials. Some emollient is generally added to these types of products, but emollients exist that do not cause comedogenic reactions. In general, these are very lightweight products that feel wet rather than creamy when applied because most are fluids, not creams. Remember to make sure the final product was properly tested for comedogenicity or acnegenicity and is intended for use on acne-prone skin.

Unfortunately, some companies still use comedogenic ingredients in products supposedly intended for acne-prone skin. If you are not sure if the product has been tested, look at the ingredient label to see if there are known comedogenic ingredients listed. You should especially check the first few ingredients, because these ingredients are present in larger concentration in the product. Check your professional products as well as the client's home care products.

acne cosmetica
Acne caused or worsened by skin care and cosmetic products.

Sometimes, simply removing the offending products from a client's home care treatment will immediately improve the client's skin. For more information about emollients and comedogenicity, see Chapter 19 or see Dr. Mark Lees' book, *Skin Care: Beyond the Basics*, which is listed in the Additional Reading section at the end of this chapter.

Acne Treatment Tip #2—Control Oil

Clients who have very oily skin need more aggressive cleansers to remove the excess oil. More aggressive cleansers are normally foaming-type cleansers. Clients should be instructed to wash their skin twice a day with a foaming cleanser that is strong enough to remove oil but not so strong that it leaves the skin feeling stripped or irritated.

Cleansers for problem skin may contain medication such as salicylic acid or benzoyl peroxide. They may or may not contain granules that help bump off dead surface cells. Some of the newer foaming cleansers also contain AHAs such as glycolic acid. AHA-containing cleansers are not a substitute for a wearable AHA gel and should not be confused by an esthetician or a client. AHAs in cleansers are usually present in very low concentrations and are there to aid in the cleansing process. They are not meant as a treatment product.

Cleansing milks can be used to remove makeup but make sure that they do not contain comedogenic fats. Oily skin may need a second cleansing after makeup removal, using a rinsable foaming cleanser. This will remove any traces of emollient from the milk cleanser and make the client's skin feel clean, which is important to a client with acne-prone, oily skin.

Toners for oily and acne-prone skin contain agents that also help remove excess sebum and residue from cleansing milks. These ingredients include SD alcohol, witch hazel (*Hammamelis virginiana*) extract, salicylic acid, or glycolic acid. They may also contain sulfur as an antibacterial. Toners for oily, acne-prone skin may also contain soothing agents such as chamomile extract or aloe. These agents can help reduce redness and are used in conjunction with the sebum-reducing ingredients.

Acne Treatment Tip #3—Use Follicular Exfoliants to Remove And Prevent Comedones

Exfoliating agents are known as keratolytics, which means keratin-dissolving. These follicular exfoliants help existing comedones to break loose and help to shed surface keratinocytes that build up on the follicle wall as part of retention hyperkeratosis. Exfoliating agents can be cosmetic or medicinal.

Medicated antibacterial agents that kill p. acnes bacteria include benzoyl peroxide gels (in 2.5%, 5%, and 10% concentrations), sulfur and resorcinol lotions, or suspensions (sometimes sulfur is used by itself), or salicylic acid in a gel or liquid. These are generally applied at night to any area affected by breakouts and acne. These agents also function as keratolytics that loosen and flush debris from the follicles.

AHAs, including glycolic and lactic acids, are also excellent follicle exfoliants. For acne-prone skin, AHAs are usually in a lightweight gel-liquid formulation. AHAs are not considered drugs by the FDA, yet they are exfoliating and help remove follicular debris. AHAs are not antibacterial, which is one way they differ from the medications listed above, but they are less irritating. The removal of debris from the follicle exposes oxygen to it and helps to control the p. acnes bacteria. For minor acne, AHAs often work just as well as the medications without irritation, and the medications can be reserved for papules and pustules only. Selective treatment of individual blemishes is called **spot treatment.**

A frequent mistake made by both clients and estheticians is forgetting that the large visible acne lesions are not the only lesions within the skin. Microcomedones are constantly forming in acne-prone skin, and they must be controlled in order to control the acne. Clients acne with, especially adults, tend to only treat visible inflammatory lesions. The uses of stronger keratolytic agents are excellent for drying up existing inflammatory lesions (papules and pustules), but when they are applied only to these lesions, they are not treating the microcomedones.

Adults are afraid of overdrying the surrounding skin, which can make sun-

spot treatment
Selective treatment of individual blemishes.

damaged skin with wrinkles look worse temporarily. The answer to this problem is to choose the right keratolytic agent and to apply it to all areas of the skin that are affected by acne. AHAs, like glycolic or lactic acid, combined with a small amount of salicylic acid, often help flush out microcomedones and prevent reformation. This helps to keep follicles consistently clear of debris. These products need a concentration of at least 8%–10% AHA in a noncomedogenic liquid or gel base.

Not only does consistent coverage help prevent formation of new comedones, it can actually help with inflammatory acne. If a client with hormone fluctuations produces a sudden surge of sebum that is inflammatory to the follicle wall, the follicle is less likely to swell to the point that oxygen is cut off if the follicle is free of cell buildup. As long as the follicle does not become occluded, a papule will not form. The bottom line here is to use an overall exfoliation product on all areas of the face to prevent comedone formation. In addition, use stronger keratolytics such as sulfur, resorcinol, benzoyl peroxide, or concentrated 2% salicylic acid to treat individual lesions and help them dry up faster.

Teenage clients with more comedones may need these stronger agents applied to the entire face. In some cases, they may need all-over applications of an AHA gel, followed by an antibacterial such as sulfur or benzoyl peroxide. The more severe a client's acne is, the more she needs stronger exfoliants.

Acne Treatment Tip #4— Do Not Irritate the Skin

Overcleansing or overusing peeling agents may strip and irritate acne-prone skin. Overuse of masks and peeling agents such as benzoyl peroxide may result in inflammation that can also contribute to more flares. There are now studies that show that 2.5% benzoyl peroxide is often just as effective as 10%, yet it is less likely to cause irritation, dehydration, and peeling. In fact, there is a type of acne known as **acne detergicans,** which is caused from overcleansing the face.

Skin should be cleansed twice a day, never more than three times a day. Explain this to your clients and include this information in your acne literature so that they understand that acne is not caused by a lack of cleansing and that overtreatment can actually worsen the condition. This is especially important for teenage clients.

Once inflammatory lesions have cleared, a client may be able to reduce the strength of her treatment. The regular use of alpha-hydroxy acid gel on cleared skin helps to remove dead cells in the follicles that can cause the development of comedones, but it is not as irritating as other keratolytic ingredients. Stronger products can be used for spot treatment as necessary.

Acne Treatment Tip #5—Avoid Environmental Aggravators

Constant exposure to greasy environments, such as the kitchen in a fast food restaurant, may contribute to acne flaring. It is ironic that eating greasy food does not flare acne, but exposing the skin to the grease in the air may worsen the condition.

Heat and humidity are also a factor in acne. Teenagers in the Deep South have more severe problems with acne than other area of the United States. High humidity does not allow oils to evaporate easily from the skin, and the sebum stays on the skin's surface. Even adults with acne-prone skin who move to a humid area quickly learn that the moisturizer they were using in Minnesota provides too much emollient in Florida.

At first, sun exposure may seem to make acne better, because the sun does have an antibacterial effect on surface acne. But the heat may inflame the skin, or it may stimulate sebum production. In addition, ultraviolet rays that eventually destroy tissues in the skin induce peeling. Most of our sun damage occurs before age 18. Therefore, sun exposure at age 16 to clear up acne will show up as wrinkles and sagging at age 40.

A tan also camouflages redness in the skin. Teenagers may neglect acne treatment while they are tan, thinking they are cured. When fall comes and the pigment from the tan fades, they will quickly realize that the acne problem is not gone and, in fact, may be worse from neglecting to treat the skin over the summer.

acne detergicans
Acne caused from overcleansing the face.

Acne Treatment Tip #6—
Reduce Stress

Stress is definitely a contributing factor to acne, mainly because of the hormonal fluctuations that stress causes. Reduction of stress, especially in adults, may significantly improve acne conditions. A regular exercise program, even something as simple as a long, daily walk, are good for your head, your body, and your skin. Just make sure to wear a noncomedogenic sunscreen while you are walking.

Analysis and Treatment Of Problem Skin

The client with problem skin must look at treatment as a program. As mentioned in the concepts section above, clients must use non-comedogenic products at home and in the salon. They should also use effective cleansers to control oiliness and keratolytics to help loosen and prevent impactions. In addition, they should have regular deep cleansing treatments in the salon. These salon treatments require visits for deep

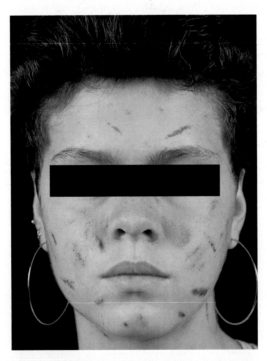

Figure 24–10 Flat, scraped lesions on a client's skin indicate acne excorieé.

cleansing with extractions, either weekly or biweekly, along with treatments to exfoliate, such as sulfur or benzoyl peroxide masks, and alphahydroxy exfoliating treatments.

During the first visit a thorough health history should be taken. Discuss with clients their history of acne-related problems. Ask if they have noticed any occurrences that fit any of the types of problems listed earlier in this chapter, such as hormone-related flares. You should also request information about their use of medications that may be related to problem skin.

Notice a client's current skin condition during the first visit. Note if a client has flat, scraped-looking lesions. She may also have small, circular tanned spots where acne lesions were once present. Flat, scraped lesions indicate that the client picks at her pimples. This condition is known as acne excorieé, which loosely means acne that has been scraped (Figure 24–10). The brown spots are from areas that have been scraped and then exposed to the sun. Scrapes, also called excoriations, on the skin remove the epidermis and may expose the dermis. Dark spots develop after these excoriations. More about treating acne excorieé can be found later in this chapter.

Feedback from clients is valuable. Because they see their skin every day, they can provide you with a tremendous amount of information about the behavior of their skin. Ask the client if she has noticed any pattern of acne breakouts, or if she has noticed anything about the frequency of the breakouts. Take a close look at the client's present home care habits and what products are being used. Check each product to see if it is appropriate for acne-prone or oily skin, and try to determine if the client is using any skin care or cosmetic products that may be comedogenic.

After cleansing the skin with a milk cleanser, carefully examine the skin. Make note of the grade of acne, how many lesions are present, and note if the lesions are in a particular area, such as the chin and jaw line, which may be indicative of hormone-related acne.

A consultation explaining the causes of acne, along with a brief description of treatment concepts, should be conducted with each client on the first visit. An explanation

SKILLS ● FOR ● SUCCESS

Joining Professional Organizations

Many students find that the exhilaration and sense of freedom that graduation brings is quickly replaced by the realization that they are suddenly out there on their own. Whether you choose to be an active or passive member, joining a professional organization is an excellent way to keep from being isolated.

One of the biggest issues students have starting out in any new career is the sudden lack of support that has been available to them through their school and their peers. Becoming involved in a professional organization that supports the field of esthetics can help maintain a sense of professional connection.

The cost of joining a professional association may vary depending upon the size of the group and its mission. However, the benefit of joining a quality organization generally outweighs any initial expense. A conscientious organization will work hard to keep its members satisfied and will have earned a reputation for promoting the vested interests of the group it represents. But before you join any organization, find out what the association dues are and what this entitles you to. Ask about the goals of the organization and request a copy of its mission statement.

Generally speaking, a professional organization should support its members by supplying such benefits and features as the following:

- Help to create and support professional standards
- Offer educational seminars led by nationally recognized experts
- Provide professional insurance, health insurance, and other special discounts that aid the professional
- Advise its members on key issues generic to the group
- Establish a forum for discussing mutual concerns
- Furnish opportunities to be in touch with other professionals

- Host events and activities that enrich you as a professional
- Maintain a resource list of other contacts, referrals, and information
- Offer journals, publications, and other information on new trends and research
- Leadership: the ability to attract industry leaders who can motivate others to make a difference and provide vision for the future
- Provide important information that impacts the group around regulations and laws
- Networking events, meetings, and directories
- Create a cohesive structure that promotes a unified voice to address matters important to the group as a whole

The following is a list of several professional organizations available to estheticians:

CIDESCO (Comite International D'Esthetique Et De Cosmetologie) / Esthetics America
National Cosmetology Association
401 North Michigan Avenue
Chicago, IL 10611

AAEA, American Aestheticians Education Association
President, Bonnie Day
1924 Westminster Drive
Carollton, TX 75007-2412
800-985-2232

AIA, Aesthetics International Association
2611 North Beltline Road, Suite 140
Sunnyvale, TX 75182
877-968-7539 or 972-203-8530
Fax: 972-203-8754

Associated Body Work & Massage Professionals
Bob Benson, President
1271 Sugarbush Drive, Evergreen, CO
800-458-2267
e-mail: expectmore@abmp.com

of step-by-step home care procedures is an important part of the treatment that should also be covered.

Home care will vary with the severity of the problem, the client's age, sun damage factors, the sensitivity of the skin, and if the client is under dermatological care as well as esthetic care. It must be emphasized that all products have to be noncomedogenic and that the client should not use any products that the esthetician is not aware of.

Basics of Home Care

The following guidelines can help treat and improve acne-prone skin.

Morning

1. Cleanse the face with a rinsable foaming cleanser. Rinse thoroughly. A soft cloth may be used if desired but not with granular cleansers.

   The cleanser will vary in strength or ingredients depending on the severity and condition of the skin. Cleansers that include exfoliants, such as polyethylene beads, glycolic or salicylic acid, or benzoyl peroxide, are reserved for oilier acne conditions. Clients with aging or sun-damaged skin or who may be using prescription exfoliants may need a nonmedicated, nonexfoliating cleanser, with a mild surfactant for effective but gentle cleansing. This accomplishes excess sebum removal without stripping the skin. If the client ever feels exceedingly dry or tight, or experiences redness after cleansing, the cleanser may be too strong. Stay clear of the eye area with this product.

2. Apply a toner/freshener with a dampened cotton ball.

   Nonalcoholic, nonexfoliating toners can be purchased in spray bottles and misted onto the face. Blot dry with a clean, dry towel. Toners vary in the content of drying agents, soothing agents, alcohol content, or keratolytic contact. More drying products are appropriate for oilier skins. Aging skin with acne problems may need a mild hydrating toner instead. Some toners may include soothing agents such as

chamomile extract, that help reduce redness. Stay clear of the eye area with this product.

3. Apply AHA exfoliating gel.

   An AHA exfoliating gel is applied and allowed to dry before sunscreen/day cream is applied. Generally, this is a liquid-gel with 10% AHA, which may include glycolic or a mixture of glycolic, lactic, or other AHAs. Salicylic acid is often added for its antibacterial and exfoliating properties. Stay clear of the eye area with this type of product. Please note that exfoliating gels are not appropriate for clients using prescription keratolytic drugs such as tretinoin, adapalene, or tazarotene.

4. Apply sunscreen/day cream.

   Any sunscreen or day cream should be noncomedogenic and designed for the appropriate skin type. Most will contain a hydrating ingredient to help improve moisture, but the emollient content may vary with the client's oiliness. All skin types should be treated with daily broad-spectrum sunscreen of SPF-15 or higher.

5. Apply eye cream as needed.

6. Apply makeup if desired.

   Foundation, powder, and blush should all be noncomedogenic. Makeup should not worsen acne if it is noncomedogenic and nonacnegenic. Foundation should be as free as possible of emollients, because this skin type makes enough of its own. Foundations that dry to a matte finish and that are low in, or free from, emollients help absorb sebaceous secretions during the day, reducing the shine associated with oiliness.

Evening

1. Makeup is removed using a cleansing milk and a soft cloth, shammie, or sponge.

   The cleansing milk should be nonoily, designed specifically for oily or acne-prone skin, and not leave an obvious residue. Eye makeup can be removed using a separate product designed for makeup removal.

2. If the face still feels oily, cleanse a second time with the rinsable foaming cleanser used in the morning.

   This will remove any residue from the milk cleanser and make the client feel completely clean. Many clients do not feel completely clean unless they have washed their face. This is acceptable, as long as the cleanser does not strip or irritate the skin. Stay clear of the eye area with this product.

3. Apply toner as in the morning routine.

   Stay clear of the eye area with this product.

4. Apply AHA gel as in the morning routine.

   Stay clear of the eye area with this product. Again, note that exfoliating gels are not appropriate for clients using prescription keratolytic drugs such as tretinoin, adapalene, or tazarotene.

5. Apply medication or a drying agent to individual blemishes as needed.

   Clients with more severe problems may need a light all-over application of this product. Stay clear of the eye area. Clients using topical medications prescribed by the dermatologist will use these drugs, instead of over-the-counter medications from the esthetician, as specifically directed by the physician.

6. Apply hydration fluid if needed.

   A hydrator designed for very oily, problem-prone skin should be extremely light-weight and very low in emollients. It should also be thoroughly tested to make sure that it is noncomedogenic, so that it does not contribute to the cell buildup that can cause acne lesions.

7. Apply eye cream as needed.

Mask Therapy

Regular use of exfoliating masks at home can be beneficial for improving acne skin. Clay-based masks with sulfur or benzoyl peroxide can be used as often as every other night on thicker acne skin. On thin skin, the mask may need to be used a little less often.

After the skin has cleared significantly, masks can be used once or twice a week for maintenance. The eye areas, neck, and other dryer areas should be treated with a hydrating mask instead of a clay mask.

Treating Acne Excorieé

Clients with acne excorieé must be treated a little differently than other clients with problem skin. It is important to tell the client, gently, that some of the problem with her skin is the fact that she scratches and picks at the lesions and impactions. Encourage the client not to obsess over her skin in the mirror, because this is when much of the picking occurs. Suggest to the client that when she is tempted to pick, she should apply a mask treatment instead, or call you, and you will try to move up her appointment.

Some clients pick subconsciously and are not even aware that they are doing it. They often do this when they are reading, watching television, or even while asleep. Suggest that the client wear cotton gloves at night so that she will not be able to scratch her skin with her fingernails while she is sleeping.

Clients who self-excoriate often come to the salon concerned about their hyperpigmented spots. It should be explained that these spots are caused by picking and that the acne and the self-picking must be brought under control to keep the dark spots from forming. The esthetician should treat the acne, not the brown spots. The spots will often fade by themselves when the acne and the picking are brought under control.

Clients who pick also tend to overtreat and overexfoliate their skin. Make sure you stress *gentle care* to the client, and be aware if the client's skin seems irritated during future treatments in the salon. Widespread redness or flaking may be indicative of overuse of exfoliating agents such as AHAs or benzoyl peroxide.

Medical Treatment for Acne

Clients with minor acne that is not responding to problem skin treatment in the salon should be referred to a dermatologist for medical treatment. A dermatologist must treat more severe forms of acne, such as grades 3 and 4. Esthetic treatment may still be of great benefit as an adjunct to medical treatment. Acne patients under dermatological care still need noncomedogenic cosmetics and skin care products, and most still need salon treatments to extract comedones.

Traditional treatment for acne by a dermatologist includes keratolytic drugs such as tretinoin (Retin-A), which is only available by prescription. It is manufactured in gel, cream, and liquid formulations, as well as a micronized form that is designed to be less irritating. Tretinoin is a keratolytic and works by normalizing the exfoliation of the follicular lining. It is a much stronger exfoliant than any of the over-the-counter medications or cosmetic exfoliants. Tretinoin has several side effects, mainly cosmetic, including redness, inflammation, irritation, dehydration, and flaking. Tretinoin-treated skin is much more sensitive to many skin care products and cosmetics. Irritants, other exfoliating agents, drying alcohols such as SD alcohol and isopropyl alcohol, mentholated products, fragranced products, essential oils, overdrying masks, and any other stimulating product should *not* be used or recommended for a client using tretinoin. Areas of skin treated with tretinoin should *never* be waxed.

Other keratolytics are used topically in a fashion similar to tretinoin. These include azelaic acid (Azelex), adapalene (Differin), and tazarotene (Tazorac). They may have side effects similar to tretinoin. Clients using these topical medications who are also being treated in the salon must be treated with special care. Their skin is much more sensitive and thinner than normal skin, and it is especially more sensitive than typical oily and acne-prone skin. Treat them with nonfragranced, noncomedogenic products that are not drying or stimulating. Scrubs, exfoliants of any type, drying clay masks, and other drying or stimulating products should be avoided both in the salon and at home.

Topical antibiotics such as erythromycin, which is sometimes combined with benzoyl peroxide (Benzamycin), are also prescribed, sometimes in conjunction with tretinoin. These are antibiotics and they kill bacteria and reduce inflammation. Another popular topical antibiotic is clindamycin (Cleocin-T). This drug is often prescribed with tretinoin or another keratolytic agent, but it should not be applied at the same time as the keratolytic agent. Another topical antibiotic is sodium sulfacetamide (Klaron, Sulfacet-R).

Oral antibiotics are sometimes prescribed for patients suffering from more inflammatory acne, such as grade 3 acne. Tetracycline, minocycline, doxycycline, and erythromycin oral medications are four oral antibiotics that are often prescribed by a dermatologist. They may have anti-inflammatory properties as well. Tetracycline and minocycline both have contraindications for sun exposure, because they increase sun sensitivity.

Accutane is an oral form of a vitamin A derivative called isotretinoin that is prescribed for severe grade 3 and grade 4 cystic acne. It is the only drug routinely effective against cysts, and it helps normalize sebum production and follicular exfoliation. Accutane has many serious side effects, and may cause birth defects and raise blood lipid levels. Routine monitoring of the blood must be performed during Accutane use. More minor side effects include dry nose and mouth, severe drying of the skin including cracked lips, and hair loss. Clients taking Accutane cannot use any exfoliating or drying agents and must be exceedingly careful with skin care products that are stimulating or possibly irritating. Many of the products they may have been using to help control their acne prior to using Accutane are no longer usable. However, nonfragranced, noncomedogenic moisturizers, lip balm, and very gentle cleansers are beneficial to the client using Accutane. These clients cannot be waxed anywhere on the body during treatment and for several months after treatment. Soothing, hydrating facials using nonfragranced, nonclogging simple hydration products can be helpful in reducing dryness. For more information on Accutane and tretinoin, see Chapter 18.

Salon Treatments for Oily And Acne-Prone Skin

The main purpose of salon treatments for oily and problem skin is to clear the follicle of impactions. In the ideal situation, problem skin clients should be advised to use their home care products for two weeks prior to their first salon treatment. The routine use of home care as described above will help loosen the comedones and impactions for easier removal through extraction. It is not always possible to wait two weeks for the client to use the recommended home care, but you will find that extraction is much easier if the client is performing proper home care before and between salon visits.

In the salon, loosening of the comedones may be accomplished through exfoliation, desincrustation, or a combination of both. Desincrustation is the softening of sebum deposits through the application of special products that loosen the hardened sebaceous material that is the binding part of the comedones. Think of a plug of hardened sebum as hardened grease in a skillet. You must soak this greasy skillet in detergent to soften it in order to clean it. Sebum is a fat, just like grease, and must be broken up to loosen the comedonal plug. Desincrustation products are made of an alkaline substance, often a complex of surfactants, that breaks up the edges of the plug that are exposed to it. For deeper penetration of the desincrustation product, galvanic current may be applied. For more information on this, see Chapter 8.

Treatment Procedures for Acne

Before beginning any skin treatment, the esthetician must put on a pair of disposable latex or vinyl gloves. This is especially important when treating problem skin. The skin is first cleansed, as any skin would be at the beginning of treatment. For extra oily and thick-textured skin, perform a second cleansing with a foaming cleanser or a mild scrub. Do *not* use toner, because it can constrict the follicle openings, which need to stay dilated for cleansing.

Apply the desincrustation product and apply steam. Check the manufacturer's instructions for the particular desincrustation product for exact instructions. Generally, the desincrustation is left on the skin for about 8 minutes during a steam. For only a few clogged pores, galvanic current may not be needed. For thicker, oilier, and more impacted skin, galvanic current is very helpful.

When choosing galvanic current, apply desincrustation fluid and leave it on the skin for about four minutes. Proceed to galvanic current on negative. Make sure that the client does not have contraindications for electrical therapy. Remove the remaining desincrustation product with wet sponges or cotton pads. Leaving the skin damp, but not wet, begin extraction in the chin area.

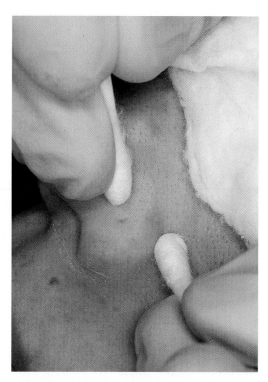

Figure 24–11 Holding the swabs as you would pencils, gently press down and in on either side of the follicle.

With your gloved hands, spread a very small area of the skin, keeping it taut between your two hands. Hold this position with the balls of the hands, just under the thumbs. Take two cotton swabs and hold them like you would a pencil, one in each hand (Figure 24–11). Gently push down and in with the cotton swabs on either side of an impacted follicle. The impaction will expel. If it does not expel readily, apply the same technique around the edges of the impaction. Do not increase the pressure. It is very important not to be overly aggressive with extractions. Too much pressure can bruise the skin and can be painful to the client. If the comedo does not expel after several gentle attempts to extract it, leave it alone and proceed to another comedo.

Follow this technique from one area to another on the face, working a bit on each area. Focus on the largest comedones first. They are more unsightly and are usually more easily extracted. Smaller impactions will loosen with proper home care.

Some estheticians are trained to use their fingertips, wrapped in thin, damp, sheet

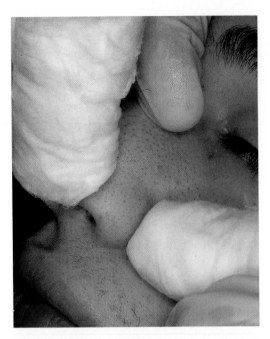

Figure 24–12 Dampened sheet cotton wrapped around the index fingers, called finger cots, can also be used for extraction.

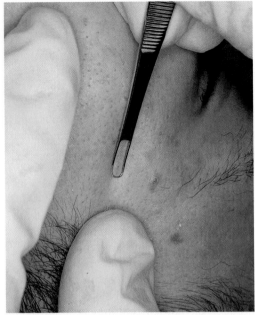

Figure 24–13 Place the loop of the comedone extractor over the lesion so that the lesion is centered in the loop area.

cotton commonly known as finger cots, to extract (Figure 24–12). This technique is certainly acceptable, but many estheticians find the cotton swab technique to be more precise and more effective due to the size of the cotton swab tip versus the size of a fingertip. The cotton swab technique is particularly useful around the nose and nostrils, where large fingertips are cumbersome.

A comedone extractor is a special metal instrument designed to apply pressure to the outside edges of a clogged follicle or open comedo. Comedone extractors have a stainless steel handle with small loops on either end. They are not designed to treat anything but open comedones or sebaceous filaments. Comedone extractors can be very effective but may be more painful than the cotton swab technique.

To use the comedo extractor, prepare the skin as you would for any other sort of extraction. Place the loop over the lesion to be extracted, so that the entire lesion is within the interior of the loop area (Figure 24–13). Press straight down on the extractor, which applies pressure to the sides of the impacted follicle and pushes the impaction up.

A lancet is a very small, sharp, disposable instrument used to dilate follicles (Figure 24–14). It is especially helpful in extracting closed comedones. Lancets must always be sterile and disposable. Most lancets are presterilized and are to be used only once. You should never actually puncture the skin.

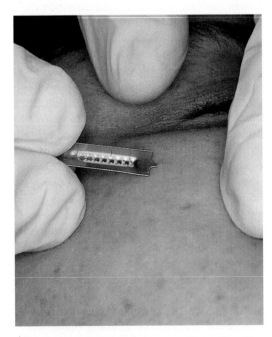

Figure 24–14 Hold the lancet parallel to the skin and gently insert the tip into the follicle opening.

The lancet is used only to dilate the follicle opening to make extraction of the closed comedo easier. By dilating the opening of the follicle, pressure is relieved on the follicle walls, making them much less likely to rupture during the extraction procedure. The dilated opening will then serve as a release for the sebaceous debris to exit the follicle.

After preparing the skin with desincrustation, remove any excess desincrustation product. Looking carefully through the magnifying lamp, find the opening to the closed comedone. Hold the lancet as you would a pencil, only with your thumbnail facing upward, with your fingers supporting the lancet. This means that the lancet is being held parallel to the skin, *never* at a 90-degree angle. Gently insert the lancet into the opening. Do not force the lancet; it should slip very easily into the opening. The technique is similar to one you would use to pull a splinter from the skin.

After you have dilated the follicle, take a pair of cotton swabs and gently press down and in around the closed comedo. You will see the impaction emerge or expel from the follicle. Move the swabs to another angle and gently press again to make sure all the debris has been expelled from the follicle. When working on many closed comedones, try dilating several in an area, and then allow them to sit for a minute before beginning the pressure technique. Dilating the follicles allows the sebaceous material lodged in the follicle to shift outward toward the surface of the skin. Waiting a minute or two before applying pressure will allow this "shifting" of the debris to occur.

Extraction should not last for more than ten minutes in one visit. Many estheticians are guilty of performing extraction marathons. Too many extractions in one session is traumatic to the skin and can result in inflammatory flares, in addition to being painful to the client. It is a better choice to see the client more often than to extract for too long in one session.

Because follicle dilation actually makes extraction a safer procedure, many states now permit the technique but some states still do not. Make sure you check with your instructor about whether this technique is permitted in your state

Extraction is one of the most beneficial parts of esthetic treatment and also one of the most difficult techniques to learn. You must practice to be good at extraction, and practice takes patience.

After you have finished the extraction part of the treatment, you must apply an antiseptic or bactericidal agent to the area that has been extracted. Often a medicated toner is applied with a cotton pad. The solution applied should have a slightly acidic pH. This helps to constrict the follicles, making the pores look smaller.

Benzoyl peroxide or sulfur-resorcinol is sometimes applied to individual extracted lesions. This is particularly effective for papules, pustules, and more serious breakouts. With grade 3 acne, it is a good idea to apply 5% benzoyl peroxide lightly to all areas affected by the acne.

Extraction sometimes causes inflammation of the follicles. This can result in minor acnegenic reactions to the procedure. The client may call the next day complaining of one or more pimples. To help prevent this surfacing reaction, many estheticians apply a soothing agent after extraction. Post-extraction serums are commercially available. They are mixtures of soothing and antibacterial agents. These serums can help prevent breakouts that may occur after the treatment. The serum can be applied with gloved hands or can be used with the high frequency machine.

High Frequency

High frequency is helpful to acne-prone skin. The current helps stimulate blood and lymph flow and works as a surface bactericidal agent. High frequency can also reduce swelling of papules and pustules.

When using high frequency for problem skin, unfold a gauze square across the face. Apply the frequency to all areas of the face using a mushroom-shaped electrode. Individual lesions can be treated by gently lifting the electrode off the skin, directly in the area of a papule or pustule. This is known as fulguration, more commonly referred to as zapping or sparking. Application of high frequency using fulguration over an individual pimple or papule causes a

Step By Step Treatment for Problem Skin

Purpose: To remove excess oils, dislodge and extract open and closed comedones, and extract sebaceous filaments in the follicles; to gently exfoliate the skin to remove dead cell buildup on the surface; to improve surface smoothness and help constrict follicles (minimize pore appearance)

Procedure

Cleanse

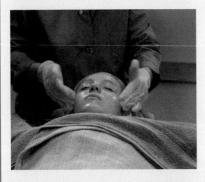

1 Remove eye makeup and lipstick with eye makeup remover.

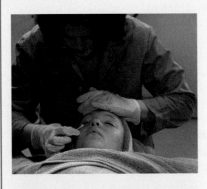

2 Apply a cleansing milk for oily skin with gloved hands. Use circular motions to thoroughly remove all makeup.

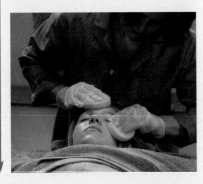

3 Rinse the skin well with wet shammies or sponges.

Analyze

3 During the skin analysis, you may evaluate the degree of oiliness or impactions. This will help determine the exact procedure for exfoliation or the strength of the products used, such as an ampoule, serum, or cleansing mask.

Second cleanse and desincrust

4 Begin steaming the skin. While steam is being applied, perform a second cleansing with a foaming, surfactant-type cleanser. Apply a small amount of foaming cleanser on dampened skin with gloved hands. Using circular movements, work up a light lather. If you choose to exfoliate the skin, you may use a rotating brush machine, but avoid this if the skin has many inflammatory lesions (papules and pustules). Instead you may apply a granular cleanser, again with small gentle, circular movements. For extra oily skin, you may choose to use an exfoliating scrub that contains an antibacterial such as benzoyl peroxide or salicylic acid. Remove the scrub thoroughly with wet sponges or shammies.

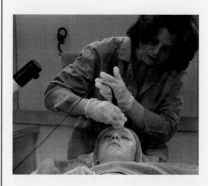

5 Apply a desincrustation lotion to all clogged or oily areas. Do not apply it to dry areas, such as the eye area or the neck. For very oily skin, you may wish to penetrate the desincrustant with negative galvanic current, assuming that the client has no contraindications for electrical treatment. Perform galvanic treatment for about 2–4 minutes. Remove excess desincrustant thoroughly with shammies or sponges. The entire desincrustant procedure should take about 8 minutes.

Extract

6 The skin should be free of all products but not completely dry for extraction. Begin extraction in the chin and neck area first and work up the face, ending at the forehead. This technique will help you avoid contact with any blood or body fluid that may have surfaced from the extraction process.

> **saponifiers**
> Soothing agents that help liquefy sebaceous materials.

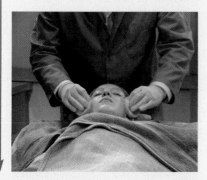

7 After extraction is complete, wipe the face with a sponge, shammie, or cotton pad soaked with a freshener or toner that contains an antiseptic such as salicylic acid.

8 Apply an ampoule or serum for oily or acneic skin on the extracted areas. This ampoule may include soothing agents or **saponifiers** that help to further liquefy any sebaceous materials left after the extraction.

Treat and correct

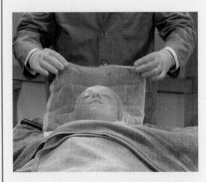

9 Unfold a 16-ply 4" × 4" square of gauze and place it across the face.

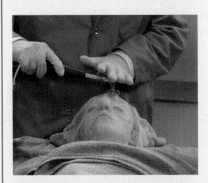

10 Apply high frequency on top of the gauze using the mushroom-shaped electrode. The high-frequency treatment should last about 2 minutes.

Massage

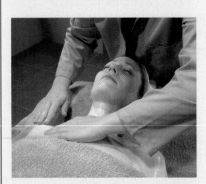

11 Massage is generally avoided on very oily and acneic skin. You may perform massage to areas not affected by acne or excess oiliness, such as the hands, the décolleté (if not affected), and the arms. Massage on oily areas may actually stimulate more sebum production and may put pressure on impactions that have not been removed.

Mask

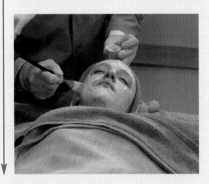

12 Apply a clay-based mask selected for the particular degree of oiliness. This mask may be applied with gloved hands or with a special mask brush. Masks for acne skin often contain sulfur and may contain soothing agents. For oily skin, they may only contain the clays, which will dry over a few minutes, helping to absorb the liquefied sebum and remove dead cell buildup on the surface of the skin. If the skin is oily and sensitive, you may prefer a gel mask designed for acne.

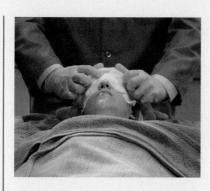

13 After the mask has dried completely (gel masks do not dry much), usually about 10 minutes, soften the mask with a warm, wet cloth or towel. Gently manipulate the skin through the towel to help loosen and remove the mask. Remove any excess mask with wet sponges or shammies.

Complete

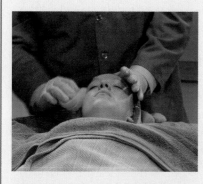

14 Reapply freshener with sponges, or you can use a cold spray machine if the freshener does not contain medication or alcohol. Allow the skin to air dry 1–2 minutes.

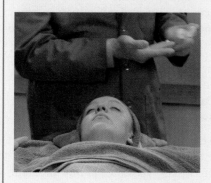

15 Apply a sunscreen/day fluid designed for oily/acne-prone skin.

Home maintenance

Clients being treated for acne-prone or problem skin should have a salon treatment administered about every two weeks until the skin is clear. Proper home care is essential and is the foundation of the program. Once the skin has cleared, monthly salon treatments should be performed.

Clients must be taught that acne-prone skin is an ongoing problem that is not *cured* just because the skin is clear. Acne-prone skin can be managed on a continual basis, but the client must be diligent.

drying effect that speeds the disappearance of the pimple.

When using high frequency, especially with problem skin, be careful not to use it over any product that contains alcohol, which can be flammable and, obviously, very dangerous.

Masks for Problem Skin

Masks are an essential part of salon treatment for problem skin. Masks for problem skin are usually clay-based and contain exfoliants and antibacterial agents. They dry and help absorb excess oils, as well as remove dead surface cells. Some are medicated with benzoyl peroxide or sulfur, which help to kill acne bacteria.

A mask should be applied to the skin after treatment with high frequency. It should be allowed to dry for approximately 10–15 minutes, and then be removed with cool, wet cotton or sponges. This is usually followed up with an application of toner to help clean up the excess mask. A sunscreen, appropriate for oily or acne skin, is applied as a final step.

Massage and Problem Skin

Massage generally should be avoided on oilier skin and especially on acne-prone skin. Massage helps to stimulate sebaceous glands, which is not helpful for acne. Massage also can put pressure on infected lesions, which can further inflame the skin. Additionally, massage oils should not be applied to acne or acne-prone skin.

Summary

Acne is a hereditary and hormonal skin condition that can be treated but not cured. Flare-ups can arise from stress, comedogenic skin care and makeup products, heat and sun exposure, and hormonal fluctuations. Severe forms or grades of acne need medical treatment, but all types of acne can benefit from salon and home care treatments that emphasize noncomedogenic and nonacnegenic products and gentle extractions.

Discussion Questions

1. Discuss the etiology of acne. What old wives' tales or stereotypical information can you think of that may need to be dispelled when helping clients understand the origin of this condition?

2. Give definitions for the following terms: papule, pustule, comedo, open comedone, closed comedone, cyst, and anaerobic bacteria.

3. Create a protocol for treating the different grades of acne. Define the best approach to developing an understanding of the contribution that estheticians make in helping dermatologists care for patients afflicted with grades 3 and 4 acne.

4. How does the production of hormones affect acne? Formulate your discussion in terms of the effect on teenagers and adults.

5. Explain the main differences between comedonal acne and inflammatory acne. Frame your answer in terms of cause and effect.

6. What is meant by acnegenic or comedogenic in reference to skin care products? Research those ingredients known to increase this factor.

7. Describe a basic protocol for treating acne, noting the best way to treat different skin types such as oily, problem skin and aging combination skin that is prone to adult acne flare-ups. What products would you recommend for home care?

8. What precautions should the esthetician take when treating clients taking prescription drugs such as topical tretinoin (Retin-A), azelaic (Differin), antibiotics (Cleocin-T) or oral medications such as tetracycline and doxycycline or Accutane?

9. Extraction is a significant component in any professional acne treatment. Create a list of best practices when performing extractions, keeping safety standards in mind.

Additional Reading

Ceaser, Jennifer. 2000. *Everything You Need to Know About Acne.* New York: The Rosen Publishing Group, Inc.

Chu, Anthony, and Ann Lovell. 1999. *The Good Skin Doctor: A Dermatologist's Guide to Beating Acne.* Great Britain: Thorsons GBR.

Lees, Mark. 2001. *Skin Care: Beyond the Basics.* Clifton Park, N.Y.: Milady, an imprint of Delmar Learning, a division of Thomson Learning, Inc.

Helpful Web Sites

http://www.acne.org
http://www.dermadoctor.com

Chapter 25
Ethnic Skin: Morphology And Treatment

Chapter Objectives:

After reading this chapter, you should be able to:

- Understand the general differences in ethnic skin.
- Identify the special challenges specific to black, Asian, Hispanic, and Native American skin.
- Describe the recommended treatments for each ethnic skin type.

Chapter Outline

Introduction
Black Skin
Asian Skin
Hispanic and Native American Skin

Introduction

Throughout the world and in all ethnic groups skin has the same function. Individuals possess skin characteristics common in their culture. In this chapter, we refer to ethnic skin types as black, Asian, Hispanic, and Native American. Each type contains various levels of melanin, which makes up its color. In a transient world, cultural distinctions are becoming less apparent in some regions. In the U.S., we are a mixed culture of nationalities resulting in a variety of different types of skin. This is why it is so important for the esthetician to understand the differences in ethnic skin, how to properly treat it, and contraindications for ethnic skin care. The main common element in all ethnic skin is the enhanced level of melanin over that of Caucasian skin.

Although all skin is susceptible to solar damage resulting in premature aging, individuals with fair skin or Caucasian skin are at a higher risk due to their decreased melanin levels. The less melanin, the more damage. The purpose of melanin in our skin is to act as a filter, thereby reducing the amount of ultraviolet (UV) radiation that is able to penetrate the skin. Even though ethnic skin has more melanin, and is generally more protected against UV damage, skin of any color can experience some degree of damage due to sun or UV radiation exposure.

As an esthetician, there are some points of caution that should be kept in mind when treating ethnic skin. Some ethnic skin may require gentle noninvasive treatments. This skin type appears to be more resilient because of its thicker appearance. However, it should be understood that even ethnic skin will have different sensitivity levels. Overly aggressive treatment can result in serious side effects that can be long lasting.

Black Skin

Probably the most misunderstood aspect of black skin is the erroneous idea that, because black skin is often shiny, it is always oily (Figure 25–1). While it is true that black skin has more and larger sudoriferous and sebaceous glands than Caucasian skin, this does not mean that black skin is oilier. Black skin

Figure 25–1 There is little difference structurally between black and Caucasian skin.

tends to be a little more acid than Caucasian skin; therefore, it can be more dehydrated and dry. It is a common perception that the oil and sweat prevent the skin from being oily. The results the client expects, and the individual needs of a client's skin will determine the correct treatment plan. Black skin should not be placed in one or two categories. As with any skin, black skin needs to be individually analyzed to determine the correct treatment procedure. It should be noted that oil-based creams will contribute to the natural shine of black skin. Therefore, unless the client wants shiny skin, the esthetician should look at products with ingredients that do not contain a lot of oil. Powders do well as long as they are not too powdery.

Challenges of Black Skin

Although there is little difference structurally between black skin and Caucasian skin, there are a few skin disorders that black skin may experience more often than Caucasian skin.

Hyperkeratosis
A common problem for black skin is hyperkeratosis, a thickening of the horny layer of the epidermis, which results in a higher rate of cell turnover. This condition is less common in Caucasian skin. Because of this increased cell turnover, black skin desquamates or "sheds" dead skin cells more

readily. The accumulation of dead cells on the surface of the skin gives an ashy cast to the skin.

Exfoliation can remove the dead cell layers more effectively as long as the exfoliation is not done too aggressively. The key would be to use an exfoliation that is highly effective but, if necessary, due to the possible sensitivity level, less irritating. Pretesting of various exfoliation products is recommended.

Pigmentation

Although the number of melanocytes is basically the same in Caucasian and black skin, the amount of melanin produced by the melanosome itself is greater in black skin. This, combined with the fact that black skin is much thicker, provides better protection from ultraviolet radiation. As a result, skin cancer is not prevalent in black skin. However, the skin can be pigmented in a blotchy manner. It is important to remember that sunscreen is necessary for black skin as well.

Black skin is often prone to a number of pigmentary disorders including vitiligo (Figure 25–2), a form of hypopigmentation where pigment is all but lost in certain areas of the skin. **Leukoderma,** the absence of pigment—partial or total—in the skin, is another form of vitiligo. Hyperpigmentation, excessive pigmentation, easily occurs when injured by trauma (postinflammatory hyperpigmentation), extractions, general facial eruptions, and sun exposure. One must be very careful doing extractions because the extracted area will often hyperpigment leaving a darkened mark for some time. Black skin is also susceptible to pigmentation problems due to hormonal imbalances. Melasma and chloasma are medical terms for hyperpigmentation due to hormones. This includes the use of oral contraceptives, hormone replacement therapies, and pregnancy. This condition is particularly common in black skin. Treatments including azelaic acid and lower concentrations of hydroquinone are generally successful for black skin with mild to moderate melasma. However, clients with more severe melasma should be referred to a physician for treatments that are more highly concentrated.

Sensitivity

Do not let the dark pigment of the skin make you think that black skin is resistant to allergic or dermatitis reactions. The skin can actually be quite sensitive and can easily react. Black skin can become inflamed and erythema can develop. Erythema will appear more bluish or purplish in black skin, and even though it is not as noticeable, it can be just as problematic. The erythema should be treated with soothing and calming procedures, as you would treat other skin types with similar problems.

Keloids

When performing extractions or anything aggressive, black skin is highly subject to keloid formation, which is a hypertrophic (raised) scarring reaction (Figure 25–3). Scars are formed through the action of the fibroblastic cells in an attempt to heal a wound. Keloidal tissue is sometimes formed by the fibroblasts continuing to deposit collagen at the wound site, which results in a disorganization of collagen bundles that thicken and pile up. This protrusion may have to be medically excised and sometimes radiation is given to prevent continued growth. Often black skin forms keloids in response to body piercing, wounds, and surgical incisions. It could be dangerous to attempt aggressive dermabrasion on postacne scars on black skins because of the tendency to form keloids. It may be just as dangerous to use a lancet or comedone extractor. Proceed with great caution when treating and extracting black skin.

leukoderma
Another form of vitiligo, the absence of pigment, partial or total, in the skin.

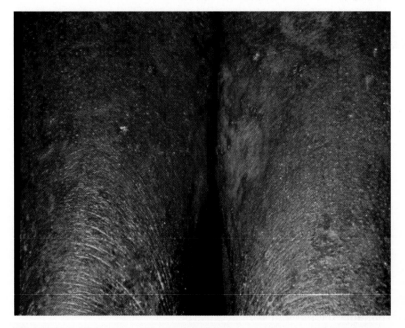

Figure 25–2 Vitiligo is a skin disorder characterized by a partial absence of pigment in the skin.

Aging and Treatment

Healthy black skin does not show the effects of aging as early as Caucasian skin. As a general rule, the connective tissue in black skin is in much better shape than the Caucasian counterpart, because of the abundance of elastic fibers and the natural pigmentary UV protection. Black skin simply does not age as quickly as Caucasian skin, so antiaging and firming treatments are not as popular among black clients.

The most effective and most desired treatments for black skin are exfoliation treatments to remove the hyperkeratinized cells and clear the ashy cast to the skin. Cleansings should concentrate on cleaning out the hair follicle opening, which is often clogged at the subsurface level with hyperkeratinized cells and sebum plugs. Finally, use caution when using brightening products to address pigmentary problems. Careless use of pigment lightening substances could cause more splotchiness in the lightening process. Sometimes, in an effort to lighten the skin, the opposite effect occurs whereby the skin becomes more pigmented or splotchy. Carefully advise your client to use such home care agents with caution and focus only on the areas needing localized lightening. As with any use of melanin-blocking ingredients, such as the most commonly used—hydroquinone, kojic acid, azeleic acid—the skin will become more photosensitive. When using any products for hyperpigmentation, advise the client with black skin to avoid *any* sun or UV exposure. These clients should also use a daily higher level SPF sunblock.

Asian Skin

Due to the elastic nature and compactness of the connective tissue, Asian skin does not show the effects of aging until long after its Caucasian counterpart. Asian skin, however, is probably the most sensitive to topical treatments of any kind. It is easily irritated and sensitized by alphahydroxy acids (AHAs) and betahydroxy acids (BHAs). One may not know what the reaction will be to these exfoliating agents. Asian skin has a great tendency to hyperpigment especially when traumatized by the use of higher levels of

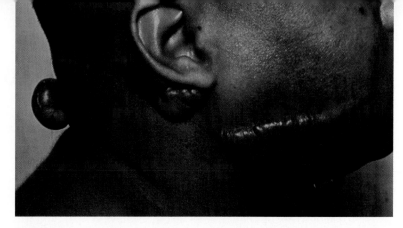

Figure 25–3 Black skin is highly subject to the formation of keloids, or raised scars.

AHAs, BHAs, Retin-A, and other fairly aggressive substances.

A better choice for exfoliating Asian skin would be slow-releasing enzymes, gommage rub-off mechanical exfoliation, or lower level AHAs or BHAs. The elastic resiliency of Asian skin makes it a good candidate for rub-off exfoliants and peel-off masks (Figure 25–4, p. 25–7). Asian skin, as stated earlier, has a tendency to hyperpigment. A great deal of care should be taken to ensure that Asian clients avoid the sun and wear a daily sunblock. If the use of acids for exfoliation is added to the treatment regime, the skin will become more photosensitive and the risk of hyperpigmentation increases. Sunscreens and sunblocks with a minimum SPF of 15 are the most important products an Asian client can use. Splotchiness and age spots are considered to be the worst facial traumas for them. Asians are constantly seeking various skin lightening and whitening treatments to remove and decrease pigmentation. Refer to Chapter 23 for additional information on hyperpigmentation.

Some commonly used products may contain hydroquinone in a 2% maximum concentration. Some of the more natural substances such as bearberry (*Arctostaphylus uva-urusi*) and melissa or lemon balm (*Melissa officinalis*) extracts are used. The more aggressive magnesium ascorbyl phosphate or kojic acid are also used.

Asians should use high-quality sunscreens or sunblocks that contain top physical blocks as well as screens with titanium dioxide. This is the number one measure to guard against pigmentation. Titanium dioxide also has anti-inflammatory properties, which is very appealing to sensitive Asian skin.

Asian skin is sometimes prone to develop keloid-type scars after injury. Much caution

SKILLS (FOR) SUCCESS

Resolving Conflict

We are all different. Some of us are sociable, some quiet and more introverted. Some of us have lots of energy; others are more laid-back. Some of us are opinionated, while others may be more tentative. Some of us are realistic and others more inclined to use their imagination. The list of comparisons is endless. That is what makes the world an interesting place.

But the important thing to remember, in terms of human behavior, is that we are in a constant state of flux. The world is a dynamic place with lots going on and many ways to interpret an action. As a result, misunderstandings and conflicts are bound to occur. To cope with stress, change, or differences in the workplace you must be willing to look at things objectively.

The mission statement of most skin care clinics and day spas is bound to include a sentence or two about establishing a caring, nurturing environment. Salons take great pride in being a haven away from the madness of day-to-day living. This does not mean that there will not be challenges in *your* day. Your job is to provide others with relief from anxiety. This supportive role will require you to develop a variety of interpersonal skills.

Learning to get along with others is an important aspect of working in a service-oriented industry such as esthetics. You will need to cope with many different personalities on a daily basis. This includes clients and coworkers. To be suc-

cessful you will need to adopt many of the standards that make a good team player—trust, unity, support, responsibility, respect, and caring. Still you will need to develop coping mechanisms that encourage cooperation when these break down. If a conflict does occur, take time to consider that we all have different styles and methods of doing things. At times you may need to

count to ten and think before you speak

distance yourself from a situation to regain your composure

avoid engaging in a no-win situation or argument

get another opinion before making a judgment

be assertive and stand your ground

direct a situation to a higher authority, if necessary

take the high road and keep from criticizing

help others meet their goals by assuming more responsibility

Whatever circumstances you are forced to deal with, trust that you have the power to make positive choices. Ultimately, if you are invested in working cooperatively with others, and practice good communication techniques, the potential for conflict is decreased.

should be taken in aggressive treatment of any kind that may break open the skin. This includes extractions, postacne dermabrasion, vacuum bruising, etc. In simple terms, all treatments for Asians should concentrate on soothing, calming, and gentle care while working to avoid or correct pigmentation splotches. Like black skin, Asians age slowly but they are still interested in antiaging treatments. As in black skin care, the most appropriate treatments for Asian skin should meet the needs of the individual's skin. Asians are very accustomed to following a good skin care regimen. They will honor a complete routine and will readily change products according to the seasons, age, and individual skin problems.

Hispanic and Native American Skin

Hispanic and Native American skin suffers from the same potential abuses as both black and Asian skin (Figure 25–5). They, too, are predisposed to pigmentary problems and should be cautious about the sun. Although Hispanic or Native American skin does not normally sunburn, like other ethnic skin, it may hyperpigment and develop uneven pigment and splotchiness. Aggressive AHA or BHA treatments may also cause temporary hyperpigmentation. It will subside, however, more quickly in Hispanic or Native American skin than in Asian or black skin.

Figure 25–4 The elastic resiliency of Asian skin delays the signs of aging longer than in Caucasian skin.

It should be noted that Hispanic skin probably has the strongest hair growth and root system. Waxing can be more difficult than on Caucasians. Hispanic and Native American skin is often thicker and has more sebaceous secretions. As a result you will notice a lot of oily, clogged, blemished skin that needs oily skin treatment concentration. Caution must be taken with extraction due to the predisposition to pigment around the extracted lesion. This skin may be a little more prone to bruising as well.

In summary, the clear common denominator in all ethnic skin is its propensity to hyperpigment. Generally, superficial peels such as AHAs at concentrations lower than

Figure 25–5 Hispanic skin has the strongest hair growth and root system.

25% are safe to enhance exfoliation and clean impacted follicle openings. However, remember that the use of any acids on the skin will photosensitize the skin and cause it to be at a higher risk for hyperpigmentation resulting from UV exposure. This is especially true of highly susceptible ethnic skin.

Summary

The differences between ethnic and Caucasian skin notwithstanding, all human skin requires care and treatment to keep it healthy and functioning properly. In order for estheticians to perform those tasks well, they must first be aware of the special needs of ethnic skin.

Discussion Questions

1. Each ethnic skin type demonstrates different needs and concerns. Create a list of concerns relevant to each of the major ethnic groups discussed in this chapter. Without stereotyping, how will you address the needs of these populations?

2. Discuss the morphology of hyperpigmentation relevant to black, Asian, Hispanic, and Native American skin. When working with these ethnic groups, what products would you suggest or avoid, based on your findings?

Additional Reading

Lees, Mark. 2001. *Skin Care: Beyond the Basics.* Clifton Park, N.Y.: Milady, an imprint of Delmar Learning, a division of Thomson Learning, Inc.

Thrower, Angelo P. 1999. *Black Skin Care for the Practicing Professional.* Clifton Park, N.Y.: Milady, an imprint of Delmar Learning, a division of Thomson Learning, Inc.

Helpful Web Sites

http://www.asds-net.org (American Society of Dermatologic Surgery)

http://www.aad.org (American Academy of Dermatology)

Chapter 26
Exfoliation

Chapter Objectives

After reading this chapter, you should be able to:

- Explain the differences between mechanical and chemical exfoliation.
- List various types of exfoliation treatments.
- Describe how enzymes work on the skin.

Chapter Outline

Introduction
Mechanical versus Chemical Exfoliation
Mechanical Exfoliation
Chemical Exfoliation
Enzymes

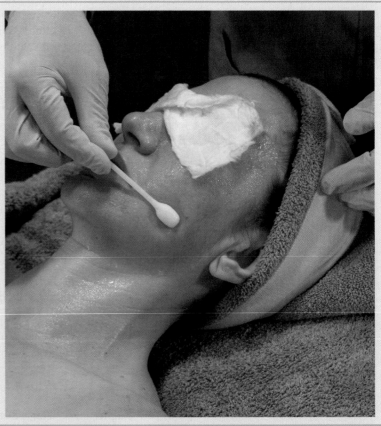

Introduction

Exfoliation procedures are an important part of an esthetician's practice. The removal of dead cells (corneocytes) has a significant effect on improving the appearance of many skin conditions. All estheticians should learn numerous methods of exfoliation to know which technique is best suited for each client and skin type.

Although both professionals and consumers generally know the word *exfoliation*, it was not that long ago when it was considered a new term in the industry. It simply means to desquamate or remove dead skin cells. According to *Webster's Ninth New Collegiate Dictionary*,

> exfoliate: vb 1: to cast off in scales, laminae, or splinters 2: to remove the surface of in scales or laminae 3: to spread or extend by or as if by opening out leaves ~ vi 1: to split into or give off scales, laminae or body cells 2: to come off in thin layers or scales 3: to grow by or as if by producing or unfolding leaves

In terms of skin care, we think of exfoliation as the means by which the keratinized stratum corneum skin cells are deliberately sloughed off for the purpose of stimulating fresh, healthy skin renewal. Natural cell growth and the renewal cycle cause skin cells to slough off. This natural process, however, may be slowed or inhibited by a number of factors. Excessive oil combines with the cells, which causes them to stick or pack together. Once stuck together, the cells do not release easily, resulting in an excessive buildup of unnecessary skin cells. Additionally, as we encounter various types of stresses—pollution, hormonal fluctuations, makeup, aging, and all sorts of other issues—this natural sloughing or exfoliation is slowed or repressed.

The natural cycle of cell desquamation may be assisted through a variety of tools and substances. While researching exfoliation concepts, it has been found that this process improves natural cell turnover. Research has also discovered that exfoliation, in many cases, actually increases the natural cell renewal rate. As we age, this natural cycle may decrease from approximately 28–30 days to 40 days or more. By exfoliating the surface of the skin, we know that the cell turnover rate from the birth of the epidermal cells (basal cells) can also be enhanced.

Although enhancing the cell turnover rate seems like a good practice, caution should be taken to not overexfoliate the skin. Excessive exfoliation creates the risk of seriously disturbing the natural process of cell turnover. It is not advantageous to destroy the very surface cells that form part of the skin's protective barrier. Any overzealous attempt to create skin renewal and reduce fine lines and wrinkles can, indeed, increase the risk of this barrier being destroyed. Subsequently, numerous problems are created. The skin may experience an increased susceptibility to sensitivity and irritation, pushing it into an actual reactive state. A drastic reduction is witnessed in the skin's ability to handle skin care products without adverse reactions. A little exfoliation is good, but when in doubt, go lightly.

Mechanical Versus Chemical Exfoliation

Two basic types of exfoliation remove dead cells from the surface of the skin. **Mechanical exfoliation** is a technique that physically removes dead corneum cells. Examples include granular scrubs, gommages, roll-off type masks, and scrubs made of ground almonds, ground apricot seeds, and other ground natural grains. As the scrub product is pressed against and passed over the skin, cells almost ready to be shed are literally bumped off the skin.

Mechanical exfoliation is a routine part of most basic facial treatments. It may be performed in the salon by an esthetician or performed at home by a client. Brushing machines, scrubs, and lift-off rubber masks are examples of techniques frequently used in a salon. Both methods should be done only occasionally; home scrubs are often recommended 2–3 times a week. Microdermabrasion, which will be discussed later in this chapter, is another good example of mechanical exfoliation.

In addition to scrubs, gommages, roll-off type masks, and other methods, we examine equipment that is used either to

mechanical exfoliation
A technique that physically removes dead corneum cells from the skin's surface.

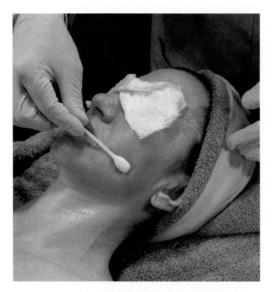

Figure 26–1 Chemical exfoliation uses chemicals to loosen dead cells from the skin's surface.

exfoliate or to increase a product's ability to exfoliate.

Chemical exfoliation uses chemicals, both natural and laboratory-designed, to loosen dead cells from the skin's surface (Figure 26–1). It is also known as chemoexfoliation. Rather than physically removing the dead cells, chemical exfoliation products help to either dissolve the keratin in the keratinocyte or loosen the bonds holding cells together. Examples of chemoexfoliation products include enzyme treatments, alphahydroxy acids (AHAs) or betahydroxy acids (BHAs), and stronger salon exfoliation treatments. Home care products integrating chemical exfoliation include AHAs, salicylic acid (BHA), sulfur, resorcinol, and benzoyl peroxide. Different products and chemicals are used for different skin conditions.

chemical exfoliation
Uses both natural and laboratory-designed chemicals to loosen dead cells from the skin's surface.

SAFETYTip

Contraindications for Scrubs
• Use as directed by an esthetician. The tendency is for consumers to use them too often and too harshly. As a professional, be sure to provide complete usage directions.
• Scrubs should not be used in conjunction with other, stronger skin-thinning substances.
• Do not scrub areas of sensitivity, redness, inflammation, pustules, or other open wounds. This includes areas of telangiectasias (couperose).

Mechanical Exfoliation

Mechanical exfoliation uses a number of granular-based products that, with friction, is effective in removing dead skin cells.

Scrubs

Granular scrubs are the most popular form of exfoliation for home care, and they have tremendous appeal to the consumer. Granular scrubs achieve cell renewal by causing a friction removal of dead cells. While there are other different and more effective chemical exfoliants available, particularly for professional use, the idea of a scrub is often desirable because it feels as if it is doing something.

Substances used in scrubs range from natural grains to high-tech polyethylene microballs. The microballs actually provide a more gentle, enhanced exfoliation. In the salon or spa, the scrub is often used in conjunction with the brush machine to further enhance the effect of exfoliation. To make the treatment a little gentler, steam is used simultaneously with the scrubbing step. This combination allows the exfoliant to glide more smoothly and gently.

Treatment Procedure—Scrub

Generally, the manufacturer prescribes how the scrub is used in the treatment room or at home. How aggressive your approach should be depends on the intensity of the grains, the formula consistency, and the skin condition. The following demonstrates a conservative usage of a scrub at the beginning of a professional facial treatment.

Cleanse
1. Remove eye makeup and lipstick with eye makeup remover.
2. Cleanse the face, neck, and décolleté by hand with the cleansing milk, cream, or lotion.

Analyze
3. Perform a skin analysis.

Exfoliate
4. Apply the chosen scrub and massage it gently onto the skin. For easier movement, it may be advisable to steam the skin while massaging the scrub around

the face. Avoid the eyes and any sensitive areas. If the skin is thick, as on a male client, or leathery, you may choose to use the electric brush machine in conjunction with the scrub for greater abrasive action. The scrub can be rubbed or brushed for approximately 2–5 minutes.

5. Rinse the skin and wipe off any residue with moistened sponges, shammies, or pads. Make sure all grains have been thoroughly removed before proceeding to the next step.

6. Continue with the next step of the facial treatment.

Gommages

Gommage is a French word that means to erase (Figure 26–2). In professional skin care, it refers to a product in a cream form that is applied to the skin by hand or brush. The cream is then allowed to become slightly dry before it is removed by rubbing. Through a friction process, dead skin cells lift off with the cream. This process is referred to as a mechanical rubbing. The rolling agent in some gommages is xanthan gum, causing the dead cells to roll off along with the residue of the product. Some gommages may include a cellular dissolving agent, such as an enzyme. The rolling action and cell removal is the same in this process.

Prior to the advent of AHAs, gommages were popular but targeted for professional use only. Currently, they seem to be having a revival in the marketplace because, to the

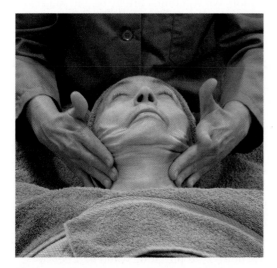

Figure 26–2 Gommage being rubbed off, removing dead skin cells.

SAFETYTip

Contraindications of Gommage
• A gommage is considered a professional product. Therefore, the gommage should be used by estheticians only. If a product line offers a consumer gommage, be sure that the client understands how to use it correctly.
• A gommage should not be used in conjunction with other, stronger skin-thinning substances.
• Do not rub the gommage off around areas of sensitivity, redness, inflammation, pustules, or other open wounds. This includes areas of telangiectasias (couperose).
• Use the gommage correctly. Overdrying the cream causes difficulty in the rub-off process, in addition to potentially causing dehydration in the area where it is being used.

consumer, the gommage as feels if it is doing something.

Newer gommages may contain encapsulated moisturizers that are released by the friction used to rub off the dead cells. These products are interesting because they claim to be able to exfoliate dead cells and moisturize at the same time.

Some product lines say to apply the gommage, let it sit, and then wash it off. This would only be of value in cases where an enzyme exfoliator is included in the ingredients. For the most part, rub-off exfoliants require friction to accomplish the removal of dead cells.

The primary caution when using a gommage pertains to the aggressiveness of the product itself in relation to the condition of the skin. Sensitive skin, rosacea, and highly exfoliated skins are completely contraindicated to treatment with rub-off gommages. It is not advisable to use steam when performing a gommage. The steam mixes with the product or skin cells and causes a temporary plumping to take place. It also causes the gommage to be gummy and makes it almost impossible to rub off.

Gommage Procedure

Cleanse
1. Remove eye makeup and lipstick with eye makeup remover.
2. Cleanse the face, neck, and décolleté by hand with the cleansing milk, cream, or lotion (see page 400).

gommage
A French word that means to erase. Also a cream product applied to the skin and rubbed off, removing dead skin cells through the friction.

Analyze

3. Perform a skin analysis.

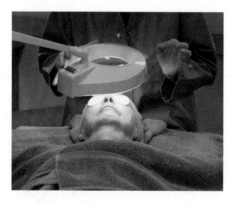

Exfoliate

4. Apply the gommage to skin that is completely dry.

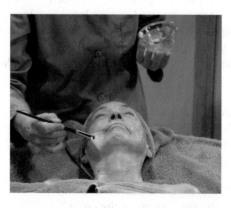

Spread the gommage gently onto the skin. Do not use steam. Avoid the eyes and sensitive areas. Time for 5–10 minutes, or according to the manufacturer's directions. Begin to roll the product off. In places where the skin seems dry, add a tiny bit of fresh gommage to begin the rolling procedure. One finger from one hand should be placed between two fin-

gers of the other hand to remove and rub the gommage off without stretching the skin. Always use one hand to hold the skin taut while rubbing off with the other hand. Some gommages have enzymes, and in certain cases, where rubbing may be contraindicated, it is better to rinse the gommage off after the timing process. Keep rolling until all flaking and residue have been removed.

5. Rinse the skin and wipe off any residue with moistened sponges, shammies, or pads.

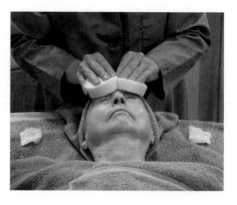

Make sure all the gommage and dead cells have been thoroughly removed before proceeding to the next treatment step.

6. Proceed with the next step of the facial treatment.

Microdermabrasion

As part of the discussion of mechanical exfoliation, we will touch briefly on the subject of microdermabrasion. Microdermabrasion is an interesting and controversial subject, due primarily to how quickly it became a strong trend in the U.S. As with all trends, pros and cons surround the treatment. Although we no longer consider microdermabrasion a new treatment, it arrived quickly in the American marketplace and with little proper training and caution.

If you have ever watched an old building being cleaned by sandblasting, the concept in microdermabrasion is quite similar. A microdermabrasion machine uses aluminum chloride, corundum, or even sodium chloride crystals. They are passed over the skin via a vacuum or air pulsating wand in order to "sandblast" dead cells off the surface of the

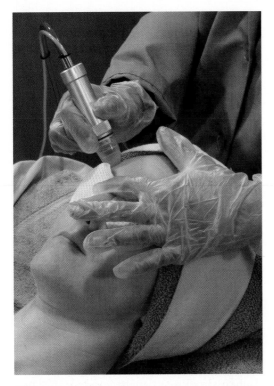

Figure 26–43 Microdermabrasion uses crystals to sandblast dead cells from the surface of the skin.

SAFETY*Tip*

Contraindications for Microdermabrasion
- Do not use on extremely dehydrated and dry skin that is sensitive to surface exfoliation.
- Microdermabrasion should not be done at the same time other abrasives or chemical exfoliations are used.
- Avoid use on areas of open lesions, wounds, and telangiectasia (couperose). Diabetics and hemophiliacs are generally contraindicated without pretesting and a well-advised consultation.
- Do not overly stress or stretch the skin.
- Proceed with caution when doing the neck area, which is normally more sensitive.
- The number of passes over the skin should be determined after careful and thorough consultation with the client.

skin (Figure 26–3). The process is a push-pull action on the skin. When the wand passes over the skin, crystals are directed in a swirling motion, abrading across the stratum corneum. At the same time, dead skin cells are picked up through a vacuum action with the crystal residue. They are delivered into a used crystal reservoir that is subsequently thrown away. Depending on the skin and the degree of dead cells, it may be necessary to pass the wand over the skin many times to achieve the desired results.

Although microdermabrasion can show immediate improvement with the removal of dead cells, dehydration, and fine lines, the procedure *can* also be overdone. The key to proper use relates to how the wand or crystals are used, how many passes are done, how often the treatment is performed, what other treatments are coordinated to complement the microdermabrasion, etc.

Training is a vital part of this concept for optimum usage and effectiveness of microdermabrasion. Rapid development of microdermabrasion devices and the expansion of this highly profitable service have placed

many of these machines into the hands of estheticians who have not had sufficient training. This has resulted in a number of microdermabrasion casualties. Refer to Chapter 38 for more information on microdermabrasion.

Chemical Exfoliation

Exfoliation versus Peeling

The words *exfoliation* and *peeling* are often used interchangeably in an esthetics practice. However, we need to establish that a big difference exists between exfoliation treatments that are performed by estheticians and medical surgical peels that are performed by plastic surgeons or dermatologists.

The Esthetics Manufacturers and Distributors Alliance (EMDA) of the American Beauty Association has recommended that all exfoliation procedures performed by estheticians be referred to as exfoliations, rather than as peels. The EMDA's recommendations are an effort to clarify the domain of the esthetician and the domain of the physician.

During exfoliation procedures, estheticians directly affect only the stratum corneum. Any procedure that removes cells beyond the stratum corneum is considered a medical peeling. The three levels of peeling are

1. **Superficial peeling** removes only the dead cells of the epidermis. Chemicals

superficial peeling
Removing only dead cells from the epidermis.

used for this type of removal include alphahydroxy acids, betahydroxy acids, resorcinol, and sulfur. Many different blends of chemicals are used in superficial peeling. Microdermabrasion is a mechanical, rather than chemical, exfoliation procedure that falls into the category of superficial peeling.

2. **Medium depth peels** are administered by dermatologists or plastic surgeons. Trichloroacetic acid (TCA) is the chemical most often used for this procedure, which essentially removes the entire epidermis and can vary in the depth of dermal tissue removed.

3. **Deep peels** are medical surgical peels performed with **phenol,** a highly acidic chemical (Figure 26–5). Phenol peels remove tissue well into the papillary dermis and are basically a controlled chemical burn. Phenol peeling is generally reserved for deeply wrinkled skin and severe sun damage.

Deep resurfacing techniques that are performed by dermatologists and plastic surgeons are included here. These do not involve chemoexfoliation but rather other modalities.

Laser resurfacing surgery uses a surgical laser to remove or **ablate** epidermal and dermal tissue. This procedure can vary in depth, depending on the needs of the patient, the type of laser, and the techniques used by the surgeon. The number of passes, or times the surgeon runs the laser over an area, affects the depth of the treatment. Refer to Chapter 36.

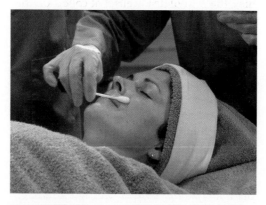

Figure 26–5 Phenol, a highly acidic chemical, is used in deep peels.

Dermabrasion is a mechanical surgical technique that uses a rotating wire brush to physically remove skin tissue. Sometimes called skin sanding by consumers, dermabrasion is most often used to improve scarring from acne or accidents, or to remove lines around the mouth in sun-damaged skin.

Alphahydroxy Acid Exfoliation

The use of higher concentrations of alphahydroxy acids (AHAs) for salon treatments is popular. This is a procedure that every esthetician should be fully trained to perform. AHA exfoliations are performed in conjunction with home care programs to treat many skin conditions. Acne-prone skin, clogged pores, hyperpigmentation, signs of aging and sun damage, dehydration, and rough-textured skin can all be helped through salon AHA exfoliation treatments.

Mechanism of Action
Alphahydroxy acids are believed to work by loosening the chemical bonds between the keratinocytes. These are chemical bonds that bind the surface corneum cells together through the desmosome, the attachment structure between the cells. AHAs also act on the surface barrier function, breaking up the lipids that make up the intercellular cement. These actions cause keratinocytes to loosen and shed from the skin's surface, which is beneficial for achieving the desired esthetic changes.

Most AHA salon exfoliation treatments are a 15% to 30% solution of alphahydroxy acid(s) in a gel formulation. Glycolic acid is the most commonly used AHA, although lactic, malic, tartaric, citric, and even betahydroxy salicylic acids are also used. It is not unusual for a formula to use a combination of acids. Sometimes the solutions are supplemented with fruit acids such as passion flower, grape, or apple extracts, all which contain alphahydroxy acids.

Acne and Clogged Pores
AHAs loosen the bond of dead cells and act on the hardened sebum that is pasting over the dead cell buildup within the follicles. It is this mix of sebum and dead cells that make up the impactions within the follicles. By loosening the cells within the impactions, the

medium depth peels
Removing the entire epidermis; the amount of dermal tissue removed can vary.

deep peels
Surgical peels performed with phenol to remove tissue well into the papillary dermis.

phenol
A highly acidic chemical used for deep peels.

ablate
To remove.

dermabrasion
A surgical technique using a rotating wire brush that physically removes skin tissue.

AHAs actually free the impactions and expel them from the follicles. Impactions that are loosened but not expelled are much easier for the esthetician to extract during a routine deep-cleansing facial treatment.

On a long-term basis, AHAs help achieve routine exfoliation of the cells located on the follicle walls. This helps greatly to reduce the formation of microcomedones. Remember, oiliness and retention hyperkeratosis are hereditary and cannot be permanently corrected through esthetic treatments. However, through the routine use of AHAs at home and in the salon, comedones can be controlled. All comedonal acne lesions begin as microcomedones. Therefore, AHAs can aid greatly in bringing oiliness and comedones under control and achieving long-term prevention of problem skin conditions.

Enlarged pores are distended from comedones and filament sebum pushing on the follicle walls, making the pores appear large. Routine use of AHAs is an excellent method for minimizing the appearance of large pores. By removing the debris from these follicles, the surface of the skin looks much more refined, and the pores look much smaller. The best results in this area are achieved after several months of regular treatment with AHAs. Pores that are affected by scar tissue, however, will not look smaller.

Acne products for home use are usually in a gel base. They may contain salicylic acid, along with AHAs, to help with inflammation and bacterial control. They should be used daily, along with other products specifically designed for acne and oily skin.

The concentration of AHAs in most AHA home care products for acne-prone and oily skin is in the range of 8%–10%. Concentrations lower than this will not be as effective in loosening impactions. However, concentrations above 10% AHA tend to be irritating and are not advisable for daily use. Likewise, home care AHA products that have pHs less than 3.5 can also be irritating. For more information, see the section later in this chapter on home care AHA programs.

Hyperpigmentation and AHAs

AHAs, used both at home and in higher percentage in salon treatments, help significantly with many types of hyperpigmentation. AHA salon exfoliations can rapidly improve hyperpigmentation by accelerating the desquamation of keratinocytes containing melanosomes. This rids the skin of splotching and reduces discoloration. The AHAs, however, do not directly affect the melanocytes, which is why the client must use a melanin-suppressive agent, such as hydroquinone, magnesium ascorbyl phosphate, or kojic acid, at home on a daily basis. The melanin suppressant helps stop the melanin-producing process, while AHAs remove epidermal cells that are already stained with melanin. Home care products for hyperpigmentation often combine AHAs such as glycolic acid with a melanin-suppressive agent to work together to exfoliate and to suppress melanin production.

It is imperative that all clients being treated for hyperpigmentation use a melanin suppressant and a broad-spectrum sunscreen on a daily basis. Sun and heat are major causes of hyperpigmentation, so direct exposure must be avoided, even when using a broad-spectrum sunscreen.

Some clients who have melasma, also known as a pregnancy mask, may also have hormonal disorders that contribute to the hyperpigmentation. These clients, or any clients who experience chronic or nonresponsive problems with hyperpigmentation, should be referred to a gynecologist or endocrinologist.

Aging and Sun Damage

The routine use of AHAs both at home and in salon exfoliation treatments is extremely beneficial in improving the signs of aging and sun damage. AHAs cause the surface epidermis to become more even and smoother, ridding the skin of dead cells that collect on the surface and make the skin look rough, dull, and old. AHA exfoliations improve fine lines and wrinkles by removing dead cells from the edges of facial lines, making wrinkles look less deep.

AHAs are also helpful in improving skin discolorations associated with sun damage. The smoothing effects, along with the effects that make the skin coloration look better, work well together in helping mature, sun-damaged skin show significant improvement and look much younger. Two weeks of home treatment using an 8%–10% AHA cream or lotion and a twice-a-week

30% AHA salon treatment for three weeks will generally show improvement fairly fast.

Effect on Dehydration

When AHAs remove surface corneum cells, they stimulate replacement of these cells. The cell renewal rate is increased as a result. This causes the increased production of intercellular lipids by the epidermal cells moving through the keratinization process. Increases in intercellular lipids increase the ability of the epidermis to hold moisture and lowers the rate of transepidermal water loss, which causes dehydration. Used correctly, AHAs can increase hydration and, therefore, improve surface smoothness and firmness.

AHA products should be used along with a good hydrator or moisturizer specifically designed for the client's skin type. Overuse or incorrect use of AHA home care or salon products actually results in dehydration. Remember that the AHA process removes surface lipids between the cells to loosen dead cells. If overused, it removes too much of these lipids, actually leading to moisture loss.

As in all other facial treatment regimes, it is imperative that AHAs be viewed as a program. Every product used in conjunction with AHAs has an influence on the success of the skin improvement program. Cleansers, toners, sunscreens, and moisturizers used with AHA products should be carefully selected for the client's skin type.

Smoothing Rough Textures

Rough-textured skin is often oily and sometimes scarred from acne. In much the same way as AHAs reduce the appearance of wrinkles, thick, rough skin can look smoother after receiving routine AHA salon exfoliations, along with proper home care.

Scar tissue is in the dermis, which is never directly affected by AHAs. Scars themselves are not improved by any superficial exfoliation, and they must be treated with surgical excision or surgical dermabrasion performed by a qualified dermatologist or plastic surgeon. However, getting the surface of the skin to reflect light more evenly can improve the appearance of scars, even though it is not directly affecting the scar tissue.

What we see when examining rough-textured skin is light being unevenly reflected from the skin's surface. AHA treatments help make the surface of the skin more even and smoother, with more uniform light reflection. It is an optical illusion but, nevertheless, does improve the appearance of scars and rough texture.

Precare for AHA Treatments

Clients should receive a thorough pretreatment consultation. During this consultation, the esthetician should determine the client's

---

SAFETY*Tip*

Contraindications for AHA Treatments

Client is currently using prescription keratolytics such as tretinoin (Retin-A or Renova), azelaic acid (Azelex), tazarotene (Tazorac), adapalene (Differin), or other drugs or cosmetics that cause exfoliation.

Client is taking Accutane or has taken Accutane in the last 4–6 months.

Client is currently being treated by a dermatologist for a facial skin disease.

Client is pregnant. Safety of AHA salon treatments in pregnant women has not been established in a formal study.

Client has a history of herpes simplex (cold sores), which may be flared by many chemoexfoliation techniques. The client should be referred to a physician for prophylactic (preventive) treatment for the herpes simplex virus. The esthetician must follow directions from the client's physician as to when treatment can be administered.

Client is not willing to stay out of the sun during the treatment, and for several weeks after the exfoliation procedure. Sunscreen must be worn daily, and tanning beds must not be used.

Client has visible redness, irritation, or inflammation.

Client is having a flare of rosacea.

Client has broken skin or scrapes on the area to be treated.

Client has extremely reactive skin, with a history of unusual reactivity.

Client has become red or very dehydrated between AHA treatments.

Client is sunburned, windburned, or severely dehydrated with irritation.

Client is being treated for a severe systemic or autoimmune disease. The client's physician should be consulted before proceeding with treatment. An example is a client who has lupus.

Any client who will not comply with the *entire* program. AHA salon treatments can be very irritating for clients who are not following home care instructions.

Any situation that you, as the esthetician, are unsure about.

---

desires for improved appearance and whether or not AHAs, or another exfoliation procedure, will achieve the desired results. It is important for the client to have realistic expectations of the program. Clients should also be screened for contraindications for AHA use.

Clients desiring to have salon exfoliation treatments using 15%–30% AHA should be treated at home with 8%–10% AHA products for a minimum of two weeks prior to receiving higher strength salon treatments.

Home Care AHA Programs

Estheticians must thoroughly evaluate the client's skin and should recommend and make the client aware of the following:

- A cleanser appropriate for the client's skin type. Clients should not use soaps or other products that are alkaline or any cleanser that is stripping. These products increase the surface absorption of the AHA product, which may cause irritation.

- A toner appropriate for the client's skin type. With the exception of very oily skin, the toner should be free of drying alcohols (isopropyl or SD alcohol). Toner should not be stimulating and should be fragrance free. Many AHA leave-on home care products have a pH of around 3.5–4.0. Use of toner before home AHA product application can reduce irritation caused by a sudden change (drop) of pH from the cleansing procedure.

- The AHA product itself may be in the form of a gel, serum, lotion, or cream. Gels are generally used for oily and combination skin, lotions and creams for dryer skin types. Products may have other additives appropriate for the client's skin type. Dry skin products will often have more emollients, and oily and acne-prone products may contain salicylic acid. Sensitive skin products may have a slightly higher pH or have an added ingredient, such as green tea extract or another soothing agent.

- A small amount of the AHA product (about the size of a dime) should be applied after cleansing and toning. Most home care products sold by salons have a concentration of AHA between 8% and 10%, with a pH no less than 3.5. This is also the directive on this matter

from the Cosmetic Ingredient Review Board (CIR), a group of scientists who determine the safety of ingredients in skin care and cosmetic products. The CIR recommendation is that any home care AHA product should not exceed a 10% concentration of AHA and should not have a pH lower than 3.5. Concentrations over 10% and pHs less than 3.5 can contribute to irritation. The CIR has a similar directive for salon-use AHA exfoliation products. These professional in-salon treatment products should have no more than 30% concentration and have a pH of no less than 3.0. EMDA, the Esthetics Manufacturers and Distributors Association, has published a safe use brochure on AHAs. You can receive one by requesting a copy from EMDA, 401 North Michigan Avenue, Chicago, IL 60611.

- Be careful *not* to apply products with 8%–10% to the thin skin around the eye area. Many companies make lower concentration AHA products especially for the eye area. The client definitely should use an AHA eye area product if you intend to use salon strength exfoliation products in the lower and outer eye areas. AHA products, even ones designed for eyes, should never be used on the upper lid and should be applied lightly and sparingly to avoid getting the product in the client's eye.

- All clients using AHA products must use a daily SPF-15 or higher sunscreen. This is also a directive by the CIR. The sunscreen, as with other products selected, should be appropriate for the client's skin type.

- A hydrating product selected for the client's skin type can be used over the

SAFETY*Tip*

- Products vary from manufacturer to manufacturer. It is important that you thoroughly acquaint yourself with and follow the techniques recommended by the manufacturer of the AHA product chosen for use in your treatments.
- Home care products should be part of the same system that is used for professional treatment. Using one AHA brand for home care and another for the professional treatment is not recommended.

AHA product at night. This will help replenish moisture lost from the exfoliation process.

- Clients with oily and acne-prone skin can also use spot treatments for pimples after the general application of AHAs.
- Remember, the AHAs primarily affect the clogged pores and microcomedones. Stronger drying agents, such as sulfur-resorcinol, salicylic acid, or benzoyl peroxide, may be used as spot treatments only on raised visible pimples.

AHA Treatment

It is strongly recommended that clients having their first salon AHA treatments be required to use the home products for the two weeks prior to their salon visit. It is also strongly recommended that clients be required to commit to a series of six treatments, usually performed twice a week for three weeks. In some cases, they may be performed once a week for six weeks. This may vary with the manufacturer of the AHA salon-use product.

Clients having only one or two treatments will not see much of a result. This is why many salons *require* that clients have a series of treatments to start. At the time of the first treatment, you should have the client sign an agreement that she understands the treatment and what she should avoid to keep from irritating the skin. This includes avoiding sun and heat exposure, avoiding other exfoliating products or treatments, and using a daily SPF-15 sunscreen. The agreement should also list the terms of the series, cost, and suggested treatment frequency. It is customary to charge less per visit for six visits bought in a series than for an individual touch-up treatment.

The following is a typical procedure for using a 30%, 3.0 pH AHA exfoliation gel in a

salon treatment. Again, this procedure may vary with the manufacturer.

How Often Should You Treat the Skin With AHA Exfoliation Treatments?

Most clients begin by having these AHA treatments twice a week for three weeks. After the series is completed, you should consult with the client about the results and her feelings about her progress. Almost every client is, at the very least, somewhat pleased with the results of the AHA series. If you and the client feel that there has been sufficient improvement, you can suggest that the client have touch-up treatments (following the same procedure) once or twice a month for maintenance of the results.

The client must understand that AHAs are superficial exfoliations. The results are not permanent and must be maintained. The client must continue to follow the home care program to keep up with the results. Failure to keep up with home care or to continue bad habits will cause the skin to return to its previous condition.

Some clients will elect to have a short series of treatments two to four times a year and maintain home care between the series. This is another acceptable plan, but it probably does not maintain results as well as once or twice a month AHA treatments.

How Do You Coordinate the AHA Treatments with Regular Salon Facial Treatments?

Clients with sensitive skin should not have any other facial treatment combined with an AHA salon exfoliation. Clients who do not have sensitive skin can have other treatments performed at the same time as the AHA treatment, as long as the other treatments do not involve exfoliation, heat, or stimulation. It is not advisable to combine treatments until the initial series is completed. Many clients who have the time visit the salon twice a month—once for an AHA treatment and another time for a deep cleansing or hydrating conditioning treatment.

If you are performing an AHA exfoliation along with a conditioning facial treatment, follow the procedure exactly as you would for a single AHA treatment, except for the application of the sunscreen. Commonly, after the AHA portion of a maintenance treatment, estheticians perform any necessary

SAFETYTip

- The AHA exfoliation treatment should be performed at the beginning of the treatment session. *Never* perform an AHA at the end of a facial treatment. To do so could result in significant irritation and redness.
- Do not wax an area that has just been treated with an AHA product.

Step By Step AHA Treatment Procedure

Purpose: To improve the texture of the skin by removing buildup and helping with cellular turnover.

Products: Cleanser, toner, moisturizer, sunscreen, and 30% AHA solution.

Tools and supplies: Large swabs, and small 2 × 2 or 4 × 4 cotton pads, round sponges, eye pads, hand towel.

Client preparation: Remove contact lenses, cover the client's hair, and cover the eyes with moistened pads.

Procedure

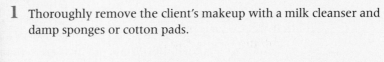

Cleanse

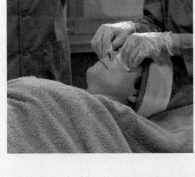

1 Thoroughly remove the client's makeup with a milk cleanser and damp sponges or cotton pads.

2 If the skin type is not thin or sensitive, apply a toner with wet sponges or cotton pads after cleansing. The more you cleanse the skin before the application of the AHA product, the stronger (and sometimes more irritating) the treatment will be. It is best not to use a toner after cleansing on the first AHA visit, until you have observed the skin after the treatment. After the first visit, you may use a toner before the 30% gel application, providing that the client has not had any irritation after the first visit. Irritation rarely occurs, especially if the client has been doing home care, and you are using a salon AHA product with a pH of no less than 3.0.

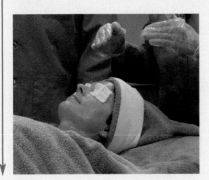

3 Place eye pads or predampened cotton pads over the eyes. The head of the client should be slightly elevated, so that the gel will not roll back into the eye.

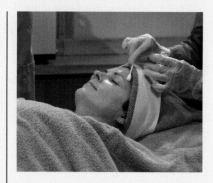

AHA application

4 Beginning with the forehead, apply the AHA 30% gel using cotton swabs. You may use two small cotton swabs or an extra large swab. Be careful not to get too much solution on the swab. Using small circular motions, apply the gel to all areas of the center panel of the face.

5 After the face has been coated in the gel, you can carefully lift the eye pads and apply a very thin coat of the AHA gel to the area under the eye. Be careful not too get to close to the lashes (stay about 1/4–1/2 inch from the lashes).

6 Clients should be told that they will feel a stinging sensation, especially during the first 2–3 minutes of the treatment. This may vary with the treatment and the client. In general, the more AHA treatments the client receives, the less they are bothered with stinging. The stinging sensation should not be so strong that the client complains much. Should the client tell you to remove the product, do so immediately. Problems are very rare, but you should take care to closely observe the client during the procedure.

7 A typical 30%, 3.0 pH salon-use AHA gel is safe to be left on for 10 minutes. These products are generally referred to as self-timing. If the instructions indicate to remove the product before 10 minutes, it is likely that the product has a concentration higher than 30% AHAs or a pH less than 3.0, and therefore the products are probably not in compliance with the CIR guidelines.

Removal

8 After 10 minutes, remove the gel thoroughly from the face with wet gauze pads. A second removal should be done with cool, wet cotton pads. *Caution*: Be careful when removing the gel around the eyes. Using damp (not dripping) cotton pads, remove the gel from the lower eye area by gently moving the cotton pad from the inner corner toward the outer eye area. This movement ensures that you do not accidentally sweep the gel into the corners of the eye. Some clients will experience a stinging feeling when the gel is removed. This is not typical, but it does happen in more sensitive skin types.

Completion

9 After the gel has been thoroughly removed, you can spray the face with cool water, not toner, which would further strip the skin at this point. Blot the face dry with a clean soft towel.

10 Apply a moisturizer and sunscreen as appropriate for the skin type. Apply the same sunscreen that the client uses at home.

Makeup application

11 It is often recommended that makeup be left off for a brief period after an AHA treatment. This is especially important for the first AHA exfoliation and for more sensitive skin types.

extractions and then a gentle massage with an appropriate hydration product. It is best to stay away from drying masks or any other exfoliating or stimulating product. Gel hydration masks, soothing gel masks, or nonstimulating cream masks for dry skin are usually fine to use after an AHA. Always end the treatment with sunscreen application. If steam is used at any point, it should be either cool steam or it should be used at a distance of at least 18 inches from the client's face.

Deeper Exfoliation

Several more aggressive and advanced exfoliation techniques are used by some experienced estheticians. These stronger exfoliation procedures should never be used as a first line of action for routine skin conditions. They should be reserved for hard-to-treat conditions that have not responded to traditional treatments. This section of this book is not designed to teach these more aggressive procedures but rather to give an overview and general knowledge about the procedures. Do *not* try any of these procedures without hands-on training from a qualified, experienced instructor.

Jessner's Exfoliation

Jessner's solution is a liquid solution of lactic acid, salicylic acid, and resorcinol in a solvent of ethanol, an alcohol. It is a much more aggressive treatment than alphahydroxy acid exfoliation and results in visible flaking of the skin. It is still considered to be superficial, because it does not directly affect the dermis, and only corneum is removed. Jessner's exfoliation should *not* be attempted without formal hands-on training by an esthetician thoroughly trained and experienced in administering this type of exfoliation procedure.

Jessner's exfoliation is appropriate for clients with rough-textured skin, fine lines and wrinkles, hyperpigmentation, or with many closed comedones. Jessner's solution should not be performed as the first technique for treating these conditions. It should be considered when other techniques have not produced the desired results.

Jessner's exfoliation produces a much more dramatic and sudden result and also comes with numerous possible side effects. Unlike alphahydroxy treatments with 3.0 or higher pH, the Jessner's procedure is much more aggressive, whereas the AHA procedure is much more gradual and user-friendly. You can look at AHA's as having small pieces of pie over a 3-week period. With a Jessner's exfoliation, you have the whole pie at once! Clients having Jessner's exfoliation procedures experience up to a week of flaking, as well as temporary hyperpigmentation and darkening of the skin. It is a somewhat uncomfortable procedure and produces a strong stinging sensation when applied. A small, handheld fan is often used during the procedure to help the client tolerate the stinging. The esthetician must be thoroughly acquainted with the possible side effects and possible reactions that can occur, and capable of handling those possible effects.

The same precautions as with AHA exfoliations should be observed for Jessner's, and the same contraindications exist. One additional long-term side effect of Jessner's is the possibility of mottling and hyperpigmentation, particularly in skin of color and darker pigmented skin. The darker the skin, the more risk of potential hyperpigmentation.

Because it is an advanced procedure, we will not discuss all the details of treatment here. The procedure for Jessner's exfoliation basically involves application of a prepping solution that removes all traces of surface skin oils. This solution is usually a stripping chemical called acetone, which is the ingredient used in nail polish remover. After prepping the skin, the Jessner's solution is evenly applied with large swabs, with the client sitting upright in a chair with her eyes completely shut. The eye area is avoided during application.

The Jessner's solution produces a strong stinging almost immediately. The skin begins turning white in patches, which is known as **frosting.** Not all areas will frost after the first coat of solution. Subsequent coats may be applied, depending on the thickness of the client's skin.

After the treatment, the skin may be slightly red. Within a day or two, the skin will begin turning brown-tan in the areas that were treated. The skin will feel extremely dry and tight, and on the third or fourth day the darkened skin will begin peeling. Clients should visit the salon daily for quick checks. No sun exposure is allowed during the procedure or for six

Jessner's solution
A liquid solution of lactic acid, salicylic acid, and resorcinol in a solvent of ethanol.

frosting
Skin that turns white in patches as a result of intense chemical exfoliation.

Customer Policies

We have all been caught unaware at one time another. Perhaps you did not read the fine print before realizing that your warranty ran out. Or maybe you failed to notice the *all sales final* sign above the markdown rack and could not return that fabulous blouse you thought would match your red suit. Chances are when you discovered your error you were not only disappointed but also a bit angry. Try to imagine your client in the same situation.

Do not wait until a client shows up late or gets charged for a missed appointment to let her know what your policy is on the matter. If the clinic or spa you are working in does not have a standard in place, suggest developing a written policy statement so that everyone is aware of the facility's policies.

Clear, concise policies are important to conducting a successful business. They also determine how you would like to be treated. Do not underestimate your value—get comfortable with it. You are a professional. Particularly in the service industry your time is extremely valuable—it may even determine your salary level.

Of course, policies must be thoughtful. After all, you are in business to satisfy customers and make money, not alienate them. How you handle the client is just as important as making a statement about your policy. Watch your tone and remember to be courteous when stating your case. Maintain a firm but pleasant demeanor and never appear condescending.

Today, most well managed salons are building clear-cut policy statements into their brochures. They are also careful to post information in highly visible areas using simple and concise language. Such information is typically posted in the most highly trafficked area, such as the reception desk. However, if you experience a problem with clients being unclear, you may want to tastefully reiterate important policies within your workplace. An attractively framed reminder usually does the trick.

The most frequent problems revolve around "no shows," "cancellations," "late arrivals," and product returns.

- **No shows:** In some salons the receptionist automatically makes a confirmation call. If not, it is a good idea to get in the habit of confirming your appointments, 24–48 hours in advance. If a client still does not show, give her a call. Chances are she simply did not get the message or "forgot" she had an appointment. If you are able to speak to the client in person remind her of your cancellation policy and note this in your record-keeping file. If you must leave a voice-mail message, simply state that the client has missed an appointment and invite her to reschedule.

- **Cancellations:** If a client cancels within the allotted policy time frame, there is not much you can do except try to book that slot. In any event you will want to note this in the client's file. If she cancels at the last minute, you need to remind her of the policy and take the appropriate action.

- **Late arrivals:** Most salons have a 15-minute rule. If a client arrives within 15 minutes of her scheduled appointment time you may offer her a choice. She can either agree to a shortened treatment session at the same price or rebook. If the client does make an effort to call and inform you that she will be late, make her aware of the same 15-minute rule. In terms of customer satisfaction, it is best not to create a situation where all of your clients will suffer the consequences.

- **Product Returns:** It is so important to educate the client. Good consultation skills and product knowledge go a long way in decreasing the number of returns. Make sure clients understand why and how to use a product. Always ask if a client has any allergies to particular ingredients. Make her aware that "dipping" into product can contaminate it. You

Customer Policies *(continued)*

may ultimately want to establish a time frame for returns, particularly if you use natural product lines that have a definite shelf life. If the manager is not aware of these conditions, it is your duty to inform her.

As an esthetician just starting out you will quickly become aware of the "rule breakers." These individuals understand the policy but feel it does not apply to them. Be gentle but firm, and know when to back off. If a good client commits a first-time offense, let it go, but let her know will she be charged next time. If it happens a second time, inform the client you will have to charge for the lost time, as you are unable to fill the time slot at the last minute. Of course, there are exceptions to every rule—be diplomatic when it comes to illness and other significant emergencies. Nevertheless, you do want to note repeated offenders in

your file; we all reach a point where we run out of empathy and may choose to be unavailable. Remember: you are in business to do business.

A final word: be consistent and wise. Clients will ultimately have more respect for your policies if they remain the same for all patrons. Hearing through the grapevine that another client was treated differently does not make for good public relations. If you feel the policies at the establishment you are working at are unreasonable, or just lacking, you may want to investigate your competitor's policies. Hopefully, management will be open to your concerns and appreciate your efforts.

---

weeks after the procedure. The client should use no other exfoliation agents in the salon or at home.

Resorcinol Paste

Resorcinol paste is a cream-form exfoliation product. The procedure for using it is similar to Jessner's, but resorcinol tends to be even more aggressive and is helpful in treating stubborn hyperpigmentation. Again, this is not a procedure for estheticians who are not thoroughly trained and experienced in the technique. This is also considered a superficial procedure, although there are possible side effects and, occasionally, allergic reactions.

"Herbal" and Other More Aggressive Techniques

Some strong exfoliation products use ingredients that are extracted from plants and herbs. They produce effects similar to the Jessner's and resorcinol paste peels described above.

Some estheticians use a diluted solution of **trichloroacetic acid (TCA)** to perform deeper exfoliation techniques. TCA is a strong acid and has many more serious side effects, and its use by estheticians is contro-

versial. Some states have laws that forbid the use of this ingredient except by qualified dermatologists or plastic surgeons.

It is generally accepted among estheticians that esthetic exfoliations should remain in the category of superficial exfoliations, as previously discussed. These are exfoliations that remove dead cells only from the stratum corneum.

Betahydroxy Acids

You should now have a good understanding of the use and function of AHAs. Although BHAs (betahydroxy acids) work in a similar manner, there are some unique applications for BHAs that should also be considered and used in your armament of exfoliants. BHA should not be confused with the preservative BHA (butylated hydroxyanisole). For the sake of simplicity, we will concentrate our BHA discussion on salicylic acid, because it is the most commonly used BHA. Even though some scientists do not consider it to be a true BHA, the industry has generally accepted salicylic acid as the most typical BHA. Sal acid is a nickname for salicylic acid.

resorcinol paste
A cream-form exfoliation product used to treat hyperpigmentation.

trichloroacetic acid (TCA)
A strong acid used for exfoliations; it has serious side effects.

Although both AHAs and BHAs are designed to slough off or exfoliate dead cells from the skin's surface, one of the most remarkable attributes of BHAs is their ability to dissolve oil-based accumulated dead cells. We refer to BHAs as being **lipophilic** or oil loving, hence their ability to dissolve oil. BHAs are recommended for oily skin either alone or in an alternating program with AHAs. Manufacturers are introducing new and effective products that combine both AHAs and BHAs.

Salicylic acids have many fine attributes. They are known for their analgesic, antiseptic, and anti-inflammatory properties. Salicylates are found in meadowsweet (*Filipendula ulmaria*), willow bark *(Salix sp.)*, sweet birch (*Betula sp.*), and wintergreen (*Gaultheria procumbens*). Aspirin (acetylsalicylic acid) is made from salicylates.

The same properties hold true in a salicylic acid exfoliation. The skin may actually undergo a mild anti-inflammatory and analgesic response. On potentially irritable skin,

salicylic acid may be a better choice for an exfoliator.

Salicylic acid also reduces hyperkeratinized cells that contribute to skin thickening and clogging. The lipophilic nature of this agent allows for the molecule to dissolve oil plugs in the follicle. This contributes to the reduction of microcomedones. It also causes stimulation of cell turnover cycles, aiding in skin renewal. It may also suppress the prevalence of Propionibacterium acnes (p. acnes), the culprit in the exacerbation of pustules, breakouts, and acne. Because of this **comedolidic** ability (capability to dissolve comedones), it is ideal to use salicylic acid a week or so prior to a facial treatment that will involve extensive extraction.

The results of the exfoliation are often visible, causing a pleasurable experience for the client because she can see the results. This enhances the client's perception of the working efficacy of the product being used.

We also have evidence of no **epidermolysis** or live cell destruction when salicylic acid is used, a problem that may be prevalent with other exfoliants. Research to date indicates that the cells in the stratum corneum are loosened with virtually no detection in blood or other tissues, making it a very safe choice of exfoliation.

And finally, due to the skin refining capability of removing surface cells, salicylic acid is also used to reduce hyperpigmentation, fine lines, and wrinkles. It is being studied for its effectiveness in softening and reducing stretch marks over protracted long-term use.

Salicylic acid's dual action—exfoliation and basal cell layer stimulation—requires that application be made in six to eight week intervals. This allows ample time for the natural cell renewal and barrier function to operate at their natural optimum levels. When there is too much interference with this natural process, there may be potential side effects, which includes increased pigmentation, irritation, and temporary sensitivity level. It is further recommended that all other skin-thinning substances, such as Retin A, Renova, glycolic acid, and Retinol, be terminated a few days prior to a professional BHA exfoliation. The recommendation may actually vary from company to company, but as a rule, it is best to allow a few days for the skin to rest prior to a BHA professional treatment.

---

lipophilic
Oil loving.

comedolidic
Able to dissolve comedones.

epidermolysis
Live cell destruction.

SAFETY Tip

Contraindications for BHA Treatment

Avoid using BHA on highly sun-exposed skins. Do not perform an exfoliation if the client is going to go out in the sun for a round of golf the next day. It is absolutely imperative for the client to apply a physical sunscreen block, such as one with titanium dioxide or zinc oxide. This means using it indefinitely at all times.

It is not unusual to experience temporary hyperpigmentation after a BHA professional treatment due to the stimulation of the basal layer. Unless treatment was performed in closer intervals than recommended, this is normal. Hyperpigmentation is considered temporary; its appearance is actually a good sign, because it visibly shows the stimulation of epidermal cell turnover.

Do not use on skin that is overexfoliated or on sensitive, tight, thin skin. All other exfoliation should be discontinued for about one week prior to the professional treatment.

Do not perform on sunburned skin.

Do not apply to the lips, eyelids, or other sensitive areas.

Do not perform this exfoliation on a pregnant woman.

Avoid any and all inflammatory conditions such as psoriasis, dermatitis, inflammatory acne, herpes simplex, etc.

Do not use when the client is taking Accutane or using other skin-thinning substances. Discontinue use of Accutane for approximately three months prior to treatment.

Step By Step BHA Treatment Procedure

Introduction: The following is a sample treatment, and the procedures may vary according to the manufacturer. Certain steps should be the same for optimum effectiveness.

Purpose: To exfoliate dead skin cells on the surface of the skin.

Products: Cleanser, toner, moisturizer, sunscreen, salicylic acid solution, and pre-treatment degreasing agent.

Tools and supplies: Large cotton swabs, 2 × 2 and 4 × 4 pads, cotton pads, shammie, fan brush

Client preparation: Complete the client health form and consultation. Obtain a signature on the release waiver. This is a vital step in having clear communications regarding the client's skin condition. It also helps to qualify the client. Some individuals may not be good candidates for this type of procedure. Some manufacturers provide a liability waiver that reminds the client of the possible side effects and the limitations of the exfoliation. The client should read, initial the details, and sign an acknowledgement of understanding. For additional safety, remove contact lenses. Cover the eyes completely with moistened pads. *Hint:* A butterfly pad will adhere to the face better than separate eyepads. It will not slip when moving the client's head from side to side. Butterfly pads are made from a rectangular piece of cotton, approximately 5" × 3". Dampen the cotton with warm water and squeeze out excess. Twist one side of the pad in half, toward yourself. This makes a natural "bridge" for the nose.

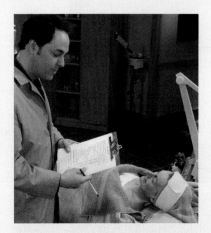

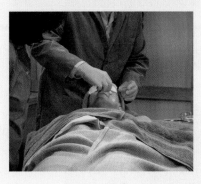

Procedure

- Do not perform any other treatments at this time, including extractions and steam. The average time for this procedure is approximately 20 minutes.
- Because there may be other variations in the treatment procedure, always follow the manufacturers instructions. When in doubt, be conservative and do not take unnecessary risks.

Cleanse

1 Gently cleanse the face and follow with a freshener. Do not be overly aggressive.

Degrease

2 Due to the lipophilic nature of salicylic acid, remove all oily residues with a pretreatment solution. In some cases this may actually be an alcohol gel that is a complete degreaser. Salicylic acid gravitates to oil, meaning that any topical residue causes the action in the follicle to be diminished or destroyed completely. The degreaser may dehydrate slightly; however, it is important to use so that the BHA can dissolve follicular debris and oil, along with the dead cells.

Application

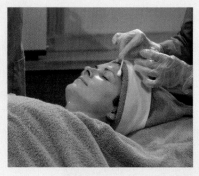

3 Apply the BHA with a large cotton swab in a well-organized fashion, moving in a consistent pattern around the face. Apply smoothly and evenly. Depending on the client's skin and the manufacturer's recommendations, two or three passes of solution may be done. Perform quickly and carefully, ensuring that no solution gets into the client's eyes. The eye pads may be lifted to allow treatment in the crow's feet area.

> Do not go any closer to the eye area than the outside of the ocular orbit.

Client communication

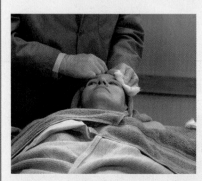

4 While applying the BHA, let the client know that there will be a very warm, prickly sensation that subsides naturally and completely in about 3 minutes. It is advisable to keep conversing with the client during this procedure so that the client remains comfortable. The BHA should self-neutralize, discontinuing its action within about 3 minutes. There may be evidence of frosting caused by the dried salicylic acid crystals. This is normal. It will wash off or come off with the application of the mask.

Rinse and mask

5 Rinse the face with cool water and remove the residue with a soft moist cloth or shammie.

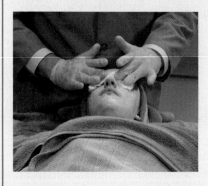

6 Apply a soothing or calming mask. Time for 5–7 minutes. Completely remove the mask with cool water.

Complete

7 Apply protective cream and a high SPF sunscreen—the titanium dioxide or zinc oxide type is preferred due to the anti-inflammatory characteristics of these substances. Some sunscreen agents are irritants and can sensitize the skin.

Home maintenance

8 Advise the client to keep the skin protected; it should be moisturized well morning and night. She should not worry too much about the degree of flaking that may or may not take place. Each individual will have her own unique reaction to this treatment depending on skin type and condition. Flaking is fine but not necessary to prove that **microdesquamation,** the removal of dead skin cells, is actually occurring.

microdesquamation
Removal of dead skin cells on the smallest level.

Step By Step Enzyme Treatment Procedure

Purpose: To exfoliate surface corneocytes in the stratum corneum. Its purpose is similar to an AHA and BHA.

Note: Read instructions carefully because procedures may vary between manufacturers.

Products: Cleanser, toner, moisturizer, sunblock, and enzyme powder.

Tools and supplies: Shammie, sponges, fan brush, eye pads.

Client preparation: Complete the client health form and consultation. It also helps to qualify the client. Some individuals may not be good candidates for this type of procedure. Obtain a signature on the release waiver. This is a vital step in having clear communications regarding the client's skin condition. Some manufacturers provide a liability waiver that reminds the client of the possible side effects and the limitations of the exfoliation. The client should read, initial the details, and sign an acknowledgement of understanding. For additional safety, remove contact lenses. Cover the eyes completely with moistened pads.

Procedure

Cleanse

1 The face is cleansed well with the cleanser and freshener but not too aggressively.

Enzyme exfoliation

2 Mix approximately 2 tablespoons of the enzyme powder with an equal amount of cool water or activating lotion. Mix well to form a creamy paste that is like softened cream cheese, not too thick and not too thin. Use a fan brush to apply the paste to the face, neck, and décolleté.

3 Moisture activates most enzymes, so do not allow the enzyme to' dry. Time according to the manufacturer's instructions, which may be anywhere from 3–4 minutes and up to 10 minutes. Use light steam directed toward the face from a distance to keep the enzyme activated.

Client communication

4 The key is to be with the client and ascertain her comfort level. If you notice excessive erythema, immediately remove the mask with cool water. Use a moistened shammie, sponges, or soft cloth. It is important to remove it gently after the proper length of time.

Enzymes

Enzyme exfoliation has existed in esthetics for over 30 years. When chemoexfoliating substances such as AHAs and BHAs became popular, the use of enzymes seemed to fade out for a time. Recently, there has been a gradual resurgence of interest in the use of enzymes.

For an excellent definition of enzymes, we will look at *Milady's Skin Care & Cosmetic Ingredients Dictionary* by Natalia Michalun with M. Varinia Michalun, which defines enzyme as biologically, a highly specific and complex protein catalyst that can accelerate or produce a chemical reaction. Without enzymes, given the temperature and pH usually found in cells, most chemical reactions would not proceed fast enough to maintain the cell's life. Enzymes are specific to the type of reaction they catalyze, and they can increase a reaction rate anywhere from 100 to 1,000 times.

The most common enzymes used in cosmetics are derived from vegetables or fruits, such as papain from papaya. They tend to be used to enhance the activity of the naturally occurring enzymes responsible for surface exfoliation of dead skin cells. Topical enzymes have a proteolytic action on the skin. A chemical reaction occurs with enzymes to exfoliate versus the mechanical action of a scrub.

Enzymes are normally applied in a creamy-type product, such as a mask, and allowed to sit in a moist state on the skin for a certain amount of time. The mask is rinsed off to reveal smoother skin.

papain
An enzyme found in papaya.

bromelain
An enzyme found in pineapple.

Enzymes such as super oxide dismutase (SOD) perform a different action in that they convert harmful and highly reactive oxygen free radicals into a less reactive form. Enzymes have also been used in cosmetics to reduce the preservative content, as some of them can protect formulations from bacterial attack.

There are any numbers of enzymes that may be used for different activities. For the sake of this section, we are concentrating on complex enzyme proteins that have a catalytic effect in exfoliating the skin. Two of the best known are **papain** from papaya and **bromelain** from pineapple. Both substances are keratolytic, meaning that they dissolve keratin or dead cells on the skin's surface. Papain and bromelain can come in a powder form that is mixed with water, or in an activating lotion, which may also contain enzymes or AHAs. Another commonly used enzyme peel is pancreatin, which is bovine-derived.

Papain and bromelain come in a powdered form, which is mixed with water to produce the mask paste. Bromelain is normally considered a bit stronger than papain but functions in the same way. When AHAs and BHAs are applied in a liquid format, a tingling or burning sensation occurs for a few minutes. Bromelain and papain are often a little less irritating to the skin when applied in a mask format, unless AHAs or BHAs are added to the wetting solution.

It is difficult to choose whether enzymes or AHAs and BHAs are better. They each have a significant action on the skin. Having these options in the armamentarium of exfoliants for professional use is quite beneficial. The best way to determine what product to use is to decide what would be most beneficial for the client's skin condition. Generally enzyme products are not made available for home use. They are marketed for professional use only.

SAFETY*Tip*

Contraindications for Enzyme Use
- Do not use on sensitive skin.
- Be cautious in using on skin that is easily reddened or inflamed. Do not use on rosacea or any other easily inflamed condition.
- Discontinue AHAs and BHAs within a few days of using enzyme exfoliants.
- Generally enzyme exfoliants are not recommended for home use. Exceptions are only in cases of weaker strength enzyme solutions.

Summary

Exfoliation, whether mechanical or chemical, is one of the most important treatments estheticians offer clients. Scrubs, gommages, AHAs, BHAs, enzymes, and other forms of exfoliation can have a wide range of effects on the skin, depending on how deep the exfoliation is. Estheticians should choose the treatment best suited for the clients' skin type and the desired results. Only properly and thoroughly trained professionals should perform more advanced techniques.

Discussion Questions

1. Exfoliation has become a primary treatment for skin renewal. Describe in skin care terms how the process of exfoliation works.

2. Explain the difference between mechanical and chemical exfoliation procedures, assigning all the exfoliation treatments discussed in this chapter into either of these two categories.

3. After reviewing the EMDA guidelines, determine the best approach to clarifying the difference between exfoliants and peels to clients. Include a description of the three levels of peeling in your discussion.

4. Clients are often not straightforward or do not understand the necessity of reporting information that may contraindicate the use of certain exfoliation agents. Simplifying information to help clients understand their eligibility may be helpful. Using clear and straightforward language, make a list of those conditions that would render a client an unlikely candidate for each of the esthetic exfoliating treatments discussed in this chapter.

5. In general, which of the milder exfoliation treatments discussed here might be appropriate for the following major skin types: normal, normal-combination, dry/dehydrated, oily/problem, and sensitive.

6. Briefly describe how AHAs work to correct the following skin conditions: acne, hyperpigmention, aging, sun damage, dehydration, and scarring. Describe a protocol for professional treatment that includes home care.

7. Review and discuss the Cosmetic Ingredient Review Board (CIR) and

Esthetic Manufacturers and Distributors Alliance (EMDA) guidelines for the use of professional exfoliation treatments and products.

Additional Reading

Lees, Mark. 2001. *Skin Care: Beyond the Basics.* Clifton Park, N.Y.: Milady, an imprint of Delmar Learning, a division of Thomson Learning, Inc.

Michalun, Natalia, with M. Varinia Michalun. 2001. *Skin Care and Cosmetic Ingredients Dictionary.* 2d ed. Clifton Park, N.Y.: Milady, an imprint of Delmar Learning, a division of Thomson Learning, Inc.

Helpful Web Sites

http://www.drugnet.com
http://www.acne-site.com
http://www.acne.com
http://www.skininc.com

Chapter 27
Holistic/Alternative Skin Care

Chapter Objectives

After reading this chapter, you should be able to:

- State the definition of the term *holistic*.
- Explain how holistic therapies work.
- Describe a variety of different holistic therapies.

Chapter Outline

Introduction
Psychological Benefits of Holistic Practices
Mind-Body Connection
Methods of Holistic Therapy

Introduction

Holistic skin care could be a book all on its own. It is so important that we cannot do justice to holism in the scope of this section. However, we will discuss the theory of, and give an overview of, the various types of holistic practices in our industry. First we will look at the word *holistic*. According to *Webster's Collegiate Dictionary, 10th ed.* the definition of holistic is:

1: of or relating to holism 2: relating to or concerned with whole or complete systems rather than with the analysis of, treatment of, or dissection into parts (~ medicine attempts to treat both the mind and the body) (~ ecology views man and the environment as a single system).

The definition of holism is:

1: a theory that the universe and especially living nature is correctly seen in terms of interacting wholes (as of living organisms) that are more than the mere sum of elementary particles 2: a holistic study or method of treatment.

When we think of the word *holistic*, we must think beyond skin care and cosmetics and consider the overall concept of holistic health care and life in general. Over the past few decades we have seen a rise in a holistic approach to thinking, in general, but particularly due to the decline in respect for Western Medicine. Western Medicine, also known as allopathic, views medicine from the inside out; it focuses on the symptoms more than the cause. Perhaps this is the result of specialization in medicine. *The Alternative Medicine Sourcebook* provides an insightful theory on holistic:

Science is inherently analytical, breaking down wholes into slivers much better than it assembles slivers into wholes (although it does both). As part of science, conventional medicine excels at concentrating on isolated aspects of health, but it seldom reaches toward embracing the entire person . . . this fault is so connected to the fundamentals of the scientific method that it is not easy to suggest a remedy. Conventional medicine is probably doomed to ever-increasing specialization. Unfortunately, this intrinsic lack of holism does not only lead to errors in treatment; it also wounds on an emotional and spiritual level. Every modern individual already suffers from a lack of holism in daily life.

In our profession, we utilize various components of holistic practices from a broader base than what was originally intended. For instance, it is easy to categorize ayurvedic practices as holistic, but is it, or any specialization really, when broken out by itself? Many believe that holistic means a desire to go back to all natural ingredients and treatment modalities. However, as we have defined holistic, to go only to natural ingredients is not enough because such an approach limits us to just one portion of a holistic approach. What is natural? *Natural* is a misleading marketing term as it applies to products. However, as it applies to the age-old practices of natural therapies, it is appropriate to be incorporated into a treatment to consider it holistic. For true holism, it is more appropriate for our approach to be a complete or whole approach, in other words, overall harmony and balance. No *one* treatment or concept is necessarily holistic on its own. What should be included in the concept of holistic is that it encompasses *all* modalities of complementary wellness practices. Focusing on the mind, body, and soul combined together is a truly holistic view.

Psychological Benefits Of Holistic Practices

An important component of holistic therapy is our own belief in the treatments and products, which is conveyed to our client. Included in this is the whole ambience or drama of the treatment, the atmosphere of the room and accessories, and the comfort level of the bed, sheets, towels, temperature, lighting, etc. If the treatment procedure is accurate in technique, but the room is a mess and unsanitary, would the desired result be achieved? Probably not. The ambience is a critical factor to help create a holistic experience.

Mind-Body Connection

The milk baths that Cleopatra so enjoyed have lasted throughout the ages. It was not until

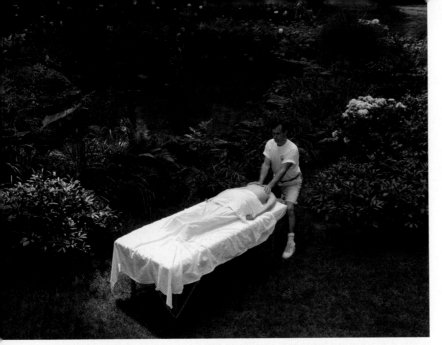

Figure 27–1 The most healing part of holistic treatments is touch.

this past century that scientific tests were developed to give us a better understanding as to why milk is so good for the skin. Milk contains lactic acid, one of our favorite alpha-hydroxy acids (AHAs). It has softening and smoothing emollients. However, what completed the treatment was the total mind-body experience. We may be so enamored of AHAs that we buy products with high levels of AHA, but forget the holistic portion of such a treatment, which provides rest and recuperation while re-energizing the body at the same time (Figure 27–1).

Certain therapies, such as some of those listed later in this chapter, are highly effective in enhancing the holistic experience and reaching a greater level of well-being and health. It is great to have the latest and best ingredients and advanced procedures; however, you do not have to wait to learn these advanced procedures to enhance your client's holistic experience. The basic things you do for the client, such as massage, is often overlooked. The reason why this is the most healing portion of a treatment is the power of touch. As estheticians we do not always realize the power of touch and the positive energy that can be transferred to the client, that is, if the esthetician is putting her heart into the massage. When reading over the list of holistic therapies the common thread in all these therapies is healing energy. Be sure of this, the effectiveness of a treatment for a client is directly proportional to the experience you give the client. If you

are cold and in a bad mood, you will not transfer positive energy. This pervades the treatment and truly inhibits the value of the overall experience and the results of the treatment itself.

Methods of Holistic Therapy

The following is an alphabetical overview of a few of the many complementary holistic therapies.

Acupressure/Acupuncture

Acupressure or acupuncture is a part of traditional Chinese medicine that has existed for over 5,000 years. It is based on the meridian system of qi (it is sometimes spelled chi) energy. The Chinese developed the principles of a sophisticated energy system called qi (pronounced chee). It is based on specific points along the meridians (energy pathways) that relate to the internal organs as well as to our emotional, psychological, and spiritual harmony. The twelve energy pathways in the body connect all the parts of the whole. The goal is to stimulate or unblock the qi along the entire meridian to enable the body to function at its best.

Acupuncture and acupressure are designed to stimulate and rebalance the qi energy (Figure 27–2). Acupressure uses pressure along the meridians to release blocked energy. Acupuncture uses fine needles along the meridians to accomplish the same. The whole point of both of these therapies lies in the Chinese belief that when the qi is out of balance, disease and disorder can occur. In

Figure 27–2 Yin and Yang – the balance of the universal elements.

Public Relations

Corporations spend billions of dollars each year shaping their image. Defining how they want the public to think about a particular idea, good, or service has become an important part of doing business. In fact, this has made public relations agencies and practitioners powerful forces in the global economy, responsible for helping businesses and governments change behavior and influence spending.

As an individual or small business owner with a limited budget, you may not be able to hire a public relations expert. However, you can use and develop some of the same basic strategies and principles that allow larger corporations to wage successful public relations campaigns.

The fine art of public relations is all about planning and developing relationships to obtain a certain desired behavior. As in any mutually satisfying and beneficial relationship, good communication skills (verbal, listening, and written) are necessary to achieve success. To communicate clearly one must first have a method for addressing the issues. As with any business venture, defining objectives, developing strategies, and setting goals must be part of the process.

But developing a public relations strategy goes beyond practical business management skills. There are also several qualitative factors that must be addressed. Developing a reputation for credibility, honesty, and exemplary business ethics are important considerations in how the world perceives you.

Understanding who you are and what you do is the first step in defining your image. Once again we are talking about value—what do you offer others that will benefit them? How can you help your clients, people you work with, other professionals and businesses, or the community as a whole? Once you are clear about your own personal qualifications you can then decide how and with whom you will share them.

Learning to think individually as well as collectively will broaden your perspective. Remember that as an esthetician or salon owner you not only represent yourself, but the entire profession. Do your goals and philosophy of doing business enhance the field of esthetics? Do you have a sense of responsibility to create a higher standard of professionalism? Do your skills represent excellence in the field? Do you work hard to increase your knowledge and skills by continuing your education? As you formulate answers to these questions you will begin to define your own public image.

How do you want to come across? Think about all those you have the opportunity to interact with. If you are a salon owner this includes employees, clients, and vendors as well as other professionals and the larger community. How do you manage these relationships? Having an appreciation for individual differences, respect for the work others do, and a good understanding of the cultural environment you have become a part of, will help foster good public relations.

Setting policies and procedures for addressing key issues such as customer service and employee relations is another important aspect of building solid relationships. Do you reward good employees for their efforts with appropriate monetary compensation as well as recognizing their good works? Do you handle difficult or unsatisfied clients with skill and diplomacy, or fly off the handle in an arrogant rage? Do you take time to foster good will in the community by doing good works? Taking the time to thoughtfully consider how you will respond to difficult situations before they arise and promoting positive relationships is a valuable exercise in diplomacy.

Figure 27–3 Aromatherapy uses many different vehicles for natural scents.

ayurvedic

The ancient Hindu art of medicine and prolonging life by a variety of methods from herbalism to massage and meditation.

shiodara

An ayurvedic treatment where warm oil is dripped over the forehead to cause deep relaxation.

essence, both are to be considered preventive as well as healing therapies. The simplicity of the Chinese system is that it is rooted in the belief that there is balance and harmony in all universal elements: dark and light, sun and moon, man and woman, etc. The concepts are based on opposites that make the whole. Chinese medicine is based on the belief that life itself is a coordinated practice of harmony between the competing forces in the universe.

Aromatherapy

Aromatherapy is the art of using essential oils for their healing and rejuvenating effects. It is used for relaxation and calming as well as for the psychological benefits derived from different aromas. Essential oils in aromatherapy are used with base oils in massage for the face or body or may be incorporated into other face and body treatments or even hydrotherapy. We also know that these essential oils can affect the limbic system in the brain, the centers of various emotions such as joy, anger, fear, and happiness. Using different essential oils to promote a sense of balance and calm can transform many basic procedures into a more holistic experience (Figure 27–3).

Ayurvedic

Ayurvedic means the science of life. It refers to practices that originated over 5,000 years ago in India. Ayurvedia indicates a universal concept of balancing all aspects of nature. It may involve many methods, from herbalism to specific types of massage, to concepts in treatments and methods of Yoga and meditation. Treatment concepts are based on three types of doshas, or mind and body types; vata represents people who are petite with a small bone structure, people who tire easily but have erratic high energy levels as well. Vata people have changeable, excitable natures. Pitta represents the moderate build, moderate bone structure, people with a sharp intelligence, but who are also easily irritated when stressed. Kaphas represent people who are heavier with well developed muscles and bone structure. Kaphas are kind and compassionate but may be sluggish and prone to fatigue or lower energy levels. These three doshas are also related to health concerns. The balance of all three doshas leads to a more healthy constitution.

Shiodara is the ayurvedic technique of dripping oil over the forehead into the "third eye" to cause deep relaxation, aromatherapeutic healing, and a general sense of wellness.

Ayurvedic therapy may consist of meditation, treatment, herbalism, massage, breathing, and diet, all balanced and combined to restore harmony in the body (Figure 27–4).

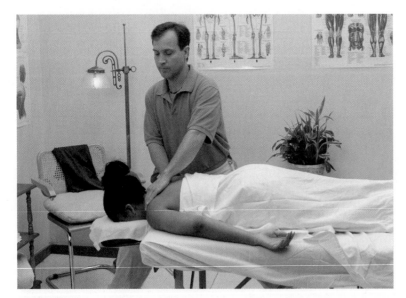

Figure 27–4 Ayurvedic treatments consist of many activities: massage, meditation, breathing, and diet.

Craniosacral Massage

Craniosacral massage is a gentle type of massage and movement of the cranium (Figure 27–5). Craniosacral massage requires a very light touch to balance the craniosacral system, the head and spinal column. It was developed in the 1970s to alleviate dysfunctions that lead can lead to neurological and sensory imbalances. This is a gentle, noninvasive massage designed to release energy blockages between the head and the spinal cord.

Lomi Lomi

Similar to Swedish massage, **Lomi Lomi** incorporates rather large movements. It is focused on finding congested areas in the body and dispersing them by moving the palms, thumbs, knuckles, and forearms in rhythmic, dancelike motions. This technique also uses spiritual, breathing, and energy components. It is practiced mostly in Hawaii.

Massage Therapies

Massage consists of using a variety of five classical European (Swedish) movements to relax and relieve stress in the face or body. More information on basic massage techniques can be found in Chapter 14. Other massage techniques are listed below.

Polarity Therapy
Developed in the 1920s by naturopath Dr. Randolph Stone, **polarity therapy** is an

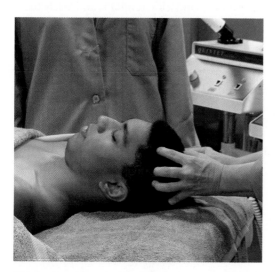

Figure 27–5 Craniosacral massage is a very gentle movement of the cranium.

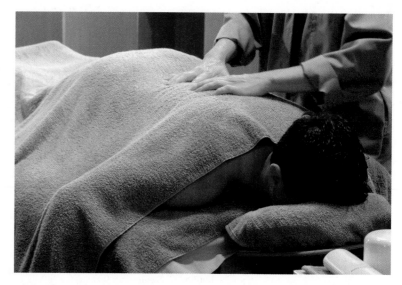

Figure 27–6 Reiki is a Japanese energy massage, more like laying-on of hands.

energy system of movement to balance positive and negative energy. The idea is to use the massage therapist's hands to rebalance the overall energy in the client's body.

Reiki
A Japanese type of energy massage, **Reiki** is a natural healing technique that feels like a flow of energy through a practitioner's hands into another person (Figure 27–6). The treatment includes placing the hands above, or on, the client's head, shoulders, stomach, and feet. It is more like a laying-on of hands. It is deeply relaxing and healing to reduce stress and balance qi energy.

Reflexology
Developed in 1988 by Eunice Inghram, a physiotherapist in the United States, reflexology massage focuses on the meridian system and balancing the organs and systems along the meridian by applying pressure to the corresponding zones on the feet or hands (Figure 27–7, p. 426). Originally the concept was based on the feet alone. Massage for the hands was added later when it was understood that there were horizontal meridians in the body as well.

In the early 1900s there was a lot of research along the same lines in Europe. Called zone therapy, it was developed by Dr. William Fitzgerald, who brought his therapy to the United States. While we call these various modalities holistic practices, in their originating countries, they were part of

craniosacral massage
A gentle type of massage and movement of the head.

Lomi Lomi
A method of massage practiced in Hawaii that is similar to Swedish massage; it incorporates large body movements, much like a dance.

polarity therapy
An energy system of movement using the massage therapist's hands to rebalance energy over the body.

Reiki
A Japanese type of energy massage.

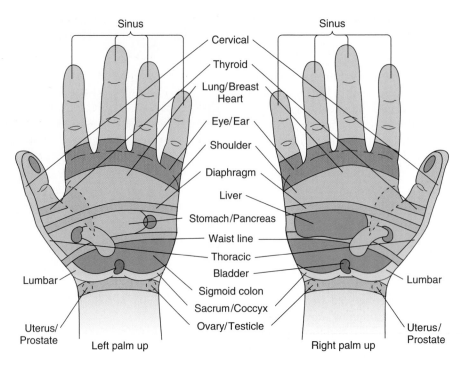

Figure 27–7 Reflexology balances the organs and systems by applying pressure to zones on the hands and feet.

comprehensive medical research and health-related practice.

Today, we in the United States frequently think of reflexology, as well as shiatsu, acupressure, shiodara, and the like as alternative therapies, more often connected with the spa or massage therapy center than with medicine.

Shiatsu

Popularized in the 1940s in Japan by Tokujiro Namikoshi, shiatsu means finger pressure therapy. It is performed similar to acupressure to relieve stress along the meridian system with the added component of meridian stretches (Figure 27–8).

The major insight and guiding principle of Chinese medicine is that health is a state of balance, while illness is a disturbance of that balance. (Refer to Chapter 1, Figure 1–9, the Chinese Model of Health). All the efforts of a Chinese practitioner tend toward restoring equilibrium.

As this concept swept across the world, the Japanese created an adaptation of the meridian system and developed a massage system called shiatsu (*shi* means finger, *atsu* means pressure). Pressure is applied to tsubo, or the motor points of nerves and muscles along the meridians that connect all the organs and systems to one whole.

Trager Method

Developed by Dr. Milton Trager in the 1920s, the **Trager method** is a mobility treatment concept where the body is gently rocked to produce positive energy stimulation. The central nervous system releases stress and leaves the client with a feeling of lightness and flexibility.

Trigger Point Myotherapy

Concentrating on relieving myofacial pain, this modality concentrates on pressure to trigger points in muscles, tendons, and fascia to

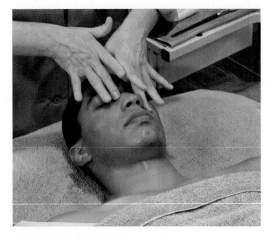

Figure 27–8 Shiatsu means finger pressure therapy.

Trager method
Mobility treatment that rocks the body gently to produce positive energy stimulation..

relieve stress and pain. Also similar to acupressure and shiatsu, the pressure exerted relieves stressed points in the meridian system.

Herbalism

We should also include another modality incorporated into many holistic treatment plans, herbalism. Herbalism has been practiced in India and China for over 5,000 years. Diets such as vegetarian and macrobiotic, exercise including tai chi, qi-gong, yoga, meditation, prayer, religion, etc. are all included in herbalism.

Other therapies such as hydrotherapy and water therapies will be discussed more fully in Chapter 34.

Please note, many of the therapies mentioned require previous specialty training and licensure such as basic massage therapy. Your state regulations determine the scope of practice under your esthetician's license. It is your responsibility to determine what training you need and which therapies you may use as an esthetician.

Summary

All of the therapies discussed concentrate on achieving wellness. These practices are based on the concept of balance and harmony. It is essential for the esthetician to believe in the procedure she performs or these treatments lose their intensity. The common theme in these holistic practices is balancing energy. It is vital to understand how important it is for the esthetician to have her own balance and positive energy. Without this essential element the holistic therapy experience becomes just another procedure. The culminating area of balance for both the client and esthetician is that of relaxing the mind, relieving stress, and producing a sense of harmony, joy, and well-being. This is the true meaning of holistic, all-encompassing and inclusive.

Discussion Questions

1. Define what is meant by a holistic approach to health care.

2. Using your analysis of a holistic approach to health care as a guideline, explain the basic differences between Eastern and Western medicine philosophies.

3. Select a topic of interest (e.g., shiodara, acupressure, or shiatsu) from one of the Eastern holistic practices that appeals to you and conduct additional research. Share this information with your classmates and discuss how this could be integrated into the esthetic practice.

4. Review several spa menus and determine those treatments that might be considered "holistic" or "alternative" in nature. Do you see a growing trend?

5. Using the same menus, select three alternative treatments and analyze them in terms of the following factors: physiological, psychological, and mind-body connection.

Additional Reading

Hess, Shelley. 1996. *SalonOvations' Guide to Aromatherapy*. Clifton Park, N.Y.: Milady, an imprint of Delmar Learning, a division of Thomson Learning, Inc.

Hess, Shelley. 1997. *The Professional's Reflexology Handbook*. Clifton Park, N.Y.: Milady, an imprint of Delmar Learning, a division of Thomson Learning, Inc.

Miller, Erica. 1996. *SalonOvations' Shiatsu Massage*. Clifton Park, N.Y.: Milady, an imprint of Delmar Learning, a division of Thomson Learning, Inc.

Notes

Merriam-Webster's Collegiate Dictionary, 10th ed. 1993. Springfield, MA: Merriam-Webster, Inc.

Bratman, Steven. 1999. *The Alternative Medicine Sourcebook*. New York: McGraw Hill.

Helpful Web Sites

http://www.holisticmedicine.org (AHMA—American Holistic Medicine Association)

http://www.ahha.org (American Holistic Health Association)

Chapter 28
Advanced Home Care

Chapter Objectives

After reading this chapter, you should be able to:

▶ Identify a more complete system of home care for your client.

▶ Know how to add advanced products to your client's home care inventory.

▶ Build a treatment plan for both professional treatment and home care recommendation.

▶ Learn how to "close the sale" with your client.

Chapter Outline

Introduction
Understanding Your Client
Advanced Product Types and Features
Introducing Advanced Products to the Client
The Home Care Treatment Form
Advanced/Enhanced Selling
Sample Advanced Product Plans

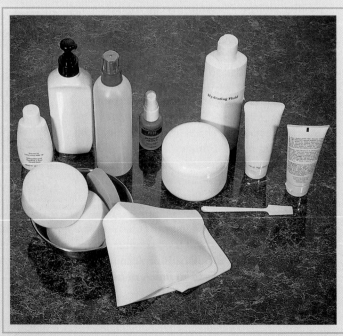

Introduction

In this chapter, we will discuss *why* and *how* to augment your client's home care product inventory to enhance the treatment results. To fully understand the home care principles of this section, it is recommended you review Chapter 16, Postconsultation and Home Care, where the basic principles of home care are outlined. This chapter presents the home care guide again. However, now it indicates step(s) for more advanced skin management and correction products. These enhanced products include deep pore cleansers, eye creams, lip treatment, and neck creams. They also may include special treatment serums or creams to give a more intense regimen for home care.

Figure 28–1 Understanding your client's needs is important when prescribing home care products.

Understanding Your Client

Your client's perception of industry trends in skin care, and her knowledge of what products are available and best to use for her particular skin treatment, may be the catalyst that brought her to you in the first place. Be aware of all popular over-the-counter (OTC) products. Know what the industry trends are. These are products that your client sees advertised constantly and has formed an opinion about. You will need to provide an informed approach in offering the most efficacious products to your clients (Figure 28–1).

A good example of this is when exfoliants first became popular. In the mid-seventies, the consumer hardly knew what the word *exfoliation* meant, that is, until the Buff Puff came out and was advertised on television and in the print media. Suddenly professionals were inundated with clients buying and overusing the Buff Puff.

Professional treatments may also be established in your client's mind through advertising. A recent noteworthy example is the interest in vitamin A or retinol products. For years, the original, pure vitamin A acid called Retinol was not available to the average consumer because of the volume of concentrate required to cause exfoliation. As a result, topical irritation was not uncommon. This is the reason Dr. Albert Klingman of the

University of Pennsylvania Medical School opted to use Retin-A, a derivative of retinoic acid. Ultimately, Dr. Klingman's work made Retin-A famous.

Eventually, it was discovered that it was possible to deliver retinol through microsponge technology resulting in little or no irritation. This newly patented delivery system, combined with retinol, was an incredible breakthrough in the skin care industry. It is one of the most sought after cell renewal exfoliation, antiaging creams on the market today. Your client has no doubt seen it advertised in professional and retail products. You need to understand what your client is exposed to. The media has brought these products to the attention of your customers; however, it is up to you, the esthetician, to bring accurate and informative education and product use to your customer.

Advanced Product Types And Features

The success of any sale depends on the strength of your knowledge about your products (Figure 28–2, p. 4). The following general product features will give you an outline

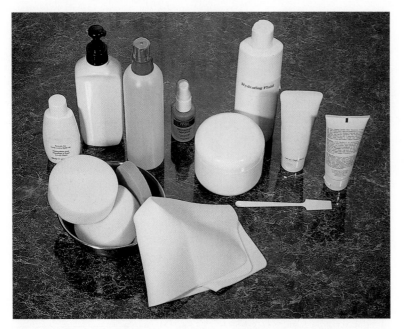

Figure 28–2 Product knowledge is key to the success of the home care regimen.

to use in building your knowledge of the product line or lines you use in your salon.

- Deep pore cleanser

  utilizes a betahydroxy acid or alpha-hydroxy acid to dissolve oil clogs in follicles

  flushes the follicle by dissolving dead cells and sebum accumulation

  use only as needed to clear clogs

- Home care strength exfoliation

  AHA or BHA special exfoliant ingredient to remove dead cells

  refines the skin

  stimulates new cell growth at the basal layer of the epidermis

- Specific-use serum

  specialized ingredients to stimulate cell turnover

  contains antioxidants to neutralize free radicals and protect the skin

  offers visible reduction in the appearance of fine lines

- Eye cream/gel

  helps reduce puffiness

  reduces the visible signs of fine lines and aging

  helps relieve dark circles by stimulating microcirculation around the eye

- Neck cream

  special liposome technology helps firm the neck tissue over several hours with each application

  softens and protects sensitive neck areas

  helps diffuse redness and "chicken skin" on the neck

- Premakeup serum or ampoule

  fills crevices and lines for a smoother look

  sets the makeup for longer lasting needs such as a photography session or special occasions

  gives the makeup foundation a smoother looking finish

  Add any additional features and benefits for your product line, keeping your points simple and easy to understand.

Introducing Advanced Products To the Client

It is important for the esthetician to take ownership in educating the client about product choices and uses. The majority of that education, as well as the sale, is done during the skin care analysis, followed by the home care consultation after the service. Discussing your client's skin care needs, as well as what you see under the magnifying lamp during the skin analysis, establishes the need for professional treatments as well as an effective home care regimen.

Explain to the client what the treatment involves and the products you will be using, including any specialty treatments and masks. Then explain what the client needs to do at home to continue the progress of the treatments and achieve the desired results. Establish a partnership with the client to improve her skin. Remember to explain to the client how important it is to follow the home care plan *daily* in conjunction with your professional treatments.

When you discuss home care during the analysis, do not identify specific products at this point. The client will not remember the names of products; however, this *is* a good time to establish the need for advanced products such as sunscreen, daytime protection, evening hydration, or deep pore cleansing. At the end of the treatment, during the home consultation write down the products you recommend for purchase.

The main principle behind the analysis or sale is not only to educate your client about what you see in her skin, but to address the client's perceived needs as well.

The Home Care Treatment Form

The home care treatment form gives a list of steps for the client to use in the home care regimen, and contains reference to the most commonly used professional retail products (Figure 28–3, p. 432). Use it as a guideline when preparing directions for your client's home care use. You can use the steps with whatever product line you choose. Other product lines may use different names for products, but the generic terms should be equivalent or similar in most product lines. As observed by the overlapping of products in the same step, there will be times when you have a client layering multiple products at the same time, such as applying eye cream, neck cream, then night cream. This is fine for the savvy, well-educated client. However, for the person who does not want an involved routine, only prescribe the most important products that will produce the most intense results. After this client sees some results, you can then build the product inventory to enhance and advance the treatment. Most of this is determined by developing a relationship with your client, and understanding her lifestyle, level of commitment to improving the skin, and the credibility and trust you have built with your client.

The **boldface** listings are directions for what is considered more advanced or enhanced product use.

Advanced/Enhanced Selling

The idea of advanced or enhanced selling is to provide a complete program. The products, including specialty items, are tools for the client to use to obtain the desired results and to educate the client on how to take proper care of the skin. Integrating these additional retail home care products as a complete program process works in tandem with your in-salon treatments. Although high-performance serums are more of an investment for home care, they are part of the total program concept, which clients come to appreciate as they notice more accelerated results.

Tips for Selling Success

Selling products, for the esthetician, is not really about selling. It is about determining the unique needs of your client's skin, product education, recommendation, and advice. It is up to you to present the most comprehensive program available to save or to manage the client's skin care problems. Without your home care recommendations, your professional service is not complete.

- Recommending home care products is about continuing the in-salon treatment at home. It results in more visible results because what the client does at home daily is so much more valuable than what happens in the salon or spa one to four times a month. Once again, it is the integration of both that makes a *complete* program.

- The closer the home care follow-up is to your in-salon treatment, the more effective the results. This enhances your credibility in your client's eye.

- Selling is not an option or just another way to make extra money, it is your professional responsibility.

- When prescribing advanced home care products such as serums, eye creams, neck creams, and deep pore cleansers, the technology is generally much more advanced. It is essential that you have a complete understanding of the product, why it exists, the technology behind it, and how it relates to the professional treatment. What specific benefits are given to your client?

- As a general rule, products that are more high tech than other companion products will be more expensive. Do not let the higher cost prevent you from offering the product. Your responsibility is to educate the client about the most advanced technology available. If the client chooses not to purchase a product, however, you can walk away knowing that you have completed your professional responsibility.

Home Care Treatment Form

1. Apply _____ eye makeup remover on a two-sided moistened cotton pad and swipe the eye area in a downward direction. Flip the pad and wipe the eyes until clean. If necessary, turn the pad inside out or use a newly moistened pad and repeat this step until the eyes are completely clean.

2. Cleanse the face with _____ by applying about a teaspoon of cleanser on your hands. Massage your hands together and then massage both hands over the entire face. Massage in circles for about 30 seconds and rinse with warm water. **or (depending on skin type/condition)**

3. Apply _____ foaming cleanser with moistened fingertips and lather over the entire face and neck well. Massage the face in upward and outward circles. Then simply rinse with warm water. Ideal to use in the shower. **or (depending on skin type/condition)**

4. **Instead of the foaming cleanser in step #3, apply _____ deep pore cleanser twice a week on clean skin (depending on the manufacturer's directions). Moisten the fingertips; massage it in and let it sit for 5–10 minutes. Then rinse well, being sure to flush skin well until all residues are removed. You may also us _____ AHA exfoliation at this step instead of a deep pore cleanser.**

5. Apply _____ freshener on a moist sponge or disposable cotton and wipe the entire face well, turning the sponges or cotton until all traces of dirt, oil, and makeup have been removed. *or (for dryer skin needing more stimulation)*

6. Apply _____ freshener again by spraying it on the fingertips and patting the skin.

7. *Apply a small amount of _____,_____ (eye cream, neck cream, or both if applicable) around the eyes or on the neck to protect and revitalize the area. Massage it in well, always working in a circular motion around the eyes.*

8. *Apply _____ (serum intensive) to the entire face and neck. Massage it in well.*

9. In the morning, apply a peanut-size amount of _____ day cream or daytime protection lotion on a clean, toned (after freshener) face and massage it in well. Wait until it is dry before applying makeup base.

10. *For a special occasion or special makeup results, do not apply the day cream before the foundation. Apply a lubricant-free makeup base under the makeup (serum or ampoule), lightly massage it in, then apply the foundation. This is the only case where day cream and sunscreen are not used.*

11. At night, the basic cleansing will remain the same as in the day but depending on the product line and the intensity of the skin problem, *there may be a special AHA product, specialty serum, or specialty treatment cream that should be applied on the freshly cleansed and toned skin and then followed with the evening treatment cream. This will allow the skin specialty treatment to nourish the skin while you rest, for whatever specific problem the skin has.*

12. *Apply _____ specialty treatment followed by _____ night cream on a cleansed and toned face and neck. The skin should feel slightly moist but not too greasy before retiring.*

13. *Apply _____ and/or _____ (insert eye cream or neck cream). Allow cream to nourish the skin during sleep.*

14. *Once or twice a week (according to manufacturer's directions) apply the _____ mask on cleansed and toned skin. The mask should be applied with the fingertips to the thickness of a dime. Do not allow the skin to show through the mask. Rest _____ minutes and rinse the mask off with warm water. Follow with a freshener again and follow the nightly treatment procedure.*

15. *Special instructions:*
   _____
   _____
   _____
   _____

Figure 28–3 Home care treatment form.

Marketing

Mention the word *marketing* and most people immediately think of advertising. However, advertising is just one aspect of marketing, which in fact, covers a much broader perspective of planning and implementing a strategy for how ideas, goods, or services are exchanged.

The key to understanding the marketing process is recognizing that it serves both buyers and sellers. Consumers (buyers) have needs or wants. Businesses (sellers) aim to satisfy these needs and wants with their products and services. In the process of marketing, something of value is exchanged between the two so that ideally each is better off after the exchange.

Formulating a marketing strategy includes developing effective communication, promotion, public relations, and personal selling skills. The first step in this process is to identify what it is you are selling and how the customer will benefit. Determining a value or price for this exchange, and how or where it will be distributed, comes next. From here you can decide on a method for promoting the exchange.

Before embarking on a method for promoting your services, it is important to gather as much information as possible about your customer. In today's competitive marketplace understanding what customers value is critical to successfully meeting their needs and wants. Whether it be convenience, service, price (low cost or exclusive high-end quality), speed, on-time delivery, or efficiency, finding the right points to target to the right population will help you achieve success. Simply stated—give clients what they want.

Providing customer value over an extended period of time is challenging. And, of course, it would be impossible to expect to be all things to all people. In this age of information, many companies spend a great deal of time and money collecting information about their clients and what they value, but fail to establish a real lasting personal relationship, an important factor in a service-oriented business such as esthetics. It is important to remember that facts and figures have no real value in isolation and must be organized and interpreted to have any real impact.

A total quality management program can help to develop strong long-term personal relationships and avoid becoming complacent. By focusing on the needs of the customer, and continually striving to understand, improve, and create new methods for meeting these needs, you can alleviate some of the challenges associated with maintaining competitive value. Customizing and managing a computer system that automatically collects and stores data for easy analysis can be extremely helpful in satisfying your customers.

Once you have a thorough understanding of whom you are marketing to, you can begin to think about how you will market. There are several methods of promotion that can be utilized, including advertising, public relations, publicity, direct marketing, personal selling, and sales promotion. These can be mixed using a variety of media such as direct mail, magazines, newspapers, radio, and television to create an effective strategy.

It is often helpful to think of the promotion mix in terms of *who, what, how,* and *where.* That is, *who* is conveying the information, or has something to sell; *what* message do they want to convey; *how* will they communicate the information; and *where* will they deliver their message? As you ponder these questions remember to think in terms of value: understand exactly what your skills and talents are, how they benefit the consumer, and what consumer population will value these services.

- Do not try to guess or manage your client's finances. Let the client make those decisions.

- Do not justify your prices for treatments or products. Your job is to present the latest technological advances in skin correction and management. Financial decisions belong to the client.

- Believing in what you do as a professional and what you sell can only be valid when you personally experience the benefits.

- Living your own philosophy and values makes a tremendous difference in successful selling. Do you use your own products? Depending on your product line, you may have the advantage of offering more than one specialty treatment, which can be alternated, such as applying one product in the morning and the other in the evening.

- Never overpromise what a product can do. Always state the benefits of the products and how they relate to the client's skin care needs. Try not to use words such as *correction*. This misleads the client into thinking that a skin care problem will be completely solved by your product. Use words such as *improvement* and *enhancement*. Point out positive aspects of the client's skin and talk about enhancement. Remember, estheticians do not cure skin problems; they enhance and improve the appearance of the skin.

Sample Advanced Product Plans

The following three examples show a generic product line with three different product divisions that provide attention to specific skin types and conditions: aging/mature/ environmentally damaged skin, sensitive/ reactive skin, and oily/problematic skin (acne). Each line includes a high-performance concentrate or serum that helps boost improvement. As you study these guidelines, notice the pattern that emerges in each section. Compare the ingredient synergy (components working together for an end result) to the actual needs of the skin type and

condition. Each has a quality that is beneficial. Notice what the physiological and biological changes are in aging and environmentally damaged skin. Look at the characteristics and conditions of sensitive, reactive skin, and then problematic/acne, oily skin. You will also note that the same ingredients may be used for many conditions due to their properties. All ingredients are placed into formulas in very small amounts. They work collectively to produce end results.

Skin Care System A

This system is designed for aging, mature and environmentally damaged skin. It contains six products—cleanser, toner, day and night moisturizers, a high performance concentrate, and a mask. Botanicals and biologicals (proteins) are performance ingredients with known properties that nourish, are regenerative (healing), firming, and toning. These are easily integrated into an antiaging program. *Note*: Intrinsic aging (associated with the normal aging process of your internal body clock) and photoaging (associated with sun damage) are key in determining how fast the skin ages. Aging skin experiences a loss of elasticity (tone) and a decrease in both lipids and water retention ability. Although circulation slows as we age, it may be even more impaired due to capillary damage from overexposure to the sun or tanning beds. The skin appears dull due to reduced cell turnover.

Goals
Notable differences in hydration levels with an increased softening and toning effect help improve the skin's appearance. The skin looks more radiant healthy, and youthful.

Key Ingredient Synergy
Table 28–1 lists the ingredients found throughout this system. These specific ingredients are included because they all help to "wake up" the skin. Aging skin needs extra nourishment to see improvement. The system also provides lipids that help balance and nourish skin that has lost some of its ability to retain moisture.

Observation of this synergy shows that there are components that help to increase sluggish circulation and calm skin that is

Table 28–1 Key Ingredient Synergy for Skin Care System A—Aging Skin

Ingredients	Known Benefits
Biologicals	
Collagen	Helps to retain and build a moisture barrier
Elastin	Firming, emollient, improves sensitivity
DNA	Strengthening, calming, restoring
Phyto (plant) Extracts	
Calendula (*Calendula officinalis*)	Regenerative, soothing, antiseptic
Cypress (*Cypress sempervirens*)	Calming, purifying, firming
Geranium (*Pelargonium sp.*)	Strengthening (capillaries), smoothes, decongests
Ginseng (*Panax sp.*)	Revitalizing, fortifying, toning
Hops (*Humulus lupulus*)	Calming, restorative, estrogenic, antiseptic, emollient, astringent
Horsetail (*Equisetum arvense*)	Anti-inflammatory, regenerative, strengthening
Jasmine (*Jasminum officinale*)	Calming, moisturizing, antiseptic, analgesic
Lotus (*Nelumbo nucifera*)	Sedative, soothes, astringent
Mandarin (*Citrus madurensis*)	Lymphatic stimulant, sedative (calming)
Pinecone (*Pinus palustris*)	Astringent (toning), stimulating, antiseptic
Rosemary (*Rosmarinus officinalis*)	Regenerative, astringent, calming
Thyme (*Thymus sp.*)	Activating, stimulating, regenerative, calming, antimicrobial
Turmeric (*Curcuma longa*)	Stimulating, regenerative, antiseptic, antioxidant, anti-inflammatory (calming)
Lipids	
Orange roughy oil	Fatty acids omega-3 and -6 to soften and nourish
Rice bran oil	Emollient, antioxidant, moisturizing, linoleic acid (vitamin F)
Soybean oil	Soothing, estrogenic, fatty acids (lecithin, sterols), vitamins A, E, K, nourishing
Squalane (olives)	Moisturizing, lubricating, soothing, regenerative
Special Agents	
Allantoin	Emollient, regenerative, soothing, desensitizing
Beta-glucans	Regenerative, softens, protective, moisturizing, restorative
Glycerin	Emollient, soothing, moisturizing
Glycoproteins	Enhances cell metabolism, boosting cells' oxygen consumption
Honey (*Mel*)	Humectant (moisturizing), softening
Hyaluronic acid	Moisture binding, softening
Sodium PCA	Humectant, desensitizing
Vitamins	
Vitamin A	Prevents tissue degeneration, antioxidant, normalizes, firms, regenerative, fortifying
Vitamin B$_5$ (panthenol)	Moisturizing, regenerative, conditions, humectant, softens
Vitamin C	Antioxidant, regenerative, stimulating, collagen synthesis
Vitamin E	Antioxidant, nourishing, soothes, hydrates

sensitive from either the aging process or environmental damage. The word *regenerative* means that the properties of an agent may help the skin regenerate fibroblastic activity. Fibroblasts are responsible for regeneration of collagen and elastin in the skin. The word *estrogenic* is a descriptive term meaning that the particular component appears to be beneficial to skin that has experienced a decrease in hormone activity.

Skin Care System B

This system addresses the needs of highly sensitive skin such as reactive, couperose, or telangiectasia. The synergy of calming botanicals, biologicals, and vitamins helps improve cell oxygen exchange, regeneration, and helps soothe and provide anti-inflammatory properties. It is an ideal system for postlaser and microdermabrasion.

Goals

Skin tones become even and less blotchy, with increased hydration. This system helps to lessen the visible cutaneous (skin) irregularities associated with poor circulation, broken capillaries, environmental damage, and genetically predisposed sensitive skin.

Key Ingredient Synergy

Table 28–2 lists the synergy of ingredients that have properties that help soothe and calm irritated, sensitive skin. Many of the components have properties that stimulate the healing process of the skin. Others are credited with helping to strengthen capillaries and balance skin tones

This system contains ingredients that support the circulation (capillary) networks. It has many anti-inflammatory and regenerative (healing) aspects. It helps calm and strengthen the skin. Remember that sensitive skin types and conditions may be oily or dry. Sun-damaged skin normally has vascular (capillary) damage most noticeable on the face, neck, and décolleté areas. Treatment for this skin type should be gradual so that maximum benefits are achieved without further sensitivity.

Skin Care System C

This system is for oily and problematic skin (acne). You will notice quite a difference in the key ingredients. The system contains six products; a cleanser, toner, oil-free day cream, and a light night emulsion. It also includes a camphor mask and a spot treatment.

Goals

The skin should appear less blotchy, more hydrated, and experience a decrease or balance of excess oil and/or breakout lesions.

Key Synergy Ingredients

Table 28–3, p. 438 lists the synergy ingredients for problematic skin. These ingredients emphasize antiseptic and calming properties. Because there is a need for moisture without excessive lipids, humectants and other proteins help soften and moisturize.

Problematic or acne skin can be sensitive, irritated, dehydrated, blotchy and have open lesions. If it is excessively oily, there may also be a buildup of skin cells and congestion in the follicles. Small amounts of AHAs help exfoliate dead skin cells. The addition of salicylic acid actually breaks through the oily, impacted comedones in the follicle. Salicylic acid is referred to as oil soluble. The agents in this synergy have both antiseptic and antimicrobial (antibacterial) properties for infected lesions. When there are open acne lesions, it is important that they are calmed and healed; therefore, the special agents and botanicals contain regenerative (healing) properties. Most botanicals do contain soothing and healing properties. Other ingredients help to control excessive oil secretion. Always be cautious when using more intense exfoliating ingredients such as those in this system for problematic skin. It is important for moisture levels be kept in balance at all times.

Summary

The first step in product knowledge is to understand the basics of your skin care line. These basics are recommended as a beginning program for the client. Familiarize yourself with each item and its function. You will use this information during your consultation and professional treatment plans as well as when making home care recommendations.

We have taken the products a step further by adding a generic skin care system that is divided into three segments:

Table 28–2 Key Ingredient Synergy for Skin Care System B—Sensitive Skin

Ingredients	Known Benefits
Biologicals	
Collagen	Helps to retain and build a moisture barrier
Elastin	Firming, emollient, calms
DNA	Strengthens, calms, restores
Phyto (plant) Extracts	
Arnica (*Arnica montana*)	Regenerative, soothing, antiseptic, stimulating
Bisabolol (from chamomile)	Anti-inflammatory, regenerative (wound healing), stimulating,
Carrot (*Daucus carota*)	Purifying, regenerative
Chamomile (*Anthemis nobilis*)	Anti-inflammatory, regenerative, bactericidal, neutralizes irritants
Comfrey (*Symphytum officinale*)	Contains allantoin, anti-inflammatory, astringent, regenerative, emollient, tonic
Cornflower (*Centaurea cyanus*)	Moisture-binding, soothing, softening, tightening, anti-inflammatory
Cucumber (*Cucumis sativus*)	Antispasmodic, anti-inflammatory, circulatory stimulant
Dang Gui (*Angelica sinensis*)	Strengthening (capillaries), smoothes, decongests
Geranium (*Pelargonium sp.*)	Antioxidant, soothing, strengthening
Grape (*Vitis vinifera*)	Anti-inflammatory, soothing
Guaiazulene (azulene)	Astringent, anti-inflammatory, strengthening to vessels
Horse chestnut (*Aesculus hippocastanum*)	Astringent, anti-inflammatory, sedative
Hypericum (*Hypericum perforatum*) - St. John's Wort	Anti-inflammatory, astringent
Hyssop (*Hyssopus officinalis*)	Healing, tonic, stimulating
Lavender (*Lavandula officinalis*)	Antiseptic, soothing, sedative, astringent Anti-inflammatory, antibacterial, antispasmodic, balancing, soothing, healing
Linden (*Tilia sp.*)	Antiseptic, skin-clearing, soothing, sedative
Mallow (*Malva sylvestris*)	Anti-inflammatory, soothing, emollient
Neroli (*Citrus aurantium*)	Sedative, soothing, stimulating to cell regeneration
Lipids	
Corn oil	Emollient, softening
Jojoba oil (*Buxeus chinensis*)	Emollient, moisturizing, nourishing
Shea butter *(Butyrospermum partii)*	Emollient, anti-inflammatory, regenerative, decongesting
Soybean oil	Improves lipid barrier, hydrates, smooths
Squalane (olives)	Desensitizing, emollient, nourishing
Sweet almond oil	Emollient, regenerative
Special Agents	
Revitalin-BT (glycoproteins)	Enhances cell metabolism, boosting cells' oxygen consumption
Hyaluronic acid	Binds moisture, emollient, soothing, moisturizing
Vitamins	
Vitamin A	Prevents tissue degeneration, antioxidant, normalizes, firms, regenerative, fortifying
Vitamin C	Antioxidant, regenerative, stimulating, promotes collagen synthesis
Vitamin D$_3$	Firms, helps support epidermal cell turnover
Vitamin E	Antioxidant, nourishing, soothes, hydrates

Table 28–3 Key Ingredient Synergy for Skin Care System C—Problematic Skin

Ingredients	Known Benefits
Botanicals	
Aloe vera	Soothing, regenerative, moisturizing
Arnica (*Arnica montana*)	Regenerative, soothing, antiseptic, stimulating
Calendula (*Calendula officinalis*)	Regenerative, soothing, antiseptic
Camphor (*Cinnamomum camphora*)	Anti-inflammatory, antiseptic, astringent, cooling, sedative
Carrot (*Daucus carota*)	Purifying, regenerative
Cucumber (*Cucumis sativus*)	Moisture-binding, soothing, softening, tightening, anti-inflammatory
Geranium (*Pelargonium sp.*)	Strengthening (capillaries), smoothes, decongests
Hops (*Humulus lupulus*)	Calming, restorative, estrogenic, antiseptic, emollient, astringent
Horsetail (*Equisetum arvense*)	Anti-inflammatory, regenerative, strengthening, softening
Lemon (*Citrus limonum*)	Antiseptic, purifying, lymphatic stimulant
Menthol (*Mentha piperita*)	Antiseptic, analgesic, calming, cooling, circulation stimulant
Peppermint (*Mentha piperita*)	Antiseptic, cooling, analgesic, calming
Rosemary (*Rosmarinus officinalis*)	Regenerative, astringent, calming,
Sage (*Salvia officinalis*)	Antispasmodic, astringent, antiseptic, cooling
Spearmint (*Mentha viridis*)	Antiseptic, cooling, analgesic
Tea tree (*Melaleuca alternifolia*)	Antiseptic, germicidal, wound-healing, anti-inflammatory
Turmeric (*Curcuma longa*)	Stimulating, regenerative, antiseptic, antioxidant, anti-inflammatory (calming)
Witch hazel (*Hamamelis virginiana*)	Anti-inflammatory, wound-healing
Yucca (*Yucca schidigera*)	Anti-inflammatory, soothing
Exfoliants	
Bromelain (Pineapple)	Exfoliates, softens, dissolves keratin buildup
Glycolic acid (AHA)	Exfoliates, softens, dissolves intercellular cement
Lactic acid (AHA)	Exfoliates, softens, water binding
Malic acid (AHA)	Exfoliates, softens
Pancreatin (enzyme)	Dissolves keratin buildup
Papain (enzyme from papaya)	Dissolves keratin buildup
Salicylic acid	Exfoliates, antimicrobial, keratolytic (keratin dissolving)
Special Agents	
Colloidal sulfur	Reduces oil activity, dissolves keratin buildup, antimicrobial
Glycerin	Emollient, soothing, moisturizing
Glycoproteins	Enhances cell metabolism, boosting cells' oxygen consumption
Oat flour (*Avena sativa*)	Soothing, anti-irritant
Yeast beta-glucans	Regenerative, hydrating, softens
Vitamins	
Vitamin A	Prevents tissue degeneration, antioxidant, normalizes, firms, regenerative, fortifying
Vitamin C	Antioxidant, regenerative, stimulating, collagen synthesis
Vitamin E	Antioxidant, nourishing, soothes, hydrates

aging/mature/environmentally damaged skin, sensitive/reactive skin, and oily/problematic skin. These are the most common types of client skin conditions you will experience. By using the aforementioned guidelines to skin type and condition, a product list with the ingredients and their properties, you will be able to build your own client treatment plans with whatever product line you are currently using.

Discussion Questions

1. Discuss techniques for helping clients adhere to a home care program. How does a written home care guide help or hinder this process?

2. Given the fact that clients will vary in their approach, brainstorm several options that could be utilized to promote a total program concept that features home care as an integral part of the package.

3. Selling products is an important part of an esthetician's job; however estheticians often have mixed feelings about selling.

Addressing sales from an educational perspective is often a viable alternative for those who are uncomfortable with a sales approach. To help discern your own comfort level, create a list of adjectives you generally associate with sales. How might an educational approach differ? Which approach are you most comfortable with?

Additional Reading

Michalun, Natalia, with M. Varinia Michalun. 2000. *Milady's Skin Care and Cosmetic Ingredients Dictionary,* 2d ed. Clifton Park, N.Y.: Milady, an imprint of Delmar Learning, a division of Thomson Learning, Inc.

Miller, Erica. 1996. *SalonOvations' Day Spa Techniques*, Clifton Park, N.Y.: Milady, an imprint of Delmar Learning, a division of Thomson Learning, Inc.

Helpful Web Sites

http://www.skindoctor.com
http://www.aad.org

Epilation

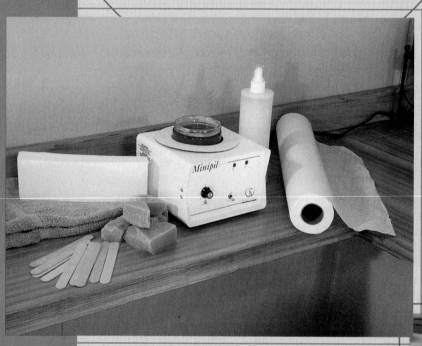

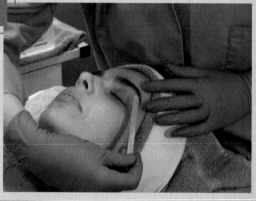

PART VIII

Part Outline

Chapter 29   Methods of Hair Removal

Chapter 30   Waxing Procedures

Hair removal makes up a large part of a salon's business. In some cases, up to 50% of the services performed involve hair removal. Understanding the techniques available for hair removal, the benefits and risks of hair removal, and how to execute the various techniques is key to an esthetician's success in this potentially profitable area.

In Part VIII, you will learn the hair removal procedures an esthetician is expected to know in the professional world. In addition, you'll learn how hair growth has been viewed in various cultures, what tools are used for each key procedure, and what is involved in room preparation. Sanitation plays an important role in hair removal, regardless of what part of the body is being treated, and the most up-to-date procedures are explained. Finally, you will be instructed on how to remove hair from nearly every part of the body.

Chapter 29
Methods of Hair Removal

Chapter Objectives

After reading this chapter, you should be able to:

- Describe hair growth as related to different ethnic groups.
- Explain the morphology of hair and its growth stages.
- Identify methods of temporary and permanent hair removal.
- Describe the proper way to set up a treatment room.
- Identify the different equipment, tools, and accessories.

Chapter Outline

Introduction
Morphology of Hair
Differences in Hair Growth and Characteristics
Hair Removal
Furniture and Accessories
Tools and Supplies
Sanitation
Room Preparation
General Hair Removal (Waxing)

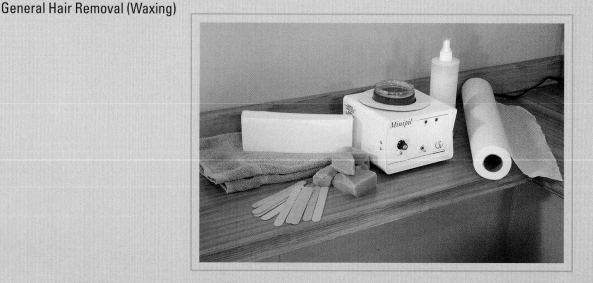

Introduction

Hair has always been part of the human experience. Since mankind crawled out of the cave and looked at his image in the nearest pool of water, people have had a preoccupation with hair: grooming it, cutting it, shaping it, and removing it to meet current social standards. From the earliest records of history, hair has been used to enhance adornment, beauty, status, and attraction.

Hair removal for cosmetic reasons became very popular after World War I. It is reported that almost $4 billion a year is now spent on hair removal products and services.

Morphology of Hair

Hair is a hard protein called keratin, which is produced from a tubular mold called the **hair follicle** (Figure 29–1). A hair follicle is a mass of epidermis, extending down into the dermis, forming a small tube. The follicle swells at the base to form a **hair bulb**, referred to as the *hair club*. The tubular mold itself is called the papilla. The hair fiber, or **hair shaft**, moves up the follicle and extends above the skin's surface.

Referred to as a pilosebaceous follicle (*pilus* means hair; pili is the plural), it contains both the sebaceous appendage and the hair shaft. Follicles grow all over the body. How much hair you have is predetermined by genetics. Not all follicles contain a hair shaft. There is generally no hair growth on the palms of the hands, the soles of the feet, the lips, or the eyelids.

Hair follicles slant into the skin, sometimes in many different directions (for example, under the arm). The largest part of the follicle, the bulb, is at its base. It contains an oval-shaped cavity filled with tissue, called **dermal papilla**, which contains the blood

hair follicle
The tubular epithelial shield that surrounds the lower part of the hair shaft.

hair bulb
The swelling at the base of the follicle that provides the growing basal part of the hair with nourishment; also referred to as the hair club.

hair shaft
The portion of hair that projects beyond the skin, consisting of an outer layer (the cuticle), an innermost later (the medulla), and an in-between layer (the cortex). Color changes are made within the cortex.

dermal papilla
The oval-shaped cavity in the bulb of the follicle; it is filled with tissue that contains the blood vessels and cells necessary for hair growth.

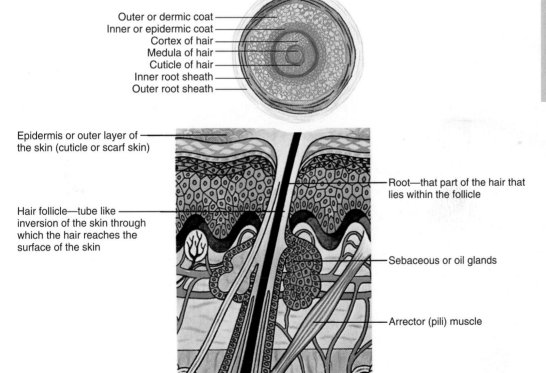

Outer or dermic coat
Inner or epidermic coat
Cortex of hair
Medula of hair
Cuticle of hair
Inner root sheath
Outer root sheath

Epidermis or outer layer of the skin (cuticle or scarf skin)

Hair follicle—tube like inversion of the skin through which the hair reaches the surface of the skin

Root—that part of the hair that lies within the follicle

Sebaceous or oil glands

Arrector (pili) muscle

Bulb
Papila

Figure 29–1 Cross section of the hair follicle and skin.

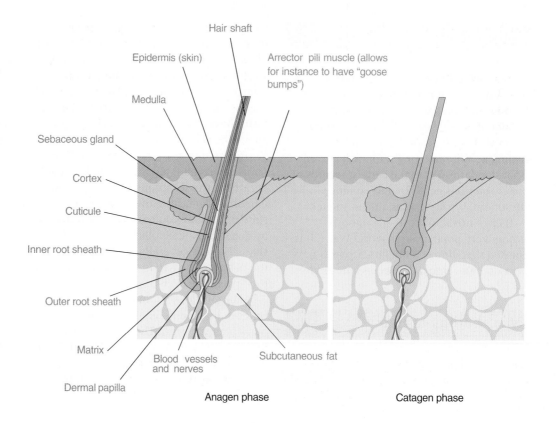

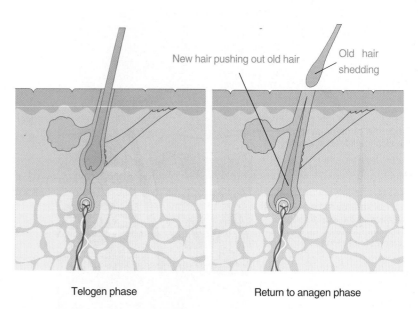

Hair shaft

Epidermis (skin)

Arrector pili muscle (allows for instance to have "goose bumps")

Medulla

Sebaceous gland

Cortex

Cuticule

Inner root sheath

Outer root sheath

Matrix

Blood vessels and nerves

Subcutaneous fat

Dermal papilla

Anagen phase

Catagen phase

New hair pushing out old hair

Old hair shedding

Telogen phase

Return to anagen phase

Figure 29–2 The three stages of hair growth: anagen, the growth stage; catagen, the regression stage; and telogen, the resting stage.

vessels and cells necessary for hair growth and nourishment for the follicle.

Oil ducts (sebaceous glands) are attached to the follicle. They are responsible for lubricating the skin and hair. Moderate amounts of sebaceous oil are necessary for healthy skin and hair. Dry skin produces less oil than oily skin. The face contains approximately 3,200 follicles per square inch.

Vitamins, minerals, and nutrients are needed for strong, healthy hair. They are brought to the hair bulb through the blood vessels. The blood vessels bring nutrients to the base of the bulb, causing it to grow and form new hair.

Hair formation actually begins before birth. The hair on a fetus is extremely soft and is known as **lanugo.** Prior to birth, the lanugo is lost and is replaced with stronger, pigmented hair after birth. The shape, size, and normal function of the hair follicle is predetermined before birth. Secretion activity and the depth of the hair shaft are also predetermined.

Hair Growth Cycle

Hair growth is a result of the activity of cells found in the basal layer. These cells are actually found within the hair bulb. Hair growth encompasses three stages: **anagen** is the growth stage; **catagen** is the regression (falling out) stage; and **telogen** is the final stage, the resting stage (Figure 29–2).

During the anagen stage, activity is greater in the hair bulb, which pushes down into the dermis and swells with cell mitosis.

In the catagen stage, the hair shaft grows upward and detaches itself from the bulb.

During the telogen stage, the hair is at its full size and is erect in the follicle. It shows above the skin's surface. The hair bulb is not active. The hair falls out. The bulb then moves upward into the dermis and begins to grow a new hair. The cycle then begins again.

Very fine, soft hair is referred to as **vellus hair.** It is found in areas that are not covered by the larger, coarse hairs found on the head, brows, and pubic area. The cheeks are a good example.

It is important to understand the three stages of hair growth. Two hairs can be growing next to another; however, they can be at a different stages of growth. When employing electrolysis or laser hair removal, the practitioner takes into consideration these stages and performs the process according to these cycles. Repeat visits are normally necessary. There is a difference between electrolysis and laser hair removal, as discussed later in this chapter.

Indicator of Health

Hair and skin are good barometers of an individual's overall state of health. Dull, lifeless hair and sallow, listless skin tone may signal a health warning. Strong, healthy hair and good skin tone are signs of good health.

Hair responds to the elements. For instance, hair grows faster in a warm climate. Excessive cold can dry the hair and reduce the luster that healthy hair should have.

The rate of secretions out of the follicle determines whether the skin is oily or dry. With the exception of acquired conditions after birth, such as disease, drugs, and the aging process, the physiology of an individual follicle size and function is established genetically. You cannot alter genetics; however, you can manage or control the hair's overall appearance.

Excessive Hair Growth

Two medical terms are applied to excessive hair growth. The first is **hirsutism,** which is hair that grows in excess on the face, arms, and legs, especially in women (Figure 29–3). The second is **hypertrichosis**, the excessive growth of hair where it does not normally grow. It is a Greek word, combining *hyper* (meaning over) and *tricho* (meaning hair).

The amount of hair an individual has differs from person to person. Genetics accounts for how much hair you will normally have on the body. What would be normal hair growth in one person might be extreme in another.

Excessive hair growth can be congenital or acquired, normal or pathological (caused by illness).

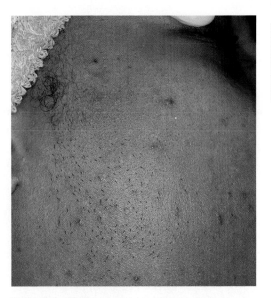

Figure 29–3 Hirsutism, or excessive hair growth in a male pattern on a female, suggests a hormone imbalance.

lanugo
Extremely soft and fine hair growth beginning before birth.

anagen
The first stage in hair growth, or the growing stage.

catagen
The second stage in hair growth, or the regression (falling out) stage.

telogen
The final stage in hair growth, the resting stage.

vellus hair
Very fine, soft hair found in areas not covered by coarse hairs, such as the cheeks.

hirsutism
Excessive hair growth on the face, arms, and legs especially in women.

hypertrichosis
Excessive hair growth where hair does not normally grow, such as the palms of the hands.

Excessive hair growth on a female body (especially when distributed like the hair on a male) suggests an imbalance in the male hormones. The normal ovary does not secrete significant amounts of male hormones and, when there is a glandular disturbance, excessive amounts of androgens may be produced, which results in hirsutism.

Other Causes of Hirsutism

Hirsutism can be caused by various factors. A normal pregnancy increases adrenocortical activity, which may cause moderate hirsutism. Vitamin deficiency, certain diseases, particular drugs, and emotional shock or stress can result in glandular disturbances, resulting in excessive hair growth. Menopause may also cause excess facial hair. The "menopause mustache," as it is often called, is not a sign of hirsutism; it is just a sign of menopause.

Differences in Hair Growth And Characteristics

Hair is indigenous (native) to all peoples. It can be either fine or thick, heavy (coarse) or smooth, or light blond or dark black. Hair protects the body from environmental elements and ultraviolet rays. It guards the nose, ears, and reproductive areas, with fine hairs acting as a filter to keep out dust and other airborne particles. Hair is a conduit of sensation for the skin, and acts as a wick in the follicle, allowing for secretions—sebum—to move up and out onto the skin's surface.

In northern regions of the world fine, delicate hair and lighter skin tones are common. Red and blond hair tends to be easy to remove. These individuals generally have fair skin and tend to be sensitive, a very important point to remember when performing hair removal.

Of course, there are variations in all regions. Darker tones were introduced through the immigration of people from other regions. After Spanish sailors became shipwrecked off the coast of Wales in the Irish Sea, they integrated among the local populations, and darker characteristics eventually become apparent. As cultures moved from region to region, individuals acquired mixed traits of hair color and thickness (Figure 29–4).

In areas closer to the equator, the skin and hair are normally thicker and darker. These characteristics help protect the body from strong ultraviolet rays. Central and South American cultures, as well as those from the Mediterranean regions and the Middle East, tend to have darker and more noticeable hair. Individuals with olive skin tones have a tendency toward pigmentation problems if epilation is not performed carefully.

Figure 29–4 There are variations in skin tone and hair color in all cultures.

Individuals from Central Europe (France, Spain, and Portugal) generally have black hair, which is average in density. Because the root is quite deep in the follicle, it can be very difficult to remove. With repeated removal, the hair regrowth tends to become thin and easier to remove.

Individuals originating from Africa and Australia tend to have black, coarse, curly hair, which has a tendency to become in-grown. The method of hair removal for these individuals needs to be chosen carefully.

Native Americans and many Asians have thinner facial hair but the roots tend to be deep.

Aging creates changes in the hair. Grey hair is a result of physiological changes, causing it to be coarse with a deep root system. Before the hair was gray, it was easy to remove. With the changes that take place during the aging process, the hair root system increases by almost 50%, making hair removal difficult.

Epilation services can provide 50% or more of a salon's total income. This market encompasses a broad spectrum of techniques originating from a variety of culturally diverse methods. It is vital for the esthetician to be well versed in a variety of methods and techniques for hair removal. Cultural orientation often influences the consumer's preferred method of hair removal.

Hair Removal

Methods of hair removal fall into two general categories: temporary and permanent. Temporary hair removal involves repeat treatments as hair grows. With permanent hair removal, the papilla is dissolved (destroyed), making regrowth impossible.

Temporary methods of hair removal include depilation, a process of removing hair at or near the level of the skin. Both shaving and chemical depilation are included in this category.

Another temporary method of hair removal is epilation, the process of removing hair by breaking contact between the bulb and the papilla. It is then pulled out of the follicle. Tweezing (manual), wax depilatories, and sugaring are all methods of epilation. The basic tools needed for waxing are shown in Figure 29–5. A summary of epilation products is presented in Table 29–1, p. 448.

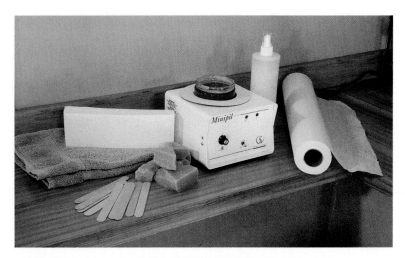

Figure 29–5 The basic tools needed for epilation by waxing.

Shaving

Shaving is a daily ritual for most men. They remove excess beard hair so that they achieve a clean-shaven appearance. Women shave the underarms, legs, and bikini area. As in any depilation method, the hair is removed up to the skin's surface. Shaving is an abrasive method of hair removal that can also irritate the skin. A common problem affecting some men is barbae folliculitis (ingrown hair), which can be corrected by changing the direction of shaving.

Chemical Depilation

Several chemical creams are available that contain ingredients to dissolve hair. Some come in a powder form that is mixed into a paste by adding water. Chemical depilatories are placed in a thin coating on the surface of the skin, such as on the legs. Any chemical depilation cream should be patch tested first to make sure that there are no allergic or sensitivity reactions. Use the inside of the arm. Normally, if there is no reaction within the first 10 minutes—swelling, itching, or redness—it can then be applied to a larger area. A chemical depilatory is generally not recommended for use on the upper lip area, because this area is very sensitive.

Tweezing

Tweezing allows for hair removal—one hair at a time—by the root. Eyebrows can be shaped and contoured by tweezing. Tweezing can also be used to touch up or fine-tune your work after waxing. To remove hair with

Table 29-1 Summary of Epilation Products

Product	Presentation	Use	Comments
Hot or solid wax	Hard state. After warmed, it becomes liquid and is easily spread. While cooling, it is removed together with the hair. Comes in blocks, disks, pellets, or beads. Lower-temperature waxes are available for sensitive skin.	Apply coating in several layers. Cool. Pick up with fingers at one end and pull. Strip-free.	A favorite for many. Most efficient substance to epilate coarse, beardlike hair. Rather high initial investment. Must purchase a wax heater with a filtering device installed.
Soft wax	A fluid and hydrosoluble depilatory. Very thick. A favorite in schools for training.	Melt in a heater. Apply a thin coat and pull off with the strip.	Adhesiveness of soft wax is considered lower than a resin. Best for longer hair. Tends to be sticky and sometimes difficult to remove. Newer versions are easier to use and remove.
Resins: clear and creamed	Classified as fluid depilatories. Not water soluble. Considered high in adhesiveness, making them suitable for relatively sparse hair. They are liposoluble (oil soluble). Considered very gentle. Newer formats have additives such as azulene, chamomile, tea tree, and lime. Comes in sensitive creams or clear format for normal skin.	Melt in a low-temperature heater so that it doesn't "cook" or become too thin. Apply a thin coating and remove with pellon strips.	Lower melting point, temperature close to body temperature. Caution must be taken not to overheat. Some are melted in the microwave first for a few minutes. Others are not recommended for the microwave and are poured directly into a heater. Use pellon or muslin strips to remove. Leaves no residue. Clean with an oily substance.
Sugaring	Liquid and water soluble.	Melts at a lower temperature. Apply a thin coat and remove with strips.	A newer method in the U.S. Removes hair efficiently and is easily cleaned with water.
Roll-on systems	Comes in a heater kit. Disposable applicators. Eliminates risk of cross-contamination.	Follow manufacturer's instructions.	Requires an initial investment; it is becoming more popular with estheticians.
Hair growth retardant	Vials: varies depending on manufacturer. Professional size and sometimes retail. Formulations vary. Research for best product.	Apply immediately after depilation. Charge separately for this service.	Normally made from a natural component. When applied immediately after waxing, it absorbs into the follicle and helps retard hair regrowth.
Electrolysis	One of the most popular hair removal methods in the U.S.	Considered a permanent form of hair removal. Performed by a licensed electrologist.	Newer machines vary. Research for best model.
Laser hair and photo light hair removal	State-of-the-art removal systems based on premise of thermal selectivity.	Performed by a medical doctor or licensed and trained esthetician under the direction of a physician.	Laws vary from state to state.

tweezers, place the tweezers at the base of a hair, and gently but firmly pull the hair at a slight angle, normally in the direction of the hair growth. Always check your work with the magnifying lamp. Some estheticians prefer to use their magnifying light while doing hair removal to allow for very detailed work.

Waxing

There are two types of waxes: hard (hot) and soft (strip). Hard waxes are applied directly to the skin in a thick, "wet" layer that hardens and shrinks as it cools. The technician then lifts the wax gently up off the skin with her fingers. Soft waxes are applied in a thin layer and covered with a strip of pellon or muslin material that is removed immediately, in the direction of the hair growth.

Waxes require a heater to liquefy them. Consistencies vary, as do melting points. A melting point is the temperature at which a substance liquefies. Some waxes are water soluble. They easily wipe off with water. Others, such as resins, are oil soluble. Excess wax is removed with an oil-based solution. They are normally not soluble in water.

Wax consistencies can be a hard, soft cream, or clear format. Formulas can be made from resins, rosins (from pine trees), sweet almond oil, beeswax, paraffin, and other substances. They may include additives to address the needs of different skin types. Azulene or chamomile may be used for sensitive skin. Tea tree oil may be added for its soothing and antiseptic benefits.

Technique and temperature are both factors in obtaining positive results. The purpose of any wax is to adhere to the hair as close to the skin as possible. When the wax is removed, it should grab the hair and remove the bulb from the follicle. If the wax is not applied correctly, at the wrong temperature, or if the skin is not cleansed well, the hair will not be removed. If the wax is too hot, it can cause skin irritation and even blistering. During removal, the skin can be pulled off as well. As with all esthetic methods, technique is the key to successful waxing.

Waxes are generally applied with small, flat, wooden disposable sticks, or with larger wooden applicators. They should be discarded after each use. Some technicians prefer to use a stainless steel 5" spatula. It can be sanitized and provides an even, thin coat of wax that is easily and quickly removed. As one becomes more proficient through practice, waxing takes less time. Gloves should always be worn during waxing services.

Hard (Hot) Waxes

Hard waxes are available as a block, disk, pellet, or bead. They are considered a no-strip wax. They must be liquefied before they can be used.

Hard waxes are applied by layering to the thickness of a nickel (approximately) in a figure eight pattern. Make a thick *lip* or *edge* on one end so that the fingers can grab it (Figure 29–6). Allow it to harden for a few moments. Pull the wax off against the hair growth. The skin is then swept clean of hair.

Hard waxes are available at different melting points to address the needs of normal and sensitive skin. The harder the wax, the more heat it requires to melt. Small, individual wax heaters are available and can be placed in each treatment room. The wax is discarded after each use.

Hard waxes are preferred by some estheticians. They are gentle enough for the face and eye area, yet strong enough on difficult-to-remove, coarse hairs. Some like to use it on the bikini area. In contrast to strip waxes, which restrict the pulling area to the size of the strip, hard waxes can be applied to larger areas. Estheticians generally use hard wax in certain areas, such as the back and legs, and soft wax in others, such as the eyebrow, lip, or underarm.

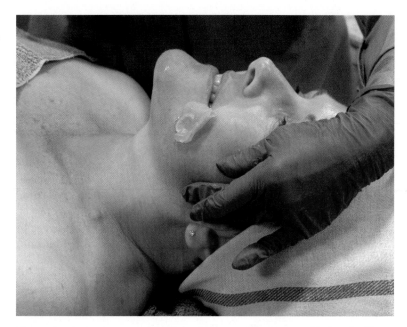

Figure 29–6 Apply wax a bit thicker at one end to form a "lip" to facilitate removal.

Soft (Strip) Waxes

In the United States, one of the most popular methods of hair removal is strip waxing, or warm waxing. Soft waxes have a lower melting point. They come in tins or plastic containers and can be melted slightly in the microwave to make it easier to pour the wax into a wax heater or warming pot. All soft waxes remain soft on the skin.

The method of application requires that a thin coat of wax be placed on the skin. Remove the wax immediately with a muslin or pellon strip or cellophane or cotton strips.

Roll-Ons

A relatively new delivery format is a roll-on container that is placed in a thermostatically controlled device that heats the product at a low temperature. It is then rolled onto the area and removed with a strip. This method is very efficient and clean. Many estheticians prefer to use a roll-on because it is so sanitary to use.

Sugaring

Sugaring is an ancient method of hair removal dating back to the Egyptians. Relatively new to the United States, it is still very popular in Arab countries. It is an alternative for those who have sensitive skin or who react to waxes with bumps and redness. Sugaring is water soluble, meaning that it is easily removed with water.

The original basic recipe is a mixture of sugar, lemon juice, and water. It is heated to form a syrup. The syrup is molded into a ball and pressed onto the skin, then quickly stripped away. It pulls the hair out at the root.

Sugar mixtures are now manufactured in large quantities and are sold in small containers ready to be placed into a heater. Melt the sugar mixture at a very low temperature. The sugar paste adheres only to the hair, making removal more comfortable, with little irritation. A thin coat is applied with an applicator. Remove with cotton or pellon strips as recommended by the manufacturer. This type of mixture is used to remove very fine hair on the face, bikini area, underarms, legs, and back. Always wear gloves when using this method of hair removal.

Threading

Another ancient method of hair removal is threading. It is used in the Middle East, India, and Pakistan. It is reported to give clean lines and good shape to the eyebrows, upper lip, and other facial areas. It can also be used on larger areas of the body.

It works by using 100% cotton thread that is twisted and rolled along the surface of the skin, entwining the hair in the thread. The thread is pulled away from the skin, lifting the hair out of the follicle. The skin usually reacts with a little redness and slight soreness. However, it is considered an effective hair removal method.

Permanent (Semipermanent) Hair Removal

Methods of "permanent" hair removal include electrolysis, laser, and photo light hair removal systems. Laser and photo light are normally performed in a medical setting. Food and Drug Administration (FDA) guidelines require that these procedures be defined as *permanent hair reduction*. While these methods are sometimes called permanent, unless the hair bulb is destroyed completely, there may be some hair regrowth. Residual growth can be remedied through occasional treatments after the original removal program is completed.

Electrolysis

Electrolysis is the process of permanently removing hair by means of electricity. It is considered the only method of *permanent* hair removal.

There are three methods of electrology:

1. Galvanic—uses direct current, which causes chemical decomposition of the hair follicle.
2. Thermolysis—utilizes high-frequency current to produce heat, which destroys the hair follicle.
3. Blend—combines both systems, sending current through a fine needle or probe.

The Galvanic method uses a multiple needle to destroy the hair by a chemical action of the galvanic current. It decomposes the papilla, the source of nourishment for the hair. The needle is connected to the negative side of a direct current (DC) power source and is inserted into the follicle. The client holds the electrode connected to the positive side of the power source. When power is applied, the electrical charge begins transforming saline moisture inside the follicle into sodium hydroxide—lye—along with hydrogen and chlorine gas. Unstable sodium hydroxide destabilizes the follicle wall through a chemical action. It weakens the hold of the follicle wall on surrounding tissue. This allows the hair to be removed easily. It is theorized that because hydrogen peroxide is unstable, at the end of a treatment it begins a process of stabilizing. During this stage, debris and hair regrowth cells left behind are saturated with the stabilizing hydrogen peroxide. The environment inside the follicle is not conducive to hair growth.

In the case of galvanic electrolysis, the moisture content within the skin is important to conduct a proper current. This method is also considered less damaging to the skin.

Electrocoagulation (thermolysis) destroys the hair by coagulating the papilla through heat. An alternating current (AC) passes through a needle, causing vibration in the water molecules surrounding the hair follicle. This action produces heat, which destroys the papilla. It is considered a one-needle method.

The blend method combines the benefits of the galvanic and thermolysis methods by passing AC and DC current through the needle at the same time. Results are reported to be quicker than the galvanic method alone. Some needles come in presterilized, disposable packages. Regular needles can also be

electrolysis
The process of removing hair permanently by means of electricity.

Developing a Plan of Action

How many times have you looked at an individual whose career status you admire and wondered how she got there? Take a private career survey at the next social gathering you attend. You will probably be surprised at some of the answers you get. People often arrive at their positions by rather unusual means.

Curiously enough, many of us do not end up working in the area we were originally trained for. Company layoffs, relocations, new interests, or opportunities within an organization are just a few of the reasons for movement.

Whether by choice or fate, many individuals will change jobs several times over the course of their working career. Perhaps you are one of those individuals who have decided to transition from another occupation into the field of esthetics. Chances are you may find a specific niche within the profession and redefine your position even further. Finding that special fit can be a challenge that calls for a definite plan of action.

As you embark on a new career in esthetics take time to think about how you arrived at your decision.

- What was the main reason you considered a career in esthetics?

- Can you list at least five reasons this field appealed to you?

- Who did you talk to about making this decision?

- Was there anyone else you needed to consider before moving ahead?

- Once you decided that esthetics was right for you what steps did you take to get the proper training?

Answering these questions will help you define your goals and objectives even further. Learning as much as possible about the many aspects and opportunities available in esthetics will allow you the freedom to make thoughtful choices as you move forward. A good way to approach this task is to list as many options as possible within the field. Looking through industry trade publications may help trigger ideas you were unaware of. Attending trade shows is another ideal opportunity for investigation.

Once you have done this, team up with a fellow student and compare notes. Armed with your list, seek out individuals who have been successful in each of the areas. If your school provides job listings they can be a good source of referrals. You should also consult your teachers and other administrative personnel for direction.

The next step is to ask those individuals whose career paths spark your interest for an informational interview. You will find that most successful people are eager to share information with those just starting out in the field. But do be prepared to be flexible; successful people are usually busy people. Be courteous and respectful of the individual's boundaries as you decide jointly if it is best to conduct the interview in person, by telephone, or via electronic mail. Keep your list of questions short and to the point, highlighting the information you desire most.

Learning more about what individuals do is a useful exercise in understanding the day-to-day requirements of a job. It is also an excellent way to decide what tasks appeal to you most. From there you can develop a time line for your own success. A key question to ask yourself is, Where would I like to be five years from now?

laser
The acronym derived from Light Amplification by Stimulated Emission of Radiation. A direct beam of radiation that penetrates the epidermis and creates a reaction.

photothermolysis
The photochemical destruction of hair follicles.

used, although they require sterilization after each use. Many prefer the packaged needles for convenience.

Electrolysis is performed only by licensed electrologists, and requires special training for licensure. Talk with your instructor for additional information about classes and licensing.

Laser and Photo Light

Laser hair removal technology has been around since the mid 1990s. As of this writing, there are a variety of lasers available: Epilaser, Epilight, Altus, diode, Nd-Yag, E-2000, GentleLase, and Softlight.

Another interesting outcome of this new technology is the ability to offer clients a choice of both treatments—epilation and laser hair removal. Large areas of hair removal can be efficiently dealt with over a longer time period with laser hair removal. Concurrently, waxing procedures can deal with the hair removal enhancements needed immediately.

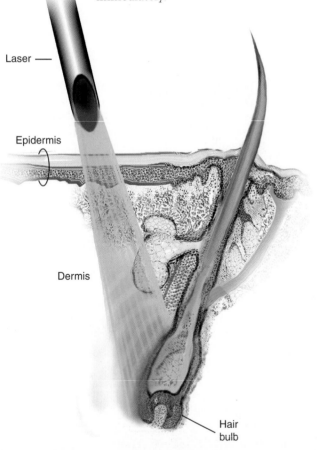

Laser

Epidermis

Dermis

Hair bulb

Figure 29–7 The laser penetrates the epidermis and the dermis, causing a reaction in which the hair bulb is destroyed.

Laser Technology

The word **laser** is an acronym for **L**ight **A**mplification by **S**timulated **E**mission of **R**adiation. A laser is a direct beam of light that penetrates into the epidermis/dermis and creates a reaction (Figure 29–7). It is regulated by controls on the machine. Light is energy. The stronger the light is, the hotter it gets, and the more intense reaction it causes.

Laser hair removal was discovered by accident in 1992 when a laser physicist zapped himself on the arm and noticed that the hair on his arm was gone. The FDA approved the first use of laser for hair removal in 1995. The treatment worked by coating the skin with a black carbon solution, which attracted the laser light, damaging the hair follicles. Claims were that it was permanent, which was not the case. The technology has improved greatly since that time.

Dark colors absorb more light, more energy. A black object gets much hotter than a white object. Earlier-generation lasers restricted hair removal to Fitzpatrick skin types I, II, and III and sometimes type IV. Darker skin ended up absorbing more energy, which could result in permanent pigmentation. Today, newer machines allow hair removal on darker Fitzpatrick skin types.

Depending on how energy is calibrated, a laser produces colored light. A correct wavelength is selected for the laser light to treat a range of skin conditions. For instance, one laser is tuned to produce a pure yellow light. Yellow light will very selectively absorb into the color red. Laser light passes harmlessly through the skin, and targets only the hemoglobin of the red blood cell. The laser energy then heats and destroys the cell, leaving the normal skin cell completely intact.

Similarly, we treat brown-pigmented lesions of the skin with a wavelength that, by design, produces a green light. This green light is then selectively absorbed into the excess pigment (melanin) in the skin. The body then absorbs the tiny particles and the color fades.

In the case of hair removal, heat energy destroys the bulb by the process of **photothermolysis.** The skin is quickly cooled through the application of a cryogen spray, circulating cool water, or a gel.

Pulsed Light

Pulsed light is different from a laser. First generation lasers were a solid beam of light.

While it is still energy, and measures similar to a laser, pulsed light (or photo light) produces a quick "flash" of light (similar to a camera flash). Pulsed lasers emit bursts of energy at intervals of a thousandth to almost a billionth of a second. These short, powerful pulses shatter their target without allowing heat to build up and burn the surrounding skin. The flash destroys the vein or hair bulb. Improved since its first introduction in the United States, it is widely used in the medical arena or in spas that are medically directed.

While there is always a risk of scarring with any laser procedure, this newer laser technology greatly reduces the risk of scarring, which in most cases is less than 1%.

Is Hair Removal Ever Permanent?

Permanent hair reduction is defined in the case of lasers as semipermanent. The laser hair removal device will permanently reduce the number of body hairs. It will not result, however, in the permanent removal of *all* hair. Clients with excess hair problems do not seem to care; laser hair removal is increasingly in demand.

Although some estheticians do perform laser services, laws vary from state to state regarding who is qualified to perform laser hair removal. It is important that estheticians understand the limits of professional boundaries and practice within the limits of the law. Lasers are powerful medical devices that must be used cautiously and respectfully. It is vital that proper training and licensure be obtained before offering these services.

All laser devices must have FDA approval. Laser or photo light hair removal must be practiced under the direct supervision of a physician. Each state regulates who can use these devices. Training should be above and beyond the manufacturers' training programs. Some advanced schools offer 60 hours of clinical training that includes skin types, Fitzpatrick Scale, and pre- and postoperative treatment care.

Hair Growth Inhibitors

Hair growth inhibitors are clear, odorless solutions that are made from a mixture of plant enzymes. They are applied directly to the skin at the end of the waxing session. Because hair has been freshly removed, the follicle is more receptive to these agents.

They work by mimicking the process that causes baldness. The structure of the hair follicle is changed and the hair becomes finer and softer until it disappears. When used according to the manufacturer's instructions, as well as having regular waxings, the length of time between waxings becomes greater.

Furniture and Accessories

Some spas and salons have separate rooms just for waxing. Others perform waxing services in the facial rooms. Waxing, especially on larger body areas such as the legs, is very labor-intensive. Furniture should be ergonomically designed so that both the technician and client are comfortable. Ideally, waxing table should be adjustable to different heights. This allows for each technician to adjust the table to the correct height for working.

Waxing heaters should be purchased from a professional distributor who offers a warranty. A multitiered, wheeled cart, commonly referred to as a trolley, is useful for holding waxing pots and supplies. The cart can be moved close to the client, keeping tools and supplies right at hand. A foot-operated, covered waste can is necessary for the proper disposal of all used supplies as you work. A step stool should also be available to facilitate the client's getting on and off the table in an easy and safe manner.

Tools and Supplies

Appropriate tools and supplies need to be replenished every day. Many items, such as applicators, are available as disposable items, which are great for convenience and sanitation.

Tweezers

Professional tweezers are available in many point sizes (Figure 29–8, p. 454) They should be made of stainless steel because it is a solid substance that will not corrode when sanitized in solution or in the autoclave. Always purchase the highest quality tweezers and accessories that you can afford. Tweezers are

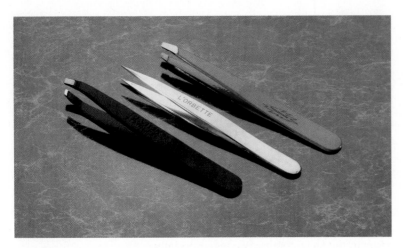

Figure 29–8 Tweezers of different sizes and point types are necessary tools for epilation.

Figure 29–9 Disposable applicators offer the best option for sanitary practices.

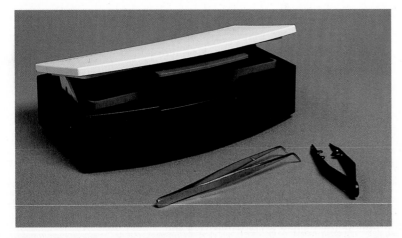

Figure 29–10 Tweezers and metal applicators should be soaked in a wet sanitizer for proper cleaning.

an important tool that will help make your work more precise. The result will be a more satisfied client.

A slanted-point tweezer is best for general tweezing. A more pointed tip is ideal for tiny hairs, ingrown hair, and difficult areas. Very fine-pointed tweezers can develop a spur on the tips if not carefully handled or if dropped. Some manufacturers offer a lifetime sharpening service. Check the manufacturer's warranty before purchasing. Make sure to choose the appropriate tweezers for your work.

Applicators

Disposable applicators offer practitioners the best option in terms of sanitary practices (Figure 29–9). Wax applicators can be disposable, wooden, flat sticks, either large or small. A stainless steel 5" spatula is ideal for spreading a thin coat on larger areas such as the legs. These must be sterilized after each use.

Sanitizer

The wet sanitizer is normally a small, rectangular box with a lid (Figure 29–10). Inside is a basket that lowers into the solutions when the lid is closed. Stainless steel tweezers should be thoroughly cleansed and placed into a wet sanitizer from 2 to 10 minutes depending on the manufacturer's instructions. Some solutions are diluted 1 part solution to 8 parts water.

Stainless steel instruments can also be autoclaved if this equipment is available. The key is to place the instruments into an approved hospital-strength disinfectant solution that is designated to kill all microbes, including staphylococcus, tuberculosis, pseudomonas (a pathogen), fungus, and the HIV virus. The solutions are often listed in catalogs for the esthetics industry or are available at a medical supply house.

Pre- and Postepilation Solutions

There are many pre- and postsolutions available for preparing and calming the skin before and after waxing. The purpose of applying a solution is to thoroughly degrease, clean, and sanitize the skin prior to waxing. Prewaxing solutions may have antiseptic and calming ingredients such as witch hazel, arnica, chamomile, and calendula. Some manufacturers offer a desensitizing lotion that helps ease any waxing discomfort. It is applied after the cleansing process.

Look for postwaxing products that contain antiseptic and soothing properties, such as safflower oil and azulene. When using a water-based product such as sugar, a calming solution of water and tea tree oil can be effective.

Be cautious when placing anything on the skin, especially after waxing, that contains fragrances or ingredients that can be irritating. The follicle and skin are very sensitive after waxing. Some clients have had reactions such as slight irritation and milia breakout.

A client health form (Figure 29–11, p. 456) should be completed by each new client and kept in the client's file folder. This form must be completed *before* epilation is performed. It can alert the esthetician to any conditions that might prevent you from providing epilation treatments. Table 29–2, p. 458 illustrates common contraindications for waxing procedures.

Strips

There are two popular types of strips: cotton muslin, which comes in rolls or precut packets, and pellon. Pellon is a fiberlike material that does not shed or stretch. It provides a clean pull and can be used several times prior to discarding.

Roll Paper

To keep the area clean, place a clean sheet of paper on the waxing table for each new client. Roll paper is normally ordered through esthetics or medical suppliers. Some roll papers have perforations so that it is easy to tear pieces off the roll.

Sanitation

Waxing rooms and the trolley (roll cart) must be kept clean and sanitized. Wax drips down the side of a heater are unsightly. The same holds true for any sticky areas on the floor or drips on linens, furniture, and even splatters on the walls! Place the waxing unit and all your accessories on a roll cart that can be pulled close to the client. Place the disposable

wooden applicators and cotton squares into glass or stainless steel cylinder containers. Tweezers should be placed in a closed sanitizer that can be opened when needed.

Always wear gloves. Use vinyl gloves rather than latex. Latex tends to get sticky and breaks down easily. Change your gloves if they become sticky from waxing.

Hair removal causes trauma to the follicle. After all, the hair shaft is forcefully pulled out of the follicle. Sometimes there is bleeding or fluids rise to the surface of the skin. All blood-stained gauze should be discarded in a hazardous waste container and disposed of properly.

When there is slight bleeding or even red bumps, place a small amount of tea tree antiseptic on a cotton 4" × 4" (or 2" × 2") pad and gently pat the area of concern. It helps stop the bleeding and calm the area. Tea tree is highly antiseptic and calming. If the skin is torn, perform the same step.

Do not use talcum powder unless recommended in the protocol provided by the manufacturer. Although powder was used in the past, newer systems are more efficient and do not require it. Many talcs contain fragrances and other particles that can cause an allergic reaction. In the case of an open, irritated follicle, more irritation may be induced. Keep epilated areas clean and free from any debris. Treat freshly epilated skin gently.

When using a strip wax, prepare your gauze or pellon ahead of time. Cut smaller strips for the eye and face areas. Trim a strip to the shape of the brow area. That way less is wasted and it ensures a more accurate pulling.

Room Preparation

Just as in performing facials, preparations for epilation should follow similar guidelines. Depending on the protocols of the spa or salon, room preparation is either done at night or early in the morning prior to opening. Between clients, reorganize and tidy the area.

A trolley is recommended for your instruments, accessories, and heater. Apply a clean piece of disposable roll paper on the shelf. The trolley can be brought close to the client so that you are not reaching across a room for supplies or wax. It helps make your work more efficient.

Client Health Form

Date _____

First name _____ Last name _____

1. Are you presently under a doctor's care? If yes, for what? _____

2. Are you currently taking any prescription medications?

   List all prescription medications you are taking in the chart below.

3. Are you presently taking any over-the-counter medications such as aspirin, Tylenol, Advil, etc. List all over-the-counter medications you are taking in the chart below.

   Drug   Frequency

   _____

   _____

   _____

   _____

3. List all vitamins and food supplements you are taking.

   Vitamins   Food Supplements

   _____

   _____

   _____

   _____

5. List all medications you are allergic to. _____

6. List any other allergies. _____

7. Have you used Accutane in the last seven years? _____

8. What skin regimen are you currently using? _____

9. Do any of the products in your skin regimen contain the following ingredients?

   ❏ Retin-A   ❏ Renova   ❏ Deferin   ❏ Glycolic acid   ❏ AHA   ❏ Salicylic acid

10. Have you ever had   ❏ Laser treatment?   ❏ Peel?

    Please describe and give the date(s). _____

11. Have you ever had an adverse reaction after using a skin regimen?

    ❏ Rash   ❏ Irritation   ❏ Peeling   ❏ Sun sensitivity   ❏ Breakout

12. Have there been any changes in your overall health or medical condition since we last met?

    If yes, please describe. _____

13. Do you have: ❏ Diabetes   ❏ Asthma   ❏ Arthritis   ❏ Hemophilia   ❏ Cancer

    ❏ High blood pressure   ❏ Heart problems

14. Have you been in a tanning bed within the last 48 hours?

   I have answered all the questions to the best of my knowledge. I understand that, because of certain health conditions, I may be refused epilation services. I also understand that there may be swelling or irritation in waxed areas. This is only a temporary condition.

   _____

   Signature

   _____

   Date

Figure 29–11 Client Health Form

Table 29–2 Waxing Contraindications

Drug/Condition	Precautions
Accutane	Do *not* wax or perform any exfoliation, whatsoever. Skin is highly sensitive and dry. If the skin is exfoliated—which includes waxing—it can be pulled off easily. Waxing can be resumed after a year of discontinuing the drug. Check with the client's physician doctor.
Retin-A	Do *not* wax or perform any exfoliation on areas receiving Retin-A. Normally, brow arching is permitted simply because Retin-A should *never* be placed that close to the eyes. Thus, it is permissible to perform an arch. But be sure to verify that the client has not used Retin-A. Client must discontinue the drug in the brow area for 5 days prior to waxing and not resume until 5 days afterward.
Antibiotics	Skin sensitivities may occur, as well as susceptibility to infection if the skin is broken. The pH and moisture content of the skin is altered. Cleanliness is vital when working on a client who is taking antibiotics. Their skin is photosensitive, so clients must wear sunblock.
Birth control or hormone replacement	Skin may be more sensitive, more photosensitive, and more susceptible to pigmentation. Pull carefully to avoid irritation.
Blood thinners, i.e., Coumadin	No waxing without a physician's authorization. Client's taking blood thinners can bleed easily.
Autoimmune diseases—lupus, AIDS	Do not wax.
Cancer therapy—chemotherapy, radiation	Do not wax.
Diabetes, phlebitis	Do not wax unless client receives a physician's authorization.
Areas to avoid	No waxing on eyelids, inside the nose, or the ear cavity. Do not apply wax to the nipples on a man or woman.
Open lesions (acne), cold sores, cysts, boils, growths, inflamed skin, sunburn, peeling or broken skin, cuts, moles, warts, active herpes virus.	Do not wax.
Exfoliators—salicylic acid, AHAs, enzymes, scrubs, depilatory creams	Depending on skin type and condition, client should discontinue use 3 days prior to waxing. Resume after 3 to 4 days, depending upon skin condition. Must not have used depilatory cream for at least 1 week or more.
Postcancer—excess hair growth	Many patients have extra hair growth around the sideburn area. Client must obtain a physician's permission to begin waxing. Perform waxing *very* carefully and gently. Follow with a cooling and soothing application.
Stimulants such as alcohol and caffeine	Skin tends to be more sensitive.
Smoking	Capillaries may be dilated and the skin may be more sensitive.
Severe sun exposure and tanning beds	Do not wax on any sunburned skin. Skin must be healed from sun lesions. Do not wax if the client has been in a tanning bed within the past 24 hours. The use of tanning bed is *never* recommended.

Prepare the following items:

1. Replace the soiled cover on the waxing trolley with a clean paper.

2. Clean off any drips on the wax heater.

3. Replace the drip collar on the heater.

4. Approximately once a month, check that the thermostat on the heater is working properly.

5. Wash all instruments and place them in the sanitizer.

6. Replenish spatulas and cotton squares.

7. Replenish or refill pre- and postwaxing skin solutions.

8. If using a soft wax, prepare it by cutting strips sized according to the area, i.e., brows, lip, chin, and face. The larger strips are normally not cut if they are being used on the leg and bikini areas.

General Hair Removal (Waxing)

Understanding the "whys and hows" of proper waxing techniques is key to providing a satisfactory, safe, and comfortable hair removal service.

EPILATION TIPS

- Don't forget to pull the skin taut when removing the wax.
- Pull the muslin or pellon strip *against* the direction of the hair growth.
- Epilated areas are sensitive. Apply pressure with your fingertips and the palms of your hands quickly and lightly.
- Remember that practice is the key to developing correct pressure, removal, and hand movements. Good hand and eye coordination comes with practice.

Room Preparation

The room should be clean and sanitized, with clean paper and appropriate covers on the waxing table, the trolley should be stocked with the appropriate wax and warmer, cleansers, pre- and postepilation solutions, tweezers, scissors, applicators, gauze 4 × 4s, and gloves. A magnifying lamp should be nearby and ready to use.

Client Preparation

First-time clients should always fill out a brief health questionnaire prior to waxing. Review the process with the client, answering any questions she may have. Provide the client with a gown, disposable panties, etc., depending on the service provided.

General Procedure

1. Skin Preparation
   Brows/face: Client's eyes should be closed. Completely remove any traces of makeup with a gentle cleanser. Follow with preparation solution to remove any greasy residue or dirt over the orbital area. Allow area to dry for a few moments.
   Other areas: Swipe the skin thoroughly with preepilation solution placed on a 4" × 4" gauze cotton.
   Excess hair: Trim any thicker or longer hair regions with scissors before applying wax. This allows the wax to adhere better and makes it more comfortable for the client.
2. Wax Application
   Strip wax: Dip the end of a small spatula into the warm wax. Beginning from the inside to the outside, apply a very thin coat along the area to be waxed. Be careful not to drip wax on areas that are not being waxed.
   Hard wax: Dip a spatula into the wax and apply it with the hair growth in a figure-eight pattern over the area to be waxed. Apply to the thickness of a nickel. Apply a thicker area on one end, making a *lip* that can be grasped between the thumb and index finger. Wait a few moments for the wax to harden.

3. Removal
   Strip wax: Apply muslin or pellon evenly and with light pressure. Smooth the strip with the palm and fingers in the same direction as the wax application. Do not use too much pressure or you could cause bruising. Leave approximately 1 inch of muslin or pellon free to grip for removing. Remove with one pull against hair growth. Because follicles are not vertically straight and grow at an angle, the hair is "popped" out at an angle, thus the pull is in the opposite direction of the hair growth. Pulling method and direction are critical. When pulling, the strip is folded or rolled back onto itself very rapidly. Immediately after you remove the strip, place your other hand quickly over the area to block nerve pain. Do not pull straight up or you will tear skin off with the hair, or you could even cause the hair to break off.
   Hard wax: Grasp the thick edge between the thumb and index finger. Pull the wax off at an angle against the hair grown. Apply your other hand over the area to sooth nerve endings.
4. Analysis
   Visually check the area with the magnifying light. All hair should have been removed in the pull. Remove any residual hair with tweezers. If there are ingrown hairs, use sanitized pointed tweezers to remove them.
5. Soothing Application
   Apply a few drops of tea tree oil or post-depilatory solution to a 4" × 4" cotton pad. Rub it into the pad. Swipe the entire waxed area, removing any wax residue.
6. Optional: If applying a hair growth retardant, apply it according to the manufacturer's direction.

Summary

Hair removal is a major service today. It is offered in spas, salons, and medical offices. Hair varies in thickness depending on genetic traits. It is important to adjust your hair removal techniques in accordance with the needs and skin type of each client. Practice basic waxing techniques until you are comfortable. Then try the more challenging areas such as the bikini area. Chapter 30 provides step-by-step waxing procedures.

Discussion Questions

1. Explain the hair growth cycle. Why is it important for estheticians to be aware of the stages of hair growth?

2. Define the terms *hirsutism* and *hypertrichosis*. What is the best approach for treating clients who have these conditions?

3. Briefly describe the options currently available to remove unwanted hair. What are the main benefits of each? Can any of these methods be considered permanent?

4. Waxing is a popular method of hair removal in most salons. What are the main differences between the hard and soft varieties?

5. Sanitation is an important consideration when performing hair removal. What precautions are necessary to provide this service in a safe and healthy manner?

6. Discuss general contraindications to waxing clients. How can the esthetician service clients who may not be eligible for this method of hair removal but are concerned about their appearance?

Additional Reading

Gio, Fino. 2000. *Modern Electrology.* New York: Hair Publishing.

Hinkle, A. R., and R. W. Lind. 1968. *Electrolysis, Thermolysis and the Blend: The Principles and Practice of Permanent Hair Removal.* Los Angeles, Calif.: Arroway.

Laird, Susan. *Electrolysis.* www.hairzapper.com

Pugliese, Peter. 1991. *Advanced Professional Skin Care.* Bernville, PA: APSC Publishing; pp. 162–165.

Helpful Web Sites

http://www.about-hair-removal.com
http://www.hairzapper.com

Chapter 30
Waxing Procedures

Chapter Objectives

After reading this chapter, you should be able to:

- Understand the uses of hard and strip waxes.
- Know the steps required for various waxing procedures.
- Understand how to treat ingrown hair.

Chapter Outline

Introduction
Eyebrow Shaping
Waxing the Ear
Waxing the Upper Torso
Waxing the Leg
Ingrown Hair Service

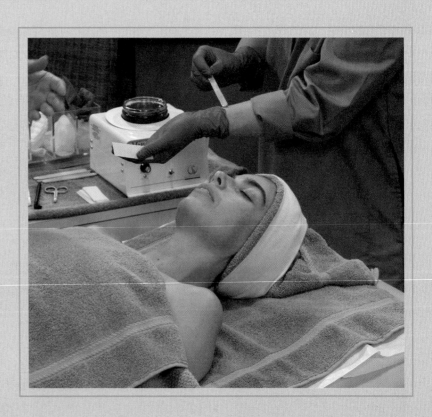

Introduction

Hair removal is a very large portion of your business. Clients are particular about these services. Waxing is a personal service and good results are important to clients. When they find a good esthetician who performs a great service, repeat business is pretty much guaranteed.

The most common problem in waxing is poor technique. We have included step-by-step procedures for you to follow when practicing specific techniques. Applying the wax, as well as learning hand coordination, takes some practice. The key is to apply the wax correctly. Hard waxes are applied thicker so that they can be pulled without a strip. Soft waxes should be applied in a thin coat so that they do not pull up skin along with the hair. Prepare the skin well prior to applying the wax. Be sure to check your work under the magnifying lamp and fine-tune with tweezers, if necessary.

Eyebrow Shaping

Eyebrow arching is the most commonly requested wax service. Once clients feel comfortable and satisfied with this service, they may very well consider waxing other areas of the body.

Shaping the brows is of great importance to improving the overall appearance of the face. In order to perform a skilled arching, specific guidelines must be followed. Each face has its natural features and shape. Brows frame the eyes. Always shape the brows according to the client's individual features. Do not try to create an arch that is unnatural or against the natural shape of the brow. The natural arch of the brow reveals itself when the orbital area is clear of superfluous hair. Also, removing hair above the brow helps to further emphasize the arch contour. Avoid going into the middle of the brow, unless it is very thick and needs thinning. Removing hair from the orbital area and above the brow normally provides enough contour. Use the magnifying lamp to get a better view and to fine-tune your work. As a new student, we suggest that you use an eyebrow pencil as a tool to mark your points, although an orangewood stick and an eyebrow brush can

also work well. Small scissors should be kept handy for trimming longer hair before waxing.

Waxing the Ear

Excessive hair on the ear lobe may be more of a problem for men than women. However, women with very dark hair may have an excessive amount of dark fuzz that is unsightly when the ears are exposed. Men tend to have longer or thicker hair growing off the top of the ear lobe or just inside the ear. Carefully trim the hair with scissors prior to waxing.

Rather than shaving or using a cream depilatory, it may be appropriate to wax. Always be careful when working around the ear area, because it is extremely sensitive.

Follow the same waxing protocols except apply very small amounts of wax to the lobe. Hold the ear lobe taut so that the procedure is comfortable for the client.

SAFETY*Tip*

Do not ever use wax to remove hair inside the ear cavity. If there are stray hairs that are unsightly and bother the client, simply use small cuticle scissors and clip the unwanted hairs.

Waxing the Upper Torso

Unwanted hair on the body is easily removed with a wax treatment. The body areas most often treated in the spa or salon are the underarm, arm, the back and shoulders, the chest, the stomach area around the navel, the bikini line, and the nape of the neck. Most of these areas are not easily accessible to the client for hair removal. Shaving is never satisfactory because the hair quickly grows back.

EPILATION TIPS

- Skin should be thoroughly prepared prior to waxing.
- Do not use too much pressure when applying the strip; this may result in bruising.
- Always pull the strip parallel to the skin in one movement against the hair growth. Do not pull the strip straight up.
- Apply hard wax thick enough to obtain a firm pull.

Work Ethic

We all want to be valued for the contributions we make. "Equal pay for equal work" has been the moral fiber of our country for decades. But it takes more than getting up in the morning and showing up at work to earn that respect. Establishing a good work ethic requires us to be thoughtful about how we approach each day and how we react to our employer's needs.

In today's competitive market, most employers are looking for people who are loyal and committed to doing a good job. Practice a positive attitude and avoid the following negative behaviors, and you will be off to a good start.

10 Things Your Boss Does Not Want to Hear

1. I am sorry, but I am going to be late this morning *or* I will not be in today.

   Esthetics is a service-oriented business. Estheticians work by appointment. If you are late, not only does your client suffer, but also the entire organization is held accountable.

2. I do not have time to clean up the treatment room. Besides, Jane left the room a mess for me yesterday, so I do not feel it is right that I should have to clean up her mess, too.

   Keeping your workstation in tip-top shape is not only a commitment to providing quality service to your clients, but also a commitment to treating your colleagues respectfully.

3. I really resent your letting so and so go home early today. You would not let me leave early to attend that concert last month.

   Learning to be a team player and accepting responsibility goes a long way in terms of building trust and gaining your employer's respect.

4. I did not know that Mrs. Jones was allergic to vitamin E.

   Taking care to understand the needs of your clients is a professional responsibility. Placing employers in the vulnerable position of being held liable for negligence is a sure way to get yourself fired.

5. I can not possibly do a good facial in under 2 hours.

   Being able to accept criticism and developing better work habits demonstrate a willingness to grow and to try new methods.

6. I am sorry I did not make my quota this week, but I really think your demands are too high, and besides I do not think your marketing strategy is a very good one.

   Criticizing your employer without offering a diplomatically stated and constructive alternative to the problem is not likely to win you kudos.

7. I cannot work one night a week. I have small children and my husband does not come home until late.

   Perhaps your personal situation has constraints, but taking an inflexible approach is likely to frustrate your employer. Think about ways you might compromise when trying to solve problems.

8. I am sorry that Ms. Smith did not like the facial. I thought I did a fine job. Oh well, you cannot please everyone. Maybe she should try going down the street to the Better Service Salon.

   A cavalier attitude toward customer satisfaction will not make you employee of the month. Before you stick your foot in your mouth, consider asking what Ms. Smith disliked about the treatment and solicit your boss's input on ways to improve the treatment next time.

9. Look I have had a really bad day. I had an argument with my husband this morning and then my son had a tantrum when it was time to go to day care. I cannot deal with this right now.

   Learning to put personal issues aside is a professional responsibility. However, if you are having trouble handling a difficult conversation, be honest. Let your boss know that you are not at your best at the moment and that you would appreciate postponing the talk until later when you can give the matter the attention it deserves.

10. I wish I could attend that seminar on new exfoliation techniques, but I do not believe in giving up my day off for work-related events.

    Keeping up with current trends shows a dedication to providing quality work. Particularly if your boss is paying for your continuing education, a lack of interest will be poorly received.

Step BY Step

Brow Waxing Using The Strip Wax Method

Purpose: To remove excessive hair, and to clean and shape the brow area.

Room setup: Prepare the waxing table or bed with fresh paper.

Supplies: Mirror, scissors, tweezers, cotton pads, cleansing solution, eyebrow pencil or orangewood stick, eyebrow brush or comb, waxing heater, applicators, and precut strips of pellon or muslin. Position the trolley near the waxing table.

Client preparation: Review the client history form making sure that there are no contraindications. Discuss how much hair is to be removed, and pull hair away from the face by using a headband and towel or a cap.

Procedure

Shaping guidelines

1 Align an eyebrow pencil along the side of the nose beginning at the outside corner of the nostril up along the inside corner of the eye. The brows should start at that point. If there is excess hair to remove, make a few dots with the pencil in that area as a guideline for removal.

2 To find the arch, line up the pencil along the outside edge of the iris.

3 Brows should always extend a bit beyond the end of the eye. Rest the pencil at the base of the nose, under the nostril, and align it along the outside corner of the eye. Align brows and determine if the brows are even and balanced. This is your basic guideline for shaping the brows.

Two exceptions to these guidelines are close-set and wide-set eyes. Brows over close-set eyes will need to be widened a bit and extended at the outside corners. Instead of lining up the inside edge alongside the nostril, remove the brow hairs just beyond the inner corner of the eye. A few less hairs will make all the difference when shaping. The desired effect is to elongate the eye and give a wide open appearance.

Wide-set eyes need to be drawn together to better balance the face. The space between the eyes should be equal to the width of one eye. Because wide-set eyes are more than one eye's width apart, we want to extend the brows to equal that distance. Resting a pencil against the side of the nose, brows should start on the inside of the pencil; brows should extend just past the corner of the eye. Find the arch and the end of the brow as described above in steps #2 and #3.

4 After you have examined the brow and determined the shape, brush the brows into a smooth line. Use the eyebrow pencil to mark where it is necessary to remove excess hairs.

5 Hand the client a mirror to discuss exactly where hair will be removed.

Cleansing and sanitizing

6 Apply 1 or 2 drops of eye makeup remover or astringent to a 2" × 2" cotton pad.

7 Completely remove makeup and cleanse the brows in a downward swiping motion, beginning from the inside of the eye to the outside.

8 Rinse the area thoroughly with warm water and a soft sponge, until all residue from the cleanser and makeup has been removed. Allow the area to dry.

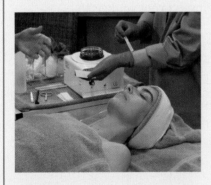

9 Trim any especially long brow hairs. This helps the wax adhere and allows you to remove the hair more easily and comfortably.

Wax application

10 Test the temperature of the wax before applying it to the client's skin by dabbing a small amount on the inside of your wrist.

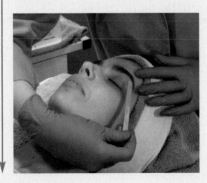

11 Dip the end of a small spatula into the warm wax (an orangewood stick works well for the brow area). Apply a thin coat of wax from the inside to the outside of the orbital bone with one swipe. Be careful to avoid dripping wax on areas that are not being waxed.

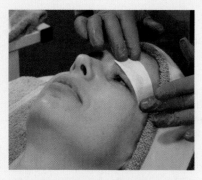

Removal

12 Apply muslin or pellon evenly with light pressure. Smooth the strip with the palm and fingers in the same direction as the wax application. Leave approximately 1 inch of muslin or pellon free to grip for removing. Use smaller strips cut to the desired length when working in the eye area. Work in small sections to avoid removing unwanted hair.

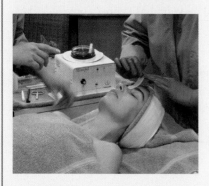

13 Remove the strip with one pull *against* the hair growth. Because follicles are not vertically straight and they grow at an angle, the hair is "popped" out at an angle, thus the pull is in the opposite direction of the hair growth. Pulling method and direction are critical. When pulling, the strip is folded or rolled back onto itself very rapidly. Do not pull the wax straight up or you will tear skin off with the hair, or even cause the hair to break off rather than pulling it out by the root. Immediately after you remove the strip, place your other hand quickly over the area to block nerve pain.

14 Check your work with a magnifying lamp. Remove any superfluous hair with tweezers.

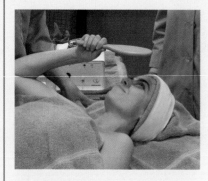

15 Give the client a mirror and have her inspect your work. Is she satisfied?

16 Pour a few drops of postwax soothing solution onto a dampened cotton pad or cotton swab.

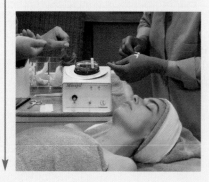

17 Swipe the area, making sure that no wax residue is left on the client's skin.

18 Remove the client's head protection.

Work neatly and cautiously to prevent mishaps. Should an accident occur, be prepared and stay calm. If a drop of wax falls into the eyelashes:

1. Ask the client to close her eyes gently, not squeeze them tight, and tell her to remain calm.
2. Apply a bit of petroleum jelly to the area with a cotton swab and roll the wax and jelly off with the cotton swab or with the end of the tweezer (the tweezer can easily retrieve the wax and jelly quickly and with no discomfort to the client).
3. Dampen a cotton pad (not soaking wet, but damp). Place the pad over the eyelid.
4. Before the client opens her eyes, use a cotton swab to absorb any excess water in the corner of the eyes.

Step By Step

Waxing the Cheek Using The Hard Wax Method

Introduction: Heavy hair at the sideburn area near the ears and peach fuzz on the cheeks and sides of the face can become caked with makeup, no matter how well blended. Give the client a mirror. Discuss with the client what effect is desired.

Clients often use a bleaching cream in these areas. The esthetician should explain that makeup will not cling to the face if the hair is removed completely, which avoids drawing attention to the area.

Purpose: To remove excessive hair in the cheek and sideburn areas.

Room setup: Prepare the waxing table or bed with fresh paper.

Supplies: Mirror, scissors, tweezers, cotton pads, waxing heater, applicators, and cleansing solution. Position the trolley near the waxing table.

Client preparation: Review the client history form, making sure there are no contraindications. Discuss how much hair is to be removed and pull the hair away from the face by using a headband and towel or a cap.

Procedure

Cleansing and sanitizing

1 Trim any overly long hair. It is less painful when removing the wax.

2 Apply a few drops of prewax sanitizing/cleansing solution to a moistened 4" × 4" cotton pad.

3 Completely clean the skin in the area to be waxed.

4 Rinse the area and allow it to dry.

Wax application

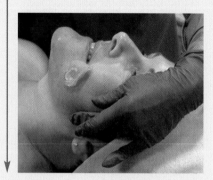

5 Dip spatula into the wax and apply it with the hair growth in a figure-eight pattern over the area. Apply the wax to the thickness of a nickel. Apply a thicker area on one end, making a *lip* that can be grasped between the thumb and index fingers. Wait a few moments for the wax to cool and harden.

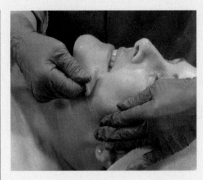

Removal

6   Place the thicker corner between the thumb and index finger. Pull the wax parallel to skin, against the hair growth.

7   Check your work with a magnifying lamp. Remove any superfluous hair with tweezers.

8   Give the client a mirror and have her inspect your work. Is she satisfied?

9   Pour a few drops of postwax soothing solution on a dampened cotton pad or cotton swab.

10   Swipe the area, making sure that no wax residue is left.

11   Remove the client's head protection.

Step
By
Step

Waxing the Chin Using
The Hard Wax Method

Introduction: Superfluous hair in this area falls into two categories: soft and fuzzy or coarse and deep rooted. The latter type can be difficult to remove. The chin area may also be sensitive. Consult with the client to discuss concerns and other options for hair removal, such as electrolysis, which may be the best option for removing deep-rooted, coarse hair.

Purpose: To remove excessive hair in the chin area.

Room setup: Prepare the waxing table or bed with fresh paper. Position the trolley near the waxing table.

Supplies: mirror, scissors, tweezers, cotton pads, waxing heater, applicators, and cleansing solution.

Client preparation: Review the client history form, making sure there are no contraindications. Discuss how much hair is to be removed, and pull hair away from the face by using a headband and towel or a cap.

Procedure

Cleansing and sanitizing

1 Apply a few drops of prewax sanitizing/cleansing solution to a moistened 4" × 4" cotton pad.

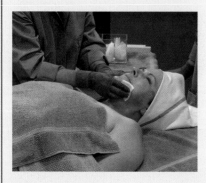

2 Completely clean the skin to be waxed. Rinse the area thoroughly and allow it to dry.

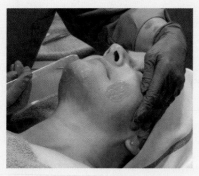

Wax application

3 Dip spatula into the wax and apply with the hair growth in a figure-eight pattern over the area. Apply the wax to the thickness of a nickel. Apply a thicker area on one end, making a *lip* that can be grasped between the thumb and index finger. Wait a few moments for the wax to harden.

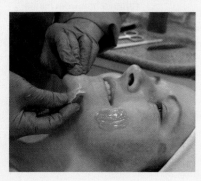

Removal

4 Place the thicker corner between the thumb and index finger. Pull the wax parallel to skin, against the hair growth. Immediately press your other hand over the waxed area to block nerve pain.

5 Check your work with a magnifying lamp. Remove any superfluous hair with tweezers.

6 Give the client a mirror and have her inspect your work. Is she satisfied?

7 Pour a few drops of postwax soothing solution onto a dampened cotton pad (2" × 2" or 4" × 4").

8 Swipe the area, making sure that no wax residue is left.

9 Remove the client's head protection.

Waxing the Upper Lip

Introduction: Excessive hair growth in this area is a common complaint among clients. Female clients may be embarrassed by hair growth here. Facial hair above the lip may cast a shadow giving the face the appearance of being dirty. If the hair is bleached it can become coated with makeup and create an untidy appearance that also directs attention to the area. The lip area is very sensitive; it may get red or even swell slightly when waxing. Be extra careful when removing the wax from this area.

Purpose: To remove excessive hair from the upper lip area.

Room setup: Prepare the waxing table or bed with fresh paper.

Supplies: Mirror, scissors, tweezers, cotton pads, waxing heater, applicators, cleansing solution, and precut pellon or muslin strips. Position the trolley near the waxing table.

Client preparation: Review the client history form, making sure there are no contraindications. Discuss with the client how much hair is to be removed, and pull hair away from the face by using a headband and towel or a cap.

> It is not advisable to remove hair from inside the nose. If, however, the client requests you remove hair inside the nose, carefully trim long hairs with cuticle scissors.

Procedure

Cleansing and sanitizing

1 Apply a few drops of prewax sanitizing/cleansing solution to a moistened 4" × 4" cotton pad.

2 Completely clean the skin to be waxed.

3 Rinse the area thoroughly and allow it to dry.

Wax application

4 Dip the end of a small spatula into the warm wax. Apply a thin coat of wax in the direction of hair growth over the lip area. Be cautious to avoid dripping wax on areas that are not being waxed.

Removal

5 Apply muslin or pellon evenly with light pressure. Smooth the strip with the palm and fingers in the same direction as the wax application. Leave approximately 1 inch of muslin or pellon free to grip for removing. Remove with one pull *against* the hair growth. Because follicles are not vertically straight and they grow at an angle, the hair is "popped" out at an angle, thus the pull is in the opposite direction of the hair growth. Pulling method and direction are critical. When pulling, the strip is folded or rolled back onto itself very rapidly. Do not pull the wax straight up or you will tear skin off with the hair, or even cause the hair to break off rather than pulling it out by the root. Immediately after you remove the strip, place your other hand quickly over the area to block nerve pain.

6 Check your work with a magnifying lamp. Remove any superfluous hair with tweezers. Give the client a mirror and have her inspect your work. Is she satisfied?

7 Pour a few drops of postwax soothing solution onto a dampened cotton pad.

8 Swipe the area, making sure that no wax residue is left.

9 Remove the client's head protection.

Step By Step

Waxing the Underarm Using The Strip Wax Method

Introduction: Removal of unwanted underarm hair is often a very satisfying service for the client. On some clients, the hair grows back slower. The span of time between waxing increases. Unlike other parts of the body, the hair under the arm grows in many different directions. Carefully note the pattern of hair growth prior to placing the wax.

Most female clients shave the underarm area. This can be irritating and can also cause ingrown hairs. Combined with a strong deodorant, the skin may become inflamed and experience a constant state of breakout. This condition is often improved by waxing.

Purpose: To remove excessive hair from the underarm area.

Room setup: Prepare the waxing table or bed with fresh paper.

Supplies: Mirror, scissors, tweezers, cotton pads, waxing heater, applicators, cleansing solution, pellon or muslin strips, and postwax soothing solution. Position the trolley near the waxing table.

Client preparation: Review the client history form making sure there are no contraindications. Discuss the procedure with the client.

> • The underarm is a breeding ground for bacteria. Thoroughly cleanse and dry the area prior to waxing.
> • Underarm hair grows in several directions. Apply smaller strips according to the growth pattern to avoid causing irritation or blood droplets.
> • If droplets of blood appear on the skin surface, this is usually normal because since the bulb has been suddenly removed and the follicle becomes traumatized. The blood naturally flows to the surface of the skin. Dispose of any strips or cotton pads in the hazardous waste container.
> • When using the hard (hot) wax, do not recycle it. Discard it in a hazardous waste container.

1 Place a small hand towel over the client's chest area to protect it from spills or drips.

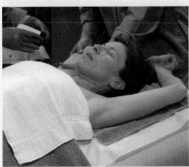

2 Ask the client to place her arms above her head, bent at the elbows with the lower arms encircling the head.

Procedure

Cleansing and sanitizing

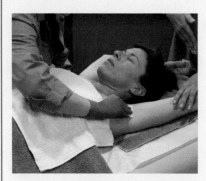

3 Cleanse the area to be waxed with a soapy cleanser. Rinse the area well. Apply a few drops of prewax sanitizing/cleansing solution to a moistened cotton pad. Allow the area to dry.

Wax application

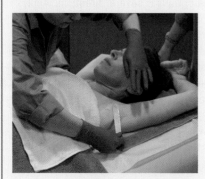

4 Dip the end of a spatula into the warm wax. Apply a thin coat of wax in the direction of hair growth. Be careful to avoid dripping wax on areas that are not being waxed.

Removal

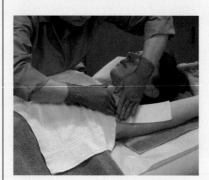

5 Apply muslin or pellon evenly with light pressure. Smooth the strip with the palm and fingers in the same direction as the wax application. Leave approximately 1 inch of muslin or pellon free to grip for removing.

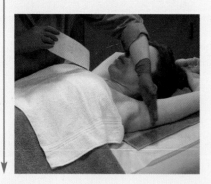

6 Remove the wax with one pull *against* the hair growth. Because follicles are not vertically straight and they grow at an angle, the hair is "popped" out at an angle, thus the pull is in the opposite direction of hair growth. Pulling method and direction are critical. When pulling, the strip is folded or rolled back onto itself very rapidly. Do not pull the strip straight up or you will tear skin off with the hair, or even cause the hair to break off, rather than pulling it out by the root. Immediately after you remove the strip, place your other hand quickly over the area to block nerve pain.

7 Check your work with a magnifying lamp. Remove any superfluous hair with tweezers.

8 Give the client a mirror and have her inspect your work. Is she satisfied?

9 Pour a few drops of postwax soothing solution onto a dampened cotton pad.

10 Swipe the area, making sure that no wax residue is left.

11 Remove the client's head protection.

Step
By
Step

Waxing the Arm

Introduction: Many clients have excess arm hair that causes them to be embarrassed or uncomfortable. Arm hair tends to grow in different directions, so closely examine the entire area before waxing. The best way to determine the growth direction is to feel the skin with your hand.

Purpose: To remove excessive hair from the arms.

Room setup: Prepare the waxing table or bed with fresh paper.

Supplies: Mirror, scissors, tweezers, cotton pads, waxing heater, applicators, cleansing solution, pellon or muslin strips (if using strip wax method), and postwax soothing solution. Position the trolley near the waxing table.

Client preparation: Review client history form, making sure there are no contraindications. Discuss the procedure with the client and arrange the client in a sitting position on the table.

EPILATION TIPS

- If skin is loose or fleshy, gently grasp the area and hold it taut so that the skin is not irritated or injured when you remove the wax.
- Keep your elbow and wrist straight and extend your arm to the full length when pulling muslin strips or hot wax off an area.
- Advise the client not to expose the waxed area to sun or a tanning bed for 48 hours.
- Advise the client not to exfoliate or expose the skin to very hot water.

Procedure

Cleansing and sanitizing

1 Apply a few drops of prewax sanitizing/cleansing solution to a moistened 4" × 4" cotton pad. Thoroughly cleanse the area to be waxed. Allow the area to dry.

Wax application

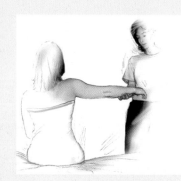

2 Strip wax: Dip a small spatula into the warm wax. Apply a thin coat in the direction of hair growth. Be careful to avoid dripping wax on areas that are not being waxed.

3 Hard wax: Dip a spatula into the wax and apply it with the hair growth in a figure-eight pattern over the area. Apply the wax to the thickness of a nickel. Apply a thicker area on one end, making a *lip* that can be grasped between the thumb and index finger. Wait a few moments for the wax to harden.

   To remove hair from the top of the forearm, elbow to wrist, extend the client's arm toward you with the palm facing downward, supported under the forearm by your hand. Because this hair usually grows sideways, apply the wax following protocol for either hard or strip wax. Note: If using strips, the best strip size to use is 3" × 6".

To remove hair from the back of the arm, elbow to shoulder, ask the client to bend the arm at the elbow and extend the elbow toward you so that the client's arm is at a right angle to her body. Place your free hand under the elbow and upper arm for support. Apply the wax following protocol for either hard or strip wax.

Removal

4 Strip wax: Apply the muslin or pellon evenly with light pressure. Smooth the strip with the palm and fingers in the same direction as the wax application. Leave approximately 1 inch of muslin or pellon free to grip for removing. Remove with one pull *against* the hair growth. Because follicles are not vertically straight and grow at an angle, the hair is "popped" out at an angle, thus the pull is in the opposite direction of hair growth. Pulling method and direction are critical. When pulling, the strip is folded or rolled back onto itself very rapidly. Do not pull the strip straight up or you will tear skin off with the hair, or even cause the hair to break off rather than pulling it out by the root. Immediately after you remove the strip, place your other hand quickly over the area to block nerve pain.

5 Hard wax: Place the thicker corner of wax between your thumb and forefinger. Pull the wax off parallel to the skin against the hair growth.

6 Pour a few drops of postwax soothing solution on a dampened cotton pad.

7 Clean the area, making sure that no wax residue is left.

Step by Step

Waxing the Shoulders and Back Using the Hard Wax Method

Introduction: Hair can be thick on the back of the shoulder area. Many men are uncomfortable or embarrassed by excessive back hair, so they often request to have it removed. The back is very sensitive, so work in small sections the first time. Always test patch a small area to check the skin's reaction. Wait a few moments. If no severe reaction occurs, you can proceed.

Skills are needed with the spatula in the shoulder area. To ensure an even application of wax to the rounded area of the shoulder, hold the spatula at an angle, which allows the wax to cover thinly, evenly, and smoothly.

When waxing only on the shoulder area, the client may sit or lie prone (face down) on the table. When waxing the entire back, the client lies prone (face down) on the table. Give the client a small pillow for face support if your waxing bed is not equipped with a headrest. When waxing the entire back, section the back into four quadrants, working in small areas, section by section.

Purpose: To remove excessive hair from the back and shoulders.

Room setup: Prepare the waxing table or bed with fresh paper. Position the trolley near waxing table.

Supplies: Mirror, scissors, tweezers, cotton pads, waxing heater, applicators, cleansing solution and postwax soothing solution.

Client preparation: Review the client history form, making sure there are no contraindications. Discuss the procedure with the client, and determine how much hair is to be removed.

Procedure

Cleansing and sanitizing

1 Trim hair if it is overly long.

2 Apply a few drops of prewax sanitizing/cleansing solution to a moistened cotton pad.

3 Completely clean the area to be waxed.

4 Rinse the area thoroughly and allow it to dry.

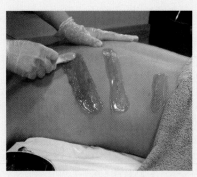

Wax application

5 Dip spatula into the wax and apply it with the hair growth in a figure-eight pattern over the area. Apply the wax to the thickness of a nickel. Apply a thicker area on one end, making a *lip* that can be grasped between the thumb and index finger. Wait a few moments for the wax to harden.

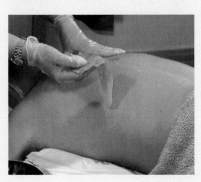

Removal

6 Place the thicker corner between the thumb and index finger. Pull the wax parallel to the skin, against the hair growth.

7 Check your work with a magnifying lamp. Remove any superfluous hair with tweezers.

8 Pour a few drops of postwax soothing solution onto a dampened cotton pad.

9 Cleanse the area, making sure that no wax residue is left.

Waxing the Leg

After facial services, leg waxing is the most popular hair removal service. Women like the fact that shaving can be eliminated completely.

Leg service is divided into four parts, upper, lower, bikini, and feet. Depending on the client's preferences and rate of hair growth, the service may vary during the year. On average leg waxing lasts 4 to 6 weeks, so you may want to schedule your client for a standing appointment on a monthly basis.

Thighs and Calves

The legs are divided into different areas, the upper leg (thighs) and the lower leg (calves). Some clients may only wish to have the lower leg (calves) epilated because some women only shave their legs on the calves because hair growth above the knee is minimal.

To begin with the calves, have your client lie on her stomach. The area is divided into three sections, the inner, outer, and middle calf. Examine hair growth carefully in all three areas.

The Bikini Line

The basic bikini line is defined as the area from the upper pubic bone to about three inches horizontally to the outside of the upper leg.

Prior to performing this service, discuss the type of bathing attire the client wears. Is it a high-cut line or regular cut? If possible, have her wear the suit, but do not perform the service with the suit on. There is a risk of damaging the suit. The brevity of bathing suits, including thongs, has made this a more time-consuming service, so plan accordingly.

The bikini line is a separate service and should not be confused with upper leg hair removal. If the client desires both, then charge for a basic bikini and an upper leg.

Brazilian Bikini

This may be considered a controversial waxing service. Bruising and skin removal can easily result. It is included here because it is a popular waxing area in various regions, especially around college campuses, major cities, and seaside communities.

You must be skilled and capable of doing this service *before* you book the appointment. Privacy is a must. Provide disposable panties for the client. Epilate one section at a time, lowering the panty for each removal. When you are ready to remove the hair from the area between the legs, follow the directions for the bikini line. The client will be asked to hold back the panty as you progress.

Have the client specify the exact area for hair removal. The client should hold the panty to cover the center of the pubis. Do not attempt to remove hair from the center of the pubic area. This is the most personal procedure in epilation, and it must be handled in a delicate manner.

Ingrown Hair Service

Some clients have a problem with ingrown hair. During your normal waxing schedule, some ingrown hairs may be removed. When they are a major problem, schedule the client for another appointment. Allow about 30 minutes to remove them correctly. Be sure to sanitize the areas very well. Use a sterile lancet to lift the hair that is imbedded. Using a blunt-edged tweezer, grasp the hair as close to the skin as possible, and pull the hair in the direction of the growth.

In some states, the use of a lancet is not allowed. Check with your State Board of Cosmetology to determine the rules in your state for using lancets. Discuss alternative methods for removing ingrown hair with your instructor.

Client Positioning for Bikini Wax

In order for the technician to successfully perform a bikini wax, the client should be relaxed and comfortable. The following client positions provide general guidelines for placing the client comfortably and allowing the technician comfortable and easy access to the waxing area.

Procedure

Position #1: The client lies face up on the table with the legs in a V spread.

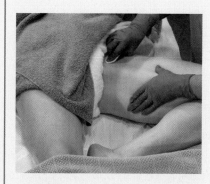

Position #2: The client lies face up on the table, with one leg straight and the other leg bent at the knee. The foot of the bent leg is placed against the inside of the straight leg.

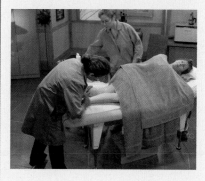

Position #3: The client turns onto the side, slightly turned out, so the natural contour of the body forms a cuplike crease at the thigh leg line for wax application. Before you begin the procedure, discuss with the client how high she would like the bikini line.

Follow waxing techniques according to protocol for a particular area.

Step By Step

Basic Bikini Waxing Using The Hard Wax Method

Purpose: To remove excessive hair from the bikini line.

Room setup: Prepare the waxing table or bed with fresh paper.

Supplies: Mirror, scissors, tweezers, cotton pads, waxing heater, applicators, cleansing solution and postwax soothing solution.

Client preparation: Review client history form, making sure there are no contraindications. Discuss how much hair is to be removed. Give the client disposable bikini panties or have the client place a clean towel between the legs and hold the end of the towel against the abdomen, keeping it taut against the skin.

Client positioning: Place client in relaxed, comfortable position. (Refer to p. 479 for the three recommended methods.)

Procedure

Cleansing and sanitizing

1 Apply a few drops of prewax sanitizing/cleansing solution to a moistened 4" × 4" cotton pad.

2 Completely clean the skin in the area to be waxed.

3 Rinse the area thoroughly and allow it to dry.

Wax application

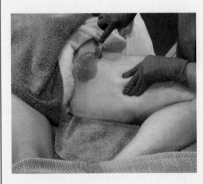

4 Dip a spatula into the wax and apply it with the hair growth in a figure-eight pattern over the area. Apply the wax to the thickness of a nickel. Apply a thicker area on one end, making a *lip* that can be grasped between the thumb and index finger. Wait a few moments for the wax to harden.

Removal

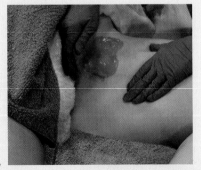

5 Place the thicker corner between the thumb and index finger. Pull the wax parallel to the skin, against the hair growth.

6 Check your work with a magnifying lamp. Remove any superfluous hair with tweezers. Remove any ingrown hair if time permits.

7 Pour a few drops of postwax soothing solution onto a dampened cotton pad.

8 Cleanse the area, making sure that no wax residue is left.

EPILATION TIPS

- Wear a clean, professional uniform or a lab coat. You may wear a protective full white apron over your uniform during a waxing service.
- Be sure the area is dry before applying the wax.
- Practice speed in applying the wax, smoothing the muslin, and removing the hot wax. Apply pressure with your palms after treatment to avoid pain in the area.
- Hold the skin as taut as possible before pulling off the muslin or pellon strips or the hot wax strips.
- Always pull the wax off *against* the direction of hair growth.
- A cool tea bag can be applied over sensitive areas to soothe any discomfort.
- Use petroleum jelly on any area where wax was accidentally dripped. The hair will not be removed.
- The upper section of the leg is normally flaccid. Show extra care by holding the area taut during epilation. It prevents skin tears and bruising.
- The back of the knee and ankle may need a special technique for the clean removal of hair. Practice makes perfect.
- Epilation wax hair removal systems should last 6 to 8 weeks.
- Suggest that the client use a loofa sponge for cleansing to prevent ingrown hairs.
- Retail products are available to apply on problematic areas for ingrown hair. They contain a small amount of salicylic acid to keep hair soft.

Summary

Waxing is a popular service. It can make up a significant portion of your spa's business. It is also labor-intensive, especially for the larger body areas. Your work should be as comfortable as possible. No matter how expensive the waxing system, its success depends on your ability to master the techniques of application, pulling (removing the wax), and care of the skin. Working in a systematic way keeps the procedure segmented and not overwhelming. Practice is your key to success.

Discussion Questions

1. Waxing clients is a very personal service. Discuss ways in which you might enhance the client's comfort level when performing these services, particularly those that involve the removal of clothing, such as bikini and underarm waxing.

2. Study the basic guidelines for shaping eyebrows. How would your approach differ when using hard wax versus soft wax?

3. Discuss pre- and post-skin care for waxing services. Does this care differ according to the areas being treated? If so, how?

4. Solicit menus (brochures) from several skin care or full-service salons and compare the costs of waxing services. What is the average cost for treating each of the areas mentioned in this chapter?

Additional Reading

Aavin, Mary. *Technical Manual for Epilation.* Bloomfield, N.J.:

Dermascope. 2001. *Professional Product and Service Guide 2001.* Sunnyvale, Tex: Dermascope.

Gambino, Henry J. 1992. *Modern Esthetics: A Scientific Source for Estheticians.* Clifton Park, N.Y.: Milady, an imprint of Delmar Learning, a division of Thomson Learning, Inc.

Gerson, Joel. 1999. *Standard Textbook for Professional Estheticians.* Clifton Park, N.Y.: Milady, an imprint of Delmar Learning, a division of Thomson Learning, Inc.

Head 2 Toe, Inc., P.O. Box 390, 167 Pleasant Street, Reading, MA 01867

Lees, Mark. 2001 *Skin Care: Beyond the Basics.* Clifton Park, N.Y.: Milady, an imprint of Delmar Learning, a division of Thomson Learning, Inc.

McCrane, Sally. 2001. "Ergonomic Problems," *New York Times,* 8 Mar. 2001, p. E10.

Michalun, Natalia, with M. Varinia Michalun. 2000. *Milady's Skin Care and Cosmetic Ingredients Dictionary.* Clifton Park, N.Y.: Milady, an imprint of Delmar Learning, a division of Thomson Learning, Inc.

Nelson, Dennis. 2001. *Safety and Health in the Salon: Facilitator's Guide.* Clifton Park, N.Y.: Milady, an imprint of Delmar Learning, a division of Thomson Learning, Inc.

Poignard, Renee. 1994. *Waxing Made Easy: A Step-by-Step Guide.* Clifton Park, N.Y.: Milady, an imprint of Delmar Learning, a division of Thomson Learning, Inc.

Pugliese, Peter. 1991. *Advanced Professional Skin Care.* Bernville, Pa: APSC.

Rayner, Victoria. 1993. *Clinical Cosmetology: A Medical Approach to Esthetics Procedures.* Clifton Park, N.Y.: Milady, an imprint of Delmar Learning, a division of Thomson Learning, Inc.

Schorr, Lia, with Shari Sims. 1994. *SalonOvations' Advanced Skin Care Handbook.* Clifton Park, N.Y.: Milady, an imprint of Delmar Learning, a division of Thomson Learning, Inc.

Skin Inc. 2001. *Symposium, January-June 2001.* Carol Stream, Il: Allured Publishing.

Thrower, Angelo. 1999. *Black Skin Care for the Practicing Professional.* Clifton Park, N.Y.: Milady, an imprint of Delmar Learning, a division of Thomson Learning, Inc.

Turkington, C., and J. Dover. 1996. *Skin Deep,* New York: Facts on File.

Helpful Web Sites

http://www.alexandriasugaring.com
(Alexandria Professional Body Sugaring,
Lockport, NY)

http://www.amberproducts.com (Amber
Products, Imperial, PA)

http://www.catherinehinds.com (Catherine
Hinds Institute of Esthetics—*300 Hour
Advanced Esthetic Curriculum Guide*, 300
Wildwood Avenue, Woburn, MA)

http://www.dermaculture.com (Derma
Culture, Newport Beach, CA)

Makeup Artistry

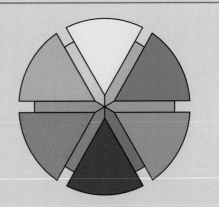

PART IX

Part Outline

Chapter 31   Color Theory, Facial Features, and Setup

Chapter 32   Makeup Applications

Since the turn of the twentieth century in the United States, the general population has taken great interest in the latest trends in fashion, jewelry and overall appearance. At the beginning of the 1900s, new trends for makeup, hairstyles, and clothing arrived from England. Evening makeup became popular to wear on special occasions and social gatherings. As moving pictures made their mark on society, what was in vogue in Hollywood became the main influence with beauty editors.

A talented makeup artist looks at the natural beauty of the client and enhances or corrects the facial features to give an individual an overall pleasing look. What many of the color theories teach today is how to work with the natural skin tone, hair color, eye color, and overall *look* of the individual. Understanding a person's lifestyle, body type, and comfort level contributes to the completeness of the recommended plan.

These chapters introduce you to the various looks that are created by the makeup artist. The color wheel and color theories are explained, providing the basics in color theory. Examples of face shapes, location of brows, and overall features are demonstrated. Makeup product descriptions and use are highlighted. Insight into the best approach to client consultation, as well as how to properly arrange the makeup station, how to choose a product line, and information on corrective and camouflage makeup, is provided. Basic, step-by-step makeup application techniques are detailed.

Chapter 31
Color Theory, Facial Features, And Setup

Chapter Objectives

After reading this chapter, you should be able to:

- Describe the theory of color and its characteristics.
- Define how dark and light colors affect objects.
- Define the meaning of *warm* and *cool* colors.
- Discuss a standard face shape and its deviations.
- Describe the key points of the face and how to create a balanced look.
- Explain each makeup product and how it is used.
- Demonstrate contouring with foundation.
- Demonstrate setting up a makeup station.

Chapter Outline

Introduction
Color Theory
Face Proportion and Shape
Facial Profile
Choosing and Using Makeup Products
Makeup Tools

Introduction

Of all the disciplines you study in this text-book, makeup artistry will allow you to develop creativity, flair, and imagination. Your clients will be thrilled that you are designing everyday looks for them that enhance their natural features. Everyone wants to appear her best. Makeup is certainly a tool to help create a *look* that radiates beauty and attractiveness.

In the past, makeup in the professional industry was regarded as an enemy of skin care. Spas and salons offered makeup because it was another expected beauty service. The professional esthetician or makeup artist would caution clients not to apply anything for at least 24 hours after a facial in order to let the skin breathe by taking a day off from the effects of daily makeup.

Over the past 10 years, clients began searching for more harmony and balance in their everyday lives. A new focus on results-oriented skin care converged with increased interest in fitness, exercise, and nutrition. Facial care products took on a new emphasis directed at skin health and wellness, and this included makeup. Clients requested options for makeup products that would allow them to leave the salon or spa looking great (Figure 31–1). The products felt great and were beneficial to their skin wellness.

Manufacturers who wanted to keep up with new health trends responded with products that were of a higher quality—in terms of skin-friendly ingredients, textures, and spreadability. They created makeup products that were beautiful in color and were also wellness oriented. Makeup formulas were transformed to include vitamins, minerals, botanical extracts, and sunscreens. Makeup was now considered healthier. The added benefits of nutrients, botanicals, unique delivery systems, moisturizing activities, and sunscreen provided a complementary benefit to the quality of the daily skin care routine. While glamour and beauty continued to be a primary concern, products also began to address and satisfy client lifestyle requirements.

The world of makeup as we know it today includes a whole range of products that are more therapeutic, skin friendly, and similar to skin care products. Now a client leaves the spa or salon wearing makeup, looking great, and feeling wonderful about

Figure 31–1 An attractive salon makeup area.

the products she is using. Makeup reaches across the boundaries of color to touch our clients in a friendly, beautiful, and healthy way. The issues of health and wellness do not limit makeup. It is considered an enhancement to the client's attractiveness. Therefore, makeup should be taken seriously and studied to bring out the best in our client's appearance (Figure 31–2).

Figure 31–2 Your client can be transformed with a makeover.

Makeup artistry permits you to work with color, mood, texture, and whimsy. Makeup brings out creativity and fun. You can transform your client with many different looks that reflect beauty, fashion, and wellness. As an artist works with paint or crayon, the esthetician also works with a palette of products such as foundations, eye shadows, lipsticks, and lip and eye pencils. A wide variety of color choices is available for all products, allowing us to obtain a perfect match with the skin tone and eyes. This unique set of tools provides flexibility in terms of a client's skin type or condition.

As in music, colors on the face should harmoni*ze* well so that your makeup selection coordinates with the look desired by the client. This can be a natural daytime look, a more sophisticated elegant look, or a sporty casual look.

Color Theory

Makeup training starts with understanding the basic principles of color theory through the use of a color wheel. Colors are placed in an easy-to-understand arrangement that highlights harmonious blends or complementary colors.

Look at the color wheel and identify the colors (Figure 31–3). Red, yellow, and blue are the **primary colors** (Figure 31–4). These are called primary colors because every other color, or **hue,** is developed from them. Hue is another name for color.

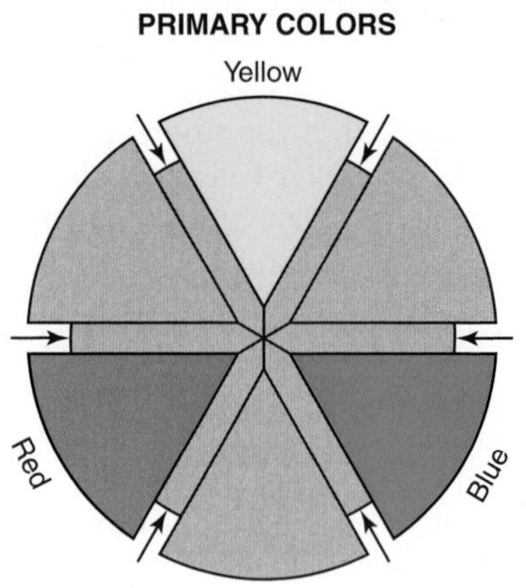

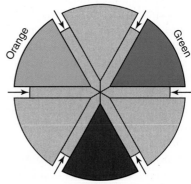

Figure 31–4 Primary colors—red, yellow, and blue.

Orange, green, and purple are known as **secondary colors** (Figure 31–5). They are achieved by mixing equal amounts of two primary colors: red + yellow = orange; blue + red = violet; yellow + blue = green.

Another designation for colors is **tertiary,** or intermediate, colors (Figure 31–6). Combining the primary and secondary colors located next to each other on the color wheel produces tertiary colors. There are six tertiary colors: red + orange = red-orange; yellow + green = yellow-green; blue + violet = blue-violet; orange + yellow = yellow-orange; green + blue = blue-green; violet + red = red-violet .

primary colors
Red, yellow, and blue on the color wheel. All other colors are made by mixing the primary colors.

hue
Another name for color.

secondary colors
Orange, green, and purple. They are developed by mixing equal parts of two primary colors.

tertiary
Intermediate, or third-level colors. They are developed by combining the primary and secondary colors located next to each other on the color wheel.

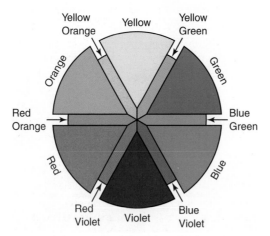

Figure 31–3 The color wheel.

Figure 31–5 Secondary colors—range, violet, and green.

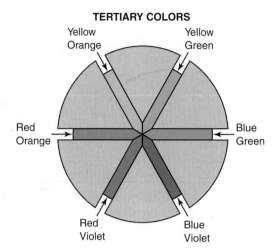

TERTIARY COLORS

Yellow Orange — Yellow Green
Red Orange — Blue Green
Red Violet — Blue Violet

Figure 31–6 Tertiary colors are created by combining a primary color with its adjacent secondary color.

On your color wheel, take a pencil and draw a line from the red to the opposite color, green. You have identified a **complementary color** (Figure 31–7). When two colors opposite one another on the color wheel are mixed, they develop neutral brown shades. We sometimes use the complementary colors to neutralize tones, such as a lavender concealer over areas that appear sallow.

When black is added to a color, a **shade** of that color is created. A darker, or lower, value of the color is achieved. If we add black

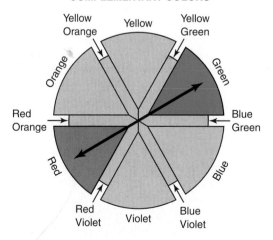

COMPLEMENTARY COLORS

Yellow Orange — Yellow — Yellow Green
Orange — Green
Red Orange — Blue Green
Red — Blue
Red Violet — Violet — Blue Violet

Figure 31–7 Complementary colors are formed by combining the colors opposite each other on the color wheel.

to blue, we get navy. Be cautious with black. When too much black is added to a color, it only makes a different shade of black instead of a darker version of that color.

A **tint** is achieved by adding white to dilute a color, thus a lighter value is achieved. For example, pink is achieved by adding white to red. **Value** is the lightness or darkness of a color.

Another way to look at color or hue is to examine its **intensity,** or the degree of purity or brilliance of a color. The strength of the saturation of a color may vary from full force at the outer edges of the wheel to completely neutral in the center of the wheel.

What Colors Do

Colors advance or recede. Bright colors advance and make the area covered appear larger. Dark colors recede and make the area covered appear smaller. This color rule can be applied to correct or to create an illusion. Light emphasizes; dark minimizes.

Color reflects other colors. Some colors tend to reflect back more than they take away. A red scarf near a ruddy complexion will make the face appear redder. A bright yellow would tend to emphasize yellow in skin with predominantly yellow tones.

Color will steal color. Bright blue placed beside light or pale blue will make the pale color appear less colorful. Darker, brighter colors steal from the lighter shade. A person with blue eyes can intensify the eye color by wearing a much lighter blue near the face.

Color Temperature

Colors have temperature and are categorized as **warm or cool tones** (Table 31–1, p. 490). Warm colors are reds, oranges, salmon pinks, yellows, corals, and browns—colors that are bright and attention getting remind us of summer or excitement. They tend to be cheerful colors that grab our attention. Think of places where you have seen lots of these colors. Eye-catching colors are often used in advertising.

Cool colors are blues, greens, violets, and grays—colors that are quiet like the sea, shaded like a mountain, or cold like an ice cube. Cool colors promote a more relaxed and quiet state of mind. Where would you find these colors?

complementary color
Developed by combining a color with the color opposite it on the color wheel.

shade
A variation in a color achieved by adding black.

tint
A variation in color achieved by adding white.

value
The lightness or darkness of a color.

intensity
The degree of purity or brilliance of a color.

warm or cool tones
Colors are categorized by temperature, with warm colors including reds, oranges, pinks, yellows, corals, and browns. Cool tones include blues, greens, violets, and grays.

Table 31–1 Color Temperature

Color/Temperature	Description
Pink—warm/cool	We think of pink as being a warm, rosy color, but a pastel (tint) is cool looking. When more red is added to white, the pink becomes warmer. Pink is flattering to skin tones unless the skin is ruddy and the pink unusually bright. Pink combines well with other shades and tints of pink, blue, black, green, yellow, gray, orange, purple, brown, beige, and white.
Blue—cool	Blue is complementary to most skin tones. Lighter blues enhance darker skin while darker blue brings out color in lighter skin. Blue combines well with almost all other colors.
Purple—cool/warm	Mixed with pale tints of orchid and lavender, purple is cool. Darker shades (plum) with red undertones are warm. Purple is not kind to blemished or reddish skin tones and should be studied carefully against the skin. Purple combines well with pink, white, gray, and soft blue, beige, black, and pale yellow.
Green—cool	Green is easy on the eyes and flattering to many skin tones. Bright green can intensify red in the skin. Blue greens are cool and generally attractive colors for both light and dark skin. Green combines well with other greens, blue, yellow, orange, beige, brown, white, and black.
Brown—warm	Brown can be kind to many complexion tones. Other reflecting or accent colors can be worn near the face if the skin is dark brown. Brown combines well with green, beige, blue, pink, yellow, orange, gold, white, and black.
Red—warm/cool	Red is a warm and exciting color, easy for most people to wear. Red with blue undertones is cool: with yellow undertones it is warm. Red of a specific tint or shade may not be kind to a ruddy complexion. Freckles will look darker when red is reflected onto the face. Red combines well with many other colors. Among them are black, white, beige, gray, pink, blue, navy, green, and yellow.
Black—neutral	Black combines well with all other colors. A black costume can create a startling contrast for light skin and light or dark hair. When the skin and hair are dark, a color contrast near the face acts as a frame or highlight for the face.
White—cool/neutral	White is easy to wear but be cautious of its undertones. Some materials reflect beige or yellow undertones while others appear slightly blue. White combines well with all other colors.
Gray—neutral	A cool, neutral gray combines well with many other colors.

Makeup Profiling

makeup profiling

Gathering the visual information needed to determine the type of makeup application and the products chosen for a particular client.

Makeup profiling is gathering the visual information needed to determine the type of makeup applications and products to choose for a client. Evaluating a potential look for a client requires asking specific questions.

Are you happy with the colors you are using now?

What are your favorite colors to wear?

Do you use any color enhancers in your hair?

What kind of look do you wish for today—natural, evening, day, sweet, etc.?

Are there any colors you would like to try?

Are there any colors you do not like at all?

Do you use color corrective lenses or glasses?

What do you think is the most colorful part of your face?

A makeup artist uses similar protocols when analyzing a client. During a consulta-tion with an image consultant, a complete client profile of overall look is discussed and recorded. This may include body measure-ments, body shape, and height. It may also include hair color, skin tones, and eye color. The consultation also takes into account age, lifestyle, and requirements necessary for developing the most complementary look for an individual. A color analysis may be the first step in the consultation. What color seems to reveal the skin tones and eye fea-tures? What colors mute or take away from the client's look? What is the overall impres-sion of that person? Does she have dark fea-tures, medium features, or is she very fair?

Have you ever noticed someone who was wearing a color that was not too flattering? Perhaps it was not very obvious, but some-how it just did not seem to enhance the indi-vidual's appearance. Perhaps the shirt color was overpowering the face or draining out the skin tone, or maybe the lipstick did not appear to match, causing the lips to look pale and washed out. Because the skin has under-lying tones of color, any color that is worn externally will either complement and brighten the skin or eyes, or give a look of being sallow, yellow, or slightly green.

Determining the underlying skin tones begins to draw a picture of that person. It helps to establish a fashion look for clothing and makeup. Generally we observe our client's skin tone, hair color, eye color, and blood tone color. Profiling places each unique person into a system or category of color tone. From that profile, we build a system of overall coloring with makeup, clothing, and hairstyle. It will complement and give the person an appealing, comfortable look.

Creating Harmony

When we think about a total, harmonious look, color plays an important role. The theme is centered on a person's hair, eye, and skin colors. Is the overall projected look warm or cool? The "Color Me Beautiful" formula of the 1980s gave great information about the client. It provided a starting point for individuals who had no idea how to choose the best colors for their wardrobe or makeup.

When we begin looking at makeup, we have more flexibility due to the fact that we are only putting makeup on a very small area of our total image—the face. Look at yourself in a mirror. View the area from the chin up to the top of your head versus the space from the chin to the feet. Sometimes a color that may not look its best for us in clothing is perfectly acceptable on the face, e.g., an eye shadow, because it is applied to a very small area. Do not place any limitations when trying certain colors on the face because it is not the *right* color. You may feel that if you practice enough, you will get it perfect; however, practice does not always make perfect.

Creativity and experimentation help you develop great ideas and great combinations of colors for a client. It brings out the wow in them. In makeup, there are no wrong colors, only artists who are afraid to try them. So now that we have learned some color basics, we will look at one way color theory helps us understand makeup.

Skin Tones

The largest area we work on is the face. Foundations and powders are matched to the

Table 31–2 Categories of Skin Tones

Tone	Undertones	Ethnicity
Ivory to fair	Fair, light skin with creamy or slightly pink undertones	Light Caucasians to light Asian, Hispanic
Beige or medium	Medium skin with pink or yellow	Medium Caucasians, medium Asian, Hispanic, black
Olive or warm	Olive skin with gold/yellow or orange/red	Tanned Caucasians, medium Asians, Hispanic, black
Deep or dark	Black skin with brown/yellow, brown/red, or brown/blue	Dark Hispanic to very black skin

skin tones. Skin tones fall into several groups (Table 31–2). Understanding how to work with different skin tones is important to achieving the desired results.

There are many skin colors in the world and within each racial group there will be individuals who have a variety of skin tones. Table 31–2 should be used as a general guide to simplify categories; however it is not all inclusive.

Face Proportion and Shape

Several basic, universal principles can be applied to analyze face shapes. For example, oval is the shape that is most often used as the standard by which all other shapes are measured. It is thought to be the "perfect" shape. This standard shape was determined by overlapping the various face shapes. The converging lines gave birth to the oval face. However, few clients conform to the perfect shape. We must work to enhance the client's face shape and highlight the features that are most pleasing.

Basic Face Shapes

The next part of understanding makeup basics is the study of the client's face shape and proportion (Table 31–3).

After the face shape has been determined, each feature must be measured to find its correct proportion and location on the face. You can measure with a small ruler or you can determine it visually after you have had some experience and fully understand the concept. Make notes as you survey the client's face, assessing its general balance.

Table 31–3 Basic Face Shapes

Face Shape		Characteristics
Oval		Widest at the temple and forehead, tapering down to a curved chin. This is considered the perfect or ideal facial shape because of its balance and overall look of symmetry. It is used as a standard for all face shapes.
Round		This face is widest at the cheekbone area, and is usually not much longer than it is wide, having a softly rounded jawline, short chin, and a rounded hairline over a rather full forehead.
Square		Starting from a straight hairline to a square chin, this face has an angular jawline and the cheekbones are not particularly prominent. The lines of this face are straight and angular.
Rectangle		This face shape is long and narrow; the cheeks are often hollowed under prominent cheekbones. An overly long angular chin, a big forehead, or both are typical for this shape.
Triangle		Like a pyramid, this face is widest at its base or jawline, tapering up to slightly narrower cheeks, and reaching its apex at a narrow forehead.
Inverted triangle		This facial shape is wide at the temple and forehead area, tapering down to a narrow chin.

Table 31–3 *(continued)*

Face Shape		Characteristics
Heart		Somewhat similar to the diamond shape, this face has a small, pointed chin and narrow jawline, but is wider at the forehead. It is usually soft rather than angular, and has some prominence in the cheekbone area.
Diamond		Widest at the cheekbones, this face has a narrow chin and forehead. It is angular in form, and the measurements of the jaw and hairline are approximately the same.

Lengthwise, the face is divided horizontally into three equal sections (Figure 31–9).

1. from the center hairline to the lowest part of the inner portion of the eyebrows
2. from the eyebrows to the base of the nose
3. from the base of the nose to the bottom of the chin

When these sections are equal, the face is considered to be in proper proportion lengthwise.

The width of the face can be determined by using the eyes as a guide. Proportionately the space between the eyes should equal the width of one eye (Figure 31–9). The distance from the corner of each eye to the hairline should equal the width of one eye. Therefore, if the width of both eyes is the same and the space between the eyes equals the width of one eye, there is correct balance.

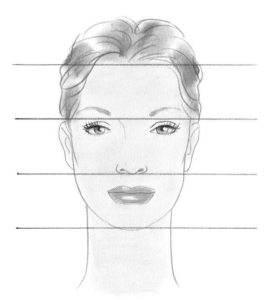

Figure 31–8 The face is divided horizontally into three equal sections.

Figure 31–9 The distance between the eyes should equal the width of one eye.

Table 31–4 Profile Features

Straight		The straight profile is considered ideal.
Convex		The convex profile is characterized by a receding forehead and chin. Highlighting the receding areas of the face will give it better balance.
Concave		The concave profile features a prominent chin and forehead. Shadowing the prominent areas of the face will give it better balance.

Facial Profile

Much can be done through illusion to alter and affect the shape of the face and the features from front view. It is more challenging to alter the profile. When using highlighting and shadowing techniques, always check to be sure that the makeup on the sides of the face matches. Table 31–4 outlines the three basic profile types.

Cheek Placement

Application of color on the cheeks should start one to two finger widths from the nostrils (depending on the width of the face), extend under the colored part of the iris, and outward to the middle of the ear (Figure 31–10). It should not extend any lower than the lip area; otherwise you cause the cheeks to drop into the jowls. Think of applying the color in a heart shape on the face, following an imaginary curved line from the edge of

the lip up and out toward the ear, around the eyebrow to the center of the brows.

Take careful notes of your findings about the client's face shape and facial proportions. Combine this information with the makeup profiling to decide what measures you are going to use to enhance or diminish your client's features. Face shape and facial proportions must serve as the basis for makeup application before considering artistic patterns and colors.

With makeup we can emphasize or diminish the individual features of the face to make changes in the overall balance. This can be done with traditional contouring, that is, highlighting (using light colors) and shadowing (using dark colors). When highlighting and shadowing, we incorporate foundations, concealers, or powders to help correct facial proportions. However, it is not necessary to highlight or shadow so much as to obliterate a client's features or proportions. In this day and age, unique features are admired as much as the standard features. In

Figure 31–10 Cheek color should cover the area in front of the ear along the jawline.

order to develop a plan of action, it is necessary to consult with your client to establish a look that pleases both the makeup artist's concept and the client's comfort factor.

Eyebrow Placement

The eyebrows should start at the inner edge of the eye. Using an eyebrow pencil, place the pencil against the nostril and hold it straight up toward the forehead. The pencil aligns with the inside corner of the eye, and along the eyebrow. Brow hairs that grow

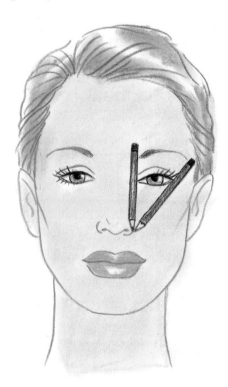

Figure 31–11 Use an eyebrow pencil to find the length and placement of the eyebrows.

beyond the pencil should be removed. To find the end of the eyebrow, hold the pencil against the nostril and angle it toward the outer corner of the eye. Brow hairs that grow beyond the pencil should also be removed (Figure 31–11).

Brow Shapes

Eyebrows are the most moveable features of the face. Think about all the emotions you can create with your face by just moving the eyebrows. Besides the moveable features of the eyebrows, the eyebrows fall into four categories (Table 31–5).

Challenges for eyebrows include loss of hairs, which is either due to age or to the client over-tweezing and/or nervous habits; i.e., pulling on the eyebrows. Hair loss or thinning is also caused from drugs such as chemotherapy. There may be loss of density, which is the loss of thickness in the eyebrow area, resulting in underlying skin showing through.

Brow shaping is an important skill for the makeup artist. Whether it is done with tweezers or waxing, eyebrows must be properly

Table 31–5 Eyebrow Shapes

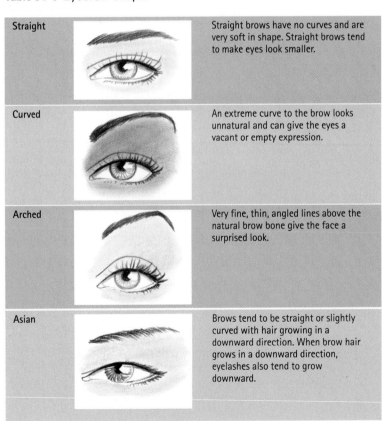

Straight		Straight brows have no curves and are very soft in shape. Straight brows tend to make eyes look smaller.
Curved		An extreme curve to the brow looks unnatural and can give the eyes a vacant or empty expression.
Arched		Very fine, thin, angled lines above the natural brow bone give the face a surprised look.
Asian		Brows tend to be straight or slightly curved with hair growing in a downward direction. When brow hair grows in a downward direction, eyelashes also tend to grow downward.

Table 31–6 Eye Shapes

Eye Shapes and Correction Techniques

Hidden lids		1. Create a crease in the middle of the upper lid. 2. Highlight the brow bone. 3. Softly line upper and lower lashes. Avoid strong colors.
Small eyes		1. Place a darker shadow over the lid, blending it out to the temple and up to the eyebrow. 2. Apply shadow to the outer corners of the lower lids. 3. Blend eyeliner softly from the center to the outer corners of both eyes along the eyelashes. 4. Apply mascara, brushing the lashes carefully.
Round eyes		1. Apply a medium shade shadow, blending it over the eyelid toward the eyebrow. 2. Apply dark shadow onto the crease and blend it toward the eyebrow. 3. Clearly line the inside of the eye with an eyeliner pencil. 4. Extend and carefully blend the colors in steps 1 and 3 toward the outer corner of the eye. 5. Apply mascara to the lashes only at the outer corners of the eyes.
Protruding eyes		1. Apply a medium color on the entire eyelid and blend it toward the eyebrow. 2. Line the inside of the eye using a brown or gray eyeliner pencil. 3. Apply mascara.
Deep-set eyes		1. Apply a light eyeshadow along the crease of the lid. 2. Blend in a medium color on the outer corners and to the temples. 3. Use a soft color to accentuate around the eyes. 4. Clearly outline the eyes along the lashes. 5. Choose a dark shade of mascara.
Close-set eyes		1. Apply a paler shade to the lid and a darker shade to the corner. 2. Line the eye from the middle to the corner and blend the shadow outward. 3. Apply mascara in an upward and outward motion.
Wide-set eyes		1. Extend a darker shadow from the inner corner of the eye toward the nose. Blend a lighter shadow from the middle toward the outer corner. Apply mascara with an inward motion.
Drooping eyes	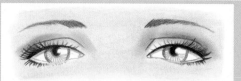	To offset the droop of the eye, which is often accompanied by a low bone structure or low lid fold, it is necessary to give the appearance of a lift to the entire eye area. 1. Tweeze the under area of the outer portion of the brow to allow a better arch. 2. Shading shadow is applied in a band across the fold and smudged outward. 3. Highlighter is placed directly under the arch of the brow. 4. Eyeliner (if used) is applied in a very thin line and thickened very slightly at the outside in a wedgelike point to give a lift to the eye.

groomed in order to achieve the optimal effect. Generally a few stray hairs may be tweezed during the makeup application. If more work is required, reschedule the makeover two or three days after you have shaped the brows.

A medium brown pencil can be used to sketch in brow hairs. A light brown eye shadow creates density. Just as there are different colors (or shades) in the hair, brows also need to appear as natural as possible. The client may have lighter and darker hairs. Other combinations from light to very dark are taupe and light brown, taupe and gray, light brown and light auburn, light brown and gray, light brown and dark brown, gray and medium brown, medium brown and dark brown, gray and dark brown, dark, brown and black. Apply very lightly, unless there is a special reason to make the brows darker. The darker the brow the more heavy it appears on the face.

Eye Shapes

The eyes are the most important focal point of the face. Eye shapes are the most commonly corrected features of the face, providing many challenges due to colors and shapes. Most clients want to learn how to choose the right colors and apply makeup to enhance their eyes.

The eye is divided into three areas:

1. eyelid
2. depth area
3. brow bone

A well-proportioned eye area measures one-third from the base of the lashes to the crease line, and two-thirds from the crease line to the eyebrow. The arc may have variations ranging from the very heavy-lidded eye to the flat-lidded eye of the Asian client.

Well-shaped eyes are the width of one eye apart. Eyes can also be close set or wide set, meaning that the distance between the eyes in less than, or greater than the width of one eye, respectively. Eyes should be corrected first in proportion to the way they fit on the face, then the shape of the eye can be addressed (Table 31–6).

To correct, always start with neutral shades of eye shadow such as ivory, brown, or gray to practice correcting the eye shape. Then you can add other colors to create variety and interest. Neutral colors are always

safe and most clients will be able to follow your directions as long as they are not confronted with too many products and/or colors. Colors can be added in small amounts or larger amounts based on the look you are creating or on the client's desired outcome.

The Nose

The nose can often disturb the balance of the face. A number of techniques are used to bring the nose shape into balance and harmony with the rest of the face (Table 31–7).

Table 31–7 Nose Shapes

Nose Shape		Correction
Crooked nose		Shade the side that the nose turns toward. Highlight in a fine line directly down the center.
Hooked nose		Shadow the hooked area then highlight directly below it. Blend very carefully.
Short nose		Place highlight down the center the full length of, and under the tip of, the nose.
Broad nose		Shadow the side of the nose and use a very fine highlight line down the center. Blend the edges well.
Long nose		Shadow the base and the tip of the nose.

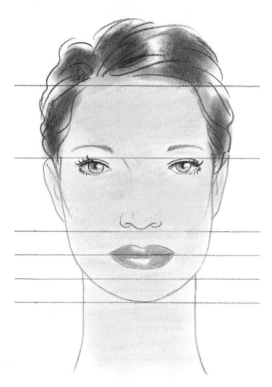

Figure 31–12 The lips fall in the lower third of the face.

Lip Placement

The proper placement and proportion of the lips can be found by dividing the lower facial area into two sections:

1. one-third from the center of the nose to the base of the lips
2. two-thirds from the center of the lips to the base of the chin

The width of the mouth may be approximately the distance between the irises of the eyes.

These basic guidelines should be used when applying makeup. After taking the dimensions of the client's face, if the proportions are not to the standard point of reference, then contouring and color sculpturing will help create the illusion that it is balanced.

The lips should fall in the lower third of the face (Figure 36–12). Then divide that lower third into thirds again so that the upper lip falls in the upper third and the bottom lip into the lower two-thirds.

Lip Shapes

Lips can be the most difficult of all features to correct, due to the skin laying over the teeth

and the color of the vermilion line or membrane of the lips. The natural texture and color of the lip line are often referred to as "hard" and "soft" lips. Soft lips are lips that do not have much natural color, making it difficult to tell where the lips begin and end on the face. Hard lips are lips that are richly colored by the vermilion in the lip membrane itself. Soft lips are more easily changed into a different shape, while the hard lip has to be completely covered before you can attempt to change the shape. Most clients have a definite opinion about their lips; usually it is better to discuss the concept of hard and soft before attempting to radically change the shape.

Lips are not the same shape but generally the upper peaks of the lips are located just below the nostrils. The end of the lips should line up with outer line of the iris (Figure 31–13).

Corrective techniques can be used to give the lips better proportion when needed, but quite often, a small or a larger mouth, or lips that are not exactly the same, give a certain individuality to the face (Table 31–8).

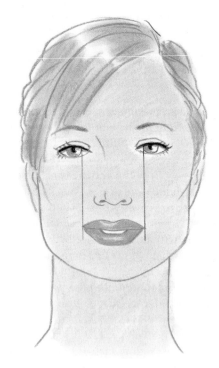

Figure 31–13 The corners of the lips should align with the inner edge of the iris.

Table 31–8 Lip Shapes and Corrective Techniques

Lip Shape	Correction
Thin lower lip	Line the lower lip to make it appear fuller. Fill in with lip color to create balance between the lower and upper lips.
Thin upper lip	Use a lip lining pencil to outline the upper lip, then fill in with lip color to balance with the lower lip.
Thin upper and lower lips	Use a lip lining pencil to outline the upper and lower lips slightly fuller, but do not try to draw far over the natural lip line. Fill in with lip color.
Cupid bow or pointed upper lip	To soften the peaks of the upper lip, use a medium lip lining pencil to draw a softer curve. Extend the line to the desired shape for the lower lip. Fill in with a soft lip color.
Large, full lips	Draw a thin line just inside the natural lip line with a lining pencil. Use soft, flat lipstick colors that will attract less attention than frosty or glossy lip colors.
Small mouth and lips	Use a lip lining pencil to outline both the upper and lower lips. Fill in lips with soft or frosted colors.
Drooping corners	Line the lips to build the corners of the mouth. This will minimize the drooping appearance. Fill in lips with a soft, flattering color.
Uneven lips	Outline the upper and lower lips with a soft color to create the illusion of matching proportions.
Straight upper lip	Use a lip lining pencil to create a slight dip in the center of the upper lip, directly beneath the nostrils. Fill in both lips with a flattering color.
Fine lines around the lips	Outline the lips with a noncreamy lip lining pencil, then fill in with a product formulated to keep lip color from running into fine lines.

Time Management

You forget to set your alarm. You have overslept by half an hour. This means you will not make the 8:40 train. More importantly, by the time you arrive at work your client will have been waiting for at least 20 minutes. And you did not bother to pull her file before you left last night. This means you have no idea what her skin care concerns are, what her last treatment was, what the next logical procedure will be, or what products she uses. Even worse, you will now be off schedule all day and your boss has already warned you twice about being late. To add to your frustration, you did not have time to prepare a lunch and you probably will not have time to step out. It will not be easy to maintain a positive disposition today.

Sound like your worst possible nightmare? Most of us can relate to at least one morning where everything goes wrong, but if you are one of those individuals who have difficulty being on time most days, you will need to work hard to develop solid time management skills.

Being on time is a professional responsibility. In the service industry, time also means money. If you cannot perform a certain number of services or allow enough time to maximize your results you will quickly fall behind your monetary goals. To achieve long-term financial success and customer satisfaction you must carefully plan each day.

The esthetician must have a solid understanding of how long each treatment will take as well as a method for maintaining an organized approach. For the esthetician just starting out, this means practicing each treatment until timing becomes second nature. At first this may require "cheat sheets" or "silent timers." Most facials will require at least one hour to perform. When combined with additional consultation and retail responsibilities, the average treatment time generally totals about one hour and fifteen minutes.

Getting used to working within these parameters requires training and discipline. Probably the most helpful advice you will receive as an esthetician is "be prepared." The following guidelines will help you do that.

1. At the end of the day begin organizing for the next day.
   - Clean and organize your treatment room and replenish supplies as needed.
   - Have enough individual supplies, such as eye makeup remover pads or palettes, prepared in advance.

2. Pull each scheduled client's record and review the last treatment.
   - Decide on possible treatment procedures based on previous notations.
   - Make sure all necessary equipment is sanitized and ready for use.

3. Note any special considerations.
   - If the client is new, make sure she knows to arrive 10 minutes early to fill out a client history form. While the client is changing review the history.

4. Look at what retail products the client is using and have them available.
   - Leave enough time to review progress on home care or to recommend a program if the client is new.

5. Build time into your schedule for making important follow-up or sales calls.

We live in a fast-paced world. We all have many obligations to meet and little time to do so. An important part of the esthetician's work that should not be overlooked is the added benefit of relaxation that most clients attribute to face and body treatments. If you are rushed and hurried your client will not be able to relax and fully enjoy the treatment. By taking time to prepare in advance you also allow your clients the consideration of your undivided attention. This is a great way to demonstrate your professionalism and provides a win-win situation all the way around.

Choosing and Using Makeup Products

If you collected every makeup product that you have and showed it to a makeup artist, you would be surprised at how much inventory you really have! Why is that? Makeup products represent many things. People buy many different products in order to create a certain look or mood, or sometimes on a whim.

Perhaps it is the color of the makeup item, but how many shades of red lipstick do you need? You can create just about any look by using your imagination and the products you already own. Makeup is not permanent, so you can change your look as often as you are willing to wash your face and reapply. It is like selecting a fresh page of paper and new crayons.

As a professional, makeup has many functions and appears in many forms. This gives the makeup artist an opportunity to choose from a variety of products and to use various techniques that correspond to the services offered at the spa or salon. You will feel more confident about the service you provide. Your clients will feel comfortable with their great new look.

Choosing makeup products carefully involves the overall design of the makeup, the client's preferences in products, ease of application, the goal of the makeup service, and future uses for the product. Also skin texture, skin type, and the client's personality determine the types and consistencies of the makeup products required. The three most commonly sold makeup items are foundations/powders, lipstick, and mascara.

Foundations

Foundations come in a variety of types. The five basic foundation types are tinted moisturizers, liquids, creams, dual cream/powder blends, and mineral powders (Figure 31–14). There are numerous reasons to purchase foundation, including to.

- cover up slight skin imperfections
- create an overall new look
- camouflage skin flaws
- create a better look for a photograph
- provide a healthy look during weather changes
- provide a sun-kissed look without the sun

Figure 31–14 One of the most commonly sold makeup items is foundation.

Tinted Moisturizers

Tinted moisturizers have a dual purpose. They provide needed moisture to the skin and give a slight natural tint to the skin. They tend to be of a medium texture (not too thin or too thick), may contain sunscreens, and come in a limited number of shades. They offer clients a convenient option when less makeup is needed. The application of this product is similar to applying a day cream: dispense some into your hand and apply it with the fingertips.

Liquids

Liquid foundations are among the most popular. They come in oil-based, oil-free, and water-based formulas. They can be layered onto the skin for a thin or thicker coverage. The thicker foundations are used to cover every crack of the skin. This is a good feature for uneven skin texture or slight scarring. This type of makeup is available in a wide range of colors. It is the most common makeup clients purchase.

Most clients need at least two or three shades of foundation to match their skin color as it changes from fall/winter to spring/summer. Application can vary from applying with a cotton swab and blending with the fingers or applying it with a makeup sponge and blending. Blending is the key to having an appearance that is smooth, even, and natural looking.

Creams

Cream foundations have the best covering ability. Choose this type for clients with sun-damaged skin or excessive unevenness. When a heavier coverage is preferred, the cream format is the first choice. It comes in a wide range of colors. It is more commonly used for video, photography, and film. It offers much heavier coverage and lasting ability when powdered and it sets well. Apply with the fingers and blend, or apply with a sponge and then blend.

Dual Cream/Powder

A foundation created from the best of two worlds, it provides the coverage of a cream with the ease of a powder. It can be applied wet with a dry or moist sponge, or dusted on with a dry brush, much like applying a powder.

When applied with a dry or moist sponge, a dual cream/powder provides a matte look. It provides a shiny look if applied dry. You can apply it with a moist sponge and then go over your face again with the dry brush. The more you apply, the more coverage you get. This type usually comes in a limited range of colors and for some skin it can be comedogenic.

Mineral Powder

Enriched, skin-friendly powdered minerals make up this great cover-up. It comes in numerous colors. It hides postsurgical skin discoloration from laser surgery, and hides general imperfections. Some clients prefer it as a general, all-purpose line with color for both foundation and other makeup needs. It is applied with either a sponge or brush depending on the manufacturer's recommendations.

Choosing Foundations and Powders

Of all the colors and products you use on the face, you must be most careful choosing a foundation and powder. They should be matched as naturally as possible to the cheeks of the face. In some situations, foundation and powder are matched to the back of the hand or the neck. This is not a good standard because one wears foundation on the face, not on the hand or neck. A client's face color may change as often as two or three times a year, based on geographical location and lifestyle activities.

It is acceptable to change foundations for skin color changes as well as for texture changes. Foundations come in a variety of textures, which dictate how it is to be used and whether it will give benefit. For example, matte foundations are better for uneven skin types. They do not reflect every uneven surface on the skin. A more moist, shiny foundation looks more appropriate on younger skins.

Caucasian skin has the smallest number of skin variations in color tones. Women of color (Hispanic, Asian, black) represent the majority of skin variations in color tones. Because they normally have many color tones in their skin, they are the most challenging to match. Look for product lines that offer a greater number of choices. It is typically necessary to blend.

Contouring with Foundation

Makeup covers irregularities and gives glow and color to the face. Expertly used, it can do more than that. It is possible to recontour a face and to create the illusion of perfection just by using various shades of foundation, highlighter, and blush (Table 31–9).

Concealers

Concealers are liquid and cream products designed to cover minor imperfections such as fine lines, under eye circles, redness, breakouts, pigmentation, and uneven lip lines (Figure 31–15, p. 504). Concealers may also be used for highlighting and shadowing the face to create a desired look. It includes shading in the cheeks for a more sculptured look, or highlighting the cheekbones for a more prominent cheek area.

Concealers can be applied under foundations for more highlighting and shadowing effects. They are quite effective over founda-

---

MAKEUPTIP

Why use a foundation?

- It provides a smooth canvas for adding color products.
- It protects the skin from sun, wind, and pollution.
- It evens out skin tones.
- It minimizes minor discolorations such as redness and a sallow look.
- It can be used to change the color tones in the skin when well blended.

Table 31–9 Using Foundation to Contour Facial Features

Facial Feature		Application
Round/square face		Use two foundations, light and dark, with the darker shade blended on the outer edges of the temples, cheekbones, and jawline, and the light one from the center of the forehead down the center of the face to the tip of the chin.
Triangular face		Apply a darker foundation over the chin and neck and a lighter foundation through the cheeks and under the eyes to the temples, and then blend them together over the forehead for a smooth and natural finish.
Narrow face		Blend a light shade of foundation over the outer edges of the cheekbones.
Wide jaw		Apply a darker foundation from below the cheekbones, and along the jawline, and blend into the neck.
Double chin		To minimize a double chin, apply shading under the jawline and over the full area.
Long, heavy chin		To make a long or heavy chin appear less prominent, apply darker foundation over the area.

(continued on next page)

Table 31–9 *(continued)*

Facial Feature		Application
Protruding forehead		Apply a darker shade of foundation over the area.
Narrow forehead		Apply a lighter foundation along the hairline and blend onto the forehead.
Wide nose		Apply foundation a shade lighter at the base to the tip of the nose. Apply darker foundation on both sides, and blend them together.
Short nose		A lighter shade of foundation is blended onto the tip of the nose and in between the eyes.

Figure 31–15 Concealers help to cover minor imperfections.

MAKEUPTIP

Why use a concealer?

- It can be used to cover up more minor imperfections such as under eye circles, fine lines, and uneven pigmentation.
- It can be used to create more shadows and highlights.
- It can be used to help correct proportion in face shapes.
- It can be used to camouflage a more serious facial disfigurement.
- It may be used to recreate lip shapes.

tions to cover minor imperfections. The lighter the consistency, the less ability it has to conceal. Concealers that are creamier in nature tend to spread easier and wear longer. They come in a variety of shades. To place it precisely where needed, use a lip brush to apply the concealer. Using a sponge or finger, press and spread the concealer evenly and lightly over the area to be concealed.

Powders

Powders come in two types—loose and pressed (Figure 31–16). Powders are designed to set foundations so they create a smoother appearance. They create a good base for topical color products such as eye shadows and blush. Loose powders come in a variety of colors and textures. Powders can help color correct a foundation that is not quite the right color. They can add color when the client wants to change her look. For example, you have a makeup line that is limited in the foundation colors and you have several shades of loose powder that, when applied over the foundation, create a better skin tone color. A client is going on vacation and wants to warm her complexion with a little more color. Choose a little darker powder to go over her foundation. This gives her the warmer color she needs without having to purchase a lot of products.

Powders are designed to pack the skin. When natural oils come onto the surface of the face, they are absorbed into the powder giving the skin a dewy quality. It generally takes about 20 minutes for this to happen.

Powders can be applied in two ways—with a brush or a powder puff. Many clients dust the powder onto the face with a brush. This is great if you have dry skin or do not want much coverage from the powder. If you want the foundation to stay on or stay true

Figure 31–16 Powders come in two forms—loose and pressed.

in color, pat on the powder with a puff. The puff will allow you to roll and pat the powder into every little crease and crevice on the skin. Afterward, brush off the excess with the powder brush.

The concept of a pressed powder compact was designed to use as a complementary makeup piece for the handbag or purse. The colors in a pressed powder compact are usually light, medium, and dark. The small sponge or puff that is inside the compact is used to do touch ups on the nose, cheeks, and forehead. Powder is placed on top of foundation. It is not designed to be worn directly on the skin. Powders are intended to set the foundation and keep it in place. Although many women prefer powder alone, the benefits of wearing a foundation are lost. Foundations are designed to color correct, protect, and smooth the complexion.

Color Products

Color products are all the products that go on the face, which has been covered by foundation, concealer, and powder. These are the colors that give expression and definition to the face. They include:

- blushes—colors that are used to enhance the cheek area
- eye shadows—colors that are used in the eye lid and brow area
- pencils—for lips, eyes, and brows
- mascaras—for the lashes
- lipsticks—to cover and enhance the lips

MAKEUP TIP

Why wear powder?

- It gives a smooth appearance to the face when applied over a foundation.
- It gives added translucency to the skin when the excess powder is buffed off.
- It helps set the foundation and concealer, giving added longevity to the overall makeup.

Figure 31–17 Blush restores a rosy glow to the face after the foundation and powder have covered it.

Blushes

Blush colors come in two categories—flush and glamour blush (Figure 31–17). Flush is still a blush. The color ranges harmonize with the client's blood tone; therefore to distinguish between blood tone colors and glamour colors, we call it *flush* and glamour blush. Flush is the color that would be naturally found in the cheeks of your client.

The foundation, concealer, and powder usually cover the natural flush color. This creates an even canvas to the skin. In order to restore a rosy glow with a flush color, examine the palm of the hand, the inside of the mouth, and the back of the ear to find the client's natural blood tone or flush color. This is the color you sell every client first. Why? Because it goes with everything! When you match a color to a client's skin tone, hair tone, eye tone, or blood tone, it should blend with the client's natural coloring. The glamour blush colors are brighter, darker, frosted colors that can be blended with the normal colors that are harmonious

MAKEUP TIP

Why wear flush and blush?
- It adds color to the face.
- It can be used with highlighters and shadows to give dimension to the cheek area.
- It creates balance between the eye makeup and the lips.
- It creates subtle changes when lightly dusted over the entire face.

with the client's blood tone. They are applied over the regular flush color to create new looks. You can create several looks. For a rosier complexion add a pink-to-pink, brown blush over the flush color. For a sun-kissed look add a bronzer (orange-brown) over the flush color. To complement your client's favorite fuchsia outfit add a lighter fuchsia blush over the flush color (if the flush color is harmonious with the client's natural color). To highlight cheeks for an evening look add a frosted blush over the flush color.

When applying blush have the client smile and start the flush and/or blush on the apple of the cheek and work back toward the middle of the ear. If your client has blond, gray, or light-colored hair, always apply the flush or blush starting at the hairline and blend out from the ear to the cheek. This prevents the flush or blush from moving into the hairline. After applying flush or blush in a horizontal direction, go back over the area with your powder brush to soften the "racing stripes." Change the face shape by applying the flush or blush in either a more vertical or more horizontal direction.

Eye Shadows

Of all the makeup products you have, eye shadows offer the most choice in color and texture (Figure 31–18). We use eye shadows to correct the eye shape by shadowing and contouring. To enhance the eye area, several shades are applied. The amount depends on the look of the client and what the makeup artist wants to accent. Some guidelines for using eye shadow are:

- Never use an eye shadow that is the same exact color as the client's eyes. Use the same color family but use a lighter, brighter, or darker shade. Otherwise the client looks like she has a giant eye all the same color.

- Use neutral colors such as ivory, tans, grays, and browns for day wear, and the more unique colors for special occasions or evening wear.

- Use eye shadow base to even out the eye area and make the eye shadow stick or keep from creasing.

- Apply a light shadow from the lash line to the area under the brow before adding a medium to darker shade.

Why wear eye shadow?

- It adds color and personality to the face.
- Eye shadow softens the eye area.
- It creates light and dark illusion for subtle image changes.
- It can be used to correct and enhance the eye shape.
- Eye shadow can be used as an accent color.

- Use fluff brushes to apply eye shadow in larger areas and angle brushes for the colors in the smaller or crease areas.

- Avoid letting the eye shadow get too far out to the sides of the eye. Some clients have more lid area that creates a little fold at the edge of the eye. Any eye shadow in that fold will cause the eye to appear aged.

- After applying the medium to dark shade for contouring in the eye area, go back over with the lighter color to soften the edges.

- Use accent colors to highlight unique colors, complement colors, or emphasize unique features of the eye.

- Use wet eye shadows for liners when the client is unable to use pencils (for whatever reason), if a client's skin is oily, a more refined line is needed, or if you want to line over false eyelashes

Eye, Brow, and Lip Pencils

Pencils are used for several different reasons. They outline, fill in, highlight, or diminish some part of the lip, eye, or brow (Figure 31–19). They also help to prevent lipstick from bleeding outside the lip area. You may do one, some, or all of these things to your client's face. Pencils come in different shades and colors, and different textures such as frosty or metallic. Some practical tips when using pencils include:

Use the right pencil for the intended area. Some brow pencils will be too hard if used to draw a liner on the eyelid.

Use eyebrow pencils to create hairlike strokes in areas of the brow that are suffering from a lack of hairs.

Figure 31–18 Eye shadows offer the most choice in color and texture.

Use eyeliner pencils to open or close the eye shape or to enhance the eye shape.

Using white or blue in the inner rim of the bottom eyelid can make the whites of the eye appear whiter. This is an effective technique for clients who have a yellow or red cast to the whites of their eyes.

For daytime looks stay with brown, black, navy, or gray eyeliners around the eyes. Keep the other colors for special wear such as evening or special occasions.

Sharpen pencils before and after each application to keep a sanitary edge.

If the pencil is too hard, soften the tip with the tips of your fingers. If the pencil

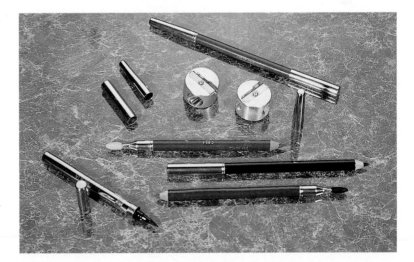

Figure 31–19 Pencils are used to outline, fill in, highlight, or diminish some part of the lip, eye, or brow.

MAKEUPTIP

Why use a liner pencil?
- Pencils bring more definition to an area.
- They can be used to change the shape or add dimension to an area.
- Lip pencils help keep lipstick in place and prevent it from bleeding into the lip creases.
- They can create the illusion of a larger or smaller size depending on the color.
- Eye pencils help make the eyelashes appear thicker.

is too soft, place it in the freezer overnight to help harden it. This is especially good if you need to sharpen a pencil that is too soft.

Use the lip pencil to correct a soft lip, create an in- or out-curve lip, and to fill in the lip area before applying lipstick. This will help the lipstick stay on the lips longer. It creates a stain underneath the lipstick, which shows after the lipstick has rubbed away.

Mascaras

Mascaras emphasize the eyelashes. They come in cake and tube form with a myriad of colors and lash enhancing formulas (Figure 31–20). Some tips for using mascara:

Figure 31–20 Mascara emphasizes the eyelashes.

Choose brown for younger teens, brown-black for general purpose, and navy for clients who already have dark eyelashes (navy makes dark eyelashes look velvety).

Keep trendy colors for an evening or fun look.

Apply brown to lashes to make them look fuller and black to the tips to make lashes look longer.

Apply mascaras with disposable applicators to avoid contamination from a shared mascara wand applicator. Trim the brush off of your demo mascara with a wire cutter to prevent anyone from using it by mistake.

Apply mascara to the bottom lashes first to avoid getting mascara residue from top lashes (this results from the open mouth and wide eye look we get in an attempt to apply mascara), and then apply mascara to the top lashes.

When applying mascara to the top lashes, start with the tops of the lashes, then go side to side, and finish with the upward, under coat of the lashes to get a really good application.

Apply two or three coats for a fuller lash look and use a clean disposable applicator brush or separator to get rid of clumps from mascara buildup.

Using an eyelash curler prior to mascara application will enhance the curl of the lashes. To avoid pulling the lashes out, it is recommended to curl the lashes with a warmed eyelash curler prior to applying mascara.

MAKEUPTIP

Why wear mascara?
- It thickens and lengthens the appearance of the lashes.
- It adds depth and character to the overall look of the eyes.
- It makes the colors of the eye shadow stand out.
- It sharpens the appearance of the eye area.
- It brings balance to the face.

Lipsticks

Lipsticks are the most fun products for the face. This is the one product that clients purchase because they like the color, are loyal to a brand, or they want to try something new. Lipsticks come in a variety of colors and textures (Figure 31–21). Creamy lipsticks tend to be more moisturizing and matte lipsticks tend to adhere more to the lip, preventing it from running into the lip crevices. Gloss adds shine but does not last very long. Lipstick is best applied after outlining and filling in the lips with your lip pencil. Lip pencils can be used to match the lipstick color, or lip pencils can be a contrasting color in order to create a more interesting lip color. Adhere to the following guidelines when applying lipstick:

To make lips appear smaller, choose a darker lipstick shade.

To make lips appear larger, choose a lighter lipstick shade.

Correct any lip shape problem first with the lip pencil, then fill in the lip with the pencil color.

To keep a lipstick from coming off, stain the lip first with the lip pencil then apply the lipstick. Blot with a tissue and apply the lipstick color again. Blot a second time or choose a lip fixative product to set the lipstick.

Never apply the lipstick directly to the client's mouth during make-up application. Always scrape off some lipstick from the side of the tube with a spatula and apply it with a lip brush. Lipstick is always more smooth and accurate when applied with a lip brush.

If a client likes a particular color, suggest that she buy two, one for home and one for her purse.

Figure 31–21 Lipsticks come in a variety of colors, textures, and forms.

Makeup Tools

Understanding the best tool for the job is important to facilitate proper makeup application, and to make the best use of your time. Using the correct tools can help you achieve the desired look.

Brushes

Brushes are the most important tools we use (Figure 31–22, p. 510). Just like sponges for facials, or blow dryers for hair, brushes are what we use to apply and blend makeup. Your personal set of brushes might include the following.

Powder Brush
The largest of the brushes, it is used to spread loose powder over the face or to brush off powder that has been applied with a powder puff after foundation has been applied.

Blush Brushes
The next largest brush, it is used to spread blush color on the cheeks, forehead, and chin to give the face a rosy glow. (One brush will be a smaller version of your powder brush, and a second blush brush may be more contoured or slanted). The second brush is a clean brush designed to sweep off any eye shadow or blush powder that has flaked into an area you did not intend to apply color to.

MAKEUPTIP

Why wear lipstick?
- It adds color to the face for a healthier look.
- It helps create the illusion of smaller or larger lips.
- It harmonizes the face between the eyes, hair, and clothes.
- It adds definition and emphasis to the lip area.
- It finishes out the makeup look.

Figure 31–22 Brushes are the most important tool for the makeup artist.

Eye Area Brushes

These brushes come in a variety of sizes and shapes to work color into the eye area, the brow area, and around the eyes, including a sharp-edged, angled, and stiff brush for applying eye shadow in the crease of the eye. To apply eyebrow powder to the eyebrow, a fluff brush is a more rounded, tapered brush designed to apply eye shadow to the eye area from the lashes to the brow. The eyeliner brush is usually very thin to allow application of eye shadow. It may be used wet or dry. The eyebrow brush is usually a duo brush with a comb on one side and a brush on the other side. The comb is used to separate lashes after applying mascara. The brush is used to help remove powder residue from the brows, or to smooth color that has been applied with another brush.

Lip Brushes

The stiffest of all the brushes, lip brushes can be used to apply lipstick as well as corrective makeup or concealer to small areas of the face. Use a fresh brush for each product to avoid mixing colors.

In the beginning, you may have one basic set of brushes. As you gain experience, add more brushes to your makeup kit. Generally in a spa or salon setting you should have enough brush sets to do three to four clients daily without reusing brushes.

Clean and sanitized brushes are also important. Clean brushes prevent cross-contamination and provide a comfort level to your client. Professional standards require

cleaning brushes between each client. This is why makeup artists need to keep several sets on hand at all times.

Liquid brush cleaners are available from suppliers. To cleanse brushes using this method, begin dipping the least color-loaded brush, powder, then blush, then eye shadow, then lip into the solution. Wipe on a paper towel to remove the color residue. This is great if you used all your brushes and need them cleaned right away. A word of caution: brush cleaners are best used occasionally. Some brush cleaners can break down the hair of the brushes causing it to fall out.

For long-term use and your client's personal use, it is recommended that the brushes be cleaned with a gentle shampoo and conditioner on a weekly basis. Spritz with a disinfectant on a daily basis. Doing so will help maintain their shape and longevity. Store unused brushes in a brush bag or in a closed container. This prevents the brush hairs from fraying and keeps your set together.

When choosing brushes, think about quality. Most big brushes are blends of pony, squirrel, and goat hair. Normally, the more expensive the brush, the better the blends. Natural hair brushes are great to use with powder and blush products. Smaller brushes tend to use blends of sable, pony, squirrel, and goat hairs. This allows the fine texture of the eye shadows to be applied better.

Lip brushes are generally sable because lipstick would be hard to apply with a softer brush. Sometimes you see brushes in all sizes advertised as pure sable. If they were really sable, they would be very expensive. They are not appropriate for applying powder, blush, or eye shadows because of the stiffness of the hair. Sometimes brushes are cut in a sable shape; however, they are not made from pure sable hair. If you cannot afford the best quality to begin with, start with some synthetic brushes. Synthetic brushes come in every shape and price range. You might prefer the shapes better than the animal blended brushes. It is likely that you will have some of each in your brush kit.

Other features of brushes are the handles. Do you prefer long or short? What handles endure frequent washings in a spa or salon setting? Acrylics and light metal handles seem to tolerate more frequent washings. Some of the heavier coated wooden handles are fine also. Some manufacturers offer handles in a variety of colors; therefore, do not settle for just one kind or look. Look around at many and purchase brushes that are compatible with the makeup you are using. When you get into a retail situation, use brushes that you plan to sell to your client. The client will always want the brush that they perceive to be the magic one that puts on the makeup in an easy fashion.

A variety of specialty brushes are also available (Figure 31–23). Mops, which are spongelike, are used to apply foundations. Fan brushes are used to apply cleaners or to sweep residues of pigment dropped onto the cheeks or other areas where you do not want color. Flat brushes are used to pat concealers or foundation onto the face. Start complementing your original set and your own personal set with new additions when you learn new techniques.

Disposables

Disposables are single-use applicators that are discarded after each use (Figure 31–24).

Plastic spatulas are used to remove products from jars or containers to avoid cross-contamination. Use a spatula to scrape lipsticks from the tube and apply lip color with a lip brush. This avoids applying lipstick directly from the tube to the lips, which invites the spread of bacteria.

Mascara wands are used to apply mascara to a client's lashes rather than using the wand that is part of the mascara packaging. Open the tester mascaras and cut off the wand with wire cutters. This will avoid spreading pinkeye or other eye irritations to your clients.

Lip brushes are mainly used with displays. This prevents clients and staff from using the

Figure 31–23 A variety of specialty brushes are good to have on hand.

tube of lipstick directly on the lips. Instruct clients and staff about the use of disposables or have a small sign to instruct them.

Puffs are used to apply powder to the face over the foundation. Unfortunately, they do not wash well. Most salons give them to the client after using. This is good public relations as well!

Sponges are either made from nonallergenic foam or latex. They are used to apply foundation, spread other cream-based products onto the face, and to pat on foundation to set it.

MAKEUPTIP

The basic brush kit should include the following:
- 1 powder brush
- 2 blush brushes
- 3 or 4 eye shadow brushes
- 2 lip brushes
- 1 to 4 specialty brushes (including fan brushes)
- brush bag

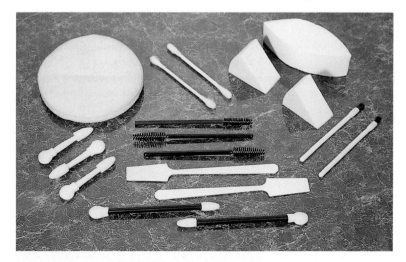

Figure 31–24 Disposable applicators help provide a sanitary environment for the client.

Miscellaneous Tools

The following tools will complete your makeup kit:

- One pair of small manicuring scissors used to trim eyebrows or false eyelashes. Soak the scissors in disinfectant between each client.

- An eyelash curler is used to curl the lashes prior to applying mascara. Clean the curler with antibacterial spray between each client. Replace the rubber lips of the curler as they begin to wear down.

- Two pairs of tweezers (pointed and slanted) to tweeze stray eyebrows. It is not recommended to wax a client on the day of the makeup application because the makeup will not adhere well and products applied over the waxed area could cause that area to break out. Tweezers are also used to apply false eyelashes. Soak tweezers in disinfectant between each client.

- Cotton swabs are used to smudge makeup products, e.g., in the eye area, or to clean makeup inadvertently applied to the wrong area.

- Tissues are used to blot the lips or lipstick between applications, absorb excess foundations, etc.

- Eye lashes and adhesive are used to create different looks in the eye area (Figure 31–25). Eyelashes come in many combinations and in two basic colors for normal wear (black and brown). The longer lashes are used on the top eyelid although some shorter lashes can be used on the top lashes or underneath the bottom lashes. Eye lashes also come in tabs. Tabs

Figure 31–26 Use professional tools and products whenever possible.

are usually one or a couple of lashes on a bud. These are used to enhance lashes. They are not as heavy or noticeable as a full strip of eyelashes. They also come in black and brown. Adhesive is made specifically for eyelashes and is applied to the bud of a tab or to the strip edge of lashes. Attach to the lash line close to the client's real eyelashes. Adhesive comes in white (transparent) and black. You should try both colors to see which you like better. White is preferred if you have applied the eye shadow and liner and want it to show through. The black is a good choice if you want the lashes to appear as a liner.

- A metal pencil sharpener with two holes—one for regular size liner pencils as well as one for a jumbo pencil. Soak the sharpener in the liquid sanitizer to clean.

- A metal makeup palette that can be used to mix makeup colors like a painter would do before applying color to a canvas. Makeup artists sometimes use the back of their hand. However, this technique could lead to blending the wrong color and worse make a client feel uncomfortable that your hand might be unsanitary. These palettes come in different sizes and are easy to clean with your sanitizer.

- A makeup kit, the professional box or container you use to store makeup and tools (Figure 31–26). Some people use a fishing tackle box, but that tends to look too unprofessional. Try to find something that makes a statement; use professional tools and professional products whenever possible. Table 31–10 lists the equipment, tools, and supplies you will need as a professional.

Figure 31–25 Eyelashes can create different looks in the eye area.

Table 31–10 Makeup Setup and Supplies

Item	Description	Comments
Equipment and fixtures	Lighting—provide the most natural possible: daylight, evening, candescent. Obtain advice from an expert in lighting or display setup for stores. Full-color spectrum lighting is available.	Mount both cool and warm lighting side by side vertically on each side of the mirror. Have separate switches for cool and for warm. Cool fluorescent lighting gives a more natural or true outside light appearance. Warm gives an office or evening look.
	Makeup station or custom cabinet	Built-in or purchase a station large enough to accommodate products, accessories, storage drawers, and overhead cabinets.
	Makeup chair	Either choose one that is hydraulic, or "bar" stool height, or one that is the correct height for you to work.
	Mirror	Wall mounted, oval or rectangular
	Trash can, covered	Keep the work area clean and tidy at all times.
	Laundry, covered soiled towel container	Do not reuse towel. Replace fresh towel with each appointment.
	Music, piped-in or a CD player	Soothing, relaxing music helps keep both you and the client focused and comfortable. It helps relax the client who may feel uncomfortable in front of a mirror.
Forms	Business cards	Display your business cards where they are visible. When designing business cards be sure to include a space for recording the next appointment time. Print your cancellation policy on the reverse side.
	Confidential makeup questionnaire	This questionnaire is an overall written survey of the client's goals including a few health questions. Be sure to maintain store records securely to maintain confidentiality.
	Makeup profile	Filled out by the makeup artist during the consultation.
	Instruction diagram—face form	Indicate direction of product placement on the instruction diagram. Include the placement of colors. List products in the provided areas. After completing, make a copy for your file. Send the client home with the original copy.
	Mail order form	If mail order service is provided by your business, include a mail order form for reordering products and accessories. It is great to use if the client goes away on vacation or travels a great deal. Be sure to include a shipping fee.
	Inventory form	This is an inventory tracking form for all your products and accessories. It helps you keep stock current on all items.
Supplies	Brush kit	Brush Bag 1 powder brush 2 blush brushes 3 or 4 eye shadow brushes 2 lip brushes 1–4 specialty brushes (including fan brushes) You may need two sets of brushes when working with multiple appointments. While one set is disinfecting, one is clean and ready to go.
	Containers: 2 stainless steel bowls	Medium size. Use for holding water and sponges when performing client facial cleansing.
	3 or 4 glass cylinder or square jars with lids	If counter room allows, place cotton, swabs, disposable wands and brushes, hair clips, etc., into these professional, tidy-looking jars.
	2 or 3 glass, custard size dishes	Pour a bit of makeup remover into a dish. Place several round cotton pads in the solution. This allows you to retrieve them without having to open the makeup remover bottle each time. Do not redip any soiled pads into the liquid. Take another clean one.

(continued on next page)

Table 31–10 *(continued)*

Item	Description	Comments
	Rectangular container	Safe place for the client's earrings or glasses
	Small set of tongs	Used to remove items from the glass jars. Do not place your fingers in the jars once you have begun working on a client.
	Clipboard and pen	Attach client forms on these. Fill out as you work.
	Hair clips	Butterfly clips to hold hair away from the face.
	Disposables:	Cotton swabs—use to apply products; clean up smudges. Cotton pads, round—moisten and use with eye makeup remover to cleanse eyes and lips. To apply freshener (toner). Lip brushes for applying lipstick. Sponges (wedge) for makeup application. Spatulas to scrape shadow powders or lipstick cylinder. Paper towel for spills. Tissues for blotting excesses from face or lips; to hold powder that was removed from container. Wands—do *not* use mascara applicator in tube. Only insert once and toss. Need more? Reinsert a new disposable wand.
	Drape for client protection during makeup session. Use white color only	3 hand towels: 2 to drape; 1 for hands. *or* 2 capes (long): to completely cover the client. One extra for replacement.
	Mirror, handheld	For client to watch closer.
	Palette, makeup	Can be found in art stores. They are round or rectangular and used for blending color. They are also used for keeping the small amount of product that you have scraped from eye shadow pan.
	Pencil sharpener	For makeup pencils only. Sharpen any used pencils to freshen for the next customer. Choose a good one.
	Small hair scissors	Trim eyebrows and false eyelashes.
	Slant and pointed tweezers	To tweeze stray eyebrows and apply false eyelashes. Always use the best professional quality that can withstand sanitation.
Skin Care	Eye makeup remover	All purpose for removing eye makeup and lipstick.
	Cleanser	Choose sensitive or normal/combination: Remove all makeup and freshen skin.
	Freshener	Sensitive or normal/combination: Helps remove excess cleanser and re-establish skin pH.
	Makeup serums	Specialized products that are designed to be a line filler or skin smoother.
	Day cream	Apply appropriate moisturizing cream according to skin type.
Makeup	Blush	3–10 colors ranging from light to dark and warm and cool.
	Concealers	2–3 lighter shades and 2–3 darker shades. Used to hide scars/flaws.
	Eye shadows	12–18 colors ranging from light to dark and warm and cool.
	Foundations	2–3 types (either liquid, creams, dual cream/powder, or 4–6 shades mineral powder.
	Lipsticks	20–25 colors total. Pick at least 1 light, 1 medium, 1 dark, 1 muted, and 1 bright in each color family of pink, orange, red, and brown.
	Mascaras	Black, brown, navy and 1 or 2 trendy colors in 1 or 2 different formulas.
	Pencils	Eye and lip: 3–5 colors in each category (eye/lip/brow).
	Powders	Loose for makeup use. Retail: compact and loose. Pick at least 2–4 shades.

Table 31–10 *(continued)*

Item	Description	Comments
Staff	Uniforms	Opinions vary, but the use of uniforms often provides a very stylish professional look. Brings conformity and unity to the staff's appearance. Should be clean at all times.
Sanitation	Hand disinfectant	Wall-mounted foam containers, disposable wipes, or gloves if you prefer.
	Surface spray disinfectants	Spray on surfaces—counter, chair—between clients to prevent any cross-contamination.
	Instrument tray	Trays are available through esthetic supply catalogues. They normally have liquid disinfectant in them with a tray at the top that is lowered into the solution when the lid is closed. Keep your clean tweezers or other reusables stored in a covered tray between uses.
	General cleaners	Keep mirrors clean. Fingerprints off handheld mirror. Choose cleaners that are low in fragrance. Keep floor clean and shiny.

Summary

The three primary colors are red, yellow, and green. Mixing two or more primary colors in equal amounts creates secondary colors. Mixing equal amounts of a secondary color with a primary color creates a tertiary or a third color. Adding black to a color creates a shade; adding white to color creates a tint. Colors are classified as warm and cool tones. An individual's skin also has basic colors made from the melanin, blood, and fluids. The tones in the skin can be warm, cool, or sometimes a bit in between. Color either enhances or diminishes. When worn, color will blend or harmonize with the skin tone, eye, and hair color, or it will appear muted, dull, and sallow. Choosing the correct color results in a more radiant appearance. Use the natural colorings of the client as a basic guideline for your makeup selection. There are many makeup tools, colors, and textures to choose from. A makeup kit provides an organized container for your makeup and brushes.

Discussion Questions

1. Discuss how makeup has changed to accommodate new trends in skin care.

2. Study the color wheel and apply the basics of color theory to explain how blending colors can be useful in correcting problems in makeup artistry. Give examples.

3. Define the following terms: hue, shade, and intensity. How are these used in makeup artistry?

4. What are the main facial imperfections that require corrective makeup? Choose three and describe the techniques for correcting each.

5. Describe the procedures for determining eyebrow placement and eyebrow shapes.

6. Describe the basic makeup techniques for enhancing the following eye shapes: small, close-set, wide set, and round.

7. What is achieved by highlighting or shadowing facial features?

8. List the different types of foundations and the most common circumstances in which each is used.

9. List the different types of necessary tools and categorize them by type.

Additional Reading

Aucoin, Kevyn. 1996. *The Art of Makeup.* New York: Harper Collins.

Fine, Sam. 1999. *Beauty Basics and Beyond for African Women.* New York: Riverhead Books.

Fornay, Alford, et al. 1998. *The African-American Women's Guide to Successful Makeup and Skin Care.* Phoenix, AZ: Amber Books.

Jackson, Carole and Christine Turner, Christine. *Color Me Beautiful.* New York: Battantine Books, Inc., Div. of Random House.

Kohoe, Vincent J.-R. 1995. *The Technique of the Professional Makeup Artist.* Stoneham, MA: Focal Press.

Chapter 32
Makeup Applications

Chapter Objectives

After reading this chapter, you should be able to:

- Discuss the objectives of consulting with a client.
- Explain the importance of cleanliness at the workstation.
- Demonstrate how to fill out a consultation form.
- Perform a client consultation including a basic makeup application.
- Demonstrate day and evening looks.

Chapter Outline

Introduction
Makeup Work Area
Client Consultation
The Closing
Choosing a Makeup Product Collection
Makeup Services
Beyond the Basics

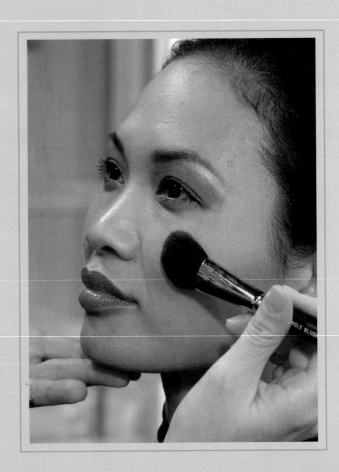

Introduction

Performing a detailed consultation is important to giving your client the appropriate service. The initial discussion builds a foundation for you to help give your client the best choice of colors and an overall look that is both attractive and pleasing to her. It is often helpful to rehearse your presentation skills with a classmate, walking through the necessary procedures step by step. When you are ready to work with a client, you will have achieved a good comfort zone for makeup application.

Makeup Work Area

The consultation process can occur in the waiting room of the spa or salon or in the makeup work area. Choose a quiet area so that you can speak freely to your client.

The makeup workstation should be spacious enough so that you can freely move around the client (Figure 32–1). The makeup chair is important. Some people use a director's chair; others select a regular makeup chair found at salon equipment suppliers. Bar stools can work fine, too, as long as they have a back so that the client does not suddenly lose her balance and fall.

The makeup work area should be immaculately clean and attractive. This helps clients feel comfortable and safe about your workstation and the tools you use. Dirty brushes and sloppiness are not appealing and may pose a concern to the client, who does not want to be exposed to bacteria or diseases. Take extra time to eliminate any issues that may cause the client discomfort.

Along with a comfortable chair, the makeup area requires a table for supply setup. Some spas and salons have custom cabinets with built-in drawers just for the makeup area. Others use pieces of antique furniture or decorative side tables. The counter or table should provide ample room to arrange your products and tools.

Client Consultation

The client consultation begins every service. It is impossible to provide a satisfactory experience without first having a thorough dis-

Figure 32–1 The makeup station should be spacious enough to allow freedom of movement.

cussion of the client's expectations, the procedures, and product use and performance.

Consultation Forms

There are three standard forms used during the consultation. The first is a short confidential makeup questionnaire (Figure 32–3, p. 519) to be completed by the client upon arrival. The second form, the makeup profile, (Figure 32–4, p.520) is filled out as you complete each step of the makeup session. Lastly, the face makeup chart, (Figure 32–5, p. 522) is a home care reference chart that lists the colors, products, and accessories used during the makeup session. The first two forms are permanent records of the client's services and

---

SAFETY*Tip*

- All tools should be clean and sanitized. Keep them covered until ready to use.
- Your hands are also tools. They should be clean and sanitized.
- Lay out all necessary tools on a covered small tray in advance.
- When applying anything powdery, avoid getting any dust into the nose, mouth, ears, or especially the eyes, because it can cause irritation to the lens or the cornea.
- Always use a new applicator (wedge sponges, cotton tip, disposable wands) when taking more product from its container, and replace the cover immediately.
- Keep your area clean and tidy. Immediately return items to their proper location.

should be kept in a secure, central file for easy access on subsequent visits.

The client should plan to arrive 15–20 minutes earlier than the scheduled appointment in order to complete the confidential makeup questionnaire. This form profiles your client's expectations and also indicates any health concerns that may prohibit the use of certain products or contraindicate the actual makeup application.

The makeup profile provides ample space to make notes regarding the client's makeup goals. The profile also reveals how much effort the client is willing to use when applying her own makeup at home. Throughout the consultation, discuss with the client what products to use, why they are chosen, and how to apply them. After the consultation, place the form in a file folder. During subsequent appointments, pull out her information and continue to record new data. The consultation time is a natural opening for rebooking.

The face makeup chart should be filled out during the service by the esthetician, charting each product, color, and accessory used, along with a sketch showing where the products were applied to the face. At the end of the service, give this form to the client as an aid to assist her in choosing products and for reference at home when applying her own makeup.

The Consultation

The client should appear for her appointment wearing makeup that was applied at home. This gives you a visual concerning her personal color selection and application technique. After the client is seated and you have placed the makeup cape for protection, proceed with the suggested dialogue.

"Mrs. Smith, this form helps me note your current look and style, so that we can adapt your makeup look to match whatever event you will be attending or a trend you would like to try (Figure 32–2). In reality, I can give you a new makeup look every month, based on these questions and observations I am making about you today.

"I will develop a plan of action for you that includes future consultation aimed at educating you to achieve your makeup goals. Also, based on what we do today, I will make some recommendations to adjust

Figure 32–2 The client must fill out her makeup questionnaire prior to beginning any service.

your current skin care and/or makeup program, so that you can repeat this process at home. When you return in a few weeks, I will introduce other products to help you continue your makeup training. I have set up a progressive system of learning so that you are not too overwhelmed in our first session. You will have some time to practice before we meet again. When you return, we will review and proceed to more advanced steps. Before you leave today, we will set up an appointment for you 3 to 4 weeks from now."

The Closing

At the end of the session, complete the face makeup chart by using cotton swabs to apply the product colors used during the makeup session. Record all products used including any skin care items. This serves as an important customized take-home referral sheet. Also record the application steps on this form in the area provided.

Confidential Makeup Questionnaire

PLEASE PRINT   Today's Date _____

First Name _____ Last Name _____ Date of Birth ___/___/___

Street _____ Apt# _____ City _____ State _____ Zip _____

Phone—Home ( ) _____ Work ( ) _____ Mobile ( ) _____

Emergency Contact _____ Phone ( ) _____

Your occupation _____

Referred by   ❏ Friend   ❏ Mailer   ❏ Walk-by   ❏ Yellow Pages   ❏ Gift Certificate   ❏ Other

1. Have you ever had a professional makeover?   ❏ Yes   ❏ No

2. If yes, what did you like (dislike) about the session? _____

3. If no, how did you learn to apply makeup? _____

4. What are some of your goals today? _____

5. What special areas of concern do you have? _____

6. Do you wear contact lenses?   ❏ Yes   ❏ No   If yes, are they   ❏ Hard   ❏ Soft

7. Do you take any medications that cause your eyes to be dry or itch?
    ❏ Yes   ❏ No   If yes, what? _____

8. Are you currently taking Accutane or have you taken it in the past?   ❏ Yes   ❏ No
    If yes, describe the course of treatment and how long. _____

9. Do you have any health condition that may cause sensitivity in your skin or eye area?
    ❏ Yes   ❏ No   If yes, what? _____

10. Do you have any allergies?   ❏ Yes   ❏ No   If yes, please indicate. _____

11. Do you have any allergies to skin care products?   ❏ Yes   ❏ No   If yes, what? _____

12. Do you smoke?   ❏ Yes   ❏ No

13. What are your favorite colors: _____

14. Describe an ideal look for your makeup. _____

    I understand that the services offered are for educational purposes only. I fully acknowledge that I do not have any known allergies to makeup products. I authorize the makeup artist to apply products to my face. He/she is free to discuss appropriate information to help me become well-informed concerning makeup application and makeup purchases.

Salon Policies

1. We require a 24-hour cancellation notice.

2. Please arrive on time for appointments.

3. There is a $25 charge for a no-show appointment

4. Health regulations do not allow us to accept returned products unless they are unopened and in their original packaging.

5. Returns are given salon credit only. *No* cash refunds.

I fully understand and agree to the above salon policies.

_____   _____
Client's Signature   Date

Figure 32–3 The confidential makeup questionnaire contains important information necessary to the service.

Makeup Profile

Name: Christiana A.   **Date:** October 5, 2002

1. Overall Look—Face & Clothes

❑ Young

❑ Youthful   She wears youthful, fun clothes in mainly blacks & reds. Is petite and has a

　　　　　　　lean body proportion

❑ Mature

❑ Aged

❑ Age Appropriate   Dresses younger than her age, more for her type of work

❑ Heritage/Ethnic Group   Hispanic/Caucasian

❑ Type of Work   Dance instructor

2. Overall Coloring—Warm & Cool Plus Specifics

a) Hair: ❑ Coloring _____   ❑ Colored Enhanced   Dark brown with red (warm)

b) Skin Tone Color: ❑ Ivory/Fair ☒ Ivory/Cool ❑ Beige/Medium ❑ Olive/Warm

　　　　　　　　❑ Deep/Dark ❑ Other Variations/Combinations _____

c) Eyes—Color   Brown (warm)

d) Blood Tone—Color   Coral (warm)

3. Face Details

Overall Face Shape ❑ Oblong ❑ Round ❑ Square ☒ Triangle

　　　　　　　　　❑ Inverted triangle ❑ Diamond ❑ Oval

4. Overall Face Proportion

a) Nose Length   Fine

b) Eye Width   Eyes are close set.

c) Lip Placement   Fine

d) Lip Shape: ❑ In-Curve Lower lip ❑ Out-Curve Upper Lip ❑ Soft ❑ Hard

e) Brow Placement: ❑ Normal ❑ Little close

f) Brow Shape: ☒ Curved ❑ Straight ❑ Arched ❑ Asian

Figure 32–4 The makeup profile charts every step of the makeup service.

g) Eye Shape: ❑ Bulging ❑ Wide Set ☒ Narrow ❑ Almond ❑ Prominent Brow

❑ Small ❑ Crepey Lid ❑ Droopy Lids ❑ Other

h) Overall Features: ❑ Balanced *Generally* ❑ Weak *Eye shape & chin*

❑ Striking *Overall coloring*

i) Chin: *Slopes inward*

j) Cheeks: ☒ High ❑ Wide ❑ Other

k) Skin Type/Condition: ☒ Oily–Combination ❑ Dehydrated ❑ Loss of Tone ❑ Wrinkles

❑ Blotchiness

5. Color Preferences

a) Are you happy with the colors you are using now?

Loves her current lipstick, can't find a cheek color that works—either too rosy or too

ketchup, foundation is close, but not enough.

b) What are your favorite colors to wear?

Red lipstick, neutral eyes, black eyeliner. Loves to wear hot pink, red & purple.

c) Do you use any color enhancers in your hair?

Yes, a violet-base to make dark brown hair a little redder.

d) What is today's look preference? ❑ Natural ☒ Day ❑ Evening ❑ Not sure

e) Are there any colors you would like to try? *Bright blue & silver*

f) Are there any colors you don't like at all? *Pastels*

g) Do you use corrective lenses or glasses? ❑ Lenses ❑ Glasses

h) What do you think is the most colorful part of your face? *Eyes*

Objectives/Observations:

1. *Concentrate on helping with a new skin care routine.*

2. *Teach her how to cover up blotchiness and under eye circles.*

3. *Critique current makeup products for appropriateness for her skin type.*

4. *Show options for new looks she could use in her dance business—elegant, jazzy.*

5. *Needs help with light contouring and shadowing to balance out her features.*

6. *She might like to try some easy-to-apply products that give her a more natural look when she is not dancing.*

Figure 32–4 *(continued).*

Face Makeup Chart

Name _____ **Date** _____

Skin Care

Makeup remover _____

Cleanser _____

Freshener _____

Moisturizer_____

Makeup

Foundation ☐ Liquid ☐ Wet/dry

Color _____

Concealer _____

Powder _____

Brow pencil _____

Eye shadows

Orbital area _____

Crease _____

Lid _____

Other_____

Eyeliner pencil _____

Lip pencil _____

Mascara _____

Lipstick _____

Special Instructions

_____

_____

_____

Next Appointment

_____
Day   Month   Year

Figure 32–5 The face makeup chart is a handy home care reference for the client.

Basic Makeup Application

Introduction: Proper application techniques are vital to the success of any makeup procedure. Once you have mastered these techniques, you can confidently teach your client how to apply her own makeup to her satisfaction.

Purpose: To develop the best makeup look for a client. The session also teaches correct color selection and makeup application.

Room setup

1. Tidy up the makeup area.

2. Place a clean makeup drape on the chair.

3. Check all lighting.

4. Place the makeup consultation form on the clipboard.

5. Gather 2 or 3 small towels.

6. Fill a stainless steel bowl with very warm water.

7. Place two sponges in the bowl and allow them to soak.

Tools and supplies: Eye makeup remover; cleanser and toner appropriate for the client's skin type; moisturizer; foundation, blush, and powder appropriate for the client's skin tone; concealer; lip and eyebrow pencils; eyeshadow—2 or 3 appropriate for client's skin tone; eye liner—pencil or liquid; mascara—cake or liquid; and lipstick appropriate for client's skin type and tone; cotton pads; cotton swabs; round sponges, assorted brushes; manicure scissors.

Client preparation: The client completes the confidential makeup profile form while in the waiting room. Greet the client and escort her to the makeup area. Seat the client and drape her with the makeup cape. Have the client pull her hair away from the face.

Assess the client's look and make notes.

Fasten the hair with butterfly clips.

Sanitize your hands with the hand sanitizer. Do it in front of your client.

Procedure

1 Remove eye makeup and lipstick with a moistened cotton pad and eye makeup remover solution. Apply a small amount of remover on a pad and proceed to cleanse.

   a. Cleanse the eyes with a downward stroke from brow to lashes and again from the outer corner of the eye to the inner corner of the eye.

   b. Cleanse off extra mascara on the lashes and under the bottom lashes with cotton swabs and eye makeup remover solution.

   c. To avoid smearing lipstick on the face, cleanse the lips with an outer to inner movement, starting on each side of the lips.

2 Beginning at the forehead, apply a small amount of cleanser and work in circular motions around the entire face to remove makeup and debris. Rinse 2 or 3 times with moistened sponges until all residue is removed.

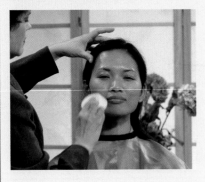

3 Apply toner on a round flat cotton pad or makeup sponge and swipe the entire face.

4 Apply a small amount of day cream or moisturizer to face and massage in circular motion until it is absorbed.

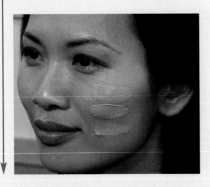

5 Choose an appropriate foundation based on skin type and condition, and the client's lifestyle requirements.

   a. Match several shades on her cheek using a cotton swab. Test three colors by applying them in narrow strips (using a cotton swab) to one cheek and lightly smudge with a makeup sponge.

   b. Stand back and squint with your eyes to see which one color disappears the best. Wipe the other strips from the cheek with the sponge.

c. Apply an even coverage over the entire face with a cotton swab or a wedge makeup sponge. Soften or feather the edges around the face using the clean side of your sponge.

Note: If using wet/dry foundation, wet your makeup sponge and apply it directly onto the face.

6 Apply concealer to needed areas—under the eyes, on fine wrinkles, and over pimples. Face proportion issues are corrected by shadowing and highlighting.

a. Apply the concealer with a lip brush to smaller face areas and a flat brush to the larger areas. Pat in lightly with the sponge until well blended.

7 Choose the appropriate shade of loose powder. Shake or remove a small amount on a facial tissue.

a. Press the powder puff, or powder brush, if preferred, in the loose powder. Rub the powder into the puff or fold up the sides of the puff (like a taco) and rub the sides together.

b. Pat and roll the powder over the face, starting with small areas. Continue applying the powder in tight areas next (around the nose), then finish with the larger parts of the face (cheeks and forehead).

c. Place a small amount of loose powder on the tip of your clean finger. Glide it over the whole face to check the completeness of the application. If you missed an area, repowder.

d. Dust off the excess powder with the powder brush.

8 Observe the brow shape. They may need some light tweezing or waxing. If they need a major clean up, then schedule your client to come back at a later time for waxing.

a. Lightly brush the powder out of the eyebrows with your eyebrow brush. Brush them up to check for long hairs. Tweeze or use small manicure scissors if needed.

b. Fill in any thinned areas in the brow using fine, hairlike strokes with the eyebrow pencil.

9 Select the most appropriate eye shadow colors for your client.

a. Apply the lightest color first as a base color.

b. Choose and apply a secondary medium or dark color for contouring the eye.

c. Choose and apply an accent color to strengthen either the light or the dark color. For example, brush a light cream color from the lashes to the brow bone using your fluff brush.

d. Apply a medium brown color in the crease of the eye with the angled brush. Begin from the outer crease of the eye and brush toward the nose (staying in the crease) Lightly go over the whole lid area again with a gold accent color. This softens the darker shades and highlights the lighter shades, giving another dimension to the eye.

10 Apply eyeliner with an eye pencil or an eyeliner brush. Observe the eye shape and note any necessary correction. Decide if you need to line both the top and bottom, or just the top. Should the liner be a thin line or smudged? Does it need to go all the way across or just part way? Pencils are a better choice when smudging. Wet liners only smudge best when they are still moist.

11 Choose an appropriate mascara color—brown/black, black/navy combination, black, or navy.

a. Apply as many coats as necessary to achieve the desired effect. Apply to the bottom lashes first and then the top lashes.

  i. After applying mascara to the bottom lashes, slightly raise the eyebrow to lift the eye area. Apply mascara to the tops and sides of the top lashes. Finish with an upward stroke to coat under the lashes.

  ii. Gently separate the lashes with a clean mascara wand.

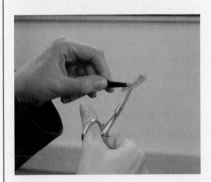

b. Optional: False eyelashes

  i. Measure and trim the eyelashes to fit. Do not apply the eyeliner.

  ii. Curl the client's eyelashes, unless they are too thin.

iii. Place an even amount of glue on the false eyelash band. Carefully affix the false eyelashes over the client's lashes.

iv. Apply mascara to the top and bottom lashes.

12 Apply glamour blush. Choose a color that enhances the blood tone and apply it with a blush brush.

Apply blush onto the cheek according to the face shape and desired effect. Soften or feather the edges of the blush with the powder brush.

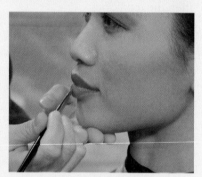

13 Choose a lipstick color that enhances the client's blood tone.

a. Using a plastic spatula, scrape off a small amount of lipstick from the side of the lipstick tube. Apply with a lipstick brush using long strokes along the curves of the lips. Continue until the contouring is satisfactory. Lipstick shades should complement blush and eye shadow colors.

The final result is one of harmony.

Makeup collections are selected according to the overall market position of the spa or salon. Its image, goals, and level of clientele play a large part in product choice. There are numerous options available, e.g., private label, custom blended, branded, or specialty lines.

Once the service menu is finalized, the owner or management along with the makeup artist/esthetician decides what is most appropriate. Tools and accessories are also selected. There are hundreds of choices available to purchase. Research the industry trade journals and magazines. Request manufacturer catalogues and view their lines at trade shows.

Private Label

Choosing a private label line is a most cost-effective way to begin; you are able to obtain a variety of items with minimal investment.

Benefits

Because of the variety of available products, private label offers many benefits, including a larger variety of color choices. Private label can also offer trendier products. You can create your own image through a variety of packaging choices. Because it is private label, there is a greater profit margin. Most private label offers a 200%–400% markup. If you purchase something for $2.00 you have the option of selling it for $12.00.

Drawbacks

One drawback to private label products is that they sometimes have look alike products because these products are widely available. This is remedied through customizing your labeling and packaging.

Private label allows for greater markup and profit, which gives you the opportunity to develop your own brand name. Marketing and support materials are something that you will normally have to produce for yourself. That, however, is exactly what branded lines do. They may have expensive, but beautiful packaging, bottles, marketing materials, and promotional campaigns. The cost for this is integrated into the cost of their products and marketing. It is passed onto the buyer. Although they may offer free training

or support materials, you are actually the one paying for it. Therefore, your cost for purchase is much higher than for private label.

Custom Blended

Using the approach of custom blending provides you the opportunity to customize formulas for your customers. Each is blended for that individual, taking into account her unique needs and preferences.

Benefits

Custom-blended products are great for those who are artistic or prefer to market their uniqueness. Custom blending can be done with foundation or powders. These products may blend well with the salon or spa's overall philosophy—both in the facial and hair care departments. Custom-blended cosmetics are produced according to a specific philosophy and system, which are coordinated with the training concepts.

Drawbacks

Purchasing products for personal customizing means a major initial investment. A wide selection of inventory must be purchased and made available for back bar products, bottles and containers for resale, and storage, etc. There may be problems with consistency in duplicating a formula; the concept comes and goes in a rather trendy manner. You must keep accurate records for each client's formula. Custom-blending suppliers generally offer little or no support materials and literature. You must create your own. More than one person should be trained to custom blend to help cover when an artist leaves or is absent.

Branded

A branded line is chosen to support other existing product lines such as hair, skin care, or nails. Several branded skin care product lines have added makeup to complement their specialty. This is the most popular way to add makeup; you have one supplier for all your needs—face, body, and makeup.

Benefits

A big benefit to a branded line is that support is available through literature, education, and samples. The range of color can be small or large depending on where the line is produced. Packaging is usually more upscale; it may even be elegantly boxed.

Drawbacks

A drawback to a branded line is that you may have inventory surpluses when the packaging concept changes. French lines are usually very weak in color products required by women of color. In addition, there may be an overage of stock in color choices that are not appropriate for your market or colors may change too often, and sometimes favorite colors disappear.

Specialty Lines

These are miscellaneous makeup lines that fit a niche or void; e.g., camouflage makeup is for a select group of people. Therefore, the companies who make this type of makeup offer a limited amount of products and colors. These lines are limited to one or two concepts, or a small group of products suited for a specific purpose. They make great add-on items for your own marketing of a free gift with a purchase promotions, focal points for holidays, special items at your checkout counter, or additions for your specialty makeovers. Medical makeup lines also fit into this category.

Makeup Services

When working in a spa or salon, it is important to be aware of what types of makeup services are offered. Make sure that they match your own skills and experience. You must also ensure that you have all the necessary products and tools. Makeup services can be grouped into four basic types:

1. touch-ups
2. makeup applications
3. makeup lessons
4. specialty makeup

Touch-Ups

A makeup touch-up provides the client with a brief application of an eye, lip, or blush product or any combination. This session offers the opportunity for the client to experience something new, such as a trendier look. For example, when visiting a depart-

MAKEUPTIP

Touch-Ups

- Apply some translucent powder over existing eye shadow or blush.
- Apply some of the new colors you wish to demonstrate on top of the powder. This visual shows the client how it will look.

ment store, a salesperson approaches and asks you if you would like to sample the latest lipstick. The goal is to sell you a new lipstick. A similar process occurs in the spa or salon, except that the lipstick is tied into another service.

- manicure—the client wants a lipstick to match her new polish
- hair color or highlights—the client has changed or added something to her hair and she wants a blush or eye shadow to complement those changes
- facial—the client's skin is glowing and she wants a powder foundation to match the glow of her skin

A makeup touch-up may be offered as a complimentary service that takes around 10–15 minutes. It can be performed at any time or anywhere in the salon. Sometimes, the spa or salon will offer touch-ups as a promotion. It is piggybacked onto another service for a period of time and for a small fee.

Makeup Application

The makeup artist can create a special new look for the client. Perhaps it is for a prom, a wedding, a new updated look, or for a career change. Makeup application services are probably the most popular makeup services you perform. Clients are already accustomed to going to a department store for free application. In a department store most makeovers are limited to the look available through a particular cosmetic line, which may not always be appropriate for a particular client. In a spa or salon environment, the goal is to provide an appealing, personalized look that is appropriate for the client. Makeup application usually takes about 30–45 minutes. It is purely a work of art by the makeup artist. It is not considered a makeup lesson for the client.

MAKEUPTIP

Application

- Follow the general guidelines for the makeup application. If an evening look is desired, focus on either the lips or eyes and increase the color in those areas. Add in some extra contouring and some different textures in the colors you use.
- To create a more interesting day look, match the foundation and powder to the skin before trying new colors on the face. Review the client's preferences for a day image.

Makeup Lessons

Makeup lessons offer the client a step-by-step approach to applying her daily makeup. Customize the lesson to meet the needs of the client. Clients who use this service may fall into one of the following categories.

- a teenager who wants to learn proper makeup application

- a mother returning to work who requires a refresher course in applying makeup

- a client who wants a new look or who wants to learn how to apply makeup for the evening.

- a bride who wants a special romantic look or a resort/vacation look.

- a college student who requires a more professional look for a job interview

A makeup lesson generally takes about an hour. The makeup artist demonstrates application on one side of the client's face.

MAKEUPTIP

The Lesson

This session requires more time than a simple makeup application. Proceed step by step through the application procedure. At each step, allow the client to mimic your actions. This is a great way to help guide and correct your client as she applies her own makeup. In this session, introduce shadowing and highlighting techniques. Take the time to answer all the client's questions.

The client copies the technique and actually does the application on the other side. This allows the makeup artist to observe how the client applies makeup and to comment and correct the client's techniques. This also helps the client build confidence and speed.

Specialty Makeup

Specialty makeup is used for special occasions. It requires more advanced skills to produce a particular look.

Wedding

Makeup application for a wedding may include makeup for the bride's wedding portrait as well as makeup for the actual wedding day (Figure 32–5). Wedding makeup generally has two looks:

1. A natural makeup look based on either warm or cool tones with extra highlights to bring out the eyes and extra gloss to highlight the lips.

2. A stronger evening look with deeper colors based on natural makeup with more accent colors on the blush, eyes, and lips. You can do extra contouring and apply false eyelashes to emphasize the bride's eyes.

You may be requested to apply makeup for the rest of the wedding party: bridesmaids, flower girls, mothers of the bride

Figure 32–5 Bridal makeup is one example of a specialty makeup service.

Compensation

Puzzled about what to expect for wages? You are not alone. How estheticians get paid continues to be a source of controversy and debate. Historically, in the United States the field of esthetics grew out of the salon industry. Because of this, skin care salons and day spas adopted the salon model of payment, which is largely percentage or commission based. However, as estheticians began to acquire separate licensure in many states, new opportunities in skin care clinics, wellness centers, and medical practices became available. These changes created a new way of thinking about how estheticians should be paid and the salon protocol began to be questioned. We will review what the options were then and also take a look at a new model of thinking.

Basically there are two ways estheticians get paid: either by commission or an hourly wage or salary. Commission-based salaries, as mentioned above, have been the salon standard. Both methods tend to incorporate some provision for sharing profits from retail sales.

Commission-based pay means that you get paid a certain percentage of whatever services you perform. Working on a straight commission basis, that could mean anywhere from 40% to 60% (the generally accepted industry standard), depending on who you work for. If your commission rate is 50% and you take in $1000 a week you get to go home with $500. You can add a percentage of retail sales, traditionally 10%–15%, to that.

The commission method of payment can actually be quite lucrative for the practitioner who enjoys finding new clients and likes to compete for work. There is generally an opportunity to build your "own clientele" with little supervision and none of the responsibilities associated with being the owner of the establishment. As long as you are healthy, show up prepared to work hard,

agree with the philosophy and practices of the establishment, and bring in new clients, you can do well. In some instances the salon will begin by providing you with clients or supply you with a certain number of clients, but for the most part *you* need to be the impetus for generating new clients. Salons who use this method tend to hire practitioners who have an established clientele. If you are just starting out you may need to start at a lower percentage rate until you develop a following.

Before you agree to a commission-based salary you should think carefully about your needs. Working on a percentage basis has its benefits, but it also has its downside. Fluctuations in the market and seasonal lows can greatly affect your income. Starting out can be difficult, particularly if marketing efforts are limited. You must be prepared to weather the highs and lows. Generally, there are few benefits, such as health insurance, sick days, or paid vacation and little opportunity for growth in terms of salary increases.

The salary or hourly wage model is gaining popularity and with good reason. As estheticians continue to develop a professional career status they are demanding more of the benefits that go along with this work ethic—guaranteed pay, health insurance, sick days, vacation, and a retirement plan. At the same time, employers are recognizing the benefit of creating an atmosphere that encourages team values and creates a more secure work environment.

Today's skin care market has also contributed to this new way of thinking. Competing with new employment options, such as medical practices, that already have professional standards in place, has forced established skin care salons to reconsider their methods for attracting talented estheticians.

Compensation *(continued)*

Still you may be wondering what to expect for a salary or hourly wage. In general estheticians just starting out can expect an hourly rate of between $8 and $10 an hour. Many skin care clinics and day spas incorporate the commission concept and also offer a service commission on top of these rates. These rates vary depending on the charge for treatments. In addition most establishments offer the standard 10%–15% retail commission. Starting salaries can range anywhere from $24,000 to $32,000 depending on the individual's experience. In some cases, where individuals are paid strictly on a salary basis, bonuses, education, and training serve as incentive.

The idea of paying estheticians a salary or hourly wage promotes the whole concept of professionalism. Guaranteed pay for guaranteed work. This sets the tone for a new generation of estheticians who are valued for their talent and work ethic. It also places more responsibility on the part of owners to set standards that promote solid business objectives. This means promoting business, encouraging teamwork, setting standards to measure performance, and rewarding individuals for good performance.

Estheticians starting out in the field today are faced with many choices. In deciding how you would like to be paid, take time to consider your own individual goals and needs, but at the same time consider how your decision affects the future of the profession as a whole.

---

and groom, grandmothers, and other members of the wedding party. They should have the appropriate natural makeup to conform to the overall look of the bridal party; however, nothing should detract from the bride.

Makeup can also be used to enhance the appearance of the male members of the bridal party. Apply foundation or bronzer to the groom for a healthy, radiant glow. Whenever makeup is performed at the wedding location, charge a fee for travel time.

Fantasy

Fantasy makeup is focused on special events such as a Halloween costume party, or a 4th of July parade, or a birthday party for children.

Corrective

A unique makeup lesson, corrective makeup helps the client identify the most positive and negative features of her face, then correctly

MAKEUPTIP

Wedding Day

The wedding day is one of the most important days in a person's life. Planning the bride's makeup naturally requires extra special care. Some brides have a definite look in mind; others need more guidance. Show the bride your portfolio of different looks so that she can choose ideas for her own look. Examine her dress and veil design. Take time to discuss the overall appearance that she wants to portray for her wedding.

MAKEUPTIP

Fantasy

This is fun makeup that ranges from face painting on the cheeks, face, or body to total effects makeup using the client's face to create a unique character. It could be a butterfly or a clown. Application of fantasy makeup follows some of the basics of general application. It uses more colorful products that are safe for the face.

Figure 32–6a Corrective makeup—before. Note the uneven pigmentation.

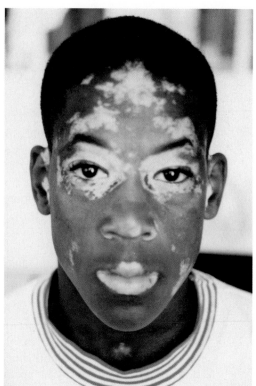

Figure 32–7a Camouflage makeup—before.

Figure 32–6b Corrective makeup—after. The complexion color has been evened out and the client's eyes are accented.

apply makeup to create the ideal look (Figures 32–6a and 6b). Her best features are emphasized with imperfections camouflaged. Shadowing and highlighting techniques can be used to achieve this. Makeup can may be directly focused on one feature, such as lip shape, eyebrow shape, or eye shape. The techniques are developed to help correct a problem.

Camouflage

Sometimes referred to as paramedical makeup, camouflage makeup uses specialized cosmetics and tools to diminish minor skin imperfections or to normalize a more serious skin disfigurement (Figures 32–7a and 7b).

Figure 32–7b Camouflage makeup—after. Note the complete coverage.

MAKEUP TIP

Camouflage

Use caution when evaluating a client for camouflage makeup. Camouflage makeup deals with more serious skin disfigurements, which may or may not be easy to cover. If you do not feel comfortable tackling this type of procedure, refer the client to another makeup specialist. Physical and emotional issues are considerations when performing this type of application. It takes time to create the perfect cover-up. Additional time is required to teach the client the actual application techniques.

These disfigurements can be the result of plastic surgery; e.g., bruising or redness from laser peels; conditions such as cancer or vitiligo; accidents such as burns or dog bites; or an elective art, such as to cover or conceal tattoos. This type of makeup can also include the use of corrective and glamour techniques. It is a very involved form of makeup beyond the scope of this chapter. Refer to Chapter 39 for more information on camouflage makeup.

Beyond the Basics

When it comes to makeup applications, there is not enough space to discuss and demonstrate all the creative techniques available. Makeup artistry is a lifelong study. There are subtle variations in techniques for stage makeup, black and white photography, and video and color photography. A good way to keep abreast of new trends and techniques is to scan the glamour magazines on a regular basis, introducing seasonal changes to clients.

You are provided with the basics in this chapter. To advance your knowledge, read, attend classes, and practice your own skills. You may even have the opportunity to study with an experienced makeup artist. You may also decide to specialize in a makeup application such as theater, camouflage or corrective makeup, or glamour.

Trends

Another area of study is that of observing makeup trends. Trends guide all aspects of the fashion world. They generally run in cycles of about one to three years. Colors or items are introduced in the first year of the cycle. Really trendy clients run with it. In the second year of the cycle, others start to catch up with the really trendy clients and those colors or items start to sell. In the third year, sales begin to decline, making way for the next trend.

However, it is important to remember that makeup does not change significantly, except for new colors, textures, and ingredients that may be introduced. For example, we will have foundations forever; however, foundation trends tend to change in cycles. To keep up with current trends in makeup, you may want to:

- Watch the local music television stations. Fashion ideas and fashion makeup often show up here first.

- Collect ideas for your clients by keeping up with the latest magazines that present current color looks for the spring/summer and fall/winter.

- Keep up to date in the professional industry by subscribing to skin care and makeup journals.

- Talk to the sales representatives from the local skin care company and find out what new makeup their companies are featuring. Or ask at your local beauty supply store. Attend beauty shows and conventions. Talented educators feature great classes in makeup and skin care. Go to the mall and check out what is happening in the department store makeup areas. Have a makeover done by a salesperson to get some ideas about what they do and say to a client.

Marketing

A beginning makeup artist has to continually practice the skills she has learned. If this is a field that you will pursue after basic esthetic school, continue training under more skilled professionals. Theatrical makeup, camouflage, and platform performance all take tremendous practice to achieve remarkable work. If esthetics is your choice for a future career with little makeup application, then you should at least understand all the basics including color theory, face shapes, and actual application.

Marketing is a twofold process that involves educating clients and recommending appropriate products. You sell the makeup you are demonstrating, and then rebook the client for an additional service. It is often difficult to rebook additional makeup services—this is less apt to generate profits than selling additional product. Informing clients of seasonal changes in makeup trends often works to encourage repeat makeup services. Planning is an important part of generating sales and contributing to the overall salon profits.

Presentation is an important aspect of marketing makeup application and products. Find the perfect space for these wonderful makeup services to happen. Makeup should not be an afterthought, placed into a small, out of the way, cramped area. When you go into a department store, what is normally the first thing you see? It is difficult to miss the long counters filled with makeup and perfumes. The owners believe it is so important that makeup counters are placed in the middle of the store or at the entrance. Everyone has to walk through the area or at least near it. These areas are sometimes the most profitable in the store.

Displays

When performing makeup services, sell everything associated with that service. If you are in charge of the inventory in your area, then make requests from the manager or owner to order specialty items such as brushes. Suggest enough choices. Do not let your client go to the local "beauty barn" to get brushes because you do not sell them. Recommend that enough inventory be ordered so that the space is inviting to retail clients.

Create an attractive display and work area. A neat and attractive area will entice your clients to explore new products and merchandise. Why should she consider any other place for her makeup supplies and services? You have everything she needs and it always looks so good. Change displays regularly to keep clients interested.

And of course, do not forget your own appearance. Do not come to the spa or salon without being totally groomed and ready to go. Personal presentation is an important part of winning client approval and confidence. What clients see is what they want to be.

Summary

Offering makeup services is a great boost to the overall service menu of a spa or salon. Instead of a client going to a department store to purchase makeup, she can obtain professional services, products, and accessories right within the domain of the spa or salon. It offers a great service to clients who would rather have makeup application in a more private, professional setting.

Makeup has evolved into a harmonious complement to our own skin care. Professional lines may offer limited colors and selections, but nevertheless, the products are high quality with excellent formulas.

We have reviewed color theory and demonstrated how to evaluate the best look for your client. It takes practice and organization to build up a loyal clientele. Furthermore, having both esthetician and makeup artist skills allows you to increase the repertoire you can offer your clients.

Your client can get a free makeover any time at a department store. However when you do a makeover, your client is going to see a difference in the way you approach makeup, the quality and kinds of products and tools you have to offer, and the sanitary conditions you provide. Consider yourself the makeup expert and she will come back again and again for your help. Makeup is the easiest and most temporary way we use to disguise or enhance our appearance. Therefore, learn all you can about your products and how they contribute to the health, wellness, and beauty of your clients. Practice the basics and learn to perform the services quickly and effectively. There are numerous opportunities for makeup artists. They are found in day spas, medispas, salons, the movie and theater industry, and the fashion industry. A more clinical setting working with disfigured clients, such as a burn center, trauma unit, or medispa, is rewarding but will require additional training. This colorful, creative art form allows you to use your imagination and become a master at making people beautiful.

Discussion Questions

1. Explain why effective communication is important to the makeup artist.

2. What is the primary goal of the makeup service? Team up with a classmate and develop a dialogue for introducing the makeup service and its benefits to a client. Practice this before trying it out on the clinic floor.

3. Name three factors in choosing a product line. Research two different product lines for similarities and differences, pricing, etc. Are they a full-service line, or do they specialize in just one or two products? Present your findings.

4. What is the purpose of the Face Makeup Chart? How does it help clients practice newly learned techniques and skills after the service?

5. Collect makeup menus from various salons and spas. Look at the types of services offered. Are they consistent from one to the other? How would you educate your clients about the different types of services?

Additional Reading

Marais, Stephanie. 2001. *Beauty Flash.* Gottingen, Germany: Berhard, Druckerei and Verlag.

Pooser, Doris, et al. 2000. *The Essential Guide To Hair, Makeup and Skin Care.* Menlo Park, Calif.: Crisp Publications.

Quant, Mary, et al. 1996. *Ultimate Makeup and Beauty Book.* New York: DK Publishing.

Robins, Cynthia, et al. 2001. *The Beauty Workbook: A Commonsense Approach to Skin Care, Makeup, Hair, and Nails.* San Francisco, Calif.: Chronicle Books.

Taylor, Pamela. 1994. *Milady's Makeup Techniques.* Clifton Park, N.Y.: Milady, an imprint of Delmar Learning, a division of Thomson Learning, Inc.

Thurdium, Laura. *Stage Makeup, The Actor's Complete Step-by-Step Guide to Today's Techniques and Materials.* Lockwood, N. J.: Back Stage Books. Imprint: Watson-Guptill Publications, Inc.

Helpful Web Sites

www.spcp.org (Society of Permanent Cosmetic Professionals)

Spa Body
Treatments

PART X

Part Outline

Chapter 33   The Value of Body Services

Chapter 34   Body Treatments

Until recently, the body treatment aspect of the esthetics business generally ranked second in importance to facial treatments. The spa boom phenomenon changed this, making body treatments more in demand. The interest in spas stems from the current state of our society. Demographics show the predominance of the population aging: Approximately 50% of the American population turned 50 in the year 2000. Along with our rapidly aging population, we have experienced problems with medical care and insurance programs, resulting in a renewed interest in preventive medicine and wellness. We have finally realized that it is far better to stay healthy than to try to fix our health once it is a problem. Body treatments are one way to help the skin maintain its health.

In Part X you will learn that facial treatments are very closely related to other services offered for the body. Just as it is important to clean, stimulate, and hydrate the face, it is equally so for the skin on the rest of the body. You will learn how to do this using the three basic steps performed in body treatments—cleansing and exfoliation, skin treatment, and body stimulation—along with descriptions of the most comprehensive treatments available in today's spa.

Chapter 33
The Value of Body Services

Chapter Objectives

After reading this chapter, you should be able to:

- Know the different types and levels of body treatments
- Understand how to address the issue of modesty with clients
- Know general body treatment principles and treatment protocols
- Understand how certain body treatments are used for metabolic stimulation
- Understand how aromatherapy can enhance body treatments

Chapter Outline

Introduction
Who Can Do Body Treatments?
Concerns
Client Health
Body Treatment Principles
Hydrotherapy
Service and Treatment Protocols
Techniques for Body Treatments
Body Masks and Wraps
Aromatherapy
Other Performance Ingredients

Introduction

It is vitally important to realize that if you can give a facial to the very small area of the face, neck and décolleté, and make a difference, imagine the benefits of applying the same principles to the entire body. If we can accomplish many changes to the skin of the face, why can't we also make similar changes to the body? If we can hydrate and moisturize the face, we can moisturize the body. Does the body need as much attention as the face? While the face poses different conditions than the body, there are valid reasons for treating both areas. For example, we do not need to worry about pigmentation and wrinkling on the hidden parts of the body. Clothing usually protects these areas from ultraviolet penetration. We do, however, concentrate much of our facial treatments on pigmentation, fine lines, and wrinkles. Conversely, we don't generally worry about cellulite or weight gain in the face, but it is of utmost concern on the body. The point here is that the body deserves just as much attention as the face.

The technology behind body treatments has grown dramatically in recent years. As a professional in this industry, you have a great responsibility in taking care of the entire body for your clients. We no longer can opt out of this responsibility by specializing only on the face, hair, or any single part of the body. A complete and holistic approach to client care must be part of our curriculum, irrespective of what our personal area of specialty is. A facial is a concept that is not just for the face. We perform back facials, scalp facials, and full body facials (Figure 33–1). It is just not appropriate anymore to refer to any of them as mere facials. The sophistication of the industry and technology lends itself better to the terms *facial treatment, body treatment, back treatment, scalp treatment*, etc.

Who Can Do Body Treatments?

Licensure for body treatments and body massage varies from state to state. In some states, only licensed massage therapists are allowed to perform body treatments (Figure 33–2). This can be an issue if the focus in a school is on massage only and it does not teach about

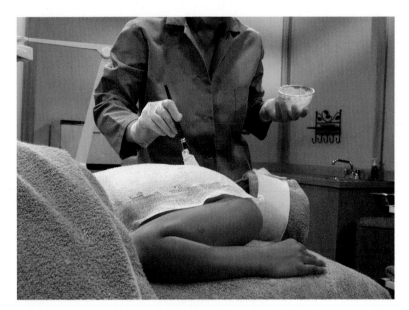

Figure 33–1 Esthetician performing back mask treatment.

other spa body treatments. Many states allow estheticians to perform body treatments but not massage, unless they hold massage licensing. Some states do not specify at all. Check with your state's licensing authorities to determine what is permissible. When you are not sure, first call the State Board of Cosmetology, then the Department of Health, or the local chapter of the Massage Therapy Association. In some extreme cases, massage and body treatments still come under the authority of the local vice squad! We will not attempt to address who is legally qualified to do body treatments. Suffice it to say, how-

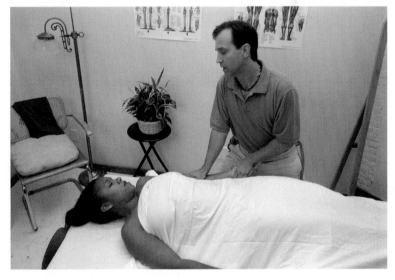

Figure 33–2 In some states, only licensed massage therapists can perform body treatments.

ever, that in general estheticians are more experienced at understanding the concepts behind treatments, products, masks, and finishing creams, etc.

The massage therapist, nevertheless, is more experienced at various forms of body massage. The ideal would be a blend of the two disciplines. It is certainly recommended that, whenever possible, professionals become properly licensed in both fields. This allows for a more holistic and flexible approach when caring for clients. It also avoids legal or licensing problems.

Concerns

Clients often express reservations about having a body treatment done. It is imperative to understand their reservations in order to put them at ease with new and difference services.

Modesty

wet rooms
A treatment room equipped for services requiring hydrotherapy treatment, such as Vichy shower, hydrotherapy tubs, etc.

Americans are more modest and shy than our European counterparts about having body treatments. Some Asian cultures, such as the Japanese, are also less modest. In countries where there is a long history of communal bathing, body care and/or massage, you will find the populace far less inhibited about removing their garments and

having a treatment performed. In Japan, for example, public baths have existed for hundreds and hundreds of years. Bathing together at the hot springs is a normal occurrence. You can go to one of the hot spring bathhouses in Germany or Hungary and experience a variety of hydrotherapy treatments without a bit of concern about communal nudity. Americans have no such history of bathing together in the nude. There is still resistance to removing clothing. The key to resolving this dilemma is to be absolutely certain that menus and client brochures address the modesty issue. Clearly stipulate protection of modesty, which includes complete body draping except the area being massaged or treated. Once a client experiences a safe treatment where her modesty has been protected, the concern is normally mitigated (Figure 33–3).

Some potential clients shy away from the spa or salon due to modesty issues. For fear of appearing ignorant, clients may not share their apprehension with you. It is important that you address this issue *prior* to their session so that they are entirely comfortable. The same occurs when using the hydrotherapy tub or Vichy shower. A thorough explanation about its benefits, how it works, and what will happen during the process will help to answer unasked questions. Listening skills are important during the initial meeting. It is important to read client body language in order to address potential concerns.

Sanitation and Hygiene

Today, sanitation and hygiene are probably the most significant issues in the spa. People generally do not ask straightforward questions about sanitary practices, or even complain if something is not clean enough. They just go away and never return! And, in addition, they tell their friends. The spa must be kept immaculate at all time (Figure 33–4). Disinfectants should be visible in all treatment areas and the use of disinfectants and sanitizing equipment must be clearly understood by all employees. There is a dichotomy between the ambiance of aromatherapy moods that we create in the spa, and maintaining an appearance of absolute, immaculate cleanliness.

Wet rooms can pose an issue. When first entering, this area should impart the

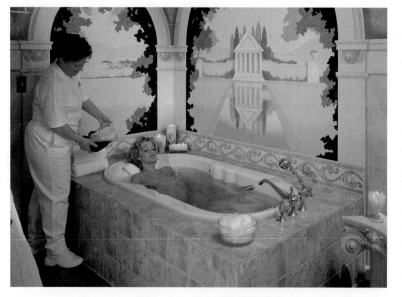

Figure 33–3 Privacy is an issue for many clients, and should be addressed prior to service.

welcoming scent of an aromatherapy candle. At the same time, there should be a subtle undercurrent of disinfectant and cleaners. It must be sanitized and dry prior to a client's entrance (Figure 33–5). Even the best spas can be rated mediocre in the areas of sanitation if cleaning and sanitation policies become lax. Sometimes therapists do not *visibly* sanitize their hands between clients and the clients are left wondering if, indeed, the therapist is practicing good hygiene. As practitioners, we become familiar with our surroundings and sometimes become inattentive. The client notices and mentally registers this concern. When clients seem to slowly dwindle, find out why. You may learn that your sanitation practices frighten them away.

Client Health

Always remember that our practice is about wellness and general health maintenance. We are not licensed to heal, cure diseases, or correct health disorders. By law, our role is about preserving and offering enhancements for a healthy person. Although we are fully cognizant of the healing and corrective aspects of many of our treatments, we must be careful not to practice medicine. As wellness practitioners, we must be cautious about doing too much, or attempting to correct disorders that are not legally within the realm of our practice. We do not take on specific client health issues that require medical intervention. Be prepared to refer clients to appropriate medical personnel for any medical issues.

Most importantly, be aware of the general health of a client. We do not perform any treatment that is deemed inappropriate for certain health conditions. There are wonderful opportunities in the body department to layer and perform multiple treatments back-to-back. Nevertheless, this cannot be done on individuals who have questionable health issues. For example, timing may have to be adjusted when performing hydrotherapy. The amount of time allowed for a hydrotherapy treatment should be adjusted according to the client's health. After one or two sessions, the client may feel comfortable enough

Figure 33–4 Treatment rooms should be immaculate at all times.

Figure 33–5 Wet rooms must be clean and dry prior to each client's use.

to extend treatment to the full 20 minutes, showing improvement in their stability and wellness level. Conversely, there are treatments that are contraindicated for certain general health issues. The health history on the intake form is not for diagnosing or treating disorders, rather, it provides us with knowledge concerning the choice, control, and timing of treatment.

Body Treatment Principles

It is just as important to cleanse, hydrate, and stimulate the skin on the body as well as the face. The approaches to body and facial treatment share three common elements:

- Cleansing and exfoliation
- Skin treatment
- Metabolic stimulation

There are many similarities and differences between body and facial treatments. The largest difference is in the scope of treatment application. The greatest similarities are the products used and the basic treatment concept. For example, the main principle of face exfoliation is to deep clean the skin, removing excessive cell buildup, dirt, and oil. This process prepares the skin for the next treatment step, such as infusing an ampoule or other product. The same principle holds true for the body. Exfoliation assists in greater penetration of the body product.

We will now examine overall treatment concepts for the body. For the novice, it is confusing to grasp how to select an appropriate product because product lines can vary considerably. Many are more focused on facial products with little to offer in the realm of body treatments. Some focus on just the body. Others offer a great selection for both. It is important to understand the concepts behind choosing the correct products (Figure 33–6).

metabolic stimulation
The application of specialized products and treatments the encourage circulatory and metabolic stimulation through vasodilation of blood capillaries.

Cleansing and Exfoliation

Cleansing and exfoliation are just as important for the body as they are for the face. Exfoliation prepares the body for a more intensive treatment. When the skin is impeccably clean, the activity of the performance ingredients is enhanced. Some treatments are performed on specific areas while others include the entire body. When choosing a product line, make certain that the manufacturer provides a variety of items for both professional and home care use that address specific needs and conditions.

Skin Treatment

This category represents a group of treatments and products that generally address skin needs. It includes procedures for body softening, moisturizing, and conditioning. Massage oils are also included. There are some sophisticated and elegant treatments available to address issues of skin conditioning. Skin conditioning and moisturization are part of the cleansing, exfoliation, and metabolic stimulation category. It may be performed as a specialized individual conditioning treatment only.

Metabolic Stimulation

Metabolic stimulation includes treatments that actually provide a subsidiary stimulation of system functions. It may be as simple as a stimulating mask that increases blood circulation, or a more complex treatment such as a cellulite treatment, bust firming and toning, body detoxification, or remineralization. **Metabolic stimulation** generally refers to the application of specialized products and treatments that encourage circulatory and metabolic stimulation through vasodilation of blood capillaries. Stimulated body systems function at a higher rate.

Once you have mastered the theory, procedures, and expected results, you will be able to expand from performing localized treatments to full body masks and wraps (Figure 33–7).

Combining Treatments

The focus of the program should be to combine all three treatments in one session: exfoliation, metabolic stimulation, and skin

Figure 33–6 Choosing the right products for home care is essential.

conditioning. Harmonizing all three components promotes better results as well as resulting in a happy customer.

Hydrotherapy

We have briefly reviewed the three larger categories of body treatments. The specifics will come later after addressing another spa concept and treatment—hydrotherapy and water usage. **Hydrotherapy**, the scientific use of water in the treatment of injuries, diseases, or mental well-being, is an integral part of performing successful body treatments (Figure 33–8). Sometimes considered a necessary component in larger spas, body treatments can be successfully offered without the use of expensive and sophisticated equipment. A shower is sufficient to remove body mud, masks, and salt. If you do not have these, hot towels work just as well. The general trend is to equip the spa with at least a hydrotherapy tub, Vichy shower, or a simple shower. However, the spa boom is well in progress, so there will no doubt be new, innovative developments in equipment, products, and technology.

Service And Treatment Protocols

Body treatments are performed for the same general health reasons as facials. The healthier a client is, the more treatments she can have simultaneously or back to back. Health weaknesses determined from your assessment of the client's health information (written and verbal) are red flags or indicators that you must choose treatments carefully. Some health issues are a total contraindication for *any* body treatment.

Beyond any health concerns, the beauty of a body session is that it provides ample opportunity to mix and match treatments. This is called **layering**. Greater benefits and results can be achieved in less time. But a client's tolerance for layering body treatments progresses slowly. Trying to do too much too soon may shock the client's system and may not be safe. The more active a

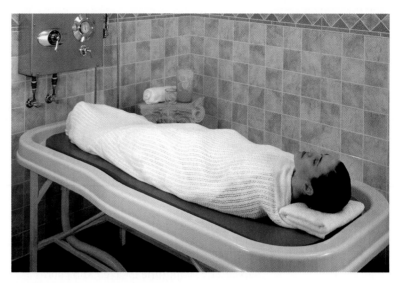

Figure 33–7 An example of a body wrap.

Figure 33–8 Hydrotherapy is an integral part of successful body treatments.

Figure 33–9 Always review the anticipated service with the client prior to beginning.

hydrotherapy
The scientific use of water in the treatment of injuries, diseases, or for mental well-being; physical therapy using water.

layering
The opportunity to mix and match treatments.

posttreatment stabilization
Relaxing after a stimulating treatment.

treatment, the more time required for **posttreatment stabilization** (relaxing after a stimulating treatment). In resorts and destination spas, relaxation rooms are available for clients to sit quietly in prior to departure. Because space in a day spa may be limited, a relaxing service may be offered instead of a relaxation room.

As you begin to understand the typical mechanics of treatments, take into account the additional time needed to perform tasks such as turning a client over or applying a body moisturizer. Layering two or three treatments saves time and product by combining steps that would otherwise be duplicated when each treatment is performed separately. Work time is saved and clients have time to receive an additional service.

Overlapping Services And Appointment Times

Most clients have hectic lives and cannot spend an entire day at the spa. Combining treatments such as a salt glow with a detox wrap can create time for additional services such as a manicure or pedicure. Blending treatments expedites client service time and brings more money to the business. Because overlapping services are so attractive to busy clients, most bestselling spa packages today are two to three hours long, not an entire day. When combining services, the time frames for each individual service are usually not indicated on the menu, listing the total time instead. Always make certain your client knows the length of time needed to complete the entire treatment (Figure 33-9, p. 545). Day spas offer many of the same experiences received at a resort or destination spa. The challenge is to provide impeccable services in less time but with equal value and benefits.

prone position
The client lies face down, usually at the beginning of the treatment.

supine position
The client lies face up, usually at the end of the treatment.

Techniques For Body Treatments

In this section we will discuss general techniques for body treatments. Most treatments have basic steps that occur no matter what treatment is being performed: table preparation, positioning the client on the table during the session, and applying product. From session to session, the procedure may change, but the basics are part of every treatment.

Table Preparation

The general order of steps for table preparation, client body positioning during product application process, and wrapping is the same for all sessions. Slight variations do occur, however, depending on the products applied and the steps needed to accomplish the desired therapeutic results. There are specific ways to set up a treatment table. Each step is dictated by the type of body treatment. The number of sheets, towels, and coverings, such as foil (Mylar) or plastic changes accordingly. For example, the setups for dry room and wet room treatments are different. When layering two or more treatments, the best way to prepare the table is to think of the basic setup. The outermost layer of materials should represent the first treatment.

Client Positioning

Each treatment requires the application of a different product, thus the positioning of the client will vary. Should a client begin the treatment face down or face up, on the left side or right side? Many treatments require that a client initially begin face down (in the **prone position**) (Figure 33–10a). Normally, at the end of the treatment, a client faces upward (in the **supine position**) (Figure 33–10b), which makes it easier to get off the treatment table. The objective is to work systematically through the treatment, requiring as little movement on the client's part as possible.

At the end of the exfoliation treatment, clients should face upward so that they are ready for the application of mud, seaweed, lotion, or another wrap. Clients should be face up for all slippery products such as a mud or seaweed wrap. Clients move from side to side, avoiding any possible safety issues. Manufacturers may provide certain protocols for product application as well as client turning.

Scrubs

For individual treatments such as gommage, salt glow, or body scrub, the steps are rather simple since the product is applied in a circular motion in an organized fashion and then removed immediately. Clients begin these treatments face down on the table. The technician then performs the treatment. Clients

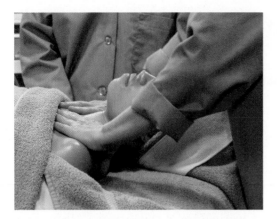

Figure 33–10a Many treatments begin with the client in the prone position.

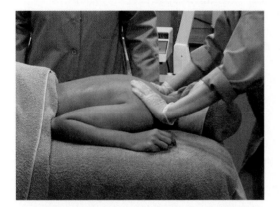

Figure 33–10b Others begin with the client in the supine position.

should be completely draped at all times, and only the area being worked on should be exposed.

Mud, Seaweed, and Wraps

Performing a seaweed or mud application followed by a body wrap is more challenging. The agents are slippery and must be applied safely to prevent the client from slipping off the table. Follow instructions for basic draping techniques (Part III, Chapter 10) to ensure that the client is covered at all times except on the area being worked.

Basic Exfoliation Techniques

Exfoliation is performed to remove dead skin cells, refine the skin, and increase the effectiveness of applied nutrients. Various types of products can be used for this purpose. The same substances may be applied as are used on the face. In full body treatments, there are more options and aggressive substances are available. Most body masks and wraps are more effective when the skin is prepared with a good exfoliation. These treatments can be booked individually or as the first step in a larger session.

Body Exfoliation—Dry Brushing

Primarily designed to stimulate blood circulation, **dry brushing** helps prepare the skin for the application of a nutrient substance and the wrap (Figure 33–11). A secondary benefit is to brush off loose, dead stratum corneum cells. Using a handheld brush, loofah, or loofah mitt, a dry brushing is performed prior to product application in a treatment such as mud or seaweed. Dry brushing is usually designated as a warm-up rub for many treatment protocols. Normally, dry brushing is a standard step in a body treatment. Occasionally, it may be performed as a separate body treatment. In this case, the body is dry brushed and the treatment is completed with the application of a body lotion.

> **dry brushing**
> Stimulates blood circulation; helps prepare the skin for application of nutrient substances and the wrap.

Salt Glow

A popular spa treatment is the **salt glow** or salt exfoliation. Some professional salts are mixed with a solvent such as a shower gel body cleanser or light oil. Aggressiveness of the salt mixture is dependent on the ratio of salt versus liquid solvent. For thicker,

> **salt glow**
> Salt exfoliation, a very popular spa treatment.

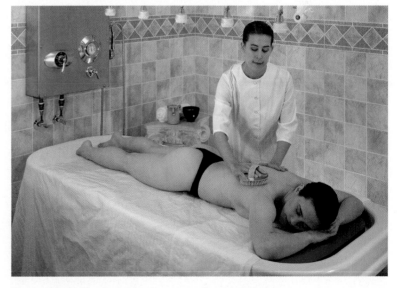

Figure 33–11 Dry brushing is an excellent exfoliation.

SKILLS **FOR** SUCCESS

Exploring the Competition

Unless you live in rural America, chances are you do not have to look too far to observe the competition. Just hop in the car and head to the nearest mall. You will be sure to find the latest in retail beauty centers, a skin care clinic or salon franchise, and perhaps even a day spa within your favorite retail store. Not to mention the rows of skin care products lined up to entice consumers at department store cosmetic counters. Better yet, you could stay home, click the remote or mouse, and tune into the home shopping network or purchase the latest in skin care technology on-line. Go to your mailbox and you may even discover a pamphlet left by your local neighborhood beauty vendor.

Yes, it is true—there is a lot of competition in today's marketplace. The skin care and spa industry has grown tremendously over the last two decades. Larger resort and day spas are cropping up all over. But fear not, in actuality the more visible skin care amenities become, the greater consumer awareness. In terms of productivity, competition can actually be considered a good thing. It is the driving force behind a healthy economy and may ultimately encourage you to become an even better esthetician.

We already know that the key to a successful marketing program is to find out what customers need and what they want, and then give them just that. It is a simple supply and demand model. But the truth is, in order to satisfy customers we must also find out what our competition is offering. Most of us would be comfortable visiting the mall to explore the retail counters. However, when it comes to checking out competitive services closer to home, most of us seem to feel a little awkward.

The quest for qualitative information can easily be developed internally. Begin by setting a high standard of quality service. What do you consider the components of a good facial or body treatment? List them. You may also want to solicit input from your clients. Use surveys or questionnaires to ask for feedback on your treat-

ments. Chances are you will not only find out what you can improve on, but you may also be positively encouraged with the many things you do well. Be open to constructive criticism. Perform a facial on a colleague or trusted friend or better still, ask your friend to send someone he knows and you do not know, and then query that person anonymously.

Do not be afraid to step out into the world. Book yourself a treatment at an established and reputable salon. Take notes and keep a list of practices that leave a positive impression on you. You may also want to join professional network organizations or trade associations that offer an opportunity to share information.

Finally, remember that there is no substitute for quality personal service. In today's impersonal society, consumers are starved for a personal connection. Corporations are spending billions to develop more intimate relationships with their constituents. As an esthetician with a license to touch, you are in a prime position to develop a personal sales relationship with your clients. Take advantage of this enviable status, demonstrate a positive caring attitude, and use each opportunity to offer sound professional advice. After all, you are the expert—learn to view yourself as such.

tougher skins, technicians use more salt and less solvent. Delicate skin requires less salt and more oil. Shower gels or body cleansers make good solvents to wash off the salt mixture. When a salt glow is performed in a dry room, and the mixture is wiped off, it is better to use extremely light, highly absorbent oil that disappears, leaving the skin as dry as possible in order to dust the salt off. Some technicians prefer to use light oil even if a shower follows. The oil has a nice slip and allows for a smooth application and easy rub. A salt glow can be a separate treatment, or used at the beginning of a larger service such as a seaweed or mud wrap.

Body Exfoliation: Scrubs

Granular scrubs, often referred to as **body polishes** in body treatments, are most popular for home care. They have tremendous appeal to the consumer. Granular scrubs achieve cell renewal by causing removal of cells by friction. A scrub or body polish is often most desirable because it feels like it's doing something. Many scrubs are in a cream base, providing the polishing feature that is absent in a salt glow.

Numerous ingredients are used for scrubs. They can be natural grains such as corn meal, oatmeal, rice bran beads, and jojoba beads or they can be more high-tech polyethylene micro balls, which are considered very gentle. More recently, AHAs have been added to scrubs and polishes to enhance exfoliation. This formula is highly effective for the body except on sensitive areas. In the salon or spa, a body brush attachment on the brush machine further enhances the effect of exfoliation. It is imperative that a body polish be followed by a good body moisturizer, especially if the scrub contains AHAs.

Gommage

Gommage is a French word that means to erase. Most skin care gommage products are in cream form. The product is applied by brush or hand and allowed to sit until almost dry. Through a friction process, or mechanical rubbing, the product is rolled off. Dead skin cells are lifted off during this process. A professional gommage exfoliation is a welcome change for the client who does scrubs or polishes at home.

Some gommages utilize xanthum gum as a rolling agent. This causes dead skin cells to roll off the skin along with the residue of the product. In some cases, the gommage may be formulated with a cellular dissolving agent such as an enzyme. The process of rubbing the gommage off the body takes longer, but it leaves the skin feeling very silky. Gommage exfoliation is wellsuited for environments that do not have showers. It is performed easily in a dry room. Keep in mind that gommage is a professional product and should not be sold to clients for use at home.

Body Masks and Wraps

When discussing a **body wrap**, we are actually referring to a **body mask** (Figure 33–12). Masks are used for the full body or are targeted for specific areas, such the upper legs in a cellulite treatment. Consumers may view the term *body wrap* as a quick weight loss method where Ace bandages or plastic wrap are tightly wrapped around each body part to constrict and cause fast vasodilation. While some of these wraps may be based on provable science with reasonable potential results, some claim unrealistic results. Hence, spas generally do not recommend this type of wrap. Clients may mistakenly believe that weight loss is associated with all body wraps. So, from a marketing standpoint, it may be best to use other terms such as *body mask* or

body polishes
Granular scrubs that are most popular for home care.

body wrap
A wrapping treatment used to treat cellulite, the condition of fatty deposits; the substances used and the wrapping technique have a diuretic effect that sometimes aids weight reduction.

body mask
Body treatment that involves the application of a mask product over the entire body. Usually used for firming the skin, or light exfoliation.

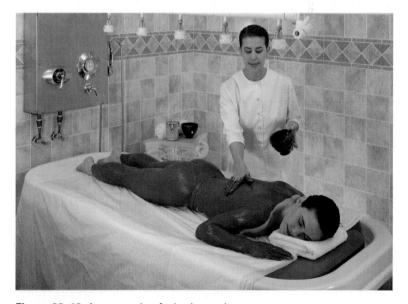

Figure 33–12 An example of a body mask.

body cocoon. Product manufacturers or professional consultants can give advice about how best to describe and market body treatments.

Skin Conditioning Versus Metabolic Stimulation

A clear distinction should be made as to whether the body mask or wrap treatment is for skin conditioning or for metabolic stimulation. Some treatments address only one of these. Others do both. Frequently, a body treatment that concentrates on metabolic stimulation will also finish with skin conditioning in the form of an application of moisturizing lotion.

Many treatments are specifically geared for softening the skin only. For example, a shea butter wrap on the market is designed purely to soften and condition the skin. Another line includes a milk and honey body mask, and yet another offers a creamy body-moisturizing mask. These treatments have no specific metabolic stimulation goals. On the other hand, most **detox treatments** are designed specifically for metabolic stimulation, which aids the body's natural elimination of toxins. To accomplish the detoxification process, seaweed and mud are typically used to dehydrate the skin. A special skin conditioner or lotion is applied as a last step.

Purpose of Body Wrapping

Why do body treatments require a wrap? A facial mask is applied to a very small area of the body, but a body mask is applied to larger areas, so wrapping prevents the client from becoming too cold and allows the product to remain in place. When working on larger areas of the body, a cover helps hold heat in as well as stimulate the activity of the treatment. Marketing photographs often display a completely uncovered body painted in nice green seaweed. This is not the way the actual treatment occurs. In reality, the body is covered after its application so that the client receives the full benefit.

Masks and Wrap Components

The theory and ingredients for masks and wraps may be long and complex. Each varies with the purpose and steps involved in the particular treatment. Discussing the components of masks and wraps is a bit like talking in general about the basic ingredients that go into all food recipes. Each product used in body treatments is based on a unique recipe. While perhaps not as long as food recipes, formulas fluctuate depending on their purpose. To simplify, only basic steps and certain aspects of the components are discussed here. For more detailed information, refer to Additional Reading at the end of this chapter or attend body classes.

Seaweed—Algae

Scientists place **algae** under the heading of seaweeds (Table 33–1). Categorized in four groups, there are over 25,000 known species. The general groups are green (*Chlorophyta*), blue-green (*Cyanophyta*), brown (*Phaeophyta*), and red (*Rhodophyta*). Algae are full of vitamins and minerals. They hold a natural affinity for the human body, making them beneficial. Properties of algae include skin-restructuring proteins, assistance in cell renewal, metabolic stimulation, antioxidant properties, stimulation of blood circulation, softening, and moisturizing.

Due to the specific properties of each algae type, they provide targeted treatments in helping correct several body conditions, such as cellulite or water retention. Algae treatments can be classified into two simple groups: the **vasodilation group**, which increases circulation by dilating blood vessels, and the **metabolic group,** which detoxifies and increases the metabolism by stimulating circulation.

Muds (Clays)

After salt glows mud treatments are probably the most popular spa body sessions. When consumers think of a spa, they normally relate it to mud (Table 33–2). As with most raw and active materials, rich mud and clay components are kept in as natural a state as possible to preserve their efficacy. Manufacturers are required by law to test all raw materials for contaminants, bacteria, and toxity levels. When processed through a manufacturer, specific consistencies and formula requirements are regulated for use in body masks and hydrotherapy tubs. Depending on mineral content, each mud has its own particular characteristics, and is chosen for targeted benefits in body treatments. Rich mud is

---

detox treatments
Designed specifically for metabolic stimulation which aids the body's natural elimination of toxins.

algae
Primitive plants found in fresh or salt water, and include seaweed, kelp, and stoneworts; considered a nutrient.

vasodilation group
A type of algae treatment that increases circulation by dilating blood vessels.

metabolic group
A type of algae treatment that detoxifies and increases the metabolism by stimulating circulation.

Table 33–1 Seaweeds and Their Use

Main Group	General Group Properties	Subgroups	Properties	Recommended Body Condition and Treatment
Algae (alginates)	Aids in skin firmness, cell renewal, and moisturization			
Chlorophyta (green)	Softening, antibacterial, anti-inflammatory	*Lichen moss*		Dry skin, irritation
Cyanophyta (blue-green)	High nutritional group, rich in vitamins A, B, C, E; stimulates cell metabolic rate	*Spirulina*	Rich source of beta-carotene, total food source, sugars (moisturizing), antioxidant	Detox, cellulite, softening, and conditioning
Phaeophyta (brown)	Probably the strongest group for blood and metabolic stimulation	*Laminaria digita*	Sugars (moisturizing); vitamins (antioxidants, etc.); provitamins (carotenoids, vitamin D, etc.); minerals (iodine, etc.); antibacterial, metabolic stimulation	More active treatments using heat and stronger stimulation, detox, cellulite, moisturizing and conditioning, revitalizing,
		Fucus *Fucus vesibulosus*	Similar to *Laminaria digita*	Similar to *Laminaria digita*
Rhodophyta (red)	Contains highly balancing emollient algae	*Chrondrus crispus*	Highly viscous (thick and stabilizing), balancing, emollient (soothing)	Moisturizing and conditioning
		Carageenan	Highly viscous (thick, slippery), emollient (soothing)	Moisturizing and conditioning

typically used by direct application, followed by wrapping the body in either plastic or Mylar. The client then rests for 30 to 60 minutes to facilitate the stimulating, detoxifying, and moisturizing effects of the mud.

In order to understand spa mud, it is necessary to examine the actual geological component referred to as *clay*. In skin care, a clay mask or pack is often designed to pull impurities out of the skin and is therefore used for oily or clogged skin. Part of its action is to pull or detoxify, and it is a welcome benefit to problematic and oily skin. Furthermore, clays are formulated with other components

that keep it moist and creamy. These are ideal for a variety of reasons, including hydration and sensitive skin. French green clay is an example of this creamy texture.

Moor Mud

Moor is a German word meaning peat. In several areas of the world, peat mud is found in bogs that are saturated with water. Peat is the result of approximately 30,000 years decaying plant material and other ground substances. Due to its high water content it is thinner at the top. It is thicker deeper in the ground. Highly rich in nutrients, moor mud is

Table 33–2 Muds and Clays

Group	Properties	Subgroup	Properties	Use
Kaolinite	Fine powder	China clay		Drawing, tightening, toning
Illite/chlorite (sea mud)	High in minerals, magnesium, potassium			
Smectites (volcanic ash)	Rich in minerals. Used to congeal thinner clays; stimulating, vasodilation	Fango mud	High volcanic content; used in Italian hot spring spas	Masks: remineralizing, detoxifying; combine with paraffin for greater benefit. Mud easier to remove when combined with paraffin
Moor (peat) mud	Obtained from bogs rich in decayed plant material, essential oils, minerals			Masks: face, body, hydrotherapy

known for its medicinal and therapeutic values. Organic substances obtained from the moor are considered rich and healing. It contains detoxifying properties and is soothing and balancing. Its many nutrients include trace elements, minerals, amino acids, enzymes, vitamins, and essential oils. Moor mud is a popular item in spa treatments. Valuable for both the face and body, it is available in professional treatments and retail.

Aromatherapy

aromatherapy
The therapeutic use of plant aromas used for beauty and health treatment purposes.

A popular treatment, especially in day spas, is the ancient art and science known as **aromatherapy** (Figure 33–13). This practice is the therapeutic use of plant aromas for beauty and health treatment purposes. It dates back to the ancient Egyptians, and there is evidence that the Romans also used essential oils. Essential oils are plant extracts that contain antiseptics, antibiotics, vitamins, and/or hormones. The oil is located between a plant's cells and causes the plant's fragrance. They are distilled from the plant for use in beauty treatments. Essential oils are not true oils such as safflower oil, olive oil, almond oil, or soy oil. Rather, they are highly complex molecular structures that contain many chemical compounds. The chemical

Figure 33–13 Different types of aromatherapy supplies.

compounds exhibit numerous properties. Essential oil blends are made specifically to target certain conditions, such as cellulite, relaxation, lymphatic drainage, and rejuvenation. A pure blend contains many essential oils working in synergy. Together the blend provides benefits. It is actually more powerful than a single essential oil.

Functions of Essential Oils

Essential oils benefit several parts of the body, including the skin, nervous system, muscles, and blood and lymph system. They are used in a variety of ways when performing body treatments. Manufacturers often predetermine how treatments are performed. Certain essential oils may be presented in a serum, blending oil, juice, or in some other format to be included for body application. Sometimes they are used before the application of the mask. They may be placed in a carrier base oil to be used in a massage before or after the mask or wrap. They are added to the mud or seaweed mixture itself for the wrap. Additionally, essential oils are added to the bath for different effects (Table 33–3). Aromatherapy baths are highly prized and are a favorite on many spa menus.

Blends versus Single Oils

Essential oils are available in pure, single forms such as chamomile, lavender, patchouli, ylang-ylang, and rosemary. Most are too strong, however, to use in their neat (undiluted) form. They are therefore added to a blending oil that is made up of natural oils. When targeted for specific results in a body treatment such as a cellulite or lymphatic massage treatment, a chemist combines more than one essential oil to create a greater effect. Note that only trained chemists should mix essential oils, which can be dangerous if overused.

When choosing blends, consideration must be given to the activity of the essential oil, fragrance, and psychological impression for the client. If the fragrance is unpleasant, it will not matter if you create a blend that fits the function; the client will not like it. It is better to employ blends developed by the manufacturer who has scrutinized this through hours of field testing. The end result must be pleasing to a majority of people. The

Table 33–3 Essential Oil Properties

Calming	Stimulating	Detoxifying
Chamomile (*Anthemis nobilis*)	Camphor (*Cinnamomum camphora*)	Camphor (*Cinnamomum camphora*)
Jasmine (*Jasminum officinale*)	Cinnamon (*Cinnamomum* spp.)	Ivy (*Hedera helix*)
Neroli (*Citrus aurantium/vulgaris*)	Clove (*Syzygium aromaticum*)	Juniper (*Juniperus communis*)
Lavender (*Lavandula officinalis*)	Rosemary (*Rosmarinus officinalis*)	Lemon (*Citrus limom*)
Rose (*Rosa*, spp.)	Sage (*Salvia officinalis*)	Lemongrass (*Cymbopogon citratus*)
Sweet orange (*Citrus sinensis*)	Spearmint (*Mentha* spp.)	Pine (*Pinus silvestrus*)
Valerian (*Valeriana officinalis*)		Thyme (*Thymus* spp.)
Ylang-Ylang (*Unona odorantissimum*)		

chemistry of essential oils also reacts differently with individual body chemistry. It must be compatible with your client.

Other Performance Ingredients

Over the past several years, numerous targeted body treatments have been developed that use specialized formulas to help correct or improve a condition such as cellulite or poor circulation. In a basic body mask or wrap, the treatment most likely requires a cleanser, an exfoliant, an essential oil, the appropriate mask chosen for the wrap, and a moisturizer to apply at the end of the treatment.

In order to enhance this process, special activators or performance agents may be included in the procedure to produce targeted stimulation in a treatment. For example, if you are doing a cellulite treatment, you may apply an activator that helps stimulate circulation. This allows for greater benefit when the mask is applied. Somewhat like an ampoule in a facial treatment, they contain more concentrated components to expedite results. Activators or performance agents are normally applied prior to mask application. In some cases, they may be applied at the end.

Activators

Certain agents are referred to as **activators** or performance agents. These formulas may include several ingredients blended to obtain a specific end result. For example, in a cellulite treatment, the main goal is to cause a

greater vasodilation effect. The blood and lymph circulation is stimulated to enhance cellular metabolism. Certain seaweeds contribute to the vasodilation effect. Essential oils also have these properties. In some cases, however, the treatment may require the essential oil, seaweed, and an additional activator. This stimulant could be in a gel or cream form. Ingredients may include climbing ivy (*Hedera helix*), caffeine, and guarana. Application is normally under the mask so that the activator enhances the cellulite treatment. All three agents—seaweed, essential oil, and activator—work harmoniously and with greater effect than applying each alone. It is analogous to adding a spice to a recipe to enhance the flavor of the food.

Activators are normally for professional use only. They are applied during treatment. Many manufacturers offer packaged professional program that gives you a step-by-step treatment. This takes the guesswork out of understanding the process.

Serums and Concentrates

Although serums or concentrates are considered the activator by some lines, in many cases serums that are commonly applied in facial treatments do not exist yet for body treatments. Any serum used for the face is certainly beneficial to the body. Serums may contain special antioxidants. However, until larger volumes are available, using serums in body treatments is cost-prohibitive. Future demands will encourage manufacturers to come out with products that are cost-effective for whole body treatments. In the meantime, a little serum can be applied before the

activators
Chemical agent used to start the action of chemical products on hair; an additive used to quicken the action or progress of a chemical. Another word for booster, accelerator, or catalyst.

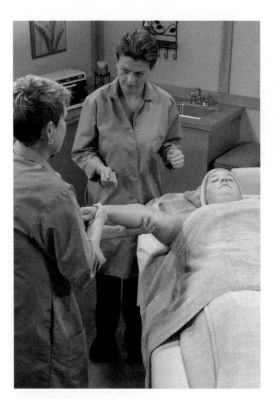

Figure 33–14 A finishing lotion is applied at the end of most treatments.

massage or mask in a body treatment. Or, a few drops of the serum can be added directly into massage oil to enhance its properties. It works well, especially if the oil is a light penetrating one. During a body treatment, add a few drops of a serum right after the exfoliation and prior to the mask or wrap. Finally, you may add a little serum to the finishing lotion or cream.

Lotions and Creams

Most body treatments conclude with the application of a finishing lotion (Figure 33–14). After a full body wrap, technicians may apply a moisturizing lotion. Cellulite treatments may conclude with a firming cream. The finishing product may be an item that is sold to the client to use at home. Because many types of seaweed have a fishy or oceanlike smell, the finishing lotion should have a light, pleasant fragrance. It adds to the ambiance of the treatment.

Certain manufacturers prefer creams to lotions. Some creams are heavier than lotion. In some cases a treatment is completed with a finishing oil. This is fine as long as it absorbs readily into the skin. Whichever is

chosen, it is important to make sure that the product is well absorbed to avoid any stains on clothing. Because the finishing phase is part of the treatment, it is not advisable to immediately shower off any excess.

Summary

As the American population ages with major issues around our health care system, individuals seek ways of supplementing their preventive care to reduce stress. Stress is the number one malady in our frenetic lifestyle. It is a catalyst to seek treatments that place our body at ease with the surrounding world. Body services are not new; they have been around since the early Egyptians. Because the main goal for many of these ancient treatments was to ward off disease, it stands to reason that today human beings are seeking some peace and tranquility to balance their body systems. The goals of body services are threefold—to cleanse and exfoliate, provide treatment to the skin, and to offer stimulation that gently helps to harmonize the body.

Discussion Questions

1. Modesty can be an issue for many spa clients. Helping clients become comfortable with removing their clothing requires sensitivity and skill. Develop a dialogue for addressing client concerns around nudity in body treatments.

2. Define the term *metabolic stimulation*. Name three body treatments that specifically target this goal. What is the value or benefit to the client?

3. The principles of cleansing and exfoliation, skin treatments, and metabolic stimulation can be applied to both face and body treatments. Discuss, in general, the main differences and similarities associated with each. How would you define the value or benefit of each to clients?

4. The client's overall state of health is a primary concern in overlapping, or layering, body treatments. What indicators should the practitioner look for on a health

questionnaire that might contraindicate multiple services?

5. To provide clients with good service, the practitioner must be aware of session versus procedure time. Make a list of all those tasks that must be incorporated into an actual session time.

6. Why should the practitioner be concerned about the "position" of the client for body treatments? Include safety issues in your discussion.

7. Make a list of standard body treatments. Differentiate between those that can be performed in a dry room and those that can be performed in a wet room. How many of these treatments fall into the category of skin conditioning versus metabolic stimulation? Can any of these treatments serve both goals? Support your reasoning.

8. Define the term *body wrap*. What is the main purpose of wrapping the body?

Additional Reading

Gambino, Henry J. 1994. *Estheticians Guide to Business Management.* Clifton Park, N.Y.: Milady, an imprint of Delmar Learning, a division of Thomson Learning, Inc.

Miller, Erica. 1996. *SalonOvations' Day Spa Techniques.* Clifton Park, N.Y.: Milady, an imprint of Delmar Learning, a division of Thomson Learning, Inc.

Miller, Erica. 1996. *SalonOvations' Day Spa Operations* Clifton Park, N.Y.: Milady, an imprint of Delmar Learning, a division of Thomson Learning, Inc.

Chapter 34
Body Treatments

Chapter Objectives

After reading this chapter, you should be able to:

- Learn the importance and proper use of the client health questionnaire.
- Review massage principles and protocols.
- Learn the difference between shiatsu and reflexology, and how they are used with certain treatments.
- Learn the importance of a complete home care guide and how to choose the best products.

Chapter Outline

Introduction
Client Charting and Consultation
Body Treatments
Spot Treatments
Paraffin
Combination Services, Packages, and Marketing
Body Massage
Shiatsu, Reflexology, and Similar Energy
Home Care

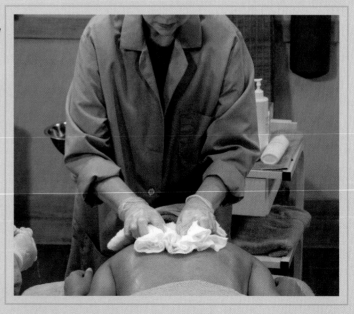

Introduction

We continue on our journey of discovering more about the world of body treatments. The safety and well-being of the client is the number one priority. All treatments begin with the initial client consultation. This is a critical time in your session because it provides an overview of your client's health and assists in reviewing any possible contraindications for treatment. Each treatment provides benefits at different levels in the mind and body. Body treatments are beneficial for everyone, especially those under stress and those seeking some time away from the world to relax and rejuvenate.

Client Charting And Consultation

Body treatments involve the entire body and as a result the potential for health risks may be high. Health concerns are of great importance and should be discussed before the beginning of a treatment. A sample form is provided in this chapter for the client to fill out (Figure 34–1). The health history must be filled out completely and reviewed before starting any treatment. This information assists you in determining whether or not a treatment will be beneficial to the client.

Body Treatments

The three main goals of a body treatment are exfoliation, skin conditioning, and metabolic stimulation. Exfoliation has already been discussed in Chapter 26. The following is a presentation of a number of body treatments, which function primarily to condition the skin or stimulate the metabolism. All body treatments offer some degree of these two benefits. Furthermore, all body treatments are contraindicated for some conditions. These conditions include systemic diseases; known allergies to the ingredients used in the treatment; high or low blood pressure; heat sensitivity; heart problems; diabetes; and vascular problems such as varicose veins. Some treatments are also not appropriate for pregnant

women, because they should avoid excess heat and essential oils. Wraps are not appropriate for clients with claustrophobia. Finally, clients with open cuts or wounds should not receive body treatments such as masks, gommages, salt glows, or anything that uses ingredients that might contaminate the wound.

The time required for skin treatments varies. Usually, a single treatment takes approximately 25 minutes, while a combination of two treatments takes 50 minutes.

Skin Conditioning

Skin conditioning is performed to exfoliate the full body and to hydrate and soften the skin. The products used for skin conditioning are gommage, hyaluronic acid serum, shea butter, and conditioning serum. Some alternatives are to use any other exfoliation for the gommage, to use another hydrating serum or activator, and to do the massage with an aromatherapy oil or emollient lightweight oil, as desired. After the exfoliation, serum, and shea butter are applied, the body is wrapped and the client rests for ten minutes to allow the shea butter to sink in. Then the wrap is removed and the client rests while the remainder of the butter is absorbed, possibly using the rest time for another treatment, such as a manicure.

Remineralizing Seaweed Wrap

The purpose of a remineralizing seaweed wrap is to relax and remineralize the body. The client is first exfoliated (most likely with dry brushing). Essential oils can be applied to the body first or to the seaweed mask. The seaweed used can be from the blue-green, green, or red groups. A warm seaweed mask is applied. Wrap the client and allow the client to rest for ten minutes. A shower or hot towels removes the wrap. A finishing lotion (which can be warmed) is applied and massaged in until absorbed. Afterward, the client rests for few minutes, possibly using this resting time for another service.

Detoxifying Seaweed Wrap

The seaweed wrap is intended to stimulate and detoxify (Figure 34–2, p. 560). It uses heat, so the client should be very warm to

Confidential Health History—Body Treatments

PLEASE PRINT　　　　　　　　　　　　　　　　　Today's Date _____

First Name _____　　Last Name _____　　Date of Birth ____/____/____

Street _____ Apt. # _____　City _____ State _____ Zip _____

Phone: Home ( ) _____ Work ( ) _____ Mobile ( ) _____

Physician/chiropractor _____ Phone ( ) _____

Emergency Contact _____ Phone ( ) _____

Your occupation _____ E-mail: _____

Referred by ❏ Friend ❏ Mailer ❏ Walk-by ❏ Yellow Pages ❏ Gift Certificate ❏ Other _____

Technician's Name _____

---

1. Is this your first body treatment ❏ Yes ❏ No

2. What is the reason for your visit today?
   _____

3. What other body treatments have you had?
   ❏ Massage ❏ Salt glow ❏ Seaweed wrap
   ❏ Moor mud ❏ Body scrub ❏ other _____

4. If yes, was it a good experience?
   _____
   _____

5. Are you presently under a physician's care for any current health problem? ❏ Yes ❏ No

6. What? _____

7. Are you pregnant? ❏ Yes ❏ No
   If yes, how many weeks?
   _____

8. Are you taking birth control? ❏ Yes ❏ No

9. Hormone replacement? ❏ Yes ❏ No If so, what?
   _____

10. Do you wear contact lenses? ❏ Yes ❏ No

11. Do you smoke? ❏ Yes ❏ No

12. What is your stress level? ❏ High ❏ Medium ❏ Low

13. Are you now using or have you ever used Accutane?
    ❏ Yes ❏ No
    If so, when and for how long? _____

14. Do you have any allergies to cosmetics, foods, seaweed, shellfish, or drugs? ❏ Yes ❏ No
    Please list_____

15. Are you presently taking medications – prescribed or over-the-counter, including aspirin?
    ❏ Yes ❏ No
    If so, please list _____
    _____

16. What products do you use presently? ❏ Soap
    ❏ Cleansing milk ❏ Toner ❏ Scrubs ❏ Mask
    ❏ Creams ❏ Sunscreen ❏ Shower gels
    ❏ Body lotions

Please indicate if you are affected by or have any of the following:

Asthma	Hepatitis	Metal bone pins or plates
Broken bones Where?	Herpes	Pacemaker
Cardiac problems	High blood pressure	Phlebitis, blood clots, poor circulation
Eczema	Hysterectomy	Psychological
Epilepsy	Immune disorders	Sinus problems
Fever blisters	Lower back or back problems	Skin diseases What?
Headaches, chronic	Lupus	Urinary or kidney problems

Head and/or neck injury? Where & how long ago?

Figure 34–1 Example of a confidential health history questionnaire.

Please explain above problems or list any other significant health concerns or issues:

_____

_____

_____

_____

Please list areas of the body that are of concern.

_____

_____

_____

_____

_____

_____

If having massage, what type of pressure do you prefer:

❑ Light?   ❑ Medium?   ❑ Deep tissue?

I understand that the services offered are not a substitute for medical care, and any information provided by the therapist is for educational purposes only and not diagnostically prescriptive in nature. I understand that the information herein is to aid the therapist in giving better service and is completely confidential.

SALON POLICIES

1. Professional consultation is required before initial dispensing of products.

2. Our active discount rate is only effective for clients visiting every 4 weeks.

3. We do not give cash refunds.

4. We require a 24-hour cancellation notice.

I fully understand and agree to the above spa policies.

Signed _____   Date _____

Figure 34–1 *(continued)*.

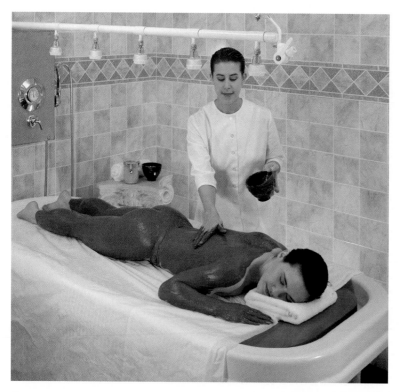

Figure 34–2 A seaweed mask will help to replenish minerals in the skin.

throughout the treatment. Like the other masks, removal is performed using a shower or hot towels and is followed by a finishing lotion and relaxation.

Detoxifying Mud Wrap

This treatment is virtually the same as the remineralizing mud wrap except it uses more heat, like the detoxifying seaweed wrap.

Stabilizing Time

It is a good practice for the client to rest for the same amount of time as for a wrap. This allows the body to regain its equilibrium (fluid balance). Detoxifying treatments are very stimulating and so it is not advisable for the client to rush out immediately. Clients should be offered a glass of water and should be advised to drink plenty of water for the next 24 hours. Also, stabilizing time allows clients to readjust if they are going on to another treatment.

Selling Tips

In the skin conditioning treatment, a gommage exfoliation is performed instead of dry brushing. The treatment is booked for 50 minutes. All seaweed and mud treatments are listed for 25 minutes. When sold in combination with an exfoliation, the service is converted to a 50-minute complete treatment. This option is a more efficient way to make both treatments more effective. It makes better use of time, and the application of the finishing lotion is not duplicated. Some abbreviated treatment combinations are described next.

allow the stimulating activity to cause vasodilation and possibly some sweating. This treatment follows the same basic process as the remineralizing wrap. However, it includes three detoxifying essential oils. The seaweed mask should contain some of the brown group seaweeds. Depending on the products chosen, the degree of metabolic stimulation of the client, and the client's propensity to sweat, oil is not recommended before the mask. Sweating will potentially interfere with the oil. During such wrap treatments, a drink of water and a cool cloth for the forehead can be offered to the client.

Remineralizing Mud Wrap

A remineralizing mud wrap is intended to cleanse and remineralize the skin. After exfoliating with a dry brushing, warmed mud is applied generously and quickly covered with foil so that the client does not get cold. If necessary, the client can have another blanket. Technicians should be extra careful about getting mud on fabrics. Both seaweed and mud can stain, but mud has a higher propensity for staining. The client then rests for 10 to 15 minutes, sipping water periodically

Combined Salt Glow and Detox Seaweed Wrap

This combination exfoliates and stimulates for greater benefits from the detox wrap. The seaweed mixture is prewarmed, and it is unnecessary to apply oil under the seaweed mask. The exfoliation salts are already combined with oil, which leaves an ideal base for either a mud or seaweed treatment.

The salt exfoliation is performed first, and then any residue is dusted off and followed by hot towels. Next, the seaweed wrap is performed. While the client is wrapped, this is a good time for a mini facial, eye treatment, or a scalp treatment. These options should be arranged prior to beginning the wrap. The entire treatment combination then concludes with a finishing lotion. As demonstrated, it is easy to combine the steps of both treatments. You have less duplication of steps and have worked more efficiently and cost-effectively. More money is generated in the same amount of time with less work.

This concept becomes even more attractive when another service, such as a cellulite treatment, is added to the combination. An important key to combinations is to understand what treatments are most appropriately combined for the well-being of clients. Body sessions should be introduced gradually so that clients can tolerate more stimulation in future treatments. Combining too many services may be more harmful than beneficial. Furthermore, the spa menu should have a balance of detoxifying and remineralizing treatments. Many spas do not understand this concept. The balance of both creates a greater selection to meet the needs of customers.

The Herbal Wrap

More popular in resorts and destination spas than day spas, herbal wraps are normally performed in a large room where several people are treated simultaneously. The room is relatively dark. An herbal wrap requires a special water heater called a **hydroculator**. Herbal sheets are infused with an herbal combination and water. They are hung in this device where they are heated to a very high temperature of 185 to 200 degrees Fahrenheit. Thick rubber gloves must be worn to remove the hot sheets from the water. Be aware also that when wet, full linen sheets can weigh up to 40 pounds, so the treatment is a very labor-intensive service for the therapist, especially when performing several treatments in one day.

Herbal wraps are designed to detoxify, invigorate, and relax the client. During the treatment, clients are wrapped in rubber sheets or thick towels, and hot, wet herbal-infused sheets are placed on top. Cool, not cold, cloths can be placed on the client's forehead. The client will stay wrapped for up to 20 minutes. The treatment is concluded with finishing lotion. If a client perspired during the treatment, a quick shower is offered

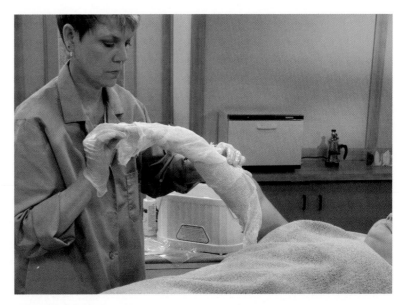

Figure 34–3 A hand and arm paraffin mask is an excellent example of a spot treatment.

before application of the finishing lotion. Clients should stabilize for 20 minutes or proceed to another treatment.

Spot Treatments

Localized treatments are called spot treatments because the treatment is designed for a specific part of the body only, not for the whole body. For example, the most common spot treatments and the ones featured here are for the back, cellulite, hand, arm, and foot (Figure 34–3). Some localized treatments can be combined with full body treatments to enhance the effects of both. Like full body treatments, spot treatments are contraindicated for certain conditions such as infectious acne or open skin lesions. These treatments also take about 25 minutes alone or 50 minutes in combination with another treatment.

hydroculator
A special water heater used in herbal wraps.

Bust Treatments

Some spas also offer bust treatments. However, the law in many states limits this treatment. Some skin care product manufacturers, especially European ones, offer bust treatments, which tone and firm the tissue around the bust area. Because the American market for this service tends to be small due to modesty concerns, the treatment is not readily available here. Most likely, as the industry continues to flourish, more women will become more interested in this treatment.

Back Treatments

back treatment
Refers to two different treatments: back facial, a back deep cleansing performed by an esthetician; back treatment, a specialized or spot treatment to relieve sore muscles in the neck, shoulders, and back performed by a massage therapist.

The term **back treatment** actually refers to two different treatments. A back facial, more appropriately called a back deep cleansing, is performed by an esthetician. The skin is either problematic, having breakouts with pustules or comedones, or would benefit from a general exfoliation treatment to stimulate, soften, and hydrate. On the other hand, a back treatment usually refers to a specialized or spot treatment to relieve sore muscles in the neck, shoulders, and back. The session is performed by a massage therapist and may consist of a hot aromatherapy pack followed by a massage targeted toward this area.

Back Treatment: Deep Cleansing
Back facials deep cleanse and rid the back area of impurities, comedones, pustules, etc. The first step is to steam the back and treat the area with a brush machine. Warmed freshener is used next to remove cleanser residues (Figure 34–4). The next step is exfoliation with deep pore cleanser and then the

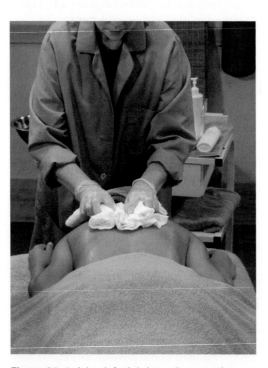

Figure 34–4 A back facial deep cleanses the skin and rids the back area of impurities.

use of galvanic current. After rinsing off the disincrustant solution, which is used for the galvanic current electrode, normal extractions are performed and the area is then cleansed and disinfected. High frequency is applied next for five minutes for additional purifying and disinfection. The next step is a massage with an oily skin moisturizer or very light hydrophilic oil for about 5 to 15 minutes, depending on the length of the treatment. A mud or oily skin mask follows and is left on for 10 to 15 minutes. Hot towels remove the mask, then freshener, light moisturizer, and sunscreen are applied.

Back Treatment: Relaxing
A relaxing back treatment is performed to thoroughly cleanse, soften, and condition skin. It is ideal for occasions when a female client will wear a low cut, backless dress. For men, the treatment is appropriate for when they desire to expose their backs, such as on the beach. This treatment is simpler than the deep cleansing back treatment. No equipment is used, no extractions are performed, and the focus of the treatment is on the massage and conditioning of the back area.

The treatment begins with a deep pore cleanser that is removed with hot towels; warmed toner is applied next. For exfoliation, AHA/BHA is used, and then rinsed off thoroughly. Next is a deep relaxing, destressing massage for about 5 to 10 minutes. A seaweed or mud mask is then applied over gauze (if desired) or directly on the skin. After 5 minutes, it is removed with hot towels and followed by a light moisturizer and sunscreen.

Cellulite

Cellulite is a condition that occurs in women. It is genetically inherited and may occur either in a thin or obese individual. Hormonal changes such as pregnancy or menopause also trigger this condition. Treating cellulite is challenging because it never completely goes away. It becomes increasingly uncomfortable with weight gain, when crossing the legs, or when sitting for long periods of time. In severe cases, adipose cells are so dense that other tissue, blood vessels, and nerves are tightly pressed against the skin, inhibiting proper circulation and sensation. The skin may feel numb to touch, highly sensitive, or even painful. Surgical procedures such as liposuction may help the condition. A new treatment called endermology is also available now. Otherwise, there is no absolute cure for this condition. But spa treatments can alleviate the discomfort and appearance of cellulite.

The general goal of a cellulite treatment is to help stimulate the circulation and metabolism through vasodilation. The body rids itself of the excess fat cells and accumulated water that cause swelling and constriction of the capillary network necessary to flush toxins. It takes several combined treatment modalities to help control and reduce cellulite, including lifestyle modification such as consuming a high-fiber diet, drinking plenty of water, performing active exercises, and receiving body treatments and passive massage. Spa treatments and products alone cannot control this condition. Furthermore, one-time treatment is not sufficient. To really control cellulite, clients will require intensive salon or spa treatments with regular home care follow-up.

In-spa cellulite treatment sessions are scheduled twice a week for a period of four to six weeks. A home care regimen helps to continue the effects of the in-spa series. For example, in order to enhance the in-spa sessions, one product line recommends that the client soak in an essential oil bath blend directed toward cellulite for 20 minutes on alternate days. A special cream is applied after the bath. Promises cannot be made for any treatment. Dedication and consistency, however, may show some improvement.

While most treatments for cellulite belong to the spot treatment group, which focuses on the area between the waist and the knees, a full body detox treatment can also be useful. The combination of the two treatments is beneficial and profitable. Note that cellulite treatments are contraindicated for numerous conditions, including clients who are pre- and post-liposuction.

Cellulite Treatments

Cellulite treatments stimulate, detoxify, and encourage vasodilation. They are directed at cellulite in the thighs, hips, and stomach (if necessary). Note that increased stimulation will cause slight erythema. First, the treatment area is cleansed. A gentle dry brushing or salt scrub can be performed to stimulate circulation. Then

the chosen anticellulite serum, gel, or cream is applied and massaged in well. A detoxifying mask and wrap follows, and the client rests for 10 to 15 minutes. After the wrap is removed with warm (not hot) towels, a soothing lotion or gel is applied. The treatment concludes with the application of firming cream that is massaged in well. Note that in order to receive results, the client must purchase the products and follow the home care regimen.

Combined Cellulite Spot Treatment With Full Body Detox

The combination of cellulite spot treatment and full body detox adds a full body-detoxifying wrap to the cellulite spot treatment just described. The main difference between the localized and full body treatment is the application of the detoxifying wrap to the whole body, followed by specific anticellulite products applied to the areas of cellulite, and finally by a finishing lotion that is applied to the rest of the body.

Hand and Foot Spa Treatments

Hand and foot treatments are offered in many ways. However, the procedure is basically the same whether it is for the hands and arms or the feet and lower legs. The key to making a hand and foot treatment more spa-like or more special than a regular manicure and pedicure is the addition of the therapeutic portion of the procedure.

Spa manicures and pedicures are normally part of the nail department. If performed in the esthetic or massage areas, then the actual nail care (cuticle work and polishing) is omitted. The emphasis changes, particularly in hand treatments, and the session is geared toward antiaging hand treatments. Age spots and extra dry hands are addressed with localized treatments that may include performance agents such as AHA, BHA, or antipigmentation and lightening. Normally, an esthetician rather than a massage therapist performs these.

Another treatment choice for hands and feet is to use special exfoliants such as a salt glow or aromatherapy massage beyond the normal massage usually done with a lotion. Seaweed, mud, or a wrap may be added. Performing any one or combination of these specialized treatments moves regular hand

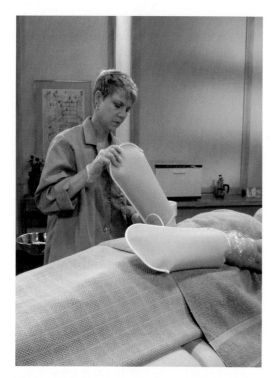

Figure 34–5 Electric mitts can enhance the effectiveness of a hand treatment, taking the place of warm towels.

and foot treatments into an enhanced, spa-like session.

Most hand and foot treatments should be kept to 25 minutes. If these treatments are done in conjunction with the nails, then the length of the treatment changes accordingly. In no case should the treatment exceed 50 minutes, even with nails. Time cannot justify the cost in most markets for anything longer than this.

Full Hand and Arm or Foot And Lower Leg Treatments

This treatment offers luxurious deep conditioning for the hands and feet. It can include age spot treatment and whitening. One contraindication for this type of treatment to keep in mind is fungus or disease of the nails.

First, the hands or feet are washed with body cleanser. An exfoliation with salt glow can follow, if appropriate. Next comes the application of essential oil–infused massage oil and a good massage to the hands, arms, feet, and legs. The massage should last about 8 to15 minutes, depending on the length of the treatment. A warmed mask is applied next and wrapped in foil or plastic. The client should rest for 10 minutes. If doing a mani-

cure or pedicure, it is a good idea to put the mask on one hand or foot, finish prepping the nails, and then do the other hand or foot. The mask is removed with hot towels, and then hand or foot lotion is massaged in well.

Paraffin

For years, manicurists have used paraffin in spas and salons. Hospitals have used it in therapeutic treatment for arthritis pain relief in the fingers and joints. Estheticians have applied paraffin during the mask phase of a facial. During a back treatment, the paraffin can be applied over a mud or seaweed mask. Its properties warm the skin and help infuse ingredients, and it softens and conditions.

Overall, warm paraffin serves as a wonderful mask for the hands, feet, back, or even full body (Figure 34–5). As a localized treatment, paraffin can be molded around the hands and feet by dipping cheesecloth into the liquid paraffin. When available, a heat lamp can be used to keep it warm. In the winter, more layers are applied than in the summer.

Paraffin Treatment

Paraffin treatments produce an occlusive warm mask in order to infuse nutrients such as performance agents and infusion of oils. The skin is rendered soft and moisturized. This procedure is usually done just prior to a normal mask (Figure 34–6).

The first step is to apply nutritional serum concentrate or cream. Then the gauze is dipped in paraffin and applied to the face, hands, feet, or back. For the latter three places, it is then covered with plastic, a liner, or a cloth. The face is just layered with the paraffin-dipped gauze. After it cools, in about 10 minutes, the mask is removed and any residue is cleaned off with hot towels.

Combination Services, Packages, and Marketing

There are innumerable variations and combinations that can be created for upscale body treatments. For the beginner, it may seem confusing at first. As you work with each treatment and feel more comfortable under-

Figure 34–6 Paraffin is an excellent product for softening the skin.

ommend limitations and suggestions. Product knowledge and treatment training is valuable; in fact it is essential for becoming a successful and efficient technician. Experience, combined with education, is the best way to learn.

Treatment Combinations

The following is a brief list of some of the more popular combinations sold as packages. Packages will include facial, hair, and nail treatments as well as a great body treatment. The following body treatments are suggested:

- Hydrotherapy tub and massage, 50 minutes
- Hydrotherapy tub, wrap, and massage, 75 minutes
- Cellulite treatment and full body detox treatment, 50 minutes
- Vichy shower, salt glow, mud wrap, and massage, 50 minutes or 75 minutes (if massage takes 50 minutes)
- Salt glow, wrap, massage, 50 or 75 minutes
- Salt glow, cellulite, and full body detox, 75 minutes (a 25-minute massage can also be added)

Anytime a client is wrapped in a full 50-minute body treatment, the wrap is timed for 20 to 25 minutes and a scalp treatment, mini facial, or an eye treatment can be added. Some practitioners prefer to offer a reflexology treatment during this time. This may not be a good idea because unwrapping the feet may cause the client to become cool and therefore lose some of the effects of the treatment.

standing why and how it is performed, your assessment of what will work for your client becomes easier.

We have demonstrated how easy it is to combine certain types of treatments. As mentioned earlier, you will only combine two or more treatments based on the general good health of the client. The healthier your client, the more services you can combine. If someone has a generally weaker health condition, then do not combine services . Doing less is always better and safer than doing more. Be cautious and combine only a few services at a time until you know how your client reacts.

It is also important to understand that combining two body treatments together is more stimulating than one. If you add a body treatment and a hydrotherapy tub treatment, there is greater stimulation. Client safety always comes first. It is recommended that combined treatments should be done at a gradual pace. However, when well tolerated, they offer more intensive benefits and results.

Performing body treatments can be exciting as well as financially rewarding. Knowing when and how to combine a treatment requires some time and practice in all the basics. Your product suppliers will also rec-

Body Massage

To cover body massage fully is not within the scope of this brief chapter. The study of massage therapy is recommended. Each state establishes what duties can be performed within the scope of an esthetics license. Because esthetics and massage therapy are so closely related, it is probably a good idea to be licensed in both. This will protect you if any future law prohibits estheticians from performing a body treatment.

Although historically an esthetician has more insight with products, masks, treatment serums, and application techniques, there may be limitations when it comes to fully understanding how to perform a correct massage. A body massage is quite different from a facial massage or facial treatment. A full massage requires the use of both hands with greater pressure on a larger surface. Massage therapists, on the other hand, understand the protocols and anatomical features of a body massage, the correct pressure, and what oils to use. Beyond that, however, they normally have little training in product application or spa body treatments such as hydrotherapy, exfoliants, masks, and wraps.

Protocols

It is always important to follow a detailed plan for treatment or procedures. These protocols help to establish a basic blueprint for performing massage treatments.

- Always sanitize hands.
- Hands and products should be as warm as possible for application to the body to avoid chilling the client.
- Most massage techniques in body treatments will include mostly effleurage and perhaps a few petrissage movements. Petrissage and friction are ideal for stimulating cellulite areas.
- Develop a regular and consistent pattern to use for massage, body treatment, and product application. For example, if you usually start on the left leg in massage and go to the right leg, then you would perform the same in a body treatment. Consistency eliminates the chance that you will have to stop and think about your movements. Technique and regularity should become second nature. This prevents mistakes from happening, i.e., forgetting to massage a particular body area. The client will feel confident and relaxed when your work is thorough and caring.
- Although both hands are used simultaneously for massage movements, only one hand is employed to apply the mask or wrap. The free hand stays clean and is used to wrap up the client in the sheets, blankets, etc. Getting used to using two hands for massage and one hand for certain product application requires some concentration.

Purpose of Massage

Massage is all about the natural benefits of touch. Physiological and psychological benefits can either positively or negatively impact a person. Your touch in treatments will either extend a great sense of well-being if performed well, or a sense of alarm if not. A firm, professional touch during a body treatment establishes a confident relationship with your client. Massage in general provides tremendous physiological as well as psychological benefits, including

- relaxing the client
- improving all natural body functions through increased blood circulation and increased metabolic rate
- increasing nutrition and oxygen to the organs and tissues of the body
- helping to relieve stiffness, soreness, and tenseness in muscles and skin
- giving the client a sense of well-being and energizing the client after the massage

Massage Movements

Just as for the face, Swedish massage has the same five classical movements for use on the body. In addition, with more training, there are numerous other beneficial modalities. To review, Swedish massage movements include the following:

- Effleurage: This gentle but firm stroking and sliding over the body is used for relaxation, application of product, and a general sense of well-being.
- Friction: This deeper, faster effleurage is designed to increase blood circulation. This movement is used to stimulate circulation in cellulite treatments
- Petrissage: This more aggressive kneading activates muscle fiber and stimulates its activities. It is also useful in cellulite and areas of stress or tension.
- Percussion or tapotement: *Tapotement* is the term we use for gentle piano or finger tapping movements on the face. In body massage, cupping, hacking, and slapping the skin helps to activate nerve endings and stimulate sensory nerve centers in the skin. Caution must be taken when doing hacking, slapping, etc., to maintain the comfort level of the client. If it begins to hurt, the muscles will tense up and the

goal will be lost.

- Vibration: Vibration deeply activates nerve and muscular tissue. The actual vibration must emanate from the shoulders not just the hands. It requires practice and effort on the part of the therapist. The addition of various electric vibrators is more effective and less stressful on the technician.

Client Positioning

Depending on your massage or body treatment training, a pattern of repeatable steps should be developed. It is better to maintain a consistent order of application or massage steps for every treatment. The only real difference is when the application of mud or seaweed or another mask changes your typical pattern. For example, you may usually start massage on the backside (client face down) and then move to the front. For safety reasons, body treatments with wraps should be performed with the client face up. Once you develop the specific order of the wrap treatment or the massage, be consistent for every treatment.

Depending on the preference of the massage therapist, as well as the appropriateness for the client, the massage is either started with the client face down or face up. Some people believe that when the massage is started with the client face down, and initial strokes are on the back, the client relaxes more readily. Conversely, others believe that if you begin with the client face up, a position that people tend to feel uncomfortable or vulnerable in, and you can get the client to relax, then the client will really move into deep relaxation and sleep once face down when the massage is performed on back. In either case, when the client feels comfortable with your professionalism and confidence, how you begin probably does not make much difference to the client. Intuitively, you should know whether your client is comfortable or not and change your routine accordingly.

Typical Order of Massage

When facing the client begin to *your* left:

1. Left foot, leg (actually the client's right foot/leg)
2. Left hand, arm
3. Chest, stomach
4. Right hand, arm

5. Right foot, leg. Turn client over.
6. Repeat, this time with the right foot, leg.
7. Right hand, arm
8. Back, buttocks
9. Left hand, arm
10. Left foot, leg

The actual order begins with the client's right foot/leg. Because you are facing the client (mirror image), you begin on *your* left side. Some people begin on the backside and do the back, buttocks, foot, arms, and legs in a clockwise or counterclockwise fashion and then turn the client over to the front side. Whatever you feel is most natural and comfortable for you to do is fine. Consistency and not forgetting to do an arm here or a leg there is the key.

Terminology/Legality

In some states the esthetician is legally permitted to do body treatments, providing the word *massage* is not used. There may be very specific issues related to what and how estheticians versus massage therapists can practice. It is up to you to know your laws, regulations, zoning ordinances, etc. Contact your State Board of Cosmetology or State Health Department. Some states have mixed regulations depending on the city, county, or state. You must be responsible and investigate these issues so that you completely understand them. Ignorance of the law is no excuse. Any and all references to massage and body treatments in this book are made without qualification as to your individual ability to legally perform these services. Furthermore, this section on massage is not designed to replace a proper course in body massage. It provides introductory, educational information only.

SAFETY *Tip*

While most of us need far more massage than we usually receive, there are some instances when massage or body treatment is not recommended:
- systemic disease or immunodeficiency issues
- clients undergoing chemotherapy for disease
- vascular (varicose veins) problems, pregnancy, diabetics (prone to bruising), open lesions, inflammations of any kind, areas of swelling, infection, lumps or bumps
- any health condition that is questionable

Shiatsu, Reflexology, And Similar Energy

Again it is impossible to address the entire subject of other modalities of massage in the scope of this chapter. Each subject could and should be a chapter or book on its own. But as we discussed in Chapter 27, Holistic/Alternative Skin Care, it is important to offer a variety of massage treatments to your clients. There is tremendous interest in energy work. There are many different forms of massage based on variations of the same energy system within the human body. Ayurvedic massage and treatments, for example, trace back over 5,000 years to a philosophy and universe concept that the body is divided into certain zones called chakras. Energy emanates from these zones. Shiatsu and reflexology, on the other hand, have their origins in China with the energy pathway system we call the meridian system. This invisible, but definitely measurable, system is much like the wind . . . you cannot see it exactly but you can see the result of the wind. You know it is there and you may hear the breeze blowing, but the actual wind is not visible to the naked eye. In the same way, the body has, depending on the school of thought you were trained in, 10 or 12 vertical energy pathways that flow from the top of the head to different spots on the bottom of the feet. Along these pathways are located motor points, acupressure points, or acupoints that are the nerve center triggers related to the muscles, nerves, organs, and tissues in the body. This is why, for example, in reflexology you will see diagrams of the bottom of the feet with corresponding organs in the human body depicted (Figure 34–7).

There is believed to be a direct connection between these points located along a specific meridian or pathway that directly relates to the organ systems along that pathway. There is also believed to be an intersecting horizontal system of pathways, some of which are vertical meridians. The meridians themselves correspond to the electrical energy field in the body. They have a direct involvement in the proper functioning of the whole body.

It is important for you to realize that these meridians are thought to flow right next to the blood and lymph system. They function as a separate electrical system that can be triggered through the motor points to relieve stress and fatigue, and to invigorate the body. When performed by a medically trained person, reflexology can alleviate disease and disorder in the body. While we are not allowed to practice medicine or relieve any true body disorder, our goal with energy treatments is primarily that of relieving tension in the body. This result alone relates quite closely to the improvement of disease and disorder. It is known that when pressure is applied to motor points, the body produces a natural analgesic effect through the release of endorphins (endogenous morphine), the body's own natural pain killers.

We know some of these things intuitively and by experience. Western medicine is just now researching the benefits of these complementary or integrative modalities for the health and wellness of the human body. Even acupuncture, believed and proven for thousands of years in Asia, is only now slowly achieving equal status in Western medicine. Our point here is not so much to discuss energy work, shiatsu, or reflexology from a medical standpoint, but rather, our focus is to perform treatments in the spa for the following reasons:

- relaxation
- relieve physical fatigue
- relieve mental fatigue
- stimulate circulation and metabolism
- relieve stress
- relieve pain or discomfort through relaxation
- increase overall well-being
- energize and invigorate the body

What is Shiatsu?

Shiatsu comes from the Japanese (shi means finger and atsu means pressure or finger pressure therapy). It obviously gained popularity in Japan even though the actual meridian system concept is Chinese. The motor points of nerves and muscles are pressed much in the same way as in acupuncture but with pressure by the fingers, palms, or balls of the hands to activate energy to the motor point. Shiatsu can be performed on the face or body as a complete face or body treatment, or a few points can be added to relieve stress when doing a regular massage. In body treatments, with training, it is good to offer a 50-minute shiatsu treatment, which would

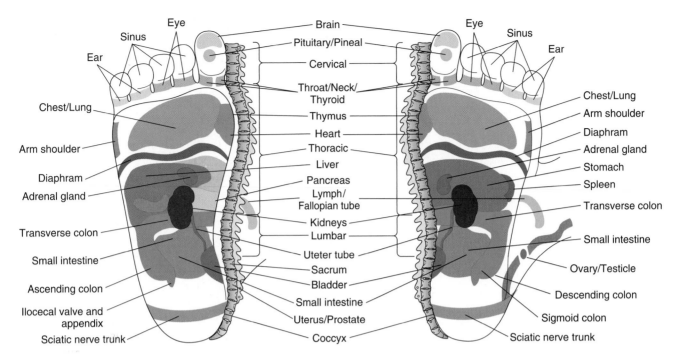

Figure 34–7 This diagram covers all the pressure points on the soles of both feet. It is particularly helpful to see how the entire body interconnects.

include an opening effleurage and shiatsu pressure points on all major parts of the body (Figure 34–8a, 34–8b, p. 570).

We might end with shiatsu or repeat the effleurage, do a little rocking of the body areas under the towel, etc. Effleurage before the shiatsu is actually not totally Japanese, but a nice addition. The Japanese typically do only the motor points.

The key to a successful shiatsu treatment lies in the smoothness and evenness of the pressure and the relief of stress without causing pain. Some practitioners believe that putting tremendous pressure on a stressed motor point is the correct way to relieve pain, tension, etc. This is actually incorrect but it is difficult to fully understand the concept of comfortable discomfort. There should be enough pressure applied for a sufficient amount of time to relieve tension in a muscle, for example. However, if it is truly painful, the muscle will tense up, not relax. If you have ever had a shiatsu treatment where you felt certain places were excruciatingly painful when pressure was applied, this was most likely a poor treatment. Slight discomfort in a comfortable way is permissible; actual deep pain is counterproductive.

Another typical misunderstanding about shiatsu is the concept that all pressure comes

from the tips of the fingers. This is erroneous. The pressure exerted on the client's body actually should come from the weight and movement of the technician's body moving into the motor point, not just heavy fingertip pressure. In fact, this method of applying pressure only with the power of the fingertips is often the reason for the beginning of carpal tunnel syndrome. This problem can prevent the technician from continuing practice. The less pressure from the fingertips themselves, and the more pressure that emanates from the body, the better the treat-

---

SAFETY*Tip*

There are many different situations and reasons why shiatsu and reflexology can or cannot be used as massage modalities in the salon or spa. Therefore, depending on the situation, the contraindications may change. But as a general rule, some of the most commonly known contraindications are:

- areas of swelling, lumps, or bumps
- known systemic disease or immunodeficiencies
- diabetes or other blood disorders due to bruising from the pressure
- pregnancy (stimulation of the abdomen and certain areas around the ankle have been known to cause early contractions)
- inflammation, infection, or open wounds
- vascular problems, varicose veins, phlebitis, couperose, etc

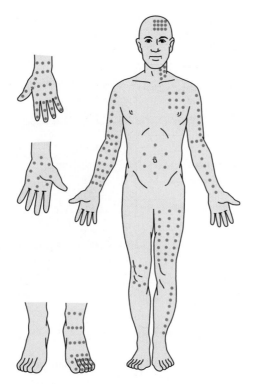

Figure 34–8a Body shiatsu for the front, noting pressure points.

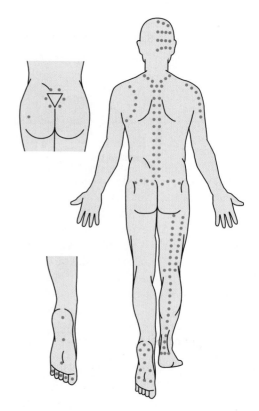

Figure 34–8b Back, noting pressure points.

ment results for the client and the safer for the technician.

Shiatsu is actually a completely natural therapy, even when performing a facial or a body treatment. You are probably naturally doing shiatsu to certain parts of the body. For example, if it is your habit to massage and press the temples in a facial massage, you are doing shiatsu. If you rub and put pressure between the joints of the fingers, you are doing shiatsu. And from a strictly human standpoint, if you bump your elbow and hit your "funny bone" you may have instinctively put pressure on it—that is shiatsu!

With some training, you will have a world of opportunities open to you to add shiatsu to what you already offer in your salon or spa. To learn a little shiatsu for wellness treatments can be done in short courses of a few days to a week, but to learn more from the healing side takes months and years.

What Is Reflexology?

Reflexology is also based on the Chinese meridian system. The concentration and focus of the treatment is strictly on the feet and hands. The term reflexology was coined by a medical assistant in Florida named Eunice

Ingham in the 1930s. She was working for a physician named Joe Shelby Riley who was a student of the concept of zone therapy and the study of reflex action from the brain to the spinal cord and extremities. Eunice realized that there was a direct corollary (effect) from all the Chinese meridians to reflex action and the souls of the feet. She wrote a book called *Stories the Feet Can Tell* with the interesting fact that her beginning reflexology theories were developed strictly for the feet as the ending of the entire meridian system. She believed that many, if not most, disorders would show up by stress and crystallizations in the feet. By placing pressure on specific points of the feet, the disorder could be alleviated, the beginning of reflexology today.

Shiatsu entered from Japan and both involve the same energy system. Depending on the training system you take, there is much more minute concentration on very specific parts of the feet and hands. The pressure taught is often generally quite painful. There are many schools of thought regarding the degree of pain and pressure. Again it may be better to realize that more treatment with comfortable uncomfortable pressure is better than causing pain and tenseness. Also, many reflexology practitioners have problems with carpal tunnel syndrome. It is imperative to be careful and take care of your hands to avoid this syndrome, which could easily end your career.

Home Care

A well-planned home care regimen for the client is just as important for body treatments as they are for facial programs. The proper home care products, coupled with detailed instructions for the client, can seriously impact the program. The principles behind selling home care products are the same for the body as they are for face. Many massage therapists and estheticians do not focus on selling body products for good home care follow-up to the salon or spa. One reason for this oversight to follow-up is a general lack of training in schools. Massage therapists often believe they are in a more healing profession. Retailing body products might not correspond with that belief. This viewpoint can actually be a disservice to the client who has come to a therapist for relaxation and education on how to continue treatment results at home.

For estheticians, the typical problem is that they are so busy educating clients about the proper things to use at home on the face, that it is often difficult to get beyond that to consider body needs. Yet selling body products is, in many ways, much easier than selling those for the face because they are easy to understand. For example, body lotion is easy to sell because everyone understands body lotion as a moisturizer and skin conditioner.

Another concern for the professional is the feeling, consciously or subconsciously, that all body products are alike. But this is not the case. Body products have the same differences in quality as any other product. When well formulated, professional body products can have as visible results as facial products.

There are certain body products that clients are all using—soap, body lotion, hand lotion, bath salts, etc.—whether they buy them from the spa or somewhere else. While technicians may forget to simply ask the client to try the spa's version, in most cases, these are better quality, perhaps more active, and maybe even more concentrated. We can save clients money and improve the skin easily by prescribing the right products!

Remember, selling body products is not about peddling. It is about educating and assisting clients in choosing the right products for home care as a follow-up to spa treatments. It is a technician's responsibility to recommend the best product. This practice increases the effectiveness of treatments and the credibility and professionalism of technicians, and it solidifies an ongoing long-term relationship of trust and improvement.

Product Recommendations

It is important to know the main body products and their benefits in order to discuss them with clients. Estheticians must know the generic characteristics of the products as well as the specifics of the product lines that the spa or salon sells.

The first category of body products is professionally designed soap. This type of product cleanses without overt alkalinity or detergents that dry the skin. Professional soaps contain emollients to condition or protect skin and have a lower pH than most grocery store soaps.

The next group is shower gel or foam bath, which is liquid bath soap for use with a sponge or puff so that it lasts longer than bar soap. Often, shower gel has nutrients to soften and condition while cleaning and may contain beneficial essential oils and fragrances to improve the ambiance of the bath experience.

Body lotions and creams are another category of body products. They soften and condition the skin. Their concentrated format allows them to moisturize effectively. While lotions quickly absorb and should be used for normal skin, creams are more emollient for drier skins.

Similarly, hand and foot lotions are specifically formulated to protect the hands or feet. Often, sunscreens are included in hand creams to protect the hands from ultraviolet light penetration and age spots; foot creams often contain antibacterial agents for foot problems. Hand lotions are designed to soften longer, and foot lotions absorb quickly and without greasiness.

Bath additives such as salts, bath rice, and bath oil condition without harsh detergents. They can cleanse, soften, moisturize, and relax. They are often made with aromatherapy for therapeutic benefits with water. These bath additives are highly relaxing or

SKILLS FOR SUCCESS

Recommending Products

It used to be that most skin care product purchases occurred at the department store cosmetic counter. That is changing. As products become increasingly more sophisticated and scientific in nature, more consumers are turning to the professional esthetician for advice.

For estheticians just starting out in the field, the idea of suggesting products can be intimidating. With new buzzwords such as *biotechnology, cosmeceuticals, antioxidants,* and *liposomes* you may be feeling like you need a degree in chemistry to keep up with the technological advancements. Explaining these processes to clients can raise the anxiety level even higher. Before pushing the panic button, stop and ask yourself three key questions:

1. What is the basic philosophy of the product line?

2. What does my customer value?

3. Are the two in synch?

Before you can build a client's trust in a product line you must first believe in it yourself. Most reputable cosmetic manufacturers are more than eager to let you know where they stand in terms of philosophy. Waiving banners of "no chemicals," "no preservatives," "all natural," and "no animal testing," they spend billions of dollars targeting, or even creating, a certain desirable consumer profile.

As you gain knowledge about different product lines you will begin to develop your own value system and understand what you can stand behind. Blending your value system with what your clients want is the key to building confidence in your recommendations. To get you started consider how you feel about the following:

state of the art ingredients

sophisticated processing such as biotechnology

medical- or pharmaceutical-grade ingredients

natural ingredients

purity of raw materials

preservatives

clinical trials

proven results

safety

allergy testing

price

fancy packaging

a product line that is sold only through professionals

Once you have decided where you stand on these issues, rate them in importance to your client's needs and wants.

If you have ever purchased a product that was packaged beautifully and pitched perfectly but didn't work, you may still be concerned about whether or not you have enough information. Here is where you must learn to rely on the credibility of the vendor. You should become familiar with every aspect of the company's efforts. Find out how long the company has been in business and who uses their products. Understand how their product is manufactured, the quality of the raw materials that are used to produce the product and what active ingredients make it effective. Keep in mind that it is the vendor's responsibility to provide you with as much education as possible to understand how their product is made and how it works. This means a commitment to whatever seminars, workshops, and support systems are necessary to answer all your questions. Once you have an understanding of how a product line works, you can begin to educate the consumer.

Manufacturers that supply additional client literature, such as brochures and posters, display units, testers, and samples are invested in helping you do your job well. Finding companies that are committed to your growth as a professional will alleviate some of the stress that you may feel starting out and help you feel confident in your recommendations.

detoxifying in conjunction with professional treatments, and they can enhance the effects of professional treatment goals.

Some body products are created with very specific target areas and results. Cellulite creams and serums are highly active products that facilitate the effectiveness of cellulite reduction treatments and stimulate the metabolism to help eliminate cellulite. They also have a diuretic effect by stimulating the metabolism to reduce water retention problems. Bust creams and serums tone and firm skin and underlying tissues by the acceleration of cell renewal. They also smooth and improve the texture of the skin. Massage oils are used during massage to soften and smooth skin, hydrate, and stimulate aromatherapeutic effects.

Finally, body powders and fragrances are a group of body products that have more concentrated therapeutic value than over-the- counter equivalents. These products offer excellent but subtle fragrance that lasts longer. These products also provide aromatherapeutic effects physiologically as well as psychologically.

Summary

This chapter has described body treatments in depth. It has provided the basics of equipment and procedures. There are numerous body exfoliation treatments including the most popular and economical salt glow. The gommage is a great dry room exfoliation because it requires *very little water*. The skin is rendered extra soft. It does cost more per treatment due to the amount of product being used. The body scrub or polish using natural grains or polyethylene beads works much like the salt glow. One has the option of choosing which is most appropriate for each treatment. There are various purposes, techniques, and protocols for each treatment. It is highly recommended that you follow each step precisely, deviating only when necessary for individual customizing. Consistency is important when you are performing so many steps and applying products. Following protocols helps you avoid missing procedure steps and also keeps you on time.

Consumer and staff education is the launchpad for successfully selling product and services. Because the therapeutic benefits of body treatments are still at the fore- front of consumer education, you, the practitioner and business owner, are in the driver's seat for promoting them. You have a tremendous opportunity to create deep inroads into the health and well-being of your client.

The more time and effort you put into learning about hydrotherapy and spa treatments, the more guaranteed your success. This is but one chapter in a field that is growing at breakneck speed. It is strongly recommended that you continue to read, research, and attend classes. There are numerous concepts to understand and it is up to you to choose the ones that serve your practice and your customers to the maximum. The field is just beginning to explode and it is fascinating to be involved with helping the future of America stay well longer and better!

Discussion Questions

1. In general, how are algaes, muds, and aromatherapy used in body treatments? What other common agents or performance products are used to condition the skin in body treatments?

2. What is a hydroculator? How is it used in herbal wrap treatments?

3. Collect menus from several spas and salons. Look at the types of body treatments offered. What names are used to describe them? Are these consistent? How can you educate clients who may be confused about the purpose of body treatments?

4. What is the purpose of body massage? Explain the use of massage within the scope of the esthetician's practice. Research boundaries and restrictions as they apply to estheticians conducting body treatments as mandated by your state's licensing board.

Helpful Web Sites

http://www.abmp.com (Associated Bodywork & Massage Professionals)
http://www.dayspaassociation.com (Day Spa Association)
Available: http://www.worldspas.com (Spa Management Journal)
www.naha.org (National Association for Holistic Aromatherapy)

Advanced Clinical Skin Care

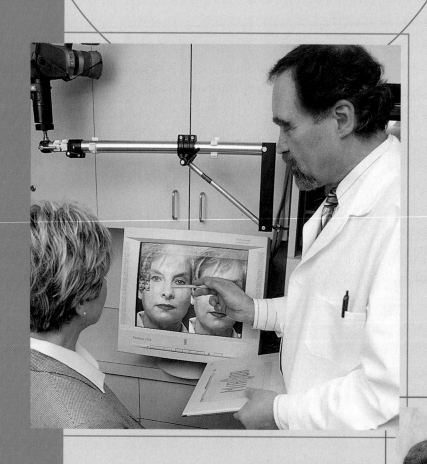

PART XI

Part Outline

Chapter 35   Career Opportunities in Medical Esthetics

Chapter 36   Plastic and Reconstructive Surgery

Chapter 37   Patient Profiles

Chapter 38   Pre- and Postoperative Care

Chapter 39   Camouflage Therapy

Thanks to the many advances in skin care treatment over the past five years, a new area of involvement for estheticians is in the medical arena. Physicians have recognized the need for and the benefit of having a trained medical esthetician as part of their treatment teams. Consequently, more physicians are opening their doors to estheticians, enhancing their practices by offering patients expanded services to complement their medical treatment.

Practicing in the medical field is exciting, but it creates more liability. In Part XI, you will learn about the career opportunities open to the trained esthetician, whether it be plastic surgery or postoperative care, and the risks involved. Information about protocols, advanced treatments, surgical procedures, medical documentation, and when to defer to the physician is included. In addition, you will learn about other responsibilities such as patient education, product knowledge, contraindications, and patient selection, as well as what results are expected for each treatment and procedure.

Part XI concludes with the importance of continuing your education as you embark on your career as an esthetician, along with tips for how to do that.

Chapter 35
Career Opportunities In Medical Esthetics

Chapter Objectives

After reading this chapter you should be able to:

- Describe the role of the esthetician in a medical setting.
- List career opportunities available in the medical skin care community.
- Describe protocols for working in the medical environment.

Chapter Outline

Introduction
Joining a Medical Team
Esthetician as a Resource

Introduction

If your career path includes working with a physician, it may prove to be a most rewarding challenge. This chapter provides an overview of advanced treatments, surgical procedures, and expectations for working in a clinical environment. As a student, we recommend that you spend your first few months mastering hands-on treatments in basic facials as well as learning to recognize skin types, disorders, and diseases. Additionally, you are encouraged to study cosmetic chemistry, conduct simple client education, be proficient in makeup and camouflage techniques, and learn basic business skills. Prior to working in a medical facility, it is advisable to be proficient in these fundamentals. They provide you with a solid foundation from which to develop and add more advanced treatments to your repertoire. After graduation, consider working with a mentor or senior esthetician in a salon, spa, or clinical skin care setting. Choose a facility that encourages routine in-service education and documented ongoing clinical training to employees.

Joining a Medical Team

Recent trends and the changing health care system are forcing many physicians to re-examine how to increase business. A beneficial way to expand business is to include **medical esthetics,** which creates a full-service environment. Medical esthetics means to integrate surgical procedures and esthetic treatments, supporting the demand for long-term age-management programs. This setting creates a full-service environment for the physician and offers in addition to surgical procedures and esthetic treatments, an ancillary profit center by offering professional clinical retail products for the face and body. They allow the physician to concentrate on surgical work while the esthetician assists in esthetic treatments. A diverse, well-trained staff offers greater control over surgical results. They closely monitor patient recovery and maintenance (Figure 35–1).

A medical team can include physician(s), physician's assistant (PA), nurses (RN, RNBS), nurse practitioner (ARNP), and LPN

Figure 35–1 The esthetician in a medical setting.

or LVN (licensed vocational nurses in some states), certified medical assistants (CMA), licensed estheticians (LE), physical therapists (PT), massage therapists (LMT), and other specialists.

Estheticians in a Medical Setting

Career opportunities for estheticians are available in many different medical settings. Some examples are listed below:

  physician's office (cosmetic surgery and dermatology)

  outpatient clinic

  hospital

  independent clinic

  laser centers

  cosmetic dentistry

  medical spa (physician directed)

Diverse Clinical Environments
Each individual setting determines the responsibilities of your position. Prior to any employment or referral program with a physician, spend time outlining and defining your relationship and tasks. Employment or affiliation may be a new venture for the physician. You may be taking a lead in educating by organizing pre- and postcare beyond current protocols. In the past, medical professionals were not familiar with the training an esthetician receives or the esthetician's potential role within their environment.

> **medical esthetics**
> Integration of surgical procedures and esthetic treatments, supporting demands for long-term age-management programs.

Physician's Office

Cosmetic Surgery

The esthetician's role in a cosmetic surgeon's office may be more entrepreneurial when compared with other settings. You may be responsible for an entire **ancillary profit center** (a separate department within the medical office that generates a profit). In addition to managing a retail center (Figure 35–2), performing routine and pre- and post-operative treatments, patient education, and camouflage therapy, you may be involved in, or responsible for, marketing. This is an ideal location for an esthetician with business savvy, or one who is a natural leader or teacher, and who is adaptive.

Dermatology

In a dermatology office, the focus of the esthetician may be more analytical. For example, you may assist in research and clinical studies as many dermatologists conduct clinical trials. You might be working in tandem with the physician by cleansing or prepping the patient for an advanced peel that the physician administers (Figure 35–3). In addition, your responsibilities may include performing routine facials, extractions, and microdermabrasion. You may also be responsible for ordering supplies.

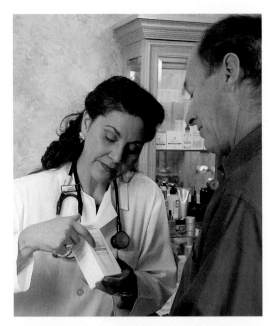

Figure 35–3 The dermatologist instructs the patient in home care and product use.

Outpatient Clinic

An esthetician working in an outpatient surgery center has responsibilities in the realm of pre- and postoperative care. The esthetician may assume the role of patient educator by establishing home care and product protocols. Responsibilities include ensuring that the patient follows home care instructions as well as complies with appointments for presurgery facials. You will most likely apply camouflage therapy and direct the patient's in-home application procedures. The position may also include responsibility for full management of the profit center.

Hospital

While new, the esthetician's role in the hospital may prove to be highly diversified, particularly if you are working in a teaching hospital. You may be involved as an assistant in research and development for clinical studies. You may provide pre- and postoperative care as a team member. There may be specific tasks that are performed independently such as peels, facials, microdermabrasion, or performing laser hair reduction treatments. Some estheticians have assumed positions in directing ancillary profit centers such as in an on-site medical spa.

Independent Clinic

This type of setting may be located near a hospital or medical facility (Figure 35–4). It caters

Figure 35–2 The retail area in a clinic.

ancillary profit center
A separate department within the medical office, such as a retail product area, generates a profit.

to patients from physician referrals. One would need advanced knowledge of medical procedures, protocols, major malpractice and liability insurance, and business acuity. Working in an independent clinic requires strong networking within the medical community. The role of the esthetician in this environment could be all encompassing and range from administrator to practitioner.

Laser Centers

Laser centers may include laser hair reduction, spider vein removal (vascular lesions), **nonablative** wrinkle treatment (bypasses the epidermis to stimulate collagen in the dermis for wrinkle reduction), and laser eye care. Specialized clinical settings of this nature offer numerous opportunities for estheticians. One focus could be taking on the role of a laser technician who is supervised by a physician, or other authorized medical personnel.

Cosmetic Dentistry

Cosmetic dentistry is a field wide open for the interested esthetician to pursue. In this setting, the esthetician may be hired to create an ancillary profit center by setting up a retail area. This may include skin care treatments, color theory, makeup, whitening toothpaste, and other dental products.

Medi-Spa

Some hospitals, medical clinics, and private physicians are setting up medi-spas to address the demands of stress and age management for their patients. A medical spa is an environment where a patient may receive spa services and surgical procedures in a medical setting (Figure 35–5). For example, in one visit a patient could receive a facial, a body treatment, a **collagen injection** (a filler, usually bovine [cow] derivative, to fill in wrinkles or make lips larger), and a presurgical consultation given by the doctor. The esthetician's role could include managing a retail center, performing pre- and postoperative treatments, assisting in protocols, and providing routine skin care.

Esthetician as a Resource

The esthetician acting as a resource is responsible for referring patients and clients to other colleagues. In this role, you will build

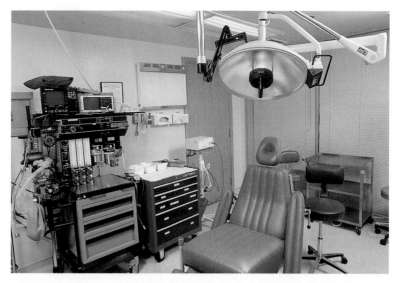

Figure 35–4 Estheticians can also work independently in a clinic located near a physician's office.

strong alliances with health care professionals, other estheticians, massage therapists, teachers, business professionals, the media, and charity organizations. As a resource person, you are greatly rewarded both in referrals, and the closer connection to your community. Recognize that a client or patient has many needs. Some clients have needs that you are not qualified to treat. Clinicians may hesitate to refer for fear that they will lose a client to another practitioner. You may be skillful in certain procedures and not so in others. It is important that you know your own strengths and limitations. Keep in mind that other professionals may, in turn, send referrals to you.

nonablative
A wrinkle treatment that bypasses the epidermis to stimulate collagen in the dermis for wrinkle reduction.

collagen injection
A filler, usually bovine (cow) derivative, to fill in wrinkles or make lips larger.

Figure 35–5 Medi-spas address the demands of stress and age management for patients.

Writing Your Resume

As you begin the final phase of your esthetic training you are probably thinking about finding employment. Looking for a job can be stressful. However, many schools offer career counseling and job placement services. Take time to access these services before you begin the job search. This will help you to set goals and develop a plan of action.

Once you have defined the kind of setting you would like to work in, you can begin to think about developing a professional resume.

However, if you are like most novices starting out in a new career, chances are the task of writing a resume is intimidating. Before you push the panic button, consider the basic rules of marketing. Your first goal will be to define your market, that is who needs or wants your services. Once you have an understanding of this you can determine what services you are able to provide. Presenting this information in a way that meets the needs and wants of the consumer—in this case a prospective employer is the key to a successful resume.

Much of what you already know about selling products and services can be applied to marketing or presenting yourself. Try to think about writing your resume as if you are developing an individual brochure or menu of services. How will you describe your mission or objective, what you have to offer, and qualifications for meeting these goals?

The first step in forming a good resume is getting organized. The most important tool you will need is a computer. This will save you time, money, and effort. If you are computer illiterate or do not have access to one, consider getting help in this area. Libraries and print or copy shops can be helpful resources. You will also want to have a handsome supply of paper and envelopes. A dictionary or thesaurus will come in handy too.

Now you are ready to think about the content of your resume. Begin by making a list of all of your accomplishment and skills. These can be broken down to into several categories including:

- practical knowledge
- people skills
- administrative capabilities
- management or sales skills

When you are clear about your qualifications you can begin to weave these into a structure. Typically, resumes incorporate the following information:

- name, street address, telephone number, and e-mail address
- your career objective
- a brief summary of your professional qualifications
- a history of your experience
- awards or achievements
- personal data such as special interests or hobbies

These are many books available that offer useful tips on formatting and style. Using a resume guide may be helpful in defining these categories and finding the personal style that works best for you. You may also want to tailor your resume or develop several formats to meet particular job requirements. However, it is important to note that any resume should be brief, yet concise, easy to read, neat, grammatically correct and error free. It is of course, always wise to be honest in your representation of yourself and include only that information which is relevant to your current search.

Writing a resume is an important part of your job search; however, you will also need to develop an employment search strategy. Take time to plan how you will access job information, keep track of your contacts, and follow-up. A simple chart that lists the contacts you have made, the date of call or mailing, and a brief summary of your results, will help you to stay organized and keep from being overwhelmed.

Table 35.1 Career Options in Medical Esthetics

Setting	Compensation	Tasks and Duties
	Most offices will have medical benefits and compensation that vary according to the individual office.	Duties will vary depending on needs of individual office
Cosmetic physician	$12 to $30 hourly Plus 15% to 30% commission on product sales and treatments	• Manage retail center/sales, buying and ordering • Pre- and postop care • Patient education • Routine skin care/facials, microdermabrasion, peels • Camouflage therapy • Laser hair reduction
Dermatologist	$12 to $25 hourly	• Routine skin care/facials, peels, microdermabrasion, extractions
Outpatient clinic	$15 to $25 hourly Plus 15% to 50% commission on product sales and treatments	• Manage retail center/sales, buying, ordering • Routine skin care/facials, microdermabrasion, peels • Pre- and postop treatments • Patient education • Camouflage therapy • Laser hair reduction
Hospital	$15–$25 hourly	• Routine skin care/facials, peels, microdermabrasion • Pre- and postop treatments • Patient education • Laser hair reduction • Research
Independent clinic	$15 to $50 hourly Plus commission on product sales and treatments	• Clinic administration • Training • Manage retail center/sales, buying • Routine skin care treatments/facials, microdermabrasion, peels
Laser centers—physician or registered nurse directed	$12 to $20 hourly	• Administer laser therapy: Hair; vascular-spider veins; intense pulsed light (light therapy for wrinkles and pigment) • Client/patient education
Cosmetic dentist	$12 to $15 hourly Plus 15% to 25% commission on product sales	• Product sales • Manage retail center • Routine skin care/facials, peels extractions
Medical spa (physician directed)	$20 to $30 hourly	• Manage retail center • Routine skin care, facials, peels, microdermabrasion • Lasers • Endermology (machine massage for cellulite)

Summary

A career in medical esthetics can be an enriching and rewarding choice, with a wide range of opportunities from which to choose. While the reasons for choosing a career in medical esthetics may differ for each person, the one common ideal is the ability to work with people who may be ill or in pain. There may be much for you to learn, but working in a medical setting can be exciting and rewarding in ways that are not possible in other areas of skin care.

Discussion Questions

1. Team up with several classmates to investigate career opportunities in advanced clinical skin care. Conduct an information interview for each of the careers listed in this chapter. Be prepared to share information. Are your findings consistent with the duties and responsibilities outlined here? What new information did you discover?

Additional Reading

Crawford, J. 2001. "The Potential of Medi-Spas." *Skin Inc.* Carol Stream, Ill.: Allured Publishing Corp., Inc. 13(5), 36–38.

Romano, J. 2001. "State of the Industry in Medical Esthetics." *Skin Inc.* Carol Stream, Ill.: Allured Publishing Corp., Inc. 13(5), 36–38.

Chapter 36
Plastic And Reconstructive Surgery

Chapter Objectives

After reading this chapter, you should be able to:

- Identify the two types of plastic surgery and how they differ.
- Describe the different specialties in plastic surgery.
- Identify the most common plastic surgery procedures for the body and face.
- Describe the benefits of laser surgery and when a laser treatment is indicated.

Chapter Outline

Introduction
The Disciplines
Common Types of Plastic Surgery
Facial Procedures
Body Procedures

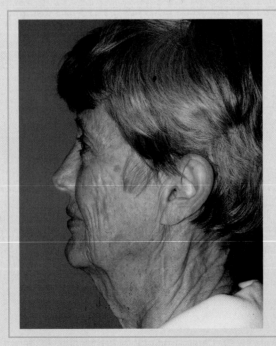
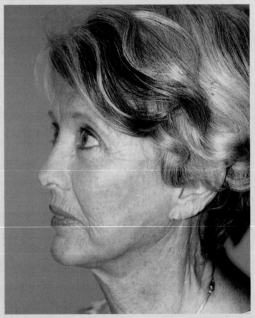

Introduction

Humankind has always tried to repair or to improve. Dating back to 800 B.C., physicians in ancient India practiced plastic reconstructive surgery by using skin grafts for facial injuries. The term *plastic* has its roots in the Greek term *plastikos*, meaning *fit for molding*. Plastic in this sense does not mean artificial. It means malleable or moldable. As treatments slowly developed throughout history, war victims sought procedures as reconstructive measures during the 1800s and 1900s. It was not until the twentieth century that elective plastic surgery became routine for the purpose of altering one's appearance, usually to look younger.

The Disciplines

Today there are two types of plastic surgery, reconstructive and cosmetic (also known as aesthetic) surgery. **Reconstructive** means to restore a bodily function, such as nasal surgery to improve breathing problems. **Cosmetic** or **aesthetic surgery** is an elective surgery for improving a feature. Specialties are as follows:

- plastic surgery
- facial plastic surgery/otolaryngology—ear, nose, and throat and facial plastic surgery
- reconstructive plastic surgery
- dermatology
- oral maxillofacial

Plastic Surgery

A general plastic surgeon is board certified by the American Board of Plastic Surgery, which is associated with the American Society of Plastic and Reconstructive Surgeons (ASPRS). General plastic surgeons perform plastic or cosmetic surgery on the face and body. They may have a practice specifically targeting cosmetic surgery, or their practice may include reconstructive surgery as well.

Facial Plastic Surgery

A facial plastic surgeon is board certified in otolaryngology (also known as head and neck surgery, or ear, nose, and throat surgery), and is associated with the American Academy of Otolaryngology. In addition to performing facial cosmetic procedures, the otolaryngologist is trained in reconstructive facial cosmetic and reconstructive surgery encompassing the diagnosis and treatment of the sinuses, throat and mouth, thyroid, cancer (including skin cancer), and otology, or ear surgery.

Reconstructive Plastic Surgery

Reconstructive surgery can be performed by either of the previously mentioned surgeons. Referred to as **reconstructive plastic surgeons,** these physicians perform procedures involving the face and body of accident survivors, and those with congenital disfigurements, cancer, or other disfiguring diseases. They are associated with the American Academy of Facial Plastic and Reconstructive Surgeons.

Dermatology

Dermatology is the study of disorders and diseases of the skin, hair, and nails. A dermatologist is board certified in dermatology, and some are surgeons as well. A dermatologist may have a specialty such as cosmetic dermatology or Mohs' micrographic surgery, which is a type of surgical procedure for skin cancers. Dermatologists are associated with the American Academy of Dermatology.

Oral Maxillofacial

Oral and **maxillofacial surgeons** are specialists treating the mouth and jaw, such as the temporomandibular joint (TMJ is a disorder of the jaw due to stress, injury, or disease). These surgeons also perform facial plastic and reconstructive surgery.

Common Types Of Plastic Surgery

Common surgeries may be performed alone, or in combination with one or more other procedures (Table 36–1, p. 585).

Facial Procedures

A large portion of cosmetic and reconstructive surgery is done on the face. Following are the most common facial surgical procedures and an explanation of each.

reconstructive plastic surgeons
Physicians who perform procedures on the face and body of accident survivors and others with disfigurements

reconstructive
Involving the restoration of a bodily function

cosmetic or aesthetic surgery
An elective surgery for improving a feature

maxillofacial surgeons
Specialists who treat the mouth and jaw, including facial, plastic and reconstructive surgery

Networking

You are at a business function with the intention of encouraging professional interaction and exchange. You learn that a colleague's business is complementary to esthetics. You approach this colleague only to be greeted with, "I am not interested in promoting or referring my clients to a skin care clinic or spa." You immediately feel disappointed and wonder why your approach was so poorly received.

Networking—the new professional buzzword—is all the rage these days, but does anyone really understand it? Networking is a separate entity that should not be confused with referral programs and special marketing promotions. With so many "hard sell" tactics and aggressive marketing and advertising techniques, all of us can empathize on some level with such an abrupt response. However, the truth of the matter is that most of us find networking a tad intimidating and often do not know what the protocol is.

If you are like most eager professionals, it is often hard to contain your enthusiasm when you recognize an opportunity to promote your business. It is only natural to get excited at the prospect of making a new and lucrative connection. However, under typical circumstances, the best approach is often a laid-back one. It is certainly appropriate to attend certain functions with the thought of increasing your contact list and gaining new clients. What is often inappropriate and poorly received is the preconceived agenda we head out the door with.

There are many ways to "network." You can participate in community functions; facilitate business roundtables; join professional organizations, small business associations, or special interest groups; volunteer for a charity project, attend industry tradeshows and educational seminars, just to name a few. But before you go, consider setting goals and thinking thoughtfully about your approach. The following are some tips for survival:

- Develop a dialogue for presenting yourself and what you do. Often estheticians are unprepared to describe what they do to the rest of the world. Practice your presentation in front of a mirror until you are comfortable with it.

- Show an interest in others. Most people love to talk about what they do—give them an opportunity!

- Set modest goals. Go with the goal of exchanging business cards with at least two others to start. This will lower your stress level.

- Think about who you want to develop relationships with beforehand. Make a list of ideal affiliations, for example, dermatologists, nutritionists, and massage therapists and then work toward developing them.

- Plan a list of possible networking activities. Find out what networking opportunities are available locally, regionally, and nationally and talk to others who have information about them.

- Keep a notebook or calendar of what is happening each month. Make a commitment to attend at least one activity per month.

- Be open-minded. Stay open to all possibilities. Many times the most unlikely person will lead to a new opportunity.

Table 36–1 Common Plastic Surgery Procedures

The Face	The Body
Face-lift/rhytidectomy	Breast augmentation
Forehead lift	Breast reduction
Eye-lift/blepharoplasty	Liposuction
Ear/otoplasty	Tummy tuck/abdominoplasty
Nose/rhinoplasty	
Laser resurfacing	
Trichloroacetic acid peel	
Phenol peel	

Face-Lift–Rhytidectomy

A **rhytidectomy** or face-lift accomplishes three things. It removes excess fat that has builtup or pooled at the jaw line, it tightens loose, atrophic muscles, and it removes sagging, draping skin (Figure 36–1). A face-lift is often combined with other procedures and primarily targets the lower face. When performed alone it may be referred to as a minilift. This procedure is often done under general anesthesia, but can be performed with intravenous (IV) sedation (Figures 36–2a, 36–2b).

Figure 36–1 Diagram of face-lift incision sites.

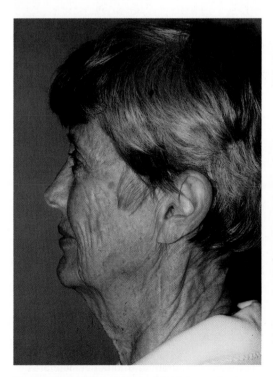

Figure 36–2a 56-year old with history of extensive sun exposure before face-lift.

Figure 36–2b Note the improvement along the neck and mandible.

> **rhytidectomy (more commonly, face-lift)**
> A surgical procedure that removes excess fat that has built up or pooled at the jaw line, tightens loose, atrophic muscles, and removes sagging, draping skin

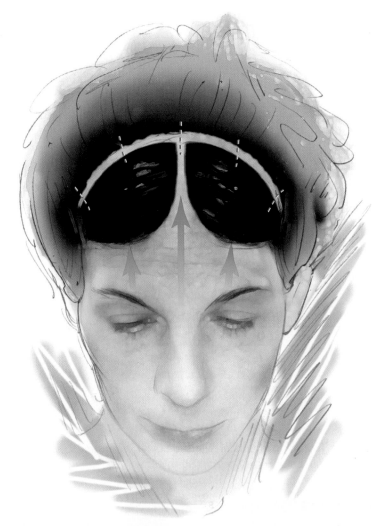

Figure 36–3 Forehead lift incision sites.

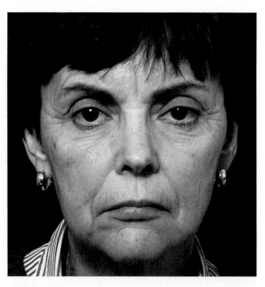

Figure 36–4a Client scheduled for both a brow lift and a face-lift.

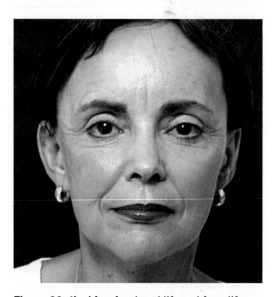

Figure 36–4b After forehead lift and face-lift.

Forehead Lift

Historically the forehead lift was considered part of a face-lift. Today it is often called the brow lift and is performed separately or in combination with an eyelift (Figure 36-4a). The procedure is performed to lift a sagging forehead, which can make the eyes look droopy, angry, or fatigued (Figure 36–4b). It involves tightening the muscles, as well as lifting and removing excess skin. This procedure is performed under general anesthesia (Figure 36–3).

Eyelift/Blepharoplasty

A **blepharoplasty** or eyelift may involve either the upper or lower lids, or both (Figure 36–5). This procedure removes the fat and skin from upper and lower lids, making them less baggy, dry and crinkled, and tired looking

blepharoplasty (more commonly, eyelift)

A surgical procedure that removes the fat and skin from upper and lower lids, making them less baggy, dry and crinkled, and tired looking

Figure 36–5 Diagram of traditional blepharoplasty, upper and lower eyelid surgery incision site.

Figure 36–6a 53-year old patient before lower eyelid blepharoplasty.

Figure 36–6b Same patient after lower eyelid surgery.

(Figures 36–6a, 36–6b). This procedure can be performed under general or IV sedation.

A **transconjunctival blepharoplasty** is a procedure performed inside the lower eyelid by making a hidden incision (Figure 36–7). It is performed on the lower lids to remove bulging fat pads, which are often congenital in nature.

Figure 36–7 Diagram of lower eyelid surgery incision site.

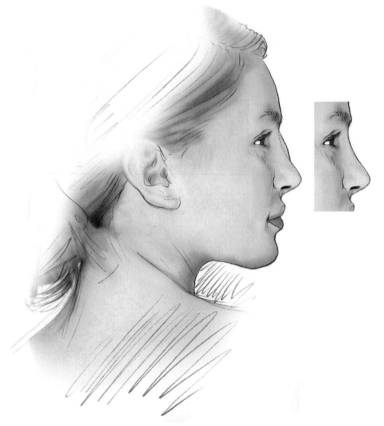

Figure 36–8 Diagram of rhinoplasty as changes are made to enhance the appearance of the nose.

Nose Surgery/Rhinoplasty

In addition to changing the appearance of the nose, surgery may be necessary to improve function and to restore the patient health. **Rhinoplasty** has been performed to make a nose smaller, larger, or less ethnic. It is often used to remove a bump on the nose, or to straighten one that is slightly bent (Figure 36–8). This procedure is performed under general anesthesia (Figures 36–9a, 36–9b, p. 588).

Otoplasty/Cosmetic Ear Surgery

An **otoplasty** is the procedure performed to flatten ears that protrude perpendicular to the face. It is often performed on children. It requires general anesthesia (Figures 36–10a, 36–10b, p. 588).

Laser Resurfacing

Laser is an acronym for *light amplification by the stimulated emission of radiation*. With the

---

transconjunctival blepharosplasty
Performed inside the lower eyelid by making a hidden incision; a surgical procedure to remove bulging fat pads, which are often congenital in nature

rhinoplasty
Surgical procedure performed to make the nose look smaller, larger, or less ethnic and most often used to remove a bump or to straighten a nose that is slightly bent

otoplasty
A surgical procedure performed to flatten ears that protrude perpendicular to the face

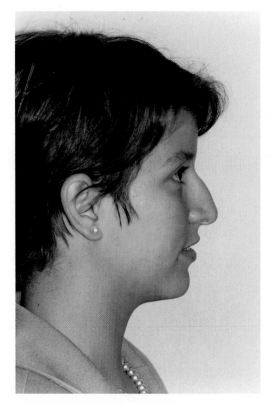

Figure 36–9a Client before rhinoplasty.

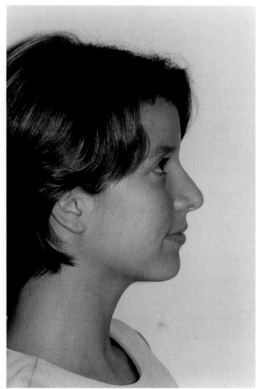

Figure 36–9b Client after rhinoplasty.

Figure 36–10a Client before otoplasty.

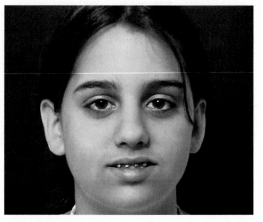

Figure 36–10b Client after otoplasty.

power of light, lasers can smooth wrinkles in the skin by vaporizing the skin layers down to the papillary dermis (Figure 36–11). It is also used to soften or lessen old acne scars, tighten skin under the eye area after a transconjunctival blepharoplasty, and to remove some skin cancers.

Commonly used lasers are the carbon dioxide, or CO_2, and the erbium. The CO_2 laser is chosen more readily for the deepest wrinkles and for **collagen remodeling**

(stimulation of the growth of new collagen in the dermis). The erbium is typically designated for rejuvenation and superficial wrinkles.

Age, Fitzpatrick skin type, and severity of the problem will direct the use, classification, and calibration of the laser. Depth of penetration is also a factor. Fitzpatrick skin types I, II, and III respond best to laser resurfacing (Figures 36–12a, 36–12b). Laser resurfacing is not recommended for darker skin types

collagen remodeling
Stimulating the growth of new collagen in the dermis

Figure 36–11 Laser treatments are effective in smoothing wrinkles and lessening scars.

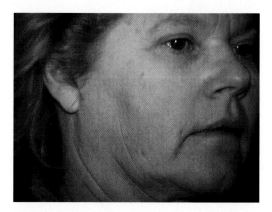

Figure 36–12a Client before laser resurfacing.

Figure 36–12b Client after laser resurfacing.

because it may cause severe pigment changes. This includes hypopigmentation (lack of pigment) or hyperpigmentation (darker pigment). Laser resurfacing is performed under general anesthesia. Some patients, however, may prefer IV sedation.

Trichloroacetic Acid Peel

Trichloroacetic acid peel (TCA) is recommended for moderate to severe sun damage, and light to moderate wrinkles. It is sometimes used to treat precancerous lesions. Because patients with darker skin pigment are not good candidates for laser resurfacing, TCA is a better choice for individuals with Fitzpatrick skin types III and IV. It is an alternative choice for patients who are not willing to spend the down time required with laser resurfacing. I.V. sedation is often used for this procedure.

Phenol Peel

Presently, laser resurfacing and TCA have overshadowed the phenol peel. In the 1960s, 1970s, and 1980s, phenol was widely used for smoothing and retexturizing the skin. It is the strongest chemical peel and can be toxic. Some physicians prefer to use this modality for skin resurfacing, however, due to longer lasting results. It is also less expensive to administer when compared with the laser. Phenol peels require general anesthesia during the procedure. The recovery period is longer than that required with either TCA or laser resurfacing.

Body Procedures

Breast Augmentation/ Mammaplasty

A **mammaplasty** is surgery that enlarges the breasts or balances a difference in breast size, or is a reconstructive technique following breast cancer surgery. The most common area of incision is to create a pocket beneath the chest muscle (Figure 36–13b, p. 590). The implant is placed into this space. Depending on the patient, the physician may instead choose to make the incision from the top. Newer procedures include the use of an **endoscope** (a long tube with a light on the end), which provides an easier method for placing the implant into the breast.

Incision scars are quite minimal for this procedure. They are usually found in the **areola** (nipple), **axilla** (armpit), or when using the older method, under the breast fold (Figure 36–13a, p. 590). Another no-scar method to breast augmentation is to enter

mammaplasty
A surgery that enlarges breasts

endoscope
A long tube with a light on the end

areola
Nipple

axilla
Armpit

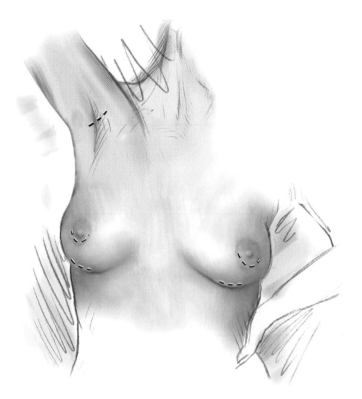

Figure 36–13a Potential breast augmentation surgery, incision site.

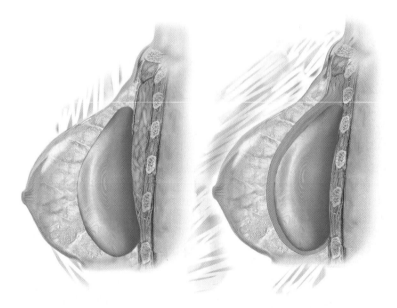

Figure 36–13b Implant locations.; (left) on top of muscle; (right) under muscle.

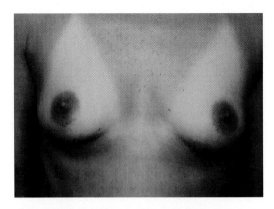

Figure 36–14a 26-year old mother of one shown before breast augmentation.

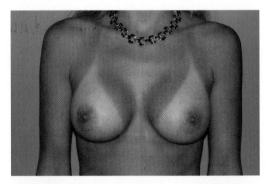

Figure 36–14b Saline implants were placed via underarm with endoscopic assistance, resulting in no breast scar.

Breast Reduction

A reduction is performed to reduce, lift, and reposition the breast, which gives a more youthful silhouette to the body (Figures 36–15a, 36–15b). This procedure is also performed for health reasons. Enlarged breasts may restrict activity and even the ability to breathe properly, especially when sleeping. Back problems are another common ailment due to enlarged breasts (Figures 36–16a, 36–16b).

Some men undergo breast reduction as a treatment for **gynecomastia** (excessive development of the male mammary glands) to remove excess breast tissue. These procedures are usually done under general anesthesia.

Liposuction/Lipoplasty

Liposuction is a body-contouring procedure performed to reduce pockets of fat in areas that have not responded to exercise or diet

gynecomastia
The excessive development of the male mammary glands

through the navel. This procedure is called the **Transumbilical Method.** The endoscopic tool guides the implant up to the breast site, where it is filled. Implants are typically filled with a sterile saline solution. They are available in a variety of shapes and sizes. This procedure is done under general anesthesia (Figures 36–14a, 36–14b).

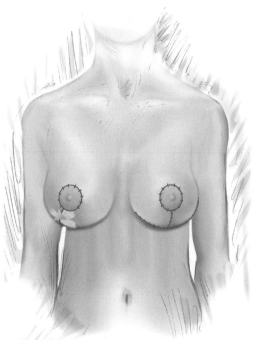

Figure 36–15a Breast reduction incision sites.

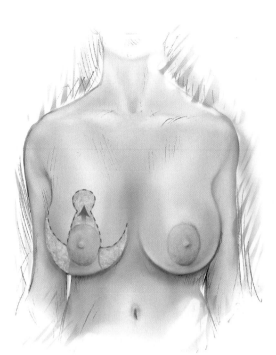

Figure 36–15b Skin above the nipple is brought down and together to reshape the breast.

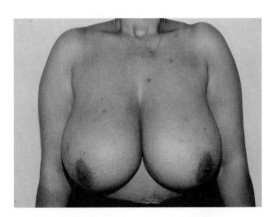

Figure 36–16a 58-year old woman before breast reduction.

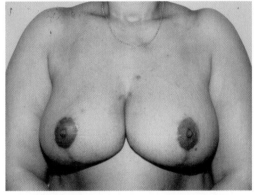

Figure 36–16b Post-operative breast reduction.

(Figure 36–17, p. 592). It is performed on the hips, thighs, arms, stomach, chin, jaw line, and buttocks (Figures 36–18a, 36–18b). Local and IV sedation may be used for this procedure. When combined with other procedures, the patient normally undergoes general anesthesia.

There are various methods of liposuction. Today the most effective and safest method is tumescent liposuction. A newer method called ultrasound-assisted lipoplasty is currently being tested.

Tummy Tuck/Abdominoplasty

During an **abdominoplasty,** excessive fat deposits and loose skin are tucked and tightened. Excessive skin is removed. The waistline is narrowed and the abdominal wall is strengthened rendering a more aesthetically pleasing appearance (Figures 36–19a, p. 592; 36–19b, p. 592). It is typically performed on patients with an extended or protruding abdomen (Figure 36–19c, p. 593). Patients undergo this surgery due to excessive muscle

transumbilical method
A no-scar method of breast augmentation, involving insertion of the implant through the navel.

abdominoplasty
A surgical procedure where excessive fat deposits and loose skin in the abdomen are tucked and tightened

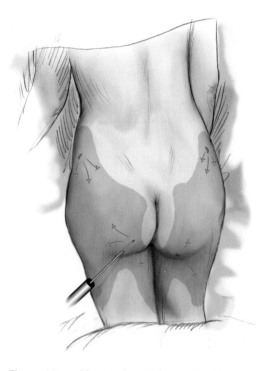

Figure 36–17 Liposuction tool insertion sites.

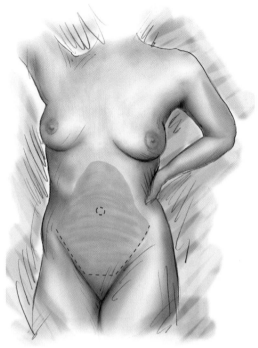

Figure 36–19a For abdominal reduction (tummy tuck), the skin is separated from the abdominal wall all the way to the ribs.

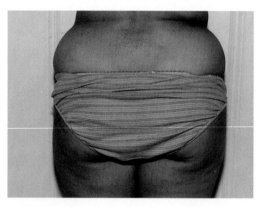

Figure 36–18a 26-year old before liposuction of hips, thighs, and buttocks.

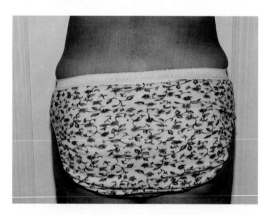

Figure 36–18b After treatment, the scars are hidden in the natural creases of the buttocks.

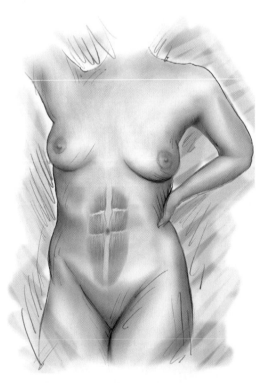

Figure 36–19b The surgeon draws underlying muscle and tissue together narrowing the waistline and strengthening the abdominal wall.

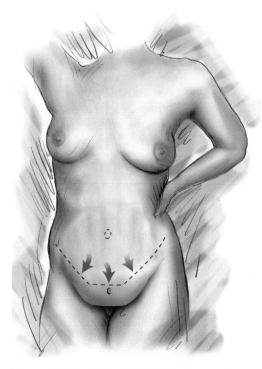

Figure 36–19c Abdominal skin is drawn down and excess removed. With complete abdomino-plasty, a new opening is cut for the navel.

stretching resulting from pregnancy, weight gain, or even a congenital disorder. The procedure requires general anesthesia (Figures 36–20a, 36–20b).

Smaller In-Clinic Procedures

Many treatments take comparatively less time to perform and can be done under a local anesthetic, or none at all.

- Botox, Collagen, injectables/implants/lip augmentation
- Spider vein removal
- Laser hair removal
- Nonablative wrinkle treatment (intense pulsed light)

Botox

Botox is a neuromuscular (nerve cell in a muscle) blocking serum, which is created from a bacterium called *Clostridium botulinum*. When this nontoxic serum is injected into a facial muscle such as the corrugator (the forehead between the eyes), it mitigates the muscle's ability to function. It decreases

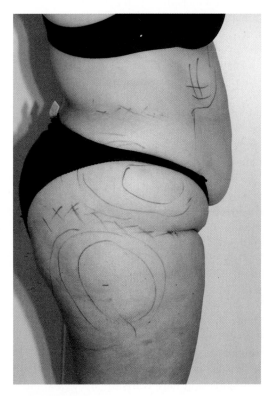

Figure 36–20a 27-year old before tumescent liposuction.

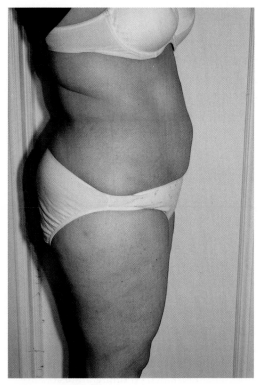

Figure 36–20b Post-operative weight loss further contributed to the result.

frowning, and eliminates the appearance of fatigue or anger. It has also been used for crow's feet and for medial forehead (middle horizontal) lines. This bacterium has been used for many years for strabismus (eyes that are misaligned) and blepharospasm (uncontrollable blinking). Recently, it was introduced as a remedy for migraine headaches and excessive perspiration.

Collagen/Fillers and Implants

Collagen fillers and fat transfers are injected or implanted to fill depressions or enlarge the lips. There are two basic types of collagen: animal and human. The latter type of collagen is grown in a tube from the patient's own cells. Animal sources include bovine (cow) or porcine (pig). Other fillers such as those acquired through cadaver tissue donation may seem controversial, but they are used routinely. Pretreatment testing should always be given (under the skin, usually forearm) to rule out adverse reactions. The length of effectiveness for collagen varies because it is not stable and requires repeat injections.

Uses for fillers are:

- chickenpox scars
- lines along the nasolabial folds (nose to mouth)
- deep furrows in forehead (corrugator muscle region)
- crows feet (periocular, around outside of eye)
- lip augmentation
- feature restoration

Based on the patient's tolerance and the area of application, the physician or nurse determines the type of material to be injected.

Spider Veins

Spider veins, or telangiectasia, are small veins that can appear on the face, legs, and ankles. Typically small, spider veins appearing on the surface of the skin can be treated with a laser. The power of the laser heats the vein in a calibrated fashion without burning the skin, collapsing the vein internally. A doctor, nurse, medical assistant, or clinical esthetician can perform this treatment. Do not perform this treatment unless you are licensed and trained. Training and licensure vary from state-to-state.

Sclerotherapy

Sclerotherapy is a procedure that helps eradicate medium-size veins. Prior to injections, an ultrasound study is performed on the patient to confirm that there are no internal blood flow problems. Injecting saline or other approved drug solutions into the vein causes it to collapse. The blood is forced to move to healthier veins. Repeated treatments may be indicated. Normally, the patient has to wear compression hose until the veins have totally collapsed. The physician sets the protocols.

Ambulatory Phlebectomy

Initially used in Europe and brought to the U.S. in the 1990s, this procedure is considered minimally invasive for varicose vein removal. Normally performed in the physician's office, local anesthesia is injected at the site of the vein. Prior to the procedure, the patient undergoes a thorough examination with ultrasound. Sometimes, the patient must undergo more intense surgery by a specialized surgeon to correct deeper vascular problems before they are ready to have this in-office procedure.

During an ambulatory **phlebectomy,** very small incisions are made along the bulging vein protruding above the skin's surface (i.e., in the leg). The problem vein is removed with a special stripping device that looks like a crochet hook. Surgery takes patience and requires several hours to complete. However, it is highly effective and creates no down time. The area is bandaged and the patient returns home immediately after surgery. After approximately one week, the bandage is checked and removed. The client is normally required to wear support hose for a small amount of time.

In extreme cases some larger or deeper bulging types of veins must be surgically removed through **ligation** (tying off veins) or stripping veins by completely removing them. These procedures are done in a hospital setting under general anesthesia.

Radio Frequency

This device is used to remove spider veins. The passage of high-frequency electrical waves can destroy the vein. It can be used for removing skin tags, warts, small cysts, some skin cancers, and moles.

sclerotherapy
A procedure that helps to eradicate medium-sized veins

phlebectomy
A procedure where very small incisions are made along the bulging vein protruding above the skin's surface

ligation
Tying off veins

Laser Hair Reduction

Hair reduction by laser is achieved through the laser's ability to disable and destroy the hair in the anagen phase of hair growth. Laser works on multiple hair follicles at a time. This procedure is a welcome change for patients who have endured hours of painful hair removal through other means. It takes a few minutes to administer the treatment. Advanced training and certification is required. Regulations for estheticians operating hair reduction lasers or photo light in physicians' offices vary from state to state.

Nonablative Wrinkle Treatment

Nonablative wrinkle treatments are relatively new. In theory, an intense pulsed light bypasses the epidermis targeting the fibroblasts in the dermis, stimulating collagen synthesis. It causes the skin to plump, reducing the appearance of a wrinkle. This treatment takes a few minutes in the office and is done without anesthesia. This creates no downtime for the patient at home. Results are minimal, but it offers a noninvasive type of procedure that can be used in addition to other superficial treatments such as microdermabrasion for age management.

Summary

Plastic surgery covers a wide range of conditions and treatments. The two types of plastic surgery include both reconstructive surgery and cosmetic surgery for the face and the body. There are several specialties, including general plastic surgery, facial plastic surgery/otolaryngology, reconstructive plastic surgery, oral maxillofacial surgery, and dermatology. Physicians must have additional board certification in some instances. You have now learned the basic definitions for many of the "traditional" procedures such as eyelifts and tummy tucks, but also for laser resurfacing, chemical peels, and nonablative wrinkle treatments, which are relatively new. The esthetician plays a key role in the pre- and postoperative preparation and care, as well as in postsurgical treatments.

Discussion Questions

1. Review disciplines within the field of plastic and reconstructive surgery. Explain the difference between the general plastic surgeon and a facial plastic surgeon. What does it mean to be "board certified" in either discipline?

2. Briefly describe the following surgical procedures: rhytidectomy, blepharoplasty, rhinoplasty, mammaplasty, abdominoplasty, and state the lay terms commonly used for each. What is the esthetician's role in working with plastic surgeons who perform these procedures?

3. Explain how "injectables" such as Botox and collagen are used in an esthetics practice. What are the main advantages and disadvantages associated with each? Conduct additional research if necessary.

Additional Reading

Gilman, S.L. 1999. *Making the Body Beautiful, A Cultural History of Aesthetic Surgery.* Princeton: Princeton University Press.

Rubin, M. 1995. *Manual of Chemical Peels: Superficial and Medium Depth.* Philadelphia: J.B. Lippincott.

Chapter 37
Patient Profiles

Chapter Objectives

After reading this chapter, you should be able to:

- Identify the five types of patients encountered most often, and the esthetician's role in working with them.

- Describe how to conduct a thorough evaluation with each type of patient.

- Describe the importance of patient education and how to deal with special needs.

- Describe the treatment protocols for various procedures.

- Define *informed consent* and tell why it is important.

Chapter Outline

Introduction
Preoperative Preparation
Postoperative Care
Survivors of Domestic Violence
Elderly
Physically Challenged
Mentally Ill, Obsessive-Compulsive,
    and Self-Abused
Pre- and Postoperative Care
Medical Documentation

Introduction

Employment in a medical environment means that you are in contact with a highly diverse population (group of people united by a common characteristic). Because you are located in a medical facility, patients tend to share information that may be beyond your scope of training. It is necessary that you remember your role as an esthetician. Although it is important to have compassion and empathy for others, it is paramount that you do not exceed your scope. Groups of patients that show up in a medical setting are

- pre- and postoperative patients
- survivors of domestic violence and other abused people
- elderly
- physically challenged
- mentally unstable

Preoperative Preparation

Prior to surgery, patients tend to be nervous about the upcoming procedure. They may have a difficult time concentrating on detailed information. Later in this chapter, we will discuss how important it is to take cues from the patient. Do not overload the patient with too much information in one setting. It is normal to be anxious, nervous, and worried. Always recommend that the patient convey any concerns to the physician.

Postoperative Care

Postsurgery patients experience varying degrees of pain. Medical personnel follow precise protocols to administer immediate care to encourage rapid wound healing and to avoid infection.

After approximately two weeks, the esthetician can begin to perform therapies, which may include massage to reduce swelling, hydration, protection, and camouflage. The patient's home care regimen is adjusted by providing instructions on postoperative products containing ingredients to expedite healing. The patient needs a knowledgeable, compassionate esthetician to perform these therapies.

Survivors of Domestic Violence

Survivors of abuse require medical and psychological therapy beyond the level of esthetic services. In such cases, it is important to maintain an open dialogue with the physician at all times. It may be tempting to be excessively helpful to this individual. You can understand and be empathetic; however, it is not appropriate to become too involved. Dependencies can be created easily, and if you do not possess appropriate training, this could become a problem for all concerned. Some guidelines for dealing with survivors of abuse follow.

1. Always work in partnership with the physician while consulting with a survivor of domestic violence.

2. Do not ask patients about their injuries or how they sustained them.

3. Do not offer counseling unless you are trained and authorized to do so.

4. Explain to patients exactly what you can do for them (such as offering camouflage skin care treatments and products).

5. Build a referral library of resources (abuse hot line, temporary safe shelters, counseling agencies, etc.) consisting of Web sites, calling cards, brochures, articles, and phone numbers to offer to the patient. The individual will realize that you have taken the time to research the matter and, because you are affiliated with the physician's office, it is appropriate for you to make the referral.

Elderly

The majority of elderly patients are delightful, compliant, and modest. Some older patients may feel that cosmetic procedures are unnecessary, even if they can improve their vision, such as in the case of a droopy upper lid. Although these are typically elective procedures, elders may feel that they are being vain if they consider a cosmetic procedure. Below are some guidelines for dealing with elderly patients.

1. Let them know that you do not think they are being frivolous.

2. Make certain that you use clear language when explaining a treatment or product.

3. Do not oversell this patient; they do not always use makeup or skin care products.

4. Share samples appropriate for their skin type, even if they choose not to buy.

Physically Challenged

Patients with physical challenges such as Parkinson disease, multiple sclerosis, or surivivors of accidents occasionally come to an office for cosmetic procedures, or for treatments and skin care products. Some key points to keep in mind when working with patients who are physically challenged:

1. Make daily rituals as easy as possible. Use fewer products to accomplish the same goal. For example, use one product for moisturizer, exfoliation, and sunscreen.

2. Do not make statements such as:

   I know what you are going through. Unless you have the specific condition that they are dealing with you do *not* know what they are experiencing.

   It's easy, just do . . . This is generally not a constructive comment to make; it will not necessarily be easy for the patient.

3. Keep in mind that a disability may be degenerative and so the condition may have worsened the next time that you see the patient.

4. Be prepared to change the room around if necessary to make access easy for the patient.

Mentally Ill, Obsessive-Compulsive, and Self-Abused

An unstable patient may not be identified until after you begin work. A simple, light facial treatment may be a trigger for someone with a compulsive disorder, such as skin picking, or in severe cases, excoriation. A patient consent form is always signed prior to beginning a treatment.

Do not be too eager to comply if an individual is anxious or insists you perform a treatment immediately. If necessary, have the physician meet the patient for evaluation. When you have justifiable reasons for not wanting to perform a treatment on someone, honor that. Although science is the basis for medical esthetics, there is room for intuition. Some observations that could help you determine that a patient is mentally ill include:

- deep scars

- anxious behavior

- many open wounds yet no real interest in a skin care program

- accusatory or blaming language such as, *you said...*

- inability to cope, crying, or extreme behavior

When you observe any of these, do not perform a treatment. Let the patient know that you want to make the best decision and you will have to refer the client to a physician.

Pre- and PostOperative Care

The first step for a successful outcome in plastic surgery is to prepare the skin to its optimum state. Improved barrier function allows for rapid healing, hence better results. The esthetician's work becomes valuable to both the patient and physician. Developing a complete surgical plan that includes both pre- and postsurgical care places the patient as a high priority. It includes protocols for care from consultation, to procedure education, in-office and home care, actual surgery, and postsurgical care. This nature of support places the patient at ease, and the physician can focus on the surgery. Preparation of a presurgical patient and postsurgical care require full attention to detail. Make accurate observations and document your findings. Protocols, documentation, and observations will guide and remind you of what is to be accomplished every step of the way.

Cosmetic Surgery Consultation

The physician conducts the initial surgical consultation and the patient is then referred

Telephone Etiquette

Voicemail, answering machines, caller ID, message services, cell phones—technology has made keeping in touch easier than ever before. With so many options available, the real challenge is communicating effectively. Although voicemail and answering machines have become standard business protocol, consumers continue to judge our customer service performance by how well we "connect" with them.

Make no mistake about it—the telephone is the most important business tool you have. Whether the skin-care clinic or spa you work in provides mechanical or human interaction or both, everyone involved in servicing clients via the telephone should be aware of these simple rules of proper telephone etiquette.

Rule #1—Don't make them wait.

Most of us are pressed for time these days, so dangling on the line waiting for someone to pick up is annoying. Learn to answer your business phone within three rings and have voicemail programmed to kick in if you cannot answer right away.

Rule #2—Be polite when placing clients in a holding pattern.

You arrive at your final destination but are forced to circle the airport waiting for clearance—annoying isn't it? Customers feel the same annoyance when they reach you by phone but are placed on hold. Before doing so always ask the client's permission. It is also a good idea to appear calm, even if the switchboard is buzzing. Giving clients the idea that your operation is hectic and out of sorts does not present the image of a calm and peaceful place to relax and rejuvenate.

Rule #3—Program your voicemail system to be user friendly.

If you are in a situation where your voicemail acts as your receptionist, make sure you provide brief but detailed instructions for the client. Let clients know they have reached your business—state the name of the company, hours of business for the day or week, reason why and how long you will be away from the telephone as well as when you plan to return calls. Ask clients to state their name, telephone number, and reason for their call.

Rule #4—Return calls promptly.

Do not let messages linger. Return all calls within a reasonable amount of time—the sooner the better; longer than 24 hours is inappropriate. You want to let clients know you appreciate their business and are eager to serve them.

Rule #5—Attitude is everything.

The telephone is the first opportunity you have to make a good impression. Make sure you receive clients with a welcoming tone of voice. There is nothing worse than letting the whole world know you are having a bad day. Be sincere, pleasant, and helpful—even if Ms. Smith tortures you with changing her appointment five times!

Rule #6—A little courtesy goes a long way.

Remember to use "please" and "thank you." Do not chew gum or eat while engaging in business calls. And don't try to carry on a conversation with anyone else while you are talking to a client. Clients expect your undivided attention—give it to them.

Rule #7—Reminder calls keep business flowing.

Most appointment-based businesses realize the value of confirming appointments—it saves time, energy, and ultimately money. Get in the habit of confirming all of your appointments 24 to 48 hours in advance, but don't forget the particulars. Whether you are leaving a message or speaking directly to the client, address him or her properly by name and always identify yourself and the name of your salon or clinic. Remind them of the exact date, day of the week, and time of their appointment.

Figure 37–1 The esthetician helps the patient understand the procedures and post-operative care protocols.

to the esthetician for preoperative facial care. Patient consultation is a key factor in building a relationship with the patient. It sets the tone for all future meetings. Whether the client is a regular, or it is your first meeting with the client, there are countless details to review after the physician's consultation.

Preoperative Consultation

During the consultation, determine the following:

- Is the patient compliant? Will the patient follow directions?

Figure 37–2 The physician conducts a thorough examination and develops a surgical plan for the patient.

- Outline your plan. What do you need to do to prepare the patient to help preparing for surgery, such as recommend or provide products, treatments, and other resources?
- If the patient decides to have the surgery, what is the return schedule for postsurgical care?

Home Care Compliance

Home care compliance is extremely important. It supports surgical results, expedites the healing process, and promotes habits for long-term maintenance. If the patient is already a client, by now you have an idea of how committed the patient is to performing a home care routine. When a patient is new, the commitment level is determined to ensure that postsurgical directions from the physician will be followed. Much of this information can be established through the initial health intake form and verbal consultation. This information gives you clues about how well you must educate the patient.

The Plan

What is your plan for the patient? The type of surgery and the physician's recommendations are some of the information that helps develop this plan. Based on the type of procedure, create a written pre- and postoperative product and treatment plan. Include how you will educate your patient to ensure adherence to *all* protocols.

Return Visits

When are return visits scheduled? For some patients, a return visit is just a matter of making sure that the patient is on track. Other patients may require treatments with an adjusted protocol according to the type of surgery and skin condition.

Patient Selection

Patient selection is not unusual in a surgical setting. It is an interesting concept, because one might assume that the individual selects a physician. Although this is true, a physician also chooses a patient. Some procedures may not be appropriate for certain individuals. After a thorough evaluation of patient history, as well as physical and psychological health, the physician makes the final decision. The ideal candidate for an elective surgery is someone who has *realistic* expectations, who has *freely* made the decision, and who is *physically* able to receive the procedure.

Experienced estheticians play a role in patient selection as well. As previously indicated, *compliance* is an important issue. It is essential to report any existing inconsistencies to the physician. A successful outcome depends upon it. Some patients may feel intimidated by the doctor and will share information with you that they do not tell the physician. Encouraging patients to have an open dialogue with the physician is healthy and professional.

Patient Education

Patient education is teaching or instructing the patient with the necessary protocols to insure a positive surgical outcome. When you are with a patient, keep in mind that the patient is not always familiar with your role or title, or with the information that is conveyed, including in-clinic and home care skin procedures, prelaser treatment, or even the correct name of the surgical procedure. Patients become overwhelmed with the abundance of information conveyed about surgery. One easy way to ensure that what you convey is understood and followed is a proven teaching concept referred to as show and tell.

1. Describe what you are going to teach.

2. Teach the patient both using verbal and visual information.

3. Have the patient repeat back to you what you have taught.

4. Go through it again in a review style.

Individuals possess unique learning styles and ways of assimilating information. Most respond to visually oriented material. When educating, use sketches, graphics, brochures, newsletters, posters, videos, CDs, and even the Internet. Color code pre- and postoperative information so that preoperative protocols are in one color, and postoperative protocols are in another color.

To reinforce information, provide a patient booklet or brochure that contains areas for the patient to write in. This education piece can contain a question and answer section that covers the most general questions regarding a particular surgery. This booklet can be used as a reference tool to refresh the patient's memory at home. Patients appreciate that you have taken the time to explain difficult information. The residual benefit is that it helps you too.

Special Needs

Patients with special needs may require you to develop different teaching strategies. Be creative. Some patients are visually impaired. You can develop an **auditory** method to help these patients learn. Using a CD or cassette tape recorder, record information for them. To help a visually impaired patient use skin care products, arrange them sequentially on a tray. Attach each product to the tray with Velcro. Make certain that each container is a different shape, so that the patient will be able to memorize the sequence and put the items back in order.

Patience

Finally, remain calm while teaching. People become overwhelmed easily with new information, especially when their attentiveness and commitment may determine the outcome of their final results. Giving undivided attention (even when you are busy) assures patients that they are receiving your utmost concern and care.

Taking Care of Yourself

Most medical environments are strenuous both mentally and physically. This even holds true for spas and salons. Daily breaks away from the office are important for eliminating or reducing stress. Physical exercise such as walking or taking a yoga class does wonders for clearing the mind.

Strict confidentiality is required when working with and discussing patient information with other medical personnel. Because you are not allowed to convey any information beyond that environment, it is recommended that you find an appropriate support person or mentor within your office. This individual helps to ease stressful experiences by providing an outlet for you. Relieving stress is vital to your health and to your practice.

Medical Documentation

A confidential medical chart is created for each patient and is generally kept in a locked file room. Normally it includes health intake forms, consent forms, and other important information such as correspondence from other physicians about the

patient education
Keeping a client fully informed of pre- and post-surgical procedures and requirements, and a full description of the treatment they will receive.

auditory
A method used to assist patients who are visually impaired by using a CD or cassette tape recorder to verbalize information to them.

patient. Initial and subsequent patient visits require documentation. This is referred to as charting. No matter what the setting—spa, salon, medical office, a patient's chart is an important legal document. All patient charts, as well as the information contained in them, are strictly confidential, and is not available to anyone except authorized personnel. Release of any information is only allowed with written consent from the patient. This is one of many laws that protect patients' rights. Consequently, it is important to be clear and concise when recording information. If necessary, you can write on another piece of paper first, then transfer the information to the patient's chart. It is vital that information be recorded when you are with the patient or immediately afterward. Do not rely on memory at the end of day to remember details. This all takes practice. As you become more familiar with the office routine and procedures, this process becomes easier.

SOAP Notes

To expedite chart writing, the medical field has made this process more scientific. The acronym **SOAP** represents a documenting process: observations (both the patient's and yours), assessment, and then planning.

S: **Subjective** data (what the patient states). Describes the problem from the patient's perspective.

O: **Objective** data (what is observed/inspected). What is presented? Without making a judgment or diagnosis, what do you see? Remember, we do *not* diagnose.

A: **Assessment** (conclusion reached on the basis of data). What is your analysis? The physician makes the diagnosis.

P: **Plan** (actions to be taken). Detail your plan. Briefly describe plans regarding possible treatments and protocols, products, sampling, etc. This may include referring the patient back to the physician.

The conventional application of SOAP simplifies chart notes, makes it easier for physicians and nurses to review your work, and remains within legal parameters.

Example of a SOAP note:

S: (subjective) Patient comes in asking for postoperative laser kit as recommended by Dr. Good.

O: (objective) Mr. Brown has recently had laser resurfacing.

A: (assessment) Mr. Brown is at day ten of his postoperative care and is now ready to begin his new home care regime.

P: (plan) He will switch from his current regime to post-laser products including: gentle cleanser, Hydration-Plus, Ultimate Sunscreen two times a day (b.i.d.), and will follow-up with Dr. Good next week to determine when to begin post-laser treatment.

(your initials here)

This guide is standard. When charting, it is not necessary to write the letters SOAP each time. Experience with this procedure becomes natural. SOAP techniques will automatically transfer into many of your written documents, for example, when writing correspondence on client cards or when recording phone messages taped to the patient's chart.

Protocol

Esthetic treatments and **protocols** are not *standardized* throughout the skin care industry. Medical offices, however, require that all office protocols and procedures be documented. This information is contained in a book called the *Standard Operating Procedures* (SOP) manual. Protocols for estheticians are also included. Additionally, it is a highly recommended professional and legal practice for any spa or salon. Regardless of the type of practice, each medical office should include this as standard procedure.

Treatment procedures include numerous steps. When charting, it is not necessary to record each step because this information is already noted in the SOP document. Record the title of the procedure and then note any variances from the protocol. Table 37-1 shows a sample treatment record.

Treatment Protocol
Treatment protocol is a written document that delineates the steps followed in a given procedure. Whenever there is a question about how to perform a treatment, refer to your *Standard Operating Procedure* manual. The following is an example of a glycolic peel procedure that may be found in the *Standard Operating Procedure* manual under Treatment Protocols.

(*text continues on p. 608*)

SOAP
An acronym that represents a documenting process: Subjective, Objective, Assessment, and Plan.

protocols
Detailed plans of a scientific or medical treatment or procedure.

SKILLS ● FOR ● SUCCESS

Collecting Client Information: Questionnaires and Consent Forms

The basic premise of client forms, whether they are focused on intake or consent, is to gather and disperse information. Two of the most commonly used forms are the client profile questionnaire and the consent form. They are both vital to the consultation process.

Ideally, questionnaires should collect as much information as possible without invading the client's privacy or making the client feel uncomfortable. The purpose of the intake questionnaire is to:

- learn as much as possible about the health or condition of the skin

- aid in providing services safely and effectively

- uncover the client's needs and wants

Before you begin working with any client you will want to be aware of any medical problems, allergies, medications, and the use of "cosmeceuticals" that could affect treatment. Beyond this critical information, some of the things you will want to become informed about are lifestyle, stress level, age, skin health habits, and nutritional status. Further skin analysis using a Wood's lamp and the Fitzpatrick Scale will help you determine the client's skin type and other conditions that may be present. From here you can proceed to recommend products and treatments. But before you do, you will want to be clear about

- what products the client is currently using on the skin

- what it is the client would like to change about her skin

- what the client's expectations are

- what services the client is interested in obtaining

Clarifying these issues will help you make the best possible decisions and create a positive course of treatment.

In our litigation oriented culture the consent form is standard practice for more aggressive treatments. However, it is important not to create a sense of apprehension around its use. What you do want to accomplish is a complete understanding of the benefits and features of the service or product in question. You also want the client to have a complete understanding of any contraindications. Making these things clear can help reduce any fears or anxiety the client may have and allow the client to feel more comfortable with the process.

When introducing the consent form take time to review with the client all the steps involved in the process and carefully explain any home care directions that may be necessary. Provide a copy of the consent form to the client and keep the original for your files. You should also maintain a client treatment log and have the client initial and date all subsequent treatment procedures. These extra precautionary measures go a long way in safeguarding both you and the client.

Table 37-1 Sample Treatment Record

TREATMENT RECORD	Patient's Name

Date _____

Treatment _____

Cleanser_____

Toner _____

Steam ❑ Yes _____ Mins ❑ No

Exfoliate/Peel _____ Mins _____

Microdermabrasion ❑ Face # passes _____

　　　　　　　　　　❑ Neck # passes _____

　　　　　　　　　　❑ Décolleté #passes _____

　　　　　　　　　　❑ Other #passes _____

Extractions ❑ Yes ❑ No

High Frequency ❑ Yes ❑ No

Mask _____

Moisturizer _____

Sun Block_____

Comments/Results_____

_____

_____

Date _____

Treatment _____

Cleanser_____

Toner _____

Steam ❑ Yes _____ Mins ❑ No

Exfoliate/Peel _____ Mins _____

Microdermabrasion ❑ Face # passes _____

　　　　　　　　　　❑ Neck # passes _____

　　　　　　　　　　❑ Décolleté #passes _____

　　　　　　　　　　❑ Other #passes _____

Extractions ❑ Yes ❑ No

High Frequency ❑ Yes ❑ No

Mask _____

Moisturizer _____

Sun Block_____

Comments/Results_____

_____

_____

Date _____

Treatment _____

Cleanser_____

Toner _____

Steam ❑ Yes _____ Mins ❑ No

Exfoliate/Peel _____ Mins _____

Microdermabrasion ❑ Face # passes _____

　　　　　　　　　　❑ Neck # passes _____

　　　　　　　　　　❑ Décolleté #passes _____

　　　　　　　　　　❑ Other #passes _____

Extractions ❑ Yes ❑ No

High Frequency ❑ Yes ❑ No

Mask _____

Moisturizer _____

Sun Block_____

Comments/Results_____

_____

_____

Date _____

Treatment _____

Cleanser_____

Toner _____

Steam ❑ Yes _____ Mins ❑ No

Exfoliate/Peel _____ Mins _____

Microdermabrasion ❑ Face # passes _____

　　　　　　　　　　❑ Neck # passes _____

　　　　　　　　　　❑ Décolleté #passes _____

　　　　　　　　　　❑ Other #passes _____

Extractions ❑ Yes ❑ No

High Frequency ❑ Yes ❑ No

Mask _____

Moisturizer _____

Sun Block_____

Comments/Results_____

_____

_____

INFORMED CONSENT FOR PEELS

Initial   I, _____ authorize _____ of

Your Medical Office/Facility Name, to perform the following peel:

❑ Glycolic   ❑ Lactic (AHA)   ❑ Salicylic   ❑ TCA   ❑ Jessner's

_____   1. This process involves application to the affected skin area with a cotton swab or small brush. Depending on the solution, it may be left on for up to _____ minutes. This is determined by product strength, skin type and condition, sensitivity, age, or prior use of any exfoliating agent.

_____   2. While other peels are neutralized and removed during treatment, I understand that TCA and Jessner's peels are applied in _____ layers and not removed.

_____   3. In order to receive maximum results, more than one application may be required, thus, it may be recommended that I participate in a series of treatments. My program is customized based on the advice of the physician and/or esthetician.

_____   4. Rate of improvement depends on my age, skin type and condition, degree of sun/environmental damage, pigmentation levels, or acne condition. I will follow pre- and/or postpeel instructions and maintain appointment schedules exactly as prescribed, including home care.

_____   5. I acknowledge that no guarantee has been made about the results of the procedure. Although it is impossible to list every potential risk and complication, I have been informed of some possible benefits, risks, and complications which may include, but are not limited to, the following:
- Softer, smoother skin
- Reduction in the appearance of lines and wrinkles
- Reduction in acne lesions
- Swelling and redness
- Scabbing or peeling of treated skin and surrounding areas
- Prolonged skin sensitivity to wind and sun
- Areas of persistent increased or decreased pigmentation

_____   6. Any potential risks and complications could result in the need to discontinue the treatment. In this case, an alternative recommendation(s) will be suggested. It is very rare that a permanent disability occurs. If the need arises, I authorize my skin care professional to perform such required treatment or procedure. I also agree to immediately inform the skin professional if I have concerns, or am overly uncomfortable during treatment, or after I return home.

_____   7. I agree to inform my skin professional when I introduce new medication(s)and/or product(s) during the course of the treatment. I attest that I have had an opportunity to ask questions and have questions answered to my satisfaction.

_____   8. I certify that I am over the age of eighteen (18), that I am not pregnant or nursing, on Accutane, or taking any other medication that may be contraindicated to having this procedure. I have read and will follow to the best of my ability any and all instructions. I understand the potential risks and complications, and choose to proceed after careful consideration of the possibility of both known and unknown risks, complications, limitations, and alternatives.

Patient's signature _____ Date _____

Esthetician's/Physicians signature _____ Date _____

Figure 37–3 An example of the informed consent form for peels.

WHAT IS MICRODERMABRASION?

Microdermabrasion has been used in Europe for many years. It was first introduced in the United States during the mid 1990s. The *NAME OF YOUR MICRODERMABRASION MACHINE* is an integrated option for advanced skin care and complements most treatment programs. Considered a gentle system, it features a dual control system and adjustable applicator head that delivers a steady, effective stream of fine crystals directly onto the skin.

The treatment removes dead surface skin cells and initiates cellular turnover at the dermis and epidermis levels in a safe controlled manner. This approach respects the integrity of the skin and promotes even healing. Maintaining even cellular growth on the surface aids in the youthfulness of the skin's appearance.

Microdermabrasion has been used to treat:

❑ Aging and sun-damaged skin
❑ Some types of acne scarring and acne
❑ Altered pigmentation

❑ Stretch marks
❑ Fine lines and wrinkles

Results may include:

❑ Improved skin tone
❑ Even skin color
❑ Refined skin pores

❑ Fewer breakouts
❑ Healthy glow
❑ Renewed elasticity

❑ Diminished appearance of scars

WHAT CAN I EXPECT?

Our protocols

Prior to your first microdermabrasion, the physician and/or esthetician perform a thorough skin analysis. If microdermabrasion is *not appropriate*, you are informed during this session. An alternative high-performance series may be recommended instead. If microdermabrasion *is* for you, maximum results are obtained by participating in a series of treatments plus following a home care regimen.

To further enhance your outcome, we require that you use products and/or medications specifically directed toward obtaining correction. Your current daily regimen and skin care products are reviewed. Every attempt will be made to incorporate current products into a more comprehensive program, which complements your in-clinic series. For example, we may tell you to continue using your cleanser and add in new corrective products to target the needs of your skin. We may also tell you that some of what you are using may not be the most appropriate for your skin.

Keeping regular appointments and carefully following your home care regimen supports your results.

During your session

Your Practice Name takes your microdermabrasion series one step further by applying additional corrective products on your skin *during* your treatment.

Additionally, we take every precaution to ensure that your skin is well hydrated and calm prior to leaving each session. In a few cases, you may experience excessive dryness or even some peeling between sessions, which may or may not be normal. Always check with us. More sensitive skin may experience some redness after the first couple of sessions. This normally goes away after 2 to 3 hours.

Figure 37–4 An example of the informed consent form for microdermabrasion.

Initials

_____

You are required to apply a hydrating gel mask or one directed by our practitioner twice within the first 24 hours of treatment. Sunblock must be worn at all times and tanning beds should never be used. You are making an investment in your face; therefore, it is to your benefit to continue to protect it long after your series is completed.

IS THERE ANY GUARANTEE?

The majority of our patients receive satisfactory to above average results with their series. *Maximum results, however, are highly dependent on your age, accumulative sun exposure, health, menopause, lifestyle, genetic traits, general skin condition, and your willingness to follow recommended protocols.*

Scars respond according to their *depth and age*. They may require laser or deeper peels. It is not appropriate to promise an unrealistic outcome.

Pore size: While we can refine and diminish their appearance, physiological size is genetically predetermined. After your facial analysis in the first session we will discuss, to the best of our ability, what you can expect.

Be aware that many changes may occur deeper within the skin over time. We find that when participating in a series, along with a commitment to your daily skin care regimen, noticeable differences may indeed be the outcome, i.e., reduction of fine lines and softening of deeper wrinkles, reduction of discoloration, softening and possible reduction in scars, and an overall improvement to the skin's tone and appearance.

_____

To continue the maintenance of your skin after you complete your treatment(s) we may inform you of long-term age-management programs. Our experience shows that the incorporation of several modalities over time and during season changes seems to be the best way to consistently maintain the suppleness and radiance of the skin.

INFORMED CONSENT

I _____ have read the above information and fully understand what to expect. If I have any concerns, I will address these with my physician and/or skin therapist. I release the physician/skin therapist, **Your practice name,** and their staff harmless from any liability that may result from this treatment.

Signed _____ Date _____

Physician and/or Esthetician _____ Date _____

Figure 37–4 *(continued).*

Standard Glycolic Peel Protocol

Purpose: To perform a superficial exfoliation of the upper layers of the stratum corneum using glycolic acid.

Contraindications: Client or patient has been on Accutane within at least one year. Herpetic breakout, open wounds, acne, or any suspicious lesion, bleeding, pregnancy, cancer, cancer therapy, AIDS, or hepatitis.

Procedure:

1. Have client/patient sign consent form.
2. Drape or gown client, and secure hair free of areas to be treated.
3. Cleanse face, throat, chest, and all areas to be treated.
4. Apply eye covers.
5. Swipe cleansed areas to be treated with prepping solution.
6. Set timer for three minutes for first peel. Then gradually increase with subsequent peels.
7. Starting at the forehead, apply peel solution toward the hairline in a counterclockwise fashion until all areas are covered with a thin veil of glycolic acid. Cover the neck and periorbital (eye area) areas last.
8. Remove with an approved neutralizing product or water when indicated.
9. Apply a hydrating serum.
10. Apply moisturizer, sunscreen, and makeup if an appropriate quality product is available and the client requests it.
11. Instruct client to refrain from using performance agents (ingredients found to cause a change in the appearance of the skin), for three to four days and no **active agents** (topical drugs such as Retin-A).

informed consent
Falls under both medical documentation and treatment protocol; a customary written agreement between the client/patient and esthetician for applying particular treatment whether routine or preoperative.

active agents
Drugs that penetrate beyond the epidermis and are prescription only.

SAFETY*Tip*

It is not appropriate to perform any treatment that could result in unnecessary irritation or a negative reaction. It is *not* appropriate to perform an independent clinical study with a new treatment or product. Pre- and postsurgical time is not the time to experiment. The only exception is when the physician authorizes it.

Communication Between The Physician and Esthetician

Consult with the physician prior to all treatment or operative phases. It is important to follow protocol using standard or scientifically measured applications. Adverse skin reactions may require that the surgery be rescheduled. This is expensive and creates an awkward situation between the patient, the physician, and you.

Once communication flow is established and the esthetician understands general procedures, future exchanges with the physician and other medical personnel may be quite brief. Sometimes both the esthetician and physician consult together with the patient to discuss a best possible course of action. Information should be shared routinely and discreetly throughout the duration of the pre- and postsurgery time frame. The physician should be able to go to the patient's chart and obtain information about treatments or products that have been administered by the esthetician without needing to question what has been documented. The patient's chart should be accurate and complete.

Informed Consent

Informed consent falls under both medical documentation and treatment protocol. As mentioned earlier, a consent form is a customary written agreement between the client/patient and esthetician for applying a particular treatment, whether routine or preoperative. It is a legal document that is kept in the patient's chart. Typically it states that the patient agrees to the treatment, application, or procedure, as well as understands and accepts all risks involved. While risks are minimal at this level, it is important to protect everyone involved. We have provided generic forms for your information.

Summary

Working with ill or anxious patients can be a real challenge to the esthetician. While it is natural to be sympathetic and to want to help, it is imperative that you stay within your range of responsibility. Most of the patients you will work with are apprehensive about their upcoming procedures, or are in pain, so their level of concentration is low. Do not overload them with information. Be encouraging and soothing in your dealings with them. If you are uncomfortable dealing with certain issues, do not forget that it is perfectly appropriate to withhold treatment and refer the patient back to the physician or to another professional for assistance. Understanding the issues you may confront, and learning how to address them, will help build confidence and foster trust in your clients.

Excellent pre- and postoperative care is imperative to the success of the procedure. The esthetician's role is of great value during this time to both the patient and the physician. Your support is necessary to assist the physician and to help the patient understand what will happen before, during, and after surgery. Establishing a comprehensive plan and abiding by it will help you to be an effective member of the team.

Discussion Questions

1. Discuss why it is important for the esthetician to be knowledgeable about working with specific populations, such as elderly or mentally ill patients.

2. How does the practice of microdermabrasion differ from chemical peeling? Describe the main benefits and features of both.

3. Compare and contrast informed consent for peels used in the medical practice with the standard form used for similar purposes in the esthetic skin care clinic. How do they differ? What similarities did you find?

Additional Reading

Lees, Mark. 2001. *Skin Care: Beyond the Basics.* Clifton, Park, N.Y.: Milady, an imprint of Delmar Learning, a division of Thomson Learning, Inc.

Rayner, Victoria. 1993. *Clinical Cosmetology, A Medical Approach to Esthetics Procedures.* Clifton, Park, N.Y.: Milady, an imprint of Delmar Learning, a division of Thomson Learning, Inc.

Warfield, Suzanne, S. 1997. *The Esthetician's Guide to Working with Physicians.* Clifton, Park, N.Y.: Milady, an imprint of Delmar Learning, a division of Thomson Learning, Inc.

Chapter 38
Pre- and Postoperative Care

Chapter Objectives

After reading this chapter, you should be able to:

▶ Describe the difference between pre- and postoperative care.

▶ State the timetables for the various procedures and treatment plans.

▶ State the importance of manual lymphatic drainage.

▶ Explain the difference between chemical peels and microdermabrasion.

▶ Describe how computer imaging is used in pre- and postoperative care.

Chapter Outline

Introduction
Procedures and Treatment Plans
Treatments Defined

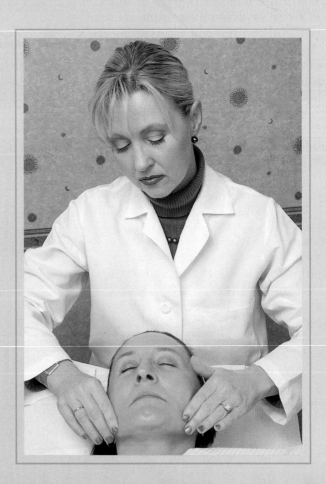

Introduction

Products and treatments used in either the pre- or postoperative stages of care are aimed at conditioning the skin to heal. In the preoperative phase, **conditioning** includes increasing the skin's metabolism and reducing the cellular debris on the surface. Postoperatively, the goal is to decrease inflammation, moisturize, nurture, and soothe. In both phases the skin is hydrated and protected from ultraviolet A and B rays emitted by the sun. Treatment plans for the most common procedures are available.

Procedures And Treatment Plans

Laser Resurfacing

Strict rules apply to the patient undergoing a laser resurfacing procedure. Patients must fully understand that the surgery results are highly dependent on their willingness to follow all protocols as directed by the medical team. All phases of the pre- and post-operative stages are labor intensive and hands on for the patient. Tables 38–1a and 38–1b provide sample guidelines for pre- and post-operative care. Each medical office will customize its own specific protocols.

> **conditioning**
> Increasing the skin's metabolism and reducing the cellular debris on the surface.

Table 38-1a Presurgery Laser Resurfacing

Timetable	In Office	Home Care
Week 8–7	Treatment plan is adapted and modified to the needs of the patient. This plan continues weeks after surgery. The patient's skin type and classification (level or degree of photoaging) will determine the plan chosen according to the physician's protocol. ❑ **Superficial chemical peel** such as AHA, BHA or Jessner's (a combination of AHA, BHA, lactic acid, resorcinol, depending on preparation) are best applied by starting with the lowest concentration and gradually increasing as patient tolerates. These peels help stimulate the home care program by exfoliating the upper layers of the epidermis and serving as an additional skin lightening measure. The patient must discontinue using retinoic acid the day before, and three days after a peel. ❑ **Microdermabrasion** can be used as an alternate to chemical peels. This is an excellent modality in superficial exfoliation for very strong, oily, thick, skin that has had extreme sun exposure. Make certain that the patient stops using retinoic acid 2-3 days prior to, and after a microdermabrasion treatment. ❑ **Enzyme peel** An enzyme called papain is found in papaya. It is a gentle exfoliant and will dissolve keratin, thereby softening and hydrating the skin. It is often used on very sensitive skin.	Prelaser kit ❑ AHAs and/or BHAs (alpha- and betahydroxy acids) for exfoliation ❑ Hydroquinone (medical-grade melanocyte suppressant-skin lightener). *Note:* There are other nonmedical-grade lighteners such as licorice extract, kojic acid, bearberry, mulberry, and ergothioteine for patients allergic to hydroquinone. Keep in mind that these must be tested for patient sensitivity ❑ Hydrating moisturizer with amino acids (enhance water retention), green tea extract (antioxidant that helps to neutralize free radicals), hyaluronic acid (natural moisturizer with water-binding capabilities). ❑ Retinoic Acid (Retin-A, Renova, Activa) is a vitamin A derivative used for exfoliation on the upper layer of the stratum corneum. It stimulates fibroblast activity. ❑ Environmental protector—sunscreen containing at least an SPF (sun protection factor) of 30, and physical barriers such as zinc oxide, titanium dioxide, Parsol 1789 (avobenzone), and broad-spectrum chemical absorbing ingredients such as octyl methoxycinnamate, and benzophenone-3 (oxybenzone). Daily regime AM 1. Cleanse 2. Lightener (hydroquinone) 3. Moisturizer with AHA and or BHA 4. Sunscreen with 30 SPF PM 1. Cleanse 2. Lightener 3. Retinoic acid 4. Moisturizer/hydrator
Weeks 6–5	Continue in-office treatment with chemical peel or microdermabrasion.	Continue home care with prelaser kit.
Weeks 4–3	Continue in-office treatment with chemical peel or microdermabrasion.	Continue home care with prelaser kit.
Week 2	Continue in-office treatment with chemical peel or microdermabrasion.	Continue home care with prelaser kit.
Week 1	Apply a soothing, hydrating facial treatment, using cool steam, high-frequency, light-to-little massage, and sunscreen. At this point the patient's skin has become conditioned, and we do not want it to be overtreated the day of surgery	Home care: Change in protocol ❑ Cleansing regime ❑ Moisturizer with AHA ingredient such as glycolic, lactic, or combination ❑ Sunscreen **Antiviral medication:** Patient begins to take medication to suppress herpetic breakout (cold sores). Routine as prescribed by physician.

Table 38–1b Postsurgery Laser Resurfacing

Timetable	In Office	Home Care
Days 1–5	Silon dressing Special sheeting is applied to freshly ameliorated/lasered skin, and occlusive ointment (petroleum) to unaffected areas such as lips. Instruct patient to call the office if this dressing falls off. It may need to be replaced.	Follow physician's directions.
Days 5–10	Once physician removes dressing, patient begins to apply solution soaks every 2–3 hours as indicated by physician. (Solution is usually 1 part hydrogen peroxide 1 part water, or 1 teaspoon vinegar to 1 cup of water.) This is followed by an application of ointment. The skin must never dry out. It must be kept well lubricated in order to prevent infection.	Follow physician's directions.
Days 10–15		Postlaser kit ❑ Gentle cleanser ❑ Hydrocortisone for itching ❑ Squalane for moisturizing (light emollient-plant lipid) ❑ Copper peptide cream (enhances wound healing) ❑ Sunscreen ❑ Continue taking antiviral medication as directed
Days 15-30	Once patient has re-epithelialized (dermis has re-established and healed) and patient has been given instruction by the physician begin: ❑ Camouflage therapy. Use mineral powder makeup for this step. It contains titanium dioxide and natural pigments, which are much less irritating to the new skin than over-the-counter (OTC) brands of makeup. Patients may exhibit pustules and milia that can be gently extracted.	Continue home care products using hydrating moisturizers, copper peptide cream, and sunscreen with SPF (sun protection factor) of at least 30.
One month postsurgery	Most patients will be tolerant of a light exfoliating AHA (less than 5% glycolic, with a high pH of 3.5) product if directed by a physician at this point. Often the skin is still peeling, which will help to further the healing process. However, all in-office treatments should be directed toward hydrating and soothing for up to 3 to 6 months. Avoid using warm steam on a post-laser patient. Continue to remind patients at every visit to use sunscreen and to avoid the sun. *Safety Note:* Do *not* use microdermabrasion, glycolic, salicylic, or lactic acids on a post-laser patient unless authorized by the physician.	

Rhytidectomy (Face-Lift) And Forehead Lift

As indicated for the laser resurfacing procedure, the patient increases tolerance for the postoperative phase when the skin is in optimum condition prior to surgery. This requires a well-orchestrated home care and in-office treatment agenda. Ideally, protocols begin 8 to 10 weeks prior to the surgery. This is an optimum program so you may need to modify according to the realistic time scheduled between the patient and physician. When a combination of procedures is scheduled, such as a face-lift and laser resurfacing, the esthetician combines both treatment plans (Tables 38–2a and 38–2b).

Blepharoplasty (Eyelift)

Modify the treatment plan when performed in conjunction with another procedure. For example, laser resurfacing is often applied periorbitally on the lower lids to tighten the skin around the eye after the fat deposits have been removed. Follow laser-resurfacing protocol if necessary. Refer to Tables 38–3a 38–3b, p. 614.

SAFETY*Tip*

Rosacea Patients
Follow the general protocol except use medication Metro-gel cream (metronidazole topical antibiotic used to fight symptoms of rosacea such as redness and swelling) first after cleanser and use a moisturizer containing chamomile or azulene, alpha lipoic acid (antioxidant and anti-inflammatory), and sunscreen. Also use enzyme peel for exfoliation in in-office treatment.

Table 38–2a Presurgery Face-Lift (Rhytidectomy)

Timetable	In Office	Home Care
Week 8	Treatments for forehead and face-lift patients can be *applied every other week,* and may include a combination of classic facials, peels, and lymphatic drainage massage. Apply treatment appropriate to skin type. At a minimum, include the following: 1. Cleansing Remove makeup with a gentle cleanser 2 Exfoliation Apply chemical peel. 3. Microdermabrasion or enzyme peel. 4. Extractions Gently perform extractions to pustules, whiteheads, blackheads, and milia. 5. Hydration Use a combination of amino acids (enhances water retention in the skin), lipids/ceramides copper peptide gel (for wound healing). 6. Protection Apply a sunscreen with antioxidants after every treatment.	Plan is adapted and modified to needs of the patient Use a minimum of products containing the following: **Cleansers** AHAs, BHAs, or papaya for exfoliation Chamomile, allantoin, or gotu kola/hydrocotyl for soothing **Exfoliators** AHAs, BHAs, vitamin-A derivatives such as retinol, retinoic acid, enzymes such as papaya/papain, and pineapple. **Hydrators/moisturizers** ❏ Alpha lipoic acid /amino acids (hydrator) ❏ Hyaluronic acid (hydrator) ❏ Green tea (antioxidant-free radical fighter) ❏ Vitamins C and E (antioxidants) ❏ Bioflavonoids (antioxidants) **Eye cream** ❏ Alpha lipoic acid (hydrator) ❏ Vitamins A, E, C (antioxidants) ❏ Arnica (reduces swelling) ❏ Sodium hyaluronate (moisturizing agent) **Sunscreen** ❏ Titanium dioxide (physical barrier against UVA/UVB rays) ❏ Zinc oxide (physical barrier against UVA/UVB rays) ❏ Parsol 1789/avobenzone (a chemical ingredient with broad spectrum protection against UVA rays) ❏ Octyl methoxycinnamate (a chemical ingredient used in a wide variety of sunscreens) **Daily regime** AM 1. Cleanse 2. Exfoliate 3. Hydrate/moisturize (sometimes exfoliators and moisturizers are combined) 4. Sunscreen PM 1. Cleanse 2. Exfoliate 3. Hydrate/moisturize
Weeks 6–3	Continue in-office treatments once a week.	Continue home care regimen.
Weeks 2–1	Continue in-office treatment, add lymphatic drainage massage (treatment massage to help reduce swelling by improving circulation and therefore lymphatic fluid flow).	Continue home care regimen.
Week 1	Perform two lymphatic drainage massages spaced 2 to 3 days apart.	Continue home care regimen.

Table 38–2b Postsurgery Face-Lift (Rhytidectomy)

Timetable	In Clinic	Home Care
Week 1	**Postoperative appointment 2-3 days after surgery** ❏ Patient comes in for postoperative appointment with the physician. The drains (which are placed below the mandible during close-up in surgery) are removed. ❏ Bandages are often replaced with a facial bra to enhance healing of newly placed skin, muscles, and nerves.	**Immediately after surgery:** ❏ Patient rests. Tylenol is taken for pain. ❏ Patient keeps jaw movement at a minimum, by having liquid meals. Using warm, soft cloth to all nonbandaged areas patient performs cleansing, and applies a light hydrating moisturizer.
Days 8-15	❏ Patient sees nurse and physician for suture and staple removal. ❏ Patient sees esthetician for lymphatic drainage massage and camouflage.	**Once bandages are removed** ❏ Gentle cleansing regime (avoid using product on all suture and staple sites). ❏ Clean suture sites with hydrogen and water ($1/2$ to $1/2$) and apply antibiotic ointment. ❏ Moisturize and hydrate (avoid suture and staple sites). ❏ Sunscreen with minimum of 30 SPF (avoid suture and staple sites). ❏ Therapy as directed by physician.

(continued)

Table 38–2b *(continued)*

Timetable	In Clinic	Home Care
2 weeks after	Lymphatic with massage 2 per week, 3 days apart ❏ Apply soothing facial mask such as azulene (German chamomile). Patients often need some exfoliation at this point. ❏ An enzyme (papaya) mask may be applied. Avoid chemical peels, microdermabrasion, heat/steam, or any treatment that may be too aggressive at this point. ❏ Physician will usually see patient for another postoperative visit during this time.	Most patients can return to their presurgery home care regime at this point. They can use AHAs, BHAs, hydrating moisturizers, and sunscreens. ❏ Many patients will feel some numbness located at or near incision sites. Lymphatic drainage massage is applied as part of a routine facial treatment.

Table 38–3a Presurgery for Eyelift (Blephroplasty)

Timetable	In Clinic	Home Care
Weeks 6–5	Skin analysis Deep cleansing facial	❏ Face—routine skin care as followed for rhytidectomy and forehead lift. ❏ Eye cream containing arnica or cucumber extract (reduces swelling), hyaluronic acid and amino acids (hydration), bioflavonoids (antioxidants), and sunscreen. *Note*: If laser resurfacing, add: ❏ Hydroquinone (lightener) AM and PM ❏ Retinoic acid (collagen stimulation and cell normalizer) PM only
Week 4	Add to routine facial, one of the following: ❏ Microdermabrasion—periorbitally for exfoliation and stimulation, followed by hydrating eye mask containing evening primrose oil (hydrating and improves barrier climate), chamomile, allantoin (soothing), and/or lady's thistle (wound healing). Follow with appropriate hydration and sunscreen. *or* ❏ Light glycolic peel for exfoliation, lightening, and hydrating. Depending on skin type and classification, follow with appropriate hydrator and sunscreen.	Continue with home care regimen.
Week 3	Continue with exfoliation treatment and eye mask.	Continue with home care *or* prelaser kit if indicated.
Week 2	Continue eye treatment.	Continue with home care as indicated.
Week 1	Use hydrating eye mask treatment only the last week.	Continue as indicated. If having laser resurfacing, stop using hydroquinone and retinoic acid.

Table 38–3b Postsurgery for Eyelift (Blepharoplasty)

Timetable	In Office	Home Care
Days 1–7	❏ Nurse or physician removes sutures at 5–7 days. ❏ If laser procedure was performed on lower lids, physician removes bandage/sheeting on day 5 (if it has not fallen off). Apply postlaser soaks (1 part hydrogen peroxide to 1 part water), then keep well lubricated with petroleum.	❏ Ice, ice, ice ❏ Apply eyedrops as indicated by physician ❏ Apply topical antibiotic at suture site (if directed by physician). ❏ Take Tylenol for pain as directed by physician.
Days 7–12	❏ Follow-up visit with physician. ❏ Camouflage makeup for bruising as directed by physician.	❏ If laser, patient follows protocol using postlaser kit items: hydrocortisone, squalane, copper peptide cream, and sunscreen. ❏ If not, use hydrating eye cream and sunscreen. ❏ If indicated by physician, light camouflage may be applied (if appropriate products are used such as mineral-based powders.)
2–3 weeks after	❏ Lymphatic drainage massage (if no laser) ❏ Hydrating/soothing eye mask as complement to routine facial treatment. ❏ Do not use microdermabrasion, glycolic, salicylic, or lactic acids on freshly ameliorated (lasered) skin. These treatments can be resumed only after several months, as indicated by physician.	❏ Return to hydrating eye cream as followed in presurgery protocol ❏ If laser resurfacing, continue following postlaser protocol. ❏ Continue camouflage makeup.

Manual Lymphatic Drainage

Manual lymphatic drainage (MLD), a treatment utilizing a series of light rhythmic movements, stimulates lymph fluid to flow through the lymphatic vessels. When vessels become blocked or congested, excess water, protein, and waste create edema (swelling) in the connective tissue. When lymph fluid is moved back through and into the bloodstream for cleansing and purifying, this process expedites the postoperative healing process. When performed preoperatively, the patient benefits from an increase in hydration, lowered levels of stress and anxiety, and general detoxification. As a clinical esthetician, studying and becoming certified in manual lymphatic drainage is one of the most valuable investments you can make in your career. You will use it, in part, or completely, just about every day on a patient. MLD has its roots in Europe. Physical therapists Emil and Estrid Vodder created MLD in 1932 for their patients suffering from chronic bronchitis, sinusitis, and arthritis.

Features

MLD involves low overhead and it is indicated treatment for most pre- and postoperative procedures.

Benefits

It serves as a soothing, relaxing massage for those in discomfort. It detoxifies tissues, improves hydration, and helps to regenerate cells.

Advanced Training

Advanced training courses are available all over the U.S., Canada, and Europe (Figure 38–1). Many are adaptations of the original method, and are excellent. The Dr. Vodder School–North America, however, is the only school in North America to teach the original method of MLD. The school is directed by Robert Harris.

Chemical Peels

Because **chemical peels** come in a variety of strengths, they are to be used carefully and cautiously depending on the esthetician's level of experience (Figure 38–2a, p. 617).

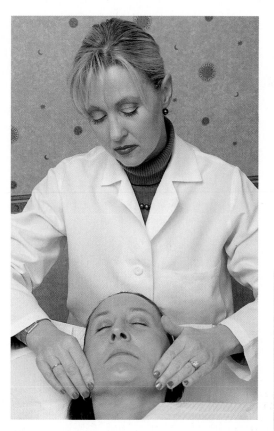

Figure 38–1 Advanced training is necessary to perform any advanced medical procedure or treatment.

> **SAFETY*Tip***
>
> Do *not* perform MLD on anyone with an infectious disease, severe sinusitis, pneumonia, basal cell carcinoma, open sores, or suspicious lesions.

Appropriate peels for an esthetician's use range from the lightest enzymatic exfoliant to light-medium. Remember to work strictly on the epidermis; any peel that penetrates further is beyond your licensure. An exception to this is when you are working in tandem with, and under the supervision of, a physician.

Alpha- and Betahydroxy Peels

Depending upon the skin type and skin conditions, these peels can be used as a preconditioning agent. These are known as lunchtime peels, and patients prefer them because they can see and feel an immediate change in the skin texture. Applying an appropriate chemical peel prior to laser resurfacing, trichloroacectic acid peel (TCA), rhytidectomy (face-lift), blepharoplasty (eyelift), forehead lift, enhances the strength and barrier function of the epidermis.

Features

Peels are reasonably inexpensive and easy to perform. Some create more discomfort than

> **SAFETY*Tip***
>
> To avoid unnecessary reactions, always patch test behind the ear for sensitivity.

> **chemical peels**
> A technique for improving the appearance when wrinkles of the skin are present.

SKILLS **FOR** SUCCESS

Continuing Education

You have finished the required number of hours for state licensure, received your esthetics diploma, and passed the state board exam. Whew—it's over! Not so quick. Education is the foundation of your career, the basis from which you will continue to grow as a professional. It is not the end of learning.

Because you have attended an accredited institution for esthetic training—one that has provided you with considerable knowledge to enter the field—you are now ready for the real challenge—keeping pace. Technology has changed the way we conduct business. From innovative advances in product and equipment to new treatments and techniques, the esthetics industry has grown tremendously over the past two decades. As a result, keeping up with the ever-increasing volume of information necessary to perform the job well has become a formidable task for the esthetician.

In today's competitive marketplace, the power of the media is astounding. Clients are continually bombarded with information that both empowers and confuses them. Estheticians must be prepared to provide savvy consumers with in-depth and knowledgeable responses to their skin care concerns.

Advanced training can be accessed from a number of different sources. Two of the best ways to stay connected to continuing education opportunities are alumni and trade associations. Most reputable esthetic schools offer advanced training courses to sustain the caliber of their graduates. Trade organizations are also invested in upholding the standard and efficacy of the profession. Maintaining affiliations with both is a good way to stay informed and connect with industry leaders who can support your learning.

Vendors and distributors are another viable source for learning. As products and techniques become more scientifically based the level of complexity has increased. Estheticians must be able to explain the theory behind treatments to sell these services to clients. Smart manufacturers understand that education is the key to generating sales and will arm you with the knowledge and support you need to use and sell their products.

Those just starting out in esthetics should be aware that the industry has undergone considerable change in the relatively short period since its inception as a unique career opportunity. The need for knowledge now goes beyond basic skin care products and processes. Today, estheticians are interfacing with a variety of health and beauty experts, such as dermatologists, plastic surgeons, massage therapists, nutritionists, and other wellness-oriented professionals. Seeking information, or attending workshops and seminars in these related fields is paramount to developing productive working relationships with these colleagues.

The field of esthetics has also witnessed a dramatic increase in the number of skin care clinics and day spas in the marketplace. This makes developing solid business skills just as important as the practical ability of maintaining a competitive edge and increasing revenues. Taking advantage of course offerings at local adult education centers and community colleges can be an easy way to access computer, accounting, and other business-related skills.

Successful estheticians understand the value of increasing their knowledge. They know that they must be proactive and responsible for their own learning. Subscribing to trade publications, purchasing books and videos, and learning to use the Internet will put you in touch with a great deal of useful information and will help you build your own resource library.

Staying on top of your game requires motivation and effort. You must be willing to expend time, energy, and money. But by continually placing yourself in professional learning situations you will meet people who can support your goals. Consider it capitalizing on your original education investment.

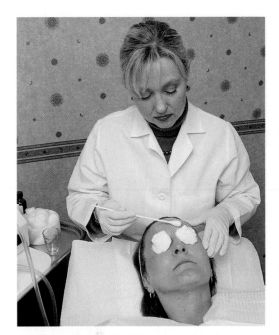

Figure 38–2a Glycolic peel.

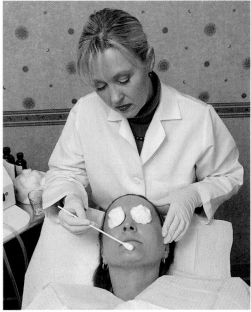

Figure 38–2c Glycolic peel.

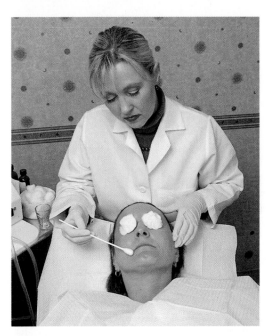

Figure 38–2b Glycolic peel.

others. Most patients, however, tolerate them well (Figure 38–2b). Patients are normally familiar with peels because of media hype.

Benefits

The skin appears smoother, softer, in some cases lighter, as glycolic and Jessner's can lift superficial hyperpigmentation (Figure 38–2c). By eliminating dead cellular debris, the skin has more clarity, luminosity, and

shows an improvement in fine lines. Conversely, this can expose blackheads and other problems which the patient may not be aware of.

Advanced Training

Lighter peel training is given in your basic program. Light to medium peel training can be sought through your physician or employer. It may be obtained as an advanced course by an accredited postgraduate school. Learn as much as you can about these peels.

SAFETY *Tip*

- Contraindications for a chemical peel of any type are
- Accutane use within one or two years (assessment made by physician)
- Fitzpatrick skin types IV–VI (may create severe hyperpigmentation)
- anyone with a herpetic breakout (cold sores)
- moderate to severe rosacea
- pregnancy or lactation
- unstable patient (If you sense that an individual may be mentally ill, have a qualified physician assess the situation prior to giving a peel.)
- anyone with an infectious disease
- open sores, suspicious lesions, or basal cell carcinoma (Always refer to a physician.)

They are used for age management, and are preferred by patients and clients because the results are remarkable!

Microdermabrasion

Microdermabrasion is a mechanical exfoliation of the stratum corneum through the use of a machine that fires crystals (aluminum oxide) through an aperture in a hand piece. The hand piece is moved in a systematic fashion across the skin (Figure 38–3a). The machine is a self-contained unit with separate modules for new and used crystals. Some machines do not use crystals, but rather diamond chips embedded into a stainless hand piece.

Microdermabrasion slightly abrades the built-up tissue, and simultaneously vacuums the crystals and matter back up into a waste bottle or filter through a separate plastic tubing (Figure 38–3b). Some estheticians use microdermabrasion for scar management. This depends on the age and nature of the scar. Patients with acne scarring (depressed scars) can also benefit from microdermabrasion. The depressions may become smoother with repeated treatments when combined with retinoids in a home care program.

Microdermabrasion can be used in a series up to one week prior to a surgical procedure. For an appropriate skin type, its beneficial aspects to enhancing a surgical procedure are limitless. As with lighter peels, it exfoliates dead skin cells in the upper layers of the stratum corneum, helps to lift hyperpigmentation, and in general smoothes out superficial lines and scarring (Figure 38–3c). A secondary benefit to using microdermabrasion preoperatively is the use of the vacuum component, which stimulates blood and lymph flow thereby conditioning the skin to heal faster.

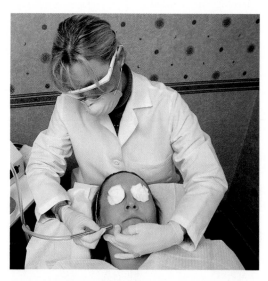

Figure 38–3a Microdermabrasion.

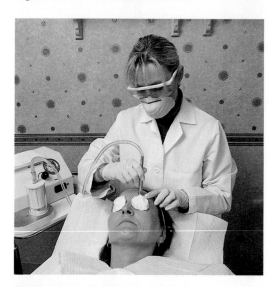

Figure 38–3b Microdermabrasion.

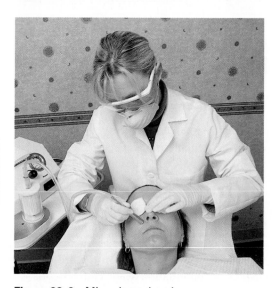

Figure 38–3c Microdermabrasion.

*SAFETY*Tip

Microdermabrasion is contraindicated for
- Accutane (must be off Accutane for 1 to 5 years, as directed by physician)
- acne type III or above
- infectious disease
- open sores or suspicious lesions (always refer to a physician)
- rosacea or presence of telangiectasias

Before Surgery

Microdermabrasion may be used preoperatively for various procedures depending upon skin types and condition. It is also used on the body to exfoliate arms, hands, legs, and feet. It is excellent as a preparatory treatment to a TCA peel on hands and arms. It can be used in conjunction with a glycolic or a TCA peel. It is considered an advanced treatment, requiring additional training as well as approval from the physician.

Features

Microdermabrasion provides a controlled exfoliation without using chemicals. It takes some experience to use it as a multitask modality, such as on heels, arms, and other body parts, but once you are trained, its uses are unlimited for superficial exfoliation.

Benefits

The benefits of using microdermabrasion are

    no down time for the patient

    can be used on people who are intolerant of chemicals

    provides an even peel

    takes a limited amount of time

    once the machine is paid for, it can be quite lucrative

Advanced Training

Operation of the microdermabrasion machine requires advanced training. The manufacturers of these systems employ estheticians, skin care professionals, educators, or nurses to train and certify in performing basic procedures as well as advanced applications. Many postgraduate programs include microdermabrasion as part of the standard curriculum.

Endermology

Endermology is a cellulite treatment given before and after liposuction. It helps stimulate the reduction of adipose tissue (fat) in areas such as the buttocks, thighs, and calves. The endermology machine provides a slight vacuum to the affected areas, thereby increasing blood and lymph flow. It helps reduce the incidence of bruising and swelling associated with liposuction. This treatment can be used both pre- and postoperatively as directed by the physician.

SAFETYTip

Contraindications and risks for endermology are
- varicose veins
- major circulatory problems
- heart conditions

Features

The endermology machine is relatively easy to operate and patients feel an immediate response to the treatment.

Benefits

The benefits of endermology are improved circulation and less cellulite. As with most of these machines, once it is paid for, it can be lucrative.

Advanced Training

Training on how to use the endermology machine is conducted at schools and trade shows, and is also given at sales presentations or by the manufacturer.

Ayurvedic and Swedish Massage

In addition to relieving stress, massage is beneficial both pre- and postoperatively due to the increased activity of the circulatory system. Simultaneously massage both calms and stimulates. Two senses are heightened: the sense of smell is stimulated by the oils that are used and the sense of touch is engaged. This treatment can reduce anxiety preoperatively, and postoperatively it helps the patient release fluids and swelling created by the surgery. It also creates a sense of well-being in the patient.

endermology
A body treatment given before and after liposuction; helps stimulate the reduction of adipose tissue (fat) in areas such as the buttocks, thighs, and calves.

SAFETYTip

Although massage can ease the stress associated with the following conditions, they must be reported to the therapist:
- active cancer
- some cardiac problems
- thyroid problems
- low blood pressure
- asthma
- pregnancy (must be done by a certified massage therapist trained in treating pregnant women)

Features

Once a practitioner has completed training by an accredited massage school, and passed the state board examinations, the massage therapist can work independently just about anywhere. There are many opportunities for a massage therapist as these services become more recognized and accepted. With some oil and a table (or chair in some cases), one can perform the job without much overhead or expense.

Benefits

Massage creates a sense of well-being, improves circulation, and reduces stress.

Advanced Training

Massage therapists must be licensed by the state to perform massage on the body. In addition to being certified and licensed to practice esthetics, many estheticians are also certified to practice massage. The American Massage Therapy Association (AMTA) offers information on schools, accreditation, certification, legislation, and continuing education.

computer imaging
Incorporates consultation, patient education, patient selection, and medical documentation; can also be used to document gradual changes during each treatment phase.

Table 38–4 Treatments at a Glance.

Procedure	Preop Treatment	Postop Treatment
Face-lift/rhytidectomy	MLD Routine facial Microdermabrasion Chemical peels	MLD Soothing facial Camouflage
Eyelift/blepharoplasty	MLD Routine facial Microdermabrasion Camouflage Peels: Pretreat if laser	MLD Calming facial Post-laser kit: Posttreat if laser
Forehead lift	MLD Routine facial	MLD Soothing facial Camouflage
Laser resurfacing	Chemical peels Microdermabrasion Prelaser kit	Postlaser kit Soothing/hydrating facial
Liposuction	MLD Endermology	MLD Endermology: After six weeks or per physician direction
Breast augmentation	MLD	Scar management Breast massage
Breast reduction	MLD Ayurvedic massage	MLD Scar management
Abdomectomy (tummy tuck)	MLD Ayurvedic massage Herbal wraps	MLD Swedish massage Scar management

Treatment Summary

Table 38–4 is a guide for suggested treatments that are administered both pre- and postoperatively. Consult with a physician to review prior to beginning any work.

Computer Imaging

Computer imaging plays a role in all phases of pre and postoperative care. It incorporates consultation, patient education, patient selection, and medical documentation. Schedule this as a separate session prior to any treatment. It can also be used to document gradual changes during each treatment phase.

Computer images can provide a means for interactive communication for all staff including the physician, nurse, patient coordinator, and esthetician. For the physician it serves as medical documentation and aids in patient selection. It is an excellent tool for patient education. Steps for a typical session include:

1. Record the patient's image with a digital or video camera. The patient's name and demographics are entered into a database.

2. Place the image on both sides of a split screen.

3. Then the artwork begins. The original photo remains stationary while the other photo is manipulated to create different images showing the patient's enhanced appearance.

4. Both photos are viewed in the split screen.

5. A photo of the enhanced image is printed and given to the patient.

Create the simulated image as realistically as possible. It is a valuable recording to keep in the patient's medical record. The physician reviews it to evaluate whether the patient's expectations are feasible. In the case of postoperative followup the patient is reimaged, and the latest image is compared to both the original image and the enhanced image.

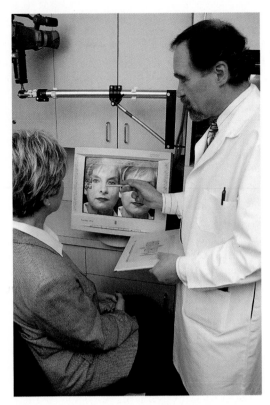

Figure 38–4 Computer imaging session.

Summary

It is imperative that thorough pre- and post-operative care procedures be established and followed to ensure the success of a procedure. Strict rules apply for many of the procedures discussed, and if followed, will help the patient to heal after surgery. Following protocols will increase the patient's tolerance for the postsurgery phase. The esthetician must understand when and how to modify treatment plans, based on the type of surgery being performed. When procedures are combined, a combined treatment plan must be instituted by the esthetician so that the patient is properly prepared for the procedures.

Discussion Questions

1. Create a list of commonly used chemical peels within a the medical esthetic practice. What are the main advantages and disadvantages associated with each? Conduct additional research if necessary.

2. How is laser technology utilized within the medical esthetic practice? Conduct additional research to determine how the FDA regulates or classifies laser equipment. Find out how these regulations affect the use of laser technology in your state. Include in your discussion the role of the esthetician and professional boundary issues.

3. How is massage therapy utilized within the medical esthetic practice? Explain the circumstances where massage might be contraindicated.

4. What role does computer imaging play in pre- and postoperative care? Discuss the pros and cons of utilitizing such advanced technology.

Additional Reading

Brody, Harold J. 1997. *Chemical Peeling and Resurfacing.* St. Louis, Mo.: Mosby Year Book, Inc.

Camezind, A. 1998. *Lymphatic Drainage.* Bellevue, Wash.: Euro-Institute.

Camiol, Paul. 2000. *Facial Rejuvenation: From Chemical Peels to Laser Resurfacing.* New York: John Wiley & Sons, Inc.

Deitz, S. 1999. *Microdermabrasion.* Torrance, Calif.: Novicom, Plastic Surgery Products.

Perricone, N. 2000. *The Wrinkle Curve.* Yale University: Rodale Reach.

Chapter 39
Camouflage Therapy

Chapter Objectives

After reading this chapter, you should be able to:

- List the different types of camouflage treatments.
- Describe the difference between temporary and permanent treatments.
- Describe how to assess when a patient is ready for camouflage treatments.
- List the medical applications.

Chapter Outline

Introduction
Short-Term Use of Camouflage Therapy
Makeup Applications for Specific Cosmetic Procedures
Medical Applications

Introduction

Camouflage means hiding, concealing, covering, veiling, or disguising something. Nature uses camouflage for protection. The basic survival of many birds, animals, and sea creatures is dependent on their coloring and appearance and their ability to hide from their predators.

Patients apply camouflage techniques for numerous reasons. For some, camouflage may be a temporary measure while recovering from a surgical procedure. For others, it is a lifetime practice of researching new products to disguise a congenital disfigurement, or even to hide the aftermath of an accident. The esthetician must carefully evaluate whether camouflage therapy is meeting the temporary or permanent needs of the patient. This determines the course of action.

All makeup applications are some form of camouflage. The same basic principles are applied when shading your own face for more definition, applying color correction to cover a hemangioma (red birthmark), or toning down a freshly abraded (lasered) skin. Shading and color enhancement principles are followed throughout. When shading, the darker a color is, the more an object recedes, or moves back into space. Conversely, the lighter a color is the more the object appears closer or to move forward. Colors have different levels of lightness and darkness known as value.

Color complements or blends a skin tone. Color can oppose and stand out by its obvious quality. Understanding the merits of applying pigment (color) combined with techniques for shading and blending enhances any face or body area. Refer to Part IX, Chapter 32.

Short-Term Use Of Camouflage Therapy

Short-term camouflage therapy is quite different from treatment due to a lifetime condition such as a congenital birth defect or a scar from a traumatic accident. Postoperative patients are normally delighted about a camouflage makeup appointment. During recovery, patients may feel exiled from their

routine lives. Occasionally, they are anxious about family and friends finding out about the surgery.

The availability of in-office camouflage makeup services is invaluable. Postoperatively, it may not be appropriate for the patient to be seen in a public place such as a department store. Many patients are self-conscious about their appearance.

Camouflage makeup should be easy to use. Instructions for application are simply taught by shading in colors on a schematic or face chart. If makeup application is not part of your expertise, there are makeup artists who specialize in working with patients in postsurgical work. Hire a freelance camouflage specialist to come to your office.

Makeup sessions should be as uncomplicated as possible. Show step-by-step application. Camouflage makeup is a thicker consistency and takes more effort to apply properly. Allow enough time to work with the patient. The patient needs to learn how to comfortably apply the makeup. Demonstrate on half the face, and then have the client apply the makeup to the other half. Remind the patient that it takes some practice. During the first visit the patient may feel more comfortable having you apply makeup to the entire face. This can be an emotional experience for some patients. It is important to have compassion and to reassure the patient that she will be able to reproduce this new look at home.

Old habits are difficult to break. When the eye area is altered through surgery, you may have to re-educate the patient on a new application process. This occurs particularly on the upper lid regions where a heavy contouring shadow had been used for a droopy eyelid. Again with compassion and an educational approach, you may show that individual why it is no longer necessary to apply dark shadow on the lid, and show her a fresh new way (and probably easier way) to apply color.

Makeup Applications for Specific Cosmetic Procedures

Application techniques vary depending upon the type of cosmetic procedure the patient has experienced. The following material

camouflage
To hide, conceal, cover, veil, or disguise something.

presents discussion on application techniques for five different surgical procedures.

Laser Resurfacing/Chemical Peel

When the patient is completely healed and ready for the next step, the physician authorizes and refers the patient for camouflage makeup. Normally makeup is allowed between ten days and two weeks after a laser treatment. The epidermis must be completely re-epithelialized with its barrier revived so that there is no danger of infection.

Today's high-tech, low-impact, sheer, inert mineral powders (titanium dioxide) work the best for camouflage postlaser. They can be lightly dusted, or gently sponged on freshly ameliorated (laser resurfacing or peeled) skin to camouflage the redness created by the procedure. The redness or erythema can last for two to four months depending on the Fitzpatrick skin type and condition of the skin. For this type of application, applying green color correcting products is no longer done. Instead, newer mineral powders and foundations that contain built-in correcting measures are used. When camouflaging redness, yellow turns out to be a better color choice. It blends in with the natural skin tones of most patients. Green color correction must be covered with an additional product, and then powder is used to set. The exception to this is when a patient requests green as a personal choice, or in the case of extreme erythema (redness).

Depending on the recovery time, mineral powders can also be mixed with sunscreens, moisturizers, eye creams, and some gels. Liquid foundations containing titanium dioxide are also available. These newer, lighter bases provide excellent coverage. When a liquid base or foundation is preferred, apply it in addition to the powder.

The following steps help ensure a successful application.

1. Always start with a fresh bottle or new powder.

2. Do not use heavy makeup or powder. Because the pores are more refined as a result of surgery, a product that is too heavy may clog the pores.

3. Use a soft, high-quality, powder brush or sponge.

4. Apply light layers of base, and gently pat in powder in areas of darker redness.

5. Make certain that the patient has an appropriate cleansing product that easily collects makeup and skin debris. It should not contain any performance agents that can overstimulate or irritate.

Rhytidectomy (Face-Lift)

Camouflage treatment for rhytidectomy (face-lift) is primarily targeted at bruising. It may be difficult to cover all the bruising. Bruising appear in various colors of yellow, green, plum, red, and dark purple, which are characteristic of a postoperative condition following a face-lift.

Bruising may involve the face, neck, and chest. The degree of bruising is dependent on the extensiveness of the surgery, the patient's skin type, and color. Full camouflage treatment can be performed at about day ten, after the sutures and staples are removed. Avoid the immediate scar site with your therapy. It must be completely healed to avoid irritation and even infection. Once healed, and with the physician's authorization, apply a base and/or powder directly on the scar to tone down the redness. Some scars will be slightly hypertrophic or have a ridge; others will be flat and smooth. This depends on the type of procedure, and the patient's ability to heal. Eventually most scars will lose color and blend in with the rest of the skin tone. Most will flatten. In any case the patient will often use products for many months to conceal the scars.

A blepharoplasty or eyelift gives an artist a rewarding challenge. Nothing can change the look of a face like the rejuvenation of a dry, crinkly, baggy, tired eye. Albeit subtle, treating the eye area with a fresh application of shadow base to lighten and brighten the lid is a welcome gift to a patient who had a hidden lid due to droopy skin, which interfered with makeup application. In some instances, it may be necessary to perform this surgery simply because the condition interfered with sight.

The first step is to cover the bruised area. With the swipe of a shadow sponge and mineral powder as a base, the redness and/or bruising can disappear. A slight yellow undertone to the powder can neutralize redness. It serves as a great base for the application of a light shadow color. Mascara and liner are recommended on days eight to ten approximately. The healing response and the physician's recommendation are the determining factors. Adding a darker color shadow on the incision in the crease may be appropriate at three weeks if substantial healing has taken place.

It is important that the patient have a gentle eye makeup remover to take off the camouflage makeup. Apply a small amount on a cotton ball and gently pat it on the lid. Do not pull across the new incision site. Instruct the patient to flush with water to make certain that the cleanser is off the eyelid. Always be very gentle around the eye area.

Long-Term Use Of Camouflage Applications

Camouflage therapy may be appropriate for a patient who has experienced disfigurement from an accident or a congenital birth defect. It is best to approach this individual with care and active listening skills. Chances are that it is possible to improve the appearance of the disfigurement (Figures 39–1a and 39–1b). If the individual has not come to terms with the scarring, it may be best to just visit with the patient with the physician in attendance.

Too Soon or Not Ready for Treatment

Some people are seriously traumatized by changes in their appearance, and feel that they are unable to cope. It is not unusual for an accident victim to be quite angry, unhappy, or unsatisfied with anything you might suggest. Also, you never want to give false hope or the impression that you can take away the disfigurement. If you have not had training or counseling yourself in this field, it may be appropriate to have the physician refer the patient to a psychologist specializing in this condition.

When the patient *is* interested in trying some camouflage techniques, be patient, pleasant, and consistent. Ask the patient the following questions.

1. What is your greatest area of concern?

2. What have you tried before? How does that work now?

3. What do you hope these sessions can do for you (then share what you may be able to do)? Proceed at the patient's pace. If the patient knows what he wants and is ready to move forward, go ahead. If the patient is hesitant, let him know that he can always return at another time when he is ready.

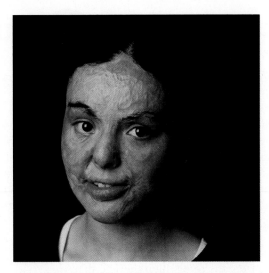

Figure 39–1a Client with disfiguring burn scars.

Figure 39–1b The client after application of camouflage makeup.

Features

One of the many features of offering camouflage therapy is to provide comprehensive care for the patients of the physician with whom you are associated.

SAFETY*Tip*

Do not perform camouflage therapy on an individual with
- open lesions
- type III acne or above
- skin that does not have an intact barrier
- infectious diseases, staph infection
- postoperative condition unauthorized by a physician

Defining Success

Congratulations! You are about to embark on a career in esthetics. All of your hard work and perseverance will soon pay off. But before you chart a course and go, take a few moments to visualize just how you would like your career to unfold.

Success means different things to different people. For some it is the knowledge of having done a job well. For others, it is about how much money they earn. Still others are inclined to measure their success from the recognition they receive or the value they gain from helping others. You will have to determine that marker for yourself.

Stephen R. Covey, author of the national bestseller *The 7 Habits of Highly Effective People* urges us to think thoughtfully about developing such skills as vision, leadership, and management on a personal level. Interpersonal skills, communication, and cooperation are also high on his list. Understanding the need to take time out to replenish your own mind, body, and spirit, he wisely acknowledges, is also an important priority.

As you create your own philosophy of what it means to be a successful esthetician, consider not only the practical skills you have worked so hard to develop, but all the business skills we have discussed. How you develop these will have as significant an impact on your career as your competence as a practitioner.

Take some time to digest the many topics we have reviewed—marketing, public relations, professional image, customer service, communication, retail skills, etc. Then think about placing them in the context of the following basic business principles.

- Understand what the customer needs and values.
- Know your competition.
- Continually strive to provide excellent service.
- Be willingly to look at yourself critically.
- Maintain flexibility and a willingness to learn.

Benefits

The benefits of camouflage therapy are numerous. You can make a big difference in helping a postoperative patient re-enter the work force feeling confident, secure in the fact that the recent surgery is not detectable. In addition, you may be able to help an individual with a facial disfigurement and greatly soften and diminish its appearance (Figures 39–2a and 39–2b).

Advanced Training

Postgraduate training is worth pursuing. It can be found at

- trade shows
- most accredited esthetic schools
- teaching hospitals
- makeup schools and qualified specialists

Micropigmentation: Permanent Cosmetic Makeup

Tattooing, permanent makeup, dermagraphics, and **micropigmentation** are all terms for permanent cosmetic makeup. Decorating the skin by applying colored dye into the dermis has been done since the time of the Egyptians, as early as 2000 B.C. Tattooing was developed as a popular form of beautifying the body. Both ancient and modern tribes have used forms of tattooing to distinguish one another, as well as in rites of passage. Cultural expressions have been realized through the use of skin markings, whether through color implantation or scar creation (slashing the skin to produce a certain marking).

Medical Applications

The modern uses for permanent makeup are vast. They are a blessing for those who have undergone reconstructive surgery due to cancer, accidents, or congenital disfigurements. When the limits of surgery are reached, micropigmentation is an additional tool to improve the appearance of individuals born with cleft palettes or for reconstructed breasts after mastectomy. Micropigmentation is used to balance out skin tones in burn survivors. It also helps to make keloids appear more relaxed and less noticeable.

Figure 39–2a Client with facial injuries.

Figure 39–2b Client after application of camouflage makeup.

micropigmentation
A part of permanent makeup, involving the placement of colorants into the skin for the purpose of cosmetic enhancement, medical correction, or aesthetic restoration. It is a separate specialty in the field of tattooing and requires specialized training.

Patients with hair loss due to cancer, alopecia, or trauma have the opportunity to recreate brows and to line the eyes to give more definition to the face. The patient's self-esteem is greatly enhanced. Permanent makeup is also useful for people with physical disabilities such as arthritis, Parkinson disease, multiple sclerosis, and visual impairments. Permanent makeup has many applications, including:

- saving time
- contact lens wearers
- individuals with diminishing eyesight, especially the elderly
- individuals with loss of mobility in the hands

Society of Permanent Cosmetic Professionals and American Academy of Micropigmentation
Membership organizations available to support industry standards, continuing education, and mentorship.

- individuals with allergies to cosmetics (to have the appearance of makeup without the irritation)
- redefining features on an aging face

Number of Treatments

Practitioners generally recommend a series of visits for micropigmentation. Color is gradually applied in a pointillist manner (small strokes or dots) or with hairlike strokes into the dermis. Advancements in topical anesthetics have made it more comfortable for the client, and are preferable to injected anesthesia, which is associated with swelling, thus rendering the treatment less feasible. Using newer modalities, such as light therapy in the 660-nm red range, can minimize swelling and postoperative healing time.

Typical Uses for Permanent Cosmetic Makeup

Eyes: eyebrows, eyeliner
Lips: lipliner, full lip color
Feature Restoration:

1. Lip
   - cleft palate
   - vermilion restoration/asymmetry
2. Breast: areola (nipple)
3. Hair simulation: eye brow (loss of hair)
4. Pigment loss: vitiligo
5. Scar camouflage: burns, accidents
6. Aging feature

Education/Training

When properly educated and certified, estheticians have an excellent opportunity to administer permanent makeup. One must have an aptitude for graphic art, good color awareness and acuity, and a background in general cosmetic principles. Strict protocols and standards must be followed for performing micropigmentation. This cannot be accomplished through a correspondence course. One should find a fully accredited program with extensive hands-on training.

After initial training, specialists recommend that you work as an apprentice. **The**

Society for Permanent Cosmetic Professionals and the American Academy of Micropigmentation are membership organizations available to support industry standards, provide continuing education, and offer mentorships. Both associations require 40-hour minimum basic training courses and recommend apprenticeships.

Summary

The choices of methodology in esthetic medicine have increased tremendously. Future opportunities for the esthetician in a clinical environment are boundless as the profession continues to be recognized and accepted. Our role in pre- and postsurgical care, as well as in advanced skin correction, has proved to be of great benefit. It can actually enhance the work of the medical practitioner. It lends itself well to supporting the efforts of the physician. Facial preparation treatments for surgery ensure a greater outcome for healing. They also open the door for postcare treatments, which are necessary to maintain the patient's investment.

The esthetician's presence in a medical setting extends an opportunity for patients to maintain and monitor their skin long after the surgery. Follow the numerous tips provided in this chapter when working with various patients and personalities. An introduction to each type of facial surgery gives you general knowledge on more advanced corrective facial work. They are a great boost to any age management program because each addresses specific concerns and issues. They can be gradual to more aggressive, depending on the skin condition, patient choice, and the physician's recommendation.

Ongoing education by a skin specialist provides accurate choice for future treatments and products. You are provided with a general summary of step-by-step care protocols for several surgical procedures. They will vary according to the physician and type of practice. The study of medical and clinical esthetics is a course in itself. However, in all settings—medical to spa—mastering the skin and its care is a lifelong objective.

Discussion Questions

1. What is camouflage therapy? Research products used for this purpose. What is the average cost of these products? Where can the patient buy such products? Share your findings.

2. What is the difference between temporary and permanent camouflage? Give examples of both, and discuss which method is best for what types of problems.

3. What are the indications that a patient is ready to begin using camouflage makeup after surgery?

Additional Reading

Rayner, Victoria. 1993. *Clinical Cosmetology, A Medical Approach to Esthetics Procedures.* Clifton Park, N.Y.: Milady, an imprint of Delmar Learning, a division of Thomson Learning, Inc.

Segal, Jeffrey Lyle. 2001, May 7. Permanent Cosmetic Makeup. E-mail personal communication.

GLOSSARY/INDEX

Note: Numbers in bold denote page on which terms are defined.

AAEA. *See* American Aestheticians Education Association (AAEA)

ABCDs of melanoma, 328

Abdomectomy, 620

Abdominoplasty, a surgical procedure where excessive fat deposits and loose skin in the abdomen are tucked and tightened, 591–593

Abducent (VI) nerve, 68, 76

Ablation, of skin, **to remove, 402.** *See also* Dermabrasion; Microdermabrasion

Abuse
    self-, 598
    therapy for survivors of, 597

AC. *See* Alternating current (AC)

Accidents
    liability in, 111
    preventing, 157

Accident victims, 598

Accutane, an oral retinoid to treat severe inflammatory and cystic acne, 175, 278–279
    acne treatment with, 380
    alpha hydroxy acids and, 404
    beta hydroxy acids and, 412
    in rosacea treatment, 255
    side effects of, 278
    use of and contraindication against, 280
    waxing contraindication against, 455

ACD. *See* Allergic contact dermatitis (ACD)

Acidic products, of iontophoresis, 127–128

Acid mantle, a barrier on the surface of the skin formed by sebum and sweat, 294

Acids, substances with a pH value lower than 7.0
    fatty, 289
    pH of, **294**

Acne, 364–388
    Accutane treatment for, 278–279
    alpha hydroxy acids and, 402–403, 406
    bacteria in, 366–367
    causes of, 273
    in client health screening information, 179
    comedonal, 370
    defined, 365
    emollients and, 289–290
    foods and, 371
    grades of, 371–373
    home treatment of, 378–379
    hormonal, 370
    hormonal therapy for, 173–174
    hormones and, 368–370
    medical treatment of, 379–380
    menopause and, 314
    nutrition and, 101
    over-the-counter treatment of, 273–275
    premenstrual, 369

rosacea as, 347
    salicylic acid and, 412
    salon treatment of, 380–388
    stress and, 370–371, 376
    tips for managing, 373–376

Acne cosmetica, acne caused or worsened by skin care and cosmetic products, 373

Acne cysts, 251, 372. *See also* Cystic acne; Cysts

Acne detergicans, acne caused from overcleansing the face, 375

Acne excoriée, a disorder in which the client purposefully scrapes off the surface skin on all acne lesions, 252, 376
    treatment of, 379

Acnegenic products, **elements that cause inflammation in the follicle and resulting acne, 370**

Acnegenic reactions, allergens versus, 180

Acne-prone skin, salon treatment of, 380–388

Acne vulgaris, 365, 372

Acquired immunodeficiency syndrome (AIDS), a syndrome caused by a virus that causes the body's immune cells to malfunction, leaving the body unable to defend itself, 80, 266–268
    in client health screening information, 177
    molluscum contagiosum and, 261
    waxing contraindication against, 455

Acrochordons, skin tags, or small extensions of the skin that look like small tags or flaps hanging off the skin, 254

Actinic damage, actinic damage General skin damage associated with sun exposure, 315

Actinic keratosis, 321
    squamous cell carcinoma and, 327

Actinic lentigenes, freckles from sun damage, 250

Activators, in body treatments, **chemical agent used to start the action of chemical products on hair; an additive used to quicken the action or progress of a chemical. Another word for booster, accelerator, or catalyst, 553**

Active agents, glycolic peel and, **drugs that penetrate beyond the epidermis and are prescription only, 608**

Acupressure massage, **the application of gentle but firm pressure to specific points of the body to release muscle tension and spasm, used on traditional Oriental medicine principles, 216**

in holistic skin care, 420–422
    shiatsu, 424

Acupuncture
    in Chinese traditional medicine, 12
    in holistic skin care, 420–422

Adapalene, also known as Differin, another prescription vitamin-A-related retinoid used to treat acne, 175, 277–278
    acne treatment with, 380

Addictive drugs, 271

Address, in health screening questionnaire, 171

Adenoids, 62

Adenosine triphosphate (ATP), a substance that provides energy to the cell, 31–32

Adhesive for false eyelashes, in makeup kit, 512

Adipose cells, **fat cells, 37**
    cellulite and, 562–563

Adipose tissue, fat tissue that helps cushion the bones and organs of the body, 36, 37. *See also* Body fat; Obesity
    in aging skin, 314
    vitamins in, 97

Adrenal glands, glands located just above the kidney that secrete adrenaline and cortisol, 59
    stress and, 179

Adrenaline, a hormone secreted under stress by the adrenal glands; it stimulates the nervous system, raises metabolism, increases cardiac pressure and output, and increases blood pressure to prepare the body for maximum exertion, 59
    stress and, 179

Adults, acne in, 369–370

Advanced home care, 426–436

Advanced ingredient technology, 302–307
    skin care systems using, 432–436

Advanced registered nurse practitioners (ARNPs)
    in clinical skin care, 577
    prescriptions by, 271

Advanced training, 616

Aesculus hippocastanum, treating telangiectasia with, 319

Aestheticians, 7. *See also* Estheticians

Aesthetics, 27. *See also* Esthetics

Aesthetics International Association (AIA), 19, 377

Aesthetic surgery, defined, 583. *See also* Plastic surgery

Aesthētikos, **perceptible to the senses, 7**

Africa, hair color in, 445

African culture, grooming practices in, 16–17

Age management programs, 6

Agents. *See* Active agents; Bleaching agents; Brightening agents; Buffering agents; Color agents; Dry sanitizing agents; Exfoliating agents; Hydrophilic agents; Lightening agents; Melanin suppressive agents; Occlusive agents; Performance agents; Special agents; Topical agents; Wet sanitizing agents

Age of Extravagance, esthetics during, 17

Aggressive massage, use of and contraindication against, 280

Aging. *See also* Photoaging
  alpha hydroxy acids and, 403–404
  of Asian skin, 394
  of black skin, 393
  discussing with clients, 328–330
  dry/dehydrated skin and, 164
  facial lines and wrinkles and, 168
  hair color and, 445
  intrinsic, 311–315
  sensitive skin and, 348–355
  Skin Care System A for, 432–434
  treating skin conditions due to, 309, 310–339

AHAs. *See* Alpha hydroxy acids (AHAs)

AIA. *See* Aestheticians International Association (AIA)

Aida Grey Beauty Book, The (Grey), 20

AIDS. *See* Acquired immunodeficiency syndrome (AIDS)

Air, in four humors theory, 15

Airborne microorganisms, germs in the air, 79

Air systems, 87

Albinism, a hereditary condition in which the body lacks pigment, including the skin, hair, and iris of the eye, 264

Alchemy, health through, 10

Alcohol. *See* Ethyl alcohol; Fatty alcohols; Isopropyl alcohol

Alcoholics, skin conditions of, 321

Algae, types of, **primitive plants found in fresh or salt water, and include seaweed, kelp, and stoneworts; considered a nutrient, 550**

Algae treatments, 550
  table of, 551

Alipidic skin, **lacking oil (lipids), 164**–165
  treatments for, 298

Alkaline products, of iontophoresis, 127–128

Alkalines, pH of, **substances with a pH value higher than 7.0, 294**

Allergens, a substance that causes an allergic reaction in certain individuals, 180, 259–260
  frequent, 346–347
  hives and, 258
  irritants versus, 180, 344–347
  sensitive skin and, 343

Allergic contact dermatitis (ACD), a type of contact dermatitis that is an allergic reaction in the skin resulting from contact with a particular substance, 257–258

Allergic reactions, 66, 276
  to fragrances, 294–296
  irritant reactions versus, 344–346
  to preservatives, 296

Allergies
  causes of, 344

in client health screening information, 180–181
  work ethic and, 460

Allopathic medicine, holism versus, 419

Almond oil, 10

Aloe vera, in treating sensitive skin, 355

Alpha hydroxy acids (AHAs), 18, 21
  in acne management, 373, 374, 375, 378, 379
  in antiaging treatments, 332
  Asian skin and, 393
  chemical peels using, 615
  dehydration and, 404
  enzyme exfoliants versus, 416
  in exfoliation, 300, 303, 398, 402–409
  first treatment with, 406
  frequency of treatment with, 406
  gommage versus, 399
  Hispanic skin and, 394, 395
  in home care programs, 405–406
  hyperpigmentation and, 359, 361–362
  Jessner's exfoliation versus, 409
  mechanism of action of, 402
  precare treatment for, 404–405
  regular facials and, 406–409
  in rosacea treatment, 257
  in scrubs, 549
  sensitive skin and, 350, 354
  in treating hyperpigmentation, 275, 403
  treatment with, 407–408
  tretinoin and, 277

Alternating current (AC), 141, 143–144
  in blend electrolysis, 448
  in high-frequency machine, 123–124
  in microcurrent devices, 129
  in thermolysis, 448

Alternative Medicine Handbook, The, 419

Alternative skin care, 418–425

Aluminum, as conductor, 141

Aluminum chloride, in microdermabrasion, 400

Ambergris, 10

Ambience, for holistic practices, 419

Ambulatory phlebectomy, 594

American Academy of Dermatology, 583

American Academy of Facial, Plastic and Reconstructive Surgeons, 583

American Academy of Micropigmentation, membership organizations available to support industry standards, continuing education, and mentorship, 628

American Aestheticians Education Association (AAEA) 19, 377

American Beauty Association, on exfoliation, 401

American Board of Plastic Surgery, 583

American Cancer Society, 330

American Institute of Aesthetics, 19

American Massage Therapy Association Foundation, 10

American skin care, evolution of, 18–20

American Society of Plastic and Reconstructive Surgeons (ASPRS), 583

American springs, 17

Amino acids, a group of molecules used by the body to synthesize protein, 31, 92

Ammonium lauryl sulfate, 291

Ampere, a measure of the amount of current flowing into a circuit, 141, **142**

Ampoules
  in facial phase IV, 208
  for home skin care, 428
  polarity of, 127–128
  serums versus, 303–304

Anaerobic bacteria, acne and, **existing in the absence of free oxygen, 273,** 366–367

Anagen phase, in hair growth cycle, **the first stage in hair growth, or the growing stage,** 442, **443**

Analysis and consultation, as facial phase II, 201, 204–205

Anaphase, 34

Anaphoresis, the infusion of a negative product during iontophoresis, 128

Ancient health practices, 9–11

Ancillary profit center, esthetician in, **a separate department within the medical office, such as a retail product area, which generates a profit, 578**

Androgens, any of various hormones that control the development of masculine characteristics, 58–59
  acne and, 368
  hirsutism and, 444
  stress and, 179

Angry clients, handling, 345

Anhydrous creams, **describes products that do not contain water, 287**

Annular lesions, **describes lesions that are ring-shaped, 248**

Answering machines, 599

Anterior facial vein, vein located on the anterior sides of the face which drains into the internal jugular vein located on the sides of the neck, 60

Anthemis nobilis, 553

Antiaging firming treatment, 338

Antiaging tips, 330–332

Antibiotics, prescription drugs that kill bacteria, 279
  in acne treatment, 273, 275, 380
  in treating perioral dermatitis, 257
  use of and contraindication against, 280
  waxing contraindication against, 455

Antibodies, a substance that is formed in response to a foreign body, bacteria, virus, or other toxic substance, 56, 63

Antigens, a foreign invader such as a bacteria, a virus, or other substances that could cause harm to the body, 63, **64,** 65

Antihistamines, a drug that works by blocking the reactions within the skin (histamines) that cause swelling, itching, and redness, 66, **276**

Antioxidants, substances (such as vitamin E) that protect the body through blocking or counteracting the damaging effects of free radical activity, 98, 100, 296
  in antiaging treatments, 330–331

Antiseptics, disinfectants designed for use in human skin, 81

Antiviral medications, 279

Aorta, the main artery coming out of the heart, 35, 60

Apocrine glands, 46

Aponeurosis, a tendon that connects the occipitalis and the frontalis, 71

Appearance. *See also* First impressions; Personal presentation; Sanitation
of skin care professionals, 8, 153
of treatment room, 148, 149, 153
Applicators
for epilation, 452, 463, 466, 469, 470, 472, 474, 477, 480
for makeup, 511
Applied science, chemistry as, **the search for practical uses of scientific knowledge, 283**
Appointments, 166, 253
work ethic and, 460
Aptitude, of skin care professionals, 8
Arched eyebrow, 495
Arctostaphylus uva-urusi, Asian skin and, 393
Arden, Elizabeth, 18
Ardennes, spas in, 11
Area of insertion, of muscles, 70–71
Areola, in mammaplasty, **nipple, 589,** 591
Argon, in electrodes, 124
Arms
muscles of, 73, 74
spot treatments for, 564
waxing of, 474–475
ARNPs. *See* Advanced registered nurse practitioners (ARNPs)
Aromatherapy, the therapeutic use of plant aromas used for beauty and health treatment purposes, 552–553
for hands and feet, 563–564
in holistic skin care, 422
sensitive skin and, 350
Aromatherapy massage, uses essential oils that penetrate the skin during massage movements, 216–218
Aromatherapy oils, highly concentrated plant oils that possess properties with various effects on the skin; also known as essential oils, 294
Arpel, Adrien, 19
Arrector pili muscle, 45, 441, 442
Arteries, 50, 60
in arteriosclerosis, 94
in lymph nodes, 63
of neck, 60
pulmonary, 35
Arteriosclerosis, fatty acids and, **clogging and hardening of the arteries, 94**
Ascorbic acid, 100
dosage, functions, and sources of, 96
Aseptic procedures, the process of properly handling sterilized and disinfected equipment and supplies so they do not become soiled or contaminated by microorganisms until they are used on a client, 83–84
Asian eyebrow, 495
Asian skin, 393–394
types of, 186
Aspirin, as allergen, 180
ASPRS. *See* American Society of Plastic and Reconstructive Surgeons (ASPRS)
Assertiveness, by skin care professionals, 345
Assessment, in SOAP notes, 602
Associated Body Work & Massage Professionals, 377
Asthma
as allergy symptom, 180
in client health screening information, 178
Asymmetry, melanoma and, 328
Atelier Esthetique, 19
Athlete's foot, 261–262

Atoms, the smallest possible unit of an element, 283
electricity and, 137–142
electron energy levels in, 284
free radicals and, 316
in molecules, 284
structure of, 137–139, 282, 283–285
Atopic dermatitis, a form of dermatitis that runs in families. It is related to nasal allergies and asthma
allergens and, 259
defined, **247**
ATP. *See* Adenosine triphosphate (ATP)
Atria, of heart, 35
Attitude
of skin care professionals, 8
work ethic and, 460
Auditory method, in educating patients, **a method used to assist patients who are visually impaired by using a CD or cassette tape recorder to verbalize information to them, 601**
Australia, hair color in, 445
Autoclave, an apparatus for sterilization by steam under pressure; it consists of a strong, closed boiler containing a small quantity of water and, in a wire basket, the articles to be sterilized, 80–81, 82
epilation and, 452
Autoimmune diseases, **a disease in which the immune system cannot distinguish between foreign organisms and the body itself, so it attacks the body's own tissues, 66,** 266–269
alpha hydroxy acids and, 404
waxing contraindication against, 455
Autoinfectious lesions, **describing a disease that can spread to other areas on the same person, 261**
Axilla, in mammaplasty, **armpit, 589**
Axis, 139
Ayurveda, the science of longevity or the science of life, 9, 10, **15**–16
in holistic skin care, 422
Ayurvedic therapy, **the ancient Hindu art of medicine and prolonging life by a variety of methods from herbalism to massage and meditation, 422,** 568, 619–620
Azelaic acid, 175
acne treatment with, 380
Azelex, 175
acne treatment with, 380
use of and contraindication against, 280
Azulene, in waxes, 446

Baby boomers, skin care among, 5, 6
Baby oil, 288
Bacilli, rod-shaped bacterium that cause diseases such as tetanus (lockjaw), influenza, typhoid fever, and tuberculosis; the most common bacteria, 78, 79, **80**
Bacillus, 78, 79
Back bar, the place used for organization and storage of professional products used during the facial, 114–115
in dispensaries, 156
supplies for, 155
Back facials, 562
Back mask treatment, 541
Back problems, alleviating, 112

Back treatment, refers to two different treatments: back facial, a back deep cleansing performed by an esthetician; back treatment, a specialized or spot treatment to relieve sore muscles in the neck, shoulders, and back performed by a massage therapist, 562
Bacteria, 30
acne caused by, 273, 366–367
antibiotics against, 279
in folliculitis, 263
impetigo and, 261
preservatives versus, 296
sanitation and, 79
sterilization and, 80
types of, 78, 79–80
in underarms, 471
Bacterial conjunctivitis, a disease that causes eye infection; also known as pinkeye, 262–263
Balance
in ancient Greek culture, 14
ayurvedic treatments and, 15–16, 422
blushes and, 506
in Chinese traditional medicine, 11–12, 420–422
esthetics in ancient civilizations and, 9–11
in eye shape, 493
holism and, 419
makeup artistry and, 487
in shiatsu therapy, 424
in treating oily skin, 165–167
Barbae folliculitis, in shaving, 445
Barber towels, 151, 152
Barrier function of skin, **provides protection against invasion of the skin by offending or injuring substances, 43,** 298, 299
alpha hydroxy acids and, 402
protecting, 331–339
salicylic acid and, 412
sensitivity and, 341, 343–344, 349
Basal cell carcinoma, a common form of skin cancer that originates in the basal layer of the epidermis, 326–327
Basal cell layer, the lower, live part of the epidermis where epidermal cell division occurs, 40, 42, 44
melanocytes in, 47
salicylic acid and, 412
Basement membrane, 39–40
Base pairs, in DNA, 33
Basic chemistry, 283–285
Basic facials, 220–224
Bath additives, body treatments and, 571–573
Bathhouses
in ancient civilizations, 9
in Middle Ages, 16
in Roman culture, 14–15
Bathing, communal, 542
Bath sheets, 150
Battery circuit, 142, 143
B complex vitamins, 99–100. *See also* Vitamin entries
dosage, functions, and sources of, 95
Beads. *See* Polyethylene beads
Bearberry, Asian skin and, 393
Beards, men's facials and, 229, 231, 235
Beauty
in ancient civilizations, 9
esthetics and, 7
evolution of American skin care and, 18–19
in Roman culture, 14–15

Bed warmers, 149
Beeswax, 10
Beige skin, 491
Belgium, spas in, 11
Belly, of muscles, 70
Benadryl, 276
Benign condition, **the term for any condition of the skin that is not cancerous, 248**
Benson, Bob, 377
Bentonite, in masks, **the main clay used in masks, 300**
Benzalkonium chloride, a preservative. With continuous use, it can cause occasional allergic reactions, 81
Benzamycin, in acne treatment, 275
Benzophenone-3, as chemical sunscreen, 272
Benzoyl peroxide, an ingredient with antibacterial properties commonly used to treat acne, 180
  acne treatment with, 273–275, 383
  as allergen, 180
Berenson, G. S., 18
Berries, 10
Beta carotene, 97, 98
  in antiaging treatments, 330
Beta-glucans, ingredients used in antiaging cosmetics to reduce the appearance of fine lines and wrinkles, 306
Beta hydroxy acids (BHAs)
  Asian skin and, 393
  chemical peels using, 615
  contraindication against, 412
  enzyme exfoliants versus, 416
  in exfoliation, 300, 398, 411–414
  Hispanic skin and, 394
  for hyperpigmentation, 362
Betula, salicylic acid from, 412
BHA. *See* Butylated hydroxyanisole (BHA)
BHAs. *See* Beta hydroxy acids (BHAs)
Biceps muscles, **the two-headed, main muscle on the front of the upper arm; lifts the forearm, flexes the elbow, and turns the palm downward, 73,** 74
Bikini line, 459, 478
Bikini waxing, 478, 479, 480–481
Biochemistry, the study of chemical reactions that occur within a living organism, 283
  of cells, 30–32
  nature versus, 306–307
Bioflavonoids
  dosage, functions, and sources of, 96
  treating telangiectasia with, 319
Biological ingredients, in sample skin care systems, 433, 435, 436
Biologically inert substances, **describes an ingredient that does not react with the chemicals involved in the skin's function, 288,** 594
Biopsies, in treating carcinomas, **a sampling of tissue taken to analyze in the laboratory, 327**
Biotin, involved in energy formation by cells, synthesis of both proteins and fatty acids, 100
  dosage, functions, and sources of, 95
Birth, hair and, 443
Birth control pills
  client health screening information on, 173–174
  waxing contraindication against, 455

Birth defects, isotretinoin and, 278
Birthmarks, 169. *See also* Moles; Nevi (nevus)
Black
  color temperature of, 490
  shade and, 489
Black bile, in four humors theory, 14, 15
Blackheads, when the sebaceous material in an open pore darkens because of oxidation; open comedones, 247, 250, 366
Black light, 118
Black skin, 184, 185–186, 391–393
  dermatosis papulosa nigra in, 260
  hyperpigmentation in, 265, 358–359
  melanosomes in, 46
Blankets, 149, 151
Bleaching agents, hyperpigmentation and, 361
Blending oils, in aromatherapy, 552–553
Blend method, hair removal via, 448–450
Blepharoplasty, a surgical procedure that removes the fat and skin from upper and lower lids, making them less baggy, dry and crinkled, and tired looking, 585, 586–587, 620
  pre- and postoperative care with, 612, 614
Blisters, 251
  in shingles, 263
Blond hair, 444
Blood, 24, 36. *See also* Clotting
  cells and, 30–31
  in circulatory system, 60–62
  in four humors theory, 14, 15
  heart and, 35
  hormones in, 56
  nevi and, 252
  in skin, 27
Bloodborne viruses, viruses that are present in blood and body fluids, 80
Blood capillaries, structure of, 24. *See also* Capillaries; Telangiectasia
Blood disorders, in client health screening information, 178
Blood pressure, in client health screening information, 178
Blood thinners, waxing contraindication against, 455
Blood vessels, for hair, 441–443. *See also* Arteries; Capillaries; Spider veins; Veins
Blue
  color temperature of, 490
  as primary color, 488
Blue-green algae, 550, 551
Blush brushes, 509
Blushes, 505, 506, 514
  in basic makeup application, 528
  tips for, 506
B lymphocytes, 65
Body
  electricity and, 137
  immune response of, 63–64
  plastic surgery of, 589–595
  in shiatsu massage, 570
  spa treatments for, 538–554, 556–573
  systems of, 50–66
  waxing of, 459
Body care therapies, 3, 538–554, 556–573
Body cocoon, 550
Body fat, skin and, 28. *See also* Adipose tissue; Obesity
Body lotions, body treatments and, 571
Body masks, body treatment that involves the application of a mask product over the entire body.

Usually used for firming the skin, or light exfoliation, 549–550
Body massage, 565–567
  client positioning for, 567
Body polishes, granular scrubs that are most popular for home care, 549
Body treatment
  client positioning for, 546
  scrubs in, 546–547
  wraps in, 547
Body treatments, 538–554, 556–573
  combining, 544–545, 564–565
  exfoliation in, 547, 549
  gommage in, 549
  history of, 541
  hydrotherapy as, 545
  layering of, 545–546
  licensing for, 541–542
  principles of, 544–545
  purposes of, 557
  salt glow in, 547–549
  scrubs in, 549
  service and protocols in, 545–546
  table preparation for, 546
  techniques for, 546–549
Body wrap, a wrapping treatment used to treat cellulite, the condition of fatty deposits; the substances used and the wrapping technique have a diuretic effect that sometimes aids weight reduction, 545, 549–550
  ingredients in, 550–552
  purpose of, 550
Bonds, 139–142, 284–285
  covalent, 140, 282, 284–285
  ionic, 140, 284
Bone
  connective tissue and, 37
  structure of, 36, 69
Bones. *See also* Skeletal system
  estheticians and, 69
  of skull, 69, 70
Booth rentals, 108
Border, melanoma and, 328
Boric acid, 82
Botanical ingredients, in sample skin care systems, 436
Botox (botulism toxin), **toxin which causes temporary paralysis; softens the scowl lines in between the eyes, or the frown lines on the forehead, 71,** 593–594
Bouffant facial caps, 152
Bound electrons, found in the inner orbits of the atom, 139
Bowls, 155
Brachial plexus, 75, 77
Brain, in nervous system, 73–75, 76, 137, 138
Branded makeup products, benefits and drawbacks of, 529–530
Brazilian bikini wax, 478
Breakouts
  in client health screening information, 179
  salicylic acid and, 412
Breast augmentation surgery, 589–590, 620
Breast reduction surgery, 590, 591, 620
Breathing, in ayurvedic therapy, 422
Brick and mortar concept, of skin cell anatomy, 42–43
Bridal makeup, 531–533
Brightening agents, 361
Broad nose, 497
Broad-spectrum antioxidants, in antiaging treatments, 331

Broad-spectrum sunscreens, **a term given to sunscreens based on how much of the light spectrum is blocked or absorbed, 271,** 323
  for hyperpigmentation, 361
Brochures, designing, 217
Bromelain, as exfoliant, **an enzyme found in pineapple, 416**
Brow. *See* Eyebrows
Brow bone, of eyes, 497
Brow lift, 586
Brow movement, in massage, 210
Brown
  color temperature of, 490
  as neutral color, 489
Brown, Monica Tuma, 11, 17
Brown algae, 550, 551
Brown skin, hyperpigmentation and, 358–359
Brow pencil, 507–508
Brow shaping, 495–497
Browtosis, the loss of elasticity in the skin of the upper eyelid, 313
Brush cleaners, 510
Brushes, 154
  applying powder with, 505
  in basic facial, 222
  in basic makeup application, 525, 526
  choosing makeup, 510
  in dry brushing, 547
  for facial mask, 212
  in facial phase III, 205
  for makeup, 509–511
  for men's facials, 232, 233
  preparing for facials, 201
  specialty makeup, 511
Brush handles, 510–511
Brush kit, 513
Brush machines, 119–120
  in facial phase III, 205
  mechanical exfoliation using, 397
  for men's facials, 232, 233
  preparing for facials, 201
Buccal nerve, 75
Buccal nodes, 62
Buffering agents, pH adjusters that are added to skin care products, 293–**294**
Buff Puff, 427
Bullae, very large vesicles, 249, 251, 252
Burch, G. E., 18
Burn scars, camouflage therapy for, 625
Business
  competition in, 548
  marketing in, 431
  public relations in, 421
  starting one's own, 253
  success in, 626
Business cards, 513
  referrals and, 267
Bust treatments, 561–562
Butterfly pads, in salicylic acid treatment, 413
Butylated hydroxyanisole (BHA), 411
Butyrospermum parkii, 16–17
Buzzwords, 572, 584

Cabinet, for makeup, 513
Caddy containers, 155
Calcium, a mineral the body requires for the formation and maintenance of teeth and bones, 100
  dosage, functions, and sources of, 96
  vitamin D and, 98
Caller ID, 599
Calming oils, 553

Calories
  in fats, 94
  necessary amount of, 101
Calves, waxing of, 478
Camellia sinensis
  in antiaging treatments, 331
  treating telangiectasia with, 319
Camouflage, to hide, conceal, cover, veil, or disguise something, 623
Camouflage makeup, 534–535, 622, 623
  tips for, 535
Camouflage therapy, 622–628
Camphor, 553
Cancellations, handling, 410
Cancer. *See also* Tumors
  in client health screening information, 179
  permanent makeup and, 627
  in sun-damaged skin, 318, 321, 326–328
  vitamin A and, 98
  vitamin C and, 100
  waxing contraindication against, 455
Candela Cool Laser hair removal system, 595
Candida albicans, seborrheic dermatitis and, 255
Capillaries, 60, 248. *See also* Lymph capillaries
  distended, 168, 169, 342
  structure of, 24
Caps, bouffant facial, 152
Carageenan, 551
Carbohydrates, the source of nutrition that breaks down the basic chemical sugars that supply energy for the body; frequently called "carbs", 92
  dieting and, 101
  as macronutrients, 91, 92, 93
Carbomers, an ingredient used to thicken creams; frequently used in gel products, 293
Carbon atom, structure of, 283
Carbon dioxide, in circulatory system, 61–62
Carbon dioxide (CO_2) laser, 588
Carbon solution, in laser hair removal, 450
Carboxymethyl cellulose, 293
Cardiac muscle, 33, 34, 35
Cardiac patients, electrical contraindication against, 174
Cardiovascular system, 54. *See also* Circulatory system
Career options, 6–7
  in medical esthetics, 576–581
  table of medical esthetics, 581
Career planning, 449
Caring, within teams, 72
Carlsbad, 11
Carotid artery, the main artery that goes to the head and face, 60
Carpal tunnel syndrome, of reflexology therapists, 571
Cartilage, a connective tissue that forms the nose and ears, 34–36
Carts, 114
  for waxing, 451
Catagen phase, in hair growth cycle, **the second stage in hair growth, or the regression (falling out) stage, 442, 443**
Cataphoresis, the infusion of a positive product during iontophoresis, 128
Catherine Hinds Institute, 19
Caucasian skin, 185–186
  ethnic skin and, 391
  melanosomes in, 46
Cell membrane, 30–31, 34
Cell migration, 44
Cell phones, 599

Cells, the basic building blocks of the human body that manufacture protein; they become the building material for making tissues and larger organs that make up the human body, 30
  biochemistry of, 30–32
  chemical communication among, 285
  in dermis and epidermis, 37, 38
  immune, 28–30
  improving metabolism of, 306
  in laser hair removal, 450
  Merkel, 37
  nutrition and, 91
  salicylic acid and, 412
  specialized, 32–38
Cellulite
  cellulitis versus, 263
  combined body treatment packages for, 565
  endermology for, 563, 619
  spot treatments for, 562–563
Cellulite creams, 573
Cellulitis, a severe bacterial infection of the skin, characterized by hot, swollen skin, 263
Cellulose, a carbohydrate that is not digested by humans, and is important in helping push wastes out of the colon, 93
Centriole, 31
Ceramides, lipids involved in forming the mortar or intercellular lipids, 43, 339
Certified colors, color agents that are inorganic; also known as metal salts, 297
Certified medical assistants (CMAs), in clinical skin care, 577
Cervical nerve, 75, 77
Cervical nodes, 62
Cervical plexus, 75
Cetyl alcohol, 289
Cevattes, poikiloderma of, 265, 319
Chairs
  for estheticians, 109–110
  facial, 107–109
Chamomile, a plant extract with clinically proven antiinflammatory and repairer properties, 180
  as allergen, 180
  in aromatherapy, 552, 553
  in waxes, 446
Charges, 140–141
  negative, 137, 140–141
  positive, 137, 140–141
Charles IV, Emperor, 11
Charting, a term in the health care industry that means to record information regarding a patient or client, 189, 602
  of body treatments, 557
  in medical documentation, 601–602
  of skin analysis, 189–193
"Cheat sheets, " in time management, 500
Cheek
  in facial profile, 494–495
  hard waxing of, 466–467
Cheek movements, in massage, 209, 210, 211
Cheilosis, 99
Chemical battery circuit, 142, 143
Chemical depilation, 445
Chemical exfoliants, contraindications against, 175
Chemical exfoliation, mechanical exfoliation versus, **uses both natural**

and laboratory-designed chemicals to loosen dead cells from the skin's surface, 397–**398**

Chemical peels, a technique for improving the appearance when wrinkles of the skin are present, 615. *See* Skin peels

Chemical reactions, 283
  with galvanic current, 126
Chemicals
  causing folliculitis, 263–264
  delivery systems for, 297–298, 304–306
  Material Safety Data Sheets for handling, 87, 88
  skin care and, 283
Chemical sunscreens, 272
Chemistry
  in aromatherapy, 552–553
  basic, 283–285
  health through, 10
  of skin products, 199, 282–300
Chemoexfoliation. *See* Chemical exfoliation; Exfoliation
Chemotherapy, waxing contraindication against, 455
Cherry angioma, 249
Chest, motor points of, 216
Chi, 11. *See also* Qi
  holistic therapies and, 420–422
Chickenpox, a contagious disease occurring most often during childhood; it is caused by the same virus that causes shingles, 263
Children
  acne and, 368–369
  sun-damaged skin of, 318, 323
Chin
  foundation contouring for, 503
  hard waxing of, 468–469
China
  ancient grooming practices in, 11
  herbalism from, 425
  holistic therapies from, 420–422
  reflexology and, 570
  shiatsu and, 424, 568
China clay, 551
Chin acne, 369–370
Chin movement, in massage, 209, 210
Chloasma, 168. *See also* Liver spots
  in sun-damaged skin, 318
  treatment of, 357
Chloramine-T, 82
Chlorazene, 82
Chlorine
  atomic structure of, 139, 284
  in galvanic electrology, 448
Chlorite, 551
Chlorophyta, 550, 551
Chlorozol, 82
Choices, in skin care services, 217
Choleric temperament, in four humors theory, 15
Cholesterol, a moisturizer and emollient that acts as a powerful emulsifier in water-in-oil systems; a fat-like substance found in plant and animal cells, 43
  fatty acids and, 94
  vitamin C and, 100
  vitamin D from, 98
Choline, dosage, functions, and sources of, 95
Chondrus crispus, 551
Chromatin, special fibers which are made of nucleic acids and proteins, 32

Chromium, a trace mineral, required in very small quantities for correct body function, 101
  dosage, functions, and sources of, 96
Chronic, an ongoing condition, 177
Chronic headaches, in client health screening information, 178
Chronic skin conditions, in client health screening information, 177–178
Chucking movement, in massage, 219
Cicatricial basal cell carcinoma, 327
CIDESCO (Comité International D'Esthetique et de Cosmétologie), international organization formed in Zurich, Switzerland, in 1946, to give estheticians the opportunity to exchange experiences with their colleagues in other countries, 19, 377
Cigarette smoking. *See* Smoking
Cinnamomum, 553
Cinnamomum camphora, 553
Cinnamon, 553
Circadian cycle, 57
Circadian rhythms, the body's natural 24-hour cycle, 12
Circles, in skin around eyes, 169
Circuit breakers, 145
Circuits, the path a current takes as it moves through a system, 142. *See* Electric circuit
Circular movement, in massage, 209, 212, 219
Circulatory system, the system that controls the steady circulation of the blood through the body by means of the heart and blood vessels, 50, 51, 60–63
  meridians and, 568
  telangiectasis and, 168, 169
Citrus aurantium, 553
Citrus limom, 553
Citrus sinensis, 553
Citrus vulgaris, 553
Classical massage movements, 218–220
Claudius Galenus, 14
Claustrophobia, body wraps and, 557
Clays
  in mud wraps, 550–551
  table of, 551
Cleaners, 515
Clean linens, for clients, 149
Cleanliness, 79. *See also* Personal presentation; Sanitation
  in ancient civilizations, 9
  policies and procedures for, 84–89
Cleanser, 514
  in acne management, 374, 378
  in acne treatment, 275
  in alpha hydroxy acid home care treatment, 405
  in basic facial, 221–222
  in basic makeup application, 524
  emulsion, 292–293
  for home skin care, 428
  for hyperpigmentation, 361
  for men's facials, 229, 232
  purpose and function of, 200
  in treating sensitive skin, 348, 351
Cleansing. *See also* Deep cleansing; Light cleansing
  during alpha hydroxy acid treatment, 407
  during arm waxing, 474
  back treatment for, 562
  during bikini wax, 480
  in body treatments, 544

during cheek waxing, 466
during chin waxing, 468
during enzyme exfoliation, 415
during eyebrow waxing, 463
during facials, 197, 202–203, 205–206
during lip waxing, 470
during salicylic acid treatment, 413
during shoulder waxing, 476
in skin analysis, 188
during thermal mask treatment, 335
in treating acne, 385
during underarm waxing, 472
Cleansing milks, 292–293
  in acne management, 374, 378, 384
Clear resins, for hair removal, 446
Cleopatra, 13, 419
Client health form, 454
  epilation and, 453
Clients
  with acne, 364–388
  advanced home care regimens for, 426–436
  analyzing skin condition of, 163–169
  antiaging tips for, 330–332
  camouflage therapy for, 622–628
  clinical skin care for, 574–581
  customer policies for, 410–411
  discussing aging with, 328–330
  draping of, 149–152
  educating, 148, 295, 305, 329, 601, 616
  epilation of, 438–456, 458–481
  exfoliation for, 396–416
  facials for, 197–225
  follow-up with, 239, 274
  handling difficult, 345
  head protection for, 152
  health analysis of, 171–182
  health history of, 161
  health of, 543
  holistic treatments for, 418–425
  home maintenance by, 215, 225, 236–243
  with hyperpigmentation, 356–362
  information gathering from, 161, 190, 191–192, 193, 603–607
  initial consultation with, 176
  makeup application for, 516–536
  makeup artistry for, 485–515
  makeup profiling for, 490–491
  male versus female, 229
  medical patients as, 596–608
  meeting with, 147–149, 153, 360
  for men's facials, 229–235
  merchandising to, 329
  networking and, 584
  plastic surgery for, 582–595
  pre- and postoperative care for, 610–621
  preparing for bikini wax, 479
  preparing for body massage, 567
  preparing for body treatment, 546
  preparing for epilation, 456
  product recommendations for, 572
  public relations for, 421
  referrals and, 267
  refusal to provide medical information by, 182
  resolving conflicts with, 394
  retention of, 198–199
  with sensitive skin, 340–355
  skin analysis of, 188–193
  spa treatments for, 538–554, 556–573
  telephone etiquette for, 599
  treating acne in young, 368–369
  treating ethnic, 390–395
  treating sun-damaged skin of, 325–339

Client wraps, 148–149
    in body treatments, 546, 547
        contraindication against, 557
Clindamycin, acne treatment with, 380
Clinical skin care, 574–581
Clinics, estheticians in, 576–581
Clipboard, 514
Clogged pores, 368
    alpha hydroxy acids and, 402–403
**Closed comedones, a comedo without a
    dilated ostium or follicular opening.
    It appears as a small bump just
    beneath the skin's surface, and
    generally has no color at all, 250**
        acne and, 366, 367
        in acne grades, 372
Close-set eyes, 496
Closing consultation, 237–239, 518
Clostridium botulinum, 593
Clothing. *See also* Uniforms
    for estheticians, 112
    ultraviolet radiation and, 541
Clotting, 61
    vitamin K and, 99
Clove, 553
CMAs. *See* Certified medical assistants (CMAs)
Coagulation. *See* Clotting
Cobalamin, 99–100
    dosage, functions, and sources of, 95
**Cocci, round, pus-producing pathogenic
    bacteria appearing in a group, 78,
    79–80**
**Coconut oil, a fatty and heavy plant oil,
    289**
Cocoon draping, 149–151
**Coenzyme Q10, an enzyme that has a
    catalytic effect on skin systems and
    revitalizes skin cells, 306**
Cold cream, 18
    first, 14
**Cold sores, sores caused by the herpes
    simplex virus that can occur on or
    around the mouth; they can be
    painful, 261**
        alpha hydroxy acids and, 404
        in client health screening information, 178
**Collagen, a protein that makes up 70% of
    the weight of the skin; collagen gives
    skin its strength and keeps it
    "young", 40–41**
        effects of microcurrent therapy on, 128
        fillers and implants and, 594
Collagen fibers, crosslinking of, 316
**Collagen injections, a filler, usually
    bovine (cow) derivative, to fill in
    wrinkles or make lips larger, 579**
Collagen remodeling, laser surgery for, **the
    growth of new collagen in the
    dermis, 588**
Collagen striations, 40, 41
Color agents, 296–297
    sensitive skin and, 350
Color products, 505–509
Colors. *See also* Skin colors
    African culture and, 16
    in basic makeup application, 524–528
    of blushes, 506
    in camouflage makeup, 623
    for cheek, 494–495
    complementary, 489
    depicted by skin scopes, 119
    of eye makeup, 496
    of eye shadows, 506–507

of hair, 444–445
    intensity of, 489
    intermediate, 488–489
    in laser hair removal, 450
    for lips, 498–499
    of lipstick, 509
    makeup and, 485, 486, 488–491
    in makeup profiling, 490–491
    of mascara, 508
    melanoma and, 328
    in micropigmentation, 628
    for nose, 497
    of pencils, 507–508
    primary, 488
    saturation of, 489
    secondary, 488
    shade and, 489
    temperature of, 489–490
    tertiary, 488–489
    tint of, 489
    value of, 489, 623
    visual impact of, 489
    under Wood's lamp, 187
Color theory, 488–491
Color wheel, 488, 489
Comb electrode, 125
Combination services, marketing of, 564–565
Combination skin, 163–164
    under Wood's lamp, 187
**Comedogenicity, the tendency of any
    topical substance to cause or worsen
    comedones (blackheads)**
        emollients and, **289–290**
        testing for, 371
Comedogenic substances, **describes
    substances that cause comedones
    (blackheads), 288–289,** 290, 370
        in acne management, 373–374
        table of, 291
Comedolidic substances, beta hydroxy acids
    as, **able to dissolve comedones, 412**
Comedolytic treatments, **a term meaning
    that a product loosens comedones,
    277**
**Comedonal acne, the most common form
    of acne, 370**
Comedone extractor, in treating acne, 382
Comedones (comedo), **more than one
    comedo,** 247, 249, **250,** 288. *See also*
    Microcomedones
        acne and, **366,** 381
        solar, 320
        tretinoin and, 277
Commission work, 532–533
Communal bathing, 542
Communication
    with clients, 274, 345, 360
    during enzyme exfoliation, 415
    nonverbal, 64
    between physician and esthetician, 608
    public relations and, 421
    during salicylic acid treatment, 414
Compacts, powder in, 505
Compensation, for estheticians, 532–533
Competency, of skin care professionals, 8
Competition
    among esthetics businesses, 548
    in skin care industry, 198–199
Complacency, among skin care professionals,
    198
**Complementary colors, developed by
    combining a color with the color
    opposite it on the color wheel, 489**

Completion, as facial phase VII, 201,
    213–214
Compliance, 601
    in home care, 600
**Compounds, the product of uniting two
    or more elements, 283**
Compulsive disorders, patients with, 598
**Computer imaging, incorporates
    consultation, patient education,
    patient selection, and medical
    documentation; can also be used to
    document gradual changes during
    each treatment phase, 620–**621
Concave profile, 494
Concealers, 502–505, 514
    in basic makeup application, 525
    tips for, 504
Concentrates, 303
    in body treatments, 553–554
**Conditioning, increasing the skin's
    metabolism and reducing the
    cellular debris on the surface, 611.** *See*
    Skin conditioning
**Conductors, a material or element that
    will easily pass an electrical current
    or flow of negatively charged
    electrons, 141**
Confidence, among skin care professionals,
    198–199
Confidential health history questionnaire, 557,
    558–559
Confidentiality, of client-professional
    relationship, 517–518
Confidential makeup questionnaire, 513, 517,
    518, 519
Confidential Skin Health Survey, 170, 172
    questions in, 171–182
Conflicts, resolving, 394
Conjunctivitis, bacterial, 262–263
**Connective tissue, tissue that helps to
    connect the bones, and provide
    a cushion between the bones, 34–**36,
    37
Consent, informed, 605, 606–607, 608
Conservatory of Esthetics, 19
Consistencies, of waxes, 446
Consultation. *See also* Analysis and
    consultation; Initial consultation;
    Postconsultation; Screening consultation
        for body treatments, 557
        closing, 237–239, 518
        for cosmetic surgery, 598–601
        in facial phase II, 204–205
        makeup, 517–518
        preoperative, 600
Consultation forms, 513, 517–518, 519–522
**Contact dermatitis, a form of dermatitis
    that occurs when the skin comes
    into contact with a sensitizing agent.
    As a result there is an immune
    response causing inflammation,**
    257–258
        defined, **247**
        vitamin E and, 344
Contact lenses, client health screening
    information on, 174
Contagious skin diseases, 260–263
Containers, 155
    for makeup, 513–514
**Contaminated, when an object or
    product has microorganisms in it, 82**
**Contamination, pollution; soiling with
    infectious matter; the spreading of**

microorganisms to an object or product, 82
    policies and procedures for avoiding, 84–89
Contests, in promotions, 230
Contouring, with foundations, 502, 503–504
Contraindication, services, activities, or products that can cause side effects or harm, or pose danger to persons who have a specific condition or are under medical care for a particular situation, 171
    against alpha hydroxy acids, 404
    against beta hydroxy acids, 412
    against body treatments, 557
    in client health screening information, 173, 174, 177, 178
    against endermology, 619
    against enzyme exfoliants, 416
    against glycolic peel, 608
    against gommage, 399
    against microdermabrasion, 401, 618
    against peels, 617
    against petrissage, 219
    against scrubs, 398
    against shiatsu, 569
    table of drugs and, 280, 455
    against waxing, 455
Convex profile, 494
Cool colors, 489–490
Cooling
    of sensitive skin, 346
    by sweat, 45–46
Cooperation, within teams, 72
Copper, a metallic element that is a good conductor of heat and electricity, 101
    atomic structure of, 139
    as conductor, 141
    dosage, functions, and sources of, 96
Corneocytes, the cells that make up the corneum, or outermost layer of the epidermis, 37, 43, 44
    acne and, 365
    exfoliation of, 397
Corneum. *See* Stratum corneum
Corporate image, 421
Correction, in facial phase IV, 208
Corrective makeup, 533–534
Correctors, intensive, 303, 304
Corrugator muscle, botox and, 593–594
Corrugator supercilii muscle, **facial muscle that draws eyebrows down, and wrinkles the forehead vertically, 71**
Cortex, of hair, 441, 442
Corticoids, 59
Corticosteroids, hormones that help to relieve inflammation, 59, 276
Cortisone, 276
Corundum, in microdermabrasion, 400
Cosmeceuticals, products intended to improve the skin's health and appearance, 286, 303
Cosmetic Act of 1938, 303
Cosmetic dentistry
    as career option, 581
    esthetician in office for, 579
Cosmetic dermatology, 583
Cosmetic physician, as career option, 581
Cosmetics, defined by the FDA as "articles that are intended to be rubbed, poured, sprinkled or otherwise applied to the human body or any part thereof for cleansing, beautifying, promoting

attractiveness or altering the appearance, " 286
    for acne, 371, 373
    as allergens, 180
    as chemicals, 283
    ingredients in, 286, 302–307
    permanent, 627–628
    skin care and, 283
Cosmetic surgery, an elective surgery for improving a feature,
    camouflage makeup following, 623–627
    consultation for, 598–601
    defined, **583**
    esthetician in office for, 578
Cosmetology, licensing of, 20–21, 29
Cotton balls, 154
Cotton muslin strips, 453
    in eyebrow waxing, 464
    in lip waxing, 470
    in underarm waxing, 472
Cotton rolls, 154, 155
Cotton swabs, 155
    in alpha hydroxy acid treatment, 408
    in extractions, 207
    in makeup kit, 512
    in salicylic acid treatment, 414
    in treating acne, 381, 383
Cotton towels, 150–152
Coumadin
    in client health screening information, 178
    waxing contraindication against, 455
Countertops, maintaining, 110
Couperose, the common name for telangiectasis, 168
Courtesy, telephone, 599
Covalent bonds, the sharing of electrons between two atoms, 140, 282, 284–285
Covey, Stephen R., 166, 626
Cranial nerves, 68, 73–75, 76
Craniosacral massage, as holistic therapy, **a gentle type of massage and movement of the head, 423**
Cranium. *See also* Head
    bones of, 69, 70
    massage of, 423
Crawford, Jane, 21
Creamed resins, for hair removal, 446
Cream foundations, 501, 502
Creams, 514. *See also* Cold cream; Day cream; Night cream; Vanishing cream
    anhydrous, 287
    in antiaging treatments, 332
    in basic makeup application, 524
    in body treatments, 554
    body treatments and, 571
    depilatory, 445
    enzyme exfoliants in, 416
    in paraffin treatment, 564
    sunscreen in, 272
Creativity, in makeup artistry, 487–488, 491
Credentials, of skin care professionals, 8
Crisscross movement, in massage, 209
Crisscross wrinkling, from sun damage, **wrinkling in a crossed pattern typical in sun-damaged skin, 319, 320**
Critical clients, handling, 345
Crooked nose, 497
Cross-contamination, occurs when touching an object like the skin, and then touching an object or product with the same hand or utensil, 82–84
Crosslinking, free radicals and, **the collagen**

fibers are bound together by free radicals, making them inflexible, resulting in the appearance of old skin, 316
Cross-merchandising, in promotions, 230
Crow's feet, 311–312
Crust, a dried body serum such as dried pus or blood, 249, 251
Cryoglobes, in treating sensitive skin, 353
Cryosurgery, dermatological treatment of actinic keratosis involving freezing the area to be treated with liquid nitrogen
    for skin tags, 254
    treating actinic keratosis with, **321**
Crystals, in microdermabrasion, 400–401
Cuboidal cells, 38
Cupid bow lips, 499
Curettage, treating actinic keratosis with, **the technique of removing a lesion with an instrument called a curette, 321**
Current
    in electrical circuits, 143–144
    galvanic, 126–128
    in high-frequency machine, 123–124
    in iontophoresis, 126–128
Curved eyebrow, 495
Custom blended makeup products, benefits and drawbacks of, 529
Customer policies, 410–411
Cuticle, of hair, 441. *See also* Nails
Cyanophyta, 550, 551
Cyclomethicone, 290
Cymbopogon citratus, 553
Cystic acne, 372
    Accutane treatment for, 278
Cysts, a pocket of fluid, infection, or other matter under the skin, 251
    acne and, 367–368
Cytology, the study of cells and cellular biology, 43
Cytoplasm, 31

Dandruff, a lay term referring to any condition causing flaking of the scalp, 255
Dark Ages, bathing during, 16
Dark hair, 444–445
Dark skin, 185–186, 491
    hyperpigmentation and, 265
Date of birth, in health screening questionnaire, 171
Day, Bonnie, 19, 377
Day cream, 514
    in basic makeup application, 524
    purpose and function of, 200
Daylight sun, skin damage from, 324
DC. *See* Direct current (DC)
Decyl glucoside, 291
Deep cleansing
    in facial phase III, 201, 205–206
    in men's facials, 232–234
Deep cleansing back treatment, 562
Deep peels, surgical peels performed with phenol to remove tissue well into the papillary dermis, 402
Deep pore cleanser, for home skin care, 428
Deep-set eyes, 496
Deep skin, 491
Degreasing, in salicylic acid treatment, 413
Dehydrated skin, lacking water, 163, 164–165, 167
    basic facials for, 221, 223

home care regimen for, 225
hydrators for, 298
under Wood's lamp, 187
Dehydration
alpha hydroxy acids and, 404
menopause and, 313
oily skin and, 165
Deimer, Robert, 18, 19
Delivery systems, chemical techniques using vehicles to make products work, 297–298, 304–306
Delmar Learning, 19–20
Deltoid muscles, **large, thick, triangular-shaped muscle covering the shoulder; lifts and turns the arm, 73,** 74
Demodex mites, rosacea and, **small mites in the skin, which may be associated with rosacea, 256**
Dentistry, cosmetic, 579
Dentists, prescriptions by, 271
Deoxyribonucleic acid, DNA, contains coding that runs the cell, and the information to pass on to daughter cells, 32. See DNA.
Depilation, chemical, 445. *See also* Epilation
Depressed immune system, 266
Depressor anguli muscle, 71
Depressor labii muscle, 71
Depth area, of eyes, 497
Derma Analysis, 18
Dermabrasion, a surgical technique using a rotating wire brush that physically removes skin tissue, 402. *See also* Microdermabrasion
Dermagraphics, 627
Dermal papilla, the oval-shaped cavity in the bulb of the follicle; it is filled with tissue that contains the blood vessels and cells necessary for hair growth, 441–442
Dermascope magazine, 19
Dermatitis, any sort of inflammation of the skin
contact, 257–258
defined, **247**
Dermatographism, sensitive skin and, **a condition in which the skin swells from the slightest touch or scrape, 342**–343
Dermatoheliosis, the technical term for sun-induced aging symptoms, 315
Dermatological terms, 247–248
Dermatologists, 247, 583
acne treatment by, 372–373, 380
Dermatology, 583
as career option, 581
esthetician in office for, 578
Dermatomyositis, an autoimmune disease that affects the immunity of the body's muscles and causes inflammation, 268
Dermatosis papulosa nigra, a condition that occurs in black skin and is characterized by many black or brown lesions that look like tiny moles, 260
Dermis, the lower, live layer of the skin, 39
aging and, 314
cells in, 37
effects of microcurrent therapy on, 128

hair in, 45, 441
laser hair removal and, 450
melanocytes in, 47
nerves in, 41
structure of, 39–41
sun damage to, 316–317
tanning and, 315
Desmosomes, small attachments that hold the upper level epidermal cells together, 42, 44
Desquamation, the normal process in which cells move to the surface of the epidermis and shed, 46–48. *See also* Microdesquamation
of black skin, 391–392
exfoliation as, 397
Detergents, the main type of surfactant used in skin care products, 290–291, 292
acne, 375
Detoxification therapy
in ayurveda, 16
cellulite treatments and, 563
in combined body treatment packages, 565
Detoxifying mud wrap, 560
Detoxifying oils, 553
Detoxifying seaweed wrap, 557–560
combined with salt glow, 560–561
Detox treatments, designed specifically for metabolic stimulation which aids in the body's natural elimination of toxins, 550
DHT. *See* Dihydrotestosterone (DHT)
Diabetes, waxing contraindication against, 455
Diameter, melanoma and, 328
Diamond-shaped face, 493
Diatomaceous earth, in masks, **a popular mask base made from sea algae, 300**
Diet. *See also* Foods; Nutrients; Nutrition
in ayurvedic therapy, 422
in herbalism, 425
Dietetics, 91
Dieticians, 91
Dieting, 101–103
Differentiate, to continually divide, 42
Differin, 175, 277
acne treatment with, 380
use of and contraindication against, 280
Digastric muscle, located under the chin; runs the length of the middle of the neck, 71
Digestive system, approximately 30 feet of tubing between the mouth, stomach, and anus responsible for complex functions including breaking down food and separating nutrients, along with eliminating waste, 57, 58
Dihydrotestosterone (DHT), acne and, 368
Dimethicone, 290
Diopters, a measure of the powers of magnification of a magnifying lamp, 117
Diplobacillus, 78, 79
Diplococci, spherical bacteria that are joined in pairs and cause pneumonia, 80
Diplococcus, 78, 79
Diplomacy, public relations and, 421
Direct current (DC), 141, 143, 144

in blend electrolysis, 448
in galvanic electrology, 448
Disaccharides, made up of two molecular sugar units, 93
Discipline, in entrepreneurship, 253
Discoid lupus erythematosus (DLE), 268
Discounts, 166, 199
in promotions, 230
Disease, 246–269. *See also* Autoimmune diseases; Contagious diseases
African culture and, 16–17
in ancient civilizations, 9, 10
ancient Egyptian medicine and, 13
ancient Greek medicine and, 14
ancient Hebrew medicine and, 13
ancient Indian medicine and, 15–16
autoimmune, 66, 266–269
causes of, 10
in Chinese traditional medicine, 11–12, 420–422
common skin, 254–258
contagious, 260–263
esthetics and, 3
immune system versus, 61
microorganisms causing, 79
during Middle Ages, 16
Native American culture and, 17
noninfectious, 254–258
proliferative, 259
Roman medicine and, 14–15
skin care professionals and, 245
symptoms of, 247
Disfigurements
camouflage makeup for, 534–535
camouflage therapy for, 622–628
Disincrustation, 126
in facial phase III, 206
heat mask and, 130
preparing equipment for, 201
in treating acne, 381, 383, 385
Disinfectants, 81, 515
hospital-grade, 81
procedures for using, 84
table of, 82
Disinfection, decontamination, nearly as effective as sterilization, but does not kill bacterial spores; used on hard surfaces, 81
Disodium laureth sulfosuccinate, 291
Disorders, 247. *See also* Blood disorders; Disease; Musculoskeletal disorders (MSDs); Neurological disorders; Skin disorders
Dispensary, an area where extra supplies and bulk products are kept, 114–115, 155, **156**–157
Displays, in marketing makeup artistry, 536
Disposable makeup applicators, 511
Disposable utensils, 81–82, 152–154, 514
for epilation, 452, 453
sharps boxes for, 82, 83
Distended capillaries, **to enlarge, 168,** 169. *See also* Telangiectasia
sensitive skin and, 342
Distillation, a main method of extracting essential oils, 13
Division of Alternative Studies, 10
DLE. *See* Discoid lupus erythematosus (DLE)
DNA (deoxyribonucleic acid), 92
in cell nucleus, 32
effects of microcurrent therapy on, 128
free radicals and, 316

replication of, 33
structure of, 24, 33
vitamin C and, 100
Doctrine of Signatures (Paracelsus), 16
Documentation, medical, 601–608
Domestic violence, therapy for survivors of, 597
Doshas, in ayurvedic therapy, 422
Double chin, foundation contouring for, 503
Drapes, 149–152, 514
Dress, for estheticians, 147
Drooping eyes, 496
Drooping lips, 499
Drugs. *See also* Antibiotics; Medications; Pharmacology
    affecting skin care, 245
    as allergens, 180
    in client health screening information, 174–177
    contraindications against, 171, 173, 280
    cosmetics as, 286, 303
    over-the-counter, 271–275, 275–276
    prescription, 271, 276–279
Dry brushing, in body treatments, **stimulates blood circulation; helps prepare the skin for application of nutrient substances and the wrap, 547**
Drying oils, use of and contraindication against, 280
Dry rosacea, 256–257
Dry sanitizing agents, 84
Dry skin, 163, 164–165, 167
    in acne management, 374–375
    in alpha hydroxy acid home care treatment, 405
    basic facials for, 221, 223
    detergents and, 291
    home care regimen for, 225
    menopause and, 313
    protecting barrier function of, 331
    sun-damaged skin and, 324–325
    treating sensitive, 344
    treatments for, 298
    under Wood's lamp, 187
Dual cream/powder foundations, 501, 502
Dyschromias, any abnormal discoloration of the skin, 264
Dysplastic nevi, 328

Earlift, 585, 587, 588
Ears, waxing of, 459
Earth
    in Chinese traditional medicine, 12
    in four humors theory, 15
    oils from, 288–289
Ecchymoses, large bruises, 248, 249
Eczema, an inflammatory disease of the skin that can cause lesions and painful itching, 177, 247
    in client health screening information, 177–178
Edema, swelling, 251
Edematous wheal, **full of fluid, 251**
Education
    career planning and, 449
    of clients, 148, 295, 305, 329, 428–429, 601
    continuation of, 616
    evolution of American skin care and, 19
    with makeup lessons, 531
    of patients, 601
    public relations and, 421

of skin care professionals, 8, 29
work ethic and, 460
Effleurage, first of the classical massage movements, effleurage is a soft, continuous stroking movement applied with the fingers or palms in a slow and rhythmic manner. This movement is often used to open or close the massage session, 218. *See also* Stroking movement
    in Swedish massage, 566
Egyptian culture
    ancient grooming practices in, 13
    aromatherapy in, 552
    medicine in, 9
    sugaring in, 447
Elasticity
    aging and skin, 312, 313, 314–315, 325
    checking skin, 325
    sun damage and, 319–320
Elastic layers, in blood vessels, 61
Elastin, the protein in elastin fibers that are responsible for skin's elasticity, 40
Elastin fibers, protein fibers that give the skin its elasticity (stretch) and ability to retain its shape, 40–41
    in aging skin, 312
Elastosis, the loss of elasticity in the skin
    of aging skin, **312,** 313
    solar, 319–320
Elderly persons, as patients, 597–598. *See also* Aging
Electrical current. *See* Alternating current (AC); Current; Direct current (DC); Galvanic current; Microcurrent machines; Sinusoidal current
Electric blankets, 129, 131–133
Electric boots, 129, 131
Electric charge, 141. *See also* Charges
Electric circuit, 141, 142–143
Electric fields, invisible influences surrounding each atomic structure, having the power to attract and repel charges, 141
Electricity, 136–145
    atoms and, 137–142
    in circuits, 142–143
    contraindications against, 174
    esthetic machines and, 144
    forms of, 143–144
    pregnancy contraindication against, 173
    properties of, 137
    safety in handling, 144–145, 157
    static, 142, 143
    in steamers, 121–122
    terminology for, 141–142
Electric mitts, 129, 131, 564
Electrocardiograph, 137
Electrocoagulation, hair removal via, 448
Electrodes, 141
    in basic facial, 223
    direct current and, 143
    for disincrustation, 126
    in facial phase III, 206
    in galvanic electrology, 448
    in high-frequency machine, 124, 125
    for iontophoresis, 126–128
    in treating acne, 386
Electrodesiccation, a treatment for telangiectasia involving the use of an electric needle inserted into the

capillaries to kill the edge of a lesion
    for skin tags, 254
    in treating carcinomas, 327
    treating telangiectasia with, **319**
Electrology, 448
Electrolysis, the process of removing hair permanently by means of electricity, 143, **448**
    hair growth cycle and, 443
    hair removal via, 446, 448–450
    licensing for, 450
    methods of, 448
    in treating sensitive skin, 355
Electromagnetism, 137, 141
Electron microscope, 137
Electrons, elementary particles consisting of negative charges of electricity that revolve around the nucleus of an atom, 137
    in atoms, 282, 283–285
    chemical bonds and, 284–285
    electricity and, 137–142, 142–143
    energy levels of, 284
    free radicals and, 316
Electron shells, 139
Eleidin, a substance in the stratum lucidum which is involved in the keratinization process, 43
Elements, a chemical that has not reacted with another element, 283
    in Chinese traditional medicine, 12
Elias, Peter M., 42
Elizabethan Age, esthetics during, 17
EMDA. *See* Esthetics Manufacturers and Distributors Alliance (EMDA)
Emollients, cosmetic ingredients that are almost always fatty agents, 287, 288–290
    comedogenic, 289–290
    dry skin and, 298
Employee handbooks, 86
Employees
    productivity of, 132
    public relations and, 421
    resumes by, 580
    work ethic and, 460
Employers
    liability and, 111
    policies and procedures by, 86
    productivity and, 132
    public relations and, 421
    resumes for, 580
    work ethic and, 460
Emulsifiers, surfactants that keep oils and water blended in a product, 290, 291–292, 292
Emulsion cleansers, 292–293
Emulsions, a product containing a mixture of oil and water bound together with an emulsifier, 86–287, **292,** 292
Encapsulation, liposomes and, 297. *See also* Microencapsulation
Endermology, a body treatment given before and after liposuction; helps stimulate the reduction of adipose tissue (fat) in areas such as the buttocks, thighs, and calves, 619
    for cellulite, 563
Endocardium, 35

Endocrine system, regulates most of the hormone producing glands including the pineal gland, hypothalamus gland, pituitary gland, parathyroid glands, adrenal glands, pancreas glands, stomach and intestines, kidneys, and reproductive organs, **56,** 58–60

End of the day protocols, 158

Endoplasmic reticulum, 31, 32

Endoscope, in mammaplasty, a long tube with a light on the end, 589, 590

Endosteum, 36

Endothelial tissue, **tissue that lines the inside of the body, and its organs, such as lungs, stomach, etc., 33**

Energy
  in Chinese traditional medicine, 420–422
  electricity as, 137
  in laser hair removal, 450
  in massage therapy, 568
  in polarity therapy, 423
  of pulsed light, 450–451

Energy levels, of electrons in atoms, **the orbits in which electrons travel, 284**

Entrepreneurship, of skin care professionals, 253

Environmental aggravators, acne and, 375

Environmental damage, to skin, 167–168. *See also* Sun

Environmental Protection Agency (EPA), disinfectant standards of, 81

Enzyme exfoliation, 415, 416

Enzymes
  as exfoliating agents, 300, 415, 416
  in hair growth inhibitors, 451

EPA. *See* Environmental Protection Agency (EPA)

Epidermal-dermal junction, 39

Epidermal strata, cell layers within the epidermis, 42–43

Epidermis
  aging and, 315
  cell migration to, 44
  cells in, 37, 38
  effects of microcurrent therapy on, 129
  in hair follicle, 441
  hair in, 45, 441
  laser hair removal and, 450
  medium depth peeling of, 402
  structure of, 39, 41–48
  superficial peeling of, 401–402
  tanning and, 315

Epidermolysis, salicylic acid and, **live cell destruction, 412**

Epilation, a hair removal treatment such as waxing, electrolysis, or laser hair removal, 171, 438–456, 458–481. *See also* Waxing
  of eyebrows, 461–465
  methods of, 445–451
  permanent, 445, 448–451
  sanitation and, 439
  semipermanent, 448–451
  temporary, 445
  tips for, 455–456, 459, 481

Epilation products, table of, 446

Epilepsy, electrical contraindication against, 174

Epiphyses, 36

Epithelial tissue, **tissue that is on the outside of the body's structures, 32**–33, 37, 38

Equipment. *See also* Supplies; Tools

electrical, 137
electrically powered, 116–134
for exfoliation, 397–398
maintaining, 110, 118, 119, 120, 122–123, 124, 128, 130, 133–134
for skin analysis, 117–119
for treatment room, 105, 106–115, 513

Erbium laser, 588

Ergonomically correct stool, **healthy for the human spine, 109**

Ergonomics, for estheticians, 110–114

Erosion, a type of scar that is a depression in the skin's surface, 249, 252

Erysipelas, a very severe form of cellulitis that can be fatal if not treated soon enough, 263

Erythema, redness indicating inflammation, 247. *See also* Redness of skin

Erythemic acne, 372

Erythemic skin, skin that turns red easily during simple esthetic procedures, 175

Erythromycin, acne treatment with, 380

Essential amino acids, 92

Essential oils, oils that are lighter than water, 13, 552–553
  in aromatherapy, 422
  sensitive skin and, 350
  in steamers, 122
  table of, 553
  use of and contraindication against, 280

Esters, 289

Estheticians. *See also* Skin care professionals
  advanced home care regimens by, 426–436
  advanced ingredient technology for, 302–307
  booth rentals by, 108
  brochures for, 217
  camouflage therapy by, 622–628
  career planning by, 449
  client health analysis by, 171–182
  client relations with, 239, 274, 295
  clinical skin care and, 574–581
  clothing and grooming for, 112
  compensation for, 532–533
  continuing education of, 616
  dieticians versus, 91
  disease and, 245, 246, 247
  as entrepreneurs, 253
  epilation by, 438–456
  ergonomics for, 110–114
  ethics of, 102
  exfoliation by, 397
  facials by, 197–225
  first impressions of, 147–149, 153
  gommage by, 399–400
  hand care for, 112–114
  holistic treatments by, 418–425
  information gathering by, 160–161, 427, 548, 601–608
  initial consultation with, 176
  joining professional organizations by, 377
  learning chemistry by, 283
  liability of, 111
  licensed, 6, 7, 29, 108, 541–542, 577
  makeup application by, 516–536
  makeup artistry by, 485–515
  makeup profiling by, 490–491
  making appointments with, 166
  marketing by, 431
  medical, 7, 575
  men's facials by, 228–235
  merchandising by, 329

microdermabrasion by, 400–401
networking by, 584
over-the-counter treatments by, 271–276
patient profiles for, 596–608
physicians and, 118, 575, 608
plastic surgery and, 582–595
policies and procedures and, 86, 108, 410–411
postconsultation with, 236–243
pre- and postoperative care by, 610–621
productivity of, 132
product recommendations by, 572
public relations for, 421
referrals and, 267
as resource, 579
resumes for, 580
sanitation and, 79
scrubs by, 398–399
self-care of, 601
setting up facilities for, 147–158
skin analysis by, 184–193
skin cancer and, 326–328
skin condition treatment by, 309
spa treatments by, 538–554, 556–573
successful, 626
sunscreens and, 272–273
supplies for, 152–155
technological tools for, 117
telephone etiquette by, 599
time management by, 166, 500
treating of acne by, 364–388
treating of aging skin by, 328–330, 330–332
treating of ethnic clients by, 390–395
treating of hyperpigmentation by, 356–362
treating of mature skin by, 332–339
treating of sensitive skin by, 340–355
treating of skin types by, 163–169
treating of sun-damaged skin by, 324–325, 325–326
treatment room for, 105, 106, 107–115
use of electricity by, 137
waxing by, 458–481
work ethic for, 460

Esthetician's stool, 109–110, 112

Esthetic machines. *See* Equipment; Machines

Esthetics, a branch of anatomical science that deals with the overall health and well-being of the skin, the largest organ of the human body, 3, 27. *See also* Skin care
  advanced education in, 616
  balance and harmony in, 9–11
  competition in, 548
  history of, 3–22
  industry conferences on, 21–22
  nutrition and, 101–103
  protocols in, 602
  standard protocols in, 602
  success in, 626

Esthetics America, 377

Esthetics laws, 29
  booth rental and, 108
  concerning massage, 567
  concerning sanitation, 87–89
  cosmetics in, 303
  liability and, 111
  in Utah, 19

Esthetics Manufacturers and Distributors Alliance (EMDA), on exfoliation, 401

Esthetics retail centers, 5, 578

Esthetic therapies, 3
  history of, 11–17

Estrogen, a female sex hormone produced by the ovaries, 59

menopause and, 313
  skin effects of, 314
Ethics, of estheticians, 102
Ethmoid bone, 70
Ethnic skin, 309, 390–395
  colors of, 491
Ethyl alcohol, 82
  aging skin and, 321
  as vasodilator, 319
Etiquette, telephone, 599
Eumelanin, 46
Europe, hair color in, 444–445
European massage, 423
European sunscreen, 273
Evening makeup, 485
Excoriations, a type of scar caused by scrapes or scratches, 249, 252
  acne and, 376
Exercise
  health through, 10
  in herbalism, 425
Exfoliating agents, 300, 303, 398. *See also* Chemical exfoliants; Keratolytics
  in acne management, 273, 374–375, 378
  Asian skin and, 393
  for home skin care, 428
  in sample skin care systems, 436
  sensitive skin and, 349–350
  waxing contraindication against, 455
Exfoliation, 300, 396–416, 427
  in antiaging firming treatment, 338
  avoiding excessive, 397
  in basic facial, 221, 222, 223
  of black skin, 392, 393
  in body treatments, 544, 546, 547, 549, 557
  chemical, 397–398, 401–414
  contraindications against, 174
  defined, 397
  enzyme, 415–416
  in facial phase III, 201, 205, 206
  in facials, 197
  with glycolic peel, 608
  for hands and feet, 563–564
  hyperpigmentation and, 359, 361–362
  Jessner's, 409–411
  mechanical, 397–398, 398–401
  in paraffin mask treatment, 333
  peeling versus, 401–402
  sensitive skin and, 349–350
  in thermal mask treatment, 336
  through microdermabrasion, 133
  in treating acne, 381
  treating oily skin with, 165
Expression lines, wrinkles or depressions in the skin developed from muscles repetitively moving in the same direction, 311–312
Extensor muscles, muscles that straighten the wrist, hand and fingers to form a straight line, 73, 74
External jugular vein, the vein located on the sides of the neck that carries blood returning to the heart from the head, face, and neck, 60, 61
Extractions
  in basic facial, 223
  of black skin, 392
  in facial phase III, 201, 205, 207
  in men's facials, 233
  in paraffin mask treatment, 333
  sensitive skin and, 343
  in thermal mask treatment, 336
  in treating acne, 380–381, 382–383, 385
  in treating sensitive skin, 352

Extrinsic aging, 315–322
Extrinsic aging factors, controllable factors that contribute to the aging of the skin, such as sun exposure, 313
Eye area brushes, 510
Eyebrow arching, 459, 461, 495
Eyebrow pencil, 459, 461, 495, 497
Eyebrows
  in basic makeup application, 526
  in facial profile, 495–497
  muscles of, 71
  shape of, 495–497
  tweezing of, 445
  waxing and shaping of, 459, 461–465
Eye cream, for home skin care, 428
Eye damage, from ultraviolet radiation, 324
Eye gel, for home skin care, 428
Eyelash curler, in makeup kit, 512
Eyelashes. *See* False eyelashes
Eyelids, 496–497
  plastic surgery on, 586–587
Eyelift, 585, 586–587, 620
  pre- and postoperative care with, 612, 614
Eyeliner, in basic makeup application, 526. *See also* Liner pencil
Eye makeup remover, 514
  applying, 202
  in basic facial, 221
  in basic makeup application, 524
  purpose and function of, 200
  in treating acne, 384
Eye movement, in massage, 210
Eye pads
  in alpha hydroxy acid treatment, 407
  in analysis and consultation, 204
  in cleansing, 205
  in extractions, 207
  in facial phase VII, 213
Eye pencil, 507–508
Eyes
  in alpha hydroxy acid home care treatment, 405
  in eyebrow waxing, 465
  in face, 493
  in facial profile, 495–497
  in salicylic acid treatment, 413–414
  sections of, 497
  shapes of, 496, 497
  skin around, 169
  width of and distance between, 493
Eye shadows, 505, 506–507, 514
  in basic makeup application, 526
  tips for, 507

Face
  bones of, 69, 70
  effects of microcurrent therapy on, 128, 129
  foundation contouring for, 503–504
  makeup for, 485, 486
  motor points of, 216
  muscles of, 70–71
  nerves of, 75, 77
  normal–combination skin of, 163
  sections of, 493
Face-lift, 585, 586, 620
  camouflage makeup following, 624–625
  pre- and postoperative care with, 612, 613–614
Face makeup chart, 518, 522
Face shapes, 491–493
Facial (VII) nerve, 68, 75, 76, 77
Facial analysis, 163
  health analysis in, 171
Facial artery, 60

Facial bed, 107, 110, 146, 194
  setup of, 149–152
Facial caps, 152
Facial chairs, 107–109
  maintaining, 110
Facial hair
  hormones and, 59
  men's facials and, 229, 231
Facial injuries, camouflage therapy for, 627
Facial lines, 168, 311–312
  near lips, 499
Facial massage, 195, 196, 215–220
  types of, 216–218
Facial plastic surgery, 583
  types of, 583–589
Facial profiles, 494–499
Facials, 6, 20, 194–225
  alpha hydroxy acid treatments and, 406–409
  basic, 220–224
  body treatments and, 541
  client health screening information on, 173
  esthetician's stool and, 109–110
  importance of, 195
  learning to provide, 197
  makeup with, 530
  mechanical exfoliation during, 397–398, 398–401
  men's, 195, 228–235
  postconsultation after, 236–243
  setting up room for, 201, 221
  seven phases of, 200, 201–215
  shiatsu massage and, 570
  skin health and, 27
  spa treatments and, 539
  supplies for, 152–155, 197–201
  technological tools for, 117, 194
  work ethic and, 460
Facial surgery, in client health screening information, 179
Facial vein, runs diagonally from the corner of the eye, across the nose to the jawline, 60
Facilities, for estheticians, 147–158
Factor, Max, 18, 19
Fad diets, 101
FAE. *See* Federation of American Esthetics (FAE)
Fair skin, 185–186, 491
False eyelashes
  in basic makeup application, 527–528
  in makeup kit, 512
  mascara and, 508
Fango mud, 551
Fantasy makeup, 533
  tips for, 533
Faraday, Michael, 129
Faradic current, 129
Fats, the third group of macronutrients. Fats can be used as energy, but not as readily as carbohydrates, 93, 289. *See also* Body fat
  dieting and, 101
  as macronutrients, 91, 93–94
Fat-soluble vitamins, 97–99
Fatty acids, acids derived from the saturated series of open chain hydrocarbons, 43, 93–94
  acne and, 367
  in emollients, 287, 289
  in plant oils, 289
Fatty alcohols, as emollients, fatty acids that have been exposed to hydrogen, 289

Fatty esters, as emollients, **emollients produced from fatty acids and alcohols, 289**

Favre-Racouchot disorder, **also called solar comedones. Large comedones developed around the eyelids and cheekbones resulting from sun damage. It is more common in men than women, 320**

FDA. *See* Food and Drug Administration (FDA)

FDCA. *See* Food, Drug, and Cosmetic Act of 1952 (FDCA)

Federal Register rulebook, 87–89

Federation of American Esthetics (FAE), 19

Feet
    in reflexology massage, 423–424, 570
    in shiatsu massage, 569
    spa treatments for, 563–564
    waxing of, 478

Femoral nerve, 75

Fetus, hair on, 443

Fever blisters, in client health screening information, 178

Fiber, as macronutrient, **a slender, thread-like structure that combines with others to form animal or vegetable tissue, 92,** 93. *See also* Carbohydrates

Fibroblasts, responsible for the formation of collagen and elastin that makes up the connective tissue, 37, 40, 41

Fifties, skin aging during, 314

Filipendula ulmaria, salicylic acid from, 412

Fillers, 594

Finances, in entrepreneurship, 253

Finger cots, in treating acne, 382–383

Fingernails, keratin in, 42. *See also* Nails

Fingers
    in shiatsu massage, 424, 569
    in treating acne, 381–382

Fire
    in Chinese traditional medicine, 12
    in four humors theory, 15

Firming treatment, for mature skin, 338

First impressions, 147–149, 153
    in skin analysis, 188

Fissure, 249

Fitch, William Edward, 17

Fitted sheets, 149

Fitzgerald, William, 423

Fitzpatrick, Thomas, 185

Fitzpatrick Scale, a method of skin typing that measures and labels the tolerance of different skin types to the sun's burning rays, 184, **185**–187
    laser hair removal and, 450

Five elements, in Chinese traditional medicine, 12

5-minute close, 237–239

Fixtures, for treatment room, 513

Flagella, 78, 79

Flares, of rosacea, sudden worsening of rosacea or redness, 255

Flash, of pulsed light, 451

Flat brushes, 511

Flat sheets, 150

Flexor muscles, **muscles that bend the wrist, draw the hand up, and close the fingers toward the forearm, 73, 74**

Fluoride, a trace mineral, required in very small quantities for correct body function, 101
    dosage, functions, and sources of, 97

Flush, 506

Foam bath, body treatments and, 571

Foaming cleanser
    in acne management, 379
    for men's facials, 229
    purpose and function of, 200
    in treating sensitive skin, 348

Folacin (folic acid), 99
    dosage, functions, and sources of, 95

Follicle dilation, in treating acne, 383

Follicles. *See also* Hair follicle
    acne and, 366
    alpha hydroxy acids and, 402–403
    in keratosis pillaris, 255
    oily skin and, 165
    puberty and, 368
    in treating acne, 383

Follicular keratinosis, a skin condition resulting from vitamin A deficiency, generally affects the body skin, 98

Folliculitis, a skin condition common in men, where instead of growing up and out onto the skin's surface, hair grows slightly under the skin, causing a bacterial infection, 231, 263–264
    men's facials and, 231
    "razor bumps" and, 235

Follow-up, in client relations, 239, 274

Food, Drug, and Cosmetic Act of 1952 (FDCA), 18

Food and Drug Administration (FDA), 245, 302, 303
    color agents and, 297
    cosmetics regulation by, 286
    disinfectant standards of, 81
    ethics and, 102
    hair reduction guidelines by, 448
    hydroquinone and, 265
    laser hair removal guidelines by, 450
    on microdermabrasion, 133
    over-the-counter and prescription drugs and, 271
    sunscreen and, 272, 273

Food guide pyramid, 90, 92

Foods. *See also* Diet; Nutrients
    acne and, 371
    as allergens, 180
    in ayurvedic therapy, 422

Foot lotions, body treatments and, 571

Footstools, for clients, 149

Forehead
    botox and, 593–594
    foundation contouring for, 504

Forehead lift, 585, 586, 620

Formaldehyde, sensitive skin and, 350

Formalin, 82

Formalin-releasers, sensitive skin and, 350

Forms, 603–607. *See also* Client health form; Confidential health history questionnaire; Confidential Skin Health Survey; Consultation forms; Health analysis form; Health screening questionnaire; Long-term skin management form; Makeup questionnaire; Medical documentation; Skin analysis form; Skin Care Management Program form; Treatment record form
    for treatment room, 513

Forties, skin aging during, 313

FotoFacial wrinkle treatment, 595

Foundations, 501–502, 514
    in basic makeup application, 524–525
    choosing, 502

    contouring with, 502, 503–504
    tips for, 502

Four humors theory, **blood, phlegm, yellow bile, and black bile, 14,** 15

Fragranced oils, use of and contraindication against, 280

Fragrances, 294–296
    as allergens, 180
    in body treatments, 573
    sensitive skin and, 350

France, origin of perfume industry in, 17–18

Freckles, 168, 248, 265
    in sun-damaged skin, 318

Free electrons, found in the outermost orbit; they are more easily moved from their orbit, 139

Free radicals, an unstable oxygen atom that tries to "steal" electrons from other atoms, 285
    smoking and, 321
    sun exposure and, 316
    vitamin E and, 98

Frequent stress, in client health screening information, 179–180

Freshener, 514
    in acne management, 378, 387
    applying, 203
    in basic facial, 221, 222, 223
    in facial phase VII, 213
    for hyperpigmentation, 361
    in men's facials, 233, 234
    purpose and function of, 200

Friction, maintains pressure on the skin while the fingers or palms are moved rapidly over the underlying muscle structures. Friction is used to improve circulation and glandular activity of the skin, 219
    in massage, 218, 219
    in Swedish massage, 566

Frontal bone, the bone which forms the forehead, 69, 70

Frontalis muscle, **anterior or front portion of the epicranium; muscle of the scalp, 71**

Frosting, of skin, **skin that turns white in patches as a result of intense chemical exfoliation, 409**

Fucus, 551

Fucus vesibulosus, 551

Fulguration, in treating acne, 383–388

Full body detoxification, cellulite treatment and, 563

Full cleanse, in skin analysis, 188

Full lips, 499

Full treatments, for extremities, 564

Fumigants, 84

Functional ingredients, in cosmetics, **ingredients in a cosmetic product that make up the majority of a product and allow products to spread, give them body and texture, and give them a specific form, 286**

Fungi, general term for vegetable parasites including all types of yeasts and mildew, 80
    in athlete's foot, 261–262
    in hypopigmentation, 265
    infections from, 80, 261–262

Furnishings. *See also* Equipment
    for epilation, 451
    maintaining, 110
    for treatment room, 107–115

Galenus, Claudius, 14
Galvanic current, 126–128, 137
    in treating acne, 381
Galvanic electrology, 448
Galvanic machine, 126
    in facial phase III, 206
    preparing for facials, 201
Gattefosse, René-Maurice, 20
Gaultheria procumbens, salicylic acid from, 412
Gauze, in paraffin treatment, 564
Gauze pads, 154
    in alpha hydroxy acid treatment, 408
Geisha tradition, 11
Gel masks
    in Accutane treatments, 278–279
    in treating acne, 386–387
    in treating sensitive skin, 353, 354
Gels
    in acne management, 374, 379, 403
    in alpha hydroxy acid treatment, 405,
        407–408
    in antiaging treatments, 332
    body treatments and, 571
    for home skin care, 428
Genes, tiny portions of chromosomes
    that determine an individual's
    features including skin coloring,
    acne factors, sensitivity, and the
    aging process, 32
    aging and, **311**
    skin condition and, 163
Genital herpes, 261
Gentleman's jacket, for clients, 148
Geographic lesions, **describes lesions that**
    are shaped like a map, 248
Germany, communal bathing in, 542
Germs. *See* Microorganisms
Gerson, Joel, 20
Glamour blush, 506
    in basic makeup application, 528
Glass, in light bulb, 136, 143
Glass tip electrode, 125
Glossopharyngeal (IX) nerve, 68, 76
Gloves, should be used during any skin
    treatment, 83
    epilation and, 453
    in treating acne, 381
Glucose, the most basic unit of a
    carbohydrate, 93
Glutaraldehyde, a dialdehyde used as a
    germicidal agent to disinfect and
    sterilize instruments or equipment
    that cannot be heat sterilized, 81
Glycolic acid, 402
    salicylic acid and, 412
    in treating hyperpigmentation, 275
Glycolic acid peels, 21, 617
    protocol for, 608
Glycolipids, 43
Glycopolypeptides, 306
Glycoproteins, yeast cell derivatives that
    have the ability to enhance cellular
    metabolism, which boosts oxygen
    uptake in the cell; also called
    glycopolypeptides, 306
Glycosaminoglycans, a group of
    chemically related polysaccharides
    that are major components of the
    extra cellular matrix (ECM) and of
    connective tissues, 41
Gold, as conductor, 141
Golgi apparatus, an organelle that is a
    storage facility, holding protein for
    future use, 31, **32**

Gommage, a French word that means to
    erase. Also a cream product applied
    to the skin and rubbed off, removing
    dead skin cells through the friction,
    397, **399**
    in basic facial, 223
    in body treatments, 549
    contraindication against, 399
    performing, 399–400
"Goose bumps, " 442
Gortex, 594
Gowns, for clients, 148–149
Grade 1–4 acne, 372
Grafts, in treating carcinomas, **skin**
    transplant, 327
Graham, Florence Nightingale, 18
Grain alcohol, 82
Grains, in scrubs, 398, 549
Granular layer, 42. *See also* Stratum
    granulosum
Granular scrubs, 397
    in body treatments, 549
    performing, 398–399
Grapeseed
    in antiaging treatments, 330–331
    in treating telangiectasia, 319
Gravity, sagging skin and, 312, 313
Gray, color temperature of, 490. *See also* Grey
    hair
Greek culture
    grooming practices in, 14
    medicine in, 9
Green
    color temperature of, 490
    as secondary color, 488
Green algae, 550, 551
Green tea
    in antiaging treatments, 331
    treating telangiectasia with, 319
Grey, Aida, 18, 20
Grey hair, 445. *See also* Gray
Grooming, for estheticians, 112
Ground substance, a jelly like fluid that
    fills the empty space between the
    collagen and elastin fibers in the
    dermis, 41
Gynecomastia, the excessive
    development of the male mammary
    glands, 590

Hacking movement, in massage, 220
Hair, 45
    anatomical structure of, 441–444
    facial, 59
    as health indicator, 443
    human preoccupation with, 441
Hair bulb, the swelling at the base of the
    follicle that provides the growing
    basal part of the hair with
    nourishment; also referred to as the
    hair club, 441
    in laser hair removal, 450
Hair clips, 514
Hair club, 441
Hair coloring, 530
Hair follicle, the tubular epithelial shield
    that surrounds the lower part of the
    hair shaft, 45, 163, **441**–442. *See also*
    Follicles
    anatomy of, 441
Hair growth
    excessive, 443–444
    geographical differences in, 444–445
    waxing contraindication against, 455

Hair growth cycle, 442, 443
Hair growth inhibitors, 451
Hair growth retardants, 446
Hair loss, permanent makeup and, 627
Hair removal. *See* Epilation
Hair root, 45, 441, 442
Hair shaft, the portion of hair that
    projects beyond the skin, consisting
    of an outer layer (the cuticle), an
    inner most later (the medulla), and
    an in-between layer (the cortex).
    Color changes are made within the
    cortex, 441, 442
Hallucinogens, in Native American culture, 17
Hammamelis virginiana, in acne management,
    374
Hand care, for estheticians, 112–114
Hand lotions, body treatments and, 571
Hands
    in massage, 566
    mobility of esthetician's, 216
    in polarity therapy, 423
    in reflexology massage, 423–424, 570–571
    in Reiki massage, 423
    skin analysis with, 188
    spa treatments for, 563–564
    in treating acne, 381–382
    use in facials, 197, 208–212
Hand towels, 150–151
    in underarm waxing, 471
Han dynasty, medicine during, 11
Hanson, Annette, 19
Hard keratin, 42
Hard wax, 446, 447
    arm waxing with, 474–475
    bikini waxing with, 480–481
    procedures for, 456, 466–467, 468–469,
        471–473
    shoulder waxing with, 476–477
Harmony
    blushes and, 506
    in Chinese traditional medicine, 420–422
    esthetics in ancient civilizations and,
        9–11
    holism and, 419
    makeup artistry and, 487, 488, 491, 528
    skin health and, 27
Harper's Bazaar, personal care products offered
    by, 18
Harris, Robert, 615
Head, motor points of, 216. *See also* Cranium
Headaches, in client health screening
    information, 178
Headbands, 150–151
    terry stretch, 152
Head protection, for clients, 152
Head wraps, 152
Healing, as skin function, 28
Healing treatments, ancient, 9–11
Health. *See also* Hygiene; Public hygiene
    in ancient civilizations, 9
    in Chinese traditional medicine, 11–12
    of clients, 543
    in early civilizations, 3
    esthetics and, 7
    four humors theory of, 14
    hair as indicator of, 443
    of skin, 167–169
    skin as indicator of, 161, 443
Health analysis form, 170, 172
    contents of, 171–182
Health history, of clients, 161
Health Maintenance Organizations (HMOs),
    skin care and, 5–6

Health practices, ancient, 9–11
Health screening questionnaire, 171–182
Heart
    anatomy of, 35
    in circulatory system, 50, 54, 61–62
Heart-shaped face, 493
Heat
    acne and, 375
    hyperpigmentation and, 358
    nerves sensing, 41
    sensitive skin and, 349
Heaters. *See also* Paraffin wax heater
    for herbal wrap, 561
    for waxing, 446, 447, 451
Heat mask, 130–131
Heavy chin, foundation contouring for, 503
Hebrew culture, ancient grooming practices in, 13
Hedera helix, 553
Heliotrope, in dermatomyositis, 268
Hematoma, a collection of blood under the skin, 248
Hemoglobin, in skin color, 46
Hemophilia, in client health screening information, **a disease in which the blood does not clot normally, 178**
Hemp, 10
Henna, a reddish hair dye obtained from the powdered leaves and shoots of the mignonette tree, an old world shrub of the loosestrife family, 9, 10
Hennessey, Sylvie, 19
Henry IV, King, 16
Hepatitis, in client health screening, 177
Hepatitis viruses, disinfectants and, 81
Herald patch, the first patch that occurs in pityriasis rosea, 260
Herald Pharmacal, 18
Herbalism, 425
Herbal sheets, working with, 561
Herbal therapies, 10, 411
    in ancient Hebrew medicine, 13
    ayurvedic, 422
    in Chinese traditional medicine, 12
    holistic, 425
    modern, 18
    in Roman culture, 14–15
Herbal wrap, 561
Heredity
    acne and, 365
    hirsutism and, 443
    melanoma and, 328
    rosacea and, 347
    sensitive skin and, 342
Herpes, in client health screening information, 177
Herpes simplex, a fever blister or cold sore caused by a virus, 178
    alpha hydroxy acids and, 404
    in client health screening information, 178
    sun exposure and, 317
Herpes simplex virus 1 (HSV1), the virus that causes cold sores, 261
Herpes simplex virus 2 (HSV2), the virus that causes genital herpes, 261
Herpes zoster, the virus that causes shingles and chickenpox, 263
Hertz (Hz), the rate at which the reversal of direction occurs in alternating current, 144
Hidden lids, 496

High blood pressure, in client health screening information, 178
High-frequency machine, 123–125
    in basic facial, 223
    in facial phase III, 207
    preparing for facials, 201
    removing spider veins with, 594
    in treating acne, 383–388, 386
Hippocrates, 14
Hirsutism, excessive hair growth on the face, arms, and legs especially in women, 443–444
Hispanic skin, 394–395
    hyperpigmentation and, 358–359
    types of, 186
Histamines, a chemical that causes inflammation and swelling of the skin during allergic and irritation reactions, 66
    hives and, 258
    sensitive skin and, 342
    vitamin B_6 and, 99
Hives, urticaria; a skin eruption, 66, 251, 258, 276
    sensitive skin and, 342
HIV positive condition, in client health screening information, 177
HMOs. *See* Health Maintenance Organizations (HMOs)
Holism, defined, 419
Holistic practices
    defined, 419
    psychological benefits of, 419
Holistic skin care, 418–425
    licensing for, 425
    methods of, 420–425
    touch in, 420
Hollywood, makeup and, 485
Home care guide, a prescription or guide that provides a detailed routine of when to apply products and in what order, 241–243
Home care products
    alpha hydroxy acids in, 403
    body treatments and, 544, 571–573
    educating clients about, 428
    enzyme exfoliants as, 416
    home care treatment form and, 429, 430
    introducing clients to, 428–429
    sample plans for using, 432–434, 435, 436
    selling of, 429–432
    types of, 427–428
Home care regimen, 236–243
    advanced, 426–436
    body treatments and, 571–573
    compliance with, 600
Home care treatment form, 429, 430
Home maintenance
    for acne, 378–379, 387
    with alpha hydroxy acids, 405–406
    by clients, 215, 225, 236–243
    for hyperpigmentation, 361
    after salicylic acid treatment, 414
    for sensitive skin, 354
Hooked nose, 497
Hormonal acne, 369–370
Hormonal changes, birth control pills and, 173–174
Hormonal therapies, 173–174
    waxing contraindication against, 455
Hormones, secretions produced in and by one of the endocrine glands, and are

carried by the blood stream and body fluid to another part of the body, or a body organ, to stimulate functional activity or secretion, 56, 58–60
    acne and, 368–370
    hirsutism and, 444
    lipids and, 93
    melasma and, 358
    menopause and, 313–314
Horse chestnut, treating telangiectasia with, 319
Hospital
    as career option, 581
    esthetician in, 578
Hospital-grade disinfectants, products that have been tested and meet specific standards for killing microorganisms. They must be able to kill hepatitis viruses and tuberculosis bacteria, 81
Host cells, for viruses, **a cell that a virus attaches itself to, or lives inside of, in order to live, 80**
Hot cabbies, 130
Hot towel cabinet, 129, 130
    preparing for facials, 201
Hot towels, for men's facials, 232
Hot wax, 446, 447
    procedures for, 471–473
Hourly work, 532–533
HPV. *See* Human papillomavirus (HPV)
Hue, another name for color, 488
Human immunodeficiency virus (HIV), the virus that causes AIDS, 268. *See also* Acquired immunodeficiency syndrome (AIDS); HIV positive condition
Human papillomavirus (HPV), the virus that causes warts, 260
Humans
    geographical differences in hair growth among, 444–445
    preoccupation with hair by, 441
Humectants, ingredients that attract water to the skin's surface; also known as hydrators or hydrophilic agents, 298
Humidity, acne and, 375
Hungary, communal bathing in, 542
Hyaluronic acid, a glycosaminoglycan; a strong water-binder that helps retain fluid content in the dermis, 41, 307
Hydration
    in antiaging treatments, 332
    in treating sensitive skin, 354
Hydrators, ingredients that attract water to the skin's surface; also known as humectants or hydrophilic agents, 298
    in acne management, 373, 379
    in alpha hydroxy acid home care treatment, 405–406
    alpha hydroxy acids and, 404
    in antiaging treatments, 332
    in treating sensitive skin, 352
Hydriatics, the study of the physiological and therapeutic properties of mineral waters upon the body, 17
Hydrocortisone, 276

Hydroculator, for herbal wrap, a special water heater used in herbal wraps, 561
Hydrogen
 atomic structure of, 137, 139, 282, 285
 fatty acids and, 93–94
 in galvanic electrology, 448
 in water, 140
Hydrogenation, the result of hydrogen atoms attaching to carbon atoms to form saturated fats, 93–94
Hydrogen ions, pH scale and, 293–294
Hydrogen peroxide, 82
 in galvanic electrology, 448
Hydrophilic agents, ingredients that attract water to the skin's surface; also known as humectants or hydrators, 298
Hydroquinone, a topical drug ingredient used in medication to treat hyperpigmentation, 265
 as allergen, 180, 275
 Asian skin and, 393
 hyperpigmentation and, 361
 in treating hyperpigmentation, 265–266, 275–276
Hydrotherapy, the scientific use of water in the treatment of injuries, diseases, or for mental well-being; physical therapy using water, 545
 client modesty and, 542
 in combined body treatment packages, 565
Hydroxy radicals, the most dangerous of the free radicals; they are formed when peroxides react with iron in the blood, 316
Hygiene, in body treatment, 542–543. See also Health; Sanitation
Hyoid, a U-shaped bone that is located in the front part of the throat, and is known as the "Adam's apple," 69
Hyperkeratosis, a thickening of the skin due to keratinocytes, 247
 acne treatment and, 273
 in black skin, 391–392
 salicylic acid and, 412
Hyperpigmentation, the over production of melanin pigment, 48, 168, 265–266, 356–362
 alpha hydroxy acids and, 403
 of Asian skin, 393
 beta hydroxy acids and, 412
 of black skin, 392
 difficulty of treating, 362
 in dyschromias, 264
 of Hispanic skin, 395
 home care regimen for, 361
 hydroquinone and, 275–276
 inflammation and, 359
 from laser resurfacing, 588–589
 postinflammatory, 187
 salon treatment for, 361–362
 in skin analysis, 357–359
 skin types and, 186–187
 in sun-damaged skin, 317–318, 357, 358
 treatment of, 359–362
 under Wood's lamp, 187
Hyperpigmented macules, a type of macule that includes freckles and lentigines, 248
Hyperplasia, sebaceous, 254

Hypertrichosis, excessive hair growth where hair does not normally grow, such as the palms of the hands, 443
Hypertrophic scars, describes an elevated scar; overgrowth, 252
Hypoglossal (XII) nerve, 68, 76
Hypopigmentation, the absence of pigmentation in the skin, resulting from missing melanocytes or from a disorder that prevents the melanocytes from producing melanin, 264–265, 318
Hypothalamus, the part of the brain that regulates many metabolic body processes, 59
Hypotrophic scars, describes an erosion or depressed scar, 252

ICD. See Irritant contact dermatitis (ICD)
Illite, 551
Imbalance. See Balance
Immune cells, cells that help identify, block, control, and eradicate germs and microorganisms from affecting the skin and entering the body, 28–30, 61
Immune response, 63–64, 65
Immune response cells, 64–66
Immune suppression, sun exposure and, 317
Immune system, patrols and defends our tissues from invasion by bacteria or other harmful substances, 36, 56, 57, 63–66. See also Autoimmune diseases
 acne and, 367
 allergic contact dermatitis and, 257–258
Immunity, as skin function, 28–30
Immunocompromised persons, 266
Immunodeficiency diseases, in client health screening information, 177
Immunosuppressed persons, 266
Impactions, alpha hydroxy acids and, 402–403
Impetigo, a bacterial infection of the skin that often occurs in young children and is extremely contagious, 261
Implants, 594. See also Metal implants; Saline implants
In-clinic plastic surgery, 593–595
Independent clinic
 as career option, 581
 esthetician in, 578–579
Indian culture
 grooming practices in, 15–16
 herbalism from, 425
 holistic therapies from, 422
 threading in, 448
Indirect electrode, 125
Industry conferences, 21–22
Inert substances, defined, 594. See also Biologically inert substances
Infection, the invasion of body tissue by bacteria that cause disease, 247
Inflammation, swelling, 247
 avoiding, 331
 free radicals and, 316
 hyperpigmentation and, 359
Inflammatory acne, acne caused by inflammation within follicles, 370
 Accutane treatment for, 278
Inflammatory acne lesion, when a lesion becomes red, 367
Information gathering, 160–161, 427
 about patients, 601–608

competition and, 548
 questionnaires for, 603–607
Informed consent, falls under both medical documentation and treatment protocol; a customary written agreement between the client/patient and esthetician for applying particular treatment whether routine or pre-operative, 608
Informed Consent Form
 for microdermabrasion, 606–607
 for peels, 605
Infra-ray heat, for heat mask, 130–131
Infundibulum, the follicular canal, 366
 of sebaceous gland, 45
Ingham, Eunice, 423, 570
Ingrown hair
 in shaving, 445
 waxing and, 478
Initial consultation, 176
Injuries, skin hyperpigmentation from, 48, 265
Inorganic material, in bones, composed of matter not arising from natural growth or living organisms; without carbon, 69
Inositol, dosage, functions, and sources of, 95
Insecure clients, handling, 345
Insulators, a material or element that does not easily pass an electrical current, such as dry wood, ceramic, and most plastics, 141
Insurance
 booth rental and, 108
 liability and, 111
 licensing of estheticians and, 29
Intensity, of color, the degree of purity or brilliance of a color, 489
Intensive correctors, 303, 304
Intercellular lipids, the substance that fills the space between the upper epidermal cells, 42, 43
Intermediate colors, 488–489
International Dermal Institute, 19
Internet, licensing of estheticians and, 29
Interphase, 34
Intimidating clients, handling, 345
Intrinsic aging, 311–315
Inventory form, 513
Inverted triangle face, 492
Iodine, 100–101
 dosage, functions, and sources of, 96
Iodine tincture, 82
Ionic bonds, the bond between two ions that have opposite charges, 140, 284
Ionic reactions, with galvanic current, 126–128
Ionization, skin reactions to, 127
Ions, imbalanced atoms that carry an electrical charge, 139–140, 141
Ionto mask, 128
Iontophoresis, the introduction of ions by means of a galvanic current, 126–128
IPL (intense pulsed light) technology, 595
Iron, 100–101
 as conductor, 141
 dosage, functions, and sources of, 96
 free radicals and, 316
Iron oxide, 283
 color agents and, 297
 free radicals and, 316

Irritant contact dermatitis (ICD), dermatitis caused by exposure to an irritating chemical, 258

Irritants
  acne and, 371, 375
  allergens versus, 180, 344–347
  frequent, 347
  hyperpigmentation and, 265
  sensitive skin and, 341, 349–350

Irritation
  allergic reactions versus, 344–346
  avoiding, 331

Isopropyl alcohol, a homologue of ethyl alcohol; used as a solvent and rubefacie, 81, 82
  use of and contraindication against, 280

Isotretinoin, 278. *See also* Tretinoin
  in rosacea treatment, 255
  use of and contraindication against, 280

Itching, sensitive skin and, 343

Ivory skin, 491

Ivy, 553

Jacquet technique, 218

Jane Crawford & Associates, 21

Japan
  ancient grooming practices in, 11
  communal bathing in, 542
  Reiki massage from, 423
  shiatsu from, 424, 568

Japanese green tea. *See* Green tea

Jars, 155
  tubes versus, 229

Jasmine, 553

Jasminum officinale, 553

Jaw, foundation contouring for, 503

Jessner's exfoliation, 409–411

Jessner's solution, a liquid solution of lactic acid, salicylic acid, and resorcinol in a solvent of ethanol, 409

Jojoba oil, 300

Juniper, 553

Juniperus communis, 553

Junk food, nutrition and, 101

Kaolin, in masks, **a popular clay used in masks, 300**

Kaolinite, 551

Kapha people, in ayurvedic therapy, 422

Keloid, a raised scar resulting from an overproduction of collagen, 40, 249, 252
  in Asian skin, 393–394
  in black skin, 392, 393

Keratin, a protein substance which fills the cells as they approach the very outer layer of the epidermis, 42, 44
  in chemical exfoliation, 398
  in hair, 45, 441
  vitamin A and, 98

Keratinization, 42, 43

Keratinocytes, the top cells of the epidermis, 42, 44, 175, 247
  acne and, 365
  alpha hydroxy acids and, 402
  in chemical exfoliation, 398
  hyperpigmentation and, 359
  of sensitive skin, 341

Keratohyalin, 44

Keratolytics, drugs that work by peeling off the top cells of the epidermis, 175. *See also* Chemical exfoliants; Exfoliation

in acne treatment, 273, 275, 374, 380
  alpha hydroxy acids and, 404
  enzymes as, 416
  use of and contraindication against, 175, 280

Keratoses, buildup of cells, 247
  actinic, 321
  seborrheic, 320–321

Keratosis pilaris, a nonpathological condition of the skin, characterized by redness and bumpiness on the cheeks, 254–255

Kidneys, blood and, 62

Killer T cells, 65, 66

Kilowatt-hour, 141

Klingman, Albert, 304, 427

Kneading movement, in massage, 218–219

Knee joint, anatomy of, 37

Kohl, 10, 13

Krause end bulbs. *See* Mucocutaneous corpuscles

Lachman, Charles, 19

Lacrimal bone, 70

Lactic acid, in Jessner's solution, 409

Lakes, names for certified colors in cosmetics, 297

Lamb black, 10

Lamellar bodies, 42, 44

Laminaria digita, 551

Lamps, magnifying, 116, 117–118. *See also* Magnifying lamps; Wood's lamp

Lancets
  in treating acne, 382–383
  in treating ingrown hair, 478

Langerhans cells, **star-shaped immune cells, 37,** 64
  sun exposure and, 317

Lanugo, extremely soft and fine hair growth beginning before birth, 443

Lard, 94

Large lips, 499

Large mushroom electrode, 125

L-Ascorbic acid, an antioxidant that helps protect the body from many forms of oxidation, and free radical induced problems, 100. *See* Ascorbic acid

Laser center
  as career option, 581
  esthetician in, 579

Laser hair removal, 446, 448, 450–451, 593, 594–595

Laser resurfacing of skin, **a surgical process that can stimulate unwanted melanin production. The beams of light emitted from the laser are absorbed superficially by the water in the skin. Depending on the wavelength, it vaporizes a thin layer of skin. When new skin grows back, it's smoother and the scars are much less noticeable, 48,** 134, 402, 585, 587–589, 620
  camouflage makeup following, 624
  postsurgery treatment after, 611
  presurgery treatment before, 611

Lasers, the acronym derived from Light Amplification by Stimulated Emission of Radiation. A direct beam of radiation that penetrates the epidermis and creates a reaction, 134, 137
  technology of, **450,** 588

Late arrivals, handling, 410

Latissimi dorsi muscles, **a broad, flat superficial muscle covering the back of the neck and upper and middle region of the back, controlling the shoulder blade and the swinging movements of the arm, 73,** 74

Lauder, Estée, 19

Laundry, 158, 513
  procedures for handling, 85

Lavandula officinalis, 553

Lavender, in aromatherapy, 552, 553

Laws. *See* Esthetics laws

Layering, of body treatments, **the opportunity to mix and match treatments, 545**–546

L-dopa, a biochemical converted from an amino acid called tyrosine, 46

Leathery skin, from sun damage, 320

Lees, Mark, 374

Legrand, Jean, 20

Lemon, 553

Lemon balm, Asian skin and, 393

Lemongrass, 553

Lens, in magnifying lamp, 117

Lentigenes, freckles, 168, 265
  in sun-damaged skin, 318

Lentigo, the singular form of lentigines, 248
  in sun-damaged skin, 318

LEs. *See* Estheticians, licensed

Lesions, any mark, symptom, or abnormality on the skin, 248–252
  acne, 366–367, 374
  defined, 248
  finding suspicious, 328
  shapes of, 248
  types of, 248–252
  waxing contraindication against, 455

Les Nouvelles Esthetiques (LNE), 20

Lessons, makeup, 531. *See also* Education

Leukoderma, of black skin, **another form of vitiligo, the absence of pigment, partial or total, in the skin, 392**

Liability, 111
  in clinical skin care, 575

Licensed vocational nurses (LPNs, LVNs), in clinical skin care, 577

Licensing, 6, 7
  for body treatment, 541–542
  in clinical skin care, 577
  of cosmetologists, 20–21, 29
  for electrolysis, 480
  of estheticians, 29, 108, 541–542, 565
  for holistic care, 425
  for massage therapy, 565

Lichen moss, 551

Ligaments, tough bands of fibrous tissue serving to connect bones or hold an organ in place, 36
  effects of microcurrent therapy on, 128

Ligation, tying off veins, 594

Light
  black, 118
  from lasers, 450
  pulsed, 450–451

Light Amplification by Stimulated Emission of Radiation, 450, 587. *See also* Laser entries

Light blankets, 149

Light bulb, components of, 136, 143

Light cleansing, as facial phase I, 201, 202–203

Lightening agents, 361
  black skin and, 393

Lighting. *See also* Magnifying lamps; Lamps; Wood's lamp

for makeup, 513
for skin analysis, 117–118
with Wood's lamp, 118
Light tapping movement, in massage, 211
Linear lesions, **describes lesions in the shape of a line, 248**
Linear movement, in massage, 208
Linens, for clients, 149
Liner pencil, 507–508
in basic makeup application, 526
Lines. *See* Facial lines
Linoleic acid, an unsaturated fatty acid prepared from fats and oils; used as an emulsifier, 93
Lip brushes, 510
disposable, 511
Lipid peroxides, a free radical formed when the cell membrane is damaged, 316
Lipids, 93–94
free radicals and, 285, 316
intercellular, 42, 43
liposomes and, 297
menopause and, 313
in protecting barrier function of skin, 331
in sample skin care systems, 433, 435, 436
in sensitive skin, 341
Lipid secretions
with alipidic skin, 164–165
skin condition and, 163
Lip movement, in massage, 210
Lipofuscin, smoking and, 321
Lipophilic substances, beta hydroxy acids as, **oil loving, 412**
Lipoplasty, 590–591
Liposomes, an example of microencapsulation, 297, 304
Liposuction, 590–591, 592, 593, 620
cellulite treatments and, 563
Lip pencil, 507–508
Lips
shapes of, 498–499
waxing upper, 470
Lipstick, 505, 509, 514
in basic makeup application, 528
tips for, 509
Liquid brush cleaners, 510
Liquid foundations, 501
Liver spots, in sun-damaged skin, 318. *See also* Chloasma
LMTs. *See* Massage therapists, licensed
LNE. See Les Nouvelles Esthetiques (LNE)
Lomi Lomi massage, as holistic therapy, **a method of massage practiced in Hawaii that is similar to Swedish massage; it incorporates large body movements much like a dance, 423**
London (Londinium), founding of, 14
Long chin, foundation contouring for, 503
Longevity, ayurvedic treatments and, 15–16
Long nose, 497
Long-term camouflage therapy, 625–627
Long-term damage, from sun exposure, 316–317
Long-term programs, for skin care, 237, 239, 240
Long-term skin management form, 240
Look Good, Feel Better program, 177
Loose powders, 505
in basic makeup application, 525–526
Lotion
in antiaging treatments, 332
in treating sensitive skin, 354
Lotions

in body treatments, 554
body treatments and, 571
Loupe, another term for a magnifying lamp, 116, **117**–118
Low blood pressure, in client health screening information, 178
Lower cheek movement, in massage, 209
Lower leg
spot treatments for, 564
waxing of, 478
Lower lip, shapes of, 499
Low-foaming cleanser, in treating sensitive skin, 348
LPNs. *See* Licensed vocational nurses (LPNs, LVNs)
Lucas sprayer, 123
Lumbar plexus, 75
Lungs, circulatory system and, 61
Lupus, an autoimmune disease resulting in a breakdown of the body's immune system, causing the immune response to be directed toward the body's own organs, 66, 266, 268
alpha hydroxy acids and, 404
in client health screening information, 178
prednisone and, 177
waxing contraindication against, 455
LVNs. *See* Licensed vocational nurses (LPNs, LVNs)
Lye, in galvanic electrology, 448
Lymph, liquid tissue that is fluid and constantly bathes the various tissues of the body, 24, 36
in lymphatic system, 62
Lymphatic drainage, 62
Lymphatic massage, 62
Lymphatic system, consists of lymph flowing through the lymphatic spaces, lymph vessels, lacteals, and lymph nodes, 62–63. *See also* Manual lymphatic drainage (MLD)
effects of microcurrent therapy on, 128–129
meridians and, 568
Lymph capillaries, 62
structure of, 24
Lymph drainage massage, uses gentle pressure on the lymphatic system to eliminate watery stagnation of tissues from the body and to stimulate the flow of body fluids, 218
Lymph nodes, filters within the lymph system, 36, 62–63
anatomy of, 38
Lymphocytes, white blood cells formed in lymphatic tissue throughout the body. In normal adults, they make up 22–28% of the total number of leukocytes in the circulating blood, 36, 37, **61,** 63
thymus and, 60
Lymphokine, 65
Lysol, 81
Lysosomes, 31, 32

Machines
electricity for, 144
for skin care, 119–128
Macronutrients, 91–94, 103
Macrophage cells, immune cells, 37
Macrophages, 36, 37, 63, 64, 66
sun exposure and, 317
Macules, any sort of flat lesion, 248–250

Magnesium, mineral used for energy release and protein synthesis, prevention of tooth decay, and in movement of muscles, 100
dosage, functions, and sources of, 97
Magnetic resonance imaging (MRI), 137
Magnetism, electricity and, 137
Magnets, 140–141
Magnifying lamps, 116, 117–118. *See also* Wood's lamp
in analysis and consultation, 204
skin analysis with, 187–188
Makeup, 484–515, 516–536
acne and, 371, 378
camouflage, 534–535, 622, 623
client consultation about, 517–518
color theory for, 488–491
corrective, 533–534
fantasy, 533
history of, 18–19
inventory of, 514
marketing of, 535–536
permanent cosmetic, 627–628
popularity of, 485
removing, 202–203
tips for, 502
touch-up, 530
trends in, 535
wedding, 531–533
Makeup application
basic procedure for, 523–528
for special occasions, 530–531, 533
tips for, 531
Makeup artistry, marketing of, 535–536
Makeup artists, 7, 485
Makeup collections, 529–530
Makeup instruction diagram, 513
Makeup kit, contents of, 512
Makeup lessons, 531
Makeup products, 487, 501–515
choosing, 501, 529–530
table of, 513–515
Makeup profile, gathering the visual information needed to determine the type of makeup application and the products chosen for a particular client, 490–491, 518, 520–521
Makeup questionnaire, 513, 517, 518, 519
Makeup services, 530–535
Makeup station, 513
Makeup supplies, 523
for estheticians, 513–515
Makeup work area, 517
Malignant condition, **the term for cancerous lesions, 248**
Malpractice, licensing of estheticians and, 29
Mammaplasty, a surgery that enlarges breasts, 589–590
Mandible, the lower jawbone, 69, 70
Manganese, a grayish-white, metallic, chemical element which rusts like iron; it is not magnetic, 101
dosage, functions, and sources of, 97
Manicures, 530, 563
Manicuring scissors, in makeup kit, 512
Manipulative clients, handling, 345
Manual lymphatic drainage (MLD) a specialized advanced form of massage; pre-surgically, it helps to prepare the skin for a facelift, or other plastic surgery; post-surgery, it helps reduce swelling or edema, dissipates bruising, and encourages the healing process of the skin, 62, 615

Manufacturers, of skin care products, 572

Margarine, 94

Marketing, 431. *See also* Retail sales; Sales; Selling
  of combination services, 564–565
  competition and, 548
  of makeup services, 535–536

Martin, Jane, 19

Mascara, 505, 508, 514
  in basic makeup application, 527, 528
  removing, 202
  tips for, 508

Mascara wands, 511
  in basic makeup application, 527

Mask ingredients, 300

Masks. *See also* Body masks; Gel masks; Heat mask; Ionto mask; Paraffin mask; Pregnancy mask; Product masks; Thermal mask; Wraps
  in acne management, 275, 379, 386–387, 388
  in antiaging firming treatment, 338
  in basic facial, 224
  in facial phase VI, 201, 212–213
  ingredients in, 550–552
  mechanical exfoliation using, 397
  men's facials and, 231, 234
  purpose and function of, 200
  in salicylic acid treatment, 414
  treating mature skin with, 333–337
  in treating sensitive skin, 353
  types of, 300

Masoprocol, treating actinic keratosis with, 321

Massage
  in antiaging firming treatment, 338
  in aromatherapy, 422
  in ayurvedic therapy, 422
  benefits of, 215–216
  body, 565–567
  in body treatments, 541–542, 544
  in combined body treatment packages, 565
  craniosacral, 423
  facial, 195, 196, 215–220
  as facial phase V, 201, 208–212
  for hands and feet, 563–564
  home care regimen and, 571
  legal terminology of, 567
  Lomi Lomi, 423
  in men's facials, 234
  order of, 567
  in paraffin mask treatment, 334
  purpose of, 566
  Swedish, 619–620
  in thermal mask treatment, 336
  in treating acne, 386, 388
  in treating sensitive skin, 352
  types of, 216–218
  use of and contraindication against, 280

Massage oils, in body treatments, 573

Massage therapists, licensed, 577

Massage therapy, 7, 215, 619–620
  in body treatments, 541–542, 565–567
  electrodes for, 125
  licensing for, 565
  skin health and, 27
  types of holistic, 423–425

Massage Therapy Association, 541

Masseter muscle, 71

Mast cells, immune cells, 36, 37

Mastery, in skin care, 7

Mastoid bone, extends from the temporal bone; can be felt just in front of ear, 69, 70

Materials, in skin care in ancient civilizations, 10

Material Safety Data Sheet (MSDS), 87, information compiled by a manufacturer listing product ranges for ingredient content and associated hazards to combustion levels and storage requirements, 88

Mature skin, treating, 332–339. *See also* Aging

Maury, Marguerite, 20

Maxillae, two bones that form the upper jawbone, 69, 70

Maxillary nerve, 75

Maxillofacial surgeons, specialists who treat the mouth and jaw, including facial, plastic and reconstructive surgery, 583

M.D. Formulations, 18

Meadowsweet, salicylic acid from, 412

Mechanical exfoliation, a technique that physically removes dead corneum cells from the skin's surface, 397, 398–401
  chemical exfoliation versus, 397–398

Mechanical folliculitis, 263–264

Mechanical irritation, of sensitive skin, 346

MED. *See* Minimal erythemal dose (MED)

Media, customer information via, 427

Medical aestheticians, 7

Medical conditions
  client health screening information on, 174, 178–182
  identifying, 245

Medical disclaimer, in client health screening information, **part of the health history form that ensures the client understands that the treatment she is receiving is for cosmetic rather than medical purposes, 181**–182

Medical documentation, 601–608

Medical esthetics, integration of surgical procedures and esthetic treatments, supporting demands for long-term age-management programs
  defined, **577**
  patient profiles in, 596–608

Medical esthetic services, 5

Medical model, for dispensaries, 156–157

Medical professionals, referrals to, 247. *See also* Physicians

Medical treatment, of acne, 379–380. *See also* Postoperative care; Preoperative care

Medications
  antiviral, 279
  in client health screening information, 174–175

Medicine
  in African culture, 16
  ancient, 9–11
  Chinese traditional, 11–12
  esthetics and, 3
  holism versus, 419
  in Native American culture, 17
  permanent makeup in, 627–628
  skin care in, 574–581
  Western, 17–18

Medi-spa, 5
  as career option, 581
  esthetician in, 579

Meditation

in ayurvedic therapy, 422
  health through, 10

Mediterranean Caucasian skin, 185–186

Mediterranean regions, hair color in, 444–445

Medium depth peels, 402

Medium skin, 491

Medulla, of hair, 441, 442

Meeting clients, 147–149

Meissner corpuscles, nerve endings that help to detect touch, pressure, and cold, 41

Melancholic temperament, in four humors theory, 15

Melanin, pigment that gives the skin color, 28, 46, 47
  alpha hydroxy acids and, 403
  in ethnic skin, 391
  hyperpigmentation and, 265, 358–359
  lasers and, 134
  in liver spots, 357
  tanning and, 315
  ultraviolet radiation and, 168

Melanin suppressive agents, 361

Melanocytes, pigment cells that determine the color of the skin and hair, 37, 46, 47
  alpha hydroxy acids and, 403
  hyperpigmentation and, 358
  in melanoma, 327–328
  in sun-damaged skin, 318, 358
  tanning and, 315

Melanoma, 327–328
  ABCDs of, 328

Melanosomes, small granules filled with melanin; manufactured by melanocytes, 46, 47

Melasma, common term to describe any disorder of hyperpigmentation, it is frequently used to describe a condition known as pregnancy mask, 168, 266
  alpha hydroxy acids and, 403
  in sun-damaged skin, 318
  treatment of, 357–358

Melissa officinalis, Asian skin and, 393

Membership programs, in promotions, 230

Membranes
  basement, 39–40
  of cells, 30–31, 34
  of nuclei, 34

Memory B cells, 65

Memory T cells, 65

Menopause
  hirsutism and, 444
  skin aging due to, 313–314

"Menopause mustache, " 444

Men's facials, 195, 228–235

Menstruation, acne and, 369

Mental disturbances, isotretinoin and, 278

Mentally ill patients, 598

Mentha, 553

Merchandising, 329. *See also* Retail sales; Sales; Selling

Mercury, as conductor, 141

Meridians
  in acupuncture, 420
  in reflexology, 423, 570
  in shiatsu therapy, 424, 568

Merkel cells, located in the epidermis, these cells are believed to be transmitters of sensory function to lower dermal nerves, 37

Message services, 599

Metabolic group, of seaweed treatments, **a type of algae treatment that detoxifies and increases the metabolism by stimulating circulation, 550**

Metabolic stimulation, the application of specialized products and treatments the encourage circulatory and metabolic stimulation through vasodilation of blood capillaries,
in body treatments, **544,** 557
wraps for, 550

Metabolism
in body treatments, 544
of cells, 306

Metal, in Chinese traditional medicine, 12

Metal implants, electrical contraindication against, 174

Metal salts, as color agents, 297

Metaphase, 34

Metastasized cancers, **to spread to other tissues or organs, 326**
from squamous cell carcinoma, 327

Metro-gel. *See* Metronidazole

Metronidazole, in rosacea treatment, **a prescription antiyeast medication, commercially known as MetroGel, Metro-Cream, or Noritate, used to treat rosacea,** 255, **256,** 279, 612

Michalun, M. Varinia, 416

Michalun, Natalia, 416

Microampere electrical neuromuscular stimulation, 128

Microballs, in scrubs, 398, 549. *See also* Polyethylene beads

Microcomedones, the beginning of the plug formation, not visible to the naked eye, 374
acne and, **366**
alpha hydroxy acids and, 403

Microcurrent machines, 128–129

Microcurrent therapy, 128–129

Microdermabrasion, a new form of mechanical exfoliation that uses a powerful electronic vacuum to spray high-grade microcrystals composed of corundum or aluminum dioxide across the skin's surface through a pressurized wand, 133–134, 397, 400–401, 618–619
Informed Consent Form for, 606–607

Microdesquamation, after salicylic acid treatment, **removal of dead skin cells on the smallest levelafter salicylic acid treatment, 414**

Microencapsulation, of antioxidants, **when an antioxidant ingredient is enveloped in a bubblelike structure, 296**

Micronutrients, 94–100

Microorganisms, microbe; microscopic plant or animal cell; bacterium; virus; fungi, 79–80
avoiding cross-contamination by, 82–84
as disease causes, 10
disinfectants for killing, 81
skin and, 30

Micropigmentation, a part of permanent makeup, involving the placement of colorants into the skin for the purpose of cosmetic enhancement, medical correction, or aesthetic restoration. It is a separate specialty

in the field of tattooing and requires specialized training, 627–628

Microsponges, a specialized delivery vehicle that releases ingredients at appropriate levels or appropriate times, 297–298, 304

Microwaves, 157

Middle Ages, grooming practices during, 16

Mideastern skin, 185–186

Milady Publishing Company, 19–20

Milady's Skin Care & Cosmetic Ingredients Dictionary (Michalun & Michalun), 416

Mildew, a disease of plants and a moldy coating that can appear on walls, fabrics, and the like; usually occurs in damp areas, 80

Milia, whiteheads, 250

Milk baths, 419–420

Milliampere meter, 141

Mind-body connection, in holistic skin care, 419–420

Mineral oil, 288

Mineral powder foundations, 501, 502

Minerals
in nutrition, 100–101
table of vitamins and, 95–97

Mineral supplements, nutrition and, 101–103

Minifacials, 225

Minimal erythemal dose (MED), 322

Minoxidil, 271

Mirror, for makeup, 513, 514

Mites, rosacea and, 256

Mitochondria, 31–32

Mitosis, the process in which the chromatin fibers line up in the nucleus and duplicate themselves, causing the cell to eventually divide into two cells with identical DNA and function, 32, 34

MLD. *See* Manual lymphatic drainage (MLD)

Models, a design, idea, specific organization, or protocol that is used as an example to copy, 156
for dispensaries, 156–157

Modesty
body treatments and, 542
bust treatments and, 561–562

Moh's surgery, a special surgical technique for the removal of tumors that takes only a minimum of healthy tissue. The tissue is examined prior to removal, is mapped, and then removed bit by bit, until the unhealthy tissue has been completely removed and the site is surrounded by healthy tissue, 583
in treating carcinomas, **327**

Moisturization, in body treatments, 544

Moisturizers, 298, 501
in acne management, 373
in acne treatment, 275
in alpha hydroxy acid treatment, 404, 408
in antiaging treatments, 332
in basic facial, 224
in basic makeup application, 524
emollients as, 287
in facial phase VII, 213, 214
in facials, 197
hyaluronic acid in, 41
origin of, 18
perioral dermatitis and, 257
sun-damaged skin and, 324–325

Molds, a fungus growth usually growing in dark, damp places; to form into a particular shape, 80

Molecular weight, permeability and, 127–128

Molecules, two or more atoms that have become linked, 139–**140,** 284
permeability of, 127–128
structure of, 282, 284

Moles, 169
melanoma and, 328

Molluscum contagiosum, a viral disease that appears in clusters of small, flesh-colored papules, 260–261
in client health screening information, 177

Molybdenum, in light bulb, 136, 143

Monasteries, medicine during Middle Ages and, 16

Monobenzone, in vitiligo treatment, 264

Monosaccharides, a one-unit molecule that all cells use for energy, 93

Monounsaturated fatty acids, 93–94

Moor mud, in mud wraps, 551–552

Mops, makeup, 511

Morphological change, in aging skin, **changes in the shape and form of the face due to gravity and other factors, 314**

Motor nerves, 75–77, 76

Motor points, chart of, 216

Mottling, a form of speckled hyperpigmentation resulting from sun exposure, 265
in sun-damaged skin, **318,** 357
treatment of, 357

Mouth. *See also* Perioral dermatitis

Mouth movement, in massage, 209, 210

Movements, in massage, 208–212, 218–220, 566–567

Moving pictures, makeup and, 485

Moxa herb, in Chinese traditional medicine, 12

Moxibustion, in Chinese traditional medicine, 12

MRI. *See* Magnetic resonance imaging (MRI)

MSDs. *See* Musculoskeletal disorders (MSDs)

MSDS. *See* Material Safety Data Sheet (MSDS)

Mucocutaneous corpuscles, nerve endings that sense pain as well as pressure; formerly known as Krause end bulbs, 41

Muds, table of, 551

Mud wrap, 546, 547, 550–552
detoxifying, 560
remineralizing, 560

Multiple sclerosis, patients with, 598

Multitier carts, 114
for waxing, 451

Murad, Howard, 18

Muscles
effects of microcurrent therapy on, 128, 129
of face, neck, and scalp, 69–73
of hair, 45
operation of, 70–71
of shoulders and arms, 73, 74
structure of, 69–71
types of, 33–34, 35

Muscular system, approximately half of the body's bulk; muscles work with the skeletal system and generate energy to move, make defined movement such as with the hands, lifting, and speaking, 51, 52–53

Musculoskeletal disorders (MSDs), esthetician susceptibility to, 216

Mushroom electrodes, 125

Muslin. *See* Cotton muslin strips

Mustaches, men's facials and, 229. *See also* "Menopause mustache"

Mycoses, fungus-related infections, 80

Myocardium, 35

Myofibrils, muscle fibers containing filaments; give muscles their contractible ability, 70–71

Myotherapy, trigger point, 424–425

Nails. *See also* Fingernails
    keratin in, 42
    trimming, 563

Name, in health screening questionnaire, 171

Namikoshi, Tokujiro, 424

Nanometers, light wavelengths in, 315

Nanosomes, smaller and thinner liposomes, capable of holding more performance ingredients and delivering them more efficiently, 304

Narrow face, foundation contouring for, 503

Narrow forehead, foundation contouring for, 504

Nasal bone, 70

Nasolabial folds, lines that form in the skin from the corners of the nose to the corner of the mouth, 312

National Cosmetology Association (NCA), 19, 377
    on cancer treatment, 177

National Institutes of Health, 10

Native American culture, grooming practices in, 17

Native Americans, hair color among, 445

Native American skin, 394–395

Natural cosmetics
    biochemistry versus, 306–307
    as chemicals, 283
    for holistic skin care, 419

NCA. *See* National Cosmetology Association (NCA)

Neat ingredients, describes an ingredient that is not combined with other ingredients, 290

Neck
    bones of, 69
    motor points of, 216
    muscles of, 71–73
    nerves of, 75–77

Neck cream, for home skin care, 428

Needles
    in acupuncture, 420
    in electrolysis, 448–450

Needy clients, handling, 345

Negative charges, 137, 140–141

Negative nonverbal cues, 64

Negative products, in iontophoresis, 126–128

Nei Ching Su Wen, 11

Neon, in electrodes, 124

Neroli, 553

Nerve chain, 138

Nerves, 73–75
    cranial, 68, 73–75, 76
    electricity and, 137
    motor, 75–77, 76
    sensory, 41, 73, 75, 137
    shingles and, 263
    in skin, 41

Nervousness, electrical contraindication against, 174

Nervous system, the basis of consciousness and creativity, 51, 55, 75, 138
    electricity and, 137
    meridians and, 568

Networking, 584

Neurological disorders, in client health screening information, **relating to the nervous system, 178**

Neutrons, particles that make up the nucleus of an atom, they have no charge, 137, 141, **283**

Nevi (nevus), a mole or birthmark, 252. *See also* Moles
    dysplastic, 328

Niacin, 99
    dosage, functions, and sources of, 95

Night cream, purpose and function of, 200

Nipple. *See* Areola

N-Lite, in nonablative wrinkle treatment, 593

Nodules, a solid bump that you can feel that is normally larger than 1 centimeter, 249, **251**
    acne and, 367, 368

Nodulocystic basal cell carcinoma, **basal cell carcinoma presenting as a pearl-like bump, usually flesh-colored or slightly pink, often with small capillaries running through it. They are generally painless, 326,** 327

Nonablative wrinkle treatment, **a wrinkle treatment that bypasses the epidermis to stimulate collagen in the dermis for wrinkle reduction, 579,** 593, 595

Noncertified colors, color agents that are organic, 297

Noncocoon draping, 151–152

Noncomedogenic substances, **describes a substance that does not cause comedones (blackheads), 290**

Nonessential amino acids, 92

Nonfoaming cleanser, in treating sensitive skin, 348

Noninflammatory acne lesions, **not red or inflamed, 366**

Nonpathogenic microorganisms, microorganisms that do not cause disease, 79

Nonsetting masks, masks that primarily moisturize and soothe, 300

Nonverbal communication, 64

Nonverbal cues, 64

Normal–combination skin, 163–164
    basic facials for, 221, 222
    home care regimen for, 225
    under Wood's lamp, 187

Normal skin, 163
    basic facials for, 221
    home care regimen for, 225
    under Wood's lamp, 187

Northern regions, hair color in, 444

Nose
    in facial profile, 497
    foundation contouring for, 504
    shapes of, 497

Nose movement, in massage, 209, 210

Nose surgery, 585, 587, 588

No shows, handling, 410

Nuclear membrane, 34

Nucleolus, of a cell, 31, 34

Nucleotides, in DNA, 33

Nucleus, the center of an atom, of a cell, 31, 32, 34
    of an atom, 137–139, **283**–285

Nudity, body treatment and, 542

Nurses (RNs, RNBS), in clinical skin care, 577

Nutrients, foods that have been broken down by the stomach and intestinal system so they may be absorbed and used by the body, 30, 91–94, 94–100, 100–101
    for cells, 30–31
    for healthy hair, 442–443
    recommended dietary allowances for, 95–97

Nutrition, 91–103
    esthetics and, 101–103
    food guide pyramid in, 90
    necessary amount of, 101
    science of, 91
    skin condition and, 163

Obesity, 101. *See also* Adipose tissue; Body fat
    cellulite and, 562–563
    fats and, 93
    skin tags and, 254

Objective data, in SOAP notes, 602

Objective symptoms, of diseases, **visible, noticeable symptoms such as edema or erythema, 247**

Observation, in skin analysis, 188–189

Obsessive-compulsive patients, 598

Occipital bone, bone that attaches to the parietal bone and forms the lower back part of the cranium, 69, 70

Occipital frontalis muscle, a broad muscle on top of the scalp, 70, 71

Occipitalis muscle, **back of the epicranius; a muscle that draws the scalp backward, 70,** 71

Occlusion, moisturizing by, **the technique of placing a layer of emollient over the skin in order to keep natural moisture from escaping from the epidermis, 287,** 288, 298, 299

Occlusive agents, ingredients such as fatty esters that cause occlusion, keeping moisture in the skin, 298, 299

Occupation, in health screening questionnaire, 171

Occupational Safety and Health Administration (OSHA), a U.S. government agency that oversees workplace safety for employees, 79
    disposal standards of, 83
    Federal Register rulebook from, 87–89
    hepatitis B standards of, 87
    sanitation guidelines of, 84

Octyl methoxycinnamate, as chemical sunscreen, 272

Octyl salicylate, as chemical sunscreen, 272

Oculomotor (III) nerve, 68, 76

Offices, medical, 578–579

Ohm, a measure of how much a material resists a flowing current, 141, **142**–143

Oil free products, in acne management, 373

Oil glands. *See* Sebaceous glands

Oil-in-water (O/W) emulsions, oil in a base of mostly water, 286–**287**

Oil of Olay, 19

Oils, 94
    in acne management, 374
    alipidic skin and, 164–165
    in aromatherapy, 422, 552–553
    in ayurvedic therapy, 422
    in body treatments, 544, 573
    dry skin and, 164
    from the earth, 288–289
    in emulsions, 286–287, 292, 293
    for massage, 208
    in men's facials, 234

from plants, 289
in salicylic acid treatment, 413
in skin care, 287–289
Oil soluble substance, **describes materials that are compatible with oil, 292**
Oily rosacea, 256–257
Oily skin, 165–167
acne and, 365–366
in alpha hydroxy acid home care treatment, 406
beta hydroxy acids and, 412
black skin as, 391
salon treatment of, 380–388
Skin Care System C for, 434, 436
under Wood's lamp, 187
Olfactory (I) nerve, 68, 76
Olive oil, 10
Olive skin, 491
Omega-3 fatty acids, a type of fat that is believed to possibly decrease the likelihood of cardiovascular diseases, 94
Opacifiers, fatty alcohols as, **fatty acids that develop a solid white color in creams, 289**
Open comedones, a blackhead, 250
acne and, 366, 367
in acne grades, 372
Operator's stool, 109–110, 112
Ophthalmic nerve, 75
Optic (II) nerve, 68, 76
Optical fibers, 134
Optional movement, in massage, 211
Oral antibiotics, acne treatment with, 380
Oral surgeons, 583
Orange, as secondary color, 488
Orbicularis oculi muscle, **a circular muscle that surrounds each eye, 71**
Orbicularis oris muscle, **a circular muscle which encircles the mouth, 71**
Orbits, of electrons, 139
Order of the Bath, The (Henry IV), 16
Organelles, in cells, 30–32
Organic material, in bones, **relating to an organ; pertaining to substances having carbon-to-carbon bonds, 69**
Organization, for estheticians, 153, 166, 500
Organs, nervous system and, 138
Origin, of muscles, 70
Ortho Pharmaceuticals, 18
Ortho-Tri-Cyclen, acne treatment with, 370
OSHA. *See* Occupational Safety and Health Administration (OSHA)
Osteoporosis, vitamin D and, 98
Ostia (ostium), many pores, 45, 366
OTC treatments. *See* Over-the-counter (OTC) treatments
Otolaryngologists, certified, 583
Otolaryngology, facial plastic surgery and, 583
Otoplasty, a surgical procedure performed to flatten ears that protrude perpendicular to the face, 585, 587, 588
Outpatient clinic
as career option, 581
esthetician in, 578
Oval face, 492
Ovaries, female sex glands that produce reproductive cells, 59
Overproliferation, a phenomenon wherein skin cells replicate themselves too quickly; it is associated with psoriasis, 259

Over-the-counter drugs, drugs available in stores without a prescription, 271
Over-the-counter (OTC) treatments, 255, 271–275, 275–276, 427
O/W emulsions. *See* Oil-in-water (O/W) emulsions
Oxidation, the loss of an electron by a chemical
acne and, 366
preservatives and, **296**
Oxygen
acne and, 366–367
atomic structure of, 282, 285
in circulatory system, 60, 61–62
in free radicals, 285, 316
ozone as, 121
in water, 140
Oxygenation, of cells, 306
Ozone, in steamers, 121–122
Ozone layer, 121

PABA (para-aminobenzoic acid), dosage, functions, and sources of, 95
Pacemakers, electrical contraindication against, 174
Pacinian corpuscles, nerve endings that sense pressure or weight against the skin, 41
Packages, of combined therapies, 564–565
Pain, nerves sensing, 41
Palettes, 154–155
in makeup kit, 512
Palm oil, a fatty and heavy plant oil, 289
Palpable nodules, **describes a nodule that can be felt and lifted away from the skin with two fingers, 251**
Pancha karma, 16
Pancreatin, as exfoliant, 416
Pantothenic acid, important in various processes involved in synthesis of fatty acids, and the metabolism of proteins and carbohydrates, 100
dosage, functions, and sources of, 96
Papain, as exfoliant, **an enzyme found in papaya, 416**
Papaya, exfoliant from, 416
Papillae, small, cone-shaped elevations at the bottom of the hair follicle in the dermis, 40, 45, 441
Papillary layer, the upper part of the dermis, also known as the basement membrane that connects the dermis to the epidermis, 39–40
anatomy of, 39
Papules, a type of raised lesion that is usually characterized by red bumps, 249, 250–251
acne and, 367
Paraben group, as allergens, 180
Paracelsus, 16
Paraffin, 565
spot treatments using, 564
Paraffin mask
spot treatments using, 564
in treating mature skin, 333–334
Paraffin wax heater, 129, 130. *See also* Heaters
Paramedical makeup, 534–535
Parfum, the international term for perfume or fragrance, 296
Parietal bones, bones that from the sides and top (crown) of the cranium, 69, 70
Parkinson disease, patients with, 598
Parotid nodes, 62

PAs. *See* Physician's assistants (PAs)
Pasteur, Louis, 10
Patches, macules larger than one centimeter, 249, 250
herald, 260
Patchouli, in aromatherapy, 552
Patch test, a test to determine a client's sensitivity to a particular product. A small amount of a product is applied behind the ear or on the inside of the arm and is then checked for a reaction, 181
for allergens, 181, 615
of depilatories, 445
Pathogenic microorganisms, microorganisms that cause disease, 79
Pathological organisms, **disease-causing, 247**
Patience, with patients, 601
Patient education, keeping a client fully informed of pre- and post-surgical procedures and requirements, and a full description of the treatment they will receive, 601
Patient profiles, 596–608
Patients
camouflage therapy for, 622–628
educating, 601, 616
elderly persons as, 597–598
mentally ill, 598
obsessive-compulsive, 598
patience with, 601
physically challenged, 598
planning with, 600
postoperative care of, 597
pre- and postoperative care for, 610–621
preoperative preparation of, 597
qualifying, 600–601
self-abused, 598
survivors of abuse as, 597
Peat mud, 551
Pectoralis major muscles, **the muscle that flexes and rotates the arm forward and inward, 73,** 74
Pectoralis minor muscles, **the muscle that draws the shoulder forward and rotates the scapula (shoulder blade) downward, 73,** 74
Pedicures, 563
Peeling. *See also* Skin peels
deep, 402
medium depth, 402
after sunburn, 317
superficial, 401–402
Peeling drugs, treating actinic keratosis with, 321
Peer pressure, acne and, 369
Pellagra, the disease associated with niacin deficiency; can affect the skin, mental functions, and the intestinal tract, and can cause death, 99
Pellon strips, 453
in eyebrow waxing, 464
in lip waxing, 470
in underarm waxing, 472
Pencils, 505, 507–508, 514. *See also* Eyebrow pencil
tips for, 508
Percussion, in Swedish massage, 566–567
Performance agents, 608
in body treatments, 553–554
in cosmetics, 286
glycolic peel and, 608

Performance ingredients, ingredients in a cosmetic product that cause a change in the skin's appearance; also known as active agents or active principals, **286**

Perfume industry, origin of French, 17–18

Pericardium, 35

Perifollicular inflammation, acne and, **swelling inside a follicle, 369**

Perioral dermatitis, an acnelike condition around the mouth that occurs almost exclusively in women, 257

Periosteum, 36

Permanent cosmetic makeup, 627–628

Permanent hair reduction, 448

Permanent hair removal, 445, 448–451

Permeability, skin that is easily penetrated by chemicals and other substances, 175
   ampoule polarity and, 127–128
   exfoliants and, 175

Pernicious anemia, a disorder caused by lack of proper amounts of vitamin B__, or from poor absorption of the vitamin caused by other diseases, 99–100

Peroxide, 82
   in free radicals, 316
   in galvanic electrology, 448

Personal presentation
   for estheticians, 147–149, 153
   in marketing makeup artistry, 536
   in networking, 584
   work ethic and, 460

Petechiae, tiny, pinpoint, red spots from trauma, 248, 249

Petrissage, a deep kneading movement of the skin between the thumb and forefinger. This highly stimulating movement stimulates sebum production, expulses excess oil, and activates sluggish skin, 218–219
   contraindication against, 219
   in Swedish massage, 566

Petrolatum, 288, 298

Petroleum jelly, 298
   waxing and, 481

Phaeophyta, 550, 551

Pharmacology, the study of medicinal drugs, how they work, and how they are produced, 270–280. *See also* Drugs
defined, **271**

Pharmacopoeias, authoritative publications designating the properties, actions use, dosage, and standards of strength and purity of drugs, 9, 10

Pharmocosmetics, 303

Phases, of facials, 200, 201–215

Phenol, deep peels using, **a highly acidic chemical used for deep peels, 402,** 585, 589

Phenyl trimethicone, 290

Pheomelanin, 46

Phlebectomy, a procedure in which very small incisions are made along the bulging vein protruding above the skin's surface, 594

Phlebitis, waxing contraindication against, 455

Phlegm, in four humors theory, 14, 15

Phlegmatic temperament, in four humors theory, 15

Phospholipids, complex fat substances that, together with protein, form the membrane of all living cells, 43

Phosphorus, mineral involved and present in DNA, and in energy release, 100
   dosage, functions, and sources of, 97

Photoaging, aging symptoms due to sun damage, 171, 315, 316

Photography, in computer imaging, 620

Photo light, 450–451

Photothermolysis, in hair removal, **the photochemical destruction of hair follicles, 450**

pH scale, 293–294

Physically challenged patients, 598

Physical sunscreens, 271–272

Physical therapists (PTs), in clinical skin care, 577

Physician care, client health screening information on, 173

Physicians
   clinical skin care and, 575, 576–581
   estheticians and, 118, 247, 608
   offices of, 578–579
   prescriptions by, 271

Physician's assistants (PAs)
   in clinical skin care, 577
   prescriptions by, 271

Physiognomy, Theory of, 14

Phyto extracts, in sample skin care systems, 433, 435, 436

Picking, acne excoriée and, 379

Pigmentation
   in albinism, 264
   of black skin, 392
   camouflage makeup for uneven, 534–535
   corrective makeup for uneven, 533–534
   in dyschromias, 264
   of skin, 168
   in vitiligo, 264–265

Pigment cells, in skin, 46–48

Pigmented basal cell carcinoma, **melanocytes are involved in the lesions and are dark in color, 327**

Pigments, in sunscreens, 271–272

PIH. *See* Postinflammatory hyperpigmentation (PIH)

Pilosebaceous unit (apparatus), the structure in which hairs grow that are commonly known as pores; the hair follicle, 45, 441

Pimples, 248
   oily rosacea and, 255

Pine, 553

Pineapple, exfoliant from, 416

Pine bark extract, in antiaging treatments, 330–331

Pine-sol, 81

Pink, color temperature of, 490

Pinkeye, 262–263

Pinus silvestrus, 553

Pitta people, in ayurvedic therapy, 422

Pituitary gland, a ductless gland located at the base of the brain, 59

Pityosporon, in tinea versicolor, **the yeast that occurs normally on everyone's skin, it can cause tinea versicolor (pityriasis versicolor), 262**

Pityriasis rosea, a skin condition characterized by red patches of skin that may be round or oval in shape, 260

Pityriasis versicolor, 262

Pityrosporum ovalli, seborrheic dermatitis and, 255

Planning. *See also* Career planning
   in entrepreneurship, 253
   in networking, 584
   with patients, 600
   in SOAP notes, 602

Plant extracts, in sample skin care systems, 433, 435, 436

Plants
   oils from, 289
   skin care products from, 283

Plaques, lesions that have flat surfaces, yet are raised above the skin, 249, 251

Plasma, the pale yellow or gray-yellow protein-containing fluid portion of the blood in which the blood cells and platelets are normally suspended, 60, 61

Plasma cells, 65

Plasma membrane, 31

Plastic surgeons, board certified, 583

Plastic surgery, 7, 582–595. *See also* Facial plastic surgery
   of body, 589–595
   defined, 583
   educating patients about, 601
   patient profiles for, 596–608
   postoperative care after, 597, 598–601, 610–621
   preoperative preparation for, 597, 598–601, 610–621
   types of, 583–595

Platelets, blood cells that aid in the forming of clots, 60–61

Platysma, extends from the upper chest and wraps the lower cheeks and chin; responsible for a firm chin and neck, 71, 73

PLE. *See* Polymorphous light eruption (PLE)

Pliny the Elder, 14

Plug, 142
   safety of, 145

Plugs, in acne, 366–367

PMS. *See* Premenstrual syndrome (PMS)

Pocks, acne and, **depressed scars, 368**

Poikiloderma of Cevattes, a combination of hyperpigmentation and teliangectasia formed in a horseshoe pattern, appearing as dark redness down the sides of the neck with a more normal-looking flesh-colored pigmentation under the chin, 265, 319

Polarity changer, 142

Polarity of ampoules, 127–128

Polarity therapy, an energy system of movement using the massage therapist's hands to rebalance energy over the body, 423

Policies and procedures
   in Confidential Skin Health Survey, 172
   customer, 410–411
   public relations and, 421
   salon, 182
   sanitation, 84–89

Polyethylene beads. *See also* Microballs
   in acne treatment, 275
   in exfoliation, 300

Polyglucans, natural substances derived from yeast cells that help strengthen the immune system and stimulate

the metabolism. A hydrophilic ingredient able to absorb more than 10 times its weight in water, it can be absorbed into the outer layers of the epidermis due to its extremely small size, **306**

Polyguard towels, 152

Polymers, in delivery systems, **new, advanced delivery systems with multiple uses, 304**–306

Polymorphous light eruption (PLE), following sun exposure, 317

Polysaccharides, made of a chain of sugar unit molecules, 93

Polyunsaturated fats, 93–94

Pond, Theron T., 18

Pond's Extract Soap, 18

Pores, 45
  acne and, 366
  alpha hydroxy acids and clogged, 402–403
  clogged, 368
  enlarged, 365–366
  in face, 164
  oily skin and, 165
  puberty and, 368
  in T-zone, 164

Port-wine stain, a type of birthmark characterized by a large, splotchy, wine-colored mark, 252

Positive charges, 137, 140–141

Positive nonverbal cues, 64

Positive products, in iontophoresis, 126–128

Postconsultation, 236–243
  maximizing, 237
  purpose of, 237

Postepilation solutions, 452–453
  in eyebrow waxing, 464

Post-fifties, skin aging during, 314

Postherpetic neuralgia, 263

Post-inflammatory hyperpigmentation (PIH), hyperpigmentation that occurs from irritation, 48, 187, 265

Postoperative care, 597, 598–601, 610–621

Posttreatment stabilization, relaxing after a stimulating treatment, 546

Potassium, an element, the salts of which are used in medicine; an essential mineral found in vegetables and fruits, necessary to the health of the skin; potassium and sodium regulate the water balance within the body, 100
  dosage, functions, and sources of, 97

Powder brush, 509
  in basic makeup application, 525, 526

Powder foundations, 501, 502

Powder puff, 505
  in basic makeup application, 525
  disposable, 511

Powders
  in basic makeup application, 525–526
  in body treatments, 573
  depilatory, 445
  makeup, 505, 514
  tips for, 505
  types of, 505

Precare, for alpha hydroxy acid treatments, 404–405. *See also* Preoperative care

Prednisone, a systemic steroid often used to treat autoimmune disease such as lupus, 177, 276
  use of and contraindication against, 177, 280

Pre-epilation solutions, 452–453

Pregnancy

alpha hydroxy acids and, 404

client health screening information on, 173

electrical contraindication against, 174

Pregnancy mask, a common hormonally determined example of hyperpigmentation that typically occurs during pregnancy. It often gets worse from sun exposure, 168, 266
  alpha hydroxy acids and, 403
  in sun-damaged skin, 318

Premenstrual acne, acne that occurs 8–10 days before a woman's period; it directly related to changes in hormones, resulting in increased sebum production and inflammation within the follicles, 369

Premenstrual syndrome (PMS), vitamin B$_6$ and, 99

Preoperative care, 610–621. *See also* Precare

Preoperative preparation, 597, 598–601

Prescription drugs, drugs that require a written order from a physician, 271, 276–279

Prescription steroids, 276

Presentation, in marketing makeup artistry, 536

Preservatives, 296
  as allergens, 180
  sensitive skin and, 350

Pressed powders, 505

Pressure
  nerves sensing, 41
  in shiatsu massage, 569

Pressure lines, 312, 313

Pressure points, in shiatsu, 569

Preston, Douglas, 20–21, 22

Preston Wynne Learning Systems, 20

Preston Wynne Spa, 5

Pretanning, 325

Prickle cell layer, 42

Primary colors, red, yellow, and blue on the color wheel. All other colors are made by mixing the primary colors, 488

Primary lesions, 248, 249

Privacy
  in bikini waxing, 478
  in body treatment, 542
  for clients, 149

Private label makeup products, benefits and drawbacks of, 529

Proanthocyanins, in antiaging treatments, 331

Problematic clients, handling, 345

Problem skin, 165–167
  Skin Care System C for, 434, 436

Product integration, 241

Productivity, 132

Product masks, 155–156

Product positioning, 199

Product returns, handling, 410–411

Professional organizations, 377

Professionals. *See* Dentists; Dermatologists; Estheticians; Medical professionals; Otolaryngologists; Physicians; Plastic surgeons; Skin care professionals; Veterinarians

Profit, with private label makeup products, 529

Progesterone, a hormone responsible for building the lining inside a woman's uterus, 59
  menopause and, 314

Proliferative diseases, diseases associated with the rate of cell turnover or cell renewal, **259**

Promotions, 166, 230, 431

Pronator muscles, **muscles that turn the hand inward so that the palm faces downward, 73,** 74

Prone position, for body treatments, **the client lies face down, usually at the beginning of the treatment, 546,** 547

Prophase, 34

Prophylactic, preventive, 178

Propionibacterium acnes, the bacteria that cause acne vulgaris
  acne caused by, **273,** 366–367
  salicylic acid and, 412
  seborrheic dermatitis and, 255

Proportions
  of eyes, 497
  of facial features, 491–493, 494–499
  of lips, 498–499

Prostaglandins, hormones that are made by linoleic acid and help with blood vessel dilation, 93

Protection, as skin function, 28, 43

Proteins, chains of amino acid molecules, which are used by every cell of the body to make other useable proteins to carry out various functions as required by the cells and the body, 92. *See also* Glycoproteins
  amino acids in, 31
  in cell nucleus, 32
  in collagen, 40–41
  effects of microcurrent therapy on, 128
  in elastin, 40–41
  immune response and, 65
  in keratin, 42
  as macronutrients, 91, 92

Protocols, a detailed plan of a scientific or medical treatment or procedure, 602
  for body massage, 566
  in body treatments, 545–546
  end of the day, 158
  for facial bed, 149
  for glycolic peel, 608
  standard medical, 602
  treatment, 602

Protons, particles that make up the nucleus of an atom; they have a positive charge, 137, 142, **283**

Protozoa, one-celled organism, 30

Protruding eyes, 496

Protruding forehead, foundation contouring for, 504

Pruritis, the medical term for itching, 248
  sensitive skin and, 343

Pseudofolliculitis, 235

Pseudofolliculitis barbae, 264

Pseudopods, a false foot, 64

Psoralen, 259–260

Psoriasis, a skin disease that causes scaly, red patches on the scalp, lower back, elbows, knees, and chest, 177, 259–260
  in client health screening information, 177–178

Psychology, holism and, 419

PTs. *See* Physical therapists (PTs)

Puberty, skin changes during, 368–369

Public hygiene
  body treatments and, 542–543
  in Roman culture, 14

Public relations, for estheticians, 421

Publishing, evolution of American skin care and, 19–20
Puffiness, of skin around eyes, 169
Pulmonary arteries, 35
Pulmonary veins, 35
Pulsed light
    from carbon dioxide laser, 588
    laser hair removal via, 450–451
    in nonablative wrinkle treatment, 593
Purple
    color temperature of, 490
    as secondary color, 488
Purpura, any form of lesion caused by bleeding under the skin, 248
    senile, 320
Pus, a fluid that is a product of infection and is a mixture of dead white blood cells, bacteria, blood, and other debris including tissue or cells that have been destroyed by infection, 250, 251
    in acne, 367
    in cysts, 368
Pus-forming microorganisms, 79, 80
Pustules, an infected papule, 249, 250, 251
    in acne, 367
    salicylic acid and, 412
PUVA treatments, for psoriasis, 260
Pycnogenol, in antiaging treatments, 330–331
Pyridoxine, 99
    dosage, functions, and sources of, 95

Q10 coenzyme, 306
Qi, a life-force energy throughout all organs of the body. Taoists believe good health depends on a free circulation of qi, 11
    holistic therapies and, 420–422
    Reiki massage and, 423
Qualifying patients, 600–601
Quarks, 137
Quaternary ammonium compounds (quats), a group of compounds of organic salts of ammonia employed effectively as disinfectants, conditioners, and other surface-active agents; nontoxic, odorless, and fast-acting, 81, 82
Questionnaires. See Forms
Quick cleanse, in skin analysis, 188
Quinone, 175

Radiation therapy, waxing contraindication against, 455
Radio frequency device, removing spider veins with, 594
Rainy days, solar skin damage during, 324
Rake electrode, 125
Ramp waveform, in microcurrent devices, 129
Rapport, with clients, 295
Rashes, in client health screening information, 177
"Razor bumps, " 235
RDAs. See Recommended dietary allowances (RDAs)
Reassessment, with clients, 148
Reassurance, of clients, 148
Receptionists, 153
Receptor sites, on cells, 31, 32
Recommendations, of products, 572
Recommended dietary allowances (RDAs), 101
    table of, 95–97
Reconstructive plastic surgeons, physicians who perform procedures

on the face and body of accident survivors and others with disfigurements, 583
Reconstructive surgery, restoration of a bodily function, 582–595
    defined, 583
    patient profiles for, 596–608
Records. See also Health analysis form
    of allergies, 180–181
    of clients, 148, 190, 191–193
    of skin analysis, 189
Rectangle face, 492
Rectangular waveform, in microcurrent devices, 129
Red, as primary color, 488
Red algae, 550, 551
Red blood cells, 60–61
    lymphatic system and, 62
Red Door, The, 18
Redness of skin, 168, 255, 276. See also Rosacea; Sunburn
    acne and, 375
    alpha hydroxy acids and, 404
    dry rosacea and, 257
    around eyes, 169
    from free radicals, 316
    sensitivity and, 341
    in skin analysis, 326
Reeducation, of clients, 148
Referrals, 267
    to dermatologists, 247
    in health screening questionnaire, 173
Reflex, 76
Reflexology massage, a form of massage that manipulates pressure points on the hands and feet that affect other parts of the body, 216, 423–424, 568, 570–571
Regimens, health through, 10. See also Home care regimen
Reiki massage, a Japanese type of energy massage, 423
Relationship, between client and esthetician, 274, 548
Relaxing back treatment, 562
Reminder calls, 599
Remineralizing mud wrap, 560
Remineralizing seaweed wrap, 557
Renaissance, esthetics during, 17
Renee, Ron, 19
Renova, the first drug ever approved by the FDA to treat visible signs of sun damage, 18, 98, 175, 277
    use of and contraindication against, 280
Repêchage company, 19
Repetitive work, ergonomics for, 110–114
Reproductive system, deals with the reproduction and the continuation of the human species, 57
Resins, for hair removal, 446
Resistance, 142
Resorcinol, an OTC-approved ingredient used in the topical treatment of acne, 273
    acne treatment with, 273, 275
    in Jessner's solution, 409
Resorcinol paste, a cream-form exfoliation product used to treat hyperpigmentation, 411
Respect, within teams, 72
Respiratory system, contains the respiratory tract that works together with the breathing muscles, to carry air in and out of the lungs, 56, 56–57

Responsibility, within teams, 72
Resumes, 580
Retail sales. See also Merchandising; Sales; Selling
    of advanced skin products, 305, 429–432
    of medical esthetics, 578
    in spa business, 241
Retention hyperkeratosis, acne and, a hereditary factor in which dead cells do not shed off the surface of the corneum and out of the follicles, causing acne, 65
Rete pegs, the epidermal side of papillae, 40
Reticular dermis, the lower part of the dermis, 40–41
    anatomy of, 39
Reticulin, collagen-related fibers that are part of the papillary layer, 40, 41
Retin-A, tretinoin; a prescription cream for acne, 18, 41, 98, 175, 277. See also Tretinoin
    acne treatment with, 380
    Asian skin and, 393
    invention of, 427
    salicylic acid and, 412
    waxing contraindication against, 455
Retinoids, skin drugs containing derivatives of vitamin A, 98, 277–279
Retinol, 97–98, 427. See also Vitamin A
    salicylic acid and, 412
Retinyl palmitate, 278
Retinyl palmitate polypeptide, 98
Retroauricular nodes, 62
Returning telephone calls, 599
Return visits, 600
Review, with clients, 148
Revlon Company, 19
Revson, Charles, 19
Revson, Martin, 19
Rheostat, 142
Rhinoplyma, 256
Rhinoplasty, surgical procedure performed to make the nose look smaller, larger, or less ethnic and most often used to remove a bump or to straighten a nose that is slightly bent, 585, 587, 588
Rhodophyta, 550, 551
Rhytidectomy, a surgical procedure that removes excess fat that has built up or pooled at the jaw line, tightens loose, atrophic muscles, and removes sagging, draping skin, 585, 620
    camouflage makeup following, 624–625
    pre- and postoperative care with, 612, 613–614
Rhytids, the medical term for wrinkles, 311. See also Wrinkles
Riboflavin, comprised of enzymes that are functional in energy production by cells, 99
    dosage, functions, and sources of, 95
Ribosomes, organelles that help build proteins required for different cell functions, 31, 32
Rickets, the result of a deficiency of vitamin D; seen in children, they do not develop bones normally, 98
Riley, Joe Shelby, 570
RNBS. See Nurses (RNs, RNBS)
RNs. See Nurses (RNs, RNBS)
Robes, for clients, 148–149
Rolling movement, in massage, 219
Roll-off masks, 397

Roll-on systems, hair removal via, 446, 447
Roll paper, 453
Roman culture
    aromatherapy in, 552
    grooming practices in, 14–15
Rosa, 553
Rosa canina, in treating mature skin, 332
Rosacea, a vascular disorder aggravated by flushing of the skin with blood, 179, 255–257
    alpha hydroxy acids and, 404
    flares of, 255
    prescription drugs for, 279
    safety considerations with, 612
    in sensitive skin, 347–348
    stress and, 179
Rose, 553
Rosemary, in aromatherapy, 552, 553
Rosins, for hair removal, 446
Rosmarinus officinalis, 553
Rotary brush, 119–120
    in facial phase III, 205
    for men's facials, 232, 233
    preparing for facials, 201
Rotary movement, in massage, 211
Rough endoplasmic reticulum, 31
Rough-textured skin
    alpha hydroxy acid and, 404
    Jessner's exfoliation for, 409
Rounded lesions, **describes lesions that are round, 248**
Round eyes, 496
Round face, 492
    foundation contouring for, 503
Rubinstein, Helena, 18, 19
Rust, 283, free radicals and, 316. *See also* Iron oxide

"Sackcloth" towels, 152
Sacral plexus, 75
Safety. *See also* Material Safety Data Sheet (MSDS); Occupational Safety and Health Administration (OSHA)
    with alpha hydroxy acid treatment, 405, 406
    with camouflage therapy, 625
    with chemical peels, 617
    with electrical devices, 144–145
    with endermology, 619
    in makeup application, 517
    with manual lymphatic drainage, 615
    during massage, 567, 619
    in medical treatments, 608
    with microdermabrasion, 618
    patch test in, 615
    for rosacea patients, 612
    with shiatsu massage, 569
    in treatment room, 157–158
    in waxing of ear, 459
Sage, 553
Sagging skin, 312
Sake, 11
Sal acid, 411. *See also* Salicylic acid
Salaries, for estheticians, 532–533
Salem witch trials, 17
Salerno, School of, 16
Sales. *See also* Merchandising; Retail sales; Selling
    of advanced skin products, 305
    of home care products, 241, 427–436
Salicylic acid, an OTC-approved ingredient used in the topical treatment of acne, 273
    acne treatment with, 273, 275

    in exfoliation, 411–412, 413–414
    in Jessner's solution, 409
Saline implants, in mammaplasty, 590
Salivary glands, 60
Salix, salicylic acid from, 412
Salomone, Barbara, 19
Salon operation, team work for, 72
Salon policies and procedures, 182
Salons. *See also* Spas; Treatment room
    alpha hydroxy acid treatments in, 402, 404, 405, 406
    compensation by, 532–533
    customer policies in, 410–411
    epilation in, 439
    makeup artistry in, 487
    makeup services offered by, 530–535
    productivity of, 132
    referrals and, 267
    in treating acne, 380–388
    in treating hyperpigmentation, 361–362
    in treating sensitive skin, 355
Salt, molecular structure of, 139–140. *See also* Sodium chloride
Salt exfoliation, 547–549
Salt glow, salt exfoliation, a very popular spa treatment
    in body treatments, **547**–549
    in combined body treatment packages, 565
    combined with detoxifying seaweed wrap, 560–561
    for hands and feet, 563–564
Salvia officinalis, 553
Sample advanced product plans, 432–436
Samples, for clients, 329
Sandblasting, microdermabrasion as, 400–401
Sanguine temperament, in four humors theory, 15
Sanitas per aquas (Spa), 11
Sanitation, the practice of cleanliness, 79, 155. *See also* Health; Hygiene; Personal presentation
    during arm waxing, 474
    during bikini wax, 480
    body treatments and, 542–543
    during cheek waxing, 466
    during chin waxing, 468
    disposable makeup applicators and, 511
    epilation and, 439, 453
    during eyebrow waxing, 463
    during lip waxing, 470
    during shoulder waxing, 476
    supplies for, 515
    during underarm waxing, 472
Sanitation policies and procedures, 84–89
Sanitizers, 84
    cleaning brushes and, 120
    dry, 84
    for epilation, 452
    wet, 81
Sanitizing, of body treatment rooms, 542–543
Saponification, a chemical reaction that occurs during disincrustation where a chemical reaction from the current transforms the sebum of the skin into soap, 126
    heat mask and, 130
Saponifiers, in treating acne, soothing agents that help liquefy sebaceous materials, 385
Sarfati, Lydia, 19
Saturated fats, 93–94
Saturation, of color, 489
SCAA. *See* Skin Care Association of America (SCAA)

Scales, flaky skin cells, 249, **251**
Scalp
    lymph nodes near, 62
    muscles of, 71
Scanner, 118–119
    skin analysis with, 188
Scars, lesions that are visible and that result from injury or infection, 169, **252**
    avoiding in mammaplasty, 589–590
    in black skin, 392, 393
    in breast reduction surgery, 591
    in laser hair removal, 451
    laser resurfacing of, 589
    in liposuction, 592
Scar tissue, alpha hydroxy acids and, 404
Scheduling of appointments, 166, 253, 500
    body treatments and, 546
School of Salerno, 16
Sciatic nerve, 75
Science
    evolution of American skin-care, 18
    holism versus, 419
    in Roman culture, 14
    skin-care, 10–11
Scientific method, holism versus, 419
Scissors, 514
    in makeup kit, 512
Scleroderma, an autoimmune disease that makes the skin very tight and thick. Internal organs and tissues are also affected, 268–269
Sclerosing basal cell carcinoma, **scarlike; most often occurring on the forehead, 326,** 327
Sclerotherapy, a procedure that helps to eradicate medium-sized veins, 594
Scowling, 73
Scowl lines, 311–312
Screening consultation, 182, 600–601. *See also* Health analysis form
Scrubs, 397
    in body treatments, 546–547, 549
    contraindication against, 398
    performing, 398–399
Scurvy, 100
Sea mud, 551
Sears, Roebuck & Company, first personal care products offered by, 18
Seaweed, 550
Seaweed mask, 560
Seaweed wrap, 546, 547
    detoxifying, 557–560
    remineralizing, 557
Sebaceous cysts, 251
Sebaceous filaments, small impactions of solidified sebaceous secretions that have oxidized, 368
Sebaceous glands, glands within the dermis that produce sebum, 39, 43, 45, 441–442
    heat mask and, 131
    menopause and, 314
    skin condition and, 163
Sebaceous hyperplasia, 254
Seborrhea, severe oiliness of the skin, primarily on the face and scalp. It is common in young males, 255
Seborrheic dermatitis, a common form of eczema that primarily affects oily areas of the face, 255
    in client health screening information, 177
Seborrheic keratosis, 321

Sebum, an oily substance that lubricates the surface of the skin, and helps prevent the surface from dehydration, 39, 43
  acne and, 273, 365–366, 366–367, 368, 369, 370
  alpha hydroxy acids and, 402
  in clogged pores, 368
  comedones and, 250
  function of, 45
  oily skin and, 165
  petrissage and, 218–219
  saponification and, 126
Secondary colors, orange, green, and purple. They are developed by mixing equal parts of two primary colors, 488
Secondary lesions, 248, 249
Second hand smoke, health problems caused by, 321–322
Secretions, skin type and, the primary determinant of skin type. They are produced between skin cells and from the sebaceous glands in hair follicles, 163
Selective permeability, of skin, the characteristic of letting some substances in and shutting out others, 30
Selenium, in nutrition, an essential mineral found in cereals, vegetables, and fish; preserves tissue elasticity and aids in promotion of body growth, 101
  dosage, functions, and sources of, 97
Self-abused patients, 598
Self-excoriation, acne excoriée and, 379
Selling. See also Merchandising; Retail sales; Sales
  of advanced skin products, 304, 305, 427–436
  of body treatments, 560
  fear of, 241
  tips for successful, 429–432, 560
Semipermanent hair removal, 448–451
Senile purpura, from sun damage, easy bruising of the skin, 320
Sensation
  nerves for, 41
  as skin function, 30
Sensitive skin, 163, 167, 340–355
  aging and, 348–355
  alpha hydroxy acids and, 404, 406
  analysis of, 341–344
  beta hydroxy acids and, 412
  black, 392
  difficulty of treating, 341
  enzyme exfoliants and, 416
  home care regimen for, 354
  products for, 298–300
  rosacea and, 347–348
  salon treatment for, 355
  Skin Care System B for, 434, 435
  sunscreen and, 324
  tips for treating, 348–355
  transient sensitivity of, 343–344
Sensitizers, sensitive skin and, 349–350
Sensory nerves, nerve endings that help the skin to sense touch, heat, pain, and pressure, 41, 73, 75, 137
Sepiginous lesions, describes lesions that are wavy and shaped like a snake, 248
Septum, in heart, 35

Serratus anterior muscles, a muscle of the chest assisting in breathing and in raising the arm, 73, 74
Serums, a user-friendly version of ampoules that are used for retailing; also called intensive correctors or concentrates, 303–304, 514, 573. See also Botox (botulism toxin)
  in body treatments, 553–554
  for home skin care, 428
  paraffin treatment and, 564
Service menus, designing, 217
Setting masks, masks that harden and dry after a few minutes of exposure to air; used for cleansing and removing surface dead cells and for absorbing sebum, 300
7 Habits of Highly Effective People, The (Covey), 166, 626
Sex hormones, 58–59
Sex organs, 59
Shade, a variation in a color achieved by adding black, 489
Shaking movement, in massage, 220
Shape, of facial features, 491–493, 494–499
Sharpener, in makeup kit, 512
Sharpening, of makeup pencils, 507
Sharps boxes, plastic box in which used needles, curettes, and anything sharp is disposed of. The top, when full, can be locked so it cannot be reopened. The full box must be disposed of as medical waste, 82, 83
Shaving, 445
  men's facials and, 229, 231
  pseudofolliculitis barbae and, 264
  in Roman culture, 15
Shea butter, 339
  in African culture, 16–17
Shedding, 442
Sheets, 151
  bath, 150
  fitted, 149
  flat, 150
Shiatsu massage, finger pressure therapy, similar to acupressure, relieves stress along the meridian system, 216, 424, 568–570
  reflexology versus, 570
Shingles, a skin disease characterized by groups of blisters; it is frequently found on one side of the face or wrapped around one side of the chest or abdomen, 263
  in client health screening information, 177
Shiodara, in ayurvedic therapy, an ayurvedic treatment where warm oil is dripped over the forehead to cause deep relaxation, 422
Short nose, 497
  foundation contouring for, 504
Short-term camouflage therapy, 623
Short-term damage, from sun exposure, 316–317
Shoulders
  motor nerves of, 77
  muscles of, 73, 74
Shower gel, body treatments and, 571
Showers, in hydrotherapy, 545
"Silent timers, " in time management, 500
Silicones, as emollients, a group of mineral-based substances used in cosmetics as lightweight emollients, 290
Silver, as conductor, 141

Simple epithelium, consists of a single layer of cells that are called squamous when they are platelike or flattened, 37
Sine wave, in microcurrent devices, 129
Sinusoidal current, alternating current, 144
  in high-frequency machine, 123–124
Skeletal system, the framework on which the rest of the body is built, 51. See also Bones
Skeletal tissue, 36
Skin, 25–48
  ablation of, 402
  alipidic, 164–165
  anatomical structure of, 26, 28
  around eyes, 169
  Asian, 393–394
  barrier function of, 43, 298, 299
  biochemistry of, 30–32
  black, 391–393
  combination, 163–164
  dehydrated, 163, 164–165, 167
  dry, 163, 164–165, 167
  effects of estrogen on, 314
  effects of microcurrent therapy on, 128–129
  effects of microdermabrasion on, 133
  environmental damage to, 167–168
  erythemic, 175
  ethnic, 309, 390–395
  exfoliation of, 396–416
  frosting of, 409
  functions of, 27–30
  as health indicator, 161, 443
  Hispanic, 394–395
  holistic/alternative, 418–425
  immune system and, 63
  laser resurfacing of, 48
  layers of, 39–48
  men's, 228, 229
  Native American, 394–395
  nerves in, 41
  normal, 163
  normal–combination, 163–164
  occupational effects on, 171
  oily, 165–167
  physiology of, 30–32
  pigmentation of, 168
  preparing for waxing, 455–456
  problem, 165–167
  puberty and, 368–369
  reactions to ionization of, 127
  rough-textured, 404
  sagging, 312
  sensitive, 163, 167, 298–300, 324, 340–355, 434, 435
  sex hormones and, 58–59
  specialized cells and tissues of, 32–38
  statistics about, 27
  sun-damaged, 167–168, 314, 317–318
  thickness of, 27
  transient sensitivity of, 343–344
  types of, 162, 163–167, 185–187
  water in, 286–287, 288
Skin analysis, 184–193. See also Analysis and consultation
  acne in, 376–378, 385
  in basic facial, 222
  of cancerous skin, 326–328
  closing, 189–193
  equipment for, 117–119, 187–188
  final review of, 192
  hyperpigmentation in, 357–359
  in men's facials, 233

procedure for, 188–189
recording, 189
of sensitive skin, 341–344
of sun-damaged skin, 325–326
in thermal mask treatment, 336
in treating sensitive skin, 351
visual checklist for, 188
Skin analysis charts, 189–193
Skin analysis form, 189, 191–192
Skin breakouts
in client health screening information, 179
salicylic acid and, 412
Skin cancer
in client health screening information, 179
in sun-damaged skin, 318, 321, 326–328
Skin Cancer Foundation, 330
Skin care. *See also* Esthetics
advanced products for, 302–307
in body treatments, 544
clinical, 574–581
evolution of American, 18–20
exfoliation in, 397
future of, 20–21
history of, 3–22
long-term programs for, 237, 239, 240
as luxury, 5–6
marketing of, 5–6
mastery in, 7
materials used by ancient civilizations in, 10
milk baths for, 419–420
problems due to poor, 322
supplies for, 514
twentieth-century, 20
Skin Care: Beyond the Basics (Lees), 374
Skin Care Association of America (SCAA), 19
Skin care machines, 119–128
Skin Care Management Program form, 240
Skin care professionals. *See also* Estheticians
advanced home care regimens by, 426–436
attitude of, 8
brochures for, 217
career options for, 6–7
career planning by, 449
client health analysis by, 171–182
compensation for, 532–533
competition among, 198–199, 548
continuing education of, 616
disease and, 245, 246, 247
as entrepreneurs, 253
equipment for, 106–115
ethics of, 102
facial massages by, 215–220
facials by, 197–225
first impressions of, 147–149, 153
information gathering by, 160–161
initial consultation with, 176
liability of, 111
makeup artistry by, 485–515
making appointments with, 166
marketing by, 431
men's facials by, 228–235
networking by, 584
origins of, 17–18
patient profiles for, 596–608
postconsultation with, 236–243
pre- and postoperative care by, 610–621
productivity of, 132
product recommendations by, 572
public relations for, 421
referrals and, 267
resumes for, 580
setting up facilities for, 147–158
skin analysis by, 184–193

successful, 626
supplies for, 152–155
treating of acne by, 364–388
treating of hyperpigmentation by, 356–362
treating skin types by, 163–169
treatment room for, 105
use of electricity by, 137
waxing by, 458–481
Skin Care System A, for aging skin, 432–434
Skin Care System B, for sensitive skin, 434, 435
Skin Care System C, for oily/problematic skin, 434, 436
Skin care treatment room, 6. *See also* Treatment room
Skin cells
desquamation of, 46–48
overproliferation of, 259
Skin colors, 46
alpha hydroxy acids and, 403–404
hair and, 444–445
hyperpigmentation and, 358–359
Jessner's exfoliation and, 409
in laser hair removal, 450
Skin conditioning
in body treatments, 557
in pre- and postoperative care, 610–621
wraps for, 550
Skin conditions, 167–169, 309
due to aging, 310–339
Skin disorders
allergic, 259–260
common, 247–248, 254–258
contagious, 260–263
noninfectious, 254–258
under Wood's lamp, 187
Skin grafts, in treating carcinomas, 327
Skin oil. *See* Sebum
Skin peels. *See also* Glycolic acid peels; Peeling; TCA (trichloroacetic) peels
chemical, 615–618
exfoliation versus, 401–402
Hispanic skin and, 395
Informed Consent Form for, 605
skin types and, 186
Skin problems, in client health screening information, 177–178
Skin products
for acne, 371
advanced, 302–307
chemistry of, 282–300
in client health screening information, 181
closing consultation and, 238
color agents in, 296–297
for facials, 197–201, 221
fragrances in, 294–296
for home care, 238, 239–241, 571–573
in home care guide, 241–243
integration of, 241
introducing new, 199
in makeup, 487
for men's skin, 229–231
positioning of, 199
preservatives in, 296
purpose and function of, 199–201
recommending, 572
surfactants in, 290–293
Skin scanner. *See* Scanner
Skin scopes, 118–119
colors depicted by, 119
Skin tags, small extensions of the skin that look like small tags or flaps hanging off the skin, 254

Skin therapies
ancient, 9
holistic, 419–425
Skin tones, 491
Skin type, characteristics of the skin from a genetic standpoint, 163
basic facials for, 220–224
comedogenicity and, 290
in Fitzpatrick scale, 184, 185–187
laser hair removal and, 450
Skull, 69, 70. *See also* Cranium; Head
Slanted-point tweezers, for epilation, 452
Slapping movement, in massage, 220
SLE. *See* Systemic lupus erythematosus (SLE)
Small eyes, 496
Small lips, 499
Small mushroom electrode, 125
Smectites, 551
Smile lines, 311–312
Smocks, for clients, 148–149
Smoking
aging skin and, 321
health problems caused by, 321–322
waxing contraindication against, 455
wrinkles and, 312
Smooth endoplasmic reticulum, 31
Soap
body treatments and, 571
saponification and, 126
SOAP notes, **an acronym that represents a documenting process: Subjective, Objective, Assessment, and Plan, 602**
Social gatherings, makeup and, 485
Society for Permanent Cosmetic Professionals, organizations available to support industry standards, continuing education, and mentorship, 628
Sodium, moves carbon dioxide; regulates water levels and the transport of materials through the cell membranes, 100
atomic structure of, 139, 284
dosage, functions, and sources of, 97
Sodium chloride, in microdermabrasion, 400. *See also* Salt entries
Sodium chloride molecule, structure of, 284
Sodium hydroxide, in galvanic electrology, 448
Sodium hypochlorite, 82
Sodium lauryl sulfate, 291
Sodium sulfacetamide, acne treatment with, 380
Soft keratin, 42
in hair, 45
Soft wax, 446, 447
Solar comedones, 320
Solar elastosis, severe sagging of the skin resulting from sun-damaged skin, 319–320
Solar lentigenes, freckles from sun damage, 250, 265
in sun-damaged skin, 318
Solar urticaria, hives associated with sun exposure, 317
Soothing ingredients, in treating sensitive skin, 355
SOP manual. *See Standard Operating Procedures (SOP) manual*
Sour milk, 10
Sparking, in treating acne, 383

Sparking electrode, 125
Spas. *See also* Medi-spa; Salons; Treatment room
    air systems in, 87
    in ancient civilizations, 9
    cellulite treatments in, 563
    home care and, 239–241
    keeping clean, 542–543
    makeup artistry in, 487
    makeup services offered by, 530–535
    in North America, 17
    origin of name, 11
    productivity of, 132
    teams for, 72
Spa therapies, 538–554, 556–573
    history of, 11–17
Spa thermal blanket, 131–133
Spatulas, flexible implements with blunt blades used for removing creams from their containers without touching them with your hands and contaminating them, 82
    for epilation, 452, 463, 466, 469, 470, 472, 474, 477, 480
    for makeup, 511
Spearmint, 553
Special agents, in sample skin care systems, 433, 435, 436
Specialized cells, 32–38
Specials, in promotions, 230
Specialty brushes, 511
Specialty line makeup products, 530
Specialty makeup, 531–535
Speech patterns, in communication, 64
Sphenoid bone, joins together all the bones of the cranium, 69, 70
Sphingolipids, 43
Spider veins, 593, 594. *See also* Telangiectasia
Spinal accessory (XI) nerve, 68, 76
Spinal cord, 75, 137, 138
    massage of, 423
Spiny layer, 42
Spiral electrode, 125
Spirilla, spiral-shaped bacteria that cause the venereal disease syphilis, 78, 79, 80
Spirochete, 78, 79
Spirulina, 551
Sponges, 155
    in acne management, 384
    in basic facial, 221, 222, 224
    in facial phase VII, 213
    for makeup, 511
    for men's facials, 231, 232, 233
Spores, bacterial, tiny bacterial bodies having a protective wall to withstand unfavorable conditions, 80
Spot treatments, selective treatment of individual blemishes, 561–564
    for acne, 275, **374**
    for full body detoxification, 563
Spraying
    in basic facial, 224
    with vacuum machines, 120–121
Springs, in America, 17
Squamous cell carcinoma, a form of skin cancer resembling a raised, crusty nodule or bump on the skin, caused by cumulative sun damage, 321, 327
Square face, 492
    foundation contouring for, 503
Square waveform, in microcurrent devices, 129
Stabilizing time, after body treatment, 560

Staff, 153, 166
    supplies for, 515
Standard Operating Procedures (SOP) manual, 602
Standard protocols, 602
Standard Textbook for Professional Estheticians (Gerson), 20
Staphylococci, pus-forming microorganisms that are grouped in clusters like a bunch of grapes; found in abscesses, pustules, and boils, 79
Staphylococcus, 78, 79
Staphylococcus aureus, in folliculitis, 263
Starches, 93. *See also* Carbohydrates
State Board of Cosmetology, 29
State of equilibrium, the state that exists when the number of protons equals the number of orbiting electrons, 137
States
    licensing of estheticians by, 29
    sanitation laws of, 89
Static electricity, 142, 143
Steamers, 121–123
    in basic facial, 222
    in facial phase III, 205
    preparing for facials, 201
    in treating sensitive skin, 352
Steam therapy, in Roman culture, 14
Stearic acid, 289
Stearyl alcohol, 289
Step stool, 110
    for waxing, 451
Sterile objects, barren; free from all living organisms; objects that have no live microorganisms present on them, 80
Sterilization, the process of completely killing all microorganisms, including bacteria, viruses, fungi, and bacterial spores, 80–84
    of electrodes, 124
Sterilizers, table of, 82
Sternocleidomastoid muscles, the muscles that run down the sides of the front of the neck, 71, 73
Steroids, 59, 276. *See also* Cholesterol
    prescription, 276
Stimulating oils, 553
Stone, Randolph, 423
Stool
    for estheticians, 109–110, 112
    step, 110, 451
Stories the Feet Can Tell (Ingham), 570
Straight eyebrow, 495
Straight profile, 494
Straight upper lip, 499
Strata, in epidermis, 42–43
Stratified epithelium, consists of more than one layer and is well adapted for protection, 37
Stratified squamous epithelium, consists of more than one layer of cells that are platelike or flattened, 37, 38
Stratum corneum, the outermost layer of the epidermis, 43, 44
    acne and, 365
    alpha hydroxy acids and, 402
    anatomy of, 39
    exfoliation of, 397
    peeling and, 401
    salicylic acid and, 412
    of sensitive skin, 341
Stratum germinativum, another term for the basal layer, 42
    anatomy of, 39

Stratum granulosum, granular layer of the skin above the stratum spinosum, 42, 44
    anatomy of, 39
Stratum lucidum, a clear layer in between the granular layer and the outermost layer of the skin, 43, 44
    anatomy of, 39
Stratum spinosum, the prickle cell layer of the skin often classified with the stratum germinatum to form the basal layer; prickle-like threads join the cells, 42, 44
    anatomy of, 39
Streptobacillus, 78, 79
Streptococci, pus-forming bacteria arranged in curved lines resembling a string of beads; found in strep throat and blood–poisoning, 80
Streptococcus, 78, 79
    in cellulitis, 263
Stress
    acne and, 370–371, 376
    in client health screening information, 179–180
    detrimental skin effects of, 179–180
Striated muscles, 33, 34, 35
Striations, in muscles, the marks within the muscles that are striped rather than smooth, 34
Strips, 453
Strip wax, 446, 447
    arm waxing with, 474–475
    eyebrow waxing with, 461–465
    procedure for, 456
Stroking movement, in massage, 210, 211. *See also* Effleurage
Subclinical inflammation, from free radicals, inflammation that is not apparent to the eye; it has no visible symptoms, 316
Subcutaneous layer, the layer of fat underneath the dermis, 41
    hair above, 45
Subcutis layer, 41
Subjective data, in SOAP notes, 602
Subjective symptoms, of diseases, symptoms that can be felt by the client or patient but are not detectable by simple observation, 247
Success, 626
Secretory coil, 45–46
Suction, with vacuum machines, 120–121
Sudoriferous glands, known as the sweat gland, its main function is to regulate body temperature, 39, 45–46
Sugaring, hair removal via, 446, 447–448
Sugars, 93. *See also* Carbohydrates
Sulfacetamide, in rosacea treatment, a topical drug frequently prescribed for rosacea, 279
Sulphur (sulfur), an OTC-approved ingredient used in the topical treatment of acne, 273
    acne treatment with, 273, 275
    dosage, functions, and sources of, 97
Sulphur waters, in Roman culture, 14
Sun
    acne and, 375
    alpha hydroxy acids and skin damage from, 403–404, 404
    beta hydroxy acids and, 412
    chloasma from, 357

discussing with clients, 328–330
facts about, 324–325
free radicals and, 316
hyperpigmentation and, 265, 358
melanoma and, 328
menopause and, 314
sensitive skin and, 349
skin and, 167–168, 185–187
skin damage caused by, 315–321, 321–325, 325–326, 328–330, 330–332
tanning and, 315
as vasodilator, 319
waxing contraindication against, 455
wrinkles and, 168, 585
Sunblock, 272. *See also* Sunscreen
Asian skin and, 393
in facial phase VII, 213, 214
in facials, 197
Sunburn, 317
Fitzpatrick scale and, 185–187
sunscreen and, 324
waxing contraindication against, 455
Sun protection factor (SPF), of sunscreens, **a numbering system applied to sunscreens that indicates how long skin can be safely exposed to the sun without burning and showing redness, 322**–323, 324
Sunscreen, 322–323. *See also* Sunblock
in acne management, 378, 387
alpha hydroxy acids and, 405, 406, 408
in antiaging treatments, 330
Asian skin and, 393
in basic facial, 224
beta hydroxy acids and, 412
broad-spectrum, 271, 323
for children, 318
choosing, 323–324
European, 273
hyperpigmentation and, 358, 361
ingredients in, 273, 322, 323
over-the-counter, 271–273
proper dosage of, 324
purpose and function of, 200
in salicylic acid treatment, 414
sensitive skin and, 349
skin types and, 185–186
sunburn and, 324
in treating sensitive skin, 353
types of, 271–272
Sunshine vitamin, 98
Superficial basal cell carcinoma, **red, flat, scaly lesions that look much like eczema. Frequently misdiagnosed, 326,** 327
Superficial peeling, removing only dead cells from the epidermis, 401–402
Superficial temporal vein, brings blood to the forehead and scalp, 60
Superior temporal artery, returns blood from the face towards the heart; situated near the temples of the head, 60
Superior vena cava, the large vein that carries blood to the upper right chamber of the heart, 60, **61**
Superoxide, in free radicals, **an unstable oxygen atom, 316**
Superoxide dismutase, in antiaging treatments, 330
Supinator muscles, **muscles that turn the hand outward and the palm upward, 73,** 74

Supine position, for body treatments, **the client lies face up, usually at the end of the treatment, 546,** 547
Supplies. *See also* Equipment; Tools
for aromatherapy, 552–553
for epilation, 451–453
for estheticians, 152–155, 513–515
for makeup, 513–515, 523
purchasing for one's own business, 253
Support, within teams, 72
Suppressor T cells, 65, 66
Surfactants, chemicals that reduce surface tension between the skin's surface and the product, 290–293
Surgery. *See also* Plastic surgery
with lasers, 134, 402
plastic/reconstructive, 582–595
postoperative care after, 597, 610–621
preoperative preparation for, 597, 610–621
treating melanoma by, 328
Survivors of abuse, therapy for, 597
Sutures, in skull, 70
Sweat
skin and, 28
from sudoriferous glands, 39, 45–46
Swedish massage, 619–620
Lomi Lomi and, 423
movements in, 566–567
Sweet birch, salicylic acid from, 412
Sweet orange, 553
Symptoms, of disease, 247. *See also* Disease
Synergy, in skin care systems, 432–436
Synthetic makeup brushes, 510
Systemic lupus erythematosus (SLE), 268
Syzygium aromaticum, 553

Table preparation, for body treatments, 546
Tables. *See* Turntables; Utility tables
Tactile roughness, from sun damage, **roughness to the feel of the skin, also associated with sun damage, 319**
Talcum powder, sanitation and, 453
Tanning, 46–48, 315
acne and, 375
misinformation about, 324
Tanning booths, skin damage from, 325. *See also* Tapotement
Tapotement, **often referred to as percussion, tapotement consists of tapping, light slapping, and hacking movements. This form of massage is the most stimulating and should be applied with care and discretion, 219**–220. *See also* Tapping movement
in Swedish massage, 566–567
Target lesions, **describes lesions that are shaped like a target. A pustule is a target lesion, 248**
Tattooing, 627
Tazarac, 175, 278
acne treatment with, 380
use of and contraindication against, 280
Tazarotene, also known as Tazorac, originally a prescription retinoid for treatment of psoriasis, now used to treat acne, 175, 278
acne treatment with, 380
use of and contraindication against, 280
TCA (trichloroacetic acid) peels, a condition involving the circulatory system; small, red enlarged capillaries that normally appear on the face and legs, 175, 402, 411, 585, 589, 615

T cells, 65, 66
Team players, 72
work ethic and, 460
Teams, 72
Team work, 72
Tea tree oil, in waxes, 446
Technological tools, 116–134
Teenagers, acne and, 368–369, 375
Telangiectasia, a condition involving the circulatory system; small, red enlarged capillaries that normally appear on the face and legs, 168, 248, 249, 249, 594
sensitive skin and, 342
in skin analysis, 326
in sun-damaged skin, 318–319
Telephone number, in health screening questionnaire, 171
Telephones, 153
etiquette for, 599
waiting on, 599
Telogen phase, in hair growth cycle, **the final stage in hair growth, the resting stage, 442, 443**
Telophase, 34
Temperature
of colors, 489–490
of wax, 447
Temperature regulation, as skin function, 28
Temporal bones, muscles on the sides of the head, 69, 70
Temporalis facial nerve, 77
Temporalis muscles, **a tendon that connects the occipitalis and the frontalis, 71**
Temporal nerve, 75
Temporary hair removal, 445
Temporomandibular joint (TMJ), 583
Terry stretch headbands, 152
Terry turbans, 152
Tertiary colors, intermediate, or third-level colors. They are developed by combining the primary and secondary colors located next to each other on the color wheel, 488–489
Tesla pulse train current, in high-frequency machine, 123
Testes, male sex glands that produce reproductive cells, 59
Testosterone, a male sex hormone, 58–59
TEWL. *See* Transepidermal water loss (TEWL)
Texturizers, 293
Thalassotherapy, 10
T-helper cells, a type of white blood cells that signal the immune system within the blood stream to react to the invasion of foreign substances or invading organisms, 64–66
Theory of Physiognomy, 14
Thermal blankets, 129, 131–133
Thermal mask, in treating mature skin, 335–337
Thermolysis, 124
hair removal via, 448
Thiamin, present in pork, beef, fortified cereals, whole-wheat products, and nuts; removes carbon dioxide from the cells, and converts carbohydrates stored as fat, 99
dosage, functions, and sources of, 95
Thickeners, 293
Thighs, waxing of, 478
Thin lower lip, 499

Thin skin, 341. *See also* Sensitive skin
    aging and, 314
Thin upper lip, 499
Thirties, skin aging during, 313
Threading, hair removal via, 448
Thyme, 553
Thymus, 553
Thymus gland, responsible for the beginning of the immune system in young persons, 60
Thyroid gland, regulates the body's metabolism, heart rate, rate of energy used, and calcium, 59
Thyroid hormone, 59
Tile flooring, 87
Time management, 166, 500
Tincture of iodine, 82
Tinea, fungal infections of the skin, 261–262
Tinea corporis, a fungus commonly known as ringworm, 262
Tinea pedis, the medical term for athlete's foot, a fungus characterized by itching, flaking, and a pink rash, 261–262
Tinea versicolor, a yeast infection, also called pityriasis versicolor, 262, 265
Tint, a variation in color achieved by adding white, 489
Tinted moisturizers, 501
Tissue, 32
    adipose, 36, 37
    connective, 34–36, 37
    effects of microcurrent therapy on, 129
    epithelial, 32–33, 37, 38
    skeletal, 36
    specialized, 32–38
Tissue respiratory factor (TRF), a natural substance derived from yeast cells that functions as an anti-inflammatory and moisturizing ingredient, 306
Tissues, in makeup kit, 512
Titanium dioxide, in sunscreen, 271–272, 322, 323
T-lymphocytes, manufactured in the bone marrow and the lymph nodes where they migrate into the body when needed, 60, 65
TMJ. *See* Temporomandibular joint (TMJ)
Tobacco, as vasodilator, 319. *See also* Smoking
Tocopherol, vitamin E; any of a group of four related viscous oils that constitute vitamin E; chief sources are wheat germ and cottonseed oils; used as a dietary supplement and as an antioxidant in some cosmetic preparations, 98. *See also* Vitamin E
Toenails, keratin in, 42. *See also* Nails
Toner
    in acne management, 374, 378, 379
    in alpha hydroxy acid treatment, 405, 407
    in basic makeup application, 524
    for hyperpigmentation, 361
    for men's facials, 229
    purpose and function of, 200
Tones, of colors, 489–490
Tongs, 155, 514
Tonsils, 62
Tools, 116–134. *See also* Equipment; Supplies
    for epilation, 451–453

for makeup, 509–512, 523
for skin analysis, 187–188
Topical agents, 174
Touch
    in holistic treatments, 420
    massage and, 566
    nerves sensing, 41
    skin health and, 27
Touch-blanching, of sensitive skin, **a technique for testing sensitive skin. Apply gentle pressure to an area of the face and release the pressure. If the skin color changes to white, the skin is sensitive, 341**–342
Touch-ups, 530
    tips for, 530
Touring of facilities, by clients, 147
Towels, 150–152. *See also* Hot towel entries
    hand, 150–151
    preparing for facials, 201
Trager, Milton, 424
Trager method, mobility treatment that rocks the body gently to produce positive energy stimulation, 424
Training
    advanced, 616
    advanced massage, 620
    in chemical peels, 617
    in endermology, 619
    for Jessner's exfoliation, 409
    for laser hair removal, 451
    in manual lymphatic drainage, 615
    for microdermabrasion, 401, 619
    in micropigmentation, 628
Transconjunctival blepharoplasty, performed inside the lower eyelid by making a hidden incision, this is a surgical procedure to remove bulging fat pads, which are often congenital in nature, 587
Transepidermal water loss (TEWL), 43
Trans fatty acids, 94
Transumblical method, a no-scar method of breast augmentation, involving insertion of the implant through the navel, 591
Transverse vein, supplies the upper cheek and facial sides with blood, 60
Trapezius muscles, muscles that cover the back of the neck and the upper and middle regions of the back; rotate the shoulder blade and control swinging movement of the arm, 73, 74
Trash cans, 513
    procedures for handling, 85
Trays, 155, 515
Treatment and correction, as facial phase IV, 201, 208
Treatment protocol, 602
Treatment Record, sample, 604
Treatment record form, 189, 193
Treatment rhythm, the smooth flow of movement that occurs during the performance of the facial, 109
Treatment room, 105. *See also* Salons; Spas; Wet room
    appearance of, 148, 149, 153, 542–543
    dispensaries for, 156–157
    end of the day protocols for, 158
    equipment for, 105, 106–115
    keeping clean, 542–543
    for makeup, 517, 523

preparing for epilation, 453–455, 456
procedures for using, 85–87
safety in, 157–158
sanitation in, 453
setting up for facials, 201, 221
setting up for men's facials, 232
supplies for, 152–155
work ethic and, 460
Treatments. *See also* Algae treatments; Body treatments; Comedolytic treatments; Detox treatments; Firming treatment; Healing treatments; Masks; Medical treatment; Over-the-counter (OTC) treatments; Postoperative care; Preoperative care; PUVA treatments; Skin peels; Spot treatments
    defined, 615–621
    table of, 620
Trends, in makeup, 535
Tretinoin, 41, 98, 175, 277. *See also* Isotretinoin; Retin-A
    acne treatment with, 380
    hyperpigmentation and, 361
TRF. *See* Tissue respiratory factor (TRF)
Triangular face, 492
    foundation contouring for, 503
Triceps muscles, the three-headed muscle that covers the entire back of the upper arm and extends the forearm forward, 73, 74
Trichloroacetic acid (TCA). *See* TCA.
Trichochrome, 46
Triethanolamine lauryl sulfate, 291
Trifacial nerve, 77
Trigeminal (V) nerve, 68, 75, 76
Trigger point myotherapy, 424–425
Triglycerides, the main fat in foods, 43, 93, 93–94
    as emollients, 289
Trimethicone, 290
Trochlear (IV) nerve, 68, 76
Trolleys, 114
    preparing for epilation, 453–455
Tropics, hair color in, 444–445
Trust, within teams, 72
Tuberculosis bacteria, disinfectants and, 1
Tubes, jars versus, 229
Tumescent liposuction, 591, 593
Tummy tuck, 591–593, 620
Tumors, 249, 251. *See also* Cancer
Tungsten, in light bulb, 136, 143
Tunica adventitia, 61
Tunica intima, 61
Tunica media, 61
Turntables, 156–157
Tweezers, 451–452, 514
    in makeup kit, 512
Tweezing, 445–446
    in treating sensitive skin, 355
Twenties, skin aging during, 313
Twentieth century, skin care during, 20
Type I–VI skins, 184, 185–186
T-zone, 163, 164
    acne in, 365
    extractions from, 207

Ulcerative carcinoma, having an indented center, 327
Ulcers, a deep erosion in which the skin surface is destroyed by infection, poor blood circulation, or cancer, 249, 252

Ultra high frequency machine, treating telangiectasia with, **a relatively new treatment for telangiectasia that releases heat into the tissues, 319**

Ultrasonic steamer, in treating sensitive skin, 352

Ultrasound-assisted lipoplasty, 591

Ultraviolet (UV) radiation, 28. *See also* PUVA treatments
  clothing and, 541
  as dry sanitizer, 84
  ethnic skin and, 391
  eye damage from, 324
  hair growth and, 444
  hyperpigmentation and, 168
  sunscreen and, 271–272, 322–323
  tanning and, 46–48

Ultraviolet A (UVA) rays, ultraviolet A rays, one type of ray contained in the light spectrum making up the sun's light. (21)Longer, more intense than UVB rays, these penetrate into the dermis, 272
  skin damage from, **315**
  sunscreen and, 322, 323
  in tanning booths, 325

Ultraviolet B (UVB) rays, ultraviolet B rays, one type of ray contained in the light spectrum making up the sun's light. Less intense than UVA rays, these only penetrate to the lower epidermis, 272
  skin damage from, **315**
  sunburn from, 317
  sunscreen and, 322, 323

Underarms, waxing of, 471–473

Uneven lips, 499

Uniforms, 515
  for estheticians, 147

United States National Electrical Code, 145

U.S.D.A. (United States Department of Agriculture), nutritional requirements established by, 101

Unity, within teams, 72

Universe, in holism, 419

University of Pennsylvania School of Medicine, 304, 427

Unona odorantissimum, 553

Unsaturated fats, 93–94

Upper cheek movement, in massage, 210

Upper leg, waxing of, 478

Upper lip
  shapes of, 499
  waxing, 470

Urinary system, eliminates wastes in the form of a slightly yellow liquid called urine, 57, 59

Urine, blood and, 62

Urticaria, red, raised lesions or wheals that itch severely; caused by an allergic or emotional reaction, 66, 251, 258
  sensitive skin and, 342
  solar, 317

Utah, esthetics laws in, 19

Utility carts, 114

Utility tables, 114
  for waxing, 451

UVA rays. *See* Ultraviolet A (UVA) rays

UVB rays. *See* Ultraviolet B (UVB) rays

UV radiation. *See* Ultraviolet (UV) radiation

Vacuoles, 32

Vacuum, in electrodes, 124

Vacuum machines, 120–121

Vagus (X) nerve, 68, 76

Valence electrons, 141

Valence shells, 139

Valerian, 553

Valeriana officinalis, 553

Valmy, Christine, 19

Valnet, Jean, 20

Value, of color, **the different levels of lightness and darkness in colors, 489,** 623

Valves, of heart, 35

Vanishing cream, 18

Van Scott, Eugene J., 18

Varicose veins, 594. *See also* Spider veins

Vascular, related to blood vessels, 252

Vascular growth factor (VGF), rosacea and, **a biochemical in the skin that is responsible for the development of new blood vessels and may be out of control in clients with rosacea, 256**

Vascular lesions, 248, 249

Vascular macules, red or purple spots that remain from former pimples or other injuries, 248

Vascular nevi, 252

Vasodilation, a sudden dilation of blood vessels, 256
  rosacea and, 347–348
  telangiectasia as, 319

Vasodilation group, of seaweed treatments, **a type of algae treatment that increases circulation by dilating blood vessels, 550**

VasuLight wrinkle treatment, 595

Vata people, in ayurvedic therapy, 422

Vegans, proteins for, 92

Vegetarians, proteins for, 92

Veins, 50, 60
  in lymph nodes, 63
  of neck, 60
  pulmonary, 35

Vellus hair, very fine, soft hair found in areas not covered by coarse hairs, such as the cheeks, 443

Vena cava, 35

Vendors
  education and, 616
  of skin care products, 572

Ventricles, of heart, 35

Vermilion pigment, **a chemical compound of mercury and sulfur, originally obtained by grinding pure cinnabar; it is now created synthetically, 14**

Vesicles, blisters, or a separation of the epidermis from the upper dermis caused by fluids released by surface blood vessels, 249, 251

Vestibulocochlear (VIII) nerve, 68, 76

Veterinarians, prescriptions by, 271

VGF. *See* Vascular growth factor (VGF)

Vibration, a shaking movement emanating from the shoulders of the esthetician by rapid muscular contractions in the arms. The ball of the fingertips are pressed firmly on the point of application, 220
  in massage, 218, 220
  in Swedish massage, 567

Vichy shower

client modesty and, 542
  in combined body treatment packages, 565
  in hydrotherapy, 545

Victoria, Queen, esthetics and, 17

Victorian Age, grooming practices during, 17

Video cameras, in computer imaging, 620

Vinegar, in cleaning steamers, 123

Violet light, in skin scopes, 118

Viruses, the causative agent of an infectious disease; any of a large group of submicroscopic structures capable of infesting almost all plants and animals, including bacteria, 80
  herpes, 261
  infections from, 80
  medications against, 279
  molluscum contagiosum and, 260–261
  pityriasis rosea and, 260
  shingles and, 263
  warts caused by, 260

Visceral muscles, 33, 34, 35

Visual checklist, in skin analysis, 188

Vitamin A, formally known as retinol, an ingredient used in some skin care products designed for aging skin, 97–98. *See also* Retinol
  dosage, functions, and sources of, 95
  Retin-A and, 427
  retinoids and, 277

Vitamin B$_1$, 99. *See also* B complex vitamins
  dosage, functions, and sources of, 95

Vitamin B$_2$, 99
  dosage, functions, and sources of, 95

Vitamin B$_6$, 99
  dosage, functions, and sources of, 95

Vitamin B$_{12}$, 99–100
  dosage, functions, and sources of, 95

Vitamin C, 100
  in antiaging treatments, 330
  dosage, functions, and sources of, 96

Vitamin D, sometimes called the sunshine vitamin; the skin synthesized vitamin D from cholesterol when the skin is exposed to sunlight, 98
  dosage, functions, and sources of, 96

Vitamin E, also known as tocopherol, primarily serves the body as an antioxidant, 98
  in antiaging treatments, 330
  contact dermatitis and, 344
  dosage, functions, and sources of, 96
  vitamin C and, 100

Vitamin F, dosage, functions, and sources of, 96

Vitamin K, responsible for the synthesis of factors necessary for blood coagulation, 99
  dosage, functions, and sources of, 96
  treating telangiectasia with, 319

Vitamin P, dosage, functions, and sources of, 96

Vitamins, 94–100
  as antioxidants, 296
  fat-soluble, 97–99
  nutrition and, 101–103
  in sample skin care systems, 433, 435, 436
  table of minerals and, 95–97
  in treating mature skin, 332
  water-soluble, 99–100

Vitiligo, a partial lack of skin pigment that appears as white or light skin patches on normal-colored skin, 264–265
of black skin, 392
camouflage makeup for, 534–535
Vitis vinifera
in antiaging treatments, 330–331
treating telangiectasia with, 319
Vodder, Emil, 615
Vodder, Estrid, 615
Vogue, personal care products offered by, 18
Voice, in communication, 64
Voicemail system, 599
Volcanic ash, 551
Voltage, the measured push or rate at which the current is being delivered, 142
Von Lee International School of Esthetics, 19

Wages, for estheticians, 532–533
Waiting room, greeting clients in, 147
Walderman, Carole, 19
Wall outlets, safety of, 145. *See also* Plug
Wand
mascara, 511
microdermabrasion with, 400–401
Warm colors (tones), 489–490
Warm paraffin, spot treatments using, 564
Warm skin, 491
Warm wax, 447
Warts, growths caused by a virus called human papillomavirus (HPV), 169, 260
in client health screening information, 177
Washable cleanser, purpose and function of, 200
Washcloth warmers, 130
Water. *See also* Hydrators
in Chinese traditional medicine, 12
in cosmetics, 286
dehydrated skin and, 164, 165
emulsions and, 292, 293
in four humors theory, 15
in herbal wrap, 561
in hydrotherapy, 545
molecular structure of, 140, 282, 285
occlusive agents and, 298, 299
in skin, 286–287, 288
in steamers, 121–122, 123
Water-in-oil (W/O) emulsions, water in a base of mostly oil, 286–287
Waterproof sunscreen, 272
Water-resistant sunscreen, sunscreens that will not wash off the skin for up to eight hours after exposure to water or rain, 272, 324
Water soluble substances, **describes substances that are mixable with water, 292**
Water-soluble vitamins, 99–100
Watt, 142
Waveform, in microcurrent devices, **helps to determine the strength of the current as well as the length of penetration, 129**

Wave therapy, also known as *microcurrent*. A passive form of exercise, this therapeutic technique helps to stimulate motor nerves to the point where a visible contraction of the muscles can be seen, 129
Waxes, 43
consistencies of, 446
types of, 446–447
Waxing, 446–447, 458–481
alpha hydroxy acid treatment and, 406
of arms, 474–475
of cheek, 466–467
of chin, 468–469
contraindications against, 177, 455
of eyebrows, 461–465
furniture and accessories for, 451
hair growth inhibitors and, 451
of Hispanic skin, 395
of legs, 478
in men's facials, 235
pre- and postepilation solutions with, 452–453
procedures for, 456, 458–481
proper technique for, 458
sanitation and, 453
sensitive skin and, 343
of shoulders, 476–477
tips for, 455–456, 481
in treating sensitive skin, 355
tweezing and, 445
of underarms, 471–473
of upper lip, 470
Wedding makeup, 531–533
tips for, 533
Weight gain, cellulite and, 562–563
Weight loss
body wrap and, 549
dieting and, 101–103
Western Medicine, holism versus, 419
Wet room, a treatment room equipped for services requiring hydrotherapy treatment, such as Vichy Shower, hydrotherapy tubs, etc., 542–543
Wet sanitizing agents, chemicals that objects are immersed in for a preset period of time to sterilize them, 81
Wheals, a plaque that is full of fluid, 249, 251
White, color temperature of, 490
White blood cells, 60–61
lymphatic system and, 62
Whiteheads, 250
acne and, 366
Whole thinking, about clients, 148
Wide jaw, foundation contouring for, 503
Wide nose, foundation contouring for, 504
Wide-set eyes, 496
Willow bark, salicylic acid from, 412
Wintergreen, salicylic acid from, 412
Witch hazel, in acne management, 374
Witch trials, in Salem, Massachusetts, 17
W/O emulsions. *See* Water-in-oil (W/O) emulsions
Women, acne in adult, 369–370
Wood, in Chinese traditional medicine, 12

Wood, Robert Williams, 118
Wood's lamp, 118, 119. *See also* Lamps; Lighting; Magnifying lamps
in analysis and consultation, 204
skin analysis with, 187
skin pigmentation and, 168
"Word of mouth" referrals, 267
Work ethic, 460
Work space. *See* Treatment room
Workstation, makeup, 517
World Health Organization, 10
Wraps. *See* Body wrap; Client wraps; Head wraps; Herbal wrap; Mud wrap; Seaweed wrap
Wringing movement, in massage, 219
Wrinkled skin, treating, 332–339
Wrinkles, 168, 311–312, 313
nonablative treatment for, 579, 595
plastic-surgery removal of, 585
salicylic acid and, 412
in skin analysis, 325–326
Wurwand, Raymond, 19

Xanthan gum, in gommage, 399

Yang. *See* Yin and yang
Yeast
seborrheic dermatitis and, 255
in tinea versicolor, 262
Yeasts, a substance consisting of minute cells of fungi; used to promote fermentation; a high source of vitamin B, 80
Yellow, as primary color, 488
Yellow bile, in four humors theory, 14, 15
Yellow Emperor, 11
Yellow Emperor's Classic of Internal Medicine, The, 11
Yin and yang, 11
holistic therapies and, 420–422
Ylang-ylang, in aromatherapy, 552, 553
Young clients, treating acne in, 368–369
Yu, Riley J., 18

Zani, A. J., 7
Zapping, in treating acne, 383
Zinc, a white crystalline metallic element; used in some cosmetics such as powders and ointments; salts of zinc are used in some antiseptics and astringents, 101
dosage, functions, and sources of, 97
Zinc oxide
color agents and, 297
in sunscreen, 271–272, 322, 323
Zits, 369. *See also* Comedones (comedo); Pimples
Zone therapy, 423–424, 570
Zygomatic arch, 70
Zygomatic nerve, 75
Zygomaticus major muscle, **muscles in the cheeks which attach the mouth to the upper cheek, 71**
Zygomaticus minor muscle, **muscles in the cheeks which attach the upper cheek to the upper lip area, 71**